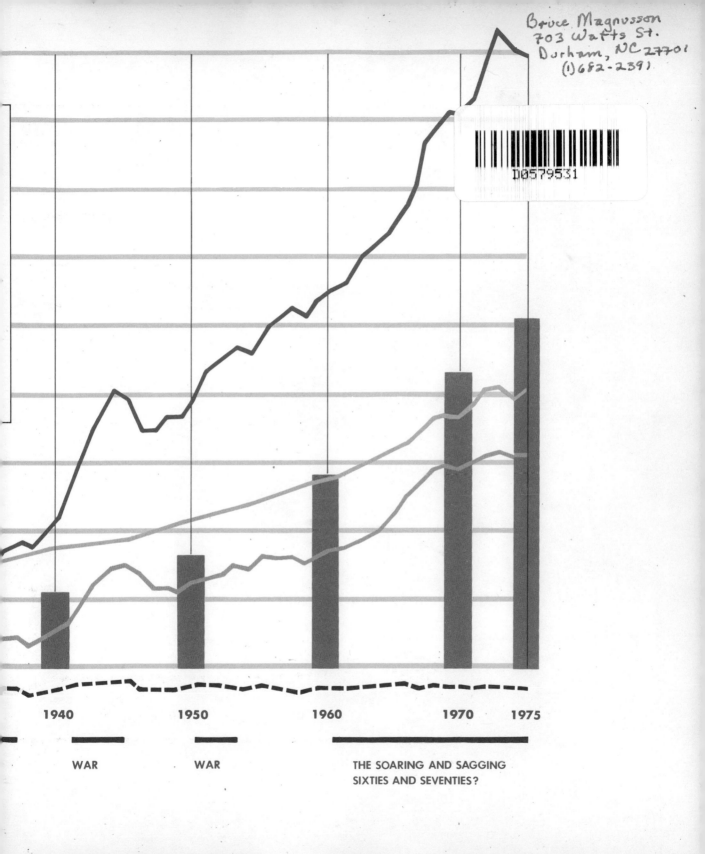

D0579531

1940 **1950** **1960** **1970** **1975**

WAR   WAR   THE SOARING AND SAGGING
                      SIXTIES AND SEVENTIES?

GEORGE LELAND BACH

Frank E. Buck Professor of Economics and Public Policy, Stanford University

Prentice-Hall, Inc., Englewood Cliffs, New Jersey   07632

ECONOMICS 9th EDITION

An Introduction To analysis and POLICY

Library of Congress Cataloging in Publication Data

Bach, George Leland, 1915–
   Economics.

   Includes bibliographical references and index.
   1. Economic policy. 2. Economics. I. Title.
HB171.B13 1977   330.1   76-45323
ISBN 0-13-227348-9

ECONOMICS ▥ 9TH EDITION
An Introduction to Analysis and Policy

GEORGE LELAND BACH

10 9 8 7 6 5 4 3 2 1

Prentice-Hall International, Inc., *London*
Prentice-Hall of Australia Pty. Limited, *Sydney*
Prentice-Hall of Canada, Ltd., *Toronto*
Prentice-Hall of India Private Limited, *New Delhi*
Prentice-Hall of Japan, Inc., *Tokyo*
Prentice-Hall of Southeast Asia Pte. Ltd., *Singapore*
Whitehall Books Limited, *Wellington, New Zealand*

contents

LIST OF CASES

SUGGESTED OUTLINES FOR alternative courses

COURSE C | One Year or Two Quarters | MACRO FIRST

First semester

(about 300 pages)

Second semester

(about 350 pages)

COURSE D | One Year or Two Quarters | MICRO FIRST

First semester

(about 330 pages)

PART

1   Some foundations

3   Markets, the price system, and the allocation of resources

4   The distribution of income and economic power

5   Public goods, income redistribution, and the public sector

Second semester

(about 320 pages)

2   National income, employment, and prices

6   The international economy

7   Economic growth

8   The changing economic world

PREFACE

This is a book focused on what the **student** does—written for students, not for teachers. The evidence is overwhelming that students retain little of what they learn in college economics courses unless they become interested enough to continue to use it as they read the newspaper and vote in elections, after they leave the classroom. If the text and the class do not kindle a real interest in economics and give them concepts and methods that they can use **for themselves** after the course is over, students will retain little.

Thus the emphasis is on:

- **A few key concepts, principles, and models—the core, no more, of essential theory; and**
- **Helping students learn to apply these analytical tools themselves to big and little real-world problems.**

Thus, the book minimizes technical apparatus.

This is a far shorter book than the comprehensive giants, which far exceed the absorptive power of most elementary students in a regular course. It is a good-sized book, not because its goal is to cram students full of information, but to provide teachers a lot of flexibility and a variety of lively applications from which they can choose to fit the interests of their students. It is designed for either a full year or a one-semester course, especially organized for instructors who wish to introduce either macro or micro first.

The edition offers a variety of innovations.

1. **A new 2-track approach to both micro and macro theory.** Track A is for those who want the bare essentials, with a minimum of technical apparatus. Track B adds more for those who want a still simple, but more thorough, foundation of theory.

2. **Thirty-eight real-world cases, each attached to a chapter where it shows the student how to apply the concepts and principles developed in that chapter.** In addition, Suggestions for Analysis for each case, segregated at the end of the book, so that students can check their own reasoning and understanding of the concepts and principles involved. Some of the cases are simple applications; others involve more complex decisions on public policy or managerial problems; still others raise broad issues for analysis and discussion, where answers hinge on value judgments and the weighting of goals as well as on economic analysis. They are real cases, not arithmetical problems.

The complete cases are listed in the Table of Contents. A sample:

- Campus Parking
- How Much For Auto Safety?
- Cash or Food Stamps for the Poor?
- Money and the Great German Hyperinflation
- Federal Reserve Independence
- Indexing—Learning to Live With Inflation
- Eggs, Copper, and Coffee
- The Battle of the Supermarkets
- The Value of a College Education
- The Voucher Education Plan
- How Much Social Security Can We Afford?
- Multinational Corporations
- Arab Oil and the International Monetary System
- Coffee, Cartels, and U.S. Development Aid

3. **Major new chapters on modern inflation (its causes and effects), the "natural rate of unemployment," and monetarism.** Has Keynesian aggregate demand policy outlived its usefulness in a world of inflation and inflationary expectations?

4. **A new organization of the micro section** that stresses the analytical power of simple supply and demand analysis; plus a framework that stresses market efficiency and market failures—with new chapters on consumer protection, government regulation, and externalities to explore the consequences of market failures.

5. **Increased emphasis on the *supply* side of the modern economy,** recognizing the pressures placed on the economy by our rising aspirations for personal income, for the macro performance of the economy, and for greater "equity" and equality.

6. **An expanded analytical comparison of the market and collective action (political processes)** as mechanisms for allocating resources, distributing incomes, and responding to individual wants in modern society.

7. **An expanded introductory section on "straight thinking in economics,"** including simple explanations of theories (models), functional relationships and graphs, correlation and causation, and how to use historical data and charts.

8. **Increased use of color to emphasize key points and to make the book interesting and inviting to students.** Again, a little help from Peanuts and a few *New Yorker* cartoons to liven things up and drive home some key points.

Again, this edition of the book is built on what we know from learning theory about how students learn:

Student motivation—cases and big and little applications to involve students and let them see how they can *use* what they are learning. Clear focus on objectives—what the student should learn and retain; see the Chapter Previews and end-of-chapter lists of key concepts.

Learning retention—through repeated explicit *use* of the concepts and principles.

Feedback—suggestions for analysis of cases, at the end of the book, let students know how they are doing and provide help in applying the theory in the text to the cases.

Beyond these, the new edition offers a package of up-to-the-minute teaching aides, for both students and teachers:

Instructors Manual and Test Bank—over 2,000 easy-to-grade objective and discussion questions; plus possible examinations and suggestions on how to use the text and the new cases in and out of class. Free to instructors on adoption.

A lively new student *Workbook and Study Guide* (by Michael Block and Henry Demmert), which includes a programmed review of every chapter, more objective questions, cases, and dozens of imaginative new problems and crossword puzzles, for all chapters. Answers are included for student self-grading and quick feedback.

Black and white transparency masters—for all charts and major tables. Free to instructors on adoption.

Economic Analysis and Policy—an experience-tested readings volume (with Myron Joseph and Norton Seeber), presenting conflicting statements and viewpoints on key policy issues and problems, designed to fit the text.

Suggested semester plans for year-long courses, putting either micro or macro first, and for different one-semester courses, are included immediately following the Table of Contents.

* * *

While the complete text is designed flexibly for use in a year-long or one-semester course, Prentice-Hall has also divided this edition into two paperbacks (*Microeconomics: Analysis and Policy* and *Macroeconomics: Analysis and Policy*) specifically for teachers who want to use only one or the other parts of the book. These paperbacks are particularly suited for one semester courses where extensive use of supplementary paperbacks is planned. Each is designed for a full one semester course, stressing the area covered by the title. Each includes all the cases applicable to its subject matter, the mathematical appendixes, and other features of the full text.

Over successive editions, my indebtedness to colleagues and friends has become so vast that it is patently impossible to list all those who deserve credit. For this ninth edition, however, a number of economists at different institutions were kind enough to make especially helpful suggestions for improvements. I must thank especially Kenneth Alexander (Michigan Technical University), Christopher Bach (Department of Commerce), Michael Boskin (Stanford), Richard Cooke (Cincinnati), Curtis Cramer (Wyoming), Bruce Dakin (Grand Rapids Jr. College), Robert Flanagan (Stanford), Blaine F. Gunn (University of California, Van Nuys), James Howell (Stanford), Dan Hoyt (Missouri Western), John Lapp (North Carolina State), Keith Lumsden (University of Edinburgh), Frank Maurer (Pace), Erwin Mayer (Western Washington State), Robert McCauley (Hudson Valley Community College), Gerald Meier (Stanford), William Mitchell (University of Missouri, St. Louis), Sam Parigi (Lamar University), Michael Peters (U.S. Military Academy), Phillip Saunders (Indiana), Stephen Shapiro (North Florida), Richard Sherman (Ohio State), Francis Shieh (Prince George's Community College), Stan Steinke (Community College of Philadelphia), David Teece (Stanford), Fred Tarpley (Georgia State), Dean Worcester (University of Washington), and W. Zeis (Bucks County Community College). Professor Michael Lovell of Wesleyan University continues to share authorship of the mathematical appendixes. The usual warning that only I am responsible for the final outcome needs to be added, however, for I have accepted only some of the suggestions advanced. Lastly, I want to add my special appreciation to Sandra Di-Somma, Robert Smith, Walter Behnke, and Marvin R. Warshaw of Prentice-Hall for their most valuable help in producing the book, to Malinda Burt and Marsha Janaes for their many uncomplaining hours with the manuscript, and to Anthony Lima for preparing the index.

CHAPTER 1

SCARCITY, PRIVATE WANTS, AND NATIONAL PRIORITIES

How is it that we in America are, by and large, well fed, well clothed, and well housed, while over two-thirds of the world's population is desperately poor—over two billion people living on per capita incomes of less than $20 per month? What explains the incomes we receive—$300,000 for basketball stars, $30,000 for a master plumber, $3,000 for an itinerant fruit-picker? Why are we plagued by repeated inflations and unemployment? Why do we have air and water pollution, when almost everyone agrees that we need a cleaner environment? How can we have a better life for all, in the United States, and in the rest of the world?

These are questions of economics, these and many others like them. There are no simple answers to most of the questions. But although economics can't give simple answers to such complex questions, it can go a long way in helping you understand the economic world in which you live and the issues on which you will have to take positions and vote.

WHAT IS ECONOMICS?

Economics is the study of how the goods and services we want get produced, and how they are distributed among us. This part we

Note: Some instructors may prefer to assign Chapter 3 first, reversing the order of Chapters 1 and 3. They are written to be usable in either order.

call **economic analysis.** Economics is also the study of how we can make the system of production and distribution work better. This part we call **economic policy.** Economic analysis is the necessary foundation for sound economic policy, and this book is about both economic analysis and policy.

Another, slightly different, definition of economics, favored by many economists, is this: **Economics is the study of how our scarce productive resources are used to satisfy human wants.** This definition emphasizes two central points. **First, productive resources are scarce,** in the sense that we are not able to produce all of everything that everyone wants free; thus we must "economize" our resources, or use them as efficiently as possible. **Second, human wants, if not infinite, go so far beyond the ability of our productive resources to satisfy them that we face a major problem in "economizing" those productive resources so as to satisfy the largest possible number of our wants.** Indeed, most major economic problems arise from this fact of scarcity, and the need to make effective use of our resources to satisfy our wants. If there were plenty of everything for everyone to have without working or paying for it, there would be no economic problem. But, alas, this is not the state of the world, even in the affluent American society, and certainly not in the poorer nations that contain most of the world's people.

SCARCITY AND AFFLUENCE

The United States is an affluent society. We are rich by comparison with other nations. In 1975, the prodigiously productive American economy turned out $1.5 trillion of goods and services, about 25 percent of the total production in the entire world, although only about 6 percent of the world's people live in the United States. Table 1–1 shows per capita output of goods and services in the United States as compared with a dozen other nations. With the Swiss and the Swedes, we lead most other nations by a wide margin. Our lead over the so-called developing countries is enormous. (Such international comparisons are very rough, and they shift substantially from year to year, but

Table 1–1

World output per capita, 1975[a]

Country	Dollars	Country	Dollars
Switzerland	$8320	Italy	$3110
Sweden	8250	USSR	2700
United States	7070	Iran	1800
West Germany	6930	Brazil	1010
Canada	6730	China	310
France	6310	Kenya	210
Australia	6250	Indonesia	160
Japan	4420	India	140
U.K.	4050	Ethiopia	100

[a]All countries in terms of 1975 U.S. dollars, converted at official exchange rates. For sources, other countries, and explanation of what is included, see Table 46–1.

they suffice to suggest orders of magnitude. We will examine them in detail later.)

In 1975, the median family income in the United States was about $13,500; half of all families received more and half less than this amount. (This is considerably less than output per family, because a large amount of total production goes into building factories, replacing worn-out productive machinery and housing, and the like that are not directly income to families.) But not all Americans are affluent. Figure 1–1 shows the distribution of income in America in 1975. About 12 percent of all families were classified as "poor" by official government statistics; a typical four-person family living in a city was considered poor if its income was $5,500 or less. By contrast, the average income of about half the world's population, about two billion people, was less than $200.

What did our huge gross national product of $1.5 trillion in 1975 include? We produced one-half billion loaves of bread and 150 billion passenger-miles of air travel; about $3 billion worth of books, $5 billion worth of frozen fruits and vegetables, $3 billion worth of toys and games, $118 billion worth of health services (over $1,600 per family), and about $80 billion worth of educational services. The auto industry turned out about 9 million cars, bringing the total on the road to over 100 million. We built 1.4 million new housing units, and over 95 percent of all existing housing had inside plumbing, a rar-

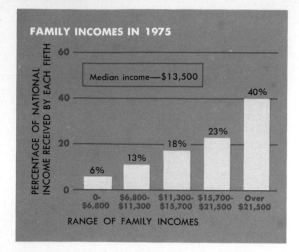

Figure 1-1
The United States has a wide range of family incomes. Each bar represents one-fifth of all families. About two-thirds of all families had incomes in 1975 between $7,000 and $25,000. Half got more than $13,500, half less. (Source: U.S. Department of Commerce; preliminary estimates for 1975 by author.)

ity among the world's nations. The economy provided jobs for 85 million people, an increasing proportion of them in retail and wholesale trade, government, and other service occupations, in contrast to agriculture and manufacturing, which had earlier provided most of the nation's jobs. Figure 1-2 presents a summary picture of what has happened to the composition of jobs in the American economy over the past century; the total number of jobs over the same period has risen by nearly 500 percent, from about 18 million in 1869.

With all this productivity, the American economy has also produced some of the world's largest slums in our great central cities, a growing amount of air and water pollution that threatens our health and the natural beauty of the land, and wide discrepancies in the quality of education provided to students of different races and different locations. The average income of blacks was only about 60 percent of that of whites, although blacks' incomes have risen more rapidly since World War II than those of whites. Defense spending in 1975 totaled about

$90 billion, enough to eliminate poverty and provide drastically improved housing and education for the American people if those resources could have been allocated to peaceful purposes.

Looking at these shortcomings, many Americans call for a redirection of our national priorities. They say we are using our resources for the wrong purposes. They call for less emphasis on the "quantity" of GNP and more on the "quality" of life. Some radicals in the "New Left" argue that modern American society is a mess, characterized by inequality of income and opportunity, alienation, capitalist imperialism internationally, and a topsy-turvy set of values. Although most Americans find these criticisms grossly overdrawn, many feel that we do need to reassess our national priorities, without giving up the demonstrated virtues of the American mixed-capitalist type of economy.

WHAT ARE OUR NATIONAL GOALS?

What are our national goals? Do we have our priorities straight? Are we producing the right things with our productive resources?

Figure 1-2
The past century has seen a dramatic change in the way Americans earn their livings. Only 25 percent now work in manufacturing, nearly 70 percent in service industries. Note the decline in agriculture. (Sources: National Resources Committee and U.S. Department of Commerce.)

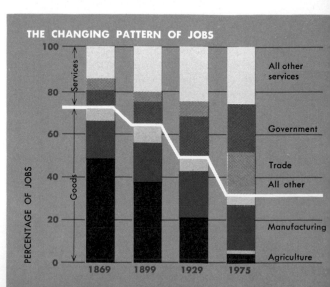

Unless we have at least a rough idea of what we want the economy to achieve for us, it is impossible to judge meaningfully whether or not it is doing a satisfactory job, and how we might improve it. Different people have different goals for the economy; this is one thing that makes it very difficult in our individual-oriented system to agree on how well we are doing. Economists often list a set of goals something like the following, focusing primarily on the economic aspects of life, as one useful way of stating the problem:

1. Progress: a rising average standard of living for the people
2. Production in accordance with individual (consumer) preferences in determining what is produced
3. Equitable distribution of income and opportunity
4. Economic security
5. Individual freedom

In the late 1960s, a group of distinguished Americans prepared for the U.S. Department of Health, Education and Welfare a thoughtful document, *Toward a Social Report.*[1] This commission chose seven major goals, or sets of goals, for emphasis:

1. Health and illness—Are we becoming healthier at a satisfactory rate?
2. Social mobility—Do we have equality of opportunity?
3. Income and poverty—How fast are we as a nation, and particular groups within the nation, becoming better off economically?
4. Physical environment—Is the environment improving or worsening?
5. Public order and safety—Does our society provide a safe, orderly environment for living?
6. Learning, science, and art—Are they enriching society as they should?
7. Participation and alienation—Is our system increasingly leaning toward participation and away from alienation for significant groups?

Other groups—for example, President Eisenhower's Commission on Goals for America in 1960—have laid out their sets of national goals. But the two above suffice to suggest what they are like. Clearly, one of the questions is how much stress should be placed on improving the standard of living of the American people and how much on other priorities that are only partially economic—for example, social mobility, health, reducing alienation, and the like. Moreover, it is clear that there may be conflicts between the goals listed, and in such cases we can obviously have more of one only by having less of another. For example, provision of complete economic security and an equal distribution of income might well reduce many people's incentive to work hard and hence slow down or reverse progress toward a higher average standard of living.

Moreover, such goals have very different meanings to different people. For example, what is "individual freedom"? You and your roommate may have quite different ideas. What is an "equitable distribution of income"? To some it means equal incomes for all; to others, incomes based on how much each produces. Does "economic security" mean a guaranteed job, a guaranteed above-poverty standard of living, protection against the loss of a job because of ill health? Setting out an agreed list of overriding national goals is a far more difficult task than it seems at first glance. Everyone is in favor of a better life. But just what that means is highly debatable.

PERSONAL WANTS, NATIONAL GOALS, AND PRIORITIES

If nature somehow provided free everything each of us wants, there would be no need to economize—no need to choose among alternative uses of resources. But alas, nature is niggardly. Affluent though we are by historical and comparative standards, our resources are far short of assuring that each of us can have all he wants without working for it. In this fundamental sense, our resources are scarce—limited in relation to our vast wants. **Given limited resources, we must choose what to have and what to forego, at both personal and national levels. We must establish priorities.**

[1] Department of Health, Education and Welfare, *Toward a Social Report* (Washington, D.C.: U.S. Government Printing Office, 1969).

Consider housing, for example. At the personal level, if you buy or rent a nice house, you have less income left for other purposes, and nice housing has become very expensive. America still has vast slums, even though nearly everyone agrees that there should be decent housing for all. We might set as a national goal a modest $30,000 house or apartment for each family in the United States, a pleasant but certainly not luxurious home. But to achieve merely this one national goal would require about $1 trillion worth of new housing—the equivalent of over thirty years of our total housing production at peak construction rates. To achieve this goal in only one year or in a few years is obviously impossible, even if we gave it a top priority.

Consider another goal that seems less farfetched. One thing the typical American wants is lots of electricity. He has a passion for gadgets that freeze, defrost, mix, blend, toast, roast, iron, sew, wash, dry, open garage doors, trim hedges, entertain with sound and picture, heat his house in winter, and cool it in summer. Residential use of electricity has been growing at about 10 percent per year, to which must be added the increases for industrial and commercial use. The whole northeastern section of the country was shut down for hours in the great electric blackout of 1965, and temporary brownouts now threaten every summer in New York City and the entire Northeast.

To increase electric-generating capacity to meet these soaring demands will require huge outlays—resources that cannot then be used for something else. Unfortunately, moreover, electric generating plants can be unsightly and may pollute the air and water around them. Electric transmission lines cut great scars across the countryside. Nuclear and fossil-fuel plants occupy scenic sights along the rivers and shores because their condensers require huge amounts of cooling water. The growth in private demand for electricity alone will, by 1985, mean that an amount equal to one-sixth of all fresh flowing water in the United States will pass through, and be heated by, the condensers of generating plants. How many new plants shall we build? If there's not enough power to go around, who shall be told no, when he wants to buy more

electricity, and by whom? If we must choose, shall we have enough electricity to fulfill our wants, or landscapes and rivers free of the pollution and unsightliness of generating plants? Actually, at a high enough cost we can have both, all the electricity people want to buy *and* clean air and water around the plants, but the resources diverted from other uses would be huge.

So it is with myriads of other things some or all of us want. Rich as this nation is, we can't have them all. We must choose.

How shall we set our priorities?

Many believe that the happiness and welfare of the individual are the primary ends of social policies. In approaching this goal, most of our individual wants are registered by purchases in the marketplace. We set our personal priorities when we decide how much we will spend on the different goods and services we buy—pizzas, automobiles, ballet tickets, haircuts. In earning our incomes, if we prefer money to leisure, we set our own priorities by taking jobs where the pay is high even though the hours are long. When one adds together these actions of over 200 million individuals in the United States today, he gets the priority-setting mechanism for most of our economic activity.

To go back to the examples at the beginning of the chapter, who decided in 1975 that we should produce a half billion loaves of bread? Answer: Millions of individual housewives voted with their dollars at the local grocery; and a complex list of farmers, truckers, bankers, bakers, and supermarkets, all actuated by the profit motive, cooperated to meet those demands. And so it is for most of the things we produce in our economy. Over three-fourths of all the goods and services produced are in response to private demands expressed through the marketplace. Less than a quarter is in response to spending by federal, state, and local governments. Thus, for the most part, our national economic priorities are set by millions of individual market preferences, not by some formal national-decision voting process.

With over 200 million consumers, no one person has much individual market power over what gets produced. Indeed, one of the virtues of the market system is that each dollar spent counts as much as every other. The "little men" who each have only a few dollars can still register their own priorities in spending those dollars, and those priorities will be met by the market if the price they are willing to pay is higher than the cost of producing what they want to buy—not precisely nor in every case, but by and large. Conversely, if consumers decide, for whatever reason, that they don't want to buy something—say, cigarettes—profits in the cigarette industry will fall, and fewer resources will be devoted to cigarette production. Thus in the private sector of the economy, the market process automatically provides direct representation of majority and minority views. There is no formal ranking of national goals, no formal ranking of alternatives, but the result seems to many observers an impressively effective one in meeting individual priorities.

The other main approach to determining priorities is through the political process. We vote for representatives who will support those goals we consider most important. If your senator or representative votes to spend what you think is too much on national defense and not enough on urban reconstruction, you can vote for his opponent in the next election. (You can also use the political process to regulate how the private sector does its job, but we shall skip over that for the moment.) You, plus 100 million or so other voters, hold the ultimate power in determining what the government should or should not do, how much of the national output shall be devoted to priorities determined through the government and how much left in private hands. For when the government taxes income away from us and uses the money to buy highways, education, and moon shots, it is in that way determining national priorities.

Once in a while, the president will establish a major national objective and mass support behind it—for example, President Kennedy's statement in 1961 that we would send a man to the moon before 1970. But mainly, the political process operates through adjustments at the margin—more for educational benefits next year, less for dams and highways, an increase in the income tax on high-income groups, a de-

crease on low-income groups. Unfortunately, it provides no simple process for reflecting minority votes on particular issues. You vote for Jones or Smith as your senator, and you have to take the bundle of preferences that is the winner, even though you like some and dislike others.

These descriptions of the market and political processes make both sound more effectively democratic than they are. In the marketplace, big corporations and big unions exert market power that sometimes overrides the wishes of consumers. The power of a billion-dollar corporation or a million-member union is constrained by competition in the market, but is by no means eliminated. Advertising can sway and shape consumer preferences. Big business and big labor unions sometimes grab off for themselves more of the increase in consumer spending than is justified by the working of competitive markets. As we shall see, the market process doesn't work satisfactorily when big "externalities" exist—for example, where the production of some good (say steel) involves social cost (dirt and smoke in the surrounding neighborhood) not included in economic costs paid by the producers and hence not included in the price of steel to consumers. Thus, the market process reflects individuals' priorities and wants only imperfectly. In such cases, people tend to turn to the government to enforce their priorities—a better deal for consumers, controls on big business and big labor, regulations to control pollution.

Similarly, governments, and the bureaucracies that often control them, also have a power of their own. "The public" is vast but generally unorganized. The political process is *ad hoc,* pragmatic. Those who are most concerned over issues take steps to get their viewpoints across to Congress and the administration, and to state and local governments. Those who feel helpless or who don't care so much are apt to be silent. Minorities who feel strongly enough can often override the majority and the "public interest." The net result is very uneven. The American democratic political system is a far-from-perfect instrument for finetuning national policy, even though it generally works, albeit often slowly, on the big issues. Most Americans feel there is no obviously superior political process that might replace it, but the practical results of government are far from the theoretical one-man–one-vote democratic model.

Which is the better way to reflect our individual interests in establishing our national priorities? Clearly, neither the political nor the economic process represents a neat, simple way of establishing and implementing our private and national goals. Both the American economy and the American political system are pragmatic, adaptive mechanisms. With over 200 million people, they both disperse power widely among many individuals and groups—although in the eyes of some, not widely enough. In the market, Madison Avenue is said to have too much power to mold consumer preferences. In the political process, legislators and bureaucrats seem inadequately responsive to what the people want.

Parts 3 and 4 examine the marketplace as a mechanism for meeting consumer wants and priorities, and some of the government interventions and controls that we have established to make the system work better. Part 5 then looks in detail at how well the political process (the "public sector") reflects individuals' wants and priorities.

As you read, formulate your own personal priorities and what you think our national goals and priorities should be. One view, emphasizing the private marketplace, denies that it is meaningful to formally list "national goals" at all in a nation of 200 million individuals where individual freedom is the overriding goal. If individual freedom is dominant, the only meaningful national goals are those that arise out of the combined free actions of individuals acting in accord with their own wishes. But others reply that somehow this doesn't get a lot of the most important things done very well—rebuilding the cities, protecting the environment, eliminating poverty, and so on—and that we need to rely on government more. Either approach we take, it is essential to remember that the fundamental problem is one of choice. Since we don't have enough resources to produce all of everything everyone wants, somehow we have to establish priorities as to what shall be done with our productive resources. And the more efficiently we use them, the better off we will all be. This is the basic problem of "economizing."

OBJECTIVES OF THE BOOK

If you're going to spend several months or a year studying a book, you deserve to know what the author is trying to accomplish. Some of the flavor of this book has been given in the preceding pages, and Chapters 1–3 are largely devoted to providing this background. The book is a mixture of analysis and policy. Specifically, it has these objectives:

1. **To provide an overview of the way our individualistic, largely private-enterprise but mixed economic system works.**
2. **To focus attention on the big problems faced by our economic system, and to arouse an interest in these problems that will last after you leave college.** If your use of the concepts in this book ends with the final exam, the book will have failed. Its real goal is to help you read the newspaper, argue understandingly with your neighbor, and vote intelligently on economic issues over the years ahead.
3. **To provide a few fundamental analytical concepts and principles that will stick with you and help you in thinking about economic problems for yourself.** You need an economic tool kit.
4. **To help you develop an orderly, systematic way of thinking through economic problems—of applying the concepts and theories in your economic tool kit.** There's nothing unique about straight thinking in economics. But straight thinking anywhere takes some real mental discipline.
5. **To provide enough descriptive material on the present economic system to give you a foundation for understanding what the problems are.** Without understanding a problem in its whole setting, there's little chance of solving it effectively. And knowing the crucial facts is a first step. But the book takes the position that your main job is to learn how to think straight for yourself, not to cram your head full of facts. A mind cluttered with transient details seldom sees the major issues. And few things will be deader ten years from now than many of today's facts. In any case, the evidence is clear that we don't remember most of the facts we memorize

anyway. So learn the main outlines of the economic system and the facts you need to understand each problem that you study. But don't make a fetish of facts.

SOME SUGGESTIONS ON HOW TO USE THE BOOK

There are some tricks in using a book like this that may help you do a better job than just plowing through each assignment.

1. Know where you're going before you start reading. Before you start a chapter, look carefully at the "Chapter Preview" on the first page. Then skim through the chapter itself. Every chapter is organized so that the major headings mark off the main parts. These headings are designed to give a summary picture of what is covered, and to provide an outline of the chapter to help you keep the main points in focus. With this framework in mind, then study the chapter thoroughly.

2. As you read, keep asking yourself, "What is the main point of this paragraph and of this section?" Try to put the ideas in your own words. Some sections are largely descriptive. Some are full of tightly reasoned analysis, usually supple-

mented by an example of how the analysis might apply. It's important to remember that the analysis is the main point; don't let the example become the center of your attention, except as an example. To help you, main ideas are set in blue type so they will stand out. In addition, the old-fashioned devices of underscoring main points in the text and making notations in the margins can help you in studying and reviewing throughout the book.

3. Much of economics is cumulative. So if you don't understand a paragraph or a section the first time you read it, don't kid yourself. **Be sure you understand as you go along.** Otherwise, as the course goes on, things are likely to get progressively foggier, not clearer.

4. When you've finished reading, review to see what you've really learned. A tough but very useful test is to shut the book, put aside any notes you have taken, and then write down in a few sentences the fundamental points of the chapter. If you can do this, you've read the right way—concentrating on the fundamentals and using the rest of the chapter as a setting for understanding them. If it takes you more than a page, you may have read the chapter well, but you had better recheck to be sure you have the central points clearly in mind.

REVIEW

Concepts to remember

This chapter has introduced some important concepts that will be reused many times throughout the book. Be sure you have especially the following firmly in mind:

scarcity	personal wants
economize	priorities
national goals	

For analysis and discussion

Throughout the text, these end-of-chapter questions are designed as a basis for class and out-of-class analysis and discussion. They are "think" questions. Drill and self-test questions and problems, to test whether you understand the mechanics of the theory presented and its use, are available in Michael Block and Henry Demmert, *Workbook in Economics* (Englewood Cliffs, N.J.: Prentice-Hall, Inc., 1977), designed specifically for use with this text.

1. Do you believe the uses of our productive resources (bread, autos, and so on) in 1975, described at the beginning of the chapter, were optimal? Who decided these were the right things to produce? What should we have produced?
2. What is your list of major national goals?
3. Can you establish priorities among those goals? If so, what are they?
4. What are your personal economic priorities? Are they different from the national priorities you list? If so, why are they different?
5. How should we as a nation set our national goals and establish operational priorities among them? Who should determine the goals and priorities? Should we use the market or the political process?
6. Are you more likely to achieve your personal economic goals if we rely on the market or on the political process to establish our national priorities—for example, on the issue of equalizing incomes and abolishing poverty?

In 1974, more than 50,000 persons were killed in automobile accidents. Over two million were injured. On the other hand, of the 200 million Americans who rode in autos that year, over 98 percent went through the year with no auto-accident injury. Until 1972, Americans were free to decide for themselves whether or not to invest in such auto passenger safety equipment as seat belts, which have been available as optional equipment on all new U.S.-made cars since the 1950s, and the vast majority decided not to. But in 1972, seat belts, padded dashboards and visors, and safety glass windshields became mandatory equipment on all new cars; and soon, automatically inflatable air bags will also be required in all new cars unless Congress modifies its recent legislation. Together, all the required passenger safety features will probably raise total cost, and hence the price, by perhaps $100–$200 per car.

Congressional action to require this safety equipment reflected widespread demands from consumer safety advocates that Congress "do something to end this needless slaughter on the highways." Ralph Nader was a leading critic of the auto manufacturers, whom he accused of being concerned only with profits, not with the welfare of auto buyers. Opponents agreed that consumers should have the option of buying such safety equipment on their cars, but denied that the equipment should be mandatory. Consumer advocates' answer to this was that experience shows that many buyers would fail to specify the safety equipment and the accident death toll would remain astronomical, whereas it could

readily be reduced by such simple steps as adding the new safety equipment on all cars. The result was a congressional requirement that new-car buyers each year spend $1–$2 billion on seat belts, air bags, and other safety features that, by the test of the pre-legislation market, most would not buy voluntarily. (New-car sales are about 10 million annually.)

Is the new auto safety legislation desirable? Should Congress have decided for all new-car buyers that they must spend $1–$2 billion annually to protect themselves against injury in possible auto accidents, or should each citizen be free to decide for himself in the market how much he wants to spend to protect himself? Two subsidiary questions: (1) Should the auto manufacturers include the safety equipment on all new cars even though not required by law to do so? (2) If Congress did not require the safety equipment on all cars, would the auto manufacturers offer it as optional equipment (that is, would the market offer consumers this option as to how much safety each wants to buy)?

Stop and analyze the issue for yourself before you go further. To help you, there are at the end of the book, for this and for each case, suggestions to help you with your analysis. But this case and all the others that follow are primarily designed to get you to use independently the concepts and principles in the chapter each follows. You will probably learn most if you work the cases through yourself, possibly in discussion with others, before you check your solution against the suggestions for analysis.

CHAPTER 2

private enterprise, Government, and the price system: an overview

The purpose of this chapter is to provide a brief overview of the way our largely private-enterprise, but mixed, system works—how its goals are set and how it uses our resources in responding to our many wants. The chapter begins by presenting the foundations of production in any economic system and the fundamental problem of economizing. It then briefly outlines the way our system solves the four big economic problems. The purpose of the overview is to provide a road map for the more detailed chapters to come, so you can see the forest while you are busily studying some of the trees of the economy. It concludes with a look at the role of government in the system. Ours is a mixed system, fundamentally capitalist and market-directed, but with a large amount of government intervention.

THE FOUNDATIONS OF ECONOMIC PROGRESS

Our standard of living depends on the resources at our disposal and the effectiveness with which we use them. The United States is rich in natural resources; it is rich in produced resources, such as factories, houses, and machinery; and it is rich in human resources, the most important of all. We have the world's most advanced technology, and vast research expenditures generate a steady stream of new products and methods. The American businessman, continually watched over by the government and consumers, uses the economy's resources to produce an immense variety of goods and services, in a way that excites the mixed envy, dismay, and sometimes disdain of his less aggressive counterparts in the rest of the world. These resources and this technology are the real foundations of the American standard of living—of our sweeping growth over the centuries.

In addition, we have developed a high degree of economic specialization and a complex exchange system. How many people do you depend on to get your everyday economic wants satisfied? You may say, not many. But think a minute. Who built the car that you drove to school, or the shoes if you walked? Where did your breakfast come from? Suppose you take in a movie tonight, or watch TV. How many people have had a hand in making this possible?

To produce all the things we want takes many people, each specializing in what he can do best. Charlie Chaplin immortalized the forlorn worker on the assembly line, day after day screwing his single bolt onto the cars as they went by. But specialization goes far deeper than this. The engineer who designs the plant is a specialist. So is the banker who lends money for its construction. So are the accountant who keeps the records and the secretary who does the typing. Only by dividing up tasks and developing highly specialized human skills and equipment can the economy obtain the benefits of "mass production."

But specialization and division of labor would be fruitless without a system for exchanging the goods and services produced by the specialists. The lawyer, the banker, the truck driver, the engineer—all would starve if the intricate system of exchange we take for granted didn't enable them to buy the food they need with the incomes they earn. Even the farmer who might eat his own carrots and potatoes would be in desperate straits if he were really cast on his own—without electricity, new clothing, gas for his car, mail delivery, and the thousand things he gets from other specialists. Every minute of our daily lives we depend on the specialization and exchange all of us take for granted. None of us would dare specialize if we couldn't count on being able to exchange our services and products for the wide range of things we want.

(1) Productive resources, (2) technology, (3) specialization, and (4) exchange. These are the four foundation stones of the productive power of the American economy—and of every other highly developed modern economy, communist or capitalist. These four basic factors make the difference between poverty and plenty. Many of the most common economic fallacies are rooted in the neglect of these simple truths.

THE NEED TO ECONOMIZE

As Chapter 1 emphasized, because resources are scarce relative to what we want from them, we must "economize" them. That is, we must choose among alternative ways of using them to satisfy the largest possible share of human wants. We need to economize time, money, and productive resources, anything that is scarce, if we are to best fulfill our private wants and achieve our national goals. This fact is the core of economics. It cannot be emphasized too much. The money you spend to buy a car can't buy a new stereo set too. It would be nice this afternoon to play golf, to go to the movies, to study, and to pick up some spare cash by working, but you can't do them all at the same time. If we use land for a shopping center, we can't use it for a school. The steel we use for autos, we can't use for refrigerators. If we use engineers to design missiles, they can't work on pollution-control devices. **Economic life is a series of tradeoffs.**

For the nation as a whole, the heavy hand of war points up vividly this fundamental dilemma of scarcity. In 1976, we spent $100 billion—about 6 percent of our total national production—on "national defense." If the government had merely left this money in the hands of taxpayers, on the average every American family would have had about $1,500 more to spend on clothes, housing, recreation, and the like.

Unemployment and depression: an exception?

Few deny the basic fact of economic scarcity in the world today. Yet in America and the other advanced Western capitalist economies, the newspaper headlines sometimes tell of millions unemployed, of auto factories idle because the public doesn't buy enough cars, of massive waste of men and machines because there isn't enough demand to buy the goods and services that could be produced with everyone at work. How can this be reconciled with the proposition that limited resources and scarcity are the basic economic problem?

Widespread unemployment of men and factories reflects a breakdown in our economic machinery. Resources are still limited relative to the vast unsatisfied human wants they might help to fulfill. People still want better houses, more food, more of almost everything. The unemployed want jobs. Businessmen want to increase production and give them jobs—if only they could sell their products. A million men involuntarily unemployed for a year means $10–20 billion worth of potential output lost forever. In depression, we mistakenly and involuntarily allocate part of our scarce productive resources into unemployment and waste. Part 2 examines the reasons in detail.

CHOOSING AMONG ALTERNATIVES

Economists are fond of illustrating the problem of economizing with an economy that must choose between guns and butter. These symbolize any competing groups of commodities for which we might use our resources. Robinson Crusoe and Friday had to choose each day whether to catch fish or search for fruits and nuts. We must choose between houses and bombers; $100 billion spent on national defense means $100 billion less of tractors, food, and education in a full-employment economy.

The production-possibilities curve

Assume that our economy has a fixed stock of productive resources (land, labor, machines, and the like) and of technological knowledge about how to use these resources in producing the things we want. With these resources and this technological know-how, we can produce houses or bombers—military or civilian goods—or a combination of the two. To simplify, assume

Table 2–1
Production possibilities for houses and bombers

Alternatives	Houses (in Thousands)	Bombers (in Thousands)
1	1,000	0
2	800	15
3	600	28
4	400	38
5	200	45
6	0	50

that only those two commodities (or groups) can be produced.

Table 2–1 shows the hypothetical range of possibilities open to us. If we use all our resources to produce houses, we can build one million a year. Or if we use all our resources to produce bombers, we can have 50,000 bombers. In between, various combinations are possible—for example, 800,000 houses and 15,000 bombers, or 600,000 houses and 28,000 bombers, and so on.

The point of this table is to show the production possibilities open to us. Of course, bombers and houses are merely arbitrary examples. We might have used highways and refrigerators, or any other pair of products to illustrate the same point. The important thing to see is that there is a tradeoff between the two commodities. We can have more of one only by giving up some of the other.

It is convenient for many purposes to put the production-possibilities table in the form of a curve, or graph. This is done in Figure 2–1.

Economists use graphs a great deal, so it is important to understand how to read them. In Figure 2–1, we show thousands of houses along the horizontal axis, and thousands of bombers along the vertical axis. Each heavy dot plots one of the production-possibility combinations from Table 2–1. For example, the top dot shows that we can produce 50,000 bombers and no houses (alternative 6 in Table 2–1). The next dot shows we can produce 45,000 bombers and 200,000 houses, and so on for the other dots. The figure is merely a graphical representation of the table, with a curve connecting the dots.

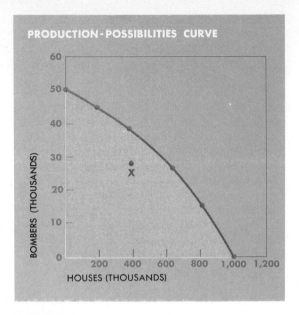

Figure 2-1
The curve shows how many houses, how many bombers, or what combination of the two we could produce with our limited resources.

Some applications

The production-possibilities curve can help illuminate a variety of economic problems. Suppose that, perhaps because of a depression, the economy produces only 28,000 bombers and 400,000 houses, as shown by the dot labeled *x* to the left of the production-possibilities curve. This dot shows that the economy is not fully utilizing its productive capacity, as in fact happens during depressions. To operate at point *x* is clearly to waste productive resources. We could have had an additional 200,000 houses and the same number of bombers, or an additional 10,000 bombers and the same number of houses, if we had employed all our resources. Point *x* shows the economy operating inside the production-possibilities frontier. We are inside the frontier when for some reason we don't fully utilize our productive capacity.

Now suppose that immigration occurs, so that we have more workers than before, or that scientists improve technology so we can obtain more output from the same amount of resources. Then there will be a new production-possibilities curve

to the right of the first-year curve. This is illustrated in Figure 2-2. The curve labelled "first year" is the same as in Figure 2-1. The curve labelled "second year" is farther out, to the right. This new curve for the second year shows economic growth. The economy can now produce a larger total output—more houses and the same number of bombers, or vice versa, or a combination involving more of both.

Suppose the economy tries to produce 40,000 bombers and 800,000 houses (shown by point *y*). Clearly, this is impossible. Production will fall short of one target or the other, or both. The economy cannot produce more than its production-possibilities curve permits.

COOPERATION AND COMPETITION IN A PRIVATE-ENTERPRISE ECONOMY

Let us focus first on the private, market-directed sector of the economy. How does it allocate our scarce production resources?

Figure 2-2
If a nation's resources expand or its technology improves, its production-possibilities curve moves out to the right. This expansion of productive capacity is the essence of economic growth.

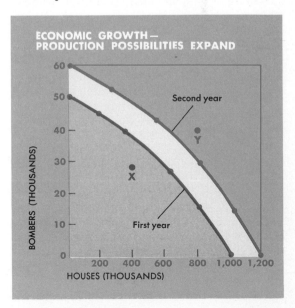

Consider New York City, teeming with eight million people crowded into a few square miles. As Bastiat, a famous economist, remarked about the Paris of a hundred years ago, here are millions of human beings who would all starve in a short time without a constant flow of provisions into the metropolis. Hardly one could support himself for more than a few days without help from the far corners of the nation. "Imagination is baffled," Bastiat wrote, "when it tries to appreciate the vast multiplicity of commodities which must enter tomorrow in order to preserve the inhabitants from falling prey to the convulsions of famine, rebellion, and pillage. Yet all sleep, and their slumbers are not disturbed for a single minute by the prospect of such a frightful catastrophe."

Every day, New York City gets hundreds of tons of meat, huge amounts of fresh vegetables, coal, oil, furniture. Every year, it gets millions of shirts, automobiles, rugs, nails, movies, and more other goods and services than you can think of. Yet no individual, business, or government agency plans it that way. The same is true, on a smaller scale, of every city and village throughout the country.

Man lives by cooperating with his fellow men. In all economics there is no more basic truth. And in the modern American economy, this cooperation is indescribably broad and complex. Yet this vast cooperative system, as a system, has not been consciously designed by man. No human director tells the 90 million workers in the United States where to work, what to do, or how to do it. On the contrary, each of the 90 million workers is motivated mainly by his own self-interest—to get the largest income he reasonably can and to get the most of what he wants by spending the money he earns. Yet somehow the system seems to organize itself, with a minimum of central planning or direction. Viewed from above, Adam Smith wrote 200 years ago, it is as if a beneficent invisible hand were guiding the competitive, private-enterprise system to allocate our scarce productive resources to produce the most of what we want at the lowest possible costs. Instead of chaos, somehow an extraordinary order comes from the attmepts of millions of citizens to look out for their own self-interests.

Man can organize, and indeed he has organized much. Tens of thousands of workers are employed in some large industrial plants. Often, many of these huge plants are joined together in a single organization. The General Motors Corporation, for example, spreads over the entire world, with more than 750,000 employees and annual sales of $45 billion. But in spite of the immense power of such huge aggregations, each business concern plays a tiny part in the total picture of organizing economic resources to satisfy human wants in our $1.5-trillion economy. And in spite of the great expansion of government controls, the private-enterprise economy still does the bulk of the job in its long-established, unplanned way—in contrast to the central plans that control our biggest rival, the Soviet economy.

HOW A PRIVATE-ENTERPRISE SYSTEM SOLVES THE BASIC ECONOMIC PROBLEMS

Even though you may be swallowing hard on the "beneficent invisible hand," patience! We shall examine the problems in due course. It is useful first to summarize in a systematic although oversimplified way, continuing to disregard government intervention, how a private-enterprise system allocates resources to solve four basic economic problems.

How it decides what to produce

Under a private-enterprise, competitive, market-directed system, consumers determine what is produced. We register our preferences by the amount of money we spend on various goods and services. The more you want something, the more you will spend on it and the higher price you will be willing to pay for it. This is how the price system decides which are the most important goods and services to produce. You vote for more Levis each time you buy a pair. Economists call this "consumer sovereignty," since consumer demands basically determine what shall be produced.

But one point is vital. In order to count, consumer demands have to be backed up with dollars. The price mechanism is hard-boiled, impersonal. It produces Cadillacs for million-aires when poor youngsters have no toys. Market demand reflects not necessarily how much consumers "need" goods and services, but how much they are willing and able to pay for them.

How it gets the goods produced

The goods and services consumers want get produced by businessmen in search of profits. They will make the largest profits by producing things whose prices most exceed their costs of production. Profit-seeking businessmen thus have an incentive to produce more when consumer demand bids up the price of anything. They equally have an incentive to reduce their costs of production, because that too will increase their profit margins. In producing more, businessmen will offer more jobs in those industries, and workers will be pulled into the production of the most-wanted goods because that is where they will be able to earn the largest incomes.

But, alas for the businessman! If competition prevails, whenever he succeeds with a high-profit venture, those high profits will lure other profit seekers into the same industry. Thus, although he may temporarily make big profits by introducing a new product or reducing costs without cutting prices, profit-seeking rivals will soon arrive on the scene to increase output and force prices down to a level where they just cover costs and a normal profit. Why does the businessman keep trying if he knows competition will eat away his excess profits? Because many businessmen are optimists, and he may make handsome profits while he leads his rivals.

Thus, the businessman is essentially a link between consumers and productive resources. His private goal is to make profits, but his social function is to organize productive activity in the most efficient (lowest-cost) way possible and to channel productive resources into industries where consumer demand is strongest. Profits are the mainspring of the system—the carrot in front of the profit seeker. In seeking profits, the businessman performs a vital social function.

This point is so important that it merits an example. In 1945, Milton Reynolds produced the first ballpoint pen. Although it only cost 80 cents to produce, he retailed it for $12.50, presumably because he thought he'd maximize profits by doing so. Consumers loved it, and profits were large. He apparently made about $500,000 per month on an initial investment of only about $25,000. But although the new pen was patented, the huge profits led others to produce similar ballpoint pens. They found they could undercut Reynolds's price and still make a juicy profit—and they did. By the end of 1946, there were nearly 100 ballpoint pen manufacturers, and retail prices were in the $3–$5 range. By 1948, ballpoint pens were everywhere and could be bought for less than 50 cents at most stores. Production costs had been reduced to 10–20 cents. Reynolds served an important social function in developing and introducing the ballpoint pen. He reaped a large reward—temporarily. Competition in the market soon made ballpoint pens available to everyone at a much lower price than Reynolds charged, partly because the competition eliminated much of the special profits on the new product and partly because costs were rapidly reduced under the pressure of competition. Adam Smith's "invisible hand" is easy to see in the ballpoint-pen case. No government plan was needed to get the job done.

How it distributes products

Who gets the goods that are produced? The market system allocates them to consumers who have the desire and the income to buy them. There are two steps in this process.

The first is the distribution of money incomes. **We earn our incomes primarily by working for businessmen, helping to produce the goods and services consumers want.** The prices we get for our services depend on how much we are worth to the businesses we work for, in helping to produce what consumers will pay for. Competition forces the businessman to pay each of us about what he contributes to the sales value of what he helps produce. **The incomes we receive in this way largely determine what we can afford to buy.**

The second step is the distribution of goods and services to those with money income to pay for them. Each consumer will pay a price that measures how important the product is to him.

The price of each commodity is bid up by competition among consumers until the buyers least able and willing to pay for it are eliminated, and the supply goes to those with the strongest demand for it. This does not necessarily mean that low-income buyers are eliminated completely. Often it means that they can afford only a few units at the price established, while higher-income groups can afford more. Poor people buy steaks, but not many. In other cases, such as mink coats and country estates, the poor are eliminated from the market. Here again, prices play a vital role; they ration final products among consumers on the basis of who will pay most for each product. Those unwilling to pay at least the full cost of producing any commodity will get none in the long run.

How it decides between present and future economic growth

We can use our productive resources either for current consumption or for capital accumulation. By building new factories and other productive facilities, we can shift the economy's production-possibilities curve out. In the same way, we can send our children to school rather than putting them directly to work, thereby investing in "human capital" and increasing the nation's future productive potential at the cost of lower present output. Here again, the private-enterprise system largely depends on the self-interest-dominated decisions of consumers and profit seekers to allocate resources between present and future.

In money terms, to grow we must save some of our incomes and invest some in building new factories and the like, rather than spending everything on consumption. In our individualistic economy, each person and each businessman decides how much of his income to save. If these savings are a large proportion of our total income, investment in factories and people can be large relative to current consumption and the economy will grow rapidly. If we save only a small proportion of our total income and investment is correspondingly small, the growth in productive capacity will be slow.

Solving all the problems simultaneously

These four major decisions are not made separately. The economic system is a huge, interconnected set of markets, each with many buyers and sellers. All four big decisions are simultaneously the outcome of millions of free, individual choices by people largely concerned with their own private welfare. How all these complex decisions are simultaneously and continuously made and how they interact in our economic system is the core of the study of economics.[1]

The organizers: self-interest and competition

The essence of the private-enterprise, market-directed economy is this: In pursuing their own self-interest, individuals unintentionally do more to advance the social good than if that had been their primary interest. Self-interest is a powerful incentive for consumers, laborers, businessmen. Indeed, it might well lead to chaos if it were not constrained and directed to the common good by the force of competition, which Adam Smith properly stressed as essential to the working of the "invisible hand." But with competition, Smith and his followers argue, in a private-enterprise economy, absence of government planning and control does not mean chaos, but rather order in an economy so complex few human minds can comprehend it—and so complex that it is government planners, however well-intentioned, who are likely to produce chaos rather than order.

Suppose, for example, that instead of relying on self-interest and the market, you were made Grand Economic Planner for the nation. How, for example, if you did not rely on Milton

---

[1]In mathematical terms, it may be helpful to think of all these interdependent markets and decisions as a large system of simultaneous equations. In fact, one of the first clear perceptions of the entire process was by Leon Walras, one of the first mathematical economists, who saw it just that way about a century ago.

Reynolds and his competitors, would you decide how many ballpoint pens to produce? How many cars, in what sizes, colors, and makes? How many airplanes? Would you run a consumer poll on each, gathering some 200 million preferences per commodity? How would you decide how each good was to be produced, and who should work at what in the economy? To whom would you allocate the dirty jobs of mining coal and collecting garbage, and to whom the pleasant ones of managing and teaching in universities—and how would you assure adequate incentives (rewards) for each? How many air conditioners would you produce, and who would get them? To suggest some of the more difficult problems, how would you plan for the machine tools, labor, and raw materials needed to produce the factory equipment and computers that in turn are needed to produce the right number of such final products as refrigerators, gasoline, and women's dresses? If you trace back the decisions needed to plan completely the production and assembly of all the parts that go into a modern jetliner, you quickly get up into the millions of separate decisions.

It is important to recognize that "self-interest" may include much more than just maximizing one's money income. I may prefer the air-conditioned comfort of a bank clerk's job to earning much more as a plumber. Or I may prefer to work as a Peace Corps volunteer at a low wage to earning much more as an auto salesman. Or I may prefer lots of leisure to a full-time job. If so, my self-interest is maximized by working in the bank, joining the Peace Corps, or taking only part-time jobs. If I am a businessman, I may get much satisfaction from producing only top-quality products, providing good working conditions in my plant, and eliminating polluting smoke from the factory stack. And I may feel that in the *long run,* profits will be maximized if I act as a good citizen in dealing with employees, customers, and neighbors, rather than squeezing out every dollar of profits I can get now. The self-interest argument does not necessarily imply that only money income and current profits serve to motivate us in individual and business activities. We will examine this point in more detail presently. For the moment, be careful not to construe self-interest too narrowly.

The incredible American economy

Understanding how a market-directed economy solves the basic economic problems is a number one task in studying economics. But this is a lesson that must not be overlearned. We can understand and admire the way the private-enterprise, market-directed system ticks on year after year, impersonally solving its millions of intertwined problems, and still not shut our eyes to its failings. For failings there are—drastic ones, some people think. The invisible hand must have slipped up, they say, to produce depressions and inflation, huge profits for billion-dollar corporations, all that smog outside the window, filthy streets, and decaying slums.

It's easy to find things wrong with a largely private-enterprise, "unplanned" economy like ours. The preceding paragraphs present a drastically oversimplified picture of reality. Today's world is different from that of Adam Smith, and a lot of people feel that Smith was way too optimistic, that any market-type economy will fall short on many scores. In particular, they cite modern technology and the huge corporations apparently now needed to obtain low-cost production. How are these consistent with Adam Smith's competition? But thoughtful observers, even including such critics as Karl Marx, have long been impressed by its remarkable efficiency in producing the infinite variety of goods and services consumers want. And don't be too quick to write off competition even among the giants. Only one of the nation's ten largest corporations in 1900 is still on the list. General Motors, Ford, and IBM didn't even exist then. International Mercantile Marine and Central Leather Company, numbers 4 and 7, are long since departed. (For the data, look ahead to Table 27-2.) And even if a firm doesn't have much direct competition, potential substitutes always lurk just around the corner—aluminum for steel, semiconductors for vacuum tubes.

THE IMPORTANT ROLE OF GOVERNMENT

We have left government out of this overview so far. But it is time now to turn to the important role government plays in the modern American economy. There are a lot of doubters about that "invisible hand." A little history can help provide perspective.

The British, French, and American revolutions that gave us political democracy provided the ideological framework for economic individualism. Political democracy and modern private-enterprise economics arose in the same historical setting, part of the same broad sweep of history. Individual freedom and self-interest were at the core of this revolution of the eighteenth and nineteenth centuries: In politics, every man should be free to vote as he pleased—to look out for his own interests at the ballot box. In economic life, every man should be free to seek his own self-interest—to work where he wished, and to spend his money on whatever he wanted most. Self-interest and individual initiative were the driving forces for the common good. The ballot box in politics and the market in economics were the ultimate, impartial arbiters of differences of opinion.

This philosophy assigned to government only a small role. The less government interfered with individual freedom, the better. This was the laissez-faire philosophy of the nineteenth century. To be sure, individualism never went so far as to exclude government intervention altogether. True freedom necessarily involves some restrictions on freedom. A society that gave you freedom to murder your neighbor whenever you felt like it would be anarchy.

So it was in the economic sphere. Clearly, the government needed to establish and enforce a few "rules of the game." One basic rule was the guarantee that no one should be deprived of life, liberty, or property without due process of law. Others were the long-standing rules against fraud and against default on contracts. But the rules should be simple, and government had no business in economic life outside these rules.

As time passed, mass production and the modern corporation swept away the possibility of an economy of tiny, highly competitive firms. Powerful unions replaced the individual worker in bargaining with big business. Throughout the economy, concentration of economic power and reliance on group activity spread. Many new products brought objectionable side effects, such as smoke from factory chimneys and polluted rivers.

Moreover, with a wealthier, more complex society, people wanted more things that couldn't be readily provided through private profit incentive in the marketplace—highways, national defense, and the like. Thus, besides setting the rules of the private-enterprise game, governments were called on to do more and more things directly. At the same time, common concern grew for the individual who couldn't take care of himself. Government "welfare" and social security largely replaced private poor relief. Willingness to abide by the impersonal income allocations of the market steadily diminished. Desire to "do something" about booms and depressions became widespread. A subtle shift in the meaning attached to the words "individual freedom" marked the changing tenor of the times. The rules of the game have grown into an intricate mass of law and administrative controls. The government has become a major participant as well as the umpire in the economic game.

The mixed economy

Today, ours is a mixed economy—still basically private-enterprise, but with large areas of government control and direct participation. It's up to you to decide whether you like what's been going on—whether you want to move back toward the traditional private-enterprise system, or on toward a more administered, planned economy, or in some other direction.

This is no ivory-tower, academic issue, dreamed up for college classrooms. It is a basic issue of public economic policy today. Clearly, the government must step in to provide national defense and highways, but how about slum clearance and public housing? How heavily should government tax upper-income families to guarantee minimum incomes for all, whether they work or not? Nearly everyone agrees that the government must act to minimize inflationary booms and depressions, but how far should it regulate private decisions on wages and prices in the process? These are big national policy issues of the 1970s and 1980s. You will have to answer them if you are to vote intelligently. The issue of how much private enterprise, how much government, is everywhere.

CAPITALISM TODAY

"Capitalism" is a term often used but seldom defined. Words so used often generate more heat than light, and over the years, "capitalism" has become a fighting word for many who advocate and oppose it. Recourse to dictionaries and learned treatises of economists and historians unfortunately does not resolve the dilemma of just what we should mean when we say "capitalism," for these authorities are far from agreement.

So this book generally uses such less colorful but more descriptive terms as the "private-enterprise" and "market-directed" system in referring to the big private sector of the modern American economy. Still, a brief note on "capitalism" may be useful. Many writers agree that a capitalist economy is marked by at least these major characteristics:

1. Private ownership of property prevails.
2. Property has been accumulated by individuals and businesses, and this accumulated "capital" provides incomes to its owners.
3. Individuals and businesses are free to seek their own economic gain; the profit motive plays a central role in economic life.
4. Some writers add to this list a highly developed banking and credit system.

This list gives the basic flavor of such a system. But the lines are hazy. How free must individuals be to own and use property if a system is to be termed "capitalism"? Is an income tax that takes away part of your income each year, depending on how much you earn, consistent with capitalism? Does a federal law that limits the monopoly power you can attain violate the essential freedoms of capitalism?

We shall be concerned with all these questions and others like them. But there is little to be gained by debating just which measures are and which are not consistent with "capitalism" when there is so little agreement on what the term means. Instead, we will concentrate on trying to decide whether particular policy measures are good or bad on their merits, taking into account the different social goals held by different groups in America today. If you like the term "capitalism," use it. But don't let your emotional attachment or antagonism toward it get in the way of thinking objectively about the issues.

ALTERNATIVE SYSTEMS

Obviously, not everyone agrees that a private-enterprise, market-directed economy is the best. Indeed, in two nations alone, China and the USSR, more than a billion people live in communist economies, with government ownership of productive resources and central planning and control of economic activity. Thus, a centrally planned, "command" economy, with the major choices made by the central government, appears the main practical alternative to the private-enterprise, market-directed economies of most Western industrial democracies.

There are two other alternatives for small, nonindustrial economies. They may make their decisions and organize their activities on the basis of custom, or tradition. Many of the early American Indian tribes used this basis; many African tribes still do. Or a very small, non-industrial economy might make its decisions in true democratic, "community" style, with everyone participating. This is the model suggested by some young people who want to opt out of our modern complex industrial society—a sort of modern Walden Pond. But neither of these alternatives offers a feasible alternative in organizing a huge, immensely complex political economy like ours.

The following chapters analyze mainly the American economy and the problems it faces. But throughout, comparisons with more centrally planned, "command" systems are suggested. And in the final chapter, we shall undertake a full-fledged comparison of the way these different systems operate as a practical matter, to place the American system, its achievements, and its shortcomings in perspective.

REVIEW

This chapter has introduced more important concepts that will be reused many times throughout the book. Recheck especially the following to be sure you have them firmly in mind:

productive resources
technology
specialization
exchange
scarcity
economizing
production-possibilities
   curve

production-possibilities
   frontier
tradeoffs
private-enterprise
   economy
market-directed system
economic growth
laissez-faire
capitalism

1. Why are we in America generally so well off (per capita annual production over $7,000) while some two billion people in the less-developed nations are so poor (per capita incomes under $200)?
2. Does this chapter help explain the wide differences in per capita outputs shown in Table 1–1? Explain how.
3. "Man lives by cooperating with his fellow men. In all economics there is no more fundamental truth than this." "The core of the competitive, free-market system is the driving urge of most men to get ahead, to rise above their fellow men."

    Are these two statements about the American economic system consistent or contradictory? If they are consistent, how do you reconcile their apparent contradiction?
4. The price system allocates resources where consumers spend their dollars. Thus the rich man has far more influence than the poor man. Is this consistent with the democratic presumption that all men are equal?
5. In a market-directed system, who decides how many jobs there will be in each industry? Who should make the decision?
6. "The economics of scarcity is obsolete in our affluent society. There's plenty for everybody." True or false? Define "scarcity," "plenty," and "everybody" in answering. Do we still face the need to economize?
7. Suppose American college students were to develop a craze for pork-chop sandwiches, instead of hamburgers. Trace through as carefully as you can the impact of this craze on the allocation of the economy's productive resources. Would such a shift be good or bad?
8. Leading TV stars receive annual salaries in the hundreds of thousands of dollars. Many baseball players receive $50,000 to $100,000 for the eight-month season. Yet an intelligent, skilled, hardworking nurse or farmer will ordinarily earn no more than $10,000 or so per year.
    a. Are such differences predictable results of the free-market system, or do they reflect breakdowns in the functioning of the system?
    b. Do you approve of such inequalities in the distribution of income? Why, or why not?

Good parking spaces on the Stanford campus, as on most campuses, are at a premium, especially on rainy days. Stanford has about 11,000 students—of whom about half live on campus—about 1,000 faculty, and perhaps 8,000 nonteaching "staff members" and other such employees. Sampling suggests that perhaps 10,000 cars may seek parking on a rainy day.

While there is no simple way to indicate the number of desirable parking spaces available (desirability depends on where one wishes to go on the campus), there are perhaps 2,000–3,000 spaces that are very convenient to different parts of the central campus. Including all outlying areas of the campus (perhaps 4–6 blocks from classrooms and offices), there are a large number of additional parking spaces available.

For many years, by tradition the best parking spaces were exclusively set aside for faculty members (via free "A" parking stickers), and the next most desirable ones for staff members (via free "B" stickers). Other reasonably close-in spaces were allocated to students at a small charge ("C" stickers). Distant campus parking was free to all. Special parking was provided for physically disabled students.

Not surprisingly, students frequently complained, as indeed did faculty and staff from time to time, since on rainy days there was an excess of cars for all three reserved parking areas. (1) Some argued that all parking should be on a first-come, first-served basis, except for physically handicapped students, faculty, and staff members. (2) Others favored maintenance of the three reserved areas, but allocating spaces within each by random lots to avoid the overflow situation. (3) Still others advocated a market price system, with stickers in each class sold to those who would pay most for them, or even (4) abolition of the faculty-staff-student distinction, with sale of stickers to anyone at a price that would roughly equate the number of stickers with the number of spaces available. Views differed widely as to what should be done with the fees collected under suggestions 3 and 4. (5) Still others argued that none of these approaches was obviously superior, and that, in accordance with democracy, students, faculty, and staff should all elect a special parking committee to decide who should get the spaces each year.

How should Stanford allocate the limited supply of desirable parking spaces?

3

ECONOMICS: FaCTS, THeory, and FanTasy

Chapters 1 and 2 have laid out some of the main problems of economics and suggested the broad outlines of the way our modern American economy goes about solving these problems. We need to turn now, briefly, to a look at how economists go about analyzing economic problems and the economy. That is the purpose of this chapter.

STRAIGHT THINKING IN ECONOMICS

Straight thinking is hard work. Few of us have acquired the careful, orderly mental habits and disciplines demanded by straight thinking.

For many people, straight thinking is especially difficult in economics. Not that economics is inherently more difficult or more complex than many other fields. But economics is so mixed up with our everyday lives that, without realizing it, we have accumulated a mass of opinions, ideas, hearsay, and half-truths that subtly dominate our minds when economic questions arise.

It's not surprising then that most people have views on economic questions. They are in the newspapers every day, and in every election campaign. Moreover, the tendency for every man to be his own economist is strengthened by the fact that economics is close to the pocket-book. It is especially hard to be objective about things that affect us intimately. But merely living in the economic world doesn't make us experts on how the economy operates, any more than having teeth makes us experts on dental health and how to fill cavities. Few people consider themselves experts on bridge building just because they drive across a bridge every day going to work, or on physics just because they live in the physical world. Yet many people somehow feel that anyone who has "met a payroll" is an expert on economics. Alas, it ain't necessarily so!

Economics as an empirical science

Economics is an empirical science; it is concerned with real-world data. Like other sciences, it has to develop theories about the complex world in which we live. But these theories, if they are to be useful, must rest on validated facts and relationships about the world they are analyzing.

The most apparent fact about economic reality is its complexity. There are millions of businesses, over 200 million consumers, hundreds of thousands of different products, multiple stages in the production of nearly every product. Faced with this overwhelming complexity, we obviously have to find some way of simplifying things to manageable proportions. Thus, the first job is to simplify.

Use of simplified models: theory

In order to simplify, the economist, like other scientists, begins by developing an analytical framework, or model, of the reality he wants to analyze. This model focuses on the main elements and relationships he is studying. **Such simplified models are often called "theories."** They make no pretense of being accurate descriptions of the economy. If they were completely accurate, they would defeat their own purpose by getting back to all the detail. Instead, they are intended as simplified abstractions of the main elements of the reality to which they apply.

The notion of a model or theory can be illustrated by a noneconomic example. Suppose you want to understand how a bicycle works—a theory of its operation. You could study every detail of a single bicycle, or a large number of them, examining the tires, the handlebars, the sprocket, the paint, and so on. But if you could instead get a simple diagram, or a stripped-down working model of a bicycle, you'd get to the essentials quicker. This diagram wouldn't be concerned with all the details of paint, style, quality of steel, and so on. Instead, it would show the fundamental parts of the bicycle—wheels, frame, sprockets, driving chain, brake—and the basic relationships among these parts.[1] People have used such a model of a bicycle many times, and its predictions have been thoroughly validated by empirical evidence. The theory, or model, is thus a good one in that it helps us to understand the way a bicycle works and to predict the consequences of changing the main variables—for example, the sizes of the two sprocket wheels. The theory "works."

So it is in economics. A model is a simplified diagram indicating the main elements in any situation, and the main interactions among these elements. The more firmly validated these relationships are by empirical observation of many cases, the safer we feel in using them in our model. Some models are very sketchy, merely identifying the main elements and loosely stating their interrelationships. Others are more elaborate.

An economic model may be stated as a diagram, and many graphs are used in the pages ahead. It may be stated in words, as in the bicycle case here. Or it may be stated in mathematical terms, but except for some simple algebra and geometry used in the diagrams, we shall use little mathematics.[2] Most economic models can be stated in any of these three ways.

Last, it is important to emphasize that the economist doesn't apologize for the fact that his

---

[1] In terms of basic physics, it might help to have explanatory notes on the diagram indicating that the principles of mechanical advantage are used, with the pedal being a second-class lever and the relative sizes of the gear wheels being crucial in determining the speed and power resulting from any given foot pressure on the pedals.

[2] However, there is a set of special mathematical appendixes at the end of the book for students familiar with calculus. References are indicated in the chapters to which these appendixes apply.

theories don't describe the real world precisely. On the contrary, like any other scientist, he says that any theory is a skeleton, a framework, to help simplify the intricate complexity he is attempting to understand and predict.

"Other things equal" and "equilibrium"

The real world is far too complex to analyze everything in it at once. Thus, in common with many other scientists, economists use the concept of holding "other things equal" in order to analyze the effects of one thing at a time.

In the chemistry laboratory, we hold "other things equal" through controlled experiments. We put two elements (say, hydrogen and oxygen) together in a test tube **under controlled conditions,** and get water if the proportions are 2 to 1. In the bicycle example above, we hold friction, gravity, air pressure, and various other factors constant as a first approximation (or assume them away altogether) in analyzing the way the bicycle works.

So it is in economics. One of the simplest and most fundamental theories in economics is that people will, other things equal, buy more of any good or service at a lower price than at a higher one. If the price of T-bone steak goes up, consumers will buy less steak. Housewives will complain bitterly, blame the greedy supermarket or farmer, and switch to lower-priced alternatives. But note that this is a safe prediction only if other things are equal. Suppose at the same time you get a big raise. Then you may well buy *more* T-bones, even at the higher price. Or suppose the prices of pork, veal, and fish all go up even more than steak. Obviously, **the "other things equal" assumption is critical.** In the real world, other factors may not stay constant; but by assuming temporarily that they do, we can analytically isolate the effects of the higher price for steak.

This idea is closely related to the concept of **equilibrium,** which is also widely used by other scientists. In chemistry, for instance, after we've combined hydrogen and oxygen to form water, this equilibrium state is maintained until something disturbs it. In the same way, economists generally think of the economic system as tend-

ing to move toward a new equilibrium whenever some disturbing change occurs. In talking about equilibrium, scientists are nearly always holding many other things constant to focus on the equilibrium of some part of the total system.

Consider a simple example. In economics, we generally theorize that people spend their incomes to get the greatest possible satisfaction from their expenditures. (Any other assumption obviously raises difficult questions as to why they don't switch to a satisfaction-maximizing spending pattern.) If people are allocating their incomes to maximize their satisfaction, given their incomes, we say they are "in equilibrium." Now suppose the government cuts taxes, so everyone's after-tax income rises. Consumers will now be out of equilibrium. With larger spendable incomes, they will start spending more, and probably saving more as well, until their new spending pattern again maximizes their satisfactions, given their new higher incomes—that is, they adjust their spending and saving until they are again in equilibrium. Similarly, suppose you are in equilibrium, buying four pizzas per week, and the price of pizzas goes up sharply. You are thrown out of equilibrium and will presumably cut back your weekly pizza consumption, substituting some other, stable-priced goody to restore your equilibrium. **By equilibrium, we mean a situation in which those involved are satisfied to keep on doing what they are doing. In equilibrium, there's nothing at work to change the economic behavior under consideration.**

To repeat, "equilibrium" and "other things equal" are purely analytical concepts. No one believes that in the real world, "other things" do always stay equal when we are trying to analyze the behavior of the economy, or that economic units are always in equilibrium. Use of these concepts simply helps us to trace through what *would* happen *if* all "other things" in the economic system remained unchanged until the disturbance (for example, the higher price for steak) had fully worked itself out. But don't think that this makes economic analysis just an intellectual game. Such analysis can give us powerful conclusions as to the **direction** in which consumers, businesses, and the economy will move in response to different private actions or government policies, even if it can't tell us precisely what the end result will be in the complex real world.

Facts and theory in economics

The social scientist, unfortunately, can seldom run controlled experiments to validate his theories. We can't get everything else in the economy to stand still while we lower income taxes 10 percent to see what would happen. Nor can we get reliable results by putting a sample of a few people in a closed room and lowering their income tax 10 percent. So how can economists be sure their theories are right—for example, that people do buy more of any product at a lower price than at a higher one, other things equal?

The answer is that when we state a theory, we then go out into the real world to see how well it works. What, for example, will happen to aggregate consumer spending in the economy, other things equal, if the government cuts consumers' income taxes by $1 billion? This is a very important question if we want the government to help get the economy out of a recession.

Suppose we theorize ("hypothesize") that the amount people spend on goods and services in any year will depend stably on the after-tax, or disposable, income they have in that year. We hypothesize that consumer spending is a "function of" disposable income—that consumer spending depends on, or is predictably related to, the disposable income consumers receive. Economists write this functional relationship:

$$C = f(DI)$$

where C stands for consumption, f for "a function of," and DI for disposable income. To say that C is a function of DI means that it depends on DI.

Suppose now that we get records showing the disposable incomes and consumption spending of a large number of families over the past ten years. Looking at these records, we find that most families have spent about 90–95 percent of their disposable incomes on consumption in most years, but there are many exceptions. For example, young families seem consistently to spend more, families in their fifties spend less, and retired families spend more. (These differences make sense: Young families are just starting out, buying new durable goods and raising babies, so they are able to save little; older families, once their homes are established and their children raised, find it easier to save out of their incomes; retired families have reduced incomes and must spend their past savings.) We also find that in years when incomes have risen rapidly, the percentage spent on consumption falls below .9. (Again, this seems reasonable, because it takes time for people to adjust their spending to new higher incomes.) And so we might find other special forces at work. But overall, for the average of all families in periods of reasonably stable, prosperous times, consumption hovers around 92–94 percent of disposable income. The value of f in the equation above will generally be .92 to .94.

From this statistical analysis we could not safely predict the behavior of any particular family without knowing a lot about that family. But on the hypothetical evidence cited, we would be increasingly comfortable in saying that, *other things equal,* in reasonably stable, prosperous periods, consumers *as a group* will spend about 93 percent of their disposable income on goods and services, given a reasonable amount of time to adjust to the new income.

This is an oversimplified theory, but it suggests the way in which we must go about building up empirical evidence on economic behavior. Actually, as we shall see later, consumer behavior is more complex than this, and we need a more elaborate theory to explain and predict it satisfactorily. Indeed, even if we found that consumers, on the average, had *always* spent just 93 percent of their disposable income on consumption in the past, we still couldn't be *sure* they would do so in the future, because they *might* change their spending–saving patterns. But through intensive empirical analysis of consumer behavior in the past, we can greatly increase our confidence in the predictions we make. And modern statistical techniques make it increasingly possible for us to use past information as a basis for predicting the future. Economics, like any other empirical science, must continually develop new theories, test them out against the real world, and reformulate them in the light of empirical evidence.

Facts and fantasy in economics

Robert Malthus, one of the first economists, saw economics as a dismal science. He predicted ("theorized") that population growth would persistently outrun the earth's capacity to feed it, so that man's standard of living would seldom rise much above the subsistence level. Malthus has proved to be spectacularly wrong in America and the Western world, but much more nearly right in many of the less-developed nations. Why did his theory largely square with the facts in some places, but turn out to be fantasy in others? Indeed, fantasy seems as common as fact in economics in the newspapers and everyday conversation. Consider some simple examples.

Even in rich America, between 10 and 15 percent of the population are "poor," with incomes below the government's officially established poverty level of about $5,500 (in 1975) for a four-person urban family. Clearly, it would be desirable to get rid of poverty. Fantasy: If Congress would only pass a law requiring that everybody receive a minimum wage of $3 an hour, poverty could be abolished in one fell swoop. Taking about 2,000 hours as a standard full-time annual job, this would provide each worker with an income of about $6,000 per year, above the poverty level. Fact: It sounds great, but it's in considerable part fantasy. Congress could pass such a law, but Congress could not make businesses keep on hiring everyone who now has a job, much less hire others looking for jobs, at the $3 hourly wage, which is much above the wage currently paid many workers. Indeed, we would predict quite the contrary from the fact that most businessmen are in business to try to make a profit. It would pay them to hire *fewer*, not more, workers at the higher wage per worker, and to substitute machinery for labor. Workers who kept their jobs at $3 per hour would indeed be above the poverty level, but unemployment would probably rise, other things equal. Moreover, of the approximately 24 million people

living in poverty in the United States in 1975, some 60 percent were children, women with small children, elderly people, and others who could not take a job. Thus, even paying a minimum wage of $3 per hour to all workers looking for jobs would leave a large portion of the poverty problem unsolved.

Second example: Nowadays, just about everybody agrees that we need to clean up the environment—cleaner air and cleaner water. Fantasy: If only greedy, profit-seeking businesses would become socially minded and stop polluting the air and water, the problem would be solved. Fact: Alas, pollution is a complex problem. The government's Council on Environmental Quality estimates that for the next decade it will take a minimum of $275 billion to clean up the environment enough to meet the minimum standards contemplated by government requirements in 1975. All corporation profits after taxes in 1975 were only about $75 billion, of which about half was paid out in dividends to stockholders. Total dividends paid by all businesses in the ten years ending in 1975 were less than $275 billion. Thus, it's clear that expecting "greedy" businesses to simply clean up all pollution runs up against some serious problems. For businesses to absorb all the costs would use all the dividends that were paid to stockholders, and would put many firms out of business. There is little reason to suppose that profit-seeking businesses will simply absorb pollution-control costs. On the contrary, they will mainly pass the costs on to consumers—that is, to all of us—which is where the burden of cleaning up the environment is going to have to rest for the most part.

Moreover, businesses account for only a fraction of the total pollution in our system. Municipal sewage, primarily handled through government agencies, does more to pollute the waterways of our nation than do industrial firms. Farmers using fertilizers and pesticides on their crops, which help to produce low-cost food for all of us, did more to make Lake Erie a "dead lake" than did the businesses pouring waste into it, as the residues of the fertilizers ran off farmland into the lake. Alas, it's the old story. With cleaner air and water, we will have more expensive food, steel, and automobiles, and we will have less of other things we would like. In economics, we are always having to choose between alternatives.

But sometimes the fact is a happy one when the fantasy is a false black cloud. Fantasy: A rising public debt means inevitable economic collapse and disaster, or at least inevitable runaway inflation. Fact: At the simple factual level, this fantasy has been persistently refuted for the last half century. The public debt has risen from less than $20 billion in the 1920s to over $600 billion today, yet the American standard of living has risen persistently over the period. Total output is about five times what it was in 1929, and per capita real income (that is, income adjusted for inflation) is about three times what it was in 1929. The number of Americans holding jobs has risen from 48 million to 85 million over the same period. The growing national debt in the United States has been associated with rising total economic activity, and the debt today equals only one-third of total gross national product, proportionately much less than in 1929. Moreover, most of the government bonds are held by Americans, so, from the point of view of the public as a whole, the debt represents a transfer among Americans when we pay interest on it or when we pay off parts of it. In a growing economy, both private and public debt can grow apace with total jobs and production without causing severe economic problems. This is not to say that there are no difficulties with the rising national debt; there are some. But it is to say, as in the other cases above, that the sweeping statements of doom here are fantasy, just as the sweeping statements of an easy road to a clean environment and the end of poverty are fantasy on the other side.

Conclusion: Economics is a field where it is easy to be led astray by the daily news and casual conversation. A major purpose of this book is to give you the analytical concepts and theories, as well as the facts, to see through a lot of the economic fantasies that you will encounter in the years ahead.

ECONOMICS IN A DEMOCRACY

Throughout your life, economics will play a major role in determining what you do and how happy you are doing it. If there are depressions or inflations, you will not be able to escape them. Your income will depend largely on how effectively you participate in the economic process. Thus, from a purely selfish point of view, it will pay you to understand how your economic system works.

But the main reason citizens in a democracy need to understand the economic system is that they are voters as well as active participants in the economy. Not long ago, governments didn't interfere much in economic life, but that time has passed. Today, almost everyone agrees that the government should provide national defense, social security, education, and a score of other services not forthcoming through the private-enterprise economy; that it should regulate the supply of money; that it should protect consumers against the excesses of monopoly; that it should prevent depressions and inflations. Many people believe the government should do more—provide medical protection for the poor, support the prices of farm products, legislate minimum wages, even guarantee full employment.

This is a book on "political economy." It is concerned with using economic analysis to find answers to the problems above and to many more. The goal is to understand how our economy works now and how to make it work better. The political economist doesn't sit on the sidelines. He is interested in what to do about the big and little problems we face.

But if you expect to find the answers in this book to what you or the government should and should not do, you're in for a disappointment. **The job of a course in economic analysis is to give you the tools and the background for making up your own mind on the important economic issues of the day, and to teach you _how_ to think about economic problems—not to tell you _what_ to think. Economics is a way of thinking, not a set of answers.** Better understanding of how the system works will go a long way toward making you a more intelligent citizen. But you should recognize from the outset that even with a thorough understanding of economics, not everyone will come out with the same answers on problems of public policy. This is because we have different ideas on where the nation ought to be headed. Some people, for example, think that avoiding inflation is the most important thing. Others believe that assuring everyone a reasonable minimum income should have first priority. Any respectable economist will advise the government to do different things, depending on which of these objectives is placed first. Such conflicts among the goals of different individuals and groups are an inescapable part of today's economic problems.

SOME TOOLS OF ECONOMIC ANALYSIS

Theories, or models, are a main tool of economic analysis. Most theories consist of an interlinked series of functional relationships, as in the theory described above that aggregate consumer expenditure is a function of (depends on) consumer disposable income. A good theory has both a rationale, or reason, and empirical support. For example, the consumer expenditure theory seems *a priori* reasonable; if people's after-tax incomes rise, it is plausible that they will spend more on consumption. And if we check the facts for recent decades, we will find that in general, the hypothesized relationship holds, other things equal. Since such functional relationships play such an important role in modern economics, they bear a little further preliminary attention.

Functional relationships and graphs

If we want to show, or examine, a functional relationship between two variables, we customarily plot them against each other on a graph. One example is the relationship between consumption and disposable personal income above, which we shall examine in a minute. But take a simpler case first.

Suppose we want to show the functional relationship between the price of pizzas and how many will be bought in a week at your local pizza parlor; $d = f(p)$, where d is the demand for pizzas and p is the price per pizza. Other things equal (that is, incomes and prices of all other products remaining unchanged), we theorize that people will buy more pizzas at lower than at higher prices. Table 3–1 shows such a relationship. We can readily show this functional

Table 3–1	
Weekly demand for pizzas at local pizza parlor	
Price per pizza	*Number bought*
$2.00	30
1.75	40
1.50	50
1.25	60
1.00	70

relationship on a graph, as in Figure 3–1, with price per pizza on the vertical axis and the number of pizzas bought on the horizontal one. The curve connecting the dots slopes down, from northwest to southeast; we call it a demand curve, since it shows how many pizzas will be bought (demanded) at each price, *other things equal.* We can obviously read the same information in the table and the graph. The downward slope of the curve shows the functional relationship between the declining price and the increasing number of pizzas sold, other things equal.

These data are, of course, hypothetical. If,

Figure 3–1
The dots and the curve connecting them show how many pizzas people will buy per week at different prices. They show the functional relationship between price and the quantity of pizzas bought.

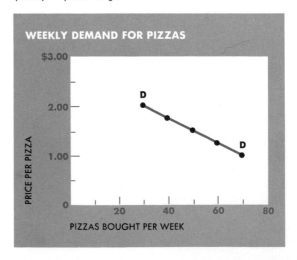

however, we wanted to determine this functional relationship in the real world, we could try to get weekly sales data for our pizza parlor at different prices, other things equal, and see whether in fact the relationship is like the one shown in Figure 3–1. (Actually, such data might be hard to come by because of the difficulty of holding all other relevant things equal, so we might have to be content with a rough approximation.)

Another, slightly different sort of functional relationship was graphed in Figure 2–1, the production-possibilities curve of Chapter 2. This showed the relationship between houses and bombers in our hypothetical economy, where to get more of one, we had to be content with less of the other.

Figure 3–2 shows a different kind of functional relationship—that between the nation's disposable personal income and consumption expenditures for ten years, with disposable income on the horizontal axis and consumption expenditure on the vertical one. Each dot shows the relationship for one year, from 1964 through 1974. For example, the highest and furthest-right dot is for 1974, when DPI was $980 billion and consumption expenditure was $902 billion. The general relationship is clear; as DPI increased, consumer spending rose roughly in proportion. But note that we have not held other things equal over the ten years, so we don't have a satisfactory test of our theory; we cannot necessarily conclude that the rising disposable income was the cause of the rising consumer expenditure. All we know is that over these years, in fact, they rose very closely together, for whatever reason.

Note that these graphs of functional relationships are of two different sorts. Figure 3–1 is a hypothetical demand curve that shows how many pizzas *would be* bought *if* prices had been as shown, other things equal. This is an analytical graph, to help us examine the relationship between the two variables. Figure 3–2, on the other hand, plots actual data that permit us to examine whether *in fact* the relationship between the two variables was as we theorized over the decade shown. Thus, we might say that Figure 3–1 is a statement of a theory, and Figure 3–2 is a test of whether the facts were consistent with the theory it states. Both purposes are perfectly

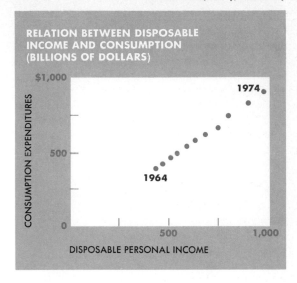

RELATION BETWEEN DISPOSABLE INCOME AND CONSUMPTION (BILLIONS OF DOLLARS)

Figure 3–2
The dot for each year shows the relationship between the nation's disposable personal income and its spending on consumption. The dots show a quite stable functional relationship between the two during the decade.

legitimate, but it is important to be sure which is being done at any given time.

Correlation and causation

When two variables move closely together, we say they are closely correlated. For example, disposable income and consumption expenditure are obviously highly correlated in Figure 3–2.[3] Price and number of pizzas sold are also closely, but inversely, correlated in Figure 3–1.

Can we, therefore, safely infer that rising disposable income has *caused* the accompanying increases in consumer expenditure in Figure 3–2, or that lower prices *cause* an increase in pizza purchases in Figure 3–1? Both theories seem plausible, but the data certainly don't prove that they're

[3] Modern statistics provides a "correlation coefficient" in such cases that gives a precise measure of the closeness of relationship between the variables. For details, see the section on correlation and regression in any elementary statistics text.

right. In Figure 3–2, for example, the close correlation between the two variables may reflect the fact that they are both determined by some third variable—for example, changes in the amount of money in the economy. Or the close inverse (negative) correlation in Figure 3–1 may reflect changes in other prices (say, at competitive restaurants) or changing consumer incomes rather than any direct causal impact of prices on sales **A high correlation between the variables involved can help to strengthen our belief in any theory, but a high correlation alone cannot prove causation. Assuming that it can is one of the commonest fallacies in dealing with economic problems.**

Some warnings on historical data and charts

Economists use historical data and charts incessantly, as they should, for history is the basis of empirical support for, or rejection of, alternative theories. But historical data must be used with care. There is an old saying that one can prove anything with statistics, and the saying has an uncomfortable kernel of truth. By selecting the right historical series for the right sample of years, one can often seem to demonstrate results quite different from those supported by other related series for different years. For example, had we plotted the years 1929–49 in Figure 3–2 (including the Great Depression and

World War II), the correlation between disposable income and consumer expenditure would have been far less close and stable. Or suppose we are interested in whether unemployment is becoming more or less volatile in recent years. Consider Figure 3–3, which shows two alternative presentations of the data for the *same* period, 1960–75. The left-hand section shows variations in the *unemployment* rate; it shows a substantial variation in the level of unemployment. But the right-hand section, which shows the percentage of the labor force *employed*, gives an impression of very little variation. Both series depict the same economy during the same period. The trick comes in the vertical scale used to show the variations in unemployment; the left-hand portion shows only the unemployment data, so changes are large relative to the 0–10 scale used. The right-hand scale shows the entire labor force, so variations in the number unemployed look very small (unemployment = labor force − number employed). And we could easily have made the unemployment variations seem even larger, by using a vertical scale for the left-hand portion that ran only from 10 percent down to 3 percent, rather than to zero. Try it for yourself and you'll see how different is the impression now given by the plotted unemployment series.

The purpose is not to warn you never to trust historical data; that would be foolish. But whenever you find historical data or charts used to demonstrate particular theories or arguments, it is a useful precaution to look carefully at the evidence to be sure it says what it seems to say.

Figure 3–3
Both halves of the figure show the same data. Note the different impression conveyed by the two ways of presenting the data; unemployment seems much larger and more volatile from the left-hand portion.

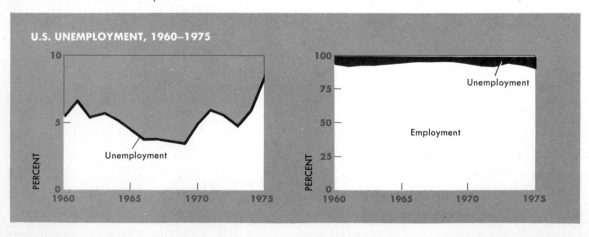

REVIEW

Concepts to remember

The following important new concepts were introduced in this chapter. Be sure you understand them:

theory (or **model,** or **hypothesis**)	**other things equal**
empirical evidence	**equilibrium**
functional relationship	**correlation**

For analysis and discussion

1. What is a "theory"? A "model"?
2. Why should we assume "other things equal" in economics when we know they aren't that way in the real world?
3. We suspect that ten-year-olds' demands for ice-cream cones depend on the temperature, their allowances, and the price of ice-cream cones. Can you write an equation showing the demand for cones (D_c) as a function of price in this case? How about demand as a function of temperature? What "other things" do you hold constant in each case? How might we go about determining the relative importance of the explanatory variables for ten-year-olds in a particular community?
4. Suppose you observe a close correlation between the annual production of corn per acre in Iowa and Illinois. Can you safely conclude that one causes the other? Can you think of a third variable that might be the cause of both?
5. According to the "laws" of probability, if you toss an unbiased penny 100 times, it will come down heads and tails about 50 times each. How does this compare with an economic "law"—for example, that, other things equal, people will buy less of any product at a higher than at a lower price?
6. "Theory is all right for college professors, but not for me. I'm a practical man. Give me the facts and they'll speak for themselves." Do you agree or disagree with this sentiment? Why? How do facts speak for themselves?
7. (*Based on the Appendix*) Analyze the validity of the following statements. In each case, explain carefully why you accept or reject the statement.
   a. What goes up must come down. (True about prices?)
   b. Human beings are all different, so you can't generalize about them. Just look at any five of your friends.
   c. In the past, booms have always been followed by depressions, so we can look forward to a real depression in the next few years.
   d. The way for farmers to get higher incomes is to raise larger crops. (Consider the position of the individual farmer and all farmers combined.)

APPENDIX

Some common fallacies

The preceding sections have outlined the positive job of straight thinking in economics. But the buzzing, booming, confusing world of economics seems to produce controversy everywhere. This appendix is intended to suggest some of the common fallacies lying in wait for the unwary, in addition to the warnings in the chapter. Many of these fallacies, incidentally, show up everywhere you go, not merely in economics.

Wishing it were so   One of the most common of human frailties is to believe the things we want to believe. The boss believes his employee-education program is opening the worker's eyes to the necessity of large profits for continued prosperity—and he may be a surprised man the next time the wage contract comes up for renewal if he's just been wishing it were so. Remember the wishful thoughts on poverty and pollution control in the text above.

This is one of the most insidious fallacies. We tend to talk to people who agree with us, to read the newspaper that reports things the way we like, and to run away from information and conclusions that are painful to us. Confronted with two interpretations of an event, one favorable and the other unfavorable, most of us will choose the favorable one. The union members believe the company could pay lots higher wages if only it would. Top management believes that all right-thinking people see that management is right and labor wrong in most wage disputes. Just wishing it were so?

Post hoc, propter hoc   Suppose there's a bad depression. The government pays out large sums on public-works projects. Six months later, we're on the way up. Was the government spending the cause of the recovery?

Many people would say yes. The government spent, and recovery came. What could be clearer? But maybe the recovery was on its way anyhow, and the government spending did no good at all. The observed evidence tells us that government spending *may* have caused the recovery. But the mere fact that one event precedes another doesn't necessarily mean the first caused the second. They may both have been caused by some third factor. To assume that causation can be determined so simply is the fallacy of post hoc, propter hoc—"after this, therefore because of it." Keep your ears open and notice how often people rely on this sort of reasoning, especially in discussing economic problems. (Note also that this is closely related to the correlation-causation trap warned against in the chapter.)

The fallacy of composition   Next, perhaps the most dangerous fallacy of all in economics—the fallacy of composition. Suppose one rancher increases his cattle production. He can reasonably expect that the increase will bring him more money when marketing time comes around. But suppose that *all* ranchers decide to raise more beef cattle this year. Will they get more money for the cattle in total? Quite possibly not. More cattle coming to market will, other things equal, push down the price of cattle. If prices fall a long way because of the increased production, the total revenue to all cattle farmers may be less for the larger output of cattle. Clearly, what is true for one rancher alone is not necessarily true for all ranchers taken together.

Consider another example. Saving is obviously a sensible procedure for most families. But suppose that in a depression, everyone decides to increase his savings. What this will mean, other things equal, is that everyone cuts down on his consumption expenditures. Unless someone spends more, merchants' sales will fall off. People may lose their jobs. Incomes fall, and with lower incomes, people may actually find they are able to save *less* than before.

There are examples elsewhere too. Suppose you're in a crowded hall and can't see the stage very well. So you stand on your chair and can see beautifully. But now suppose everyone else stands on his chair too. As a result, no one is better off. You can't conclude that what worked for you will work for the whole crowd.

To assume that what is true of one part will necessarily be true of the whole is the fallacy of composition. It may not seem reasonable that when we aggregate everybody together, everything may go topsy-turvy from the way it looked when we considered one person alone. But it does in economics, in a surprising number of cases. It's easy but fallacious to assume that what you know about the individual family or business is necessarily true for the whole economy.

Reasoning by analogy   One of the most effective ways to explain something is to use an analogy. For example, in trying to explain the effect of continued repression on human behavior, you may say, "Not letting someone express his feelings is like building up steam in a boiler." This conveys a vivid impression; if those feelings aren't let out, the person is going to burst like an overheated boiler.

Is the analogy a useful means of communication, or a fallacy? It may be either, depending on how closely a human being with repressions actually corresponds to a steam boiler. It would be difficult to communicate without using analogies, but don't let the analogies lead you farther than can be justified by careful analysis. Analogies are everywhere. For example, are big businessmen in economic life robber barons?

Generalizing from small samples   "I know that businessmen are greedy; my grocer is always trying to palm off wilted vegetables and overripe fruit, and look at the huge profits big businesses make." Or, "I know that dogs like bones, because I've seen lots of dogs and they all like bones!" Such statements are a favorite way of backing up your position that you "know for a fact."

To generalize about all businessmen or about all dogs on your personal small sample is extremely dangerous, unless you have some convincing reason to suppose that this tiny sample is representative of the whole universe of grocers or dogs. There is probably no commoner fallacy than that of generalizing unthinkingly from small samples. We are continually learning from what we see and do; this is the commonest way of extending our knowledge. Thus, we inevitably build up tentative generalizations about the world from our everyday experience. But anyone's limited experience may or may not be typical. The safest generalizations have been established by careful, systematic observation of a large number of cases. When is a fact a fact? The problem of empirical evidence again.

Black, or white, or gray   There is another, related fallacy. If you are not wary, you can go astray by (explicitly or implicitly) assuming that there is no middle ground between two extremes. On a foggy day, someone asks, "Is it raining?" You reply, "No." "Oh," he retorts, "you mean it is sunny." But of course it may just be cloudy. Often there is a perfectly logical middle ground between what appear at first glance to be two mutually exclusive alternatives; the alternatives stated may not exhaust the possible situations. The wise observer of the economic scene is one who sees the grays in their proper shadings—not one who sees everything as black or white, true or false.

CHAPTER 4

BUSINESS FIRMS AND MARKET SUPPLY

In a private-enterprise economy, the profit-seeking business firm is at the center of the economic process. The businessman decides what will be produced in response to market demand, and how much of it. In the process, he decides how many employees to hire and how much he is willing to pay them. Within the rules established by society, his decisions most directly determine how effectively the private-enterprise economy utilizes its resources.

Anybody can see that many business firms in the modern economy are a long way from the myriad of small competitors envisaged by Adam Smith two centuries ago. Not only are General Motors, Ford, General Electric, AT&T, and other such well-known firms industrial giants, but hundreds of other firms like them have sales of hundreds of millions or even billions of dollars per year. They employ thousands of people, and obviously have some degree of market power in setting wages and market prices. At the same time, small firms, not unlike those envisaged by Smith, number in the millions—especially in agriculture, retail trade, and the service industries (for example, dry cleaners, doctors, lawyers, and so on). Over the last century, very large firms have accounted for a slightly increased share of the total economy's activity. But this increase has come almost entirely in manufacturing, which now provides only about 25 percent of all the jobs in the country. In the services, which are the most rapidly growing sector of the economy, small businesses have prospered and the dominance of the giants is far less widespread. It is this potpourri of large and small businesses that has the job of responding to consumer demands and using our resources effectively to produce what consumers most want.

It is the purpose of this chapter to describe briefly the major forms of business enterprise that supply most of the goods and services in the modern American economy, with some attention to small businesses but more to the huge corporations that dominate the news headlines. If you want to understand the role of big business in America and how much economic power it really has, you need to know something about what corporations are and how they operate. Especially if you sympathize with the critics of big business—that it holds too much power over both economic and political life—you need to know something of how such businesses are organized, how they are managed, and how you can understand their financial statements.

ENTREPRENEURS, PLANTS, FIRMS, AND INDUSTRIES

Business enterprises are called "firms." John Brown and his family run a farm; the farm is a firm. United States Steel is a firm, with steel mills in many cities, with iron and coal mines, with ore ships on the Great Lakes. The important characteristic of the firm is that it is owned and controlled essentially as a unit, however diverse its parts.

The function of making fundamental policy decisions in a firm is generally called "entrepreneurship." The entrepreneur decides when to establish a firm, what goods to produce, how the concern will be financed, what price policies to follow, when to expand or contract, and so on. A firm is thus a business unit under one coordinated "entrepreneurship."

In the independent corner grocery store, the proprietor is the entrepreneur. He decides whether to borrow funds to remodel his store, what prices to set on his merchandise. In bigger businesses, it is harder to pick out the entrepre-

neur. For example, who is the entrepreneur of AT&T? The three million stockholders? The board of directors? The finance committee of the board? The president? Here it is impossible to pick out any person or group of persons as the entrepreneur; the functions of the entrepreneur are performed in a coordinated way by the various individuals and groups concerned.

A "plant" is a building or a group of buildings, along with other more or less fixed physical equipment, that are used together in producing something—such as a shoe-manufacturing plant or an auto-assembly plant. The Ford Motor Company is a firm with plants in Dearborn, St. Louis, Kansas City, and so forth. John Brown's farm, on the other hand, is a firm with only one plant.

An "industry" is harder to define. Usually, we use the word to mean all the producers of any "commodity." Farmer Brown is part of the wheat industry if he produces wheat, part of the corn industry if he produces corn; he may be in both simultaneously. General Motors is part of many industries; it produces a wide range of autos, trucks, diesel engines, refrigerators, and hundreds of other products. The trouble comes when we try to be precise. Shall we consider a "motor-vehicle industry," or an "auto industry," or a "low-priced auto industry"? For many purposes, how finely we divide up commodities is not a major problem. You will seldom get in trouble if you let common sense be your guide and if you stick to the same definition of "commodity" and the associated "industry" in analyzing any problem.

The shifting legal organization of firms

The legal forms of business firms have changed with the times. When small-scale business was the rule, the individual proprietorship was dominant. This is a simple arrangement in which an individual puts up the money, starts his own business, runs it himself, and has the profits and losses to himself. There are still more individual proprietorships in the United States than any other form of business organization—some nine million in all. Of these, three million are in agriculture, and most of the rest are small-scale retail concerns and service enterprises, such as cleaning establishments, filling stations, doctors, lawyers, and so on. Ninety-nine percent of all farms are still single proprietorships, but the 1 percent that are corporations do about 25 percent of all the business. In wholesale and retail trade, the 80 percent of all firms that are single proprietorships do only about 25 percent of the business; remember Sears and the big grocery chains.

As the need for larger capital funds increased, partnerships became popular. In these, two or more people become joint proprietors—usually with joint provision of funds, joint management, and joint financial responsibility. This arrangement has substantial advantages over the single proprietorship, especially in raising funds, but it still falls short of providing enough capital for really large-scale business operations. And it shares one serious drawback with the single proprietorship: The partners are personally liable for all the debts of the business. Thus, in most cases, each partner is personally liable to an unlimited amount for the deeds of the other partners—a somewhat precarious position at best, and definitely not suited to drawing in funds from absentee investors. Partnerships are not very important in the United States today, although there are some 900,000 in existence. About half of them are in retailing; the rest are widely scattered.

THE MODERN CORPORATION

The modern corporation, which was conceived to meet the financial-managerial needs of large-scale business and to avoid the drawbacks of partnerships, has become the dominant form of American business enterprise. Although there are only about 1.5 million business corporations, they do the bulk of the nation's business, employ over 50 percent of the workers, account for about two-thirds of the nation's privately produced income, and pay out over 50 percent of the total national income. They do virtually all the business in public utilities, manufacturing, transportation, and finance; around half in trade and construction; but less than a quarter in services and agriculture.

The biggest modern corporations are Goli-

aths. In 1975, for example, the assets of the American Telephone and Telegraph Company (the world's largest business) were $80 billion. Those of Exxon (formerly Standard Oil of New Jersey) and of General Motors were $33 and $22 billion, respectively. Their 1975 sales of $45 and $36 billion, respectively, were larger than the entire gross national product of most of the world's nations. In all, in 1975 there were 203 nonfinancial corporations with sales over a billion dollars.

Many financial corporations (banks and insurance companies) are as large, even though most of their assets consist of investments in corporate and government securities and of direct loans to businesses and individuals. In 1975, the total assets of the Prudential Life Insurance Company, the largest insurance company, were $37 billion. Those of the Bank of America, the biggest bank, were $70 billion. Thus, modern finance and industry are heavily concentrated in the hands of large firms (more details in Chapters 26 and 27).

Nevertheless, there are still many more small firms than large ones. Only about one American worker in four works for a large corporation. The share of the total national income produced by all private corporations is now only about 52 percent, and has declined gradually since hitting a peak of 55 percent in the 1950s, as government and other nonprofit service industries (for example, health and education) have expanded. The market share of the giants in manufacturing has grown gradually since World War II, but their profits haven't grown as fast as their sales. Ours is still a very mixed economy, not one dominated only by giant corporations.

What are corporations?

A corporation is an organization that exists as a "legal person" apart from the individuals who own and control it. A corporation may carry on business in its own name, enter into contracts, sue and be sued, own property, borrow and lend money. In general, it may as a business unit do all the things that any individual person may legally do in business.

As was indicated above, the corporate form of organization was developed mainly to facilitate financing and management of large business firms. Briefly, its advantages are the following:

1. Stockholders who invest money in corporations have no liability for the debts of the corporation; at worst, they can lose their original investment. Thus, corporations can obtain funds by selling "stocks" and "bonds" to many investors who merely want to earn a return on their investments without further financial involvement. These advantages are spelled out below.

2. In a corporation, management is delegated to a board of directors elected by the stockholders. The directors in turn supervise the salaried officials who actually run the business. Thus, the individual stockholder need not concern himself with the details of managing the concern unless he wishes to—quite another story from the continuous attention required in a single-proprietorship or partnership. Freedom to delegate power and responsibility to expert "managers" is essential to the operation of today's mammoth business enterprises.

3. Corporate securities are readily transferrable. No matter how many individual stockholders die or lose interest in the corporation, the business can go on unaffected.

Financing corporate enterprise— stocks and bonds

Corporations obtain funds by selling "stocks" and "bonds" to savers. Individual investors who buy these securities may be part owners of the corporation, or they may simply lend money to the business. Stocks represent ownership in the corporation. Bonds represent money lent to the corporation by bondholders. There are many variations within each class, and at the margin they run together. The most important differences are (1) the priority of the security owner's claim on the income of the enterprise, and (2) the owner's right to vote on personnel and corporate policy, and hence his power to control the corporation.

Common stockholders are the owners of a corporation. They own the company's stock. They have the right to elect the board of directors and hence to control the policies of the corporation. They are entitled to any income

remaining after prior claims of creditors have been met. If the corporation is dissolved, they get all that remains (if anything) after everyone else has been paid. The common stockholders are the "residual claimants" to the corporation's income and property. They gain the most when income is high, and they are the first to lose when things go badly.

Profits paid out to stockholders are called "dividends." Although the profits of the business "belong" to the stockholders, often the corporation does not pay them all out, but instead reinvests part in the business. This is called "plowing back" earnings. Whether the profits are paid out or reinvested, however, they accrue to the benefit of stockholders, since reinvested earnings increase the value of the business.

Bondholders are creditors of the corporation. When corporations want to borrow large sums for long periods, they commonly issue bonds that are sold to people or institutions with funds to invest. Bonds are promises by the corporation to repay the funds to bondholders at some specified future date, with a set rate of interest.

If you own a bond, you are merely a creditor. You ordinarily have no voting power to elect directors and control the corporation's policies. You take less risk than the stockholders do, since the interest on your bonds must be paid before they get any dividends. On the other hand, you will receive only your set rate of interest no matter how big profits are. Bondholders also have a prior claim on the assets of the corporation in case of liquidation.

Preferred stockholders have a position intermediate between common stockholders and bondholders. Preferred stock sometimes carries a vote; more often it does not. Typically, it has a set rate of dividends—say, $6 per share—that must be paid before any dividends can be paid on the common stock. It also has priority over common stock in case of liquidation. But preferred stock stands behind bonds in priority of claim on income and assets.

Who controls the corporations?

Suppose you own 100 shares of General Electric stock. How much control do you have over how General Electric is run?

The answer is, for practical purposes, none. Not because anyone is cheating or hoodwinking you—least of all the GE management, which makes a continuous effort to keep stockholders informed and to get them interested in company affairs. It is because of a combination of factors. In the first place, you own only a tiny fraction of 1 percent of the company's stock. Moreover, you don't and can't know much about the operations and internal policies of GE, a $15 billion corporation producing thousands of products, most of them involving complex scientific processes and know-how. Besides, GE pays good dividends on your 100 shares, and that's what you bought them for. You haven't the slightest intention of spending a lot of money and time on an obviously fruitless trip all the way to Schenectady, New York, to try to tell the management how to run GE, or to throw them out for a new management.

Even if you don't go to the annual stockholders' meeting, you are entitled to send a "proxy," a person of your choice whom you designate to vote for you. Before each annual meeting, you will receive from the management a proxy form, suggesting that you designate someone to vote for you in case you don't plan to be present. You may throw the proxy in the wastebasket. If you do send it back, the chances are you'll designate the person suggested—partly because you don't know anyone else to designate—thereby giving the present management the votes to reelect themselves.

Surprisingly enough, you will be acting like the typical stockholder when you do this, even though you may assume there are many other interested "big" stockholders who are keeping a sharp eye on the operating management from a stockholder viewpoint. AT&T now has three million stockholders, no one of whom owns as much as 1 percent of its stock. U.S. Steel has over 300,000 stockholders; Westinghouse, over 175,000. Many big corporations now have more stockholders than employees. On the other hand, a few well-to-do people and large investment institutions (like pension and trust funds) own large blocks of stock in many well-known companies.

This widespread dispersion of stock ownership, coupled with the lethargy of most stock-holders, goes far to explain the substantial control over most large corporations exercised by small groups of active stockholders, and often by the operating management "insiders" who may themselves own very little stock. This divorce of active control from ownership is a major development of modern business enterprise. It is probably inevitable in the large corporation. It certainly does not provide a "democratic" government of corporation affairs in most cases, however good the intentions of the management on this score.

Of course, stockholder lethargy does not always exist. In some smaller companies, stockholders take an active interest in the conduct of the business. Even in large corporations, conflicts and sharp struggles for proxies sometimes occur, with control of the corporation at stake. But for the most part, management or other minorities retain effective control without holding more than a small fraction of the voting stock. They are on the scene; most of the stockholders are far away and little interested. Less than 10 percent of the voting stock is enough to assure working control of most major corporations.

A 1966 study of the 200 largest nonfinancial corporations in the United States found that in 85 percent of the companies, control was exercised by the management without material stock ownership. None of the corporations was directly controlled by a private family through ownership of over 50 percent of the stock, and in only 12 percent was direction exercised by a particular family or other special group of stockholders with a substantial share of the stock—say, 20 to 50 percent. By contrast, in 1929, 50 percent of the top 200 companies were controlled by families or other special groups through substantial blocks of stockholdings, while only 44 percent were management-controlled. Clearly, there has been a change in the way our major corporations are controlled.[1]

What proportion of the public owns corporation stock? There are now about 25 million individual stockholders in "publicly owned" corpo-

[1] The data are from R.J. Larner, "Ownership and Control in the 200 Largest Nonfinancial Corporations," *American Economic Review,* September 1966. See also R.A. Gordon, *Business Leadership in the Large Corporation* (Washington, D.C.: The Brookings Institution, 1964), Chap. 2.

rations, plus probably one to two million more in "privately owned" companies whose stock is held entirely by family or private control groups. The comparable total for 1955 was only six or seven million. Thus, perhaps 20 percent of all adults now own stock in business corporations. But most of them own only a few shares. Many more own stock indirectly, because part of their insurance and pension-fund reserves are invested in common stocks.

The bulk of corporate stock is held by a small number of well-to-do families. In 1971, the richest 1 percent of all families owned about 50 percent of all stock owned by individuals, and nearly 40 percent of all stock. The richest 10 percent held about 75 percent of all individually owned stock and almost two-thirds of the total.[2] Thus, although this concentration of ownership has been persistently lessening for several decades, voting *power* (although not necessarily *control*) over the corporate sector is held by a small proportion of the public.

Financial control groups in the modern economy

By means of large investments, mergers, interlocking directorates, and "insider" control, a few major financial groups may exercise substantial control over groups of large corporations.

Some are family groups—the Rockefellers, Mellons, and du Ponts. Others are alleged to work through linkages between banks and the concerns they help to finance. Such financial control groups today are said to operate mainly through interlocking directorates, which include directors of banks and nonfinancial businesses. But modern antitrust laws and Securities and Exchange Commission (SEC) regulations have substantially circumscribed their power, certainly their power to abuse their positions. For example, no individual can now serve as a director of competing corporations.[3]

A huge and growing volume of corporate stock is held by financial institutions—pension funds, bank trust departments, mutual funds,

[2] For details, see "Stock Ownership in the United States," *Survey of Current Business,* November 1974.
[3] See P.C. Dooley, "The Interlocking Directorate," *American Economic Review,* June 1969.

insurance companies, and the like. They probably now hold nearly a third of all stock. To date, such financial institutions have seldom intervened directly in corporate management. But as savings pile up in such institutions, their potential power becomes enormous, far exceeding that of the wealthiest families. Even corporations' and unions' own pension funds, amounting to billions of dollars, are now being invested in corporation stocks, posing intriguing problems of future corporate control. Who should watch over the managers of these vast accumulations of funds?

CONCLUSION

Some critics of modern capitalism and big business argue that the U.S. economy is dominated by corporate giants and a few greedy capitalists who control them. They say there is no resemblance between this reality and the competitive forces on which Smith's "invisible hand" relied to regulate the avarice of businessmen.

The facts of business size are reasonably clear; we shall return to them in detail in Chapters 26–27. There are, indeed, many huge corporations that produce a wide variety of necessities and luxuries. There are also many markets supplied by multitudes of smaller firms. The American trillion-dollar economy is so vast that even corporate giants are tiny by comparison. GM's total sales are only about 3 percent of GNP. Exxon, the world's largest industrial corporation, nonetheless has only 7 percent of the U.S. gasoline market. As we shall see, absolute size confers some types of economic power, but it is the intensity of competition that matters most for getting consumer demands met efficiently. Where large firms must compete actively with others, as many must do domestically and internationally, their economic power is greatly constrained. The degree of competition in different markets will thus be a recurring, central question in the chapters ahead.

This is not to say that corporate size per se does not give other types of power to managerial and financial control groups. It does. But again, it is important to look at the facts with care.

Many big business concerns are now managed both more efficiently and with a greater view to the social welfare than they were under the direct control of owner-operators. If you have $5,000 invested in IBM, it is doubtful that your interests would be better protected were Messrs. Frank Cary and John Opel (the top executives of IBM) larger stockholders than in fact they are, or if you could personally participate in the management of the business. Similarly, today's growing group of professional managers seems more concerned with serving the public well than was the typical captain of industry a half century ago. Nor is there much evidence that most dominant large stockholders use their positions to exploit other stockholders. Indeed, many investors prefer such companies as du Pont and Alcoa partly because they want the watchful guidance given these companies by the duPont and Mellon families.

There is little likelihood that the modern corporation, with its vast accumulations of capital and its professional management divorced from most stockholders, will soon disappear from the American scene. Its advantages are too great. The problem is how to make such businesses efficient suppliers of the goods and services we as consumers want. This is the problem to which we now turn in examining how demand and supply interact in different markets.

REVIEW

Concepts to remember

The concepts in this chapter deal largely with institutions and legal forms. Be particularly sure that you understand the following:

entrepreneur	corporation
plant	common stock
firm	dividends
industry	"plowed-back" earnings
individual proprietorship	preferred stock
partnership	bond

For analysis and discussion

1. Explain the difference between stocks and bonds.
2. Suppose you are planning to set up a small dry-cleaning shop. Will you be better off with a single proprietorship, a partnership, or a corporation as your legal form of business? What are the main considerations involved in choosing?
3. Single proprietorships and partnerships predominate in retailing and agriculture, while corporations dominate the manufacturing industries. How do you account for these differences? How can you reconcile the statement above with the great success of such retail corporate giants as Sears, Roebuck and J.C. Penney?
4. Public-opinion polls repeatedly indicate that the majority of the public view common stocks as a speculative and somewhat uncertain investment. How do you account for this fact, in view of the great growth in the aggregate value and earnings of American corporations over the past century?
5. If you are a stockholder in General Motors, would you prefer to have earnings paid out to you as dividends or directly reinvested by the management? Why?
6. Should individual stockholders in business concerns take a more active part in the management of the concerns involved? Why, or why not?
7. (*Based on the appendix*) Construct the profit-and-loss statement of the Amalgamated Widget Company for 1976 from the following data:

	(000's omitted)
Materials used	$ 400
Net sales	2,500
Selling costs	150
Dividends on common stock	50
Provision for income taxes	180
Wages and salaries paid	400
Interest paid on bonds	20
Real estate taxes	50
Administrative costs	300
Depreciation	150
Dividends on preferred stock	0
Maintenance and repairs	200

8. (*Based on the appendix*) ABC Corporation reports the following data on its position as of December 31, 1977. Construct its balance sheet. Note that the figure for retained earnings is missing and must be computed.

	(000's omitted)
Buildings and equipment	$ 400
Inventories on hand	200
Bonds outstanding	250
Cash	200
Accounts payable	250
Common stock	400
Accounts receivable	450
Goodwill	10
Retained earnings	
Reserve for taxes	60
Loan from bank	180
U.S. government bonds	50

APPENDIX

The elements of business accounting

In order to understand the workings of modern business, you need to know something about the elements of business accounting. Although the details of accounting are complex, its fundamentals are simple. Only a knowledge of these fundamentals is essential for our purposes.

The Balance Sheet A balance sheet is a cross-section picture of the financial position of a firm at some given point of time. It is an instantaneous snapshot. A second sort of picture, discussed below, is an "income" or "profit-and-loss" statement that summarizes the firm's operations over some period of time.

The balance sheet of any business rests on a fundamental equation. One side of the balance sheet shows what the business owns—its assets. Exactly corresponding to the value of these assets must be their ownership, which goes on the other side of the balance sheet. Obviously, the two are always equal—the balance sheet always balances.

It is not easy to say just *who* "owns" the assets of the business. At the one extreme, the common stockholders are considered the "residual owners"—that is, the ones who would receive all the cash left over if the business were liquidated and its debts (liabilities) were paid off. But this statement makes it clear that the various creditors of the business (for example, the bank that has loaned it funds or the supplier from whom it has bought on credit) also have a claim on the assets. Such creditors, to whom the business owes money, are at the other extreme of the claimants on the business's assets—they get their funds first. Bondholders, whose interest is contingent on satisfactory earnings, have a less-preferred claim on the assets. Plainly, the line between "creditors" and "owners" is indistinct. The two groups shade into one another as a continuum of claimants on the business's assets.

Fundamentally, the balance sheet reflects the basic accounting equation (or identity) that Assets = Liabilities + Net worth; or, put the other way around, that Net worth = Assets − Liabilities. That is, the business is worth to the stockholders what assets they would have left over if all the liabilities were paid off.

Table A is the balance sheet of the General Electric Company, as of December 31, 1974. (A number of smaller items are omitted, to simplify the picture.) The left-hand side lists all the assets of the company—everything of value that it owns. The right-hand side lists all claims against these assets, broken down into two groups: first, its liabilities (what it owes), and second, its "capital" or "owners' equity" accounts (sometimes called its "net worth" or "proprietorship") on that date.

ASSETS   Once you see the basic equation underlying the balance sheet, most of its items are self-explanatory. For convenience, assets are often arranged beginning with the most liquid (the most readily convertible into cash) and ending with the least liquid.

The amount shown for each asset is its estimated value as of the date of the balance sheet. Cash was obviously worth exactly the amount shown. But inventories, for example, are often carried at their cost, which may turn out to be higher or lower than their actual value on that date. Accounts receivable may

---

Table A

GENERAL ELECTRIC COMPANY[a]

Balance Sheet, December 31, 1974
(In Millions of Dollars)

Assets			Liabilities & owners' equity		
Current assets:			Current liabilities:		
Cash	$ 315		Short-term borrowings	$ 645	
Marketable securities	57		Accounts payable	696	
Accounts receivable	2,594		Accrued taxes, etc.	1,465	
Inventories on hand	2,257		Other	1,074	
Total current assets		$5,223	Total current liabilities		$3,880
			Bonds outstanding & other		1,465
			Total liabilities		$5,594
Other assets:			Owners' equity:		
Investment in affiliated companies	$1,005		Common stock	$ 704	
Plant and equipment	2,616		Retained earnings	3,000	
Other	562		Total owners equity		3,704
Total assets		$9,369	Total		$9,369

[a]Based on GE annual report. Some minor items are combined for simplification and numbers are rounded, so they may not add exactly to totals.

include some noncollectible items, so they are not necessarily worth quite what they are listed at, and so on. The value placed on plant and equipment, as we shall see, is particularly susceptible to the vagaries of managerial and accounting judgment, because the current value shown is generally nothing but the original cost of the assets less an estimated amount of depreciation.[4]

Some companies show as an asset "patents and goodwill," which is obviously an estimated figure, a more or less arbitrary valuation determined by the company's officials and accountants. The item is so obviously intangible, even though of tremendous importance for such well-established products as Coca-Cola and Lucky Strike, that it has become accepted conservative business practice to place a very low value on it. GE carries such "intangible" assets at a nominal figure.[5]

LIABILITIES AND OWNERS' EQUITY The liability side seems a little more tricky at first glance. "Short-term borrowings" are mainly funds borrowed from banks. "Accounts payable" are debts owed to suppliers. "Accrued taxes, etc." are tax liabilities and other liabilities that have been incurred but have not yet been paid. "Bonds outstanding" are liabilities that may not come due for a much longer time.

"Owners' equity" (net worth) consists of two main items on this balance sheet. Part of the company's funds were obtained by sale of common stock. The amount shown is the amount for which the stock was originally sold (although this is not always so).[6] GE has issued no preferred stock. "Retained earnings" are profits of the company that have not been paid out as dividends to stockholders, but instead have been reinvested in the company.

There is no reason to suppose that these past profits now repose in the cash account. More likely, as

[4]See the discussion of "depreciation" charges in the following section.

[5]United States Steel and American Tobacco (Lucky Strike), for example, carry "goodwill and patents" at $1. Coca-Cola, on the other hand, carried goodwill, trademarks, formulas, and so on, at their cost—$56 million in 1974.

[6]In the 1800s, it was common practice to set a fictitiously high value on the capital stock issued. Part of this stock was issued to original founders who provided not money but goods and services that were overvalued. The term "stock watering" in reference to this practice came from the then-common practice of inducing cattle to drink as much water as possible just before being marketed in order to temporarily increase their weight. Although supervisory control now exercised by the U.S. government's Securities and Exchange Commission has made such watering very difficult for stocks "listed" on the major exchanges, it can still be done with unlisted stocks.

part of the firm's regular operations, they have been "plowed back" into inventory, plant and equipment, or some other assets. Or they may be reflected in a reduced level of the firm's liabilities. **It is essential to understand that there is no direct correspondence between individual items on the two sides of the balance sheet. Any attempt to link up individual items directly will lead to fallacious conclusions.**[7]

The income (profit-and-loss) statement The income or profit-and-loss statement is the accountant's summary view of a firm's operation over some period of time—say, a year.

Table B shows General Electric's profit-and-loss statement for 1975, the year following the balance sheet shown in Table A. This is a straightforward account of the income received during the year and what was done with it. The first line shows GE's income from sales in 1975. Then the expenses of producing the goods and services sold are deducted, which gives GE's operating profit for the year.[8] GE had some other income (mainly, from its investments in other, partially owned companies and interest on consumer credit extended), and some other expenses (mainly, interest on its bonds). These figures are shown separately. This gives total profits before income taxes. Then federal income tax liability is deducted, which gives GE's net profit after taxes of $581 million for 1975.

The last part of the statement shows how GE allocated this profit. About half was paid out as dividends; the other half was reinvested in the company, shown as retained earnings. Thus owners' equity (net worth) is now $288 million higher than if all the profits had been distributed to the stockholders. Common stockholders—the corporation's "owners"—may thus be as well off one way as the other. In one case, they get cash dividends; in the other, the value of their investment accumulates. Such plowing back of earnings has long been commonplace in American industry, and some industrial giants such as Eastman Kodak and Ford have grown almost entirely through reinvestment of earnings.

One warning about the profit-and-loss statement: The income and costs shown are not necessarily **cash** receipts and outlays; the profits are not necessarily **cash** profits. The distinction between cash transac-

[7]The common argument that higher wages should be paid out of accumulated retained earnings is an example of such an inadequate understanding of the elements of accounting.

[8]The "Net sales" item corresponds to the revenue from sales shown by the "demand curves" in the following chapters; the expenses correspond to the costs analyzed in Part 3.

Table B

GENERAL ELECTRIC COMPANY

Income Statement for Year Ended December 31, 1975[a]
(In Millions of Dollars)

Net sales		$13,399
Manufacturing and selling costs:		
Materials	$6,749	
Labor cost	5,042	
Depreciation	419	
Taxes (other than income taxes)	126	
Other	142	12,478
Net profit from operations		$ 921
Other income—interest and dividends		198
Less interest charges on own bonds outstanding		169
Net income before federal income taxes		$ 950
Provision for federal income taxes		368
Net income (or profit)		$ 581
Allocation of net income:		
Dividends on common stock		$ 293
Increase in retained earnings		288

[a]Some minor items are combined with items listed. For more detail, see GE Annual Report for 1975.

tions and accounting records is illustrated by the "Materials" item. The materials used may have been purchased long before and already have been in inventory at the year's beginning. Or materials purchased during the year might have been larger than the $6,749 million shown, if GE had chosen to build up its inventories during the year. The materials cost shown is the accounting figure for materials **used,** not for materials **bought** during the year, although some firms show inventory changes separately while others do not.

The same point is illustrated by the cost item "Depreciation." Every engineer and accountant knows that plant and equipment depreciate. If a truck bought in 1975 is expected to last five years, after five years it will have only scrap value if the original estimates were accurate. The concern will not have to buy another truck until 1980, but if it does not figure the using up of the truck as a current expense, it is obviously understating its costs and overstating its profits in the intervening years. If no current depreciation is charged, in 1980 the entire cost of the new truck would have to be charged against 1980 income. Hence, accountants "charge" depreciation annually, even though no cash outlay is involved. Thus, one-fifth of the value of the truck

might be charged off as a current cost each year, or some more complicated depreciation formula might be used. There need be no cash expenditure that matches the depreciation shown.

Since cost and income items are accounting entries rather than cash transactions, obviously there is no necessary cash accumulation at the year's end equal to net profit earned during the year. The firm's cash may be higher or lower, depending on what has seemed to the managers the best use of available funds. (As we shall presently see from Table C, GE increased its cash on hand by about $338 million during 1975.) Managers need only be sure they have cash on hand to meet their obligations, one of which is dividends. Dividends may be paid in years when no profits have been made. AT&T, for example, paid its regular cash dividend of $9 per share each year straight through the depression of the 1930s, even though annual profits fell well below $9. Retained earnings, of course, then declined by the excess of dividend payments over net profits.

Relation between income statement and balance sheet These observations tell us a good deal about the relation between the income statement and the balance sheet. Suppose now we draw up GE's balance

Table C

GENERAL ELECTRIC COMPANY

Balance Sheet, December 31, 1975
(In Millions of Dollars)

Assets			Liabilities & Owners' Equity		
Current assets:			Current liabilities:		
Cash	$ 753		Short-term borrowings	$ 650	
Marketable securities	100		Accounts payable	738	
Accounts receivable	2,597		Accrued taxes, etc.	1,431	
Inventories on hand	2,115		Other	1,073	
Total current assets		$5,566	Total current liabilities		$3,963
			Bonds outstanding & other		1,732
Fixed assets:			Total liabilities		$5,695
Investment in affiliated			Owners' equity:		
companies	$1,050		Common stock	$ 781	
Plant and equipment	2,562		Retained earnings	3,288	
Other	585		Total owners' equity		4,069
Total assets		$9,764	Total		$9,764

sheet at the end of 1975—another spot picture, linked to the earlier one by the 1975 income statement.

During the year, assets have been continually used up in the production of current output; sales or other sources of funds have continually rebuilt the firm's assets. Since a net profit of $581 million after taxes was made during 1975, total owners' equity (net worth) was up by this amount at year-end before payment of dividends. As was emphasized above, the increase in assets over the year may have come in cash, inventories, accounts receivable, or any other item—or there may have been a decrease in liabilities. All we know from the income statement is that, on balance, assets less liabilities are up $581 million.

This $581 million is reduced to $288 million by the payment of dividends. On the asset side, the reduction is in the cash item when cash is paid out; on the other side, it is in retained earnings, which would have shown a steady increase through the year if monthly balance sheets had been made. This leaves the retained earnings account up $288 million over December 31, 1974. Together, the income statement and balance sheets provide an overall accounting of the firm's operations and changing status over the period.

Corporate profits and the stock market Throughout this appendix, we have been primarily concerned with the mechanics of business accounting. Stop now and look for a moment at what this all means economically. During 1975, GE had a good year. It made $581 million of profits on its average owners' equity (investment) during the year. This is a 15 percent return, even after paying taxes. Before taxes, the return was twice as high. If you compare this rate of return with that of other leading American corporations, you will find that it looks very good.

How did this good year show up for the common stockholders? They collected $293 million of dividends on their (average) equity of about $3,850 million, a return of nearly 8 percent. We can safely assume that the price of GE stock has been bid up in the market by investors to reflect this high rate of return. If you had bought one share at the end of 1975, you would have had to pay about $50 for it, more than double the $22 "book value" per share of stock outstanding (obtained by dividing the 183 million shares outstanding into total owners' equity). Although market prices of common stock fluctuate widely, depending on many circumstances, in 1975 no "blue chip" stocks like GE could be bought to give a dividend yield of anything like 8 percent. About half that was more usual, and the $50 price to which GE stock had been bid up gave a 3.2 percent yield on the 1975 dividend of $1.60 per share.

But of course, the stockholders also gained from

the $288 million of profits plowed back into the business, which shows up on the December 31, 1975, balance sheet as additional retained earnings. This means that the company now has either that many more dollars' worth of assets, or that much less debt, or some combination of both, which should make it a more profitable company in the future, with larger total profit figures in the years ahead. Thus, savvy investors look at the total earnings of companies, not just at the dividends they pay. They calculate another ratio (the "price–earnings ratio") in comparing stocks to buy. For example, GE's price–earnings ratio at the end of 1975 was about 15 to 1; that is, you had to pay about $50 for a share of stock while GE's earnings per share were $3.17 in 1975. This was a high "P–E ratio" (as financial experts call it), reflecting GE's long record of solid growth and good profits, and the presumption of more good years to come. Stocks in less stable, successful companies could be bought at much lower P–E ratios; 5:1 or 6:1 was not uncommon in 1975, which meant that your current return per dollar invested would be higher than in GE. But don't rush out to buy the lowest P–E-multiple stock you can find. Chances are that it's very risky, and that its low price relative to current earnings reflects precisely this fact. With millions of investors constantly looking for bargains, P-E ratios tend to reflect the relative prospective earnings of different companies fairly accurately, and it's hard to get rich quick by outguessing other investors.

REVIEW

**Concepts
to remember**

This appendix has introduced several important new concepts. You will meet many of the following terms not only throughout the course but in the newspaper as well:

balance sheet	income statement
assets	dividends
liabilities	depreciation
owners' equity	retained earnings
net worth	price–earnings ratio
profit-and-loss statement	

Get a copy of the most recent General Electric Company annual report, or that of some other company in which you are interested. On the basis of your review of the report, what are your answers to the following questions? (On financial information, concentrate only on the profit-and-loss (or income) statement and the balance sheet (usually toward the end of the report), since the details in many corporate statements go beyond the points covered in the preceding appendix to Chapter 4.)

---

1. What are the main lines of business in which the company is involved?

2. Does the annual report give you a good picture of what the company does and how well it is doing it?

3. Last year, did the company do a good job for its stockholders? for its customers? How, if at all, can you tell?

4. What rate of return did the company earn on its stockholders' investment? (Use owners' equity as the measure of stockholders' investment.) What were the company's earnings as a percentage of its sales?

5. What part of its after-tax earnings did the company pay out in dividends? Plow back into the company? If you had been a stockholder, would you have preferred a different allocation of the earnings? Why?

6. Was last year a good or bad year profitwise, compared to the preceding years?

7. Look up on the New York Stock Exchange page of your newspaper the current price of GE stock (or of whatever company you are using). What was the ratio of the stock price to last year's GE earnings (often called the price–earnings ratio)? For you as an investor, is this ratio or the rate of return on stockholders' investment in question 4 above a better measure of what you can earn on your money if you now invest in GE stock? Why should the price–earnings ratio for GE stock be higher than that for many other stocks (as it in fact is)? (*Hint:* Look at the growth of GE earnings over the years in the "Historical Review" section of the report.)

8. Does GE have more stockholders or employees?

consumers and market demand

By and large, businesses can make profits only by producing goods and services that people want to buy—autos, houses, dry cleaning, air travel, dog food. If there is no consumer who is willing and able to buy, the businessman is out of luck. Maybe the government will temporarily come to his rescue with a subsidy, or maybe he can keep going by using up his own invested capital. **But over the long pull, it is customers who are willing and able to buy who direct production in a private-enterprise economy.**

THE SOVEREIGN CONSUMER?

Consumers direct production by the way they spend their money. If consumers demand yellow refrigerators, businesses will produce yellow refrigerators. If consumers want to rent cars at airports, the rent-a-car agencies will prosper. If consumers develop a taste for artichokes, enterprising farmers will soon be raising artichokes to gain a profit by meeting that demand.

Note: Some instructors who wish to emphasize here only a broad picture of supply, demand, and markets, may prefer to assign only pp. 50–55 of Chapter 5 here, assigning the rest at the beginning of Part 3 on microeconomics, preceding Chapter 20.

Also note that this chapter has a mathematical appendix at the end of the book, for those who want to assign it.

Consumer demand is the mainspring of economic activity. But never forget—it is the consumer *with money to spend* who counts! Many of us would like to have a Cadillac, and filet mignon for dinner. But unless we have the money and are willing to spend it on these objects, our desires have little significance for General Motors or for the local supermarket.

Thus, your "vote" on what gets produced in a private-enterprise economy is largely determined by your income, unless you have accumulated funds to supplement your income. The mill hand has a lot less influence than the rich man, even though the former may be a virtuous, hardworking father of five needy children and the latter a ne'er-do-well who has inherited his money through no effort of his own. This is not to imply that virtue resides in poor rather than rich souls, but merely to emphasize that the private-enterprise economy responds to what people have to spend, not to who they are.

Figure 5–1 shows who has the buying power in America. It emphasizes the huge buying power of the "middle class." Two-thirds of all families fell in the $5,000–$20,000 income group in 1975,

Figure 5–1

In 1975, three-fifths of all families fell in the $6,800–$21,500 income range, and they received about 55 percent of the national income. But the top fifth, receiving incomes of $21,500 and up, had about 40 percent of the total buying power. (Source: U.S. Department of Commerce; preliminary estimates for 1975 by author.)

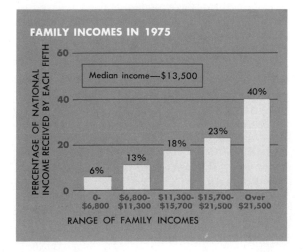

Table 5–1

Percentage breakdown of consumer spending

Spending category	1929	1975
Food and drink	28	21
Housing	14	15
Clothing	12	10
Household furnishings	6	6
Medical services	4	8
Recreation	3	7
Autos and operations	3	13

and the average income of this group is steadily moving up.

But Figure 5–1 points up the extremes too. Ten million families, one family out of five, had an income below $5,600. These families received only 6 percent of total personal income—far less than their proportionate say over what gets produced for the market. At the other extreme, about one million families (2 percent of the total) received incomes over $40,000, giving them a larger leverage over what the system produces.

The consumer is a powerful, and sometimes capricious, sovereign. Table 5–1 shows what he spends on some major categories in the American economy. He still spends the biggest chunk of his income on food, housing, and clothing. But the proportion spent on food and clothing has dropped sharply since 1929 (to only 31 percent, as against 42). Spending on services (medicine, transportation, recreation, and the like) has grown rapidly as we have become richer and able to devote more of our incomes to "nonessentials." The bottom three items show what kind of living consumers now like.

Most of us are not coldly calculating "economic men." Still, most of us face a real problem of how to allocate our incomes among far more goods and services than we are able to pay for. Perhaps the Aga Khan buys everything he wants without concern for what it costs. But most of us have to calculate how to divide up our incomes among the things we want to buy. You may devote most of your income to nourishing foods, college tuition, and durable clothes; I may spend most of mine on books, stereo albums, and air-

plane trips; our neighbor may prefer a dissolute life of wine, women, and song. None of us is a human calculating machine, but all of us face the need to allocate our limited incomes to maximize our satisfactions from spending them.

The economist does not pass judgment on which pattern of expenditure is the proper one. Nor does he pretend to tell you how you should spend your income to lead a happier, healthier, more learned, or other kind of life. What he does do is assume that normally you spend your money on the things you want most. Thus, if you spent a dollar on a hamburger this noon, he takes that as evidence that you preferred that over a pizza or a paperback at the same price. If you stop and think about it, any other assumption leads to very strange results, as long as we assume freedom of individual action in spending incomes.

These rather obvious observations become important later on when we try to evaluate how well the economic system works. Unless we can assume that consumers' expenditures generally reflect what they want most, we will be at a loss for any measure of how well the system does in fact allocate its scarce productive resources to satisfying consumer wants. So we shall generally assume that people spend their money on the goods and services they want most, wisely or not.

Advertising and the management of demand

"Consumer sovereignty" is just establishment rhetoric, say some critics of the U.S. economy. Reality is just the opposite, they argue. Businesses decide what they can make the most profit producing; then they convince consumers, through advertising and other high-pressure selling, that that's what they want to buy. Businesses, helped by Madison Avenue, are the sovereigns; consumers' wants are managed, manipulated, indeed created outright.

Insofar as the critics are right, the basic argument for an individual-oriented, free-market economy is undermined, since the whole system rests on the notion of consumer wants directing the use of society's resources. Does big business in fact dictate your wants, as a consumer? Clearly, modern advertising influences what a lot of people buy. In 1975, businesses spent over $28 billion on advertising—on TV and billboards, in newspapers, magazines, stores, and by direct mail. Procter & Gamble was the nation's largest advertiser, on soaps, detergents, and a myriad of household products; it spent 7 percent of its sales income on advertising. General Motors was second, with only 0.9 percent of its sales income spent on advertising. Sears, Roebuck was third, General Foods fourth. Twenty-eight billion dollars is a very large amount, but it's less than 2 percent of the gross national product. It's hard to see how that percentage could dominate all our "wants." Moreover, a lot of the advertising is primarily informational, not merely want-manipulating; nearly a third of the total is newspaper advertising, with huge ads by supermarkets on weekend grocery prices and the like, presumably useful information for the housewife. Some advertising is seriously misleading, or dishonest; some is illegal, and not all of it is caught.

Obviously, advertising is a complicated problem, and there's a major section on it in Chapter 25, including both factual data and analysis of the major issues. There is surely some truth to the critics' charges, and the recent upsurge of "consumerism" shows that a lot of people are concerned. At the same time, the charges are easy to blow up into emotional overstatements; the facts just don't support some of the wilder ones. So remember that for the next few chapters, we're oversimplifying by assuming that consumers decide for themselves what they want and freely express these preferences in the market. But it's a useful first approximation, and there'll be plenty of opportunity to alter it in Chapters 25 through 27.

INDIVIDUAL DEMAND

Since consumer demand largely directs production in a private-enterprise system, it is important to define "demand" accurately at the outset. **"Demand" is the schedule of amounts of any product that buyers will purchase at different prices during some stated time period.** This definition takes some explaining, since it obviously isn't quite what the word means in everyday conversation.

What is your demand for pizzas? A little thought will tell you that this is a meaningless question until you ask, "At what price, and over how long a time?" You'll surely buy more at 50 cents than at $1.00 each; and obviously, you'll buy more in a year than in a week. Recognizing this need to specify prices and a time period, we might construct a hypothetical "schedule" of the numbers of pizzas you would buy at different prices during a week, as in Table 5–2. The table shows how many pizzas you will buy during the

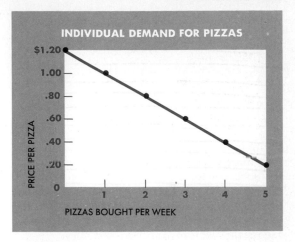

Figure 5–2
The demand curve shows how many pizzas this individual will buy in a week at different prices. He will buy more at lower than at higher prices.

week at each price shown, **assuming that other things (especially your income and the prices of other commodities) remain unchanged.**

When we speak of your "demand" for pizza, we mean this entire schedule of amounts that you would buy at various prices, other things equal. It is meaningless to say that your demand is one or three pizzas a week. By "demand" we mean instead your entire state of mind as to how many pizzas you would buy at different prices, other things remaining unchanged. In principle, we might list every possible price from zero to infinity. Table 5–2 pictures your demand only over the price range shown.

This state of mind (your demand) can be shown graphically, as in Figure 5–2. If we plot price on the vertical axis and pizzas bought on the horizontal axis and connect the points, we can read off the resulting curve how many pizzas you will buy during the week at any price shown, continuing the assumption of other things equal. Thus, at $1.20 you will buy none, at $1.00 you will buy one, and so on down the curve. If you haven't had much experience with graphs, check how Figure 5–2 is plotted from Table 5–2. The top dot is at a price of $1.20 and 0 number of pizzas bought. Similarly plot each point from Table 5–2. Then connect the dots with a line, which gives you the demand curve.

Table 5–2

Individual demand for pizzas

Price per pizza	Pizzas bought per week
$1.20	0
1.00	1
.80	2
.60	3
.40	4
.20	5

Whether we use the schedule or the demand curve is a matter of convenience.

But watch out for one tricky point, whether you use schedules or graphs! Going back to your demand for pizzas, suppose the price is $1.00 and you are buying one per week. Now the local pizza parlor lowers the price to 80 cents and you step up your weekly purchases to two. **This is not a change in demand.** Your demand (your state of mind toward pizza) has not changed. You have merely moved to a different point on your demand schedule, or curve, as a result of the lower price, as the original demand schedule or curve says you would do. Your increased purchase at a lower price is merely a reflection of the downward slope of your demand curve.

Why demand curves slope downward

It seems obvious that you will buy more of anything at a low price than at a high one. Thus, on the kind of graph we have drawn, the demand curve will slope down, from northwest to southeast. Why? First, at a lower price for anything, you can afford to buy more of it out of any given income. Second, at a lower price you are likely to want to buy more of it, because it becomes relatively more attractive compared with other things you might buy, given unchanged prices of other things. You will want to substitute pizza for hamburger another night each week as pizzas become cheaper.[1]

Many economists associate downward-sloping demand curves with the "law of diminishing marginal utility." The additional, or marginal, utility (satisfaction) you obtain per unit falls as you consume more units within the stated time

period. Marginal utility is the want satisfaction obtained from having one additional unit of some commodity per unit of time. Since marginal utility from an additional unit declines as you get more units, you will be willing to pay less for each additional unit; hence, your demand curve slopes downward. Try applying the law to yourself—for oranges, movies, airplane trips home. And see the box on "consumer's surplus."

Changes in demand

Remember that your "demand" for pizzas is your entire set of intentions about buying pizzas. These depend on how much income you have, your taste for pizza compared with other things, and the prices of alternatives. Now suppose that you get tired of pizza and develop a taste for seafood. You will now buy fewer pizzas than before at each of the prices shown. **This change in attitude is a change in demand. Your demand for pizzas has decreased.**

A change in demand is easily illustrated by using demand curves. Begin with curve *AA* in Figure 5–3. Your *lower* demand for pizzas would be reflected in a new demand curve, to the left of, or

Figure 5–3
Curve CC shows an increase in demand from AA, curve BB shows a decrease. How many pizzas would consumers buy at $1.00 per pizza in each case?

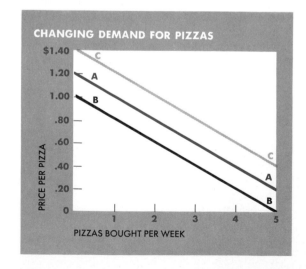

CHANGING DEMAND FOR PIZZAS

---

[1] Three exceptions should be mentioned: (1) "Prestige goods," such as mink coats and exotic perfume, may be bought largely because their price is high. A decline in price might lead rich people to buy less as the goods come down into a price range open to the less wealthy. (2) Some goods, called "inferior," are bought by poor people simply because they are cheap and useful. Potatoes in Ireland are the classic example. If the price of the food staple, potatoes, goes up, the Irish peasants may have to buy even more potatoes, which are still the cheapest food, because they have even less left than before to buy other, more expensive foods. (3) When price drops, people may buy less because they expect the price to decline still further. But this is a dynamic effect that depends not on whether price is high or low but on the way it is changing.

AN APPLICATION— CONSUMER'S SURPLUS

When a consumer is in equilibrium, he is usually receiving a "consumer surplus" on most commodities he buys. Figure 5–4 shows a typical downward-sloping demand curve—say, for bananas. The market price is 10 cents, and you buy five per week. But your demand curve shows that you would have been willing to pay 20 cents for the first banana, 17 cents for the second, and so on. The price you would have paid for each banana indicates the marginal utility you expect to receive from that banana. Thus, you get a "consumer's surplus" of utility on each of the first four bananas, since you have to pay only 10 cents for each. The light blue area provides a measure of this consumer's surplus.

(*Brainteaser:* How much consumer's surplus do you get on each gallon of water you drink? On each cubic foot of air you breathe? *Hint:* The answer depends on the difference between total utility and marginal utility.)

Figure 5–4

The consumer pays only 50 cents (gray rectangle) for his five bananas, but his demand curve shows he would have been willing to pay more than 10 cents for each of the first four. Thus, the light blue triangle measures how much more he would have been willing to pay to get the total utility provided by five bananas, and hence measures the "consumer's surplus" he obtains free.

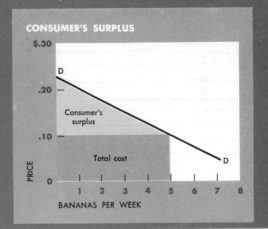

below, the old curve. You will now buy only one per week at 80 cents, and none at any higher price; only two at 60 cents; and so on. This new, *lower* demand curve is shown in Figure 5–3 as curve *BB*. If something increases your demand for pizzas—say, a fatter paycheck to finance such delicacies—the new, *higher* demand might be indicated by *CC*. **A change in demand is shown by a move to another demand curve.**

Why would your demand for pizzas, or Porsches, or neckties change? There are three major reasons. **First, your tastes may change.** You simply decide you don't like pizza, or that you now prefer Porsches to other cars. **Second, your income may change.** As a beginning office clerk, you may have to be satisfied with a secondhand Volkswagon. With a doubled paycheck, you may be in the Camaro class. **Third, changes in the availability and prices of other commodities may change your demand.** If hamburger prices soar, your demand for pizzas

may rise, because you'll buy more pizzas than before now that the alternatives cost more.

It is important to distinguish between movements along the same demand curve and shifts in the curve itself. Many economic fallacies are perpetrated through slippery use of the concept of "demand." Try checking your own grasp with these questions: (1) Production of sheep rises, prices fall, and consumers buy more mutton. Is there an increase in the demand for mutton? (*Hint:* Does the demand curve itself shift, or do customers merely buy more mutton on the same demand curve at lower prices?) (2) Chrysler comes out with a new engine, and Buick sales decline. Has demand for Buicks dropped? (3) Philco raises the price of its TV sets, and sales drop off. Is there a drop in demand? (4) Congress puts a new tax on movie admissions, and movie attendance drops. Is there a drop in demand?[2]

[2]Answers: (1) no; (2) yes; (3) no; (4) no.

EQUILIBRIUM OF THE CONSUMER

It is useful to have a general theory of consumer demand. If we assume that consumers (households) generally try to maximize the utility (or satisfaction) they get by spending their incomes, two important propositions follow:

1. First, each consumer will change the pattern of goods and services he buys whenever he can get more utility by spending an extra dollar on item A than on item B. He will maximize his total utility when he allocates his income so that the marginal utility he receives from the last dollar spent on each item he buys is identical. When he so allocates his income, the consumer is "in equilibrium," in the sense that he is maximizing the satisfaction he can obtain by spending his income. He has no incentive to change to another spending pattern.

This is only common sense. If you can get a larger marginal utility by spending a dollar on A than on B, obviously you should spend it on A. Whenever the marginal utility of the last dollar spent on different commodities is unequal, you can increase your total utility by switching from the lower to the higher marginal utility commodities. If, to simplify, we assume that the price of every commodity is the same, you should so allocate your income as to obtain the same marginal utility from every commodity you buy. We could write this in equation form as follows: $MU_x = MU_y = MU_z$, and so on, where $x, y,$ and z are the commodities bought.

If the prices of different commodities differ, the consumer in equilibrium would not expect to get the same marginal utility from each commodity, but only from the last dollar spent on each commodity. It would be nonsense to think of so allocating your income as to obtain the same marginal utility from a movie and an automobile. But if we divide the marginal utility from each by the price of each, we make them comparable. Then we can state our central proposition again: For the consumer to be in equilibrium, the marginal utility of the last dollar spent on each commodity must be equal. In equation form, the equilibrium condition is, therefore:

$$\frac{MU_x}{P_x} = \frac{MU_y}{P_y} = \frac{MU_z}{P_z}, \text{ etc.,}$$

where P is the price of each commodity.[3]

We can extend this reasoning to other uses of households' incomes. You may save part of your disposable income rather than spending it. To be in equilibrium, you must so allocate your income between saving and spending that the marginal utility obtained from a dollar saved is equal to that obtained from a dollar spent on each item you buy. Equating marginal utilities works for all uses of the dollars we have to spend or to save.

2. When consumers spend their incomes this way, their demand curves for different products accurately reflect the relative marginal utilities they think they will obtain from different products they might buy. If you spend $5 for a necktie rather than for a movie ticket, we assume you prefer the tie to the movie. Your preferences are reflected in your demand curves for the two products, and your demands will reflect to producers the relative values you place on neckties and movies. This is an extremely important point, since in our system we rely largely on consumer demand to give signals to producers on what should be produced and in what quantities.

MARKET DEMANDS— SIGNALS TO PRODUCERS

Millions of consumers, each allocating his income to provide the greatest satisfaction to himself, provide the basic signals to producers telling what consumers want pro-

[3] Wouldn't this lead the consumer to allocate all his income to x instead of y or z, if x has the highest marginal utility? No, because of the law of diminishing marginal utility. Remember that the marginal utility obtained from an additional unit of each commodity declines as the consumer gets more of it in any time period. Thus, spending more dollars on x will produce diminishing marginal utility for x, and this will keep the consumer from switching all his expenditures to x (that is, to any one commodity).

duced. The local department store isn't much concerned with your personal demand for shirts. But it is very much concerned with the aggregate market demand for shirts in its market territory. Aggregate, or market, demand is the sum of all the individual demands in each market. Such market demand provides the main signal to producers as to what they should supply to make the largest profits by meeting consumers' wants. Market demand tells the local grocer the relative importance its customers attach to getting more pounds of sugar at different prices (given their incomes and the prices of other products).

Consider the market demand for sugar at the crossroads store of an isolated village that has only three families. The demand schedules of the three families, and total demand, might look something like Table 5–3. The market demand schedule for sugar, as seen by the crossroads grocer, is the sum of the individual demands of his customers. It could be plotted on a graph just like the individual's demand schedule. The total expenditures column shows the grocer's total weekly sales of sugar at different prices. (For the moment, disregard the right-hand column.)

ELASTICITY OF DEMAND

The preceding sections say the most important things about consumer demands as signals to producers. But demands for individual products vary widely, and it is useful to be able to describe some of these differences precisely in

analyzing how well the economic system responds to changing consumer demands.[4]

Consider salt. Suppose ordinary table salt sells for 10 cents a pound and you use about a pound a month. If the price goes up to 15 cents, how much less salt will you use? Probably no less at all. Unsalted beans and potatoes don't taste very good, and the fraction of a cent saved each day by not salting your food is trivial compared with the better taste of flavored cooking.

This is a case where quantity bought responds very little, or not at all, to price changes. A higher price doesn't weed out very many buyers. Plotted on a graph, the demand curve for table salt at the local grocery store would be substantially vertical over the 10- to 15-cent price range. We say that the demand for table salt is very "inelastic" over this price range. Quantity bought changes very little in response to a change in price.

At the other extreme, take your demand for steak at the local A&P if you are substantially indifferent about whether you eat beef or pork. Suppose the price of beef jumps 10 percent. The chances are that you will cut back your steak purchases sharply and substitute pork. Here your demand for steak would be highly "elastic." You would cut your purchases a lot in response to an increase in price.

"Elasticity" is a measure that tells how much the quantity bought will change in response to a

[4]Mathematical Appendix I at the end of the book provides a precise mathematical statement of demand elasticity, which may be helpful to students who think readily in mathematical terms.

Table 5–3
Crossroads demand for sugar

Price per pound	PURCHASES PER WEEK BY:			All three	Expenditures	Demand
	A	B	C			
20 cents	3 lb	1 lb	2 lb	6 lb	$1.20	Elastic
15 cents	4 lb	2 lb	4 lb	10 lb	1.50	Unitary
10 cents	6 lb	3 lb	6 lb	15 lb	1.50	Inelastic
5 cents	6 lb	4 lb	7 lb	17 lb	.85	

change in price. Thus, elasticity of demand is a measure of the responsiveness of quantity bought to changes in price. (It is defined precisely on page 59.) Elasticity is one characteristic of any given demand curve or schedule. To say a given demand is elastic or inelastic is merely to describe it, just as you might describe your next-door neighbor as tall or short.[5]

Total revenue and elasticity of demand

The concept of demand elasticity helps us predict what effect price changes will have on total expenditure for a commodity. Look at the last column of Table 5–3. Suppose the grocer cuts the price of sugar 25 percent, from 20 to 15 cents a pound. Sales jump from six to ten pounds per week, a 67 percent increase, and his total revenue from sugar goes up from $1.20 to $1.50 per week. The increase in quantity sold more than offsets the decrease in price. Looking at what happens to total expenditures (revenue) gives us a precise measure of elasticity. If demand is elastic, total expenditures will change in the opposite direction from a change in price. If demand is inelastic, total expenditures on a commodity will change in the same direction as a change in price. Examine the reasoning.

1. Elastic demand—total revenue moves in the opposite direction from price. This is the sugar case just described. Although the storekeeper gets 25 percent less per pound, he sells 67 percent more pounds, and total revenue increases. Demand is elastic. Reverse the process over the same price range and you will see again that total revenue moves in the opposite direction from price.

2. Inelastic demand—total revenue moves in the same direction as price. Now observe what hap-

pens when the grocer cuts the price from 10 to 5 cents. He gets 50 percent less for each pound of sugar, but he sells only 13 percent more pounds. The volume increase, with inelastic demand, is not great enough to offset the lower price per pound sold. Total revenue drops with a cut in price. Demand is inelastic. Now reverse the process over the same price range. Total revenue will rise if he raises the price from 5 to 10 cents.

3. Unit elasticity—total revenue is unaffected by price changes. The borderline case between elastic and inelastic demand is called "unit" elasticity. This occurs where an upward or downward shift of price is just offset by a proportional change in quantity bought, so that total revenue remains unchanged. The crossroads demand for sugar between 10 and 15 cents is a case in point. Total expenditure on sugar is identical at either price, since the shift in amount bought just offsets the change in price.

A warning: Note that the same demand curve may be elastic in some price ranges and inelastic in others. In most cases, it is not correct to speak of a demand curve as elastic or inelastic as a whole. You need to specify at what price.

The real-world importance of elasticity

The elasticity of demand for his product is a prime concern of every businessman, whether or not he uses that technical term. Consider two important real-world examples that will show why.

First, the farmer. Modern studies show that the demand for most basic farm products is inelastic over the relevant price ranges. What does this mean if farmers all work hard, the weather cooperates, and a bumper crop rolls out? It means that the *total revenue* farmers get from selling their crops will be *lower* as a result of this bonanza, because the bigger crop can be sold only by cutting prices more than proportionately. This simple fact goes far to explain the continuing stream of government-sponsored crop-reduction plans, beginning with the New Deal AAA program, all aimed at raising total farm income. With inelastic demand, even a small crop restriction may induce a substantially

---

[5] Strictly, we should call this concept "price elasticity of demand." There is a related concept, "income elasticity of demand," that measures the response of quantity bought to a change in income received. However, throughout this book we shall use "elasticity" to mean "price elasticity." At a more advanced level, we can also speak of "cross-elasticity" of demand. This is the percentage change in the amount of product *A* that will be bought in response to a given percentage change in the price of product *B*.

higher price and more total revenue from crop sales.

Contrast this with the depression-period attempts of the railroads to increase their total revenues by raising passenger fares in the 1930s. Unfortunately for the railroads, the customers stayed away in droves. Either they stayed home, or they traveled by bus or car. Demand turned out to be elastic, and total revenue moved down, not up. Only when fares were *cut* did total revenue actually rise. The impossibility of filling the coffers by raising price in an elastic-demand market is plain to see, once you understand the concept of elasticity.[6]

A quantitative measure of elasticity

For some purposes, it is useful to be able to say just how elastic or inelastic demand is. A ready measure can be worked out from the previous reasoning. Elasticity depends on the relative changes in quantity and price. If the percentage change in quantity bought (Q) is more than the percentage change in price (P), total revenue moves in the opposite direction from price; demand is elastic. Thus, we can easily get a numerical value for elasticity by the formula:

$$\text{Elasticity} = \frac{\%\ \text{change in } Q}{\%\ \text{change in } P}$$

For example, if a cut in the price of steel ingots from $80 to $76 per ton (5 percent) leads to an increase in sales from 100 million to 101 million tons (1 percent), by inserting the 5 percent and 1 percent in the formula we get an elasticity of demand of .2. Any value less than 1 (unity) is

Table 5–4	
Estimated elasticities of demand	
Furs	2.6
Autos	1.5
Refrigerators	1.1
Local phone calls	1.0
Luggage	.8
Movie tickets	.4
Electric light bulbs	.3
Matches	0

Source: Treasury estimates presented before House Ways and Means Committee, 1960.

called inelastic demand. Any value of more than 1 is called elastic demand. Unitary elasticity of demand means exactly offsetting changes in quantity and price.[7]

Econometric estimates have been made of the elasticity of demand for many products, although many of these are very rough. Table 5–4 gives estimates for several common products (for price variations near their then prices). The preceding footnote on what makes demand elastic or inelastic should help you explain the elasticities of the different products. Another study recently found the present demand elasticity for butter to be about 1.3, compared to a pre–World War II estimate of about .6. Can you explain the difference? (*Hint:* Consider possible substitutes then and now. Margarine came into general use in the 1940s.)

---

[6]What makes demand elastic or inelastic? Demand is likely to be inelastic when (1) your outlay on the object is small, (2) your want for it is urgent, (3) good substitutes are unavailable, and (4) it is wanted jointly with some complementary item. Conversely, demand is likely to be elastic where (1) the outlay involved bulks large in your total expenditures, (2) your want is not urgent, (3) close substitutes are available, (4) the commodity is durable or repairable, and (5) the commodity has multiple uses. The availability of satisfactory substitutes is crucial. For example, nobody's want for Exxon gasoline is likely to be terribly urgent as long as a similar grade of Gulf can be had for the same price across the street.

[7]Since price and quantity move in opposite directions, elasticity will always be a negative figure. The minus sign is customarily dropped in using elasticity measures.

Strictly, our formula needs to be applied only to very small changes in price and quantity. Notice, for example, that the percentage change in price from 10 to 5 cents is different from that from 5 to 10 cents—50 percent compared with 100 percent. This is because the base with which we compared the 5-cent change varies with the direction in which we calculate. The difference really doesn't matter for our purposes, since the effect on total revenue will always give the right answer. (If you always take the percentage change on the bigger price or quantity figure, you can avoid this directional problem.) Obviously, the discrepancy between the two ways of figuring percentage change will gradually vanish as we take smaller and smaller price intervals—for example, a price change between 99 cents and $1.00. There is a more precise formula, using calculus, in the mathematical appendix.

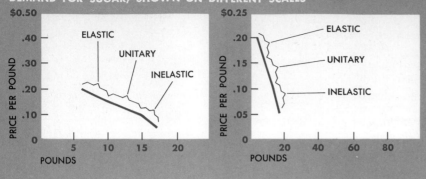

DEMAND FOR SUGAR, SHOWN ON DIFFERENT SCALES

Figure 5-5
Trying to judge elasticity of demand by looking at the slope of a demand curve is tricky. These two curves show identical demands, plotted on different scales.

Elasticity in graphical presentations

A perfectly inelastic demand curve would obviously be vertical; the same quantity would be bought at every price. An example might be your demand for insulin over a wide price range if you needed the insulin to stay alive. Highly elastic demand would be a nearly horizontal demand curve. Very small changes in price would lead to very large changes in the quantity bought. But in between these extremes, trying to read elasticity by the slope of a plotted demand curve is dangerous business. Look, for example, at the two charts in Figure 5-5. Both show the demand schedule seen by our old friend the crossroads grocer, but they use different horizontal and vertical scales. Exactly the same demand is shown on both.

Because the left-hand graph uses an extended horizontal scale, the demand curve is relatively flat throughout. Yet it is exactly the same demand as in the right-hand graph, and the elasticity at every point along it is identical with the corresponding points on the right-hand graph. Both curves are marked to show the elastic and inelastic areas. This example emphasizes the danger in trying to generalize that flat demand curves are elastic, whereas steep ones are inelastic. You have to remember that elasticity is a matter of **relative** (percentage) changes in price and quantity. Elasticity changes continuously along a straight, diagonal demand curve. Check

it for yourself if, as is likely, this statement seems to you intuitively wrong.[8]

INTERACTING DEMANDS

If you buy a car, your demand for gasoline is pretty sure to increase. But, assuming that your total income stays unchanged, your demand for some other things (say, bus rides) will drop. This example illustrates the two main kinds of interrelationships among demands for different things: (1) complementary, or joint; and (2) substitutive, or competitive. When you buy a car, you take on a "complementary" demand for gasoline to run it. But now you don't need to ride the bus. Bus rides are "competitive" with cars in your demand pattern.

In the broadest sense, if your income is a given amount, every expenditure is competitive with every other. More of anything means less of something else. But in many instances, this effect is quite remote; for example, your car purchase may have little effect on your demand for potatoes. By contrast, the substitution of car rides for bus rides is very direct. Thus, in many cases it is important to recognize complementary demands, even though in the broader sense all are competitive, given the budget constraints nearly all of us face.

[8] For mathematicians: The curve that shows unitary elasticity at all points is a rectangular hyperbola. The equation is $xy = $ constant.

REVIEW

Concepts to remember

This chapter has presented a string of important new analytical concepts that will be used repeatedly. Check to be sure you have them clearly in mind:

demand
individual and aggregate demand
marginal utility
total utility
law of diminishing marginal utility
equilibrium of the consumer

elasticity of demand
elastic demand
inelastic demand
unit elasticity
competitive demands
complementary demands

For analysis and discussion

1. Is price a good measure of the marginal utility of a good to each buyer? Explain.
2. Do you act like the mythical "economic man" in allocating your income among alternative uses to maximize your satisfaction from it? If your answer is no, are you saying that you are irrational?
3. Calculate roughly how big a voice people in your own family's income group have in the allocation of the economy's resources. Does it seem to you to be a fair share? (Check the income data in Figure 5–1.)
4. Explain the concept of "equilibrium of the consumer." How useful does this concept seem to you in understanding consumer behavior? If you don't think it is useful, can you suggest a better model?
5. "Every individual is different. Thus it makes no sense for economists to lump them all together in talking about aggregate market demand." True or false?
6. "Since consumers' demand signals what is to be produced in America, it follows that consumers are responsible if our economy produces 'wasteful' products like elaborate chrome trim on automobiles." Do you agree or disagree?
7. How elastic is your demand for the following, at the present price for each?
   a. Beer
   b. Stereos
   c. Porsche roadsters
   d. Required textbooks
   e. Gasoline
   f. Airplane tickets home

   In each case, see if you can isolate the factors that make the elasticity what it is.
8. If the demand for wheat is inelastic, would a bumper crop raise or lower wheat farmers' total income?
9. What effect would a successful advertising campaign by the Gulf Oil Company have on the elasticity of consumer demand for Gulf gas? Explain your answer.
10. Suppose unsold stocks of gasoline are piling up in the storage tanks of the major refineries. If you were regional sales director of one of the major companies, would you recommend a marked reduction in the filling-station price? How would you go about deciding?

One controversial part of the government's overall program to aid the poor has been the food-stamp program. Following its introduction in the 1960s, the program was expanded rapidly, and by early 1976, nearly 20 million people were receiving benefits, with a total annual cost to the federal government of almost $6 billion. Under the program, the government provides participants with stamps that can be used to purchase food in most stores, and then redeems the stamps from the grocers who take them in payment for food.

Congress has raised the value of the food stamps provided, at roughly the same pace as inflation. By 1976, an eligible family of four could receive free $162 in food stamps monthly (about $2,000 annually) if its "net" annual income was under about $3,600. Similar families with higher "net" incomes, up to about $7,000, could receive food stamps by paying up to 85 percent of their value. "Net" income was calculated by subtracting from gross money income $3,600, plus taxes, medical expenses, rent, utilities, mortgage payments, school tuition, and several other items. Thus, a $3,600 "net" income corresponded to a substantially higher gross income. In extreme cases, families with gross incomes up to $15,000 could qualify for food stamps, but the bulk of the stamps have gone to families and individuals with current money incomes below the early-1976 federal "poverty" level of about $5,500; and there is a complex regulation disqualifying families with substantial holdings of earning assets.

The stated purpose of the program is to ensure that poor families, especially those with children, receive a reasonably adequate diet. By giving the poor food stamps instead of money, proponents argue, we ensure a minimum level of nourishment for poor families at a much lower cost than if we gave the poor money aid, because food stamps must be used for food and cannot be diverted to liquor, gasoline, drugs, paying off old debts, or other less urgent needs.

Others, including some of the poor themselves, disagree. It is insulting and inefficient, they say, to give food stamps rather than money, restricting the recipients' freedom to judge for themselves what is best for them. It is inefficient, they argue, because if the government gave the poor the same amount of money, the poor could not possibly be worse off, and would almost certainly be better off, since they would be free to allocate their incomes so as to maximize their own utilities. The poor recipient could buy all food with his money grant if food is what he wants and needs most, or he could use the funds for something else if other needs are more urgent. The plan is insulting because it implies that the poor cannot be trusted to know and to do what is best for themselves and their children. Moreover, as a practical matter, many food-stamp recipients sell their stamps (illegally) to others and spend the funds as they please.

Who is right? Should we scrap the food-stamp plan and go to a system of cash grants only for the poor? The question is an important one not only because of the size of the food-stamp program, but also because the same basic issue arises with many other types of government assistance. For example, rent supplements to provide better housing, free public education, and subsidized public health benefits under Medicare and Medicaid all parallel food stamps as "in-kind," rather than cash, aid to the poor.

6

SUPPLY, DeManD, and market prices

Chapter 2 provided a bird's-eye view of how producers respond to consumer demands in a private-enterprise, free-market economy. Chapters 4 and 5 looked briefly at businesses and households, the main suppliers and demanders in the economy. This chapter examines in more detail the role of the market and market prices in connecting consumers and producers. If you thought economics was going to be about "supply and demand," this is it.

THE ROLE OF MARKETS AND MARKET PRICES

In a loose way, it is easy to see how consumer demands get the goods and services produced that consumers want. If consumers buy more paint, the immediate result is increased retail sales, and paint stores order more paint from wholesalers to replenish their stocks. Wholesalers in turn order more paint from the manufacturers; and manufacturers, with joyous hearts, produce more paint, because their profits depend on producing and selling paint. The linkage may be jerky and imperfect, but each participant has an incentive—the profit incentive—to do his part.

Sometimes the linkage between consumer and producer is direct. An example is the barber who cuts your hair. More often, consumer demand has to pass through many links before it hits the ultimate producer. An example is consumer demand for automobiles, which goes through the local auto dealer back to GM or Ford, and through them to literally thousands of different suppliers of parts and productive equipment—machine tools, steel, tires, electrical switches, wire, brake linings, shock absorbers, spark plugs, batteries, and so on. And behind each of these lies an array of suppliers to them, involving other raw materials and components. Moreover, at each stage, the supplier must hire the labor he needs (engineers, accountants, stenographers, janitors, salesmen, technicians, assembly workers, and others). Add on arranging transportation, storage for inventories, and financing, and you begin to get a picture of what's involved.

What ties all these decisions and operations together? What brings order out of the potential chaos in an economy that includes millions of different products demanded by millions of consumers? The answer is, an intricately interlinked net of markets and market prices. The grocer knows you want sugar when you walk into his store and buy ten pounds at the prevailing price. Similarly, there is a market that links grocers to wholesalers; one that links wholesalers and sugar refiners; one that links sugar refiners and sugar growers; one that links each of these to the workers needed at each stage.

In each market, price acts as the adjuster between demand and supply. When you demand more, price tends to move up. When price rises, there is an increased profit incentive to produce more. It is this interaction among demand, supply, and price that is the core of the self-adjusting mechanism of the private-enterprise system. A good understanding of the much-cited "law of supply and demand" is a powerful tool indeed for understanding how the modern economy works—how it produces order rather than chaos in allocating scarce resources.

SUPPLY

Businesses are the main suppliers of goods and services in our economy. Some suppliers are huge corporations, like GE. Others are

individuals, like the barber or the corner grocer. All are seeking profits by meeting consumer demands. To understand more precisely how they respond to consumer demands, we need to define "supply" carefully, as we did "demand."

Supply is a schedule of amounts that will be offered for sale at different prices during some time period, other things remaining unchanged. Like demand, supply can also be plotted on a curve with amounts on the horizontal axis and prices on the vertical one. But it differs from demand when it is plotted, since the supply curve ordinarily slopes uphill, whereas the demand curve ordinarily slopes downhill. The upward slope of the supply curve reflects the fact that more units will usually be offered for sale at high than at low prices, in contrast to the reverse demand relationship.

Upward-sloping supply curves may seem obvious to you. The higher the price, the greater will be the profit inducement to produce and to sell more. Or they may seem anything but obvious. You may think of the economies of mass production and suspect that more units will be produced when demand increases, without any rise in price. This may, of course, be true under some circumstances, and sometimes—for example, in the auto industry—to a significant extent.

The relation between firms' costs and the supply curves for their products is analyzed in detail in Chapters 20–22. For the moment, take it on faith that most supply curves are flat or upward-sloping. And even if supply curves should turn out to be downward-sloping in some cases, the type of interaction among supply, demand, and price described in the following pages will still be useful.

Individual and market supply

Individual consumers and households are the basic economic decision makers underlying market demand curves. Similarly, individual suppliers are the basic decision makers underlying market supply curves. For consumer goods and services, business firms are the main suppliers; for labor and other productive resources, individuals (sometimes through unions) are the main suppliers.

We aggregate individual supplies to obtain

Table 6-1
Supply schedule for milk

PRICE PER QUART	NUMBER OF QUARTS SUPPLIED PER WEEK BY:			
	A	*B*	*C*	*All*
20 cents	50	50	20	120
15 cents	40	50	20	110
10 cents	40	40	0	80
5 cents	30	35	0	65

market supply curves. Suppose there are three dairy farms. At various milk prices, each will produce and offer different amounts for sale, as in Table 6-1. This is the market supply schedule for milk in this area.[1]

This supply schedule can be plotted on a graph just as the demand schedule was. Again putting price on the vertical axis and quantity on the horizontal one, we get the market supply curve shown in Figure 6-1.

It is important to remember some of the same warnings on supply that apply to demand: (1) Supply is a schedule, not a single amount. Thus, more output at a higher price may merely

[1] Farmer *C* is what some economists call a "marginal producer." He comes into the market only if the price rises to a relatively high level.

Figure 6-1
The supply curve shows how many quarts will be supplied each week at different prices.

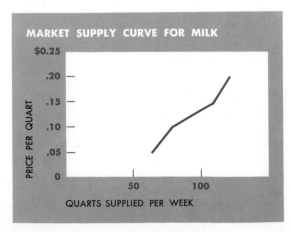

MARKET SUPPLY CURVE FOR MILK

be a movement to a new point on the supply schedule, not an increase in supply. A change in supply is a change in the schedule (a shift of the curve). (2) Supply has meaning only with reference to some time period. The period should always be specified. (3) A supply schedule or curve is always drawn on the assumption of "other things equal"—for example, costs of labor and raw materials, technology, and the like. Just what "other things" we hold constant will vary from case to case, depending partly on the time period involved. For a one-day period, the number of cows and the amount of mechanical equipment the farmer has must be taken as constants. If we're talking about supply per year, obviously such factors become variable. This would lead you to suspect that the supply curve per year might look quite different from the supply curve per day—and it does, as we shall see next.

Elasticity of supply

Supply can be elastic or inelastic, just like demand. This is true of both individual producers' and market supplies. If the amount put on the market is highly responsive to price changes, the supply is elastic. If the amount offered is little affected by price variations, the supply is inelastic. Except that the amount supplied and the price ordinarily move in the same rather than opposite directions, the concepts of demand and supply elasticity are similar. You can calculate a precise measure of supply elasticity by using the same percentage change formula as that given for demand, back on page 59.

Elasticity of supply varies with the time period involved. Take an extreme case of inelastic supply first. Suppose you have a strawberry patch and a roadside stand, but no overnight refrigeration. If you picked twenty quarts this morning, you must sell them today at whatever price you can get or let them spoil (neglecting the possibilities that you may eat them fresh yourself or preserve them). Thus, your supply curve *for the day* may be completely inelastic—a vertical line at twenty quarts of strawberries. By the end of the day, if you have them left, you're willing to sell your twenty quarts at any price from zero up—the higher the better, of course. Figure 6-2 pictures this simple assumption, in

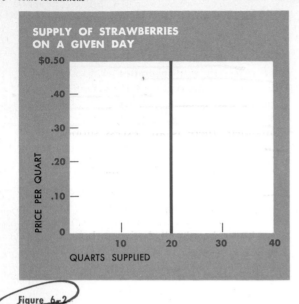

Figure 6-2
The chart shows completely inelastic supply. The same number of quarts is offered at any price shown.

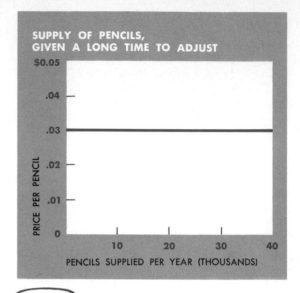

Figure 6-3
This chart shows infinitely elastic supply. Given a long time to adjust, any number of pencils can be produced for sale at 3 cents a pencil.

which, incidentally, cost of production appears to play no role in determining your supply curve for the day.

Now take a case at the other extreme. Suppose some simple commodity like lead pencils can be produced almost without limit at a certain cost—say, 3 cents per pencil—merely by duplicating existing manufacturing facilities, materials, and workers. *Given enough time to build new facilities,* almost any given number of pencils will be produced for sale at a price of 3 cents or above. Thus, the long-run supply curve might be completely elastic—a horizontal line, at 3 cents per pencil, as in Figure 6–3.

This case, like that of the strawberries, is oversimplified; cost per pencil may not be quite constant in the real world, and the resulting supply curve may not be perfectly flat. Most cases and most time periods, of course, fall somewhere between these two extremes.

SUPPLY, DEMAND, AND MARKET PRICE

You may have visited the "wheat pit" at the Board of Trade in Chicago, which is one of the world's major wheat-trading markets.

Here, millions of bushels of wheat are bought and sold daily by a relatively small number of men, acting largely as dealers and agents for others. Suppose the supply and demand for wheat in the pit on some particular day are as shown in Table 6–2, and that these schedules are constant for the entire day.

In effect, each of these men acts as an agent for people wanting to sell or buy wheat. Imagine that each seller tries to auction his wheat off at the highest possible price. Suppose that the first

Table 6–2

Supply and demand for wheat, Chicago, on a given day

Bushels offered (in millions)	Price	Bushels demanded (in millions)
18	$3.00	8
16	2.50	11
14	2.00	14
12	1.50	17
10	1.00	20

bid on this day is $1.50 a bushel for 1,000 bushels. It is readily filled, but it's clear that at this price there's going to be trouble, because buyers will demand 17 million bushels, whereas sellers are willing to offer only 12 million bushels. Table 6–2 shows that a lot of buyers are willing to pay more than $1.50 if they have to. And most of them soon discover they have to, because offerings are 5 million bushels short of demand at $1.50. We say there is an "excess demand" of 5 million bushels at $1.50. As buyers bid higher prices to get the wheat they want, the price will move up toward $2.00. As the price rises, those unwilling to pay the higher price will drop out and new sellers will come in, until at $2.00 the amount offered for sale just matches the amount demanded. There is no reason to suppose that the price will be bid higher this day, because everyone who is willing to pay $2.00 is getting his wheat and everyone who has wheat for sale at $2.00 sells it.

Try starting with a price of $3.00 to see whether that price could last long in this market. Where does the price stabilize?

This same analysis can be done graphically just as well. Figure 6-4 graphs these same demand and supply schedules. **The curves intersect at a price of $2.00 with 14 million bushels traded.**

Figure 6–4
With these supply and demand curves, the equilibrium price will be $2.00, with 14 million bushels exchanged.

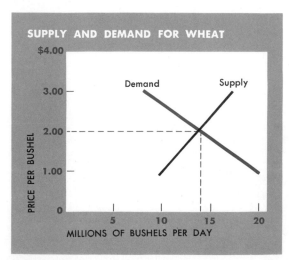

SUPPLY AND DEMAND FOR WHEAT

This is the only price at which the amount demanded just matches the amount supplied, and it is the price that will be reached through bargaining in the market. The reasoning is the same as with the schedules. Try any higher price—say, $3.00—and you can see from Figure 6-4 that it can't last. At $3.00, 18 million bushels will be offered but only 8 million bushels demanded; there is an "excess supply" of 10 million bushels. Competition among sellers will push the price down. At any price higher than $2.00, there is excess supply. There will be too many sellers for the buyers, and sellers will shade their prices in order to find buyers. At any lower price, buyers won't be able to get the wheat they demand and will shade up the prices they offer.

Equilibrium price and market equilibrium

When a price is established that just clears the market, economists call it an "equilibrium price." The amount offered just equals the amount demanded at that price. Price is in equilibrium when, with given demand and supply curves, it stays put at that level. At any other level, price will not be in equilibrium, because there will be excess supply or excess demand that will drive price up or down toward a level that will eliminate the excess supply or excess demand.

When an equilibrium price has been reached, with given demand and supply curves, we say the market is in equilibrium. At the prevailing price, there is neither excess supply nor excess demand. Unless either demand or supply changes, price will remain unchanged, as will the amount bought and sold in each time period.

Consumer demands and producers' responses to those demands are thus meshed together through market adjustments toward equilibrium. Once a market has reached equilibrium, it has impersonally and automatically accomplished the following:

1. It has reflected the wants of all consumers willing to spend their dollars in that market, weighting each want by the number of dollars that particular consumer will spend at different prices. If each consumer's demand schedule

truly reflects the marginal utilities of different amounts of the product to him, the market has given him the largest utility obtainable for his dollars.

2. It has led firms to produce as much of the product as consumers will buy, when the price is high enough to cover the costs of producing the commodity. These costs are reflected in the supply curve; the higher costs of production are, the less will be produced at each price offered by consumers.

And we can be reasonably sure this equilibrium accurately reflects the preferences of all parties concerned, buyers and sellers, because the exchanges are voluntary. If any individual saw the purchase or sale as against his best interests, he would not have bought or sold at that price.

Changes in demand and supply

Suppose that on the following day, the demand for wheat increases, to D^1D^1 in Figure 6–5. The supply curve remains unchanged. Common sense tells you that with constant supply and increased demand, the price will be bid up—and it is. With increased demand D^1D^1, the price is bid up to $2.50 with 16 million bushels bought. Although the supply curve is constant, more wheat is supplied at the higher price. The result of the increased demand is *both* a higher price and more wheat traded. Suppose now that on the third day, demand rises again, to D^2D^2. The price is then bid still higher—up to $3.00 with 18 million bushels bought. The demand curve slides up the fixed supply curve.

Now try holding the demand curve constant and increasing or decreasing supply. Figure

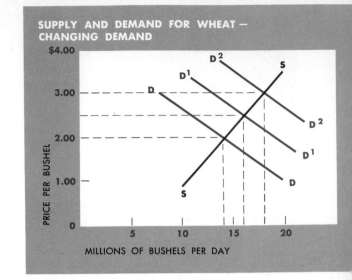

SUPPLY AND DEMAND FOR WHEAT — CHANGING DEMAND

Figure 6–5
Increases in demand D^1D^1 and D^2D^2 cause increases in both price and quantity traded. The new equilibrium with D^2D^2 involves a price of $3.00 and 18 million bushels exchanged daily.

out the effect on price and sales of each shift in supply.

Last, consider a case in which both demand and supply shift simultaneously. Suppose the price of turnips is 10 cents a pound and 2,000 pounds are being sold daily, with curves SS and DD in Figure 6–6. Now both supply and demand increase, to $S'S'$ and $D'D'$. The result is a big increase in sales, to 4,000 pounds, and a rise in price to 12 cents. Try shifting the curves to other positions, and with steeper and flatter slopes. The market price and quantity sold will automatically adjust to reflect the preferences of both buyers and sellers.

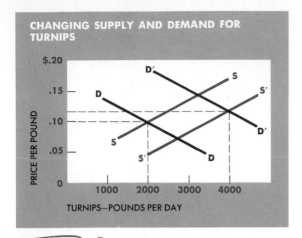

CHANGING SUPPLY AND DEMAND FOR TURNIPS

Figure 6-6

When both demand and supply shift simultaneously, as shown by the dashed lines sales rise to 4,000 pounds and price rises to 12 cents. Try shifting the curves to other positions.

Supply and demand: some special cases

Completely inelastic supply. Some extreme cases may help to clarify what is involved in market adjustments to different demand-and-supply relationships. First take a case in which the amount supplied is absolutely fixed. A favorite economists' example is that there are only four corners at State and Madison Streets in Chicago, sometimes called the busiest corner in the world. The supply curve for building space on this corner is thus completely inelastic—there's no more land available on the corner no matter how high land prices or rents may go. Suppose we graph the supply of land on this corner in square feet, and the demand (*DD*) for it on either a purchase or a rental basis. The picture might look roughly like Figure 6–7, with annual rents in equilibrium at $1,000 per square foot.

Now suppose the demand for space on the corner increases. The demand curve moves up to D^1D^1. Property owners can now charge $1,100 per square foot. The amount of land rented is identical before and after the increase in demand. This outcome is very nice for the landowner, not so good for the consumer. But if demand falls, the full burden falls on the land-

owner. The price (rent) going to the supplier (landowner) is determined solely by the demand. Supply in this extreme case, and only in this case, has no active role in determining the price. Note that supply may be inelastic for many products **in the short run,** but long-run inelastic supply is uncommon.

Completely elastic supply with "constant costs". Now take the other extreme—the pencil industry described before, where the amount supplied could be increased at a constant cost by merely duplicating productive facilities. Given a long enough time period, the supply curve here would look perfectly flat, as in Figure 6–8. If *DD* is the demand, the price of pencils will be 3 cents, and 10,000 per day will be made and sold. If demand increases to D^1D^1, the price remains unchanged while production and sales rise to 12,000 daily. This is a case of "constant costs." Since more pencils can be produced at the same cost per pencil, increased demand will simply call forth more pencils without bidding up the price.

Most real-world cases lie between the land and pencil extremes—although many commodities approximate the pencil case, **given a long**

Figure 6-7
With completely inelastic supply, increased demand means merely a higher price.

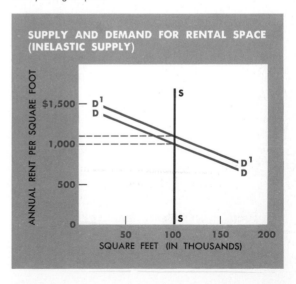

SUPPLY AND DEMAND FOR RENTAL SPACE (INELASTIC SUPPLY)

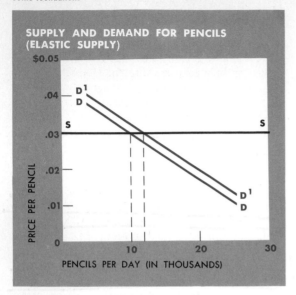

**SUPPLY AND DEMAND FOR PENCILS
(ELASTIC SUPPLY)**

Figure 6-8
With infinitely elastic supply, increased demand leads to more output with no increase in price.

enough time period for adjustment. If increased output can be obtained only by constructing more expensive factories, or by paying higher prices for raw materials and labor, the supply curve will slope upward. This is the case that economists call "increasing costs," and it is a common one.

Try working out graphically the results of increased demand in constant and increasing cost cases. You will see that it makes a good deal of difference to you, the consumer, which kind of product you want more of. In the elastic-supply case, you get more at the same price; in the inelastic-supply case, you get more only at a higher price. (With **decreasing** costs and a **downward**-sloping supply curve, which we have temporarily ruled out, you could be happier still, since then increased demand could mean more goods at a **lower** price.)

THE SOCIAL FUNCTIONS OF MARKET PRICES

It is easy to get bogged down in the mechanics of demand and supply curves. Stop and be sure you understand the three big social functions of market prices as they move to equilibrate demand and supply in different markets. Note that they serve these functions automatically, in response to many buyers and sellers each intent on looking out for his own self-interests.

Suppose, to take a case recently much in the news, the demand for gasoline and other oil products grows, beginning from a market equilibrium like that for wheat in Figure 6–4. Suppose, using the figures there, the equilibrium price is $2.00 per barrel of crude oil (about what it was before the formation of the OPEC cartel and their escalation of oil prices), with 14 million barrels sold per day. Demand grows by 1 million barrels per day. What will the results be?

The demand curve moves out, or up the supply curve, by 1 million barrels at each price. In Table 6–2 and Figure 6–4, add 1 million barrels to the amount demanded at each price. Thus, the price of oil will rise to a new equilibrium level of about $2.15, with about 14.8 million barrels bought daily. (Note that the amount bought does not rise a full million barrels, because at $2.15 per barrel the short-run supply curve says that suppliers will offer only about 14.8 million barrels, not 15 million.) Note the three functions of the rising price.

1. **The higher price calls forth more production. (a) It immediately calls forth 800,000 additional barrels of oil per day in response to increased consumer demand, given the short-run supply curve indicated. (b) With more time to adjust (that is, in the long run), the higher price will also stimulate further drilling for oil, moving the entire supply curve out, to the right.** This is a long-run supply increase, whereas (a) was a short-run increase in output, given the short-run supply curve.

2. **The higher price rations the available supply of oil to those who want it most, and induces them to economize on its use as it becomes more expensive.** As Table 6–2 indicates, the public wants vastly more oil than there is to go around; the table shows a demand for 20 million barrels daily at $1.00 a barrel, and the amount would be still larger at lower prices—perhaps almost infinite if oil were free. Price is the rationer of scarce supplies in a market system; it

leads users to economize on the use of the increasingly expensive commodity. If, for example, the supply of oil is reduced (as it was by the OPEC cartel in 1974), rising prices will ration the less urgent demanders out of the market, determining who gets the increasingly scarce oil, and stimulating the use of substitutes.

3. Although it is not shown on our chart, the higher price for oil will increase the demand for substitute energy sources (such as coal, natural gas, and nuclear energy). This will raise their prices too and stimulate greater production of them in both the short and long runs. A higher price for any product stimulates the production of substitutes, an important effect indeed, as some natural resources are exhausted and society needs to stimulate the production of substitutes. (Note that this effect may stimulate research seeking currently unknown substitutes, as well as more output of currently known energy sources.)

To summarize, rising market prices, reflecting excess demand, serve three vitally important social purposes: (1) They increase the amount of the scarce product produced by profit-seeking suppliers; (2) they ration out less urgent demanders, leading users to economize their use of the scarce commodity; and (3) they stimulate the production of substitutes.

THE ECONOMICS OF PRICE FIXING

The law of supply and demand states that market price and quantity sold are determined by supply and demand under competitive conditions. But lots of times, people—labor unions, farmers, businessmen, congressmen—don't like the prices and quantities set by market demand and supply. And they want to do something about it. What then?

Price ceilings and "shortages"

Most people don't like to pay high prices. When prices rise, the pressures mount on Congress and the president to hold them down. "How can I pay $1.00 a pound for butter and $200 a month rent for a poor apartment when my income is only $5,000 a year?" asks the mill

hand. And he's not going to be very happy about getting an answer from the politicians in Washington that the law of supply and demand says it has to be that way. He wants something done, or he's easy picking for the other party next election.

So sometimes Congress passes a law to keep prices down. Suppose it slaps an 80-cent price ceiling on butter, below the equilibrium level. The demand for and supply of butter are shown in Figure 6–9. The equilibrium price would be $1.00 a pound.

At the legal price ceiling, clearly there is excess demand of about 600 pounds; people want a lot more butter than there is to buy. The amount demanded daily is 2,200 pounds; that offered is only 1,600. There is, in short, a "shortage."

Who gets the butter? The price system is tied down—it can't ration the butter by equilibrating supply and demand through a higher price.

"First come, first served" may be the answer. Housewives get the children off to school early and head for the grocer's. They stand in lines in the grocery store. This solution is not calculated to make anyone very happy, least of all the grocer, who loses his friends fast when there isn't enough to go around, and the working wives, who can't do their shopping till evening. We had

Figure 6–9
When the government sets a legal maximum price below the market equilibrium price, there's trouble. There is excess demand for butter at the artificially low price.

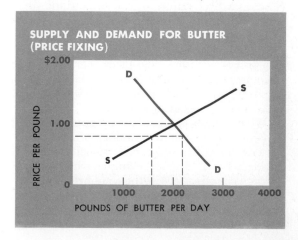

a painful experience sitting in long gasoline lines in 1974, when the OPEC oil embargo plus a government price ceiling created a temporary gasoline "shortage."

In frustration, grocers may set up informal butter rationing systems of their own—say, only a half pound to a customer. Or they may decide to protect their regular customers, so they put away a few cases of butter for them. This is hard on wives who shop around, and disastrous for families that move to new neighborhoods.

If enough people become unhappy enough, the government may have to step in with a formal rationing plan, whereby the customer has to have a government ration ticket as well as money to buy a pound of butter (or his weekly ration of gasoline). Nobody is very happy about being rationed, and everybody complains about the red tape. Unless the government officials are both skillful and lucky, the number of ration tickets issued won't exactly match the supplies available, and mixups can be counted on.

Finally, the price system may sneak in the back door again and take over part of the equilibrating job outside the law. "Black markets" may develop. It's pretty hard for well-to-do consumers not to offer the corner grocer a little extra for an extra pound of butter. And it's pretty hard for the grocer, pinched between rising costs and fixed price ceilings, to refuse. Short of a regimented system like Hitler's Germany, it's very hard to enforce rigid price ceilings when excess demand is large. In World War II, such ceilings worked reasonably well in the United States, partly because of intense patriotic pressures and partly because the government gradually raised ceilings as pressures built up on various commodities. The surprising thing to most economists was not that black markets developed, but that the public's sense of fair play was so strong that the price-control system didn't blow apart faster than it did.

Whether the job is done by informal seller rationing, government rationing, or black-market price increases, someone or something has to decide who is to get the butter when a price ceiling is imposed below the equilibrium market price. A price ceiling works no magic. It just transfers the rationing job to some other channel, and it eliminates the stimulus to supply that higher prices would produce. You can't get rid of the basic supply-and-demand forces at work by passing a law.

Rent controls and housing shortages

In recent years, rents on apartments and houses have risen rapidly almost everywhere. This reflects growing pressures of population in many areas, rising construction costs, higher taxes and maintenance, and many other factors. Rent is a big part of many family budgets, especially for poor families, and it is not surprising that many cities have felt strong pressures to impose rent ceilings, particularly since it is commonly believed that landlords are high-income individuals and businesses that gouge renters whenever they are able to do so.

Rent ceilings were widely used during World War II, and three large cities—New York, Stockholm, and Moscow—provide interesting case studies of the effects of retaining these ceilings over extended periods. Let us assume that the rent ceiling is set below the market equilibrium level; otherwise, there would be no point in applying it. The immediate result, our supply-and-demand analysis tells us, will depend on the supply and demand curves involved. In the short run, presumably the supply of rental apartments in, say, New York City is substantially fixed; the supply curve is almost a vertical line. If the legal rent ceiling is below the market-clearing level, there is little the landlords can do (if they obey the law) other than complain and see part or all of their profits shifted to renters. What renters get the benefit of the lower rents? Presumably those who are lucky enough to be in the controlled apartments. There will be an excess demand for apartments at the controlled price (a "shortage" of apartments), and newcomers looking for places to live will have a tough time, since they can't get apartments by bidding them away from present tenants through offering to pay higher rents. But all in all, the rent-control program seems to be providing lower rents at the expense of those well-to-do landlords. (*Query:* How would you ration the apartments among the excess demanders in such cases when present occupants moved out?)

Not only the rationing but also the supply-increasing effects of higher prices are tied down by the rent-control laws. If you were a landlord, what would you do? As your after-costs profit on rented apartments fell, you would transfer your investment out of rental housing to some uncontrolled activity where you could make a normal profit. If you couldn't sell the property outright (which would be difficult, because potential buyers would know about the rent controls too), you would probably do this by skimping on maintenance and repairs. Above all, you certainly wouldn't invest in constructing new rental housing if it were also rent-controlled. The long-run supply would be far more elastic than the short-run.

Precisely these things happened. In New York, for example, there has been wholesale undermaintenance and actual abandonment of older apartments that would have been maintained in livable condition without rent controls. In 1975, for example, 50,000 apartments were simply abandoned as unlivable in spite of the drastic housing "shortage." New apartment construction was virtually zero in the late 1960s, until the city began to relax the rent-control laws and exempt new housing. Families holding leases on controlled apartments went to great lengths to keep their apartments, whose rents were far below free-market levels. They were passed on within families, or sold for (often illegal) side payments where leases were transferable. Hopeful renters perused the obituary columns of the local papers, and arrived ahead of the first mourners. The subsidy was large for those who benefited; but the cost to newly married, families who had to move, and all those who would have benefited from new housing construction was large. Not least, massive undermaintenance of rent-controlled apartments contributed significantly to the rapid decay of New York City slum areas.

In Stockholm, the results of long-continued rent controls were similar. World War II rent controls were maintained, with only slow rises permitted to meet rising costs. By the mid-1960s, over 40 percent of Stockholm's entire population was registered in the city government's official queue, which is supposed to govern priority as to who gets the controlled housing as it becomes available. Stories abound of children being given official-queue list certificates as christening gifts, and obituary columns are a closely watched source of rental openings. The average waiting time on the official government queue has approached ten years. However, much new housing is outside the rent-control system, and most residents find their housing at higher rates through more usual market arrangements now.

Moscow (and the USSR generally) is the extreme case of such controlled rents. Housing is very scarce and generally poor in quality. Since it is virtually all owned by the state, the issue is merely one of how the available supply is rationed. Rents are very low (often less than 5 percent of family income, compared to about 25 percent in the United States), so there is an enormous shortage of (excess demand for) housing, which is allocated by government fiat, with preference given to Communist party members, good workers, and others who meet special standards set by the government. Most families must share their apartments with others, and young people often wait for years after marriage before getting an apartment of their own. Activities aimed at finding apartments in New York and Stockholm are nothing compared to the desperate plans devised by Muscovites.

Price controls, shortages, and rationing

Is there a "shortage" of good apartments in New York? Was there a shortage of gasoline in 1974 when OPEC embargoed the United States and the government here applied price controls? Is there a shortage of Porsche sportscars, of filet mignon, of fine whiskies? In each case, there obviously isn't enough to go around to everybody who would like to have some. But the appropriate question in each case is, At what price? You may say there's no "shortage" of Porsche sportscars. But suppose the government fixed the price at $2,500? It is easy to predict that there would be long waiting lines of potential buyers. Or suppose Congress decreed that the price of filet mignon could be no more than 50 cents a pound. A huge "shortage" would predictably develop overnight.

You may say that, in some moral sense, there is a shortage of adequate housing for poor families. But if we define "shortage" (as most economists do) to mean "excess demand," a shortage arises only when there is unsatisfied demand at the existing price. And this condition cannot last in a free market. An economic "shortage" will arise and continue only when the price is fixed below the equilibrium market level.

Whenever there is a shortage, with the price system tied down, some other form of rationing must be found. Many have been devised, officially and unofficially—government ration tickets; illegal black-market payments; first come, first served; friendship with the rationing officials; social acceptability of claimants' behavior. Price rationing rewards those with money; first come, first served rewards those with patience and free time; and so on. It has been pointed out that some of the most desirable things on university campuses are rationed largely on the basis of personality and good looks. Each of these rationing systems may have its advocates as being the most equitable and efficient.

Troublesome as the rationing problem may be, outlawing the supply-increasing effects of rising free-market prices where supplies are scarce is likely to create even more serious economic problems. In the New York rent-control case, for example, many critics argue that the cost in apartments abandoned or not built far exceeds the "equity" advantages to protected renters.

Farm price supports

Some people—usually sellers—worry because prices aren't high enough. Labor unions often try to set wages above free-market levels. Some business firms do the same thing with their prices. The government is a large-scale participant in the game of putting floors under prices above the free-market level; farm price-support programs and minimum-wage legislation are big examples.

Suppose the government decrees that wheat shall not sell for less than $3.00 a bushel when the market-clearing price would be only $2.00, as pictured in Figure 6–10. It's clear that there will be a lot of unsold wheat around—excess supply at the $3.00 price is 30 million bushels.

Suppose the government price floor is enforced and nobody undercuts the stated $3.00

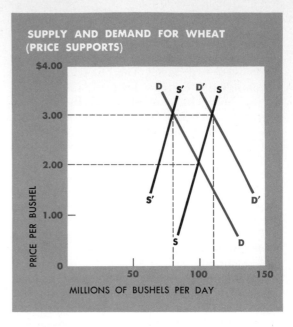

SUPPLY AND DEMAND FOR WHEAT (PRICE SUPPORTS)

Figure 6–10
When the government sets a minimum price higher than the market equilibrium price, there's also trouble. At $3.00, there is an excess supply of 30 million bushels. D'D' shows the new demand curve if the government buys up the excess; S'S' the new supply curve if the government induces farmers to restrict their output.

price. Are wheat farmers better or worse off as a result? First, only about 80 million bushels will be bought. Another 30 million bushels are offered, and either the government will have to buy them up or strong price-cutting pressures will develop among the farmers with the unsold wheat. Second, our old friend elasticity of demand reenters. If demand is inelastic (as in Figure 6–10), total expenditures on wheat are larger at the higher price, and total farm income is up (even though consumers get less wheat to eat). But if demand is elastic, the higher price leaves everyone worse off; then, farmers get less total income from their wheat, and consumers get less wheat.

But even if demand is inelastic over the price range involved, this simple form of government price edict won't prove very satisfactory. If you are one of the farmers with the millions of bushels of wheat that nobody bought, the higher total income of wheat farmers is small solace to you when you have no income at all. You want the government to help you, too.

So the government program will probably take one of two basic courses: (1) The government may support the legal price through buying up the extra 30 million bushels of wheat. This would in effect move the total (private plus government) demand curve to the right (to $D'D'$ in Fig. 6–10), so the equilibrium price is $3.00 with 110 million bushels sold. Or (2) the government may restrict wheat production (maybe through a "soil-conservation" program) to reduce supply to a point where the new market price is $3.00 with sales of 80 million bushels. This policy would bring supply and demand into equilibrium by shifting the supply curve to the left (to $S'S'$ in Fig. 6–10).

In approach (1), the government ends up buying the 30 million bushels of wheat at $3.00 a bushel—at a cost of $90 million to the taxpayers. Who gains? Farmers. Who loses? Taxpayers, and consumers who end up with less wheat and a higher price for what they buy. Moreover, unless something changes, the government will keep on piling up wheat indefinitely.

In approach (2), this continuing "surplus" situation is avoided by requiring that 30 million fewer bushels of wheat are produced. If the government merely required everybody to cut production by the required percentage, this would be the end of the matter. But the government pays farmers for not producing. Here again, taxpayers pick up the bill for the subsidy paid to farmers for not producing the 30 million bushels of wheat. And as under approach (1), consumers pay more and get fewer bushels of wheat. Strikingly, under both plans, it is the big, rich farmers who get most of the benefits. Under (1), the big farmers get most of the higher price benefits because they have more output to sell. Under (2), they get the biggest government payments for cutting back production, since they begin with the biggest production to cut back. The farm-income price programs have increased mainly the incomes that were already highest.

The government can keep the price up—if it's willing to eliminate excess supply by buying it up or by restricting output. But laws that fix prices above or below market-equilibrium levels

without dealing with excess demand or supply soon face painful problems of which simple supply-and-demand analysis can give ample warning.

Minimum wage laws

In conclusion, to check your grasp of supply-and-demand analysis, try the following. As was suggested in Chapter 3, a popular remedy for poverty is getting the government to pass a minimum wage law that will ensure all workers an above-poverty annual wage. For example, if Congress were to set a legal minimum wage of $3 per hour, given an average annual work year of 2,000 hours, this would provide an annual income of $6,000 for all workers—not magnificent, but well above many incomes now, and above the federal "poverty level." Would the proposed minimum wage law eliminate poverty? (*Hint:* Draw a hypothetical demand curve of a typical business firm for low-skilled or unskilled workers, and a hypothetical supply curve for such workers. Suppose the market-clearing equilibrium wage is now $2.50. What would you predict as the effect of the new law? Who would gain and who would lose?)

CONCLUSION: SUPPLY, DEMAND, AND MARKET PRICES

Continuous interaction among demand, supply, and prices in a myriad of markets for goods and services is the core of the private-enterprise, market-directed economic system. In each market, the spending and work decisions of individuals combine with the profit-seeking activities of businesses, large and small, in movements toward equilibrium that, when combined with thousands of other markets, allocate society's scarce productive resources to producing the goods and services that consumers want. Part 3 will provide a more detailed and rigorous analysis of this process. But the preceding sections provide a rough overview of how self-interests of millions of different individuals and businesses are meshed together through the market system to do the job.

Supply-and-demand analysis provides a sim-

TWO MORE APPLICATIONS

Who really pays the taxes?

Suppose the government imposes an additional $1.00 tax on each fifth of whiskey distilled for sale. Assume that the long-run supply curve before the new tax is SS in Figure 6–11 (same in both halves). The left-hand diagram shows a highly elastic demand curve for whiskey, the right-hand diagram a highly inelastic one. Before the new tax, the price is $5.00 per fifth, and 100,000 fifths are being sold weekly in both diagrams.

The new tax raises the effective cost of producing whiskey by $1.00 per fifth; hence the supply curve moves to the left by $1.00 at each level of output. Less will be produced at each price. S'S' represents the new supply curve (after tax) in both halves of the diagram. But as supply is restricted, the results are very different with the two demand curves.

With highly inelastic demand (right-hand diagram), as price moves up, consumers continue to buy nearly as much whiskey; the new equilibrium shows nearly as much whiskey produced and sold as before the tax, with the price to the consumer higher by nearly the full amount of the tax. Nearly the whole $1 tax has been shifted onto consumers. With highly elas-

Figure 6–11

A new tax on whiskey is largely passed on to consumers with little drop in consumption if demand is inelastic (right-hand portion), but results mainly in reduced output and consumption if demand is elastic (left-hand portion).

tic demand (left-hand diagram), the amount bought drops rapidly as price rises. The new after-tax equilibrium shows mainly a reduction in production and purchases, with the new price (including tax) only a little above the old $5.00 level. The main result is that consumers get less whiskey, while producers share $1 of the $5+ price with the government. Simple supply-and-demand analysis can produce illuminating results if we use it to examine particular markets.

"Free goods"

How is it that air, without which we should all die, is free, whereas most other things, which are much less essential, command a price? The answer is obvious, once you try a demand-and-supply analysis. What is the supply of air? It is substantially unlimited at zero cost. The supply curve would rise above the zero-cost line only at some very high quantity figure for most real-world situations. Thus, even though we might be willing, if necessary, to pay a very high price for air, it just isn't necessary. Draw a demand curve, probably highly inelastic, wherever you wish and it will still intersect the zero-cost supply curve at a price of zero.

But now suppose pollution threatens to reduce breathable air below healthy standards. Then the supply of acceptable air is no longer infinite at a zero cost. The supply curve will slope up, reflecting the cost of providing enough clean air, and we shall have to pay a price to get the acceptable air we need.

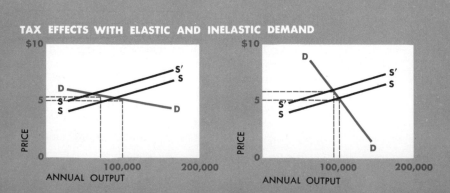

TAX EFFECTS WITH ELASTIC AND INELASTIC DEMAND

ple but powerful tool for thinking through a wide range of economic problems—both those of individual markets and those of the economy as a whole. The preceding pages provide a variety of examples of how supply-and-demand analysis can illuminate everyday problems. Over and over in the chapters ahead we shall be asking, What determines demand and supply in this market, how do they interact, and what is the equilibrium outcome toward which they move? These questions are the core of analytical economics.

REVIEW

Concepts to remember

Recheck your understanding of the important new concepts introduced in this chapter. They are:

equilibrium price	excess demand
supply	excess supply
supply curve	shortage
elasticity of supply	rationing
market price	constant costs
market equilibrium	increasing costs

For analysis and discussion

1. Define supply carefully. What is a change in supply?
2. Is it demand or supply that primarily determines price? If your answer is, "Different in different cases," give an example in which you would expect each to be the dominant force.
3. Explain carefully what is meant by saying that an equilibrium price "clears the market."
4. When demand is large, we can be sure the price of the commodity will be high. True or false? Why?
5. Why are diamonds so high-priced, when they serve for the most part only as decoration, while air is free?
6. Are the factors determining the price of a Picasso painting the same as those determining the price of potatoes? Explain your answer.
7. Is there a shortage of T-bone steaks? Would there be if the government set a price ceiling of 50 cents a pound? How about hamburger?
8. Go back to Figure 6–9, and assume that the demand for butter increases. Explain what will happen.
9. Suppose that the demand for cigarettes is very inelastic and a new tax is imposed on cigarettes. Would the tax be passed on to consumers through higher prices? Compare this with a product for which the demand is highly elastic.
10. How does elasticity of demand help to explain why, historically, governments often imposed a salt tax when they wanted to obtain more revenue?

Throughout the Middle Ages, to charge interest for the use of money was improper under Catholic church doctrines (most lending was done by Jews) and was prohibited by law in many kingdoms—with violation sometimes punishable by death. Such laws were commonly evaded by borrowers and lenders because of the obvious benefits to both of borrowing and lending, and, with the Protestant Reformation and the commercial and industrial revolutions, official antagonism to lending at interest faded rapidly. Yet, today, most states still have laws limiting the interest rates that can legally be charged on loans, presumably to safeguard borrowers against greedy lenders.

State laws have varied widely, but many have had a general ceiling (say, 10 percent or so on business and mortgage loans), with an escape provision permitting higher rates where (as on small loans to consumers) extra costs or risks of lending can be shown. In such cases, upper limits of 30–42 percent are not uncommon. The volume of such lending is large—nearly $200 billion of consumer credit was outstanding in 1975 on department-store installment credit, credit cards, bank loans, auto-purchase loans, and the like.

In response to the recent wave of "consumerism," the National Uniform Credit Act was passed to limit to 1.5 percent per month (18 percent per annum) the interest rate that department stores, credit-card companies, auto dealers, banks, and others can charge borrowers. This was well below the going rate for many borrowers, especially high-risk, low-income individuals and families. Moreover, in the early 1970s, several states went still further and reduced the legal ceiling rate to 10 (Arkansas, Montana, and Tennessee) or 12 percent (Minnesota, Washington, and Wisconsin). Consumer protection groups are pushing such legislation in other states.

Parallel pressures to impose lower interest-rate ceilings on mortgage loans (which now total $400 billion) arise each time money becomes "tight" and interest rates rise. The following news item is an example.

TUNNEY URGES 6% HOME LOAN INTEREST LIMIT

Los Angeles—"The economy needs a bang to shock it back into economic health," Senator John Tunney says, and one big help would be a mandatory six percent interest rate upper limit on home loans.

"We're really on the brink of depression," the California Senator said Saturday, at the conclusion of a three-hour conference he called with representatives of labor, business, and the League of Women Voters. Home buyers need more money at reasonable rates.[2]

[2] *San Francisco Chronicle*, April 7, 1975.

Should your state lower its ceiling on consumer and mortgage loans? What do you predict will be the results of these new consumer-protection laws? Who will gain and who will lose?

CHAPTER 7

THE macroeconomy: an overview

We now have, from Chapters 1 through 6, an overview of the way a basically market-directed economy handles the big economic problems. This analysis is often called "microeconomics," because it focuses on the way individual households and businesses behave, and the way their interactions govern the uses society makes of its productive resources.

We turn now in Part 2 to an examination of the "macroeconomy"—the totals of output, employment, income, and prices, when we add together all the individual economic units in the economy. Where microeconomics looks at the output and prices of shoes or pizzas, macroeconomics looks at the **total** national output of all goods and services added together, at the **total** national income earned by everyone in the economy, at the average price level for all goods and services. Clearly, macroeconomics must build on the foundation of microeconomics, for the national totals are nothing but the sum of the individual parts. And we shall find that the concepts of aggregate demand and aggregate supply (when we add together all households and businesses) help in understanding the outcome of excess supply and demand at the national level, much as supply and demand do for individual products and services. But combining individual demands as supplies into national aggregates raises some important new problems.

THE CIRCULAR FLOW OF SPENDING AND PRODUCTION

In a market-directed economy, goods and services are produced only when there is a market demand for them. If businesses produce more than customers buy (that is, if there is excess aggregate supply), unsold inventories pile up, prices fall, and businessmen cut back on production, laying off workers. Conversely, if customers try to buy more than is being produced (that is, if there is excess aggregate demand), prices are bid up (there is inflation), and businesses increase output and employment.

Total money spending is the flow that controls the level of aggregate production, employment, and prices. Businesses pay wages, interest, and other income to the public in producing what consumers want to buy. The public, as consumers, channels the income back to businesses in payment for finished goods and services. This demand, in turn, leads businessmen to hire workers to produce more goods and services for consumers.

Figure 7–1 shows this circular flow of income. The inner circle shows consumers' spending to businesses for goods and services (top half) and businesses' spending back to the public through wages and interest (bottom half). The outer circle shows the corresponding reverse flow of productive services and final products. On the bottom half, labor and other productive services are being hired by businesses from the public. On the top half, finished goods are moving from businesses to consumers.

Which comes first, business hiring and wage payments, or consumer spending? This is a chicken-and-egg question. The main point is that neither can go on for long without the other. Economic activity in a private-enterprise system is a continuous flow of productive services and finished products, called forth by a matching counterflow of money spending and guided by the price system into thousands of different product channels within the main streams shown in the diagram.

You can readily see that this picture is oversimplified. Again, the government has been left out. And the diagram omits savings and production of capital goods that aren't sold to consumers. But the simple picture points up the central role of the circular flow of spending. Unless there is a continuous flow of money-spending by businesses to the public and by the public to businesses, we're in trouble. If some-

Figure 7–1
Dollars flow from consumers to businesses and back in a continuous circle, in payment for final goods and productive services, respectively.

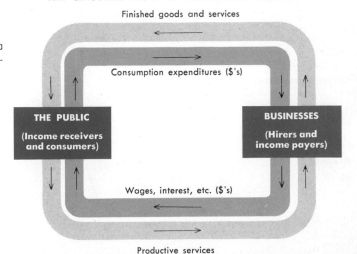

THE CIRCULAR FLOW OF ECONOMIC ACTIVITY

Finished goods and services

Consumption expenditures ($'s)

THE PUBLIC
(Income receivers and consumers)

BUSINESSES
(Hirers and income payers)

Wages, interest, etc. ($'s)

Productive services

thing dams up the flow of spending (say, either households or businesses don't respend the incomes they receive), there is excess total supply; depression and unemployment result, and the economy wastefully operates inside its production frontier. Conversely, if households and businesses spend more than the economy is producing (say, by drawing on past savings or borrowing new money from banks), there is excess demand.

Thus, in macroeconomics, the levels of both aggregate demand (total spending) and aggregate supply (total capacity of the economy to produce goods and services) are very important. In the short run, the potential full-employment output of an economy is roughly fixed, set by its production-possibilities frontier. Thus, in the short run, the major focus of macroeconomics is on aggregate demand, for that largely determines the level of current production, employment, incomes, and prices. But in the long run, we can increase the economy's capacity to produce—by saving and investing in new machines and factories, by training workers to produce more efficiently, and the like. Thus, in the long run, the major focus is on expanding potential aggregate supply, for that determines the rate at which society's output and standard of living can rise.

GROWTH AND FLUCTUATIONS IN THE AMERICAN ECONOMY

Viewed macroeconomically, how well has the American economy performed? The answer can be summed up in three statements:

1. Total national output has grown rapidly and vigorously over the past two centuries.
2. Output has grown far more rapidly than the number of people at work—that is, output per person (and hence the average standard of living) has also risen rapidly.
3. Real growth has been spasmodic and uneven, interrupted by intermittent inflationary booms and recessions.

Growth in total output

Figure 7–2 shows the growth in national output over the past century. National output (often called gross national product, or GNP) in actual prices rose from $7 billion to $1.5 trillion. If you take out the price inflation, the growth is less, but it's still phenomenal—from $30 billion to about $1.2 trillion in constant dollars (at 1972 prices). This is a more-than-thirtyfold increase. Total real output grew between 3 and 3½ percent per annum. This rate

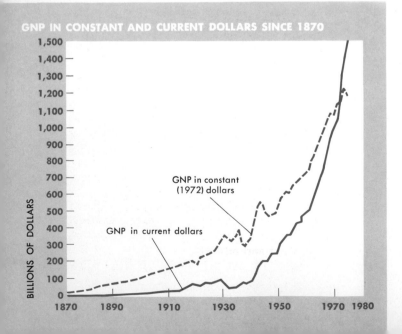

GNP IN CONSTANT AND CURRENT DOLLARS SINCE 1870

GNP in constant (1972) dollars

GNP in current dollars

BILLIONS OF DOLLARS

Figure 7–2

Total national output has grown rapidly, but in spurts, over the past century. The solid line shows GNP in current dollars, while the dashed line shows GNP in dollars of constant (1972) purchasing power. The latter thus shows the growth in real output. (Sources: National Bureau of Economic Research and U.S. Department of Commerce.)

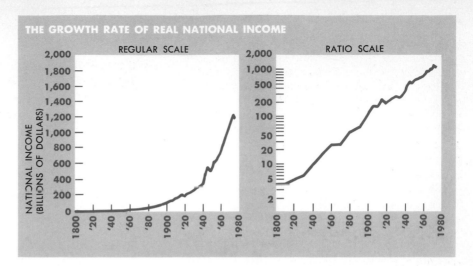

Figure 7-3
Both halves of the chart show the same data—total national output since 1800 in constant (1972) dollars. But the ratio scale shows that the annual growth rate has been quite stable over the past century, not rising sharply as the regular (left-hand) scale suggests. (Sources: National Industrial Conference Board and U.S. Department of Commerce.)

doesn't sound like much in a single year, but it compounds fast as the decades go by. An annual growth rate of $3\frac{1}{3}$ percent will more than double GNP every two decades.

Growth rates—a digression

Figure 7–3, which takes an even longer look at American economic history, emphasizes the importance of considering annual growth *rates*—that is, the percentage increase per year. The left-hand portion shows real national income—in constant prices—from 1800 to 1975. This chart makes it look as if the growth rate had speeded up enormously in the last half century. The line goes almost straight up, with an increase of over $500 billion in the last fifty years.

But look at the right-hand portion. This shows exactly the same data (national income since 1800, in constant prices) on a "ratio," or "logarithmic," scale. In contrast to regular charts, which give equal vertical distance to equal **absolute** increases, this ratio scale on the vertical axis gives equal distance to equal **percentage** increases. Thus, on the ratio scale, an increase from 5 to 10 takes about a third of an inch vertically, and an increase from 100 to 200, or from 500 to 1,000, takes exactly the same distance.

A ratio scale permits easy comparison of annual growth rates over a long period. A constant **percentage** increase—say, 3 percent per year—will show as an equal vertical increase each year—a steadily rising straight line. If the growth rate is 4 percent, the line will be steeper. If it is only 2 percent, the line will be flatter.

Thus, when we look at the right-hand section of Figure 7–3, we see the past in a different perspective. What looks on the regular-interval scale like a big increase in the recent growth rate turns out on the ratio scale to be just about the same annual growth rate as over most of our history.

Growth in output (or income) per worker and per capita

This growth in national output in part reflects the steady increase in the number of people working. But over the past century, only somewhat over 1 percent of the 3+ percent annual growth in real output has come from more workers. The other 2+ percent a year represents increased output per worker, which in turn reflects more capital, improved technology, and better management, as well as improved worker skills and education.

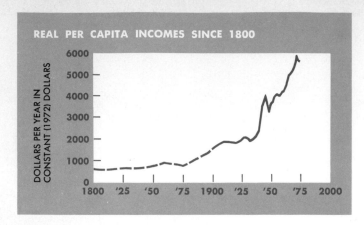

REAL PER CAPITA INCOMES SINCE 1800

Figure 7–4
Per capita real output has grown rapidly but erratically over the past century, apparently less rapidly during the early 1800s. Note the big recent spurts, but remember that this is not a ratio scale. (Data from Figure 7–3 divided by population.)

Figure 7–4 shows the growth in real output (and income) *per capita* since 1800. As in the other charts, data before the present century are rough, and are plotted only once each decade to give a picture of major trends. Note the big increase in recent decades—but remember that this is a regular-interval, not a ratio, scale. On a ratio scale, the speedup has been moderate, between ½ and 1 percent per annum.

Some international comparisons

Look back at Table 1–1 to see the results of this prodigious growth in U.S. production. Our production per capita (which is our average economic standard of living) is near the highest in the world.

Table 7–1 shows comparative growth rates in per capita output for major industrialized nations over the past century. Growth rates have varied widely even among these industrialized nations. Although some rates are surprisingly close (for example, those of the United States and Sweden), don't forget the enormous difference that even a fraction of 1 percent annually can make when compounded over an entire century. A dollar invested at 1.5 percent per annum grows to $4.43 in 100 years; one invested at 2 percent, to $7.25; and one invested at 3 percent, to $19.22. We shall look at the problem of growth in detail in Part 7. Growth has dominated U.S. economic history, although we focus first on the shorter-run problems of business cycles, inflations, and unemployment.

INSTABILITY—UNEMPLOYMENT AND INFLATION

Over the long run, growth in output, employment, and incomes dominates the macroeconomic picture. But in the short run, unemployment and inflation are often the problems that fill the headlines. Although over the long

Table 7–1

Long-term growth rates in output per capita[a]

	Annual percentage increase
Japan	3.0
Sweden	2.2
United States	2.1
USSR	2.0
Canada	1.8
Denmark	1.7
France	1.6
Germany	1.6
United Kingdom	1.2
Italy	1.2

[a]Based on data for approximately 100 years. Exact beginning date varies slightly; for example, U.S. data begin in 1871, to avoid Civil War period.

Sources: D. C. Paige, "Economic Growth: The Last Hundred Years," *National Institute Economic Review*, July 1961; Simon Kuznets, "The Pattern of U.S. Economic Growth," *The Nation's Economic Objectives*, E. Edwards, ed. (Chicago: University of Chicago Press, 1964); and United Nations.

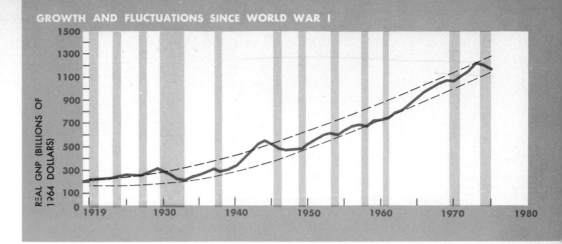

GROWTH AND FLUCTUATIONS SINCE WORLD WAR I

Figure 7–5
The shaded areas show recessions and depressions since 1919. Most recessions since World War II have been mild, hardly more than a flattening out of the growth in real GNP, although quarterly data would show sharper fluctuations. (Sources: U.S. Department of Commerce and National Bureau of Economic Research.)

run the economy has grown impressively, growth has come in surges (inflationary booms) followed by recessions and unemployment. At their worst, these recessions develop into major depressions, with massive unemployment of men and machines.

Figure 7–5 shows our intermittent booms and recessions since World War I, superimposed on the strong growth trend in total output. The dashed lines roughly connect the peaks of the booms and the troughs of the recessions.[1] The vertical shaded areas are periods officially labeled recessions, when output was actually falling, or at least growing so slowly that unemployment was piling up. Clearly, periods of recovery and prosperity exceed those of recession. But if we think of the top dashed line as roughly the growing full-employment productive capacity of the economy, it is equally clear that much of the time we have wasted potential output by operating inside the economy's production-possibilities frontier. How far the actual output curve falls short of the top dashed line gives a rough picture of the potential output wasted by operating below full employment.

Growth, booms, and depressions are thus part and parcel of the same economic process. However, it is convenient to consider them separately, and the remainder of Part 2 primarily focuses on

[1] The top of the World War II boom (1942–45) is shown above the dashed line because the economy was then clearly operating beyond its normal capacity level. Housewives, old people, and children were temporarily pulled into the labor force, and workers were called on for vast amounts of overtime to meet wartime production goals.

the determinants of production, employment, income, and prices in the **short run,** postponing to Part 7 the **long-run** problem of economic growth. Let us first look briefly at the two big problems that short-run economic instability has frequently posed—unemployment and inflation. What are they, and what are their effects?

UNEMPLOYMENT

The case for high-level employment of men and machines is clear. Involuntary unemployment wastes productive capacity. It means less housing, fewer refrigerators, highways, and factories than we could otherwise have. It means human misery, decay of skills, degrading deprivation for the unemployed and their families. It means a lower average standard of living for the nation today and in the future. In 1974, our last recession year, total output was $150–$200 billion short of the economy's high-employment capacity.

What is unemployment?

Unemployment is defined in the official U.S. statistics to include all those in the labor force who are not employed or self-employed. The labor force includes all those sixteen years old or over who have a job, are self-employed, or are looking for a job. In essence, the unemployed are those over sixteen who don't have a job and are looking for one.

How do we decide who is unemployed? We ask. A large scientific sample of the entire population in the relevant age group is asked, "Do you have a job?" If the answer is no, the respondent is asked, "Are you looking for a job?" If the answer is no, the respondent is not in the labor force and is not considered unemployed. If the answer is yes, he is in the labor force and is unemployed. The interview probes somewhat further, but this is the core of the matter. A person may be in the labor force, and unemployed, even though he is looking for only a part-time job; large movements of students into and out of the labor force often account for big swings in the unemployment totals during the summer and other vacation periods.

How low can unemployment be?

Back in the Great Depression of the 1930s, the unemployed exceeded 25 percent of the labor force, and millions of others held only part-time or makeshift jobs. National output in 1932 and 1933 wasn't much over half of potential, an enormous human and economic waste. During the 1965–75 decade, which saw two recessions, unemployment varied from 3.5 to 9 percent. This unemployment meant that we wasted over $500 billion in potential real output (at current prices)—or in terms of wasted manpower, the equivalent of some 30 million man-years of work.

Clearly, there is some unavoidable minimum of unemployment. In a large, free economy like ours, there are always millions of people on the move. In 1975, for example, some 20 million people changed jobs. It takes time for people to move from one job to another; such unemployment is often called "frictional." Moreover, there are always some essentially "unemployable" people looking for jobs—individuals with very poor health, very low mental capacities, no training, and the like. Still others are potentially employable, but their skills and locations are

badly out of line with job openings, or their wage demands are unrealistically high for what they can offer; these are the "structurally" unemployed.

How large is unavoidable minimum unemployment? There is no precise answer. With enough pressure of aggregate demand (as in World War II), unemployment can be reduced to almost zero, and indeed, millions of new workers can be drawn into the labor force by high wages—if we are willing to accept the accompanying inflation. Careful empirical studies suggest that perhaps 2–3 percent of the labor force may be taken as a reasonable approximation of frictional unemployment, in addition to job seekers who are, for practical purposes, unemployable under normal conditions.[2] As a practical matter, many observers consider 4 percent or so a reasonable high-employment target for an economy such as ours, and this figure is often used in assessing the economy's performance relative to its "high-employment" potential. Others say from 3 to 6 percent. Our aspirations on the minimum-unemployment level vary with recent experiences.

Other nations set us as a goal to shoot at. In Western Europe since World War II, unemployment rates have generally been lower than ours, in most cases varying between 1 and 6 percent of the labor force over the past decade. But these results have generally been achieved at the cost of somewhat higher inflation than in the United States.

The human costs of unemployment

Fewer than 15 percent of today's 200 million Americans were adults at the onset of the Great Depression of the 1930s. Thus, most Americans today have no memory of that period and its devastating impact on human morale and well-being, as well as on the aggregate production of the economy.

Figure 7–6 presents the cold statistics. Unemployment reached a peak of over 25 percent of the labor force in 1933, and it averaged between

[2]See, for example, *The Extent and Nature of Frictional Unemployment*, published by the Joint Economic Committee of Congress in 1959, and *Economic Report of the President*, January 1975, Chap. 3.

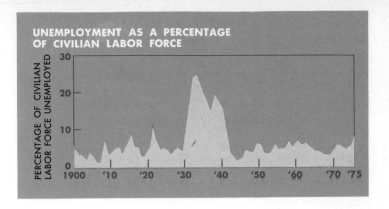

Figure 7-6
Unemployment soars in depression, and even in recessions. What is a reasonable minimum unemployment level for us to shoot at? (Source: U.S. Department of Labor.)

15 and 20 percent for the entire decade of the thirties. Moreover, many of the people employed were working on a part-time basis at drastically reduced rates of pay, and there were millions of "hidden unemployed" barely eking out an existence in agriculture. At the bottom of the depression, not more than two-thirds of the total labor force had regular full-time jobs, and some estimates put the figure nearer one-half.

But statistics are bloodless things. Listen to the testimony given by an economist before a Senate subcommittee investigating unemployment in 1932:

MR. deSCHWEINITZ: When I appeared before the subcommittee last December, I stated that there were 233,000 persons out of work in Philadelphia. . . . There are now 298,000 persons out of work. . . . In December I told you that 43,000 families were receiving relief, today 55,000 families are receiving relief.

In December, our per family grant was $4.39 per week per family. It is now $4.23 per family. Of this $4.23 per family, about $3.93 is an allowance for food. . . .

I want to tell you about an experience we had here in Philadelphia when our private funds were exhausted and before public funds became available. . . . There was a period of about eleven days when many families received nothing from us. We have received reports from workers as to how these families managed. The material I am about to give you is typical, although it is based on a small sample.

One woman said she borrowed 50 cents from a friend and bought stale bread for $3\frac{1}{2}$ cents per loaf, and that is all they had for eleven days except for one or two meals.

One woman went along the docks and picked up vegetables that fell from the wagons. Sometimes the fish vendors gave her fish at the end of the day. On two different occasions this family was without food for a day and a half.

The gas company was careful not to turn off gas in the homes of a great many of these families, so in some instances food could be cooked.

Another family did not have food for two days. Then the husband went out and gathered dandelions and the family lived on them.

I should also like to say that when we talk to people to ask about unemployment, they say, "Well, people manage to get along somehow or other, don't they? You do not have very many people who really drop dead of starvation." That is true. Actually, death from starvation is not a frequent occurrence. . . . They live on inadequacies, and because they live on inadequacies the thing does not become dramatic, and we do not hear about it. Yet the cost in human suffering is just as great as if they starved to death overnight.[3]

Now listen to the testimony of another witness, given before a House subcommittee at about the same time:

MR. AMERINGER: The last thing I saw on the night I left Seattle was numbers of women searching for scraps of food in the refuse piles of the principal markets of that city. A number of Montana citizens told me of thousands of bushels of wheat left in the field uncut on account of its low price that hardly paid for the harvesting. In Oregon I saw thousands of bushels of apples rotting in the orchards. Only absolutely flawless apples were still salable, at from 40–50 cents a box containing 200 apples. At the same time,

---

[3] *Federal Cooperation in Unemployment Relief,* Hearings before Senate Committee on Manufactures, 72nd Cong., 1st sess., 1932, pp. 20–26. This testimony and that which follows is reproduced more completely in D.A. Shannon, *The Great Depression* (Englewood Cliffs, N.J.: Prentice-Hall, 1960).

there are millions of children who, on account of the poverty of their parents, will not eat one apple this winter.

While I was in Oregon, the *Portland Oregonian* bemoaned the fact that thousands of ewes were killed by the sheep raisers because they did not bring enough in the market to pay the freight on them. And while Oregon sheep raisers fed mutton to the buzzards, I saw men picking meat scraps in the garbage cans in the cities of New York and Chicago. I talked to one man in a restaurant in Chicago. He told me of his experience in raising sheep. He said that he had killed 3,000 sheep this fall and thrown them down the canyon because it cost $1.10 to ship a sheep, and then he would get less than a dollar for it. He said he could not afford to feed the sheep, and he would not let them starve, so he just cut their throats and threw them down the canyon.

The roads of the West and Southwest teem with hungry hitchhikers. The campfires of homeless are seen along every railroad track. . . .[4]

Most American families were not in such desperate straits. But fear was everywhere. Many fought to maintain respectability. For many others, long-continued failure wiped out self-respect and the will to try. Parks were sprinkled with desolate men in shabby clothes, merely sitting. Many more stayed home.

Is such evidence on the human cost of unemployment relevant today? Today, unemployment is far more modest even at the depths of our postwar recessions. Nationwide unemployment insurance provides temporary financial support for most workers who have been laid off. Government relief payments help others. Many unions have obtained private unemployment-compensation plans. Thus, modern unemployment is far less devastating than during the desperate days of the 1930s.

But most unemployment-insurance plans provide only a fraction of regular wage incomes, and all have time limits, some as short as thirteen weeks. Moreover, to receive unemployment-insurance benefits, one must have held a regular job, and many unemployed persons fail to qualify on this test. In depressed areas—for example, the soft-coal fields of the Appalachians—many workers have been jobless for years.

[4] *Unemployment in the United States,* Hearings before House Committee on Labor, 72nd Cong., 1st sess., 1932, pp. 98–99.

Discouragement, and then despair, take over when no job is available month after month.

Who are the unemployed today? Table 7–2 gives the answer for 1975, a year with the highest unemployment level since the 1930s. Unemployment averaged 8.5 percent of the labor force—eight million people.

Note that nearly a quarter of all the unemployed were teenagers, although many of them were seeking only part-time jobs. They had by far the highest unemployment rate of any age group, 20 percent compared to 7 percent for adults. Minority groups (mainly blacks) consistently showed unemployment rates about twice those for whites; unemployment averaged 37 percent for minority-group teenagers.

Why were the unemployed out of work? Table 7–3 provides one set of answers. Over 25 million people were unemployed at some time during the year, although the average at any given time was only eight million. Rapid technological change, shifting consumer demands, and seasonal patterns in some industries all lead

Table 7–2

Unemployment, 1975

	Number unemployed (in thousands)	Rate (percent)
Total unemployment	7,830	8.5
Age:		
Teenagers, 16–19	1,752	19.9
Nonwhite teenagers	467	37.2
Adults, 20 and over	6,078	7.4
Race:		
White	6,371	7.9
Black and others	1,459	13.8
Type of worker:		
Blue-collar	3,713	11.7
White-collar	2,100	4.7
Sex:		
Male	4,385	7.9
Female	3,445	9.3
Marital Status:		
Married men	2,044	5.1
Other	5,786	11.2

Source: U.S. Department of Labor, preliminary data.

Table 7–3

Reasons for unemployment, 1975

Reason	Number unemployed (in thousands)	Percentage distribution
Total unemployment	7,830	100
Lost last job	4,341	55
Voluntarily left last job	812	10
Reentered labor force	1,865	25
Entered labor force, first time	612	9

Source: U.S. Department of Labor.

to continually shifting job patterns. But only about half had actually lost their last job; the rest had either quit voluntarily or had just recently begun looking for a job; and in prosperous years, such as 1972 and 1973, quits far exceeded layoffs even though average unemployment was nearly 5 percent. Many of the unemployed, especially younger people, quit jobs frequently to look for better positions. Many quit jobs that they find unsatisfactory or consider dead-end. The data are not consistent with the common impression that the unemployed are a large, stable mass of people who are unable to find any job. In more prosperous years, like 1972 and 1973, less than 40 percent of the unemployed had lost their jobs.

Variations in unemployment are thus closely linked to variations in its duration. As Table 7–4 shows, in 1975, 37 percent of all the unemployed were out of work only one to four weeks. Only 1.2 million (15 percent of the total) were out of work for as long as six months. The average duration of unemployment for all unemployed was about three months, up sharply from the preceding years. In 1973–74, for example, well over half the unemployed had been out of work one month or less, and the average duration of unemployment was a little over two months.

These data show that unemployment is relatively short-lived for most workers, as long as major depressions are avoided. For many, it reflects preferences for quitting to look for a better job elsewhere or the need to adjust to a constantly shifting economic scene. An eight-million unemployment figure does not mean that eight million people were out of work for the whole year; very few were. But this fact is of little solace if you are one of the unemployed, with no job and little hope of finding one.

INFLATION

Nearly everyone agrees that most involuntary unemployment is bad. But the case against inflation is less obvious.[5]

What is inflation?

When you use the word *inflation* to mean a rise in the price level and your neighbor

[5] For a more complete analysis of the causes and effects of inflation, see G.L. Bach, *The New Inflation* (Englewood Cliffs, N.J.: Prentice-Hall, 1973).

Table 7–4

Duration of unemployment, 1975

Weeks	Number (in thousands)	Percentage of unemployed
Less than 5	2,894	37.0
5 to 14	2,452	31.3
15 to 26	1,290	16.5
27 and over	1,193	15.2

Source: U.S. Department of Labor.

uses it to mean more money printed by those irresponsible fellows in Washington, it's no wonder you don't succeed in talking sensibly about it—especially if neither of you bothers to make clear how you are defining inflation. Socrates said, "If you want to argue with me, first define your terms." And he was right. There are several common definitions of inflation, so you must be clear about which you are using.

"Inflation," in this book, means a rise in the average price of all currently produced goods and services. Note that this definition does not include higher prices of existing assets, such as houses or stocks and bonds. It does not include rising wages or money and credit. All these are usually found when inflation, as we define it, occurs; but inflation per se is merely a rise in the price level of currently produced goods and services. Figure 7-7 presents the evidence on inflation over the past century.

Hyperinflation

When inflation runs away and reaches astronomical proportions, it is often called "hyperinflation." Every American schoolchild learns about the great hyperinflation in Germany following World War I. The government had to make huge expenditures (including heavy reparation payments to the victorious Allies), and it financed its expenditures by printing paper money rather than by increasing taxes. This new money increased total spending and sped the price spiral upward, for the war-torn German economy could not rapidly increase its output of goods. As prices spiraled up, so did government costs, requiring further recourse to the printing presses. People receiving money spent it as fast as they could, to convert it into goods before it fell further in value. Prices, government spending, and new money soared to fantastic levels.

Near the peak of the inflation in 1923, a box of matches sold for more than 6 billion marks, the total amount of German marks in circulation ten years before. Before the war, all mortgages in Germany totaled 40 billion marks; at the peak of the inflation 40 billion marks were worth only one U.S. cent. Things happened as in a feverish dream. No one wanted to lend, everyone wanted to borrow, because it would soon be so easy to pay off today's debts as the value of money fell. Interest rates rose to 900 percent, and even then, lenders were not protected. Wages, as well as prices, came to be adjusted daily, then several times a day. Savings invested in fixed-income securities were completely wiped out, and many of the middle class became paupers while skillful speculators became fabulously wealthy. Prices rose so fast that productive activity was disrupted and real output was reduced. The distribution of income and wealth was cruelly and arbitrarily altered. At the end, the German government in effect repudiated its paper money; it exchanged one new mark for one trillion old ones. (See Case 6.)

Inflation can be a terrible thing. Happily, there have not been many hyperinflations, and

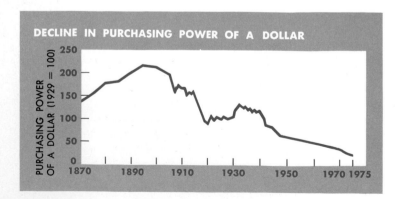

DECLINE IN PURCHASING POWER OF A DOLLAR

PURCHASING POWER OF A DOLLAR (1929 = 100)

250 200 150 100 50 0

1870 1890 1910 1930 1950 1970 1975

Figure 7-7
Inflation has repeatedly eroded the purchasing power of a dollar, with the biggest price increases coming during and after wars. (Source: U.S. Department of Labor.)

"My client would like to point out, Your Honor, that he would only be charged with petty larceny were it not for spiralling inflation." (Drawing by Modell; © 1973. The New Yorker Magazine, Inc.)

interestingly, two common elements have linked them all. They were associated with war or its aftermath, especially in defeated countries; and they were financed by great issues of new money to cover huge government expenditures.

One other introductory fact. You often hear the statement that we can't have "just a little" inflation—that inflation, once started, inevitably builds up and runs away. This assertion is simply wrong on the evidence of history. Both here and in other nations, there have been many periods of moderate or creeping inflation, followed by stable or moderately declining prices; few inflations have turned into hyperinflations. Most economists agree that inflation has some self-feeding elements, mainly the expectation that price increases will accelerate. But they need not do so.[6]

---

[6] Many of the less-developed countries have had repeated periods of rapid, although not hyper-, inflation. Brazil, for example, has had inflation varying between 20 and 100 percent annually over many decades.

THE EFFECTS OF MODERATE INFLATION

What are the effects of moderate (creeping) inflation of only a few percent a year, the kind most major industrialized nations have faced since World War II? Who gains, and who loses? Does such inflation rob everyone except big business and a few sly profiteers?

Everyone complains about having to pay higher prices in inflation. But clearly, this is too narrow a view of the situation, because incomes (wages, interest, profits, and so on) rise in inflation along with the prices we all have to pay. If your dollar buys less but you have a lot more dollars of income, you may be better off in terms of real buying power, not worse.

Because it is the public's real buying power that matters, what happens to our total output of goods and services is the best single measure of whether the nation as a whole is better or worse off in a period of inflation. We need to peer through the veil of money and prices to real output and real buying power. Second, because each of us is concerned with his individual welfare, total national output provides only part of the answer. To see what inflation does to each individual or group, we need to know what happens to his **share** of total output—whether his individual income rises faster or slower than the prices he has to pay. So we need to ask two basic questions: (1) Does moderate inflation increase or decrease total national output? (2) How does it affect the distribution of real income and wealth?

Effects on total national output

In principle, inflation can increase or decrease national production. In the short run, inflation clearly can increase real output only if there are unemployed resources; if we are already fully utilizing our productive resources, more spending can only mean more inflation. If there is unemployment, more spending may lead businessmen to hire more workers and increase output—if in the inflation their selling prices rise faster than wages and their other costs of production. In that case, they have an incentive to increase output. But if wages and other costs rise faster than selling prices, profits are cut and businessmen will reduce employment and output.[7] Do wages lead or lag selling prices in moderate inflations? Sometimes one, sometimes the other. There is no consistent relationship over history, but since World War II, the wage lag that characterized many earlier inflations appears to have generally given way to a wage lead in this country.

Inflation can also decrease output in the short run if prices rise so fast that they disrupt business and individual economic planning and operations. As noted above, this clearly happened in the great German hyperinflation, and may have occurred in the U.S. "double-digit" inflation of 1974–75. But there is not much evidence of such disruption from the moderate inflations in the United States since World War II, although inflation may trigger speculative price rises that increasingly set the stage for a collapse.

Conclusion: In the short run, moderate inflation

[7]A more precise statement is provided in Chapter 19.

may help to stimulate more output in times of unemployment, but this effect is uncertain. In full-employment periods, it can do little good and may do harm by upsetting planning or precipitating recession. Either way, remember, it's the impact on the employment of real resources—on jobs and real output—that counts.

In the long run, we can increase the economy's growth rate—productive capacity—by saving and investing more in factories, machinery, and human beings (through education and training), by spending on research and development, and the like. If inflation induces people to save and invest more, it will speed the rate of economic growth; if it reduces saving and investment, the opposite will occur.

What is the evidence on the growth issue? Mixed. But the data seem reasonably clear on three points: First, hyperinflation cuts down on saving and productive investment. Second, moderate, or creeping, inflation has little effect one way or the other on the level of saving and investment. Third, again the critical relationship in determining the effect of moderate inflation on growth is the one between selling prices and wages, because wage lag tends to stimulate profits and investment. More details on this problem in later chapters.

Effects on the distribution of income

In a full-employment economy, inflation cannot increase total output. But it can change who receives the output. Think of total national output as a big pie. With full employment, inflation cannot increase the size of the pie (except possibly over a long period, through speeding growth), but it can affect the size of the pieces that different people get.

First, a very fundamental fact. **Given the size of the real pie, inflation does not make people in the aggregate either better or worse off economically. If someone gets a smaller piece, someone else is bound to get a bigger one.** Moving up from a $900-billion to a trillion-dollar GNP merely through higher prices does not make the economy either better or worse off in terms of real output and income if the same level of employment prevails before and after.

The central principle about how inflation

affects the distribution of income for a given real GNP is this: Those whose incomes rise faster than the average get bigger pieces of the real GNP, and those whose incomes rise slower or not at all get smaller pieces.[8] In a full-employment economy, inflation usually means that prices rise at about the same rate as money GNP. The man whose income just keeps pace with rising prices will keep about the same-sized piece of pie. The man whose income lags behind rising prices will get a smaller piece. Those whose incomes rise faster than prices will get bigger shares. Remember, however, that in an under-employed economy, real GNP may expand with inflation, and everyone's piece may increase.

The importance of anticipations.

Whose income lags and whose leads depends heavily on how accurately different people anticipate the amount of inflation ahead. If everyone expected prices to rise 10 percent annually, everyone would presumably try to build this anticipation into his actions. Unions would demand 10 percent higher wages to avoid losing real purchasing power; lenders would demand 10 percent increases on interest rates they charged on loans; businessmen pricing their products would add on 10 percent, recognizing that costs would rise that much. At the same time, businesses would be more willing to give big wage boosts, borrowers would pay the higher interest rates, and the like, because they would expect their incomes to be 10 percent higher owing to the inflation. In principle, if there were no market barriers (such as long-term wage or interest-rate agreements) and everyone were equally able to adjust, all prices would be adjusted upward by 10 percent in accordance with inflation anticipations. Real incomes would remain unchanged. Inflation would have no effect on real output and employment, since all prices, costs, and asset values would increase proportionately.

[8]To be strictly accurate, the principle must be modified to recognize that different people buy different things whose prices may rise faster or slower than the average. So how an individual is affected depends on the increase in his income relative to the increase in the prices of the goods he buys, not relative to some general price index. But the simple proposition in the text provides a good first approximation in a full-employment economy.

In fact, of course, inflation anticipations are far from perfect, and abilities to adjust vary greatly. The uneducated, the poor, the unsophisticated are likely to be badly informed and unable to adjust effectively, compared to the educated and well-to-do. But others also face difficulties in adjusting. Bondholders are stuck with a real loss on their fixed-interest bonds. So are workers with long-term wage contracts and others with fixed commitments.

Shifts in income shares.

It used to be said that interest receivers and wage and salaried workers had lagging incomes and were hurt by inflation, while businessmen and stockholders gained. But even if this was once so, the recent picture of leads and lags is more complex. Consider 1950–72, a period of nearly continuous mild inflation, beginning after the special forces of World War II had worked themselves out; and then, separately, 1972–75, which saw a burst of more rapid inflation.

Just about everyone's real income went up. Total output in the economy more than doubled. Table 7–5 shows what happened to different income shares. Within the rapidly growing total, the wage-and-salary share rose by a whopping 6.6 percent (from 61 to over 67 percent of the total) between 1950 and 1972; while the corporate-profits share fell by 6.2 percent (from 15.7 percent to only 9.5 percent of the total). Farms and other unincorporated businesses (retail shops, legal firms, and the like) fared no better than corporations. Moreover, the big income shifts to wages and salaries against corporate profits were concentrated in the three surges of inflation: 1950–52, 1955–57, and 1965–72, shown in the three middle columns. Note that labor's share grew by 7.9 percent in these three inflation surges but by only 6.6 percent in the total 1950–72 period. Thus, the labor share eroded in 1953–54 and 1958–64, the substantially noninflationary years in the 1950–72 period. Conversely, the corporate-profits squeeze was concentrated in the inflationary surges.[9]

[9]In fact, corporate profits fared even worse than Table 7–5 shows, because traditional accounting methods understate inventory costs and depreciation charges in inflation and hence overstate real profits.

Table 7–5

Changes in percentage shares of national income, 1950–75

	1950–72	1950–52	1955–57	1965–72	1972–75
Wages and salaries	+6.1	+2.6	+1.4	+3.4	+1.0
Unincorporated business profits:					
Farm	−4.0	−0.5	−0.4	−0.5	+0.1
Nonfarm	−3.5	−0.7	−0.2	−1.6	−1.2
Corporate profits[a]	−6.2	−2.0	−1.7	−4.1	−2.3
Rents	+1.1	+0.1	−0.2	−0.6	−0.6
Interest	+3.6	+0.1	+0.3	+1.2	+2.8
Transfer payments to persons[b]	+4.1	−1.8	+0.6	+3.4	+3.5

[a] After inventory adjustment, before corporation income taxes.
[b] Not a part of national income.
Source: U.S. Department of Commerce.

The last column (1972–75) shows what happened in a period of less-expected, much more rapid inflation. The general pattern was the same, but the shift from profits to wages was less pronounced; farmers' share rose slightly, reflecting the big 1973–74 burst in food prices; and the interest share rose sharply, reflecting high interest rates in the inflationary boom.

The bottom line of Table 7–5 bears special attention, in addition to these regular income-share shifts. Transfer payments to persons are largely government Social Security and welfare benefits. These transfer payments further augmented the big increase in the share going to individuals rather than businesses; the large increase in Social Security payments has occurred since 1965.

The fact that income shares changed in favor of wage and salary workers and against corporate profits during the past two decades of inflation does not, of course, prove that this shift was due to the inflation. Nor does it prove that a similar shift will occur in any future inflation. But the facts do emphasize that the widely held wage-lag hypothesis is not applicable to modern America, nor is the presumption that businesses generally gain from inflation.

There are other distributional effects of inflation. Except for Social Security increases, older persons are hard hit, because they are retired, with no wages to be raised in order to offset the higher prices they must pay. So are others without marketable services to sell or other means of raising their incomes. Inflation's effects vary widely among different individuals.

Effects on distribution of wealth

Inflation also affects the ownership of existing wealth. It transfers real purchasing power from creditors to debtors.[10] If you borrow $1,000 for a year and an unexpected inflation of 10 percent occurs, even though you repay the full $1,000, you have in fact repaid only $900 of real purchasing power for the $1,000 you received. As a debtor, you have gained from inflation; the lender has lost part of his principal to you.

The same effect occurs if you hold money during an inflation. If you hold $1,000 in your safe deposit box while prices rise 5 percent, you have effectively lost 5 percent of your $1,000. Even if you have invested in a safe security, such as a government bond, which pays you interest, inflation erodes the real buying power of both

[10] More accurately, we must calculate the *net* debtor or creditor position of each economic unit. For example, if a family has $10,000 of money and bonds but owes $6,000, it is a "net creditor" by $4,000.

Table 7–6

Half-life of a dollar with inflation

Annual rate of inflation	Years to lose half its purchasing power
1 percent	70
2 percent	35
3 percent	23
4 percent	18
5 percent	14

the interest and the principal you receive when the bond comes due.

Don't be tricked into thinking that the loss doesn't amount to much as long as inflation only creeps. Table 7–6 shows how long it takes for a dollar to lose half its purchasing power at different small rates of inflation. At only 5 percent inflation a year, half its purchasing power is gone in fourteen years.

Table 7–7 shows the main net debtors and net creditors in America. Households are the main net creditors exposed to inflation, and governments (mainly the federal government) are the biggest net debtors, followed by business firms. Of course, we need to peer through both governments and business firms to the people behind them, but crudely we can say that unanticipated inflation transfers wealth from households to taxpayers and owners of business firms.

Although households are clearly the main net creditors, they vary widely. Some are heavily in

Table 7–7

Net debtor and net creditor groups, 1972[a] (in billions of dollars)

Households	+856
Unincorporated businesses	−115
Nonfinancial corporations	−228
Financial corporations	−130
Governments	−399

[a] + shows net creditor; − shows net debtor.

For details, see G. L. Bach, *The New Inflation* (Englewood Cliffs, N.J.: Prentice-Hall, 1973), p. 25.

debt; others have few debts and many monetary assets susceptible to inflation's erosion. Table 7–8 shows which families are most likely to lose, and which to gain, from inflation on wealth account. Families with a high proportion of their assets in money and other such fixed-money-value assets as bonds (monetary assets) are vulnerable to inflation; those with high ratios of debt to total assets tend to gain from inflation. Loosely speaking, very low- and very high-income families appear most vulnerable to inflation because of their relatively high monetary-asset and relatively low debt ratios; middle-income families tend to be gainers because of the reverse situation. More clearly, inflation helps the young at the expense of the aged. Young people are heavily in debt and hold relatively few monetary assets, while old people have virtually no debts and have a big proportion of their assets in monetary forms.

As was emphasized above, if everyone anticipated inflation correctly, bargains between borrowers and lenders would reflect those anticipations, and interest rates would rise to take expected inflation into account. If the noninflationary interest rate was 4 percent, and a 5 percent inflation was expected by both parties, the interest rate would be raised to 9 percent to allow for the inflation. Thus, neither party would gain or lose from the inflation. In periods of continuing inflation, some such adjustment clearly takes place, but much past inflation has not been fully anticipated by many borrowers and lenders. One recent estimate suggests that inflation has transferred half a trillion dollars of real purchasing power from creditors to debtors since World War II. About $4 trillion of monetary assets are now in existence, susceptible to erosion by inflation. A 1 percent unanticipated inflation would thus transfer $40 billion from creditors to debtors. Of course, this huge transfer of purchasing power did not represent a loss of real wealth to society as a whole. But it was a capricious and inequitable redistribution of real wealth that is hard to justify.[11]

[11]Inflation may have further complex, painful wealth effects. For example, the profit squeeze of the 1960s and 1970s apparently helped reduce the prices of common stocks, whose aggregate market value fell by over $600 billion in the early 1970s.

Table 7–8

Assets and Debts of Households

Income level:	Percentage of all households	PERCENTAGE OF TOTAL ASSETS Monetary assets	Debts
Under $3,000	17	20	8
3,000–4,999	14	20	15
5,000–9,999	33	18	23
10,000–14,999	24	14	29
15,000–24,999	9	12	21
25,000–49,999	2	14	18
$50,000 and over	0.4	18	10
Age of head of household:			
18–24	10	14	49
25–34	21	8	48
35–44	18	9	37
45–54	17	13	22
55–64	15	21	9
65 and over	19	23	3

Source: G. Katona et al., *1969 Survey of Consumer Finances* (Ann Arbor: University of Michigan, 1970), p. 310. Data are for 1969.

International effects

If costs and prices in one country rise faster than elsewhere, that country will have increasing trouble meeting competition in international markets. Conversely, as its own incomes rise, its people will import more from abroad. Thus, it will end up with an international "balance-of-payments deficit"—it will owe more abroad than it has to collect from foreigners. For any nation heavily dependent on foreign trade (for example, most of Western Europe and many of the less-developed countries), this fact constitutes a major barrier against accepting more rapid inflation than other countries with which it trades. We postpone detailed consideration of the international aspects of inflation to Part 6, but it is important to recognize that inflation may involve major international costs to any country whose prices rise faster than those abroad.

How bad is inflation?

How bad is inflation, putting all these effects together? Try the following exercise to test your understanding. Evaluate this statement by a well-known senator: "Inflation reduces the buying power of every dollar, and impoverishes the American people. It is a national disaster!"

The first half of the first sentence is true by definition. Inflation is rising prices, and higher prices do reduce the purchasing power of any dollar. But it does not necessarily follow from this that inflation impoverishes the American people.

Consider the decade of the 1960s. The price level rose from 100 to 130, using 1960 as the base year, or by 30 percent. In 1960, total national income was $415 billion; in 1970, it was about $800 billion. If we adjust the 1970 national-income figure downward to eliminate the effect of inflation, we get a 1970 real income of $615 billion in constant (1960) prices. This was an increase of $200 billion (almost 50 percent) over the 1960 real income. Even allowing for possible error in the price index, it is hard to see how this inflation impoverished the American people as a whole. Although one dollar would buy less in 1970 than in 1960, the increase in money incomes received far outdistanced the loss caused by rising prices. Real output rose, it didn't fall.

However, this historical evidence doesn't prove that inflation *caused* the increase in output, so we are not justified in giving inflation credit for the extra goods and services produced. Moreover, even though the public as a whole had 50 percent more real income in 1970 than in 1960, some people were absolutely harmed by the inflation—people whose money incomes were relatively fixed and who were net monetary creditors—and others saw their relative income positions worsen. Inflation was certainly no national disaster in the 1960s, but it's easy to understand why a lot of people object to it strongly.

Moreover, in 1973–75, rapid inflation was accompanied by a *decline* in real output (both in total and per capita). Current GNP rose 15 percent over the two years, but the price level rose 18 percent, so *real* GNP fell about 3 percent. How much the inflation contributed to reducing real output is uncertain, but a lot of people felt they were being hurt by it. Their real incomes were falling because their money incomes rose less than the prices they paid. Moreover, note that in inflation, everyone has to pay higher prices, while the burden of unemployment is concentrated on only one group of people.

CONCLUSION

Whether we have prosperity or depression will go far to determine what kind of job you have and how well you live when you graduate—indeed, perhaps whether you have any job at all. With this overview of the macroeconomy and its problems, we turn now to some problems of measuring national output and price level changes, and to a detailed examination of what determines the levels of national production, employment, incomes, and prices—of why we sometimes have good times, sometimes bad. Equally important, we shall consider what can be done to reduce the amount of both unemployment and inflation. Some economists feel that we will probably have to choose between high employment and stable prices—that we can have one or the other, but not both. But others deny this dilemma and argue that proper policies will permit both simultaneously. This issue runs through the following chapters. On the basis of this preliminary overview, how would you weigh high employment and avoidance of inflation as goals of national macroeconomic policy?

REVIEW

Concepts to remember

The following important new concepts were introduced in this chapter:

macroeconomics	structural unemployment
circular flow of spending	inflation
growth-rate	hyperinflation
ratio scale	redistributional effects of
unemployment	inflation on income and
frictional unemployment	wealth

For analysis and discussion

1. Looking at Figures 7–2 through 7–7, how well would you say the American economy has performed over the past century? How do you rate it on the two criteria of growth and stability?

2. In setting goals for the economy, is it more important to avoid unemployment or inflation, if we must choose?

3. Who are the main sufferers from "moderate" unemployment such as we have had in recent years? Use Tables 7–2, 7–3, and 7–4 in answering.

4. Should students looking for part-time jobs be counted as unemployed? (They are.) Discouraged workers who have given up looking? (They are not.)

5. In 1973, unemployment averaged just over four million people. Of these, only about 300,000 were out of work for as long as half a year; over half were out of work for a month or less; and the unemployment rate was below 3 percent for married males. Would you consider this a satisfactory approximation to full employment? Look back at Table 7–2 for comparative data.

6. Who are the main sufferers from "moderate" inflation such as we have had in recent years? Use Tables 7–5, 7–7, and 7–8 in answering.

7. Explain why anticipations play a crucial role in determining who is hurt and who is helped by inflation.

8. If unemployment wastes real output while moderate inflation mainly redistributes income and wealth, how can you explain why the general public seems to consider inflation the major problem in periods like 1972–73, when inflation and unemployment both averaged 4–5 percent? (Consider both the number of people affected and the importance of the impact on each in answering.) Would your answer be different for 1973–75, when inflation averaged about 9 percent and unemployment about 7 percent, while total national output fell about 3 percent?

In March 1976, substantially the following story appeared in leading newspapers. What were the major issues at stake? Why did the various persons quoted take the positions they did? If a reporter had asked you whether unemployment or inflation was the greater danger for the nation, what would you have said? If you had been running for Congress in the 1976 elections, which side would you have taken?

WASHINGTON—The Labor Department announced yesterday that unemployment continued its steady decline last month, falling to 7.6 percent, more than a full percentage point below its peak of 8.9 percent last summer. The spokesman said that this is a rapid rate of decline, and appears to confirm the solid recovery of the economy, although unemployment remains high by historical standards. He noted also that consumer prices continued their rise last month, but that the 5 percent increase was slower than for any year since 1972.

The AFL-CIO, however, said that the Labor Department's figure understates the true unemployment picture in the nation. The labor federation said that the real unemployment rate is 10.5 percent, and that 9.9 million, not 7.1 million, people are unemployed. The difference is in discouraged workers who have given up looking for jobs and hence are not considered unemployed in the official statistics, and in part-time workers officially counted as employed but unemployed by the AFL-CIO count. Labor spokesmen urged that the government focus on creating more jobs, rather than combatting inflation.

This recommendation was echoed by Prof. Walter Heller, chief economic advisor to Presidents Kennedy and Johnson. Heller said the danger of stimulating further inflation now is slight, with so many people out of work, and that the cost of unemployment is great in human misery and wasted potential output.

However, Arthur Burns, chairman of the prestigious and powerful Federal Reserve Board, the nation's central bank; warned that although unemployment is still too high, it is too soon to drop the battle against inflation. In a recent speech, he said, "Our nation cannot now achieve the goal of full employment by pursuing spending and monetary policies that rekindle inflationary expectations. Inflation has weakened our economy; it is endangering our economic and political system. America has become enmeshed in an inflationary web, and we need to gather our moral strength and intellectual courage to extricate ourselves from it."

Labor Department spokesmen, while avoiding confrontation with the AFL-CIO, questioned the 10.5 percent unemployment figure. Regular Labor Department surveys place the "discouraged workers" total at only 1 million or so, and some contend that elimination of part-time workers from the employment totals would also require elimination from the ranks of the unemployed of those seeking only part-time jobs. Many teenagers, students, and older women look for only part-time work but are nonetheless officially considered unemployed if they don't have jobs. Labor Department spokesmen would not comment on whether unemployment or inflation is the more serious problem.

8

THE national income accounts and economic welfare

Modern economics is an empirical science. To understand and regulate the behavior of an enormously complex economy, we need measures of its performance—just as a business needs accounts to measure its performance. We need measures of the nation's total output of goods and services, and of the total income received by all its people. We also need more detailed measures—of how much people have left to spend after paying their taxes, of corporate profits, of family and business savings, and so on.

Over the past half century, the United States and most other economically developed nations have evolved detailed sets of "national income accounts" to provide such measures. They are the topic of this chapter. For our elementary purposes it is not important to know all the details of these accounts. But the gross national product (GNP), national income (NI), disposable personal income (DPI), consumption and investment, and consumer price index (CPI) not only are vital in analyzing how the macroeconomy works, but have become part of America's standard newspaper and TV news vocabularies. Many people use these figures as measures of general economic welfare, although their use for this purpose is sharply debated. Be sure you understand the basic GNP accounts.

Note: This chapter can be used ahead of Chapter 7 by instructors who wish to do so.

MEASURES OF NATIONAL PRODUCTION AND INCOME

Economic production defined

To begin, a basic question: What do economists mean by "production"?

To the economist, production is the creation of any good or service that people are willing to pay for. Raising wheat is production, and so is making the wheat into flour, and the flour into bread. It is also production for the local grocer to have the bread on his shelf when you want it, or to deliver it to your door. The agricultural, manufacturing, and marketing services all satisfy human wants, and people are willing to pay for them.

In fact, over half the people employed in the United States today render services rather than manufacture or raise anything. Over half of what you pay goes for middlemen's services— those of the retailer, the wholesaler, the banker, the trucker, and many others. Lots of people object to this situation. "There are too many middlemen!" they say. Maybe there are. But if you stop to think about it, you'll run head-on into this question: Are there too many manufacturers, or too many farmers? **The real economic test for all producers of goods or services is whether they satisfy a consumer demand—not how many pounds of physical stuff they produce.**

Production as the economist defines it is thus not a moral or ethical concept. Making and selling cigarettes is production, just like raising and selling food. The test of the private-enterprise economy is the test of the market. If an act helps satisfy a want that someone is willing to pay for, that act is production.

Gross national product

Gross national product is the nation's total production of goods and services (usually for a year) valued in terms of the market prices of the goods and services produced. This concept goes directly back to the definition of production above: Production is whatever people will pay for, and what they pay is an economic valuation of the worth of the product or service. GNP includes all the economic production in the country in any given time period. It can also be thought of as all the current production that provides jobs in any time period.

Gross national product is stated in money terms, because this is the only meaningful way of adding together the output of such diverse goods and services as carrots, machine tools, maid service, air travel, and Fords. Strictly, then, GNP is the money value of total national production for any time period.

GNP is also the nation's total expenditures on goods and services produced during the year. Each unit produced is matched by an expenditure on that unit. Most goods and services produced are bought outright. But how about the ones produced but not sold? Economists regard these as having been bought by the producers who hold them as inventories. Then it is clear that the production and expenditure totals are identical. Viewed as total expenditure, GNP is the very important concept "aggregate demand," which we shall use repeatedly in the chapters ahead.

GNP is also the total income received by all sellers of goods and services. What someone spends on current output, someone else receives as income. This is GNP seen from the receipts side.

Thus, national output = national expenditure = national (gross) income. We get the same total each way we calculate GNP.

Estimating GNP. There are two ways to calculate GNP, each designed to avoid the danger of double-counting in a complex economy. One way is to sum up all expenditures on *final* products sold to consumers or to businesses for final use as producers' goods—all spending on potatoes, factories, missiles, legal services, and so on. Note the word "final"; we must be careful not to double-count. Miners dig iron ore out of the ground and sell it to U.S. Steel. The latter makes the ore into steel and sells the steel to Westinghouse. Westinghouse makes refrigerators and sells them to us. We don't count the value of the iron ore, plus the value of the steel, plus the value of the refrigerator. That would involve counting the iron ore three times. Instead, everything that is used in another product during the year shows up and is counted only in the *final* product (in this case, refrigerators), since the value of the final product will reflect the value of all the raw materials, labor, and other productive services included in it.

Producers' goods, like machinery, which are bought by businesses, pose an obvious problem, because they are not directly incorporated into the final consumers' goods the way raw materials are. We count machinery and other producers' goods once, when they reach their final buyer— for example, when Westinghouse buys a new machine tool. This process of summing up all final purchases is called the "final-products approach" to estimating GNP.

GNP can also be estimated by the "value-added" method. Here, the estimators establish the value added by each producer at each stage of production, then sum up all these values. For example, in converting the iron ore to steel, U.S. Steel adds value to the product it passes along. This added value is the difference between what it pays for the ore, coal, and other products that it uses and the price at which it sells the steel to Westinghouse; roughly, it is the wages, interest, and rents paid by U.S. Steel plus the profit it earns. Similarly, we can compute the value added by Westinghouse. And so on for each productive unit in the economy. By summing up all the values added, we come out with the gross national product, again avoiding double-counting.

Composition of GNP.   Table 8–1 shows who buys the goods and services in the GNP, a useful breakdown in a market-directed economy. Buyers are divided into three big groups: consumers, businesses (buying "investment," or "producers'," goods), and governments. To provide historical perspective, Figure 8–1 then presents the same data from 1929 through 1975. Take a look at the three major segments.

1. The biggest part of total production is goods and services for consumers—turnips, stoves, dresses, movies, medical services, hats, and all the other things that consumers buy.
2. The next group is "producers'" or "capital" goods, in which businesses invest. These are

Table 8–1

U.S. Gross national product, 1975

Components	Amount (in billions)
Consumer purchases	$964
Private investment expenditures (including foreign)	205
Government purchases	331
Total	$1,500

Source: U.S. Department of Commerce.

buildings, machinery, equipment, and other capital goods used in the production of further goods or services. Such producers' goods are purchased primarily by businesses. But houses are also included in the investment-goods category, on the ground that they are so durable that in effect they represent investment goods owned directly by consumers.[1] Business investment also includes—as inventories—any increase in unsold goods in process or final form.

Three important warnings about the private-investment category:

First, "investment" means the purchase of investment goods (buildings, machinery, and so on) produced during the year. For example, if someone buys a ten-year-old factory, this is not investment; the factory was included in the gross national product ten years ago, when it was built.

Second, investment does not include mere financial transfers, such as the purchase of stocks and bonds. For example, if you buy a share of General Motors stock from GM or me, this is not investment for purposes of the national income accounts, because it does not pay for any new production.

Third, note that investment includes gross purchases of investment goods. It includes production that merely replaces depreciating buildings, machinery, and equipment, as well as production that represents a net increase in society's

[1] Although it is reasonable to treat new private housing as investment, note that houses differ only in degree from such durable consumer goods as autos, refrigerators, and vacuum cleaners, which are treated as consumption goods.

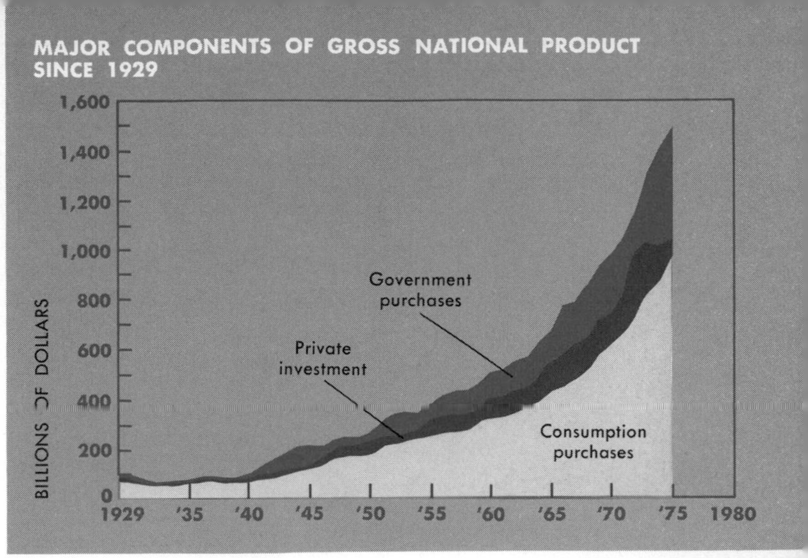

MAJOR COMPONENTS OF GROSS NATIONAL PRODUCT SINCE 1929

Figure 8-1
Consumers buy most (two thirds) of the GNP. The other third is divided between private investment and government purchases. (Source: U.S. Department of Commerce.)

stock of capital goods. We come to the **net** increase in the nation's capital goods in the section on "net national product" below.

3. Government purchases of goods and services include both consumption and investment goods. Federal, state, and local governments buy food, police services, and other current consumption items, as well as investment goods such as roads, buildings, and parks. But note that government purchases of goods and services do not include all government expenditures. Governments also spend large sums on "transfer payments" (such as unemployment insurance and Social Security payments) that are not payments for currently produced goods and services and are hence not included in GNP.

4. We have included $21 billion of "foreign investment," or "net exports," in private investment here, although it is often shown as a separate item. If, for example, the United States exports more than it imports, we include this net difference in GNP. It provides jobs in the U.S. economy even though it does not increase U.S. consumption or investment goods. Conversely, a net excess of imports over exports is deducted in computing GNP. We will take a more thorough look at this item in Part 6, on the international economy.

To summarize, GNP is made up of (1) consumer goods and services bought by individuals and households, (2) investment goods bought mainly by businesses, and (3) both consumer

and investment goods and services bought by federal, state, and local governments. **In all three categories, remember that only goods and services produced during the current year count; transfers of existing assets are excluded. GNP may be thought of as the total national pie of goods and services produced each year, with the big slices going to consumers, businesses, and governments.**

Net national product

GNP includes some investment each year that just replaces already-existing producers' goods that are "depreciating," or wearing out. As we saw in looking at the individual corporation (in Chapter 4), if a truck lasts ten years, we might say that one-tenth of it is used up every year, and the business that owns it would consider this tenth as an annual cost that year.[2] So it is with all other producers' goods; they wear out. Before a firm or the economy as a whole adds anything *net* to its stock of producers' goods, part of each year's production must go to replacing depreciating capital goods.

Net national product (NNP) is the net national production of goods and services. It is GNP, less those goods that merely replace depreciating buildings and machines. In 1975, for

---

[2]Accountants have more complicated depreciation formulas, which recognize the fact that buildings and machines do not necessarily wear out at constant rates.

example, GNP was $1,500 billion. Depreciation (sometimes called "capital consumption allowances") was estimated at $153 billion. Thus, *net* national product was $1,347 billion, about 10 percent less than gross national product, because 10 percent of our total output went to replace depreciating producers' goods and houses. Net national product measures the total production of goods and services available for current consumption and for adding to our stock of producers' equipment, including housing.

National income

National income is the total of all income earned by the "factors of production"—land, labor, capital, and management. The national income is basically the net national product viewed from the income side, but with one difference. The factors of production (laborers, managers, machinery, and so forth) do not receive as income the full value of their output, because businesses that hire them must pay indirect taxes (sales taxes, excises, and property taxes) to the government, which reduce the income left to pay to the factors of production. If we subtract indirect business taxes from NNP, we have left the "national income" that goes to

Table 8-2
U.S. National income, 1975

Source of income	Amount (in billions)
Total	$1,210
Wages and salaries	921
Net income of unincorporated business[a]	83
Corporation profits[b]	102
Interest	82
Rental income	21

[a] Mainly farmers and professional men in business for themselves, plus small retail stores.

[b] Of which $47 billion was paid out in income taxes and $40 billion was plowed back as reinvested earnings. Dividends paid out to stockholders were $30 billion.

Source: U.S. Department of Commerce.

Table 8-3
U.S. personal income, 1975

		Amount (in billions)
Total personal income		$1,246
Less: Personal income taxes	$169	
Equals: Disposable personal income		1,077
Of which:		
Consumer outlays[a]		987
Personal saving		90

[a] Consumer outlays include $23 billion of consumer interest payments, which are excluded from the "consumer purchases" shown in Table 8-1. The Department of Commerce defines "consumers' expenditures" to include only consumer payments for goods and services.

Source: U.S. Department of Commerce.

all factors of production. In 1975, indirect taxes were $137 billion. Deducting this from net national product, we get national income of $1,210 billion.[3]

Table 8-2 shows the share of the national income earned by each major factor of production. Note the large share of wages and salaries—76 percent in 1975. This percentage has risen substantially since World War II.

Personal income and disposable personal income

For many purposes, we need to know how much income households (individuals) have to spend on consumer goods. For this, we need "personal income" and "disposable personal income." **"Personal income" is the total income received by all individuals in the country— what individuals actually have to spend, save, or pay taxes with.** It differs from national income mainly because national income includes total corporation profits before taxes, whereas only part of these profits are paid out to individuals in dividends, and because personal income includes large transfer payments (especially Social Security and other government benefits)

[3] This omits some minor items that explain the apparent discrepancy in subtraction.

that are not payments for productive services and hence are not in national income. As the footnote to Table 8–2 indicates, nearly half of corporation profits go to Uncle Sam as corporation income taxes, and half of what's left is plowed back into businesses rather than paid out to stockholders. We must subtract these amounts from national income to get income actually paid out to individuals. On the other hand, "transfer payments" to individuals (Social Security, interest on the national debt, and so forth) more than offset the corporate profits not paid to individuals, so personal income was larger than national income. (Table 8–4 shows the calculation in detail for 1975.)

Table 8–3 shows what people did with their total personal income in 1975. First, they paid their income taxes. What they had left we call "disposable personal income." Most of this they spent on consumption, and the rest they saved. **The concept of "disposable personal income"**

(what people have left after they pay their taxes) will be important later on in analyzing consumer spending and saving behavior.

The integrated national income accounts[4]

Table 8–4 summarizes the complete set of interconnections for 1975 just explained, beginning with the gross national product total. Figure 8–2 shows the same set of interconnections as a flow diagram, tracing the entire income-and-payments flow. This figure ties the

[4]Within the last few years, a new set of social accounts has been released by the Federal Reserve System. These are called the "flow of funds accounts." They include all financial transactions in the economy, including payments in the stock market, for other financial transfers, for existing assets, and for a variety of other purposes not included in the national income accounts. These new money-flows accounts can be integrated with the national income accounts, and now provide a complete picture of money payments throughout the economy.

Table 8–4

National income accounts for 1975

		Amount (in billions)
Gross national product		$1,500
Deduct: Capital consumption allowances (depreciation allowances)	$153	
Net national product		1,347
Deduct: Indirect business taxes	137	
National income		1,210
Deduct: Corporation profits taxes	47	
Corporate savings (undistributed profits)	40	
Social Security taxes	108	
Add: Transfer and interest payments[a]	214	
Personal income		1,246
Deduct: Personal taxes	169	
Disposable personal income		1,077
Of which: Consumer outlays[b]		987
Personal saving		90

[a]A few minor items are omitted, which explain the apparent discrepancies in the table.
[b]Includes $23 billion of interest paid by consumers, not considered an expenditure on goods and services.

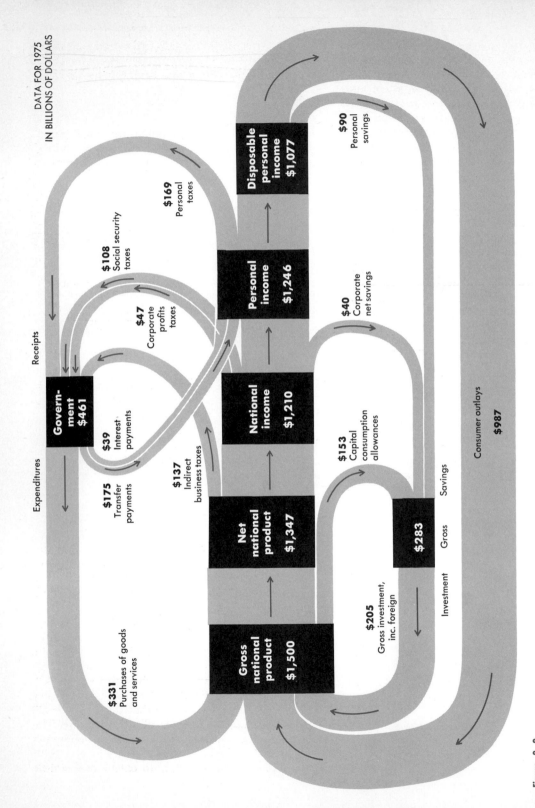

Figure 8-2
National income and expenditure make essentially a circular flow, with many side loops. This is a more complete version of the simple circular money flow illustrated in Figure 7–1. Some minor items are omitted, and "consumer outlays" include $24 billion of consumer interest payments generally excluded from "consumer expenditures" and GNP, so figures will not add exactly to GNP and some subtotals. Note that government spending exceeds tax receipts, and private saving exceeds private investment.

circular flow of gross national product back to the simple, fundamental circular-flow diagram in Figure 7–1. (A few minor items are omitted, which explains the apparent discrepancies.)

In Figure 8–2, begin with the GNP of $1,500 billion, as in Table 8–4. Then, $153 billion of capital consumption (depreciation) allowances drains off as a form of private saving, leaving $1,347 billion of net national product. From NNP, another $137 billion drains off to the government through indirect business taxes, leaving national income of $1,210 billion. From this, corporate income taxes, Social Security taxes, and corporate saving (undistributed profits) are drained off, while interest on the government debt, Social Security, and other transfer payments are added back into the income stream, to make up $1,246 billion of personal income. The resulting personal-income total is reduced to personal disposable income by the payment of personal income taxes, and then part of disposable income drains off into personal savings while the bulk flows on into consumption expenditures and into GNP.

Now add back the private-investment and government-spending flows out of private savings and government tax receipts. Together these three types of spending make up GNP, the three big components of aggregate demand for currently produced goods and services—consumption, investment, and government spending. Remember these, for they are at the center of the analysis of Chapters 10 and 11.[5]

CHANGING PRICE LEVELS
AND PRICE INDEXES

When prices change, GNP expressed in terms of dollars is no longer an adequate measure of the real goods and services produced. A 100 percent increase in real national output would mean a great rise in the national standard of living. But doubling GNP merely by doubling prices is no real economic gain at all. In order to

[5]Note that private investment need not equal the private-saving flow in the bottom loop, nor need government spending equal tax collections in the top loop. Either sector may run a surplus or a deficit, as will be explained in Chapter 11.

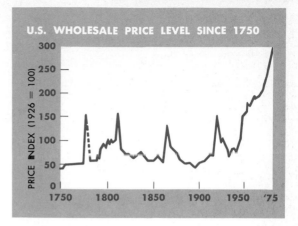

U.S. WHOLESALE PRICE LEVEL SINCE 1750

PRICE INDEX (1926 = 100)

Figure 8–3
Prices have fluctuated sharply throughout our history. Until recently, the big peaks have come during or just after major wars, but we have had more inflation since World War II than ever before in peacetime. (Source: U.S. Department of Labor.)

separate "real" from merely "dollar" changes in individual and national incomes, we have to make an adjustment for price-level changes.

Figure 8–3 indicates the big fluctuations in prices in the United States over the last two centuries. The problem of price-level changes is no minor one.

What is a price index?

In 1929, a family income of $1,300 would have bought a group of goods and services called a "subsistence standard of living." In 1933, you could have bought the same collection of goods and services for about $900. By 1976, you would have needed about $4,000.

If all prices changed in the same proportion in the same direction at the same time, measuring price-level changes would be simple. But the world of real prices is not simple and orderly. Even in the big price rises shown in Figure 8–3, some prices declined and others rose at very different rates. Yet we say that the "price level" rose, because the average of all prices rose. The price of the same market basket of goods was higher than before.

Table 8–5 shows how to calculate a simple

Table 8–5

Price index for 1975 with 1970 as base year

Product	1970	1975
Eggs, each	5¢ = 100%	6¢ = 120%
Hamburger, per lb.	40¢ = 100%	50¢ = 125%
Turnips, per lb.	9¢ = 100%	6¢ = 67%
Apples, per lb.	10¢ = 100%	12¢ = 120%
	4)400%	4)432%
	100% = price level in 1970	108% = price level in 1975

} of the 1970 price }

"price index" for a market basket of four commodities, to show whether their price level went up or down between 1970 and 1975. A price index is a measure of price-level changes.

With 1970 as the "base year," the price of each item in that year is 100 percent of itself. This is what people mean when they say, "Take 1970 as 100." Then we compute what percentage each 1975 price is of the 1970 price. For example, eggs at 6 cents each are 120 percent of the 1970 price. This 120 percent is the 1975 "price relative" for eggs, since it shows the 1975 price relative to that in 1970. To find the change in the price level (the average of all four prices), we simply take the average of the four 1975 price relatives, which gives us 108 percent for the 1975 price level. (The percentage sign is usually omitted for convenience.) Of course, most price indexes include more commodities, but they are made in a generally similar way.[6]

This simple method of calculating price-level changes may give misleading results, however. It tacitly assumes that eggs, hamburger, turnips, and apples are equally important. A 10 percent change in the price of hamburger influences the index exactly as much as a 10 percent change in the price of turnips. Actually, hamburger is more important than turnips in most budgets, and it

seems logical that the price of hamburger should affect the index more.

Thus, in most price indexes, each price is "weighted" according to its importance. For example, the U.S. Bureau of Labor Statistics weights the prices in its widely used consumer price index (CPI) as follows. The statisticians take a "market basket" of the goods and services bought during the 1960s by typical urban wage earners' families. Choosing some 400 of the most important prices, they weight each in accordance with the proportion of the families' total expenditure for that commodity in the base period. If the families bought lots of auto repairs then, such repairs make up a sizable part of the weekly market basket; rent is a big item in the basket. In effect, the market-basket approach weights the price of each commodity according to the weekly amount spent on that commodity in the base period.

Then the BLS gets its price index by comparing the cost of the basket from one week to the next. If the index uses 1967 as a base period (100), a weekly index reading of 120 means that the cost of the market basket is up 20 percent from the 1967 price level for those goods and services.

The Bureau of Labor Statistics updates and revises the CPI periodically to reflect changes in consumer spending patterns. For example, consumers spent 35 percent of their income on food in 1935–36, but this had dropped to about 20 percent by the early 1970s. Thus, 1930s weights would give far too much emphasis to food prices if the old weights were used in the 1970s. The

[6]The final index numbers merely indicate relative average prices in the two years. We could just as well have taken 1975 as 100, in which case the 1970 index would have been 93. Although the actual index numbers would have been different, either set shows equally well the relative price levels in the two years: 93/100 = 100/108. Thus, the year chosen as 100 has little significance.

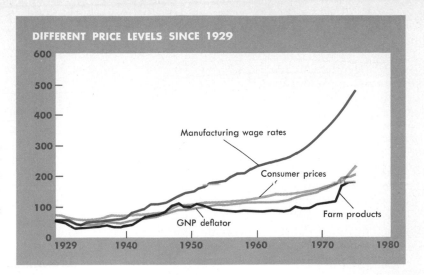

600

500

400

300

200

100

0

Manufacturing wage rates

Consumer prices

GNP deflator

Farm products

1929   1940   1950   1960   1970   1980

Figure 8–4
Different prices move diversely in the American economy. The GNP deflator comes closest to showing price changes for all currently produced goods and services. Note the rapid rise of the wage-rate index. (Sources: U.S. Department of Labor and Commerce.)

BLS has recently conducted a major revision of the CPI, shifting the base year from 1964 to 1973–74 and adding a new index covering all lower-middle-income-level urban dwellers to the older index, which covered only urban wage earners and clerical workers. The narrow index will be continued, especially for use in union wage-contract "escalators," while the new, broader index will reflect prices paid by all lower-middle-income urban families.[7]

Price indexes for different price levels

A price level is merely an average of some group of prices, so we can speak of many different price levels. One may reflect the prices paid by a group of consumers; another, the level of wages in manufacturing; and so on.

Figure 8–4 shows the movements of four important price indexes from 1929 through 1975. What price level is most significant depends on what you are talking about. If you want to measure changes in the cost of living for a particular group, the logical choice is an index of the prices of the goods and services the group buys. Given the wide diversity of price movements, it is hard to devise a single price index that will be a significant measure for the whole

economy. The closest approach is an index developed by the Department of Commerce to eliminate the effects of price-level movements from the gross national product. This adjustment is spoken of as "deflating" the GNP. In it, first, special indexes are determined for the different major sectors of GNP, and then these are combined to obtain a "GNP deflator." The result is a price index for all goods and services in the gross national product.

If we had an index for *all* prices, including all those not included in GNP, we would have an index of the changing purchasing power of the dollar. Clearly, the value of money (the purchasing power of one dollar) varies just inversely with the general price level. If all prices double, one dollar will buy just half as much. But remember the warning in Chapter 7 against confusing the purchasing power of one dollar with that of all dollars in the economy.

Figure 7–2 compared GNP since 1870 in the actual (current) prices that prevailed each year with GNP in constant (1964) prices.[8] We often speak of the constant-price GNP as "real" GNP, because with the elimination of price-level changes, the GNP index measures real changes in output of goods and services. Actual current

[7]For a description of the new indexes, see J. Shiskin, "Updating the Consumer Price Index," *Challenge*, November 1974.

[8]Remember from above that we could have chosen some year other than 1964 as the "base" year for calculating constant-price GNP over the years. Another base year would give different absolute levels for the constant-price GNP but would not change the relative movements in the two curves.

109

GNP without adjustment for inflation is often called "nominal" GNP. In periods of rapidly changing prices, nominal-GNP changes give a seriously misleading picture of what is happening to real GNP.

How good are the price indexes?

How accurately do the well-known price indexes mirror the price changes they are intended to summarize? The most widely used indexes are prepared by the government—the consumer price index, the wholesale price index, and the GNP deflator. These are the product of years of hard work and millions of dollars, and they're as good as the experts can make them. Many privately made indexes fall short of these standards of excellence, even though they may serve useful purposes. Others are extremely accurate, but they measure only a few prices—for example, the well-known Dow Jones index of a small group of leading stock prices.

Millions of workers' wages are adjusted periodically under their union-contract escalators for increases in the "cost of living," which are usually measured by the CPI. In 1959, President Eisenhower appointed a group of the country's leading economists and statisticians to restudy the CPI. Their report gave the index high marks but pointed to some tough statistical problems yet to be solved. For example, they found that the index probably doesn't recognize quality improvements as effectively as it should. Suppose Ford ups the horsepower in next year's models and adds a new type of carburetor, but doesn't change the price. The index should not show the price of Fords unchanged; it should show price as lower (because you get more car for your money). But how much lower? Some economists believe the CPI shows prices rising perhaps 1 percent a year too fast, because of the difficulty of promptly reflecting such changes due to new products and quality improvements, but this is a debatable issue.

GNP AND ECONOMIC WELFARE

GNP was devised as a measure of economic output. It is, however, often used as a measure of economic welfare; more GNP means we are better off. More real GNP per capita does indeed suggest that, on the average, we are economically better off, but GNP has some serious weaknesses as a measure of economic well-being. Indeed, modern supporters of "zero economic growth" (ZEG) argue that growth in GNP worsens, not improves, the nation's economic well-being, because growth in production destroys the quality of life, even though it means more quantity of output.

This controversy is an important one, and we shall look into it in detail presently. First, however, eight warnings on the use of GNP as a measure of economic welfare.

1. Be sure the figures used are *real*—that is, price-level-adjusted—GNP. Changes in GNP merely because of changes in prices obviously do not reflect changes in real output.

2. GNP per capita or per family is generally more useful as a welfare measure than are the national totals. Ultimately, economic welfare must refer to the situation of individuals. A big nation like China is poor with a large GNP; a small one like Switzerland is well off with a tiny GNP.

3. GNP places no value on leisure. Over the past century in the United States, the average workweek has been cut in half—from 75 to 39 hours; vacations have lengthened greatly; people start working later in life and retire earlier. Although it is difficult to value this great increase in leisure, to say that it has made no contribution to our economic well-being would obviously be foolish.

4. GNP includes for the most part only production that passes through a market transaction. It takes no account of such important items as nonpaid housewives' services, and home labor such as painting, gardening, and the like. If a bachelor marries his maid, GNP is reduced. If Mrs. A and Mrs. B simply did each other's housework and paid each other $5,000, GNP would be $10,000 higher, with no change in real activity. In only a few cases, such as the estimated value of services from owner-occupied homes, has it proved practicable to include real production that is not sold in the marketplace.

5. GNP counts durable consumer goods, such as autos, when they are produced, although their actual services are consumed over their entire

lives. If production and consumption run at even rates, this causes no problem. But in depressions, when few new durables are produced, GNP understates real consumption, because consumers continue to use the services of existing durables. Conversely, GNP overstates real consumption in booms, when consumers' durables are produced faster than they are used.

6. GNP says nothing about *what* goods and services are produced. A dollar spent on one thing counts the same as a dollar spent on anything else. Many critics argue that in fact some kinds of output are more valuable to our well-being than others are, dollar for dollar. For example, they say that a dollar spent on nourishing food is more valuable than one spent on whiskey or bombs. But this is far from obvious; think back to Chapter 5 on consumer behavior. If GNP production is in response to free consumer choices, presumably the marginal dollar spent by each consumer on each thing he buys gives roughly equal satisfaction; otherwise, he would spend his dollars so that they do.

The biggest problem comes with goods and services provided by the government. If we assume that democracy works well, the government presumably provides public services and requires people to pay for them through taxes in accordance with the public's wishes. But in this case, the individual can only vote for his representative; then he must go along with the particular taxes and expenditures Congress votes, whether he likes them or not. Clearly, the public sector provides only a rough response to individual wishes, but to handle government taxes and spending in any other way in the GNP accounts would seem even less satisfactory. So GNP says that a dollar spent on anything by individuals or governments counts the same as any other dollar. Ask yourself: Should a dollar spent on schools or national defense be considered more or less important to our economic welfare than one spent on steak or cigarettes?

A further problem arises as modern life becomes more complex. Now we build elaborate subway, elevated, and highway systems in our cities. They provide incomes to thousands and serve millions daily, contributing billions to the annual GNP. Do these billions reflect increased well-being for our city dwellers, or do they reflect instead a huge amount of resources devoted to

the painful necessity of getting around in crowded cities? Some economists call them "regrettables," and argue that our larger GNP gives a misleading picture of how much better off we actually are than, for example, a rural nation with lower expenditures on regrettables.

7. GNP gives no *negative* weight to those side effects of GNP that do harm rather than good. Air and water pollution are vivid cases. Factories that spew out smoke and dirty water as well as wanted products get overcounted. Their products increase GNP dollar for dollar, but there is no negative charge for all the damage done by pollution. Such side effects (called "externalities" by economists) are common in our modern, crowded, high-technology society.

Nor does GNP give any negative weight to the sheer disamenities of living in dirty, noisy, crowded cities and slums, compared to more open, pleasant surroundings.

8. GNP measures only *economic* production, which is only one part of what makes us happy or unhappy, contented or alienated. Critics of modern life point to high suicide rates, alienation, and what they see as the dull monotonony of middle-class American life. But defenders counter that comfortable homes, modern plumbing, healthy children, automobiles, and well-paying office or factory jobs look very good compared to the lives of our grandfathers—and that the alienated critics had better be careful not to throw out the baby with the bath water. Clearly, GNP doesn't measure everything that contributes to human happiness—peace, health, friendship, and so on. But focusing on the economic issues, are we happier—better off—with our high GNP per capita than if we were poorer? This controversy will seldom be far from the surface through the chapters to come.[9]

GNP, growth, and net economic welfare

To introduce more reason into the somewhat feverish rhetoric of debate on economic growth and the quality of life, Yale's James Tobin and William Nordhaus have at-

[9]For an interesting study concluding that the answer is yes for improvements in each individual's income, but not necessarily so if all incomes go up together, see R. Easterlin, "Does Money Bring Happiness?" *The Public Interest,* Winter 1973.

Table 8–6

GNP and net economic welfare, 1929 and 1965 (in billions, 1958 prices)

	1929	1965
GNP	$204	$618
NNP	184	563
Add:		
Leisure	340	630
Nonmarket activities	86	295
Other services of private and government capital	30	79
Deduct:		
Regrettables	−17	−94
Disamenities	−13	−35
Other capital consumption and growth requirement	−65	−195
Net economic welfare	544	1,241

Source: W. Nordhaus and J. Tobin, *Economic Growth* (New York: National Bureau of Economic Research, 1972), p. 12.

tempted rough estimates to convert the GNP accounts into a usable measure of economic welfare. Table 8–6 summarizes their attempt to make some order-of-magnitude judgments for 1929 and 1965 about what has really been happening to economic welfare in American economic growth.

Beginning with the regular GNP figures, they estimated the value of leisure and nonmarket activities in both years, and added them, plus services of capital not usually included in GNP, to the GNP totals. They then subtracted from the total the "regrettables" (such as national defense, police, and other resource uses that really don't add to our well-being even though they may be necessary) and "disamenities" (dirt, smoke, noise, and other externalities, mainly associated with urban life). They also subtracted the large amount of capital use each year devoted to keeping the economy growing in per capita income at about the rate it is used to; large additions to our capital stock are needed each year just to keep per capita incomes growing, or even from declining as population grows. The result is a rough dollar measure of net economic welfare (NEW) in the two years.

The results, although very rough, are striking.

The dollar measure of economic welfare each year is far larger than GNP. The estimated dollar value of leisure and of nonmarket activities exceeds the entire GNP. Although the estimated costs of regrettables and disamenities, plus the heavy use of capital just to keep total output growing, are large, they are far less than the additions from valuing leisure and nonmarket activities. In total, the measure of economic welfare in 1929 was nearly three times GNP, in 1965 more than twice GNP. And total U.S. economic welfare in 1965 was more than double that in 1929, in spite of the costs of economic growth stressed by its critics. But economic welfare did grow at a slower rate than GNP, which tripled over the same period. We shall return to these issues on growth in Part 7.

Tobin and Nordhaus emphasize that different underlying assumptions can greatly change the results of such calculations. For example, how leisure time and nonmarket labor are valued obviously makes a huge difference to the results. And valuation of the disamenities of modern life is clearly arbitrary. So use the estimates only as suggestions. But they do indicate something of the extent to which the national income accounts can reasonably be used as indicators of economic welfare.

ESTIMATES OF NATIONAL WEALTH

Work is under way on estimates of the total national wealth of the United States. Table 8–7 shows the estimates of the nation's real net national wealth in 1925 and 1975, pre-

Table 8–7

Net national wealth of the United States[a]

	1925	1975
Net national wealth (Billions of 1975 dollars)	1,626	5,684
Per capita wealth (1975 dollars)	13,943	26,516

[a] Source: John Kendrick, Measuring America's Wealth," *The Morgan Guaranty Survey.* May, 1976.

pared by John Kendrick. The total was $5.6 trillion in 1975, not quite four times our net national product for the year, and about $26,000 per capita. Real net national wealth approximately quadrupled over the half century, a growth rate of about $2\frac{1}{2}$ percent per annum. These figures eliminate debts owed by one part of the nation to another, to avoid double-counting. If we construct a national balance sheet showing all assets and liabilities of all individuals, businesses and governments, the total assets exceeded $10 trillion in 1975, about double the net wealth total.

REVIEW

Concepts to remember

This chapter introduces some of the most important concepts in economics. The following checklist is to help you make sure that you have them firmly in mind:

production	personal income
gross national product	disposable personal income
"real" GNP	personal consumption
nominal GNP	personal saving
"value-added approach"	private investment
"final-products approach"	producers', or capital, goods
net national product	per capita income and output
capital consumption allowance	price level
depreciation allowance	price index
national income	net economic welfare

For analysis and discussion

1. Define *production.* Which of the following are production, as defined by the economist?
   a. Delivering milk
   b. Making steel
   c. Selling cigarettes
   d. Playing golf
2. In the national income accounts, production is measured by what people pay for it. Is it therefore true that a dollar spent on liquor, one on bombs, and one on bread are all equally important?
3. Using Figure 8–2, explain each diversion from the main circular flow of income, and trace through the way in which it returns to the main stream. Did government add to or deduct from the flow of spending in 1975?
4. A recent congressional investigation found that over half the consumer price of many food products went to middlemen at different levels—retailers, wholesalers, and so on; in some cases, as little as 20 percent to the farmer. Farm and consumer groups testifying before the committee urged action to rectify this situation.
   a. Do you agree that Congress should take some action? Why, or why not?
   b. If Congress should act, what should it do?
5. Is gross national product, net national product, or disposable personal income after taxes the best measure of the overall performance of the economy? Why?

6. Should we substitute the Tobin-Nordhaus measure of net economic welfare for gross national product in our official government statistics? Why, or why not? (See Case 7, on following pages.)

7. The steady growth in service workers is a sign of weakness in our economy, because they produce no *real* goods output comparable to farm output of food and raw materials. (True or false? Why?)

8. From the following data on disposable personal income and the consumer price index, compute disposable personal income for the years shown in constant (1947–49) dollars. Did "real" disposable income fluctuate more or less than money disposable income?

	Disposable personal income (in billions)	Consumer price index (1947–49 = 100)	DPI in 1947–49 dollars
1929	$ 83	73	—
1933	46	55	—
1939	70	60	—
1959	337	126	—
1975	1,077	210	—

9. Suppose that prices for certain products in 1970 and 1975 were as follows:

	1970	1975	
Round steak (per pound)	$ 1.70	$ 2.00	117.6
Butter (per pound)	1.00	.95	95.0
Men's suits (each)	100.00	160.00	160.0
Ford sedans (each)	2,600.00	4,000.00	153.8
Student notebooks (each)	1.00	1.00	100.0

P .108

a. Construct a price index showing the change in the price level of these commodities from 1970 to 1975. If you feel you need further data, explain why, make a reasonable assumption on the data, and then construct the index.

b. Does this index give a reasonably good picture of the change in the cost of living between 1970 and 1975? Why, or why not?

In 1971, the *Survey of Current Business,* which publishes the government's official national income accounts, was fifty years old. To celebrate the occasion, a number of distinguished economists wrote evaluative reviews of the accounts. One of the most interesting was addressed to the producers of the national income accounts by Arthur Okun, former chairman of President Johnson's Council of Economic Advisors. Okun argued strongly against trying to convert the nation's economic accounts into a measure of economic welfare. Evaluate his arguments as you read them. What is your conclusion: Should GNP be revised to try to measure social welfare?

The national accounts system is a great accomplishment of modern quantitative economics; it supplies an intelligible, integrated, and invaluable body of information about the functioning of the nation's economy. Its big summary number—the gross national product—has become a household word and has even been enshrined in a clock in the lobby of the Department of Commerce.

Yet, even as your numbers are receiving greater use and attention than ever before, they also are receiving more criticism. Put simply (perhaps caricatured), the fundamental criticism is that, even after correction for price and population change, the gross national product does not yield an unambiguous measure of national welfare; a rise in real GNP per capita does not necessarily mean that the nation has become better off. This diagnosis may be followed by either of two prescriptions: (1) ignore GNP, or (2) fix GNP so that it does measure social welfare.

I know you will not ignore the GNP. I urge you to bear the criticism with pride as a symbol of your success. I urge that you not try to "fix" it—to convert GNP into a purported measure of social welfare. You are doing your job so well that people are asking you to take on a different and bigger job. Resist at all costs, for you can't do that job; indeed, nobody can. Producing a summary measure of social welfare is a job for a philosopher-king, and there is no room for a philosopher-king in the federal government. . . .

Obviously, any number of things would make the nation better off without raising its real GNP as measured today. We might start the list with peace, equality of opportunity, the elimination of

injustice and violence, greater brotherhood among Americans of different racial and ethnic backgrounds, better understanding between parents and children and between husbands and wives, and we could go on endlessly. To suggest that GNP could become *the* indicator of social welfare is to imply that an appropriate price tag could be put on changes in all of these social factors from one year to the next. This would hardly be a minor modification of the national accounts. As I have suggested, it would be asking the national income statistician to play the role of philosopher-king, quantifying and evaluating all changes in the human condition. And it is absurd to suggest that if the national income statistician can't do that job, the figure he writes for GNP is not interesting. . . .

What you can and do measure as national income statisticians is the output resulting from market-oriented activity. The key to market-oriented activity is the presence of price tags—the essential ingredient in an objective standard of measurement. Price tags enable you to sum up physicians' prescriptions and phonograph records and pounds of steak and packages of beans, or all the things that money can buy. But if you were to be seduced by your critics into inventing price tags that neither exist nor can be reasonably approximated for things that money can't buy, you would have sacrificed the objective yardstick.

. . . . Let me run through some examples of changes you should *not* make.

Imputation of the value of housewives' services and of leisure For good reasons, you violate the normal institutional boundary between business and consumers when you include in GNP the imputed rental value of owner-occupied housing. You do this because the owner-occupant is short-circuiting the market that tenants go through. You do the same for the food farmers produce and consume within their own households rather than sending to market. Why, so the argument goes, should you not similarly treat the housewife as short-circuiting the market by providing services that other families obtain by hiring domestic workers? I find it a compelling argument that a housewife is not a maid—and that this difference is of a higher order than the difference between the title to a house and a lease. The valuation of the housewife's hourly services by the wage rate of maids, or any multiple thereof, would not really translate her activity into dollars and cents.

I have never been disturbed by the well-known paradox that when the bachelor marries his cook, the national product goes down. The GNP measures the output of market-oriented activity, and the market-oriented activity is reduced by the cook's marriage. Why is this any more paradoxical than the fact that the national product will go down if I take a month's unpaid vacation in order to travel around the world? In both cases, the nation's marketable output is reduced, but that doesn't mean that welfare is reduced.

The vacation example brings us to the largest element of what might conceivably be viewed as potentially marketable services that do not show up in the national accounts—that is, time allocated to everything but work. . . . Leisure is a good thing, but it is one of many good things that do not bear a reasonably determinate price tag. It is an important subject for analysis and research, but it does not belong in GNP.

"Regrettable necessities"   It is obvious that many of the things consumers buy are not intended for pure enjoyment, but are rather a means of avoiding discomfort or preventing deterioration of physical and human capital. Yet you count them all as final product. You have been urged to try to eliminate "regrettable necessities" from final product and thus to classify them as a cost of living rather than a source of satisfaction. Don't start down that path. If you should do so (regrettably and unnecessarily), you would find that it winds along forever. Costs of physicians' services and other medical care are obviously regrettable necessities. So are the services of lawyers, policemen, firemen, sanitation workers, and economists (including national income statisticians). So are heating and air-conditioning outlays. Except for the few people who live to eat rather than eating to live, food is a regrettable necessity. Indeed, it is hard to imagine any output that clearly serves the purpose of pure, unmitigated enjoyment. But even if you could invent some arbitrary definition that kept final-product consumption from falling to zero, the exclusion of regrettable necessities would make no sense. . . .

Imputations for externalities   It is obvious that the producer does not incur all the costs of producing certain types of output, nor does the consumer get all the benefits. The producer whose factory belches smoke or sends effluents into the river is imposing a cost on society that is not reflected in private costs of production. On the other hand, draining a swamp or building a park may create benefits that are equally absent in your measure of the gross national product. Why, then, should you not try to estimate the net deterioration (or improvement) of the environment as a cost of productive activity, netting it out of GNP?

Again, I must ask how such a valuation could be made, if the market and the democratic process didn't provide price tags. Following your present rules, you will report the costs and benefits that society recognizes and responds to. If a ban is placed on activity that is inherently dangerous, or fees and taxes are imposed, you will follow the signals and properly reflect them in your valuation of output. If society changes its mind, you will make some rather puzzling changes in your definition and coverage of outputs. But any puzzles that arise concern the volatility of the nation's collective judgment, not of your practices. Your principle of excluding the output of illegal activity from the national product abides by the social judgment that some activities have such important negative externalities that they subtract from society's output even though somebody is willing to pay for them as an ultimate consumer. However sensible or foolish it was for the nation to decide that the sale of alcoholic beverages was illegal and then that it was legal again, it was completely sensible for the national income accountant to follow those verdicts. . . .

In short, the GNP is not the whole story of our society or even of our economy, and no conceivable redefinition can turn it into the whole story. You can help in many ways to put together some of the other pieces required to develop the whole story about social performance. But you would not assist by compromising on the proposition that GNP is *not* a measure of total social welfare. The beauty of your present practice is that no sensible person could mistake it for such.[10]

[10] Arthur Okun, "Should GNP Measure Social Welfare?" *Survey of Current Business,* Part II, July 1971.

9

AGGREGATE SUPPLY and AGGREGATE DEMAND

What determines how fast an economy grows? Why do we have booms, depressions, inflations, and unemployment? For over a century, economists have examined these problems. Today, we have a reasonably good understanding, although some important unanswered questions remain.

This and the next six chapters present the basic theory of income, employment, and prices—the general analytical model that has proved most useful in understanding what determines the overall level of income, employment, and prices in the American economy. No section of the book is more important to understand thoroughly. Chapters 16–19 then turn to the question of stabilization policy—how to avoid unemployment and inflation, and how to have a prosperous, stably growing economy.

A SIMPLE MODEL

To understand the complex real economic world, it is useful to begin with a very simple model. You will recall from Chapter 3 that the essence of a model is that it focuses on a few critical variables and the relationships among them, abstracting from many details in order to highlight these essentials. We want to understand the determinants of real GNP, of aggregate employment, and of price level. Let us begin by focusing on two major variables—aggregate demand and aggregate supply—which underlie the entire analysis.

Aggregate demand is the combined expenditures of consumers, businesses, and governments, which make up GNP. In our basically private-enterprise economy (leaving government production aside for the moment), goods and services are produced only when they can be sold at a profit. If there is no market demand, businesses will soon stop producing. And businesses will not invest in new factories and other productive capacity unless they expect to be able to sell their increased future output at a profit. Thus, the level of aggregate demand is crucial in determining both current output (GNP) and growth of productive capacity through new investment. It will be useful later to analyze separately consumption, investment, and government spending (the major components of aggregate demand), but for the moment, simply consider it as total spending.

Aggregate supply is the total amount of goods and services that will be produced (supplied) in response to different levels of aggregate demand. We can think of it as a schedule of different amounts of real GNP that will be produced in response to different levels of aggregate demand. At any given time, the maximum possible output (capacity) of the economy is determined by the amount of labor, land, machinery, and other productive resources, and the state of technology. At full employment of all those resources, the economy reaches its capacity for producing real GNP; more demand does not increase output, it only bids up prices. But if demand falls short of that level, less than full-capacity GNP may be produced.

Obviously, as we look back on any time period, aggregate demand (the amount bought) and aggregate supply (the amount produced) will be the same. What is produced (measured in dollars) is identical with what is spent on it. This is simply GNP looked at from the production and expenditure sides. **But whether the two sides are equal at a high or low level of GNP—whether at full employment or depression—is the vital question we need to examine.**

AGGREGATE SUPPLY AND AGGREGATE DEMAND

What determines the economy's aggregate supply schedule? The "real" productive capacity of any economic system sets the upper limit to its real GNP at any time. This productive capacity—the economy's production-possibilities curve for total output, from Chapter 2—depends on its underlying real productive resources, its technology, and its economic organization.[1] But an economy may not achieve this full-production potential. History shows that nations often fall short of obtaining the maximum production possible from their economies—for example, in the Great Depression of the 1930s. This failure primarily reflects a shortage of aggregate demand. There is not enough total spending by consumers and businesses to buy all the goods that could be produced at full employment.

Conversely, aggregate spending may exceed the productive capacity of the economy at existing prices. If that occurs, prices are bid up and there is inflation, because no more can be produced as demand rises.

The short-run supply schedule and supply curve

At any given time, the production-possibilities curve for an economy is given. Keeping this fact in mind, let us construct an aggregate-supply schedule for the economy, assuming that the full-employment prodcution limit is $400 billion. Column 1 in Table 9–1 first shows different assumed levels of aggregate demand; column 2 shows the amount that will be produced in response to each level of demand. **As long as the economy is below its capacity limit, rising demand calls forth more output, dollar for dollar. But after full capacity is reached, more demand cannot increase output further. The result will be inflation, but this**

[1]Over time, some economies have been able to increase their productive capacity rapidly, while others seem to get nowhere. But for the moment, we take the nation's production-possibilities curve as given. This is reasonable, because we want to begin by analyzing the behavior of the economy at a given point in time.

Table 9–1
Aggregate demand and aggregate supply

Aggregate demand (in billions)	Aggregate supply (in real terms, in billions)
$100	$100
200	200
300	300
400	400
500	400
600	400

doesn't show in Table 9–1, because the aggregate-supply schedule there is in real (constant-price) terms. Above $400 billion of aggregate demand, total real output is unchanged at $400 billion, although nominal GNP rises with inflation.

It is useful to represent this aggregate-supply schedule graphically as an "aggregate-supply curve" for the economy. This curve will show how much will be produced (supplied) in response to different levels of aggregate demand.[2]

In Figure 9–1, we show on the horizontal axis the amount supplied—that is, real GNP (in initial prices). On the vertical axis, we show aggregate demand—total spending by all those who buy goods and services in the economy in this period. Equal distances show equal amounts on both axes.

At one extreme, if there is no demand, nothing will be produced in our profit-motivated economy. If demand is OD_1, businessmen will produce OQ_1, and so on for different levels of demand. If demand is OD_3, output is OQ_3, the maximum real output possible for the economy in this period. Output OQ_3 corresponds to $400 billion in Table 9–1. No matter how much people spend, more than this cannot be produced.

[2]We shall see that the terms "supply schedule" and "supply curve" are used somewhat differently here from Parts 1 and 3, in which they apply to individual business firms and markets. Here, the supply schedule shows the aggregate amounts that will be produced in response to different levels of aggregate demand. There, supply schedules for individual firms show the amounts produced in response to different prices for the product concerned.

Thus, if we imagine the output levels called forth by all possible levels of aggregate demand from zero to OD_3, we would have the line OA, rising at a 45° angle from the zero point. It rises at a 45° angle because for each level of OD, real output on the horizontal axis is an identical amount. **We call this line OA the economy's aggregate-supply curve; it shows how much the economy would produce at each different level of aggregate demand.**

But once the economy has reached its full-employment GNP (here, OQ_3), it cannot increase output further. Thus, the aggregate-supply curve OA becomes perpendicular at that point; it becomes OAB. Further increases in demand—say, aggregate demand of OD_4—will simply bid up prices rather than call forth more output.

Figure 9–1
Curve OA suggests that as aggregate demand rises, output will be increased proportionately without any price increase (inflation) up to full-employment output OQ_3. If demand increases further, however, the result will be purely rising prices, since output cannot be expanded further in the short run.

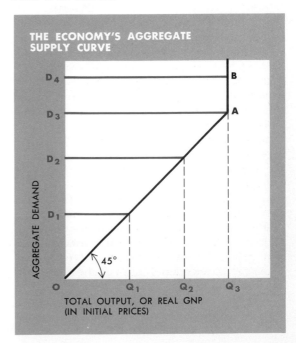

It is important to recognize that, by the same reasoning, if aggregate demand falls, the results are exactly the reverse. Given the aggregate-supply curve OAB, when aggregate demand falls from OD_4 to OD_3, the result is purely lower prices. But when demand falls from OD_3 to OD_2 or to OD_1, the result is purely reduced real GNP, not falling prices. **That is, we assume temporarily that below full-employment output, rising or falling aggregate demand will alter only real GNP, while after full employment has been reached, changes in demand will affect only the price level.** We shall see later that this is not necessarily true, but it is a useful temporary assumption.

AGGREGATE DEMAND, UNEMPLOYMENT, AND INFLATION

Our model is, of course, a highly oversimplified representation of the real world. Let us now make it a little more realistic, to analyze more fully when rising demand will call forth additional output, when inflation, and when a mixture of both.

In the real world, it is not true that rising aggregate demand will always call forth solely dollar-for-dollar increases in real GNP up to full employment, and pure inflation thereafter. Actually, some prices would begin to rise before full employment is reached, because increases in demand might cause production bottlenecks and shortages in some sectors of the economy before full employment occurred in others. Demand would normally rise faster for some products than for others.

To show this situation, Figure 9–2 reproduces the aggregate-supply curve from Figure 9–1, as solid line OAB. But it adds a dashed segment that rounds off the corner where solid OAB has a sharp kink at A. **This dashed segment shows that prices will begin to rise before we reach full employment. Put otherwise, it shows that we can reach full-employment output OQ_3 only with aggregate demand OD_4 and the considerable inflation that that implies.**

Try using Figure 9–2 to predict the consequences of different levels of demand. If demand rises from OD_1 to OD_2, the result is still purely

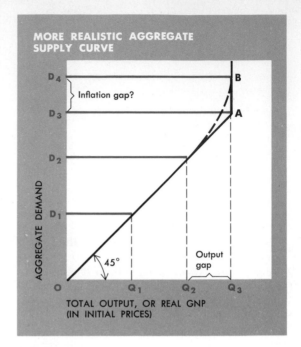

Figure 9–2

As the dashed section of OB shows, when an economy approaches full employment, prices ordinarily begin to rise before full-capacity output is reached. Here, full-employment output, OQ_3, can be achieved only with aggregate demand, OD_4, which would imply substantial inflation.

rising output and employment as before. But if demand moves on up to OD_3, now some of the growth in demand will induce more output, but some will go into higher prices. To push the economy all the way to its full-employment output of OQ_3, we must now have aggregate demand of OD_4, and with it a lot of inflation. Demand OD_3 won't do the job any more.

This situation can pose a difficult dilemma for economic policy makers. As we approach OQ_3, should the government expand aggregate demand further in order to reduce unemployment to a bare minimum, even though this brings on some inflation? Or is it better to keep aggregate demand at a lower level, accepting some unemployment but also avoiding inflation? This will be a central issue in Chapters 16–19.[3]

[3]A second modification of this Figure 9–1 model is in order if we want more realism. In the real world, full-

The output gap and the inflation gap

If aggregate demand falls short of the economy's full-employment capacity level, unemployment of men and factories will result. For example, if aggregate demand is only OD_2 in Figure 9–2, output will be only OQ_2 and there will be an "output gap" of $Q_2 - Q_3$ by which output falls short of full capacity. Sometimes this is called the "employment gap." In a depression, this gap is large.

If, on the other hand, aggregate demand exceeds full-employment capacity output at existing prices, there will be an "inflation gap." If demand is D_4, for example, prices will rise. Thus, the inflation gap would be $D_3 - D_4$, showing the rise in prices as a result of excess aggregate demand. Actually, as Figure 9–2 suggests, the concept of the inflation gap is a slippery one. Because prices would begin to rise once demand exceeded D_2, we might call $D_2 - D_4$ the inflation gap even though output Q_2 is far short of full employment. But usually, $D_3 - D_4$ is called the inflation gap. The question mark in Figure 9–2 reflects this ambiguity.

GROWTH IN PRODUCTIVE CAPACITY: ECONOMIC GROWTH

The aggregate-supply curves in Figures 9–1 and 9–2 are for a given time period—say, a year. They are what economists often call short-run supply curves. Over longer periods, of course, the productive capacity of an economy can grow—for example, through investment in new factories, increases in the labor force, and technological progress. In that event, full-employment output each year is larger than the year before; the production-possibilities frontier moves out. It is important to note that if productive capacity grows this way, what is full-

employment GNP (OQ_3) is never as rigid a limit as is shown in the diagram. As prices rise, housewives, students, and older people enter the labor force. Workers put in longer hours. Production managers push plants beyond their rated capacities. The full-employment ceiling on output is a mushy one. To reflect this accurately, the vertical segment of OAB should bend over a little to the right.

employment aggregate demand for one year will be inadequate to call forth full-employment output the next year.

We can readily show this in Figure 9–3. It reproduces supply curve OAB from Figure 9–1, and adds on extended segments ACC and ADD to show how potential real GNP moves out year after year with new investment, more labor, and advancing technology. By the same token, Figure 9–3 shows that larger aggregate demand will be needed each year to call forth full-employment GNP.

Thus, the aggregate-supply curve for year 2 is OCC. Potential real GNP has moved out to OQ_4, and demand OD_4 is required to ensure full employment. In year 3, the aggregate-supply curve becomes ODD, and aggregate demand OD_5 is needed for full employment. In terms of Chapter 2, the economy's production frontier moves out. **This is economic growth.**

Figure 9–3
With more productive resources and improved technology, an economy's productive capacity increases. With increased capacity, more aggregate demand is required to call forth full-employment output. In years 2 and 3, full-employment capacity has risen to OQ_4 and OQ_5 respectively.

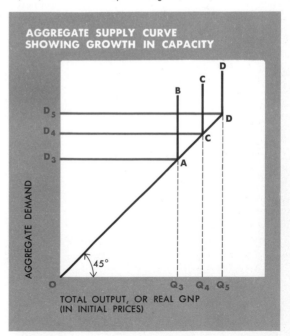

AGGREGATE SUPPLY CURVE SHOWING GROWTH IN CAPACITY

AGGREGATE DEMAND

TOTAL OUTPUT, OR REAL GNP (IN INITIAL PRICES)

Chapters 9–19 are primarily concerned with the short-run behavior of the economy. They generally take the productive capacity of the economy as substantially fixed, even though this is not quite accurate, and focus on aggregate demand as the major determinant of the level of output and prices. Part 7 later focuses on long-term economic growth, and there the expansion of aggregate capacity will be the center of attention.

REVIEW

Concepts to remember

This chapter introduces new basic concepts that will be used over and over. Be sure you understand:

aggregate supply	inflationary gap
aggregate demand	output gap

For analysis and discussion

1. Why does the economy's aggregate-supply curve slope upward as demand rises?
2. Explain the relationship between an economy's production-possibilities curve and its aggregate-supply curve.
3. Does the aggregate-supply curve in Figure 9–1 or that in Figure 9–2 make it easier for the economy to achieve full employment without inflation? Explain.
4. In a private-enterprise, profit-motivated economy, why is it reasonable to say that aggregate production will depend on the level of aggregate demand?
5. After an economy reaches full employment, raising aggregate expenditure must always cause inflation. True or false? (Does the time period involved influence your answer?)
6. What are the main ways by which a nation can move its production-possibilities curve out (to the right)?

CHAPTER 10 AGGREGATE DEMAND, income, and EMPLOYMENT

We turn now, in the rest of Part 2, to analysis of the forces that determine the levels of GNP, employment, and the price level in the short run. Since the productive capacity of any economy is substantially fixed in the short run (say, a year or so), GNP, employment, and the price level will then be determined largely by the level of aggregate demand, and this is the central focus of this and the next four chapters.

Economists have stressed two different approaches. One, often called the income-expenditures, or neo-Keynesian, approach, emphasizes that spending depends largely on the incomes people and businesses receive. It focuses on household consumption, business investment, and government spending decisions, using the major categories of the GNP accounts. Chapters 10 and 11 present this analysis, which provides the foundation for the use of government "fiscal

NOTE: The following macro-theory chapters, like the micro theory in Part Three, are written on a 2-track basis. Track A, for instructors and students who want only the bare-bones essentials of macro theory, includes only Chapters 10, 11, and 13, as a foundation for the policy chapters beginning with Chapter 15. Track B, for those who want a more thorough theoretical foundation, adds Chapters 12, 14, and 15.

For either Track A or Track B, Chapters 10 and 11 are actually a unified whole, and some instructors may wish to assign them together. The presentation is broken into two chapters because many students learn such multipart analysis better when it is divided into smaller subunits.

CHAPTER PREVIEW

Simple static GNP model
   Algebraic presentation
   Verbal presentation
   Graphic presentation
   The consumption and saving schedules
   Equilibrium not necessarily full employment

policy" (variations in government taxes and spending) to stabilize the economy.[1] The other, often called the "monetarist" or neoclassical approach, emphasizes the stock of money as the dominant force determining aggregate spending. It provides the foundation for the use of "monetary policy" (variations in the stock of money and interest rates) to avoid economic instability. (We shall continue to ignore international considerations temporarily, postponing their discussion to Part 6.)

In focusing so heavily on aggregate demand and the use of fiscal and monetary policy to control it, we are, as we shall see in later chapters, oversimplifying the complex forces that actually determine the levels of GNP, employment, and prices at any time. But this simple approach can provide a useful first approximation, as long as we remember the need for more detailed analysis before our results can necessarily be applied to the "real world."[2]

SIMPLE STATIC GNP MODEL

Aggregate demand consists of consumption, investment, and government spending. If we focus first on the private sector of the economy, we might begin by analyzing separately the factors controlling household and business spending decisions on consumption and investment. Chapter 12 does just that, and some instructors may prefer to begin that way, using Chapter 12 first. Here, however, we begin by making some very simple assumptions about the determinants of consumption and investment,

[1] This approach was first popularized by a noted economist, John Maynard Keynes, during the depression of the 1930s. Keynes achieved wide fame because he was one of the earliest advocates of fighting depressions with deficit spending. Whatever you think about that issue—it's examined in detail presently—you should understand that the present chapter deals only with neutral analytic tools that can help you understand the determinants of aggregate demand, but they don't necessarily tell you what is the best way to fight depressions and inflations.

[2] Section II of the Mathematical Appendix, at the end of the text, presents the central argument of this chapter in mathematical terms. Students who know calculus and find mathematical formulations helpful may find the appendix a useful aid; it is recommended for use after the following text sections have been read.

and focus first on the way they interact to determine GNP and the price level under different conditions, using what economists call a simple static model. Then, using this simple model as a framework, we can take into account the more complex forces that determine actual household and business spending decisions. Let us therefore begin with some simple assumptions and see how business and household spending decisions would then interact to determine GNP and the price level. Here, as in the supply-and-demand analysis of Part 1, we use the analytical concept of an "equilibrium," toward which households, businesses, and the system as a whole all tend. As in Part 1, there is no guarantee that such an equilibrium would be reached and maintained in the real world, but the model gives us a manageable approach to predicting directions of change and the probable consequences of different private and public policy actions in a complex world.

To simplify, first temporarily assume that there is no government spending or taxation. Thus, aggregate demand is the sum of consumption (C) plus investment spending (I). Because aggregate demand is also equal to gross national product, we can say that GNP equals $C + I$. (Economists typically use Y to represent national income or GNP, and so will we. Thus, $Y = C + I$.)

Second, assume (what many economists consider a first approximation to reality) that consumption spending depends entirely on the incomes that people receive. Moreover, the portion of their income that households don't spend on consumption, they save. Because saving is defined as simply that income received that is not spent on consumption, saving also depends on the amount of income people receive. Obviously, saving equals income minus consumption ($S = Y - C$). **Thus, both consumption spending and saving are "induced" by the level of consumer income.**

Third, assume temporarily that business investment spending is autonomously determined. That is, businessmen decide how much to invest on the basis of considerations other than consumer spending and saving, and get the needed funds outside the model, perhaps by borrowing at banks or using accumulated savings of their own. The independently determined, "autonomous" nature of investment thus contrasts with the dependent, induced nature of consumption and saving.

This contrast between autonomous and induced expenditure is a critical one for the analysis that follows. Be sure you understand the difference. Autonomous expenditure is completely determined by forces outside our system, or model; induced expenditure is determined by the forces at work inside the model.[3]

Given these assumptions, we can readily show how consumption and investment spending will interact to produce an equilibrium level of aggregate demand (GNP) each year. The reasoning can be presented algebraically, verbally, or graphically. It's done all three ways below, because different people find different approaches most helpful. Note, therefore, that the following three sections repeat substantially the *same* analysis in these different forms.

Algebraic presentation

We have defined aggregate demand as identical with GNP, which is equal to consumption plus investment spending. Let Y stand for aggregate demand and GNP. Then:

$$Y = C + I$$

Now assume that consumption spending is always just .75 of income (that is, people spend three-fourths of their incomes on consumption and save one-fourth), so that:

$$C = .75 \cdot Y$$

Saving (S) is the portion of their income that people do not spend on consumption. (Think of them as hiding S in a mattress, so it does not return to the spending stream as either consumption or investment.) Thus:

$$S = .25Y$$

Remember that investment (I) is autono-

mous; it is independently determined. Suppose that business investment spending is 100 this year, so:

$$I = 100$$

Now, substitute the values for C and I in our original equation, $Y = C + I$. We get:

$$Y = .75Y + 100$$

Using the rules of elementary algebra, move the .75Y to the left side of the equation. This changes the sign from plus to minus, and we have:

$$Y - .75Y = 100, \text{ or}$$
$$.25Y = 100, \text{ or}$$
$$Y = {}^{100}/_{.25}, \text{ and}$$
$$Y = 400$$

Equilibrium aggregate demand, or GNP, will be 400 if investment is 100 and people spend three-fourths of all the income they receive on consumption. Households will be spending 300 each year on consumption, and saving 100—just the $3/4 : 1/4$ ratio they wish. They are in equilibrium. And so is the whole economy. At a GNP of 400, consumers save 100, just enough to match the 100 of new investment that businesses spend into the GNP stream each year. **Thus, the GNP flow is stable (in equilibrium) at 400 annually, as long as our assumed conditions stay unchanged (see Figure 8–2).**

Verbal presentation

Let's put the reasoning in words. Given our assumptions, when GNP is 400, everyone is content to keep on doing what he is doing. With total income of 400 each year, people are consuming .75 of the income they receive, and saving .25, or 100, just enough to match the 100 that businesses are spending each year on investment. And businesses are selling just the 400 of output they produce each year, 300 to consumers and 100 to businesses as investment goods (such as machinery).[4]

---

[3]As we move later to more complex models, we shall see that, actually, both consumption and investment are partly autonomous and partly induced, and must then be broken down into these separate parts for analysis.

[4]Note that this is not precisely right, because total productive capacity of the economy would rise each year with net investment. But to simplify matters temporarily, we shall neglect this fact over short periods like a year or two.

But wouldn't some other GNP be equally stable? The answer is no. Try 500, for example. Then businesses are producing 500 of output each year. But on the demand side, buyers would purchase only 475—that is, 375 of consumption goods (three-fourths of 500) plus 100 of investment goods. Unsold inventories would pile up, and businesses would reduce production (GNP). And so it would be for any other GNP above 400. Conversely, if we assume a GNP less than 400, then demand ($C + I$) would be larger than production. For example, suppose GNP (production) were 300. Then demand would be $325 - 100$ of investment, plus the 225 that people would consume if their incomes were 300. Inventories would be drawn down, and businesses would have to increase production to meet the larger demand. GNP would thus rise toward 400.

Work out as many examples as you like and you'll always get one and only one equilibrium value of aggregate demand and GNP; with our assumptions, it is 400. **Equilibrium requires that the public decide to save just the amount businesses have decided to invest; the savings withdrawals from the income stream just offset the autonomous investment spending inserted each year. Then the circular flow of income is continuous and stable.**

Of course, the particular numbers in our example are arbitrary. If business investment is higher—say, 150—the equilibrium GNP is higher. If consumers spend 80 instead of 75 percent of their income on consumption, equilibrium GNP will be higher. Try it and see. But the reasoning—the underlying economic adjustment process—is unchanged.

Graphic presentation

The same reasoning can be presented in graphical terms. But in doing so, let us change the numbers and introduce a more realistic "consumption function," which is what economists call the relation between people's spendable income and their consumption spending. The only difference from the preceding example is that people now consume a lower percentage of their incomes at high than at low incomes, instead of always just three-fourths. This shift will, of course, change the equilibrium level of GNP. Again, consumption and saving depend entirely on GNP and investment is autonomously fixed at 100.

The consumption and saving schedules

Figure 10–1 shows these new consumption and saving functions. On the left-hand chart, line CC shows consumption spending at different levels of GNP; for example, consumption spending (vertical axis) would be 200 if GNP were 300 (horizontal axis).

In addition, the chart has a 45° line, every point on which is equidistant from the two axes. Thus, if line CC coincided with the 45° line, consumers would spend all their income (GNP) on consumption; there would be no saving. Whenever the consumption curve (CC) is below the 45° line, part of GNP is being saved. For

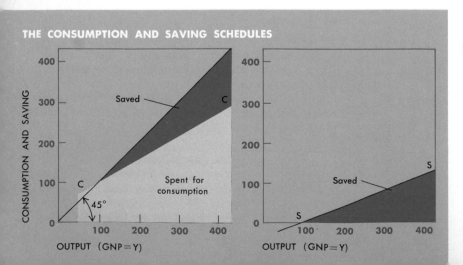

THE CONSUMPTION AND SAVING SCHEDULES

Figure 10-1
The left-hand portion of this figure shows that people will spend a smaller proportion of their income on consumption as income rises, and will save a larger proportion. The right-hand portion shows the same saving behavior by itself.

example, at a GNP of 200, the economy would spend 160 on consumption and save 40. Note that if GNP were as low as 50, people would spend more than their full incomes on consumption; they would "dissave" by borrowing or drawing on past savings.[5]

The right-hand part of Figure 10-1 shows the corresponding saving schedule (SS). This is drawn simply by taking the amount saved at each level of GNP from the left-hand portion. Saving will be negative at low income levels when CC exceeds total GNP, and will be positive at higher income levels. The SS curve will, of course, cross the zero line at the same income level where the CC curve cuts the 45° line, where all GNP is spent on consumption—at GNP of 100 on Figure 10-1.

We can show graphically in two ways how equilibrium is determined. First, plot the saving curve (SS) in Figure 10-2, from the right-hand portion of Figure 10-1. Now add investment (II). It is a horizontal line at 100, because we have assumed that investment is fixed at that level. II intersects SS at a GNP of 350, and this is the equilibrium level. Note that equilibrium GNP here is different from the preceding example, because we have assumed a different consumption function. People no longer spend just 75 percent of their incomes on consumption.

Why is 350 the equilibrium level? The reasoning is the same as before: because at this level of GNP, the amount businessmen invest is exactly offset by the amount people want to save. Thus, the circular flow of income will be complete and stable. Consumers will receive 350

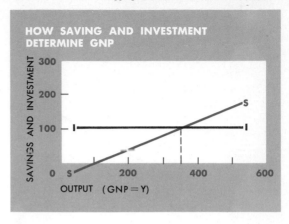

Figure 10-2
Equilibrium GNP is established where the public wishes to save just enough to match the amount being invested.

of income each year from producing the 350 GNP, and they will save 100 and spend 250 on consumption. Each year, businesses will invest 100, just offsetting the amount people save; and so on indefinitely.

There is a second way of showing the same result graphically. Figure 10-3 shows the consumption and investment functions on the same graph. It adds to consumption spending (the CC curve of Figure 10-1) 100 of investment spending at each income level each year. Thus, C + I is the amount that households and businesses will spend on consumption plus investment at each level of GNP (total output and income). Now, because consumption and investment spending are on the vertical axis, and total GNP is on the horizontal axis, the 45° line shows all the points at which aggregate demand (C + I) will just equal total production (GNP).

In Figure 10-3, aggregate demand (C + I) just equals GNP (cuts the 45° line) at 350, the equilibrium GNP for these investment and consumption assumptions. At 350, and only at 350, does the sum of consumption and investment demand just equal GNP (output).

Test the result. As before, assume any GNP lower than 350 (say, 300), and you will see that it can't last. At a GNP of 300, consumption plus investment spending, shown by C + I, would be above the 45° line. Thus, total demand would exceed production, business inventories would be

[5]For readers who like mathematics, the equation of this consumption function is $C = a + b(Y)$, where a and b are constants, with $a = 40$ and $b = .6$. Therefore, $C = 40 + .6Y$. That is, consumption is always 40 plus .6 of the amount of income received. The basic $Y = C + I$ equation can be solved just as before by making the new substitution for C. Thus:

$$Y = (40 + .6Y) + 100, \text{ or}$$
$$Y - .6Y = 40 + 100$$
$$.4Y = 140, \text{ so}$$
$$Y = 350$$

Mathematical Appendix II, at the end of the book, and the appendix to the next chapter, on "Econometric Models," show more fully how simple mathematical systems can be used to determine equilibrium GNP levels under more complicated conditions.

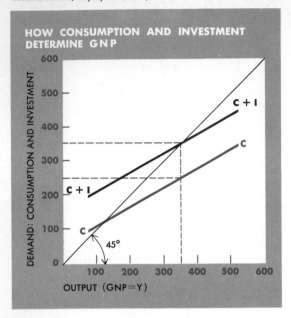

Figure 10-3
Equilibrium GNP is established where the sum of consumption and investment spending (on the vertical axis) just equals GNP (on the horizontal axis). This gives the same equilibrium level as Figure 10-2.

drawn down, and businesses would increase production. GNP would rise toward 350. The opposite is true if we assume GNP is anything higher than 350—say, 400. At a GNP of 400, $C + I$ would be less than 400; people would not buy all the goods being produced; unsold inventories would pile up; and production would be cut back toward 350.

A crucial reminder: All the analysis above assumes that consumption and saving are func-tions solely of income received. **If consumption spending changes for any other (autonomous) reason, the equilibrium level of income will be changed.** In the model, such a change would be shown as a shift in the consumption function (a shift of the CC line to the right or left).

Equilibrium not necessarily full employment

It is important to recognize that an equilibrium GNP does not necessarily imply that there is full employment. Look back at the short-run aggregate-supply curve in Figure 9–1. It shows that if aggregate demand is less than OD_3 and equilibrium GNP is less than OQ_3, the economy will be operating inside its production-possibilities frontier. This will be an underemployment equilibrium with an output gap. If equilibrium GNP is above OD_3, the result will be inflation; there will be an inflation gap. "Equilibrium" GNP as we have defined it is thus a neutral analytical concept. It does not imply anything, either good or bad, about the level of employment or how well the economic system is performing. You can think of the 45° line on Figure 10–3 as the economy's short-run aggregate-supply curve up to the full-employment output, at which point the supply curve would rise vertically. It shows what the economy's equilibrium response will be to different levels of aggregate demand.

(We shall see in later chapters that there are serious questions as to whether equilibrium will be stable with either an output or an inflationary gap, but accept the statements in the preceding paragraph as a first approximation for the time being.)

REVIEW

Concepts
to remember

This is an important chapter. Its analytical concepts and models are used throughout the rest of the book, although they will need to be complicated somewhat. Be sure you understand the basic reasoning in the chapter and the following new concepts:

income-expenditure approach
autonomous and induced
   expenditure
consumption function

saving function
equilibrium GNP
underemployment equilibrium

**For analysis
and discussion**

1. Assume a private economy with no government spending or taxes. In this high-saving economy, people save half their incomes and spend half on consumption. Suppose business investment (autonomously determined) is 1,000.
   a. What will be the equilibrium level of GNP? (*Hint:* GNP $= C + I$)
   b. In equilibrium, how much will be spent on consumption, and how much saved?
   c. Will there be full employment at the equilibrium GNP? If you can't tell from the information given, what further information would you need in order to answer?

2. Suppose the public in question 1 increases its consumption/GNP ratio from .5 to .75. Compute the new GNP equilibrium. What has been the effect of the shifting consumption function?

3. Again assume a private economy. In this economy, the public's consumption function is $C = 1,000 + .8$ GNP. Investment, again autonomously determined, is again 1,000.
   a. Using simple algebra, determine the equilibrium level of GNP (by substituting the values for consumption and investment in the equation GNP $= C + I$, and solving for GNP).
   b. On a sheet of graph paper, first draw a 45° line between the axes. Then plot the economy's consumption spending for each level of GNP between 5,000 and 15,000, at intervals of 1,000, joining the plotted consumption points together with a straight line to form a consumption function. Next, add 1,000 of investment to consumption spending at each level of GNP. Now determine equilibrium GNP from your graph. (It will be the level at which your $C + I$ curve cuts the 45° line.) Explain why this is the equilibrium level.

4. Double the level of investment in each of the preceding questions. What does this do to the equilibrium level of GNP? (For further explanation of the results, which may surprise you, go on to the next chapter. The questions at the end of Chapter 11 also review the present one.)

Answers: 1a. 2,000; 1b. 1,000 and 1,000; 1c. Depends on the full-employment capacity of the economy. 2. 4,000. 3. 10,000. 4. 2,000 increase; 4,000 increase; 5,000 increase.

11

AGGReGaTe DemanD, THe mULTIPLIer, anD FISCaL POLICY

This chapter extends the simple static equilibrium analysis of the preceding chapter in two important ways. First, it investigates the effects of changes in investment (autonomous) spending on GNP. Changes in investment produce multiplied effects on the equilibrium level of GNP, other things equal. Second, it explains how modern neo-Keynesian economists employ such analysis as the basis for using changes in government spending and taxes to control GNP. In our simple model, government spending can, other things equal, have the same effect on equilibrium GNP as do changes in private investment; and through analogous reasoning, changes in tax rates can have similar, although somewhat different, effects. Such changes in government spending and tax rates in order to influence real GNP and the price level are called fiscal policy.

CHANGING INVESTMENT AND THE MULTIPLIER

Suppose now that businessmen decide to increase their investment spending, perhaps because of a new invention. The result, common sense tells you, will be a higher equilibrium level of GNP after the increase in investment. Conversely, a decrease in investment spending would lead to a lower equilibrium level.

But the size of the effect is less obvious. **Under our assumptions, each dollar of increase in investment (autonomous spending) will increase aggregate demand and GNP by a larger, or multiplied, amount.** This is because each new dollar of investment, as it is spent, becomes income to a consumer who saves part but respends the rest on consumption. This induced consumption spending constitutes income to someone else, who in turn saves part but respends the rest. And so on. The number of times the final increase in income (GNP) exceeds the new investment is called the "multiplier." For example, if one additional dollar of investment spending generates four additional dollars of GNP, the multiplier is 4.

Marginal propensity to consume (MPC)

To explore this process more fully, we now need to distinguish between the "average" and the "marginal" propensity to consume. Suppose that total income (GNP) is 100 and people are spending 75 on consumption and saving 25 each period. Then the **average** propensity to consume is .75. However, it does not necessarily follow that if people receive additional income, they would maintain this same consumption–income ratio. Suppose their incomes now rise to 110, but they only consume .5 of this additional 10 of income. Then the **marginal** propensity to consume is .5. **The marginal propensity to consume (MPC) is the proportion of additional, or marginal, income that is spent on consumption.** It is the marginal propensity on which we need to focus our attention when we are analyzing *changes* in the level of GNP.

The multiplier

Begin with an equilibrium GNP of 350, as in Figure 10–3, and assume that the *marginal* propensity to consume is .75. Suppose now that businessmen increase their investment spending by 10. When the 10 is spent on new investment (say, building a new plant), it becomes income to the recipients, who then spend 7.5 on consumption and save 2.5. The 7.5 of

consumption spending becomes income to someone else, who in turn respends 75 percent (5.6) on consumption and saves 25 percent (1.9). The 5.6 becomes income to someone else, and so the process goes. Remember that savings are withdrawn from the income stream and are *not* respent in this model; nor do they induce more investment, because investment is autonomous. We get a table like the following:[1]

	New income	New consumption	New saving
Initiating New Investment	10.0	7.5	2.5
On Round 2	7.5	5.6	1.9
On Round 3	5.6	4.2	1.4
On Round 4	4.2	3.2	1.0
.	.	.	.
	40	30	10

The table shows only the first four rounds, but it gives the general picture. The 10 of new investment generates a chain of respending on consumption, the "multiplier" effect. Each round makes a smaller net addition to income than its predecessor does, because part of the new income is drained off into saving by each recipient. If you carry the arithmetic to its conclusion, you will find that the total new GNP generated is 40 (including the 10 of new investment). Of this total, 30 is spent on consumption and 10 is saved, in accordance with our marginal propensity to consume of .75. The expansion has continued until the amount people want to save of their higher income just offsets the 10 of new autonomous investment. Adding these increments to the original equilibrium values, we get a new equilibrium GNP of 390. **The multiplier is 4, since GNP has risen by 40 in response to 10 of autonomous investment.**

This result is shown graphically in Figure 11–1. The *CC* and *C + I* curves before the increase in investment are reproduced directly from Figure 10–3. Now we add 10 more of investment at each level of income, so the new

---

[1]Assume for this example that the businesses get the funds for the extra 10 of investment by borrowing newly created funds from the banks, rather than by saving out of their own current incomes.

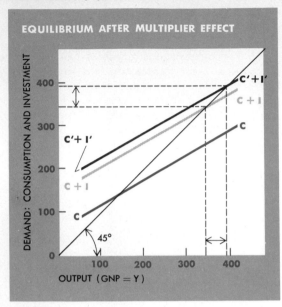

EQUILIBRIUM AFTER MULTIPLIER EFFECT

(Vertical axis) DEMAND: CONSUMPTION AND INVESTMENT

C' + I'
C + I
C
C' + I'
C + I
C
45°

(Horizontal axis) OUTPUT (GNP = Y)

Figure 11-1
An additional 10 of investment raises the C + I curve to C' + I' and brings a new equilibrium level of GNP of 390, up 40 from the previous equilibrium. The investment multiplier is 4.

$C' + I'$ now represents consumption plus 110, instead of plus 100. The CC line is unchanged because the consumption function is unchanged. The new equilibrium level of GNP is 390, up 40, where the new $C' + I'$ curve cuts the 45° line.

If this looks like graphical trickery, consider the economic reasoning. There are four important points:

1. The multiplier effect hinges on the fact that people respend on consumption part of each increment of income they receive. If at any point they save *all* their new income, the respending spiral stops short.

2. The larger the proportion of its additional income that the public respends each round, the larger will be the multiplier.

3. The size of the multiplier is given precisely by the formula:

$$M = \frac{1}{1 - \text{Marginal propensity to consume}}$$

Thus, if the marginal propensity to consume is .75, the multiplier will be:

$$M = \frac{1}{1 - .75} = \frac{1}{.25} = 4$$

If the economy's marginal propensity to consume out of GNP were .90, the multiplier would be 10. (Work out the .90 case in the equation for yourself.) An easy way to look at it is this: The multiplier is the reciprocal of the marginal propensity to save, *given our simple assumptions*. Thus, if consumers save one-fourth of their new income, the multiplier is 4; if one-tenth, the multiplier is 10; and so on.

4. Last, review again the economic reasoning behind this formula. A dollar of autonomous spending will set off an induced spending spiral that will continue until the public's income is enough higher that it wants to save just enough to offset the increased amount of autonomous investment. Only when these two just match will the circular flow of income be continuous and stable.

This is the basic multiplier process. But a warning is needed. In the real world, with government taxes and spending and with business as well as consumer saving, the picture becomes more complex. To calculate real-world multipliers, see the box, "The Multiplier in the Real World."[2]

---

[2]This multiplier reasoning suggests a curious paradox, sometimes called the "paradox of thrift." If consumers decide to save a larger percentage of their incomes, this increased propensity to save, other things equal, will lead to a lower multiplier, lower consumption, a lower GNP, and a *lower* level of aggregate saving in the new equilibrium. Here is an example of the fallacy of composition. More saving out of any given level of income may be a very good thing for the individual household, but a simultaneous attempt by many households to save more out of their incomes may throw the economy into a recession that makes us all worse off, and in which we actually save less because of our lower incomes.

But note that an increase in the economy's propensity to save *need not* throw us into recession. If the increased thriftiness comes in a period of inflation, it can help reduce inflationary pressure. And even in noninflationary periods, the increased propensity to save may be offset by higher private investment or government spending.

THE MULTIPLIER IN THE REAL WORLD

Suppose the economy is in recession, with widespread unemployment. The preceding pages on the multiplier suggest something the government can do about it—increase expenditures without raising taxes. Suppose it increases expenditures by $10 billion to fight unemployment this year. What will the multiplier be? How much will GNP rise?

Your first question presumably will be, What is the consumption function? Looking ahead to the next chapter, you can find that households have quite consistently spent about .9 of their disposable personal income on consumption and saved about .1. So the multiplier would be a powerful 10, raising GNP by $100 billion. Right? Wrong! The real-world multiplier would probably be far less, more like 2. Why?

1. First, the multiplier depends on the *marginal*, not the average, propensity to consume, and experience suggests that consumers are generally slow to adjust to sharp increases in income. Thus, their marginal propensity to consume this year out of the new income is likely to be lower than .9.

2. Even if households were to consume .9 of each dollar of disposable personal income, saving .1, there are numerous other leakages from the $10 billion of autonomous government spending. First, corporations also save, by retaining part of their profits and their depreciation accounts. Second, government tax collections will rise with rising in-

comes, even though tax *rates* are kept unchanged. Thus, part of the new income will drain off to the government through all kinds of taxes. Look back at Figure 8–2 and trace the $10 billion down the path from GNP to disposable personal income. Taxes and corporate saving are likely to drain off a quarter to a third of the $10 billion before it gets to disposable personal income. So, even if the marginal propensity to consume were .9, it would apply to only, say, $6 or $7 billion, not $10 billion, of new disposable income. Another way to look at it is, the marginal propensity to consume *out of GNP* is likely to be more like .5 than .9, so the multiplier on GNP will be more like 2 than 10.

3. This chapter has omitted money and interest rates from the analysis. As we shall see in Chapter 14, government borrowing to get the money to spend may well bid up interest rates, thereby discouraging private investment and inducing a negative multiplier effect that partly or fully offsets the positive multiplier effect of the autonomous government spending.

All this is not to say that government fiscal policy can't help fight depressions. As we shall see, it certainly can. But to apply multiplier analysis reliably to the real world requires that we take all the complications into account. And the result is a much smaller multiplier than a casual application of the .9 average propensity to consume out of disposable personal income would suggest.

INDUCED INVESTMENT
AND DYNAMIC PROCESSES

Thus far, we have assumed that investment decisions are autonomous—that is, determined independently of the levels of consumption, saving, and GNP. Actually, business investment decisions rest on many factors, fundamentally on sales and profit expectations, as we shall see in Chapter 12. If sales rise, so will the level of plant and equipment needed to produce

more in the future. But if savings fall, this, other things equal, will raise interest rates that businesses must pay to borrow funds to finance new investment.

The level of sales (consumer expenditures) is thus clearly one important determinant of business investment plans. For example, the new equilibrium GNP level in Figure 11–1 in response to more investment would probably not be a stable equilibrium, since the rising consumer spending would, other things equal, in turn induce more business investment. The new induced investment would in turn lead to a further multiplier effect on consumption and GNP. Such additional investment is "induced" by the rising sales in the preceding period, in what economists call a "dynamic" process. Intuitively, you might expect such a process to spiral upward indefinitely—and under some conditions, it would. But under others, the spiral will die out, or even reverse itself and start downward in a recession.

Such dynamic processes are the essence of booms and depressions (business cycles). An upswing started by new investment will raise income through the multiplier. More income leads to more consumption, and that improves business sales, which leads to more investment. But, as noted above, the process is more complex than this, and we shall postpone the dynamic analysis of business cycles until Chapter 15. For the moment, stick to simpler equilibrium analysis.

GOVERNMENT TAXES AND EXPENDITURES (FISCAL POLICY)

Now let us put government taxes and spending into our model, to bring it into closer correspondence with the real world and to demonstrate how such government action can stabilize, or destabilize, the economy. Government spending is part of aggregate demand, and taxes take away part of the spendable income of households and businesses. Thus, we need to add government on both the spending and saving sides of the picture.

We can treat government spending on goods and services as similar to autonomous private investment spending, determined by forces other than the current level of GNP. Government spending constitutes effective demand for goods and services. We can treat government tax collections as similar to private savings; they constitute a withdrawal from (leakage out of) the responding stream, with their amount determined (induced) by the level of GNP, given any set of tax rates.

This is easy to see in a circular-income-flow picture of the economy (as in Figures 7–1 and 8–2). Larger taxes drain income away from the basic GNP flow into the upper (government)

loop in Figure 8–2. Larger government expenditures put more into the basic GNP flow (aggregate demand).

Alternatively, we can add government into the algebraic explanation. We now have a slightly more complex model, in which both private investment and government spending are autonomous, whereas consumption spending is an induced expenditure; and on the other side, both private savings and government tax receipts are withdrawals from the income stream. Thus, the new equation is:

$$C + I + GE = C + S + GT$$

where GE is government expenditure and GT is government tax receipts. That is, if the sum of private investment plus government expenditures (autonomous spending) exceeds the "leakages" from the spending stream through private savings and tax receipts, GNP will rise. Conversely, GNP will fall if investment plus government spending is less than the leakages through saving and tax receipts.

Fiscal policy

This suggests a way the government can raise aggregate demand in a depression or reduce it in an inflation. The government can increase aggregate demand by spending more than it collects in taxes, or reduce it by spending less than it collects in taxes.

An autonomous increase in government expenditures raises GNP, other things equal. The increase per dollar of government spending is determined by the multiplier. Each additional dollar of government spending on goods and services adds directly to GNP and becomes income to an individual or a business, thereby inducing more consumption spending, just as private investment does. If the multiplier for the economy is 3, for example, each dollar of additional government spending will generate a $3 increase in GNP.

An autonomous increase in tax collections reduces GNP. The decrease per dollar of tax collections again depends on the multiplier. When individuals or businesses pay taxes out of their incomes, they reduce their disposable incomes and their spending on goods and services.

This reduction has a negative multiplier effect, the reverse of the positive multiplier associated with government expenditures.

The net multiplier effect of the government budget on the economy depends on the net result of these plus and minus factors. The larger the excess of government expenditures over tax receipts (that is, the larger the deficit), the larger will be the effect of government fiscal policy on total GNP, other things equal. Conversely, the larger the excess of tax receipts over expenditures (that is, the larger the government surplus), the lower GNP will be, other things equal. Such government tax and expenditure changes to influence aggregate demand are called fiscal policy. These propositions will need to be qualified somewhat presently, but they provide a powerful first approximation. When we want the government to exert strong expansionary pressure on GNP, a larger government deficit is desirable.

Figure 11–2
Net new government spending of 10 increases autonomous spending by 10 and, with a multiplier of 4, raises GNP by 40—up to a new equilibrium of 390. This is identical with the multiplier effect of 10 of new private investment in Figure 11–1.

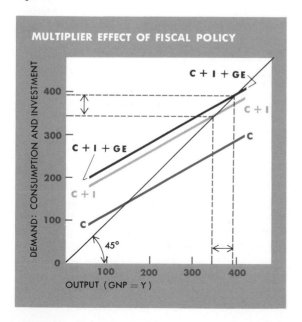

MULTIPLIER EFFECT OF FISCAL POLICY

C + I + GE

C + I

C + I + GE

C + I

C

C

400

300

200

100

0

DEMAND: CONSUMPTION AND INVESTMENT

45°

100   200   300   400

OUTPUT (GNP = Y)

Figure 11–2 presents the analysis graphically. Let the CC and $C + I$ lines be identical with the lines in Figure 10–3. Equilibrium income would then be 350, where $C + I$ cuts the 45° line. Now suppose the government enters the picture and begins to spend 10 each year without collecting any taxes (perhaps borrowing at the banks). We can thus draw a new government-spending layer (GE) on top of the $C + I$ curve. This new $C + I + GE$ curve is 10 higher at every point. The autonomous government spending becomes income to the private economy and has a multiplier effect through inducing new private consumption, just as private investment does. If the marginal propensity to consume is .75, the new equilibrium level of GNP in Figure 11–2 will be 390, as the multiplier raises total income by four times the original government spending. Note that this new equilibrium income is identical to that in Figure 11–1, in which the additional autonomous spending of 10 was private rather than governmental.

The balanced-budget multiplier

It may appear intuitively that a balanced government budget (that is, tax collections just equal to government spending) will always be neutral with respect to GNP. But this is not quite correct. An increase in government spending matched by an identical increase in tax collections provides some net expansionary multiplier effect, and conversely for a decrease in government expenditures exactly matched by a tax reduction. This is called the **balanced-budget multiplier.** It works this way:

Assume that the government increases its spending by $10 million, and that the public's marginal propensity to consume is .5. The $10 million of new government spending immediately constitutes $10 million of new GNP, to which the multiplier of 2 adds another $10 million through respending. This gives a total increase in GNP of $20 million in the new equilibrium level of GNP.

Now, trace through the deflationary impact of an identical $10 million tax increase to finance the expenditures. With a marginal propensity to consume of .5, private spending will fall by $5 million in the first round, $2.5 million in the second, $1.25 million in the third, and so on as in the preceding example. The total sequence of induced spending cuts ($5 million plus $2.5 million plus $1.25 million plus . . .) adds up to a total reduction of $10 million in spending from the tax increase.

Note that this negative tax multiplier is just $10 million less than the positive expenditure multiplier, just the amount of the budget increase. The respending effects after the first impact of the new government spending and of the new government taxes are the same, but the $10 million increase in government purchases of goods and services become a direct part of GNP, whereas the tax payment by the private economy to the government was simply a transfer of purchasing power that is not part of GNP. The "balanced-budget multiplier" is thus just 1 in this example; GNP rises by precisely the amount of the increase in government spending financed by an identical increase in government tax receipts.[3]

Most economists agree that a balanced-budget multiplier effect of this sort occurs. But this precise result of 1 depends on three assumptions: that the government spending is on goods and services rather than on transfer payments; that the propensity to consume out of disposable personal income is the same for taxpayers and recipients of government spending; and that neither government spending nor taxes induce any change in private investment. In any event, the balanced-budget multiplier is, at most, only 1. Most economists believe that deficit-financed government spending is a far surer road to a higher GNP.

Surpluses and deficits—public and private

There is no reason, of course, why government taxes and spending must exactly balance in each time period. Neither, once we introduce government into our model, is there any reason why private saving and private investment must exactly balance in each time period. Our basic equation is now:

[3] It follows from this reasoning that the tax multiplier will always be smaller than the expenditure multiplier per dollar of tax reduction or expenditure increase. Can you explain why?

$$C + I + GE = C + S + GT$$

Thus, the private part of the economy may be investing more than it saves at equilibrium GNP, while the government is collecting more taxes than it spends. In that case, the private economy is running a "deficit" and the government a "surplus." Conversely, the private economy may run a surplus by saving more than it invests, while the government runs a deficit by spending more than it collects in taxes.

It should be clear then that it is total autonomous spending (here, $I + GE$) that is the base for the multiplier effect. And the equilibrium condition now is: GNP must be such that private savings plus government tax collections just offset autonomous expenditure (here, private investment plus government spending). Figure 8–2 provides an example. The government in 1975 ran an $84 billion deficit, while the private sector ran a roughly offsetting $78 billion surplus.[4]

Three warnings

Fiscal policy is a powerful tool for the government against unemployment and inflation, and the preceding simple model provides the essential analysis. Neo-Keynesian economists consider fiscal policy our main weapon against economic instability. But you may suspect that there must be some problems or we would already have eliminated unemployment and inflation. And there are. Three major warnings are in order:

1. Remember that the real-world multiplier is far smaller than in the preceding examples. (See the box on "The Multiplier in the Real World.")

2. We have assumed that consumption is completely induced, a known function of income, and that private investment is autonomous, independent of government spending and taxes. But, as the next chapter emphasizes, consumption is often partly autonomous and fluctuates in its relationship to income. Moreover,

[4] For an explanation of why the sectors do not exactly offset each other, see the caption to Figure 8–2.

government borrowing to finance deficit spending may take funds away from private investment, thereby partly or completely offsetting the autonomous government spending. This is called the "crowding-out" effect.

3. We have said nothing about the role of money in determining aggregate demand. Many economists believe that the stock of money plays a—perhaps even *the*—dominant role in determining total private spending, overriding the fiscal effects discussed above. Nearly everyone agrees that we need to add money to the model to understand the real world. So keep an open mind on the effectiveness of fiscal policy until Chapters 13 and 14 on money.

Fiscal policy, its strengths, and its weaknesses are considered in detail in Chapter 16.[5]

[5] Some instructors may wish to go directly on to Chapter 16, on fiscal policy, at this point. The chapters are written to be usable in either order.

REVIEW

Concepts to remember

This chapter adds more important analytical concepts to those of the preceding chapter. Be sure you understand the basic reasoning on multipliers and fiscal policy in the chapter and the following new concepts:

> **average and marginal propensities to consume**
> **average and marginal propensities to save**
> **fiscal policy**
> **the multiplier**
> **balanced-budget multiplier**
> **private- and public-sector surpluses and deficits**
> **paradox of thrift**

For analysis and discussion

1. Assume that gross national product is $1,100 billion. Investment is $200 billion. Consumption expenditures are $900 billion. Assume no government participation in the income stream.
   a. If investment rises to $225 billion, with the marginal propensity to consume at .8, what will be the new equilibrium level of GNP?
   b. Explain why this will be an equilibrium level.
2. Would you expect that decisions to save for the year ahead in the economy would ordinarily be about the same as decisions to invest? Why, or why not?
3. What is the multiplier? Explain why the real-world multiplier will always be smaller than

$$\frac{1}{1 - \text{MPC out of disposable personal income}}$$

4. What is the "paradox of thrift"? Explain why its strange result occurs.
5. Suppose that in a hypothetical economy, GNP is running at an annual rate of $1,200 billion. Other major items in the national income accounts are as follows:

Consumption . . . . $800 billion
Investment 140
Savings 200
Government expenditures 260
Taxes 200

The marginal propensity to consume is three-fourths. (For purposes of this problem, take the three-fourths marginal propensity to consume against income before taxes.)

Suppose that the government now balances its budget through a reduction in government expenditures while maintaining taxes at the level of $200 billion. Private investment remains unchanged. What will be the effect on the levels of (a) GNP, (b) consumption, and (c) savings? Explain.

6. Assume the following conditions in an economy that includes a government sector:

Government spending . . . . $100 billion
Government tax receipts (obtained from a tax that
    is independent of the level of GNP) 100
Consumption expenditure = $30 billion plus .8 of the
    GNP remaining after payment of taxes . . . .
Investment expenditure 50
GNP = C + I + G

a. Calculate the equilibrium levels of GNP, consumption, and savings.
b. Investment increases to an annual rate of $75 billion and remains constant at that level. Calculate the new equilibrium levels of GNP, consumption, and savings.
c. Under the conditions described in (a), government spending increases to an annual rate of $200 billion and annual tax receipts are raised to $200 billion. Both figures then remain constant. Calculate new equilibrium levels of GNP, consumption, and savings.
d. What is the balanced budget multiplier in (c)?

7. Explain why, if the private sector runs a "deficit" (that is, invests more than it saves), the public sector must run an exactly offsetting "surplus" (that is, collect more in taxes than it spends).

Answers: 1. 1,225. 5a. −240; 5b. −180; 5c. −60. 6a. 500, 350, and 50; 6b. 625, 450, and 75; 6c. 600, 350, and 50; 6d. 1.

Marxist critics assert that without war spending, modern capitalism would collapse into disastrous depression. Without massive defense spending (about $100 billion in 1976), they say, aggregate demand would collapse, because consumers would receive incomes too small to buy all the goods capitalism produces.

Are the Marxists right? Leaving aside the details of their argument, suppose that the United States and the USSR agree tomorrow on a massive arms-reduction program, and, happy day, we can cut our defense spending immediately by $50 billion. Would the result be disaster—massive unemployment and depression? Or would the arms reduction be a great boon to Americans, both because of its promise of peace

and because it would make possible a $50 billion increase in the civilian goods and services (schools, stores, houses, health services, and so on) in the United States?

Your congressman, no economist, asks your advice on the problem. In early 1976, there were 2.5 million persons in the armed services, so a 50 percent cut in the military budget might throw perhaps 1.3 million people onto the job market. Apparently 6–7 million civilian jobs are dependent on the government's defense spending. He is understandably concerned about growing unemployment if the big cut in government spending is actually carried out. What do you advise him to do to make the best of the situation?

APPENDIX

Econometric models

Modern economics, like other sciences, has increasingly come to use precisely stated analytical models, which are often most conveniently put in mathematical form. Modern economics also has become increasingly empirical—that is, concerned with measuring its variables in the real world, as distinguished from merely theorizing about them. Thus, "econometrics" has become an increasingly important branch of economics.

Econometrics deals with the science of economic measurement, as is obvious from its components, "econo" and "metrics." Broadly, econometrics involves setting up precise models of economic phenomena in mathematical form; then measuring in the real world the variables and relationships included in the model; and then solving the model to see how closely it conforms to or can predict actual economic behavior.

Simple income-determination models.[6] The simple model back in Chapter 10 provides an example. We specify a model:

$$Y = C + I, \text{ and}$$
$$C = f(Y), \text{ where } f \text{ stands for "function"}$$

This equation says that C is a function of (or depends on) Y. The model is obviously too simple to represent the real world precisely, but assume for the moment that it does. Next, we have to measure in the real world the crucial variables and relationships specified by the model. Suppose we find that I is always 100 and is independent of Y and C; and estimate that C is always just .75 of Y. Then we can insert these values in $Y = C + I$, and get our final equation: $400 = 300 + 100$.

But note that our model, if it is a true model of the real world, can tell us other things. If I rises to 125, we can predict that, other things remaining unchanged, GNP will rise to 500; this follows directly by inserting the new value for I in the model—since we know from empirical evidence that C is always .75 of Y, I must always be .25 of Y. So an econometric model is in effect a forecasting device, which says that *if* we know the values of some of the crucial variables and relationships, *then* we can predict others—in this model, GNP and consumption.

More complex simultaneous-equation models.[7] More complex econometric models involve precisely the same basic steps: specification of the model, measurement of the relationships and variables, and solution of the model (system of equations). Some years ago, *Business Week,* while poking a little fun at econometricians, summed up the method of econometrics effectively in the sketch on the next page.

Note that the basic model is stated in the system of multiple equations in #3. Equations 1, 2, and 3 are "behavioral" equations; that is, they describe the behavior of units in the economy. Equations 4 and 5 are "identities"; that is, they merely state what we have defined as being identical. For example, we define GNP as the sum of consumption plus investment plus government spending. Obviously, equations 1 through 3 are the critical ones. The solution of the model (that is, the value of GNP) depends on solving the set of five equations simultaneously, just as in the real world all the factors are interacting simultaneously to determine GNP.

This is a more complex model than was used in Chapter 10, although it is still too simple to represent the real world effectively. The government is added, and investment is made a function of profits in the proceding time period. (P_{-1} means profits in the preceding time period; most econometricians label all their variables with time subscripts, since time is so important in most economic relationships.) This

---

[6]These are technically called "single-equation" models, since, although they begin with more than one equation, they reduce to one equation for statistical fitting to the real-world situation they represent.

[7]These are called "simultaneous-equation" models because several equations must be fitted statistically on a simultaneous basis.

The Junior Econometrician's Work Kit.

Predict the U. S. Economy for 1956.
Build Your Own Forecasting Model.

DIRECTIONS:

1. Make up a theory. You might theorize, for instance, that (1) next year's consumption will depend on next year's national income; (2) next year's investment will depend on this year's profits; (3) tax receipts will depend on future Gross National Product. (4) GNP is the sum of consumption, investment, and government expenditures. (5) National income equals GNP minus taxes.

2. Use symbols for words. Call consumption, C; national income, Y; investment, I; preceding year's profits, P_{-1}; tax receipts, T; Gross National Product, G; government expenditures, E.

3. Translate your theories into mathematical equations:

$$(1)\ C = aY + b \qquad (4)\ G = C + I + E$$
$$(2)\ I = cP_{-1} + d \qquad (5)\ Y = G - T$$
$$(3)\ T = eG$$

This is your forecasting model. The small letters, a, b, c, d, e, are the constants that make things come out even. For instance, if horses (H) have four legs (L), then $L = aH$; or $L = 4H$. This can be important in the blacksmith business.

4. Calculate the constants. Look up past years' statistics on consumption, income, and so on. From these find values for a, b, c, d, and e that make your equation come out fairly correct.

5. Now you're ready to forecast. Start by forecasting investment from this year's profits. Look up the current rate of corporate profits — it's around $42-billion. The model won't tell what federal, state, and local governments will spend next year — that's politics. But we can estimate it from present budget information — it looks like around $75-billion.

6. Put all available figures into your model. (We've put in the constants for you.)

$$(1)\ C = .7Y + 40 \qquad (4)\ G = C + I + 75$$
$$(2)\ I = .9 \times 42 + 20 \qquad (5)\ Y = G - T$$
$$(3)\ T = .2G$$

7. Solve the equations. You want values of C, I, T, G, Y. Hints: Do them in this order — (2), (1), (4), (3), (5). In solving (1), remember that I and E are both part of G, $Y = G - T$, and $T = .2G$.

8. Results. (See if yours are the same.) For 1956, consumption will be $260.0-billion; investment, $57.8-billion; GNP, $392.8-billion; tax receipts, $78.6-billion; national income, $314.2-billion. These results are guaranteed — provided that the theories on which they're based are valid.

Reprinted with permission from *Business Week*, September 24, 1955 model will predict this year's national income and consumption **if** we know last year's profits (to predict I in equation #2) and government expenditures. These two—last year's profits, and government spending—turn out to be the crucial "independent variables" that control the predicted level of national income, given the relationships specified in the model. In fact, if we want to predict more than one year ahead, we need a more complex model, since profits this year will obviously depend partly on the levels of C, I, and G this year (as well as on other variables). Thus, a more complete model would need a behavioral equation to integrate the determinants of profits into the system. Then, only government spending would remain a truly autonomous variable; and even that might turn out to depend on some of the other variables, such as tax receipts of the government. If so, the model would then require another behavioral equation to specify government spending.

All this may begin to sound complex, and it is. There are now several working econometric models of the economy involving 20 to 400 equations.[8] For more

[8]A substantial econometric model of the economy is described in nontechnical language in "A Quarterly Econometric Model of the United States," *Survey of Current Business,* May 1966.

information on the big econometric forecasting models, which are now widely used by the government and private businesses, see Chapter 15.

Problems of statistical estimation. Building an econometric model requires an underlying theory. But equally it requires careful statistical estimation of the variables and relationships in the equations. A good econometrician is thus as much a statistician as an economist. Statistical estimation of complex economic relationships is a difficult job indeed. Interactions among important variables in our economy—for example, among personal consumption, disposable income, the money stock, holdings of liquid assets, and the like—are complex and sometimes shifting. Although most of the preceding discussion is about constructing models, the bulk of econometricians' work is studying the empirical behavior summarized in the individual equations that make up the models.

Modern statisticians are gradually developing methods to handle such complex interrelationships and forecasting problems. They are too intricate to consider here. But remember that progress in understanding what determines what in the economy depends heavily on this kind of behind-the-scenes interacting theoretical and empirical work.

CHAPTER 12

THE DETERMINANTS OF CONSUMPTION AND INVESTMENT

The income–expenditures model of Chapters 10 and 11 oversimplified by assuming that consumption is entirely induced—a function of the level of income—and that investment is entirely autonomous—unaffected by the level of income and consumption spending. In fact, the determinants of both consumption and investment are more complex. While consumption depends heavily on income, people sometimes change their consumption spending for quite different reasons. And business investment depends greatly on recent and expected sales, interest rates, and numerous other forces influencing profit expectations. Thus, both consumption and investment are partly induced, partly autonomous. This chapter examines in more detail the determinants of both consumption and investment.

CONSUMPTION EXPENDITURES

The consumption function

It seems intuitively reasonable that consumption expenditures depend heavily on people's disposable incomes, and they do. As far back as our data go, they show consumption rising and falling with aggregate disposable personal income. Figure 12–1 plots this relationship

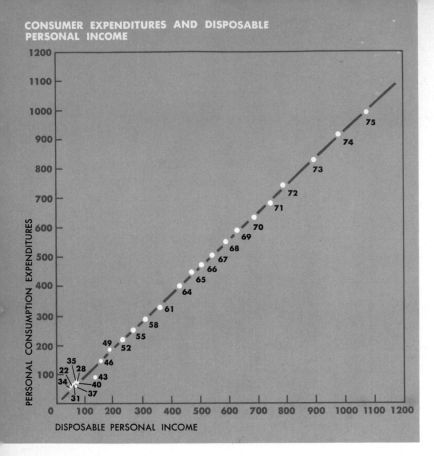

CONSUMER EXPENDITURES AND DISPOSABLE PERSONAL INCOME

since the 1920s. For example, in 1973, disposable personal income was $900 billion and consumption expenditures $830 billion. For 1933, the lowest year, DPI was only $45 billion while personal consumption expenditures were $46 billion, actually more than disposable personal income. People used accumulated savings and went into debt to keep themselves fed and housed when incomes fell in the depression.

The line running from southwest to northeast on the chart is drawn to "fit" the dots plotted. The fact that most years fall about on the straight line shows that the relationship between disposable income and consumption spending has been a rather stable one. But the fact that some years are substantially off the line shows equally that the stable relationship has not always held. During World War II, for example, consumption spending fell far below what would normally have been expected for the high incomes received during those years.

Put in commonsense language, this evidence says that the percentage of DPI spent on consumption rose as incomes fell in the depression; people tried hard not to cut back their living standards as much as their incomes fell. In generally prosperous periods (for example, most years since 1950), the percentage spent on consumption hovered around 92–94 percent. And under special circumstances such as World War II, when many goods were unavailable and the government urged everyone to save more to avoid inflation, the consumption percentage fell sharply—down to about 75 percent in 1943 and 1944. The fact that the "fitted" line leans over toward the right shows that the percentage relationship is not a constant one, like $C = .9$ DPI. Such an equation would give us a line that shows zero consumption at zero DPI. But we see that households in fact raised their consumption to over 100 percent of DPI in 1932, when income was well above zero. Try fitting a shorter straight line to the years through 1945 only, and you will see that it leans over considerably more to the right, reflecting experience in a more sharply cyclical period.[1]

The saving function

By definition, consumers save that portion of their disposable income that they do not spend on consumption. The relationship between consumer saving and disposable personal income is shown in Figure 12–2, which gives the percentage of DPI *saved* each year. The underlying data are the same as those for Figure 12–1. The percentage saved is, of course, 1 minus the percentage consumed for each year.

Figure 12–2 indicates vividly the high percentage of DPI saved in the war years, and the negative savings in the years 1932 and 1933 at the bottom of the Great Depression. But more significantly, it stresses the quite stable percentage saved (about 6–8 percent) during the reasonably stable, prosperous times since 1950.

What determines consumption expenditures?

The preceding data reinforce our intuitive presumption that consumption spending

[1]The equation that approximately fits the solid line is $C = a + b(Y)$, where a and b are constants that show the relationship between consumption (C) and disposable income (Y). This is the consumption function used in Chapter 10, footnote 5.

depends mainly on DPI. But they also warn us that other forces may shift the consumption function, slightly or dramatically. We need now to take a more detailed look at the forces that determine consumption.

Income—present, past, and future. The generally close relationship between current income and current consumer spending is obvious. But sophisticated statistical work over the past decade has suggested that adding past income and income expectations gives a better explanation of consumer spending than does present income alone.

The influence of past income is persistent. Once families have become used to any real consumption level, they are reluctant to slide back down to a lower level, even if their income drops. Rather than reduce their standard of living as income falls, they will (at least temporarily) reduce their saving levels to well below the amount they would have saved at that income on the way up. Similarly, when incomes rise sharply, consumption spending rises more slowly. That is, with rising incomes, the marginal propensity to consume is lower in the short run than in the long run.

Figure 12-2
Personal saving has been a quite stable percentage of disposable personal income in peacetime prosperity, but has fluctuated sharply in depressions and wars. (Source: U.S. Department of Commerce.)

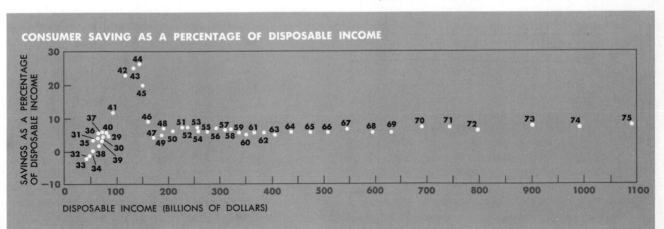

CONSUMER SAVING AS A PERCENTAGE OF DISPOSABLE INCOME

Recently, some research workers have advanced a more sophisticated hypothesis. **They suggest that consumption spending is a substantially constant and similar proportion of DPI for average families at all income levels—*if*** we exclude major disruptions like war and mass depression, *if* we include consumer durables (houses, autos, and household furnishings) with saving (investment),[2] **and if we consider their "permanent" or "life-span" incomes rather than the particular income of any given year, which may be distorted by special factors.**

One version of this approach (the life-cycle hypothesis) holds that families, consciously or subconsciously, estimate their long-range income over their entire life cycle, and adjust their current consumption spending to their expectations for the entire period. During their early married years, most couples spend most of their income and even go into debt to start families and to set up households. Later, as income rises and these special expenses have passed, they begin to save more, for retirement, to send their children to college, and so on. After their houses are well furnished and their children are educated, they commonly save at a much higher rate. Late in life, after they retire, the saving ratio drops again and often becomes negative. Averaged over this life span, the ratio of consumption to income is, if the investigations of this group stand up under further scrutiny, surprisingly similar for typical families at different income levels. By the same token, this suggests that consumption is a quite stable function of income for the population as a whole.

The "permanent-income" hypothesis is similar. It holds that families base their consumption on what they expect their "permanent" income to be. Temporary deviations in income up or down from this permanent expectation will usually not affect consumption much. Rather, if income falls temporarily, the family will cut back its savings, use up its liquid assets, or go into debt to maintain consumption. If income bulges temporarily, the bulge is likely to go mainly into saving and investment (including purchases of consumer durables).

[2]That is, families consume only the current services rendered by durable goods, just as businesses use each year only the current services of their factories and machinery.

What is the evidence on the life-span and permanent-income models? Good statistical evidence is hard to get, and interpretation of the data in relation to these models is tricky. There is some evidence that supports the models, but enough contradictory data to require a suspended judgment as far as practical use of the models is concerned.

Wealth.   Other things equal, a family with large wealth (ownership of economic assets such as money, stocks, bonds, and houses) will spend more on consumption than will a low-wealth family with the same income. For example, suppose a family receives an annual income of $10,000 and has accumulated wealth of $25,000. Now imagine that a wealthy relative dies and leaves the family another $25,000, or the stock market soars so its wealth doubles. We would expect its level of consumption to rise even if the father's salary stayed at $10,000. Note, incidentally, that this effect is closely related to the "permanent-income" hypothesis above. With more wealth, the family's permanent, or lifetime average, income has increased, because the family's income now includes the interest, dividends, or other yield on the additional $25,000 of wealth. But it also faces the permanent-income test if it's the stock market that increases wealth; will stock prices stay up permanently?

Money.   Money is one form of wealth, and more money, other things equal, will surely lead households to spend more on consumption (and possibly on other things as well). But money is a special form of wealth—the only one that can be freely used to buy other goods and services. Some economists (the "monetarists") argue that this special quality of money makes it an especially powerful determinant of consumer spending. They contend that the stock of money in the economy is the main determinant of consumption, and indeed of total aggregate demand.

This alternative approach to explaining aggregate demand is examined in detail in Chapters 13 and 14. In the meantime, remember that money may be a very important variable, which is being temporarily set aside here.

Consumer credit.   One way of getting around

the limitation of income is to borrow money or to buy on credit. A net increase in consumer credit correspondingly increases consumer spending power beyond that provided by current income. Until the last few decades, consumers did little credit buying except in purchasing homes. But since World War II, a huge volume of houses and consumer durables (especially automobiles) has been bought on credit. By 1976, households were $625 billion in debt on houses and durables.

But there is a counterforce at work here too. The deeper you are in debt, the bigger are the interest and debt repayments you must meet before current income can be devoted to new consumption expenditures. In 1976, the proportion of current disposable income committed in this way exceeded 15 percent.

Consumer stocks and availability of durables. Sometimes, as during World War II, you just can't buy lots of "hard goods" like refrigerators and automobiles because they are unavailable. Thus, in 1943–44, the economy's consumption ratio dropped to below 75 percent of DPI. By 1946, consumers had accumulated an enormous backlog of demand for such consumer durables, which undoubtedly helps explain the big postwar buying surge.

The converse effect occurs when consumers have built up unusually large stocks of durable goods. Thus, after consumers engage in a big buying spree on durables (for example, twelve million autos in 1973), they are likely to slack off their buying until the new durables are at least a few years old, even though consumer income holds up.

Inflation and price expectations. If you expect inflation, the time to buy is now, before prices go up. Immediately after the outbreak of the Korean War in 1950, for example, current consumer saving dropped almost to zero as consumers rushed to stock up before prices skyrocketed and goods vanished from the market. Such drastic shifts in price expectations are rare, but when they do occur, they can dominate the more stable consumption–income relationships that generally prevail. Unfortunately, there is no one simple price–expectations–spending

relationship. Repeated consumer-polls tell us that many consumers *reduce* buying of nonessentials when they expect inflation, to conserve their funds for the most urgent needs.

Modern econometric evidence

Although the generalizations above give us some guides to consumption behavior, they are too rough to be satisfactory for national forecasting purposes—for example, when we want to predict the probable effects of a tax cut or tax increase on consumption and GNP. Thus, modern econometricians have devoted a great deal of attention to analyzing precisely the empirical relationships between the various causes listed above and consumption.

One approach is to break down consumer spending into a number of major components—spending on services, on nondurable goods, on automobiles, on other durable goods, and the like. One well-known econometric model, for example, relates spending on automobiles and their parts to real disposable personal income, the relative price of autos, average weekly working hours in manufacturing, and strikes in the auto industry, plus a catchall factor for all other variables. In fitting this equation to the real world for 1953–65, the following results were obtained:

$$\text{Auto exp.} = +.104\,\text{DPI} - 11.0\,\frac{P_a}{P_c} + 129.0\,h_w + 1.85\,d_a - 134.0$$

In this equation, DPI is real disposable personal income; P_a is a price index for autos and parts; P_c is the consumer price index; h_w is an index of average weekly working hours in manufacturing; d_a is a special variable for strikes in the auto industry, which is 0 if there is a strike and 1 if there is none; and the final figure is the catchall for other variables. Thus expenditures on autos and parts in any quarter was, over the period studied, .104 times real disposable income, minus 11.0 times any increase in relative prices of autos, plus 129.0 times an index of weekly working hours in manufacturing, and so on. Similar equations have been fitted for the other major components of aggregate demand and other important economic variables. The exact "fits" vary for different periods and with the explanatory variables included in the equations.[3]

Where do all these considerations leave us on the determinants of consumer spending? At the risk of oversimplification, we can say that the long-run ratio of consumption to disposable personal income has been quite stable. At high-employment levels, it has seldom varied from the 92–94 percent range, moving outside that range for long only in response to identifiable special forces. The short-run (monthly or quarterly) marginal propensity to consume is much more variable. But in spite of short-run fluctuations in business cycles, consumers as a whole appear to adjust their consumption upward roughly in proportion to rising incomes. Will this tendency persist over the years ahead? Nobody knows. But the historical relationship has prevailed long enough to make it a reasonably good bet.

[3] See "A Quarterly Econometric Model of the United States," *Survey of Current Business,* May 1966, p. 30. The article explains in relatively nontechnical language how the entire model is constructed and used.

INVESTMENT EXPENDITURES

Private investment has been the most dynamic and unstable major component of the gross national product. Most economists think it plays a central role in explaining both economic growth and fluctuations. Figure 12–3 shows the fluctuation in private investment since 1929. The top line is gross, or total, investment, as in the GNP accounts. The lower line is net investment, which subtracts the allowance to replace capital goods worn out (depreciated) during that year. Although investment appears to have boomed in the 1960s and early 1970s, a substantial part of the dollar increase has been merely inflation. When inflation is eliminated, real net investment as a percentage of real GNP has fallen substantially since the mid-1960s.

Private investment expenditure is partly autonomous, but it also depends partly on the level of consumer spending. That is, rising consumption may induce more investment, as well as the other way around. Thus, a more thorough look at the system will require us to complete the circle: investment spending → more consumption → more private investment → more consumption . . . and so on. To do so, we need to ask

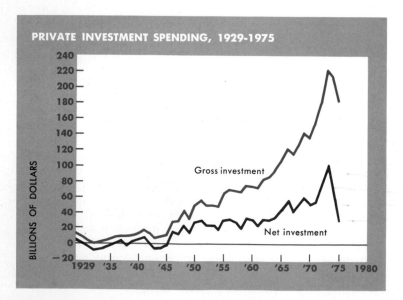

PRIVATE INVESTMENT SPENDING, 1929–1975

Figure 12–3
Private investment fluctuates sharply. It reached new peaks in the early 1970s, but much of the increase was merely inflation. New investment as a percentage of GNP has declined since the mid-1960s. (Source: U.S. Department of Commerce.)

specifically, What controls businessmen's decisions to invest?

As with consumer expenditure, the answer is gradually being clarified through both theoretical and empirical work. Begin again with a simplified theoretical model of a profit-maximizing business. Then we shall look at some of the modern empirical evidence.

Fundamentally, expected profit determines how much a business will invest in any given year. When a businessman thinks he can invest in a new machine and get back over the life of the machine what it costs, plus running expenses, plus interest on the money invested, plus some extra return (profit), he will make the investment. He will invest when the expected rate of return on his invested capital exceeds the going rate of interest (cost of capital) he must pay for funds to make the investment.

The marginal efficiency of investment

Economists call the expected rate of return on investment the "marginal efficiency of investment" (MEI). Suppose, for example, a businessman is thinking of buying a new milling machine for his plant. He knows the machine will cost $10,000, and his engineers estimate that it will increase the annual output of the plant by about $2,000, with unchanged costs for labor and materials. To maintain the machine, however, will cost about $500 a year. (To make the example easy, assume that the machine lasts indefinitely.) Thus, the expected annual net return on the $10,000 investment in the machine will be $1,500. The marginal efficiency of investment would thus be 15 percent (that is, $15 return annually on every $100 invested). If the businessman can borrow money at, say, 5 percent to buy the machine, it looks like a good investment.[4]

The businessman's estimate of MEI (the expected rate of return) obviously plays a central role in his decision. What factors determine the marginal efficiency of investment in typical cases? Some of the major ones follow.

---

[4] For a more complete analysis of how to compute the net rate of return on investments and how businessmen look at the investment problem, see Chapter 33.

Expected product demand. The dominant consideration is the expected demand for the firm's product. Note that it is **expected** return on investment that matters. Thus, whenever a businessman **expects the demand for his product to** rise, this anticipation increases the **expected** rate of return he can get by investing in new plant and equipment that will increase his output or improve the quality of his product. The fact that expectations govern the marginal efficiency of investment makes it subject to wide fluctuations, depending on how things look to the businessman. If the world looks black, down goes the marginal efficiency of investment. **Note the tie back to consumer spending. One of the big forces influencing the expected return on new investment is consumer spending—the demand for business's products.**

Technology and innovation. Research and development push the marginal efficiency of investment up. If a new machine promises to lower costs or to improve product quality, this promise will be reflected in a larger expected net return on the investment. Technological advance is the foundation of most present-day investment in plant and equipment.

Taxes. Businessmen are primarily concerned with the expected rate of return on investment **after taxes.** Big corporations pay income taxes of about 50 percent on their profits. (If we take this factor into account, the milling-machine investment above loses a lot of its glamor.) An increase in corporation tax rates or other corporation taxes, other things equal, will lower MEI; a decrease will raise it.

General outlook. A businessman can never estimate precisely all the factors involved over the life of a major investment. Will demand for the final product really be what he expects? Will the government step in and regulate his business? Will a new machine come along that will make this one obsolete? With all this uncertainty, the general outlook of the businessman often plays a big role in his final decision on whether or not to invest, and it is very hard to specify all the other factors which may influence businessmen's attitudes.

Interest rates—"the cost of money"

The other side of the picture is the interest rate—the cost of the money needed to make the investment under consideration. If the businessman has to borrow the funds needed, we can get a direct figure for the cost of money—maybe it's 5 percent. But even if he has the money already, possibly in retained earnings from previous profits, he must still figure "implicit" interest on the funds used, since, when he ties them up here, he will be foregoing interest he could earn by investing them elsewhere. Then the proper interest rate to charge is harder to estimate, but he must settle on some figure for his calculation.

The investment schedule and investment decisions

At any time, many alternative investment opportunities are open to any business, some promising high rates of return, some low. We can graph these investment opportunities as in Figure 12–4. Suppose we list all the possible investment opportunities that the firm foresees for next year, beginning with the most profitable. A few projects will promise a high rate of return; more will promise at least a medium rate; many will be available that promise at least a very low rate. Plot these in curve *II*. A few investments (about $140,000) promise 5 percent or more; about $300,000 promise 4 percent or more; and so on. Note that the $300,000 includes all that promise 4 percent *or higher;* it includes the $140,000 that promise 5 percent or more.

Now we can easily see how much a rational, profit-seeking businessman will invest. Suppose the interest rate he must pay or charge himself is 4 percent. Then any investment opportunity on his investment schedule that will yield above 4 percent is profitable. Figure 12–4 shows that this business should invest about $300,000 if the interest cost is 4 percent, taking on all the projects promising to yield 4 percent or higher. If the interest cost is 5 percent, it will only pay to invest $140,000 this year—only in those projects above where the 5 percent line intersects *II*. Each point on *II* shows how much will be invested at that

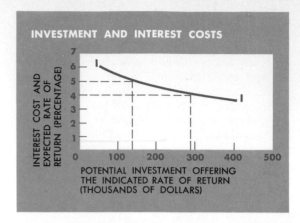

Figure 12–4
The curve II shows the amount of investment it will pay to undertake at each level of the interest rate.

interest rate. It shows investment as a function of the interest rate: $I = f(i)$.[5]

To summarize: Business investment spending in any given time period is determined by the marginal efficiency of investment in relation to the interest rate (cost of capital). Many business firms consciously go through the type of analysis outlined above for each major investment considered. Others make their calculations much more roughly. Some operate by hunch and intuition. For present purposes, assume that our model gives a rough approximation for the economy as a whole.

[5] Many businessmen introduce a "safety factor." They require an expected return of 15 or 20 percent on new investment before taking action, even though they can go to banks or the open market and borrow at 6 or 7 percent. Why?

Taxes are part of the story. They take about half of most business profits. A second answer is risks; businessmen say they never know whether things will turn out as well as expected. Third, some businessmen are reluctant to go into debt, even when it is directly profitable to do so. Fourth, many businessmen calculate the effective cost of money to themselves as much higher than current market interest rates, especially if they must issue new stock to get funds. These facts do not change the general principle in the text, but they do reduce the number of investment opportunities that many businessmen will consider attractive at any given time.

Business investment in inventories

The analysis of business investment above applies basically to business investment in plant and equipment—buildings, machinery, and the like. Business investment in inventories (raw materials, goods in process, and finished goods still on hand) raises other special problems, which become especially important when we consider short-run economic fluctuations—booms and depressions. For the moment, only a warning that inventory investment is a special problem, one we will examine in more detail in Chapter 15 on business cycles.[6]

MONEY IN THE INCOME-EXPENDITURES MODEL

Money has entered the analysis of the last three chapters only peripherally. In conclusion, it is important to clarify the role of money in the income–expenditures (neo-Keynesian) model.

In this model, changes in the stock of money influence the interest rate and, through the interest rate, the level of investment. An in-

---

[6]Net exports have also been neglected throughout this chapter, even though they may have a multiplier effect on GNP similar to that of domestic private investment. Net exports have been relatively small since World War II, and it is more convenient to consider them in Part 6, "The International Economy."

creased supply of money lowers its price (the interest rate), and a decreased supply raises the interest rate, other things equal. A higher or lower interest rate in turn decreases or increases investment.

The way money fits into the income–expenditures model can be seen easily from the following causal chain. If the government adds more money to the system, it affects GNP as follows:

$$+M \rightarrow -i \rightarrow +I \rightarrow +GNP$$

where M stands for money, i stands for interest rate, and I stands for investment. Note that in this approach, more money does not directly stimulate consumption spending; its only effect is to lower the interest rate, thereby stimulating investment.

Moreover, Keynes argued, often changes in M won't affect interest rates very much, especially in depressions (for reasons to be explored in the next chapters). Besides, he argued, fluctuations in interest rates are generally smaller than variations in the marginal efficiency of investment, which depends on expectations of profits and other factors in the future—and these may swing widely. Thus, moderate changes in the stock of money, bringing about only moderate changes in interest rates, generally have a limited influence on investment spending. But the sensitivity of investment to interest-rate changes is a factual issue, on which the evidence is mixed. (Some of the relevant information is presented in Chapters 15 and 18.) Many economists argue that changes in M affect investment powerfully.

REVIEW

Concepts to remember

Be sure you understand the following new analytical concepts introduced in this chapter:

"permanent income"
"life-cycle income"
marginal efficiency of investment
interest rate

implicit interest
"cost of capital"
investment schedule

**For analysis
and discussion**

1. What are the main factors that determine your personal consumption expenditure? What forces would you expect to shift your consumption function over the next ten years?

2. How would you expect the marginal propensity to consume to compare for families at the same income level (say, $15,000 per year) at the following ages for the head of the family: 25, 40, 60, 75? Explain your answer. How does it relate to the permanent-income hypothesis?

3. Consumer surveys have found that when people expect inflation, some raise their MPC, others lower it. Which seems to you rational behavior? Which would you do if you expected a higher rate of inflation over the next year?

4. Investment spending has often fluctuated sharply during booms and depressions. Using the model of business-investment decision making in the chapter, can you explain why this is likely?

5. Explain how you would decide whether to invest in a new set of store furnishings if you were the owner of an ice-cream parlor.

6. Would you expect higher interest rates to stimulate or retard business investment? Explain why, using a graph like Figure 12–4.

For many years, Congressman Wright Patman of Texas, chairman of the House Banking and Currency Committee and senior member of the House in years of service, argued that high interest rates damage the nation's economy and impose a needless burden on taxpayers when the government borrows at higher-than-nominal interest rates. He believed that the government, which has the power to create money, should hold interest rates low, presumably through creating enough money to achieve this result. Then it could borrow at low interest rates, avoiding the heavy interest burdens it has faced since World War II and holding the national debt far below present levels.

Many economists who testified before Mr. Patman's committee disagreed with this position, pointing out that plentiful money to hold interest rates low in periods of high employment would stimulate more investment and consumption spending, and hence more inflation. Thus, the apparent saving in interest costs to the government would be illusory, because its total expenses would rise by far more than the interest savings as inflation pushed up the prices of everything it buys.

In reply, Congressman Patman said that higher interest rates raise prices rather than holding them down. Interest is a cost to businessmen, and they just pass the higher costs on to consumers if the Federal Reserve attempts to restrain business investment through tight money and high interest rates.

The issue is posed by the following interchange at hearings before Representative Patman's committee in 1964:

CHAIRMAN PATMAN: It should be mentioned that if the [$2\frac{1}{2}$ percent] interest rates that prevailed after the war had been continued and had not increased, we would have a national debt . . . $40 billion less than it is today. . . . Did you look with favor upon those higher interest rates, Dr. Bach?

DR. BACH: It seems to me that there is a good case for higher interest rates when one wishes to restrain the level of economic activity. . . .

CONGRESSMAN BROCK: On the question of interest rates . . . what would have happened if we had kept that [$2\frac{1}{2}$ percent] ceiling on interest rates from 1951 until this time?

DR. BACH: If we had continued to peg the long rate at $2\frac{1}{2}$ percent . . . we would have had a lot more inflation between 1951 and now. . . .

I do not think that low interest rates or high interest rates per se are good. The interest rate is a . . . very important price because it [greatly influences] the level of total borrowing, investment, and consumer spending in the economy. . . .[7]

Who was right, Congressman Patman or Dr. Bach?

---

[7] *The Federal Reserve System after Fifty Years,* Hearings before Subcommittee on Domestic Finance, House Banking and Currency Committee, March 11, 1964, pp. 1402ff.

CHAPTER 13

MONEY, AGGREGATE DEMAND, OUTPUT, AND PRICES

Chapters 10–12 explained aggregate demand with little mention of money. There, spending depended largely on incomes received. But we receive our incomes in the form of money, and somehow it seems that money must be more than peripheral. It is! This chapter and the next now focus on money and the important role it plays in determining aggregate demand, real output, and the price level. This chapter presents an analysis of the role of money, and Chapter 14 combines the neo-Keynesian and monetarist approaches in a modern synthesis of macroeconomic theory.[1]

THE FACTS

What is money? What controls its supply? What are the facts about money in relation to aggregate demand, real output, and the price level?

What is money, and who controls it?

In today's economy, money is composed of bank demand deposits (which we spend

---

[1] Teachers who want their students to understand monetary mechanics (the operations of the banking system) before considering money in relation to aggregate demand should assign Chapter 17 before Chapter 13.

by writing checks) and currency (coins and paper money). Together, as of early 1976 they totalled about $300 billion. Contrary to the common impression, bank deposits make up the bulk of our money (about 75 percent); currency plays a relatively minor role.

It is important to distinguish between money and income. A man with an *income* of, say, $10,000 annually may possess only a few hundred dollars of *money* at any given time. Money is a form of wealth, an asset; income is a flow or stream of payments made by exchanging money. Each dollar of money may thus be spent many or a few times a year, creating "income" each time it is spent on transactions that enter the national income accounts.

For example, in 1975, the average amount of money outstanding (currency and checking deposits) was about $290 billion, while GNP was $1.5 trillion. Thus, on the average, people and businesses held money equal to only about one-fifth of their total incomes at any given time. Put another way, on the average, each dollar of money was spent on a GNP transaction about five times during the year.

The Constitution gives Congress the power to create money and regulate the value of it. Congress has delegated this power, with certain restrictions, to the U.S. Treasury and the Federal Reserve System, the nation's "central bank." The Treasury mints coins, a routine function. The Federal Reserve issues paper currency, and, more important, regulates the supply of bank deposits by controlling the "reserves" that commercial banks must hold behind their deposits.

Broadly speaking, therefore, the government (including the Federal Reserve) controls the supply of money. This is not entirely accurate, as we shall see, but it will do as a first approximation until Chapter 17.

Some historical facts

Figure 13–1 summarizes some important relationships among money, aggregate demand, real output, and prices since 1900. The bottom line shows the growth in the stock of money, averaging $5\frac{1}{2}$ percent per annum since 1900. The next two lines show that "real" gross

national product (that is, GNP in constant prices) rose at about $3\frac{3}{4}$ percent per annum over the same period, while nominal GNP rose at about $6\frac{1}{4}$ percent annually. The top line shows that the price level rose by an average of about $2\frac{1}{2}$ percent annually, the difference between nominal gross national product and real gross national product.

It is clear that on the average, the growth in *nominal* GNP paralleled closely the increase in the money stock; and that about two-thirds of the growth in nominal GNP was growth in real output, while about one-third of the growth was inflation.

Deviations from these average (trend) growth lines are as interesting as the trends themselves. The big inflation of World War I is clearly visible. The money stock shot up from 1915 to 1920 as new money was created to finance the war, and prices soared, at roughly the same pace. About 1927, the money stock began to fall below the economy's 3 + percent real long-term growth rate, and the long depression of the 1930s began two years later. The great collapse (in both output and prices) came between 1929 and 1933, when the money supply was contracting very sharply.

World War II was financed by newly created money, and both nominal GNP and prices rose rapidly. After World War II, the growth rate of the money stock slowed down, as did nominal GNP and prices, but with the Vietnam War of the late 1960s, money, nominal GNP, and prices all again rose more rapidly.

Some economists infer from these facts that the money supply exercises a powerful effect on the level of both real output and prices. When the money supply rises much faster than the growth in the economy's real output potential, inflation results. Growth in the money supply parallel to growth in potential real GNP (about 3 + percent per annum over the past half century) would go far to ensure stable economic growth. Slower growth in money means recession. But others say that this is too simple an analysis of a highly complex problem, and that it overstates the role of money. We now turn to the monetary theory developed by the classical economists to explain how money affects aggregate demand and prices.

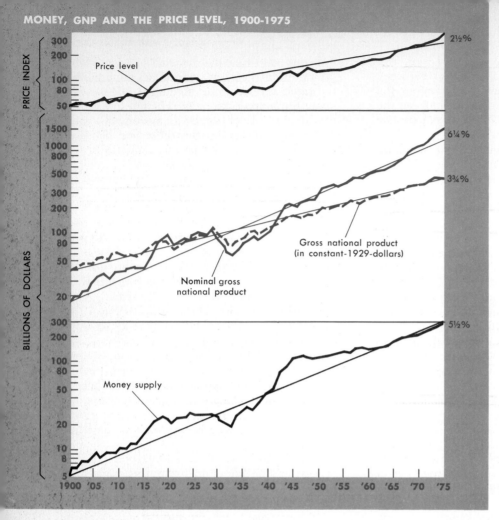

Figure 13-1
The money stock has risen about 5½ percent annually, and money GNP a little faster. GNP in constant prices has grown only about 3¾ percent annually, however, and a price rise of about 2½ percent per annum accounts for the difference. Has the excess of money supply over the growth in real GNP caused the inflation? (Sources: Federal Reserve Board, U.S. Department of Commerce, and National Bureau of Economic Research.)

MONEY AND PRICES—THE CLASSICAL VIEW

The classical economists—the long tradition from Adam Smith through David Ricardo and Alfred Marshall, up to the decade of the 1920s—gave money a central role in explaining aggregate spending and prices. They had two main points. First, the amount of

money will determine aggregate money-spending; and second, variations in aggregate money-spending will generally affect the price level but not real GNP and employment, except for temporary aberrations.

1. If people have more or less money, they will generally spend proportionately more or less. In general, the rate at which people spend the money they receive will be stable, or change only gradually. Thus, changes in the amount of money will generally lead to proportional changes in total spending. **This analysis is called the quantity theory of money, because in it, the quantity of money determines aggregate spending and, as we shall see, generally the price level as well.**

2. These variations in total spending will mainly just bid the price level up or down, without permanently changing the level of real output and employment. The classical economists argued that a free-market economic system would ordinarily tend to be self-equilibrating at approximately full employment. They reasoned that whenever resources are unemployed or unsold, their market price will move down until it falls low enough so that everything offered is hired or sold—just as will the price of wheat or coal. There may be temporary deviations from full employment and, indeed, these deviations may involve booms and depressions. But they will be aberrations, explained largely by special external factors such as wars or famines; by cumulative, herdlike sweeps of expectations that lead to gluts of overproduction and depression; and especially by the erratic behavior of the monetary system. Over the long pull, the economic system will always tend toward full employment. More or less money will change spending proportionately, and thus lead to a correspondingly higher or lower price level, not to a change in real output.

In terms of our earlier diagrams, this classical position can be put as follows: The economy will always tend to operate on its production-possibilities frontier—at full employment. Thus, in Figure 9-1, the economy's short-run aggregate-supply curve is, as a practical matter, not OAB but instead a vertical line rising from the horizontal axis at OQ_3. This is because the economy will tend to operate at full employment whatever the level of aggregate demand is. If aggregate demand falls, prices will fall, but output and employment (real GNP) will be unchanged; if aggregate demand rises, prices will rise, but real GNP will remain unchanged. It is important to see that the classical proportionality of changes in the price level to changes in money depends on the special aggregate-supply assumptions made. If supply conditions instead are as in Figure 9-1, full employment will not always prevail, and more money will lead to higher prices only when there is full employment.

Indeed, as we shall see in Chapter 19, many modern "monetarists" argue that there is a "natural rate of unemployment" set by the relation of the average wage rate to the productivity of labor, and by the fact of many imperfections in labor markets (lack of information about jobs, immobility of workers, mismatches between worker skills and job requirements, and the like). They argue that the system will tend toward this natural rate of unemployment, not toward full employment. But either way, these economists argue, the quantity theory will be correct in explaining aggregate demand (number 1 above). How much of the effect is on output–employment and how much on prices depends on the supply responses of the system (number 2 above).[2]

Money, velocity, output, and prices

Just how do changes in money lead to changes in aggregate demand (nominal GNP)? To explain, the classical economists asked, (1) How much money do people have, and (2) how fast do they spend it? A simple "equation of exchange" (proposed by Prof. Irving Fisher a half century ago) points up the relationships involved in this approach. The equation is:

$$MV = PT = \text{(nominal) GNP}$$

M stands for the amount of money in the hands of the public; V for the average "velocity of circulation," or the number of times each dollar is spent per time period; P for the price level, or average price per unit sold; and T for the number of units sold during each time period. If we think of T as the real goods and services produced in any year, it becomes the real GNP of the economy; and P can be thought of as the "GNP deflator" from Chapter 8. Then V is called "income velocity," because it shows the

---

[2] These remarks do less than justice to the classical economists, but the purpose here is merely to sketch in their view of money's role, not to paint a complete picture of what different economists thought. In particular, they realized that severe booms or depressions could occur while these long-run forces were gradually moving the economy back toward full-employment equilibrium, and that "sticky" prices (because of monopoly or other market imperfections) could keep the equilibrating price adjustments from occurring.

average number of times a dollar is spent each year on income-creating transactions in the GNP accounts.[3]

For example, in a very simple hypothetical economy, suppose M is $1,000. Suppose further that during some year, 2,000 units of physical goods are sold, and that their average price is $2. The T (real GNP) in our equation would then be 2,000, and the P would be $2; PT (or nominal GNP) equals $4,000, the total amount paid for the goods sold. The V, the average number of times per year each dollar is spent, is then obviously 4, since total expenditures were $4,000, so each of the 1,000 dollars must have been spent four times during the year on the average. The whole equation is then:

$$MV = PT, \text{ or}$$

$$\$1,000 \times 4 = \$2 \times 2,000$$

The two sides of the equation are defined so that they will always be equal. MV is simply the total amount *spent* on goods and services during the time period—the total number of dollars

[3]Obviously, we could include in T, *all* transactions during the period, adding in purchases of stocks and bonds, of existing houses, of secondhand autos, and so on. Then MV and PT would be equal to a much larger total that would include sales of existing assets as well. In 1975, nominal GNP was about $1.5 trillion, whereas total expenditures on all transactions were estimated roughly at over $15 trillion—perhaps ten times GNP. If we use this broader approach, V reflects spending on all transactions, and is called "transactions velocity."

multiplied by the average number of times each dollar is spent in the period. PT is the total amount *received* for goods and services during the period—the number of units sold multiplied by the average price per unit. The two are identical; what someone spends, someone else receives.

The equation of exchange is obviously a truism. Why, then, is it a useful analytical tool? The answer is, because it sets out four important variables for analyzing booms and depressions, inflations and deflations. The equation certainly doesn't provide any answers, but it is a framework for looking at the complex real world. It skips over the whole detailed analysis of consumer and business spending decisions in Chapters 10–12. But it suggests that behind the scenes, the quantity of money may be the basic factor controlling the level of spending.

The classical economists argued that, by and large, the receipts side of the equation is passive. If this is so, the equation says that changes in the stock of money will lead to corresponding changes in nominal GNP, unless changes in M are offset by changes in the velocity at which money is spent. Thus, if V were stable, changes in M would be a good predictor of GNP. And Professor Fisher argued that, by and large, his V (which was a little different from ours) was relatively stable over long periods, so that changes in M would have roughly proportionate effects on PT, although V might be highly volatile in short-run booms and depressions.

Has the evidence borne Fisher out? Yes and

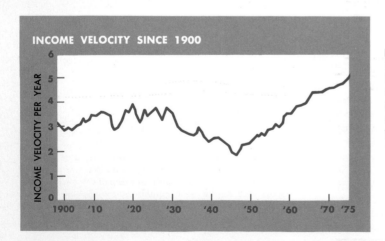

INCOME VELOCITY SINCE 1900

INCOME VELOCITY PER YEAR

1900 '10 '20 '30 '40 '50 '60 '70 '75

Figure 13–2
Income velocity has shown a gradual updrift over the long run. It rises and falls sharply in booms and depressions, and sometimes falls dramatically for special reasons—note the World War II period. (Calculated by dividing M into nominal GNP for each year.)

no. Figure 13–2 provides the data since 1900. *V* dropped sharply in depressions and increased in booms. But over the long pull, if we eliminate the long dip from 1930 to the early 1960s, *V* was reasonably stable, with a gradual upward trend that may reflect increasing efficiency in our payments mechanism (for example, use of credit cards and computers).

Equilibrium and the demand for "real-money" balances

Suppose that uncertainty increases and we all decide to build up our "real-money balances" by decreasing our expenditures relative to our incomes. That is, as a group, we want to hold more purchasing power in the form of money balances. That is what we mean by "real-money" balances.

When we all cut our expenditures to build up our real balances, will we succeed in holding more money? If your inclination is to say yes, stop and think again. One family can clearly build up its cash balance by holding back part of its income from spending. But with any given stock of money, there can be no change in the total amount of nominal money balances (*M*) held by the public as a whole. There isn't any more or less money for the public to hold, and every existing dollar must always be held by someone. If A's nominal cash balance goes up, B's must go down. Thus, the result of a general attempt to build up money balances is a decrease in total expenditures as each person reduces his rate of spending: *V* decreases. There is no increase in nominal money balances if the stock of money (*M*) is unchanged. *M* stays the same and *V* decreases, reducing nominal GNP. (Remember the fallacy of composition.)

Will the public's attempt to accumulate buying power over goods and services be completely thwarted? The answer is no. By the reduction in total expenditures, this slowdown in *V* will ultimately decrease prices (and probably production and employment as well). As prices fall, the existing amount of money will command more real goods and services. Thus, even though *M* remains unchanged, the public will succeed in increasing its **real** balances. People don't plan it that way, but they increase the real value of their money balances by bringing on deflation. When

prices have fallen enough to give existing nominal money balances the desired higher amount of real purchasing power, the public's demand for money balances will again be in equilibrium. People (households, businesses, and others) will again be satisfied to hold just the amount of money that exists.[4]

This can be put in equilibrium terms. Suppose there is some fixed amount of nominal money (M). If people have more money than they want to hold, M^s will exceed M^d. That is, there will be an excess supply of money, which people will spend on goods, bonds, or whatnot, to reduce their real balances to the desired level (M^d). Spending and prices will thus rise until $M^s = M^d$; that is, until the amounts of money demanded and supplied are equal. Only then is there monetary equilibrium.

Conversely, if M^d exceeds M^s, people will try to build up their real balances. They will reduce their spending and prices will fall until, at the lower prices, M^d just equals M^s. **Thus, in this classical, or "monetarist," analysis, the interaction between government changes in the money supply (M^s) and the public's demand for money balances (M^d) plays the key role in determining aggregate demand (GNP).**

Why do people hold money?

Since the public's (that is, individuals' and businesses') demand for money balances plays a key role in determining aggregate demand, many modern economists ("monetarists" or "neoclassicists") view explaining this demand as the key to explaining aggregate output, employment, and prices. They try to explain the demand for money by a combination of theoretical and empirical work.

Presumably, people are primarily interested in the real buying power of their money, and research has focused on the demand for **real** money balances. Theorizing suggests that the

---

[4]It is important to note that if prices are flexible downward as spending falls, the attempt to increase real balances will succeed without any decrease in real output and employment. But if prices and costs are inflexible downward (say, because unions resist wage cuts), the result is likely to be a big decline in output and employment before prices fall far enough to satisfy the increased demand for real balances.

larger an individual's income or the more wealthy he is, the more money he will usually hold for normal transactions purposes, as well as just to have some spare funds (liquidity) on hand for unforeseen contingencies or because he expects prices to fall in the future. But why does he hold money instead of maintaining that liquidity by holding bonds or other dividend- or interest-yielding securities? The answer is that securities aren't as liquid as money—they involve some risk that you can't convert them into cash on short notice without loss, and in any event, there is often a transactions cost (in time and money) in converting them into cash when you need it. So people will hold some money, even though it yields no interest return; it provides utility even though it provides no interest. But the higher the interest rate available on securities (close money substitutes), the more reluctant people will be to hold money and forego that interest.

Thus, it seems plausible that the demand for money is a function of two variables, the public's income or wealth, and the interest rate on close money substitutes (say, U.S. government securities). And empirical research confirms that this is generally so. The demand for real money balances is:

$$M^d = f(Y, i)$$

where Y is real income and i is the interest rate. Wealth (W) can be substituted for Y with about equally good results. These results suggest that if we know the public's income and the interest rate, we can predict its demand for money (or V), assuming that people behave in the future as they have in the past. They also say that, other things equal, if incomes rise, so will the demand for money, and that the demand for money to hold will vary inversely with the interest rate.[5]

These are powerful findings. But the public's behavior varies somewhat from time to time, and the empirical results are not consistent enough to permit us to predict precisely what V

will be for any period ahead. The equation gives us a first working approximation for estimating the effects on aggregate demand of changes in M under different income and interest-rate conditions, but only an approximation, because we never know just how the public will behave in the future, especially if circumstances are out of the ordinary.

MONEY, PORTFOLIO BALANCING, AND AGGREGATE DEMAND

Extending this reasoning, modern monetarists have developed a more systematic and complete theory to explain the public's demand for money. The reasoning is precisely parallel to the model in Chapter 5, where consumers maximized their utility by allocating their incomes so the marginal utility obtained from the last dollar spent on each product was identical. Just so, they will maximize their utility from their total assets, or wealth, by allocating their wealth (their "portfolios") among assets so that the marginal utility obtained from the last dollar invested in each asset is identical. Each household and business will be in equilibrium when it has allocated its total wealth (assets) among money, other liquid assets (bonds, savings accounts, and so on), and real assets (houses, durable goods, and so on) so that the marginal utility from the last dollar invested in each asset is the same. If this were not so, it would pay to shift out of the low-yield assets into higher-yield assets.

For example, suppose a family receives an unexpected gift of $10,000 cash from a forgotten aunt. It now has more money than it wants to hold and will use this "excess" money to acquire other assets, such as an auto, clothes, or bonds. It will spend down its money balance until the marginal satisfaction obtained from the last dollar held in money just equals that received from the last dollar invested in bonds, housing, and any other asset the family wants. Then its asset portfolio will be in equilibrium. If MU is the marginal utility, or satisfaction, obtained from the last dollar invested, then equilibrium is obtained when:

---

[5] If we take Y to stand for "permanent," or average lifelong, income, the accuracy of the equation improves, because people's demand for money apparently does not vary with all short-run fluctuations in incomes received.

$$MU \text{ (money)} = MU \text{ (bonds)} = MU \text{ (equities)}$$
$$= MU \text{ (clothing)} = MU \text{ (autos)} \ldots \text{ and so on}$$

for all assets held.

Note that this implies that holding money provides utility (a return) even if the money yields no money interest return. Clearly, this is correct. Money provides generalized, riskless, immediately available buying power. Other assets provide different returns. Securities provide interest or dividends and possibly the expectation of capital gains, although they also involve some risk. Capital goods (like machinery) provide a direct contribution to business profits. Consumer goods provide services to their users. All these assets are in the portfolio that must be balanced to maximize the total utility obtained. And the same portfolio-balancing model holds for business firms as well as households.

It should now be easy to see how putting more or less M in the system will increase or decrease spending on other assets. Your aunt's $10,000 gift leads you to buy a $1,000 government bond, ten shares of AT&T stock, and a new car, as well as to increase your checking balance at the local bank (that is, to hold more money). Note that an increase or decrease in the stock of *any* asset, or a change in its yield, will logically lead to a reshuffling of portfolios. Whenever individuals or businesses find that the marginal returns on different assets are different, they will always move toward equilibrium by shifting out of assets with lower marginal yields into higher-yielding ones. Thus, more M will lead them to spend more on other assets.

It is important to note that increased spending induced by more M may or may not directly increase aggregate demand (GNP). If you reduce your money balance by buying General Motors stock, U.S. bonds, or an existing house, this is merely an exchange of existing assets. Your expenditure does not directly increase GNP (current production and employment). But if you buy a new coat, or have your car repaired, your money expenditure does directly increase GNP. Similarly, a business may shift out of money into new plant and equipment, thus directly increasing the investment component of GNP; or it might simply invest its excess money

in bonds. It is this portfolio balancing that provides the linkage between money stocks on the one hand and the flows of consumption and investment spending in the GNP accounts on the other.[6]

THE FOUNDATIONS OF MONETARY POLICY

The government has no very effective way of controlling the public's demand for money. But it can control the supply of money reasonably closely. By doing so, it can create an excess supply, or deficiency, of money relative to the demand for money ($M^s > M^d$, or $M^s < M^d$), and thereby increase or reduce the public's spending. In this monetarist model, the supply of money plays a central role in determining aggregate demand, far more important than under the neo-Keynesian model described at the end of Chapter 12, where changes in M affect only the interest rate, which in turn may or may not greatly affect investment spending.

Looking ahead, classical analysis leads toward two main policy conclusions, one reassuring, the other discouraging. First, the quantity theory says that aggregate money demand can be roughly stabilized by maintaining a stable quantity of money. We can avoid big fluctuations in aggregate demand if only we keep the money stock growing at a stable rate. Since population and the productive capacity of the economy grow over time, it will be desirable to increase the money stock gradually, roughly at the same pace as the growing full-employment-output capacity of the economy; otherwise, prices will fall steadily as output increases. If inflation prevails, slow the growth in M. If deflation is the problem, increase M faster.

The second, discouraging policy implication of the classical analysis is that monetary policy can't do much to eliminate unemployment, except possibly temporarily. Note that this conclusion follows from the classicists' assumption about the economy's aggregate-supply curve, not

---

[6]Chapter 14 considers more thoroughly the question of when more M will lead to a larger GNP (more production and employment) and when only to shifts into other existing assets.

from the quantity theory of money. Although more M can increase aggregate demand, the long-run levels of employment and unemployment are not determined by aggregate demand. More M to raise aggregate spending will mainly increase prices rather than provide more jobs.

Many more modern monetarists accept the quantity-theory linkage between M and nominal GNP than accept the thesis of the natural rate of unemployment. They argue that certainly in the short run, more M can help reduce unemployment and increase output, and probably it can help in the long run too, as well as raising prices. They see control over the growth rate of the money stock as the government's main stabilization-policy weapon, more powerful than fiscal policy. The following chapter turns to the task of integrating neo-Keynesian and monetarist analysis, and of providing a foundation for stabilization policy that will use the best of both fiscal and monetary approaches.

Money in perspective

But first, a preliminary perspective on the question, How important is money? Clearly, money matters—and matters a lot. Money has played a vital role in all the big inflations. Runaway increases in the money stock have invariably been associated with soaring prices, usually in a dog-chasing-his-own-tail upward spiral where more money leads to higher prices, which leads the government to print more money to pay its bills, which leads to still higher prices, and so on. The expected yield on M becomes negative because people expect inflation to erode its value. People reduce their holdings of M to the barest minimums needed for transactions and precautionary purposes.

Just how important changes in M are in explaining smaller business fluctuations is less clear. Although changes in M and in GNP are quite closely correlated, V fluctuates substantially in the short run, and it is not always clear whether changes in M cause changes in GNP, or vice versa. But one historical fact stands out: Real GNP has grown stably in this country only when the money supply was growing at least **roughly** at the same rate as the productive capacity of the economy. Nearly everyone agrees that a growing money supply is a **necessary** condition for a growing real GNP. Some believe that it is a **sufficient** condition to induce stable growth in our economy. The implications of the two conclusions for long-run monetary policy are, happily, similar. But until we have clearer evidence, most economists are not prepared to rely solely on stable growth in M to provide stable growth in aggregate demand and real output.

REVIEW

Concepts to remember

The following new concepts in this chapter are worth careful review:

money
difference between money
 and income
velocity of circulation
equation of exchange

nominal money
real-money balances
demand for money
quantity theory of money
portfolio balancing

For analysis and discussion

1. By and large, would you expect prices to rise in proportion to any major increase in the supply of money? Explain.

2. Suppose the government holds the stock of money roughly constant over the next decade. Would you expect constant, rising, or falling price and income levels? Explain.

3. Is your own spending rate primarily a function of your recent income, your cash balance, or other factors?

4. Suppose the 1980 full-employment potential GNP is $2 trillion. How big a money supply do you estimate will be needed to finance this GNP?

5. Suppose the public's demand for money balances increases because of fear and uncertainty at the beginning of a recession. If the government wants to keep prices and employment stable, what should it do about the stock of money?

6. "In depression, an increase in the money supply leads to more jobs; in prosperity, to inflation." Is this quotation correct? Does the equation of exchange help in analyzing it?

7. Figure 13–1 shows that growth in nominal GNP closely parallels that in money. Does this demonstrate that the monetarists are right—that changes in M are the main causes of changes in nominal GNP? Is the possibility that changes in GNP cause changes in M also consistent with the evidence? Do you need a theory to decide between the hypotheses?

8. Explain why the public's demand for real money depends largely on its real income (or wealth) and on the interest rate of money substitutes (like government securities)—that is, $M^d = f(Y, i)$.

9. Explain how the portfolio-balancing analysis links changes in the stock of money with changes in nominal GNP.

MONEY AND THE GREAT GERMAN HYPERINFLATION

Following World War I, Germany suffered one of the greatest hyperinflations in recorded history. The war put a severe strain on the German economy, and the Treaty of Versailles imposed heavy reparations burdens on Germany, requiring massive transfers of real goods to the victorious allies. The weak German government found it increasingly difficult to raise enough money by taxes to pay its internal bills, including servicing its internal war debts, and to obtain the resources required to meet reparations requirements.

Increasingly, the government resorted to the expedient of printing new paper money (marks) to pay its bills. The government also increasingly issued "bills" (government bonds) to the Reichsbank (the nation's central bank), which then in effect created new money to lend to the government. Table 13–1 shows the course of events, as the nation became more and more discouraged. The occupation of the Ruhr by France in 1923 seemed the last straw, and the issues of paper marks reached unheard-of heights.

Table 13–1

Treasury bills discounted by the Reich, paper currency issued, and index of wholesale prices, 1919–1923 (value figures in millions of marks)

End of month	Total amount of Treasury bills discounted by the Reich[a]	Total issues of paper currency (except emergency currency)	Index of wholesale prices[b] 1913 = 1
1919 Dec.	86,400	50,065	8.03
1920 June	113,200	68,154	13.82
Dec.	152,800	81,387	14.40
1921 June	185,100	84,556	13.66
Dec.	247,100	122,497	34.87
1922 June	295,200	180,169	70.30
July	308,000	202,626	100.59
Aug.	331,600	252,212	192.00
Sept.	451,100	331,876	287.00
Oct.	603,800	484,685	566.00
Nov.	839,100	769,500	1,154.00
Dec.	1,495,200	1,295,228	1,475.00
1923 Jan.	2,081,800	1,999,600	3,286.00
Feb.	3,588,000	3,536,300	5,257.00
Mar.	6,601,300	5,542,900	4,827.00
April	8,442,300	6,581,200	5,738.00
May	10,275,000	8,609,700	9,034.00
June	22,019,800	17,340,500	24,618.00
July	57,848,900	43,813,500	183,510.00
Aug.	1,196,294,700	668,702,600	1,695,109.00
Sept.	46,716,616,400	28,244,405,800	36,223,771.00
Oct.	6,907,511,102,800	2,504,955,700,000	18,700,000,000.00
Nov.	191,580,465,422,100	400,338,326,400,000	1,422,900,000,000.00
Dec.	1,232,679,853,100	496,585,345,900,000	1,200,400,000,000.00

[a] Practically all government borrowing after 1919 was in the form of discounted Treasury bills. The figure for November 1923 is as of the 15th of that month.

[b] The figures in the table are for the latest available date in each month.

Source: F.D. Graham, *Exchange, Prices and Production in Hyperinflation: Germany: 1920–1923* (Princeton, N.J.: Princeton University Press, 1930).

As more paper money was issued to pay the government's bills, total (government plus private) spending power was correspondingly increased, since there was no corresponding reduction in private spending power through taxes. The result, predictably, was soaring prices, as the table shows. And the higher prices rose, the more new money the government had to print to pay its bills. As prices spiraled upward, the value of each paper mark fell correspondingly. Soon, prices were rising so rapidly that marks would lose most of their value in only days or, by 1923, hours; and a major occupation of the public was spending the money it received immediately, before its value fell even further. This increase in velocity, of course, further sped the upward spiral of prices. (For some of the consequences, see the section on "Hyperinflation" in Chapter 7.)

The end came in November–December 1923, when the government, with the help of some foreign nations, simply repudiated the paper marks it had issued (officially, it offered to exchange one new mark for each trillion old marks). This was followed by the Dawes Plan, reducing Germany's reparations burden to more reasonable levels, and the issue of new marks was rigidly limited to maintain their value. Prices in terms of the new currency fell to about one-trillionth of their levels in terms of old paper marks, and they remained fairly stable thereafter.

Using the analytical concepts of this chapter (both the equation of exchange and modern equilibrium analysis), analyze the great German inflation. In particular, consider the following questions:

1. What caused the inflation?

2. Was the inflation consistent with the quantity theory of money?

3. How do you explain the fact that prices rose faster than the money stock increased?

4. Does the equation of exchange or the portfolio-balancing theory provide a more helpful analytical approach? Are their results consistent? (In answering, to simplify, assume that real output of the German economy was roughly constant over the period shown. In fact, output grew substantially until about 1923, when the inflation increasingly disrupted real production.)

CHAPTER 14

AGGREGATE DEMAND, EMPLOYMENT, AND INFLATION: THE MODERN SYNTHESIS

Both the income–expenditures and monetarist models of the preceding chapters provide plausible explanations of how aggregate demand is determined. They stress different variables, and to some extent they are in conflict. But modern economists have increasingly tried to integrate them into one modern theory of aggregate demand, employment, and inflation—one that will provide the best analytical foundation for stabilization policy. This modern synthesis is the subject of this chapter.

THE MODERN SYNTHESIS

The income-expenditures model says that equilibrium can be attained only when households are consuming and saving in relation to their incomes at the rates they prefer, and only when businessmen are investing at the rate they judge will maximize their profits. This is an analysis in terms of income flows—through consumption and investment expenditures—not in terms of equilibriums between supplies and demands of assets held. Money (an asset) is ignored or introduced only indirectly through its effect on the interest rate and investment.

The monetarist (portfolio-balancing) model says that the system will be in equilibrium only when households and businesses are content to

Keynes

hold just the existing stocks of money and other assets. That is, equilibrium requires that $M^s = M^a$, and similarly for other assets. This equilibrium will occur when each household and business has allocated its total wealth so that it is maximizing its total yield, and so that all economic units together are content to hold just the existing stock of every asset, including money. In this approach, the emphasis is on assets, with spending flows derived from people's decisions about what assets to hold.

Thus, for equilibrium to be obtained in the economy, both the "flows" of the income-expenditures model and the "stocks" of the portfolio-balancing model must be in equilibrium. Unless all economic units are in equilibrium on both accounts—that is, unless they are content to keep on doing what they are doing—they will change their behavior and bring about a movement in spending, output, and prices toward the desired equilibrium state. The synthesis consists of seeing that both sets of equilibrium conditions must be met simultaneously.

M increases wealth and aggregate demand: an example

Consider now two experiments to illustrate both the differences in the two approaches and their synthesis. First, suppose the government simply prints up some new money and gives it to the public—say, in the form of unemployment relief. This increases the money and total assets (wealth) of the public and simultaneously increases disposable personal income. Let us trace through the effects of this increase in M on nominal GNP.

1. **Consider first the monetarist analysis.** The public now has more money than previously. If it was previously satisfied with its money holdings (that is, its asset portfolios were balanced), it now has too much money compared to other assets, such as consumer goods and securities. The marginal satisfaction from holding money has fallen relative to that from other assets, because the public has more money but no more of other things. It therefore will spend some of the new money for other existing or newly produced assets. This will bid up prices of other things and thus gradually decrease the

satisfaction obtainable by spending an additional dollar on them. (Note that the total stock of M does not change; what A spends, B receives.) The public will continue to spend its new money balances until rising prices restore an equilibrium in the rates of return provided by a marginal dollar held in money and in all other assets. Thus, **on the asset side,** more M leads to more spending, as people act to rebalance their portfolios.[1]

2. **In income-flows analysis,** the increase in disposable income will lead to more consumption and, through the multiplier, to a higher GNP. Equilibrium is reestablished when GNP rises to a new level where consumers are at their desired consumption–income ratios and businesses are at their desired investment levels relative to their receipts and profit expectations given their larger income.

Now the synthesis. Thus, households and businesses throughout the economy adjust both their asset portfolios and their current spending patterns until they are content with new equilibria attained on both fronts. Both adjustments go on simultaneously.

But note an interesting difference between the monetarist and Keynesian conclusions. The monetarists predict a *continuing* higher level of GNP, consistent with the new permanently higher level of M. But the Keynesians predict that there will be only a *temporary* increase in GNP, unless the higher autonomous relief payments are repeated in succeeding periods. The increased aggregate demand is based on the increased autonomous spending, in their theory, not on the increased M. Thus, the higher GNP will continue only as long as its higher autono-

[1] To see why a rise in the price of a security or other asset is the same thing as a decline in the yield on it, consider the following. Suppose the security is a $100 government bond paying 3 percent (that is, $3 a year) and due in ten years. If the price is bid up to $110, the annual real yield falls to about 2 percent. This is because, offset against the annual interest payment of $3, the bond buyer must consider the $10 he will lose when he gets back in ten years only $100 instead of the $110 he paid. Spreading this "capital loss" evenly over the ten years takes away $1 return per year, lowering the effective annual yield to $2, which is an effective interest rate of 2 percent. (Actually, it is a little less than 2 percent, since you get $2 per year on an investment of $110.) This same type of effect holds for other assets that provide a fixed dollar yield.

mous spending base is continued; the increase in *M* is only incidental, except insofar as it may indirectly stimulate more investment.

M increases without increasing wealth

Now, a second experiment. Suppose the government increases *M* by buying up bonds owned by the public. This increases the public's money balances and reduces the interest rate through bidding up the price of bonds, but it does not increase the public's total wealth. Does this lead to more spending, via either the income-flows or portfolio-balancing route?

The neo-Keynesians would say no, or at least, only indirectly. It would have no effect on disposable income and hence no effect on consumption. It could indirectly increase GNP by stimulating investment through the lower interest rate, but this effect is often weak. The monetarists concur that the stimulus to money GNP would be less than in the preceding increased-wealth case. But they argue that the new money will spill over at least in part to other assets, like consumer and investment goods, raising nominal GNP directly. This difference of opinion is again an important one for government monetary-policy makers who must determine how much money we should have and how to introduce it.[2]

THE MODERN SYNTHESIS AND STABILIZATION POLICY

Nearly everyone agrees that both money and income-flow factors are important determinants of aggregate demand, and that we must take both into account. But which is more powerful, and which relationship is more stable, so we can rely upon it in predicting the future behavior of the system? Suppose, for example, there is unemployment and we want to raise aggregate demand by $10 billion. One ap-

proach: We might print up $2 billion of new money and give it out in the form of relief payments, on the reasoning that income velocity recently has been about 5, so the new money would raise GNP by about $10 billion. Another approach: We might not change *M* at all but instead increase government spending by $4–$5 billion without correspondingly raising taxes. Neo-Keynesians suggest that the multiplier on autonomous spending is about $2–2\frac{1}{2}$, given stable interest rates. Thus, the result should be an increase of about $10 billion in GNP. Which approach is better? Is the figure for income velocity (5, in this example) more reliable than the figure for the multiplier ($2–2\frac{1}{2}$, in this example) in predicting the new GNP?

The answer from econometric studies is mixed. Neither income velocity nor the multiplier is as predictably stable as their advocates would like. As a practical matter, if we want an increase of $10 billion in aggregate demand, to use either increased *M* or decreased taxes alone risks partial success. For example, the increased government spending will increase GNP, but if *M* is unchanged, rising income will increase the demand for money and interest rates, which will partially check the upswing by reducing businesses' incentive to invest. Moreover, the government will have to borrow money to finance its new deficit, which will further increase interest rates. On the other hand, to increase *M* alone (say, by buying up outstanding bonds with new money) does not increase anyone's disposable income or assets, and the income-expenditure advocates say the policy may do little more than slightly reduce the interest yield on bonds. Depending on either the tax or the monetary approach alone may be dangerous. Thus most experts agree that it is safer to use them both simultaneously.

More research is needed to clarify the quantitative importance of the income and money factors in household and business behavior. The simple income–expenditures model of Chapters 10 and 11 (before money was introduced) implicitly assumed that either the stock of *M* or *V* (that is, the demand for money) would passively adjust to permit the equilibrium level of GNP predicted by the income–expenditures model. If, for example, we raised government spending by

---

[2]Note that neither theory gives a clear-cut answer as to how much of the increased expenditure will go into existing assets vs. newly produced goods (although the neo-Keynesians say it will be mainly existing assets in our second case) or into higher prices vs. new production if nominal GNP is increased. More on this presently.

$1 billion but did not change the money stock, a multiplier of, say, 2 would necessarily imply that V automatically rises to permit the $2 billion increase in GNP. Conversely, the monetary approach implicitly assumes a passive adjustment in MPC to permit GNP to follow changes in M. Suppose, for example, we increase the money stock by $1 billion but make no change in taxes, government expenditures, or the other income-flow variables. The monetary approach tells us that, if V is stable at, say, 5, GNP will rise by $5 billion. But this increase necessarily implies a corresponding upward adjustment in the public's marginal propensity to consume or in businesses' marginal propensity to invest. To decide whether fiscal or monetary policy is a more powerful device to regulate aggregate demand, we need to know more about the relative stabilities of the demand for money and the economy's propensity to spend out of disposable income. The evidence is not yet conclusive. Clearly, both the income and asset adjustment processes go on simultaneously whenever the system is out of equilibrium. Some economists are pure monetarists or pure Keynesians. But most see the combined adjustment process as the best description of reality.[3]

---

[3] Modern econometricians are working hard to determine the relative influence on GNP of changes in M and in autonomous expenditure (often roughly defined as private investment plus most government spending). For example, to oversimplify, they say: Suppose we statistically relate changes in GNP to changes in M, and then separately relate changes in GNP to changes in A (autonomous expenditure). The results look like this for the decade of the 1960s. (In the equations, t stands for time period, so t is this quarter, $t - 1$ is one quarter back, and so on; and Δ stands for "change in.")

$$(1) \quad \Delta GNP_t = 5.61b. + 3.94 \, (\Delta M)_{t-3} \qquad r^2 = .553$$
$$(2) \quad \Delta GNP_t = 4.94b. + 1.08 \, (\Delta A)_{t-1} \qquad r^2 = .400$$

Equation (1) says that the quarterly change in GNP equaled $5.61 billion plus $3.94 for each $1 increase in M three quarters previously. Put otherwise, a $1 increase in M was associated with a $3.94 increase in GNP three quarters later. Equation (2) says that a $1 increase in A was associated with a $1.08 increase in GNP one quarter later. The r^2 in each case is called the "coefficient of determination." It shows how much of the total actual change in GNP each quarter is explained by the M or A, respectively. Thus, ΔM in the simple test explained a little more of ΔGNP than did ΔA.

But actually, of course, both M and A exert influence on

DYNAMIC ADJUSTMENTS AND DISEQUILIBRIUM ANALYSIS

Although the economy never reaches full equilibrium adjustment, it is continually moving *toward* equilibrium. Thus, understanding the dynamic process of adjustment toward equilibrium is often as important as the equilibrium conditions themselves. Some economists call these dynamic adjustments "disequilibrium analysis" and stress them rather than the analytical equilibrium results.

Differential lags in adjustment

The real world is full of market imperfections and other special factors that slow or block adjustments toward equilibrium. For example, we know that when aggregate demand falls, unions resist wage cuts and many businesses are reluctant to cut prices. Thus, output and employment are likely to be cut first, while prices (including wage costs) fall more slowly. Often, workers thrown out of jobs in one industry by shifting consumer demand don't have the skills needed to meet the new demands, and they find it difficult or impossible to transfer to the

---

GNP simultaneously. If we put both variables in the same equation, we get:

$$(3) \quad \Delta GNP = 4.00b. + 2.52 \, (\Delta M)_{t-3} + .670 \, (\Delta A)_{t-1}$$
$$r^2 = .658$$

This equation shows that ΔM and ΔA together explain appreciably more (65.8 percent) of ΔGNP than does either alone. Quarterly changes in GNP (annual rates) over the ten years were $4 billion plus $2.52 for each $1 increase in M and 67 cents for each $1 increase in A, with the time lags shown.

This example suggests how econometricians go about using historical evidence to judge how much different factors influence GNP. But the example is greatly oversimplified, and it is important to remember that the figures shown do not provide a satisfactory answer on the relative importance of M and A for real-world use. Different time periods and different definitions of M and A give significantly different results. And a dispute rages among the experts as to whether more meaningful answers are obtained from relatively simple models like this one or complex models including many more variables.

For references to more complex models, see the appendixes to Chapters 11 and 15.

expanding sectors of the economy. Similarly, information on new jobs elsewhere may be imperfect, or workers may lack funds to move themselves and their families to new jobs.

Market imperfections occur in product markets as well. On the monetary-fiscal-policy front, increased M and lower interest rates may take a long time to stimulate business investment spending. Businessmen must plan their new investments, arrange to borrow the needed funds, and let contracts before new investment actually occurs, a process that may take years for big investments. Conversely, higher government spending or lower taxes may affect consumer spending promptly, but long political lags may occur before the president and Congress see the need for action and pass the needed legislation. In long-run equilibrium, all these differential lags would wash out. But the long run may be a very long time. Thus, most modern economists emphasize the need to recognize short-run, disequilibrium problems as well.

We shall look at some of the most important of these differential lags in adjustment in detail in the following chapters, in particular as they affect the paths of booms and depressions.

Rigid prices and costs

As Chapter 6 emphasized, when a price is held above its market-clearing level, excess supply will result and not all of the product will be sold. In fact, both many wages and many product prices are resistant to downward pressures when aggregate demand falls short of high-employment levels. Thus, disequilibrium analysis stresses, demand inadequacy is likely to lead more to unemployment than to falling prices, at least in the short run. If wages and prices adjust upward slowly when demand rises, again changing aggregate demand will influence mainly output and employment, rather than prices—but this upward wage-price lag is less common than its downward counterpart. Interest rates are also sticky. When aggregate demand falls sharply, interest rates often fall more slowly; and many lenders are very resistant to lending at rates near zero when risk and liquidity problems are present. Insofar as some prices (especially wages and interest rates) are inflexible down-

ward, there is no logical reason that the economy need tend to either full employment or a definable natural rate of unemployment. Much more on this in Chapter 19.[4]

Money, interest rates, and expectations

One further complication produced by the realities of dynamic disequilibrium analysis deserves mention. In fact, interest rates generally rise when M is increased rapidly, rather than falling, as Keynesian analysis predicts. Why?

Everyone agrees that the **first**, direct effect of introducing more money into the economy will, other things equal, be to reduce the interest rate—directly if the government introduces the money by buying up bonds, or indirectly through portfolio balancing if the money is inserted some other way. But one of the main lessons of economics is, Don't stop with the first effect; second and third effects may also be important! And so they may be here.

More M will almost certainly raise money incomes. This, in turn, will increase the demand for money, and this **second** effect will tend to **raise** the interest rate, partially offsetting the original downward pressure of more M. This is called the "income effect." But there may be a still further, **third** effect—the "inflation effect." Especially if the rising income comes at a time of high employment, it will stimulate further inflation. If this leads the public to expect more inflation, it will lead lenders to demand higher interest rates to offset the expected inflation. It

---

[4] A technical point: You may ask, Wouldn't an economic system of fully flexible prices suffer a complete breakdown before full employment is restored if aggregate demand falls and cumulative deflation of prices, output, and employment sets in? Not so, say the classicists. Even if a cumulative price deflation set in, as prices fell the real purchasing power of any *fixed* money stock would rise, checking the deflation. This is often called the "Pigou effect," after the famous British economist who stressed it in answering Keynes' argument that underemployment equilibrium could persist in the modern economy. In perspective, much of their difference can be explained by the different assumptions each made about wage and interest flexibilities. As a practical matter, both schools increasingly agree on the crucial importance of avoiding big reductions in M and nominal GNP, whatever the theoretical case that the economy would automatically restore full employment *in the long run*.

will also make borrowers willing to pay higher rates because they can repay in dollars of reduced buying power. The third effect of more M may, therefore, be higher interest rates, not lower ones, as both lenders and borrowers include an "inflation allowance" in their bargains. The final combined effect will depend on the relative size of the three effects.

In fact, rapid increases in M have generally been associated with rising, not falling, interest rates. The 1965–76 period is an example. M, commodity prices, and interest rates all rose rapidly, apparently reflecting strong expectations that more M created by the government would lead to more inflation and hence to substantial inflation allowances by both lenders and borrowers in interest-rate bargains. This direct relationship between changes in M and interest rates is often called the "Gibson paradox." M and interest rates move together rather than in opposite directions, as was postulated in the basic Keynesian analysis.

THE COMPLEX CAUSES OF UNEMPLOYMENT AND INFLATION

Thus, the causes of unemployment and inflation in the real world are more complex than is suggested by the basic neo-Keynesian and monetarist models outlined above. Disequilibrium analysis must be added to them (giving the dynamic business-cycle analysis of Chapter 15); and often unforeseen special factors, like the OPEC oil embargo of 1974, play important roles.

Nearly all economists agree that big swings in aggregate demand are likely to generate big inflations (from excess aggregate demand) and big depressions (from deficient aggregate demand). But this is far from the full story. Neo-Keynesians generally stress changes in aggregate demand in explaining general unemployment. They either play down individual market rigidities as unimportant or accept them as given if they are important, stressing that they can be overcome by assuring the right amount of aggregate demand. The neo-Keynesians generally care most about short-run problems and solutions, not about long-run equilibrium conditions.

By contrast, many neoclassicists consider individual market adjustments the key to understanding why we have unemployment and what must be done to get rid of it. They agree that aggregate demand should be kept growing stably, roughly in step with the growth of productive capacity, since short-run swings in nominal GNP may generate both temporary unemployment and inflation. But increasing aggregate demand, by whatever means, is unlikely to reduce unemployment more than temporarily below its natural rate. To reduce the natural rate of unemployment requires reducing real wage rates relative to demand, and reducing the market imperfections that bar effective matching of workers with jobs. The neoclassicists look primarily to individual markets and long-run equilibrium tendencies.

On inflation, nearly everyone agrees that excess aggregate demand is the biggest immediate cause of big inflations. But again, this is only the beginning of an explanation. What causes the excess demand? The monetarists say, too much money; the neo-Keynesians stress excess private and governmental spending financed by borrowing. But events of the past decade suggest a crucial political-economic process that underlies both. Workers, businessmen, farmers, the elderly, students—nearly everyone has come to want more than he has, and to feel that the government should help him get it if it isn't forthcoming through the market. Unions push for higher wages; farmers and businessmen raise their prices to increase their incomes. When they are unsuccessful in the marketplace, they turn to Washington or their state capitals for help, and very often get it—through farm-aid programs, price-support programs for their commodities, minimum wage laws, welfare payments, food stamps, housing subsidies. Groups unable to raise their incomes through the marketplace—the elderly, students, the poor, many others—turn directly to the government, and government spending goes up accordingly.

If these higher wages and prices threaten to produce recession and unemployment because people price themselves out of markets and jobs, the public now insists that the government raise aggregate demand (through fiscal and monetary policy) to avoid substantial unemployment. And the increased government spending and new M "validate" the higher prices and support the new round of inflation. But everyone then discovers that the inflation has eroded his hoped-for increase in real income, and the stage is set for another round of cost-push and demands for higher government benefits. Thus, the inflation is partly cost-push, partly demand-pull—a combined economic-political process fueled by public insistence on ever-higher real incomes, and by its insistence that these income claims not be permitted to generate unemployment.[5]

Beyond this complex set of forces, special events may intervene. Worldwide bad weather and bad crops in 1972–73, coupled with boom conditions throughout the industrialized world, drove food prices up sharply; and the OPEC oil embargo of 1973–74, following the Arab-Israeli war, quadrupled the world price of oil. These individual price increases should be sharply differentiated from general inflation (an increase in the average of all prices). But they were so large and so important that the government apparently felt it must put more money in the system to avoid the downward pressure on other prices that would have occurred had aggregate demand been held constant as food and energy prices took growing shares of incomes. The result was unprecedented "double-digit" (above 10 percent) inflation.

The political and economic dynamics of inflation are intimately interrelated. Both illustrate the need for attention to the disequilibrium dynamics of individual situations and to special *ad hoc* developments. But these warnings notwithstanding, the basic macroeconomic models of the preceding chapters provide the best simple analytical frameworks for understanding inflation and unemployment in the modern world.

[5] This analysis is developed more thoroughly in Chapter 19, and in G.L. Bach, *The New Inflation* (Englewood Cliffs, N.J.: Prentice-Hall, 1973), Chap. 3.

REVIEW

Concepts to remember

The following new concepts in this chapter are worth careful review:

income vs. asset adjustments
the modern synthesis

interest yields and security prices
disequilibrium analysis
Gibson paradox

For analysis and discussion

1. Suppose the public considers money and bonds to be very close substitutes, but money and goods to be distant substitutes. Would this tend to support the monetarists, or the advocates of the income-expenditures model? Explain.
2. Explain why an equilibrium-level GNP requires equilibrium in *both* the "flow" decisions that consumers and businesses make about their spending *and* their "stock" decisions as to the form in which they hold their assets.
3. In a period of inflation, would you expect an increase in the money stock to lower or to raise interest rates? Would your answer be different in a recession period?
4. Keynes wrote, "In the long run we are all dead. . . ." Is this a fair criticism of equilibrium analysis? Does it convince you that we should concentrate on short-run disequilibrium analysis rather than equilibrium analysis?
5. Explain why differential lags in adjustment to decreases in aggregate demand for wages–prices as against output–employment tend to undercut the classical full-employment equilibrium analysis.
6. If the final section of this chapter is correct, would you describe inflation as primarily an economic or a political phenomenon? Explain.

A severe recession has hit the economy. Unemployment has risen to 7 percent and profits are sagging. Just about everyone agrees that we need more aggregate demand.

Your congressman, no economist, is home from Washington, sounding out public opinion. He says that, as usual, the experts can't seem to agree on what to do. They agree that another $40–$50 billion of aggregate demand is needed quickly to get unemployment back down to 5 percent, but they propose at least three different approaches to getting it. One group says, "Increase government spending on urban renewal, the environment, public health, and the like. They're all high-priority social goals, and another $20 billion of government spending with a multiplier of 2 should just about do the job, helping everyone and hurting no one, since, of course, taxes should not be raised."

A second group says, "No way! The government is spending too much already. The thing to do is cut taxes by $20 billion or so. With the same multiplier of 2, this will give the desired increase in aggregate demand, and will give back to the people the freedom to spend their incomes on what they want most, rather than having the government tell them what they ought to want."

A third group has a different angle. "Let monetary policy do the job," they say. "Let the Federal Reserve increase the money stock by $10 billion or so. Given the nation's income velocity of about 5 for the last several years, this will increase aggregate demand by about $50 billion. Either the Fed can put the money in circulation by buying up bonds from the public, or the money can be lent to the government (the Treasury) and given out in the form of unemployment relief—or, indeed, in any other way you like, since the basic objective is to get the money into the public's hands."

What is your advice to your congressman? What policy, or combination of policies, do you propose? Be specific in your proposal, as to the amount of any action to be taken and your reasons for believing it will do the job better than the other approaches will.

CHAPTER 15 BUSINESS CYCLES

The long pull of American economic growth is impressive. But that growth has come spasmodically, in spurts separated by recessions and sometimes major depressions. In perspective, the booms and depressions of American history are fluctuations around a long-term growth trend. And this is the right way to look at them. For seldom has the trough of a recession been lower than the peak of the next boom before it. Growth dominates fluctuations in our history. But this doesn't mean that repeated booms and depressions have been unimportant. Far from it!

We turn now to look at business cycles—at a dynamic world of cumulative upward and downward sweeps that generate inflation and unemployment in repeated booms and depressions. It is a disequilibrium world.

GROWTH AND FLUCTUATIONS IN AMERICA

The long sweep of growth in America, interrupted by repeated recessions, is shown by the top lines of the graph inside the front cover. Figure 7–5, in the introductory overview of macroeconomics, pointed up both characteristics another way; look back at it. The fluctuations of real GNP around its growth rate of some 3–4 percent per year are bounded on the top and bottom by two trend lines, roughly connecting the peaks of the booms and the troughs of the depressions. Growth is the basic process, with the economy pushing up toward the bounds of productive capacity in boom periods and falling short in recessions. The vertical shaded areas are recession periods. Note that the upswing periods are substantially longer than the shaded (recession) areas.[1]

One way of studying economic fluctuations is to separate the fluctuations from the long-term upward trend, or growth. Figure 15–1 does this for industrial production, a volatile sector of the modern American economy. To construct the figure, we first draw a "trend" line through the actual monthly data for industrial production (per capita) over the period, a rapidly but irregularly rising series. A trend line is a line drawn roughly through the middle of the fluctuating series—so that the readings on the industrial-production curve above the trend line about equal those below it.[2] If, then, we lay the trend line out flat, it becomes the zero line in Figure 15–1. Thus, periods when industrial production was above the trend line are shown above zero, and conversely for those below.

All the data are shown as percentage deviations from trend. Thus, moderately prosperous 1964 runs about 10 percent above "normal," as do the similar years 1905–07. In absolute terms, of course, industrial production in 1964 was many times more than in 1905–07. The vast area below normal in the 1930s and that above nor-

mal in the 1960s on the chart are thus far smaller in comparison with earlier cycles than they would be plotted as absolute, rather than percentage, deviations.

The anatomy of economic fluctuations

The big booms and depressions in America have all involved major swings in real GNP, employment, and money income. The great depressions, like that of the 1930s, have meant massive unemployment, vast idle factories, financial disaster for millions, endless days of desperate job hunting, hunger, and malnutrition. Most college students today cannot remember a great depression, for they have never seen one.[3] Perhaps there will never be another, but we cannot be sure. The big booms have been the opposite—more jobs than workers, soaring wages and prices, big profits, speculation on the stock market, good times for nearly everyone, but uncertainty about how long it will all last. Happily, business fluctuations since World War II have been much milder than during the 1930s and 1940s.

Figure 15–2 shows unemployment and three major components of real GNP in the United States over the past half century. Production of durable goods (steel, electrical machinery, automobiles, refrigerators) fluctuates far more than

---

[1]The top of the World War II boom (1942–45) is shown above the dashed line because the economy was then clearly operating beyond its normal capacity level. Housewives, old people, and children were temporarily pulled into the labor force, and workers were called on for vast amounts of overtime to meet wartime production goals.

[2]Any elementary statistics book will provide information on the statistical techniques used in "fitting" trend lines to data. There are several techniques, which may be considred substantially equivalent for our purposes.

[3]Some "feel" of the Great Depression is provided by Chapter 7. For more detail, see "Black Depression," in Frederick L. Allen, *Only Yesterday* (New York: Harper & Row, 1939); and the dreary, desperate saga, "Job Hunters," in E.W. Bakke, *The Unemployed Worker* (New Haven, Conn.: Yale University Press, 1940).

Figure 15–1
The curve shows percentage deviations from the long-term upward trend of U.S. industrial production. Areas above the zero line are above the trend, and conversely for areas below it. (Source: Cleveland Trust Company.)

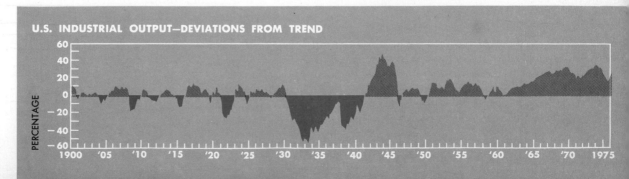

U.S. INDUSTRIAL OUTPUT—DEVIATIONS FROM TREND

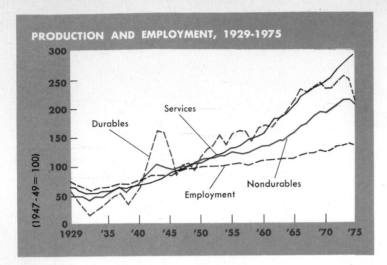

300
250
200
150
100
50
0

(1947-49 = 100)

Services

Durables

Employment

Nondurables

1929 '35 '40 '45 '50 '55 '60 '65 '70 '75

Figure 15-2
The major components of production and employment fluctuate roughly together, but with very different amplitudes. All curves except "Employment" show actual production, with 1947–49 = 100. Note the big fluctuations in the production of durables. (Source: U.S. Department of Commerce.)

the other series. Fluctuations are much milder in shoes, clothing, food, and other nondurable consumer goods. And the stability of spending on services is remarkable; the growth curve hardly wobbles since the 1930s. This does not mean that services and nondurable-consumer-goods industries are unaffected by cyclical fluctuations, but the heart of the problem lies in the durable-goods industries. In analyzing business cycles, many economists prefer to focus on a few big, critical measures, like real GNP, employment, industrial production, investment, and prices; but it is important never to forget the great complexity of the real world.

Are there business cycles—regularly recurring booms and recessions? By now the answer should be clear. It is no, if you stress the "regularly." Some upswings are long and strong, others short and weak. Some recessions are mild, others become massive depressions. But the answer is yes, if you mean only that there are intermittent periods of prosperity and recession.

BUSINESS-CYCLE THEORY

Ever since booms and depressions began, people have been trying to figure out why they occur. Different writers have emphasized everything from sunspots to Wall Street as the primary cause of booms and depressions. A theory that seems to explain all business cycles

176

simply and neatly is heady stuff. But alas, no one has come up with one simple theory that does the job. However, there is substantial agreement among many economists on an analytical framework for looking at the dynamically interacting variables.

This is the framework provided by Chapters 9 through 14. It tells us to focus on changes in aggregate demand relative to the economy's growing productive capacity. Aggregate demand is made up of consumption and investment spending (if we temporarily ignore government spending), and these in turn are influenced by the supply of money and interest rates. Booms are dynamic, cumulative processes in which increased investment stimulates more consumption, which in turn raises business sales and profits and stimulates more investment. This upsweep of demand often outruns productive capacity, generates inflation, and overshoots sustainable levels, precipitating a downturn. Similarly, depressions are cumulative downward processes in which the dynamic interaction between contracting consumption and contracting investment is the core of the downswing. In both booms and depressions, money plays an important role, both in stimulating swings in aggregate demand and in checking cumulative swings in either direction.

We shall, therefore, focus on these three major variables (consumption, investment, and money) and on their dynamic interactions. They comprise a dynamic disequilibrium system, where movement toward equilibrium in consumption, investment, and money balances changes the equilibrium values themselves. It is the dynamic interaction among these three major variables, sometimes strongly affected by government policy and by random shocks such as wars, that is the essence of "business cycles."

The model above leaves the government out, since we want to consider government policy separately in the following chapters. But don't forget that government purchases and transfer payments total over 30 percent of GNP, and taxes withdraw a comparable amount from the payments stream. Moreover, government control of the money supply exerts a major influence on the economy. And, as we shall see, sometimes the government's fiscal and monetary policies can be destabilizing as well as stabilizing.

THE CUMULATIVE UPSWING

Assume that something happens to start an upswing from a recession—perhaps a new product is developed. In examining the upswing, note how each expansive factor gradually develops self-limiting tendencies, which increasingly act to put a ceiling on the prosperity and to turn the economy down into recession.

Rising consumption

Rising incomes are the main foundation for rising consumption spending in the upswing. Consumption spending rises primarily because incomes rise. If new investment spending triggers an upswing, this will generate more income and consumer spending through the multiplier. Just how much consumption rises for each dollar of new investment depends, of course, on the "leakages" through saving (and taxes) in each round of spending. Apparently a multiplier of 2 or so is probable in the American economy; remember, it's the relation of consumption spending to GNP, not to disposable personal income, that provides the relevant multiplier for explaining GNP.

The ratio of consumption to disposable income tends to be high in depressions; people are able to save very little. If the *marginal* propensity to consume is high, the multiplier will be relatively large. As incomes rise into prosperity, though, the marginal propensity to save typically rises, reducing the multiplier on each additional investment dollar.

As the economy comes out of a depression, more spendable income is the only thing likely to give a major boost to consumption spending. But consumption is not completely passive. If the revival takes hold, at least three special factors may increase the marginal propensity to consume and the resultant multiplier.

First, consumers may have a backlog demand for consumer durables—refrigerators, stoves, autos, and radios—piled up from the depression. You can use the same refrigerator a long time if you're good at minor repairs and don't mind foregoing the latest improvements. But try as you will to avoid it, the day will come when you have to buy another refrigerator or have the food spoil in hot weather. The postponement of purchases of durable goods is one reason why recessions last. Catching up on these postponed purchases is one of the big lifts in revival.

Second, as prices begin to rise in revival, consumers may begin to expect still higher prices ahead. Expectations of rising prices can speed consumer buying, but this is a boost we can't count on with any confidence until the upswing is well under way.

Third, as times improve, consumer credit may become more readily available to marginal borrowers. Such credit premits consumers to spend more in relation to current income than they otherwise might.

But remember: Rising consumption in the upswing depends largely on rising incomes, and thus indirectly on rising investment or government spending.

Rising investment

The "accelerator." Rising consumer spending means rising sales for businesses. This will deplete inventories and push firms toward capacity limits in factories and stores. Thus, rising sales sooner or later will stimulate more investment. This effect of more consumption spending in inducing more investment is called the "accelerator." It provides the link to complete the cumulative interaction in the upswing: more investment → more income → more consumption → more investment, and so on. In summary, the upswing is a cumulative multiplier-accelerator process.[4]

Unless the original burst of investment and its multiplied effect on consumption in turn induce more investment, there will be no cumulative upswing—only a hump on the floor of the depression. But if the rise in consumer spending does produce a substantial accelerator effect, then the revival is on. The further induced investment in turn produces its multiplier effect, which in its turn induces further investment. If both the multiplier and the accelerator are large, any revival that gets started will be an explosive one, with consumption and investment interacting vigorously. If either is zero, that's the end of the upswing.

How strong will the accelerator in fact be? The answer is, different at different times. Rising incomes and sales will induce new investment whenever they make the **desired** amount of plant and equipment larger than the **actual** amount on hand. Thus, if sales rise and the producer has no excess productive capacity, his desired stock of plant and equipment will clearly exceed his present stock, because without more capacity he can't meet the expanding demand. But if he begins with excess capacity, he has more plant and equipment than he currently needs, so even increased sales won't necessarily raise his desired stock above what he has.

Pragmatically, when the economy is just emerging from a serious recession, the outlook for a large accelerator effect from rising sales is bad, for two reasons:

1. Idle capacity is widespread during depression, and moderate increases in demand can often be met by using existing idle equipment.
2. Businessmen, whatever the capacity situation is, may cautiously wait to see whether the increased demand is permanent. If they do, no acceleration effect will occur. Their desired stock of capital depends on the permanence they attach to the increased demand.

But if revival progresses and idle capacity vanishes, further increases in consumer spending are more and more likely to stimulate new investment. History and theory both suggest that the acceleration effect can be powerful.[5]

The accelerator can account for a substantial part of increases in investment as consumption rises. But not for all of them. Some other determinants of the cyclical behavior of investment may be at least as important.

Shifting Cost–Price Relationships. Early in the upswing, profit margins expand as selling prices rise faster than costs, but as the upswing continues, this relationship reverses. Thus, shifting cost–price relationships (differential legs in adjustment) first stimulate business investment, but later discourage it.

When a revival is just beginning, businessmen can increase output and build new plants without incurring higher construction or unit operating costs—because there is still a lot of unemployed plant capacity and manpower in the economy. Costs stay low as demand and prices rise in the upswing; unemployment tends to hold wage rates down, and higher plant-operating rates tend to reduce costs per unit of output in existing plants. Profit margins widen, increasing the marginal efficiency of capital and providing more funds to finance new investment.

But as the boom sweeps upward, excess capacity and unemployment vanish. Increasingly, both operating costs (for example, wages and materials) and the cost of money (interest rates) rise. Thus, the return on investment is squeezed by rising costs as the boom progresses. Businessmen complain about the "profit squeeze," and about the shortage of profits to finance new plant and equipment.

Rising labor costs in prosperity also stimulate businessmen to invest in labor-saving equipment.

---

[4]Appendix B to this chapter presents a formal model of the cumulative multiplier-accelerator process that shows that under certain (not unrealistic) conditions, the combination of accelerator and multiplier effects can induce cyclical fluctuations in GNP even when the original stimulus of investment does not fluctuate.

[5]In some cases, as more advanced texts explain, an increase in comsumer demand may stimulate a much more than proportional increase in investment spending on plant and equipment.

This fact helps account for large business investments sometimes even when there is substantial excess manufacturing capacity. Such investment does not contradict the comments about the acceleration principle above; it merely indicates that there are many different factors that influence investment decisions.

Innovation and the development of new industries. Historically, most big booms have centered around the development of a few important new industries. For example, during the 1800s, railroad building, with the resultant demand for iron and steel products, was especially important. The boom of the 1920s centered around the auto and electrical industries. Actually, the inventions underlying these industries had been made years before. It was the utilization of these inventions on a large scale through developmental investment that produced the booms they dominated. And when the investment opportunities surrounding these new industries were temporarily exploited, the central thrust of the boom was gone.

Was the development of new industries at those particular times induced by the revivals then beginning, or were the revivals created by new industries? Both. Whether such innovations actually set off a revival or not, they play an important role in most major booms. Once a few entrepreneurs have successfully braved the uncertain paths by introducing new products and new methods, others are eager to follow. With big new industries, booms are long and lusty. Without them, prosperities are weaker and growth slows down.

Inventory investment and the inventory cycle. Many business cycles are predominantly inventory cycles. When inventories become scarce relative to rising sales, businessmen try to build inventories back up to desired levels. Businesses tend to overbuy in building them up, because at first, sales continue to grow faster than they can replace their falling inventories. Thus, businessmen sharply increase their orders and usually overshoot what they consider desirable inventories when inventories do begin to catch up with sales. Trying to unload these excess inventories, they generally overshoot again, but downward, plummeting themselves into a position where inventories are short—and they're all ready to start up again.

When businesses are accumulating inventories, production is running ahead of consumption. Obviously, this can go on only for so long; the day of reckoning must come. Conversely, when business inventories are declining, consumption is running ahead of production. Obviously, this too can go on for only so long. Over the long pull, inventories can be expected to rise roughly with the growth in total sales—perhaps 4 percent a year, assuming no inflation. You can be pretty sure that inventory accumulation a lot faster than that won't last for long. And you can equally suspect that if inventory growth falls far short of that rate, inventory investment will fuel an upswing in the near future.

Figure 15–3 shows the persistence and vigor of these inventory fluctuations. Note that the chart shows changes in *net* inventory investment, in accordance with the national income accounts. Thus, any figure above the zero line shows inventories building up; any figure below zero shows inventories being depleted. If you compare Figure 15–3 with the earlier data on total investment and GNP, you'll see that net inventory investment changes alone account for much of the recession drops of 1949, 1954, 1958, 1960, 1970, and 1974, and for the upswings in 1950, 1955, 1958, 1961, 1966, and 1973. If, as some argue, we are beginning to get major cyclical fluctuations under control, the inventory cycle may be our stickiest remaining cyclical problem.

Money in the upswing

The cumulative upswing in production, employment, and income may be financed by the existing money stock for a while, as businesses and consumers draw on "idle" balances and V rises. But before long, new money is needed to finance the growing volume of business. Businesses need more working capital to expand operations, and longer-term funds to finance new investment in plant and equipment. With higher incomes, consumers want to hold larger money balances. On all sides, the demand for money rises.

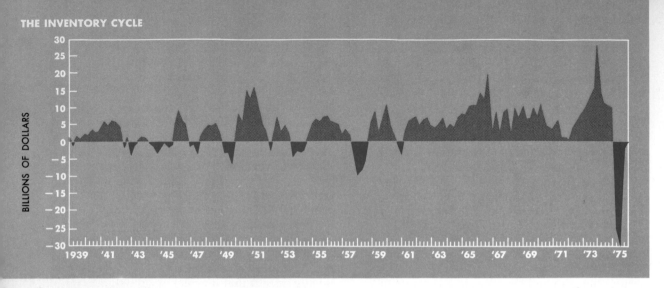

Figure 15-3
The inventory cycle shows large, sharp fluctuations in inventory investment, which are a major factor in most smaller swings in aggregate economic activity. Note especially the 1974–75 swing. (Source: U.S. Department of Commerce.)

Will the rising demand for money be met by more M, or will it result in higher interest rates and a growing drag on the upswing process? The commercial banks and, behind them, the government (through the Federal Reserve) are the only source of new money for the system as a whole, as we shall see in Chapter 17. Early in the upswing, as demands for loans increase and as better times lessen the apparent risks in lending, bankers are glad to expand loans. But as revival progresses and banks' excess reserves are used up, interest rates rise and bankers begin to "ration" their remaining credit to preferred borrowers. As businesses and households pile up ever-larger debts, they become less attractive borrowers for new loans. Unless the Federal Reserve provides more money for the system, credit stringency will gradually impose a ceiling on the upswing as businesses cannot borrow the money they need to expand, and consumer credit tightens.

The ceiling is not a firm one. As money tightens and interest rates rise, businesses and families increasingly economize on the money balances they hold. When working capital is scarce, corporate treasurers squeeze their idle cash down to the lowest possible levels. Households put their unneeded money to work in securities or other ways when interest rates offered on such investments rise. Thus, V rises and partially offsets the credit ceiling imposed by a shortage of money. But there are limits on how small cash balances can be and still meet the needs of expanding businesses. Only provision of more money by the Federal Reserve can keep the boom going. **Every major upswing has been marked by a substantial increase in the volume of bank credit and money, and in velocity.**

UPPER TURNING POINTS: CAN PROSPERITY CONTINUE FOREVER?

Prosperity is wonderful. Why can't it go on forever? If only we ensure enough M, won't the cumulative multiplier-accelerator process move the economy up to full employment, and keep it there? Both theory and history warn us against too much optimism.

The cumulative upswing is many-sided and interacting. Early in the rise, everything seems to work together toward prosperity. But as the boom continues, the economic system becomes increasingly vulnerable to shocks that may precipitate a downturn, especially if the upswing is a rapid one. Inflationary booms in particular typically produce distorted patterns of activity that are difficult to maintain indefinitely.

What actually turns economic activity downward? Sometimes there is a spectacular financial crisis, as in 1907 and 1929. But economic change

is complex, and often some phases of economic activity turn down while others are still moving strongly upward. Sometimes it is hard to say whether the economy is still moving up or has turned down; it depends on where you look.

So the experts are wary of predicting just what particular factor will trigger the downturn. Rather, a series of developments gradually sets the stage for a downswing, and in such a setting it becomes increasingly likely that something will give the push that turns the economy down, even though we may not recognize it until months later.

The main limiting factors on the upswing appear to be:

1. Accumulation of large stocks of new durables in consumers' hands, including housing
2. Consumer resistance to rising prices
3. Piling up of business inventories
4. End of the upward "acceleration" effect, and resulting slowdown in investment spending[6]
5. Rising costs and profit squeeze
6. Accumulation of new productive capacity
7. Utilization of available new technological developments, and growing scarcity of promising large-scale investment outlets

[6] In the multiplier-accelerator model in Appendix B to this chapter, the accelerator alone is sufficient to generate upper and lower turning points in GNP.

8. Pileup of business and consumer debt
9. Exhaustion of excess bank reserves
10. Weakening of confidence and expectations

Sometimes a boom keeps going until it faces all these hurdles simultaneously. Sometimes the downturn comes when only two or three seem to present serious problems. Basically, the boom ends when the entire conjuncture gradually shifts over from favorable to unfavorable—when the driving forces of the upswing (especially spending on investment and consumer durables) give way to disappointed expectations in the face of increasingly saturated markets. In general, the faster and stronger the rise in GNP, the more likely it is to overshoot.

All this has left the government out of the picture. Yet increasingly, government action is a critical consideration in turning points. Government fiscal and Federal Reserve monetary policy may help avoid a downturn and recession; but badly timed, they may make matters worse instead of better. Such government action is the focus of attention in the next five chapters. If we are to achieve stable high employment without inflation, it's clear we will often need positive government assistance to turn the trick.

"And so, extrapolating from the best figures available, we see that current trends, unless dramatically reversed, will inevitably lead to a situation in which the sky will fall." (Drawing by Lorenz; © 1972. The New Yorker Magazine, Inc.)

THE DOWNSWING

A recession looks much like a boom in reverse. Once the downturn occurs, the multiplier and accelerator work downward instead of upward. Decreasing investment pulls out the support for a multiplied amount of income. Falling incomes mean falling consumption expenditures, which in turn reduce the incentive to invest. Once-attractive loans turn sour. The upward spiral that made hearts glad seems diabolically designed as it races downward into depression.

Once a downswing gets under way, the path toward depression may be direct and cumulative. Businessmen, somewhat disappointed in sales and profits as prosperity levels off, are uneasy. Under such conditions, it takes only a downturn in expectations to undermine investment and production plans. Attempts to unload inventories and to obtain cash lead to the very price declines that sellers are trying to "beat," and to still worse expectations for the future. Banks call for repayment of loans, and the money stock declines or grows more slowly. Once it is well started down, a downward-spiralling disequilibrium system may be very hard to check.

On the other hand, not all downturns turn into major depressions, just as not all recoveries soar into full-fledged booms. Since World War II, sustained consumer spending on non-durables and services has proved a massive block against a downward spiral. Business investment in plant and equipment has become more resistant to panic cutbacks. Government spending now provides a big, stable block of demand, and government tax and expenditure systems automatically lead to quick tax-liability reductions when incomes fall and to increased unemployment-compensation transfer payments. Private unemployment-insurance plans supplement this support. And the Federal Reserve has learned to keep the money stock growing to avoid financial collapse.

SOME SPECIAL FACTORS

The role of the stock market

In spite of its prominent position in the public eye, the stock market has generally played only a modest role in business cycles. Rising security prices do help to speed the upswing, and a collapse of prices on the stock market may help set off or intensify a downswing. But often these events bring more newspaper headlines than are justified by their importance in determining real output and employment.

The stock market has four main channels of impact. First, one big effect is psychological—a symbol of better or worse times for businessmen and the general public. Second, rising stock prices mean paper profits (increased wealth) for stockholders. With more wealth, at least on paper, stockholders may spend more out of their incomes or out of capital gains. Conversely, the big stock-market drop of 1973–74 wiped out over $500 billion of nominal wealth, and may have reduced consumption substantially. Third, from the point of view of corporations, higher stock prices mean a lower cost of capital for expansion. If a firm needs long-term funds, it can sell new stock at a higher price; that is, it can obtain new funds at a lower cost for the money obtained. Fourth, if rising stock prices have been heavily financed by borrowed money, a downturn in the market may precipitate a major collapse in stock prices as lenders call for cash, and may place serious financial pressure on banks and other lenders. A high market based on credit is thus far more vulnerable than a "cash" market, and is more likely to be a cyclically destabilizing force.[7]

Stock prices have usually led cyclical movements in general business, although by no definite lead. And financial crisis has often characterized the upper turning point of the cycle. But with reforms in our financial system since the crash of 1929, financial crises seem likely to play

[7]For a lively, popular account of the crash of 1929, see J.K. Galbraith, *The Great Crash* (Boston: Houghton Mifflin, 1955).

a less prominent role in the future. For example, severe stock-market breaks in 1962 and 1970 failed to trigger major depressions.

International aspects of business fluctuations

One component of gross investment omitted above is net foreign investment. Current excess of exports over imports represents a net demand for U.S. output. It represents jobs and goods produced in this country that do not move into current U.S. consumption, like inventories accumulated by domestic businesses. Such a net export balance provides employment and incomes in the United States, just as does domestic investment; it is called the "foreign-trade multiplier." The main difference is that with foreign investment, the goods produced go abroad rather than being used domestically, and, as we shall see later, there are some special forces limiting the foreign-trade multiplier.

How important is the foreign-trade multi-plier? Not very, most of the time. The U.S. net export surplus has seldom exceeded $5-$10 billion, a fraction of 1 percent of GNP. But the world's economies are increasingly linked together through trade and investment, so business cycles in any major country are likely to be exported to other nations. We shall return to the whole problem of international interactions in detail in Part Six.

BUSINESS CYCLES AND STABILIZATION POLICY

Can we have rapid, stable growth without booms and depressions in our basically private-enterprise, profit-motivated economy? Look back at Figure 15–1. History warns against overoptimism, unless we've learned how to turn the trick through government monetary and fiscal policy. Some economists think we have. The time has come to look in detail at the prospects and the problems of stabilization policy.

REVIEW

Concepts to remember

This chapter reuses most of the important concepts introduced in Chapters 9–14. In addition to those, be sure you have a firm understanding of the following:

business cycle	inventory cycle
boom	innovation
recession and depression	cycle turning points
deviations from trend	foreign-trade multiplier
accelerator	

For analysis and discussion

1. Explain how consumption and investment interact in an upswing, and also at upper turning points of business cycles.
2. What is the accelerator? What, if any, is its relationship to the multiplier?
3. Why do businesses often face a "profit squeeze" as full employment is reached in strong booms?
4. Why can't a boom go on forever? Or can it? If your answer is yes, what change promises to make the future different from the past?
5. One group of business-cycle analysts argues that booms and depressions are caused

by expansions and contractions in the quantity of money. Can you see any important weaknesses in this argument? If so, what are they?

6. "The bigger the boom, the bigger the bust." Is this often-heard statement true or false? Support your answer by a careful analysis of reasons why or why not.

7. The following factors, it is generally agreed, play important roles in cyclical upswings. Analyze how the force of each changes as national income rises from depression levels to prosperity, and how each gradually helps set the stage for the upper turning point:

    a. The public's propensity to consume

    b. Consumer and business price expectations

    c. Induced investment (the accelerator effect)

    d. Cost–price relationships as they affect investment

    e. Inventory levels

    f. Consumer and business "psychology"

    g. The banking system

8. How many factors can you list that might reasonably be expected to provide a strong impetus to an upswing from a long, deep depression? Evaluate the likely force of each.

During the sharp recession of 1974–75, the following special report appeared in the *New York Times,* arguing that massive inventory liquidation was worsening the recession but that at the same time it was a bright omen for the future. Was the *Times* analysis good economics? Can inventory liquidation simultaneously be the cause of deepening recession and a source of recovery to come?

Impact of inventories[8]   In almost every recession there comes a time when the tail wags the dog. For the current recession, the deepest in decades, that time is now. The tail, so far, is a $36-billion swing in inventory levels. The enormous United States economy, with a gross national product of $1.4 trillion, is the dog.

For the next year or so, what happens to the tail is going to be most important to the dog.

That, say the analysts, was the meaning of the first quarter's record-breaking 10.4 percent slide in overall economic activity, announced recently by the Commerce Department.

[8] By Soma Golden, *New York Times,* April 25, 1975. Reproduced by permission.

Without the dramatic cutback in business inventories that occurred during the first quarter, the economy would have remained flat at December's depressed level. Instead, in the effort to unload unwanted inventories, business cut production further, unemployment rose higher and the recession moved into its second spring.

Analysts comment   Yet economists were cheered. "The inventory figures are absolutely marvelous—the best thing that could have happened," said Morris Cohen, chief economist with the investment management firm of Schroder, Naess & Thomas.

"It's the most important news of the last month," said A. Gary Shilling, first vice-president and economist with White, Weld & Co., an investment banking firm. "A big inventory liquidation is the source of a big recovery later on," said the economist.

According to such logic, the economy will not charge ahead until the inventory correction that is under way slows down. Business activity will not pick up, analysts say, until firms have managed to trim their inventories enough to match sluggish sales.

APPENDIX A

Economic forecasting

All economic policy, public or private, involves making forecasts about the future. If the government is to help stabilize the economy, it must know whether next year promises unemployment or a boom. The businessman must forecast his sales for months ahead to plan purchases of materials, inventory levels, and sales quotas for his marketing department. He must forecast years ahead if he is to make his long-range plans soundly—when to expand plant and equipment, when the firm will need to obtain additional capital funds, what his needs will be for managers, engineers, and the like. Thus, both the government and the businessman have to make economic forecasts, like it or not.

How well can we forecast? How well can we forecast, using the models of the preceding chapters or other approaches as a foundation? First, no one can forecast **precisely** very far into the future, no matter how glibly he talks or how much he charges for his services. Second, real experts, using the latest tools and the mass of statistical data now available, can do a reasonably reliable job for perhaps six months to a year ahead for overall activity (say, GNP), but the reliability goes down rapidly as the distance into the future increases. Third, especially for longer-term forecasts, it is realistic to recognize that ranges (say, a GNP between $200 and $210 billion higher for two years hence) are more reliable forecasts than those that pick a specific figure. Your economics should tell you that economic fluctuations are complex, ever-changing phenomena, and that there is no foolproof way to predict the economy, even six months ahead. Beware of the forecaster who has the surefire answer!

GNP models—judgmental forecasts Most economists (in industry, government, and universities) now use the GNP accounts as a framework, and try to estimate each major component separately. Then they fit the parts together to see whether they are consistent, and check for likely interactions that may

have been missed in studying the individual parts. Chapter 8 provides the breakdown commonly used (although many forecasters look in considerably more detail); and Chapters 10–15 indicate most of the interrelationships among the major variables that forecasters typically work with.

For example, nearly everyone forecasts separately private investment, consumer expenditures, and government expenditures to get GNP. Then they need separate estimates on government taxes and depreciation accounts to get to national income, and estimates of transfer payments and personal income taxes to get to disposable personal income.

How, for example, do they forecast that volatile item, business investment? For plant and equipment spending, we now have businessmen's own forecasts of their investment spending a year ahead, collected and published regularly by the U.S. Department of Commerce and others. These figures give a fairly good short-run bench mark. Forecasters check them to see whether projected spending is way out of line with historical relationships to, say, consumer buying of final goods. We know that investment seldom booms when there is substantial unused capacity. And we know that businessmen typically underestimate their reactions to upturns or downturns in aggregate demand.

For investment in inventories, we also have the published plans of businessmen from time to time. But these forecasts have proved less reliable. We need to look at the ratio of inventories to sales in relation to historical standards, at whether purchasers are facing full-capacity production conditions that may force them to wait for deliveries, and at how fast businesses have been accumulating or using up inventories over the past year or two. Over the long pull, businesses won't continue to produce large inventories they don't sell. Nor will they be willing to deplete their inventories below what they consider sound business levels. On the average, we can expect that total inventories will grow at somewhere near the same rate as total sales in the economy.

To finish forecasting private investment, forecasters do a separate analysis of home construction, of foreign investment, and so on in detail for all investment categories.

Similarly, they estimate consumer spending from different sides, and thus cross-check. The University of Michigan's Survey Research Center examines consumer buying attitudes and intentions quarterly and publishes the results. These give some clues. But consumer spending mainly depends on the disposable income consumers receive, plus the special factors noted in Chapter 12.

Then they look at the government—at tax and expenditure rates, at monetary-policy expectations, at special government activities in any field that might affect economic activity. The federal budget calls for careful attention, because federal spending and tax receipts exercise such a big effect on the economy. Happily, the government publishes detailed estimates semiannually.

Put this analysis of the individual categories together in the national income accounts, cross-check to see whether the individual estimates appear consistent with one another, apply liberal doses of judgment if something doesn't look reasonable, and you have a fairly typical GNP judgmental forecast.[9]

Large econometric models The fastest-growing modern forecasting method evolves out of the preceding one. It is the use of econometric models. It uses the same variables and relationships as those in the preceding paragraphs, but bases the relationships on statistical studies of past experience, and then obtains final estimates of the dependent variables (say, GNP and unemployment) by using a computer to solve the set of equations in the econometric model, which, in essence, assumes that the statistically validated relationships of the past will hold in the future.

The method of econometric models was outlined in the appendix to Chapter 11. Modern forecasters have put together large models, including as many as 200–300 equations describing the behavior of different parts of the economy. Each of these equations is "estimated" by statistically analyzing past experience. Then they are all combined and solved simultaneously on a large computer, producing estimates of future GNP, all its major components, and a multitude of other variables, such as prices, interest rates, and the like.[10]

There are about a half dozen such basic large econometric models now in operation, plus a number of modifications of them. Some of the best known are the Federal Reserve Board's model in Washington (which is only partly revealed to the public), a much smaller model run by the Department of Commerce, and four private models—those of a group of MIT and Penn economists (who also cooperated in developing the Federal Reserve model); Data Resources, Inc. (developed and run mainly by Harvard economists); Chase Econometric Service (connected with the Chase Manhattan Bank); and the Wharton Econometric Model (developed and run mainly by University of Pennsylvania economists). The last three sell use of their models to many business and financial firms—either as simple forecasts, or on a more complex basis in which the buyer can specify his own assumptions and investigate alternative forecasts. There are other smaller models.

It is important to see that even with such large econometric models, forecasting is far from a mechanical task in which one just plugs in the computer and out comes the answer. Each large model has dozens of key equations and autonomous variables on which reasonable experts can differ for the year or years ahead. And the experts using the big models make judgmental adjustments all the time, when answers come out that don't look reasonable or when they believe key relationships have changed. A big part of success in forecasting still lies in these judgmental adjustments.

How good are the big models? For forecasting such global variables as GNP, pretty good, but no better than simpler ones that use only a few equations. Often, in fact, shrewd, simple-model judgmental forecasters do better, because the big-model users can't figure out just why the assumptions fed in are producing the strange results they sometimes get; the human mind simply can't trace through that many simultaneous interactions. But for examining the interrelationships of dozens of lesser variables, the big models are essential. And the method is clearly one that promises better ultimate understanding of the economy. Only hard empirical testing of the relationships among the key variables can give us a reliable basis for making forecasts in our complex economic system.

Leading indicators A last approach emphasizes leads and lags. The National Bureau of Economic Research has studied the behavior of hundreds of economic series in business fluctuations since the middle 1800s, and has found that some economic series usually lead others. Typically, leading series include construction contracts, new orders for pro-

---

[9] The "Business Roundup" in *Fortune* each January provides a good example of this approach.

[10] A reasonably simple description and explanation of such a model is given in "A Quarterly Econometric Model of the United States," *Survey of Current Business,* May 1966.

ducers' durables, new business incorporations, length of the workweek in manufacturing, common-stock prices, and business failures (inverted). No one alone is reliable, but if most or all of the so-called leading indicators are moving up or down together, this suggests that other parts of the economy will probably follow. Since most leading series exhibit irregular jags from month to month, it's often hard to separate out the false signals from the real ones. For very short-range forecasts, the leading indicators now provide valuable forecasting evidence, especially when interpreted by the experts. But don't be misled by the newspaper accounts; the leading indicators fall far short of providing a layman's guide to the future.[11]

Input-output models Economists have also developed elaborate "input-output" models of the economy that show, for past U.S. census years, the interrelations among the sales, materials, and labor utilization of hundreds of different industries. These

[11] The leading, coincident, and lagging series are now published monthly by the U.S. Department of Commerce in *Business Conditions Digest,* together with a substantial amount of related information.

interrelations are shown as matrices, listing the industries involved across the top and down the side of the matrix. One cell then shows, for example, how much steel the auto industry buys from the steel industry to produce $1 million worth of autos. The relevant steel-industry cell shows how much coal the steel industry would buy to produce that steel, and so on for thousands of interlinkages in the economy.

While the statistical work involved in making such an input-output matrix is enormous, the principle is simple. If the interindustry relationships are reasonably stable over time, the matrix can forecast the effects of, say, a billion dollars of new government spending on highways next year on all the industries in the country that will be affected. The same is true for any other change in demand. Input-output, or interindustry, economics is one of the exciting new frontiers of economic forecasting.[12]

[12] For further information, see W. Leontief, "Structure of the American Economy," *Scientific American,* April 1965. A good recent text on forecasting is W. Butler, R. Kavesh, and R. Plant, *Methods and Techniques of Business Forecasting* (Englewood, N.J.: Prentice-Hall, 1974), especially Part II.

APPENDIX B

A formal multiplier-accelerator model

This appendix presents a simple formal model to illustrate the types of dynamic interaction that may occur between the multiplier and the accelerator. It will be most interesting to those who like precise, theoretical reasoning, and especially to those who know some mathematics.

Suppose, in Table 15–1, that we begin with national income at 1,000. Now (say, because there is a temporary war scare), businesses increase their investment rate by 100 in periods 1 and 2. The war scare then vanishes, and businessmen are prepared to drop their investment spending back to the original level. What will be the impact of this temporary surge of new investment?

Assume, for this example, that the marginal propensity to consume is .8 out of the income of the **preceding** period (perhaps a more reasonable as-

sumption than that consumption is related to **current** income). Assume also that businessmen are led to make new investments in inventories and plants when sales improve, and that such new induced, accelerator-type investment is just equal to the rise in consumption during the preceding time period.

On the basis of these **illustrative** assumptions, now trace through the dynamic results of this original surge of assumed autonomous business investment.

In Table 15–1, the 100 of new autonomous investment in period 1 becomes income to its recipients in that period, raising the period 1 total-income level to 1,100. The rise in income increases consumption in period 2 by 80, which is .8 of the new income in period 1. The burst of autonomous business investment continues in period 2, by assumption. Adding together the new investment and new consumption in

Table 15–1

Dynamic income–expenditures model

	Total income (1)	CHANGE FROM ORIGINAL LEVEL IN:		
		Investment (2)	Consumption (3)	Income (4)
Original level	1,000			
Period 1	1,100	+100		+100
Period 2	1,180	+100	+ 80	+180
Period 3	1,224	+ 80	+144	+224
Period 4	1,243	+ 64	+179	+243
Period 5	1,229	+ 35	+194	+229
Period 6	1,198	+ 15	+183	+198
Period 7	1,147	− 11	+158	+147

Assume: Original autonomous investment of 100 in periods 1 and 2 (in col. 2).

Thereafter: To obtain change from original level: Consumption equals .8 of income during preceding period.

Investment equals the increase (+ or −) in consumption (that is, business sales) in preceding period over the next preceding period. For example, investment in period 3 is +80, because consumption was 80 higher in period 2 than in period 1.

Thus: Col. 1 equals 1,000 (original income) plus col. 4 (change in income).

Col. 2 equals 100 in periods 1 and 2 (new assumed investment), and changes in col. 3 in preceding period for all succeeding periods (since induced investment equals the preceding change in consumption).

Col. 3 equals .8 of col. 4 during preceding period (since consumption is always .8 of the national income of the preceding period).

Col. 4 equals col. 2 plus col. 3 (since national income equals investment plus consumption).

The same model in equations (as explained in appendix to Chapter 11, on Econometric Models):

$$C_t = .8Y_{t-1}$$
$$I_t = C_{t-1} - C_{t-2}$$
$$Y_t = C_t + I_t$$

where C = consumption, I = investment, Y = income, and the subscript shows the time period. Thus $_t$ is any time period, $_{t-1}$ is the preceding period, and so on.

period 2, we get new income 180 above the original level; this gives a total income of 1,180 for period 2. The higher income in period 2 in turn raises consumption in period 3; in addition, the preceding rise in consumption induces 80 of new business investment, raising total income to 1,224. And so the process goes.

This cumulative upward expansion arises out of the interacting multiplier and accelerator effects. Common sense tells us that if we increase the strength of either the multiplier or the accelerator, we will get a more rapid income expansion. If we weaken either, the rise in income will be slower. And these results can be checked readily by substituting a different propensity to consume or a different accelerator in the table.

Once it's started, why does GNP ever stop going up or down? Notice that income rises ever more slowly from period 1 through period 4. Since induced investment depends on the **change** in consumption, induced investment gradually falls and the acceleration effect gradually weakens, in spite of the continued upward multiplier effect of whatever new investment there is. By period 5, new investment has dropped off substantially, and the drop in investment is enough to more than offset the continued rise in consumption. Thus, total income falls slightly in period 5, and the expansion has passed its upper turning point. Moreover, once consumption begins to fall, investment becomes a negative figure (by our accelerator assumption). This sets off a negative multiplier effect, and the downswing is under way. Moreover, if you trace the process further, you'll see that it also reverses the downswing a few periods later.

The model can be put in the simple system of equations shown under Table 15–1. These are "difference equations," and the solution of the system mathematically gives the pattern of changes in income worked out arithmetically in the table.

This dynamic model gives some idea of the possible results of interacting multiplier and acceleration effects. But don't be too impressed with it. Changing the values of the accelerator and multiplier can substantially change the pattern you get for national income over a series of time periods. If you increase both—the multiplier to a very high marginal propensity to consume, and the accelerator to 3 or 4—you will find that national income "explodes" upward once anything starts it up. If you trace out the model given in Table 15–1 for about fifteen periods, you will find that income "damps" back down toward the original income level of 1,000. If you use lower values for the multiplier and accelerator, national income will return to the 1,000 level faster. Moreover, if you make induced investment a function of the **level** of national income in the preceding period, rather than of the **change** in national income, you will get still a different pattern of interaction.

Thus, the purpose of this simple dynamic model is not to show how business fluctuations really work. Rather, it is to show how a simple mathematical model can be used to analyze economic problems.

CHAPTER 16 FISCAL POLICY and THE national DEBT

We turn now to fiscal policy—what the government can do through its expenditures and taxes to maintain a stably growing economy without unemployment or inflation. All the Western democratic societies now take it for granted that when the economy gets off a prosperous growth path, the government should step in to help provide more income and jobs if the problem is depression, or to check rising prices if the problem is inflation. Indeed, Congress, in the Employment Act of 1946, declared that "it is the continuing responsibility of the federal government . . . to promote maximum employment, production, and purchasing power," and this statement has been a keystone of the government's economic policy ever since.

Back in the pre-1930 days, government expenditures and taxes were only about 10 percent of the national income, and there was widespread agreement that little government was the best government. Almost no one questioned the wisdom of balancing the federal budget every year. Sometimes the government didn't manage to do it, but everyone was apologetic about the

Note: Some instructors may prefer to assign Chapter 35, which presents a summary of government taxes and expenditures, before Chapter 16, to provide further background for the discussion of fiscal policy. Also, monetary policy (Chapters 17 and 18) can equally well be assigned before fiscal policy by instructors who prefer that order.

failure. But as the depression deepened in the 1930s, the federal government just couldn't balance the budget, try as both Presidents Hoover and Roosevelt would. We had federal deficit financing because we couldn't avoid it. However, an increasing number of people, led by economist John Maynard Keynes, began to argue that government deficit spending was actually a good thing during depression. So modern fiscal policy is a child of the Great Depression, only four decades ago.

Many economists consider fiscal policy to be one of the major advances in the history of economics. But others, as we shall see presently, consider it overrated, both theoretically and practically. Even though it is only a lusty infant historically, they argue that it may have already outlived its usefulness.

THE THEORY OF FISCAL POLICY

The basic theory of fiscal policy was laid out in Chapter 11. In the short run, aggregate demand largely determines national production, incomes, and prices. Private spending on consumption and investment fluctuates substantially around a stable growth path, but government spending is also part of aggregate demand (GNP = $C + I + G$). To keep aggregate demand growing roughly along the economy's full-employment growth path, the government can increase or decrease its own spending, and influence private spending by raising or lowering taxes. It can increase total expenditures by spending more than the amount by which it reduces private spending by collecting taxes. Conversely, it can reduce GNP by taxing away more than it spends. Either way, the net change in autonomous spending triggers a multiplier effect.

This potential of fiscal policy was shown visually in the circular GNP flow diagram in Figure 8–2. The government may spend back into the income stream either more or less than it withdraws in taxes. A more complete and sophisticated theory of fiscal policy is shown in Figure 16–1, reproduced from Figure 11–2. Let the CC and C + I lines be identical with the lines in Figure 11–1. Equilibrium income would then be

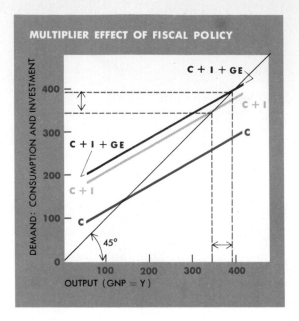

MULTIPLIER EFFECT OF FISCAL POLICY

Figure 16–1
Net new government spending of 10 increases autonomous spending by 10 and, with a multiplier of 4, raises GNP by 40—up to a new equilibrium of 390.

350, where $C + I$ cuts the 45° line. Now suppose the government enters the picture and begins to spend 10 each year without collecting any taxes. We can then draw a new government spending layer (GE) on top of the $C + I$ curve. This new $C + I + GE$ curve is 10 higher at every point. The new government spending is income to its recipients and has a multiplier effect just like private investment. If the marginal propensity to consume is .75, the new equilibrium level of GNP in Figure 16–1 will be 390, as the multiplier raises total income by four times the original government spending. The result is the same as if the 10 of new autonomous spending had been private investment or consumption spending.

To this basic theory of fiscal policy we must add three provisos, which may be important in applying the theory in particular cases. First, remember that it is only *net* autonomous government spending that has a multiplier effect. If the new government spending reduces private investment, this reduction of private spending must be subtracted from the government expenditure in calculating the overall multiplier effect. Such a reduction in private investment may occur, for example, if the government borrowing to finance the deficit "crowds out" private borrowing to finance private investment. This result is especially likely if the Federal Reserve keeps M stable, so interest rates rise with more borrowing and the scarce funds go to the government rather than to private borrowers. Thus, successful expansionary fiscal policy generally depends on a supportive monetary policy to increase M at the same pace and hold interest rates down. Second, remember that even if fiscal policy increases *nominal* GNP, there is no guarantee that it will produce more jobs and output rather than inflation. Third, although government spending financed by increased taxes will normally produce a balanced-budget multiplier, as Chapter 11 suggests, this multiplier will not exceed 1. The major expansionary effect of new government spending is likely to depend on its being financed by a government deficit, preferably through new money creation.

AUTOMATIC FISCAL STABILIZERS

Although we normally think of fiscal policy as discretionary changes in taxes and government spending to stabilize the economy, some of the most powerful fiscal stabilizers work automatically, calling for no special action by either the president or Congress. There are two big built-in automatic fiscal stabilizers in the modern fiscal system, plus a variety of smaller ones.

1. Automatic changes in tax receipts. If national income falls, unchanged tax rates (especially on personal and corporation income taxes) will bring lower tax receipts to the government. With present tax rates, each drop of $100 in national income reduces tax receipts by about $35. Thus, if Congress maintains government spending unchanged, falling tax receipts will automatically produce an expansionary budget deficit. Conversely, if national income rises, so will tax receipts, automatically damping the rise in income. The government budget will

automatically run a surplus, collecting more in taxes than it spends.

Note that this built-in stabilizer works both ways. It automatically slows any decline toward recession, but it also slows economic expansion, whether or not we have already reached full employment.

2. Unemployment compensation. Since the Great Depression, we have developed a nation-wide government unemployment-insurance system, under which workers automatically draw unemployment benefits if they lose their jobs. Thus, government expenditures rise automatically when recession strikes and unemployment rises. When workers get jobs again, these benefits stop. Because the payments go only to unemployed workers, this automatic stabilizer is much less powerful than the economy-wide automatic changes in tax receipts noted above, but it does work automatically with no reliance on Congress or the administration to do the right thing at the right time. The special payroll taxes to finance unemployment benefits, incidentally, also work in a stabilizing way. Because they are a fixed percentage of workers' wages, tax collections rise with increasing employment and fall when unemployment strikes.

Figure 16–2 shows unemployment insurance at work as an automatic fiscal stabilizer. Benefit payments rise sharply in each recession (shown by the shaded vertical areas), while tax collections are much more stable, rising gradually in good times and falling in recessions. The system thus produces automatic deficit spending in each recession and a drag on the economy when it is moving up.[1]

A number of other special government programs work as built-in stabilizers. The farm-aid program increases benefit payments to farmers when farm prices and incomes fall, and reduces them when the incomes and prices rise. "Welfare"

---

[1]Unemployment insurance has some special weaknesses. For example, if unemployment rises through new additions to the labor force, there is no automatic countercyclical effect, because the new entrants have built up no claims for unemployment-insurance payments. Also, as we shall see in Chapter 19, unemployment benefits plus related tax advantages are big enough in some instances to reduce the cost of unemployment almost to zero and thereby lessen the inducement to look for another job promptly.

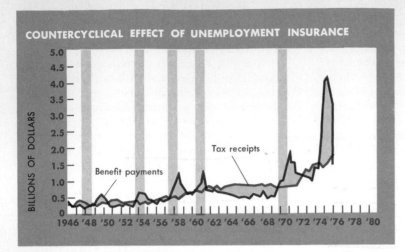

COUNTERCYCLICAL EFFECT OF UNEMPLOYMENT INSURANCE

Benefit payments

Tax receipts

BILLIONS OF DOLLARS

1946 '48 '50 '52 '54 '56 '58 '60 '62 '64 '66 '68 '70 '72 '74 '76 '78 '80

Figure 16–2
Unemployment insurance provides a strong, automatic countercyclical force. While payroll tax collections are fairly stable, benefit payments build up rapidly in recessions and fall rapidly as recovery develops. Data plotted quarterly. (Source: U.S. Department of Labor.)

and relief payments to poor families have an element of automatic countercyclical stabilization policy. So do other government expenditures that are automatically geared to increases and decreases in the recipients' incomes or in prices.

Limitations of built-in fiscal stabilizers. The automatic fiscal stabilizers provide a powerful first line of defense against major swings in the economy. Together, they now offset perhaps a third of swings either way in national income. Against minor destabilizing forces, alone they may be enough to keep the economy near an even keel.

But against major destabilizing forces, there is no guarantee the automatic stabilizers will be enough to prevent a major depression or major inflation. To fight such disturbances, we clearly need to turn to discretionary policy—to congressional and administration policy decisions to vary tax and expenditure rates enough to slow or reverse unwanted swings in output, employment, and prices.

DISCRETIONARY FISCAL POLICY
Government spending: public works and transfer payments

Back in the 1930s, when discretionary fiscal policy was introduced, spending on public works seemed the sensible way to "prime the pump" of private spending, as the problem

was first seen. Highways, parks, post offices, and the like were obviously useful in their own right, and they provided new jobs in their construction. They both gave us "something to show for our money" and helped to maintain the morale, self-respect, and skills of otherwise unemployed workers.

But experience taught some bitter lessons. Many of the public-works projects were ill-designed and wasteful (make-work jobs such as leaf-raking were prominent). More important, flexibility in public-works spending is hard to achieve. Apartment houses, highways, and the like are slow to get started—they need years of planning, blueprints, land acquisition, and so on before actual construction begins. And they are hard to stop promptly when the need is past; a bridge halfway across a river or a schoolhouse half built must be completed to avoid flagrant waste, even if recession has turned to a boom. Because most recent business-cycle recessions have lasted only a year or two, there is a good chance that public works planned to fight unemployment will start too late to do much good and will be carried out mainly in the boom phase of the cycle, although advance planning of a "shelf" of public works can help some.

A further objection to public works is that they may compete with private investment. This objection is advanced most strongly against low-cost housing projects, public power plants, and the like, which might have been built by private capital. But this objection can be met fairly easily. There is a wide range of public investment outlets, such as schools, highways, parks, and resource conservation, that is clearly noncompetitive with private investment.

Although public works per se are, in many people's eyes, a valuable use of society's resources, the problem of achieving countercyclical flexibility has turned many economists against them *for stabilization purposes.* Direct government transfer payments to the unemployed are generally easier to get started fast and to shut off when the need is past. Moreover, they are guaranteed to help the unemployed directly—rather than construction companies and already-employed workers, as public-works projects often do.

The unemployment-insurance plans noted above provide a big built-in block of countercyclical transfer payments without relying on discretion, and the "negative income tax" (see Chapter 37) would do an even broader automatic countercyclical job. A variety of cash and in-kind discretionary grants to unemployed (or all poor) people have been suggested. While the transfer-payments multiplier (like the tax multiplier) is smaller than that for government spending on goods and services, the flexibility argument turns most economists toward transfer payments.

Recently some economists and political leaders have proposed a government guarantee of a job for everyone willing and able to work. The government would act as an employer of last resort. As to the jobs to be provided, there is wide disagreement. They range from standard public-works prescriptions to manpower training and pure make-work ("leaf-raking") jobs. Such a sweeping federal job guarantee still seems extreme to most American observers. It would be very costly compared to direct money-transfer payments, and clearly less flexible than unemployment insurance. And many worry about its disincentive effects; would people in government jobs move on to private work? But several European nations come close to the government-guaranteed-job plan.

Changes in tax rates

Many economists favor change in tax rates over variations in spending on grounds of flexibility. Compared to public works, which may take years to get started, tax rates affect disposable income almost immediately once Congress acts. Most income taxes are withheld from wages and salaries each payroll period, usually every week or month, so the impact of tax changes is quick. Moreover, tax cuts leave households and businesses free to spend their new disposable income as they wish, in contrast to government control over resource allocation implied by increased government spending.

What are the drawbacks to relying on tax changes? First, the tax multiplier is smaller than the government-expenditure multiplier. Second, if people see tax changes to fight inflation or recession as temporary and if the permanent-income hypothesis is right, the public may primarily vary its saving rate rather than its consumption expenditure. This happened with the Johnson 10 percent income surtax in 1968, which was designed to check inflationary consumption spending. The saving rate dropped temporarily, but there was little evident restraint on consumer spending. Third, those who generally favor a larger government budget are reluctant to see taxes cut to fight recessions, because they believe it will be difficult to get Congress to raise taxes again when prosperity returns with the need for increased public services.

Politics, lags, and fiscal flexibility

Finetuning the economy for stable economic growth depends on accurate timing of fiscal policy: knowing when to do what, and then doing it. For discretionary fiscal policy to work well, the administration must recognize promptly what fiscal policy is needed. Then Congress must act promptly to change expenditures or tax rates, whichever it chooses. Although there have been some cases of successful, prompt action (for example, the excise-tax cut of 1965), these have been the exception rather than the rule. The two big income tax bills of the 1960s were both based on modern fiscal theory. But it took nearly three years, first to convince President Kennedy and then to get the widely applauded big tax cut of 1964 through Congress. The Johnson antiinflation surtax of 1968 was nearly as slow in coming. Variations in government expenditures to combat economic fluctuations have also lagged notoriously behind the apparent need for them.

Thus, the lag in using fiscal policy effectively is largely an "inside lag"—inside the government. Once the administration and Congress act, the impact of tax or expenditure changes on income and expenditure is prompt. (By contrast, we shall see in Chapter 18, with monetary policy the problem is more an "outside lag"; the Federal Reserve can act promptly, but the effects of changes in M on income and employment are lagged and may spread out over a long period.)

Good timing for fiscal policy is thus a two-part problem—economic and political. Any honest economist will admit a lot of uncertainty about just what policy measure should be adopted and when. Economic forecasting is an imperfect art. And even when we're sure what lies ahead, we're not sure about the exact timing and size of the impact of different fiscal actions. But a lot of the problem is political, too. Both the administration and Congress have to be convinced of the need to change taxes and spending to fight the boom or recession, and then they must act. It's a slow total process, especially if the need is to damp an overheating boom. Prosperity is nice: What elected official wants to risk turning it into depression?

The record in using fiscal policy for stabilization has thus been a mixed one. As often as not, fiscal policy has been destabilizing. Fiscal policy, determined by a slow-moving, bickering Congress, is part of the stabilization problem as well as of its solution. It is important to remember that the ultimate fiscal authority lies with Congress, not with the president. The president proposes, but Congress disposes.

One way to reduce these lags would be for Congress to delegate limited power to the president to cut or raise tax rates temporarily in case of rising unemployment or inflation. Recent presidents have asked Congress for this power, to be exercised for a six-month period, subject to congressional veto at any time. But Congress has shown no interest in giving away its exclusive power to set tax rates.

The most fundamental reform would be to persuade Congress to consider stabilization budget proposals promptly as such, and not to let them get bogged down in the usual tax and expenditure legislation procedures. The typical tax bill is subject to long hearings before House and Senate committees, with enormous pressures from lobbies and special-interest groups, each understandably out to protect its own interests. On the expenditure side, appropriations are largely controlled by some 25 powerful subcommittees, each dominant over its section of the budget, and often controlled by a congressman of long seniority who rules his domain almost as a private fiefdom. Little wonder that prompt overall budget swings to offset economic instability have proved difficult to obtain in the Congress.

In 1975, Congress, stung by such criticisms, moved modestly to reform its budgetary processes. A new budget committee each spring will review the entire budget from a stabilization perspective and tentatively set a total spending ceiling for the year. This ceiling will be reviewed in the autumn, and Congress will (presumably) vote to impose the limit on itself. Thereafter, if appropriations for the year exceed the ceiling, Congress will be obliged to either raise taxes to match the excess or cut back expenditures. Clearly, the new procedure is an improvement, for at least it makes Congress look explicitly at the stabilization consequences of its expenditures. But whether it will obey its own self-denying ordinances remains to be seen. A similar act just after World War II was simply disregarded after a couple of years.

Economists and political scientists look for still sharper ways to focus the need for specific congressional budget action against instability. To many, the tax side looks more promising than action to focus the multicommittee expenditure process on stabilization as a major goal. Perhaps Congress might be persuaded to consider **separately as a stabilization proposal** annual presidential recommendations for a flat percentage surtax (positive, negative, or zero) on personal and corporate income taxes, set solely to help stabilize the economy, avoiding the issues of relative tax burdens and "inequities," which usually bog down tax bills.[2]

---

[2] For a more detailed analysis with recommendations for change, see G.L. Bach, *Making Monetary and Fiscal Policy* (Washington, D.C.: The Brookings Institution, 1971), Chaps. 7 and 8.

DOES FISCAL POLICY WORK?

Some critics of modern fiscal policy argue that, however logical it all may sound, it just doesn't work, even aside from the political lags. Who is right?

First, note the evidence. During the 1930s, unemployment rose to a peak of about thirteen million people by 1933, over 25 percent of the total labor force. During the decade, unemployment averaged over 18 percent of the total work force. The federal government ran a deficit each year from 1931 through 1940, averaging about $3 billion annually—although President Roosevelt clearly tried to avoid deficits until the last three or four years of the decade. The unemployment rate fell rapidly only after 1939, when aggregate demand (and government deficits) rose with the onset of World War II. More recently, the Vietnam War period was a fiscal-policy debacle: President Johnson and Congress loaded vast war and "Great Society" expenditures onto an already high-employment economy, and the result was an inflationary boom. Government spending soared again in the Nixon 1970s, leading to an overstimulated economy and a sharp cyclical downturn in 1974–75, against which an enormous budget deficit, reaching $70 billion in 1975, could barely bring unemployment back below 8 percent.

On the other hand, in the early 1960s, President Kennedy's advisers urged a large tax cut to raise aggregate demand to fight persistent slack and unemployment in the economy—in spite of the already substantial federal deficit. The economists predicted that the $10 billion tax cut would raise GNP by $20–$25 billion, through a combined multiplier-accelerator effect. And in fact almost exactly the result predicted by the economists occurred following the 1964 tax cut.

How shall we assess this evidence? Defenders of fiscal policy contend that the 1930s were not a fair test of their proposals. First, what deficits did occur were the result of haphazard, unplanned actions. Indeed, government expenditures were **cut** and tax rates **increased** during the first three years of the decade when the depression was spiraling downward. Moreover, state and local governments were actually running surpluses big enough to offset the complete federal deficits until the mid-1930s. Even during the latter part of the decade, when President Roosevelt and the New Dealers finally became convinced that deficit financing was a sensible thing, deficits were still small, only 2 or 3 percent of GNP. With such a massive unemployment problem, they understandably didn't eliminate unemployment.

Again in the 1950s, early 1960s, and early 1970s, government deficits were not part of a planned attack on unemployment. Rather, they reflected haphazard fiscal measures on both tax and expenditure sides. They reflected a series of political failures, not reasoned use of stabilizing fiscal policy.

The high-employment budget

But the main argument of the fiscal-policy supporters is this—that government fiscal policy in the 1930s, 1950s, early 1960s, and mid-1970s was **not** expansionary, in spite of the deficits. They argue that the deficits during these years were mainly the **involuntary** results of a depressed GNP that pulled tax receipts below government spending levels. Tax rates were too **high** in spite of the deficit. Each time GNP rose, rising tax receipts would have swung the budget to a surplus before full employment was reached, given those tax rates.

To understand what really happened in those years, we need a new concept—the "high-employment surplus."[3] This is the surplus (or deficit) that would have occurred with the existing tax rates and government spending **if the economy had been operating at high employment—say, 4 percent.** Although actual federal deficits occurred in most of the years noted above, in all of them except 1975 there was a large high-employment surplus. The federal budget on balance exerted a drag on the economy before it could reach full employment, because with existing tax rates, receipts would have exceeded government spending before high employment was achieved.

[3] Also often called the "full-employment budget." Usually, high or full employment is taken to mean 4 or 5 percent unemployment.

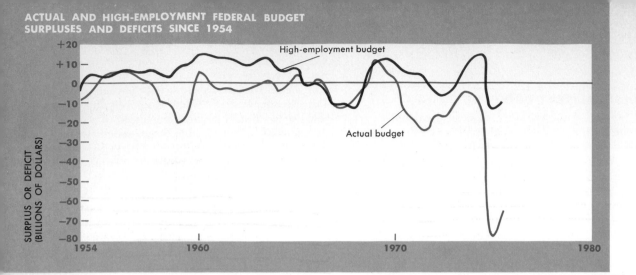

Figure 16-3
The "high-employment" and actual budgets give very different pictures of the impact of the federal budget on the economy. Most economists believe that the former gives a better indication of the government's net fiscal stimulus or drag on the economy. Data are seasonally adjusted annual rates, plotted semiannually. (Source: Federal Reserve Bank of St. Louis.)

In fiscal 1975, for example, the realized government deficit was $35 billion. Yet, then-existing tax rates would have produced a federal budget **surplus** of $17 billion, had the economy been at high employment. That is, existing tax rates put a heavy "fiscal drag" on the upswing long before it reached full-employment levels.

Figure 16-3 shows this effect. The dark curve shows the actual recorded federal deficits and surpluses over the last two decades—deficits for most years. The light curve shows what the budget situation would have been had the economy been at high employment each year. In every year except 1966-68, 1972, and 1973, the federal budget would have shown a substantial surplus at high employment.[4]

It is important to recognize that the high-employment surplus is a more meaningful measure of government fiscal policy than is the actual reported surplus or deficit. But it is also important to see that a balanced high-employment budget is not necessarily desirable. If at

[4]Many economists now think of the federal budget as "neutral" when the high-employment surplus is zero.

198

high employment, private investment would exceed private saving, then the ideal government high-employment surplus would be just large enough to offset the private-investment excess. Conversely, if, at high employment, private saving would exceed private investment, the government high-employment budget should show an offsetting deficit.

Last, with both the actual and the high-employment surplus (or deficit), it is important to see that it is only changes in the level of the surplus that will induce changes in GNP. A large government surplus will mean a lower GNP, other things equal, than would a smaller surplus or a deficit. But if we want to *raise* **aggregate demand, it is necessary to** *increase* **the government's deficit or** *decrease* **its surplus, and conversely to move the budget toward surplus if we want to lower GNP.**

THE "FISCAL DRAG" AND THE "FISCAL DIVIDEND"

Critics and advocates of modern fiscal policy alike agree on one major point: With our rapidly growing economy, if we keep any given level of government spending and set of tax rates, the federal budget will rapidly move toward surpluses as GNP increases. With a 4 percent annual increase in GNP (about our real growth potential), federal tax receipts rise by about $15 billion annually. Thus, a budget in balance one year will show a $15 billion surplus only a year later if federal spending stays unchanged. To avoid this "fiscal drag" resulting merely from the growth of the economy, we must cut federal tax receipts by $15 billion annually, increase federal expenditures by this amount, or some combination of the two. Actually, with inflation added to real growth, the fiscal drag over the years ahead will substantially exceed $15 billion annually.

Looked at another way, this fiscal drag can be seen as a huge "fiscal dividend" we can obtain by merely holding tax rates constant as the economy grows. This would generate an annual surplus of nearly $100 billion by 1980, assuming continued growth, unchanged government spending, 4 percent unemployment, and no inflation. This potential surplus could finance a vast increase in federal spending on education, urban renewal, health, and the like. Alternatively, it would permit large tax cuts if we maintain an unchanged level of federal spending. But the fiscal-drag analysis above warns us that we will build up massive deflationary pressure over the decade if we neither cut tax rates nor increase federal spending, and the expected dividend will not materialize.

Actually, Congress' and successive administrations' spending plans have already used up the anticipated fiscal dividend (wiped out the potential fiscal drag) for several years to come. They have already committed the government to large, growing expenditure programs, like Social Security, military pensions, and the like, that will use all the dividend at least until 1980.[5]

ALTERNATIVE BUDGET POLICIES

This reasoning suggests that government deficits and surpluses are powerful tools in fighting unemployment and inflation. Yet many people still believe a balanced budget is the best thing. Are they all wrong?

[5] See, for example, B. Blechman et al., *Setting National Priorities: The 1976 Budget* (Washington, D.C.: The Brookings Institution, 1975). Chapter 7, and corresponding volumes for later years.

Annual budget balance

A balanced-budget policy is, in one sense, a "neutral" government policy. The government feeds back into the income stream just what it withdraws—no more and no less. Thus, a balanced budget seems appropriate when we are satisfied with the existing level of GNP—roughly, in periods of full employment without inflation.

But suppose recession appears. What does the annually balanced budget policy call for then? With falling GNP and unchanged tax rates, the government's tax receipts will fall. A deficit will automatically be created unless offsetting steps are taken. To avoid the deficit, the annual-budget balancers would say: Raise tax rates to get more money, or reduce spending. If you believe that the government ought to try to **expand** total spending in order to check the recession, the balanced-budget prescription is clearly wrong. To **reduce** tax rates and **increase** government spending would help raise the level of total spending, but the balanced-budget policy calls for exactly the opposite actions under recession conditions.

Similarly, inflation would generate a budget surplus; an annually balanced budget policy would call for tax **reductions** and **increased** spending to avoid this surplus. Again, this clearly seems the wrong prescription for stabilization purposes. It would speed the inflation, rather than check it.

If an annually balanced budget fiscal policy is likely to give the wrong answer so often, why did it take so long to discover its weakness? There are probably two main answers: (1) a belief that budget deficits always lead to inflation; and (2) an analogy that if private individuals should balance their own budgets, the government should do likewise. You should be able to form your own judgment on (1) by now; government deficits do tend to raise aggregate demand, but whether this leads to inflation depends on a variety of factors, especially how near the economy is to full employment. On (2), we shall have more to say in the next section. For the moment, keep an open mind.

A cyclically balanced budget

The obvious difficulties of annual budget balancing led, during the 1930s, to the proposal that the budget should be balanced not annually but over the length of the business cycle. There seemed no great virtue in one year as an arbitrary accounting period. A cyclically balanced budget would permit government fiscal policy to play a positive stabilizing role, running a deficit in depression and paying it off with a counterbalancing surplus in the following boom.

But history suggests one major problem. What if the government runs a big deficit fighting a long, severe depression, and then the following boom turns out to be a weak affair that never gets up to full employment? Should the government then try to collect a large surplus to offset the preceding deficit, even though to do so would depress the economy again? The advocate of a cyclically balanced budget policy would presumably say yes, but common sense rebels at the idea of a big government surplus when the problem is to get out of a recession.

If inflationary booms just offset depressions, a cyclically balanced budget could work out just right. But if the two needs for fiscal policy turn out not to balance at all, the cyclically balanced budget philosophy exposes us to the same false prescriptions as annual budget balancing.

Functional finance

"Functional finance" is the logical outcome of the new Keynesian fiscal economics. The "functional finance" advocates say: Forget about balancing the budget as a separate goal. Use the government budget as needed to help provide full employment without inflation. If the private economy stagnates, more federal deficits than surpluses are appropriate; if the private economy is too buoyant, we need continued government surpluses. This approach is called "functional finance" because it views the federal budget functionally, as a means toward the goal of stable economic growth. If aggregate demand at present tax rates is too small to provide prosperity, to paraphrase Admiral Farragut, "Damn the deficits, full speed ahead!"

High-employment budget balance plus built-in flexibility

One last middle-of-the-road budget proposal is worth attention. It proposes that we should first determine federal spending on non-stabilization grounds; then set tax rates to cover those expenditures at roughly full employment; and then, foregoing discretionary countercyclical fiscal policy, rely on built-in flexibility to keep the economy from swinging to either unemployment or inflation.

For example, suppose federal spending is set at $400 billion because that's the volume of public services we want the government to provide, on the assumption that we must pay for them through taxes. Then tax rates would be set to yield $400 billion when GNP is at roughly high employment. With stable tax rates, tax yields would vary directly with any fluctuations in GNP. Stabilizing deficits and surpluses would automatically result from holding government expenditures constant. The plan would thus combine "built-in budgetary flexibility" with the basic virtue of making Congress face up to the need to balance expenditures with taxes—at high employment.

Proponents of this plan claim that they are facing political and economic realities that other approaches gloss over. The built-in-flexibility plan would require no action on the part of Congress or the administration in forecasting business developments and in changing tax and expenditure policies to counter changing economic conditions. There would be no need to delegate congressional power over tax rates or spending to get quick action. Congress would need only to establish annually the basic level of government spending and set tax rates to cover those expenditures at high-level employment. The rest would be automatic; just don't try to change tax rates or expenditures to stabilize the economy, because, as a practical matter, you'll probably do more harm than good.

But this plan has weaknesses too. First, there's no guarantee that the automatically created deficits and surpluses would be enough to keep small swings from developing into big booms or depressions. Second, if the private economy is basically stagnant or overbuoyant, federal high-employment budget balance won't compensate for this private under- or overspending. In those cases, the economy needs positive federal stimulus or restraint, not the neutrality of high-employment budget balance.

THE UNFULFILLED PROMISE OF KEYNESIAN ECONOMICS

All this makes clear both the potential of Keynesian fiscal policy and the complexities involved in using it effectively. In the two decades following World War II, many economists proclaimed the demise of the business cycle and the imminent arrival of stable growth at full employment without inflation. Modern fiscal policy would do the job; all we needed was some experience in using the new tool, and broad education (especially of Congress) as to its potentialities. And the record of the economy was generally good—relatively stable economic growth with only moderate fluctuations.

But the late 1960s saw an old-fashioned inflationary boom, fed by inflationary fiscal policy as the president and Congress refused to heed the warning of economists. Worse, the recession of 1970 failed to halt the inflation, and unemployment remained stubbornly high in the following years while inflation retreated only slowly. Then the food and oil crises of 1973 and 1974 triggered an outburst of double-digit inflation while unemployment stuck well above 4 percent. The inflationary boom plus Federal Reserve monetary restriction to fight the inflation brought the worst recession since the 1930s, with unemployment rising to nearly 9 percent. But the inflation rate stubbornly hovered around 8 percent, far above acceptable prewar levels.

What went wrong? More important, have we learned from this painful experience how to use fiscal policy more effectively in the future?

Clearly, part of the answer is the political process. Economists can honestly claim that they foresaw the inflationary results that were inevitable if the president and Congress loaded Vietnam War plus "Great Society" spending onto an already high-employment economy in the 1960s. And the political policy makers paid only moderate heed to economists' advice in the 1970s. But more than the political process was at fault.

The economy simply wasn't behaving the way the traditional theory predicted. Prices continued to rise rapidly in spite of widespread unemployment and slack. Rising aggregate demand triggered continuing inflation rather than reducing unemployment, even when unemployment was already high. Moreover, without supportive monetary policy, fiscal policy seemed largely impotent, since it would trigger offsetting changes in private investment as public and private financing competed for the same credit.

Chapter 19 will consider these questions in detail, after we have examined monetary policy more thoroughly. In the meantime, keep a suspended judgment on the new fiscal policy—high potential, but lots of uncertainties yet to be resolved.

FISCAL POLICY AND THE PUBLIC DEBT

Much of the controversy over fiscal policy arises because people fear the rising public debt that comes with deficit financing. Since the 1920s, the public debt has risen to over $600 billion. Should we view this debt with alarm? The answer is, not with as much alarm as most people have, but with some. The first step toward an objective assessment of the problem is to look at the facts.

The facts about the public debt

Figure 16–4 shows the public debt (the heavy black line), and the debt as a percentage of the GNP (dashed blue line), since 1920. It is clear that much of our present $600 billion federal debt came from World War II, and a lot from spending in recent years. It's also clear that as a percentage of GNP, the federal debt has steadily drifted downhill from a peak of about 130 percent at the end of World War II to below 40 percent now.[6]

Another useful way of looking at the federal debt is in terms of the interest charges it involves.

---

[6]Over $250 billion of the national debt is held by the government's own trust funds (for example, in pension funds) and by the Federal Reserve. Thus, the national debt held by the public in 1976 was only about $350 billion, or about 20 percent of GNP.

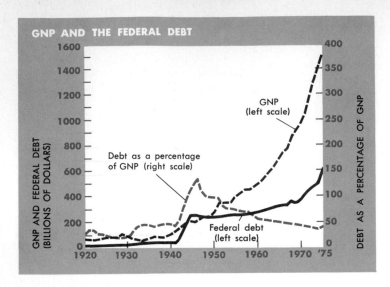

Figure 16-4
The federal debt has spurted upward in war periods, but has declined persistently relative to GNP since World War II. (Source: U.S. Treasury and Commerce Departments.)

Figure 16–5 shows annual interest payments on the federal debt since 1920, and again those payments as a percentage of GNP. Interest rates have risen persistently since World War II, and the annual interest payments on the debt have grown to $35 billion. This growth has roughly matched the steadily growing GNP, so that interest payments have run about 1.5–2 percent of GNP over most of the last decade.

It is also instructive to compare public and private debt. Figure 16–6 shows dramatically that private (corporate, household, and farm) debt accounts for most of the massive growth in total debt since 1929, and far exceeds the public debt in size. Of the private debt increase, about half is corporate debt and the other half is debt of individuals and unincorporated businesses. The biggest single item is real estate mortgages, which now exceed the federal debt. There's far more private than public debt to worry about.

Against these facts, consider eight common objections to a large federal debt.

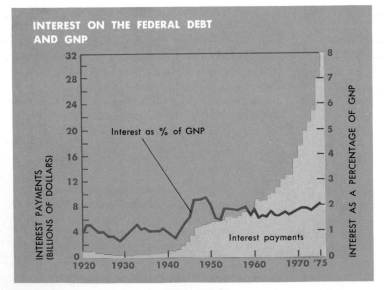

Figure 16-5
Annual interest on the federal debt has shot up in recent years, and now exceeds $35 billion. But it is still only about 2 percent of GNP, only a slightly higher percentage than during the 1920s. (Source: U.S. Treasury Department.)

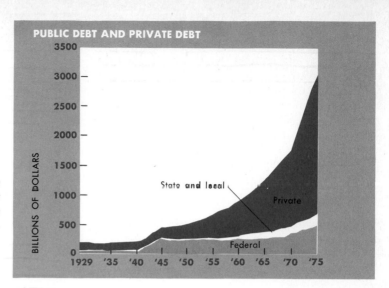

Figure 16-6
Net public and private debt combined are now over $3 trillion, but private debt accounts for three-fourths of the total and for nearly all the huge increase since World War II. (Source: U.S. Department of Commerce.)

The danger of bankruptcy and economic collapse

May a big government debt bankrupt the government and lead to economic collapse? "Bankruptcy," as the word is generally used, means inability to pay one's debts when they are due. In this sense, the federal government need never go bankrupt, because it always has the power to tax, and the economic capacity of the entire economy to produce provides fundamental ability to pay taxes. Beyond this, the federal government has the power to create money to service or repay the debt. It never needs to default.

But can a big public debt bankrupt "the economy"? Extremely unlikely, is the answer, although extreme cases like post–World War I Germany might be considered counterexamples. Payment of interest and principal essentially involves a redistribution of income and assets within the economy, **as long as the debt is domestically held,** as ours is.[7] It is conceivable, of course, that a purely domestic government debt might be so large as to lower drastically the credit standing of the government among investors. But U.S. government bonds are still the world's ultimate gilt-edged investment. Even

---

[7] If the debt is held by foreigners (as in the German case), then payments on interest and principal involve actual costs to the domestic economy rather than merely a redistribution.

with its huge debt, the government obtains funds in competitive markets at the lowest interest rates of any borrower. And whatever interest rate the government must pay to borrow, there is nothing involved that will "bankrupt the economy," whatever this vague term actually means.

In regard to the problems raised by a large government debt, most economists emphasize the need to look at the debt relative to current GNP. As the preceding section indicates, on this score the burden of the debt has steadily declined since World War II, while interest payments have remained a roughly constant percentage of GNP. If real GNP grows at only 4 percent annually over the years ahead, the increase will be over $60 billion annually. Thus the public debt could increase by over $20 billion a year and still merely maintain the present ratio of the debt to GNP.

Surely the dire predictions of economic collapse because of the public debt are overdone. But there are more worries to consider.

A big public debt must cause inflation

Closely related to the economic-collapse argument is the assertion that a big public debt must necessarily cause inflation, sooner or later.

A government deficit, other things equal, has an expansionary effect on aggregate demand because government spending adds more to the income stream than taxes subtract. But the result may or may not be inflation, depending largely on how near the economy is to full employment. There appears to be an inflationary bias in the modern economy, and growing public debt financed by new money helps to finance the inflation. But it is important to recognize that any inflationary effect arises from the *current* expansion of total spending generated by the government's deficit spending, not from the existence of public debt per se.

The "public-debt-causes-inflation" claimants often argue that the larger debt must cause inflation sometime in the future, even if it doesn't now. This argument too is a dubious one. The expansionary pressure of the deficit occurs when the government spending occurs, as was indicated above. The mere existence of the resulting debt a decade later has little or no expansionary effect on total spending. Indeed, the transfer burden involved in interest charges may well be somewhat deflationary, because the transfer is generally from lower- to higher-income groups.

Is there no validity to the "inflation-in-the-future" fear? Some argue that the government, saddled with the public debt, will someday create new money to pay it off, and the newly created money will then create inflationary pressures. Obviously, this argument is difficult to rebut or support. How much weight you give it will depend heavily on your faith in governmental processes to produce responsible fiscal behavior. Certainly history shows that there **need** not be repudiation of a large debt through inflation, although some government debts have been eliminated this way.

It just passes the burden on to future generations

Many people say that borrowing to pay our government bills just passes the cost on to future generations. But this concern is largely fallacious, as a little careful reasoning will show. Suppose we are fighting a war. The **real** economic cost of war consists of the resources used up. If we use steel to produce jet engines and missiles, we can't use it for autos and refrigerators. A further real economic cost is the wartime disruption and destruction. However the war is financed—by taxation, by borrowing, or by just printing new money—these real costs are substantially the same. They are borne by the war generation. They cannot be passed on to future generations except insofar as wartime destruction may impoverish future generations because we pass on less real capital to them. If the new debt is accumulated through antidepression deficits that succeed in putting unemployed resources to work, there is little real burden of any sort on the generation involved.

But may not borrowing impose a burden on future generations,[8] even if it cannot remove the burden from the present generation? The answer is that payment of interest and principal by any future generation is just a transfer or redistribution of income within that generation. If the debt is paid off, the future generation is taxing itself to pay itself. If the debt is refunded, the result again is a redistributional one. Although the redistributional effects may be important, the crucial factors determining the economic well-being of the future generation are its accumulated real capital and its current real output. Having a money debt from earlier generations does not reduce either, and hence imposes no aggregate real burden on the future generation.[9]

There is one way that borrowing instead of taxing **can** pass a real burden on to future generations, even with an internal debt. This is if people who buy bonds consider them as wealth, and base their **lifetime** consumption levels on the higher wealth they now hold. Then, holding bonds from war financing, after the war the present generation would consume more than if it had been taxed, and would accumulate correspondingly less capital to be passed on to following generations. In this way, borrowing rather than taxing might burden future generations and lessen the real consumption given up by the present generation because of the war. Some

[8] To simplify matters, a "future generation" is assumed to be one that does not overlap with the present generation. The basic reasoning is similar if the generations overlap, but the results are more complicated, because then we need to consider the relative positions of working and retired people in the two generations.

[9] If the war generation borrows outside the United States, and the future generation has to pay foreign bondholders, then it may be justifiable to speak of a burden of payment being placed on the future generation in the United States.

economists believe this is the way people behave; others are doubtful. In any event, the **main** real costs of government spending and use of resources are as indicated above.

The transfer burden of interest payments

Large interest costs on a big public debt may impose a real burden, even though these are only transfer payments within the economy—from one of our pockets to the other, considering the nation as a whole. The taxpayer and the interest receiver may be different people. To the individual taxpayer, higher taxes to finance interest payments seem a very real cost.

Heavy taxation tends to distort people's behavior. If the government takes a big chunk of each additional dollar earned, your incentive to work may diminish. Taxes on particular items raise their cost relative to other items and shift consumption away from the taxed goods. Nobody knows just how important such distortions are, but they look substantial. And they surely increase as the tax share of the national income goes up.

Last, given our present tax system, taxing to pay interest on the debt tends to shift income from active earners to rentiers. Taxing the workers to pay bondholders sounds unjust to many people.

Psychological deterrents to private investment

Many writers allege that concern over the government debt deters private investment. Direct facts on the issue are hard to come by, but most evidence suggests that the danger is easy to overstress. Business investment depends far more on consumer demand and on expected profits than on the size of the public debt.

The business community and the general public adjust surprisingly quickly to changes in the economic environment. One of the writer's first memories of economics is the bitter controversy that raged during the 1930s over whether a public debt as huge as $50 billion could conceivably be borne without utterly destroying organized economic activity. No one seriously dreamed the debt would ever go so high—the argument concerned a hypothetical ultimate

upper limit. By the 1940s, the debt of $50 billion was forgotten in the mad scramble for materials, labor, sales, and profits as government and private spending soared with the war. Soon the question, no longer an issue of burning interest, was, What about a $200-billion debt?

With the present national debt at over $600 billion, per capita income at new highs each year, and the economy growing persistently, public concern over the debt is far less than it was a generation ago. Conservative financial circles still complain that the debt is too big. But there is little reason to believe that we will not adjust "psychologically" to further increases as we have in the past. The businessman who foregoes otherwise profitable investments because of the debt item on the Treasury daily statement is hard to find.

Debt management and monetary policy

A big federal debt may increase the difficulty of using monetary policy effectively, as we shall see in the next chapters. This may be a serious problem, but it is not an insuperable one.

Encouragement of government waste

As a matter of practical politics, too-easy reliance on borrowing invites easy spending. Experience has shown that when Congress doesn't feel obliged to raise taxes to pay the bills, waste and inefficiency are likely. This is a homely but powerful argument against too-easy reliance on continued deficit financing.

How big can the public debt be?

How big can the public debt be? There is no simple answer to this question. **The most important principle is that changes in the level of public debt—either increases or decreases—ordinarily exercise a much more direct effect on the level of current GNP than does any given level of existing debt.**

Current fiscal policy (which may increase or decrease the public debt) is thus generally more crucial than the level of existing debt. If our major aim is to maintain high-level output, the level of public debt becomes a residual effect of stabilizing fiscal policy. Paying off the debt, viewed in this fundamental fashion, is a secondary reason for running a budget surplus. Whether a budget deficit or surplus is desirable depends predominantly on whether a deflationary or expansionary effect on current GNP is needed. Once we have the public debt, its major

effect has been felt. Similarly, the effect of paying off the debt will be largely through the impact of the current budget surplus. The national debt per se has played a bigger role in the public's worries than is justified by the facts and careful analysis.

REVIEW

For analysis and discussion

1. You are asked to speak before a local voters' group on whether federal taxes should be increased, lowered, or left unchanged for the next year. Outline the talk you would give, indicating briefly how you would develop each of your major points.

2. If GNP is $50 billion short of a full-employment level and the public's marginal propensity to consume is .8, about how much additional government investment, financed by borrowing, would be necessary to raise GNP to a full-employment level? Explain, indicating clearly any assumptions you make.

3. "Since government officials can't forecast accurately what fiscal policy will be needed and when, we are better off to rely entirely on built-in fiscal stabilizers." Do you agree? Explain.

4. Does the "high-employment-budget surplus" analysis convince you that federal fiscal policy can work effectively, in spite of the coexistence of large deficits and unemployment in the past?

5. Are economists or politicians mainly to blame for the failure of Keynesian fiscal policy to produce a stably growing economy?

6. State carefully all the advantages and disadvantages you can think of in balancing the federal budget (a) weekly; (b) annually; (c) over the cycle; (d) over a fifty-year period; (e) only when business conditions are at the desired level, regardless of how often this occurs. Which alternative is best on the basis of your analysis?

7. Assume that international tensions require a $50-billion increase in military expenditures over the next two years. Would you recommend that the federal government raise the $50 billion by borrowing, or by increasing tax rates? Why?

8. The National Association of Manufacturers has stated, "A government cannot continue indefinitely to run at a deficit without creating a serious inflationary trend." Do you agree or disagree with this statement? Why?

9. You are asked to give an hour's talk before a businessmen's club on the subject, "What Should We Do about Our National Debt?" Outline your talk indicating briefly under each point how you would develop it.

10. Is public debt more dangerous than private debt, or vice versa? Why?

Reproduced here is the substance of a 1973 broadcast by a well-known TV commentator (name omitted to avoid prejudicing you for or against his argument). Is his analysis convincing? What, if anything, should Congress and the administration do about it?

Today the administration announced that before the end of this year, the public debt will exceed $500 billion. That's half a trillion, in case you have trouble with how many zeros to add on big numbers. The administration says this is nothing to worry about, that the economy's in good shape—prosperity, low unemployment, inflation under control, highest standard of living in our history.

How long are we going to go on kidding ourselves this way? If you divide up half a trillion dollars of debt, that's about $10,000 of debt for every family in the United States, on top of what you already owe the local banker or moneylender. We're in debt up to our necks, and you know perfectly well what happens when you go on a binge by buying more on credit than you can afford to pay for. You feel great while you're enjoying the high life—but it's a painful time when the bill collector comes around. And he comes, never doubt. That's one of the sure things about life, like death and taxes!

We're not living in the greatest era of prosperity known to mankind. We're living in one of the biggest counterfeit jobs the world has seen—living high by keeping one step ahead of the bill collector. Every time the debt comes due, borrow some more to pay it off plus a bigger and bigger interest burden. Ten thousand dollars—some bag of stones to carry around on your back, if we're willing to face up to reality and admit that it's there.

CHAPTER 17 MONEY AND THE FEDERAL RESERVE

The purpose of this chapter is to explain the operation of the American monetary and banking system, as a foundation for further analysis of the use of monetary policy to stabilize the economy.

Without financial intermediaries like banks and savings and loan associations to link savers and investors, the circular flow of income would stagnate. Without money, our complex exchange economy would grind to a halt. Think for a minute about what life would be like under a barter economy. Suppose you have a pig. But what you really want is a spool of thread, two new shirts, a movie, and a newspaper. You hear that B down the road has made some shirts. But unless B happens to want some pork chops, you're still out of luck. Your neighbor, C, wants a pig, but he has only lumber to trade. If you're lucky, you may be able to get lumber from C and swap that to B for shirts. But it's going to take some fancy haggling to work out a fair trade with such indivisible products, even if you all have a basic desire to swap. With money as a medium of exchange and as a standard unit for quoting exchange prices, it's easy to avoid this kind of difficulty. Money is a universally accepted unit of purchasing power, freely spendable, and easy to store if you want to postpone spending your income.

When you hear the word "money," you think

of coins and paper bills. But many other objects (oxen, wampum, beads) have served as money, and today we have largely substituted bank checks for currency. Computer entries will almost certainly be next.

A useful definition of money thus must be based on what money does, not on what it looks like. Actually, over 75 percent of all payments in the United States today are made by bank checks, less than 25 percent by currency (that is, coins and paper money). We have become so accustomed to using bank checks as money that for practical purposes, payment by check is the equivalent of payment by currency, even though the check is a "credit" instrument that is good only if the bank will pay the sum indicated. Money, therefore, is defined here as the total of currency and bank checking deposits, because these two constitute the nation's generally acceptable media of payment. The top part of Table 17–1 shows the amount of these two major types of money in existence in 1976. (This is often termed M_1.)

Only a thin line separates actual money from a variety of "near-monies," shown in the bottom half of the table, which are readily convertible into currency or checking deposits. Bank savings deposits, savings and loan shares, and U.S. government securities redeemable within a year are the most important of these near-monies. But there are many more that are only a little less easily convertible, including a great mass of longer-term government bonds. (M_1 plus savings and time deposits at commercial banks is often termed M_2. M_2 plus S&L and mutual savings bank deposits is called M_3.)

Any of these near-monies serves one function

of money reasonably well—that of a store of value. In one way, they are better than money, for the holder receives interest on most near-monies and none on money itself. Balanced against this, the near-money must be converted into actual money before it can be spent. This always involves some inconvenience or delay, and sometimes a risk that the near-money can be converted only at a loss—for example, when government securities must be sold before maturity. The factors that induce people and businesses to shift back and forth between money and near-monies sometimes play an important role in determining aggregate demand.

Table 17–1

Money and near-monies in the United States[a]

		Amount (in billions)
Money		$ 303
Currency	$ 75	
Checking deposits	228	
Important near-monies		1,042
Savings deposits	448	
Savings and loan shares[b]	394	
Liquid U.S. government securities	200	

[a] As of January 1, 1976. Currency shown is that held by the public outside banks. Only government securities redeemable on demand or due within one year are included.
[b] Includes mutual savings banks.
Source: *Federal Reserve Bulletin.*

PART A

PRIVATE FINANCIAL INSTITUTIONS AND THE MONEY SUPPLY

Many kinds of private financial institutions have developed over the years to meet people's changing needs. Some of these, such as savings and loan associations and insurance companies, receive long-term savings and channel them into real investment in buildings, equipment, and the like. Others, such as the ordinary ("commercial") banks, serve as depositories for both currently used funds (demand deposits) and longer-term savings.

Banks

There are now about 14,600 "commercial" banks in the United States, which accept both "savings" (or time) accounts and "checking" (or demand) accounts. The presumption is that savings accounts represent funds put in the bank for relatively long periods of time, while checking deposits are funds that you may want to use promptly. Thus, banks generally feel freer to make long-term loans when their savings deposits go up than when their checking accounts increase. Technically, the banks can require depositors to give thirty or sixty days' notice before withdrawing savings deposits, but they almost never do. Actually, the dividing line between savings and checking deposits is not very sharp once the funds have been deposited in the bank. **But there is one important difference: Checking deposits are spendable money, since depositors can write checks on them. Depositors cannot write checks on savings deposits. A savings deposit can be spent only by withdrawing it in the form of hand-to-hand currency or by transferring it to a checking account.**[1]

Other financial intermediaries

Financial middlemen have grown up to accommodate about every imaginable type of saver and borrower. Savings and loan associations are much like the savings departments of commercial banks; they draw mainly the savings of individuals, make loans mainly for home construction, and have grown enormously since World War II. Life insurance, consumer finance, and sales finance companies are other important intermediaries. So are federal, state, and local governments, although they're out of place in this section on private institutions. Whenever governments borrow from private savers to

finance their expenditures, they're behaving much like private financial middlemen in linking savers with investment.

In everyday conversation, the term "investment" sometimes means *financial* investment—that is, the process of taking funds and "investing" them in stocks, bonds, or the like. Sometimes it also means "investing" in real assets, like houses, as when you buy a new or used house. Each usage is justified by the dictionary, but it is important to remember that in the national income accounts, the term "investment" means *real* investment in *currently produced* capital goods—factories, machinery, and the like. Thus, if you buy a government bond, this is often considered investment in the newspapers and everyday conversation, but it is not investment as the economist defines the term. In economics, if I use my savings to build a new house, that's real investment. But if I buy General Motors stock, that's only a financial transfer, which passes my savings on to the man who sells me the stock, or to GM if it's a new stock issue.

THE SUPPLY OF CURRENCY (GOVERNMENT-ISSUED MONEY)

Currency (government-issued coins and paper money) makes up only about a quarter of our money supply, and it is used primarily to finance small transactions. As a practical matter, whenever you have a bank deposit account, you can readily get currency, merely by writing a check on your account. Indeed, this is the way currency is placed in the hands of the public. Although it is formally issued by the government (mainly the Federal Reserve Banks, to be explained presently), new currency is made available to the general public through providing it to the banks, which in turn pay it out to depositors on demand. In essence, the Federal Reserve always stands ready to print up enough currency to permit the public to get currency in exchange for any deposits it has.

Thus, it is the public's demand for currency that determines how many coins are minted and how much paper money is printed. The Federal Reserve always prints enough paper money to give bank depositors all they want in

---

[1] Even this distinction is breaking down. In some states, customers of banks and savings and loan associations can now in effect write checks on savings accounts, since the bank or S&L will automatically shift funds from savings to checking accounts whenever such transfers are needed to pay checks written on the customer's checking account. More on this later.

exchange for their deposits. Once the public has deposits, it can obtain more currency at will. If for some reason the public has more currency than it wants to hold, it simply puts the currency back in the bank and receives a deposit in exchange.

People ordinarily keep about one-quarter of their total money holdings in the form of currency, and about three-fourths in demand deposits. Although this ratio varies from time to time, as a general rule the monetary authorities can predict that if households and businesses receive $100 of additional deposits, they will withdraw about $20–$25 of it in the form of new currency.

THE SUPPLY OF BANK MONEY: CHECKING DEPOSITS

The great bulk of our money is created by the commercial banks in their day-to-day business of making loans and "investments."[2] The distinguishing feature of modern commercial banking is its ability, through making loans and investments, to "monetize" the debts of others, and thereby in effect to create demand deposits (checking acounts) that serve as money.

Thus, the commercial banks (that is, the banks we all know and deal with) in good times

[2]When banks make "investments," these are financial investments in government bonds or other securities. Banks make very few direct *real* investments in the GNP sense.

generally lend out more than customers have previously deposited. In bad times, they may insist on repayment of the same loans, wiping out the deposits created when the loans were made. Far from being a passive link in the savings-investment process, commercial banks may drastically affect the flow of funds from savers into real investment.

To understand this rather startling statement that commercial banks "create" checking deposits, you need to know something about how a commercial bank works. The easiest way to get this picture is to look at a simplified balance sheet of a bank, and then to trace through a few transactions. This will give you an understanding of the nature of deposits and how they get created.

The bank's balance sheet

Banks, like other business institutions, keep a running financial record of what they own and what they owe to other people. What they own and what is owed to them are their assets. What they owe to other people are their liabilities. The difference between the two is the net worth of the business to its owners, its capital and surplus, just as with any other business. Surplus is retained earnings.

A typical bank balance sheet looks like the one below, except that we have omitted a lot of minor items to make the essential categories stand out.

What this balance sheet says is that on June 30, 1977, the bank owned cash of $400,000,

---

REPORT OF CONDITION
LOCAL BANK AND TRUST COMPANY
June 30, 1977

Assets		Liabilities and net worth	
Cash	$ 400,000	Demand deposits	$ 900,000
Bonds	800,000	Savings deposits	600,000
Loans outstanding	400,000	Capital and surplus	150,000
Building and fixtures	50,000		
	$1,650,000		1,650,000

bonds valued at $800,000, and a building and fixtures valued at $50,000. In addition, it had loaned out $400,000 to customers, who owed the money back to the bank. These are its **assets.**

Offsetting these assets, the bank had deposits of $1,500,000, partly demand and partly savings deposits. These deposits are **liabilities,** because they are sums the bank promises to pay to the depositors on demand or on due notice. The difference between the assets and liabilities is $150,000, which is the estimated net worth of the bank, partly originally paid in by the stockholders as capital and partly surplus (retained profits plowed back into the business).

POTENTIAL CREATION OF CREDIT
BY AN INDIVIDUAL BANK

If we make some highly simplified assumptions, the basic operations of the Local Bank are laid bare. Assume for the moment that (1) the bank is on an isolated island where there are no other banks and no communications with other countries; (2) all payments on the island are made by bank check and no currency is used by the public (the "cash" item on the balance sheet may, for example, be gold); and (3) there are no laws to control the volume of loans the bank can make.

Suppose now that you, a substantial businessman on the island, go to the banker and ask to borrow $1,000. Your credit is good, and he agrees to make the loan. What happens to the bank's balance sheet?

On the assets side, "Loans" go up $1,000, and on the liabilities side, "Demand Deposits" go up the same amount. Remember that all payments are made by check, so you will simply take your loan as an addition to your checking deposit at the bank. Instead of giving you currency, the banker gives you a checking account. The balance sheet still balances, as it always must. **But now there is $1,000 more spendable money (checking deposits) in existence as a result of the bank's making a loan to you. There is no change at all in the amount of "cash" in existence. The bank has taken your promise to pay (which could not serve as money) and has given you its promise to pay on the order of your**

check (which is widely acceptable money). It has "monetized" your debt.[3]

This result is shown readily by a simplified bank balance sheet (sometimes called a T-account), listing only the **changes** that take place in this transaction. It shows that loans increase $1,000 on the assets side and that deposits increase $1,000 on the liabilities side of the balance sheet.

Assets		Liabilities	
Loans	+ $1,000	Deposits	+ $1,000

Chances are you've borrowed the money because you want to spend it. What happens when you do spend it? Say you buy some machinery from John Jones and write him a check for $1,000. When Jones presents the check at the bank for payment, $1,000 is taken out of your account and put in his. Since all payments are made by check, he will not want any currency. The new $1,000 of checking deposits has been spent once and is now available for Jones to spend again.

A few days later, Jones buys a new roof for his house, and pays for it with the $1,000. Then the $1,000 is transferred again, from Jones's to the roofer's account. Now the $1,000 has financed $2,000 of transactions (its velocity is 2), and the money is as ready for spending again as if the bank had printed up a thousand one-dollar bills and lent them to you. Obviously, the new deposit can be spent over and over as long as it is in existence.

In the meantime, what has been happening on the bank's balance sheet? Nothing. The $1,000 checking deposit has been moving from one account to another, but the overall totals on the balance sheet remain unchanged. The additional deposit created by the loan to you remains

[3]Banks ordinarily deduct interest on loans in advance. Thus, the bank would give you perhaps $970 and keep the other $30 for interest; you would repay the full $1,000. This process of deducting interest in advance is called "discount" rather than charging "interest." Assume for simplicity, however, that the bank gives you the full $1,000.

outstanding until the loan is paid off, and may be spent (transferred) any number of times in the meantime.

Some day your loan will come due. If you're a sound businessman, you will have built up your own checking account in preparation for the day by holding on to receipts you get from your customers. On the due date, you go in to see the banker and write him a check for $1,000 on your own account. He returns your promissory note to you, and the loan is paid off. But look at what this does to the bank's balance sheet.

Loans are down by $1,000, since the loan to you is paid off. And deposits are down by $1,000, since you have written a $1,000 check against your account payable to the bank, and this amount is not transferred to any other depositor. Repayment of the loan just reverses the original entries that were made when you borrowed the money. The whole transaction has been perfectly businesslike. It has thousands of counterparts every day in the United States. Yet, in effect, the bank has acted like a little mint, monetizing your debt and creating the checking deposit it lends you, and wiping the deposit out when you repay the loan.

Look at the T-account now. Before you repay, it still shows the $+\$1,000$ in loans and deposits from the initial loan. But now we add a $-\$1,000$ for both deposits and loans. The balance sheet is back to its original position, but the economy had an extra $1,000 of money while the loan was outstanding.

Assets		Liabilities	
Loans	+$1,000	Deposits	+$1,000
	− 1,000		− 1,000

How many other loans can the banker make simultaneously? Obviously, there is no reason why he has to stop with you. Because the public does all its business by check, and because there is no other bank on the island, he need not worry about currency withdrawals or loss of deposits to another bank. It is hard to see what will put a ceiling on the volume of loans the banker can

extend. And he could just as well extend credit by buying bonds. Suppose that instead of lending $1,000 to you, he buys a new $1,000 bond issued by the island government. The bank enters a $1,000 checking account for the government, which the government can spend when it pleases. The checking deposit is created in exactly the same way, and it stays in existence (however often it is spent) until the bank is repaid for the bond. Since the bank collects interest on every loan or investment made, this looks like a very good thing indeed for the banker and his stockholders.

But it all sounds a little like never-never land. You probably suspect there's a catch in it some place. If people could draw out currency, you say, the banker couldn't go around creating money like that just by writing down entries on his books. And you'd be right—partly right. We need to explore what happens when people *can* withdraw currency. But before you throw out this simplified example, remember that nearly 80 percent of all transactions in the United States today are made by bank check. The example is not far off on that score after all.

LIMITS TO CREDIT CREATION BY AN INDIVIDUAL BANK

Why don't banks keep on expanding their loans and earning more interest indefinitely, if all they have to do is create new checking accounts by making entries on their books? To answer, remove the simplifying assumptions of our island economy, one by one, to get a real-world situation like the one that exists in the United States today. But still assume there is no Federal Reserve to regulate the banks and to provide more currency; the amount is fixed. Assume now that the island's money-using habits are like those in the United States today. Say, the people want to hold about a fifth of their total money supply in the form of currency, and the bank's "cash" account consists of currency.

Currency withdrawals

Now the banker has to be more careful. His balance sheet shows $400,000 of cash (currency). If he is reasonably sure that the 4-to-1 ratio between deposits and currency wanted by the public will continue, he can calculate how far he can safely go in extending new credit. Every time he adds $5 to his deposits, the public will withdraw $1 of it in currency. Thus, he might be safe in expanding his deposits by nearly $2,000,000, of which he would expect to lose about $400,000 in currency, if he didn't mind seeing his cash account go down to almost zero.

Actually, the banker wouldn't want to run that close on his currency lest the bank be unable to meet unexpected demands of depositors and "go broke"; bankers are traditionally conservative people. The basic relationship of currency to potential credit expansion is clear. Whenever there is a chance of a currency withdrawal, the bank must be sure it has enough currency to meet the requests of depositors.

What if people lose confidence in the bank and all want their money in currency right now? The answer is painfully clear. The depositors who demand the first $400,000 can be paid off, but the rest are out of luck. In a fractional-reserve banking system—that is, one where the total cash reserves are only a fraction of the system's deposits—the banks cannot pay off all their depositors in currency, for the simple reason that they don't have that much currency. This sad fact was faced with regularity during past financial crises and depressions in the United States up through the 1930s.

This situation reemphasizes the basic fact: Bank deposits largely represent credit extended through the making of loans and investments by banks, not the deposit of currency in banks. This is obviously true in the Local Bank, since it has only $400,000 in currency, but deposits of $1,500,000. It is equally true in the United States today; here the total "cash" reserves of all commercial banks are about $100 billion and total deposits (demand plus savings) are about $700 billion.

Legal reserve requirements

Suppose now that the islanders get to worrying about whether their bank is sound (or maybe they hear about the way things are done in the United States), and they pass a law requiring the bank to hold cash reserves equal to at least 20 percent of its deposits.

This legal requirement (like the one imposed by the Federal Reserve in the United States) puts a limit on the bank's expansion possibilities. With $400,000 of cash, the bank can have only $2,000,000 of deposits. It already has $1,500,000, so the limit of its new deposits (credit extension) is $500,000. The actual working limit is less, because the banker needs to worry about likely currency withdrawals as well as about the legal reserve requirement. Thus, a legal cash-reserve requirement against deposits puts an upper limit on the amount of credit the bank can extend, since new loans or investments mean new deposits.

How many deposits can be supported on any given cash reserve depends on the level of the reserve requirement. With a 20 percent reserve requirement, the bank can legally have five times as many deposits as it has reserves. If the reserve requirement is 10 percent, deposits can be ten times reserves. The actual legal reserve requirement now averages about 14 percent for banks in the United States.[4]

The real function of bank reserve requirements is, thus, to limit the total volume of bank credit that can be extended. In other words, it is to limit the amount of money banks can create. Although bank reserve requirements do serve the purpose of protecting the security of customers' deposits to some extent, it should be clear by now that nothing short of 100 percent reserves would guarantee the continuous availability of cash for all depositors. With much smaller cash reserves, the thing that really keeps the banking system solvent is the confidence of the public in each other's checks. As long as nobody wants much more currency than usual, the banks get along fine. But if everyone tried to get currency for his deposits at the same time, the legal reserve requirement would be of only minor help in paying off the depositors.

When a bank has more cash reserves than the law requires, the excess is termed *excess reserves*.

---

[4]Only "cash" is counted in computing banks' legal reserves. Government securities and other assets may be nearly as liquid as cash, but they are not part of a bank's legal reserve.

Whenever a bank has excess reserves, it feels pressure to expand its loans and investments. Reserves earn no interest. Thus, the banker generally tries to keep his reserves at the lowest level that is consistent with his liquidity needs and the availability of safe loans and investments.

Adverse clearing balances

Now drop the last special assumption—that there is only one bank—and put the Local Bank in the United States. Here there are lots of other banks in operation, and the Local Bank needs to take this fact into account. If the bank makes loans to its customers, there is a good chance that they will write checks to people who do business elsewhere. And when this happens, the Local Bank has to pay cash to the other bank. This is an important change in the bank's position.

In a many-bank system, the most important limitation on the power of an individual bank to expand credit to the legal limit permitted by its reserves is the fear that it will lose reserves to other banks. If bank A has to pay cash to bank B when they settle up the checks written back and forth between their customers, we say that bank A has an "adverse clearing balance." And to bank A, an adverse clearing balance is just like a currency drain—it takes away cash reserves.

Ordinarily, the checks written against any bank and the checks it has to collect against other banks roughly balance off. You send $500 to Philadelphia to pay a bill, and your neighbor gets a payment from Philadelphia. But if one bank expands its credit more rapidly than other banks do, it's likely to lose reserves on balance. Recognizing this fact, few bankers would make new loans and investments amounting to anything like $5,000 on $1,000 of excess reserves (assuming a 20 percent reserve requirement). Indeed, bankers ordinarily hesitate to extend new credit much beyond the excess reserves they have on hand.

To summarize what we have said so far about banks and the supply of money: (1) One function of financial institutions is to channel savings to borrowers. This activity has no direct effect on the volume of money. (2) Commercial banks are distinguished from other savings in-stitutions in that they do not simply lend out the money that people have deposited. They actually "create" money by giving borrowers current spending power in exchange for future promises to repay the bank. (3) The power of an individual commercial bank to expand credit on its reserves is limited by (a) legal reserve requirements, (b) the dangers of currency withdrawals by customers, and (c) adverse clearing balances.

CREDIT CREATION AND CONTRACTION BY THE BANKING SYSTEM

Any one bank that expands loans when other banks are not expanding is checked by adverse clearing balances. But when we view the banking system as a whole, the limitation imposed by adverse clearing balances disappears. This is because the reserves one bank loses, another gains. Since the banking system as a whole loses no reserves through adverse clearing balances, it can create deposits through lending up to the multiple permitted by the legal reserve-requirement ratio, just like the island bank above. If, for example, the legal reserve requirement against deposits is 20 percent, the banking system can expand deposits up to five times its reserves.

Of course, the banking system faces limitations from the withdrawal of currency by depositors and from increases in reserve requirements, just as did the Local Bank above. For currency withdrawals reduce the volume of total reserves in the banking system. And higher legal reserve requirements reduce the multiple by which deposits can exceed reserves. But the apparent check of adverse clearing balances vanishes when we consider all banks together.[5]

It is easy to see that adverse clearing balances don't limit the expansion power of the banking system. But since individual banks normally do not lend much beyond their excess reserves, the banking system normally only gradually ex-

---

[5] Because the Federal Reserve imposes higher legal reserve requirements against demand deposits than against savings deposits, the power of the banking system to expand credit depends to some extent on whether the public chooses to hold its deposits in demand or savings accounts.

pands deposits to the legal limit on new reserves.[6]

The money-creation process works in reverse,
too. If one dollar of reserves is the basis for five
dollars of outstanding bank deposits created by
loans and investments, the loss of each dollar of
reserves can force contraction of five dollars in
deposits. Indeed, if banks are fully "loaned up"
to their legal required-reserve limit, loss of reserves must cause a contraction of deposits, and
hence of loans and investments. Such a contraction is brought about when banks reduce their
loans or investments; remember the $1,000 re-
duction in deposits when your Local Bank loan
was paid off above.

Sometimes, as with credit expansion, credit
contraction snowballs in a massive way. In the
Great Depression of the early 1930s, for example,
nearly one-third of the nation's money supply
(mainly demand deposits) was wiped out through
the contraction of bank loans and investments.
Banks lost reserves as the public withdrew currency in a scare wave, and this forced the banks
to call for payment of loans and to sell off their
government bonds. Bank deposits plus currency
fell from $46 billion to $30 billion between 1929
and 1933, a 35 percent contraction in M. Remember that each dollar of currency withdrawn
removes the reserve base for several dollars of
deposits and loans and investments.

MONEY AND THE CREATION
OF NEAR-MONIES

Only commercial banks can
"create" money by monetizing others' debts,
because by law only banks can hold demand
(checking) deposits. But savings deposits, savings and loan shares, and other near-monies are
close substitutes for money as a store of purchasing power. And other financial institutions
can "create" near-monies, as banks "create"
demand deposits. Moreover, by shifting their
savings between checking deposits and time

deposits at banks and savings and loan associations, the public can change the amount of
checking deposits and near-monies in existence.

Suppose John Doe, seeing an ad promising 6
percent interest at a savings and loan association, saves part of his paycheck and deposits
$100 in the S&L. Or he may just withdraw $100
from his own bank checking account and transfer it to the S&L. Either way, he transfers $100
from a commercial-bank demand deposit to the
savings and loan association. Bank demand deposits are down, S&L savings deposits are up
correspondingly. But the S&L association will
probably soon redeposit the $100 in its own
checking account at a commercial bank so that
it can spend or lend the money itself.

Look now at the results: First, commercial-
bank reserves and demand deposits are unchanged in total; the S&L has returned John
Doe's deposit to the commercial bank. But second, John has a fine $100 money substitute in his
savings and loan account; this will presumably
decrease the amount of actual money (currency
and checking deposits) he needs at any given
time to have an adequate margin of liquidity. It
thus frees a bigger share of demand deposits for
"active" use in making payments for goods and
services. Third, the savings and loan association
has a new $100 deposit, most of which it will
now feel free to lend out to new borrowers.
John's decision to substitute a near-money for
actual money in his own financial position has
both increased the nation's total supply of
money plus near-monies, **and** increased the total
lending power of all financial institutions, since
the commercial banks have lost no reserves and
the savings and loan association has gained $100
in additional lending power (less whatever part
of the total it feels it must hold as a ready cash
reserve).

Thus, we must add to the money-creating
powers of the commercial banks a similar power
of other financial intermediaries to "create"
near-monies, as individuals and businesses
transfer money holdings into near-monies. In
total, therefore, the power of the financial system
to generate money plus near-monies far exceeds
its power to create money alone. Moreover, the
money stock is, therefore, not entirely under the
control of the government, although it is clear

---

[6] For doubters, the appendix to this chapter explains in
detail how the banking system can expand deposits fivefold
on new reserves, assuming a 20 percent reserve requirement,
even though no individual bank ever lends out more than its
excess reserves.

that by regulating the volume of reserves the government can generally control the volume of deposits that banks create.

Following the recommendations of a special presidential commission in 1973, Congress has been considering major changes in the laws governing financial institutions. Competition among banks and other financial institutions has blurred the distinctions between them, and between money and near-monies. It seems likely that Congress will soon, in substance, permit checks to be written on savings deposits; if so, savings and demand deposits may both need to be included in the "money supply." Currently, M_1 is commonly used to denote money (currency plus demand deposits), while M_2, M_3, and other such symbols are used to denote money plus near-monies such as commercial-bank savings deposits, S&L deposits, and so on.

PART B

THE FEDERAL RESERVE SYSTEM AND THE MONEY SUPPLY

The Constitution gives to Congress the power to "coin money and regulate the value thereof." Congress has since delegated most of this power to the Federal Reserve system, which was established in 1914 after years of painful experience with repeated financial crises. The following pages first describe the Federal Reserve System and indicate briefly how it carries out its day-to-day activities. Then we analyze more fully how the Federal Reserve influences interest rates and the supply of money, the "Fed's" main channels for regulating the level of aggregate demand.

THE FEDERAL RESERVE SYSTEM

The Federal Reserve System is the major agency established by Congress to provide currency for the nation; to furnish a wide variety of financial services to the government and to the economy; and, most important, to regulate the total amount of money and to maintain "monetary and credit conditions favorable to sound business activity in all fields—agricultural, industrial and commercial."[7]

Organization and service functions

The Federal Reserve System is made up of the following:

1. The Board of Governors
2. The twelve Federal Reserve banks
3. The Federal Open Market Committee
4. The member banks

1. The Board of Governors is composed of seven members, appointed by the president and confirmed by the Senate. Members are appointed for fourteen years. One term expires every two years, an effort to safeguard the board as far as possible from political pressure groups. In most matters, the Board of Governors is ultimately responsible for the major policies of the twelve Federal Reserve banks; and, since the Federal Reserve banks in turn supervise and regulate the member banks, ultimate responsibility for the entire system is largely centralized in the Board.

2. Each of the twelve Federal Reserve banks serves a certain district in the United States. The banks are located in Boston, New York, Philadelphia, Cleveland, Richmond, Atlanta, Chicago, St. Louis, Minneapolis, Kansas City, Dallas, and San Francisco. Each Federal Reserve bank was founded by the sale of stock to member banks, which are required to buy stock. Although technically they are thus privately

[7] *The Federal Reserve System: Its Purposes and Functions* (Board of Governors of the Federal Reserve System), p. 23. This booklet provides an authoritative statement of the aims and operations of the Federal Reserve System.

owned, the Federal Reserve banks are operated in the public interest, not for profit. Most profits are returned to the U.S. Treasury.

3. The Federal Open Market Committee consists of the seven members of the Board of Governors, plus five of the presidents of the Federal Reserve banks. This twelve-member committee determines the system's policy on open-market operations—that is, the purchase and sale of government securities in the open market. These operations, explained below, are the primary means by which the Federal Reserve authorities attempt to control the volume of bank credit. Although the Board of Governors does not determine open-market policy independently, its seven members constitute a majority of the Open Market Committee.

4. The member banks include all national banks (chartered by the federal government) in the United States and those state banks that agree to conform to the requirements set up for member banks. In 1976, about 5,800 of the 14,600 commercial banks were member banks, but the nonmember banks were almost all small ones, holding only about 25 percent of the total deposits of the banking system.

In addition to its major policy functions, the Fed has important service functions.

Holding member-bank reserves.   Each member bank must by law keep its legally required reserves on deposit at its Federal Reserve bank.[8] These reserve balances are essentially checking accounts that the member banks maintain with the Federal Reserve, just as an individual has a checking account with a commercial bank. A member bank must always keep the reserve required by law, but beyond this requirement, it is free to draw on, or add to, its reserve account as it wishes.

Furnishing currency for circulation.   All currency in the United States is issued either by the Treasury or by the Federal Reserve banks. Treasury currency—mainly coins—makes up about 15 percent of the total. The Reserve banks

themselves issue our paper money, Federal Reserve notes. These are liabilities of the issuing Federal Reserve bank, and also of the federal government. Each Federal Reserve note must be fully backed by collateral—gold, government bonds, or other designated acceptable security—but in essence, the Fed has virtually unlimited power to issue new Federal Reserve notes.

Currency in circulation grows gradually as the economy grows, and increases temporarily at certain periods of the year, such as Christmas and the Fourth of July, when people and businesses want more hand-to-hand money. The banks get currency by drawing on their reserve accounts at the Reserve banks and pay out the currency to customers who make withdrawals from their deposit accounts. If the public has more currency than it wants, it simply redeposits the currency in commercial banks, which in turn redeposit the excess in their reserve accounts at the Federal Reserve banks.

Clearing and collecting checks.   Most payments in the United States are made by means of bank checks. And most bank checks drawn on out-of-town banks are "cleared" through the Federal Reserve system to avoid shipping currency. Suppose Jones in Chicago sells a $100 bill of goods to Smith in Detroit, and Smith pays by a check on his Detroit bank. Jones deposits the check at his bank in Chicago. Since both banks keep their reserves with the Chicago Federal Reserve bank, the check is cleared simply by increasing the reserve account of the Chicago bank and decreasing the account of the Detroit bank. No currency has to be shipped around the country. When Jones and Smith are in different Federal Reserve districts (say, Chicago and New York), the process is identical except that the New York and Chicago Federal Reserve banks must settle their accounts. They offset the checks due to each other through an "Interdistrict Settlement Fund."

In 1975, the Federal Reserve System handled 13 billion checks, involving total payments of $5 trillion.

Supervising member banks.   Banks in this country are supervised by several authorities.

---

[8]Except for the "vault cash" (currency) it keeps in its own vaults.

The Federal Reserve supervises all member banks. Its examiners make detailed reports on the management, the loans and investments, and the general condition of each member bank. If any member bank refuses to conform to the standards of sound banking practice specified by the Federal Reserve, the Board of Governors may remove its officers and directors or take away its right to make use of Federal Reserve credit facilities. However, these sanctions are seldom used.

Fiscal agent for the federal government. The Federal Reserve banks are bankers for the federal government. They carry most of the government's checking accounts, handle the issue and redemption of government securities, and act as fiscal agent for the government in numerous other ways. These activities are a major part of the Federal Reserve's operating responsibilities.

THE FEDERAL RESERVE, INTEREST RATES, AND THE SUPPLY OF MONEY

In the United States, the Federal Reserve is the "central bank." Its major job is to maintain monetary conditions that will help achieve a stably growing, prosperous economy. Federal Reserve control over the supply of money and interest rates is exercised largely by controlling the volume and use of member-bank reserves. Without excess reserves, commercial banks cannot extend more credit. Excess reserves make possible (but do not ensure) expansion of bank earning assets and deposits. Thus, Federal Reserve powers are designed largely to provide or reduce excess reserves.

The fundamental nature of central banking

A Federal Reserve bank is a central bank—a banker's bank. Member-bank reserves are member-bank deposits at the Reserve banks. Thus, Federal Reserve control over the volume of member-bank reserves is, in fact, control over the volume of its own deposits. And the Fed can create or destroy the reserves that underlie commercial banks' powers to lend and invest.

Before the establishment of the Federal Reserve as a central bank in 1914, the nation's commercial banks faced periodic crises. Mass currency withdrawals by depositors in times of panic exhausted reserves and forced widespread bank failures, because there was no way to convert good but illiquid loans into currency on short notice. The Federal Reserve was established largely to remedy this situation. The Reserve authorities were given power to provide new reserves for member banks in times of need.

The ability to create new bank reserves and to provide liquidity to commercial-bank assets is the distinguishing feature of a true central bank. The Federal Reserve can create new reserves (member-bank deposits) by buying bonds or making loans to member banks, just as member banks create deposits by buying bonds or making loans to businesses and individuals. It gives deposits (new reserves) to member banks in exchange for bonds or the banks' promises to repay at a later date. Thus, if a member bank wants more reserves (that is, deposits at the Fed), it can borrow at the Fed, giving its own promise to repay. Or it can sell some of its government bonds to the Fed, receiving reserves (deposits at the Fed) in payment. In either case, the Fed "creates" the new reserves by giving the member bank a new deposit (reserve) in exchange for the assets it receives from the member bank.

The Fed authorities attempt to control the volume and direction of commercial-bank lending and investing, and hence the volume of bank deposits, through the following seven major channels. The first three (open-market operations, reserve requirements, and the discount rate) are aimed largely at controlling the total supply of credit and deposits, through regulating the commercial banks' excess reserves. The others are aimed more at controlling the flow of credit to particular uses, such as speculation. These latter are thus called "selective," or "qualitative," credit controls. In regulating the supply of credit, the Fed also influences interest rates—the "cost" of credit.

Open-market operations

Purchase and sale of U.S. government securities in the open market is the major device used by the Fed to control the volume of member-bank reserves. By buying "governments," the Fed increases member-bank reserves; by selling "governments," it reduces member-bank reserves. To understand how this works, consider first the combined balance sheet of the Federal Reserve banks, shown at the bottom of this page.

This shows the two big assets of the Federal Reserve banks, gold and government securities. The offsetting major liabilities are member-bank deposits and Federal Reserve notes. It is essential to remember that the "cash reserves" shown on commercial-bank statements are mainly not actual currency but are instead deposits held at the Federal Reserve banks.

1. The Federal Reserve can create new reserves for the commercial banks by buying government bonds in the open market—thereby stimulating the commercial banks to make new loans and investments. If the Fed wants to encourage more bank loans, it buys $1,000 worth of U.S. government bonds, say, from a commercial bank.[9] To pay for these bonds, it simply gives the bank a $1,000 deposit credit (new reserve balance) at the Federal Reserve. The commercial bank has $1,000 of new reserves, and they are all excess reserves, since its deposits have not been changed by the transaction. The Federal Reserve has created a $1,000 member-bank deposit (reserve account) against the government bond. Because the commercial

bank now has $1,000 of new excess reserves, it is in a position to expand its loans by four or five times that amount, depending on legal reserve requirements.[10]

Consider the T-accounts for the commercial and the Federal Reserve bank. They show the $1,000 addition to excess reserves on the books of both the commercial bank and the Fed.

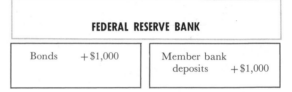

COMMERCIAL BANK	
Cash + $1,000 Bonds − 1,000	

FEDERAL RESERVE BANK	
Bonds + $1,000	Member bank deposits + $1,000

Does all this seem a little like black magic—new commercial-bank reserves created out of nowhere by the Federal Reserve banks, reserves that in turn can provide the basis for a much larger amount of commercial-bank deposits, also created out of nowhere? In a sense, it is. But each

[9] Remember that the Fed does not issue any bonds itself, but merely buys and sells government bonds that have been issued previously by the Treasury.

[10] There is substantially, but not quite, the same effect if the Fed buys the bond from a business or individual. Trace through the effect for yourself. The following section suggests the analysis if you need help.

FEDERAL RESERVE BANKS			
January 1, 1976			
(In Billions)			
Gold	$ 12	Member-bank deposits	$ 26
U.S. securities	` 88	Federal Reserve notes	77
	$100		$103

[a] Does not balance because other (minor) items are omitted.

dollar of new member-bank reserves at the Fed is matched by a newly acquired government bond, and each new deposit at the commercial bank will be matched by a borrower's promise to repay. There is no magic. But through this process the Fed is able to "create" new member-bank reserves, which are often called "high-powered money," because they can in turn serve as the reserves behind a larger volume of newly created deposits at commercial banks.

Is there a limitation on how many new reserves the Federal Reserve can create in this way? No direct limit. Until 1968, the Fed was required to have a specified gold reserve against member-bank deposits and Federal Reserve notes respectively, but now there is no such requirement. Fundamentally, the reserve-creating powers of the Fed are now limited only by the good judgment of the Federal Reserve authorities, **and by the discretion of Congress, which can repeal or alter the Fed's powers anytime it wishes.** Thus, control over the nation's money supply is ultimately subject to the control of the democratic process, just as are other government powers.[11]

How effective is the Federal Reserve in lowering interest rates and stimulating new commercial-bank loans when it provides new reserves? More reserves push a banker to extend new credit, for no banker likes to lose the interest he might earn on idle reserves. In those rare cases where excess reserves are already large because bankers don't see any "sound" borrowers looking for loans, still more excess reserves may not help much. But banks can also increase the volume of deposits by buying up government bonds. Bankers do vary the amount of excess reserves they wish to hold under different circumstances, but with rare exceptions, commercial bankers have increased their loans and investments about as far as their excess reserves permit. The big exception was the depression of the 1930s, when the commercial banks held billions of dollars of excess reserves for nearly a decade.

Note that the Fed's open-market purchases also directly push down interest rates on govern-

ment securities. Fed purchases will bid up the prices of bonds, which is equivalent to forcing down on the interest yield on the bonds. (See Chapter 14, footnote 15 if you don't remember why.) Since lower interest rates help to stimulate the economy, open-market purchases are a two-pronged weapon against recession.

2. **When the Open Market Committee wants to decrease member-bank reserves, it sells government securities in the open market to whoever bids for them—individuals, businesses, or banks. This reduces commercial-bank reserves when the Federal Reserve is paid for the bonds.** Consider how.

If a member bank buys the bond, it pays by giving $1,000 of its reserves to the Federal Reserve; on the member bank's balance sheet, "cash" goes down and "bonds" go up by $1,000. Thus, the bank loses a full $1,000 of excess reserves, since its deposits remain unchanged. If a business or individual buys the bond from the Reserve, the effect is almost the same. He pays by a check on his bank. His bank's reserves are reduced by $1,000 when the Federal Reserve presents the check for collection. The member bank's deposits also drop by the $1,000 transferred from the bond buyer's account to the Federal Reserve. Since the bank loses $1,000 in both deposits and reserves, its required reserves are $200 lower but its excess reserves drop by $800. Excess reserves contract a little less than in the bank-purchase case, but the general effect is similar.

If the bank buys the bond, the T-account entries at the commerical bank are as shown above the dotted line. If an individual buys it, the entries are as shown below the dotted line.[12] Either way, the commercial bank's lending power is reduced.

Cash	− $1,000		
Bonds	+ 1,000		
....		....	
Cash	− $1,000	Deposits	− $1,000

[12]If the buyer pays in currency, he reduces the amount of currency in circulation, also a reduction in the money stock. But payment in currency is very unusual.

Discount-rate changes

When a member bank runs short of reserves, it may borrow from its Federal Reserve bank, just as you and I borrow at a commercial bank. In such a case, the member bank could "discount" notes. It can borrow reserves from the Fed, using customers' notes (promises to repay loans) or government securities as collateral. The rate of interest charged by the Federal Reserve to member banks is called the "discount rate." In discounting, the initiative is in the hands of the commercial banker to increase his reserves, while open-market operations are at the discretion of the Fed.

The Fed raises the discount rate to discourage member-bank borrowing and lowers the rate to encourage it. But the Fed discourages member-bank borrowing except on a temporary basis. Thus, the discount rate is of relatively minor direct importance. But changes in the rate have an important psychological effect on the banking and business communities, because they are viewed as evidence of the Fed's general position on monetary expansion or restraint.[13]

Changes in member-bank reserve requirements

In 1933, a drastic new power was given to the Board of Governors—the power to raise and lower legal reserve requirements for member banks. By raising reserve requirements, the Board wipes out member banks' excess reserves and directly restricts credit expansion. Suppose a member bank has $1,000,000 deposits and $200,000 reserves, and the required legal reserve ratio is 16 percent. It has a comfortable $40,000 of excess reserves. If the Board raises the legal requirement to 20 percent, the bank's excess reserve is wiped out. Conversely, lowering legal reserve requirements increases excess reserves.

Changing reserve requirements is a blunt tool of credit control, compared with the gradual,

---

[13]Sometimes you see the term "free reserves." These are excess reserves *less* commercial-bank borrowing from the Fed. Because each commercial bank must repay its borrowing promptly, many experts believe that free reserves are better than excess reserves as an indication of commercial banks' ability to extend new credit. When free reserves are negative, they are called "net borrowed reserves."

flexible way open-market operations can be used. Thus, the Reserve authorities change reserve requirements only infrequently, depending instead primarily on open-market operations.

"Selective" credit controls

The preceding general controls over bank reserves control the total volume of bank lending, the level of interest rates, and the stock of money, but they leave the private banker free to allocate his funds as he wishes among different borrowers. In addition, the Fed has smaller "selective" controls over particular bank loans and uses to which bank credit is put. These permit the Fed to influence directly the uses of bank credit. Many economists question the effectiveness of such controls, because money, once created, flows freely from one sector of the economy to another, and it is very difficult to control any one sector by limiting lending directly to it. But such selective controls may have important temporary effects.

Maximum interest rates paid on deposits. The Fed has the power to set maximum interest rates on different classes of deposits, and other regulatory agencies have similar powers over other financial intermediaries, such as the savings and loan associations. By setting different ceilings on interest rates at different institutions, the bank supervisors can influence their relative competitive positions, and thus indirectly influence where savers' funds go.

For example, in the 1960s, the S&Ls bid many deposits away from the commercial banks by offering higher interest rates, and channeled these funds into mortgages to finance home building, especially in the West. Originally, there were no government ceilings on the rates that S&Ls could pay their depositors, but commercial banks had maximum rates on their savings deposits. In the mid-1960s, the Fed raised the maximum rates that commercial banks might pay, and thus permitted them to compete for deposits with the S&Ls. This channeled funds away from the housing industry toward the more diverse borrowers from commercial banks. Rate ceilings were also used to affect the competitive power of big U.S. commercial banks vis-à-vis European capital markets.

Once detailed direct controls are instituted that influence the competitive position of different financial institutions, difficult questions of equity arise, and there is an unfortunate tendency for such direct controls to proliferate. We shall return to this issue in the next chapter.

Control of stock-market credit: margin requirements. Often customers buy stocks and bonds "on margin." That is, they pay the broker a cash "margin" (down payment) and borrow the rest of the purchase price from the broker, leaving the newly purchased securities as collateral for the loan. The broker, in turn, typically borrows from commercial banks what the security buyer does not put up as margin (cash). The smaller the margin required, the more the buyer can borrow of the purchase price. If margin requirements are raised, therefore, the use of bank credit for purchasing securities is restricted. If margin requirements are lowered, it becomes easier to buy securities on credit.

The Fed has power to set minimum margin requirements for dealings on the major securities exchanges, ranging up to 100 percent cash payments. In the wild stock-market speculation of the late 1920s, most stock was bought on margins of 10 percent or less, so speculators found it easy to bid up prices on borrowed money; but they could also be wiped out by only a small decline in the price of the stock. Now, margin requirements are generally set between 50 and 100 percent. Most economists believe that Federal Reserve margin requirements exercise a healthy retraint on speculative stock purchases under boom conditions.

"Direct pressure" or "moral suasion." When the Fed wants to discourage bank lending, it may use "direct pressure" or "moral suasion," on the bankers. Bank examiners may be instructed to tighten up their requirements for "good" loans and investments. Reserve officials may frown when member banks come to the discount window for temporary loans. They may also make public statements warning against inflation and overexpansion of credit. In extreme cases, the Reserve banks may simply refuse to lend to offending member banks. There is not much evidence that such moral suasion is very effective. There is even less hope that it can do

anything to persuade bankers to make more loans in hard times.

Consumer-credit controls. During World War II and in the Korean War, the Fed was temporarily given power to regulate consumer credit (on installment purchases and charge accounts) and real estate credit. On both housing and consumer credit, the Fed imposed minimum down payments and maximum repayment periods. Raising down payments made it hard to buy without cash in hand; shortening the total payment period increased the monthly payment required. These were controversial controls, and they have found little support in the peacetime economy. Although they were powerful, they mainly restrained the purchases of lower- and middle-income families, who needed to buy on credit.

CONCLUSION

In perspective, the Fed has enormous powers to check any credit expansion—indeed, to force mass contraction—if it chooses to use them. By dumping all its nearly $100 billion of government securities on the market and by raising reserve requirements to their legal limits, the Fed could bring on a massive deflation sure to send the entire economic system into chaos. Of course, the Federal Reserve officials would never consider such a foolish action. But this points up the great power inherent in the Fed to restrict growth in *M*.

The Fed's ability to stimulate bank lending is also great, and it has substantially unlimited power to create new reserves through open-market operations. But success on the expansion side is less sure. Banks need not necessarily make new loans in recession merely because they receive new excess reserves, although they are almost certain to increase the money stock by buying more bonds if they don't expand their loans. How effectively this will stimulate aggregate spending depends on the issues outlined in Chapters 13 and 14.

Even with these limitations, the Fed's powers are great. The real issue is how to use these powers most effectively to achieve a stably growing, high-employment economy without inflation. How to do this is the subject of Chapter 18.

REVIEW

**Concepts
to remember**

This chapter has introduced several important concepts and institutions. Be sure you understand the following:

money	adverse clearing balance
currency	credit contraction
demand (checking) deposits	Board of Governors
savings and time deposits	Open Market Committee
near-monies	Federal Reserve banks
bank credit	member banks
commercial bank	"creation" of bank reserves
financial intermediary	open-market operations
credit creation	discount rate
bank reserves	selective credit controls
excess reserves	interest-rate ceilings
reserve requirements	margin requirements

**For analysis
and discussion**

1. Why is currency worth more than its value as paper and ink?
2. Get a copy of a recent balance sheet from one of your local banks. What main types of credit does this bank extend? Which of these types of credit would you expect to be most liquid (most readily convertible into cash) in case of a business recession?
3. If banks hold reserves equal to only a small fraction of their deposits, are you safe in depositing your money in a bank? Explain why, or why not.
4. If you were a banker, would you hold excess reserves? Why, or why not?
5. In a small, isolated economy (that is, no foreign trade) with money-using habits comparable to those of the United States, there are five identical banks. Each bank's balance sheet is as shown below. The law prescribes that banks must hold a 10 percent cash reserve against deposits. There is no central bank.

Cash	$ 7,000,000	Deposits	$30,000,000
Loans	14,000,000	Capital and Surplus	4,000,000
Government Securities	13,000,000		
	$34,000,000		$34,000,000

    a. A customer of bank A mines $1 million of gold (considered as cash for reserve purposes) and deposits it in his bank. Trace through any *likely* expansion of the money supply by bank A and by the entire banking system. What would be the *maximum* expansion possible? Specify clearly any assumptions you make, and state your reasoning carefully and precisely.

b. Is the banking system in a more or less *sound* position as a result of the gold deposit and the consequences you have predicted above? Explain.

6. Explain how the transfer of your $100 deposit from a commercial bank to a savings and loan association can increase society's stock of liquid assets (money plus near-monies).

7. In what ways are the objectives of a central bank (like the Federal Reserve) different from those of a commercial bank?

8. Explain the main weapons the Fed has to check an inflationary boom.

9. Suppose the Federal Reserve takes the following actions. In each case, explain what will be the likely effect on the total money stock.
   a. It sells $1 billion of government securities to the banks.
   b. It raises reserve requirements from 10 to 15 percent for all member banks.
   c. It buys $1 billion of government securities from individuals and business concerns.
   d. It buys directly from the U.S. Treasury $1 billion of newly issued government securities.
   e. It raises the discount rate by 1 percent.

10. Suppose the economy is in a recession. What steps would you advocate that the Federal Reserve take to help stimulate lending and recovery?

APPENDIX

The individual bank and the banking system

If no individual bank lends more than its excess reserves, how can the banking system expand credit fivefold on its excess reserves (assuming a 20 percent reserve requirement)? An example can show how it works.

Assume, first, that the Local Bank has $1,000 excess reserves, and that all other banks are loaned up to their legal limits. As the Local Bank makes new loans and investments, its reserves are gradually drawn away to other banks, and its credit-expansion possibilities are limited. But the reserves the Local Bank loses, some other bank gains.

Suppose Local makes a new loan of $1,000, just the amount of its excess reserves. The T-account then looks like Stage 1, including the original $1,000 of excess reserves but excluding the rest of the original balance sheet. Consider first only the entries above the dotted line.

Soon the borrower writes a check for the entire $1,000, and the check is deposited in bank *B*. This action transfers both the $1,000 deposit and the matching $1,000 cash reserve from the Local Bank to

LOCAL BANK—STAGE 1			
Excess reserve	$1,000		
Loans	+ 1,000	Deposits	+$1,000
Cash	− 1,000	Deposits	− 1,000

B. On the Local Bank T-account, deduct $1,000 from cash and from deposits, as shown below the dotted line, to see the bank's new position. Local is left with $1,000 of increased loans, on which it happily earns interest.

Bank *B* now has $1,000 of new reserves and $1,000 of new deposits. We can set up a T-account for bank *B*, showing (Stage 2) +$1,000 for both the new cash and deposits, above the first dotted line. Of the new reserves, only $200 is required to back the new $1,000 deposit, so $800 is excess. Obviously, *B* is now safe in

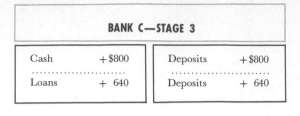

BANK B—STAGE 2			
Cash	+$1,000	Deposits	+$1,000
Loans	+ 800	Deposits	+ 800
Cash	− 800	Deposits	− 800

BANK C—STAGE 3			
Cash	+$800	Deposits	+$800
Loans	+ 640	Deposits	+ 640

extending at least $800 of new loans, since it has that much excess reserves.

So *B* makes a new $800 loan, creating $800 of additional deposits. This is shown on *B*'s T-account, below the first dotted line.

Now the borrower spends the money to a customer of bank *C*. Bank *B* loses the $800 of deposits and reserves to bank *C*. The loss is shown below the second dotted line on *B*'s accounts. Note that on the liability side, *B* still has the $1,000 original deposit created by Local Bank; on the asset side, it still has a matching $200 of new reserves from Local, plus $800 of its own new loans. It is earning interest on its new $800 loan.

But *C* now has $800 of new deposits and the $800 of new reserves from *B* (Stage 3). This is shown in a new T-account, set up for *C*; the items are shown above the dotted line in Stage 3.

The total of new deposits has now risen to $1,800 ($1,000 in *B* and $800 in *C*), matched by $1,800 of new

loans, even though no bank has lent a penny beyond its available excess reserves. Bank *C*, moreover, now has $640 of excess reserves ($800 new reserves, of which only $160 is required to back its $800 of new deposits). On these excess reserves it can safely make at least $640 of new loans, shown below the dotted line on its T-account. This will raise the total of new deposits to $2,440 against the original $1,000 of excess reserves. (The $2,440 total includes $1,000 in bank *B* and $1,440 in bank *C* at this stage.) And the expansion process can obviously continue. Trace it another stage for yourself, assuming that *C*'s borrower spends his deposit to someone who banks with *D*; or the effect is the same if the reserves go back to Local Bank, or to any other. The expansion can continue until total deposits have risen to $5,000 against the $1,000 of excess reserves. Each individual bank rightly hesitates to lend out more than its excess reserves, but the reserves it loses go to some other bank.

This process of cumulative deposit expansion is diagrammed in Figure 17–1. Assume that bank *A*

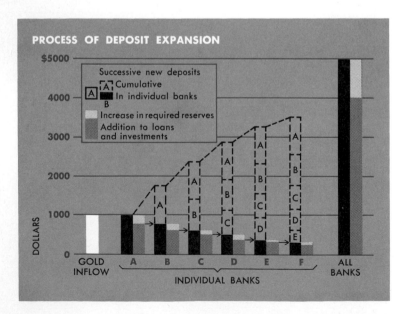

Figure 17–1
One thousand dollars of new reserves (gold) ultimately serves as the foundation for $5,000 of new deposits, as banks make new loans and investments—even though no bank ever lends out more than its own excess reserves.

receives $1,000 of new reserves, say, because $1,000 of newly mined gold is deposited. This $1,000 deposit requires only $200 of new reserves, so bank *A* is entirely safe in expanding its loans and investments by $800, as shown in the dark-colored bar for bank *A*. (Note that the bank letters don't match those in the preceding example.)

Now bank *A*'s new borrower writes a check to a customer of bank *B,* and the $800 is transferred to bank *B*. Bank *B* now has $800 of new deposits and $800 of new reserves, which means that it has excess reserves of $640, since required reserves increase by only $160. It is perfectly safe in lending out an additional $640, and does so, as shown in the diagram. This $640 may now be transferred to a customer of some other bank (*C*), which then has new deposits and excess reserves on which to expand its loans. At each stage, the deposits created by previous transactions are piled on top, in the dotted sections, to show the cumulative increase.

As the diagram shows, this process can continue, piling up new deposits that arise from new loans, until a total of $5,000 of new deposits is reached (the tall dark-colored bar at the right), including the original $1,000 deposit produced by the gold deposit. This is just what we would expect: $1,000 of new reserves has been able to support $5,000 of new deposits, given a 20 percent legal reserve requirement against deposits and no currency drain. The tall light bar at the right shows the $4,000 of new loans and the $1,000 of new required reserves, just using up the original $1,000 of new gold reserves, so the growth must now stop. Moreover, this expansion has taken place even though no individual bank has ever lent out more than the excess reserves it actually has on hand. So when your banker tells you that he would never lend out more money than he has in excess reserves, he may be quite correct. Yet the banking system as a whole creates deposits equal to many times its cash reserves—in this case, equal to five times its new reserves.

The critical point is that the banking system is not limited by adverse clearing balances. For the banking system as a whole, the only overall drain on reserves comes from currency withdrawals, from international gold flows, or from Federal Reserve or Treasury policies.

CHAPTER 18 MONETARY POLICY

Monetary policy is the second big gun in the government's arsenal against economic instability. This chapter examines the theory and practical operations involved, and concludes with a look at the optimal mix of monetary and fiscal policy.

THE THEORY OF MONETARY POLICY

Under the "gold standard" that prevailed in the Western world during most of the century preceding World War II, the stock of money was loosely controlled by an impersonal mechanism. The money supply increased and decreased when gold flowed in or out of a nation. But now, most economists argue against leaving the supply of money to this mechanism. Instead, they say that the government or a "central bank" should control the money stock so as to minimize inflations and depressions.

Monetary policy, interest rates, and the money stock

Chapters 13 and 14 provided the analytical foundation for monetary policy. If we want to increase or decrease aggregate demand, the central bank should increase or decrease M. Remember the main channels of effect.

The neo-Keynesian model suggests that more M will act only by increasing investment spending through reducing the rate of interest. Then the chain of effects runs like this:

$$+M \rightarrow -r \rightarrow +I \rightarrow +\text{GNP}$$

That is, an increase in M leads to a lower interest rate, which in turn leads to more investment, which in turn leads to a higher GNP directly and through the multiplier.

The monetarists argue that money has a broader and more direct effect. More M will lead not only to more investment through lower interest rates, but also directly to more consumption and investment spending. This occurs because an increase in M will lower the marginal return on money relative to other assets and will lead consumers and businesses to spend down their real money balances, acquiring other assets (including both consumer and investment goods) instead.

What is the right amount of money?

If GNP were a constant multiple of the stock of money, then the task of monetary policy would be relatively simple. Determine the desired level of GNP, and then move the stock of money up or down to obtain that desired level. But even if M causes changes in money GNP, we know that the public's demand for money balances also varies, that the V in $MV = PT$ varies. Thus, to determine the right M to produce any desired level of aggregate money-spending, we must take into account changes in the public's demand for money balances. Figure 13–2 pictured the fluctuations in income velocity since 1900.

The public's demand for money balances depends on its level of income (or wealth) and on interest rates on money substitutes. The higher the income (or wealth) of the public, the larger, other things equal, will be the money balances it wishes to hold. The higher the interest rate on money substitutes, the less money it will want to hold, because higher interest rates will lead people to shift their assets out of money (which yields no interest) into securities or other assets. Thus, for any level of aggregate demand we want to achieve, the right amount of M is that amount that the public wants to hold at that desired level of GNP and at existing interest rates. More M than this amount will lead to higher spending than we want; less M will lead to lower spending.

In a growing economy, the amount of money needed will gradually rise. Prima facie, we might expect the need for more money to grow apace with the growth in real-output potential—say, about 4 percent a year. But just how fast M needs to grow will depend on how fast the public's demand for money balances rises at full-employment levels.

Even if the Fed could keep aggregate demand growing at exactly the desired rate, this would not guarantee full employment without inflation. Sometimes, especially in the upsweep of a boom, more spending leads to rising prices when substantial unemployment remains. But we shall focus attention here on the control of *nominal* GNP, leaving to Chapter 19 the further difficult problem that arises when we simultaneously face inflation and unemployment.

Summary: The right amount of money depends both on the desired level of real GNP and on the public's demand for money balances at that level of GNP and of interest rates. A rising GNP without an increase in M will tend to raise interest rates and limit the growth in GNP. Thus, it is important that M grow gradually over the long pull—at roughly the growth rate of the economy's productive capacity, but probably with variations to offset short-run disturbances.[1]

Should the Fed watch M or interest rates?

The Fed's big job is to regulate aggregate demand. But monetary theory provides no decisive answer as to whether the Fed should focus on M or on interest rates in doing so. The monetarist says M, since V will normally be relatively stable. The neo-Keynesians say interest

---

[1] Some economists argue that the Fed should concentrate on M_2 instead of M_1. M_2, the broader concept of money that includes time and savings accounts as well as demand deposits, grows somewhat faster than M_1, is somewhat more stable, and has a somewhat stabler relationship to GNP ($V_2 = $ about 2.5) than does M_1.

rates, since interest rates influence the rate of investment, which in turn dominates GNP, and the multiplier is relatively stable.

If the public's demand for money varies, the Fed can fix the stock of money, or interest rates—but not both. It must choose. Suppose the economy is growing satisfactorily at 4 percent along a high-employment growth path, and the money stock is growing at the same rate. Now interest rates begin to rise. The Keynesians say, increase M faster to check the rise in interest rates before they reduce investment and bring recession. But the monetarists say, just keep on increasing M at 4 percent per annum, since to speed that rate would increase the growth rate of GNP and generate inflation. Which is right?

The answer is, it depends on the cause of the increase in interest rates. If the cause is an increase in the public's liquidity demand for money, then V will fall and there will be a recession unless more M is provided to offset the lower V; the Keynesians are right. But if the cause is a rise in the transactions demand for money (for example, because businesses want more bank credit to expand their inventories and make new investments), to provide more M will permit this faster rise in aggregate demand, and inflation will result; the monetarists are right. In principle, both can agree on the proper monetary policy *if* we know what is causing the higher interest rates—but often we don't know. The monetarists generally presume that the public's demand for M is stable (that is, V is stable), so the Fed should concentrate on providing the right growth in M, letting interest rates move as they will. The Keynesians presume that interest rates influence investment spending, so the Fed should keep interest rates stable when the level of investment and GNP are satisfactory, varying M as need be to achieve this result. In any given situation, the Fed must choose, and which presumption is right is no idle question.

Often no dilemma exists. For example, everyone agrees that in depressions, both more M and lower interest rates are needed; conversely, to fight inflation, both tighter M and higher interest rates are appropriate. But sometimes the dilemma does arise—whether to be guided by interest rates or the money stock. The late 1960s were a painful case in point when, in retrospect, the Fed concentrated on interest rates too much, and the result was too much M and too much inflation. Today, the Fed watches both M and interest rates—and, until the dispute is resolved, tries to analyze each case on its own merits when the two indicators conflict.

POLICIES TO REGULATE AGGREGATE DEMAND

Monetary restraint to check inflation

If the Fed wants to restrain aggregate demand and inflation, it can sell bonds in the open market or raise reserve requirements to reduce excess reserves. Since commercial banks typically operate with small excess reserves, either action can have a direct and powerful restrictive effect on the extension of bank credit. The Fed can also raise the discount rate, which makes it more expensive for commercial banks to borrow additional reserves when they run tight. This is a less powerful restraint, since banks are still able to borrow additional reserves if they are willing to pay the higher rate. But the discount rate is widely viewed as an indicator of the Fed's attitude on credit conditions, and thus has an important symbolic, psychological impact. The Fed has plenty of powers to restrain aggregate demand if it wants to use them. Its problem is rather how to use its powers so as to have the desired effects on real output, employment, and the price level, when all it can do directly is regulate bank reserves and short-term interest rates.

When the economy is expanding, businesses need more money for "working capital" to finance larger inventories, to meet higher payrolls, to buy more materials, and to finance new factories and equipment. Consumers' demand for money also rises with their incomes. In an expanding economy, therefore, if the Fed merely does nothing to provide additional reserves, this policy of inaction implies a gradual tightening of the money markets and a rise in interest rates, since demand for M rises but its supply does not.

What do banks do when their excess reserves are squeezed? They often raise their interest rates—the prices they charge on loans. Banks also often "ration" credit to their customers. Instead of using higher rates to eliminate the customers least willing to pay more for loans, they allocate their scarce credit to their oldest and best customers. They consider this sound long-run policy, just as many businesses don't try to squeeze the last penny out of good customers in periods of temporary shortages. Either way, tight money tends to check the growth in output, employment, and prices.

On their side, businesses and consumers try to avoid the pinch by economizing on money balances—that is, by reducing their money balances to the barest minimum needed to carry on their transactions and meet precautionary needs. The same amount of money thus does more work; V is speeded up, and the restraint of tighter money is partially avoided. The higher that interest rates are forced by the credit squeeze, the greater the inducement is to put "idle" (non-interest-bearing) money to work.

Figure 18–1 shows this effect clearly. The dot for each year shows the average interest rate on "prime" short-term loans and the average turnover (or velocity) of demand deposits at banks in some 200 cities outside New York City (which is eliminated to avoid the huge volume of stock-market transactions there). Velocity varies directly with interest rates. For example, note the low interest rates and velocity during the depression years. These velocity figures include many transactions not contained in the GNP accounts and thus are only a very imperfect approximation to changes in income velocity. But in some respects they are more interesting, because they show what happens to the total use of demand deposits when interest rates rise or fall. If we plot income velocity against interest rates for the same years, the same general relationship is revealed.

But there are limits on how far working-cash balances can be reduced. The public and the banks can avoid the pressure of Federal Reserve restraint temporarily, but only temporarily if the Fed keeps the pressure on. Ultimately, the Fed can have as strong an impact as it wishes, by raising reserve requirements sharply and by selling a large enough volume of government securities.

But the Fed's job is not easy. Too-drastic action may throw the baby out with the bath water. Its task is to check the inflation and level off the boom, not to plunge the economy into depression. Tightening up credit just enough to keep consumption and investment growing at exactly the right rate is a difficult and delicate task.

Figure 18–1
As interest rates rise, the turnover of demand deposits goes up. It pays people to economize on the use of money and to reduce their idle balances. (Source: Federal Reserve Board.)

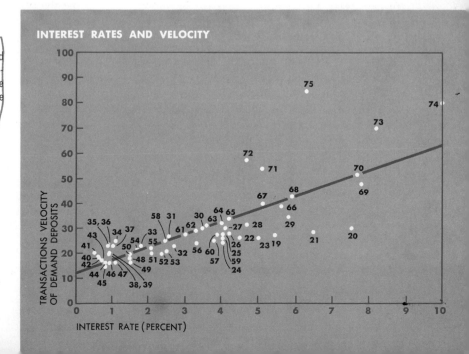

INTEREST RATES AND VELOCITY

The differential effects of tight money

The job is even tougher for another reason. When money tightens, some borrowers are squeezed more than others. Banks naturally tend to allocate their scarce funds to established customers. Conversely, new small firms and individuals tend to be squeezed out, especially when their credit rating is not high. Tight money especially squeezes home construction, because high interest rates bulk large in total monthly mortgage payments and because many banks rank such loans below those to businesses that they see as long-run customers. Bitter claims of inequity can be expected from potential borrowers who are shut out when interest rates rise and there aren't enough loans to go around. There is no way to restrict aggregate demand without turning away somebody, and the big, grade-A borrowers aren't likely to be the ones shut out.

A further complication arises when the monetary authorities use direct controls (interest-rate ceilings) to regulate the flow of savings to different financial institutions. Savings and loan associations, for example, lend almost entirely to builders and home buyers. Thus, if they are permitted to pay high rates to their depositors while commercial banks are limited to lower rates, both S&Ls and the housing industry are favored relative to commercial banks and industries that borrow from the banks. But in tight-money periods, interest rates obtainable elsewhere by savers rise above the rates S&Ls can pay, and funds are channeled away from the housing market.[2] Housing is thus a prime victim of tight money in most cases. Tight money must shut out someone from credit if it is to do its job. There is no way it can avoid restraining some potential borrowers more than others.

Monetary expansion to increase spending

If aggregate demand is inadequate, the Fed's first job is to be sure that banks have

[2]This is called "disintermediation," because funds are channeled away from such financial intermediaries as the S&Ls into direct investment in higher-yield securities like Treasury bills and "commercial paper."

plenty of reserves. It can reduce reserve requirements and buy government securities in the open market, providing new bank reserves in paying for its purchases. In addition, it can lower the discount rate. It can guarantee liquidity to the banking system and eliminate the possibility of another debacle like that of the years 1929–33, when mass liquidation of bank loans occurred as the banks lost reserves through currency withdrawals, forcing the downward spiral ever deeper.

If the Fed provides generous excess reserves, what will the bankers do? They will want to lend, because idle reserves earn no interest. If times are reasonably good, bankers will usually increase their loans promptly. But in depression, acceptable borrowers are scarce.

Even in this case, however, bankers can put their reserves to work by buying government securities. These are always substantially safe, and they pay interest. And buying government securities increases the money stock, just as making new loans does. So flooding the banks with reserves will increase M, bidding up the price of bonds and (what is the same thing) bidding down interest rates.

History presents one big counterexample. After 1933, in the Great Depression, the inflow of gold plus Federal Reserve policy built up large excess reserves at the commercial banks. Although bank credit in fact expanded rapidly as reserves built up, it did not expand nearly as rapidly as did reserves. Thus, for the first time in history, the banking system held a huge volume of excess reserves over an extended period of years. Some economists suggest that this indicates a "liquidity trap" that we can expect to face again if we get into another serious depression. More excess reserves or more M will simply pile up in the idle balances, so monetary policy is a very weak stimulant to expansion under such conditions. But monetarists reply that the large excess reserves of the 1930s were the exception to the rule. More important, they stress that pumping reserves into the banking system did in fact increase M rapidly, and that in turn both money and real GNP rose rapidly, once the great contraction of both reserves and M in the period 1929–33 was reversed.

Everyone agrees that easy money is a good

thing in recessions, even though there is disagreement over its precise effects. The evidence suggests that lower interest rates are more likely to stimulate long- than short-term investment. On a long loan, like a 30-year mortgage, a small reduction in the interest rate makes a big difference in the monthly payment. Thus, lower interest rates may be a substantial stimulus to long-term projects like houses, public ultilities, factories, and the like. Low short-term interest rates are less likely to stimulate investment. Cheaper money lowers the cost of borrowing for working-capital purposes—to meet payrolls, carry inventories, and so on. But here, interest is a tiny part of the relevant costs. And the short-run marginal efficiency of investment depends heavily on volatile customer demand and profit expectations.

Since everyone agrees that easy money may help somewhat to expand aggregate demand, why not just flood the banks with reserves to get whatever stimulus more M can produce? The answer is that here, as in fighting inflation, there may be danger of too much as well as too little. If the Fed pours excessive M into the economy, given the lags in policy effects, it may be very hard to check the ensuing boom without very strong restrictive measures if the economy "overheats." The timing problems faced in fighting recession are roughly comparable to those in fighting an inflationary boom. Just right is what's needed, neither too much nor too little!

The problem of timing and lags

The Federal Reserve's problem is deciding what is the right thing to do at the right time. In large part, it's the same problem faced by the fiscal authorities, but with some important differences. The problem breaks down into two big questions: First, what is the state of the economy now, and where is it going in the absence of further monetary-policy action? Second, what shall we do to mold this pattern into one of stable economic growth without inflation? Look at Figure 18–2, which provides a very rough picture of a business cycle, and imagine you are a Federal Reserve Board member.

First, you have to decide where you are now. At A, B, C, or D? You don't know for sure, and

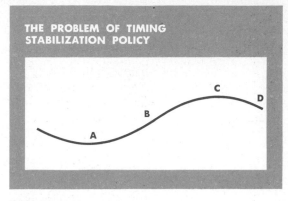

Figure 18–2
The Federal Reserve authorities seldom know where we are in the cycle, or just how long it will take their actions to exercise their full effects. What is the correct monetary policy if you think we're probably at B, but there's a good chance it may be C instead?

neither does anybody else. Suppose you think we're probably well along in a strong business upswing—say, at about B. Then the problem is, How near the top? Is the boom weakening, with a downturn just around the corner? Or does the upswing have months or years of booming prosperity left in it? If only you knew![3]

Second, given your best decision as to where we are and where we're headed, you have to decide what the Fed should do now. Suppose that you suspect we're at B, and that potential inflation poses a serious problem. Should you raise reserve requirements? Sell bonds in the open market to tighten reserves? Or is the safe thing just to wait till we're clearly at D if that comes, and then fight the recession, on the ground that it's better not to risk killing off prosperity by mistaken stabilization policy?

Note that here you have two subproblems. One is, *How much* effect will any Federal Reserve action have on business activity? If you sell $1 billion of government bonds, will this drastically check bank lending, or only slow it slightly? The second problem is *lags.* Even if you know what the effect will be, *how long* will it take for the full impact of tighter money to be felt? If you sell

---

[3]For a discussion of how government and other economists forecast, look back at the first appendix to Chapter 15.

bonds tomorrow, this may only gradually shut off lending, and that in turn may reduce C and I still later. Thus, the full effects of your action will be spread over months, probably over a year or two. By that time, the boom may have turned down. Then the lagged effect of tight money would be to speed the downturn, rather than to help check an excessive boom.

The lags and uncertainties between Federal Reserve actions and their final impact on total spending are substantial. How long will it take the banks to react to tighter reserves? How fast will businesses react to tighter credit and higher interest rates? Will the Fed's action have a strong psychological effect that reduces business investment? Most economists estimate the total lag between Federal Reserve action on reserves and the ultimate major effect on GNP to be as long as 12 to 24 months and suggest that the lag varies depending on prevailing conditions. Part of the effect is felt immediately, and the rest spreads over 6 to 30 months. Researchers are hard at work on the problem, but the Fed doesn't know for sure. And it has to act, or let things go their way without control. *Question:* Suppose the average lag in the effect of monetary policy is a year. Is a policy of acting to offset current booms and recessions a sound one at all times?

THE DANGERS OF DESTABILIZING POLICY

Given the uncertainties outlined above, it is not surprising that the monetary authorities sometimes make mistakes. The monetarists, who generally support reasonably stable growth in M, criticize the Fed for overreacting to short-run disturbances with big swings in M as it tries to keep interest rates and money-market conditions stable. The neo-Keynesians, on the other hand, criticize the Fed for letting interest rates swing too widely in misguided attempts to keep M growing stably.

The inflation burst of 1973–74 provides a lively example. The consumer price index, which had been rising about 4–5 percent annually in a generally prosperous economy, took off like a skyrocket in 1973, reflecting, first, worldwide crop failures, and then the Arab oil embargo. By early 1974, the CPI was rising at over 12 percent annually, as consumer hoarding and scare-buying drove up food, energy, and other commodity prices. Business demand for bank loans rose sharply, especially to carry inventories, as businesses too tried to accumulate stocks of scarce commodities. Reflecting both rising loan demand and soaring inflation expectations, interest rates shot up. Commercial banks' "prime rate" (charged to the lowest-risk business borrowers) rose from 5 to 12 percent in a little over two years. However, unemployment, which continued to fall gradually to about 5 percent in 1973, began to rise again in 1974 in spite of the swelling nominal consumer spending and business profits. Increasing unemployment was mainly concentrated in the auto and energy-related industries, reflecting the energy "shortage."

What should the Fed do? Its first problem was to decide whether to fight inflation or rising unemployment. The second was, in assessing the impact of its policies, whether to watch interest rates or the money stock. The Fed compromised on both. Throughout 1973, the money stock, although fluctuating sharply, grew at about a 5–6 percent annual rate, not far from the average for the preceding year. But combined with rapidly growing business-loan demand, this produced soaring interest rates.

Many neo-Keynesians cried out against what they termed drastically tight money (peak peacetime interest rates) that they argued would soon bring a major recession, if continued. But monetarists saw the Fed's policy as too easy; M was growing at a rate far above the real long-term growth rate of the economy. Similar dilemmas have confronted the Fed repeatedly in recent years.

A few decades ago, monetary policy seemed relatively simple. If there was inflation, tighten money; if there was unemployment, ease it. The job was seen as largely one of fighting business-cycle booms and recessions. But in the last two decades, inflation and unemployment have persisted at the same time. (Some economists call it "stagflation"—a situation combining stagnation and inflation.) It is no longer possible unambiguously to fight *either* one *or* the other. We must fight them simultaneously, or decide which one is the primary evil and concentrate on it, quite possibly worsening the other. And at best, the Fed can only control *nominal* GNP. Even if it is 100 percent successful in this, it cannot be sure how much of the impact will be on real output and how much on the price component of GNP. Monetary, like fiscal, policy, however well meant, may be destabilizing as well as stabilizing.

STABLE GROWTH IN THE MONEY STOCK?

Some monetarists, led by Chicago's Milton Friedman, suggest a simple rule for monetary policy. Just increase M about 4 percent a year through thick and thin. (The 4 percent is based on the assumption that this is about the rate of growth in the full-employment capacity of the economy. If the growth rate of the economy is more or less, the growth rate of the money stock could be adjusted accordingly, and a reduction could be made for long-term increase in V.) These economists argue that, even with the best intentions in the world, the Fed cannot forecast business conditions effectively. Moreover, the lag in effect of monetary policy is uncertain, and the Fed generally pays too much attention to short-term interest-rate fluctuations. Thus, Federal Reserve discretionary action has been destabilizing on many occasions in the past. A major example is the collapse of 1929–33, when the Fed permitted the money stock to shrink by nearly one-third; another is too much M in the inflationary boom of 1966–68.

Suppose we automatically increase M at about the full-employment growth rate of the economy, eschewing all attempts to forecast and to offset every real or imagined fluctuation. To be sure, this might not keep the economy exactly on a stable growth path. But the policy would avoid big booms and big depressions. Whenever the economy began to fall into serious recession, continued increase in the money stock at the annual 4 percent rate would provide a massive support against collapse. Conversely, if inflation began, limitation of the growth in M to 4 percent annually would be a powerful restraint on the inflation. A constant-growth-in-M rule is not a counsel of perfection; it is advanced as a sensible precept of action that would give by-and-large good results and would avoid the danger of serious errors by fallible monetary authorities.

Few economists or laymen take seriously the proposal to abolish the Federal Reserve and to substitute a completely inflexible rule of a stably growing money stock. But many economists who have studied the evidence believe that the reasoning behind the rule has much to offer the Federal Reserve authorities. Whenever M is growing much faster or slower than the full-employment growth rate of the economy, that's a warning flag, and there ought to be a good reason for the divergence.

THE MIX OF MONETARY AND FISCAL POLICY

Fiscal and monetary policy must be effectively coordinated for optimum results. Unless they are, one may offset the other.

The 1964 experience shows the importance of such cooperation. A big tax cut led to rising incomes, to rising demands for money balances, and to upward pressures on interest rates owing to direct federal borrowing to finance the deficit. But simultaneously, the Fed provided new bank reserves that permitted the money stock to grow about 5 percent during the year, which kept interest rates roughly stable and helped induce more spending. Whether monetary or fiscal policy deserves more credit is not the issue here; we needed coordinated use of *both*.

The 1960s and early 1970s demonstrated the problems that arise if monetary policy has to do the whole job of checking an inflationary boom. In 1965–66, fiscal policy was highly expansionary, reflecting big increases in both domestic and Vietnam spending. The Fed had to undertake single-handed the job of slowing the inflationary boom. In 1966, the Fed halted the expansion of M. The result was big increases in interest rates and a "credit crunch." Available funds went to the government and to the highest-quality business and household credit risks. New credit for home construction nearly vanished. Similarly, rising interest rates made it very difficult for local governments to borrow; many were forbidden by law to pay more than stated rates, which were below soaring market rates. New and small businesses also found funds very hard to obtain. Exclusive reliance on tight money threw the brunt of restriction on particular sectors of the economy.

Substantially the same scenario was repeated in 1970, when the credit crunch threatened to throw big business borrowers into bankruptcy and generate a major financial crisis. The Fed delicately eased the credit markets to avoid disaster, but inevitably softened its antiinflation programs in doing so. A more balanced stabilization program, including restrictive fiscal policy, would have permitted a broader, more equitable spreading of the burden in both cases, and would have greatly lessened the risk of a major financial crisis.

The monetary-fiscal policy mix also influences the rate of economic growth. Suppose we want to stimulate faster growth when we already have high-level employment. We can do so by an easy-money policy, because low interest rates will stimulate investment. But this policy would also produce excess aggregate demand and inflation. However, if we simultaneously raise taxes to generate a budget surplus, we can restrain demand and counteract the undesired inflationary pressure. Thus, an easy-money policy of low interest rates combined with a budget surplus could stimulate growth while maintaining high-level employment without inflation.

The need to mesh international and domestic consideration raises different problems of determining the right policy mix. During the early 1960s, for example, our international position called for high interest rates to pull funds here from abroad, while at home, unemployment called for increased aggregate demand. Thus, many economists urged tighter money to raise interest rates in order to solve our international problem, combined with an expansionary fiscal policy to stimulate the domestic economy.

Meshing multiple policy goals calls for imaginative, flexible use of our policy tools. Moreover, history shows that the world has an unpleasant way of throwing up new problems every time we think we have the old ones well under control. Prudent economic policy will require a cooperative, flexible mix of monetary and fiscal policies to cope with new situations as they arise.

FEDERAL RESERVE INDEPENDENCE

In 1914, Congress set up the Federal Reserve to be substantially "independent" of the president and the Treasury. Modern fiscal policy had not yet been invented, and the purpose was to keep control of the nation's money supply "out of politics." But since the Keynesian revolution of the 1930s, the need for coordination between monetary and fiscal policy has been clear, and, as a practical matter, Federal Reserve authorities have worked fairly closely with other government stabilization officials—although the degree of coordination has varied widely.

Traditionally, as its founding fathers had hoped, the Fed has been more concerned with inflation than has the government itself (Congress and the administration). Frequently, the Fed has taken the responsibility of checking inflation with tight money when Congress and the president were still in a big-spending mood. These periods (for example, the 1960s and 1970s) led to bitter criticism of the Fed, as insensitive to human needs and unduly concerned with keeping interest rates high. Many critics argue that the Fed should be stripped of its "independence" and brought under stricter control by the president and Congress, who are elected by the people and must answer for their policy decisions every election. Monetary policy is vastly powerful, they argue, and it should be directly under the control of the people, not of a banker-oriented semi-independent central bank.

Congress has provided few directions to the Fed for conducting monetary policy—mainly, the Employment Act of 1946, which specifies "maximum employment, production and purchasing power" as the goals of stabilization policy. But Federal Reserve officials, especially the chairman of the Board of Governors, are called to testify before congressional committees many times each year, and they get lots of advice on these occasions. Congress recently specified that the Fed must report quarterly on its past operations and its general policy plans for the future, and the Fed is sensitive to both congressional and presidential pressures. Some critics, notably liberal Democratic political leaders, push legislation to shorten Board members' terms of office, to require that the Fed follow objectives specified by the president each year, to make the Fed come to Congress each year for operating funds, and to specify in detail Federal Reserve goals and operating rules (for instance, increase the money stock at a 5–7 percent annual rate).

How independent should the Fed be—from the president and from Congress? The case against independence is suggested above: In a democratic society, the health of the economy is of great importance, and those controlling it should be directly responsible to the public, as represented by the elected president and Congress. Almost no one denies that the Fed must work closely with other government officials to coordinate monetary policy with other steps to produce a stably growing economy. But the argument for considerable Federal Reserve independence stresses three points: First, dispersion of power is fundamental in the U.S. system of government. A partially independent Federal Reserve may contribute to a significant broadening of the total base of macroeconomic decision making in the federal government. Second, history warns that governments tend to err on the side of inflation. They often turn to money issue to pay the bills they are reluctant to cover by taxes. A central bank at least partially insulated from day-to-day political pressures can provide a buffer against the inflationary biases of U.S. democratic political processes. Third, while Congress clearly has, and should have, the ultimate power to direct or even abolish the Fed, 500 busy congressmen, most of them unskilled in economics, would surely be an inefficient group to run the nation's complex monetary and banking system. Surely Congress' main role should be to specify goals and general rules for the Federal Reserve authorities to follow—not to prescribe a rigid rule or detailed operating procedures.

How independent should the Federal Reserve be? Take a look at Case 14, for the issue as it currently faces Congress.[4]

[4] For a more detailed analysis of the politics and economics of the monetary-policy-making process, see G.L. Bach, *Making Monetary and Fiscal Policy* (Washington, D.C.: The Brookings Institution, 1971), Chap. 8, especially pp. 205–22.

GOLD AND MONETARY POLICY

We have said little about the fact that the United States lives in an increasingly interdependent economic world, and that gold has frequently played an important role in determining monetary policy. Although you can understand the importance of gold and the balance of payments only through a detailed analysis of international economic relations (in Part 6), a few words about gold are useful here.[5]

What was the "gold standard"?

The "gold standard" prevailed in the United States and most major European nations over a good share of the century preceding the 1930s. Although it varied from country to country and from period to period, it had two major characteristics. First, changes in the total amount of money in each country were to be roughly proportional to changes in its gold holdings. Gold itself was not the only kind of money. But as new gold was received by a country, it would serve as the basis for additional money issued in the form of currency or deposits. On $1 worth of new gold, $2, $10, or some other number of dollars of new money might be issued. Conversely, an outflow of gold would reduce the nation's money supply.

Second, each unit of money was "worth" (freely convertible into) a certain number of grains of gold. Until 1934, for example, each U.S. dollar "contained" 23.22 grains of fine gold; that is, the price of gold was fixed so that 23.22 grains of gold could always be obtained at the Treasury for $1, and vice versa.

Thus, the gold standard in its pure form was an essentially automatic regulator of the supply of money. M would be largely dependent on the stock of gold in each nation. Actually, the gold standard was never as automatic in operation as in theory. But it did provide a strong constraining framework for almost all monetary-policy thinking and action over a long period of years.

[5] This section can be omitted by those who will study Part 6.

History presents an unending series of cases that illustrate the problems faced in monetary policy making. In each of the following historical vignettes, ask yourself what you would have done if you had been a policy maker.

The 1930s—dealing with depression

As the economy spiraled down in 1930, it was far from clear whether this was a major depression or merely a temporary setback. The Fed reduced discount rates to ease credit in the deflation, and by early 1931 there was evidence that the worst was over.

But European financial crises in mid-1931 set off worldwide gold hoarding. Facing this gold loss, the Reserve authorities adopted a tight-money, high-interest policy to keep our gold from flowing abroad. The spiral of financial liquidation resumed. Unemployment soared. Runs on banks developed everywhere. Franklin Roosevelt's first major act as president was to declare a nationwide ''bank holiday,'' closing all banks until the panic could be calmed and arrangements could be made to keep the financial system operating.

Following 1933, with Roosevelt's new appointees running the system, the Federal Reserve adopted easy money and low interest rates to fight the depression. Excess reserves were pushed up rapidly, and then, as prices began to rise, pulled back down to $1 billion in 1937. Soon after, the boomlet of 1936–37 crashed precipitously back to mass unemployment in early 1938. Again there was widespread criticism of the Federal Reserve increases in reserve requirements to restrain rising prices in spite of continued heavy unemployment.

From then on, the banks were flooded with reserves. Total bank credit and the money stock rose in response. But by 1939, GNP was still only back up to the level of 1929; eight or nine million people were unemployed; net private investment for the entire decade was a negative figure.

Lessons: (1) When mass deflation sets in,

don't hesitate to flood the economy with liquidity. Hindsight makes it clear that the Reserve authorities made a fatal error in moving so slowly. (2) When times are bad, it's still hard to know what is the best policy vis-à-vis minor fluctuations. (3) In a major depression, flooding the economy with liquidity at least checks further financial liquidation and helps to stimulate total spending; but bankers and the public may pile up idle cash rather than lending and spending. The life of a central banker is not easy!

Monetary Policy and the national debt—1946-51

At the end of World War II, over $275 billion of government debt was outstanding, nearly $100 billion of it held by the banking system. Between $50 and $75 billion of this debt came due for refunding each year. The Federal Reserve faced a dilemma: (1) If it tightened bank reserves and raised interest rates to check the postwar inflation, the squeeze would induce banks to dump their low-yield government securities on the market to get new reserves in order to make higher-yield business loans. This would force down the price of government bonds, with cries of anguish from the Treasury and the public. (2) On the other hand, if the Fed continued to provide plentiful reserves to finance bank loans to private borrowers, it could ease the Treasury's job of refinancing the national debt by keeping bond prices up and interest rates down; but then it would be lying down on its job as the nation's defender against inflation.

At first, the Fed chose the latter path. It stood ready to buy all government bonds from the commercial banks at par, maintaining their price against decline. This meant that the banks' huge holdings of government securities were as good as excess reserves, since they could be converted into money with no loss at any time.

The Treasury, anxious to maintain confidence in the government's credit, liked this policy. If government-bond prices fell, present holders might dump their bonds and refuse to buy others except at much higher interest rates. Political repercussions from government-bond holders could be very unpleasant for the administration in power if bond prices slumped. Many economists and others argued, however, that higher interest costs and sagging bond prices were a proper price to pay for the restoration of effective monetary restraint against inflation. The Fed increasingly took this view. If monetary policy was to check inflation, it argued, the Fed must tighten the overall credit supply, including a rise in interest rates to the federal government itself.

Thus, the Federal Reserve authorities gradually tightened up the money markets. Finally, in 1951, in an open break with the Treasury, the Fed withdrew its support for government-bond prices. Bond prices fell below par, but bank credit was tightened and Federal Reserve control over the money supply was partially restored.

But even then, the Federal Reserve officials made it clear they would continue to work closely with the Treasury. Why? In spite of their "nonpolitical" status, Federal Reserve Board members are appointed by the president and are responsible to Congress. They recognize fully their primary role as part of the government. Their job is to work with other agencies to produce a stably growing economy. With a major portion of the nation's money supply outstanding against Treasury bonds, it is clear that Federal Reserve monetary policy and Treasury policy in handling the federal debt must be made cooperatively.

Lesson: Many considerations must be weighed in forming wise monetary policy. One of the most difficult problems is the weight to be given to Treasury financing needs when they conflict with other stabilization objectives. The life of a central banker is not easy!

The sagging-soaring sixties and seventies

During the first half of the sixties, growth was slow and unemployment persisted until after the big tax cut of 1964 and the easy money that accompanied it. But with the Vietnam War and bulging spending on civilian programs, the problem soon became inflation. In 1966, to slow inflation with rising employment, the Fed hauled the growth rate in M down to zero for a six-month period. The result was soaring interest rates and a temporary credit crunch, as many borrowers were unable to obtain the loans they had expected. The boom was checked, and the Fed quickly released the reins on M to avoid a slide-off into recession.

But victory was short, and before long the inflationary boom was on again. With soaring government spending and no tax increase, the whole burden of slowing the boom fell on the Fed, already smarting from criticism that it had dangerously risked precipitating collapse in the crunch of 1966. The period 1967–70 was a repeat of the preceding years, with sharp restraint in 1970 generating another credit crunch. Again, the medicine worked, and again there were anguished cries from opponents of the restrictive action. Again, the Fed relaxed the reins as soon as the slowdown was obvious. But again the inflation persisted through the credit crunch.

A few years later, we were off on the same cycle again. This time, prosperity was aided by worldwide crop failures and the OPEC oil embargo in generating inflation in 1973–75, but unemployment crept up to 9 percent in the face of double-digit inflation. What would you have done in 1974–75, with that inflation and the worst recession since the 1930s?

Lesson: Managing aggregate demand is very difficult when the economy is in the high-employment area. Tight money can check a boom; but if the dose is too strong, a credit crisis and recession may be the result. And if inflationary expectations are deep-seated, monetary restraint is apt to slow real growth and employment before it makes much headway against rising prices. The old refrain: The life. . . !

The gold standard as a safeguard against inflation

The main argument for the gold standard in most people's minds was that it would safeguard the economy against overissue of money and inflation. Because the government must have gold to back each dollar, gold sets a limit to how much money can be created and provides value for the money issued.

But U.S. history shows clearly that as a practical matter, the gold standard was no guarantee against inflation. Figure 7–5 showed the big inflation that took place during and following World War I, the precipitous drop following that inflation, and the sharp drop from 1929 to 1933—all while we were on the gold standard.

On the other hand, it is true that adherence to the gold standard would insure against any such runaway inflation as occurred in Germany after World War I, if sticking to the gold standard were politically and economically possible under such circumstances. Then the limited stock of gold would prevent a vast overissue of money. However, it is hard to imagine that under such drastic circumstances, any country would remain on a gold standard. The extreme monetary disturbances of that period were as much a symptom as a cause of the difficulties of the German economy.

Most economists today deny that gold flows provide an acceptable guide to how much money the economy needs. There is no reason to suppose that the optimal supply of money will correspond to how much gold is mined each year and how much goes into or out of speculators' hoards. Moreover, rigid adherence to a gold standard would tie the monetary authorities' hands against monetary action to combat unemployment and depression.

Gold today

It was the desire to "do something" about the depression that largely explains the worldwide abandonment of the gold standard in the 1930s. Countries were increasingly loath to accept deflation as they lost gold. Getting men back to work became the major national goal. European countries faced huge gold drains into private hoards and to the United States. In 1931, England, long the financial center of the world, went off the gold standard. Remaining on gold meant intensified deflation as gold was withdrawn. Within a few years, all the major Western nations, including the United States, had gone off gold. The price of contracting domestic money supplies as gold was lost was too high. Avoiding unemployment by expansionary monetary policy was more important in the dark days of worldwide depression.

Gold flows no longer control monetary policy in the world's major nations, nor do governments promise to redeem their money in fixed amounts of gold. Gold is little used as domestic money, and the international role of gold has greatly decreased.

But gold has not vanished from the monetary scene. It is still used as international money among governments and central banks to a limited extent, and in many nations individual citizens hold gold in coins or other forms. International monetary arrangements have been in a state of flux since the late 1960s, and we shall postpone to Part 6 more detailed analysis of the international role of gold today. In the United States, at least, you will not go far wrong by omitting gold from the analysis of domestic monetary policy, as we have done.

REVIEW

**For analysis
and discussion**

1. How would you rate the following for quick action to fight a recession? (a) monetary policy; (b) tax reductions; (c) increased government spending.

2. Suppose you were a banker with a balance sheet like that of the Local Bank in Chapter 17. The Federal Reserve raises reserve requirements to tighten credit just when the demand for loans from your long-standing business customers is rising. What would you do?

3. Suppose that prices are rising but 7 percent of the labor force is still unemployed. As a member of the Federal Reserve Board, what would you do?

4. When inflation and unemployment coincide, sensible Federal Reserve action would be to raise reserve requirements while buying bonds in the open market. True or false? Explain.

5. If the Treasury must borrow to finance a federal budget deficit designed to stimulate the economy, what should the Federal Reserve do? Suppose it holds the stock of bank reserves constant. What would you expect to happen to interest rates and credit conditions?

6. Suppose an inflationary boom is under way, but Congress and the administration do not raise taxes to check it, as in early 1973. Should the Fed assume the full burden by drastically tightening money, even recognizing that monetary restraint alone can probably check inflation only by precipitating a "credit crunch" that may lead to a recession? What if it does not act?

7. If the Fed wishes to encourage stable growth in real GNP and employment, can you see any serious objections to merely increasing the money stock about 4 percent each year?

8. When tight money is needed to check inflation, should the Fed provide special loopholes for housing borrowers, to avoid limiting home construction? If so, why, and who else should bear the burden of restriction?

9. How independent should the Federal Reserve be?

10. Explain the gold standard and how it was supposed to guard against inflation.

Representative Wright Patman of Texas, for forty years perhaps the most outspoken critic of the Federal Reserve System in Congress, repeatedly proposed legislation to eliminate, or reduce significantly, the "independence" of the Federal Reserve. In literally hundreds of committee hearings, to which Federal Reserve Board chairmen and other Fed officials were summoned, he strongly denounced the Federal Reserve as a threat to high employment and economic stability in the United States, beholden to the big-city bankers, insensitive to the needs of the common people, outside the control of either Congress or the president, and heavily slanted toward tight money and high interest rates, with an almost psychopathic fear of inflation.

Few other senators and representatives have been as critical as Congressman Patman. But he had many supporters in his campaign to reduce the independence of the Fed and to push it toward more expansionary policies, especially in times of slow growth and unemployment.

H.R. 11, introduced into Congress in January 1965 by Congressman Patman, is typical of legislation he proposed as long-time chairman of the House Banking and Currency Committee:

1. The Federal Open Market Committee would be abolished and all policy powers concentrated in the Board of Governors, to eliminate the influence of private bankers exercised through the Federal Reserve banks, which are represented on the Open Market Committee.

2. The membership of the Board of Governors would be reduced from seven to five, and the terms of office reduced from fourteen to five years; thus every president would, within one four-year term, be able to appoint a majority of the Federal Reserve Board.

3. The term of the chairman of the Board would be made coterminous with the term of the President of the United States, so the chairman would always be appointed by the president in office.

4. The Federal Reserve System would be required to operate on funds appropriated by Congress annually, like any other government agency. (The income of the Fed now comes mainly from interest on the government securities it holds; but the Fed returns these funds to the Treasury after paying its expenses out of them.)

5. The Federal Reserve would be audited each year by the comptroller general, who reports directly to Congress, thereby bringing the Federal Reserve under the direct operating control of Congress.

6. Private stock in the Federal Reserve banks, now held by the member banks, would be eliminated, and the Fed would become entirely a government agency.

7. The law would direct the Federal Reserve to conduct its open-market operations and other policy operations in accordance with the programs and policies of the President of the United States, and the President each year would specify the monetary policy he expected the Fed to follow that year.

The net effect of this legislation would be to make the Federal Reserve a regular operating agency of the government, like the Treasury or the Department of Commerce, directly responsible to the president and Congress for daily operations. Some other congressmen have modified the Patman position to eliminate the requirement that the Fed follow a monetary policy laid out by the president, and have substituted a statement that the Fed must follow a policy specified by Congress each year, reporting regularly to Congress on its operations under the congressional directive. A modified form of such a statement was adopted by the House and Senate in 1975, but attempts to specify a given growth rate in the money stock or any other specific congressional directive were voted down, although they were supported by the Democratic leadership in both the House and Senate.

Expert opinion has been mixed on how far Congress should go toward the Patman proposals. On one side, President Eisenhower said in 1956, "The Federal Reserve is set up as a separate agency of government. It is not under the authority of the President . . . and I believe it would be a serious mistake to make it responsible to the political head of state." On the other, some economists support Patman. One wrote recently:

The basic premise behind this independence is so obvious—or so embarrassing—that it is seldom mentioned: The general public is either too ignorant or too immoral to be trusted with money management. Having risen above the musky depths of politics, as the "Supreme Court of Finance" the Fed is regally beyond the influence of the citizen. Fed officials can exert their power over the economy with no need to take account of the various special interest groups—or if the truth be known, the general public. . . .

The public acquiesces in monetary management without representation, despite the fact that what the Fed decides touches almost everyone, almost every day. . . .

The effect of these [Patman's] reforms would be to exhume the Federal Reserve from solitary confinement and make it a political institution, subject to appropriate pressures from the public at large rather than permitting it to cater to the positive preferences of a small coterie.[6]

Should Congress adopt the Patman legislation?

[6]E.R. Canterbery, "The Awkward Independence of the Federal Reserve," *Challenge,* September 1975.

19 CHAPTER INFLATION AND UNEMPLOYMENT: THE MODERN DILEMMA

Reducing both unemployment and inflation to a sustainable minimum is the main task of monetary and fiscal policy. Either unemployment or inflation alone can be attacked readily. The former calls for easy money and an expansionary budget, the latter for the reverse actions. But when unemployment and inflation occur at the same time, there's trouble. And recently, they have occurred simultaneously a large share of the time in most of the Western industrialized nations, something that shouldn't happen in a well-behaved neoclassical or Keynesian world. How to maintain high employment and a stable price level simultaneously seems to be the big unsolved problem of macroeconomic policy.

WHAT'S NEW?

In a perfectly competitive economy, increasing aggregate demand would generally lead to more output and employment whenever unemployment existed, and to inflation only after full employment was reached, as in the simple model of Chapter 9. As long as unemployed workers competed for jobs, wage rates would stay down and no firms could raise prices without losing sales to competitors. To be sure, as Chapter 9 pointed out, even in such an economy, some inflation would occur before full employment was reached, because demand rises faster for some products than for others, and bottlenecks would be reached in some industries and areas while excess capacity remained in others. But these bottlenecks would be local and temporary, and could be alleviated by approaching full employment gradually, to give resources time to shift in accordance with consumer demand patterns. One lesson for monetary-fiscal policy is clear: Don't be greedy and try to eliminate unemployment too fast when the economy is approaching high-level employment.

But the unemployment-inflation dilemma is more basic than just the speed of increasing demand. We do not live in a purely competitive world. And increasingly, inflation seems to be a political as well as an economic process. Recently, inflation has persisted even when unemployment is widespread. The recession of 1970 scarcely slowed the rapid inflation inherited from the preceding years. Prices soared to double-digit annual inflation in 1973–74 in spite of growing unemployment, and they continued to rise in 1975–76 in spite of 8.5 percent unemployment. Something new seems to be happening. To understand it, we need to look at modern inflation and unemployment in more detail.

THE NEW INFLATION[1]

Inflation, it is often said, is too much money chasing too few goods. Without excess aggregate demand, substantial inflation will not long continue. But costs, especially wages, may push upward on prices, even though there is no general excess demand; the last decade has provided repeated examples of this situation. A dynamic interaction between demand-pull and cost-push can easily develop that makes it very difficult to separate the two interacting causes of inflationary pressure. But unless aggregate demand is growing, price increases reflecting cost-push will not go very far. We must, therefore, look at both the forces that generate upward cost-push on prices and, more important, the

likely level of total spending against the level of potential real GNP to understand modern inflation.

Figure 8–3 showed that in America, inflation has come with every major war—and deflation (falling prices) has come *after* every major war, *except* for World War II. In the last quarter century, prices have simply gone on up from their World War II peaks. Six big socio-political-economic changes seem to underlie the new inflation.

1. **The sanctity of high employment.** In the United States—indeed, in all the Western world—maintenance of high employment has become not only a goal, but probably the main goal, of economic policy. Following Keynes's prescriptions of the 1930s, nearly everyone, Republican and Democrat alike, now agrees that above all, we must avoid another major depression like that of the 1930s. There is, of course, much argument over what is the practical level of unemployment at which to aim. But major unemployment must not be tolerated.

2. **The apparent World War II demonstration that massive government spending can produce high employment.** World War II showed vividly the power of government spending, when it is big enough and when it is financed largely by deficits, to put millions of unemployed people back to work. To many, the 1940s were convincing evidence that Keynes was right. Thus, the generation of the 1930s found an escape from its greatest economic disaster. For generations maturing in the postwar years, history seems to show clearly that widespread unemployment need not be tolerated.

3. **The increasing political and economic strength of major socio-economic groups.** In all democratic countries, trade unions have become much stronger since the Great Depression. This means an increasingly powerful upward push on wages, the major component of costs in the industrial economies. Most industrial prices are not set impersonally in highly competitive markets; many are administered, set by leading firms and by bargains between leading buyers and sellers. Thus, within limits, businesses may push up prices, just as unions push up wages, even without excess demand. Other important

[1] This section is based on G.L. Bach, *The New Inflation* (Englewood Cliffs, N.J.: Prentice-Hall, 1973), Chap. 3.

economic groups have discovered their power in the market—and, at least equally important, their power to achieve goals through the political process that they cannot achieve through the marketplace. If farmers cannot get higher prices through the free market, they can do it through Congress. If workers cannot get livable wages through the market, they can put great pressure on governments for higher minimum wages, protection against foreign competition, and the like. If businessmen cannot get high enough prices through the market for their coal or milk, they can usually get help from Washington, or their state capital. If the elderly have none of these ways to raise their incomes, they can turn to Congress for bigger Social Security benefits.

The import of this discovery is far-reaching. With recognition of their powers, sellers need not be content with what the market gives them. Strong sellers generate higher costs and higher prices in the market. And Congress intervenes to provide higher prices and incomes for effective political groups.

4. **Increased government responsibility for the welfare of the masses.** Modern democracy is established to maximize the responsiveness of the government to the common man and his wants. The economic group in trouble, especially if it is a group of "little men," can turn to the government for help with a reasonable expectation that it will not go away empty-handed. Such help costs money—and democratic governments enjoy spending more than they do taxing.

5. **War, hot and cold.** Modern war, hot or cold, is immensely expensive. History shows that all modern wars have brought inflation. "National defense" costs now exceed $100 billion annually. Government spending of this magnitude for an "unproductive" purpose cannot avoid pushing upward on prices in a democratic society.

6. **The end of the gold standard.** The gold standard had many failings. But it did provide a monetary "religion" that brought the government and public up short when they felt the urge to spend more than they were taking in, through the check it provided on domestic expansion of the money supply, and through the discipline imposed by international gold flows if

our rate of inflation exceeded the rate in other countries. While governments often avoided the restraint imposed by the gold-standard rules, those rules provided red warning flags in plenty. Governments felt obliged to explain why they were spending more money than they were taking in, and the public looked for that explanation. But no more!

How do these factors combine to generate persistent inflation? The government is committed to maintaining high employment. Economists, government officials, labor leaders, businessmen, and ordinary citizens are convinced that government spending financed by new money can produce higher employment. Many important wages and prices are set on a bargained or administered basis, and large organizations and power groups recognize the power they have through the political process to achieve what they may not be able to accomplish unaided in the market. Price and wage setters and other income-seeking groups all seek bigger income shares in the market and the political process—more than are consistent with stable prices.

A half century ago, there was a clear ceiling on such excess-income claims of businesses, workers, and other claimants. If they kept on pushing up wages and prices and pressing for more government help, they risked pricing themselves out of the market and pushing the government into unacceptable deficits. When bank reserves were used up and no more gold was available, tight money laid its cold hand on the boom.

Today's monetary and fiscal authorities could play this same role in limiting the inflationary upsweep of wages and prices—if the government were not under pressure to ensure high employment. But if the government essentially bails out inflationary wage, price, and other income claims, the result is a validation of the inflationary excess-income claims, and an implicit invitation for all groups to try for even larger income shares next time around. Thus, the new inflation tends to be a stair-step process. Excess-income claims are followed by the injection of new money by the monetary-fiscal authorities to avoid unemployment. The resulting inflation is followed in turn by further wage, price, and income demands to catch up with the inflation and to restore (enlarge) individual income shares. These are followed by more money to avoid unemployment, and so on in an upward spiral.

This socio-political-economic theory of inflation is, of course, oversimplified. But it provides a foundation for intermittent but persistent inflation in the modern Western democracies. Other factors must be added. First, both prices and wages have become increasingly resistant to downward pressures. Unions successfully resist wage cuts. Many businesses are equally reluctant to cut prices when demand weakens, preferring to take reductions in volume instead. Thus, when anything increases wages or prices in one sector, they are unlikely to be offset by corresponding decreases in other sectors. This is often called "sectoral" inflation. Again, the willingness of the monetary-fiscal authorities to insert money to keep the higher prices from generating widespread unemployment is crucial. In 1973–74, for example, when double-digit inflation exploded in the American economy, the immediate causes were worldwide food "shortages" (reflecting bad crops all over the world in the face of prosperous demand conditions everywhere) and the enormous increases in oil prices imposed by the OPEC countries. With constant aggregate demand, these big price increases would have forced corresponding decreases in other sectors of the economy, but the monetary-fiscal authorities chose to increase aggregate demand in order to lessen downward pressures on other sectors.

Even if restrictive monetary-fiscal policy does check inflation, some income groups will have lagged behind in the circular process. They will understandably want to "catch up." Thus, any attempt to check the inflation spiral must reckon with strong cost-push catch-up forces that may continue over years before powerful wage-, price-, and income-setting groups feel that they have restored a "fair" position for themselves in the dynamic struggle for income shares. This helps to explain continuing wage and price increases in the face of widespread unemployment and absence of excess demand in 1974–75. Modern inflation is a complex process.

AGGREGATE DEMAND, THE "NATURAL RATE," AND THE STRUCTURE OF UNEMPLOYMENT

The Great Depression produced a huge, solid core of unemployment, totaling over 25 percent of all workers. Hunger and want were widespread. Look back at Chapter 7 for a brief review of what unemployment was like then.

Unemployment is still a major social waste. But, as Chapter 7 indicated, unemployment in the moderate recessions since World War II has been very different from that in the Great Depression. First, unemployment rates have been much lower. Only in 1974–75 did unemployment go above 8 percent for long. And most of the unemployed now receive private or government benefits to reduce the economic impact of joblessness. In 1975, with unemployment averaging about 8 million workers (8.5 percent unemployment), an average of 5.5 million drew unemployment compensation from the government, with about 2 million more receiving benefit payments under private unemployment-insurance programs. Total government benefit payments were $18 billion. In addition, the government provided, for unemployed workers as well as for other beneficiaries, food stamps costing $5 billion to 18 million people; $9 billion of cash benefits to families with dependent children; $15 billion of medical-aid benefits to the elderly and poor; and $6 billion of supplementary-income security payments to the elderly. While benefits vary widely, many unemployed workers, especially those on short layoffs, received benefits totaling from 75 to nearly 100 percent of their regular on-the-job take-home pay—although these benefits dropped substantially when private unemployment benefit funds were exhausted in many industries.

Equally important, the structure of today's unemployment is different from that of the 1930s. Of the 8 million people unemployed in 1975, only about half had actually lost their jobs. Only 15 percent (less than 2 million people) were unemployed as long as six months. The average period of unemployment for each unemployed worker was about three months. During the year, more than 20 million people were unemployed at one time or another; the unemployed are a constantly changing group. Eight million unemployed does not mean 8 million people out of work for the year.

As Chapter 7 emphasized, relatively few "mature" male heads of families now experience substantial unemployment. Even in times as bad as 1975, their unemployment rate was less than 5 percent at its peak. On the other hand, teenagers and minority groups experience very high rates of unemployment; teenage unemployment reached 20 percent in 1975, but a third of these were students seeking part-time jobs, and the job turnover rate for other teenagers was high. Large numbers of unskilled women have recently entered the labor force.

Modern econometric models of the economy suggest that an increase in aggregate demand that would reduce unemployment among adult males to prosperity levels of, say, 2 or 3 percent would leave high unemployment rates among teenagers and new female entrants to the labor force. Conversely, enough aggregate demand to eliminate unemployment among teenagers and new female entrants would generate intense inflationary pressures and sharp wage increases for adult males. If this conclusion is correct, it suggests the need for special labor-market policies to deal with the problems of teenage and low-skilled female unemployment rather than relying entirely on aggregate-demand policy.[2]

Given the situation, many modern economists emphasize that there is now a higher "natural rate of unemployment" than previously. Employer demand for workers depends on the real wage rate in relation to the productivity of the workers involved. If the labor force includes many unskilled teenagers, women, and others with weak attachments to their jobs, the natural rate of unemployment will be higher for any given average wage rate for the economy than if the labor force were made up of highly skilled, trained workers with strong job attachments. Higher minimum wage laws, larger unemployment benefits, and the like also increase the natural rate of unemployment by raising effective real wage costs. Trying to reduce unemploy

ment below the natural rate by increasing aggregate demand will only produce more inflation. It will bid up the wages of higher-skilled workers, but will create jobs for marginal workers only if their real wage is reduced by having prices rise faster than money wages increase—that is, by reducing the natural rate of unemployment.

THE UNEMPLOYMENT-INFLATION DILEMMA
Is there a short-run tradeoff?

When substantial unemployment exists, pouring aggregate demand into the economy is almost sure to increase employment at least temporarily—if we don't care how much inflation we generate. If unemployment is widespread, inflation may be minor. At the extreme, in a major depression, jobs may increase with no rise in prices at all. But the nearer we are to full employment, the bigger the share of rising nominal GNP that will be higher prices rather than real output as labor and product markets tighten. And, as was noted above, the *faster* the growth in aggregate demand, the less time there will be for markets to adjust, and the more inflation is likely. **Thus, in the short run, it seems plausible to expect that stimulating aggregate demand will produce more jobs, although increasingly at the expense of inflation as output rises and unemployment falls. This is generally called the unemployment-inflation tradeoff. We can have more employment, it says, if we are willing to accept more inflation.**

These predictions rest on the theory of the firm, which will be considered in detail in Part 3. To maximize profits, a business firm will hire more workers to increase output if demand increases, so it can sell more at the same or a higher price—unless its costs of production rise. If costs rise, then the firm will increase output only if selling prices can be increased at least enough to cover the higher costs. Thus, whether wages (the biggest cost item for most firms) rise faster or slower than selling prices is a crucial question.

If unemployment is widespread, wages are apt to lag behind rising prices. But the stronger unions are, the shorter such lags are likely to be.

---

[2]For a fuller account, see the *Economic Report of the President,* January 1975, Chap. 3.

And the more generally inflation is expected, the more workers will insist on bigger wage increases to offset rising prices. Then the wage lag that makes it profitable for firms to hire more workers with rising prices vanishes, and the growth in aggregate demand generated by monetary-fiscal policy produces merely inflation with higher wages and higher prices, but no growth in jobs and real output. **Fundamentally, the trade-off between inflation and unemployment rests on this wage lag: If prices rise faster than wage costs, real wages will be reduced and it will pay to hire more workers. If wage costs rise faster than prices, inflation provides no incentive to hire more workers; indeed, the number of jobs may be reduced if real wages rise.**[3]

Thus, in the short run, a rapid increase in aggregate demand will usually increase employment; wages will generally lag temporarily, or at least not rise faster than prices. But acceptance of inflation as a price of expansionary aggregate demand policy does not guarantee a lower level of unemployment even in the short run. And whether any increase will last is uncertain. If the wage lag is only temporary, the new inflation-induced jobs will presumably be eliminated when wage costs catch up with the higher prices, and the result will be only inflation with no lasting increase in employment.

Is there a long-run tradeoff?

A pioneering study by A.W. Phillips of the London School of Economics in the 1950s showed that in England over the past century, whenever unemployment fell below about 5 percent, wage rates rose faster than was consistent with stable prices. Some American economists believed they found the same general relationship in our economy. This apparent tradeoff between unemployment and inflation, when shown graphically, is often called a "Phillips curve." Figure 19–1 plots the rate of inflation against unemployment for the United States since 1950. A curve is roughly fitted to the points

[3]This is only a rough statement of the theory involved, but it presents the central issue. A more rigorous statement is provided in Parts 3 and 4.

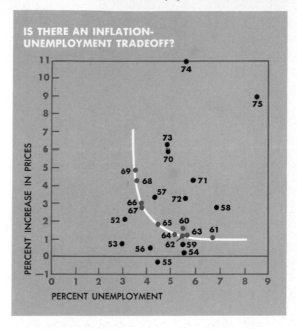

IS THERE AN INFLATION-UNEMPLOYMENT TRADEOFF?

Figure 19–1
During the 1960s, prices generally rose fastest when unemployment was low, as is indicated by the curve fitted to data for the 1960s. But when data for the 1950s and 1970s are included, this simple relationship no longer holds. Note the dots for the 1970s. (Source: U.S. Department of Labor.)

for the 1960s, which suggests the unemployment-inflation tradeoff noted by Phillips.[4]

But economists have increasingly questioned this apparent long-run tradeoff for at least three reasons: (1) If you look at the dots for the 1950s and 1970s as well as the 1960s, it is obvious that there is no simple Phillips-curve fit. The dots look almost like a random scatter; there are numerous cases of high inflation with high unemployment, and the converse. The data for the 1970s especially are inconsistent with the simple tradeoff hypothesis. We had both high unemployment and high inflation simultaneously. (2) Look back at Table 7–5, showing wages and profits since 1952. The wages-salaries share of

[4]Actually, Phillips plotted the increase in wage rates against unemployment. But since wages are a big element in costs, many economists plot prices directly against unemployment, although logically this slides over a complex relationship between wage rates and prices.

national income *rose* during every inflation period, while profits were squeezed. Although these figures show wage incomes, not wage costs, they certainly don't support the hypothesis that wages have lagged during recent inflations. (3) In a world where inflation is increasingly expected, theory tells us that wage lag will tend to vanish. As both workers and businesses come to expect inflation, workers include an inflation allowance in their wage demands, and businessmen are increasingly willing to grant such inflation allowances to buy labor peace. As inflation is built into anticipations, the wage lag vanishes, and with it, businesses' incentive to hire more workers. Thus, inflation, **once it has become anticipated,** will not increase employment. The long-run Phillips curve becomes a vertical line; the level of unemployment is unaffected by the amount of inflation. Only an ever-increasing rate of inflation that continually runs ahead of anticipations can further reduce unemployment. It's hard to fool most of the people all the time that yesterday's inflation will be the last. **Indeed, this reasoning suggests not only that monetary-fiscal policy cannot guarantee full employment without inflation, but that it is more likely to guarantee inflation without full employment.**

How much of a long-run tradeoff actually exists between inflation and unemployment is a complex, unsettled issue, on both empirical and theoretical grounds. Clearly, expectations adjust, but how fast and how completely is uncertain. Certainly we are unsafe in counting on more inflation to buy a continuing increase in employment. Two distinguished experts on the problem have summarized the situation as follows: "Authors of Phillips curves would do well to label them conspicuously: '*Unstable. Apply with extreme care.*'"[5]

[5] A. Rees and M. Hamilton, "The Wage-Price-Productivity Perplex," *Journal of Political Economy,* February 1967, p. 70. For a good nontechnical summary of the controversy, see "The Relation Between Prices and Employment: Two Views," *Federal Reserve Bank of St. Louis Monthly Review,* March 1969, which also includes references to more detailed studies on both sides.

IS KEYNESIAN POLICY OBSOLETE?

The Keynesian revolution of the 1930s suggested that unemployment need not be tolerated if only combined monetary and fiscal policy were sufficiently aggressive to expand aggregate demand appropriately. But the preceding sections suggest that it is not so easy. Although in the short run monetary-fiscal expansion may help reduce unemployment if we are willing to accept some inflation, over a longer period the result may be merely more inflation and no less unemployment. Thus, expansionary monetary and fiscal policy (the Keynesian revolution) may end up mainly creating more inflation with little impact on the level of unemployment that it was intended to fight. The critics say that Keynesian economic policy is bankrupt—it simply doesn't do the job any more. It may have been appropriate for the depression world of the 1930s, but it won't work in the world of the 1970s, where unemployment is less disastrous, wages and prices are more volatile upward, and inflation expectations are everywhere.

The crucial question is whether workers think in real terms. If so, the government may be able to trick them in the short run into temporarily taking lower real wages by pushing up prices faster than wages; but soon workers will reassert their minimum desired real wage, and Keynesian expansionary monetary-fiscal policy will be impotent to reduce the level of unemployment below the natural rate.

How good a description of reality is the neoclassical picture? We're not sure. Many economists continue to place a lot of faith in expansionary monetary-fiscal policy to get rid of unemployment, and nearly everyone agrees it will work in periods of massive unemployment. Then wage rates will stay down even if total spending rises. But the continued rapid inflation of the last decade has clearly reduced the power of Keynesian policies. **The best conclusion is probably something like this: Expansionary monetary-fiscal policy can help reduce unemployment when unemployment is widespread, and especially when a lot of the economy is** nonunion. But continued expansionary policy, once inflationary wage and price increases have begun, is increasingly likely to be offset by inflationary expectations, so the result is mainly inflation rather than increased jobs and output.

WAGE-PRICE (INCOMES) POLICIES

Today, monetary-fiscal policy alone seems unable to guarantee full employment without inflation. Thus, nearly every major Western nation has sought other means to supplement aggregate-demand policy. One approach is direct controls to hold down wages and prices while expansionary monetary-fiscal policy generates full employment. If expansionary monetary-fiscal policy is thwarted by unions and businesses that raise their wages and prices, the answer of the "man in the street" is simple: Pass a law forbidding inflationary wage and price increases. And nearly every major government has tried it at one time or another—but with limited success. The other approach is manpower policies to increase the employability and employment of the unemployed, especially teenagers, minority groups, and others who lack marketable skills. Both are designed to reduce the level of inflation and increase the level of employment related to any given level of aggregate demand—to shift the Phillips curve to the left. Let us consider them in order.

The Kennedy wage-price guideposts

In 1962, President Kennedy's Council of Economic Advisers suggested a set of wage-price "guideposts" for unions and businessmen, to keep wages and prices in line so aggregate-demand policy could be used to bring full employment without inflation. The administration did not propose legislation to force unions and businesses to adhere to the guideposts, but it did urge them as guides to acceptable private behavior.[6]

In essence, the guideposts suggested that annual wage increases in all industries should

[6] See *Economic Report of the President,* January 1962, Chap. 4.

roughly equal the average increase in output per man-hour in the economy. With such wage increases, prices of final products should be kept stable. Bigger wage increases would be inflationary, while smaller ones would give an undue share of the benefits of increasing productivity to profits. The guideposts were based on the general position that wage rates should behave about as they would in a highly competitive market where supply and demand would tend to produce wage increases equal to increases in "productivity."[7]

Consider a simple example. Assume a stable population and an economy where all income goes to wages and profits. Total output is $300, of which wages are two-thirds and profits one-third. Now suppose the total output increases by 3 percent (that is, $9), and that wages are increased by 3 percent, as suggested by the productivity guidepost. Wages will now rise by $6 (that is, 3 percent of $200), leaving $3 for increased profits (that is, 3 percent of $100). Thus, the average-productivity-increase guide would increase both wages and profits by the same percentage, maintaining whatever distribution of income prevailed before. Don't make the common mistake of assuming that increasing wage rates in proportion to productivity increase would give all the increase to labor.

[7] Three details may help spell out the implications of the guideposts:

1. Wages in particular industries *should not* be directly related to productivity changes in that industry. Thus, if productivity in the automobile industry increases 5 percent per year, but only 3 percent for the economy as a whole, this does not justify a 5 percent wage increase in the auto industry. Rather, it calls for a decline in the price of automobiles.

2. Prices should remain approximately stable in industries that have an average rate of productivity increase. Where productivity increases faster than the national average (that is, where per-unit costs fall faster than the average), selling prices should decline. Prices should rise where productivity increases more slowly than the average.

3. Some exceptions are justified. Wages should rise less than the national average in industries where unemployment persists, to discourage additional workers from entering the industry and to encourage employers to use more labor in that industry. Wages should rise faster than the average where labor is especially scarce. (Again, these are the results to be expected from highly competitive markets.) Moreover, individual wages could rise more or less than the national average where deviation is needed to correct major inequities.

Critics of the guideposts made three points: First, if you don't think the present income distribution between wages and profits is fair, preserving it won't be very attractive. Many union members believe that profits are already exorbitant. Many businessmen believe profits are already too low. And at any time, individual wage rates in particular firms or industries may seem unfairly out of line, too high or too low.

Second, some economists said that government price and wage setting would lead to distortions and inefficiencies. By restricting the free play of market prices, the guideposts would block the proper responses of resources to market forces.

Third, the critics said guideposts just won't work. Both unions and businessmen told the government to keep its nose out. They wanted no government control over wages and prices. If productivity rises 5 percent annually in the auto industry, the auto workers are understandably reluctant to settle for only a 3 percent wage increase, just because productivity elsewhere has increased less than theirs. If you were head of the auto union, would you agree to a 3 percent increase when by hard bargaining you could get 5 percent? If you were president of General Motors, would you reduce prices just because the guideposts say to, when you could make bigger profits by keeping prices up? Would you take a costly strike to hold wages down to help the nation fight inflation, when the customers will pay higher prices? Without government sanctions, some unions and businesses may follow the guideposts, but compliance is almost sure to be uneven and to erode as time goes on.

In retrospect, both the advocates and the critics were partially right. Most studies conclude that the guideposts did help modestly to hold down wages and prices during their early years. But their impact was uneven and, in spite of extensive "jawboning" against violators by President Johnson and his Council of Economic Advisors, they became increasingly futile as aggregate demand soared in 1965–66, when they were abandoned.

The Nixon administration tried wage-price controls again in 1971–73, this time on a mandatory basis. A Pay Board and a Price Commission were established to administer the controls.

The initial "price freeze" was effective, but it soon became clear that, short of a massive new bureaucracy, there was no way to enforce ceilings on every wage and price in the United States, and the Nixon Administration had little taste for such extensive intervention. In early 1973, Nixon announced the end of mandatory direct controls, but he kept a "big stick" in the closet to reimpose controls over big firms and unions that raised prices or wages too rapidly. But this system had little impact, and prices shot upward in 1973, led by farm prices, reflecting a worldwide crop failure, and in 1974 by oil prices, which were quadrupled by the OPEC cartel. Peacetime U.S. wage-price controls merit at best a B– or C in the grade books of most economists.

European incomes policies

Since World War II, the unemployment-inflation dilemma has been everywhere. Every major European nation has experimented with some form of wage-price, or "incomes," policy, some with several, in attempts to reconcile low unemployment with low inflation. Some countries have tried nationwide formal legal controls over all wages and prices—for example, the Netherlands and the United Kingdom. Others have tried "voluntary" plans, more like the Kennedy wage-price guideposts. Most have been somewhere in between.

Most European incomes policies have differed from the two U.S. experiments in one major respect. In most European moves, the wage-price guidelines or incomes policies have been developed with extensive consultation among all the major parties concerned—business, union, agricultural, and government leaders. This reflects two major facts of life in democratic nations. First, any sweeping wage-price control plan necessarily involves setting the relative income shares that will go to the major groups in the economy—hence the name "incomes policies." Second, no plan affecting such a vital economic interest of everyone involved can succeed for long without the working agreement of the major parties, whether the program is "voluntary" or legally mandatory. Unless the unions are willing to moderate their wage demands, the plan will blow up. If millions of workers strike, as they did in the United Kingdom in 1972 and 1974, no democratic government can make them go back to work for long at what they consider unacceptable wages. Involving all the major interests in devising the guidelines has thus seemed to most governments essential to obtaining a national consensus with which labor, business, agriculture, and other major groups will go along.[8]

How well have European incomes policies worked? Results have varied, but two conclusions seem merited. First, they have generally helped to hold down wages and prices temporarily, for a matter of months or even years in some cases, especially where a good consensus was reached that such restraint was essential to the national welfare. Second, in all cases they have failed to restrain wages and prices for long where large excess aggregate demand was permitted to develop. The force of the market and the self-interests of the millions of individuals in it are very strong, and no country has found a way to keep most workers, farmers, and businessmen content for long with less income than they think they ought to have, when the market invites them to raise their wages and prices.

These European results closely parallel those in the United States. Although European incomes policies have generally involved more consultative planning, they face the same basic dilemma as the two American plans. In the showdown, most people want more, and long-continued control over millions of individual wage and price transactions is almost impossible through either legal enforcement or "voluntary" compliance if the controlled prices and wages are substantially below market levels. Incomes policies can help temporarily when there is little or no excess demand. And they can help to dramatize to everyone concerned the fact that self-defeating inflation can be avoided only if all parties keep their income demands roughly consistent with the total real GNP producible at existing prices. Thus, incomes policies can play an important educational and political role. But

on the evidence to date, they cannot take over from aggregate-demand policy the main job of preventing inflation.[9]

MANPOWER AND LABOR-MARKET POLICIES

Policy makers have sought other ways to move the Phillips curve to the left—to decrease the level of unemployment associated with any given level of aggregate demand. Better job-information exchanges, training programs for the unemployed, government emergency employment, and reduced monopolistic barriers to entry by unions are examples of such measures. All are aimed at improving the efficiency of labor markets; all whittle away the core of unemployed for any level of aggregate demand; all are complementary, not competitive, with aggregate-demand policies for high-level employment.

Aggregate demand and structural unemployment

Unemployment that seems impossible, or very difficult, to eliminate through more aggregate demand is often called structural unemployment. Workers whose skills are obsolete (for example, uneducated, middle-aged displaced coal miners in West Virginia), whose IQs are very low, who have little education or marketable skills, or who have physical disabilities are examples of the structurally unemployed. The preceding analysis suggests that many teenagers may also be almost structurally unemployed now, given their attitudes about the jobs they are willing to take and keep. There is some level of aggregate demand that will pull the structurally unemployed into jobs, but it may be very high and would produce rapid inflation

---

[8]For an authoritative account of the European experiences, see L. Ulman and R. Flanagan, *Wage Restraint: A Study of Incomes Policies in Western Europe* (Berkeley: University of California Press, 1971).

[9]During World War II, mandatory general wage and price controls were used, complete with rationing of consumer goods and allocation of materials and labor. Even with such extensive government controls and wartime patriotic pressures for cooperation, inflation could not be eliminated when government war spending soared. Many black markets developed, controls were widely evaded, and the authorities were forced to adjust legal wage and price ceilings upwards repeatedly during the war. Moreover, much of the inflation that was suppressed during the war exploded when controls were removed after 1945.

Table 19–1

Unemployment rates for different groups when rate for mature white males is 1.5 percent

	Unemployment rate[a]
All males, 16–19	11.4
All females, 16–19	13.7
Whites, 16–19	10.8
Non-whites, 16–19	24.5
Non-white males, over 20	3.3
White females, over 20	3.2
Non-white females, over 20	6.1

[a] Estimates by Martin Feldstein, "The Economics of the New Unemployment," *The Public Interest,* Fall 1973, p. 7. "Mature males" includes ages 24–65.

before such unemployment was eliminated.

Table 19–1 shows estimates of the unemployment rate that would have remained for various demographic groups in the early 1970s if aggregate demand had driven the unemployment rate for mature (over 24) white males down to 1.5 percent. The obvious answer seems to be to retrain, educate, and move those structurally unemployed groups to fit the jobs available.

Harvard's Martin Feldstein, who is responsible for the estimates in Table 19–1, argues that, while shortage of aggregate demand may be the major cause of unemployment in serious recessions, for most postwar years the basic problem has been a mismatch between unemployed people and available jobs. Reducing unemployment for the groups shown in Table 19–1 calls for retraining, educating, and moving the unemployed to fit the jobs available, and for making the available jobs more attractive so as to increase the job attachment for workers who now quit low-level, dead-end jobs in large numbers, or simply refuse to take them at all. Even with unemployment rates of 10–20 percent, the want-ad columns of city newspapers are full of openings for common laborers, dishwashers, clerk-typists, and the like.

But a warning is in order before turning to manpower and labor-market programs to remedy these situations. It is easy to underestimate the power of prosperity to provide jobs. The experience of Pittsburgh in the 1960s is a good

example. In 1961, the unemployment rate in Pittsburgh was over 11 percent, compared to a national average of about 6 percent. Employment in the steel mills had been declining persistently since World War II. The steel companies could produce one-third more steel than ten years previously, with fewer men. Pittsburgh was cited as a classic case of structural unemployment—unemployed steelworkers whose jobs were gone forever and who were ill equipped to take on other jobs and unwilling or unable to move to other areas.

But after the strong economic expansion of 1964, Pittsburgh unemployment at year-end was only 3.7 percent, compared to over 5 percent for the nation. Rapidly growing aggregate demand boomed needs for steel in the economy. Mills called displaced workers back to their jobs. Even more important, over the years 1960 to 1964, more than 100,000 people emigrated from the Pittsburgh industrial area as more jobs opened up elsewhere in the United States. The "hard core" of unemployed workers was of ice, not of iron; much of it melted away under the sun of strong aggregate demand. When private employers need labor, they usually manage to provide the training needed to fit unemployed workers to the jobs, better than special government training programs can do.

Government manpower and labor-market programs

The Kennedy and Johnson administrations developed numerous programs to fit unemployed workers to jobs. Better employment exchanges, government job-training centers, subsidies to private firms to train workers, special help for minorities, and a wide variety of educational programs were all aimed at improving the fit between the unemployed and the jobs available. At their peak in 1972, federal manpower and employment program expenditures totaled nearly $4 billion annually; this was nearly $1,000 per unemployed person, and did not include either education programs or additional manpower expenditures by state governments.

Results of these manpower programs have been disappointing, although their effects are hard to evaluate precisely. Many affected workers have not found jobs, or have not kept them if they were placed. Only training programs leading directly to known permanent jobs in private industry appear to have been generally successful. Government emergency jobs have led to only a few permanent private jobs. Many workers who were placed complained that their jobs were low-level and dead-end, which partially accounts for their high quit rates.

The Nixon and Ford administrations reduced federal expenditures on such programs, allocating about half the previous funds to the states and localities through revenue sharing, on the ground that local programs would have a better chance of matching workers to jobs. They believed that the most efficient way to provide job training is through assuring adequate demand that will induce private firms to train the unemployed for jobs that open up.[10]

Feldstein suggests focusing on the groups with highest unemployment rates, especially teenagers. He urges a special Youth Employment Service similar to that in the United Kingdom, to counsel high school graduates and help move them into suitable jobs. High school programs directed toward developing vocational skills could help. Modification of the minimum wage law to permit employers to pay lower beginning rates to teenagers would remove an important barrier for many young people, who are not at the outset worth to employers the $2.30-per-hour minimum they must be paid under existing (1976) law. Some have suggested special federal subsidies to employers hiring such youths to lower their effective wage costs.

While unemployment insurance is an important built-in fiscal-policy stabilizer and provides major benefits for the unemployed, it obviously may reduce the incentive to find another job promptly and thus may increase the unemployment rate. This effect rises as total unemployment benefits rise relative to wage incomes.[11] In 1973, the average duration of unemployment was fourteen weeks for those on unemployment insurance, compared to ten weeks for others.

Unemployment insurance may merely give the worker more time to look around carefully for another job, but it increases the level of unemployment at any given time. The answer, most economists argue, lies not in eliminating unemployment insurance, but in changing the total benefit system to increase the incentive to find a new job promptly.[12]

When unemployment rises and manpower training programs seem ineffective, some, including labor and political leaders, propose that the government act as employer of last resort by directly providing jobs for those who can't get them elsewhere. Ideally, such jobs would provide useful services (cleaning up parks and streets, unskilled help in schools and hospitals, and the like), rather than the make-work, leaf-raking kinds of activities that characterized much work relief in the 1930s. Pay rates would be high enough to provide a decent living standard, but below private job rates to maintain an incentive to shift to private employment. Critics point out that such government direct employment has been expensive per job provided in the past and has not succeeded in moving most workers on into private jobs. Instead, in many cases, it has merely substituted public for private jobs. They argue instead for subsidies or other measures directly aimed at stimulating employment in the private sector if aggregate demand plus labor-market improvements won't do the job. Nonetheless, many Democrats, in Congress and out, advocate a government guarantee of a job for everyone willing and able to work.

Most Western European nations, especially in Scandinavia, have government manpower and labor-market programs that go far beyond ours, and they have generally managed somewhat lower unemployment rates than ours, although generally at a cost of higher inflation. Sweden, for example, provides complete job retraining at full pay plus full moving allowances for workers who the government thinks will need to move to

---

[10] For a brief report on these experiences, see A. Sorkin, *Education, Unemployment, and Economic Growth* (Lexington Books, 1974), Chapter 7.

[11] Reflecting this situation, some union contracts (for example, in the auto industry) now contain "inverse seniority" provisions, giving workers with the longest seniority the right to be laid off first in seasonal cutbacks and the like.

[12] A related reform would be to alter the way in which employers are taxed to support unemployment-insurance payments, so as to increase the employer's inducement to minimize seasonal and cyclical unemployment. The present employer "experience rating" system provides a very weak inducement. Martin Feldstein, "The Economics of the New Unemployment," *The Public Interest,* Fall 1973, provides a more detailed analysis of the issues raised in this section.

other jobs a year or more hence. Most European educational systems place more stress on occupational training, and job turnover is generally much lower in Europe than here, especially among young people. European manpower and labor-market programs are expensive, and higher U.S. job turnover rates reflect Americans preferences for individual freedom and mobility. But most observers feel the European policies have generally worked well. American manpower policy will be a source of both experimentation and controversy over the years ahead.

MORE DRASTIC (FUNDAMENTAL?) MEASURES

In a perfectly competitive economy, neither workers nor businesses would have any market power to set wages or product prices. In such a world, therefore, the unemployment-inflation dilemma would vanish, except for short-run problems when demand approached full-employment levels too fast to permit unemployed resources to adjust to shifting patterns of demand. The solution to the unemployment-inflation dilemma, therefore, some economists argue, is simple but drastic: Eliminate monopoly in the American economy! Outlaw all unions and firms large enough to have any appreciable individual market power. Goodbye to both General Motors and the United Auto Workers, to General Electric and the Electrical Workers, indeed to nearly every business firm and union we know, beyond small local establishments.

Not many Americans take such a dramatic remedy seriously. It would, in most people's eyes, involve throwing out the baby with the bath water. But the underlying analysis suggests that less draconian measures toward more effectively competitive markets could help. Not least, abolition of such government-imposed barriers as import quotas and tariffs that protect domestic producers against lower-price foreign competition, and the Davis-Bacon Act requirement that all government-sponsored construction projects must pay prevailing peak union wage rates, could help significantly to obtain the price-reducing effects of competition.

Many steps have been suggested to lessen the unemployment-inflation dilemma. Some of them would surely help. But alas, the fact seems to be that the Western democratic economies have not yet found a real solution to this nagging problem of macroeconomics. Here, as so often, the problem is not one of economics alone, but of economics and politics together. And solutions to such problems cannot be found in economic analysis alone.

CONCLUSION ON STABILIZATION POLICY

At the end of this long analysis of stabilization policy, where do we stand? What are our chances of avoiding major depressions and inflations in the future?

In spite of the problems, the history of the last thirty years or so is encouraging. We weathered three wars, three reconversions to peace, and a wide variety of other economic shocks without a major bust, albeit with a good deal of inflation and more unemployment than we like. The post–World War II growth in real GNP has been quite steady compared to its earlier roller-coaster performance. And we surely know a lot more than we did about what makes business cycles tick and how to damp them down. The optimists list the following specific factors, in roughly ascending order of importance:

1. Businessmen now plan their investment on a longer-range basis. Thus, investment plans are less susceptible to short-term swings in expectations. Long-run growth is widely recognized as a dominant factor in business planning, and this factor reduces the likelihood of serious short-run collapses in investment.

2. Consumers have become adjusted to a high and rising standard of living, and they will not be panicked into cutting back their spending even though business conditions weaken. If incomes slide, they draw on liquid assets and borrow to protect their living standards, looking to a resumption of better times in the near future. This fact has been demonstrated repeatedly during the postwar years.

3. Federal, state, and local government spending of over $600 billion annually provides

a massive, stable component of demand. Never before has there been such a huge, stable block of spending.

4. Federal tax and spending arrangements now have a large element of built-in counter-cyclical flexibility. All things considered, built-in federal fiscal flexibility will automatically absorb maybe a third of the shock of any drop in national income.

5. The banking and financial system has been greatly strengthened since the crash of 1929. We need never again have the enormous credit contraction that was the core of the 1929–33 collapse. Federal insurance of bank deposits has substantially removed the danger of runs on banks, and the Federal Reserve now stands ready to convert bank assets into cash reserves in case of any major banking crisis, so a general financial collapse like that of 1929–33 is no longer thinkable. And monetary policy can be used as a major countercyclical tool.

6. We have learned how to fight booms and depressions through government fiscal policy. We now understand business slumps far better than in 1929, and there is now general recognition that government deficit spending can provide massive buying power if private spending slumps.

How convincing are these arguments? We're surely in better shape than ever before to avoid major depressions. But although we have powerful cannon to wheel up against big depressions, our small artillery to fight minor fluctuations merits less confidence. The inventory cycle alone is big enough to give us some nasty bumps, and we have yet to demonstrate our ability to fine-tune the economy effectively. Moreover, the preceding discussion of the unemployment-inflation dilemma suggests a world of uneasy swings between the two when times are reasonably prosperous, and a serious danger that inflation may become an ever-more-disruptive force.

Yet to end on a negative note would be a mistake. Combined monetary and fiscal policy, plus improvements in our institutional arrangements, provide a powerful arsenal against instability that should eliminate massive depressions and help substantially to smooth out smaller fluctuations. And experience plus concentrated analysis may teach us how to tame, or live with, the unemployment-inflation dilemma that looks so difficult today.[13]

[13] More thorough support for this analysis is presented in G.L. Bach, "The Search for Stability—What Have We Learned?" in *Public Policy and Economic Understanding* (Washington, D.C.: American Bankers' Association, 1970).

REVIEW

For analysis and discussion

1. Is the "new inflation" analysis in the text a convincing prediction that we face a world of persistent, if intermittent, inflation? To what extent does the analysis rest on political, as distinct from economic, predictions?

2. As a practical matter, is the present level of unemployment as low as we can expect without more inflation? Explain.

3. Look back at Figure 19–1. Using all the data plotted, can you see a Phillips-curve tradeoff in the United States since 1950?

4. Explain how there could be a Phillips-curve tradeoff in the short run but not in the long run. Why are inflation anticipations central to the analysis?

5. In the last four decades, labor unions have become much more powerful. Under these circumstances, according to some economists, government assurance that total spending will be kept up to high-employment levels would be, in effect, a guarantee of continued inflation. Why, if at all, would this be so?

6. How high would you expect unemployment to have to be in order to permit aggressive monetary-fiscal policy without stimulating inflation?

7. Do the Kennedy wage-price guideposts provide an equitable solution to the persistent quarrel between management and labor over income shares? Do they provide an effective means of solving the inflation-unemployment dilemma? Do they represent a dangerous intrusion of government into the private economy?

8. If neither monetary-fiscal policy nor incomes policies can assure high employment without inflation, what should we do?

9. Are big depressions and big inflationary booms obsolete? How would you rate the six arguments at the end of Chapter 19?

Your congressman—still no economist, but learning—is home again from Washington, feeling the public pulse. This time it's inflation he's worried about, and he asks your advice.

Just about everyone complains about inflation—rich and poor, businessmen and consumers, workers and farmers, old and young. Yet the standard remedy of tightening up on monetary and fiscal policy seems likely to make unemployment worse—a cure that's apt to be worse than the disease.

Recently, some economists have testified in favor of "indexing"—tying all wages and prices to the cost of living—as a way of taking the inequities and abuses out of inflation. If you can't lick 'em, join 'em, seems to be the solution suggested. But as usual, the economists differ. Two have recently testified on the issue, roughly as follows:

Economist A: The price we must pay for fighting inflation is simply too high. We would do better to recognize that we will probably have persistent, intermittent inflation for many years to come, and set up safeguards to see that the evil effects of that inflation are largely negated. Inflation has been called the silent robber. But its effects can, in principle, be largely neutralized by helping everyone to rob everyone else at about the same rate. Ideally, everyone should be told what the rate of inflation will be; then everyone could make his bargains taking the inflation into account, and its inequitable redistributional effects would be largely avoided. In the absence of this advance knowledge, we could get much the same results by "indexing"—by tying virtually all wages, prices, and economic contracts to changes in the cost of living, so if the cost of living goes up 5 percent, everything else goes up 5 percent too. Specifically, this would mean:

1. Wages and salaries should be tied to a cost-of-living index. This would immediately immunize something like two-thirds of the entire income structure against loss from inflation on current income account.

2. Business accounting practices should be drastically changed to tie costs and prices to the cost-of-living index. Specifically, depreciation charges should be reckoned in terms that will replace depreciating assets at current prices; and all inventory should be valued on a current replacement basis. Moreover, the current value of assets and liabilities on each business' balance sheet should be adjusted to the changes in the price level. This would state costs in indexed terms, and would make accounting profits reflect the realities of a world of inflation, unlike the present situation, where accounting profits may grossly overstate "real" profits in inflation periods.

3. All taxes should be adjusted for changes in the cost of living. Now, with inflation, people's money incomes rise, pushing them into higher tax brackets although their real incomes are not increased. This siphons off resources to the government, but it is grossly unfair to taxpayers. The same kind of adjustment should be made for business taxes.

4. Where the government regulates the economy (for example, with public utilities), it should tie both wages and utility prices to changes in the cost of living, as it expects the private sector to do.

5. In borrowing money, both the government and private borrowers should issue securities on a constant-puchasing-power basis. That is, bonds should be repayable in a variable number of dollars, but in a constant amount of purchasing power.

If these five measures were adopted, the inequities of modern inflation would be largely eliminated, even though they would not protect every individual from all the bad effects of inflation. Although inflation would still rob the holder of money of part of its value, the program would see that most of the fraud of inflation was offset by giving everyone more income to buy at the higher prices.

Economist B: The case for indexing has a good deal of appeal. Inflation is inequitable, and indexing would be a major attempt to help. But it has two vital flaws:

1. As a practical matter, there is no way of indexing everything. While the government might introduce indexing on its own transactions (for example, it has already put Social Security benefits on an indexed basis, which increases them as inflation goes up), it has no way of enforcing such a rule on all private transactions. To even approach this would call for an army of bureaucrats that staggers the imagination. If strict government enforcement of such indexing were not involved, we would be back where we are now—the shrewd and well informed will best the uneducated and ill-informed in adjusting to inflation. Moreover, there is no possible way to index all prices and income shares—for example, profits.

2. In attempting to protect everyone's income from loss due to inflation, indexing would remove the strongest present barriers to inflation. There would be no incentive left for many people to oppose it. Instead, indexing would guarantee that every price and wage increase would spread on to others. As a practical matter, unions, businesses, and everyone else would begin trying to get ahead of the indexed adjustments, just as they now try to get ahead of the non-indexed rises in the costs and prices they must pay. Thus, indexing would escalate the very inflation whose harm it is intended to reduce. It would, incidentally, eliminate any possibility that monetary-fiscal policy could effectively reduce unemployment. With indexing, money wages would rise as fast as prices, real wages could not be reduced; and there would be no incentive for employers to increase employment with rising aggregate demand.

Too bad! Indexing sounds great, but not after you think about it a little.

What do you advise your congressman to do? Which economist is right? If you don't agree with either, is there a better alternative?

APPENDIX TO PART 2

Current research

The main job of an elementary economics textbook is to stir an interest in economic problems, to present the central analytical tools of economics, and to provide some guided experience in using them to reach independent judgments on current economic developments and public-policy issues. I hope that the preceding pages have conveyed some sense of the lively urgency of the problems with which economics deals, and some sense of the manner in which modern economics helps to solve them.

Economists spend much of their time using the tools presented here and helping to devise public policies that will make our economic system work better. But one of the further things that makes economics exciting is research—the fascination of probing for new knowledge and new insights into how the economic system works. Economics is far from a dead, stable body of theory and knowledge. It is the research of today that will make the better textbooks and the better world of tomorrow.

It is the purpose of these appendixes at the end of each Part to convey a brief impression of the kinds of research currently under way in economics. Some of the research cited is readily understandable by a good student at the elementary level; other parts are more difficult. But the purpose is not to provide references that all beginning students should read. Rather it is to suggest some samples of economic research that may be intriguing to students who want to look beyond the text and who want to know more about what economics is and what economists do. Pick out two or three and look at them. If they don't hit the spot, try another. The goal is to interest you and make you want to read further.

The following paragraphs briefly report a small sample of research on some major problems covered by Part 2. There is no intention to imply that they represent the best, or the most important, research under way on the problems covered. They are merely samples of research that one economist thinks might be interesting to curious students getting acquainted with economics. A major criterion in selection has

been variety. A half dozen other comparable lists could readily be provided—and, indeed, your instructor may be happy to provide one he feels is superior.[1]

Inflation and unemployment. A good start on the inflation problem is provided by Robert Solow, "The Intelligent Citizen's Guide to Inflation," *The Public Interest,* Winter 1975; Milton Friedman, "The Role of Monetary Policy," *American Economic Review,* March 1968; and W. Nordhaus, "The Worldwide Wage Explosion," *Brookings Papers on Economic Activity,* 1972:2. On the unemployment problem, begin with M. Feldstein, "The Economics of the New Unemployment," *The Public Interest,* Fall 1973. The Brookings Institution's *Papers on Economic Activity* (published three times annually) present numerous research analyses of macroeconomic policy, at a relatively nontechnical level; see, for example, G.L. Perry, "Unemployment Flows in the U.S. Labor Market" (1972:2), and R.E. Hall, "Proposals for Shifting the Phillips Curve through Manpower Policy" (1971:3). Barbara Bergmann analyzes the difficulties of attaining full employment through aggregate-demand policy, with stress on the problems of minorities and women, in "Curing High Unemployment Rates among Blacks and Women," Joint Economic Committee, U.S. Congress, *Reducing Unemployment to 2 Percent,* October 17, 1972. A broader approach, which combines economic, social, and political factors, is G.L. Bach, *The New Inflation* (Providence, R.I.: Brown University Press, 1973). Chapter 2 analyzes the effects of recent inflation on different groups. Gardner Ackley's *Stemming World Inflation* (The Atlantic Institute, 1971) stresses the international aspects of inflation. Finally, California's Lloyd Ulman and Stanford's Robert

[1]A number of the following references, in this and other appendixes on current research, have been reprinted in M.L. Joseph, N.C. Seeber, and G.L. Bach, eds., *Economic Analysis and Policy,* 4th ed. (Englewood Cliffs, N.J.: Prentice-Hall, 1974).

Flanagan provide an authoritative but discouraging analysis of incomes policies in *Wage Restraint: A Study of Incomes Policies in Western Europe* (Berkeley: University of California Press, 1971).

Monetary and fiscal policy. The great debate between the monetarists and neo-Keynesians has spawned a huge literature. For a starter, try "Two Views of the Role of Money," by Yale's James Tobin and Carnegie-Mellon's Allan Meltzer, in *Controlling Monetary Aggregates* (Federal Reserve Bank of Boston, 1969). Milton Friedman's *A Program for Monetary Stability* (New York: Fordham University Press, 1969) is an authoritative statement of the monetarist viewpoint. Arthur Okun provides an excellent example of applying modern fiscal analysis to recent situations in "Measuring the Impact of the 1964 Tax Reduction," in W.W. Heller, ed., *Perspectives on Economic Growth* (New York: Random House, 1968). Herbert Stein provides a fascinating account of the development of modern fiscal policy, with some surprises, in *The Fiscal Revolution in America* (Chicago: University of Chicago Press, 1969). G.L. Bach's *Making Monetary and Fiscal Policy* (The Brookings Institution, 1971) is a study of the political and economic interactions that occur in real-world policy making; see especially Chapters 5–8.

FORECASTING. If you're interested in some of the newer developments in economic forecasting and know a little mathematics, two recent studies will give you a good introduction; "A Quarterly Econometric Model of the United States," *Survey of Current Business,* May 1966; and I. Friend and P. Taubman, "A Short-Term Forecasting Model," *Review of Economics and Statistics,* August 1964. W.W. Leontief's "The Structure of the U.S. Economy," *The Scientific American,* April 1965, describes "input-output analysis." A survey of modern forecasting techniques is provided by Part One and pp. 161–89 of W. Butler, R. Kavesh, and R. Platt, eds., *Methods and Techniques of Business Forecasting* (Englewood Cliffs, N.J.: Prentice-Hall, 1974).

markets,
the price system,
and the allocation
of resources

THE BUSINESS FIRM AND ITS COSTS

Chapters 1–6 presented an overview of the way a competitive market economy solves the big economic problems—how it allocates society's limited economic resources to meet consumers' wants. Consumers spend their money on what they want most. Businessmen, seeking profits, have an incentive to produce the goods and services consumers want most because that is how they will generally make the biggest

CHAPTER PREVIEW

NOTE: The first three chapters of Part 3 (Chapters 20–22) comprise a unit, analyzing how a highly ("purely") competitive system would work in responding to consumer demands. The following chapters then compare these results with those where varying degrees of monopoly, with big corporations, exist. Some teachers and students will want to concentrate mainly on the "big picture"—on a general overview and comparison of these different kinds of markets. This is provided by Track A. Others will want to analyze them in considerable detail and more rigorously. This is provided by Track B. Chapters 20–22 are written to be usable either way.

Those who want Track A should use only Parts A of Chapters 20 and 22, skipping Chapter 21 entirely. This presents merely an overview of the theory, stressing the main results. Those who want Track B should add all the rest of Chapters 20–22, using them completely. This will provide a more detailed, rigorous statement of the basic theory and its implications.

profits. In Part 3, we now want to examine in detail how, and how well, this process works, building on the simple demand-and-supply analysis of Part 1. How far can we rely on the market process to use our limited resources efficiently? Is big business now so powerful that it diverts consumer dollars into its own pockets, and through advertising manipulates consumers so they buy what yields the biggest business profits rather than what they really want? Should we turn more to government to decide what to produce, how to produce it, and who should get it?

The foundation of the system is consumer demands for the millions of products that different consumers want. So first look back at Chapter 5 if the analysis there of consumer demand isn't fresh in your mind. For in studying "microeconomics" in Part 3, we are largely studying how, and how effectively, different types of business firms and markets respond to consumers' demands.

PART A

COSTS—THE BARE ESSENTIALS

WHY STUDY COSTS?

Why study costs? Because a businessman's costs largely determine how much he will produce in response to different demands, and the lowest price at which he can sell and stay in business. If customers won't pay more than $1 for a widget and the minimum cost of producing widgets is $1.25, you don't need to be an expert economist to see it won't pay to produce widgets. How far any business will go in producing what consumers want will depend on how much that article costs to produce, relative to how much buyers will pay for it.

Business costs are important for another reason. **Looked at as wages, salaries, rent, and interest payments, business costs are the incomes of workers and of resource owners. In explaining business costs, therefore, we are simultaneously explaining why most people receive the incomes they do.**

Most important, the basic fact of scarcity (limited resources) means that the "real" cost of producing anything is the alternatives foregone that might have been produced with those resources. For example, the real cost of producing an auto is the other things given up that might otherwise have been produced with the same steel, glass, rubber, and labor. **The real cost is an** "alternative cost"—the alternative uses of the resources that are given up when the resources are used in producing autos. Sometimes, alternative cost is called "opportunity" cost.

This concept of opportunity cost can be put into money terms. Thus, the cost of producing one TV set is the amount of money necessary to get the factors of production needed for the set away from alternative uses. The TV manufacturer has to pay enough to engineers to get them away from auto and radar plants, enough for copper wire to bid it away from telephone companies. And so it is for every resource he uses. **In economic terms, the cost of the TV is the amount necessary to bid all the required resources away from the strongest competing uses.**

Accounting and economic costs

Business money costs of production include wages, materials, rent, interest, and all the other items listed in the profit-and-loss statement in the Appendix to Chapter 4. But the alternative-cost concept leads economists to somewhat different cost figures from the ones that businessmen and their accountants work with—primarily because the economist includes several items that the accountant ordinarily doesn't consider as costs when he draws up his profit-and-loss statements.

A simple example is the independent corner grocer, who has bought a store with his own money and runs it himself. In addition to the regular business costs in the profit-and-loss statement, the economist would say:

How about a return on your own investment and a salary for yourself? If you didn't have your money tied up in the store, you could be earning 5 percent on it in another investment. If you weren't working in the store, you could earn $10,000 a year working for Kroger's. You ought to account as costs a 5 percent return on your investment and a $10,000 salary for yourself before you compute your profit for the year, because these reflect real alternatives that you're giving up when you stay in your business.

If the grocer does not include these costs and finds he's making a $9,000 annual "profit," he may think he's doing well—but actually he's kidding himself. The $9,000 doesn't even give him the salary he could earn working for someone else, much less the return he could get by doing that and investing his money somewhere else. If his investment was, say, $20,000, his interest foregone elsewhere at 5 percent would be $1,000 annually. His accounting "profit" would have to be $11,000 on the store just to break even—that is, to cover his own $10,000 salary plus $1,000 interest on his money.

A similar, although less obvious, situation is found in business corporations. Corporations pay salaries to their officers and employees, so there's no problem there. And they pay interest to their bondholders, which is considered a cost in computing profits. But they don't consider the interest on the owners' (stockholders') investment to be a cost. Dividends to stockholders are treated as a *use* of profits, *not as a cost.*

The economist, however, includes in the firm's costs a reasonable ("normal") rate of return on stockholders' investment (measuring the alternative return that is foregone elsewhere). He therefore considers as "economic profit" only the excess income over and above this basic alternative cost, because this normal rate of return is part of the cost required to keep funds invested in any business. Thus, part of dividends to stockholders should be counted as costs.[1]

Throughout the rest of this book, we shall use the alternative-cost concept. Thus, costs of production will include the normal rate of return (profit) on investment necessary to keep the funds invested in that concern rather than elsewhere. Costs will include the entrepreneur's salary if he is self-employed, and dividends equal to a normal return on capital invested by stockholders. Broadly, they will include all costs required to get and keep resources in the firm being considered. Most costs will be the same as those used by the accountant, but the differences noted above must be kept in mind. **Especially, remember that the cost data and curves used here include a "normal" return, or profit, on investment, if you want to avoid some dangerous pitfalls later on.**

Costs of production and the rate of output

It is important to distinguish among some different measures of cost incurred by firms, even though you don't plan to study costs in detail. **They are (1) "sunk," (or committed, or fixed) costs; (2) "average" cost, or total cost per unit produced; and (3) "marginal" cost.**

Suppose you run a guided fishing service on a large nearby lake. You have leased five fishing boats for the summer, and you hire local college students to serve as boat operators and fishing guides for wealthy visiting fishermen. Your lease cost for the boats, plus your own time and rental on a wharf, comes to $50 per day, or $10 per boat. Your operating cost per boat per day (guide plus gas and oil) is $20, incurred only when a boat is rented out for the day. Note the following different measures of costs.

---

[1] In economics, costs that show up in the usual accounting procedures are often called "explicit" costs, while alternative costs (such as a return on stockholders' investment) that are not usually recorded in modern accounting are called "implicit" costs.

CASH VERSUS ECONOMIC PROFITS: A MANAGERIAL APPLICATION

A simple managerial example may help show the importance of these distinctions, as well as give you an impression of how basic economic analysis can help in day-to-day business. Suppose you're in business for yourself, doing miscellaneous repairs (carpentering, electrical wiring, and so on) at a minimum charge of $10 per call and $4 per hour additional after the first hour. Your only equipment is your family station wagon; you have converted the back to carry your working tools. You are prepared to answer calls anywhere in your general area. You've spent $20 for an ad in the local paper and for a supply of mimeographed postcards mailed at random to names from the phone book.

After a month, you've collected a large amount of experience, considerable boredom waiting for the phone to ring, and $620. Have you made a profit? Should you stay in business?

The answer to the profit question hinges on what your costs have been. If you deduct the original $20 outlay, you have $600 left. Not bad for a summer month. But look again. There is clearly gas and oil for the station wagon, and wear and tear on it, which may be appreciable from this use. Then, aside from any materials (for which you may have charged extra), there's the question of your own time.

Suppose gas and oil allocable to this work have cost $80. And you make a rough estimate of $50 a month extra depreciation on the car. That still leaves you $470. Is that more or less than a reasonable wage for your own full time and energy for the month? Here the concept of opportunity cost provides a guide to the answer. What could you make elsewhere, doing work you consider about equally interesting, difficult, and convenient? If the answer is above $470, you've made a loss, even with $520 in the bank. If it's less than $470, you've made a profit, although maybe a very small one. Central concepts: the distinction between cash and income, and opportunity cost. Without them you're apt to pull a real boner.

Your *fixed,* or committed, or "sunk," *costs* for the summer are $50 per day, or $10 per boat. You are committed to these costs, whether or not you have customers for your fishing-guide service.

Average cost is your total cost divided by the number of units produced (boat-days rented). Suppose you rent out only one boat with guide today. What is the average cost of boat-days sold to customers today? Answer: $70. Your total cost has been $50 of sunk costs, plus $20 for one guide plus gas, or $70. Since you have rented only one boat for the day, the average cost per unit (boat-days) produced is $70. But suppose you rent all five boats. Then your total cost is $50 sunk costs (same as before) plus $100 for five guides and gas, amounting to $150. If you divide this by the five boats rented, the average cost per unit rented is obviously $30, far less than when you rented only one boat. You have spread your $50 fixed, or "sunk," cost over all five boats, instead of concentrating it all on one. Average cost thus clearly varies with the number of units produced. In this simple case, it falls steadily as the number of units produced per day rises. In more complex cases, this is also commonly true over a considerable range of output, but average cost generally turns up after a firm has reached roughly the production "capacity" for which it was designed (details in Part B of this chapter). Average cost is also frequently called "total cost per unit."

Marginal cost is the additional cost incurred in producing one more unit. For your guide service, this is obviously $20 per unit, the extra outlay in putting one more boat into service for a day. Note that the $50 sunk lease cost is not involved, since it does not increase or decrease when we produce one more unit. In this simple example, marginal cost is the same ($20) whether we are renting out the first or last boat for the day. In more complex cases, this may not be true.

As we shall see, these three cost concepts are important ones for economic analysis. Looking ahead, four brief suggestions may be helpful. **First, once "sunk" costs are committed, they should not affect our decisions on pricing and** production for the period of that commitment—for example, in deciding how much to charge in renting out our boats.

Second, the difference between average cost and selling price per unit determines the profit per unit sold. In a competitive economy, whenever price is above average cost, other firms will have an incentive to enter the industry to obtain some of the profits.

Third, marginal cost, which is often different from average cost, provides a useful tool for deciding whether or not we will gain by producing and selling one more unit. **If marginal cost is below the extra, or marginal, revenue obtained by selling the additional unit, you will increase profits by selling the additional unit.** Suppose we can rent out an additional boat today for $40. Since our marginal cost is only $20, clearly we will increase total profit by selling the additional unit; it adds $40 to income and only $20 to costs. But if marginal cost is higher than marginal revenue, we would reduce our total profit by renting the additional unit, since it would add more to total cost than to total revenue.

Fourth, to reemphasize, all costs except sunk costs vary with the rate of production. Thus, it is generally meaningless to say that *the* cost of producing anything is some fixed amount; the cost will normally vary depending on the number of units produced per day or week or year.[2]

[2] It is recommended that students doing only Part A also read "Social Costs and Private Costs," on p. 273 of this chapter.

PART B
MORE DETAILED ANALYSIS—COSTS

COST OF PRODUCTION AND THE RATE OF OUTPUT—ANALYSIS

Let us turn now to a more detailed and rigorous analysis of costs in relation to the rate of output.[3] Imagine a somewhat more complex company but still one that produces only a single product—say, it assembles luxury-level stereos. Suppose the company's only costs are raw materials, labor, depreciation on plant and equipment, maintenance, and return on stockholders' investment. Suppose further that, if we look at costs over the period ahead, we find that depreciation and a normal (implicit) return on stockholders' investment are fixed (sunk) for the next year—they go on whether the company operates at full capacity or partial capacity, or shuts down. The other costs are "variable," depending on the company's rate of output.

[3] The appendix to this chapter, "Physical-Production Relationships Underlying Cost Curves," provides the logical foundation for this cost analysis. It should be assigned here by those instructors who wish a rigorous analytical foundation for this and the following chapter, but students can grasp the central points in the text without it.

Assume that the fixed costs amount to $1,000 per week, and that the variable costs vary with changes in output as in Table 20–1. Total cost is simply the sum of fixed and variable costs.

These same costs are plotted in Figure 20–1. Cost is shown on the vertical axis, output on the horizontal one. The fixed cost totals $1,000, the same no matter what output is produced. On top

Table 20–1
Fixed, variable, and total costs

Output per week	Total fixed cost	Total variable cost	Total cost
1	$1,000	$ 2,000	$ 3,000
2	1,000	2,500	3,500
3	1,000	3,100	4,100
4	1,000	4,000	5,000
5	1,000	5,000	6,000
6	1,000	6,600	7,600
7	1,000	10,000	11,000
8	1,000	16,000	17,000

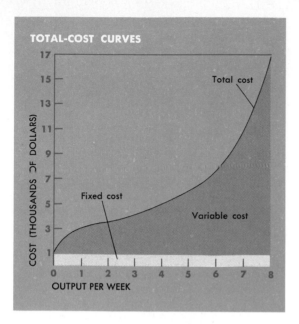

TOTAL-COST CURVES

Total cost

Fixed cost

Variable cost

COST (THOUSANDS OF DOLLARS)

OUTPUT PER WEEK

Figure 20-1
Total fixed cost is $1,000 at all outputs. Total variable cost rises as output increases. Total cost for any output is the sum of fixed and variable costs; it rises rapidly once the "capacity" of the plant is reached.

of this, we need to put total variable cost—zero at zero output, $2,000 for one set, $2,500 for two, and so on. The total-cost curve (top line) thus shows the sum of total fixed and total variable cost at each level of output.

It is easy to see that total cost does not rise at an even rate. It doesn't cost much more in total

Table 20-2

Total and marginal costs

Output	Total cost	Marginal cost
1	$ 3,000	$ 500
2	3,500	600
3	4,100	900
4	5,000	1,000
5	6,000	1,600
6	7,600	3,400
7	11,000	6,000
8	17,000	

to produce two sets than one, or three than two, once you've invested in the plant. But as the firm gets up to six or seven sets per week, total cost begins to rise much more rapidly. Total variable cost shoots up. The company was set up with a capacity of only five or six sets a week, and to exceed this capacity involves expensive readjustments in equipment, hiring more workers or overtime labor, and other special problems. Nearly all firms see their variable costs soar if they try to produce beyond their plant's planned capacity.

Marginal cost

Marginal cost is the addition, or increment, to total cost involved in expanding output by one unit. In this firm, for example, the total cost of producing three sets per month is $4,100 and that of producing four sets $5,000, so the marginal cost of expanding production from three to four units is $900. That's how much *extra* it costs us to get the fourth set produced. This calculation is shown in Table 20-2, using the cost data from Table 20-1. Note that, unlike the earlier, fishing-boat case, here marginal cost varies with changes in output.[4]

Marginal cost is a very important concept. Most economic decisions involve choices—comparisons of alternatives "at the margin." Shall we increase output another unit? Shall we paint the house this year? Shall we raise the tax rate to increase Medicare benefits for the poor? In making such choices, the logical procedure is to compare the marginal cost of the change with the marginal income, or benefit, from it, to see whether the net result is positive or negative. Be sure you understand marginal cost and the basic process of comparing alternatives at the margin.

Costs per unit of output

Except for marginal cost, the Table 20-1 data don't show costs per set produced, and you probably think of business output in terms

[4] For students who study the appendix to this chapter: Marginal cost is the cost counterpart of marginal productivity. Other things equal, marginal cost will be lowest when marginal productivity is highest.

Table 20-3

Fixed, variable, and total costs per unit

Output	Fixed cost per unit	Variable cost per unit	Total cost per unit (average cost)
1	$1,000	$2,000	$3,000
2	500	1,250	1,750
3	333	1,000	1,333
4	250	1,000	1,250
5	200	1,000	1,200
6	167	1,100	1,267
7	143	1,430	1,573
8	125	2,000	2,125

of cost and selling price per unit. You may already have divided the total-cost figures by the number of stereos produced to see what the cost per set (average cost) is at different levels of output. If you haven't, it's a sensible thing to do. The result is shown in Table 20-3.

Fixed cost per unit will always be a steadily decreasing series, because the constant total-fixed-cost figure (here, $1,000) is divided by a steadily rising volume of output. This is what is commonly known as "spreading the overhead." The drop in fixed cost per unit is very rapid at first, but as volume grows, the additional cost reduction per unit steadily decreases in importance.

Variable cost per unit will generally fall at the outset, then flatten out, and then rise again as plant "capacity" is approached. To produce one set, the company has to have labor and materials of all the types needed for the set. It will clearly be inefficient to try to call in each type of skilled labor just long enough to work on one set. If we try to use two or three jacks-of-all-trades, we get less efficient work. Similarly, it may be cheaper to buy materials in larger quantities, and so on. It's not efficient to produce only one or two sets a week.

At the other extreme, once the "capacity" for which the plant was planned has been reached, costs will shoot up if we try to produce more sets per month. "Capacity" is seldom an absolute limit in a plant. For example, steel plants may operate above 100 percent of capacity; rated capacity allows for an average amount of shutdown time for maintenance and repairs, which can be postponed temporarily. But expansion of output beyond plant "capacity" often means expensive overtime work, hiring of lower-skilled workers, more spoilage under pressure of speed-up and a variety of other such factors.

Thus, with any given plant, variable costs per unit will rise rapidly at some point beyond "capacity" output. Just where this point is reached depends, of course, on the individual firm. In many industries, variable costs per unit are apparently flat over a wide range of output. In others, where small-scale operations are advantageous, increase in output beyond low levels leads quickly to rising unit costs.

Total cost per unit (average cost) is simply the sum of fixed and variable costs per unit. It can also be obtained by dividing total cost by the number of units produced. The decreasing fixed cost per unit will always pull down on average cost as output rises. At first, as long as both fixed and variable costs per unit are declining, clearly the total cost per unit is declining. But at some point, total unit costs will begin to rise, when variable cost per unit turns up more than enough to offset the downward pull of spreading the overhead (fixed cost). This point is at the sixth unit in our stereo plant. Total unit cost is relatively stable over the output range of three to six units, with the minimum cost per unit at an output of five sets per month.

This simple stereo example should warn you

against the common fallacy that each firm has a cost of production for its product. In every firm, cost of production per unit varies with output. This is certain at the extremes of very low and above-capacity output. It often also occurs over the range of normal variation in operations.[5]

All these per-unit-cost data can readily be plotted on graphs as cost curves. Figure 20–2 shows the average cost data for our stereo firm. Fixed cost per unit falls steadily as the constant total cost is spread over more and more units. Variable cost per unit and total cost per unit are both U-shaped, for the reasons explained above. In most firms, the *TUC* (total-unit-cost) curve is probably flatter than in this hypothetical case. That is, there is a wider range of output over which total cost per unit is substantially constant, between the low-output inefficiencies shown at the left of the graph and the above-capacity inefficiencies at the right. (For a large, real-world plant producing hundreds of sets weekly, the cost curves would be smooth and continuous, without the corners shown in the curves for our very small firm.)

Be sure you know just what the graph shows. For example, at an output of five sets, the fixed cost per set will be $200 and the variable cost per unit $1,000, for a total of $1,200. This happens to be the lowest point on the total-unit-cost curve. It is called the "least-cost combination." It is the lowest average cost at which these stereos can be made, given the existing plant and the firm's other commitments.

Reading the marginal-cost curve (plotted from Table 20–2) takes special care, since it shows the *extra* cost involved in increasing output from one level to another. For example, the marginal cost of increasing output from two to three sets per week is $600. Read the marginal-cost curve at 6 sets; this point shows it would cost an *additional* $1,600 to raise output from five to six sets.

[5]Many firms now use what they call "standard costs" in pricing their products. A "standard cost" for our stereo would be an estimate of how much it would cost to produce one set at a normal, or typical, rate of output. If we think of four sets weekly as about normal operation, our standard-cost figure would be $1,250 per set. It is important, however, to remember that "standard cost" is only an estimate of unit cost at some selected level of output, not necessarily the minimum unit-cost level.

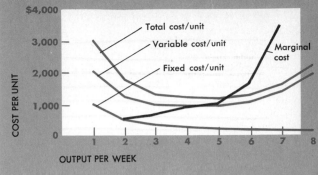

AVERAGE (UNIT-COST) CURVES

Figure 20–2
Unit-cost curves are derived by dividing the corresponding total-cost curves by total output. Here, fixed unit cost slopes continuously downward as the constant total fixed cost is spread over more units of output. The variable and total average-cost curves are U-shaped, and are cut by the marginal-cost curve at their lowest points.

"SHORT-RUN" AND "LONG-RUN" VIEWS OF COSTS

Economists speak of the "short run" and the "long run." Time is an extremely important variable in the analysis of economic problems, and this distinction is an attempt to clarify the assumptions being made about the time period involved in any case. **We mean by the "short run" any time period in which some costs (such as rent and interest on borrowed funds) are fixed and do not vary with changes in the firm's output. We mean by "long run" a time period long enough so that all costs become variable. Thus. the distinction is an analytical one. In calendar time, the short run for one firm may be longer than the long run for another, depending on how long the cost commitments run in different cases.**

Some examples will clarify this distinction. For our firm, next week is clearly a "short run." During that week, certain costs are fixed no matter how many stereos we produce—depreciation on the factory building, for example. Given a longer time period, the existing plant will depreciate fully, or it may be sold, so the capital tied up in the plant becomes available for other uses. Similarly, the manager's salary is a fixed cost for the next month, but over some longer time period, his contract will expire and his salary will become a variable cost. If a firm

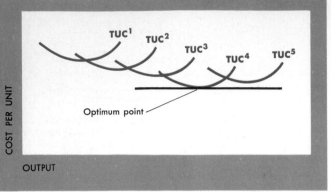

Figure 20-3
Larger firms have lower minimum total-unit-cost points until the optimal scale of firm is reached. Then, still larger firms face higher minimum TUCs.

has commitments for fixed costs extending for years ahead, the "short run" for that firm will be a long time.

In the "long run," by contrast, all the firm's costs become variable. The entrepreneur can decide to build a new plant of different size if he likes. He can transfer his investment to another industry. He has complete freedom to move.

The optimum scale of enterprise

The "long run" is thus a planning period, free from the short-run limitations imposed by fixed plant and other commitments. The big long-run planning problem is, What is the "optimum scale of enterprise" for the firm? How big a fixed plant, how big a labor force, how much equipment? The questions involve everything related to planning the enterprise's scale of operations in the future.

Businesses seldom find themselves in a position to make all these decisions on future scale at one time. But they are continually making changes, so that in essence they may replan their overall scale of enterprise much more frequently than would appear from a superficial glance.

A set of five possible planning curves, showing expected costs for five different scales of enterprise, is given in Figure 20–3. Each *TUC* curve corresponds to a given scale of enterprise—a plant of certain size, equipment of certain sorts, and so on. The scale of enterprise at the extreme left would be advantageous only for a very small

market. In this figure, the scale corresponding to the fourth cost curve gives the lowest possible least-cost point. A firm of this size is the "optimum scale of enterprise," in the sense that it provides the possibility of the lowest cost per unit of output of any possible scale of enterprise. Note, however, that, if total market demand is small, it may not be economical to build and operate a firm of this scale.

How big is "optimal"?

The optimal scale of enterprise varies widely from industry to industry. In some, very large plants and firms are required to obtain peak efficiency—for example, in autos, cigarettes, petroleum, and steel. But the evidence is also clear that in many industries, medium-sized or even small firms manage to achieve costs as low as those of the giants. Rates of return on invested capital do not appear to be consistently larger for huge than for medium-sized firms, although many of the giants are among the most profitable firms. An indirect test of the optimal scale of firm is provided by the size of firm that grows fastest. Here again, the evidence is mixed. For the economy as a whole, the share of market obtained by the largest firms is growing in some industries but not in others—even though nearly all firms are getting bigger as the economy grows. The empirical evidence shows clearly that there is no single, pat answer to the question, How big is optimal?

Do businesses operate at optimal scale?

If we look at all the firms in any particular industry, we will probably find a wide divergence in size. Why aren't all firms the "optimal" size? There are many reasons. For example:

1. In some cases, the market isn't big enough to permit all firms to operate at optimal scale. In such industries, a firm may operate at lower costs per unit with a small plant than it would with a large plant used at only partial capacity.

2. Some firms become overexpanded as part of a drive to attain dominance in their industry. Men with dreams of industrial empire may expand beyond optimal scale in their drive for

bigness and prestige. It is hard to measure this factor, but the last century of U.S. history has produced many cases where this motive appears to have been important.

3. Sometimes, fear of government action holds firms back from profitable expansion—for example, when a firm fears that further growth may bring government antitrust action to break it up. It is often alleged that this fear is what keeps General Motors from taking a still larger share of the auto market.

4. Probably most important of all, errors and delays in adjusting to changing conditions mean that at any time, most firms will not be at optimal scale. Plans in establishing a new plant are inevitably imprecise on many factors: new technology, future wage rates and prices, scale of market available, and so on. And even if the estimates could be precise, change is inescapable in economic life. Before long, new situations will arise, new technological changes will appear. Replanning optimal scale is a continuous process for the well-managed firm.

SOCIAL COSTS AND PRIVATE COSTS

Large profits in an industry are a signal that resources can profitably be moved into that industry from elsewhere. Losses are a signal that resources can earn more elsewhere and should be moved away. Profits and losses are thus crucial signals in the working of a free-market economy.

If the signals are to be correct, costs of pro-ducing goods should reflect fully the alternatives foregone. Generally, the private costs incurred by the firm in obtaining resources (wages, rents, raw materials, and so on) are a good measure of what it takes to get resources away from other industries. But in some cases, additional costs are involved in the production of a good or service. If, for example, a steel mill produces steel for $100 per ton, but also spews out smoke and soot that cover the surrounding neighborhood, the $100 is not a complete measure of the total social cost of producing the steel. The extra cost involved in grimy windowsills and curtains, discolored paint, and smoke-filled lungs are all real costs for the people in that community. They are social costs ("negative externalities" imposed on the community), even though they are not included in the money costs that the steel company must pay to produce steel at $100 per ton.

In such a case, total social costs including the externalities exceed the private costs faced by the steelmaker. The $100-per-ton price does not cover the full cost, so, as we shall see, steel consumers pay too low a price and get too much steel, at the expense of those who suffer from the externalities.

There may be positive external economies as well as diseconomies; that is, production may involve side benefits to the community instead of side costs. For example, a company may build an attractive new facility that improves the appearance of the neighborhood. Possible government policies vis-à-vis both positive and negative externalities will be examined in detail in Chapter 27 and Part 5.

REVIEW

Concepts to remember

This is another chapter of important concepts that will be used throughout the analysis of business-firm behavior. Be sure you understand the following:

In Part A:
alternative cost
opportunity cost
real costs

In Part B:
variable costs
total costs
fixed cost per unit

accounting costs
money costs
fixed (sunk) costs
total cost per unit (average cost)
marginal cost
marginal comparisons

variable cost per unit
least-cost combination
short run
long run
optimal scale of enterprise
social costs
externalities (positive and negative)

For analysis and discussion

For Parts A and B:

1. Define opportunity, or alternative, cost. Explain why the dollar cost of producing an auto is a measure of the alternative uses of the resources foregone.
2. If you were operating a grocery store, would there be any significant difference between your cash outlays per month and your costs per month? If so, what items would account for the difference?
3. You are considering the possibility of setting up a pizza parlor near the campus. Make a list of all the costs you ought to have in mind in estimating whether the expected demand will produce a profit. Which of the costs would be fixed regardless of how many pizzas you sold, and which would vary from week to week with sales volume?
4. In the fishing-boat example in the text: (a) Explain why marginal cost is independent of (does not depend on) the level of fixed cost. (b) How many boats would it pay you to rent out today at a price of $25? $15?

For Part B only:

5. The ABC company has the following costs. From this information, prepare a table showing the following: fixed cost per unit, variable cost per unit, total cost per unit, and marginal costs. Then plot your data on a graph.

Total fixed cost per month	$1,000
Total variable costs:	

Units produced	Variable cost
10	$ 500
11	1,000
12	1,400
13	1,750
14	2,000
15	2,400

6. Make a list of the reasons why manufacturing concerns are typically bigger than dry-cleaning establishments. Can you reconcile your list with the observed fact that some dry-cleaning establishments are bigger than some manufacturing companies?
7. "By and large, the competitive system sees to it that every firm is near the optimal size for producing its product." Do you agree with this statement? Explain carefully why, or why not.
8. List three cases of external diseconomies of business firms. Do such diseconomies seem to you rare, or pervasive?

Professor Polly Poet of the English Department plans to spend next year traveling, and is trying to decide whether to put her house up for rent. She has never studied economics, and indeed is rather uncomfortable with figures. She has, nevertheless, compiled the following list of monthly costs that she is using to decide whether to rent the house and what rent to charge if she does so.

Assuming that the list is complete and that no other factors affect her decision (for example, the increased probability of burglary if the house is empty), what is the lowest rent she should be willing to accept rather than leave the house unoccupied? (*Note:* It is customary in this area to include the price of gardeners in the rent.) Explain your advice so that she will fully understand your reasoning.

Property taxes	$200
Insurance	15
Mortgage payments	100
Gardener (for lawn and trees)	50
Depreciation and maintenance:	
With house empty	40
With house occupied	80
Total: (house empty)	$405
(house occupied)	$445

APPENDIX

Physical-production relationships underlying cost curves

This appendix provides a brief statement of part of the "theory of production," which underlies the cost of production in a firm and provides a foundation for understanding the distribution of income to different factors of production. Its purpose is to examine rigorously the physical and technological relationships involved as the businessman combines the various factors of production in turning out his product. It is intended for those who want a rigorous physical-output foundation for the previous and following sections on business costs. It can be omitted by others.

The simplest case arises when one variable factor of production (say, labor) is applied to a fixed amount of some other factor (say, land). Consider the results of applying an increasing number of units of labor to a fixed plot of land, abstracting from any other factors of production, such as fertilizer and tools. Table 20–4 shows what might happen in such a case. The physical outputs obtainable from various combinations of productive factors are what economists call a "production function."

Column 1 shows the number of laborers used. Column 2 shows the total production—say, bushels of wheat—obtained as more workers are added. Total product rises until at some point (twelve workers with 3,300 bushels of output, in this example), so many laborers are being used on this small plot of land that they get in each other's way, and thereafter there is an actual **decrease** in the total output of wheat. Obviously, no intelligent farmer would ever carry

Table 20–4
Variable output with increasing inputs

Units of input (labor)	Total output (bushels)	Average output per unit of labor (bushels)	Marginal output of labor (bushels)
1	100	100	100
2	350	175	250
3	702	234	352
4	1,152	288	450
5	1,700	340	548[a]
6	2,190	365	490
7	2,604	372[a]	414
8	2,908	364	304
9	3,114	346	206
10	3,240	324	126
11	3,300[a]	300	60
12	3,300	375	0
13	3,250	250	−50
14	3,080	220	−170

[a]Denotes highest point for each output series.

production of wheat beyond this point, because by hiring more laborers, he would actually decrease the total crop he obtained.

Column 3 shows the average product (bushels of wheat) per worker on the land. This average product rises at first, because total product rises faster than in proportion to the number of workers used. But the average output per worker reaches a peak (at seven workers and 2,604 bushels in this example, which gives the maximum output per worker of 372 bushels). Thereafter, even though total product continues to rise for a while, the average output per worker falls.

Column 4 shows the "marginal product" as more workers are used. This column shows the **additional,** or *marginal,* output obtained by adding each extra worker. Thus, adding the first worker increases total product by 100 bushels. For the second worker, the marginal product is 250 bushels, as total product rises from 100 to 350. Marginal product reaches its peak at five workers. After this, adding workers (up to eleven) continues to increase total product, but not as rapidly as before; so the increment per additional worker falls.

These relationships can be seen readily in Figures 20–4 and 20–5. Figure 20–4 shows total product as additional workers are hired. It rises rapidly at first as production becomes more efficient, then gradually levels off, and finally (after twelve workers and 3,300

bushels) turns down, for there are just too many workers to avoid getting in each other's way.

Figure 20–5 plots average product and marginal product from Table 20–4. Marginal product reaches its peak first, and then turns down as the rate of growth of total product begins to slow. Average output per worker shows a similar inverted U, but the peak is reached with more workers, as Table 20–4 shows.

Note that the marginal-product curve cuts the average-product curve at the latter's highest point. This is necessarily true because as long as marginal product is higher than average product, each additional worker is adding more to total product than the average of all workers up to that point. As soon as the marginal worker adds less to total product than the average up to that point, the marginal-product curve will be below the average-product curve. Thus, it will always cut the average-product curve at the latter's highest point.

The other significant point is the one at which marginal product becomes zero. Comparing the two figures, we see that this is at twelve workers, **which is just the point where total product turns down.** This clearly must be so, because marginal product is merely the amount by which total product increases as additional workers are added. Thus, when adding another worker decreases total product, marginal product becomes negative.

Figure 20–4
Total output rises fast at first as variable factors are added to a fixed factor, then levels off, and eventually turns down.

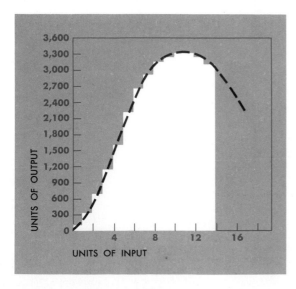

The law of diminishing returns, or variable proportions. The preceding paragraphs provide a statement of Ricardo's famous "law of diminishing returns." They show just what happens when additional units of one factor of production are combined with a fixed stock of some other factor or factors.

Modern economists have come to a more general statement of these relationships, which they call the "law of variable proportions." **As the proportion of one factor of production to other fixed factors increases, the average product of the increasing factor will first rise and then fall persistently; and the marginal product of the increasing factor will also first rise and then fall, cutting the average-product curve at its highest point.**

Thus, if all factors increase in proportion, there is no reason to expect Ricardo's law of diminishing returns to set in. This is a critical fact, for it says that neither an individual firm nor an economy need face diminishing returns just because it gets bigger.

Production foundations of cost curves. These production relationships underlie the cost data for the firm. Assume that the market prices of all factors of

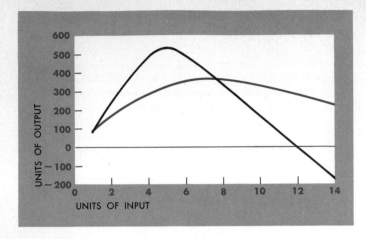

Figure 20-5
Marginal product shoots up rapidly as total output grows fast when the first variable factors are added. It turns down as the growth in total output slows, and becomes negative when total output turns down. Check it against Figure 20–4.

production are fixed—labor and land in our case. Then the total-fixed-cost curve (as in Figure 20–1) is obtained directly by multiplying the fixed amount of land used (fixed factor) by its rent per acre. The total-variable-cost curve is obtained by multiplying the number of workers (variable factors) by the wage per worker.

These total costs can readily be converted to the **per-unit** cost curves of Figure 20–2 by dividing through by the number of units produced. Thus, the variable-unit-cost curve will be the inverse of the average-product-per-worker curve, because wage per worker is constant. When average product per worker is rising, variable cost per unit of output falls (we continue to assume that workers are the only variable cost involved). When average product per worker

begins to fall, variable cost per unit of output begins to rise. Fixed cost per unit (rent on the land, in the example above) steadily falls as more bushels are produced with the same total fixed cost for land.

The combination of the persistently declining fixed-cost-per-unit curve with the U-shaped variable-unit-cost curve gives the (flatter) U-shaped total-unit-cost curve. Thus, given the prices of the factors of production, the physical-production relationships determine the shape of the fixed-cost-per-unit, the variable-cost-per-unit, and the total-cost-per-unit curves in any situation. The unit-cost curves are the inverses of the physical-production curves in Figure 20–5. The marginal-product curve is the basis for the marginal-cost curve.

21

THE BUSINESS FIRM: COMPETITIVE OUTPUT AND PRICE IN THE SHORT RUN

This chapter examines how business firms, given their costs, respond to consumer demand in competitive markets in the short run. We postpone until later a look at the partially monopolized sectors of the economy.

THE THEORY OF THE FIRM

Let us assume, as a first approximation, that firms in highly competitive industries try to maximize their profits. Profits are the difference between total cost and total revenue. Hence, the firm does what it can (within the legal rules and mores of society) to maximize this difference. It tries to sell more of its own product when the price is high enough to cover costs, and it tries to keep its costs as low as possible—that is, to produce as efficiently as possible. Whenever the firm can increase its profits by increasing its revenues or by reducing its costs, it will do so.

Note: This chapter should be omitted by instructors assigning only the overview readings on the response of a purely competitive system to consumer demands—i.e., Track A, using only Parts A of Chapters 20 and 22.

Section III of the Mathematical Appendix at the end of the text provides a concise mathematical statement (for students who know calculus) of the detailed cost relationships of the preceding chapter and of the profit-maximizing behavior of the firm in the short run, as stated in this chapter.

When it is maximizing its profits to the best of its ability, the firm will be in "equilibrium"—in the sense that it will not change its own actions unless conditions change. Actually, external conditions (for example, consumer demand and wage rates) do change frequently, so business firms seldom reach equilibrium and stay in it for long. But we assume that the firm will always be aiming at this maximum-profit position in conducting its day-to-day affairs and in its long-run planning.

We know, of course, that not all firms behave this way. But for the moment, assume that firms in our highly competitive industry have the single goal of maximizing profit.

THE COMPETITIVE FIRM IN THE SHORT RUN

The individual firm in a highly competitive industry (for example, one wheat farmer, or our small stereo maker) is so small that it has no appreciable influence over the price of its product or the prices it pays for its inputs (labor, materials, and the like). As a practical matter, our small firm must take the market price as given—fixed in the market by total demand-and-supply conditions over which we have no significant control. Under this assumption, we can't charge a higher price than the one prevailing in the market for such sets. If we do, we won't sell any goods, because consumers can get all they want at the prevailing price from other sellers. **In sum, our firm is a "price taker," not a "price maker."**

This means that the firm sees the demand curve as a horizontal line at the prevailing market price. This assumption may seem to you extreme, and it is the limiting case of what economists call perfect competition. But it is an instructive case with which to begin. We will modify the assumption later.

Comparison of total costs and total revenue

Our stereo firm from Chapter 20 wants to maximize profits. **Assume that the market price is $1,800.** We can compare total cost with total revenue at each level of output, and thus determine the most profitable number of sets to produce. This is done in Table 21–1. Total revenue is merely output multiplied by the price. The table shows that the maximum-profit output is six sets per week. Total profit is $3,200. At only one set per week, total revenue doesn't cover costs. When the plant gets up to eight sets a week, cost shoots up so fast that it exceeds even the big sales income. In between, any output is profitable, but some more so than others. Profit is the largest if we produce and sell six sets.

To check your understanding, assume that the price drops to $1,500. What will be the new maximum-profit output level? Calculate a new total-revenue column and compare it with total costs. (*Answer:* five sets per week, with a profit of $1,500.)

Maximizing profits—marginal analysis

We can make the same maximum-profit calculation by using marginal analysis,

Table 21–1

Total cost, total revenue, and profit when price is $1,800

Output	Total cost	Total revenue	Profit
1	$ 3,000	$ 1,800	−$1,200
2	3,500	3,600	100
3	4,000	5,400	1,400
4	5,000	7,200	2,200
5	6,000	9,000	3,000
6	7,600	10,800	3,200
7	11,000	12,600	1,600
8	17,000	14,400	−2,600

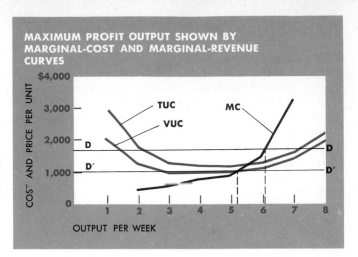

MAXIMUM PROFIT OUTPUT SHOWN BY MARGINAL-COST AND MARGINAL-REVENUE CURVES

Figure 21-1
Profit is maximized by carrying production up to the intersection of the marginal-cost and marginal-revenue curves—if you operate at all. Horizontal price lines are also marginal-revenue curves for this producer under perfect competition.

which is simpler than calculating all possible profit positions. The rule is: **We will maximize profits by continuing to increase output as long as marginal cost is less than marginal revenue, and no further.** That is, as long as producing more units adds more to total revenue than to total costs, it clearly pays to keep increasing output. **Conversely, we will reduce total profits if we produce more when marginal cost is higher than marginal revenue.** (Remember the fishing-boat example of Chapter 20, and Polly Poet in Case 16).

Check this by referring back to Table 20-2, which shows marginal costs for our stereo firm. If the price (marginal revenue) is $1,800, clearly we will add more to revenues than to costs (that is, our profits will increase) by producing each set up to and including the sixth. But to produce the seventh set would add $3,400 to costs but only $1,800 to revenue. Our profit would thereby be reduced by $1,600, the amount by which *MC* exceeds *MR*. As Table 21-1 shows, we would still be making a profit with output at seven sets monthly, but a smaller profit than by producing only six sets.

Marginal analysis using graphs

This analysis can readily be put graphically with, of course, the same answers. The cost curves in Figure 21-1 are the same as in Figure 20-2, except for the omission of the fixed-cost-per-unit curve. The marginal-cost curve shows the increment to total cost involved

in increasing output by one unit at each stage. For example, the marginal cost involved in stepping up output from four to five units is $1,000; in going from five units to six, it is $1,600.[1]

On Figure 21-1, line *DD* shows the demand curve as seen by our firm when the market price is $1,800. The demand curve is the marginal-revenue curve, and also the price. It is a horizontal line; we can sell all we make at $1,800 a set, but none if we ask a higher price. (Think of the firm as one small wheat farmer if the stereo case seems unreal to you. The farmer can sell all the wheat he produces at the going market price, but none if he asks more, since his wheat is identical with millions of other bushels offered at the going price.)

The principle in using the graph is the same as before. **To maximize profit, increase output as long as marginal revenue is above marginal cost.** With *DD* (marginal revenue) at $1,800, the maximum-profit output is clear. Through six units, the marginal-cost curve is below $1,800, so each additional set adds more to revenue than to cost. But the seventh unit adds more to cost than

---

[1] Note that the marginal-cost curve will always cut the *TUC* (average cost) curve at its minimum point. This is so because marginal cost is the increment to total cost. Whenever this increment to total cost is less than the existing average cost per unit, the average cost per unit must be falling. Whenever the increment is larger than the existing cost per unit, the average cost per unit must be rising. The same reasoning holds for the relationship of the marginal-cost and variable-unit-cost curves. For mathematically inclined readers: Marginal cost is the first derivative of total cost; for more details, see the Mathematical Appendix.

281

to revenue, because the marginal-cost curve is above *DD*. Therefore, six is the maximum-profit output.

Ask yourself one more question, to be sure you understand. Wouldn't we be better off to produce seven units instead of six, getting the profit on the seventh, since the $1,800 price exceeds the average cost of $1,573 at seven units of output? The marginal-cost–marginal-revenue comparison gives the answer. The seventh set adds $3,400 to total cost and only $1,800 to total revenue. The fact that price is above total unit cost tells us that we can make a profit at that output level, but not that we will make our **maximum** profit at that level. Trying to pick up the profit on a seventh set would be a mistake, because it would actually involve adding more to cost than to revenue; average cost per unit would be higher on all seven units if we increase output to seven. Compute the total profit at seven units and you'll see that it's only $1,600 ($12,600 revenue less cost of about $11,000), less than at six units.

Minimizing losses in the short run

With the market price at $1,800, we're in clover. But suppose consumer demand for stereo sets nosedives, and the market price falls to $1,100, shown by *D'D'*. A quick look at Figure 21–1 shows that we're going to lose money at this price, no matter what we do. The lowest total cost per unit at which we can produce is $1,200, at an output of five units, and the price is only $1,100.

What should we do to minimize our losses? One possibility would be to shut down. This way we'd lose $1,000 a month, the amount of our sunk costs, which continue whether we operate or not. But if we operate, producing three, four, or five units, we'll be getting $1,100 per set produced and only having to spend $1,000 per set in variable (out-of-pocket) costs. This income will provide $100 per set left over to apply on our $1,000 of fixed costs, which we have to pay in any case. So we'd better operate as long as we're stuck with the fixed costs, even though we lose money. By operating, we lose less than by shutting down.

The marginal-cost–marginal-revenue princi-

ple still tells us how many units to produce. The answer is five. Producing every unit up to and including the fifth adds more to revenue than it does to costs. Marginal revenue for the fifth unit is $1,100; marginal cost is only $1,000. But marginal cost for the sixth set is $1,600, above marginal revenue. The principle for minimizing loss is the same as for maximizing profit: **If you operate at all, carry production up to the point where marginal costs equal marginal revenue, and no further.**

The decision to shut down in the short run

Would it ever pay us to shut down in the short run? Obviously, yes. If price falls below $1,000, which is the lowest variable unit cost we can manage at any output level, we'd better close up shop. Suppose price falls to $900. No matter how many units we produce, our income is not even enough to cover our variable costs, much less provide anything to help cover the $1,000 of fixed costs. Suppose we produce three units. They will cost $4,000 but will bring in only $2,700, leaving a loss of $1,300 compared with only $1,000 if we just shut down. **At any price below the lowest variable-cost-unit point, we will minimize losses by shutting down altogether.** This rule does not contradict the marginal-cost–marginal-revenue principle for maximizing profits, since that principle tells us only what to do *if* we operate at all.

Short-run equilibrium of the firm

When will the business firm be in short-run equilibrium? When it is maximizing its profit or minimizing its loss, given consumer demand and given its fixed costs that it cannot alter in the short run. It will then be in short-run equilibrium when it is producing just up to the point where marginal cost is equal to marginal revenue (price).

This concept of the equilibrium of the firm parallels the concept of the equilibrium of the household (or consumer) developed in Chapter 5. Both tell us the situation **toward which** an economic unit will move in trying to improve its economic position. In a real world of constant change, we will seldom find firms actually in equilibrium for long. But whenever a household or firm is out of equilibrium, we can expect it to move to maximize its satisfaction or profit.

PROFIT MAXIMIZING IN THE SHORT AND LONG RUNS

A firm may be in short-run equilibrium and still be making substantial profits or losses. But such a situation will not last. If there are large profits, other firms will invade the industry, increasing supply and forcing down prices. If there are losses, the losing firm must do better or ultimately go broke. Hence, short-run losses lead firms to move resources to greener pastures unless demand rises or costs can be reduced in the long run. Short-run equilibrium in such cases is clearly only a temporary equilibrium.

In the short run, managers may be inefficient; they may over- or underadjust to change; they may guess wrong about consumer wants and production costs. But not in the long run, when there is time for new competitors to enter the industry and for firms to go broke. Adam Smith's "invisible hand" will be at work, and other profit seekers will enter to produce more cheaply (efficiently) if existing firms have high costs. If losses prevail, better profit prospects elsewhere will lure resources away from the loss-ridden industry. In the long run, excess profits and losses will tend to be eliminated by competition, and prices will tend to be just high enough to cover all costs, including a normal profit. Chapter 22 examines these long-run adjustments in detail.

SHORT-RUN COST CURVES AND SUPPLY CURVES

If firms try to maximize profits in the short run, we can tell from any firm's cost curves what output it will produce at any given price. **The firm's marginal-cost curve will be its short-run supply curve anywhere above the minimum point on the variable-unit-cost curve.** Look at Figure 21–1 or Table 21–2. At any price below $1,000, our firm will supply zero units. At

Table 21–2
Short-run industry supply schedule

Price	Output of typical firm	Industry output
Under $1,000	0	0
$1,000–1,599	5	5,000
$1,600–3,399	6	6,000
$3,400–5,999	7	7,000
Over $6,000	8	8,000

prices from $1,000 to $1,599, it will supply five units. At prices from $1,600 to $3,399, it will supply six units. And so on, up the marginal-cost curve. **The short-run marginal-cost curve is the firm's short-run supply curve.**

If this is true for all firms, it is easy to get a short-run market supply curve for any industry. Just add together the short-term supply curves (or schedules) of all the individual firms. Suppose there were 1,000 identical firms in the stereo industry. Then the short-run industry supply schedule would look like Table 21–2. At each price, the supply offered would be 1,000 times the supply offered by our own little firm.

THE FIRM AS A BUYER OF PRODUCTIVE SERVICES

Before ending this chapter, it is important to look at the short-run output policies of the firm from a different angle. Whenever businessmen decide to produce 1, 10, or 1,000 units of output, they simultaneously decide to buy or hire the "inputs" of productive services needed to produce those units—labor, raw materials, machinery, and so on.

We can, therefore, analyze the most profitable level of output in terms of units of productive inputs used, as well as in terms of units of output. For example, assume that our plant needs only labor and raw materials, and that these are conveniently hired in units costing $100 per unit—perhaps one worker per week plus the material he uses. For each input, there will be some corresponding output of stereo sets. Thus, our cost schedules above could have been stated in terms of costs to hire different inputs rather than in terms of producing one, two, three, or more sets per week as output.

How many units of labor–materials input should we hire each month at $100 per unit? The marginal-cost–marginal-revenue principle holds here as before. Whenever adding one more unit of input adds more to revenue than to cost (that is, when it adds more than $100), it pays to increase inputs and hence output. As soon as marginal cost exceeds marginal revenue, stop expanding, because you have reached your best profit level.[2]

In explaining the firm's output decisions, we have thus explained simultaneously its demand for inputs (labor, capital, and so on). Because workers' wages depend on supply and demand forces, just like other prices, the theory of the firm here gives us half the picture of what determines wages, as we shall see when we come to explaining in Part 4 why people receive the incomes they do.

---

[2] The marginal revenue from hiring an additional unit of variable input is based directly on its "marginal product," as described in the appendix to Chapter 20, although, of course, the marginal product needs to be converted to dollar terms to become marginal revenue.

REVIEW

Concepts to remember

The essence of this chapter is the way a profit-seeking firm would try to maximize profits in the short run by carrying production up to the point where marginal cost equals marginal revenue and no further, if it operates at all. Check your understanding of the following concepts:

profit maximization	equilibrium of the firm
marginal revenue	price taker

For analysis and discussion

1. Fixed costs are often substantial and real. Why then do economists assert that businessmen should disregard them in short-run decisions on setting price and output?
2. A competitive firm will always maximize profits by producing at the lowest possible total unit cost. True or false? Explain.
3. Explain carefully why a firm will maximize its profits by carrying production up to the point where marginal cost just equals marginal revenue. If there are any exceptions to this rule, specify them.
4. You operate a roadside fruit stand. You have been selling raspberries at $1 a quart; they cost you 40 cents to produce. It is now midafternoon and raining. With customers scarce, you now estimate your demand schedule for the rest of the afternoon as follows:

Price	Quarts
60¢	30
50	40
40	50
30	70
20	80

You have 80 quarts on hand and no storage facilities to avoid spoilage before tomorrow. What price should you charge to maximize profits? Explain. What is the importance of your costs in this case?

5. You are managing the stereo plant shown in Figure 21–1 and are now producing four sets a month. You have an order for one additional set a month, but the customer will pay only $1,050 a set, less than your minimum total cost per set. Should you accept the order? Show both graphically and through arithmetical calculations why your answer is sound.

6. Explain why the firm's short-run marginal-cost curve is its short-run supply curve. Is this always true?

Continental Air Lines, Inc., last year filled only half the available seats on its Boeing 707 jet flights, a record some 15 percentage points worse than the national average.

By eliminating just a few runs—less than 5 percent—Continental could have raised its average load considerably. Some of its flights frequently carry as few as 30 passengers on the 120-seat plane. But the improved load factor would have meant reduced profits.

For Continental bolsters its corporate profits by deliberately running extra flights that aren't expected to do more than return their out-of-pocket costs—plus a little profit. Such marginal flights are an integral part of the overall operating philosophy that has brought small, Denver-based Continental—tenth among the eleven trunk carriers—through the bumpy postwar period with only one loss year.

This philosophy leans heavily on marginal analysis. And the line leans heavily on Chris F. Whelan, vice-president in charge of economic planning, to translate marginalism into hard, dollars-and-cents decisions.

Getting management to accept and apply the marginal concept is probably the chief contribution any economist can make to his company. Put most simply, marginalists maintain that a company should undertake any activity that adds more to revenues than it does to costs—and not limit itself to those activities whose returns equal average or "fully allocated" costs. . . .

Whelan's work is a concrete example of the truth in a crack by Prof. Sidney Alexander of MIT—formerly economist for Columbia Broadcasting System—that the economist who understands marginal analysis has a "full-time job in undoing the work of the accountant." This is so, Alexander holds, because the practices of accountants—and of most businesses—are permeated with cost allocation directed at average, rather than marginal, costs.

In any complex business, there's likely to be a big difference between the costs of each company activity as it's carried on the accounting books and the marginal or "true" costs that can determine whether or not the activity should be undertaken.

The difficulty comes in applying the simple "textbook" marginal concept to specific decisions. If the economist is unwilling to make some bold simplifications, the job of determining "true" marginal costs may be highly complex, time-wasting, and too expensive. But even a rough application of marginal principles may come closer to the right answer for business decision makers than an analysis based on precise average-cost data.

Proving that this is so demands economists who can break the crust of corporate habits and show concretely why the typical manager's re-

---

Marginal analysis in a nutshell:

Problem: Shall Continental run an extra daily flight from City X to City Y?

The facts: Fully-allocated costs of the flight $4,500
Out-of-pocket costs of this flight $2,000
Flight should gross $3,100

Decision: Run the flight. It will add $1,100 to net profit—because it will add $3,100 to revenues and only $2,000 to costs. Overhead and other costs, total $2,500 [$4,500 minus $2,000], would be incurred whether the flight is run or not. Therefore, fully allocated or "average" costs of $4,500 are not relevant to this business decision. It's the out-of-pocket or "marginal" costs that count.

---

[3]Reprinted from *Business Week*, April 20, 1963, with permission of the publisher, © 1963, McGraw-Hill Book Company.

sponse—that nobody ever made a profit without meeting all costs—is misleading and can reduce profits. To be sure, the whole business cannot make a profit unless average costs are met; but covering average costs should not determine whether any particular activity should be undertaken. For this would unduly restrict corporate decisions and cause managements to forgo opportunities for extra gains.

Whelan's approach is this: He considers that the bulk of his scheduled flights have to return at least their fully allocated costs. Overhead, depreciation, and insurance are very real expenses and must be covered. The out-of-pocket approach comes into play, says Whelan, only after the line's basic schedule has been set.

"Then you go a step farther," he says, and see if adding more flights will contribute to the corporate net. Similarly, if he's thinking of dropping a flight with a disappointing record, he puts it under the marginal microscope: "If your revenues are going to be more than your out-of-pocket costs, you should keep the flight on."

By "out-of-pocket costs" Whelan means just that: the actual dollars that Continental has to pay out to run a flight. He gets the figure not by applying hypothetical equations but by circulating a proposed schedule to every operating department concerned and finding out just what extra expenses it will entail. If a ground crew already on duty can service the plane, the flight isn't charged a penny of their salary expense. There may even be some costs eliminated in running the flight; they won't need men to roll the plane to a hangar, for instance, if it flies on to another stop.

Most of these extra flights, of course, are run at off-beat hours, mainly late at night. At times, though, Continental discovers that the hours aren't so unpopular after all. A pair of night coach flights on the Houston–San Antonio–El Paso–Phoenix–Los Angeles leg, added on a marginal basis, have turned out to be so successful that they are now more than covering full allocated costs. . . .

Continental's data-handling system produces weekly reports on each flight, with revenues measured against both out-of-pocket and fully allocated costs. Whelan uses these to give each flight a careful analysis at least once a quarter. But those added on a marginal basis get the fine-tooth-comb treatment monthly.

Is Continental Airlines right in using marginal analysis to decide whether to add flights? What if each flight, looked at individually, more than covers marginal cost, but added together they don't cover the firm's total costs? Would this latter case invalidate the marginal principle?

CHAPTER 22

LONG-RUN COMPETITIVE EQUILIBRIUM AND ECONOMIC EFFICIENCY

Building on our detailed analysis of individual households, firms, and markets in the short run, we need now to see how they all fit together in the long run. The main purpose of this chapter, then, is to analyze how a purely competitive economy would work *in the long run*—how well the long-run competitive pressures of Adam Smith's "invisible hand" would guide the economy, and how efficiently it would allocate society's scarce productive resources to satisfy consumers' demands as expressed in the marketplace. On the basis of this examination, you can judge for yourself whether Smith set economists off on the right track with his talk about the "invisible hand"—or whether he gave us a bad steer.

Here again, as in Chapter 20, Track A presents the analysis in summary, nontechnical form for those who want only the essential, big picture, and to minimize the detailed technical analysis. Others should study the entire chapter: Part B adds a more complete, rigorous analysis of the way Smith's "invisible hand" would work in a purely competitive economy.

But first we need to be clear on two important points that have been glossed over so far. Precisely what do we mean by "pure competition" and by "long-run equilibrium"—two key analytical concepts?

PART A

THE COMPETITIVE SYSTEM—OVERVIEW

COMPETITION IN
THE MODERN ECONOMY

No business firm is free from competition. Even AT&T, which is often cited as a complete monopoly in the field of telephone communication, faces lively competition from other forms of communication. There are only six major firms that produce aluminum today. But quite aside from the competition among the six, steel, copper, and other metals are potential substitutes for aluminum, and Alcoa and the other aluminum companies are acutely aware of this fact. Competition is inescapable in business.

Nevertheless, it is obvious that competition is a lot more active in some industries than in others. At the competitive extreme, we find the individual farmer producing such standardized products as wheat, corn, and hogs. He has thousands of competitors, and his product is so standardized that the buyer has no interest in who the producer is. If Farmer Jones prices his No. 2 hard northern wheat at 1 cent a bushel more than other farmers do, he just won't sell any.

There is a whole spectrum of market positions between the protected monopoly position of the public utility and the extreme competition of farmers. Most of the real world lies somewhere between these two extremes, and we will look at the less competitive sectors later. Here we want to examine how the economy would function under "pure competition"—roughly the situation of the wheat farmer above, without government intervention.

Pure competition

The essence of pure competition is that no single seller is important enough to have any appreciable influence over market price.

Specifically, pure competition is characterized by:

1. Many sellers, each acting independently and each so small relative to the market as to have no appreciable effect on market price.
2. An identical product, so that the consumer is indifferent about the seller from whom he buys.[1]
3. Freedom of entry for new sellers who wish to enter the market. (This assumption is not logically necessary where characteristics 1 and 2 hold, but most economists include it in analyzing pure competition.)

The same conditions define pure competition on the buyers' side of any market.

When there are many sellers of identical products, and when no one of them **acting alone** can exert a significant influence on the market price, each producer must adjust his activities to the market price. The individual firm is a "price taker," not a price setter or price maker. It takes the market price as given and, considering its costs of production, decides how much to produce in order to maximize its profit.

But although no one firm alone can significantly influence market price, the **summation** of all the individual producers' actions can and does. If prevailing costs and market price lead each individual firm to restrict output, the summation of all the thousands of individual cutbacks will reduce market supply and, other things equal, raise the price. Thus, quantity produced and the market price are "automatically" determined by the impersonal mechanism of the competitive market as it responds to consumer demand. No one has to plan how much cabbage should be produced. The profit motive and the competitive market together determine

---

[1]The added assumption is also usually made that all buyers and sellers have full knowledge of prices being quoted over the entire market.

how much, as farmers respond to what consumers buy in the market.

Why study pure competition?

There aren't many purely competitive industries in the modern American economy. Even agriculture, which has long been the standard example, doesn't quite represent pure competition any more, since the government has frequently intervened to control prices and output levels. Why study pure competition, then? There are two main reasons:

1. Economics is concerned with the overall performance of the economic system, and with how well it allocates society's scarce resources among alternative uses. To get at these problems, we must have an overall picture of the way the various parts of the economy fit together. The purely competitive model, with all competitive markets, has the great virtue of providing a reasonably simple picture of the way markets signal consumer demands to producers and producers respond to those demands. Many economists believe that this picture also provides a rough approximation of the "ideal" way in which a private-enterprise system ought to work. They thus use the model as a standard of comparison to ferret out those areas of the actual economy that aren't operating as well as they ought to.

2. Pure competition, although limited, does provide a rough approximation to the behavior of major sectors of the modern economy. Most of agriculture, broad areas of retailing, wholesaling, and service establishments, and important sectors of manufacturing where a moderate scale of plant is big enough for efficient production—all come reasonably close to the pure-competition model. To be sure, their products are not quite identical, and each producer has some control over the price at which he sells his product. But the pressures of competition are strong, and if he gets far out of competitive line, the individual producer finds himself steadily losing out in the market.

Long-run equilibrium

Long-run equilibrium is a situation that would be reached and maintained indefinitely unless some external force came along to disturb it. Suppose we want to know how a purely competitive system, beginning from an equilibrium position, would respond to an increased consumer demand for strawberries. Assume that we can hold everything else constant—the supply of productive resources, consumers' other wants, society's technological know-how, all legal and social factors. The new position to which the system would move in response to the changed demand would be its new long-run-equilibrium position.

To be complete, we should consider all the millions of interrelated effects throughout the economic system. But once we get far from the strawberry industry, for example, these effects are likely to be negligible. When the demand for strawberries rises, people may also buy more cream to put on their desserts and fewer paperback books because they have less disposable income left for other products. If we took all these effects into account, we would be looking at the **general equilibrium** of the whole economy. But most of these effects are small and distant, and we shall generally concentrate our analysis on the strawberry industry and others closely related to it. For this purpose, it is useful to look mainly at the long-run **equilibrium of firms** involved and at the long-run **equilibrium of the industry** they comprise (the strawberry industry).

When we talk about long-run equilibrium, therefore, we are talking about the new situation **toward which** industry is moving and would ultimately reach if no other forces interfered. Long-run analysis provides guides to the **ultimate** effects of particular changes. **Long-run equilibrium gives us a picture of how well off consumers, workers, businesses, and others would be in a highly competitive system—how efficiently such a system would use our scarce productive resources.**

LONG-RUN EQUILIBRIUM:
THE CONTINUOUS SEARCH FOR PROFITS

The mainspring of the private-enter-prise economy is the businessman's continuous search for profits. This does not imply that the proprietor of the local grocery spends every waking hour worrying about how to squeeze the last nickel out of his business, or that the farmer doesn't decide to visit his friends some afternoons when he could be working. But it does imply that, by and large, the desire to earn profits is a dominant one among businessmen, and that business concerns generally adopt those policies that they think will produce the largest profits for the company.[2]

In the long run, all costs become variable. Existing plant and equipment wear out. Wage and salary contracts come up for renewal. Long-term contracts for supplies and materials expire. With all costs variable, the entrepreneur is completely free in making his output decisions. He can expand, contract, change the nature of his productive processes, or go out of business altogether, moving his resources to a more promising industry.

Thus, in the long run, firms will move into or drop out of any purely competitive industry until expectations of profits or losses have been substantially eliminated—until it is no longer possible for anyone to better his position by moving into or out of the industry.[3] Thus, as long as the expected market price is above the expected minimum cost of producing a commodity, firms will move into the industry and present firms may expand. Output will increase,

and the price will gradually be forced down to about the minimum-cost point. But if the expected market price is below the minimum expected cost of production, firms will drop out of the industry, output will decline, and price will gradually rise toward the minimum-cost level. **Under pure competition, with firms free to enter and leave the industry, market price cannot in the long run stay higher or lower than the minimum total cost per unit of producing the commodity. This is the long-run equilibrium price and output level toward which the industry will move.**

Each firm and the industry will be in long-run equilibrium when there is no advantage to any firm in increasing or decreasing its output, either by varying utilization of existing plant or by changing the scale of plant. This equilibrium will be reached when (1) each firm is producing in the most efficient way available (otherwise there would be an advantage in shifting to more efficient operations), and (2) market price is just equal to the least-cost point on the cost curve for that scale of enterprise. In this equilibrium position, profits have been eliminated by competition (remember that costs include a "normal" return on investment), and each firm will continue using just the same amount of all productive resources that it now uses.

Survival of the fittest and
pressures toward cost minimization

The competitive market is an impersonal arbiter of who survives and who vanishes from the business scene. With a standard product, such as oats, the buyer is indifferent to who the producer is. Any farmer whose production cost is above the market price simply makes a loss, and in due course will vanish from the scene unless he improves his efficiency or receives a subsidy from someone. The fact that he may be a hard-working farmer with a good wife and six small children is irrelevant in the market. In long-run equilibrium, only those who can and do produce at a cost as low as market price will survive, and this price will be no higher than the least-cost point on the cost curve of firms using the most efficient methods.

---

[2]To assert that most businesses try to maximize profits each day, or month, or even each year, would be naïve indeed. Any alert businessman will tell you that it is the long pull that matters. The businesses that last and pay good dividends to their shareholders year after year are seldom out to "turn a fast buck." They are the ones that hold back new products until they have worked out the bugs, even though short-run profits are foregone. They are the ones who say that the customer is right, even when they're burned up at his unreasonable demands on return privileges. But this is not to say that the search for profits is not pervasive in the long run.

[3]Remember that a "normal," or "going," rate of return (or profit) on investment is included in the costs of each firm.

LONG-RUN EQUILIBRIUM—THE RESULTS

A brief summary now of the results of the competitive process. Would a purely competitive economy do a good job? In purely competitive equilibrium:

1. Each consumer would be getting as much of every product as could be produced at the cost he was willing to pay for it.

2. Each productive resource (labor, capital, etc.) would be used in that industry and occupation where it would contribute most to satisfying consumers' demands; and (as we shall see presently) in so doing, it would be earning the largest income consistent with its ability and willingness to help produce what consumers want to buy. The cost of each product would thus reflect the occupational and industry preferences of workers and other resource owners.

3. Each business would be producing in the most efficient way possible, so consumers would be getting their products with the smallest feasible use of resources in producing each; and each business would be earning just a normal rate of return on its investment.

Any system that achieved these results in allocating society's scarce productive resources would deserve a high mark indeed for economic efficiency. But, as you no doubt suspected, there are some problems we have glossed over so far, which may make a highly competitive, market-directed economy less attractive than this summary suggests. They are summarized in the final section of this chapter,[4] and will be examined in detail in the chapters to come.

[4] That section, "Purely Competitive Economy—Evaluation," is recommended reading at this point for users of Part A who are skipping Part B.

PART B

THE COMPETITIVE SYSTEM—MORE DETAILED ANALYSIS

Let us turn now to a more detailed and rigorous analysis of the results of a purely competitive economy. A careful look at how such an economy would adjust to a change in consumer demand can provide useful insights.

ILLUSTRATION OF RESPONSE
TO AN INCREASE IN DEMAND

Suppose that the purely competitive pencil industry is in long-run equilibrium and that consumer demand for pencils increases. How will the industry respond?

The **immediate** effect will be (1) a higher price for pencils, with improved profits. (2) Then each firm will increase its output, because with a higher price, it is now profitable to produce more pencils. (This is a move upward along the industry short-run supply curve, before there is time for new firms to move in.) (3) In the new **short-run** equilibrium, price will be higher, output

larger, and profits in the industry greater than before the increase in demand.

This **short-run** adjustment is pictured in Figure 22–1. The left-hand portion shows the short-run industry supply of pencils (S^1S^1). D^1D^1 is the original demand for pencils, while D^2D^2 shows the increased demand. The result of the increased demand is to raise the price from 6 to 8 cents. At this higher price, each firm can increase its profits by increasing its output from 400 to 500 units, as indicated on the right-hand portion of the graph. That is, each firm increases output to the point at which marginal cost (its short-run supply curve) equals the new higher price of 8 cents.

The right-hand portion shows the happy result for each firm; it is now producing more and making the profit indicated by the shaded area. The summation of all these increases is shown in S^1S^1 on the left, which indicates the total increase in pencils supplied at the higher price of 8 cents. Consumers are now getting 62,500 pencils

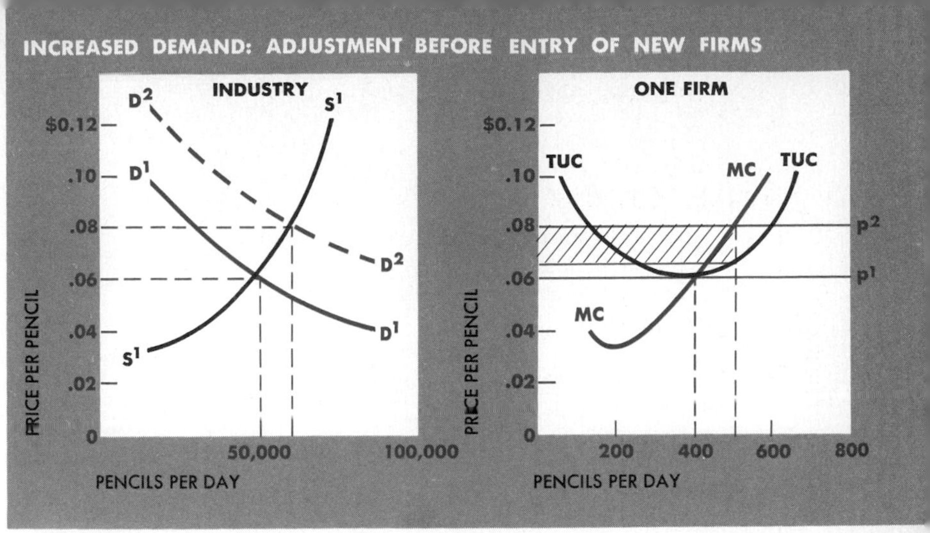

Figure 22-1
New increased demand (D^2D^2) raises the market price and makes increased output profitable for the individual firms.

instead of the original 50,000, but they have to pay 8 instead of 6 cents per pencil. This increase results automatically from the independent actions of hundreds of purely competitive firms producing pencils.

But this situation is obviously unstable. New resources will be attracted to the industry by the generous profits. As new firms enter and productive capacity is expanded, the industry supply curve (S^1S^1) will gradually move to the right; more will be produced as more resources move into the pencil industry **in the long run.**

With more pencils produced, the price will gradually fall back toward its original level. **If unlimited productive resources can be attracted without the necessity to pay more for them (that is, if new firms can enter without bidding up costs in the pencil industry), the new long-run equilibrium will be back at the original price but with more pencils being produced. This would be a case of long-run "constant costs"** for the industry. If, however, the entrance of new firms raises costs for all firms, because higher payments are necessary to attract labor, materials, and other resources from other industries, we have a case of **"increasing costs."** Either way, as the price of the product falls back and costs rise, profits are gradually squeezed out. When the price is again equal to the lowest total unit cost, there will be no further inducement for new firms to enter. The new long-run equilibrium will probably be at somewhat higher costs and price than originally, with a larger industry output because most industries probably face long-run increasing costs.

These long-run adjustments are shown in Figure 22-2. S^2S^2 is the new short-run aggregate-supply curve after new firms have had time to come into the industry; it has shifted to the right. Under these new conditions, supply and demand are equal at a price of 7 cents per pencil, with an output of 70,000 pencils in the industry as a whole. This is the new long-run industry equilibrium; price is now just equal to the new higher *TUC* curve at its minimum point, shown in the right-hand portion of Figure 22-2. Thus, there is no longer any incentive for resources to move into or out of the industry. Note that the cost curves of the typical firm have risen, because the increased production of pencils has bid up the price of labor and raw materials. On the demand side, price first rose from 6 to 8 cents, and then fell back to 7 cents, the lowest point on the *TUC* (average-cost) curve. In the new long-run equilibrium, the typical firm is again producing about the same amount as before, again at just its lowest total-unit-cost point.[5] But since there are more firms than before, the aggregate

---

[5] Figure 21-2 shows the new equilibrium output of the firm identical with the old—that is, the new average-cost curve is merely raised by 1 cent for each level of output. This will be the result if the costs of all factors of production rise in the same proportion. This need not, of course, be the case, and the particular type of cost increase shown is not important for the basic analysis of the industry's response to an increase in demand.

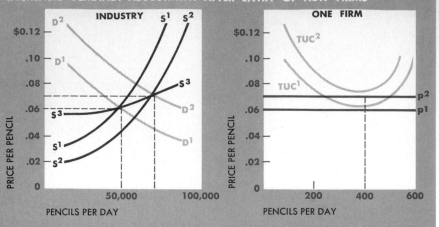

Figure 22-2
Increased demand draws new firms into the industry and produces new equilibrium for the firms and the industry at a price of 7 cents. S^3S^3 is the long-run industry supply curve.

output of the industry is greater than it was initially. **In response to their increased demand, consumers are getting 20,000 more pencils, and are getting them at the lowest price that will cover costs. But they have to pay 1 cent more per pencil, because that much more was necessary to attract more productive resources from other uses into pencil making.**

Long-run industry supply curves

S^3S^3 in Figure 22–2 is the long-run supply curve for the pencil industry. It joins the points at which the demand and supply curves intersect before and after the increase in demand. More fundamentally, it joins the lowest points on the typical firm's average-total-unit-cost curves as more firms enter the industry.

This is shown in Figure 22–3, patterned after Figure 20–3, which considered the optimal scale of enterprise for firms. The little *TUC* curves show the average-total-unit-cost curves for the typical firm as more firms enter the industry. The *SS* curve in this figure corresponds to the S^3S^3 curve in Figure 22–2. The industry is one of constant costs between 15,000 and 30,000 pencils, and one of gradually increasing costs above 30,000 pencils.

THE DEMAND FOR PRODUCTIVE SERVICES: WAGES AND OTHER INCOMES

When a business expands output to meet consumer demand, it hires more workers, rents more land, and uses more capital as long as

marginal cost is less than marginal revenue. Thus, the business hires more workers, for example, as long as the marginal cost of labor (its wage) is less than its marginal revenue.

Competition among businessmen for productive resources will bid up the return (wage, rent, and so on) on each productive resource to roughly its marginal revenue, or "marginal product," and no higher.[6] Whenever the price of any productive service (say, the wage of a par-

---

[6]Marginal product is the addition to total output made by using one more unit of labor or capital. A slightly more precise statement of this paragraph will be presented in Chapter 30.

Figure 22-3
This figure shows the relationship between typical individual-firm average-cost curves and long-run industry supply curves over a wide range of outputs. SS corresponds to S^3S^3 on Figure 22–2.

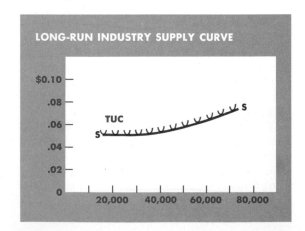

LONG-RUN INDUSTRY SUPPLY CURVE

COMPETITIVE ADJUSTMENTS—SOME FINER POINTS

What to maximize—profits, or present value of the firm?

This chapter assumes that businessmen try to maximize profits, and this is a satisfactory approximation for our elementary purposes. But if you take more advanced courses in economics or finance, you will find that we are sliding by some more sophisticated points that real-world managers and investors must take into account.

First, we have not specified exactly what we mean by profits. Is it total profits of the firm? Profits per share of common stock? Rate of return on stockholders' investment? And over what time period? For our elementary analysis we need not distinguish. But the goals are all somewhat different, and if you become a corporation manager or investor, you will need to be more precise.

Second, profit maximization as a goal will not help us choose between alternative actions whose profits accrue at different times. For example, is an investment that yields $500 annually beginning this year more or less profitable than one that yields nothing now but $600 annually beginning in five years? Which would you prefer?

Third, profit maximization as a goal ignores the ''quality'' of different investments. Some are riskier than others.

Many economists and financial analysts therefore now substitute for profit maximization the goal of maximizing the present value of stockholders' investment in the firm. This involves discounting back to the present the value of all expected earnings in the future. The longer one has to wait for future profits and the riskier they are, the less will be their present value. All these factors are presumably taken into account by investors buying and selling the firm's stock, so the market value of all the common stock outstanding can be used as an approximation of the present value of the firm at any given time.

Issues like these are what make the lives of businessmen and investors lively and challenging. But we can safely leave them to more advanced courses.

Do all firms minimize costs under pure competition?

At any time, every industry includes firms of varying efficiency, with different levels of profits and losses. This is partly because in the dynamic economic world, some firms are on the way up, some on the way down. Partly it is because many industries are far from purely competitive; some markets are not open to new firms. But in purely competitive long-run equilibrium, all firms in any industry would be driven to produce at the same minimum average (total per-unit) cost. This must be true, since any firm with a higher cost would have been driven out of business, and any firm with a lower cost would be luring business away from others.

It is easy to see that in the long run inefficient firms will be eliminated by competition. But we need not assume that all remaining firms would become identical. Some entrepreneurs are more efficient than others. Some firms are located near good markets and pay high rents, whereas others are more distant but pay lower rents. Some firms are small and obtain efficiency through close personal supervision; others are large and count on mass-production methods to provide low costs. It is not necessary that all firms be identical. It is only necessary that the method of production used by each permit it to produce at a total unit cost as low as that of its competitors.

For example, suppose that one manager of a textile firm is more effective in organizing production than anyone else in the industry is. Won't his firm continue to make a juicy profit even in the long run? The answer is no. When the manager is hired, his firm will have to pay him a higher salary than other managers receive, in order to keep him away from other firms. Assuming active competition among firms, his salary will be bid up until it is higher than that of a less efficient manager by the differential advantage of his services. If the entrepreneur himself is the efficient manager, to calculate accurately he must charge as a cost a salary for himself equal to what he would be able to get in alternative opportunities.

ticular grade of labor) is lower than its marginal product, businessmen can increase their profits by hiring more of that factor, and this competition will bid the wage up. Whenever the price of a productive service is higher than its marginal product, businessmen will cut back on hiring that factor, and its price will fall until it just equals its marginal product. **In the long-run equilibrium, each worker's wage will be just equal to his marginal product (or marginal revenue).**

Moreover, each productive resource will have its highest marginal product when it is in the industry where its contribution is greatest in producing the products consumers want. Thus, each productive factor will earn the most when it is contributing most to satisfying consumer demands. And each resource (worker) will be drawn to the use where its marginal product is highest if it wishes to maximize its income. The invisible hand again! A more detailed look at this in Part 4.

GENERAL EQUILIBRIUM OF A COMPETITIVE ECONOMY

The concluding section of Part A, "Long-Run Equilibrium—The Results," provided a summary view of the results of the competitive process. We want now to provide a more complete and precise picture of the results of a purely competitive economy, to see just how well such an economy would allocate society's scarce resources. Suppose the entire pattern of consumer demands for the economy is frozen, and a full "general-equilibrium" adjustment to these demands has worked itself out in a purely competitive economy. What would be the main characteristics of the resulting long-run general equilibrium?

1. **Each consumer (household) is in equilibrium, where it maximizes its utility.** In this equilibrium, each household spends its income on the different goods and services it wants most, given the prices it must pay. Each household buys different products until the marginal utility derived from the last dollar spent on each is equal. **Hence, consumer demand in the marketplace provides an accurate measure of how much satisfaction each commodity yields, and an accurate signal to producers as to how much of each commodity consumers want produced at different prices. The relative price paid is a measure of the relative marginal utility of each product to consumers who buy it.**

2. **Each business firm is in equilibrium, producing at the minimum feasible average cost and earning just a "normal" rate of return on its investment.** Each firm, to achieve this maximum-profit position, carries its output up to the point where marginal cost equals price. Remember that the marginal-cost curve necessarily cuts the average-cost curve at the latter's minimum point, which is also equal to price in long-run equilibrium. Thus, when competition has forced price down to its minimum feasible average cost of production, $MC = \min. TUC = P$ for each firm, a critical outcome of the competitive adjustment. The price is set by overall market conditions—by consumer demand and by the costs businesses must incur to produce the goods consumers want.

3. **Each industry is in equilibrium.** The price of every commodity has been forced down by competition to the lowest point on the average-cost curve—to the lowest total cost of production that is consistent with known technology, with the prices of productive resources used in the industry, and with the size of consumer demands. **Hence, the minimum possible amount of society's scarce resources is being used in producing each commodity demanded by consumers.**

4. **Each market is in equilibrium.** In each, the amount being supplied is equal to the amount being demanded at the existing price. There is no unsatisfied (excess) demand or supply in any market.

5. **The income received by each resource owner (laborers, capitalists, and the like) is equal to its marginal revenue product and is the largest possible, given the ability and willingness of each to help in producing the goods consumers demand.** Each owner of productive resources and each resource market is thus also in equilibrium.

In this general equilibrium, we have demonstrated that:

1. Each consumer is getting as much of every good demanded as can be produced at the price that that consumer is willing to pay for it, given the costs of producing the good.

2. Each business is producing each good in the most efficient (lowest-cost) way possible, so consumers' demands are satisfied with the smallest feasible use of resources.

3. Profits have served as an incentive to produce desired goods in the most efficient way, but no firm is earning more than a "normal" return ("profit").

4. Each productive resource (labor, capital, etc.) is used in that industry and occupation where it contributes most to satisfying consumers' demands, consistent with its occupational and industry preference. Thus, the costs of producing each good reflect the income demands and occupational and industry preferences of workers and other resource owners.

5. In doing so, each productive resource is receiving an income equal to its marginal contribution to producing the goods and services consumers demand—the largest income consistent with its ability and willingness to help produce what consumers demand.

How can we be *sure* that each resource is being used most efficiently in satisfying consumers' demands? Note that price is a measure of the marginal utility received by consumers from the last unit of each product brought. Price is also equal to, or a measure of, the marginal cost of the last unit each good produced, where costs reflect the income, occupational, and industrial preferences of all resource owners. Thus, for each pair of goods: $MU_1/MU_2 = P_1/P_2 = MC_1/MC_2$. Additional resources have been used in each industry up to the point where the marginal utility obtained from the last product produced by each is just equal to the marginal cost of that additional output. To produce more of any good (raising costs to bid resources away from other goods and reducing its marginal utility) would mean a marginal cost greater than the marginal utility provided by more of that good. (For a more rigorous proof, see the appendix on pages 394–395.)[7]

[7]Some economists describe general-equilibrium conditions in mathematical terms. Because general equilibrium involves considering a vast number of demands, costs, mar-

PURELY COMPETITIVE ECONOMY—EVALUATION

Such is the case for an individual-initiative, market-directed, purely-competitive economy. It is an impressive one, especially if we want to avoid authoritarian control over what gets produced and where we work. The purely competitive private-enterprise system offers a nonpolitical, individualistic way of making the millions of interrelated compromises required among the different interests involved. Each individual, as consumer, laborer, or business-man, looks out for his own self-interest. No individual consumer or resource owner has any appreciable influence over what gets produced and how much of it, but in the mass they efficiently determine the allocation of society's resources among all possible alternative uses. The result is an organization of our scarce resources that looks amazingly as if it had indeed been guided by some invisible hand for the welfare of society as a whole. And the Western, democratic, largely market-directed economies have in fact done very well in raising the standards of living of their people over the last two centuries. Only one of the top twenty nations as measured by per capita income falls outside this group, and that one (the USSR) is only fifteenth on the list. (See Tables 1–1 and 46–1 for the data.)

But there are problems. Even a purely competitive economy, for all its virtues, would fall short of satisfying at least some people's personal and social goals on three major fronts. We will look at these problems in detail in the following chapters, where you can make up your own mind whether they would be serious shortcomings; people disagree strongly. Here they are merely indicated to round out this evaluative overview of an individualistic, market-directed, purely competitive economy.

kets, prices, and productive factors simultaneously, we can view the system as a large set of simultaneous equations and investigate the effects of different changes mathematically. Leon Walras, a French economist, was one of the first, a century ago, to use mathematics in analyzing economic problems, and apparently the first to state precisely the essential general-equilibrium conditions for such a competitive economy.

Problems in making competitive markets
work effectively

***Resource allocation when social costs exceed
private costs.*** To get the optimal allocation of
resources among different products, the price of
each product to the consumer should cover the
total cost of producing it. In some cases, there are
hidden costs ("externalities") that are not paid
by the producer and hence do not enter into the
commodity's price but nevertheless are borne
involuntarily by others. Pollution is a leading
example. In such cases, price is lower than it
should be and output is larger than is socially
justifiable; a market system fails to produce an
"ideal" pattern of resource allocation. Most
economists believe that in such cases, we should
take collective (government) action to bring results nearer to the competitive ideal.

***Imperfect information, immobility, and demand
manipulation.*** For a competitive system to work
optimally, consumers must be well informed
about the goods and services available at different prices, and resource owners must be well
informed about employment opportunities that
are open to them. If farm workers in Montana
know nothing of available jobs in Detroit's
auto-assembly plants, or secretaries in Chicago
don't know about better jobs in St. Louis, the
optimal allocation of resources is blocked. Perhaps the Montana worker would prefer to stay
out on the range even if he knew about the
higher-paying Detroit jobs, but we can't be sure
unless he knows about them.

A similar misallocation may result if resources
are immobile, even though information is available. If our farmer has a big family and no
savings, he may be unable to take the better
Detroit job, no matter how badly he wants it.
Both the farmer and society would be better off
if he could somehow get over the hump into the
new industrial job.

Another problem is perhaps even more serious, if we temporarily drop the assumption of a
perfectly competitive economy. In the modern
world, advertising influences, and sometimes
even determines, what consumers want. Some

people say that big business tells us what we
should want, rather than responding to our own
wants. If so, the basic assumption of free consumer choice is unacceptable. This is an important and complex issue, which will come to center stage in Chapter 25.

***The problem of minimum size for efficient
production and dynamic progress.*** Pure competition requires that no one seller be large enough
to have appreciable influence over market price.
If one gets very big, there is a danger that he
may respond to increased consumer demand by
raising price and trying to shut out new competitors, rather than by expanding output. For pure
competition, there have to be lots of firms in
every industry.

But in many industries—for example, autos
and steel—firms have to be big in order to produce efficiently. Moreover, much of the research
and development underlying our new products
and methods is done in big businesses. In such
industries, we face a difficult choice. We can
insist on many small firms to assure competition,
but this will mean higher production costs, and
possibly less research and development spending,
than a smaller number of large firms would
involve. Or we can tolerate some degree of monopoly, but lose some of the pressures of competition obtainable with large numbers of producers. More on this dilemma in Chapters 26 and
27. We certainly don't need *pure* competition to
get the benefits outlined above, but just how
many firms are needed in each industry for
workable competition is a debatable issue.

Public goods and the public sector

There are some public, or collective,
wants that cannot be satisfactorily provided
through the marketplace. National defense and
the court system are examples. We agree that
they are essential and, through the political
process, legislate taxes (compulsory payments) to
hire resources to provide them. There is no practical way to leave it up to each individual to buy
in the marketplace the amount and kind of
national defense or general law and order he
wants. The special characteristics of public goods

are that they are widely agreed to be essential and, if provided, cannot practically be withheld from any citizen just because he doesn't pay.

What we do directly through government action, we often call the "public sector" of the economy. This now totals over $500 billion annually, nearly a third of the total gross national product. Just how far we should go in using compulsory taxes to "buy" public goods and services is another highly debatable issue. The lines defining public goods are sometimes far from clear. Is slum clearance a "public good," not salable through the market? For true public goods, there is no practical alternative to turning to the political process for making decisions, but lots of cases are marginal.

We will take a detailed look at how big the public sector is and should be, in Part 5.

Equity in the distribution of income

Many observers believe that the distribution of income (wages, interest, profits, and the like) produced by a purely competitive economy would be inequitable, however "efficiently" the market might allocate resources in response to consumer demands. In a purely competitive economy, every man's income would rest on his own and his property's economic contribution. And this would mean an unequal distribution of incomes. In a competitive race, some win and some lose. Moreover, we don't all start equal in the race. Some individuals inherit large fortunes, from which they obtain large incomes in the form of interest and dividends. Some people have higher intellectual abilities than others. Some are born into higher-income families, which means they get better educations and broader opportunities. Even a purely competitive economy would have rich and poor (although less inequality than in a more monopolistic system), and many Americans believe we

should reduce these inequalities through government action.

On the other hand, others argue that an income distribution based on "economic contribution" would be both just and efficient. It would provide both incentives and a fair income for all. Whether you agree or not, you can decide for yourself. What is the most equitable distribution of income and buying power is a third highly debatable issue and is a main topic in Parts 4 and 5.

CONCLUSION

Public-opinion polls in recent years have shown increasing antagonism toward big business, big labor, and big government. Big business especially is criticized for being too powerful and for concentrating too much on making profits rather than serving the public interest.

Four questions on these public attitudes toward business may serve as a useful conclusion to this chapter, and lead on to the ones that follow:

1. Is the criticism that businesses try to make profits rather than advancing the public welfare justified? Should businessmen "serve the public interest" rather than attempting to make profits?
2. Is there a conflict between attempting to maximize profits and serving the public interest?
3. Would these criticisms be more or less appropriate if the American economy were one of pure competition?
4. If we did not count on businesses and the market to make most of the decisions as to what should be produced and how, who would make these decisions and carry them out? Would the alternative produce results that would serve the public interest better?

REVIEW

Concepts to remember

Be sure you have a firm grasp of the new analytical concepts introduced in this chapter:

pure competition
long-run equilibrium
equilibrium of the firm
equilibrium of the industry
general equilibrium
economic efficiency

constant-cost industry
increasing-cost industry
long-run supply curve
price taker
public goods

For analysis and discussion

1. Explain briefly but concisely how individuals and businesses, each pursuing its own self-interest, interact to produce a widely beneficial outcome under competitive market conditions.
2. "Under pure competition, the consumer is king. The price of what he wants to buy can never stay for long above the minimum cost of producing any article." Is this quotation sound?
3. Under a purely competitive system, what incentive, if any, would remain for businessmen to do an efficient job, since competition would eliminate profits?
4. Pure competition, strictly speaking, does not prevail in any part of the economy. Then why study it?
5. "A purely competitive economic system would be ideal." Do you agree? Why, or why not?
6. (*Part B only*) Suppose a tax of 1 cent per pencil has been included in the costs of all pencil producers. Now the tax is removed. Beginning from the situation in Figure 22–1, with the price at 6 cents and demand D^1D^1, trace through the adjustment to a new equilibrium.
7. (*Part B only*) As a consumer of widgets, would you prefer that the industry be one of constant or increasing long-run costs? Why?
8. Chapter 22 demonstrates that under pure competition, price will be set equal to the minimum cost of production. How, if so, do you explain the cost of a Picasso or Rembrandt painting? (*Hint:* Is there pure competition among sellers?)
9. "Most people would agree that a dollar means more to a poor man than to a rich man. Since this is so, an economic system that merely reacts to the number of dollars spent is a grossly unfair system in the way it allocates resources." Do you agree or disagree? Why? If you agree, how should we modify the system to get around the problem?
10. What would be the main weaknesses, if any, of a purely competitive system? Should we use public policies to move further toward such a system?

APPENDIX

General equilibrium and economic efficiency

A purely competitive system of the sort described above would provide the most efficient possible allocation of resources in the sense described in the text of the chapter. More precisely, we can show that such a purely competitive system would allocate resources most efficiently, in the sense that no possible reallocation would increase the welfare of anyone in the system without harming someone else. This condition, which economists call "Pareto optimality" (after the famous French economist who first stated it precisely), seems to some observers a weak claim for an optimal system. But it is a major claim indeed, if you stop to think about it. For if Pareto optimality does not prevail, we could make someone better off without harming anyone else, thus unambiguously increasing the public's total utility. **Any system that does not provide Pareto optimality is producing a socially inefficient allocation of resources that holds total utility for the economy below what it could otherwise be.**

It is possible to demonstrate precisely that Pareto optimality will prevail under competitive general equilibrium (that is, no one can be made better off without injuring someone else); while under other market arrangements (for example, with some degree of monopoly), it is generally possible to increase the welfare of someone without injuring anyone else. For simplicity, consider only two goods, x and y, although the argument can be generalized to many goods.

Assume that competitive general equilibrium prevails. We know then (from Chapter 5) that when a consumer is in equilibrium, maximizing his utility, he spends his income so that the marginal utility obtained from the last dollar spent on x is the same as that obtained from the last dollar spent on y. Alternatively, we can say that the marginal utilities of the two products must be proportional to their prices. In equation form:

$$\frac{MU_x}{MU_y} = \frac{P_x}{P_y} \qquad (1)$$

We also know (from Chapters 21 and 22) that in long-run competitive equilibrium, each producer in each industry maximizes profits by producing up to the point where marginal cost equals price. Thus:

$$P_x = MC_x \text{ (for industry } x) \qquad (2a)$$

$$P_y = MC_y \text{ (for industry } y) \qquad (2b)$$

Combining equations (1) and (2), we can then write:

$$\frac{MU_x}{MU_y} = \frac{P_x}{P_y} = \frac{MC_x}{MC_y} \qquad (3)$$

Equations (1), (2), and (3) state the conditions under which, with the competitive prices P_x and P_y, every consumer and business firm is in the best position it can achieve. No one can increase his utility or profits by changing his behavior. Equation (3) also emphasizes that prices provide the basic equilibrating link between consumers (expressing their preferences through expenditures) and businesses (maximizing their profits by hiring resources up to the point where marginal cost equals price).

Now, consider any situation where perfect competition does not prevail—for example, where a monopolist is restricting output and raising price to enlarge profits so that he holds his selling price above marginal cost. (We will demonstrate rigorously in Chapter 24 why he will do so in order to maximize his profits, once he is free from competitive pressure.) Suppose, for example, that monopoly prevails in industry y, so marginal cost in y is less than price. Then equation (2b) will not hold, and hence neither will equation (3).

Suppose, for example, that

$$\frac{MU_x}{MU_y} = 2$$

but that

$$\frac{MC_x}{MC_y} = 3$$

because marginal cost is below price in industry y, while MC equals price in industry x. Thus, the marginal utility of one unit of x is twice that of one unit of y, but the marginal cost of producing one more y is only one-third that for x. This means that in terms of costs, producers could make three additional units of y by giving up one of x. By so shifting resources to produce one less x and three more y, we can make consumers better off, by giving them more than the two units of y they view as equivalent to one unit of x in their utility functions. Similarly, for any other condition than the (competitive) one specified in equation (3), it will be possible to make someone better off without injuring anyone else. When equation (3) is satisfied, Pareto optimality will prevail.

Competitive equilibrium provides Pareto optimality, and monopolistic equilibrium does not, except in some unlikely hypothetical cases that need not concern us here. Thus, economists presume that a monopolistic situation that holds price above marginal cost will generally lead to a less efficient allocation of resources than would a competitive system.

But remember that a Pareto optimal competitive system would not necessarily be the best system, even though it provided the most "efficient" allocation of resources in response to consumer demands. You might still object to its failure to take into account externalities, to provide enough public goods, or to produce an "equitable" distribution of income. The substantial benefits from purely competitive markets do not necessarily imply that, economically, no government is the best government.

CHAPTER 23

AGRICULTURE:
a CASE STUDY
in COMPETITION

Agriculture is the area of the American economy that comes closest to the model of pure competition. For most major farm products—wheat, cotton, hogs, and many others—the conditions of pure competition substantially prevail except insofar as the government has stepped in to alter them.

This chapter has three main parts. First, it asks, How well has substantially pure competition worked in agriculture? How close have the results come to the picture painted by Chapter 22? Second, what have been the causes and consequences of government intervention in agriculture over the past half century? Government has intervened repeatedly, and these government policies provide excellent opportunities to apply the supply-and-demand analysis that you have learned thus far in predicting their consequences. Third, after over a half century of repeated government attempts to raise farm prices and incomes by restricting farm output, the last few years have seen a dramatic change in the place of American agriculture in the world economy, and these changes, too, call for supply-and-demand analysis as American agriculture looks to the future. Agriculture provides a fascinating case study of competition at work, and of the political economy of a major industry in our democratic society.

RESPONSES TO CHANGING DEMANDS

Table 23–1 presents data on spending for, and production of, food in the United States since 1929. How well has agriculture responded to changing consumer demands over the past half century? Using Table 23–1 and what you have learned about competitive markets thus far (especially from Chapter 22), try to answer this question for yourself before reading on.

Suggestions for analysis

Although Table 23–1 provides only a small subset of the data for a complete answer, it has the crucial information on most of the important points.

First, what has happened to consumer demand for food since 1929? Line 1 shows that consumers bought over three times as much food in 1975 as 1929. (Total spending on food rose more, but a part of the increase was merely higher prices, and this inflation has been eliminated by converting all years to the same [1967] prices.) Thus, the line shows both growing consumer demand (mainly more people) and farmers' increased production in response to that demand. But line 2 shows an equally important fact about demand. Demand for food grew much less rapidly than demand for other goods and services: Food's share of total consumer spending fell from 29 to 22 percent as the American people became more affluent.

How did agriculture respond? We know from line 1 that production grew to meet growing demand. Lines 3 through 8 tell us more, that people have persistently moved out of farming to the rest of the economy where consumer demand has grown more rapidly, as the competitive model predicts—but that fewer and fewer farms and farmers nonetheless managed to produce the big increase in food demanded. Lines 3 through 5 show the big exodus from farming to the rest of the economy, and line 9 suggests why. Average incomes from farming have persistently been far below those in nonfarm occupations. Millions of farm proprietors and workers have moved out of low-profit and low-income farming to other industries where income prospects are higher, just as economic theory says they will. A half century ago, a quarter of the labor force was in farming. Now it is only 4 percent.

Lines 6 through 8 tell how the farm industry managed the big increase in food production. Land devoted to farming remained virtually unchanged, but farmers invested large sums in tractors, chemicals, and other modern capital equipment that dramatically raised output per worker and per acre. Investment per worker in farming is more than double that in manufacturing. And modern technology has been spec-

Table 23–1

Food in the United States, 1929–75

	1929	1947	1975
1. Consumer expenditures on food (billions of 1967 dollars)	$ 38	$ 72	$130
2. Food as percentage of total consumption	29	28	22
3. Number of farms (millions)	6.2	5.5	2.8
4. Number of farm workers (millions)	13	10	4.3
5. Farmers as percentage of total population	25	16	4.2
6. Output per farm worker (1967 = 100)	17	33	136
7. Investment per farm worker (1967 = 100)	34	71	115
8. Acres devoted to farming (millions)	974	1,055	995
9. Per capita farm income as percentage of nonfarm[a]	29	37	34

[a] Farm income excludes government payments and nonfarm earnings.

tacular on the farm. New fertilizers, hybrid seeds, plant-disease control, and modern farm machinery have revolutionized food production. A century ago, one farmer fed five people; today he feeds nearly fifty. Output per man has grown about 6 percent per year, about twice as fast as in manufacturing. As part of this revolution, the average farm nearly tripled in size; increasingly, only very large farms can produce at the lowest costs per unit. Today about half of all farm products come from the largest 6 percent of farms, with over $50,000 of annual sales and utilizing advanced modern machinery and technology. But although farm experts estimate that it is a rare farmer selling $10,000 or less annually who can cover his costs in basic crops, over 35 percent of all farms still have total sales (not profits) of less than $2,500 annually—clearly far too small to produce efficiently with modern methods. (Part of the reason for this is that many "farms" are small plots farmed by people who have full- or part-time jobs elsewhere.)

Line 9 is perhaps the most striking of all. In spite of a large, continuing exodus of young people from farming, per capita income from farming (excluding government subsidies) remains only about one-third of nonfarm incomes. Figure 23–1 shows the picture in more detail. The bottom line shows per capita incomes from farming. The middle line adds government subsidies and nonfarm income of farmers (dividends, interest, and so on), but even that brings farm incomes up to only about 75 percent of nonfarm. Farm incomes have risen dramatically in the last few years, especially with the world food "shortage" of 1973–74, and there are some very rich farmers. But most farmers are small and many are poor.

So, all things considered, how well would you say agriculture has responded to changing consumer demands?

ARGUMENTS FOR AID TO AGRICULTURE

For many years, farmers have argued that, as the producers of society's food, they deserve higher incomes than their highly competitive markets give them. And much of the public has agreed. What are the main arguments supporting special government aid to farmers, over and above what they can earn in the market?

Figure 23–1
Per capita farmers' incomes from farm sources have long been far under nonfarm incomes, but many "farmers" receive substantial incomes from nonfarm occupations and government payments. (Source: U.S. Department of Agriculture.)

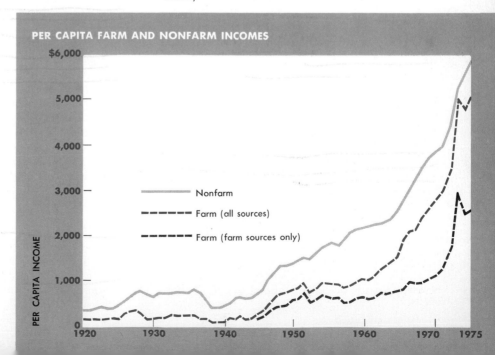

PER CAPITA FARM AND NONFARM INCOMES

— Nonfarm
- - - Farm (all sources)
- - - Farm (farm sources only)

PER CAPITA INCOME

$6,000
5,000
4,000
3,000
2,000
1,000
0

1920   1930   1940   1950   1960   1970   1975

1. **Low-income status.**   Low farm incomes are a major argument. Farmers say they deserve a reasonable living and a fair return for a hard day's work, just as high as anyone else's. If you believe that everyone should have at least some minimum income, this plea is understandable. But remember that while many farmers are poor, many others are not.

2. **Special susceptibility to business cycles.** Farmers are hard hit by depressions; their incomes drop sharply as food prices fall in highly competitive markets where demand is generally inelastic. (It's not so often mentioned, but they also prosper especially in booms.) This argument, you should note, is easy to confuse with the general low-income argument above. Don't count the same thing twice.

3. **The weather.**   Farming is especially exposed to the vagaries of nature, to droughts and floods.

4. **Special aid to offset advantages of other groups.**   Farmers claim that they are injured by special privileges for other groups and that they deserve offsetting special assistance. For example, the American tariff on industrial products has long forced the farmer to pay higher domestic prices. Monopolistic conditions in business and labor have been tolerated by government officials in many industries. These raise the prices paid by farmers and restrict movement from farms to urban occupations.

5. **Soil conservation.**   Much of the farm-aid program has been justified as soil conservation (for example, conserving soil by not planting part of the land each year).

6. **Agriculture as a way of life.**   Some people look on agriculture as a stable, sound way of life, harking back to the ways of our fathers—an anchor to windward in a hectic world of assembly lines, tenements, skyscrapers, and neuroses. The farmer is still an individual, not just a cog in a huge economic machine. This, they feel, is a way of life worth preserving.

This case raises some economic dilemmas, because the very traits of the farmer and his life that are admired most in this view are the ones associated with small-scale, often inefficient, family farming. A closely related argument hinges on large farm families. There is no provision in the price system, some say, for paying farmers for the outlays of money and effort they make in bearing, rearing, and educating a large number of children who later move into other economic areas. Economically, the argument runs, human beings are capital resources of the nation just as much as are buildings and machines. (Note that on closer examination, this, like the low-income argument, is logically a personal, not an industry, argument. If we want to encourage and pay for large families, presumably the aid should be based on size of family, not on where they live.)

All these claims face substantial counterarguments. But they have convinced enough congressmen to produce a large farm-aid program from the 1930s to the early 1970s, involving widespread government intervention in farm-markets. How well did it work?

THE ECONOMICS OF FARM AID

Parity

Since the New Deal, "parity" between farm incomes and prices and those in the rest of the economy has been the foundation of the farm-aid program. To be fair, it is argued, farm prices and incomes should rise at least as fast as nonfarm.

As it was developed in the New Deal legislation, farm parity meant that prices paid and received by farmers should be in the same ratio as in the "normal" years 1909–14. If farm prices drop *relative to* other prices (or don't rise as fast as other prices), government action should push the farm prices back up to parity.

If you're a skeptic, you will recall that the period 1909–14 was the golden age of agriculture. You may ask, why not a parity program for buggies and women's high-buttoned shoes, based on the years 1905–06, which saw the peak for the buggy and high-button-shoe industries? But parity was the foundation of most farm-aid programs.

Output-restriction programs

One major approach to raising farm prices and incomes has been government restriction of farm output. The demand for most farm products is inelastic, so reducing output will,

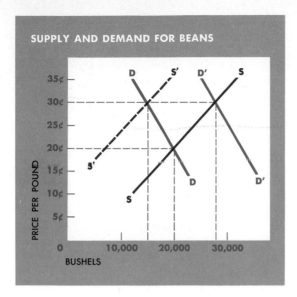

SUPPLY AND DEMAND FOR BEANS

Figure 23-2
The market-clearing price for beans is 20 cents, given the original demand and supply curves DD and SS. If price is fixed at 30 cents, there are 13,000 bushels of unsold beans, which the government must either buy up (D'D') or keep from being produced (S'S') to maintain the price.

bushels. Those farmers who sell at 30 cents per pound may be very happy, but there are a lot of unhappy farmers holding the unsold 13,000 bushels of beans.

The government, considerate of the bean farmers' plight, offers to pay them to cut back production to 15,000 bushels. It might, for example, provide a "soil conservation" payment of 10 cents per bushel for beans, to reduce bean acreage so that no more than 15,000 bushels are produced by the industry as a whole. This, in effect, moves the supply curve back to the left, so that the total amount supplied at 30 cents per pound is just the 15,000 bushels that the private market will take. This movement of the supply curve is shown by S'S'.

How do the various parties fare? The bean farmers should be happy. They are getting 30 cents a pound for their beans, and they are permitted to either produce, or be paid for not producing, a total of 28,000 bushels. But tax-payers end up spending 10 cents per pound on subsidies for 13,000 bushels of beans not produced under the output-restriction plan. And consumers must pay 30 cents per pound for beans, getting only 15,000 bushels at that price—they are now paying more for 15,000 bushels than they were for 20,000 bushels before the farm-aid program, since demand is inelastic. Clearly, there are too many bean farms and farmers in the industry, but they are paid to stay there by the "soil conservation" subsidy paid by the government to reduce supply.

other things equal, raise both price and total consumer expenditure on farm products.

Suppose that *SS* in Figure 23–2 is the supply curve and *DD* the demand curve for beans. Given these curves, the equilibrium price will clearly be 20 cents per pound, with 20,000 bushels of beans produced each year. All farmers producing beans will be doing so at a cost of no more than 20 cents per pound, because at any lower price, their incomes would not cover their costs. Everyone who is willing to pay 20 cents per pound for beans is getting all he wants to buy at that price.

Suppose, however, that bean farmers protest that the price is too low, below parity, and they are not making a decent living at that price. They lobby for a price-support program for beans, and they get it—at a price of 30 cents per pound, which they allege will give them a decent living. What is the result?

The first result is that there is a large excess supply in the market. At 30 cents per pound, roughly 28,000 bushels of beans will be produced, but buyers will only take about 15,000

Government purchase or loan programs

Alternatively, the government could maintain the bean price at 30 cents by buying up the excess supply (13,000 bushels) left by private buyers at that price. This would move the total private-plus-government demand curve to the right by 13,000 bushels at the 30-cent price in Figure 23–2 (as shown by D'D'), clearing the market and ensuring bean farmers their desired prices and incomes. This is fine for bean producers, but bad for consumers, who are again paying more for fewer beans, and for taxpayers, who have to pick up the bill for 13,000 bushels of beans. The government could not sell the beans on the open market, because to do so would undercut the price it is trying to support. Thus, in all probability it will store them, at least temporarily.

Sometimes the government, instead of buying up the overhang, merely lent the farmers the parity price on the excess crops, with the beans as security—say, 30 cents a pound on unsold beans. Then the farmer could pay off the loan and sell the beans if the price later rose above 30 cents, or default on the loan and turn the beans over to the government if the price stayed below 30 cents. It was a heads-I-win, tails-you-lose deal for the farmer, much like the outright purchase plan for consumers and taxpayers.

If, under such a plan, the government ended up with lots of beans in storage, which it couldn't sell here without depressing the market price, it could recoup part of its investment by selling them abroad at the competitive world-market price, well below the 30-cent-supported domestic price. But if it did so, it would encounter cries of "dumping" by foreign bean producers who found themselves in competition with a government-subsidized price from the United States. If the government couldn't sell the beans abroad, perhaps it could at least give them away to hungry countries or to the hungry poor at home. This would make the cost of the gifts

quite clear, and the full amount of the subsidy would be seen as a cost to the government. But don't forget that even then, domestic consumers were only getting 15,000 bushels in the market and had to pay 30 cents per pound for them.

The farm-aid program in action

The core of the farm-aid program over the past half century was the effort to keep up prices and incomes by preventing crop "surpluses" or buying them up if they occurred. The resulting pile-up of government-held surpluses is shown in Figure 23–3. Figure 23–4 shows the percentage of the annual crop bought up or loaned on by the government each year from 1952 to 1974 for wheat, cotton, and corn. Some twenty crops were covered by the price-support program in 1974.[1]

Table 23–2 summarizes the cost of these programs to the government and the beneficiaries. Note that this does not include the costs to consumers in the form of higher prices.

Nor does the table convey the concentration of federal aid payments to a relatively small number of large farmers. For example, in one

[1]The others were barley, beans, butter, cheese, dried milk, honey, peanuts, flaxseed, sorghum, oats, rice, rye, soybeans, tung oil, tobacco, wool, and mohair. Surpluses were sold mainly abroad (where the world price was under the U.S. support price) and at low prices domestically when deterioration threatened. The average loss was about 25 percent of the C.C.C. (government) investment.

Figure 23–3
This chart shows the amount of government funds tied up in farm-crop loans and surplus stocks each year. Tobacco and soybeans account for most "Other" in recent years. (Source: Commodity Credit Corporation.)

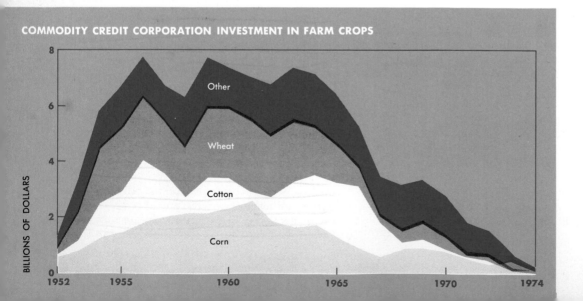

COMMODITY CREDIT CORPORATION INVESTMENT IN FARM CROPS

BILLIONS OF DOLLARS

Other

Wheat

Cotton

Corn

1952   1955   1960   1965   1970   1974

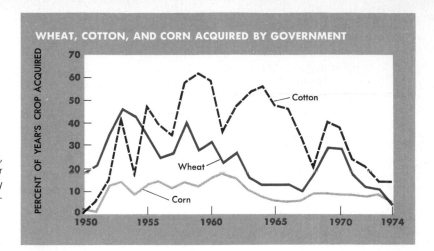

Figure 23-4
A big proportion of the cotton, wheat, and corn crops has been bought up or loaned on by the government in many years. (Source: U.S. Department of Agriculture.)

recent year, one farm in Kern County, California, received a federal farm-subsidy payment of $4.4 million for not growing cotton; this reflected crop-reduction payments on a farm covering 83,000 acres. In four San Joaquin Valley counties in California, 2,300 cotton farms received a total of $65.4 million in federal farm subsidies. Although these are extreme cases, most poor small farmers, who needed help most, got tiny subsidy payments because benefit payments were based on the acreage or crop cut back, usually some proportion of previous output levels. In 1970, the smallest 50 percent of all farms received only 9 percent of total government benefits. In 1973, Congress limited payments per crop to each farmer to $20,000, although many large farmers had earlier avoided such limits by breaking up farms into smaller legal units and by diversifying crops.

The effects of nearly a half century of price support and production-control plans are hard to assess precisely. It is not clear, for example, that farm output was in fact reduced by all these payments; farmers greatly increased output per acre when their acreage was reduced, and they substituted noncontrolled crops for the forbidden ones in many cases. But two results are clear.

First, in the two decades following 1950, federal agricultural expenditures, mainly through price- and income-support programs, amounted to more than the entire increase in farm income over the period, although even this support was insufficient to raise average farm incomes to equal nonfarm ones. Second, the huge farm surpluses piled up by the government have been expensive evidence of the difficulties of trying to maintain prices above market levels through government action, even when billions were spent paying farmers not to produce. To a man from Mars, the American farm program would have seemed a strange phenomenon. It would be hard to explain to him why we should pay farmers not to produce food, and buy up available food to hold prices so high people won't consume it, when so many people are hungry.

Table 23-2

Federal government aid to agriculture

	Federal aid (in billions)	Percent of total federal budget	Farm population (in millions)
1950	$3.0	6.9%	23.1
1955	4.1	5.9	19.1
1960	3.7	4.0	15.6
1965	4.8	4.1	12.4
1970	6.2	3.2	9.7
1972	5.3	2.3	9.6
1974	2.3	0.9	9.3
1976	2.0	0.6	8.7

Source: U.S. Budget and *Economic Report of the President:* Figures are for fiscal years.

Programs to promote agricultural efficiency

Long before the government set out to raise farm incomes by restricting production, the Department of Agriculture was busy telling farmers how to increase production. A broad program of scientific research, on-the-ground help for farmers through nationwide agricultural experiment stations, advice on soil-conservation practices, and a variety of other measures have played a major role in raising the efficiency of American agriculture to a level unparalleled in most other nations.

But by carrying out this eminently sensible program, the Department of Agriculture has persistently sabotaged its own crop-restriction programs. The American farmer is nobody's fool, and he took full advantage of modern methods to increase yields even while he was cutting back acreage under the income-support programs. Would you do differently if you were a farmer?

U.S. AGRICULTURE AND THE WORLD FOOD PROBLEM

More than two billion people in the less-developed nations live with inadequate diets, millions of them literally on the brink of starvation. In such a world, U.S. farm programs devoted to paying farmers not to produce food have long seemed anomalous to many observers. Years ago, Secretaries of Agriculture Brannan (under Truman) and Benson (under Eisenhower), frustrated by the expensive and ineffective farm policies they administered, proposed a modification that would substitute direct cash subsidies to farmers for the elaborate crop-reduction plans, and both the Johnson and Nixon administrations more recently urged Congress to move in this direction.

The new farm legislation of 1973 came in the midst of the greatest farm boom in U.S. history—and in the first U.S. peacetime "food shortage" in living memory. Worldwide crop failures in 1971 and 1972; record prosperity in the industrial nations, which led to big increases in food demands (especially for meats); massive U.S. grain sales to Russia, Western Europe, and other nations; nationwide food hoarding by U.S. consumers, in the near-panic that developed as farmers temporarily held back meat from the market when the Nixon administration temporarily froze meat prices; and international speculation in grains—all combined to shoot grain and meat prices up to unprecedented levels. Wheat, which for years had averaged below $2 a bushel, soared to over $5 a bushel. Soybeans rose even more. Beef and pork prices doubled.

Faced with soaring prices and domestic shortages of meat, President Nixon removed planting restrictions on wheat, and proposed a return to a free market in farm products. Congress, after long debate, enacted a new farm program for major products, even though it continued traditional price-support programs for many minor ones.

Direct income-support subsidies

The core of the new program was to free production and prices from controls and to provide direct cash subsidies to farmers to keep their incomes up to "target" levels. Production controls were lifted and price was freed to respond to market forces. Using the bean example above, in Figure 23–2, price would move to 20 cents a pound, and 20,000 bushels would be produced in a free market. But Congress specified "target" prices for basic farm products and provided that cash subsidies will be paid to farmers if market prices fall below the target prices. Thus, even in the face of the highest farm prices in history and soaring farm incomes, Congress inserted guarantees that would give unlimited subsidies to farmers should basic farm products fall below their target prices. And target prices, while well below then-prevailing record market levels, were set well above previous market and parity levels. And Congress retained the old, lower parity prices, providing that production controls could be reinstituted should prices fall to those levels.

Consumers are clearly better off under the new program, since prices are relatively free to respond to market pressures, and if inflation and record farm prosperity continue, taxpayers will have low bills for farm subsidies. But if farm prices fall below target levels, farmers will have an unlimited claim on the federal Treasury for cash subsidies to keep incomes up. And, as in the past, the income subsidies will go mainly to big, already-prosperous farmers, since they will be paid in proportion to the crops each has to sell (up to the $20,000 limit). The little, low-income farmers will receive only small subsidies.[2]

U.S. food power and the world economy

U.S. agriculture, with its labor, capital, land, and modern technology, can produce vastly more food and fibers than the U.S. public will buy at prices high enough to provide anything like a competitive return on the labor and other resources involved. We export annually nearly two-thirds of our total production of wheat and about half our oilseeds, rice, and cotton. Perhaps more important, our grain exports in 1975 totaled 80 million tons, about two-thirds of total world grain exports. Canada, the second largest exporter, shipped only about 15 million tons. By contrast, the USSR, Japan, Great Britain, Italy, and the other major industrialized nations imported significant parts of their total food, ranging from about 25 million tons for the USSR downward for the other nations. U.S. farm exports rose from $7 billion in 1970 to $22 billion in 1975, paying for a huge volume of U.S. imports (see Figure 39–1). While we usually think of America as an industrial power, it is now the one great source of grain exports to feed the rest of the world.

While the highly competitive farm sector has apparently responded very effectively to U.S. and other Western industrialized nations' demand for food and fibers, should we fault it for not meeting the needs of two billion undernourished people in the "third world"? Why hasn't it met their demands as well? Why should the United States not produce all the food it can and sell the "surplus" above our needs to the hungry less-developed nations? A thorough analysis must wait for Parts 6 and 7, on the international

economy. But the main answer is that the less-developed nations can't afford to pay for it at anything like world prices. American farmers haven't volunteered to produce the extra food free, and neither Congress nor most American citizens appear willing to pay American farmers to produce the food and then give it to the less-developed nations. Poor people abroad are in much the same position as poor people in the United States, except that Congress hasn't enacted as many special programs (like "welfare" and food stamps) to help them get food.

In fact, the United States has given away every year, during the past two decades, a large amount of "surplus" food, accumulated under the U.S. farm-price-support program. During the 1960s, for example, food aid to the less-developed nations averaged between $1.0 billion and $1.5 billion annually.[3] More recently, the total has declined gradually, reflecting partly a reduced congressional willingness to provide foreign aid, and partly the smaller surpluses being accumulated by the U.S. farm program. Presumably the government will accumulate no more huge surpluses under the new target-price program, and we will have to buy food outright if we want to give it to the less-developed nations. What this will mean to the level of U.S. foreign aid remains to be seen. If you believe the American taxpayer should see clearly where his dollars go, you will probably prefer the new situation. If your main goal is to get food to the third world, you may prefer the P.L. 480 process. Either way, it is clear that the United States occupies an extremely powerful international

[2]For a simple description of the new act, see G.E. Brandow, "Agricultural Policy: Different Now?" *Challenge*, March 1974.

[3]Much of this food aid was provided under "Public Law 480," which, in essence, permits the United States to sell surplus food to less-developed countries and accept payment in local currency, which the U.S. government promises not to take out of the country by converting it into dollars. Thus, for example, huge stocks of wheat have been provided to India for many years in exchange for "payment" in rupees. But since the United States accumulated vastly more rupees than there was any likelihood we would be able to spend in India for the foreseeable future, the food was, in effect, a gift. Part of U.S. government expenses overseas have been met by P.L. 480 funds; "Fulbright aid" to American students and teachers to spend time in the countries involved is a well-known example in university circles. Recently, the United States has made substantial direct dollar loans to less-developed countries to permit them to buy U.S. food in world markets.

position as the bread basket for the world, because of the enormous productivity of American agriculture.

Agriculture in the political economy

In fiscal 1973, the federal government spent $6 billion on aid for agriculture. In the same year, total farm income from farming (excluding income from investments and other nonfarm sources) was about $19 billion. Thus, nearly 40 percent of total income from farming was accounted for by federal government aid. Yet in 1973, there were fewer than three million farm families in the United States, out of a total of over 60 million family units. By 1976, budgeted federal aid to agriculture had dropped to $2 billion, reflecting both a sharp worldwide rise in food prices and the new U.S. farm policy. Whether this downtrend will continue or be reversed when the 1973 farm act expires in 1977 remains to be seen.

In perspective, three big facts stand out about the farm legislation of the past half century. One is the farmers' success in getting what they want. As one Washington correspondent put it, "As long as they act together, the farmers can get anything out of the government short of good growing weather—and Washington is working on that through cloud seeding." Some observers believe the political force of agriculture is weakening, and recent reductions in annual farm-aid budgets support this analysis. But if farm prices and incomes fall again, as they may well do, it is far from clear that Congress will not return to earlier aid patterns.

Second, forty years of massive federal aid haven't solved the basic farm-income problem. The worldwide boom of the 1970s swept farm prices upward, reflecting the highly unusual set of circumstances outlined above. But even then, small farmers' incomes remained at poverty levels. It was the big, efficient farmers who prospered. Moreover, the productive capacity of U.S. agriculture, once unleashed from government production restrictions, is huge indeed, and there is little reason to suppose that the farm dilemmas of the past half century have vanished permanently. There are still too many resources in American agriculture to earn competitive returns without either strong boom conditions, government aid, or new ways of channeling food to the less-developed nations.

Third, there has been widespread failure to distinguish between the economic problem of efficiency in resource allocation and the ethical problem of ensuring minimum income levels. Fundamentally, the American farm problem is rural poverty. The underlying purpose of farm-aid programs is not higher farm prices per se, but higher farm incomes. Yet farm-aid legislation has by and large required farmers to stay in farming as a condition of receiving aid. They have been paid for not raising crops and have been guaranteed prices that include government subsidies. If they leave agriculture, they lose the subsidies.

Thus, tying benefit payments to products, not to people, has failed to channel aid to poor families, and it has produced a domestically inefficient allocation of resources. By raising farm prices, the program has given the biggest benefits to the biggest farmers, because they have the most to sell. By paying farmers for cutting back production in proportion to acres farmed, the program has handed the biggest benefit checks to the highest-income farmers, now including many huge corporate farms. This adds up to the anomalous result of passing out benefits in inverse relation to need. The program has fallen short on both efficiency and equity criteria.

REVIEW

**For analysis
and discussion**

1. Has pure competition in agriculture worked as Chapter 22 says it should?
2. In a competitive economy, resources are supposed to move where consumer demand is strongest, as individuals seek higher incomes. In the light of the comparative incomes shown by Figure 23–1, how do you explain the fact that so many families stay in agriculture?
3. In agriculture, output per man has recently grown at the rate of 6 percent per annum, twice that for the rest of the economy. Since we apparently face a situation of continuing farm "surpluses," would decreased productivity in agriculture be a desirable solution to the farm problem?
4. Are there too many farmers?
5. Who has gained and who has lost the most from Congress's shift to the new target-price, direct-subsidy farm-aid program?
6. Does agriculture's failure to provide food for the third-world countries represent a failure of Adam Smith's "invisible hand"?
7. There are fewer than three million farm families in the United States. Yet Congress has repeatedly voted to grant large subsidies to agriculture. How do you explain this fact?
8. If you were a congressman, what legislation would you support on the "farm problem"?

On January 8, 1975, substantially the following story appeared in West Coast newspapers:

> California egg producers decided yesterday to continue diverting 5 percent of the state's weekly egg production from the consumer market to keep egg prices up.
>
> The 16-member State Egg Advisory Board, on a 9–5 vote with two abstentions, turned down a motion from consumer representatives to quit diverting 10,000 cases of eggs a week—30 dozen eggs to the case—from the consumer marketplace for later sale abroad at lower prices. The policy, in effect since November, helps hold prices up to about 72 cents a dozen in San Francisco.
>
> Inflation-squeezed egg farmers, hurt by soaring grain and feed prices, said that ending the diversion policy would depress prices, probably as much as 5 to 8 cents a dozen, and would force smaller egg producers out of business.

A few days earlier, substantially the following two stories had appeared:

> The government of Chile announced today the closing of one of its major copper mines for six months, in order to help halt the downward slide of copper prices. Three other major copper-producing countries—Peru, Zaire, and Zambia—recently announced plans to cut their copper exports by 10 percent, with the same goal.

> Latin America's coffee-exporting countries met together in Caracas last week, they announced today, to discuss plans for withholding 20 percent of the new coffee crop from world markets. The announcement stressed rising costs of production and rising prices of other products which coffee-producing countries must pay in world markets with continuing inflation. While coffee prices have risen sharply in the past two years, the spokesman said that many coffee producers are losing money, and that coffee-producing countries face serious problems in paying for their imports.

---

1. Should the state of California legalize and support agreements of egg farmers to restrict supply in order to keep prices up? If not, should the state take any other steps to ensure the farmers reasonable prices and incomes? Would consumers be better off if "cutthroat competition" prevailed?

2. Assuming that the state gives permission through the Egg Advisory Board, if you were an egg farmer, would you favor diverting eggs from the domestic to the overseas market, as described in the news story?

3. Do you see any significant differences between the case of eggs in California and those of copper and coffee in the other stories?

4. Suppose hi-fi stereo manufacturers applied to the government for exemption from antitrust laws to arrange together to limit production so as to avoid the surpluses that periodically lead to price wars in the hi-fi field, with losses for many companies. Would you favor granting the request, with a Hi-Fi Advisory Board (comparable to the Egg Advisory Board) with government-appointed members, to pass on industry plans? What, if any, difference do you see between the egg and hi-fi cases?

CHAPTER 24

MONOPOLY and PUBLIC UTILITIES

Monopoly is something like sin. Everyone says he's against it, but a lot of people aren't very clear just what it is they're against. Like sin, monopoly has to be defined before one can talk much sense about it, or decide what, if anything, ought to be done about it.

THE SPECTRUM FROM COMPETITION TO MONOPOLY

Monopoly is generally defined as a market in which there is only one seller. But this is deceptively simple. There is no commodity that doesn't have some substitute, more or less close, and we have no sharp criterion of how close the substitute can be before we no longer have a monopoly. The Aluminum Company of America, until World War II, was often called a monopoly in this sense; there was no other American producer of basic aluminum. But steel, wood, copper, and other materials are possible substitutes for aluminum, if the price of aluminum gets too high. Or consider General Motors: It has a monopoly in producing Chevrolets, but there is Ford next door producing close substitutes. In one sense, every producer who isn't in a purely competitive market has a monopoly in selling his own product. But the closer the substitutes produced by others, the less he has a "monopoly" as a practical matter.

Pure monopoly

In spite of this problem, economists have defined a situation they call "pure" monopoly. Consider the local power company in a small town as an example. It is the only producer of electricity in the town; it has an exclusive franchise from the city government; and the substitution of candles, oil lamps, or gas lighting by consumers who rebel at high prices is not a very serious likelihood. A pure monopoly is characterized by:

1. Only one seller of the good or service
2. Rivalry from producers of substitutes so remote as to be insignificant

Under these circumstances, the pure monopolist can set the market price himself, and customers don't have close substitutes to turn to. He is a "price maker," unlike the wheat farmer who is a "price taker." But even the monopolist has to face up to the realities of elasticity of demand. He can put his price where he wishes; but unless demand is perfectly inelastic, the higher he puts his price, the less he will sell. In large part, the elasticity of demand for any product reflects the presence of potential substitutes, and there is no monopoly so pure that it can escape completely the possibility of partial substitutes. Thus, pure monopoly in the textbook sense is never quite found in the real world, and pure monopoly shades into competition, just as pure competition shades into lesser degrees of competition. But many public utilities come close to the pure monopoly case.[1]

Monopolistic competition and oligopoly

There is a spectrum from pure competition to pure monopoly. Where there are many sellers of only slightly differentiated products, but not enough to make the market perfectly competitive, we call the situation "monopolistic competition." There may be a dozen or a hundred sellers of substantially identical products. But the products vary somewhat. For example, breakfast-food manufacturers don't make just breakfast food. They make Wheaties, Cheerios, and all the rest. Even corn flakes aren't just corn flakes; Post and Kellogg put them in differently colored boxes under different names, and to the buyer they are at least somewhat differentiated. Or stores may provide different services with the same product—say, free delivery. The degree of "product differentiation" gets to be more substantial for, say, television sets. Philco, RCA, and Sylvania may all show the same picture on the same-sized tube when tuned to Channel 4, but neither the makers nor the customers believe the sets are identical.

Where there are only a few competing producers and each producer must take into account what each other producer does, we call the situation "oligopoly," which means few sellers. In the auto industry, with only a few big producers, obviously General Motors, Chrysler, and Ford have to pay a lot of attention to each other's policies in setting prices, even though their products are all somewhat differentiated. Firms in oligopolistic industries may compete actively, or they may get together ("collude") formally or informally to agree on prices and on sharing the market.

Most of the American economic system lies in between pure competition and pure monopoly. Each industry seems to be a little different. Yet we need to classify this huge "in-between" area into some major groups if we are to make any headway in analyzing how it operates. Most economists use a division something like this, emphasizing the number of sellers, closeness of substitutes, and vigor of competition among firms:

I. **Pure competition**—many sellers of an identical product (wheat)
II. **Monopolistic competition**—a substantial number of sellers of closely substitutable products
   a. Price competition (vegetables in local grocery stores)
   b. Nonprice competition and "demand creation" (beer, men's suits)

---

[1] The analogy to pure monopoly on the buyer's side is sometimes called "pure monopsony," which means one buyer. This case might prevail where there is only one buyer for labor services—say, the mill in an isolated mill town. But like pure monopoly, pure monopsony is hard to find. For instance, workers are free to move to another town if the monopsonist exploits his position too much.

III. **Oligopoly**—a few sellers of closely substitutable products[2]
   a. Competition—on prices and through non-price competition and demand creation (television, autos)
   b. Collaboration
     1. Formal collusion on prices and on output—"cartels" (nickel, internationally)[3]
     2. Price leadership or informal price stabilization (steel, gasoline)

IV. **Pure monopoly**—one seller of a product without close substitutes (local water company)

The examples are intended merely to provide some concrete impressions to go with the analytical categories. Few real-world cases fit neatly and exclusively into any one of the intermediate categories. For example, there is some demand creation, and quality competition as well as price competition, in groceries (case IIa). Broadly, most of the "service" industries (retail trade, legal services, banking, and so on) fall into the monopolistic competition category, as do a good many manufacturing firms. Much of manufacturing (probably over half) falls under the oligopoly head. Only public utilities, like the local water company, provide major examples that approach "pure monopoly."

THE BASES OF MONOPOLY

The basic test of an effective monopoly is its power to exclude competitors from the market. If a firm can keep out potential competitors, it can raise prices with relative impunity. The nearer the substitutes that competitors can put on the market, the weaker is the firm's monopoly position. The ideal monopoly (from the monopolist's viewpoint) would cover an absolutely essential product with no substitutes.

Government action
as a basis for monopoly

The strongest monopolies are the public utilities. An exclusive government franchise is about as airtight protection as any monopoly can hope for. This arrangement is found in most localities for water, electricity, gas, and telephone companies. Having granted this enviable monopoly position, however, governments invariably regulate the prices the monopoly can charge. Otherwise, the stockholders of the local water or gas company would be in a happy position indeed.

Governments intervene in other ways to provide partial bases for monopolies. The farm-aid programs of the past three decades have supported prices and induced farmers to behave like a cartel in restricting output. Government licensing of doctors and other professionals is manifestly intended to protect the public against such things as incompetent medical service, but in fact also provides a basis for monopolistic practices by the doctors and others where supply is restricted by licensing. The entire federal patent system, discussed below, protects the monopoly position of the inventor. Federal legislation establishes the right of workers to combine in unions that in essence act as monopolies in selling their labor to employers.

Patents and research

The patent law gives the inventor exclusive control over his invention for 17 years, to stimulate and reward inventions. Key patents underlie the industrial position of many major American concerns. Research has become part of the American industrial scene, and the "blue chips" of American industry come automatically to mind when we think of technological advance—IBM, General Electric, du Pont. These firms maintain their leading positions in oligopolistic industries in no small part by being first with the best in research. Over the past twenty years, almost two-thirds of all patents have gone to corporations. General Electric alone, for example, received about 13,000; AT&T about 10,000. Research is an expensive and cumulative process. It's hard for the little firm to compete, quite aside from the patent laws.

Control of raw materials

If you can get exclusive control over the raw materials needed to make your product,

[2] Where there are only two sellers, "duopoly" exists. This is a special case of oligopoly.
[3] Formal collusion in setting prices or dividing up markets is illegal under the Sherman Act, as we shall see in Chapter 27.

you're sitting pretty—at least until someone figures out a substitute material. For example, the International Nickel Company of Canada for years owned more than nine-tenths of the world's known reserves of nickel, and produced more than 90 percent of the world's output of nickel.

Financial resources and the capital market

The money needed to set up an efficient firm in many industries today is tens and even hundreds of millions of dollars. Not very many people have this much money, and it's hard to borrow $10 million unless you're already a very well established person or firm, no matter how engaging a picture you paint of your prospects.

In a "perfect" capital market, funds would be available whenever the prospective borrower was willing and able to pay the going rate of interest on loans of comparable risk. In fact, however, it is hard for newcomers to raise funds in the market. Lenders are skeptical of unknown faces. Moreover, borrowing is more expensive for small, new borrowers, even when they can get the funds. These facts give an important advantage to established monopolists, who are likely to have a well-established credit position.

Advertising

Advertising by itself would have a hard time establishing or even maintaining a monopoly on any product. But the entrenched positions of names like Westinghouse and RCA in the mind of the American consumer are a cause of dismay to prospective competitors. Modern advertising has become increasingly "institutionalized." That is, ads aim primarily at building up the company's name and prestige, rather than at selling a particular product. Large-scale prestige advertising (for example, national TV advertising) costs big money, and only big and successful companies can afford it. On the other hand, advertising offers potential competitors a way of luring customers away from established firms; advertising works both ways on the monopoly problem.

Unfair competition

Running the little fellow out of business by unfair price cutting, after which price is raised to a monopolistic level, is one of the charges commonly brought against big business. If Safeway prices groceries very low, it is accused of a devious intent to run the independents out and then to boost its own prices when competition is gone. Some observers say that the old Standard Oil Company of the 1800s provided some spectacular cases of such behavior. The accusation is commonly levelled at big businesses.

Such predatory price competition is now illegal. But the line between legitimate and unfair price cutting merely to eliminate competition is hard to draw in many cases. The more efficient producers always tend to eliminate the inefficient.

Large-scale production and decreasing costs

Low-cost mass production is the pride of American industry. In many industries (steel, electrical equipment, autos, chemicals, and so on), maximum efficiency can be obtained only by large firms, each producing a substantial share of the market. In local areas, taking advantage of the economies of large-scale production may mean one or a few monopolistic firms—for example, the one grocery store a small town can reasonably support. In such cases, until a firm reaches this optimal scale, it is operating in its range of "decreasing costs." That is, by increasing output, it can cut its cost per unit produced.

Figure 24–1 represents such an industry. The TUC curves are simply total-unit-cost curves for different scales of enterprise for a firm in the industry—say, a local gas company. Scale TUC^3 is the most efficient scale in this case; its least-cost point is the lowest of any possible scale of enterprise. This is a decreasing-cost industry if demand is small relative to the first three scales of enterprise—for example, if demand is D^1D^1 or D^2D^2. It is a "decreasing-cost" industry because the economies of scale within the single firm have not yet been fully exploited at any output less than OM, the least-cost point on TUC^3. Up to output OM it has an obvious cost advantage from increasing its sales.

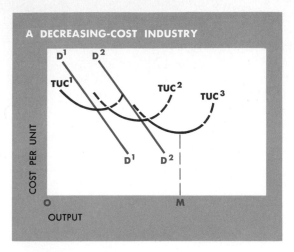

A DECREASING-COST INDUSTRY

Figure 24–1
The industry has decreasing unit costs up to output M. For any demand short of that amount, competition is unlikely to work effectively.

Clearly, competition with many firms is not going to work in this industry. If there are several firms and demand is, say, D^2D^2, each firm will cut price to increase its share of the market and increase its profit. This price competition will persist until one firm has driven out the others, and has a monopoly.

The social advantage of limiting such an industry to one firm is obvious; this is the basis for most exclusive public utility franchises. To insist on several firms would obviously mean higher costs and higher prices if they all stayed in business. But it would be equally foolish to expect the one firm not to exploit its monopoly position to obtain high profits unless it is regulated.

PURE MONOPOLY[4]

In the American economy, except for the public utilities, we seldom find in a market only one firm, no available substitutes for the commodity produced, and no possibility that

[4]Since this section rests directly on the marginal-cost–marginal-revenue analysis of Chapter 21, instructors who assigned only Track A of Chapters 20–22 may wish to skip the remainder of the chapter.

other firms may invade the market. Yet looking at such an extreme case is useful, because it gives some insight into what the world might be like if pure monopolies were tolerated without regulation. It suggests rules for controlling public utilities. And it may be a quite realistic description of the temporary monopoly position in which firms sometimes find themselves because of special advantages of location, development of new products ahead of competitors, patents, or other such circumstances.

Imagine a single electric-power company in an isolated community, free to charge whatever rates it pleases. Suppose you are the owner-manager of this hypothetical concern. You are a price maker; you can set your price where you wish. Waiving the fear that the local government will begin to regulate your rates, how would you maximize your profits?

The answer, as you have probably predicted, is: Increase output up to the point where marginal cost equals marginal revenue. Let us consider the answer in more detail.

Total and marginal revenue

Suppose your market research people estimate demand as shown in columns 1 and 2 of Table 24–1. Column 3 shows the total revenue obtained at different prices. But as a monopolist, you need to face a new fact. You are a price maker, and you can sell more electricity only by lowering your price, unlike the (perfectly elastic) to him infinitely large demand, faced by the stereo manufacturer under pure competition. Under pure competition, price and marginal revenue were identical; if you sold one more stereo set for $1,000, you increased your total revenue by $1,000. But not here.

Now you face a downward-sloping demand curve. To sell more you must cut price, not only on the extra sales but on all the electricity you sell.[5] **For the monopolist, marginal revenue is always less than price. This is because he must lower his price to sell more units, and he must lower it not just on the marginal unit but on all units sold.**

[5]This assumes that you sell at the same price to everyone, not discriminating between residential and commercial users, or others.

Table 24–1

Hometown Electric Company—customer demand schedule

Kilowatts (1)	Price (2)	Total revenue (3)	MARGINAL REVENUE	
			Per 100,000 kilowatts (4)	Per kilowatt (5)
1,000,000	8.0¢	$80,000	$3,600	3.6¢
1,100,000	7.6	83,600	3,400	3.4
1,200,000	7.25	87,000	2,700	2.7
1,300,000	6.9	89,700	1,300	1.3
1,400,000	6.5	91,000	500	.5
1,500,000	6.1	91,500	−300	−.3
1,600,000	5.7	91,200		

For example, Table 24–1 says you can sell 1,000,000 kilowatts at 8 cents per kilowatt. (To simplify the language, we will use the word kilowatt for kilowatt hours.) To increase sales to 1,100,000, you must reduce the price to 7.6 cents on all 1,100,000 kilowatts. Thus, your marginal revenue is your income from selling the extra 100,000 kilowatts (100,000 times 7.6 cents = $7,600) **minus** the .4 cent loss on each of the other 1,000,000 kilowatts (1,000,000 times .4 cents = $4,000). The marginal revenue from the extra 100,000 kilowatts is thus only $3,600 (not $7,600), as shown by column 4. To convert to marginal revenue per kilowatt, we simply divide the figures by 100,000, getting a marginal revenue per additional kilowatt of 3.6 cents (in column 5). And so it is all along the demand schedule. Marginal revenue is always less than price, and it even becomes negative when you must cut price to 5.7 cents in order to increase sales to 1,600,000 kilowatts.[6]

This relationship between price and marginal revenue is fundamental for every seller who is not in a perfectly competitive market. Whenever he faces a downward-sloping demand

curve, to sell more he must cut price both for the extra units he hopes to sell and for the units he could otherwise sell at a higher price. **His gain from cutting prices is never as big as it appears at first glance.**

Maximizing monopoly profits

Suppose your costs are as shown in Table 24–2; total cost for the outputs shown is in column 2 and marginal cost, converted to a per-kilowatt basis, in column 5. What price should you set to maximize your profits?

One answer is: Compare total cost and total revenue at each different level of output to find where the difference is biggest. As columns 2, 4, and 7 show, you should set price at 6.9 cents per kilowatt, which gives the maximum profit of $32,500.

Another way is: Equate marginal cost and marginal revenue. MC and MR are shown in columns 5 and 6. As long as the marginal revenue from selling an additional unit of output is greater than the marginal cost of producing the unit, obviously profit is increased by producing the extra unit. Up through 1,300,000 kilowatts, this is so; MC is below MR. But moving to 1,400,000 kilowatts adds more to cost than to revenue. The maximum-profit output rate is 1,300,000 kilowatts, which can be sold at a price of 6.9 cents per kilowatt.

Still a third way would be by comparing

[6]Marginal revenue is always zero when elasticity of demand is unity, positive when demand is elastic, and negative when demand is inelastic. Why? From this proposition it obviously follows that no perceptive monopolist will ever increase his output into the range where demand is inelastic, because in this range, cutting price to increase output would *reduce* his total revenue from sales.

marginal cost and marginal revenue per 100,000 units, instead of on a per-kilowatt basis.

Which way is better? Take your pick. All three give the same result.

Graphical analysis of profit maximization

The same calculation can be shown graphically. Figure 24–2 plots the relevant per-unit data. *DD* is the estimated market-demand curve. *MR* is the associated marginal-revenue-per-unit curve. *TUC* is the estimated total-unit-cost (average-cost) curve. And *MC* is the associated marginal-unit-cost curve. The solid part of each curve represents the data from Table 24–2; the dotted lines extend the curves hypothetically beyond the range of data we have. Note that, as was emphasized above, the *MR* curve is always below the downward-sloping demand curve.

Using the *MC* and *MR* curves, you can easily determine the maximum-profit position. It will be the output where marginal cost just equals marginal revenue. This is a little above 1,300,000 kilowatts, which you could sell at a

Figure 24–2
The monopolist maximizes profit by equating marginal cost and marginal revenue—here, at an output of about 1.32 million kilowatts to be sold at a price just under 7 cents.

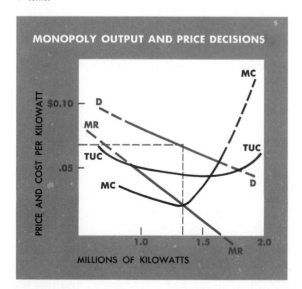

price of about 6.8 cents, reading off the demand curve at that output. If you want to compute your total profit from this graph, first take the distance between the selling price and the *TUC* curve, and then multiply this profit per unit by the total number of units sold. This would give a profit of roughly 2.5 cents per kilowatt on 1,320,000 kilowatts—about $33,000 at the best level.

Note that this is a slightly higher profit than the peak shown by Table 24–2. The graph, which gives you estimated data for **all** levels of output rather than just figures for each 100,000 kilowatts, tells you to produce an extra 20,000 kilowatts beyond the prescription of the table. The continuous curves on the graph give you a quick guide to the maximum-profit level of output and prices, which includes all levels of output, not just the ones shown in the table.

PURE MONOPOLY—EVALUATION

Monopoly leads to an inefficient allocation of resources from the consumers' point of view. The monopolist restricts output and raises price to maximize his profits, holding price above marginal cost. But Chapter 22 told us that *MC* = Price is the condition for achieving the socially most efficient allocation of productive resources to satisfy consumers' demands. Thus, monopoly price is too high, and too few resources are hired into the monopolized industry. Consumers get too little of the monopolized product. Conversely, too many resources are used in other sectors of the economy, since resources shut out from the monopolized industry must seek employment elsewhere. Thus, prices are too low and output is too large elsewhere.[7]

Are there limits, other than legal regulation, to how much the monopolist can exploit consumers? The answer is yes. He faces two limiting factors. First, even a monopolist faces a down-

---

[7]The difficulty in making a precise comparison with competitive price and output in such a case should be clear. Because the market is not large enough to support a large number of producers, each with a least-cost point as low as the large monopolist's, we cannot demonstrate rigorously that monopoly price is higher than competitive price would be.

Table 24–2

Hometown Electric Company—profit calculations

Kilowatts (1)	Total cost (2)	Price (3)	Total revenue (4)	Marginal unit cost (5)	Marginal unit revenue (6)	Total profit (7)
1,000,000	$50,000	8.0¢	$80,000	2.8¢	3.6¢	$30,000
1,100,000	52,800	7.6	83,600	2.4	3.4	30,800
1,200,000	55,200	7.25	87,000	2.0	2.7	31,800
1,300,000	57,200	6.9	89,700	3.0	1.3	32,500[a]
1,400,000	60,200	6.5	91,000	4.3	.5	30,800
1,500,000	64,500	6.1	91,500	5.9	−.3	27,000
1,600,000	70,400	5.7	91,200			20,800

[a]Maximum total profit.

ward-sloping demand curve, reflecting basically the fact that every product has some substitutes if its price becomes high enough. Second, if the monopolist does not have a government-bestowed, airtight franchise, the larger his profits become, the greater will be the incentive for new firms to enter, even though the cost may be high and the risks great. Thus, while an unregulated pure monopolist would be in a strong position to bleed the public through high prices, even he would face the increasing likelihood of competition and substitutes the further he exploited his position.

But American law is firmly set against unregulated monopolies. As we shall see in Chapter 27, the Sherman Act specifically forbids monopolizing and attempting to monopolize, and the prices and services of all public utilities are regulated. Nevertheless, especially in the recent inflationary period, nearly everyone complains that electricity, gas, and water (all regulated monopolies) have soared in price, while the big privately owned utility companies show big profits. Even government regulation may not be enough to satisfy consumers. How would you set public utility prices if you were in charge? (See Case 19, at the end of this chapter.)

Monopolies are also likely to be inefficient and slow to introduce technological change. Pure competition forces each firm to be efficient or perish. If new production techniques are developed, the laggard who fails to keep up with the leaders soon loses out in the market. Under monopoly, these pressures are weak. It does not necessarily follow that monopolies are inefficient or uninterested in progress. But many observers feel that the absence of strong competitive pressures does often lead to inefficiency and lessened interest in meeting consumer needs. We hear a flood of complaints that AT&T doesn't provide the newest telephone equipment as fast as it should, that the local utility is full of bureaucrats and red tape. But the utilities have their defenders too, and utility prices have risen much more slowly than the cost of living over the past century.

REVIEW

**Concepts
to remember**

Most of the major concepts used in this chapter were introduced in earlier chapters. But there are a few important new ones:

pure (simple) monopoly   oligopoly
monopolistic competition   decreasing-cost industry
price makers

**For analysis
and discussion**

1. Why do economists say that the basic *economic* criticism of monopolies is that they hold price above marginal cost?
2. If a monopoly is not making excessive (above-normal) profits, it is doing no serious harm to the public. True or false? Explain.
3. Why do many Americans distrust both monopolies and big business? Is there any significant economic distinction between the two?
4. The post office and your local water company are cases that are close to pure monopolies. How would you go about deciding whether they are doing an efficient job of serving the consumer at reasonable prices? Do you have a better way of evaluating the performance of such big partial monopolies as General Motors and Alcoa?
5. Chicago's George Stigler has argued that without government support, there would be few serious monopoly problems in America today. He cites public utilities, government support of unions, government-sponsored cartelization in agriculture, and local building codes that hold up construction costs. How sound is this argument? Can you cite counterexamples?

In recent years, the newspapers have been full of protests that public utility prices, especially for natural gas and electricity, are too high. Every public utility company request for higher rates in order (the company says) to meet higher costs is met by angry protests of aroused citizens' groups that the big privately-owned utility companies are unconscionably and brazenly bleeding the poor consumers. They argue that utility company profits are huge, and that the companies should be made to provide better service at lower costs, not poorer service at higher costs. The companies reply that their costs are rising rapidly, especially since the so-called energy crisis of 1974, and that their rate of return on investment has slid steadily in recent years, as regulatory commissions have persistently held rate increases behind rapidly rising costs. They plead that they are not responsible for the growing energy shortage—that, on the contrary, they have long warned of its imminence, and that higher energy prices are one important way to stimulate energy production and the search for new energy sources. (A few bold ones suggest that higher energy rates would also help induce consumers to use less energy.)

Suppose you are on your state regulatory commission and you must decide the right price for the Hometown Electric Company of this chapter to charge its customers. To make it easy, suppose you know that demand and costs are as shown in Table 24–2 and that they will stay put (that is, you can disregard the inflation problem). What price would you decree?[8]

---

[8] This case is, in effect, an extension of the analysis in the chapter. Most students will need the help of the suggestions at the end of the book to work out the analysis.

CHAPTER 25 MONOPOLISTIC COMPETITION AND ADVERTISING

Almost no one has a pure monopoly. But many firms have partial monopolies. The corner druggist has a partial monopoly in his neighborhood. He can charge several cents more a quart for ice cream than the big dairy stores downtown do. And he can get it—because he is so conveniently located for people in that neighborhood.

Coca-Cola has a partial monopoly. No one else can make a drink exactly like Coca-Cola without infringing the law, and for years "a Coke" has been the habitual drink of millions. But Pepsi-Cola, Royal Crown Cola, and a good many others look and taste enough like Coca-Cola to have shrunk Coca-Cola's share of the soft-drink market greatly in the last two decades. The Coca-Cola people will tell you they're in a highly competitive field.

As was emphasized above, a large part of the American economy is in the range between competition and monopoly—a substantial number of firms, each partly protected from competitors by trade names, location, tradition, and product quality, but far from perfectly protected; exposed to new competitors, but less exposed than the wheat farmer is. This is the area of "monopolistic competition." In it, each firm's product is "differentiated" from its competitors', but not enough to forestall active competition—on prices, selling costs, quality, or all three.

How much of the economy is in the monopolistic-competition category? The lines are hazy, but a fair, although very crude, answer would be, perhaps a third to a half of the private sector. This would include most wholesale and retail trade, real estate, and personal services (legal, medical, and the like);[1] a substantial sector of manufacturing (for example, apparel, lumber, and printing); and most of construction and trucking. By contrast, a large part of finance and manufacturing (for example, autos, steel, heavy electrical equipment, glass, and tobacco products) is oligopolistic, but these industries have an important monopolistic-competition element, and the oligopoly and monopolistic-competition areas overlap. It's a complex world, but "monopolistically competitive" describes a big part of it.

PRICES AND OUTPUT UNDER MONOPOLISTIC COMPETITION

The bases for product differentiation

The essence of monopolistic competition is a substantial number of firms, with each firm's product a little different from those of its competitors, but not very different. Each producer tries to differentiate his product and to increase the demand for it. To the extent that he succeeds, he can get away with charging a little more for his product.

Sometimes product differentiation involves actual physical differentiation. For example, Schlitz beer tastes different from Pabst; a Frigidaire is different from a GE refrigerator. But often, the differentiation hinges on the things that go along with the product—convenience of location, thick carpets on the floors, well-groomed waitresses, easy credit terms. Sometimes the differentiation is largely illusory—it exists in the mind of the customer but not in fact. If you can really tell the difference between the various high-test gasolines in your car on the road, you're better than most of the experts. Often, when you think you're getting special easy credit terms, you're paying just what is normal in the trade.

[1] Insofar as lawyers and doctors agree (collude) to set minimum fees, they are also behaving like oligopolists, in "cartels" (see Chapter 26).

Whatever the reason, whenever one seller is differentiated from others in the customer's mind, that seller is able to charge a price higher than his competitors' without losing all his market. **His demand curve slopes downward; it is not horizontal as under perfect competition.**

Short-run output and prices

The monopolistic competitor's problem is to set his price to maximize his profits. He has some freedom to raise price above what his competitors charge for similar products, but if he goes too far, his share of the market will drop sharply. The more successful he is in differentiating his product, the less elastic his demand curve will be. With an inelastic demand curve, he can boost his price without a corresponding drop in sales. But it's hard to convince customers that no substitute will do.

The firm's optimal price–output decision in the short run is hard to specify under these conditions. What any one firm's demand curve looks like is hard to estimate. For it depends **both** on what this firm does through selling expenses to change consumer demand **and** on what competitors do that also affects the demand for our firm's product. The demand curve we face will depend on consumers' total demand for the whole group of slightly differentiated products, and on our share of the total. Palmolive can increase and steepen the consumer demand curve for its soap either by getting customers away from Lux, Sweetheart, and the rest, or by somehow increasing total consumer demand for soap. If Palmolive succeeds in convincing people they should wash their faces more often, this may increase the demand for other soaps as much as for Palmolive. The trick is to be sure you get the big share of the benefit if you go in for this kind of advertising. Conversely, increased advertising by Lux may leave Palmolive with a lower, flatter demand curve, even though Palmolive soap is just as good as before. And if Palmolive's advertising steals Lux's customers, retaliation is almost certain. **Thus, it should be clear that under monopolistic competition (and oligopoly), the level and elasticity of any firm's demand curve depend both on what it does and on what the other firms in the industry do. It is** not possible to draw a stable, unambiguous demand curve for the individual firm's product.[2]

Presumably, any monopolistic competitor will increase his expenditures on advertising and other demand-creating activities as long as he estimates that this will add more to his income than to his costs. But under monopolistic competition, uncertainty about what competitors will do makes short-run output and price behavior very hard to predict. Thus, as with pure competition, we are on much safer ground when we look at long-run adjustments than when we try to predict short-run behavior.

Long-run adjustments
under monopolistic competition

In the long run, new firms enter industries and old firms leave. The search for profits goes on, with productive resources freely transferable throughout the economy. Monopolistic competition is like pure competition in that new firms can enter the industry. It is different in that new firms cannot exactly duplicate the product of existing firms. A new drugstore across the street from an established one might provide very close substitutes. But a new women's-wear store that sets up in competition with Saks Fifth

[2] *Given* the firm's cost and demand curves, the technical conditions for maximizing profit in the short run are identical with those for the monopolist described in Chapter 24. Thus, in the figure below, to maximize profits the firm will set price and output where marginal cost equals marginal revenue. This gives output O to be sold at price P as the optimal position. But when we say *given* the demand curve, we are assuming away a big piece of the problem, as is explained in the text.

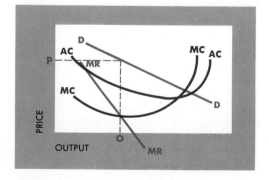

Avenue will have a tougher time. For one thing, drugs, candy, and ice cream are relatively standardized as compared with women's clothes. For another, few drugstores have the prestige of Saks.

But even though newcomers face problems, high profits in any monopolistically competitive field will draw new competitors. As more firms enter, the total market is divided up more ways (temporarily disregard the added costs of advertising). The demand curve for each established firm is moved downward (to the left). Profits per firm are reduced by this sharing of the market. Gradually, as more firms enter, profits tend to be eliminated, just as under pure competition. A new (unstable) equilibrium with excess profits eliminated may be achieved.

This sounds just like pure competition. But in this temporary equilibrium, under monopolistic competition each firm is restricting output a little to take advantage of its product differentiation. The demand curve is tangent to the cost curve to the left of the minimum point, and marginal cost is less than price. Each firm is thus operating below its optimal capacity and producing at a cost above the least-cost point on its optimal-cost curve. From a social point of view, too little of the product is being produced and sold, since price is being held above marginal cost.

This is illustrated in Figure 25–1. Case *A* pictures a typical firm making a profit. Its demand curve is above its total-unit-cost curve over a substantial range. The demand curve is downward-sloping, because this product is differentiated from its competitors.

What will happen? Competition will pick up. As new firms enter the market, the demand curve for each old firm moves downward as its share of the market falls. Eventually, the demand curve for a typical firm will be pushed down far enough to be just tangent to the cost curve. All profit will be eliminated, and there will be no further incentive for new firms and new resources to enter the industry. Neither will there be any incentive for existing firms to leave, unless some especially attractive opportunity opens up elsewhere in the economy. This is case *C* in Figure 25–1.

Case *B* shows firms making losses. Here, firms

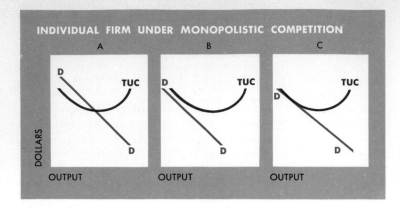

INDIVIDUAL FIRM UNDER MONOPOLISTIC COMPETITION

Figure 25-1
This figure shows a firm making money on left, losing money in middle, and in no-profit, temporary equilibrium on right.

will gradually drop out of the industry, and the demand for the products of each remaining firm will gradually rise. This process will continue until a no-loss situation has been reached, when there is no further incentive for resources to move out of the industry. Again, the firm will be in a case *C* equilibrium position.

Equilibrium unstable under competitive demand creation

But this is not the end of the story; the equilibrium is almost surely unstable. If you were running a drugstore and were in position *C* in Figure 25–1, what would you do? Maybe you'd just sit, but probably you'd try to figure a way to get more business. You might try improving your service to customers. Or putting in air conditioning. Or advertising more. All these attempts would cost you money. They might bring you more customers—that is, they might raise your demand curve—probably by drawing customers away from competitors. And they would upset the equilibrium situation shown in *C*. Such attempts to increase demand are apparent everywhere, keeping equilibrium (with the demand curve tangent to the cost curve) from being achieved or maintained.

Imagine a monopolistically competitive milk industry in a large city, with fifteen milk companies of about equal size and no advertising. Company *A* begins an advertising campaign. It gets more customers by luring a few away from each competitor. *A*'s costs are now higher, but its profits are up with the increased volume.

It doesn't take a business genius to predict the

reaction of the other companies. After expressing a few well-chosen words about the manager of Company *A*, they will get busy on their own advertising campaigns, designed to get their customers back and to lure new customers into the fold. If every company just matched *A*'s advertising, we might think of a new equilibrium situation, with each producer getting back just his original customers, but with every company's cost higher by the amount of the advertising and with price correspondingly higher to the consumer.

But having tasted success, *A* is not likely to sit quietly at the restored higher-price equilibrium. Nor are *B*, *C*, and *D*. Each will be busy contriving a new and better advertising campaign. If another round of advertising starts, or trading stamps with each gallon of milk are introduced, the result is likely to be similar. **Everybody's costs go up. Nobody ends up with many more customers, or with any more profits. And consumers end up with higher prices. Now they're buying advertising and trading stamps along with their milk—without having anything to say about whether they really want to buy them or not. And nobody can tell where the whole process will stop.**

Even in the happy event that the advertising campaign increases **total** spending on milk, a similar problem remains. Where do the additional funds for milk come from? Maybe the milk advertising stimulates total spending and raises the level of total spending and GNP, but as we saw in Part 2, this is unlikely. If total spending is unchanged, more spending on milk must mean less spending on something else. Producers in these other industries will fight back to regain sales. This will cause another reshuffling of demand, with still other industries (possibly including milk) losing customers to the newest advertisers.

QUALITY COMPETITION

Every housewife knows about quality competition. She knows which stores have the freshest vegetables, and where there are enough clerks to provide quick service. When you buy a suit, you go to a store you know will stand behind it if something goes wrong. These are examples of quality competition.

Alert businessmen are very much interested in knowing how much quality consumers want. They spend thousands of dollars on market research to find out whether consumers want softer seats in autos, cellophane around fresh vegetables, more carbonation in ginger ale, a new look on auto models each year. A shrewd businessman will improve the quality of his product whenever he believes customers will want the improvement enough to pay the extra cost—and something more. He will reduce product quality—for example, by putting his store on a cash-and-carry basis—whenever he believes that most customers would prefer to pay less and go without delivery service.

Some observers believe that quality competition is the pervasive form of competition in modern America, and that price competition is of secondary importance. There is evidence to support this point of view. Filling stations long ago learned that a clean rest room is more important to a touring family than a half cent off the price of gas. The first air-conditioned movie had an enormous quality advantage; now they're all air-conditioned.

Such is often the case in quality competition. Once one firm pioneers, others feel they must follow—or risk losing their customers as a consequence of holding out. If GM comes out with new auto models each year, Ford and Chrysler can't stick with last year's look without losing their share of the market. The result is higher "quality" all around, and higher prices to cover the higher costs involved in providing it,

whether or not all consumers want to pay for the changes. Then every manager starts scratching his head to figure out a new change that will give him at least a temporary jump on the field again.

Quality competition can be a perfectly valid type of competition, just as much as price competition. Sometimes people don't want the extra "quality" built into new products. But if there is active competition, there's always a competitor to provide a cheaper, "lower-quality" product—witness the success of discount stores and of compact cars.

ADVERTISING

Recently, social critics have leveled their big guns on advertising as big business's and Madison Avenue's main device for manipulating consumer demand. Certainly advertising plays a major role in many markets, and it deserves a further look.

In 1975, American business spent about $28 billion on advertising, and the total has risen persistently over the last two decades. In 1940, it was only $2 billion. Figure 25–2 summarizes these facts, and shows the composition of the total each year.

Twenty-eight billion dollars is a lot of money, and it represents a lot of persuasion. It would have bought a lot of other goods and services, had consumers had the cash to spend instead. On the other hand, it was only about 2 percent of the total gross national product.

Who were the big advertisers? Table 25–1 shows the top seven for 1974, plus a few others that may be of special interest. Strikingly, it was not the big-ticket companies like autos and appliances that spent a large proportion of their sales dollars on advertising; autos averaged only .7 of 1 percent, electrical appliances even less. Drugs, cosmetics, soap, packaged foods, and other such small consumer items spent the highest percentages; drugs and cosmetics averaged nearly 20 percent. P&G is by far the world's largest advertiser; AT&T, Exxon, and General Motors, the world's largest companies, lag far behind in their use of the sales dollar to persuade customers away from their competitors.

Advertising and information

The most important positive product of advertising is information. Each household maximizes its utility from the income it receives when it allocates that income among all the things it buys so as to equate the utility received from the last dollar spent on each good and service. To make this allocation most effectively, the household needs the best possible information on the alternatives available to it. Thus, insofar as advertising provides information on the alternative goods and services available (as to price, quality, or other relevant characteristics), it helps buyers maximize the utility obtainable from their incomes. In a rapidly changing world, it may be especially useful; if a firm comes along with a better product or lower price,

how else can consumers learn of them? Insofar as advertising provides erroneous information, of course, it has the opposite effect. If advertising simply alters consumer wants (for example, if it convinces people to prefer wine to beer), it is hard to say whether that advertising increases or decreases consumer satisfaction.

The information content of advertising varies widely. Many advertisers are more concerned with attracting consumers away from competitors and with building a "corporate image" than with providing information on which consumers can make more intelligent choices. Watch TV for a whole evening and record all the information you get that is of value in helping you decide among the products advertised. Read a copy of one of the big-selling magazines. Try the morning newspaper. How much useful information does each provide?

Figure 25–2 showed the relative importance of different kinds of advertising. Newspaper advertising, which contains a lot of useful information (grocery and clothing ads, want ads, and so on) makes up about 30 percent of the total. TV and magazine advertising, which are more com-

Figure 25–2
Advertising has grown rapidly and persistently, although more slowly in recession years. Newspapers get the biggest share, followed by TV and direct mail. (Source: *Advertising Age.*)

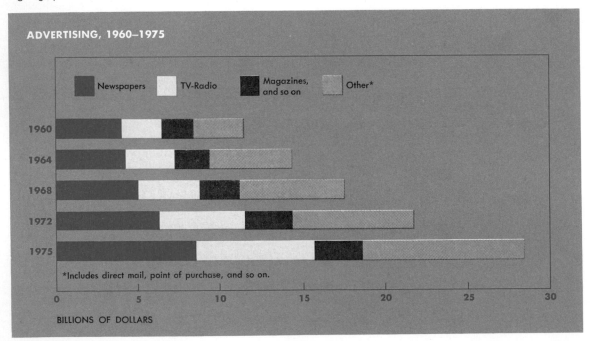

monly aimed at brand emphasis and prestige building, account for another third. The remainder is a wide variety of types, some of which (for example, in trade magazines) include significant customer information, while others have limited informational value.

While brand-loyalty advertising may make entry by new firms more difficult, as was suggested above, advertising can also serve as an important weapon for competitors who want to enter a market by stressing lower prices. For example, a much-quoted study by Chicago's Lee Benham found that the prices of eye examinations and glasses were much lower in states that permitted advertising by optometrists—$29.27 in Texas and the District of Columbia, against $49.87 in North Carolina and California.[3] Information on prices is essential to effective competition and consumer sovereignty. Without advertising, how would competitors wishing to tell about lower prices or new products get the information to potential consumers? The livelier competition may more than offset the costs of informative advertising, and some information economists argue that most advertising of goods that the consumer can evaluate easily (for instance, simple consumer products) does provide useful information. Moreover, such advertised

products are generally better buys than unadvertised brands; to provide misleading information on such products would be self-defeating for the advertiser.[4]

The use of resources in "demand creation"

As the preceding pages have emphasized, in a fully-employed economy, we must choose between alternative uses of resources. For our advertising dollar (paid in the price of the product), we get information on products, TV shows and sport events, billboards, the Metropolitan Opera, and a wide variety of other services, the worth of some of which might be disputed vigorously. Advertising expenditures make possible 15-cent daily papers, and a 75-cent *Newsweek* magazine. But with these services financed through advertising, little effective choice is left to the consumer as to how much of each he buys. The beer drinker pays for TV

[3]"The Effects of Advertising on the Price of Eyeglasses," *Journal of Law and Economics,* October 1972.

[4]For a nontechnical summary of these new developments, especially as presented by Phillip Nelson of SUNY (Binghamton), see *Business Week,* December 2, 1975, pp. 48–54.

Table 25–1
Advertising expenditures, 1974

Rank	Company and products	Amount (in millions)	Percent of sales
1	Procter & Gamble (soaps, etc.)	$325	7.3
2	General Motors (autos)	247	0.9
3	Sears, Roebuck (general retail)	220	1.7
4	General Foods (packaged foods)	189	6.9
5	Warner Lambert (drugs and cosmetics)	156	14.3
6	Bristol-Myers (drugs and cosmetics)	150	9.4
12	AT&T (communications)	97	0.4
21	General Electric (electrical products)	80	0.6
57	Alberto Culver (drugs and cosmetics)	40	26.2
66	Carter Wallace (drugs and cosmetics)	35	31.3
83	UAL (air travel)	25	1.1
88	Exxon (oil products)	24	0.1

Source: *Advertising Age,* August 18, 1975.

westerns even though he never watches TV. Still, almost everyone buys many advertised products and enjoys some of the fruits of advertising. Most people benefit from cheap newspapers and other news sources largely financed by advertising. Perhaps aside from cases of misleading advertising, everything pretty much evens out and consumers get just about the information and "entertainment" with their advertising dollars they would have bought anyway. But you may—understandably—have your doubts.

How much does advertising actually increase demand for advertised products? As was emphasized above, a large part of the total is counteradvertising, where the companies involved largely just offset each other's advertising. When TWA takes full-page newspaper ads to extoll the virtues of its 747 coach lounges, it is trying to increase the demand for its product by convincing (1) more people to fly, and (2) those who do fly to fly TWA instead of United or American. But United's and American's full-page ads about their 747s appear in the same papers. A 747 is pretty much the same airplane, whichever of the three big companies flies it. It gets there as fast with one as the other; prices are the same, set by government regulation; and it's hard to make your coach lounge much plusher than your competitors'. Demand may not be changed much, but in the long run, air fares have to be enough higher to pay for the advertising. Do the ads increase total air travel? Possibly so, especially if they provide useful information on fares and service to possible customers. But then there's the question of offsetting counteradvertising designed to lure people's dollars into other industries. Counteradvertising is everywhere in today's economy—but don't forget the preceding section on information.

Last, does advertising help everyone by increasing *total* spending and thereby providing more jobs and more total gross national product? The answer, if the economy's resources are already fully employed, is obviously no. If there are unemployed resources (for example, in a recession), more advertising might increase aggregate demand and consequently the amount of goods produced. But even if it could, monetary and fiscal policy, as you saw in Part 2, are more powerful ways to increase demand, and they do not use up resources in the process.[5]

Do advertisers manipulate consumer wants?

Radical critics of today's scene, and some not so radical, argue that the American consumer has little real freedom of choice—that his "wants" are created and manipulated by big business and Madison Avenue, mainly through advertising. Businesses decide what will make the largest profits, and convince consumers to "want" that. To some extent, the problem is dishonest and misleading advertising; there has always been a fair amount of this, although such advertising is specifically forbidden by law. But more fundamentally, advertising and TV mold our very style of life—we learn to want what the TV dangles before us. The best-known critic along these lines is Harvard's J.K. Galbraith, in his best-selling *The New Industrial State.*

This attack challenges the foundation of private-enterprise economics. If consumers merely respond to what businesses tell them to want, the whole intellectual case for an individualistic consumer-directed economy falls.

Stated in the extreme form above, this argument is obviously unacceptable. Something under 2 percent of the total gross national product hardly seems adequate to govern the entire pattern of "wants" of every consumer in America. Moreover, there is a long history of business firms gone broke trying to convince consumers through advertising and other selling campaigns to buy products that the consumers stubbornly refuse to purchase. The classic case is Ford's Edsel in the 1950s, which flopped colossally in spite of an enormous advertising campaign. Less than a dozen of the fifty best-known automobile brands of the past half century are still with us, in spite of the best advertising assistance Detroit and Madison Avenue have been able to provide over the years. Much-advertised Camel, Chesterfield, and Lucky Strike held 42 percent of the cigarette market in 1956, only 18 percent in 1966, and even less in 1976. The history of

---

[5] It is doubtful that advertising has much influence on total consumer spending in the economy, but the evidence is not conclusive.

American business is littered with well-advertised products that just didn't sell.

On the other hand, it would be ridiculous to argue that advertising has no effect on how consumers spend their incomes. TV is indeed pervasive in American life, and it is full of "beautiful people" and beautiful things to want. Just how far advertising does influence the expenditure pattern of the American public is a much-argued issue. Alas, there is no evidence that can give a simple, clear-cut answer. Look back at Table 5–1, which summarized what consumers buy, and make your own judgment on how much of it is dominated by the kinds of advertising you see around you.

Finally, whatever your answer, there's a basic issue involved as to the meaning of truly "independent" consumer wants. Galbraith's argument suggests that we have a basic set of wants that are good, while wants influenced by advertising are suspect and incompatible with maximization of consumer satisfaction. But beyond the most basic wants for food and shelter, all our wants are heavily conditioned by our environments. Suppose I prefer Chopin and champagne, while you choose beer and baseball. Does the fact that my tastes were developed largely independent of advertising while yours were heavily influenced by advertising make yours somehow less valid than mine?

Conclusion

With advertising, as with almost everything else, the principle of marginalism applies. It would be surprising indeed if we were to come to the conclusion that advertising is all bad or all good, that we should completely eliminate advertising or increase it to some very large amount. From a social point of view, the decision as to whether we want more or less advertising is a marginal one. We need to weigh the gains from the last dollar spent on advertising against alternative possibilities for that dollar devoted to other uses. Clearly, some advertising has high social value—for example, if it tells consumers about a new, highly desirable product. Conversely, misleading advertising has a negative marginal value. And the marginal value of the last dollar spent on some types of advertising may seem to you very low, particularly when the effect is simply to offset someone else's advertising. As to how much advertising we ought to have in our society, marginalism is the principle to follow.

REVIEW

Concepts to remember

Many of the major concepts used in this chapter were introduced in earlier chapters. But there are important new ones, too:

product differentiation	demand creation
quality competition	unstable equilibrium

For analysis and discussion

1. Explain why equilibrium in a monopolistically competitive industry is likely to be unstable.
2. Is the absence of high profits in an industry satisfactory evidence that monopolistic competition is not injuring consumers of the product concerned? Explain your answer to a noneconomist.
3. Advertising by lawyers and doctors has long been forbidden as unethical by local

bar associations and the American Medical Association. Recently, however, some young lawyers and doctors have challenged this tradition, openly advertising the prices they charge for standard services. Should such advertising be supported by consumers? What are the arguments on both sides?

4. "As long as there is relatively free entry to an industry, I can't get worried about the dangers of monopoly in that industry." Do you agree or disagree? Explain.

5. Some critics argue that we now have "producers sovereignty" rather than "consumer sovereignty," because advertising determines what we think we want. Marshal the evidence for and against this argument.

6. "If we had adequate 'Truth-in-Advertising' legislation, I wouldn't worry about excessive advertising or manipulation of consumer wants by Madison Avenue." Do you agree or disagree?

7. As a consumer, would you like to see aggressive price competition among sellers of all the products you buy? Under such competition, would you get the same breadth of display, return privileges, and charge-account arrangements now provided by major department stores?

8. Do you get your money's worth out of the advertising for which you pay? If not, what specific steps would you propose to improve the situation?

Ralph Nader and other consumer advocates urge a wide range of new measures to protect consumers in the marketplace. Some advocate direct government regulation of product quality. Others favor stronger laws controlling advertising. Still others believe that present legislation is generally adequate but that we need a more strongly consumer-oriented government agency to enforce the laws protecting consumers.

Present law, reaching back to the Federal Trade Commission Act of 1914 and broadened several times since, specifically forbids "dishonest or misleading" advertising and directs the FTC to enforce the law, to protect both consumers and other sellers from unfair competition. "Truth in lending," "truth in packaging," and several Food and Drug Acts have extended consumer protection beyond the original FTC Act. Over the years, the FTC has undertaken many thousands of investigations to halt deceptive advertising, most of which have ended in informal agreements that the advertiser will halt the challenged behavior.

Recently, one consumer protection group proposed that Congress and/or all state legislatures pass legislation providing that:

1. No advertising be permitted that does not provide information useful to consumers.

2. No firm be permitted to spend on advertising more than 10 percent of its income from sales in the preceding year.

3. No firm be permitted to engage in dishonest or misleading advertising, and that any firm doing so be liable to triple damages to all injured consumers through class-action suits, brought by either consumers or the government.

4. The Federal Trade Commission, or appropriate state agencies, be enpowered to enforce these rules.

Would you recommend that your representatives vote for the proposed legislation?

CHAPTER 26 OLIGOPOLY, COLLUSION, and market power

Three companies—General Motors, Ford, and Chrysler—make nearly all the automobiles produced in the United States. Over 90 percent of all flat glass and electric light bulbs are produced by the top four companies in those industries. In dozens of major industries, from half to three-fourths of the total business is done by only a few firms. These are the oligopolies—industries in which a few firms dominate, even though there may be many small firms that generally follow the leaders, or take what is left over. Figure 26–1 summarizes the market domination by the leading four firms in a number of major industries.

These examples are on a national scale. The number of oligopolists in local markets is far larger. Building materials (such as cement and bricks) are produced by hundreds of different firms scattered all over the country; but in any one local market, production is usually concentrated in one or a few firms. The more important transportation costs are and the harder it is for customers to shop around, the more likely local oligopolies are to be found.

Economists consider "concentration ratios" (the percentage of total sales concentrated in the largest four, or sometimes eight, firms) an important indication of likely market performance. But it is important to recognize that this is only one measure of the degree of monopoly power

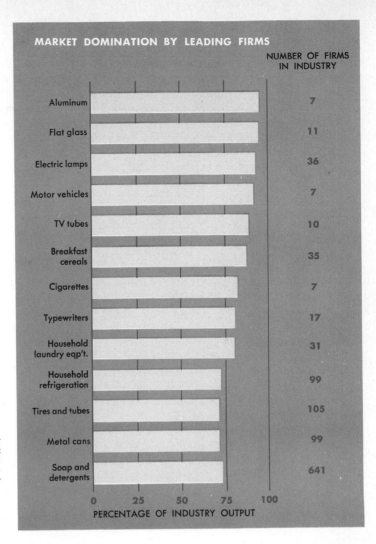

MARKET DOMINATION BY LEADING FIRMS

NUMBER OF FIRMS IN INDUSTRY

Industry	Number of firms
Aluminum	7
Flat glass	11
Electric lamps	36
Motor vehicles	7
TV tubes	10
Breakfast cereals	35
Cigarettes	7
Typewriters	17
Household laundry eqp't.	31
Household refrigeration	99
Tires and tubes	105
Metal cans	99
Soap and detergents	641

PERCENTAGE OF INDUSTRY OUTPUT

Figure 26-1
The largest four firms dominate the industry's output in some leading U.S. industries. The total number of firms varies greatly from industry to industry. (Source: U.S. Department of Commerce; data are for 1970.)

held by the leading firms. Probable price–output behavior may be quite different, for example, in two industries with the same concentration ratio of 80 percent, if in one case the biggest firm has 60 percent of the market while in the other it has only 25. Similarly, the total number of firms in the industry outside the leaders may make a difference. The soap and match industries have similar four-firm concentration ratios, with the additional industry characteristics shown in the following table. Which would you say is more concentrated? In general, economists suspect that monopoly-like results are more likely in highly concentrated industries. But this measure provides only a rough presumption.

	Soap	Matches
Total number of firms	267	14
Percentage of total industry sales by:		
Largest 4 firms	85	74
Largest 8 firms	89	93
Largest 20 firms	95	100

The degree of concentration in different industries has varied substantially over the years. But some industries, with the characteristics noted below, have been dominated persistently by a few large firms, and overall data on concentration show a surprisingly stable pattern for a dynamically changing economy.

International data on concentration are also illuminating. Table 26–1 compares concentration ratios for leading industries in five industrialized nations. Overall, the patterns are strikingly similar, which suggests common underlying factors in the industries concerned. But here again, there are numerous cases that don't fit the general pattern.

These observations stress the size of firms relative to their markets. But some observers are more concerned with absolute size. Exxon is the biggest industrial corporation in the world, with $33 billion of assets and $45 billion of sales in 1975. But the gasoline industry is not highly concentrated in the United States, and Exxon has only a modest 7 percent of the retail gasoline market; the biggest four firms accounted for only 30 percent of total sales. Yet Exxon's sales and assets made it bigger than many of the world's nations. In fact, it, like such other corporate giants as GM and GE, produces many products, in many different industries. Vast power, economic and political, must go with such size, many critics contend—power over jobs, wages, products, prices, and governments at home and abroad.

Clearly, power over market output and prices depends primarily on size relative to that market; a small firm may have great monopoly power in a tiny market, while Exxon's is limited by competition. And as economists we shall be mainly concerned with market power in this chapter. But in the following chapters, we shall turn to nonmarket powers of giant corporations, which may be of greater concern to many Americans than is the danger of monopoly prices and output.

THE FOUNDATIONS OF OLIGOPOLY

At bottom, most oligopolies rest on one or both of two factors: (1) the necessity of large-scale production (relative to the size of the market) for low-cost output, and (2) barriers against the entry of new firms into the industry.

If total market demand will support only a few firms of optimum size, clearly the competitive struggle will tend to make a few big firms the winners. This situation rests fundamentally on the economies of large-scale production—on modern technology. In each of the industries in Figure 26–1, large-scale production is essential to obtain low unit costs.

How do these big firms maintain their positions, once attained? As we shall see presently, aggressive price competition is unlikely. Instead,

---

Table 26–1

Concentration ratios in five nations[a]

	U.S.	U.K.	Canada	France	Japan
Primary aluminum	100	43	100	100	100
Autos	98	74	100	79	76
Cigarettes	82	74	85	100	
Trucks	77	86	100	78	
Matches	74	86	98	100	74
Steel ingots	64	32	81	40	52
Flour	40	46	35	12	53
Petroleum refining	32	93	79	72	41
Beer	27	11	49	25	98
Cement	31	89	100	52	48
Cotton textiles	18	4	60		7

[a] Ratios are for four firms in the United States, three firms in other nations. Figures show percent of total sales accounted for by leading firms. Data vary between 1950 and 1960 for different nations, but have apparently changed little since then.

Source: J. Bain, *International Differences in Industrial Structure* (New Haven, Conn.: Yale University Press, 1966), pp. 67–106.

the oligopolist often tries to increase his market share and his profits by improving his product, by demand-creating activities, and by setting up barriers against the intrusion of new competitors. Patents, an established marketing organization, or control over raw materials may be the key to keeping out newcomers. The bases for oligopoly power are similar to those for other monopolies indicated in Chapter 24. But dominant firms in an oligopoly are seldom safe from potential competition. It is the rare oligopoly that escapes for long the pressures of competition from new firms and new products. Even patents, large size, and technological dominance provide only partial and temporary insulation.

OLIGOPOLY POWER, PRICES, AND PROFITS

Analytically, the crucial thing about an oligopoly is the small number of sellers, which gives each one substantial market power and makes it imperative for each to weigh carefully the reactions of the others to its own price, production, and sales policy. Given the wide range of possible reactions of competitors in most oligopolistic markets, it is difficult to predict precisely what these reactions will be, and therefore difficult for the oligopolist to determine what price–production levels will give him the largest profits. We have, therefore, no simple oligopoly theory to tell us reliably just what prices and output will be in equilibrium. The outcome will be different depending on how each businessman assesses the likely reactions of his competitors to his own policies.

While many reaction patterns are possible, history suggests some central tendencies in oligopoly price–production decisions. In oligopoly. one attractive alternative for the rivals is collectively to establish the profit-maximizing price for the industry as a whole, and then divide up the market and profits among themselves. The law forbids collusion of this sort, so oligopolists must make secret agreements or rely on the willingness of all to "go along" with avoiding price competition. But in such a situation, it will also generally be to the self-interest of each individual producer to get a bigger share of the market for himself, which he might hope to do by cut-

ting prices and luring away some of his competitors' customers. On the other hand, if he cuts price, there is always the danger that competitors will meet the price cut, and the only result will be a lower price and lower profits for all the oligopolists.

Oligopoly theory:
avoidance of aggressive price competition

Suppose that you are the manager of a local brick factory, and that you have two competitors in the area. You are making a reasonable profit, and so are your competitors. Each of you sets the price at which he sells. You are price makers. Each of you knows he could make a larger profit if he could manage to increase his share of the market, because each of you is operating below capacity. Will you cut your price to lure customers away from your competition?

Maybe you will. But you'd better think twice before you try it. Your competitors will almost surely retaliate by meeting your price cut. Maybe they'll undercut you if you stir them up by disturbing the stability of the market. Your price advantage can't last more than a day or two before they know about it, and you can't get very rich in that length of time. Heaven only knows just what will happen if you start a local price war, but three things look reasonably sure: All three of you will end up with lower prices; none of you will have lured many customers away from the others; and everyone's profits will have taken a beating. In the end, you might just glower at each other in the local Rotary Club meetings, but you'd probably get together and agree to put prices back to some reasonable level near where you started.

This is only a small-scale, hypothetical example. But the questions are the same ones that the presidents of huge corporations ask when they consider cutting prices in oligopolistic markets in steel, automobiles, cigarettes. With only a few firms in the industry, the forces toward letting well enough alone are strong. Price reductions are likely to come only to meet a competitor's cut or under severe pressures—in recessions, for example. When firms do cut, they usually do so in the expectation that their cut will be met by rivals. Thus, the cut is made with the intention of moving the whole industry price scale to a lower level, in the hope of stimulating overall demand for the industry's product. In many cases, one major firm in an oligopolistic industry acts as a "price leader" in this way, although there may be no formal agreement.

Such a "live-and-let-live" policy makes sense to most producers. It leaves room for each firm to try quality and advertising competition to increase its share of the market. It leaves room for some price shading when times are hard or when one firm is losing out badly in the market. But aggressive price competition will probably blow the situation wide open. Cigarettes are a good example: The leading firms almost never compete on prices, but spend huge sums on advertising and other demand-creating activities.

Oligopoly theory: the kinked demand curve

Economic theory helps present the price problem that faces the oligopolist. Go back to the brickworks case above. The current price is 20 cents a brick, and you are selling 10,000 bricks per week. As you sit in your office, you try to imagine what your demand curve looks like, as a basis for deciding whether to change your price. Chances are you will decide it is something like Figure 26–2, a "kinked" demand curve.

It says that if you raise your price and the others don't follow, your sales will fall off sharply because your customers will desert you; your demand curve looks highly elastic if you raise your price above 20 cents. On the other hand, if you cut the price, you can be almost sure your rivals will follow to avoid losing customers to you. Thus, a lower price may increase sales a little, because the market will take some more bricks at a lower price; but there's little reason to suppose you'll get a bigger share of the market away from your competitors. Your demand curve looks very inelastic if you cut your price below 20 cents. This situation puts a high premium on keeping the price where it is, just as the common-sense reasoning above suggested.

Note now the critical assumptions. The first is that if you **raise** price, your rivals **will not** follow. It is this assumption that underlies the highly elastic curve to the left of the "corner" *P*. If, by

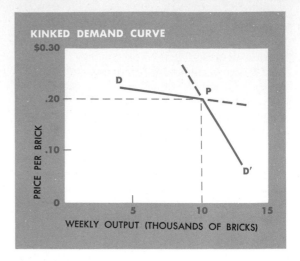

Figure 26–2
Kinked demand curve suggests that you will lose total revenue if you either raise or lower price. Demand is elastic above 20 cents, inelastic below it.

contrast, you are a price leader and your rivals will follow your increase, the *DP* section of the curve will be much less elastic and will probably just extend directly on up from *D'P*, as in the dashed line. This is because you won't lose share of the market to the others; the only loss in sales volume comes because fewer bricks will be bought at the higher price.

The second crucial assumption is that if you **cut** price, the others **will also** cut. If they do not, then *D'P* of your demand curve will probably be highly elastic, as your rivals' customers switch to you. Then the "corner" in the demand curve would again vanish and your demand curve will just be an extension of *DP*. This would be a wonderful situation for you, but it is not very likely unless you can hide your price cuts from your rivals. And that's difficult in an oligopoly.[1]

In summary, then, the kinked demand curve

---

[1]Where the demand curve is kinked, the corresponding marginal-revenue curve has a break, or discontinuity. The following graph shows the demand and marginal-revenue curves from Figure 26–2. Note that given this marginal-revenue curve, a marginal-cost curve (*MC*) could move up or down considerably without logically leading the firm to change its price. This fact may further explain the observed oligopoly tendency toward price stability, even when costs

exists because you assume a **different** reaction from your competitors when you raise and when you lower your price. If you are the recognized price leader, there will be no kink, and you are merely moving price up or down along the demand curve for the whole industry. If you are so little that nobody reacts to your price changes, there is also no kink—but this case is really a violation of the oligopoly situation, because the essence of oligopoly is so few competitors that each must be concerned with the others' reactions. Last, your freedom to move price without immediately risking rivals' reactions is larger the more differentiated your product is.[2]

change substantially. (The lower half of the *MR* curve need not be negative, although of course it will be if *D'P* shows inelastic demand.)

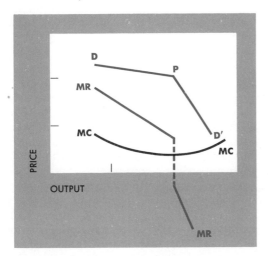

[2]Another approach to understanding oligopoly behavior is through "game theory." This likens competing oligopolists to participants in a game—a contest for market share and profits. In an oligopoly of, say, five leading firms, there are many possibilities of partial collusion and different forms of competition. If you change your price, will all the others react together? May they "gang up" on you? If you have been the price leader, will they follow you this time? Game theory systematically explores the outcomes of different strategies and coalitions. But the combinations and permutations of different assumptions mount rapidly, so unfortunately, game theory gives no simple predictions of what profit-seeking oligopolists will do, although it helps to suggest some likely limiting cases.

Oligopoly theory: cartels

If oligopolists collude, they can set price and total output to maximize profits for the industry as a whole, and then divide up the profit by sharing the market. Such a price-fixing market-sharing arrangement is called a "cartel."

This practice is illegal in the United States. But analyzing a formal cartel can suggest the consequences of today's informal cartel-like price-stabilization arrangements. And the line between not competing aggressively and agreeing to stabilize price is nebulous. In the brickworks example above, there was no open collusion on prices, but the result was much the same as if there had been. Moreover, formal cartels are a dominant form of market organization in many European countries, and are widely used in international trade. Witness the famous OPEC oil cartel of Middle East and other producers to dramatically raise oil prices in the 1970s.

Assume a hypothetical furnace industry, in which there are only ten firms. What are the long-run results of a cartel in the industry, if the ten firms agree to "stabilize" prices and to share the market equally?

In effect, the firms will act like one pure monopoly in setting price and then divide up the business and profits.[3] Assume that the competitive price for furnaces would be $400, the lowest point on the total-unit-cost curve of each producer. At $400, consumers would buy 30,000 furnaces monthly. But by restricting output, the ten firms can make substantial profits. So they agree to raise the price to $500, at which level 20,000 furnaces can be sold monthly, this price being estimated to maximize profits for the group as a whole. Then each firm sells only 2,000 furnaces monthly, but at the higher price it reaps a profit of about $75 per furnace (the difference between the $500 price and the $425 total unit cost at the 2,000 output level). The situation is pictured in Figure 26–3.

[3]Logically, the cartel would maximize its profits by setting price and output where marginal cost equals marginal revenue for the industry as a whole. See Figure 24–2.

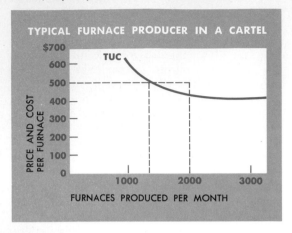

Figure 26-3
At the cartel price of $500, a firm first makes $75 profit per furnace. As more firms enter, each firm's market share and profit diminish.

Price is now higher than the competitive level; output is lower; use of labor and raw materials is lower; and production is less "efficient." Consumers pay more; price is well above marginal cost. If the furnace makers can keep new competitors out, they're sitting pretty.

But suppose new firms can't be kept out. Oligopoly profits lure them in. The entry of new firms will divide up the same total sales among more and more firms. Thus, profits are eliminated as new firms enter, not by price reduction but by rising unit costs as each firm reduces its output to a less and less efficient level. New firms will continue to enter, cutting down the market available to each, until finally the cost per unit has risen to equal the cartel price of $500 at an output of 1,333 for each of fifteen firms.

This is shown in Figure 26-3. The original cartel members agreed to stabilize the price at $500, so each producer could sell 2,000 furnaces monthly and make $75 per furnace. But as more firms enter, building similar plants, the sales allotted to each producer fall until with fifteen producers, each can sell only 1,333 furnaces monthly and rising costs have eliminated profits.

Consider the results. Producers are no better off than under competition; consumers suffer all the results of monopoly, with price still up at

$500 and total output restricted to 20,000 furnaces; and society bears the loss of extensive "overinvestment" in the industry, because far more productive facilities have been built than are required. **Such a cartel arrangement with free entry, it might thus be argued, is not a halfway point between competition and monopoly, but rather an arrangement that combines the worst characteristics of each and the benefits of neither.**

Obviously, this fifteen-firm "equilibrium" would be highly unstable. Each producer sees a big potential gain from cutting his price, and he has little inducement to remain in the agreement, since profits have been eliminated. Cartels without effective restrictions on entry seldom last long.

Nations, as well as private sellers, may form cartels. In 1973, the OPEC (Organization of Petroleum Exporting Countries) oil cartel, made up of the major Middle East and other oil exporters, shocked the world by raising the price of oil from about $2.50 to over $10 per barrel. OPEC included most of the world's major oil producers except for the United States, Canada, and the USSR. The short-run elasticity of demand for oil was, as the cartel hoped, inelastic. Consumption dropped somewhat as nations and private users tried to economize on the use of oil and shift to alternative energy sources, but these responses to higher prices took time, and OPEC profits soared. By 1975, however, the rate of growth in world oil consumption had dropped sharply, from about 4 percent annually to near zero, and output of both oil and other energy sources increased in other nations. To keep prices from falling, the OPEC countries had to reduce their production sharply, and strains began to develop among the cartel nations as to how these cutbacks were to be shared.

On the basis of the cartel theory above, how long would you expect the OPEC cartel to be able to maintain very high oil prices? On what factors does your answer depend? (*Hints:* Will demand be more or less elastic in the long run? How fast will new oil sources be developed—in Alaska, the North Sea fields, Indonesia, U.S. offshore waters? What alternative energy sources—coal, shale, natural gas, nuclear power, solar power, and so on—become economically and technologically feasible at the new higher price for oil?)[4]

Oligopoly theory: restrictions on entry

The preceding section points up the importance of restrictions on entry of new firms in determining the price–output performance of an oligopolistic industry. If the original ten furnace producers above had had some effective way of keeping new firms out of the industry, their cartel would have worked out very nicely for them in terms of continuing profits—although there would always be the danger that one firm would become dissatisfied and cut prices to increase its share of market and profits. If OPEC had controlled all the world's energy sources, it would have had a secure position. But once outsiders are free to enter, profits are eroded for everyone as more firms enter, and the pressure toward price cutting becomes almost irresistible.

Thus, oligopolists try hard to insulate themselves against new competitors, by product differentiation, by patents, by developing secret production know-how, by bringing out new products that are hard to reproduce. And in many cases they are helped by modern technology and the high cost of entering such businesses. Where large-scale investment and production are required for efficient output, it's hard for newcomers to break in.

Recent research confirms that barriers to entry do protect above-average profits, at least temporarily. When industries are classified by the barriers they have against new entrants, the average rate of return is highest for those with the highest entry barriers.[5] The drug industry's continued success in marketing brand-name prescription drugs at prices two to ten times as high as the same drugs sold under their generic names is a notable case in point. For example, Pfizer Terramycin in 1973 sold at wholesale for $20.48 per 100 capsules, while as oxytetracycline (its generic name), the same drug sold for $1.95 per 100 capsules; Squibb's Pentids sold for $10.04 per 100 tablets, but as penicillin G for only $1.45. The rate of return on investment in the ethical-drug industry has persistently been among the highest.[6]

Try one last check on oligopoly theory. Suppose the ten barbers in Hometown are pricing haircuts at $3 and making what seems to them a very bad living. So they get together and agree to raise the price of haircuts to $4. Predict the results of this cartel-type agreement—for barbers and for customers. *Hints:* What is the elasticity of demand for haircuts? What will happen to the number of barbers in Hometown?

RESEARCH, DEVELOPMENT, AND INNOVATION

Oligopoly gets poor marks on the criterion of efficiency in the allocation of resources. But there is another important kind of efficiency—efficiency in using resources to promote economic progress.

The general presumption of static economic theory is against monopoly on this score as well. The pressure of competition is the greatest prod to progress, Adam Smith and his successors tell us. The more protected from competition any businessman is, the less likely he is to work hard at producing new and better products.

But there is another side to the issue. Progress in the modern economy depends heavily on research and development spending. And only big firms have the resources to afford large R&D expenditures. Thus, as a practical matter, only with oligopolistic market structures are we likely to get the heavy R&D spending on which modern industrial progress depends.

What do the facts show? Table 26–2 details R&D done in industry in 1974, financed by both federal and industrial funds. Of all industrial R&D expenditures, less than 5 percent was in industries dominated by small firms—for example, textiles and construction. Conversely, the great bulk of R&D is done by big firms, and by

[4] This states only part of the complex issues involved in the OPEC cartel. See also Case 36.

[5] See H.M. Mann, "Barriers to Entry and Long-Run Profitability," *Antitrust Bulletin,* Winter 1969; and J. Bain, *Barriers to New Competition* (Cambridge, Mass.: Harvard University Press, 1956).

[6] See "Hearings before the Senate Monopoly Subcommittee," 1973.

DO PARTIAL MONOPOLISTS
MAXIMIZE PROFITS?

Do partial monopolists, operating with various degrees of protection from market competition under monopolistic competition and oligopoly, produce efficiently and maximize their profits? If businessmen in highly competitive industries don't make a good stab at this behavior, competition will remove them from the scene in due time. With the monopolist, and partial monopolist, we can't count so fully on competition to exert this pressure.

There are several reasons why a businessman may not be maximizing profits at any time:

1. It's the long run that matters, and he may be willing to absorb a short-run loss for long-run gain.

2. It takes time to adjust to changes in demand, costs, and the like.

3. Businessmen never know what costs and demand in the future will be. They can only estimate, and often they're wrong.

4. Sometimes managers just aren't very efficient. They don't do a very good job of either minimizing costs or increasing revenues.

5. Unusually large profits may be an invitation to new competitors, lured by the hope of winning some customers away. Thus, the partial monopolist may think twice before reaching for more profits that may invite more competition.

6. Unusually large profits may bring unwanted scrutiny from the government's antitrust officials.

7. Historians point to many firms that have grown big as a result of the promoters' and managers' desire for bigness per se. They focus on growth in total sales and share of market, rather than on profits per se.

8. Some managements engage in "business statesmanship." They concentrate on improving the community and on social responsibilities. These things cost money and may or may not help long-run profits.

9. Last, the modern hired manager (as distinct from the owner-operator) may have important objectives in addition to profits—the desire to get along well with others in the company; to avoid ulcer-producing arguments with the union; to avoid looking foolish by being wrong when he takes risks. Management has more freedom to follow these other motives if it is sheltered from vigorous competition. (There is some evidence that owner-controlled firms do achieve a higher rate of return on investment than do similar management-controlled firms. Between 1952 and 1963, owner-controlled firms earned a 12.3 percent rate of return on investment as against 7.3 percent for management-controlled firms.)*

There are clearly wide differences among firms on all these scores. We assume in this chapter that, by and large, making profits is a dominant goal for partial monopolists. But in using profit-maximizing models, don't forget these other possible motives and problems.

*R.J. Monsen, J. Chin, and D. Cooley, "The Effect of Separation of Ownership and Control on the Performance of Large Firms," *Quarterly Journal of Economics*, August 1968, p. 441.

the same token in oligopolistic industries—for example, aerospace, chemicals, and electrical equipment, although much of this research is ultimately financed by government funds. Only in agriculture among the industries approaching pure competition is there large R&D spending, and this is financed almost entirely by the government and conducted largely in the universities, not shown in Table 26–2.

But the picture is more complex. Among the large firms that do have research and development organizations, the medium-large ones spend as large a fraction of their sales dollars on research as do the huge ones. Although modern industrial research is heavily concentrated in oligopolistic industries, increasing firm size above a certain level doesn't seem to increase the relative stress on research.

Table 26–2

Industrial research and development spending, 1974[a]

Industry	R&D spending (in billions)	Percentage of all R&D	Federal funds as percentage of total
Aircraft and missiles	$5.8	27.2%	82.1%
Electrical equipment	5.4	25.4	51.7
Chemicals	2.1	10.0	10.1
Machinery	2.1	10.0	16.7
Autos, transport equipment	2.1	10.0	15.5
Instruments	.8	3.8	19.7
Petroleum and extraction	.5	2.4	4.0
Food products	.3	1.4	1.0
Rubber products	.3	1.4	10.4
All other[b]	1.9	8.4	N.A.
Total	$21.3	100.0%	42.5%

[a]Estimates by National Science Foundation. This series excludes certain commercial-product-development activities sometimes included in R&D estimates.
[b]Includes mining, construction, transportation, public utilities, agriculture, and others.

Whose research contributes the most to innovation and economic progress? We have few clear measures of success. Researchers have looked especially at three measures—patents received, important innovations achieved, and the rate of increase in productivity.

A few giants dominate the total number of patents awarded (Bell Labs, GE, and du Pont), but in general, big firms receive patents only in proportion to their larger expenditures on research. If anything, the middle-sized firms appear to have done a shade better in relation to their research spending, except for the few research giants.

A more important, but more difficult, measure is the number of important innovations actually produced by different-sized companies. Here, Penn's Edwin Mansfield has studied three major industries intensively. He finds that in petroleum refining and coal mining, the larger firms have produced a larger proportion of the important innovations than their share in industry sales. But in steel, the reverse was true. He speculates on the basis of his evidence that large, but not giant-sized, companies are the most promising sources of R&D innovations—although this statement must be recognized as only a very tentative judgment. Many of the major advances have originated outside the big business labs, in universities and small firms.

Which industries show the highest rates of growth in productivity? Broadly speaking, the oligopolies—chemicals, aerospace, and communications. Productivity has grown more slowly in industries dominated by small firms—the services, construction, and textiles. Agriculture is a major counterexample, with a very high growth rate in productivity, but its research is mainly financed by the government and disseminated through state agricultural extension services.

How about the influence of entry barriers on the rate of innovation? As was indicated above, profits on invested capital tend to be higher where barriers to entry are high, which might suggest that oligopolists have been progressive in reducing costs. However, numerous well-protected oligopolists have failed to introduce major innovations until the way has been charted by others. Examples are the introduction of radio outside GE and Bell Telephone, the dominant communication firms, and the development of jet engines outside the established aircraft-engine manufacturers. But there are numerous counterexamples. Pending more conclusive research, we

SOME PRACTICAL ASPECTS OF
BUSINESS PRICING

Businessmen frequently have inadequate information on future costs and revenues. Yet decisions have to be made, day in and day out. Many managers thus look for some reasonable rules of thumb to avoid the necessity of starting from scratch on each price problem.

Standard costing

Cost per unit of output varies at different output levels. Yet you can't quote everybody a different price and be jiggling your price up and down all the time. So a lot of businessmen ask their accountants and engineers to estimate the total cost of one unit of output at near-capacity operations. They call this estimate the "standard cost," and use it for price setting, even though actual output may vary markedly from day to day and month to month.

"Standard costing" may not be very precise, and many economists explain that it may lead the firm to less than maximum profits on some orders. But standard costing is a rule-of-thumb shortcut for getting the day's business done when there are thousands of different customers and orders. The alternative might well be utter confusion rather than a more perfect approach to profit maximization.

Cost-plus pricing

Using standard costs as a basis, many firms engage in "cost-plus," or "full-cost," or "markup" pricing. They price their product by taking their standard-cost estimate and adding on some standard markup—10, 50, or 100 percent—to provide a reasonable profit. They are likely to use this same markup to quote prices on all orders, regardless of substantial variations in the actual cost of filling the orders. This approach leads to reasonable simplicity in business operations, but it is easy to see how it may also lead to less-than-maximum profits on individual orders.

Actually, businessmen are often better economists than this would suggest. When standard-cost pricing gets them too far out of line with the results they would get through maximum-profit pricing, they often modify their standard-cost pricing. For example, in booming markets where standard-cost pricing clearly undershoots what the market will bear, larger markups are common. In depression, price cutting under "full-cost" prices is widespread. And big buyers often get price concessions on large orders.

Return on investment

Increasingly in recent years, big corporations use some "target" return on capital investment as a rough guide to pricing policy (and to capital investment in new ventures as well). General Motors, for example, shoots for 20 percent on invested capital after taxes. This, of course, doesn't give any automatic guide to setting prices, but it provides some guidelines. Thus, current pricing and plans for expansion are all wrapped up in the same general process, in which the test of effective performance is whether it meets this profit-rate standard.

Why does GM choose 20 percent as the target rate? U.S. Steel is reported to use 8 percent after taxes; Alcoa, 20 percent before taxes. Maybe each is out to maximize profits, and their target rates are merely about the peak they think they can earn. Certainly we need to know more about how the targets are set to evaluate their impact on pricing. But for better or worse, lots of big businesses use this approach as one major guide in pricing and investment planning.*

*There is a large literature on business pricing practices. For easy-to-read accounts, see A.D.H. Kaplan, J. Dirlam, and R.F. Lanzillotti, *Pricing in Big Business* (Washington, D.C.: The Brookings Institution, 1958); and G. Burck, "The Realities of Corporate Pricing," *Fortune*, April 1972.

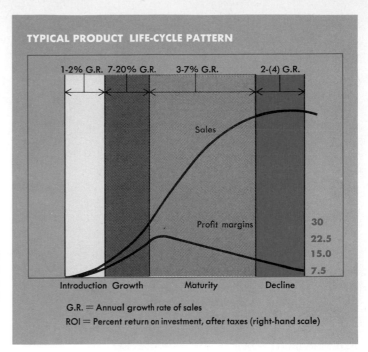

TYPICAL PRODUCT LIFE-CYCLE PATTERN

G.R. = Annual growth rate of sales

ROI = Percent return on investment, after taxes (right-hand scale)

Figure 26–4
Typically, sales of successful products grow rapidly at first, then gradually level off, and ultimately turn down. Profits peak earlier. (Source: Economic Concentration, Hearings before the Senate Subcommittee on Antitrust and Monopoly, 1964, p. 138.)

are left with only a general theoretical presumption that pressures to innovate will be strongest where firms are not protected against the threat of new entrants.

What is the conclusion on oligopoly and economic progress? Clearly, firms of substantial size are needed in most industries to undertake substantial R&D activities, if we expect the research to be done by private firms.[7] But just how big firms should be for optimal progress remains an unsettled issue.[8]

The Dynamics of oligopoly

Many rapidly growing industries are dominated (led) by one or a few firms. Rapid growth tends to come with the introduction of new products or new methods, and understandably the firms that innovate achieve a leader-

---

[7]Some observers suggest introduction of government-financed research and dissemination for the business sector, to parallel the arrangements that have worked so well in the small-firm agricultural sector.

[8]For surveys of the evidence, see M. Kamien and N. Schwartz, "Market Structure and Innovation: A Survey," *Journal of Economic Literature,* March 1975; and E. Mansfield, *The Economics of Technological Change* (New York: Norton, 1968).

ship position. Figure 26–4 shows a typical life-cycle curve for a new product. After introduction, sales grow slowly as it becomes better known on the market. Then, as it catches on, it grows rapidly, often reaching rates of 10–30 percent per year, or even higher. Profits soar, both because new products are often priced to "skim the cream" off the market and because of the rapidly rising sales volume.

As the product matures and other producers come into the market, the growth rate tends to slow. Profit margins for the innovating firm tend to level off. As the product reaches "maturity," the sales growth rate slows and finally turns down, as new products and new methods tend to replace this one.

Figure 26–4 is, of course, only illustrative. Many products never catch on in the market at all; others have short lives and are soon outpaced by competitive products. But the success stories usually look something like Figure 26–4, and in such cases, one or a few firms very often dominate the market.

Table 26–3 shows some of the success stories of modern times. These are firms that pioneered new product lines, and then stayed ahead of competitors during the rapid growth of their

Table 26–3

Growth rates of innovative industries, 1945–74

		AVERAGE ANNUAL GROWTH RATE	
Company	*Product line*	*Sales*	*Jobs*
Texas Instruments	Transistors, integrated circuits	29%	11%
Xerox	Photocopiers	28	19
IBM	Computers, office systems	18	13
3M	Tapes	15	8
Polaroid	Instant photography	15	8
Total economy		3.6 (GNP)	1.6

Source: U.S. Department of Commerce, *Technological Innovation: Its Environment and Management* (1967), p. 5; and *Fortune.*

industries. Each firm was dominant in its industry during this rapid growth period.

The fact that each industry grew around one pioneering firm is not a coincidence. Competition developed only as the successes became apparent. Oligopoly thus often comes with rapid growth, but oligopolies, of course, do not guarantee rapid growth.

One last observation on the dynamics of oligopoly. Alert firms know that spectacular growth rates for individual products must end. Thus, most large firms try to diversify with many products. They try always to have a new growth product in the wings as established lines reach maturity. Otherwise, they may fade as competitors' new products make them obsolete. The most successful oligopolists are those that manage to keep a step ahead of their competition with new products.[9]

[9]This suggests that oligopolists often make their biggest profits on new products, and they do. During the rapid-growth period, price may be set far above marginal cost to "skim the cream" of market demand, and the wide profit spread continues as costs fall with production experience and rising volume. As the product reaches maturity and competition intensifies, profit spreads narrow. Then the innovative firm may be willing to accept small profits or even losses, continuing production from its fixed plant as long as price exceeds variable cost. The total profits of multiproduct firms may thus reflect a combination of large and small profits, and even losses, on different product lines in any given year.

OLIGOPOLY IN THE AMERICAN ECONOMY

Big business has been a favorite target of radical—and some not so radical—critics of the American economy in recent years. High prices, pollution, poor products, misleading advertising, dehumanization of work, manipulation of consumer demand, international imperialism—big business is said to be the devil in the piece for all. And when such critics say "big business," they generally mean the big oligopolies in the industries we've been talking about. We shall examine some of these wide-ranging charges further in the following chapters. Here, a concluding note on merely the *market* powers of oligopolies.

Decreasing-cost oligopolies have filled the American economic-history books. The railroads operating between New York and Chicago before rates were regulated by the federal government are an interesting example. There were four main routes. Each had an enormous fixed investment in right-of-way, stations, rolling stock, and so forth. Variable costs associated with adding a few more cars to any given train, or even adding whole trains, were inconsequential compared with the fixed costs. The average-cost curve for each (for ton-miles of freight or for passengers) was downward-sloping far beyond the traffic level any one of them could realize. Thus, marginal costs were low and the incentive was great to cut prices in order to get more of the available traffic. The New York Central could boost its profits spectacularly if it could get traffic away from the Pennsylvania, and vice versa. Cutthroat competition, not surprisingly, therefore broke out intermittently.[10]

You might suppose that after about the third price war, the railroads would get together and agree on a cartel (market-sharing, price-stabilization) policy. And they did periodically. But the lure of profits was great, and those were the days of the swaggering industrial tycoon. It was not until the government stepped in with the Interstate Commerce Commission in 1887 to regulate rates that the price wars were ended and price discrimination against short-haul shippers was eliminated.

Most of the industries listed in the tables and charts of this chapter face similar decreasing cost and demand situations. The cost of a modern steel mill, for example, has to be spread over an enormous tonnage to keep the cost per ton down to a reasonable figure. Steel demand is highly sensitive to business fluctuations, and only in good times do the steel companies run near capacity. Thus, much of the time, each company can increase its profits markedly by increasing volume, since its TUC·curve is downward-sloping and marginal cost is low until reasonably high-level operation is reached. The pressure to shade prices is great, and few firms resist it when demand is weak.

Some oligopolies have managed to avoid open price competition for many years without illegal collusion; cigarettes are an example, with lots of "quality" competition and advertising. But the pressures toward illegal collusion are great. A spectacular case was the heavy electrical equipment industry in the 1950s, where executives of GE, Westinghouse, Allis Chalmers, and others were found guilty of elaborate price fixing and market-sharing arrangements.[11] But as we shall see in Chapter 27, antitrust enforcement has now made formal collusion a dangerous and little-used policy for oligopolies. Price leadership, go-along attitudes, and heavy demand-creation outlays are the rule of the day in most modern oligopolies—with more price competition than many of them like. Even in oligopoly, the pressures of competition are never very far away.

It is a complex picture of the big oligopolies that emerges from the preceding pages. Giant corporations have great power; yet on all sides they face actual and potential competition. They are said to gouge consumers by restricting output and raising prices; yet most evidence suggests that growth in sales and share of market is a dominant goal of most big firms. Oligopoly theory suggests that too little oligopoly output results when prices to consumers are kept up; yet Professor Galbraith urges that by creating and manipulating consumers' demands, the great corporations dominate the use of society's resources and have grown far too big, both absolutely and relative to the rest of the economy. What, if anything, to do about big business is a fascinating problem, to which we shall turn in Chapters 27 and 28.

---

[10]Throughout, the railroads kept up their short-haul rates to shippers who were served by only one of the four roads and who therefore had no alternatives. In many cases, it cost more to ship freight a few hundred miles between intermediate points than to ship the same freight all the way from Chicago to New York.

[11]For a vivid account, see "The Incredible Electrical Conspiracy," *Fortune,* April and May 1961.

REVIEW

Concepts to remember

This chapter reuses most of the analytical concepts introduced throughout Part 3. Beyond these, be sure you understand the following new ones:

administered prices   price leadership
cartel   price stabilization
concentration ratio   kinked demand curve
standard costs   cost-plus pricing

For analysis and discussion

1. "The big oligopolies like General Motors, General Electric, and Alcoa have been primarily responsible for making better goods available to consumers. Breaking them up into smaller units to obtain more active price competition would be counterproductive." Do you agree or disagree? Support your position against a critic.
2. Is the rate of profit earned on invested capital a good indication of whether an oligopoly is abusing its position?
3. Suppose you were manager of one of the furnace firms originally forming the cartel described in Chapter 26. What would you do to promote your own best interests as additional new firms entered the industry?
4. Consider the international coffee-producers' cartel described in Case 18 (Chapter 23). What would you predict would be the crucial factors determining how successful the cartel would be?
5. What are the main forces that determine whether there will be few or many firms in any given industry?
6. In many of the major oligopolistic industries, entry is difficult for new firms because of both the technical know-how and the large financial investment required for effective competition. Can you suggest desirable ways to overcome these difficulties?
7. Suppose that you are president of the largest firm in an industry in which the great bulk of the business is done by the largest five firms. As the industry leader, your firm ordinarily initiates any price changes in the industry.
   a. How would you go about deciding what price to charge for your product?
   b. Is there a conflict or community between your interests and those of the other four firms in the industry?
   c. Would consumers be better off, by and large, if active price competition were enforced rather than price leadership in the industry?

In early 1972, there were 288,000 retail food stores in the United States, down from 313,000 five years earlier. In 1971, sales of the top four supermarket chains totaled about $17 billion, somewhat under 20 percent of total retail food sales (excluding tobacco and liquor) of about $90 billion. A total of fourteen supermarket chains reported sales of over a billion dollars each, and their combined sales of about $30 billion were about one-third of total national sales.

	Sales (in billions)
A&P	$ 5.5
Safeway	5.4
Kroger's	3.7
Food Fair	2.1
	$16.7

Very small stores have accounted for almost all the dropouts from the industry; some have merged together.

At the national level, food retailing was thus a highly competitive industry as measured by the number of firms, but in some areas a few big supermarkets dominate, with local oligopolies. As judged by profits as a percentage of sales, the industry is highly competitive. Average profit per dollar of sales has recently been less than 1 percent.

For half a century, the Great Atlantic and Pacific Tea Company (A&P) had been the world's largest food retailer. But late in 1971, culminating a long, rapid growth, Safeway edged past A&P in total sales. A&P, which markets largely in the eastern half of the country, had steadily slipped in market share and profitability over the preceding decade, while its chief competitors, marketing more heavily in the West and South, gained. Some of the regional chains (Albertsons, Jewel, Winn-Dixie, and Safeway itself) have done especially well, although, as the table shows, none except Safeway and Kroger's approach A&P in total size.

In 1971, the A&P management took a dramatic step. In what some competitors labeled a desperate move to regain market leadership, they converted most of their stores to a new "Where Economy Originates" (WEO) "discount-store" format. Prices were slashed by 10–20 percent on thousands of products to lure the customers back.

The results were dramatic. By 1972, A&P sales had jumped 15 percent, but profits nosedived. The company lost $41 million during the first half of 1972. Between 1968 and 1972, the price of A&P stock fell from 40 to 15. With the market leader cutting prices, smaller stores had to cut too or lose customers, and most cut. Customers smiled happily at the price cuts in the middle of inflation, but in October 1972, the *New York Times* reported:

> Five of the 10 largest supermarket chains in the country are in "bad financial shape" while half a dozen food chains in the metropolitan New York area are on the brink of insolvency, Clarence Adamy, president of the National Association of Food Chains, declared yesterday. He attributed the situation to:
>
> One of the most dramatic and widespread price competitions that we have had in the retail food field since the 1930s. . . .
>
> Inflation, which is particularly difficult for such a tightly-competitive industry. Stores are being forced to absorb rising costs. . . .
>
> Earnings in the supermarket industry will probably fall to less than 0.50 percent of sales by the year's end, he added, down from 0.86 percent during the summer and 1.41 percent in 1965.

As the price war spread in 1972 with more stores converting to "discount" pricing, profits turned to losses for many of the leading supermarket chains—and apparently for many small retail stores, although accurate published data are not available for such small retailers. Nearly all supermarket stocks nosedived on the security markets. Accusations and counteraccusations of unfair price cutting filled the air. Joseph Binder, president of Bohack, a large New York supermarket chain, charged, "The truth of the matter is this: The Great Atlantic and Pacific Tea Co. didn't know how to run its own business, so it decided to run everybody else out of business." But A&P shrugged off the complaints. William Kane, A&P's chairman, said the charges levelled by competitors "seem a little strange in an economic system that prides itself on being based on competition."

---

1. Why did cutthroat competition break out in this oligopolized industry in a period of generally rising prices and inflation?

2. Did A&P management act wisely in its own self-interest in adopting its new policy?

3. If you were head of one of the competing supermarkets, would you meet the A&P price cuts?

4. If you ran a small corner grocery near a supermarket, what would you do?

5. How long would you expect this war of the supermarkets to last, and how would you expect it to end?

6. If you were a supermarket-chain head, what would you do to restore reasonable stability and profits to your firm? To the industry?

7. Are customers (at A&P and elsewhere) likely to be better or worse off as a result of A&P's policy change? In the short run? In the long run?

8. If price cutting continues, would you expect more or less investment in food retail stores in the future?

9. What, if anything, should the government do?

CASE 22
SOME MANAGERIAL APPLICATIONS[12]

Elasticity of demand and product pricing Demand is often elastic. And when it is, a price policy that doesn't recognize this fact can mean disaster. But a price policy founded on full knowledge of demand elasticity can make life pleasant for the stockholders, and unpleasant for competitors.

The record industry is a classic case. For decades, classical records were high-priced luxury items, aimed at a small market. In 1938, Columbia broke the oligopoly price pattern, cutting the price per record (on the old shellac 78-rpm records) from $2 to $1. The response was overwhelming. Total expenditure on classical rec-

ords, to the amazement of almost everyone else, rose drastically. Demand turned out to be highly elastic, and the competition was left behind. Soon other companies had to meet the cut.

About the same time, the railroads, desperate for revenue, **raised** their fares. The result was equally impressive. The customers switched to cars and buses, or just stayed home in droves; total revenue dropped as the railroads learned about elastic demand the hard way.

Of course, individual product demand is sometimes inelastic. But over and over again, businessmen have underestimated the gain to be had from reducing prices and expanding markets in which elastic demand prevails. Economists sometimes describe this as "elasticity pessimism." Mass markets based on low costs and low prices have been the foundation of the growing American economy.

[12] For more detailed analyses of the use of economic analysis in managerial decision making, see M. Spencer and L. Siegelman, *Managerial Economics* (Homewood, Ill.: Richard D. Irwin, Inc., 1968); and D.S. Watson, *Price Theory in Action* (New York: Houghton Mifflin Company, 1972).

New-product decisions—marginal cost versus average cost Suppose you manage a filling station. You have handled only gasoline, oil, and a few miscellaneous supplics like auto polish, windshield-wiper blades, and so on. The local wholesaler approaches you to put in a line of batteries and tires. He argues that there will be very little extra expense because you're not pressed for space, and that you have a small but ready-made market in your regular customers, who don't want to go to the inconvenience of shopping around for these items.

You've had a course in economics and you know about costs. So you calculate carefully what the marginal (extra) cost of putting in these lines would be, compared to the likely increase in revenue. The answer looks good. The only marginal cost you can see is the money tied up in keeping an inventory on hand, and it looks as if you might sell $200 to $300 a month worth of tires and batteries. At a markup over wholesale that will keep the final price roughly competitive with other retailers, this should yield an extra $50 to $75 a month even after allowing for interest cost on the money tied up in inventory. On the other hand, if you allocate against the tires and batteries their proportionate share of other costs (space, your time and that of the help, taxes, electricity, and so on), the line would probably show a small loss. **Should you put in the tires and batteries?**

The answer clearly hinges on whether you use marginal or average costs, assuming your estimates are reasonable. Adding the line will clearly increase revenue more than cost for the enterprise as a whole, unless you've overlooked some new costs associated with the tires and batteries. Following the principles of Chapter 21, you'll increase your total profit by expanding, even though when you compare the average total cost of the batteries and tires against their selling prices, they wouldn't appear to provide a profit. If it's total profit that matters to you, the comparison based on marginal cost and marginal revenue will point to the best answer.

But this is a rule to be used with care. It depends on being sure of what is truly marginal and what is not. Suppose you add the tires and they seem a great success, selling better than you'd expected and taking up more and more

space and time. You have to add a new man and expand your building. Where do you allocate the cost—to the gasoline, the tires, where? You can look at any one part of your output first, and then the rest looks marginal.

Many businessmen use this kind of marginal (or incremental) analysis in adding products, but only when the addition is small relative to their total activity, and understandably so. When any product line becomes relatively large, they expect it to carry its regular share of the "overhead," or the "burden," as indirect costs of running the business are sometimes called. In principle, comparing marginal cost with marginal revenue always gives the right answer in deciding whether or not to take on a new product or to expand output. The trick lies in applying the principle carefully, and being sure which costs are really marginal in both the short and long runs. Remember Continental Airlines in Case 17.

Sunk costs and operating decisions Try another case—similar but different. You manufacture men's suits. Your costs fall roughly into two groups—variable (mainly labor and materials), and fixed (rent, management salaries, and so on). You know that for the range of output in which you usually operate, you must add about 30 percent to your variable costs to get a price that permits you to break even; you normally price by adding 40 percent to variable costs, with the prices of individual suits varying largely with differences in cloth and the amount of hand labor.

This season, demand has been slow and you are operating well under your normal rate. It has been a bad year, and you probably will not even break even. You have a chance to make 1,000 suits on a special order from a wholesaler who is not a regular customer. However, he will only pay a price that would cover variable costs plus 20 percent. **Should you take the order?**

Your fixed costs are "sunk." That is, they go on and must be paid, at least for the short run, whether you operate or not. Because they are sunk, economic analysis says they should have no effect on your decision to accept or reject the order. By taking the order, you will cover all your variable costs and will have the 20 percent addition to apply on your fixed costs. You may not make a profit on your total operations, but your loss will be smaller than without the order, as was explained in Chapter 21.

The logic is right. But many businessmen would think a long time before taking the order. They worry about the long run, and properly so. Suppose you cut the price on this order and your regular customers hear about it. Might this break your whole price line, with dire results for profits over the longer run? Or might it lead your competitors to cut their prices? If the answer is yes, looking only at the particular gain from taking this order would be wearing blinders to the long-run result. *In the short run,* you may minimize losses by taking orders at less than total cost, but both economic analysis and managerial common sense say that *in the long run,* your price has to cover all costs or you'll end up in bankruptcy.

The nature of costs: depreciation   You operate a fleet of taxicabs. With the hard use the cabs receive, you estimate that after three years they will have depreciated to the point where it is no longer economical to operate them. At that time, you anticipate, you will be able to sell or trade them for about 10 percent of the original cost of $3,000 each. Thus, you account as a cost an annual depreciation charge of 30 percent ($900) per cab, in addition to regular operating and maintenance costs.

At the end of three years, you have fully depreciated the cabs, except for the small turn-in value. Yet they seem to be still in reasonably good condition. **Should you turn them in on** new cabs, using the accumulated depreciation reserve to finance the new cabs, or continue to use the old ones?

The forward-looking nature of economics, and the principle above that "sunk costs are sunk," suggest the answer. The fact that you estimated a three-year life and have now accumulated a 90 percent depreciation reserve does not give you an answer to when you should replace these particular cabs. Don't be overimpressed by the bookkeeping. The optimal choice depends on analyzing the cost and performance of new cabs against the cost and performance of continued use of the old cabs. If the total profit by continuing to use the old cabs exceeds the profit with new cabs,[13] then keep the old ones. If not, buy new ones. The crucial point is the importance of the forward-looking decision, not the fact that three years is the end of your estimated depreciation period. If you made a mistake in estimating the cabs' useful life, it may pay you to replace long before the cabs are fully depreciated or to wait until long after. Depreciation charges represent only an estimate of the proper cost to be currently charged for the use of durable assets, not a determinant of when assets should be replaced.[14]

[13] Remembering possible consumer preferences for new models and all such relevant considerations, and recognizing that the money can temporarily be used another way if it is not used to buy new cabs.

[14] For a precise analysis of how to decide the best time to replace durable plant and equipment, a more advanced text is needed. See, for example, E.L. Grant and W. Ireson, *Principles of Engineering Economy* (New York: Ronald Press, 1970), Part II.

CHAPTER 27

BUSINESS, ANTITRUST, AND THE PUBLIC INTEREST

Business, especially big business, is a favorite target of critics of American capitalism. As noted in the previous chapter, some critics blame just about everything on big corporations and corporate executives—high prices, pollution, concentration of economic power, poor products, manipulation of consumers, racism, sexism, dehumanization of workers, international imperialism. Others see much virtue in the American economic system, but still raise serious questions about big business's power and the need for more effective government regulation. Still others argue that individual self-interest is the most powerful incentive of all—the driving force that has made the American standard of living the highest in the world—and that more regulation and government controls risk killing the goose that lays the golden eggs.

Communism or a massive government takeover of the businesses that now produce our goods and services seems very unlikely in America. But continuing change in government controls and regulation of businesses is very likely indeed. The closing section of Chapter 22 summarized the probable "market failures," or problem areas, that are likely to arise in a market-directed economy, and each of these has led to widespread demands for government action or other steps to improve the way the economy works. The next three chapters explore the three big problems in making competitive markets work effectively: how to maintain effective competition, especially where large firms are required to obtain the economies of large-scale production (Chapter 27); problems of imperfect buyer information, demand manipulation, and consumer protection (Chapter 28); and what to do where social costs exceed private costs because of externalities, as with pollution (Chapter 29). The other two big shortcomings of a competitive system noted in Chapter 22 (failure to produce desired "public goods," and undesirable inequality of incomes) are considered in Part 5, which focuses on the government's own direct economic activities in the "public sector."

BIGNESS, MONOPOLY, AND PUBLIC OPINION

Why should government intervene at all in business affairs? Adam Smith had one answer: Because self-seeking will be channeled to the common good only if *competition* prevails. Seldom do merchants gather together, he wrote, that their talk does not turn to means of obtaining higher prices for their products. It is the job of government, representing all the people, to see to it that competition prevails.

Everyone agrees, moreover, that in an individualistic society there have to be some rules of fair play in economic life, just as in personal behavior. Without common consent to eliminate fraud, to respect property ownership, and to honor legal contracts, economic dealings would be carried on under a great handicap. By general agreement, it is the job of the government to establish and enforce these basic rules to enable men to work effectively together. Among Adam Smith's nineteenth-century followers, "laissez faire" never meant that the government should do nothing, but rather that it should leave economic affairs alone *within* a framework of basic moral and governmental rules of the game.

But economic theory gives no clear answer as to just how much competition is optimal—just how the public interest is best served where the extreme of Adam Smith's pure competition is not feasible. Moreover, the issue of monopoly power shades almost imperceptibly into the

problems of bigness and power per se. Consider the following comparison between General Electric and an isolated country grocery.

In 1975, the General Electric Company had assets of $7 billion, and reported profits after taxes of $570 million on sales of $15 billion. It had about 400,000 employees. Although no exact figures are available, GE apparently accounted for about half the total sales in the country of heavy electrical machinery, light bulbs, and other major categories of electrical equipment. It was rivaled only by Westinghouse, another giant about half the size of GE. Big companies like Allis Chalmers in heavy equipment and Sylvania in bulbs and lighter equipment absorbed another sizable chunk of the market, but they were far short of the two leaders in overall size and market power. GE did business all around the world. Does GE have too much monopoly power? Should it be broken up into several smaller concerns in the public interest?

Now consider Jones's Grocery Store, at the crossroads corner of an isolated village in northern Minnesota—population 150. Jones's total sales in 1975 were about $30,000, on which he realized a return after paying all costs (except his own salary) of about $7,000, as near as he could figure it. Jones had one employee—himself. His service was so-so. There is no other grocery store within 35 miles. Is Jones's Grocery Store a monopoly? Should it be broken up into several smaller concerns in the public interest?

No reasonable person would answer that Jones's store ought to be broken up to provide more competition in the village. The market can't support one respectable grocery, let alone two or three. Yet Jones's monopoly power over the customers in that village may far exceed GE's power over its customers. If Jones takes advantage of Widow Smith down the street and slips a bad potato into every peck, she's pretty much out of luck. Let GE treat one of its customers that way, and Westinghouse will get a phone call the next day from the outraged purchasing agent.

How about GE? If you think it should be broken up or subjected to more government control, why? Because GE clearly has a dominant position in its major products, with around half the market for many of them? Or just because GE seems too big—because you feel that no one business ought to control so much wealth, with the far-reaching economic and political power that goes with it?

Analytically, it is important to distinguish between these two reasons, even though they are closely intertwined. The degree of monopoly power depends largely on the size of the seller *relative* to the market in which he sells. Broader economic and political power depends more on *absolute size,* which bears no necessary relationship to the degree of monopoly the firm possesses. Jones's Grocery has a pretty effective monopoly in its market, according to the economist's definition, but it's a tiny concern. GE clearly holds some monopoly powers too—it's an oligopolist. But the striking difference is GE's absolute size. Its managers exert economic power—the power of $15 billion—over the lives of 400,000 workers, over the communities in which they live, over millions of consumers. And, some would add, political power over what happens in Washington and in state capitals.

This difference between absolute and relative size is illustrated vividly by the oil industry. Six of the ten largest industrial corporations in the United States are oil companies—Exxon, Mobil, Texaco, and so on—and together they had assets of over $100 billion in 1975, some ten times those of GE. Yet no one of them had more than 8 percent of the domestic gasoline market, and together they accounted for only 39 percent of total sales.

The public-opinion pollsters have repeatedly sampled the man in the street's feelings about big business since World War II. Although views vary with the times (for instance, many people blame inflation on big business "greed" for profits), surveys have persistently found that Americans (1) on the whole believe that good business and good profits are good for the economy, and that, on balance, business does a good job of turning out good-quality products; (2) don't trust big business, and want the government to keep an eagle eye on the big businessman to see that he doesn't abuse his enormous potential power over consumers, workers, and smaller competitors. The last few years, reflecting the national wave of dejection and cynicism

from Vietnam and Watergate, have seen a strong upswing in criticism of big businesses. Polls report that large majorities say businesses concentrate too much on making profits rather than serving the public interest, that they charge too much, and that they should do more to eliminate unemployment, rebuild the cities, and eliminate racial and sex discrimination, pollution, and poverty. Ninety percent of the public feels that monopolies are a real danger.

IS ECONOMIC CONCENTRATION GROWING?

Is monopoly growing? Are big firms dominating the economy more and more? The answer is mixed, and it's easy to cite figures that seem to prove the answer either way.

If we look at the manufacturing sector alone, the answer seems to be yes. Table 27–1 shows that the market share of the biggest firms has risen substantially since 1948, although most of the increase occurred early in the period and shares haven't changed much in the last two decades. If we use sales instead of assets, the picture is similar.[1]

However, even in manufacturing, the picture is complicated. The profit share of the giants has fallen relative to the rest of the top 500, even though the 500 have increased their share of

[1]Concentration statistics are tricky, and it is possible to convey significantly different pictures by changing the groupings of products and measures used (assets, sales, value added, and so on). When reading such statistics, it is generally wise to probe for possible biases of the writer.

Table 27–1

Concentration in manufacturing

| | SHARE OF TOTAL ASSETS IN: | |
	1948	*1974*
Largest 5 firms	10%	13%
Largest 20 firms	21	27
Largest 100 firms	39	50
Largest 200 firms	48	65

Source: Federal Trade Commission and *Fortune.*

Table 27-2

Ten largest industrial firms, 1909–1975

RANK		
1909	*1974*	
1	13	U.S. Steel Corporation
2	1	Standard Oil Co. (New Jersey) (now Exxon)
3	a	American Tobacco Co.
4	a	International Mercantile Marine Company
5	a	Anaconda Co.
6	33	International Harvester Co.
7	a	Central Leather Company
8	a	Pullman Inc.
9	a	Armour & Co.
10	a	American Sugar Refining Co.

a No longer in top 100 firms.

Source: A.D.H. Kaplan, *Big Enterprise in a Competitive System* (Washington, D.C.: The Brookings Institution, 1964), and *Fortune*. Rankings based on total assets.

total manufacturing profits. Moreover, the top is a slippery pinnacle. Table 27–2 shows the largest ten industrial firms in 1909, and what happened to them by 1975. Only one was still in the top ten, and eight had vanished from the list of the largest 100. General Motors, Ford, and IBM, three of the top five now, didn't even exist in 1909.

One other warning: Most of the giants now produce many products, not just one. Thus, the firm concentration figures don't necessarily tell us the degree of monopoly exercised by that firm in the different industries in which it competes. GM, for example, has over half the automobile market, but it is far behind GE in home appliances, which it also produces. Exxon is the leading petroleum company, but lags far behind several of the chemical firms in chemical sales, which also make up a substantial part of its business. The big "conglomerates," like ITT and Litton Industries, operate in dozens of different industries, in some of which they play only a minor role.

If we look at the whole economy, not just manufacturing, there is little evidence of increasing market concentration. In the rapidly growing services area, markets are widely divided among large and small sellers. Construction continues to be dominated by relatively small firms. There are still millions of farmers, even though the market share of big commercial farms has been rising steadily. But the biggest development has been the explosive growth of the government (see Part 5) and nonprofit sectors, especially in the service areas—hospitals and Blue Cross, private education, research institutes, and the like. The share of the national income produced by profit-seeking corporations apparently reached a peak of 55 percent in the mid-1950s. By 1970 it was back down to 53 percent, its level of twenty years earlier. The problem of growing economic concentration, if we eliminate the already highly regulated public utilities, appears to be centered in the manufacturing sector, if it exists anywhere.

Mergers to form huge conglomerates, sometimes called megacorps, were the big news of the 1960s. From only 219 in 1960, corporate mergers rose to nearly 2,500 in 1969, when assets of the acquired companies totalled $13 billion. But the glamor of such mergers faded as many of the new conglomerates showed low profits or losses, and as the Justice Department's Antitrust Division challenged the legality of several. Mergers have continued, but at a far slower pace over the last few years.[2]

THE WELFARE COST OF MONOPOLY

What is the cost to the public of the inefficiencies induced by monopolies? How much could we hope to gain by reducing the amount of monopoly in the system? Unfortunately, there are no reliable estimates of these costs, but some approximations have been attempted. They suggest that the costs arising purely from misallocation of resources (allocative inefficiency) are probably quite small, not above a few billion dollars. But the costs arising from internal technological and bureaucratic inefficiency (sometimes called "X-inefficiency"), because monopolists aren't forced to reduce costs

[2] See "What We Learned from the Great Merger Frenzy," *Fortune*, April 1973.

as much as under competition, may be much larger.

Many economists are skeptical of the small estimates of allocative inefficiency, but the possible gain from competition on this score is the difference between the productivity of the resources employed in two different businesses producing what consumers want. By contrast, X-inefficiency has no such obvious limits; more competitive pressure might force partial monopolists to lower costs substantially (to operate more efficiently) and thereby reduce unit costs and prices substantially.

More reliable estimates of the welfare costs of monopoly would provide a better basis for judging how hard we ought to try through public policies to reduce monopoly. Most estimates of allocative inefficiency find that these costs are probably largely concentrated in a few mining and manufacturing industries—metal mining and fabricating, petroleum extraction and refining, plastics, drugs, tobacco manufacturing, office machinery, photographic equipment, and, most important, automobiles. This suggests focus of antitrust activities on these areas. But as to the potentially more important savings in technological efficiency we have few systematic comparisons, but rather many studies of particular firms and industries. As we shall see, application of antitrust laws has apparently not been guided primarily by such estimates of the probable relative efficiency gains in different industries.[3]

THE LAW, COMPETITION, AND MONOPOLY

The law is what is written down in the statute books, and more. It is what the courts say it is, what the long rows of past court decisions suggest, altered as the judge thinks proper in any particular case. It is what the Justice Department thinks it is; most law is enforced without ever coming near a courtroom. It is what the president and his advisers think it is,

[3]On the probable size and locations of allocative inefficiency, see J. Siegfried and T. Tiemann, "The Welfare Cost of Monopoly," *Economic Inquiry,* June 1974; for a broader review, see H. Liebenstein, "Allocative Efficiency versus X-Efficiency," *American Economic Review,* June 1966.

through the way they instruct the government's law-enforcement branches. Above all, it is what the people will obey and support. In our democratic system, no law that does not command widespread public support can long be enforced. Sometimes the law is changed when it loses support, but equally often its enforcement varies to mirror the times.

This description is especially accurate in the field of government–business relations. Here, much of the law is in the mass of court decisions and in the policies of the government's administrative agencies. Both reflect (with lags) what the public wants—often more accurately than we realize. Our antitrust laws seldom change by formal congressional action. But in fact they alter constantly—with changing congressional appropriations for enforcement, changing personnel in the antitrust agencies, and changing judicial attitudes.

The common law

Until 1890, there was no federal legislation that declared monopoly illegal. Nor did the states have any antimonopoly laws of consequence. Under the common (unwritten) law inherited from England, contracts to restrain trade unreasonably or to raise prices were unenforceable. But the common law did not hold monopoly practices to be criminal, nor did it even provide for damages to those harmed by the restraint of trade. The contracts were merely unenforceable. Thus, the common law provided little protection to the consumer or to the little competitor who got squeezed out by combinations in restraint of trade.

Legislation

The last half of the nineteenth century saw the development of the great trusts. Standard Oil, American Sugar, American Tobacco, and dozens of others amassed huge empires that held almost complete monopolies over the products concerned. Standard Oil at its peak controlled over 90 percent of the country's oil-refining capacity, and the bulk of the pipelines. American Sugar controlled 98 percent of the country's sugar-refining capacity. American Tobacco had virtually complete control of tobacco manufacturing.

Moreover, the means used to build up these monopolies aroused widespread ire and fear. Standard Oil, for example, is said (although historians differ) to have driven small competitors to the wall by cutthroat competition, bought them up cheap, and then raised prices. Competitors who resisted found themselves up against ruthless force.

The Sherman and Interstate Commerce Commission Acts. With half a hundred trust giants on the American scene, popular resentment was reflected in two major acts—the Interstate Commerce Commission Act (1887) and the Sherman Antitrust Act (1890)—which established the pattern of U.S. regulation of monopoly for the century to come. The I.C.C. Act established federal control over railroad rates and services for the first time, making them a public utility since effective competition was unfeasible. The Sherman Antitrust Act was aimed at preventing monopoly and enforcing competition in the great bulk of the economy, where effective competition seemed feasible.

The Interstate Commerce Commission Act called for strict, comprehensive government regulation of industries that cannot operate satisfactorily on a competitive basis. By the late 1800s, it was abundantly clear that regulation of interstate railway rates and service through market competition was impracticable. Most markets were simply not big enough to support several railway systems, each operating near its minimum-cost level. Thus, the ICC Act made the railroads regulated public utilities. General operating responsibility was left with the management elected by the private stockholders, but prices and the amount and quality of service had to be approved by the ICC to protect the public interest. Under this approach, the railroads are guaranteed monopoly positions, but how they use their monopoly powers is carefully regulated.[4]

---

[4] With modern truck, bus, pipeline, and airline competition, many economists now suggest that the day has come to try freer competition again, on the argument that competition provides more stimulus to efficiency and good service than does government regulation.

The Sherman Act was aimed at the other part of the economy, where competition could reasonably be expected to do a good job of regulating prices, output, and quality for the public good. Here, in order to enforce active competition, protecting both consumers and small competitors, the Sherman Act outlawed restraints of trade and attempts to monopolize, as follows:

> Section 1. Every contract, combination in the form of a trust or otherwise, or conspiracy, in restraint of trade or commerce among the several states, or with foreign nations, is hereby declared to be illegal. . . .
>
> Section 2. Every person who shall monopolize, or attempt to monopolize, or combine or conspire with any other person or persons to monopolize any part of the trade or commerce among the several states, or with foreign nations, shall be deemed guilty. . . .

This was broad and sweeping language. Inevitably, a wide range of questions arose over the years as to just what was actually outlawed. As with all such legislation, such questions have been answered primarily through a long series of court rulings interpreting the law. No legislation regulating the complex modern economy can hope to specify in detail every case and situation that is to be covered.

The Clayton and Federal Trade Commission Acts. In 1914, two new acts were passed—the Clayton Act and the Federal Trade Commission Act—to clarify the Sherman Act by specifically prohibiting certain practices, regardless of the group or individual engaging in them, and by setting up new enforcement procedures. The Clayton Act listed specifically as illegal (1) discriminatory price cutting; (2) tying contracts, which require buyers to purchase other items as a condition of getting the item they want; (3) acquisition of stock in competing companies to obtain monopoly powers; and (4) interlocking directorates in competing corporations. But each of these was prohibited only "where the effect may be to substantially lessen competition or tend to create a monopoly. . . ." Thus, the Clayton Act cleared the picture by defining some illegal acts. But it still left open the basic problem of interpretation for the courts in many individual cases.

The Federal Trade Commission Act created a commission to act as a watchdog against unfair competitive practices aimed at creating monopoly or injuring competitors—for example, through predatory pricing or misleading advertising. The commission was given power to hold hearings and to issue "cease and desist" orders that require offending firms to discontinue illegal practices. When the first major appeal from a commission ruling reached the Supreme Court in 1919, however, the Court held that it is for the courts, not for the FTC, to make the ultimate decisions in interpreting the law. The FTC, nevertheless, plays an important role in policing cases of seller misrepresentation (for instance, through false advertising), and in arranging voluntary agreements among business competitors on fair-trade practices.

New Deal legislation of the 1930s.

During the Great Depression of the 1930s, the New Deal was mainly concerned with recovery, greater economic security, and helping the little fellow. It sought to halt falling prices and cutthroat competition. The National Recovery Act (NRA) led businessmen to band together in formal cartels, aimed at raising prices. In agriculture, the Agricultural Adjustment Administration (AAA) had a similar purpose—to raise farm prices and incomes by government-sponsored cartel-like agreements to restrict production. The Bituminous Coal Act did the same thing for soft coal. In labor markets, the Wagner Act threw the full force of the government behind workers' right to unionize and bargain collectively. Both the NRA and the AAA were later declared unconstitutional, but the powerful competition-restricting effects of the agricultural and labor programs have become central parts of our government policy on market·structure and performance.

This desire to help the small competitor and avoid "destructive" competition was reflected in two other new pieces of legislation. The Robinson-Patman Act of 1936 strengthened the prohibition against price discrimination that might help such large buyers as chain stores to undersell small retailers. In 1937, the Miller-Tydings

Act guaranteed protection from Sherman Act prosecution to manufacturers and retailers who participated in "fair-trading" arrangements, whereby the manufacturer specifies that no retailer may sell his product below a specified price. Too much competition was feared more than too little.

The Celler Antimerger Act of 1950.

After World War II, many corporations found that acquiring other companies outright was a profitable way to expand. Such extension of market power through merger was not limited by earlier antitrust legislation. To close this loophole, in 1950 the Celler Antimerger Act was passed forbidding the acquisition of, or merger with, other companies where the effect "may be substantially to lessen competition, or tend to create a monopoly."

The law in operation

Antitrust law is what its administrators and the courts make it. And its administrators and the courts by and large make it what the public wants, albeit often very roughly and with a considerable lag. The first big enforcement campaign under the Sherman Act was President Theodore Roosevelt's, conducted with a total staff of seven lawyers and four stenographers. With this tiny staff, but with the big stick of aroused public opinion, the government tackled the biggest trusts. In 1911, the Supreme Court required both Standard Oil and American Tobacco to divest themselves of a large share of their holdings and to desist from numerous specific unfair competitive practices. But there, too, for the first time, the Court enunciated the now-famous "rule of reason." Only trusts that "unreasonably" restrained trade were illegal. In a series of earlier cases, the Court had given a broad interpretation to the interstate-commerce clause, permitting federal regulation to apply to all firms that had any direct dealing across state lines or (later) in products or materials crossing state lines; this interpretation brought most big businesses within the purview of federal antitrust legislation.

By 1920, the attitude toward big business had altered, with the checking of the flagrant abuses of the 1800s. In the *U.S. Steel* case of 1920, the Supreme Court refused to dissolve the company. It held that neither mere bigness nor unexerted monopoly power was illegal as such; that actual unreasonable restraint of trade must be proved under the Sherman Act. The tenor of the 1920s was one of prosperity and "leave well enough alone." The total budget allocated the Antitrust Division averaged only $250,000 annually for the decade. Big business was popular.

With the strong antibusiness sweep of the New Deal, the last major change in the application and interpretation of the antitrust laws began in the late 1930s. Under Thurman Arnold, Antitrust began an aggressive drive in the late 1930s against several of the industrial giants. Its budget was upped to $1 million (to police the entire economy). Succeeding administrations have continued active prosecution under antitrust legislation. Appropriations to both the Federal Trade Commission and the Antitrust Division of the Department of Justice have been greatly increased. The Antimerger Act has become a powerful barrier to business growth through price fixing or acquisition of competitors. The government does not win all the antitrust cases it initiates, but under the Warren Court it won most of them. The new, more conservative Burger Court appears to be less certain in its support of antitrust action.

Not all economists, understanding the theoretical presumption against monopoly, agree that antitrust always serves the public interest. Some economists, for example, argue that the courts' strong interpretation of the Antimerger Act can give topsy-turvy results. To prevent mergers among relatively small firms may hinder useful, cost-saving combinations and protect small inefficient competitors more than it protects consumers. In the 1966 *Von's Groceries* case, the court forbade a merger between two Los Angeles grocery chains that together held less than 8 percent of the Los Angeles market. (See Case 23, at the end of this chapter.)

Where does antitrust law stand now, as a practical matter? First, all price-fixing agreements are illegal per se. Second, oligopolies in which a few firms dominate the market are probably legal as long as no leading firm tries to expand its market share by merger or by aggres-

"It so happens, Gregory, that your Grandfather Sloan was detained by an agency of our government over an honest misunderstanding concerning certain antitrust matters! He was not 'busted by the Feds'!" (Drawing by W. Miller; © 1971. The New Yorker Magazine, Inc.)

sive competition that endangers small firms.[5] Third, growth through merger in the same industry is virtually forbidden, except among very small firms—although growth without merger is generally permissible. The IBM case now in the courts raises this issue squarely. How far the law prohibits conglomerate mergers remains to be determined by the courts. Fourth, many specific practices (price discrimination, tying clauses in contracts, misleading advertising, and the like) are illegal when they may tend to create a monopoly or significantly reduce competition. Fifth, a growing number of consumer protection laws have been passed recently, regulating sellers' behavior; these, which are not primarily antimonopoly acts, are considered in Chapter 28. But the Miller-Tydings "Fair Trade" Act was repealed in 1975.

Why has antitrust again become a potent force since the 1930s? First, the budget given the Antitrust Division by Congress is now about $18 million, larger than ever before; Antitrust now

---

[5] J.K. Galbraith has argued vigorously that the effect of present antitrust is to let the big, established oligopolies go untouched while applying the Antimerger Act to smaller firms trying to grow through mergers.

has some 300 lawyers to police the economy. Looked at another way, however, this is still a tiny sum compared with the vast resources of the billion-dollar corporations it has to police. The budget reflects America's ambivalent attitude toward antitrust. We want the advantages of big business, but we also want to be sure that big business doesn't abuse its powers.

One last point on the law in action: The main impact of the antitrust law is preventive, not punitive. Since 1890, only about 1,600 suits have been brought under the Sherman Act. Of these, the government has won about three-fourths, with a large proportion settled out of court through "consent decrees." Total fines paid by defendants over the eight decades were only $30 million dollars—very little compared to the billions of dollars of assets in the companies concerned. But a company convicted of antitrust violation is also liable for triple damages if customers or competitors can show they were injured by the illegal acts. GE and Westinghouse were sued for hundreds of millions of dollars by customers after they were found guilty of price fixing in 1961. Moreover, no business likes to be called criminal. It does not like to have its affairs dragged into open court, even though it thinks it may win out in the end.

WHERE TO FROM HERE?

Nobody thinks the modern American economy can look like the economist's perfectly competitive model. It never has, even back in the pre–Civil War days, and it certainly doesn't now. We're in for a mixed economy of some sort. How shall we ensure that business performance is efficient and in the public interest?

Antitrust and economic efficiency

Would stronger antitrust action really produce a more "efficient" economy, in the sense of giving consumers the largest possible amount of what they want at the lowest feasible prices? The presence of more firms creates a general presumption of more active competition. But no magic number of firms is needed to ensure effective competition. Sometimes (for ex-

ample, in the auto industry) there is aggressive competition with only three or four big firms. But most observers agree that the presence of more firms generally increases the likelihood of strong price and quality competition.

If more firms are generally good for competition, we need to face the issue of whether this is consistent with having firms big enough to take advantage of modern technology. Clearly, business has to be big for efficiency in many industries. But it's also true that business can get too big from the cost standpoint. In many industries, middle-sized to large companies have lower costs than gigantic ones. But not always.

It is important to remember that most technological economies of scale come at the *plant* level, so no more production efficiency is gained by combining similar-sized plants in one *firm*. Some critics argue that U.S. Steel, for example, is little more than a number of Inland Steels put together in one firm, although Inland is big enough to be technologically efficient. But bigger firms may yield marketing, financial, and managerial efficiencies. Nothing but a detailed analysis of each industry is likely to provide clear answers on such issues.

Professors George Stigler and Thomas Saving suggest that the market will settle the issue for us if we just let firms battle it out.[6] They postulate that, by and large, the most efficient sizes of plant and firm will win out in the competitive race. During the postwar period, medium-sized plants (relative to their total markets) have survived most effectively in most industries. This test therefore suggests that in most industries, plants small enough to permit effective competition can produce efficiently. But in some industries—for example, computers—the biggest firm is clearly the most efficient by this test.

In some industries (such as autos, cigarettes, oil refining, and steel), the cost of an efficient plant is so high that there is little point in pretending that competition can be readily open to new producers. This means that relying on competition to regulate output and prices in these industries is risky, but that government action to

[6]See, for example, T.R. Saving, "Estimation of Optimum Size of Plant by the Survivor Technique," *Quarterly Journal of Economics,* November 1961.

break up the oligopolies would also risk insisting on inefficiently small firms.

Many economists are critical of the Robinson-Patman Act, designed primarily to protect small competitors against large ones, even when the large competitors are more efficient in satisfying consumer needs. Recent Supreme Court decisions applying the Antimerger Act are open to the same criticism. They tend to protect small competitors, not competition. From the economist's and the consumer's point of view, it's not clear why price cutting isn't just what competition is supposed to produce, as long as it isn't used as a device for driving out competitors by temporarily selling below cost just to gain a monopoly position.

Antitrust and economic progress

The other big question about monopoly and partial monopoly is what they do to the rate of economic progress—whether they contribute to or impede a dynamically growing economy. The issues and some of the facts were presented in the concluding sections of Chapter 26. Broadly speaking, those industries with the highest growth rates tend to be oligopolies—big firms with large R&D expenditures. Most research and development spending is done by large firms. Productivity has grown more slowly in industries dominated by small firms (except agriculture, with its government financing and distribution of research). But the picture is far from uniform; there are numerous exceptions, and industries protected against entry by new competitors clearly have the power to suppress innovations that might otherwise have been forced by competition.

What is the implication for antitrust? Not clear. It seems certain that we can generally not expect much R&D spending from small firms in industries that approach perfect competition, however aggressively they may compete for the consumer's favor. If we want R&D in such industries, the pattern of government financing and dissemination of results in agriculture may be the best way. But remember that firms far short of giant size can spend heavily on research and obtain results that compete with the giants' in many industries. Even on the score of economic progress, few industries require such large firms

for efficient R&D that they cannot support numerous sellers and substantial price competition.

The dilemma of modern antitrust policy

The dilemma of antitrust policy in the modern economy is a painful one. How can we have both the efficiencies of size and the benefits of active competition among many sellers? Recent antitrust enforcement has generally sought a compromise, but one leaning toward more firms and more competition. Business claims of cost economies from large-scale production have been ruled inadmissible as protection against application of the antitrust laws.

By contrast, *Fortune* magazine has urged a major revolution in our antitrust laws and philosophy, as follows:

> Congress should amend the antitrust statutes to make it clear that the national policy is to foster competition by punishing restraints of trade, including conspiracies to fix prices, limit production, allocate markets, and suppress innovation; but that it is not the national policy to prefer any particular size, shape, or number of firms to any other size, shape or number; and that mergers— horizontal, vertical, or conglomerate—are entirely legal unless they spring from a manifest attempt to restrain trade.[7]

Would this be a good substitute for our present antitrust policy? How is the public interest best served?

BIGNESS AND THE CONCENTRATION OF ECONOMIC POWER

Can antitrust do anything about the problem of the sheer power of bigness? Should we break up the giant corporations or regulate them more just because they're too big, whether or not they violate the Sherman Act? This is the most basic question of all for some people. Political power, economic power, power over other people's lives, just the power that goes with a billion dollars—these are the things that worry many people most about big business.

The power of big business seems espe-

[7] Max Ways, "Antitrust in an Era of Radical Change," *Fortune,* March 1966.

cially alarming to some observers because in many firms "inside management" has a substantially free hand. Although stockholders theoretically direct the management, as a practical matter few stockholders know much about the details of management or have any interest in interfering in it. To whom is big management really responsible in the exercise of its economic power?

A.A. Berle, a long-time observer of the business corporation, pointed up this problem. Only 500 corporations control nearly two-thirds of the entire manufacturing sector of the American economy, he wrote, and within each of those 500, a relatively small group holds the ultimate decision-making power. "Since the United States carries on not quite half of the manufacturing production of the entire world today, these 500 groupings—each with its own little dominating pyramid within—represent a concentration of power over economies which makes the medieval feudal system look like a Sunday School party. In sheer economic power, this has gone far beyond anything we have yet seen."[8] Berle's solution: more effective antitrust action.

J.K. Galbraith, in his best-selling *Economics and the Public Purpose,* goes even further—arguing that big-business planning and control have substantially replaced market competition in modern America. He updates Berle's data on the role of the largest corporations in manufacturing, and argues that the big oligopolies have become self-perpetuating bureaucracies, whose main goals are growth and security, not profit maximization. They manage consumer demand through advertising, and largely avoid outside control through the capital markets by using undistributed earnings to expand. Long-range planning and solid, prosperous growth are the keynote, without undue, disruptive, old-style competition. The government generally cooperates by providing a stable growing economy, free education for new employees, and expensive R&D to aid further growth. The military-industrial complex is an extreme case of the way big business cooperates with (manipulates) government to obtain special concessions and lead a comfortable, profitable life. With these policies, the big quietly grow bigger and more powerful.

In essence, government, increasingly under the influence of corporate leaders, protects and approves this secure, stable world for the giants, unless they abuse the mores unduly or openly try to aggrandize their positions by acquiring or squeezing out smaller firms. Antitrust acts mainly to prevent open collusion and mergers among the smaller competitors, which, as a practical matter, are probably their only way of challenging the concentrated power of the giants.

Galbraith's solution? Not to break up the giants, for that would waste the economic benefits of modern technology that underlie the success of big firms. Rather, he says that the answer is increasing government ownership and operation of the big oligopolies to return control over them from the bureaucrats to the people; and increasing government participation throughout the economy to provide the good life—more and better public services in the modern affluent society. A national health program, slum clearance, better housing, state-supported symphonies and drama—through a bigger public sector with more taxes and more government spending, we can improve the quality of modern life, not merely the quantity of GNP.

Most economists believe that Berle and Galbraith have overdrawn their case. Competition in most markets is far too pervasive in most industries to permit the comfortable life for the giants that Galbraith paints. Manufacturing now accounts for only about a quarter of total GNP and 22 percent of all jobs; big firms are far less dominant in the nonmanufacturing sectors of the economy. The turnover in firms at the top is too fast and the number of failures too large to support Galbraith's picture of comfortable security. Moreover, one may ask whether government operation of major sections of the economy would not just substitute government bureaucracy for private bureaucracy, when, so far at least, government bureaucracy has not proved notably efficient or responsive to the wishes of the people. Who would make the decisions under government operations?

Yet Galbraith has touched a sensitive nerve. Many Americans are uneasy about the concentration of economic power in the big corporations, even though they support the predominantly capitalist American economy. What is your answer?

[8] A.A. Berle, *Economic Power and the Free Society* (New York: Fund for the Republic, 1958), p. 14.

REVIEW

1. Does big business have too much power? (Define "power" carefully in your answer.) If so, who should do something about it, and what should they do?
2. How should we decide whether it is in the public interest for any industry to consist of a large or a small number of firms?
3. Many businessmen argue that vigorous government prosecution under the anti-trust laws is a sign of government antagonism toward business and profits. Is this a proper criticism? If you think it isn't, how would you convince such a critic?
4. Critics of big business often argue that the majority of large modern corporations could be broken up into several competing units without loss of productive efficiency, because as a rule they control many plants, each of which could just as well operate as a separate, competitive business. Is this argument a sound one? If so, how should we go about implementing the proposal?
5. Should conglomerate mergers be challenged under the antitrust laws, even though the merging firms handle noncompeting products?
6. Would you favor direct government conduct or support of all basic research, with the results freely available to all? List the advantages and disadvantages. Who should pay for the research?
7. Would you favor tripling the congressional appropriation to the Department of Justice for antitrust enforcement?

In 1966, the Supreme Court, by a 6–2 decision, found that a merger of Von's Grocery Company and Shopping Bag Food Stores in Los Angeles violated Section 7 of the Clayton Act (often called the Celler Anti-Merger Act). The following extended excerpts summarize the majority and minority decisions. Which do you think was right? (See the questions at the end of the case.)

The majority decision   On March 25, 1960, the United States brought this action charging that the acquisition by Von's Grocery Company of its direct competitor Shopping Food Stores, both large retail grocery companies in Los Angeles, California, violated #7 of the Clayton Act which, as amended in 1950 by the Celler-Kefauver Anti-Merger Bill, provides:

> No corporation engaged in commerce shall acquire the whole or any part of the assets of another corporation engaged also in commerce, where in any line of commerce in any section of the country the effect of such acquisition may be substantially to lessen competition or to create a monopoly.

The market involved here is the retail grocery market in the Los Angeles area. In 1958 Von's retail sales ranked third in the area and Shopping Bag's ranked sixth. In 1960 their sales together were 7.5 percent of the total two and one half billion dollars of retail groceries sold in the Los Angeles market each year. For many years before the merger both companies had enjoyed great success as rapidly growing companies. From 1948 to 1958 the number of Von's stores in the Los Angeles area practically doubled from 14 to 27, while at the same time the number of Shopping Bag's stores jumped from 15 to 34. During that same decade, Von's sales increased fourfold and its share of the market almost doubled while Shopping Bag's sales multiplied seven times and its share of the market tripled. The merger of these two highly successful, expanding and aggressive competitors created the second

largest grocery chain in Los Angeles with sales of almost $172,488,000 annually.

In addition the findings of the District Court show that the number of owners operating a single store in the Los Angeles retail grocery market decreased from 5,365 in 1950 to 3,818 in 1961. By 1963, three years after the merger, the number of single-store owners had dropped still further to 3,590. During roughly the same period from 1953 to 1962 the number of chains with two or more grocery stores increased from 96 to 150. While the grocery business was being concentrated into the hands of fewer and fewer owners, the small companies were continually being absorbed by the larger firms through mergers. According to an exhibit prepared by one of the Government's expert witnesses, in the period from 1949 to 1958 nine of the top 20 chains acquired 126 stores from their smaller competitors. . . . These facts alone are enough to cause us to conclude contrary to the District Court that the Von's Shopping Bag merger did violate #7. . . .

From this country's beginning there has been an abiding and widespread fear of the evils which flow from monopoly—that is the concentration of economic power in the hands of the few. On the basis of this fear, in 1890, when many of the nation's industries were already concentrated into what Congress deemed too few hands, it passed the Sherman Act in an attempt to prevent further concentration and to preserve competition among a large number of sellers. . . .

Like the Sherman Act in 1890 and the Clayton Act in 1914, the basic purpose of the 1950 Celler-Kefauver Bill was to prevent economic concentration in the American economy by keeping a large number of small competitors in business. In stating the purpose of the bill, both of its sponsors, Representative Celler and Senator Kefauver, emphasized their fear, widely shared by other members of Congress, that this concentration was rapidly driving the small businessman out of the market. As we said in *Brown Shoe Co.* v. *United States*, 370 U.S. 294,315,

[9]384 U.S. 270.

"The dominant theme pervading congressional consideration of the 1950 amendments was a fear of what was considered to be a rising tide of economic concentration in the American economy." By using terms in #7 which look not merely to the actual present effect of a merger but instead to its effect upon future competition, Congress sought to preserve competition among many small businesses by arresting a trend toward concentration in its incipiency before that trend developed to the point that a market was left in the grip of a few big companies. Thus, where concentration is gaining momentum in a market, we must be alert to carry out Congress' intent to protect competition against ever-increasing concentration through mergers. . . .

The facts of this case present exactly the threatening trend toward concentration which Congress wanted to halt. The number of small grocery companies in the Los Angeles retail grocery market had been declining rapidly before the merger and continued to decline rapidly afterwards. This rapid decline in the number of grocery store owners moved hand in hand with a large number of significant absorptions of the small companies by the larger ones. In the midst of this steadfast trend toward concentration, Von's and Shopping Bag, two of the most successful and largest companies in the area, jointly owning 66 grocery stores, merged to become the second largest chain in Los Angeles. . . .

Appellee's primary argument is that the merger between Von's and Shopping Bag is not prohibited by #7 because the Los Angeles grocery market was competitive before the merger, has been since, and may continue to be in the future. Even so, #7 "requires not merely an appraisal of the immediate impact of the merger upon competition, but a prediction of its impact upon competitive conditions in the future; this is what is meant when it is said that the amended #7 was intended to arrest anticompetitive tendencies in their 'incipiency.'" (*United States* v. *Philadelphia Nat. Bank,* 374 U.S., p. 362.) It is enough for us that Congress feared that a market marked at the same time by both a continuous decline in the number of small businesses and a large number of mergers would, slowly but inevitably, gravitate from a market of many small competitors to one dominated by one or a few

giants, and competition would thereby be destroyed. . . .

The minority dissent   First, the standards of #7 require that every corporate acquisition be judged in the light of the contemporary economic context of its industry. Second, the purpose of #7 is to protect competition, not to protect competitors, and every #7 case must be decided in the light of that clear statutory purpose. Today the Court turns its back on these two basic principles and on all the decisions that have followed them.

The Court makes no effort to appraise the competitive effects of this acquisition in terms of the contemporary economy of the retail food industry in the Los Angeles area. Instead, through a simple exercise in sums, it finds that the number of individual competitors in the market has decreased over the years, and, apparently on the theory that the degree of competition is invariably proportional to the number of competitors, it holds that this historic reduction in the number of competing units is enough under #7 to invalidate a merger within the market, with no need to examine the economic concentration of the market, the level of competition in the market, or the potential adverse effect of the merger on that competition. This startling per se rule is contrary not only to our previous decisions, but contrary to the language of #7, contrary to the legislative history of the 1950 amendment, and contrary to economic reality. . . .

The concept of arresting restraints of trade in their "incipiency" was not an innovation of the 1950 amendment. The notion of incipiency was part of the report on the original Clayton Act by the Senate Committee on the Judiciary in 1914, and it was reiterated in the Senate report in 1950. That notion was not left undefined. The legislative history leaves no doubt that the applicable standard for measuring the substantiality of the effect of a merger on competition was that of a "reasonable probability" of lessening competition. The standard was thus more stringent than that of a "mere possibility" on the one hand and more lenient than that of a "certainty" on the other. I cannot agree that the retail grocery business in Los Angeles is in an incipient or any other stage of a trend toward lessening of competition, or that the effective level of concentration in the industry has increased. Moreover, there is no indication that the present merger, or the trend in this industry as a whole, augers any danger whatsoever for the small businessman. The Court has substituted bare conjecture for the statutory standard of a reasonable probability that competition may be lessened. . . .

I believe that even the most superficial analysis of the record makes plain the fallacy of the Court's syllogism that competition is necessarily reduced when the bare number of competitors has declined. In any meaningful sense, the structure of the Los Angeles grocery market remains unthreatened by concentration. Local competition is vigorous to a fault, not only among chain stores themselves but also between chain stores and single-store operators. . . . The record simply cries out that the numerical decline in the number of single-store owners is the result of transcending social and technological changes that positively preclude the inference that competition has suffered because of the attrition of competitors. . . .

Section 7 was never intended by Congress for use by the Court as a charter to roll back the supermarket revolution. Yet the Court's opinion is hardly more than a requiem for the so-called "Mom and Pop" grocery stores—the bakery and butcher shops, the vegetable and fish markets—that are now economically and technologically obsolete in many parts of the country. No action by this Court can restore the old single-line Los Angeles food stores that have been run over by the automobile or obliterated by the freeway.

The transformation of American society since the Second World War has not completely shelved these specialty stores, but it has relegated them to a much less central role in our food economy. Today's dominant enterprise in food retailing is the supermarket. Accessible to the housewife's automobile from a wide radius, it houses under a single roof the entire food requirements of the family. Only through the sort of reactionary philosophy that this Court long ago rejected in the Due Process Clause area can the Court read into the legislative history of #7 its attempt to make the automobile stand still, to mold the food economy of today into the market pattern of another era. . . .

The District Court found that Von's stores were located in the southern and western portions of the Los Angeles metropolitan area, and that the Shopping Bag stores were located in the northern and eastern portions. In each of the areas in which Von's and Shopping Bag stores competed directly, there were also at least six other chain stores and several smaller stores competing for the patronage of customers. . . . The actual market share foreclosed by the elimination of Shopping Bag as an independent competitor was thus slightly less than 1 percent of the total grocery store sales in the area. . . .

Moreover, it is clear that there are no substantial barriers to market entry. . . .

In your judgment, should this merger have been allowed—under Section 7 of the Clayton Act? Was forbidding the merger in the public interest, whatever you think about its legality?

CHAPTER 28 CONSUMER PROTECTION AND GOVERNMENT REGULATION

Where there is active competition among sellers, that competition for consumers' dollars protects consumers. If seller *A* doesn't give consumers what they want, they can turn to *B*, who will be happy to do so, assuming that consumers are willing to pay the cost of producing the good. The consumer is king, and competition guards his interests. Well-meaning attempts to protect consumers through government regulation are both unnecessary and often harmful. So say many economists, reminding you of Adam Smith's "invisible hand."

But lots of consumer advocates, led by Ralph Nader in recent years, say, "No way!" First, they say, active competition doesn't exist in many markets. Second, even where it does, consumers aren't able to protect themselves adequately from the greed and wiles of sellers, especially big corporations. Most of the goods consumers buy, they argue, come from giant businesses that hold all the cards in dealing with individual consumers. They twist consumers' wants through advertising, often misleading or downright dishonest. They offer only the goods on which they can make big profits, not the ones consumers would like to have. Many products are complicated, and there's no effective way for consumers to detect the poor ones until after they've spent their money. The giant firms produce cars that are "unsafe at any speed," as Nader's first book was titled; toys that endanger children who play with them; drugs and pesticides that threaten the health of all of us; shoddy products that wear out too fast and don't do what they're supposed to. As the final section of Chapter 22 stressed, "market failures" occur when consumers lack accurate information on products available, where advertising distorts their wants, and so on. The invisible hand falters, the critics argue.

Since the turn of the century, new legislation has intermittently been passed to protect both consumers and small competitors against unfair competition through misrepresentation, misleading advertising, and the like. The Food and Drug and the Federal Meat Inspection Acts of 1906 and 1909, and the Federal Trade Commission Act of 1914, were early examples. The New Deal spawned a whole set of new regulatory agencies—for example, the Securities and Exchange Commission (SEC), Federal Aviation Administration and Civil Aeronautics Board (FAA and CAB), Federal Communications Commission (FCC), and Federal Power Commission (FPC)—and gave new powers to others. With the advent of modern "consumerism," the past decade has seen a flood of new consumer protection measures, ranging from auto safety to honest packaging, product safety, truth in lending, and occupational licensing. This has produced a new alphabet jungle—EPA, CPSC, NEFP, OSHA, NHTSA, and many others. The American instinct seems to be, if you don't like it, regulate it.[1]

What has been the outcome of these new controls and regulations? The basic case for them has been to protect consumers where they cannot protect themselves in the market, and, to a lesser extent, to redistribute incomes. In short, they have presumably been designed to correct market failures. How well have they done? Consider a sample of them: (1) some consumer protection measures, (2) government licensing of occupations, and (3) some of the regulatory commissions themselves.

[1] For a summary of such measures, see Clair Wilcox, *Public Policies toward Business* (New York: Richard D. Irwin, 1966), Chaps. 24–25.

CONSUMER PROTECTION
Auto safety

Purchasers of new cars produced in the United States in 1975 paid perhaps $2 to $3 billion extra for the equipment and modifications necessary to meet federal safety requirements—mandatory buzzers and harnesses, padded dashboards, safety glass, impact-absorbing bumpers, and the like. The stated goal was to protect consumers. Nader's Raiders were pleased, although unhappy that so many lives had been lost before the measures were passed. Many consumers were also pleased. A lot of others complained bitterly, and the mandatory buzzer-harness interlock that kept the car from starting until the driver was fastened in lasted only about six months. Most car passengers, especially drivers, while potentially safer than before against serious injury, continued not to fasten their seat belts.

As an economist, how would you evaluate the consumer protection legislation? Your economics should lead you to a familiar question: Did the marginal gains exceed the marginal costs? This is a difficult question to answer, partly because we don't have all the relevant information, and partly because the people paying and those benefiting are not the same and we have no satisfactory way of comparing costs and benefits as between different people. If you say that a life is priceless and the new legislation saves lives, you will presumably rate it high. But if, as seems more reasonable, safety is something each of us considers very important, but hardly of infinite value when the chance we will be involved in an auto accident is quite small, we face a cost–benefit tradeoff. Is the extra safety I get from each safety component worth what I have to pay for it?

As Case 1 emphasized, moreover, your economics should lead you to ask another question: Why should the government require everybody to buy this set of safety devices rather than leave to each person the option of deciding for himself whether it's worth the price? We don't require everyone to buy warm woolies for winter, or gloves and scarves, even though those would presumably help keep him healthier. Why auto safety? One answer might be that the government knows better than each of us what is good for him—but that line doesn't read very well. Another answer might be that auto safety equipment has important externalities. It protects others against my bad driving; hence, I should have to pay for it whether or not I want to buy it for my own protection. If we consider safety equipment to include headlights, good brakes, and the like, this is a compelling argument. I shouldn't be free to endanger the lives of others by driving without good brakes. But for seat belts, air bags, padded dashes, shock-absorbing bumpers, and the like, the case is different. These mainly, or entirely, protect the occupants of the car, not the innocent other party.[2] Perhaps you can stretch the argument that without the safety equipment, the car's occupants would be more likely to be injured, and society would have to take care of them if they could not pay for their own medical attention; but that is carrying the reasoning on externalities quite a way. Many economists, using the reasoning of the preceding chapters, would say that unless there are clearly substantial positive externalities from adding the safety equipment, the presumption is that each individual is the best judge of whether the extra benefits are worth the extra cost to him. This has the further advantage that we don't need to balance out marginal cost against marginal benefit for society as a whole—a very difficult task—since we can leave the choice up to each individual to decide for himself, which he is presumably competent to do.

Mandatory auto safety equipment is an interesting example of government regulation to protect consumers. The problem is more complex than it may seem. For example, suppose that without legislation, most consumers would not buy today's safety equipment, but some would like it. Would auto manufacturers offer the option to those who want to buy? If so, at what price?

[2] Indeed, some economists argue that the added protection for the driver makes him more likely to take risks and hence to injure others, so the safety equipment probably leads to no reduction at all in total injuries and deaths. See S. Peltzman, "The Effects of Automobile Safety Regulation," *Journal of Political Economy*, August 1975.

Drugs

The worst horror stories supporting the case for government protection of consumers have been those of untested, unsafe drugs. Consumers have little competence to protect themselves in such cases; they must rely on doctors' recommendations, hearsay, or hunch, and are easy prey to unscrupulous drug manufacturers and panacea salesmen. Modern drugs have revolutionized the practice of medicine, but they have also brought great dangers.

The best-known example is thalidomide. During the late 1950s, this new sedative was widely used in Europe, where it seemed highly effective and free of unwanted side effects. Dr. Frances Kelsey, of the U.S. Food and Drug Administration, in considering thalidomide for use in the United States, noted German reports of nerve inflammations where the drug had been heavily used and held up U.S. approval to check the facts further. Within a year, major birth defects began to appear everywhere that thalidomide had been used by pregnant women, although the connection was not recognized for some time—with the poignant results that became worldwide news as thousands of deformed babies were born. Dr. Kelsey was a heroine in the United States. The Food and Drug Administration's regulations on approval of new drugs, the most stringent in the world, seemed clearly validated. Helpless consumers certainly need protection against dangerous drugs.

But consider another case: High blood pressure (hypertension) afflicts millions of people in the United States, bringing disability or death to many. A powerful new drug, guanoxan, has been widely used in England since 1964 to reduce high blood pressure, but it has serious side effects on the functioning of the liver in a substantial fraction of people who take it, although these side effects can be reversed if the drug's use is stopped. Many British doctors believe the liver risk is worth taking for hypertension patients who don't respond to other treatment. In the United States, however, guanoxan is illegal; the FDA has decided it is too dangerous to use. Although an estimated 25 million Americans suffer from hypertension, the FDA has approved none of six new drugs that have come into wide

European use in treating the disease over the past decade.

Has the FDA protected consumers, or condemned an unknown number of hypertension sufferers to pain and earlier death than they might otherwise have faced with use of the new European drugs? Economics cannot answer the question. But it does suggest that drugs, like almost everything else, involve tradeoffs between costs and benefits. To look at only the "protection" provided Americans against liver dysfunction from taking guanoxan is to look at only one side of the problem. The possible gains to hypertension sufferers that are lost by the FDA's prohibition need to be measured against the possible costs. Clearly, one alternative would be a more permissive approach by the FDA, which would permit individual doctors and patients more choice in such cases as guanoxan.

The FDA has a long history of stricter barriers to the introduction of new drugs until they have been proved "both safe and effective" than comparable agencies have in West European nations. Most estimates put the approval lag behind European nations at two to five years. Before 1962, when FDA rules were tightened substantially after the thalidomide episode, some 40 to 50 major new drugs were approved each year. In the following decade, the number fell to 15, even though U.S. drug manufacturers greatly increased their spending on research. American drug manufacturers complain that FDA approval requires extremely long, expensive test procedures, which hold health-giving drugs off the market for years and seriously underrate the costs to potential patients. They argue for quicker provisional approval with continued close surveillance during early years of use. They report years of testing and literally thousands of pages of test results required for approval of new drugs in recent years. Moreover, they argue that sometimes rigid test requirements may do great harm. For example, all drugs must be tested first on animals. But penicillin, one of mankind's greatest lifesavers, will kill hamsters and guinea pigs if repeatedly administered. Thus, penicillin would probably never have been approved if the FDA had the same standards 30 years ago that it uses now.

On the other hand, other legislators and consumer advocates argue for more, not less, stringent procedures to protect the American people from unsafe, inadequately tested, overpriced new drugs. They accuse the drug companies of being interested only in profits, not patients' welfare. They cite a long history of new drugs with disastrous results for users before FDA rules were tightened up.

Economic analysis suggests an approach to weighing such arguments. Again, comparing marginal costs and benefits is the key, but be sure you've included *all* the relevant costs and benefits. Clearly, the consumer needs protection in the drug case, but equally clearly, too much protection may involve a higher cost than he may want to pay if he considers all the costs and benefits.[3]

Building codes

Nearly every city has building codes which specify minimum standards for plumbing, electrical wiring, building materials, and the like in all newly constructed or renovated houses. The stated purpose is usually to protect buyers against shoddy construction and unsafe buildings. Often the codes specify that major plumbing and wiring must be done by contractors or workmen licensed by the city, to ensure that the work will meet code standards.

To many consumers, government protection against shoddy, unsafe construction makes sense. They don't know enough about construction to be sure otherwise that they are getting good quality construction, and safe plumbing and wiring. Is this a consumer protection regulation that everyone can support?

Alas, no. The situation should bring the auto safety case above to mind. Unless there are important externalities involved, why should the government tell you that you must buy grade A, expensive plumbing, wiring, and other materials, when grade B might meet your standards adequately? Why should the government tell you that you must have an expensive licensed plumber or electrical contractor, using expensive union labor, do your work rather than permitting you to hire less expensive workers or do it

[3]For a popular analysis of the drug-regulation problem, see W.S. Ross, "The Medicines We Need—But Can't Have," *Reader's Digest*, October 1973.

yourself? You're the one who is going to live in the house, and who will pay the cost if you have to replace the plumbing in five years, or suffer the damage if faulty wiring leads to a fire.

Perhaps there are positive externalities for the rest of the community from your using the code-specified, high-cost materials and labor, but it's not apparent what they would be in most cases, beyond meeting minimum fire-protection standards. Or one might argue that the code will protect future buyers of your house, who otherwise might innocently buy a house with inferior wiring and plumbing. But this gives little credit to the intelligence of the future buyer. If he has any sense at all, unless he's competent to judge for himself, he'll surely want to get an expert appraiser to come in and look over the house before he buys it, which will readily disclose the state of the plumbing and wiring.

While many codes have been passed by city councils with the best of intentions, often they have become highly effective means of protecting the quasi-monopoly positions of materials suppliers, licensed contractors, and union labor in the city. Attempts to relax codes to permit use of new, cheaper materials and methods have generally met bitter resistance from entrenched suppliers and labor unions. Thus, not surprisingly, the "protection" the code gives consumers costs something, because it prescribes high standards. No less, it costs because it effectively shuts out cheaper materials, contractors, and labor that might have done the work for less. Whether the extra "quality" is worth the extra cost to each home buyer or renovator will depend on his comparison of marginal costs and benefits. But unless he violates the law (a risky practice, since the city building inspector may require any "substandard" work to be torn out and replaced according to the code), the buyer has no option. He must buy the code-approved, expensive materials and construction, whether or not he thinks they're worth to him what they cost.

Conclusion: Should city building codes be eliminated? Not necessarily, of course. Some may provide minimal standards necessary to the public health and safety, and no more. But economics suggests comparing marginal costs and marginal benefits again—a careful look at just how much of the prescribed standards are unnecessary or outdated, how much can safely be left to individual choice, and how much the code has in effect been taken over by local suppliers, contractors, and unions to protect partial monopoly positions.

Gasoline prices

In late 1973, the OPEC countries (mainly the Middle East Arab nations) clamped an embargo on oil shipments to the United States and other oil-importing nations, especially those that had supported Israel in the Arab-Israeli war. The resulting "energy crisis" was a complex problem, and here we want to consider only one aspect of it—the temporary "shortage" of gasoline and the government regulation of prices and supplies adopted to deal with it.

It was quickly apparent that, if the embargo was effective, there would soon be not enough gasoline for everybody to have as much as he had been using; we were importing about 15–20 percent of our gas consumption. The government therefore imposed a price ceiling on gasoline and an allocation system that it hoped would provide each oil company and each section of the country about the same share of the available total as it had been getting. Thus, the burden of reduced consumption would fall roughly equally on different parts of the country and different companies. The price ceiling, according to many congressmen and news writers, was intended primarily to protect consumers against the rapacity of the giant oil companies.

What happened? The simple supply-and-demand analysis of Chapter 6 should give you most of the answer. When government regulation to "protect the consumer" fixed the price below the market-clearing level, the price system was barred from its usual rationing function of dividing up the available gas among buyers. With the price of gas fixed too low to clear the market, there was excess demand, a gas "shortage." Some other way of rationing the limited supply had to take over. Long lines formed at gas stations as everybody tried to get the gas he wanted. Tempers flared as people tried to sneak into lines, or as suppliers ran out before all those waiting were served. Service-station operators set limits of 5 or 10 gallons to a customer, and some hopeful buyers used as much gas sitting in line as they got when they arrived at the pumps. Millions of hours were wasted sitting. A few service stations contrived imaginative plans. One announced a price of $10 for each car wash—with a tankful of gas thrown in at the legal price. Another formed a club whose members got a new stuffed radiator mascot each month for a mere $25, with a tank of gas thrown in each week at the legal price. There was no price ceiling on car washes, mascots, or clubs. The air was full of talk of plans to institute formal gas rationing with government-determined quotas for different classes of drivers. Farmers, doctors, and others immediately asserted that they had a priority claim for adequate gas, since only that way could they serve the public. Others contrived more elaborate schemes, including salable ration tickets, with the government making a market in them.

At the national level, allocation problems developed rapidly. "Independent" oil companies protested that they weren't getting enough gas from the big integrated producers to permit them to stay in business. Spot shortages developed all over the country, while spot surpluses were reported in other areas. New York and other big eastern cities were particularly hard hit, while small western communities seemed to have more gas than they could sell, partly because people were reluctant to leave home on long trips when they might run out of gas en route. Vacation areas protested bitterly that they were being ruined. The Federal Energy Administration in Washington reshuffled company and area quotas frantically, and produced regulations to avoid the worst crises as fast as they could, but they usually seemed to be about two weeks behind each developing crisis.

Should the government have simply let the price rise to ration available gas, rather than imposing price ceilings and allocations? Many economists thought so, pointing to the "crises" that predictably arose everywhere under the rapidly devised set of controls. Others argued strongly against the free-market solution because, they said, price would then rise very sharply, the rich would get all the gas, and the

big oil companies would make huge profits off the helpless public. Some economists countered with a proposal to tax excess oil-industry profits, with the proceeds to be rebated to the public.

Finding the best solution was a complex problem. The planners had to consider, in addition to the immediate crises, the longer-run need to lead people to economize on the use of energy, and to stimulate production of more gasoline and alternative energy sources, where rising prices could also provide a powerful incentive toward both goals. More government regulation is an appealing answer to any nasty problem that comes along. But history attests that regulating any part of the complex American economy gets rapidly into hundreds, and then thousands, of interacting decisions that have to be made in replacing the price system. Government regulation may protect consumers better than relying on the market for price, allocation, and rationing decisions, but even elementary economics confirms that the regulators had better be prepared for geometrically expanding complexities and a flood of unhappy protests from across the land.

OCCUPATIONAL LICENSING

Nearly every state licenses architects, barbers, beauticians, chiropractors, dentists, embalmers, lawyers, pharmacists, physicians, registered nurses, and veterinarians. Without a state license, practice of any of these occupations is illegal. Many states also license a wide variety of other occupations—bail bondsmen, garage operators, pest controllers, plumbers, tree surgeons, junk dealers, and others. The stated purpose is generally to protect the public against incompetent, shoddy, or unsafe work. Before the turn of the century, the number of licensed occupations was far smaller. What accounts for their rapid increase, and what have been their main effects?

Although consumer protection is commonly advanced as the main goal, most of the arguments for more and stricter licensing have, strikingly, come from the occupations themselves, not from consumers. And little wonder, if you stop to think about it. Government licensing is a powerful way indeed to restrict entry into an occupation, and the higher the "consumer protection" standards, the harder it will be for new practitioners to enter and drive down prices and incomes. Chicago's George Stigler has compared incomes in a list of licensed occupations with those in nonlicensed occupations requiring roughly comparable education and skills, and finds, to no economists' surprise, that median incomes in the former are about 50 percent higher.[4] Restrictions on entry apply to individual occupations as well as to big oligopoly firms.

This is not to suggest that all members of licensed occupations are greedy, self-seeking souls who merely want to pad their pockets. On the contrary, many of them honestly believe that the public needs protection from untrained incompetents and quacks in their fields. And such may indeed be the case. But the same questions as in the preceding section recur: Should consumers have the option to decide for themselves whether the extra "protection" is worth the extra cost? And note that the extra cost may be not only the cost of higher-quality services but also the monopoly cost of higher prices because of restricted supply. If we don't permit individual consumers to make this choice, is the social marginal benefit of the "consumer protection" provided larger than the social marginal cost?

Many requirements for obtaining licenses are sensible and important. But in some instances, the licensing seems primarily to raise the incomes of the licensees by keeping down the number of competitors. In most cases, not surprisingly, the occupations themselves exercise substantial influence over the entrance standards set. They are the ones most deeply concerned, whereas—as in most other aspects of lawmaking and government regulation—any individual consumer is likely to be affected only slightly by how the standards are set. Most men go to the barber mainly to get a haircut, and have little interest in his competence in dermatology, which is part of the long training many states require for a barber's license. But they aren't affected enough to mount a major campaign to reduce the license requirements, which would probably

reduce the price of haircuts. Most women can make their own judgments as to which beauticians do their hair best, without wanting to pay for a long training period that has little direct relevance to hair styling—but it's not worth a major undertaking to modify state licensing requirements for beauticians.

The case of physicians is perhaps the most striking and interesting of all. Nearly everyone agrees that some form of government licensing is desirable for doctors—but how much, and how exercised? Entry to the medical profession in America is largely controlled by state accreditation of medical schools, but the states in turn rely heavily on the recommendations of the Council on Medical Education and Hospitals of the American Medical Association. Thus, it is largely the AMA (the present doctors) who determine the standards that new doctors must meet, and to a substantial extent how many new doctors will be trained each year.

Not surprisingly, the standards set for new physicians by doctors already in the profession are high. In 1974, nearly 100,000 hopeful students took the standard national entrance exams for admission to medical school, but fewer than 14,000 were admitted to the approved schools. The effect on physicians' incomes has, again not surprisingly, been spectacular. The mean income of physicians and surgeons in 1960 was $15,000; in 1975, it was over $70,000, reflecting both restrictions on supply and a sharply rising demand for physicians' services, partly financed by dramatic increases in government funding through Medicare, Medicaid, and medical research activities. This was far greater than the rise in other professional incomes. Strikingly, advertising quoting prices, which would permit the potential patient to compare costs, is strictly forbidden as nonprofessional.

Some observers express surprise that doctors are so "greedy" as to restrict entry and to collect these high incomes for a service so essential to the mass of people. But why should one be surprised? Doctors understandably believe that only thoroughly competent physicians should be permitted to treat the public. They properly argue that they are, on the average, now more highly trained than ever before, and that the road to such high incomes is long and slow. But

[4] Stigler, "The Theory of Regulation," *Bell Journal of Economics and Management Science,* Spring 1971.

more important, if society bestowed on shoe or machinery manufacturers the legal power to restrict entry into their fields and thereby to set prices, should we expect them to open up the industry to many new competitors and thereby drive down the prices of their products?

Even with their restrictions on entry, present medical licensing arrangements don't adequately protect the public from incompetence and poor medical service. For one thing, most doctors now practising have not had to meet today's high entrance standards. More important, doctors are scarce, and the best way to ensure adequate medical care for the public is to increase the supply of doctors. This is unlikely to happen as long as the doctors themselves are given the power to determine the supply of medical services—as is true with most other occupational licensing. The problem of providing the public the optimal level of medical service and the right amount of protection is, of course, more complex than these few paragraphs suggest. But the application of simple supply-and-demand economics throws some of the main issues into sharp relief.[5]

THE PRACTICAL POLITICS OF REGULATION

When Americans are unhappy with the behavior of business, they cry for government regulation. The man in the street's faith in more competition to provide consumer protection against business is limited. When he thinks business is unreasonable, he wants the government to do something about it.

This attitude has spawned a large group of government regulatory agencies, big and small. Their history has varied. In general, new commissions have moved with vigor to carry out their duties during their early years. The legislation is new, the mission seems clear, strong appointments are made to the commissions, and there is enthusiasm for getting the job done. Often the businesses being regulated have pro-

[5] Some economists argue that the social costs of government regulation (largely aimed to protect consumers) are substantially larger than the social costs of monopoly per se. See Richard Posner, "The Social Costs of Monopoly and Regulation," *Journal of Political Economy,* August 1975.

tested that the regulators are overenergetic, even antagonistic. In a few cases, this attitude of vigorous enforcement and protection of the public interest has persisted; the SEC is sometimes cited as an example, although many disagree. But in most cases, after a decade or two the inaugural enthusiasm wears off, new appointments to the regulatory commission are often less than distinguished (often payment of political debts by the administration in power), and gradually the agency develops more "understanding" of the problems of the regulated industry, to the point that it serves as much to protect the industry itself as it does the public interest.

Who regulates whom?

The Interstate Commerce Commission is an example. During the early decades of its existence, the ICC developed an enviable reputation for honesty, expertness, and impartiality. It moved strongly to eliminate railroad-rate discrimination against farmers, other small shippers, and short-haul traffic. Down to World War I, support for the commission came largely from those responsible for its establishment, dissatisfied farmers and commercial shippers. But with the 1920s, this gradually changed. The worst discriminatory practices were gone, "normalcy" was the tone of the times, the railroads had been convinced that they must live with the commission, and their enthusiasm for rampant rate competition had faded. They and the commissioners came to understand each others' problems, new commissioners were appointed from the industry, and retiring commissioners predominantly moved to positions in the industry. The railroads and the commission have both praised their harmonious relations. And the railroads have increasingly looked to the commission for support and defense against new forms of competition.

Since World War II, as rail transport has gradually lost business to trucks, buses, airlines, and pipelines, the ICC has increasingly worked with the railroads to avoid active price competition among themselves and with other carriers. Procedures have become more and more complex and cumbersome, a veritable sea of red tape. The commission must approve each rail-

and truck rate change, and each year thousands of miniscule changes of rates on particular products between particular points clog ICC dockets. The commission has shown little ability to deal with the major problems of transport policy that confront the nation. In recent years, it has increasingly moved toward a more understanding relationship with the trucking industry, similar to that with the railroads. It has been widely criticized for its red tape, its failure to represent the interests of shippers (including, not least, those families at the mercy of truckers in moving their household goods), and its general support of the status quo. Truck rates are much higher on regulated routes than on nonregulated ones. Many trucks are prohibited from carrying cargo on return trips, and must follow long, roundabout routes with certain cargoes, to avoid "excess competition" with established lines. Safety rules are loosely enforced. Unauthorized price competition is forbidden.

Increasingly, economists argue that competition among different carriers (trucks, buses, airlines, railroads, and pipelines) would now be substantial if they were freed from ICC and other government restrictions, and that the ICC should be abolished. Its current social product is negative, they say. It stifles innovation and mainly protects the cartel practices of the common carriers, which can continue only with the legal support given by supportive commission rules on rates and practices.[6]

Similar criticisms have been levied at other major regulatory commissions—the CAB, FCC, FPC, and the commissions that control state and local public utilities. The central problem is the same. Consumer interests often fall by the wayside as the regulated firms and the commissions work together over the years. Generally, the firms have found it more rewarding to cooperate with the commissions than to fight them. Moreover, understandably, the firms have a strong interest in bringing all the political pressure they possess to bear on getting regulations and rulings

that are workable for themselves. History records a long list of generous political contributions from the regulated industries to key state and national legislators who oversee the regulatory commissions. By contrast, individual consumers seldom have enough at stake to mount major attacks on commissions that fail to support their interests aggressively.

But there are many exceptions. Especially in inflationary periods, public utility commissions have usually lagged in permitting higher prices to cover rising costs. In all periods, the rate of return to investors has generally been low in regulated compared to unregulated firms, which may indicate that the regulated firms are less successful in influencing commissions than the analysis above suggests. But your economics from Chapters 25 and 26 should suggest that where price competition is largely eliminated, "service" and advertising competition will take over, raising costs to eliminate profits even at government-supported high cartel prices.

Airline competition is a classic example. The CAB has not licensed a single new major carrier since the 1930s and has generally refused to approve direct price competition, even when suggested by the carriers. But massive advertising and repeated "customer-service" battles on meals, hostesses, passenger lounges, and the like have reduced profits to very low (even negative) levels. This is an oversimple picture of the airlines' plight, but it suggests some results of regulatory price-fixing practices.

A strong counterexample: The Federal Power Commission has for many years held the price of natural gas sold in interstate commerce far below free-market competitive levels, resulting in massive consumption of gas because it has been such a cheap fuel. Today, as a result, the nation faces severe gas "shortages," and the federal government has at last moved to deregulate natural-gas prices in order to discourage consumption and encourage production.

Submerged in a sea of trivia?

Congress established the Federal Trade Commission in 1914 to mount a major attack on the antitrust front, with sweeping

---

[6] For a highly critical, detailed study of the ICC, see the Ralph Nader Study Group Report, *The Interstate Commerce Omission* (New York: Grossman, 1970). A shorter, more balanced criticism is L.M. Kohlmeier, *The Regulators* (New York: Harper & Row, 1969), Chapter 7.

powers of investigation. It also gave the commission a secondary task of protecting both competitors and consumers against unfair competitive practices, deceptive advertising, and the like. When the commission's first major ruling was appealed to the Supreme Court, that body held that all FTC rulings were reviewable by the courts, and the FTC's potential antitrust powers were drastically limited.

Over the years, the FTC has often seemed submerged in a sea of trivia. Each year it has issued hundreds of rulings dealing with such matters as how manufacturers of aluminum storm windows can advertise their product, that lace made elsewhere can't be called Irish lace, that Ipana toothpaste can't claim to prevent pink toothbrush, and the like. In the course of a year, its Bureau of Deceptive Practices examines more than 250,000 printed advertisements and 500,000 radio and TV commercials.

Perhaps its most famous defense of consumers was the Rapid Shave case. Rapid Shave shaving cream produced a TV commercial showing a New York Giants football star, "a man with a problem just like yours . . . a beard as tough as sandpaper," and then a separate picture showing a razor shaving clean a piece of sandpaper lathered with Rapid Shave. But, the FTC found, it wasn't real sandpaper at all. Real sandpaper, it turned out, looks just like plain colored paper on TV, so the advertiser had substituted Plexiglas sprinkled with sand. Real sandpaper, like what the Plexiglas seemed to be, could be shaved as Rapid Shave claimed, but only after prolonged prior soaking. Colgate-Palmolive, the manufacturer, argued that it hadn't committed any material sin, and the FTC examiner agreed that the case should be dismissed. But the FTC overruled the examiner, and two years later the Supreme Court finally upheld the conviction of guilt.

The commission spent sixteen years on the Carter's Little Liver Pills case. Carter's pills had been a household laxative for seventy years when, in the midst of World War II, the FTC challenged the word "liver" in the name because, it alleged, there was nothing of therapeutic value to the liver in the pills. Moreover, the commission staff claimed, the pills would not, as

advertised, "keep one smiling and happy," clearing away "dark clouds of listlessness." Hearings before the FTC examiner ran on for two years, producing a hearing record of 15,000 pages, not including more than 2,000 exhibits. In 1946, the examiner, in a 267-page decision, found Carter's guilty of misleading advertising, and in 1951, six years later, the full commission affirmed his finding. Carter's appealed to the courts, and both the court of appeals and the Supreme Court agreed that the company had not received a fair hearing, remanding the whole affair to the commission. In 1955, after extended further hearings, the FTC examiner once again determined that Carter's was guilty, and in 1956 the full commission issued its new 50-page finding that the company was indeed guilty. Back to the courts went the case, and the court of appeals this time upheld the commission, noting the record of "monumental proportions." The case was closed in 1959 when the Supreme Court refused to review the company's appeal. Out came the word "liver" at last.

In spite of the commission's preoccupation with relatively minor consumer protection matters, Congress has continued to load still more such responsibilities on it. The FTC, with the FDA, is responsible for enforcing the Fair Packaging and Labeling Act, the Wool Products Labeling Act, and a variety of other new consumer protection laws. Intermittently, the commission has attempted to emerge from this sea of detail to deal with larger issues. But it has had limited success, partly because of a long-lived, status quo–oriented staff. In the 1970s, the commission has again moved to expand its work on major antitrust issues, focusing studies and legislative recommendations on the oligopoly problem. It attacked headon as illegal the pervasive oligopoly practice of failing to compete actively through price reductions, even where no collusion was involved. It has pushed for a big budget increase and has hired a core of new, lively economists and lawyers to spearhead the new push. Whether it will overcome the hardening of the arteries of which it has been widely accused remains to be seen.

The practical politics of maintaining a vital, responsive government regulatory agency are difficult indeed to manage. Not least, success requires a continuing public and congressional interest strong enough to ensure the dominance of broad consumer protection goals over the predictable day-to-day drift toward comfortable consensus with the regulated industry and over primary concern with comfortable, safe, and often trivial regulatory issues. Lots of consumers

need protection. The problem is how to provide it effectively.[7]

[7] For a more detailed, lively examination of six consumer protection problems, see the series of articles in *Fortune* on phosphates, toys, food additives, auto safety, appliances, and packaging, during the first half of 1972, reprinted in *Consumerism: Things Ralph Nader Never Told You* (New York: Harper & Row, 1972). For a more scholarly analysis, see Roger Noll, *Reforming Regulation* (Washington, D.C.: The Brookings Institution, 1971).

REVIEW

For analysis and discussion

1. Some free-market advocates argue that government should restrict itself to ensuring that consumers receive honest information on products offered for sale, leaving each consumer free to decide for himself what he is willing to pay for. Do you see any important weaknesses in this position? How much information should the government require sellers to provide on each product, if any, to make it possible for each consumer to protect himself? Would it be desirable to apply your rule to food and drugs?

2. Many consumerists argue that much more government protection is needed for consumers. If you accept this position, what criterion would you use in deciding how safe manufacturers should be required to make lawn mowers? automobiles? Draft the legislation you would favor on this point.

3. The president of the American Bar Association was recently quoted by news reporters as objecting to advertising by lawyers: "Unrestricted advertising would be a disservice to the public. It would mean that some people would retain an attorney on the basis of who mounted the best advertising campaign or who charged the lowest fees, factors which are not relevant to performance." Should the ABA drop the antiadvertising rule from its Code of Professional Ethics? Who would gain and who lose?

4. Do consumers need more protection from advertisers? If so, how would you advocate providing it?

5. Trucks, buses, pipelines, and airlines are now at least as important as railroads in freight and passenger transportation in most areas. Has the time come to abolish the Interstate Commerce Commission and turn the transportation field back to open competition, to provide more effective incentives to efficiency and progress?

In terms of sheer abundance, one of the great economic success stories in this promised land of industrialism has been the outpouring of clever machines for home use. Americans own more than a billion of them, servant mechanisms that grind, cool, moisten, wash, stir, steam, spray, fan, dry, shave, freeze, carve, blend, sharpen, stitch, warn, pop, perk, pick our teeth, shine our shoes, toast our English, keep us informed and entertained, tan our hides, and warm our beds.

Yet nobody seems very happy about it all—not the manufacturers, not the retailers, not even the repairmen, and certainly not the consumers. The White House Office of Consumer Affairs has received thousands of letters complaining about appliances. Only recently did automobiles overtake appliances as the foremost generator of complaints. And the tone of the correspondence suggests not simple anger at fallible appliances, but bitterness and something akin to despair at a great promise broken.

Consumers start feeling helpless about appliances even before they own them. Shopping for appliances is about as confusing for most people as picking the right abstract painting. It sometimes seems that makers and vendors of appliances create confusion deliberately.

Unlike automobile manufacturers, most makers of appliances do not exert much real control over the distribution of their products, and retailers' selling floors typically exhibit a number of competing brands, standing side by side. All the larger appliances are fairly neuter objects, white or avocado shells with gleaming interiors and gadgetry. The customer can neither try the item on and look in a mirror nor demonstrate-drive it, so he is a perfect subject for a hypnotic salesman and a cut-rate price tag. . . .

All three administrators of the Office of Consumer Affairs have urged legislation on several fronts that would affect appliances. One recurrent source of complaint is inadequate regard for safety. . . . "On opening day of the grass mowing season," said the commission report, "the rotary mower begins its work of trimming lawns, fingers, and toes."

Another source of complaint is the well-hedged warranty. Manufacturers' warranties were investigated in 1968 by a presidential task force, which observed that in many cases their legal language actually limited that guarantee rightfully presumed by the buyer for fitness and merchandisability of the product. . . .

. . . The conking out of an appliance is likely to bring a series of irritations for the owner. He may tinker with the machine at first, thinking he can fix it, but almost inevitably he has to telephone for professional assistance. Then the usual complaints about servicemen begin to accumulate, ranging from their casualness about keeping appointments to their bothersome habit of so often not having the needed new parts on the truck. When it is the appliance owner who is paying, the very keenest of the complaints have to do with the cost of repair service. In most communities it is comparable to the cost of a physician's consultation; frequently it is higher. . . .

What, if anything, should the federal or state government do to protect buyers and users of consumer appliances? Among the actions suggested have been these:

1. Establish minimum standards of performance and durability for all consumer appliances.

2. Establish a Consumer Appliance Protection agency to develop and enforce standards for all major appliances and for service work on them. (Alternatively, assign this responsibility to some existing agency.)

3. Make all appliance manufacturers and sellers responsible for triple damages to all consumers if any of their products is shown to be unsafe.

4. Require that detailed information be attached to all appliances, covering their cost of operation, performance specifications, and likely life.

5. License all appliance service firms, approving only those that meet established standards of reliability, satisfactory service, fair price, and guarantee of work done.

[8]Reproduced by permission of Editors of *Fortune, Consumerism* (New York: Harper & Row, 1972), pp. 80–83.

29

EXTERNALITIES, POLLUTION, and THE environment

Chapters 27 and 28 considered government intervention to prevent or alleviate market failures—antitrust laws to limit monopolies and a variety of regulations to protect consumers from misleading information and other producer distortions. This chapter considers another, and major, possible market failure—the existence of "externalities"—which may require government intervention if the market system is to serve us effectively. These three comprise the first big class of "market failures" listed at the end of Chapter 22. The other two—failures to produce "public goods" and an acceptable distribution of income—are considered in Part 5, on the public sector of the economy.

In the United States, we have a strong tradition of trying private enterprise first and calling on government or government regulation only when private enterprise falls short. As long as trade takes place voluntarily between a buyer and a seller and affects only those two, we can be confident that their satisfactions and the general welfare are increased by each trade. Both buyer and seller must believe they are better off from the trade; otherwise they would not have traded. And no one else is harmed, so total satisfaction must be increased. This is summarized by Adam Smith's famous argument that it is not from his benevolence that we get our meat from the butcher, but out of his regard for his own self-interest. He buys beef and cuts it to sell to you because he feels he will be better off by doing this. You buy the meat because you would rather have the steak than the money you give him in exchange.

Unless you believe that super-wisdom resides in dictators or elected leaders, it is hard to imagine a system that will guard the interests of both you and the butcher better. One of the system's most important advantages is the freedom it provides for individual choices, and its minimization of others' power over you and other individuals. However, when the world becomes complex and your bargain affects the interests of others, the answer is less clear.

THE PROBLEM OF EXTERNALITIES

If I sell you cement made in a plant that pollutes the air for miles around, we can be reasonably sure that you and I both gain from the trade; otherwise we would not have traded. But our transaction, in effect, worsens the lot of people who live near the cement mill, and they have had no say in our transaction. Thus, we can no longer be sure that the general welfare is increased by the transaction. This is the case of "externalities," noted in Chapter 22 as an important market failure. An external effect, or externality, occurs when your behavior affects the well-being of someone else without his agreement. Externalities can be either positive or negative; your action can either improve or worsen the lot of others without their assent. The cement case produces negative external effects; but if I hire a landscaper to beautify my lot, this produces positive external effects for my neighbors.

Consider the cement-plant case more thoroughly. What are the crucial variables? **First,** this is a case of complex exchange where third parties are affected by the exchange. There are externalities. **Second,** one of the important goods, or resources, is not privately owned. The air over the land surrounding the plant is publicly owned; private rights to its use are ill-defined. For the most part, it is treated as if it were a free good, available for anyone to use (pollute) as he wishes without payment. **Third,** since there are numerous landowners and resi-

dents affected by the dust from the cement plant, there would be substantial "transactions costs" involved in their all getting together to work out some voluntary group solution to the problem. **Note that if the air over the surrounding land were privately owned, the externalities problem would probably not arise.** Private owners would not permit the cement plant to violate their air rights without payment for the dirt it imposed. Thus, the cost of using the surrounding air to discharge cement dust would be a cost of production, just like raw materials and labor, and it would enter into the price charged for cement produced by the plant. The price would cover total costs, and the market system would provide the optimal level of cement output. The division between private and additional social costs noted in Chapter 22 would simply not arise.

Since the air is treated as a free good, it is not surprising that the cement plant uses it for dumping its dust; disposing of the dust in some other way would cost more. Any resource, good, or service that is free, or underpriced, will be overused. One major function of prices, as earlier chapters have repeatedly emphasized, is to ration, or limit the use of, the resource or good in question. Similarly, suppose the Ohio River, a heavily polluted stream, were privately owned—say, by General Motors, or by the thousands of people whose property lines the river. You can safely predict that polluters would be charged for using the river as a dumping ground for their effluents.

This case raises the third point noted above, the problem of "transactions costs." If GM owned the river, a price would promptly be set. But if thousands of river-rights owners and possible dumpers were involved in working out a charge for using the river to dump effluents, we can safely bet it would be a long and complex process; indeed, there is a good probability that they would never all be able to agree on an acceptable price and set of controls. Where only two or a few parties are involved, usually transactions costs are relatively small, and the parties are more likely to reach a voluntary agreement.

To summarize: **Where externalities exist, private property rights are ill-defined, and transactions costs are large, a socially satisfactory solution to the pollution problem is almost cer-**

tain to require collective (government) intervention. The same is true for other cases of both positive and negative externalities. For example, we will get the socially optimal amounts of education and noise (which have substantial positive and negative externalities, respectively) only with government intervention.

POLLUTION AND THE ENVIRONMENT

Pollution provides the most prominent, but by no means the only, example of externalities and the problems we face in dealing with them. Indeed, some observers argue that externalities are everywhere; that they are a pervasive market failure that requires equally pervasive government intervention in the market system. Whether or not this is true, pollution provides a major, timely case study.

National concern for the deteriorating quality of the environment has snowballed in recent years. Concern for economic growth has been supplanted by the question, Growth for what? Air and water pollution are pervasive by-products (externalities) of modern industrial society. On every side there are cries for the government to "do something" to halt pollution.

Water, air, solid wastes, noise, and the ecological system per se are the main elements of the pollution problem. Many of our rivers and lakes are contaminated and dangerous from sewage, industrial wastes, farm chemicals, and other pollutants. Each year America's industries, cars, and homes spew over 200 million tons of smoke and fumes into the air. Each year we throw away 60 billion metal cans, 20 billion bottles, 150 million tons of garbage, and 3 billion tons of mine tailings and debris. Especially in big cities, noise is reaching ever-higher levels of intensity. A typical subway train produces 95 decibels, a power mower 110 decibels, and a jet aircraft at takeoff 140 decibels. Electronically magnified rock-and-roll music reaches well above 100 decibels. Most broadly, ecologists, who study the interactions of entire systems of living things, go far beyond the problems above. They suggest that population growth and modern technology have gone so far so fast that they threaten man's very existence on this globe.

Deterioration in the quality of the environ-

ment is not confined to the United States, although our massive increases in real GNP and modern technology make the problem especially vivid for us. Nor is the problem confined to capitalist systems. Soviet newspapers complain of the same conditions in the USSR, and Soviet cartoonists are equally caustic in their drawings of pollution as it envelopes the Russian man in the street. Their rivers vie with ours for the title of dirtiest.[1] Japan's environmental problems are already worse than ours. And the Rhine, fabled in song and verse, is possibly the dirtiest of the world's major rivers.

Moreover, pollution is far from new. Early Roman writers complained of filthy drinking water. Early Spanish explorers noted that campfire smoke hung thick and low in what is now the Los Angeles basin. Open sewers and polluted water are daily threats to health and life itself in the world's less-developed nations, many of which are neither rich nor capitalist.

Pollution in the United States is largely a problem of high levels of consumption coupled with externalities, although governments themselves are often major polluters, especially through inadequate sewer systems. In responding to market demands, businessmen do not charge the full social cost of their operations in their prices to consumers. The result is that the price of these products is too low; consumers buy too much paper and steel produced by the polluting plants. In effect, we make those harmed by pollution subsidize users of steel and paper. In the same way, the price of autos does not reflect their full cost to society; car users do not have to pay for the air pollution they create.

In principle, to provide an optimal allocation of society's resources in response to the public's wishes, costs should include both private and by-product social costs. If the price system doesn't do the job, we must turn to collective action if we want pollution reduced.

Put another way, manufacturers and auto drivers treat clean water, clean air, and quiet as if they were free goods, when in fact they are increasingly scarce and are overconsumed at a

[1] For example, see K. Iosifob, "The Vokhna River Flows," and O. Volkov, "A Writer's Notes: A Trip to Baikal," reprinted in M. Goldman, ed., *Controlling Pollution* (Englewood Cliffs, N.J.: Prentice-Hall, Spectrum Books, 1967).

price of zero. We should be able to charge users of clean air and clean water for the privilege of making them dirty.

SOLUTIONS TO POLLUTION
Pollution, population, and economic growth

Pollution, population growth, and economic growth are intimately related. But this does not mean that the way to reduce pollution is to stop economic growth. Economic growth, as we shall see in Chapter 43, means growth in total economic output per capita—it is growth in generalized productive capacity. We may use the increased capacity to produce things that pollute (for example, leaded gasoline), things that involve no pollution (art museums), or things that reduce pollution (smoke filters on chimneys). Even though output of some goods inescapably involves pollution (solid waste from many products), in general we can use our productive capacity to produce the combination of goods, services, and cleanliness we want and are willing to pay for. The choice of more clean air will mean less steel and auto transportation from the resources available, but more steel and autos need not mean dirtier air if we are willing to pay for "clean" methods of production. GNP in total and per capita will not then be as large as with pollution, because cleaner air (less pollution) doesn't get included as we measure GNP; but this does not change the fact that we can allocate our productive resources as we wish to maximize our satisfaction from them. Indeed, the more we grow (increase productive capacity), the greater will be our ability to have *both* cleaner air and water *and* more of the other goods and services we want. To oppose economic growth because that seems the only way to lessen pollution is shortsighted indeed. (More details in Chapter 45.)

Population growth is different. More population, other things equal, means *less* output *per capita*—a lower standard of living. It also inescapably means more crowding of the environment, because the total amount of space to be shared is substantially fixed.

As a practical matter, combined population and economic growth have brought a devastating amount of environmental pollution over the last half century. But this does not mean that zero economic growth (ZEG), or even zero population growth (ZPG), is the best way to clean up the environment. On the contrary, we need to be careful not to throw the baby out with the bathwater.

Controlling water pollution—an example

There are, broadly, four approaches to pollution control—voluntary action, direct government regulation, effluent charges, and subsidies. Let us consider briefly how each would work in controlling water pollution.

Voluntary action. To many environmentalists, pollution is a moral issue. Those who pollute are immoral, especially if they are large corporations. They ought to stop. Economics cannot pass judgment on people's moral and ethical values. But it must warn such moralists that their approach is not likely to get very far in cleaning up the nation's lakes and streams. First, the notion that big corporations are the devil in the piece is a half-truth. Much of the worst water pollution comes from public sewer systems, from private homes. Much comes from use of chemical fertilizers, pesticides, and the like on farms. And, although a lot does come from big corporations, much comes from little firms as well. Second, and still more important, elimination of pollution from industrial and agricultural production will be very expensive for many firms and farms. Thus, if only one paper mill along a river, voluntarily or under social pressure from its critics, spends the money to treat or recycle its effluents that have been polluting the river, it will find its costs higher than those of its competitors, and that it is pricing itself out of the market. Alone, it can do little good in reducing the overall level of water pollution, and it is likely to go broke trying. Only if other paper mills are required to meet similar effluent standards is any one firm economically safe in spending the money to reduce its pollution.[2]

[2] Similarly, it would be unreasonable to expect the individual consumer to invest voluntarily in an expensive smog-control device for his car when other car users were not required to do so. Alone, he could do no measurable good in reducing smog. Only if all, or most, car users are required to add smog-control devices can the individual be sure that cleaner air will in fact result.

To rely on voluntary action by businessmen to eliminate pollution, therefore, is to misconstrue the nature of the competitive process. Effective action to alleviate pollution (to internalize the externality) must, in most cases, be collective action. Moral pressure and persuasion may help, but by themselves they are unlikely to produce major changes against the pressures of market competition.

Direct regulation. To reduce water pollution, the government may simply order all industries to reduce the amount of effluents they discharge into the lakes and rivers concerned. First, it must decide how clean it wants the lake or river to be—say, 90 percent cleaner than now. Then it orders each firm to reduce its untreated discharges by 90 percent. This would appear to be the simplest approach.

In fact, however, direct regulation faces many problems, even if a law is passed ordering a cleanup of the waterways. Under the 1956 and 1965 Amendments to the Water Pollution Control Act, first, the government was to determine the standard of cleanliness needed in each lake or stream to meet the overall goal; then it was to determine how much each polluter contributed to the excess pollution, and order each to cut back its pollution to meet the prescribed standard. But there are some 40,000 individual industrial sources of water pollution. Some firms have previously dumped few effluents, some many. The former understandably argue that they pollute little, that they should not have to reduce their effluents by a further 90 percent; and they are likely to go to court against the Environmental Pollution Agency if it applies the 90 percent rule to them. Moreover, it is obvious that the most efficient way to achieve the 90 percent overall reduction goal would be to concentrate cleanup action where the cost of reducing effluents is the least, not across the board. But either way, individual firms will protest that they are not in fact responsible for the pollution observed, and long court battles have ensued over the reasonableness of the regulatory actions.

Effluent charges. Increasingly, economists and conservationists favor special taxes, or effluent charges, per unit of effluent discharged, to limit water and air pollution. As with direct regulation, the first step is to decide how much pollution is to be reduced. Then an across-the-board tax per unit of effluent discharged is levied (for example, 2 cents per pound of solid waste dumped into the stream). The level of the tax is set to reduce pollution to the desired level; by reducing their effluents, firms can avoid the tax. The higher the tax, the more it will pay the firm to avoid discharging effluent into the stream.

This approach has three big advantages over direct regulation: (1) It avoids the necessity of making a special administrative decision as to the limit to be placed on each separate firm; each firm pays the tax in proportion to its own polluting. (2) It achieves the desired reduction in total pollution at a lower cost. The incentive to reduce effluents will be greatest for those who can reduce their pollution at the lowest cost. Those firms that face a very high cost of reducing pollution may prefer to pay the tax, although since all firms face rising costs per unit as they eliminate more and more pollution, we can be sure that the effluent charge will lead virtually all polluters to reduce their effluents to some extent. The result will be that the cost (price) of goods produced by the polluters will rise as little as is consistent with reducing pollution to the desired level.[3] (3) With direct regulation, once a firm meets the legal standard, it has no incentive to reduce pollution further. But with an effluent charge, it always has an incentive to reduce pollution further—for example, if technological advance reduces the cost of cutting back on effluents, it will pay the firm to reduce its pollution further to reduce its effluent tax. Conversely, with direct regulation, the firm has no incentive to reduce effluents further, even if it becomes cheaper to do so.

Some critics have called effluent charges "licenses to pollute," because a firm may choose to pay the tax and continue polluting. But the same charge can be levied against a regulatory

---

[3] If the effluent tax *rate* is the same for every firm and each firm reduces its effluent discharge to the point where the marginal cost of reducing discharge is equal to the effluent fee per unit of discharge, the marginal cost of reducing discharge is the same for all firms, and the total cost of obtaining the desired reduction in pollution is minimized. The marginalist principle gives the right answer again!

"Now maybe they'll be moved to do something about water pollution!" (Drawing by Chas. Addams; © 1969. The New Yorker Magazine, Inc.)

limit; then all firms have a free license to pollute up to that limit. Precisely the same pollution reduction can be obtained under either approach, but more cheaply with effluent charges. Effluent charges can be set high enough to discourage any amount of pollution we want to eliminate. The only way to eliminate completely any license to pollute would be to forbid pollution completely, by either regulation or a prohibitively high effluent tax.

Subsidies. The fourth way to deal with pollution is to subsidize polluters to stop polluting. The government might pay polluters to install the equipment to clean up discharges before they enter the stream. In that case, taxpayers rather than customers pay the bill.

Economists are generally unenthusiastic about such subsidies, because they have the wrong incentive effects. If the government pays for the antipollution devices, the private firm incurs no costs and has no incentive to minimize the cost of cleaning up the effluent. More important, since costs and therefore prices are not raised, the consumer of the product involved has no incentive to consume less of the more costly product. Thus, more is produced, and the total cost of resources devoted to pollution control will be larger with subsidies than with either direct regulation or effluent charges. In both the latter cases, the cost of cleaning up the effluent is included in the higher price the consumer must pay when he buys the product, and less will be produced and sold. Thus, subsidies may be convenient where it would be difficult to enforce direct regulations or effluent charges, but they are economically costly. For example, it may be more workable to pay consumers to return their used bottles and cans than to tax them for each bottle or can thrown away to litter the environment, even though this is not, in principle, the most efficient way of dealing with the solid-waste problem.

Who should pay?

The preceding sections generally presume that consumers should pay the full cost of the products they buy, including any related cost of pollution control. Most experts feel this is ethically desirable as well as economically sound. But suppose city A decides it wants exceptionally clean air or water, well above the standards of other cities. If it imposes either effluent charges or direct regulations on local industries to attain this goal, those firms will have higher costs than competing firms in other cities, and hence will lose sales. If A wants cleaner air than its neighbors, it will have to subsidize the local firms to meet these standards, or see those firms lose sales and ultimately be driven out of business by competitors elsewhere. Local taxpayers, rather than consumers elsewhere, will end up paying for the exceptionally clean air in A. See if you can devise a way to make the local firms and their customers bear the costs of extra cleanliness in the long run. Will it make a difference whether the firms involved sell in highly competitive or quasi-monopoly markets?

Marginalism—how clean is clean enough?

It should be clear by now that the cost of clean water depends substantially on how clean we want the water to be. If we want all our streams and lakes to meet distilled-water standards, the cost will be astronomical.

Urban sewage disposal, an unglamorous but central part of the water-pollution problem, illustrates this point. In many American communities, raw sewage is dumped directly into flowing streams. In about 35 percent of the cases, sewage is passed through a one-stage treatment; in another 25 percent, through a two-stage treatment, which removes perhaps 90 percent of the pollutant qualities of the sewage before it is dumped into streams. In virtually all cases, common sewers are used for rainwater runoff and sewage waste. Thus, heavy rainstorms may produce such flooding that the combined sewage plus rain runoff must be bypassed around the treatment plants, pouring directly into flowing streams or lakes without any sewage treatment at all.

Use of sewers for both waste and rain runoff works well most of the time; both sewage and rainwater are funneled through the sewage-treatment plants. To protect against infrequent overloads would require either a new, dual sewer system or new sewage-treatment plants so large that they would handle even the massive runoffs in large storms. These would be extremely expensive. For industrial wastes, costs soar similarly as firms try to clean up their effluents to higher and higher standards of cleanliness. Cost estimates vary, but a total additional annual cost of $25–$30 billion would possibly suffice to provide two-stage sewage treatment for all major municipalities. This would, of course, fall substantially short of 100 percent water purification for the nation. To move the standard up to 95 percent cleanliness with three-stage treatment would probably increase the additional cost astronomically. In virtually all cases, the cost of additional cleanliness rises far more than proportionately as absolute cleanliness is approached.

How clean is clean? Clean water is not an all-or-nothing proposition. As almost everywhere in economics, the question is one of degree, a tradeoff between cleaner water and higher costs. Sensible policy involves comparing the marginal cost of each additional unit of cleanliness against the marginal benefits of that unit. And, to repeat, in most cases marginal costs rise sharply as cleanliness standards go up.

A simple example may emphasize this point.

Johnny's mother tells him to wash his hands before he comes to dinner. When she sees the result, she says he has not *really* washed his hands. Johnny protests that he has; he has passed his hands through a stream of cold water before coming to the table. His mother sends him back, to use hot water, soap, and a towel, and then his hands pass inspection. Yet Johnny's hands, even after a two-stage treatment, are far from clean enough to meet a surgeon's hospital-operating-room standards. The surgeon would demand a third-stage process. To insist on this third level of cleanliness in day-to-day life for most of us would be incredibly expensive in terms of time, energy, and money—and pointless. So it may be with many pollution issues.

THE ECONOMICS AND POLITICS OF POLLUTION

Reducing pollution, we have learned painfully over the past few years, is a complex, expensive job. The economic analysis involved is simple in principle, but complicated in its application to individual situations. Much of the difficulty arises from the fundamental fact of conflicts of interest that can be compromised only through the political process.

The last decade has seen a vast surge of concern for the environment. Congress has passed a series of major acts to protect the environment. Yet progress has seemed painfully slow to many environmentalists. In its 1975 report, the Council on Environmental Quality said, quoting figures on cleaner air, that "we are winning the battle against air pollution," but that progress on the water-pollution front is mixed. The sewage and industrial-effluents situation is clearly improving, but pollution from agricultural fertilizers and other chemicals may be worsening. In 1975, business firms invested $6 billion on pollution control, about 5 percent of their total investment. The Council on Environmental Quality estimated in 1974 that during the decade ahead, the nation, mainly private firms, will need to spend about $275 billion to meet 1974 legal standards for cleaner air and water, assuming no further inflation. The council emphasized that, although this is a huge sum, it would rep-

resent only about 2 percent of total GNP over the decade, and well under half of the growth in GNP over the period. But it might also equal a quarter of business's total net investment for the decade.

In 1973, Congress passed a new Water Pollution Act, over President Nixon's veto, further tightening the standards to be met. This reflected disenchantment with progress under the 1956 and 1965 regulatory approach; the job of dealing individually with over 40,000 industrial firms seemed insuperable as a practical matter. Congress decreed that by 1977 all companies must install the "best practicable" pollution control technology, by 1983 the "best available" technology, and by 1985 have reached "zero discharge," complete elimination of water pollution—with heavy fines for violators. What this new legislation will mean as a practical matter remains to be seen. Although most environmentalists and many economists agreed on the need for a change, many doubt that the new bill will prove workable—and Congress registered its own doubts by simultaneously establishing a new National Study Commission to investigate the "total economic, social, and environmental effects" of meeting these standards. Experts question whether the new legislation will get around the problem of dealing individually with standards for many different firms and industries (what does "best practicable" mean in any particular case?), point out that "zero discharge" may be more than we will really want to pay for, and reemphasize the advantages of a flexible effluent-charge approach.[4]

The battle against air pollution has also been a shifting one. Congress has passed stringent bills

[4]Effluent-charge systems have proved workable in action. For example, water pollution in the Ruhr River valley in Germany, one of the world's most concentrated industrial complexes, has for over forty years been controlled by such a set of charges—and very effectively, in the eyes of most observers. For a brief description, see L.E. Ruff, "The Economic Common Sense of Pollution," *The Public Interest,* Spring 1970, pp. 84–85. Excellent, more detailed treatments of the pollution problem are presented in E.G. Dolan, *TANSTAAFL* ("There Ain't No Such Thing As a Free Lunch") (New York: Holt, Rinehart & Winston, 1971); and Chap. 11, "The Environment," in C. Schultze et al., *Setting National Priorities: The 1973 Budget* (Washington, D.C.: The Brookings Institution, 1972).

requiring all communities to meet much higher standards, and auto manufacturers to improve dramatically their emission-control performances. But difficulties in meeting these standards at acceptable costs (ultimately to consumers and taxpayers) have led to repeated extensions of time deadlines. Public enthusiasm for pollution control, not surprisingly, moves inversely with the cost of achieving the desired results.

REVIEW

Concepts to remember

This chapter reemphasizes some concepts introduced earlier and adds two more that are central to the analysis of certain types of "market failures":

externalities	**ill-defined property rights**
transaction costs	**effluent charges**

For analysis and discussion

1. Explain why you would expect "market failure" in cases of large externalities?
2. Explain why effluent charges will generally be the most efficient way to achieve any pollution-control goals.
3. Should the Ohio River be cleaned up so that it is again attractive for swimming, boating, and fishing? If so, how, and who should pay for the reclamation?
4. Many critics argue that the auto manufacturers are responsible for smog and air pollution in the cities. They argue that the auto companies should be required to bear the cost of eliminating the auto-exhaust contribution to smog.
   a. Is this a correct analysis of responsibility?
   b. If you believe the cost of eliminating auto air pollution should be placed on the auto manufacturers, how would you accomplish this? (Remember your price theory from Chapters 22–26.)
5. Your city has an air-pollution problem, primarily from autos, private furnaces, and industry. Devise an acceptable program to clean up the air to acceptable standards. Will direct effluent limits or effluent charges work better?
6. Should the federal government pay for upgrading the sewage systems of cities that do not meet the new federal water-cleanliness standards? Why?
7. Should the federal government spend more to improve the environment? How do you decide how much is the right amount, and who should pay?
8. Should students picket corporations that cause air or water pollution?

On February 21, 1973, the Mobil Oil Company placed the following full-page advertisement in major newspapers throughout the country. The problem outlined then is still with us. Do you agree with Mobil's analysis and recommendations?

In 1970, Congress passed a series of amendments to the Clean Air Act. One of them said that all cars sold in the United States after 1974 must be near-zero polluters.

It sounded fine. Near-perfect emission control seemed not only desirable, but imperative. At that time, people widely assumed that the air was getting steadily dirtier because of the automobile. Most people also assumed that industry could solve any technical problems that might be encountered—and at a reasonable cost.

The goal has proved elusive. Despite the expenditure of hundreds of millions of dollars and uncounted hours of research and development time, no control system that meets all the requirements of the federal standards has yet been proved.

Bad news? Not necessarily. Today both industry and government have the benefit of research results and other information that were simply not available when Congress passed its amendment in 1970. Today we know that:

• Total air pollution from cars has already been rolled back to the level of about 1960, and is continuing to drop.
• Cars that met the federal standards would probably be poor performers and gasoline-guzzlers. They also could need costlier maintenance than today's cars.
• A less restrictive level of controls on automotive emissions would do very nearly as much for air quality as the federal standards would.
• Meeting the federal standards could cost $100 billion over ten years starting in 1976; meeting the less-restrictive standards could cost $34 billion. The difference could be a $66 billion mistake.

If not perfection, what? The only way to completely eliminate auto pollution would be to do away with the auto itself. Since this would be neither practical nor desirable, what percentage reduction of emissions should we aim at? By what date? And at what cost?

The goal should be to make the auto as small a contributor to air pollution as technology allows—but without incurring exorbitant costs for dubious results. Since technology does not stand still, this would be a moving goal. Today's impractical dream often can be tomorrow's reality.

Today's reality in automotive-pollution control is, in fact, yesterday's dream: As Chart 1 indicates, emissions of hydrocarbons, carbon monoxide, and nitrogen oxides have been drastically reduced from the days (not long ago) when exhaust emissions were uncontrolled. Changes in engine design plus pollution-control devices have reduced emissions by 1973-model cars an average of 66 percent.

This is quite an achievement. And as a result,

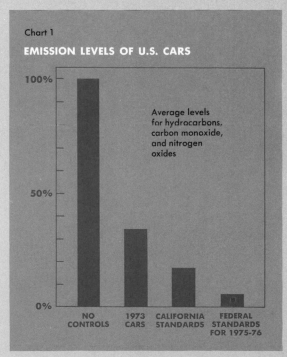

Chart 1

EMISSION LEVELS OF U.S. CARS

Average levels for hydrocarbons, carbon monoxide, and nitrogen oxides

100% — NO CONTROLS
50%
0% — 1973 CARS — CALIFORNIA STANDARDS — FEDERAL STANDARDS FOR 1975-76

total air pollution from automobiles has been declining in the United States since 1968, and is now down to the levels of about 1960. It would continue to decline for several more years even if no further controls were imposed, as old cars with few if any controls are scrapped.

So, how much further should we go? And by when?

California has a better way   The Air Resources Board of the State of California has proposed automotive emission-control levels based on air-quality standards calculated to restore the atmosphere of Los Angeles to its quality of the early 1940s. California proposes to cut the three principal auto emissions by an average of 83 percent. . . .

The California standards are similar to those proposed by the federal government's own Department of Health, Education and Welfare in 1970.

The HEW standards were not accepted. Instead, Congress voted for the last bar on Chart 1. The Clean Air Act now mandates that the three emissions be reduced by 97, 96, and 93 percent—for an average of 95 percent. These levels must be reached by 1975 for hydrocarbons and carbon monoxide, and by 1976 for oxides of nitrogen, unless the federal government grants an extension.

A 95 percent reduction in emissions may not seem much more difficult to achieve than an 83 percent reduction. But did you every try to wring the last drop of water out of a wet towel? One good twist and most of the water flows out. Another hard twist and a little more dribbles out. But now the law of diminishing returns sets in. It's just plain impossible to wring the towel dry, and not worth the effort.

Similarly, the last few percentage points of automotive emission control are far costlier and far more difficult to achieve than the first 80 to 85 points.

Mobil sells gasoline, but we have no desire to see our products wasted. Cars built to the federal standards could consume as much as 15 percent more gasoline per mile than cars built to the California standards. That 15 percent would require refining an extra 30 million barrels of crude oil in 1976, and an extra 150 million barrels a year by 1980. All that crude oil would have to be imported, with a substantial drain on our country's balance of payments.

Up the Matterhorn   Which brings us to Chart 2. The one with a curve that looks like the southeastern slope of the Matterhorn.

Control equipment to meet the 1973 standards adds about $65 to $100 to the cost of a new car. Not excessive, considering how far the cars have come in reducing harmful emission.

The price curve turns up to meet the California standards—to a range of $175 to $300 per car for the control equipment. Perhaps still not too expensive, considering the extra gains in pollution reduction. But to reach the federal standards that are now the law for 1975 and 1976 models, the cost curve heads almost straight up. These systems could cost $500 to $600 a car—and maybe more. We can't deter-

Auto emission reductions below pre-control levels			
	Hydro-carbons	*Carbon monoxide*	*Oxides of nitrogen*
1973 Cars	80%	69%	50%
California	94	81	75
Federal	97	96	93

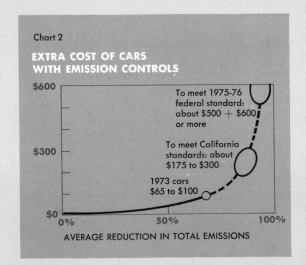

Chart 2

EXTRA COST OF CARS WITH EMISSION CONTROLS

To meet 1975-76 federal standard: about $500 + $600 or more

To meet California standards: about $175 to $300

1973 cars $65 to $100

AVERAGE REDUCTION IN TOTAL EMISSIONS

mine the exact cost, since systems to meet the 1976 standards have not been proved.

These are just the initial costs of the emission-control systems. Add the extra maintenance, and throw in the additional gasoline, and the grand total for meeting the federal standards comes to $100 billion over the decade starting in 1976.

What would $66,000,000,000 buy?

The program Mobil outlines in this report could save the American consumer $66 billion over ten years. . . . Here are a few things $66 billion could do:

• Build the water-treatment plants needed for all the country's household, municipal, and industrial sewage and waste water—and maintain those facilities for more than five years.

• Nearly pay the annual U.S. expenditures for all health and medical care ($67 billion in 1970).

• More than finance all new private and public housing construction in this country for two years (1970 total: $30 billion).

• Almost pay the total cost of all types of education in the United States, at all levels, for a year (1970 total: $67 billion).

• Buy various combinations of subways, BART systems, commuter trains, longer-haul railroads, and express lanes for buses on freeways.

Add the same expenses for the California standards, and the grand total is $34 billion. (All these figures are Mobil engineers' estimates, expressed in today's dollars.)

Our calculations do not include a cost for the special kind of gasoline that would be needed to meet the federal standards.

Clean air and public transportation Is there a better way to spend all or part of $66 billion to reduce total automotive air pollution?

There is indeed. Public transportation. Public transportation clean enough, safe enough, fast enough, and priced attractively enough to induce Americans to use their automobiles less and public transportation more.

More and better public transportation can go a long way toward several desirable objectives: Less air pollution. Less waste of gasoline. Less pressure on the U.S. balance of payments as our imports of oil inevitably rise. And maybe less emotional strain on motorists and fewer accidents.

Under such a program, motorists could drive better-performing, less expensive, and safer cars. A substantial drain on the U.S. balance of payments, for crude oil and platinum, would be avoided. A vital and scarce natural resource— petroleum—would be conserved. And the advance of technology would enable automakers to meet even stricter control standards—if they were found necessary at some future date—with durable, trouble-free, and reasonably economic systems.

Not to mention avoiding a $66 billion mistake.

Do you agree with Mobil's analysis and recommendations? If not, what is your program for handling the auto air-pollution problem? Under Mobil's proposal and yours, who are the main beneficiaries, and who would pay most of the costs of cleaner air?

APPENDIX TO PART 3

Current research

As with the appendix to Part 2, the purpose here is to suggest a sample of recent research in economics that may be of interest to students who want to know more of what economists do, and especially of the excitement that goes with research—the search for new knowledge and new understanding. Here again, the items listed are merely a sample. They are not necessarily the best, or even a cross section, of current research in the area. They are chosen because I hope some of them may be intriguing to you and may make you want to look further. They vary widely in approach, substance, and difficulty.

The most controversial and lively study of modern business is J.K. Galbraith's best-selling *The New Industrial State* (New York: Houghton Mifflin, 1967). For equally lively antidotes, see the review of Galbraith's book in *Fortune,* July 1967 (pp. 90ff.), and the amusing but penetrating exchange on the analysis by R. Solow, R. Maris, and Galbraith in *The Public Interest,* Fall 1967 and Spring 1968. In 1973, Galbraith published an equally controversial follow-up book, *Economics and the Public Purpose* (Boston: Houghton Mifflin), which argues that the federal government should buy out owners of the big industrial corporations.

For different, broad looks at the issues involved, try Edward Mason's Introduction to his *The Corporation in Modern Society* (Cambridge, Mass.: Harvard University Press, 1959); Chapter 8 of Milton Friedman, *Capitalism and Freedom* (Chicago: University of Chicago Press, 1962); and Neil Jacoby, *Corporate Power and Social Responsibility* (New York: Macmillan, 1973).

Industry and Market Studies. You can find a research study on just about every major industry. Brief studies of all the major industries, with a bibliography on each, are collected in Walter Adams, ed., *The Structure of American Industry* (New York: Macmillan, 1971). Two more extended analyses are L.J. White, *The Automobile Industry since 1945* (Cambridge, Mass.: Harvard University Press, 1972), and M.A. Adelman, *A&P: A Study in Price-Cost Behavior and*

Public Policy (Cambridge, Mass.: Harvard University Press, 1959). For a very different industry (music, the theatre, and ballet), see W. Baumol and W. Bowen, *Performing Arts—The Economic Dilemma* (New York: Twentieth Century Fund, 1966). Broader coverage is given in *Pricing in Big Business: A Case Approach,* by A.D. Kaplan, J. Dirlam, and R. Lanzilotti (Washington, D.C.: The Brookings Institution, 1958); and Kaplan's *Big Enterprise in a Competitive System* (Washington, D.C.: The Brookings Institution, 1964) provides a further readable overview.

Antitrust Policy, Mergers, and regulation. A sample of leading economists' analyses of antitrust policy is provided by J.F. Weston and S. Peltzman, eds., *Public Policy toward Mergers* (Pacific Palisades, Calif.: Goodyear, 1969); and by Edwin Mansfield, ed., *Monopoly Power and Economic Performance* (New York: Norton, 1968). For more detailed analyses of the conglomerate merger problem, which is a central issue of modern antitrust policy, see *Economic Report on Corporate Mergers,* by the Staff of the Federal Trade Commission (1969), which is generally antimerger; J.S. McGee, *In Defense of Industrial Concentration* (New York: Praeger, 1971); and *Conglomerate Merger Performance: An Empirical Analysis of Nine Corporations,* a further report by the FTC Staff (November 1972), which finds that the major conglomerate mergers of recent years have had little or no anticompetitive effects.

Public utilities and other partial "natural monopolies" are customarily governed by government regulatory commissions. Paul MacAvoy's *The Crisis of the Regulatory Commissions* (New York: Norton, 1970) collects recent research studies and policy statements on this approach to market regulation. See also Roger Noll, *Reforming Regulation* (Washington, D.C.: The Brookings Institition, 1971). At the competition end of the spectrum, Charles Schultze analyzes *The Distribution of Farm Subsidies: Who Gets the Benefits?* (Washington, D.C.: The Brookings Institution, 1971) when a different approach is taken to markets that don't function satisfactorily on their own.

Pollution and externalities. A. Kneese and R. d'Arge's "Pervasive External Costs and the Response of Society," in the Joint Economic Committee's *The Analysis and Evaluation of Public Expenditures,* 1969 (Vol. 1), is a penetrating analysis of externalities. L.E. Ruff's "The Economic Common Sense of Pollution," *The Public Interest,* Spring 1970, and M. Boskin and R. Gilbert's "The Economic Common Sense of Controlling Nuclear Power Development,"

in *The California Nuclear Initiative* (Stanford, Calif.: Stanford University Institute for Energy Studies, 1976), apply the principles understandably and well. From the flood of recent books on pollution, Kneese and Schultze's *Pollution, Prices and Public Policy* (Washington, D.C.: The Brookings Institution, 1975), and E.G. Dolan, TANSTAAFL ("There Ain't No Such Thing as a Free Lunch") (New York: Holt, Rinehart & Winston, 1971), are among the best.

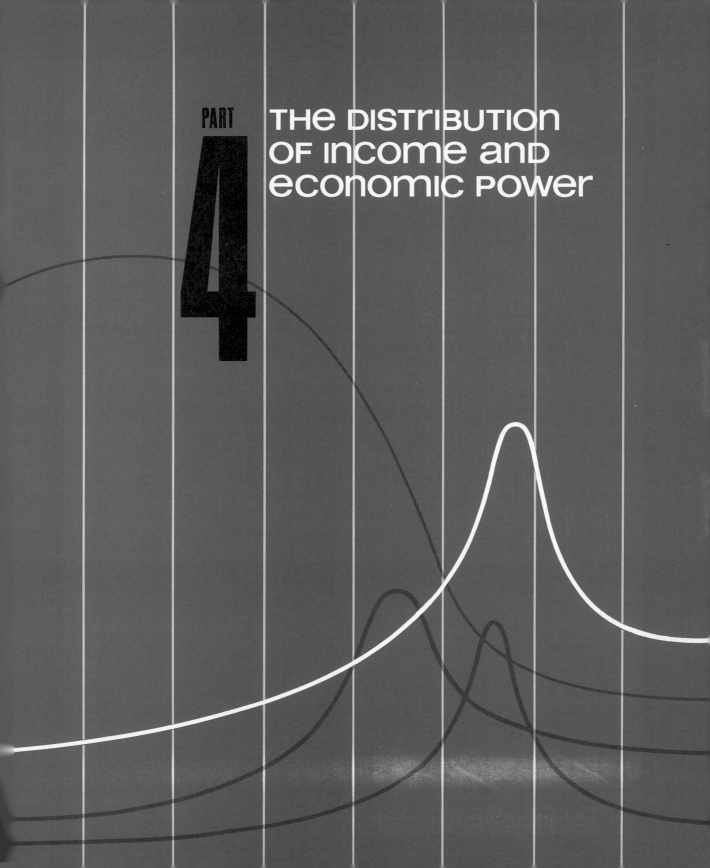

PART 4
THE DISTRIBUTION OF INCOME AND economic power

30 CHAPTER incomes: THE PRICING OF PRODUCTIVE services

One of the hottest issues in economics has long been the distribution of the national income—between wages and profits, rich and poor, farmer and industrial worker, the "haves" and the "have-nots." Governments have risen and fallen on the struggle for income shares. The revolutionary doctrines of Karl Marx centered around the "exploitation of the worker" by the "rich, greedy capitalist." In a different setting, this same struggle over income shares is the issue when the United Steelworkers fight the steel companies for wage increases. It is the issue behind the race riots in the cities. History tells a recurrent story of the "have-nots" fighting for more and the "haves" struggling to protect their share.

Thoughtful observers of the private-enterprise economy point out that we're all in the same boat. If everyone pulls together—labor, capital, management—total output will grow and everyone can have more. No one who understands the basic interdependence inherent in the modern economy would deny this. There is an enormous community of interest in making the private-enterprise economy work effectively, and the spectacular growth of U.S. total output, with rising income for every group, is the great success story of economic history.

But part and parcel of that community of interest is a basic conflict, rooted deep in our ethics and traditions of self-interest and competition. This is the struggle of each individual to get more for himself and his family. It is the struggle over who gets how much of the economic pie. However rich the nation is, we're all interested in our own shares—relative and absolute. Nothing is gained by refusing to face this fact.

This chapter has two major sections. First, the facts—who gets how much income in the United States today? Second, the theory of income distribution—why do people receive the incomes they do? Then the following chapters apply this theory to explaining wages and salaries, rents and interest, and profits.

WHO GETS HOW MUCH?

The income revolution

American incomes have risen persistently and rapidly for over two centuries, and nearly every group has participated. Our standard of living is one of the highest in the world.

Table 30–1 summarizes the facts since World War II. Total real national income (that is, the sum of all incomes adjusted to eliminate rises due only to higher prices) has nearly tripled—from $470 billion to $1,246 billion (in 1975 prices). In 1947, median family income was $7,100 in 1975 dollars; in 1975, it was about

Table 30–1
Family incomes in 1947 and 1975

ANNUAL INCOME (In 1975 dollars)	PERCENT OF FAMILIES	
	1947	1975
Under $3,000	22	5
3,000–5,000	25	7
5,000–10,000	36	28
Over $10,000	17	60
Median family income	$7,100	$13,500
Total income—all families	$470 billion	$1,246 billion

Source: U.S. Census Bureau. Preliminary estimates of distribution for 1975 by author.

Table 30–2
Family income shares, 1929–75

	PERCENT OF TOTAL INCOME RECEIVED			
	1929	1950	1960	1975
Bottom fifth	3.5	4.5	4.8	5.4
Second fifth	9.0	12.0	11.7	12.0
Middle fifth	13.8	17.4	17.4	17.6
Fourth fifth	19.3	23.5	23.6	24.1
Top fifth	54.4	42.6	42.6	41.0
All families	100.0	100.0	100.0	100.0
Top 5 percent	30.0	17.0	16.8	15.3

Source: U.S. Census Bureau. Preliminary estimates for 1975 by author.

$13,500.[1] In 1975, about 60 percent of all families earned over $10,000, compared to only 17 percent 25 years earlier. The other big element of the U.S. income revolution was the rise of the huge middle class. In 1975, about 60 percent of all families received incomes between $7,000 and $20,000. But the extremes are interesting, too, as Table 30–2 shows.

Figure 30–1 poses an interesting question about the distribution of incomes in America. The regular, bell-shaped curve shows what statisticians call a "normal" distribution. Intelligence, physical traits, and many other phenomena seem to approximate closely this type of normal distribution, when large numbers are considered. More people are at the midpoint of the curve than at any other level, and those above and below the average shade off about equally either way.

We might assume that general ability is normally distributed among the total population at birth. But incomes received, shown by the white line, are "skewed." That is, there are many more relatively poor than rich people. These account for the big hump in the curve toward the lower-income end of the scale. There are a few very rich, who give the curve a long "tail" out to the right. Why are incomes less "normally" distributed than human abilities at birth?

[1] The median is the figure that divides the total number of families in half. Thus, in 1975, half of all families received more than $13,500, half less.

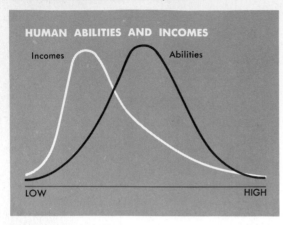

Figure 30-1
Ability and most other human characteristics seem to be "normally" distributed through the population at birth, as shown by the regular bell-shaped curve. Incomes are much more unequally distributed. Why?

Is income becoming more or less equally distributed? Since the 1920s, more equally. (Before that, the data are highly unreliable, although apparently the same conclusion would apply.) The facts are shown in Table 30–2.

Another way of measuring changes in income distribution is shown by the "Lorenz curve" in Figure 30–2. The income of all families is cumulated along the horizontal axis, beginning with the lowest-income family; the percentage of total income received by those families is cumulated along the vertical axis. For example, in 1929, the bottom 40 percent of all families received about 12 percent of the total national income, the lowest 90 percent received about 60 percent. By comparison, in 1975, the bottom 40 percent of families received about 18 percent, and the bottom 90 percent received about 75 percent.

If all family incomes were equal, the points plotted would all fall on the diagonal. That is, the lowest 10 percent would receive 10 percent of the total income, and so on up the line. Thus, the more bowed out the Lorenz curve is, the **more**

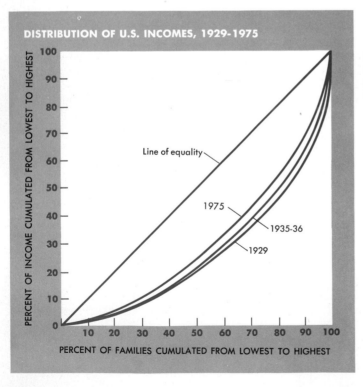

Figure 30-2
Incomes are somewhat more equally distributed now than in 1929 or 1935–36. The more bowed the curve is, the less equal the distribution of income was in that year. (Source: U.S. Census Bureau.)

unequal the distribution of income is; the nearer it is to the diagonal, the **more equally** incomes are distributed.

Figure 30–2 thus shows that incomes are somewhat more equally distributed now than either in 1929 (the peak of the boom) or in 1935–36, the Great Depression years. It also shows that the distribution has changed only moderately over that tumultuous period.

One last historical observation: Are the very rich—the millionaires—being squeezed out by high income and inheritance tax rates? Apparently not. Invested capital continues to be the main source of most very high incomes. In 1969 (the last reliable study), the bottom 80 percent of all families held only 22 percent of the wealth. At the other extreme, the richest 1 percent held 24 percent of all wealth, but this share has declined persistently from 36 percent in 1929. In 1970, there were some 50,000 millionaires in the nation in terms of wealth, compared to only a few hundred in the 1920s; and in 1970, about 1,000 people had annual incomes exceeding $1 million. Still, the richest 1 percent (families with incomes over $50,000) received only 6 percent of the total national income. Families with incomes over $100,000 received only 2 percent of total income.[2]

Occupational and educational differences

What jobs provide the best incomes? Table 30–3 gives part of the answer. It shows rough estimates of median incomes for a sample of occupations in 1975.

Physicians, lawyers, and other highly trained professionals top the list. The median figures for managers and proprietors don't look like the huge salaries you read about for corporation presidents. *Answer:* There are some huge salaries, but many middle-level managers earn lots less. Nor do many people who are in business for themselves get rich quick; some succeed, many don't. At the bottom of the list, it's clear that low-

[2] For details on the distribution of income and wealth, see D. Radner and J. Hinrich, "Size Distribution of Income in 1964, 1970, and 1971," *Survey of Current Business*, October 1974, especially pp. 21–23; and J. Smith and S. Franklin, "The Concentration of Personal Wealth," *American Economic Review*, May 1974, pp. 162–67.

Table 30–3

Median incomes in different occupations, 1975[a]

Physicians and surgeons	$60,000
Dentists	36,000
Lawyers	31,000
Engineers	22,800
Economists	22,000
Managers and proprietors	17,600
College and university teachers	17,500
Accountants	17,500
Foremen	16,500
Postal clerks	13,700
Manufacturing operatives	13,600
Secretaries, typists	9,100
Retail salesclerks	8,800
Waiters	4,700
Unskilled workers, farm	4,100

[a] Males only; female incomes were substantially lower in all occupations shown. 1975 figures are extensions of 1970 census data (except for physicians, based on special studies), assuming that interoccupation differences remained substantially stable; *thus, 1975 figures are only rough approximations.* Some figures are averages of diverse groups (for example, managers and proprietors). Figures do not include "fringe benefits."

and unskilled laborers in business or agriculture don't do very well. Women's incomes in the same occupations were lower throughout—for example, only $16,500 in engineering (their highest-paid occupation), and $3,600 as retail sales-clerks.

Table 30–3 suggests a high correlation between incomes earned and the amount of education workers have. Eight of the ten top occupations in the Census Bureau's detailed list of income receivers involved schooling beyond a college degree, averaging 17+ years of school. Figure 30–3 shows this clearly. The estimated lifetime earnings (as of 1972, in 1972 prices) for all males with only an elementary school education was only $390,000. They were $540,000 for high school graduates, $710,000 for college graduates, and $820,000 for holders of advanced degrees.

Women and minority groups

The average income of working women is about 70 percent that of working men.

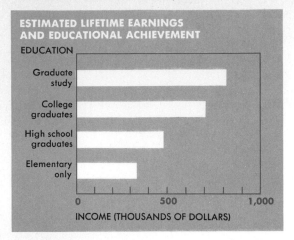

ESTIMATED LIFETIME EARNINGS AND EDUCATIONAL ACHIEVEMENT

Figure 30-3
The biggest earned incomes go to physicians, dentists, lawyers, and other professionals with postgraduate schooling; the smallest to unskilled and low-skilled workers with high school educations or less. (Estimates based on 1970 census data.)

Women generally get paid less than men do for similar jobs. But more than that, the difference reflects the heavy concentration of women in low-paying jobs—especially clerical and service work, and unskilled labor. Women are now increasingly showing up in higher-paid occupations—the professions, skilled labor, and middle management. But there are still relatively few in peak-income jobs.

Similar income differentials prevail for minority groups, of which blacks are the largest. The median black household income in 1974 was only $7,200; compared to $11,600 for white households (which include individuals living alone). About 18 percent of all black households had incomes over $15,000, compared to 35 percent for whites. Conversely, 18 percent of all black households had incomes under $3,000, while only 6 percent of whites had incomes below this figure. Apparently slightly smaller income gaps prevail for Spanish-origin Americans, but somewhat larger ones for American Indians, for whom we have less detailed information.

But the income status of minority groups has improved markedly. In 1947, the median black-family income was only 51 percent of that for whites; by 1975, it was 62 percent. Much of this rise was related to a massive move of blacks from the South to the North, where higher wages prevail. The overall figures mask dramatic differential movements for men and women. Since 1939, black male full-time earnings rose from 45 to 65 percent of their white counterparts, mainly during the tight labor market of World War II; but black full-time female workers' incomes rose from 38 to 90 percent of their white counterparts over the same period, including a big advance in the 1960s and 1970s.

Why do these differences exist, and why are they changing? To answer these questions, we need a theory of income distribution, to which the last half of this chapter is largely devoted.

WAGES AND PROFITS— FUNCTIONAL SHARES

Most very rich people get a big part of their incomes from invested capital—from interest and profits. Most low- and middle-income families receive almost nothing from such investments, except for the use of the houses some own. Yet the American economy today doesn't look much like Karl Marx's picture of capitalism in its death throes, with the workers poised to seize ownership of the means of production. American labor and management do exchange some violent words, and strikes are sometimes long and bitter. But in the showdown, management and labor get together; production goes on, with the worker's rights still intact and the capitalist's control over his investment substantially maintained. When the workers go to the polls, they vote Republican or Democratic, not Communist. The radicals who want to destroy the capitalist system have usually been students and other revolutionaries, who have found themselves lined up against management **and** workers defending the economic system.

But within this framework, labor and management wrestle constantly over the division of the consumer's dollar between wages and profits. Figure 30-4 gives an overall picture of the outcome of this wage-profit bargaining during the last four decades. The left-hand part plots the

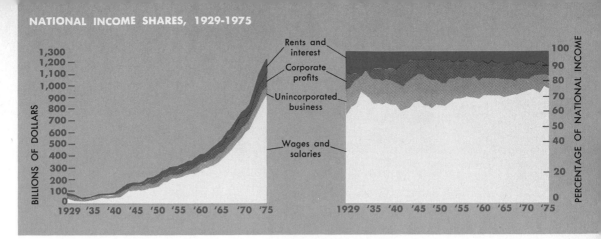

actual dollar shares of national income that go to wages and salaries, corporate profits, unincorporated business incomes (a mixture of salaries and profits), rents, and interest, all before payment of income taxes. The right-hand portion shows the percentage shares that go to these various groups.

The first lesson comes from the left-hand chart. Everyone's income has grown rapidly, and in a serious depression we're also all in the same boat—everyone takes a beating. The second lesson, from the right-hand chart, is the dominance of wage–salary incomes and the general stability in the major income shares, except during big business fluctuations. The wage and salary share persistently hovered in the 65–75 percent range, with a gradual upward trend. Partly, the rising wage share reflects the steady population shift from farms to urban jobs, but beyond this, there has apparently been some tendency for the profit-plus-interest share to be squeezed. Look back at Table 7–5 for additional evidence.

A rather different picture of the outcome of the labor–capital struggle for income shares is given if we compare the return *per unit* of labor and capital used in the economy. Real wages per hour are four times as high as they were in 1900, while the real long-term interest rate (a crude measure of the return per dollar of capital invested in the economy) is still about the same. The profit rate appears to be about the same as a half century ago, or somewhat lower. Looked at this way, it appears that virtually all the fruits of increased output have gone to labor and virtually none to capital.

Figure 30–4
Everyone's income has grown since 1929, but wages and salaries by much the biggest amount. They have also gradually increased their share of the total. Note that profits vanished in the Great Depression. (Source: U.S. Department of Commerce.)

How are these different ways of looking at the same world to be reconciled? (The answer is given in detail in Chapters 43–44, on economic growth.) (1) The total capital stock has grown much faster than the labor force. Thus, the law of diminishing returns has reduced the return per unit of capital relative to that per unit of labor (see the appendix to Chapter 20). (2) But improving technology has helped increase total output faster than the combined inputs of labor and capital, so diminishing returns have not reduced the return per unit of capital, but merely kept it from rising with technological advance. (3) The relatively stable total shares of labor and capital in GNP thus reflect the rapid growth in income per unit of labor, and a correspondingly faster growth in the capital stock than in the labor force, with the two factors just about offsetting each other to keep the total labor and capital shares in GNP relatively stable. Figure 44–2 provides the data.

THE THEORY OF INCOME DISTRIBUTION

Why do people receive the incomes they do—some large, some small, some stable, some insecure? The answer is complex, as with most other important issues in economics. But the core of the answer is summarized in the

INEQUALITY, OPPORTUNITY, AND UPWARD MOBILITY

Have industrialization, big business, and modern technology increased economic and social stratification in America? Does today's inequality of income and wealth mean that only the children of the rich have a chance to become rich and powerful in their generations?

These answers are complex and the evidence is mixed. Clearly, the poor face a tough path in trying to rise from poverty. But it has always been tough to rise from the lower-income classes, and today's concentration of income and wealth is clearly less than it was a century ago. Overall, the evidence suggests that economic stratification is less rigid today than it was fifty or a hundred years ago.

A recent study of the sources of top business exectives found:

> Only 10.5 percent of the current generation of big business executives . . . [are] sons of wealthy families; as recently as 1950 the corresponding figure was 36.1 percent, and at the turn of the century, 45.6 percent. . . . Two thirds of the 1900 generation had fathers who were heads of the same corporations or who were independent businessmen; less than half of the current generation had fathers so placed in American society. On the other hand, less than 10 percent of the 1900 generation had fathers who were employees; by 1964 this percentage had increased to nearly 30 percent.[a]

The post–World War II period brought the greatest increase in the proportion of those from economically poor backgrounds (from 12.1 percent in 1950 to 23.3 percent in 1964) who entered the top echelons of American business; and there was a corresponding decline in the percentage from wealthy families. The replacement of family-owned enterprise by the public corporation, the bureaucratization of American corporate life, the recruitment of management personnel from the ranks of college graduates, and an increasingly competitive promotion process were all important factors. Because of the spread of higher education to the children of the working classes (almost one-third now attend college), the ladder of bureaucratic success is increasingly open to those from poorer circumstances. Business and professional families are still the largest sources of business leaders. Privileged family and class backgrounds continue to be a big help in the quest for corporate success, but training and talent can increasingly make up for their lack.[b]

Other recent sociological studies reach the same conclusion, although with some vigorous dissenters from the communist–socialist wing. But to say that apparently more opportunity now exists for upward mobility than a half century ago is not enough. Particularly, members of minority groups, such as blacks, Spanish-speaking Americans, and American Indians, have made very little progress in reaching top economic positions, even though their incomes have risen relative to those of whites.

[a]See S.M. Lipset, "Social Mobility and Equal Opportunity," *The Public Interest,* Fall 1972, for a summary and references to a number of students.

[b]See G. Burck, "A Group Profile of the Fortune 500 Chief Executive," *Fortune,* May, 1976.

remainder of this chapter; then it is applied specifically to wages, interest, rent, and profits in the following chapters. You will find that you already have the central analysis from Part 3.

The income you get (leaving aside gifts, Social Security benefits and other transfer payments) depends on the productive services you have to sell—your labor and your capital, if you have any. Most people get nearly all their income as wages or salaries, but owners of capital also get income from rent, interest, and profits.

The price of each productive service (for example, the wage of a worker) is set through supply and demand, roughly equal to the mar-

ginal productivity of that productive resource—that is, equal to the contribution that
that worker makes toward producing what consumers demand. Whenever the price of, say,
labor is below its marginal product (what one
more worker would add to the firm's salable
output), businessmen can increase their profits
by hiring more labor. Competition among businesses for workers will bid up the wage rate
toward the marginal productivity of that type of
labor. Conversely, if the wage rate is more than
labor's marginal product, it will pay businessmen to hire fewer workers, and the wage rate
will fall. Only when the wage rate just equals
labor's marginal product will business firms and
the labor market be in equilibrium.

Each person's earned income, therefore, will
depend on his marginal productivity and on
how much he works, plus the marginal productivity of capital multiplied by the amount of
capital he owns. His education and training, his
IQ, his family background, how hard he works,
his race and sex, the match of his interests with
what consumers will buy, and luck—all these
and more will determine his wage or salary. Add
how wealthy his parents were, how much he
saves, his skill in investing or in running a business, and again luck, for his income from capital.
Some of these factors are clearly under the individual's own control; others, he can't do much
about. In the simplest language, he has to have
something to sell that consumers (or businesses
catering to consumers) want to buy.

"Distribution theory," explaining why different productive resources earn the incomes
they do, is thus merely price theory from Part 3,
viewed from the reverse side. There, we focused
on the pricing of final products, like autos; here,
we focus on the pricing of productive services,
like labor and capital used to produce autos.
Obviously, when the businessman decides to
produce 10,000 autos this week, he is, ipso facto,
deciding to hire the labor and to rent or buy the
machines he needs to do the job. When we compare this demand with the supply of labor or
machines offered, we can determine the prices set
for productive services through the same supply-and-demand mechanism as in Part 3. Obviously, the degree of competition or monopoly in
the market will affect the outcome.

The supply side

To determine the price of any productive service, first we need a supply curve, or
schedule. Consider the supply of some type of
labor in your town—say, carpenters—as an example. The supply this month may be highly
inelastic—fixed by the number of carpenters
there and by their preference to work about forty
hours a week. Or the supply may be elastic, if
carpenters can readily be drawn in from neigh-
boring areas. Or overtime work may be feasible.
All these things together produce a labor-supply
curve for the market for the time period under
study, probably an upward-sloping supply curve
indicating that more labor hours will be supplied at higher than at lower wage rates. In
general, the more unattractive the job and the
lower the promise of advancement, the higher
the wage will have to be to lure workers in.

Labor-supply conditions vary widely for different jobs, and over different periods of time.
The supply of neurosurgeons is highly inelastic
in the short run and only moderately elastic in
the long run. That of waitresses or store clerks is
highly elastic, because their jobs require little
training, and workers can be drawn quickly
from other jobs by higher pay. In general, the
elasticity of supply goes up as more time is allowed for training, education, and movement of
workers from other areas.

The supply of labor for any occupation can
be increased by investment in "human capital"
through education and training, just as the supply of machinery, factories, and other forms of
nonhuman capital can be increased by investment. Thus, as we shall see in Chapter 31, the
value of an individual's services over his lifetime
will reflect how much investment he has made in
himself through education, experience, and the
like, to prepare for the jobs he seeks.

The demand side

The demand for productive services
is primarily a derived demand.[3] The local drug-

---

[3] The appendix to Chapter 20, "Physical Production
Relationships Underlying Cost Curves," provides a rigorous

store hires clerks because customers want to be waited on—not because the druggist wants clerks in the same way that he wants consumer goods. Businesses' demands for productive services are thus derived from ultimate consumer demands. If consumers want lots of prescriptions filled, the demand for prescription clerks will be strong. But if the customers stay away, the druggist doesn't need many clerks.

How many workers (or other productive resources) will a firm demand at any given wage rate? The familiar marginal-cost-equals-marginal-revenue rule gives the answer. **If it is to maximize profits, the firm will hire additional workers as long as each additional worker adds more to the firm's income (marginal revenue) than he adds to its costs (marginal cost). If the wage of another worker is more than that worker adds to revenue, to hire him would lower the firm's profits. If the wage is less than the worker's marginal product, hiring him will increase profits. Profits will be maximized by hiring additional productive resources until the marginal cost just equals marginal revenue.**

The marginal revenue obtained from hiring productive resources is often called "marginal-revenue product." To understand the determinants of marginal-revenue product of any productive resource (and hence business firms' demand for it), we need to separate two components. Additional **physical** output ("marginal physical product") is what the worker adds to total output. But from management's point of view, it is the increase in sales dollars that matters. Hence, it is the marginal **revenue** product in which we are most interested, so multiply the marginal physical product by its price.[4]

Be sure you understand that this is merely a repetition of the central profit-maximizing propositions from Part 3. There, we thought of the firm's planning in terms of units of output; here, the firm plans in terms of units of inputs of productive services used. But the rule of

$MC = MR$ to obtain maximum profit applies either way, and the equilibrium position is the same either way you go at it.[5]

The interaction of supply and demand

We now have the broad outlines of the market for productive services—a supply curve and a demand curve for each type of productive service in each market area, local or national. Employers will compete for more workers as long as their wage is below their marginal-revenue product, but no employer will pay more than labor's marginal-revenue product. **Thus, competition will bid wages up to about the level of labor's marginal productivity, and no higher. And so the wage will be set.**

Figure 30–5 pictures a simple supply-and-demand market equilibrium for one type of labor (say, electrical engineers) in a local market this week. The supply curve is inelastic; in this period, not many more labor hours will be supplied at moderately higher wage rates. The demand curve slopes down for the reasons suggested above. A weekly wage of $200 just clears the market, at 400 engineers per week demanded and supplied. At a higher wage, more would be supplied but less demanded; at a lower wage, the reverse.

Give your theory a workout to explore some implications of this analysis. Suppose Figure 30–5 pictured the market for heart surgeons. The total supply is highly inelastic (substantially fixed in amount) in the short run, a bit more elastic to any given community. Now suppose Congress greatly increases appropriations to support research in this area and to finance heart operations for needy patients. What will happen to the incomes of heart surgeons in the short and

---

logical foundation for this section. If you studied that appendix, it may be useful to review it before proceeding. The "marginal product" of that appendix is identical with the "marginal physical product" of this chapter.

[4]The existence of monopoly raises some special problems, which will be considered in the next chapter.

[5]Although the statements above indicate only how much of a single resource it will pay the business to hire, this approach can readily be generalized to cover *all* the productive resources the firm hires. It will pay to hire more of *each* resource as long as its marginal cost is less than its marginal-revenue product. In equilibrium, therefore, each resource will be hired up to the point where its marginal cost just equals its marginal-revenue product, which is the same as saying that marginal cost equals marginal revenue for the firm as a whole, the profit-maximizing condition stated in Chapter 21. (For a more complete statement, see the appendix to this chapter.)

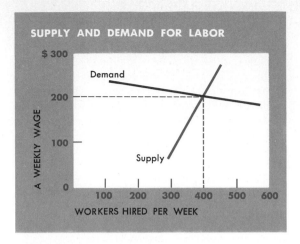

Figure 30-5
Wages, like other prices, are determined by supply and demand forces. Here, the equilibrium wage is $200 per week, with 400 workers hired.

in the long runs? (*Hint:* The median income of physicians in 1975 was about $60,000, up from $24,000 in 1960; total expenditures on health services rose from $13 billion to $118 billion over the period, while the number of physicians per 100,000 population remained roughly constant.)

THE INTEGRATION OF PRICE AND DISTRIBUTION THEORY

The preceding section emphasized that price theory and distribution theory (Parts 3 and 4) are substantially the same. They both look at the pricing process and at the allocation of resources and incomes in response to consumer demands.

To see how the total general equilibrium system fits together, go back and reread the section "General Equilibrium of a Competitive Economy," in Chapter 22. It is the analytical core of this section as well. The pricing of productive services is part and parcel of the general equilibrium pricing process. The costs paid out by business firms **are** the incomes received by the factors of production. Thus, the profit-maximizing decisions of businessmen simultaneously provide the goods most desired by consumers at the lowest feasible prices **and** provide to resource

owners the largest incomes consistent with their abilities and willingness to contribute to producing what consumers demand. The whole system relies on each individual (worker, consumer, businessman, capitalist) to look out for his own self-interest; it relies on competition to see that the end result is in the best interests of all.

Wages, rents, profits, and prices simultaneously determined

Wages, rents, profits, and product prices are all *simultaneously* determined in the competitive market system.[6] Economists are fond of quoting the following little rhyme by H. J. Davenport, a famous economist, to point up the interdependent determination of all product and factor prices:

> The price of pig is something big;
> Because its corn, you'll understand,
> Is high-priced, too; because it grew
> Upon the high-priced farming land.
>
> If you'd know why that land is high,
> Consider this: Its price is big
> Because it pays thereon to raise
> The costly corn, the high-priced pig.

Consider the jingle. It tells an important truth.

TOTAL INCOMES: EARNINGS AND TRANSFER PAYMENTS

This chapter has emphasized that people's earned incomes depend on the services that they and their capital provide. This accounts for most of most people's incomes. But many people also receive substantial transfer payments from the government—Social Security benefits, unemployment payments, "welfare," veterans' benefits, food stamps, Medicare, Med-

[6] The appendix to this chapter provides a more rigorous statement of the marginal-productivity relationships involved. Mathematically inclined readers are referred to Mathematical Appendix IV at the end of the book, where the preceding theory of income distribution (factor pricing) is stated rigorously and some of its interconnections with the macro explanations of relative income shares are explored.

icaid, and a variety of others. In 1975, these transfer payments to individuals from the federal government totalled $154 billion, about 12 percent of all personal incomes. By 1977, such transfer payments were scheduled to rise to over $175 billion. For the last decade, they have been the fastest-rising share of the federal budget.

Who gets these transfer payments? Mainly members of the big middle class; Social Security benefits are by far the biggest single item. But as a percentage of total income received, they bulk largest for poor families, for some of whom such payments constitute most of their incomes. Look ahead to Figure 35–6 for estimates of the shares of income received from government transfer payments at different income levels.

Thus, the preceding pages have been right in stressing marginal productivity as the main factor explaining the incomes we receive. But this explanation needs to be supplemented by a look at the massive transfer payments that now go to many individuals and families. These transfer payments will be a major focus of attention in Part 5, on the public (government) sector of the economy.[7]

[7]In terms of the GNP accounts, the major portion of this chapter has been concerned with the *national income* (how the national income is earned), while this final section focuses on *personal incomes* (how much income people have for paying taxes, spending, or saving).

REVIEW

Concepts to remember

Check your understanding of the following new concepts introduced in this chapter. You ought to be able to relate them directly back to Part 3, especially to the various cost and demand concepts developed there:

derived demand
marginal-physical product
marginal-revenue product

distribution theory
Lorenz curve

For analysis and discussion

1. Are most people's incomes a good measure of what they are worth?
2. The two biggest shares of the national income are wages and profits. Are the basic interests of wage earners and of their employers competitive or complementary?
3. Explain carefully how incomes are distributed in a highly competitive, market-type economy.
4. Would a distribution of income based purely on marginal productivity give everyone about what he is worth? Explain. If you don't think the market properly measures people's worth, how would you measure it?
5. Would the equalization of incomes in the United States, as is proposed by some socialists, solve the problem of poverty? Use the figures on national income (in Chapter 8) and those on income distribution (in this chapter), insofar as you think they are relevant, to support your answer.
6. According to Table 30–3, farm and other unskilled laborers have made substantially lower incomes than the other groups shown. If this is so, why do people continue to be farmers and unskilled laborers?
7. "The distribution of incomes to factors of production is no problem to one who has studied the behavior of business firms. In determining what prices to charge and what output to produce, the firm simultaneously determines how many workers to hire and what wages to pay out, what rents and interest charges to incur, and so on for the other income shares." Can you show how your analysis of Part 3 has in effect explained the distribution of incomes?

APPENDIX

Production theory, price theory, and distribution theory

This **optional** appendix provides (for those who studied Chapter 21) a more rigorous statement of what economists call the theory of production and the way in which it underlies price theory and distribution theory.

The theory of production   The theory of production is concerned with the physical relationship between the factors of production used (input) and the product produced (output). The central principle is the law of diminishing returns, or of variable proportions. This law states (appendix to Chapter 20) that as the proportion of one input to other inputs rises, the additional units of output per unit of that input may rise at first, but will sooner or later begin to fall, and will fall persistently thereafter (other things, such as technology, being unchanged).

Because the law of diminishing returns applies to each productive factor as more of it is used relative to others, it constitutes a powerful analytical tool for deciding the optimal proportions among factors of production if we want to obtain the most efficient (least-cost) production of any commodity. As more of each factor is added relative to the others, its marginal physical product will decline. To obtain the minimum cost of production for any given output, we should add more of each productive factor until the last (marginal) dollar spent on each provides the same addition to total output—that is, the same marginal physical product. This is so because under any other condition, more physical product could be obtained for the same cost by switching a dollar from a lesser-contributing factor of production to a higher-contributing factor. Thus, in equilibrium:

$$\frac{\text{Marginal physical product of } A}{\text{Price of } A}$$

$$= \frac{\text{Marginal physical product of } B}{\text{Price of } B}, \text{etc.}$$

Another (equivalent) way of saying the same thing is that in the least-cost condition, the marginal physical products of the factors of production must be proportional to their prices. That is:

$$\frac{\text{Marginal physical product of } A}{\text{Marginal physical product of } B}$$

$$= \frac{\text{Price of } A}{\text{Price of } B}, \text{etc.}$$

This proposition implicitly underlies the discussion of the unit-cost curves in Chapters 20 and 21. The U-shape of the firm's cost curve derives in part from the physical relationships described by the law of variable proportions. Most important, assuming the prices of factors of production to be given, the minimum-cost point on the firm's unit-cost curve can be achieved only when the factors of production are used in the proportions indicated above.

This theory of production also provides the answer to how a change in the price of any factor will affect its use. If the price of one resource (say, labor) falls, its use will be increased until its marginal physical product falls to the same proportion with other marginal physical products as the new proportion among the factor prices concerned. In other words, more labor will be hired until the marginal dollar spent on labor again produces the same marginal product as when spent on any other factor of production. Hiring more labor becomes desirable even though this reduces labor's marginal physical product under the law of diminishing returns.

Maximum-profit positions in price theory and distribution theory   The statement of the least-cost conditions above does not necessarily specify the maximum-profit position of the firm. It only specifies the conditions for obtaining the least-cost production for any given production level. The condition for maximum-profit (or minimum-loss) production is to increase production as long as marginal cost is less than marginal revenue (up to $MC = MR$). This is identical with the proposition that maximum profit (or minimum loss) will be obtained by adding units of each factor of production as long as its marginal cost (price, under competitive conditions) is less than its marginal-revenue product. The statement in terms of individual factors of production merely specifies in more detail the **mix** of productive factors that must be used in arriving at the maximum-profit position. The $MC = MR$ proposition of earlier chapters is silent on the optimal factor combination; it implicitly takes the optimal combination for granted. We can now add the proposition that for maximum profit, the marginal cost of each factor used must be equal to its marginal-revenue product and that the marginal costs of all the factors used must be proportional to their marginal-revenue products:

$$\frac{\text{Marginal cost of factor } A}{\text{Marginal cost of factor } B}$$

$$= \frac{\text{Marginal-revenue productivity of } A}{\text{Marginal-revenue productivity of } B}$$

Or, to put it another way, that:

$$\frac{\text{Marginal cost of } A}{\text{Marginal-revenue productivity of } A}$$

$$= \frac{\text{Marginal cost of } B}{\text{Marginal-revenue productivity of } B}$$

CHAPTER 31

wages and salaries: applying the theory

Wages and salaries account for over two-thirds of the total national income, and for nearly all of most people's incomes. By the same token, they constitute about two-thirds of total business costs. So it is not surprising that people have long been spinning out theories to explain why wages and salaries are what they are.

Economists' theories mirror the times in which they live, and several different theories have been widely accepted over the last two centuries. Today, we do not yet have a fully satisfactory theory of wages. Yet most economists agree that the simple marginal-productivity, supply-and-demand theory stated in the last half of Chapter 30 provides a fruitful way to examine why individual wages are what they are. **This chapter is primarily an application of that theory—to explain why different people get the wages and salaries they do.**

SOME DUBIOUS THEORIES

But first let us consider briefly three theories of wages that attained widespread acceptance during the last century, and that still have considerable influence in lay thinking, even though most economists today consider them to be largely fallacious, or at least of dubious value.

The subsistence theory. Nearly two centuries ago, Thomas Malthus argued that wages for the masses would never long remain above the subsistence level—the so-called "Iron Law of Wages." Malthus said that population will tend to grow geometrically—2, 4, 8, 16 . . .—while the food it can produce is limited. Thus, the growing supply of labor will always tend to force wages down toward the subsistence level. Wages cannot permanently stay below the subsistence level, for obvious reasons. But they will not for long stay above it in the absence of artificial means to limit the rate of population growth. Marx accepted much of the theory and predicted the downfall of capitalism, as workers become increasingly unwilling to accept their menial existence while capitalists appropriate the "surplus value" created by the workers whose wages fall increasingly short of the total value they create.

But history has shown an escape from this bitter prospect. In most Western industrialized nations, technological advance and capital accumulation have saved us from Malthus and Marx. In fact, real wages have risen rapidly and (except for cyclical fluctuations) steadily over the past century. Moreover, in the nations with the highest living standards, birthrates have fallen far below the rates in less-advanced countries.

But don't write off Malthus too fast. For the less-developed nations, Malthus's predictions on wages look perilously close to right. Total output has grown in most nations, but for over half the world's population, little faster than the number of mouths to feed, and starvation looms on the horizon each bad crop year.

The "lump-of-labor" theory. Another widely held, but almost completely fallacious, theory is that there is some fixed amount of work to be done in the short run, so more people seeking work will merely bid wages down and steal jobs from those already at work. This theory, often unarticulated, lies behind widespread opposition to letting new workers into the labor market— foreigners, women, apprentices, and so on. It lies behind union restrictions on entry to many occupations, and behind widespread resistance to "automation"—to the introduction of machines that appear to replace human beings.

What is the fallacy in this "lump-of-labor" theory? A big part of the answer was given in Part 2. We can always—through government monetary and fiscal policy—ensure enough demand to provide jobs for as many workers as enter the labor market. At the level of the individual industry, the demand for labor is a function of the marginal productivity of that labor. Workers willing to work for a wage at or below their marginal productivity can always be employed profitably if we ensure the right amount of total national demand. The total amount of labor that will be hired is thus a function of both ultimate demand and the price (wage) of the labor. **There is no fixed amount of work to be divided up; the number of jobs depends on aggregate demand and the real wage that workers demand.**

The bargaining theory. A third theory, one with an important element of truth, is that wages depend on the relative bargaining power of employers and employees. Clearly, relative bargaining strength does matter sometimes—for example, when the United Auto Workers sit down to bargain with General Motors. But the bargaining theory leaves one big question unanswered: What are the limits within which the bargaining can vary the wage, and what sets those limits? If the union is very strong, does that mean there is no upper limit as to how high it can push its members' wages? Obviously not. At some level, the employer would have an economic incentive to substitute nonunion labor or machinery for the high-cost union members, or eventually go broke. If there is no union, does that mean the employer can drive down the wage virtually to zero? Obviously not. If his wages go far below prevailing levels, his employees will look for jobs elsewhere. Thus, to say that wages depend on relative bargaining strength is an obvious half-truth. The following pages should go a long way toward defining the limits within which bargaining power may dominate under different conditions.

But to point out the inadequacies of these theories does not provide a satisfactory explanation of what does set wages. We need a theory that will encompass the cases where Malthus appears to be right, where "automation" occurs,

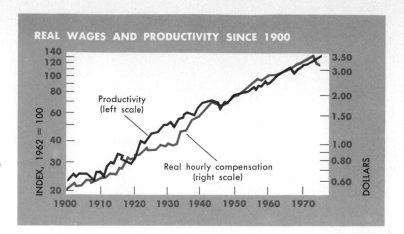

Figure 31–1

Rising productivity has made possible the steadily rising real wages of American workers. (Source: Council of Economic Advisers.)

where bargaining power varies, and where new workers enter the labor market.

WAGES IN COMPETITIVE MARKETS

Supply and demand for labor, with marginal productivity determining the demand, goes a long way toward explaining all the cases in market-type economies. The wage earned by each class of labor will tend to equal its marginal-revenue productivity, for the reasons outlined in Chapter 30.

Figure 31–1 shows the close correspondence between output per man-hour and real wages in the American economy since 1900. It emphasizes a basic fact: **It is rising productivity that has made possible the steadily rising wages of American workers. Even though there are many more workers seeking jobs now than in 1900, their productivity is so much higher now that businesses demand the larger number— even at much higher wages.**

But before applying the theory in detail, two preliminary warnings: First, there are nearly 100 million people in the American labor force, no two exactly alike. Thus, we cannot talk of "labor" and "wages" as if they were homogeneous. We need to look separately at many different types of labor, at people with different capacities, different education and training, different attitudes, living in different places.

Second, we shall be looking at the determinants of individual wages, or wages of particular groups of workers, in contrast to the "macro"

issues of wage-profit shares in the total national income. **Thus, this is a chapter mainly at the "micro" level. It takes the level of aggregate demand (GNP) as given, determined by the forces described in Part 2.**

Begin with a simple case. What determines the wage received by William (Bill) Welder, a hypothetical laborer who works for the Acme Plumbing Company, a small plumbing-fixtures manufacturer. There is no welders' union in the area. Bill's abilities are substantially undifferentiated from those of other welders. There are many companies in the area that hire welders. And there are many plumbing-supplies manufacturers in the United States who compete actively with each other in the product market. So there is active competition at three levels— among welders for jobs, among businesses for the services of welders, and among businesses for the consumer's sales dollar.

What determines Bill's wage? He gets the going hourly rate for welders—say, $6 an hour. Acme Plumbing doesn't haggle over wage rates with each man it hires. It pays the going rate.

Something beyond Acme determines the "going wage" for welders in the area. By now, the answer "supply and demand" ought to come easily to you as the framework for looking at this price—the price of labor.

The supply side

What determines the supply of welders in the area? In the short run, it depends largely on the number of welders in the area, the

413

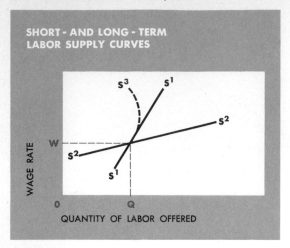

SHORT- AND LONG-TERM LABOR SUPPLY CURVES

Figure 31–2
The short-run supply curve for labor (S^1S^1) is typically much less elastic than the long-run curve (S^2S^2). If OQ labor is offered now at wage OW, a higher wage will increase the labor offered only slightly in the short run, much more in the long run. The dashed portion (S^3) of the short-run supply curve shows the special case where a higher wage calls forth less, not more, labor.

availability of additional welders from nearby areas, and the willingness of welders to work longer hours. In the long run, supply will be more elastic. Welders may be drawn from long distances; workers may shift from other occupations; new labor-force entrants may learn welding. Plumbing manufacturers, the government, or workers themselves may invest in human capital by training nonwelders to become welders.

Figure 31–2 pictures the general relationship between short-run and long-run labor-supply curves. Short-run supply is usually inelastic. Except for overtime and the possibility of getting workers away from other areas or occupations, higher wages won't greatly increase the amount of labor offered. See curve S^1S^1. But in the long run, there are many new sources of supply; the curve is more likely to look like S^2S^2. Everywhere, long-run supply elasticity is greater than short-run. But the facts vary greatly among different occupations.[1]

---

[1] Sometimes labor-supply curves are "backward bending," as indicated by the dashed extension of S^1 to S^3 in

The nature of the supply curve in each industry depends in part on the kind of work involved, working conditions, promise of advancement, and the like. The less attractive, pleasant, and promising the job, the higher the wage will have to be to bribe workers to accept that package of wages, working conditions, and promise for the future. Many people are surprised that even in periods of widespread unemployment, city newspapers are full of ads for dishwashers, household help, messengers, and the like. But a common reaction to such jobs is that they're low-pay, unattractive, and dead-end—why take them? "Job attachment" in such occupations is low. People, especially young people, often quit after only a brief stay. Try applying this kind of supply analysis to the job of "sandhogs"—men who drill tunnels under rivers. The work is dangerous, unpleasant, and difficult; the pay is high. Or to lifeguards at your local beach in summer.

The demand side

The demand for welders' services is a derived demand—derived from the ultimate consumer demand for the plumbing fixtures Acme produces. Acme (and other businesses) will demand more welders whenever it has unfulfilled demand for its product at profitable prices. More precisely, Acme will demand more welders as long as the wage is below welders' marginal-revenue productivity. Other firms will do likewise. By aggregating the demands of all firms, we could draw a market-demand curve for welders' services. The lower the wage (marginal

---

Figure 31–2. This is fairly common in the less-developed countries. Workers, accustomed to very low standards of living, simply stop working after they have earned enough in, say, a week to meet their minimal needs. They prefer leisure to more money with the additional work required to get it. Thus, raising the hourly wage will get less work, not more, because workers will earn their desired minimum income by working *fewer* hours.

Backward-bending labor-supply curves are less common in countries like the United States. But you may know people who simply prefer leisure to work once they have the current income they need to buy what they most want. At a high enough wage rate, they will feel able to afford to work less, not more, even though the money opportunity cost of each extra hour of leisure is higher.

cost), the more welders the market will demand.

Marginal-revenue productivity for most workers is compounded of marginal physical productivity and a product-price factor. Bill Welder's marginal *physical* product is the additional physical product Acme Plumbing turns out by having Bill on the job, compared with the output without him, all other productive factors being identical. This marginal physical product depends on Bill's own mental and physical abilities, training, morale, and so on. It also depends, probably even more, on the capital (other productive agents) with which he works. The average U.S. worker in manufacturing is supported now by a capital investment of over $40,000, which goes far to explain his higher marginal productivity.

The production manager is mainly interested in the number of sinks turned out per day. But the president and the stockholders are more interested in profit figures—in dollars and cents, rather than in numbers of sinks and faucets. For them, productivity figures have to be converted into **marginal-revenue (sales-dollar) terms.**

Will's marginal-revenue productivity is the additional sales dollars brought in by employing him. If his marginal physical product is two sinks per day, and the wholesale price of sinks is $30, then his marginal-revenue productivity at Acme Plumbing is $60. Marginal-revenue productivity is found by multiplying the marginal physical product by marginal-unit revenue (price under pure competition). Consumer demand for the ultimate product is just as important as the worker's physical output in determining his value to the business.

The marginal-revenue productivity of welders will eventually decrease as more welders are put to work producing sinks—because of the law of diminishing returns, and because, as more sinks are produced by this and competing firms, their price will fall, consumer demand remaining unchanged, although Acme alone is too small to influence market price. Thus, the demand curve for workers will generally be downward-sloping, as in Figure 31–3. Starting from any equilibrium position, firms will hire more labor only as wage rates fall, given an unchanged demand for sinks. The marginal-revenue-product curve for welders

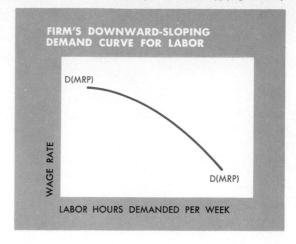

Figure 31–3
The competitive firm's demand curve for labor is downward-sloping. The demand curve is labor's marginal-revenue product in the firm, since it will pay to hire more workers as long as marginal-revenue product is more than wage.

in the firm is that particular firm's demand curve for welders.[2]

SUPPLY, DEMAND, AND PURELY COMPETITIVE WAGES

To demonstrate rigorously that the wage will equal marginal productivity, assume (1) that welders are all identical, (2) that employment conditions are similar at different plants in the area, and (3) that information on wages at different plants is circulated freely. Then all plants will have to pay about the same wage to get welders, just as there tends to be a single price for any identical commodity within any given market area.

Suppose that the going wage for welders is $50 a day, but that Acme Plumbing and other plants figure that welders' marginal productivity is around $60 per eight-hour day. What will

[2]Note that if firms are prepared to increase the capital with which welders work (for example, by increasing the scale of plant), the effect of diminishing physical productivity can be avoided. But the declining-price effect will nevertheless pull down marginal-revenue productivity.

DOES DEMAND REALLY DEPEND ON MARGINAL-REVENUE PRODUCTIVITY?

In a purely competitive labor market, the individual employer is a wage taker, not a wage maker. He has to pay the going wage; his problem is how many men to hire at that wage. This depends on the marginal product an additional worker will provide. But how can businessmen estimate anything as complex as a worker's marginal-revenue productivity?

In a small firm like Acme Plumbing, with only a few employees, the boss will have a good idea of how much his daily output will go up if he puts on an extra man. And he knows the price of sinks. This was the kind of situation economists had in mind when they developed the marginal-productivity approach to explaining the demand for labor.

But what about the marginal-revenue productivity of a welder at U.S. Steel? It has nearly 300,000 employees scattered over the United States, with hundreds of welders among them. Welders work on jobs many steps removed from the ultimate products sold to customers. For example, one welder may do repair work on the company's railway cars that shuttle materials around the mills. What is his marginal productivity?

Obviously, no one knows precisely. It would be impossible to isolate the effect on the ultimate production of steel of laying off that one welder. And there are millions of workers in American industry who present similar problems in estimating marginal productivity.

Still, U.S. Steel has to decide how many welders it will hire. Company officials might tell you that they simply hire enough welders to get the steel produced for which they have orders. But this answer drives us back to the question of the price at which U.S. Steel will book orders.

Clearly, this decision depends in large part on the costs estimated by the steel people for producing steel sheets. All these interrelated variables have to be put together, and somehow the managers at the plant level have to decide when it will pay to hire another welder.

Where does all this leave us on the demand for labor? First, it's clear that no very precise estimate of marginal productivity is possible in many cases. Second, hard as the estimating job is, businessmen have to make some such calculation (consciously or subconsciously) in their hiring and pricing decisions if they are intelligently trying to maximize profits. Third, often several types of labor must be hired as a group to operate as a production unit. You either have the people it takes to run a modern assembly line, or you just shut the line down. In such cases, it is very difficult to separate out the marginal product of each kind of laborer.

Out of all this emerges a rough notion that businessmen are willing to pay workers only what they are "worth," sometimes viewing them as individuals but often as groups required for an integrated operation. What workers are worth **logically** boils down to a notion of marginal-revenue productivity. Although this figure can't be estimated precisely in most cases, many businesses use their cost-accounting systems to get working ideas of when it pays to take new orders and to hire more workers. Behind these money-cost estimates are time-and-motion studies of how much labor time should turn out how much product. Using such studies, the businessman can get a rough estimate of the "productivity" of different types of workers.

happen? Those firms will try to hire more welders. When they do, (1) the wage rate will be bid up, and (2) the marginal-revenue productivity of welders in these plants will fall as more welders are added, because of the law of diminishing returns and a lower price for sinks. Each firm will bid for additional welders as long as the rising wage is lower than its estimate of the welders' falling marginal product. At some wage between $50 and $60 (say, $55), a new equilibrium will be established, with market supply and demand in balance at that new wage.

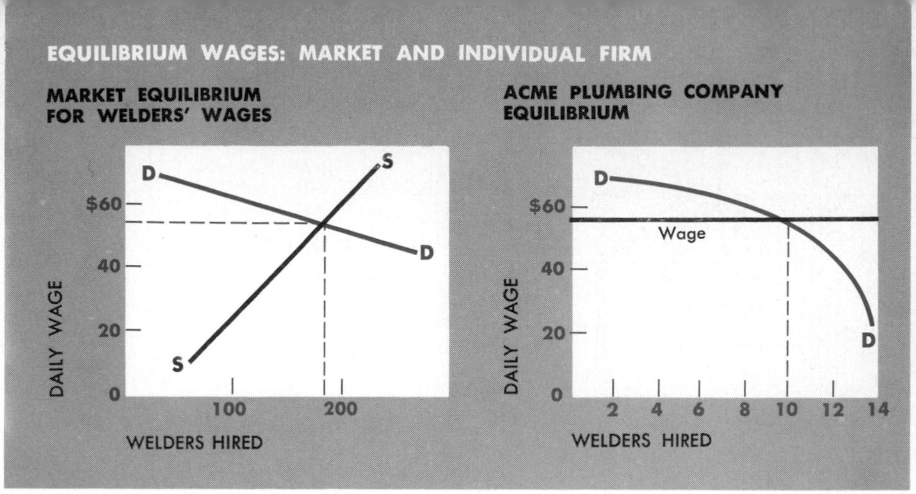

Figure 31-4
Welders' wages are set in the market, much like other prices (left-hand side). At a market wage of $55, Acme maximizes profits by hiring ten welders, at which point their wage equals their marginal-revenue productivity to Acme (right-hand side).

MARKET EQUILIBRIUM FOR WELDERS' WAGES

ACME PLUMBING COMPANY EQUILIBRIUM

The left-hand portion of Figure 31-4 shows the equilibrium for the entire labor market; this is a summation of all the firms demanding welders as against the total supply of welders in the area. The right-hand portion of the figure shows that Acme hires ten welders when the daily wage is set by the market at $55; remember that Acme simply pays the going wage rate to get the welders it needs.

In this equilibrium situation, we would expect to find the following:

1. The wage rate is equal to welders' marginal-revenue productivity in the plants where they are hired.
2. Welders' wages are identical at all plants in the area.
3. Each firm is hiring as many welders as it "can afford" at that wage, because each firm continues to hire welders as long as the wage is lower than welders' marginal-revenue productivity.
4. All welders in the area who are seeking work at that wage are employed. If any were still looking for work at that wage or less, the market wage rate would be bid down, since employers could hire unemployed workers at less than they were paying employed welders.

Thus, each worker earns what his labor is "worth," as measured by its marginal contribution to producing the goods and services consumers demand. But remember: Each individual's marginal-revenue productivity, and hence his wage, depends on a lot of forces outside his own control—on shifts in consumer demand,

changing technology, the efficiency of management, the state of the business cycle.

Now try applying the same analysis to a related question. What will *your* starting salary be when you are graduated from college? Five years later?

WAGE DETERMINATION IN MONOPOLIZED INDUSTRIES

What difference does it make if the plumbing-supplies industry is monopolized by one or a few major producers? Continue the assumptions that each firm does the best it can to maximize profits, and that firms in this and other industries compete actively for welders.

As under competition, each firm will continue to hire more welders as long as the wage is lower than welders' estimated marginal worth to the concern. But the total number of welders hired in this industry will be lower than under competition, because the monopolist restricts output to get higher prices and higher profits.

Thus, fewer welders will have jobs making plumbing supplies. If welders could work only there, clearly wages would be forced down by their competition for the reduced number of jobs. But since (we assume) welders are mobile, those unemployed will compete for jobs elsewhere, forcing down welders' wages there. Welders' wages will again be identical everywhere in the new equilibrium, but at a lower level than without the monopoly. **By restricting output**

417

"Leave it to good old G.M. to break the monotony of the assembly line!" (Drawing by Alan Dunn; © 1972 The New Yorker Magazine, Inc.)

below the competitive "ideal," the monopolist forces an inefficient allocation of labor, and this produces a lower wage for welders than under competition, both in the plumbing-supplies industry and elsewhere. Too few workers are employed in making plumbing supplies, too many

[3]The argument can be stated rigorously, as follows: Since the monopolist always faces a downward-sloping demand curve, marginal revenue is always less than price. The marginal-revenue product obtained by hiring more labor is therefore always less than marginal physical product times the product price; instead, it is marginal physical product times marginal revenue. Since the marginal-revenue-product curve is the firm's demand-for-labor curve, the firm's demand for labor under monopoly will always be less than in a comparable competitive case.

in the rest of the economy. They are not efficiently allocated.[3]

WAGE DETERMINATION UNDER EMPLOYER MONOPSONY

Now assume a different situation, where there is no competition among employers for labor. An example might be an isolated company mining town, where there is no significant alternative to working in the mine. The mine operator has a substantially complete "monopsony"—that is, a monopoly in hiring workers. Such a business is a wage maker, not a wage taker. There is no competition to make it pay a wage as high as the workers' marginal-revenue productivity. If the workers are immobile, the manager may "exploit" them—that is, he may pay them a wage below their marginal-revenue productivity to him.

How much can the monopsonist exploit his workers? It depends mainly on their mobility. If his wages get too far below rates elsewhere, workers may move away to other areas where they can earn more. If he has to go outside his monopsony area to hire more workers, competition with other employers is likely to eliminate his ability to exploit the workers.

Economists define **exploitation** as a wage below a worker's marginal-revenue productivity. Although such cases may seem unethical or improper to you, "exploitation" in economics is an analytical, not a moral, term. Willie Mays or a corporate executive may be exploited in this sense, just as may a secretary or an itinerant fruit picker. (Note that this is quite different from Marx's definition of the term.)

To hear workers tell it, monopsony is a common case, often because employers agree not to compete for labor. Thus, the worker needs a union to protect himself against exploitation. According to employers, this is a rare case. The evidence suggests a mixed world. But everywhere, the strength of monopsony positions diminishes as job-information channels improve, and as workers' mobility increases. For example, even though waitresses' wages are low in most cities, it is very difficult for employers to exploit them. There are hundreds of restaurants, so collusion is difficult, and any waitress will soon move elsewhere if her boss pays wages below the going competitive rate.

WAGE DETERMINATION UNDER
BILATERAL MONOPOLY AND OLIGOPOLY

The next model is one that comes close to real-world conditions in some of the current big-union–big-business areas. "Bilateral monopoly" is the case where employers with monopsony power bargain with unions with monopoly power in selling labor. A simple case would be the mining-town example above, after the workers formed a union to represent them as exclusive bargaining agent. A more realistic example, a case of bilateral oligopoly, is wage bargaining in the steel industry, where the United Steelworkers represent most of the workers, and the major firms in the industry in effect act together in bargaining for new contracts.

Under bilateral monopoly or bilateral oligopoly, the wage outcome is logically uncertain. The employer will be unwilling to pay more than the labor's marginal-revenue productivity without cutting back the number employed; he will pay less if he can get the labor he needs at a lower wage, and without a union he can exploit the workers to some extent in this way. The union, with a monopoly in the sale of its members' services, pushes up wages as far as it can. If the wage is pushed above labor's marginal-value product at the present employment level, fewer men will be hired. But the exact wage level is indeterminate between this marginal-value-product ceiling and a wage floor above which the employer could (without a union) get all the labor he needs. The outcome will depend on the relative bargaining strength of union and employer, on how badly the employer wants to avoid a strike, on the size of the union's strike fund.

WAGE AND SALARY DIFFERENTIALS—
THE RICH AND THE POOR

Now turn to another application of the marginal-productivity theory—the explanation of wage and salary differentials. Why should TV stars, corporation presidents, and home-run hitters get over $100,000 a year, when most of us have to be content with a small fraction of that? And especially, why should they get it when their work, by and large, looks so pleasant compared with ditchdigging or typing, which pay only a few dollars an hour?

Supply and demand again

The most fundamental things about wage and salary differentials can be seen by using the same supply-and-demand, marginal-productivity model again. Give your theory a workout.

Salaries are extremely high where the supply is tiny and the demand is large. Wages are low where there are lots of workers relative to the demand. How hard, how unpleasant, how tedious the job is—such considerations aren't very important except as they influence the supply of workers to the job. But sometimes, such supply differentials have a big impact on the "wage structure." The wage structure must be a set of relative wages in different occupations and industries that equalizes supply and demand conditions for all different workers in all different occupations in equilibrium.

Why has Jack Nicklaus collected over $3 million just for playing golf on warm summer afternoons? Mainly because he is better at playing golf than anyone else; and we Americans lay our dollars on the line with enthusiasm to watch good golf players in person and on TV.[4] How can a surgeon get away with charging hundreds of dollars an hour? Because his skills are very scarce, and the demand for them is relatively very large. His marginal-revenue productivity is very high. In contrast, it's easy to be a delivery boy or a retail clerk, and lots of people try these jobs. Their marginal productivity is low. So are wages and job attachment.

The biggest factor accounting for wage differentials thus lies in the ability and willingness of the individual to do something that few others can do—something that is demanded by consumers with money to pay for it. There are big differences in the capabilities of different people, some reflecting innate physical and mental differences, others the amount of investment in human capital through education, training, and experience. Mohammed Ali's split-second timing was largely born, not made, in spite of the years of training that went into it. Psychologists tell us that our basic intelligence apparently changes little over the years, no matter how hard we study. But our capabilities also depend on family environments, the amount and quality of education, hard work, and other things that are,

to at least some extent, controllable. Not least, luck often plays a big role—certainly as to what kind of family environment you are born into. To understand the incomes different people earn, we therefore need to analyze their basic abilities, how these abilities have been modified by environment, education, and training, and the markets for the particular workers.

Psychologists dispute bitterly over the relative importance of heredity and environment in making people what they are. Here, we can look only at the economic factors involved in determining marginal productivities.

Education and investment in human capital

Clearly, most of the highest-paying occupations have high educational requirements. Look back at Table 30–3. The best-paid occupations are professional or managerial, averaging over seventeen years of schooling. Salary studies consistently show a high rate of return on investment in education—over 10 percent, in most cases. In other words, every year of additional schooling beyond the eighth grade seems to be worth an extra $500 or so a year over one's working lifetime; college may be worth $100,000 or so in extra earnings, a tidy return. (There is some trickery in these figures, of course, since we know that those who go on to college are generally more able and would presumably earn above-average salaries even without the extra schooling. But even making a rough allowance to eliminate that factor, higher education pays well on the average.)

Figure 30–3 showed the relationship between education and earning power more sharply. There is a consistent rise in income with increased education, for both whites and nonwhites. While there is a lot of individual variation, low-education families are concentrated at the lower-income levels; very few reach the higher levels. Interestingly, however, the rate of return declines steadily with each year of additional education, other things equal. It is extremely important to get through grade and high school, a little less important for each additional year of schooling. Education is an income equalizer. The income gap between whites and nonwhites decreases at high-education levels.

---

[4]Anomalously, athletic stars like Willie Mays and Babe Ruth may have been more susceptible to wage exploitation than most common laborers. This is because there was little active competition for their services to force the Giants and the Yankees to pay them their full marginal product. Under organized baseball's "reserve clause," other clubs couldn't hire Mays or Ruth away; they would have had to "buy" them from the Giants or Yankees. But Mays and Ruth each obviously had a monopoly in selling his own services. Thus, each situation was one of bilateral monopoly.

Don't fall into the trap, however, of thinking that formal education is the only important form of investment in human capital, or that education determines the incomes people receive. On the contrary, we learn basic habits and skills in everyday life, at home and on the job, and recent sociological studies suggest that for most people, especially in the below-median-income groups, nonschool forces dominate the learning process. Moreover, most highly skilled jobs (medicine, law, management, engineering, and so forth) require continued learning after formal education has been completed. Some of this further investment in human capital is financed by employers; a lot is the result of drive and hard work by those who win out in the highly competitive race for the best-paying jobs. The importance of continued investment in human capital is confirmed by the lifetime-earnings patterns of different occupations. The annual earnings of doctors, lawyers, managers, and others with extensive education and continued learning by experience peak in their fifties and sixties, while the annual earnings of low-education, unskilled workers who depend largely on simple physical labor peak in their twenties or thirties and slide downhill thereafter. Figure 31–5 shows the combined importance of age and investment in human capital on lifetime-earnings patterns.

Four concluding questions for discussion: (1) How much education should each individual invest in, assuming he wants to maximize his lifetime income? (Remember that education has costs as well as benefits, including the earnings foregone during years spent in college and graduate school.) (2) If education pays off so well, should we count on people to finance their own education, by borrowing if need be? (3) How much should the government spend on education, who should get the subsidized education, and who should pay the bill?[5] (We shall return to these questions in Part 5, on government policy and the provision of public services.) (4) Do existing differentials (for TV stars, surgeons, corporation presidents, schoolteachers,

[5]For example, the average family-income level of students at the University of California at Berkeley is substantially larger than the average family-income level of California taxpayers.

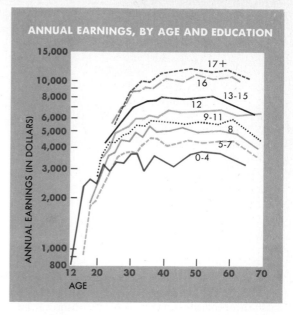

Figure 31–5
Annual earnings vary widely with age and education. Numbers on curve show years of schooling. Data for white males, 1959. Source: J. Mincer, *Schooling, Experience and Earnings* (New York: National Bureau of Economic Research, 1974), p. 68.

nurses, factory workers, farm laborers) reward most highly those who make the greatest contribution to human welfare? If your answer is no, how do you explain why we pay some people enormous incomes? (See Case 26.)

Discrimination and inequality

Table 31–1 summarizes the income differences among white and nonwhite families, and those headed by males and by females. Table 31–2 presents a more direct comparison between white and black full-time, full-year workers. The data suggest substantial discrimination against both nonwhites and women, although Table 31–2 shows less job discrimination against black women than black men.

For economic analysis, we need to define discrimination precisely. If an employer can hire a black or a woman for wage W, but he in fact acts as if the effective wage were $W + D$, then D can be called a coefficient or measure of discrimina-

Table 31–1
Household incomes, 1974

| | | | PERCENTAGE RECEIVING INCOMES: | | | | | |
	All	Under $5,000	$5,000 to $9,999	$10,000 to $14,999	$15,000 to $24,000	$25,000 to $49,999	$50,000 and over	Median Income
Total	100.0	21.1	23.7	22.0	23.7	8.6	0.9	$11,101
White	100.0	19.2	22.9	22.7	24.9	9.2	1.0	11,604
Nonwhite	100.0	36.2	28.4	17.2	14.6	3.4	0.3	7,180
Male head	100.0	12.0	22.0	25.0	28.9	10.8	1.2	13,135
Female head	100.0	50.5	28.8	12.6	6.6	1.3	0.2	4,937

Source: U.S. Census Bureau. Households include individuals living alone.

tion. For an employer who completely refused to hire blacks at any wage, however low, D would be infinitely large. If the employer discriminates in favor of blacks or women, his D is negative.

Let us analyze the *economic* effects of discrimination. Discrimination clearly harms the group discriminated against—say, black workers. They are partly or completely shut out of some jobs, which means they are forced to compete for less-attractive jobs, forcing down the wage for those jobs. White workers in the jobs from which blacks are excluded clearly gain, since fewer workers compete for the jobs, and white wages are therefore higher. But discriminating employers lose, rather than gain, economically from their discrimination. They presumably feel better by not having blacks in the jobs, but they are foregoing profits by not hiring blacks up to the point where their wages are equal to their marginal products. They are paying higher wages to the whites than they could have paid blacks for the same work. This conclusion is in striking contradiction to the standard Marxist argument that employers discriminate in order to increase their profits.

In effect, discrimination shutting minority workers out of some jobs sets up "dual labor markets"—with the best jobs reserved for whites. Then each market must be analyzed separately, although there is clearly some spillover between them. Note, for example, that any white workers who must compete for jobs in the lower (minority) job areas will suffer from the antiminority discrimination because wages are forced down in those areas.

Employers may discriminate not because of their own prejudices, but because they believe customers or other workers would object to being served by, or working with, minority groups or women. If this belief is correct, it is less clear that discriminating employers forego maximum profits by discriminating; the result then depends on the particular circumstances, mainly on how strong the prejudices of customers or other workers are.

Discrimination in the United States now seldom takes the form of paying lower wages to minority groups or women than to white males for the same job in the same place, because this is

Table 31–2

Black workers' earnings as percentage of whites—full-time, full-year workers

Year	Males	Females
1955	.56	.56
1960	.59	.68
1965	.60	.80
1970	.65	.83
1974	.65	.87

Source: U.S. Census Bureau.

a clear violation of the law. Instead, discrimination usually involves refusing to employ minorities or women in jobs for which they are qualified, or insisting on higher qualifications than for white males for the same job. But the overall economic result is similar in either case. Nor does the economic analysis of discrimination against women differ in essentials from that against minority groups.

A substantial part of the lower earnings of minorities and women reflects not current discrimination but their lower productivity. Employers argue, often correctly, that few blacks and few women are currently qualified for many of the highest-paying jobs. Exclusion of minorities and women from the best jobs thus often reflects past rather than present discrimination, in both education and on-the-job training. Differences in education are hard to measure, and they clearly do not account for all, or perhaps even most, of the relevant differences in productivity. But we know that minorities have substantially fewer years of education than whites on the average, and there is much evidence that the quality of their education is generally inferior. Minority groups are closing the education gap, but they are still far behind. In 1975, 80 percent of all whites had completed high school, and 20 percent had completed college. The comparable figures for nonwhites were 60 and 12 percent, but in 1940, only 12 percent of nonwhites had completed high school, and 2 percent college.

All things considered, what is the economic cost of being black? Only the roughest estimates are possible. Some suggest that perhaps a third of the total shortfall of black income, equalizing for age, education, and location, is due to current discrimination. Another study estimates that the annual income cost of being black averaged about $1,000 in the 1960s, after adjustment to equalize age, education, and the like. Obviously, the estimated cost of discrimination can be raised or lowered substantially by attributing more or less of existing education and training differences to past discrimination.[6]

[6]For more details, see B. Schiller, *The Economics of Poverty and Discrimination* (Englewood Cliffs, N.J.: Prentice-Hall, 1972), Chaps. 9–10; L. Thurow, *Poverty and Discrimination* (Washington, D.C.: The Brookings Institution, 1969),

Unions and barriers to entry

Unions have some influence on wage differentials, as we shall see in Chapter 32. Where employer monopsony exists, clearly unions can improve workers' positions compared to nonunion shops. By shutting out nonmembers through restrictions on entry into particular occupations (for instance, the building trades), unions can clearly raise their members' wages in those occupations while lowering the wages of workers forced to compete in nonunionized areas.

Generally, only the craft unions have exercised effective barriers to entry. Many craft unions have traditionally excluded blacks, but most industrial unions (such as autos and steel) have open-door policies for minorities. Much evidence suggests (see Chapter 32) that unions have generally raised the wages of the unskilled relative to the skilled, so despite the discriminatory policies of some craft unions, unions on the whole have probably somewhat narrowed wage differentials by race.

AUTOMATION AND WAGES

Technological advance is a dominant force in the American economy. New methods, new machines, new products are the lifeblood of a dynamic, growing economy. Without the linotype, we'd still be setting type by hand, and books and newspapers would still be for the elite few. Without the electric light bulb, we'd still be lighting our houses with candles, oil, and gas.

But "automation" (as technological advance is sometimes called when new automatic machines replace men) is often blamed for widespread unemployment. Computers replace thousands of clerks in processing checks and keeping records in banks and businesses. Modern chemical plants are almost fully automated. On a humbler level, spray guns and rollers get work done a lot faster than the old-fashioned paint-

Chaps. 7 and 9; and M. Blaxall and B. Reagan, *Women and the Workplace* (Chicago: University of Chicago Press, 1976).

brush. Everywhere, new factories produce more goods with fewer workers.

Technological progress increases output per unit of input—output per worker, output per unit of capital, or both, whichever way you wish to divide up total output. Thus, we might expect it to raise both wages and the rate of return on capital—and so it generally will, other things equal. But how much of the gain goes to each under what circumstances is a more complex question.

Some facts

Figure 31–1 showed the steady parallel growth in output per man-hour and wages in the American economy. Moreover, the growth in total output has been much greater than the total input of labor and capital combined. Look ahead to Figure 44–2 for the facts. The total incomes of both capital and labor have risen greatly over the past century, but the return per unit of labor (the real wage rate) has gone up much more than the return per unit of capital (the real interest rate), as the bottom half of Figure 44–2 shows dramatically. The average real wage now is about 500 percent of what it was in 1900, while the real interest rate is substantially unchanged. Labor has apparently been the great gainer from technological advance as measured this way. However, as Figure 30–3 showed, the percentage share of the total national income going to labor has grown only gradually, because the quantity of capital has grown much faster than the quantity of labor.

Analysis

Against this factual backdrop, let us examine the impact of automation on wages in a particular industry and occupation. Look back at Bill Welder. Suppose a new machine is invented that stamps out metal sinks, eliminating the need for welding. Let us trace through the results, assuming that all markets are perfectly competitive and all prices flexible both upward and downward.

1. Sink producers will adopt the new method if it's cheaper per unit produced than the old one, and competition will force sink prices down to the lower cost level.

2. Some welders will lose their jobs in plumbing-supply companies. Welders' wages will fall as they compete for jobs elsewhere.

3. Employment will increase in plants that manufacture the new stamping machine, in industries producing raw materials and parts, and in plumbing-supply companies that need men to install, service, and operate the new machines. Wages will rise for those workers.

4. At the lower price of sinks, more sinks will be produced and sold, and consumers will be better off, with more sinks and more other goods, since sinks are now cheaper (note, though, the importance of elasticity of demand). More goods in total can be produced because technical advance has made it possible to produce the same number of sinks with less resources, so some resources (welders) can make something else instead.

In all this, what has happened to the wages of different labor groups and to the wage share in the national income?

First, welders' wages drop. Welders thrown out of work look for other jobs. If they stay unemployed, average wages of all welders are clearly down. Even if they get jobs as welders elsewhere, welders' wage rates and incomes will be pulled down as more welders seek jobs there.

Second, the demand for other types of labor rises—for workers to make the new machines and to service and operate them. Wages will rise in those other industries and occupations.

Third, if we assume constant aggregate demand in the economy, no long-run unemployment need result. Welders thrown out of jobs will get work elsewhere or at different jobs in the plumbing industry, as consumers buy more sinks and other products. Consumers will spend more on other products if they spend less on sinks, and more jobs will open up in other industries. This pleasant conclusion, however, depends on two critical assumptions: that workers are mobile in moving to new jobs, and that individual wages are flexible, so that the displaced workers can be absorbed elsewhere. Thus, it skips lightly over the big short-run retraining and readjustment problems facing individual workers. Probably the biggest help in providing jobs and incomes elsewhere in the face of "automation" is government assurance of prosperity and continued high aggregate demand.

Fourth, what happens to the total wage share in the national income will depend largely on the elasticity of demand for the product concerned and on the ratio of labor to capital used in the innovating industry, relative to the rest of the economy. This gets pretty complicated. But since labor clearly benefits along with all of us in its role as consumer, in the real world it's reasonably clear that labor's aggregate real income is raised by technological advance, whatever happens to its **relative** share of the national income. The real wage per worker has grown rapidly. And the gradually rising share of wages and salaries in the national income over many years of rapid technological advance suggests that while both labor and nonlabor incomes share the benefits of technological progress, wage earners have benefited greatly from such advance.

MARX AND THE RESERVE ARMY OF THE UNEMPLOYED

One last application of the theory: Marx put great emphasis on the "reserve army of the unemployed" as a force inevitably driving wages down to a minimum subsistence level—his "iron law of wages." The final result would be revolt and the overthrow of capitalism. How about it?

Suppose the demand for and supply of labor are as shown in Figure 31-6. Suppose the wage rate is W^1; then there is indeed unemployment (excess supply of labor), as shown on the chart. This unemployment, presuming competitive markets, will indeed push wages down, incidentally providing jobs for some of the unemployed workers at the lower wage rate. But will wages fall to W^3, assumed to be the minimum level of subsistence? Clearly not. They will fall to W^2, the level at which the amounts of labor demanded and supplied are just equal, but there is nothing to make them fall further. Quite possibly employers would like to pay still lower wages, but competition among them will pre-

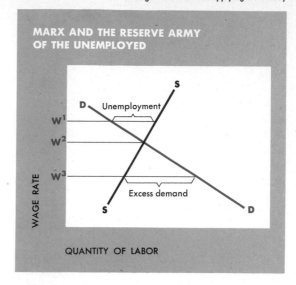

Figure 31-6
Marx argued that unemployment would always force wages down to the minimum subsistence level (W^3). But if we assume unemployment shown at some wage rate (W^1), competition for workers will keep wages from falling below W^2.

vent this outcome. Workers, on the other hand, might like to have wages higher than W^2, but at a higher wage, fewer men will be hired and competition among the unemployed will push the wage rate back down to W^2.

Suppose, to examine Marx's argument, wages were somehow depressed to W^3, the subsistence level. Would they stay there? They would not. At wage W^3 there would be a large employer excess demand for labor, and competition among employers would bid wages up. Only if competition among either employers or laborers is eliminated by collusion or government action can the wage rate stay far below or above W^2 in the economy shown in Figure 31-6. Is this conclusion contradicted by the minimum-subsistence wage levels found in some of the less-developed economies, such as India? No. The minimum-subsistence wage level is the equilibrium level there because productivity, given their populations, lack of education, and lack of capital, is at about that level. Marginal productivity is the fundamental determinant of the real wage level in both economies. The higher average wage in our Western economies reflects higher productivity; and given the productivity, the average real wage cannot be forced down to a minimum-subsistence level by greedy capitalist employers as long as there is substantial competition for labor among them.

REVIEW

Concepts to remember

Be sure you understand the following important concepts:

monopsony	wage structure
exploitation	discrimination
investment in human capital	dual labor markets
wage taker	"automation"
wage maker	

For analysis and discussion

1. Suppose you want to maximize your lifetime income. What factors should you take into account in selecting your occupation and in timing your entry into it? How much should you invest in your own human capital?
2. "Labor is just another commodity, and wages are its price. All we need to explain wages is a basic understanding of supply and demand." Do you agree with this quotation from an economics textbook? Is it immoral? Explain.
3. Wilt Chamberlain was reported to get $600,000 annually for playing basketball for the Los Angeles Lakers. Can you explain this huge salary by the marginal-productivity theory of Chapter 31?
4. Look at Tables 31–1 and 31–2. Are the income differentials between whites and nonwhites shown there a measure of discrimination? What other factors may help explain the differences?
5. Is "automation" good or bad for workers in the industries in which it occurs? for workers elsewhere? for consumers? Explain.
6. Malthus argued that population would tend to outrun the world's food supply, and that wages would tend to be forced back down toward a bare subsistence level.
   a. Is this an acceptable theory of wages?
   b. How would you differentiate between its usefulness in explaining wages in America and in India?
7. One theory holds that wages are the result of bargaining between workers and employers, and that the only important determinant of the outcome is the relative bargaining power of the two parties. Is this theory correct?
8. Is inequality of economic opportunity a major factor in the present unequal distribution of personal incomes in the United States? If it is important, what, if anything, should be done to reduce such inequality of opportunity?
9. Define "exploitation" as it is used by economists. What are the factors that determine whether or not any worker is likely to be exploited?
10. Can you explain to a confirmed Marxist why greedy employers will not force workers' wages down to subsistence levels?

During the post–World War II era, a college education seemed the royal road to success. For the individual, investment in college education was indisputably profitable. Both starting salaries and continuing incomes of college graduates rose much more rapidly than for those who had only high school degrees. Figures 30–3 and 31–5 and Table 30–3 provide some of the evidence. Not only individuals, but society as a whole, rode the boom in college education. Economists estimated that at least 20 percent of the increase in GNP in the 1950s and 1960s was attributable to college-level education of the work force. They emphasized that college education is both investment in human capital and "consumption." The acquisition of learning and the broadening of attitudes and interest not only help to increase real output and make for a better society, but also provide human satisfactions comparable to other forms of consumption.

College enrollment rose from two million in 1946 to ten million in 1972, college graduates from 157,000 to over a million during the same years. At first, a major cause was returning veterans using their GI benefits, but enrollments continued to grow as this source decreased. The gray bars in Figure 31–7 show this spectacular growth since 1960.

But the rising demand for college graduates seemed insatiable. Businesses, governments, and educational institutions themselves wanted holders of college degrees or, better yet, of graduate degrees. Scholars felt that in the new "post-industrial" economy, the unskilled would find jobs increasingly scarce while demands for the college-educated would rise ever more rapidly. Economists' calculations of the rate of return on investment in human capital through college education generally suggested that a heart-warming return of 11–15 percent annually seemed probable over the forty-year normal work span following college. In the early 1950s, it cost an average of about $10,000 for a student to get a college degree; by the late 1960s, the cost was up to $17,000. In both cases, a big part of

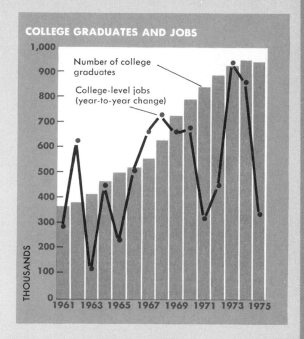

COLLEGE GRADUATES AND JOBS

Number of college graduates

College-level jobs (year-to-year change)

Figure 31–7
New "college-level" jobs have recently risen more slowly than the supply of new college graduates.

the cost was the income foregone while students were in school.

But something happened on the way to the good life! Beginning in the late 1960s, growth in the number of jobs that seemed to require a college education slowed, while the supply of college graduates soared. The heavy line in Figure 31–7 shows the number of "college-level" jobs opening up in the economy year by year during the 1960s and 1970s. During the 1960s, the growth was substantial, especially during the later, boom years of the decade, but this growth substantially stopped in the 1970s and the demand nosedived during years of recession. The rate of return on investment in college education fell to perhaps 7 percent by 1973–74, and getting a job became the number one problem for many college graduates. The National Education Association estimated in 1973 that a record 340,000 persons completed college-level teacher-training degrees, but that only 197,000 new teachers were needed. In the recession of 1974–75, unemployment was 15 percent for new degree holders in the humanities and social sciences, although less than half that for graduates in engineering, business, and the sciences. Starting salaries for college graduates had risen steadily since 1950 relative to salaries of all employees in the industries needing high-skilled employees, especially in engineering and business. But after 1970, this ratio turned down. While college graduates still received higher starting salaries than the average for all employees, the spread narrowed.

As the bloom wore off the boom in college education, the growth in freshmen entering college slowed substantially in the 1970s, and junior colleges and community colleges gained students relative to four-year colleges and universities. From a high of 63 percent in 1968, the percentage of all male high school graduates entering college fell to 48 percent in 1975. There was a flight to vocational training. Comparing incomes of plumbers and librarians, many high school students found the advantages of going on to college less than obvious. At last, 1975 showed the first actual decrease in the number of college graduates over the long postwar boom. Student interest increasingly followed the market. Enrollments in economics, business, and "practical" subjects boomed; those in the "impractical" liberal arts and humanities nosedived. Some economists were quoted to the effect that "self-interest works; students will go where the jobs are—where the rate of return on their investment in human capital is the highest."[7]

Does your economic analysis explain the changing fortunes of college education and college graduates over the past quarter century? How well can it help you predict what will happen to the value of a college education over the decade ahead? Given the apparent oversupply (at least in market terms) of college graduates in many fields now, should society cut back its rate of investment in human capital through college programs by reducing its backing of publicly supported colleges and universities? Should it follow the market in deciding what kinds of college programs to support and which ones to abandon?

---

[7] For more data and an economic analysis of the problem, see R. Freeman, *Overeducated Americans* (New York: Academic Press, 1976). The 1970s spawned a bevy of reports on the education problem. See, e.g., M.S. Gordon, *Higher Education and the Labor Market* (New York: Carnegie Commission on Higher Education, 1974).

CHAPTER 32

UNIONS, COLLECTIVE BARGAINING, AND PUBLIC POLICY

Labor unions loom large on the current American scene. On the economic front, they exercise great pressures on wages, hours, and working conditions. They are behind the worker in his differences with the foreman, the day-to-day arguments that seldom reach the public's eye. Their votes are felt in elections—usually on the Democratic side. Their lobbyists are among the most effective in Washington and the state capitals, and it is a secure congressman who can afford to disregard what organized labor thinks.

Important as unions are, don't overrate their importance. Unions do indeed influence wages and hours. But supply and demand still set a confining framework for labor–management negotiations. Although the combined AFL-CIO loosely joins together many unions, the member unions are still separate, often disputing among themselves. Less than one-fourth of all workers are unionized, and union membership has grown little in recent years outside the public sector, although the labor force has expanded steadily. Throughout the services, agriculture, and clerical and professional areas, unions have little hold, although in recent years they have grown rapidly among government workers and teachers. Politically, the divisions within organized labor weaken the power it can exercise, and since World War II, labor has gone down to defeat on some of its most bitterly fought issues—notably the passage of the Taft-Hartley Act.

HISTORY OF AMERICAN UNIONISM[1]

The foundations of labor unionism
in America lay in the skilled crafts during the
early 1800s. But it was not until the 1870s that
the first loose nationwide labor association appeared. This was the Knights of Labor, founded
as a secret society to avoid public antagonism
and employers' reprisals against members. A
decade later, the American Federation of Labor
(AFL) became the first effective national union
organization. Under the leadership (1886–1924)
of Samuel Gompers, a remarkable figure in
American labor history, the Federation became
a significant force, with an outspoken philosophy
of "practical" unionism. Gompers reflected the
spirit of the times in organized labor—"Get
more, now." Only this pragmatic, typically
American attitude began to win a little grudging
acceptance for unionism from employers and the
public at large.

But it was Franklin Roosevelt and the New
Deal that gave unions their place in modern
industrial society. Depression was everywhere—
massive unemployment, low wages, low purchasing power. Higher wages and higher prices
to promote recovery were cornerstones of the
New Deal. The National Industrial Recovery
Act for the first time gave workers the right to
organize and bargain collectively with employers. Although NIRA was soon declared unconstitutional, the Wagner Act of 1935 was passed
shortly thereafter, to become the foundation of
modern union powers. It spelled out workers'
rights vis-à-vis employers, put teeth in the unions' powers to bargain collectively, and forbade
prevalent employer antiunion practices. Unions
were guaranteed recognition if they won a majority vote among the workers.

The labor history of the middle 1930s was
stormy. The newly formed Congress of Industrial Organizations (CIO), with the fiery John L.
Lewis as its first president, opened big organization drives—violent, spectacular, and successful.
Open defiance of management rather than
workers' traditional subservience was the tone.

[1]For a good account, see U.S. Labor Department, *Brief
History of the American Labor Movement* (Washington, D.C.:
U.S. Government Printing Office, 1964).

The famous sit-down strikes, when the unions
seized possession of the major auto plants,
rocked the companies and the public. But in the
bloodshed and bitterness that ensued, the unions
won recognition time after time—with the open
support of the Roosevelt administration and
local Democratic government officials. The
Who's Who of American industry fell to CIO
organizing drives one by one—U.S. and Bethle-
hem Steel, General Motors, General Electric,
Goodyear, and so on down the list. By 1940,
union membership had more than doubled, to
about ten million. By 1945, it was nearly fifteen
million, about one-third of the nonagricultural
labor force.

Public sympathy during the 1930s was by
and large prolabor, although many friends were
lost by the sit-down strikes. But strong union
wage demands during World War II, interunion
jurisdictional quarrels and strikes, and open defiance of the federal government by a few leaders
convinced the bulk of the public that organized
labor's power had gone too far. In 1947, Congress passed the Taft-Hartley Act, restricting the
powers of unions and restoring some rights that
employers had lost during the preceding decade.
And the years since World War II have seen a
definite leveling of union power.

Figure 32–1 shows the picture. Union membership (excluding Canada) rose above seventeen million in the mid-1950s, but then leveled
off. Unions have made slow headway with
white-collar workers and employees of the rapidly growing service industries. The bottom half
of the chart shows the union problem more
strongly. Union membership as a percentage of
the total civilian labor force hit a peak of 28
percent in the 1950s, and has declined since
then.

In 1955, the merger of the AFL and the CIO
into one loose organization (the AFL-CIO)
marked a major step toward a united labor
movement. But interunion rivalries have kept
the new organization from acting as an effective
unit, economically or politically. Neither the
United Auto Workers, the Teamsters, nor the
United Mine Workers now participate. Jurisdictional disputes have been a persistent source of
quarrels.

Moreover, the unions face a new problem.
The average union member has a good job, and

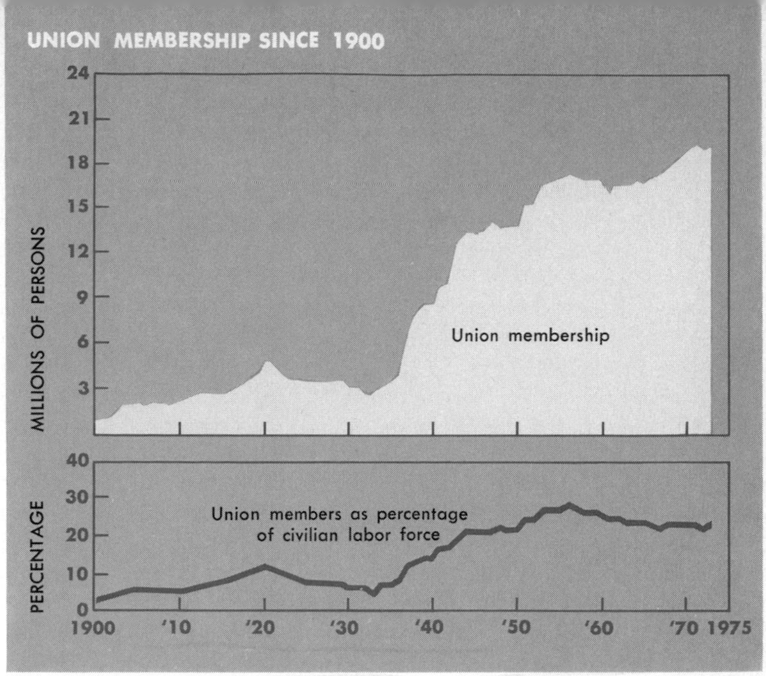

UNION MEMBERSHIP SINCE 1900

Figure 32-1
The big growth period for unions was during the 1930s and 1950s. Since then, union membership has declined somewhat as a percentage of the civilian labor force. (Sources: National Bureau of Economic Research and U.S. Department of Labor.)

often a house in the suburbs. He belongs to the big middle-income class, well above the insecurity and poverty that threatened during the 1930s. He wants more pay, longer vacations, better fringe benefits. But the old class solidarity that once united workers against the capitalist employers is gone. There is an increasing gap between the goals of young union members and the militancy that motivated the now-aging leaders. Many younger members feel little tie to the union. And unions can hope for big gains only among white-collar workers in the services, education, government, and the like. Total employment in manufacturing has been slowly declining over the last decade.

Where is union power concentrated today? In transportation, contract construction, autos, metals, paper, electrical machinery, and mining, if we judge by the percentage of workers unionized. The Teamsters, Air Line Pilots, Longshoremen, Carpenters, Plumbers, Painters, Steelworkers, Papermakers, Electrical Workers, and United Mineworkers all have unionized 75 percent or more of the workers in their industries and possess a large degree of monopoly power. Most of the other big, well-known unions are in manufacturing, with membership varying between 25 and 75 percent of the workers involved. The degree of unionization in the service indus-

tries is generally less than 25 percent—retail clerks, hotel workers, teachers, local government employees, secretarial-clerical workers. Their market power is a lot less.

UNION WAGE POLICY

From one point of view, a union is merely a monopoly that sells the labor services of its members. Neglecting for the moment all the other things that unions do, how effective are they in raising wages for their members? And how does the public fare?

The analytical models of the last chapter provide a simple framework for examining the problem. Let us first assume that the union is an effective organization in controlling its workers. It speaks for them all, and it need not worry about defections from the ranks. Assume also, for the moment, that aggregate demand in the economy is constant, unaffected by the behavior of individual unions and employers.

Competition

First, consider the case where employers are highly competitive with one another both in selling products and in hiring work-

431

ers—for example, waitresses in a large city. Here, in the long run, all economic profits will tend to be eliminated. Price will be forced down to about the minimum average cost at which each product can be produced. From the labor side, wages will be roughly equal to the marginal-revenue productivity of each class of labor hired.

Suppose now that a union comes in and organizes all waitresses in the area. It demands a wage increase and gets it. This raises costs, and forces up meal prices. At the higher prices, consumers will buy fewer restaurant meals (remember that aggregate spending is constant). With less meals, there are fewer jobs for waitresses; how many less will depend on the elasticity of demand. Thus, with a higher wage but the same marginal product, it pays employers to hire fewer waitresses. Union wage demands lead to higher wages for members who keep their jobs, but fewer jobs. In a highly competitive industry, unions can't push up wages without reducing employment in the long run (unless aggregate spending is somehow increased). The workers who keep their jobs are better off, but those laid off bear the brunt. And it becomes harder for new job-seekers to find work as waitresses.

Monopoly and partial monopoly

Second, consider the case where there is monopoly or monopolistic competition in selling products, but still active competition among firms for workers. Suppose, for example, there are only a dozen or so restaurants or stores in the area, or at the extreme, only one. Can the new union now force the stores to pay higher wages without reducing the number of jobs? Our theory tells us, probably not. If the firms are maximizing profits before the union, they will be hiring workers up to the point where the wage equals the workers' marginal product. If the union raises wages, it will, logically, pay employers to cut back on the number of workers hired and to raise prices; the new maximum-profit output will be smaller than before. Again, logically, the union can obtain higher wages only at the cost of less employment.

But partial monopolists—especially oligopolists—may not be maximizing profits in the precise sense above. Oligopoly is the world of live

and let live, of price leadership, of partially protected markets. Under these conditions, the effect of a wage increase on prices and employment is harder to predict. If firms have a protected profit position, this special profit provides a melon over which the union and management can bargain, and higher wages need have no effect on either product price or output and employment. In oligopolies where firms behave as if they faced kinked demand curves, the union may have a considerable range over which it can force up wages without inducing higher prices and reduced employment. But wherever the union makes substantially the same bargain for all major firms in the industry, it faces much the same likely result on employment and prices as with a single monopoly firm; higher wages for union workers will generally mean fewer available jobs.

Monopsony and bilateral monopoly

Where workers are being exploited through a wage less than their marginal-revenue productivity, a union can push the wage up without decreasing employment.[2] The employer is making a special profit by exploiting the workers, and theoretically the union can grab this sum back for the workers. But the employer isn't going to be enthusiastic about turning his profits over to the workers. He'll fight to keep wages down. Where this struggle comes out is indeterminate so far as economic theory is concerned. To guess who will win, look at the relative bargaining power of employer and union. How big is the union strike fund? How adept are both parties around the bargaining table? How badly does the employer want to get his customers' orders out on time? This is a case of bilateral monopoly, where the union (a monopolist in selling labor) meets a single employer (a monopsonist in buying labor).

[2] In fact, the union theoretically might *increase* employment by eliminating exploitation. Without the union, the employer bargains wages down and gets as many workers as possible at his low wage. With a union, he must pay the going wage and he can get as many workers as he wants at that wage. Thus, he hires workers up to the point where the wage equals their marginal-revenue productivity; there is no longer any incentive to restrict output and employment to get the advantage of low wages.

Impact of unions on nonunion wages

If unions reduce the number of jobs in unionized industries, they force wages down elsewhere by increasing the number of workers who must seek work in nonunionized industries. A substantial part of union gains thus comes at the expense of nonunion workers. But in some cases, unions may also indirectly raise nonunion wages. If nonunion employers want to keep unions out (perhaps to protect other managerial prerogatives), they may, and often do, raise their wages at roughly the same pace with union increases. This is known as the "union-threat effect." It works most strongly where employers are exposed to possible union organizing drives, and in prosperity when labor is scarce.

Union wages and capital substitution

The short-run effect of union wage pressures on the number of jobs in an industry is often hard to predict accurately. But one longer-range effect is highly predictable. Higher labor costs will lead businessmen to invest in labor-saving machinery more rapidly than they otherwise would. It will pay to shift to coal-mining machinery to replace miners as hourly wages rise, to install mechanical dishwashers in restaurants, to replace farm laborers by automatic vegetable pickers. Higher union wages clearly speed automation.

Do unions really raise wages?

This may sound like a silly question. Everyone has read of many cases where union demands for higher wages have finally been granted by employers. But such instances don't really answer the question. Maybe supply and demand would have produced the same raises in the market without any union. Don't forget the fallacy of *post hoc, propter hoc.*

Although any union man and most employers will tell you that of course unions raise wages, the dispassionate, objective evidence is less clear. One careful study estimates that unions raised the wages of their members by about 25 percent relative to nonunion workers in 1933 at the bottom of the depression (reflecting temporary union resistance to wage cuts), by about 5 percent in the inflationary boom of the late 1940s when all wages were bid up rapidly in tight labor markets, and by 10–15 percent during the 1950s.[3] Another concludes that in perhaps one-third of all cases, unions have raised wages by 15–20 percent; in another third by perhaps 5–10 percent; in the other third not at all.[4] The unions' effects are greatest during recessions when union contracts hold up wages, least in booms when strong employer demand bids up all wages rapidly. In the latter case, nonunion wages rose faster, because union wage increases were slowed by three-year contracts made earlier.

Unions have raised unskilled wages relative to skilled wages. Economic theory doesn't explain this completely. In part, it seems to reflect industrial union pressures to raise low wages relative to high ones. They have also pressed to eliminate interfirm and regional differentials by leveling up the lower rates.[5]

Note a commonly cited but unconvincing bit of evidence, that union wages are nearly always higher than nonunion ones. This is true, but many unionized industries were high-wage industries before they were unionized—big companies with lots of highly skilled labor. One other interesting piece of evidence is that labor's share of the national income has increased persistently since the 1920s, before the big modern union increase. But the shift is not enough to provide clear evidence that unions have raised the aggregate wage share.

COLLECTIVE BARGAINING AND LABOR–MANAGEMENT RELATIONS

The big wage negotiations and strikes make the headlines. But the great bulk of union–management collective bargaining and

[3]H.G. Lewis, *Unionism and Relative Wages in the United States* (Chicago: University of Chicago Press, 1963), p. 193.
[4]A. Rees, *Wage Inflation* (New York: National Industrial Conference Board, 1967), p. 27.
[5]G.E. Johnson, "Economic Analysis of Trade Unionism," *American Economic Review,* May 1975, provides a balanced summary of the evidence on all types of union effects since World War II.

negotiation goes on unheralded behind the scenes. After a union contract is signed, the day-to-day relations of the foreman and his workers take over. Wage rates have to be set for individual jobs; broad contract wage provisions must be translated into elaborate wage structures in large firms. Decisions must be made as to which jobs are on a flat hourly pay basis and which "on incentive," where the pay depends on the number of units turned out. Arrangements have to be agreed on for handling the introduction of new machinery and new methods. Wrangles between foremen and individual workers have to be adjudicated. A thousand and one problems arise in a big plant that involve disputes between labor and management.

In these disputes, the union steward is the worker's first-line negotiator, just as the foreman is management's. Good feelings and cooperation between foremen and stewards can do more for effective union–management relations than almost any amount of fine top-level policy making. Down in the plant is where the work gets done and where most of the disputes arise, except for the major wage and hour negotiations at contract-expiration dates.

Some union–management agreements provide elaborate machinery for handling worker–management disputes that can't be settled by the foreman and the worker. These often culminate in calling on an impartial arbitrator, paid jointly by union and management, whose decision is final on disputed issues under contract. Such agreements usually try to set up a body of rules under which workers and management can minimize friction and disagreement. The contract is something like the laws under which we operate our democratic system. This procedure has gone far toward creating stability and order in employee–management relations in thousands of industrial plants. But in industrial as in political democracy, the rules alone can't make the system work. They only provide a framework within which men of reasonable goodwill can work peaceably together.[6]

[6]"Union-shop" and "right-to-work" laws cause much controversy. Under a union-shop agreement, everyone who works in the firm covered must join the union. The union's big argument for this arrangement is that if workers get the benefits of union activities (higher wages, better working

Union and management motivation in bargaining

You don't need a course in economics to tell you the main reason why unions fight for higher wages. They want more pay! But some other things aren't so easy to explain.

Why will unions strike for an extra few cents an hour in pay, when third-grade arithmetic will show that it would take months or even years at the extra rate to make up for the pay lost in a long strike. Why are the union leaders willing to keep the men out over a few dollars? The same question can be asked the other way around, too. Why doesn't the company give in and end the divisive strike?

Try putting yourself in the workers' shoes. You'd probably think, "That so-and-so who runs the company! He gets a big salary and has everything. His plushy stockholders are getting big dividends. Yet we have to scrape along on pay that just keeps the wolf away from the door. He won't even give us a few cents extra when he could save himself profits by doing it instead of trying to break this strike. We'll fight it out and lick him yet!"

Now turn around and see how you'd feel as the employer. You see the wages your company is already paying as generous. You see the workers stubbornly holding out for "unreasonable" demands. You may see the union leaders as self-seeking hypocrites, out to protect their own jobs. The whole business is just one more step in the union's attempt to dictate to management. Would you give in if you were the employer?

Now put yourself in the union president's shoes. You know that your best bet in the long

conditions, and so on), they should have to pay dues and bear their share of the union costs. Otherwise they get a "free ride," which makes no more sense than permitting a citizen to benefit from government but decide for himself that he won't pay taxes.

The counterargument says that union shops take away the individual worker's right to work without joining a union, and that this abrogates an important individual freedom. Make up your own mind. The union shop is legal under federal law, but prohibited in a number of southern and western states that have enacted state "right-to-work" laws. Such right-to-work laws are fought bitterly by the unions.

run lies in getting along with management. But you also know that there's never enough money to go around, and that you're going to have to push hard to get the wages to which your members are (in your eyes) clearly entitled. You know a strike is costly to everyone, but you know too that a threat often repeated but never carried out loses its force.

You know that unless you produce for your members, you're likely to be just another ex-president. If other unions have been getting 30 cents an hour plus fringe benefits, you'd better get that much too. You know that your chances of rising in the union ranks, say, to a position in the international, depend on your success in getting more than other unions do. As you sit across the bargaining table from management, with tempers frayed by a long strike, would you give in?

The issues at stake in a labor negotiation are seldom simple. The quarrel that the public sees in the newspapers is only part of the real issue. The fine speeches made by both sides—about the need for wage increases to prevent recession and the like—sound good on the news broadcasts but often have little to do with settling the dispute at the bargaining table. To look at the issue in terms of a simple dollars-and-cents comparison is naïve. The issues are real, and no purpose is served by pretending that nothing but a common interest is involved. Unfortunately, there is seldom a clear, objective, right-or-wrong answer.

The changing role of strikes

Collective bargaining is a process of challenge and response. For the most part, it settles the disputes between employers and unions. But sometimes they can't, or won't, reach agreement. Tempers fray. Bitterness grows. Finally the union goes out on strike.

Strikes are rare events. With over 150,000 collective-bargaining contracts in force, strikes over the last five years have caused a loss of only one-fifth of 1 percent of the total working time involved. Table 32–1 shows the record since 1935. Time lost exceeded 1 percent in only one year—1946.[7]

Moreover, most of today's strikes are orderly and nonviolent, in sharp contrast to the bitter, bloody battles of thirty years ago. Strikes now arise largely over renewal of contracts and most often involve wage and work-rule arguments, far less explosive issues than the life-or-death organizing conflicts of the 1930s. Arbitration is now largely used to settle disputes that arise during

[7]A Department of Labor study shows that higher wages were the main issue behind 44 percent of all strikes between 1964 and 1974; work rules or conditions, 15 percent; union recognition or union shop, 13 percent; and union jurisdictional differences, 11 percent.

Table 32–1

Time lost in strikes, 1935–75

Period	Number of strikes (annual average)	Workers involved (annual average) (in thousands)	Percentage of working time lost
1935–39	2,862	1,130	0.27
1940–44	3,754	1,386	.16
1945–50	4,210	2,940	.61
1951–55	4,540	2,510	.31
1956–60	3,602	1,620	.29
1961–65	3,560	1,365	.14
1966–70	5,032	2,653	.27
1971–75	5,735	2,485	.20

Source: U.S. Department of Labor.

the life of the contract. International officers generally try to help avoid or settle "wildcat" strikes, in which local unions strike in contravention of contract arrangements.

Thus, conflict resolution between labor and management has been moved increasingly to an orderly, peaceful procedural basis. But conflicts do persist, and the strike remains organized labor's weapon of last resort to enforce its views. Sometimes big strikes are enormously disruptive—for example, a long steel or public utility strike. But many labor observers feel that an occasional strike in most industries does no great harm and indeed may be a useful incident in the continuing bargaining relationship between labor and management. A strike is a device for letting off steam, for reasserting bargaining powers. It is not necessarily a symbol of the failure of collective bargaining. Thus, few labor experts favor laws to outlaw strikes, except possibly strikes that clearly threaten the public interest. For to outlaw strikes would not resolve conflicts but merely force them into other channels. But public tolerance of disruptive strikes has been strained in recent years, and better devices are needed to settle labor disputes within less costly, more orderly channels. (More on this subject in the next section.)

GOVERNMENT AND LABOR

Many labor–management disputes are now a test of strength between equals—sometimes equals of prodigious strength. When Leonard Woodcock sits down to bargain for the United Auto Workers, he speaks for a million men. Literally billions of dollars are at stake in these bargains; not only wages, but also the pensions of tomorrow's retired families, workers' health and disability insurance, their working hours, their vacations. A nationwide Teamsters strike could bring the economy to a grinding halt in a matter of days. In local areas, small groups of union workers can achieve comparable results; a mere dozen bridge-tenders nearly shut down New York City in 1971.

Is union power excessive? Many say yes; they stress that antitrust laws do not limit union power. Most union members say no. Do we need

more stringent laws to limit union powers? Should government intervene when disruptive strikes occur, or when wage settlements threaten the government's antiinflation programs? Labor–management relations have many unanswered questions.

Major legislation

The Norris-LaGuardia Act of 1932 was the first major national prolabor legislation. Employers had long been able to get court injunctions against labor groups to prohibit just about anything—for example, striking or picketing. Once the injunction was obtained, labor was the wrongdoer in the eyes of the law. Norris-LaGuardia outlawed the injunction in federal courts as an employer weapon against a wide variety of union activities—strikes, joining a union, peaceful picketing, or giving financial aid to unions. The intent of the law was clear. It was to give unions support in achieving a more equal bargaining status with employers, and to eliminate one of the most powerful employer weapons.

The New Deal, a year later, was frankly and aggressively prolabor. The Wagner Act of 1935 is the cornerstone of modern prolabor legislation. The act:

1. Affirmed the legal right of employees to organize and bargain collectively, free from employer interference or coercion.

2. Required employers to bargain with unions of the workers' own free choosing.

3. Specifically prohibited a list of "unfair" employer practices.

4. Set up the National Labor Relations Board to provide a mechanism through which workers could gain recognition for unions of their own choosing, and to act as a quasi court to protect workers against unfair labor practices. (The NLRB does not act directly to mediate or settle labor–management disputes.) Employer intimidation, antiunion discrimination in hiring and firing, company attempts to influence union elections, and a variety of other employer practices were soon outlawed as unfair practices as NLRB and court decisions interpreted the new law.

By the early 1940s, the bitterest union organizing struggles were over, and industrial unionism in the mass-production industries was firmly entrenched. In the courts, labor also fared better. The Supreme Court, reflecting the changing temper of the times and the presence of several Roosevelt-appointed judges, in the *Apex* and *Hutcheson* cases (1940 and 1941) reversed a long line of judicial precedent and granted unions virtual immunity from the Sherman Act, although in the *Allen Bradley* case of 1945, an exception was made where they conspired with employers to fix prices or divide markets.

The federal *Fair Labor Standards Act of 1938* established minimum wages, maximum basic hours, and other fair-labor standards for all labor in interstate commerce. FLSA has been periodically amended since 1938, both to widen its coverage and to raise the minimum wage.

All through the 1930s and during World War II, labor rode high. But the pendulum had swung too far. More and more middle-of-the-roaders began to feel that labor had overstepped its bounds, first in the sit-down strikes of the 1930s; then in the spreading jurisdictional disputes and strikes that the public and employers seemed powerless to halt; in its persistent wage demands during the World War II fight against inflation; and last, in its outright defiance of the federal government itself in disputes of critical importance to the national economy. The Taft-Hartley Act of 1947 was passed to redress the balance of power between management and labor.

Taft-Hartley defined unfair labor practices of unions to parallel those of employers. It clarified the powers of employers to speak against unions; it prohibited the closed shop; it contained provisions to protect the individual workers against the union; it empowered the president under conditions of national emergency to obtain an 80-day cooling-off period before a strike, and required a secret union ballot on the latest company offer before the end of that period.

By 1950, labor racketeering had become a national scandal, and Congress passed the *Landrum-Griffin Act,* again over the violent objections of union leaders. Landrum-Griffin included a new "bill of rights" for individual union members, requirements for more detailed financial reporting by unions, and a requirement for secret-ballot elections.[8]

Labor and the antitrust laws

Unions are substantially exempt from the antitrust laws, except as they may collude *with employers* to restrict output or to fix prices. The Wagner Act put the National Labor Relations Board in the position of granting official patents of monopoly to the unions it certified as exclusive bargaining agents. Most businessmen, and many economists who believe in the efficacy of competitive markets, believe that the antitrust laws should, at least in part, be applied to unions as well as businesses.

But unless a union has exclusive power to bargain for its members, it has limited market power. One proposal is to forbid industrywide bargaining, just as firms may not collude to fix prices and output. Union supporters retort that this would *de facto* emasculate unions, moving back to the old relationships where all the power was on the employer's side. Another proposal would forbid union pressures on employers to restrict output and union "featherbedding" (for example, by work rules that prohibit use of paint sprays in place of brushes). But such distinctions have proved very hard to enforce. Only legal reforms that command widespread public support have much chance of enactment and enforcement on such emotionally charged issues. And such widespread public support is hard to mobilize when the issue seems to be the working man against business, even where indirectly the ultimate consumer pays the bill.[9]

The government as watchdog and wage setter

Congress has long been quick to investigate labor–management affairs. The biggest issues arise around disruptions of the national

[8]For a fuller account of the changing legal foundations of unions and collective bargaining, see L.G. Reynolds, *Labor Economics and Labor Relations,* 6th ed. (Englewood Cliffs, N.J.: Prentice-Hall, 1974), Chap. 5.

[9]For an economic survey of the antitrust laws in relation to unions, see G. Hildebrand, "Collective Bargaining and the Antitrust Laws," in J. Shister, ed., *Public Policy and Collective Bargaining* (New York: Harper & Row, 1962).

UNIONS AND STRIKES IN THE PUBLIC SECTOR

Strikes have long been illegal in the public sector—at the federal level and in most states. Only recently has the right of public employees to join unions been widely recognized. Yet today, collective bargaining between public employees and governments (or quasi-government agencies like school boards) poses the most difficult problems in labor relations.

A few public workers—for example, postal employees—have long had unions. But membership in public-service unions and "associations" (for example, the National Education Association of over one million teachers) has soared in recent years. Today, probably 40 percent of the nation's twelve million public employees belong to either unions or associations that are increasingly acting like unions in collective-bargaining relationships, and membership is growing faster than anywhere in the private sector. Public-sector salaries have risen much faster in the last decade than those in the private sector.

Until the 1950s, strikes by public employees were virtually unheard of. But as resort to power tactics spread in society, especially during the 1960s, public employees began increasingly to use strikes to achieve their wage goals, just like other unionized workers, albeit illegally. The New York subway workers, then bus drivers, airport traffic controllers, postmen, garbage collectors, teachers, and even firemen went out, and often achieved their demands when important services were crippled and public attitudes were divided. Government employees elsewhere followed suit. Antistrike laws were discretely disregarded by public officials, or quickly amended in some cases. Sometimes, nonstrike actions are used to get the same results. If airport traffic controllers just work "according to the rule book," the result can be to slow down air traffic dramatically without their violating any antistrike provision. If

teachers report in sick, it is very difficult to teach the school-children.

Should public employees have the same rights to strike and to bargain collectively as private workers have? Most people apparently still say no, although attitudes toward public unions are far more permissive than they were two decades ago. Clearly, this issue goes far beyond economic analysis, into ethics and politics. Shutting down the schools, or air travel, or subway service, or fire protection imposes a cost many people are unwilling to tolerate. But if we deny these powers to public workers, how are they to be sure of getting a fair deal, comparable to private employees? Indeed, as a practical matter, how are we to keep them from striking, law or no law, if they just go ahead and strike? Bringing in the army to teach school, run the subways, or collect garbage is not a very attractive alternative.

The answers, if there are any, lie in considerable part outside economics. Some would tie public-employee salaries to comparable private salaries. Many urge compulsory arbitration if disagreement persists. Increasingly, when penalties are levied by the government, they are in the form of heavy fines against unions, not widespread punishments against individual employees. Fining or firing many individual public workers is generally neither realistic nor popular.

How do *you* believe we should handle the snowballing problem of public-employee demands and strikes? What should the law say? Perhaps even more important, what should the relevant public officials do if and when the public employees strike anyhow?*

*For a survey of the issues, see J. Stieber, *Public Employee Unionism: Structure, Growth, Policy* (Washington, D.C.: The Brookings Institution, 1973); and *Collective Bargaining in American Government* (New York: The American Assembly, 1971).

economy. Suppose a nationwide steel strike is in progress. The union, pointing to rising living costs, high profits, and increasing productivity, argues that 50 cents an hour more in pay and fringe benefits is the lowest raise it will even consider. Management in the steel industry's Big Six say they won't offer a penny more than 20 cents. They say that profits are down, that foreign competition is murderous, and that steelworkers are already among the best-paid in the nation. The strike has gone on now for two long months, and the steel shortage is shutting down not only civilian production but also arms production. If you were President, what would you do?

You might say, let the strike go on; it's none of the government's business. But with the economy grinding to a halt and with critical defense needs, you probably wouldn't.

You might invoke the national-emergency provision of the Taft-Hartley Act. This probably would get the union back to work and would give you eighty days to bring all the pressure you could on both sides to settle their differences. You'd focus as much public pressure as you could on the negotiators. If you felt strongly that right was mainly on one side, you might tell the American people so and build up pressure on the other side to capitulate. But your position is especially tough if you're also worried about inflation, so you fear a settlement that would lead the companies to raise steel prices.

The power of the federal government is great, and this kind of pressure might well bring some kind of settlement, optimally noninflationary. But suppose neither the companies nor the union will give in. So the workers go out on strike again at the end of eighty days, more bitter than ever. What then?

Then is the tough time. By now, tempers are really frayed. Labor and management have been over the issues *ad nauseam*. Each has been provoked into saying a lot of things better left unsaid. Everybody's dirty linen has been thoroughly aired before 200 million Americans.

You might decide to seize the steel industry and ask the workers to stay on the job. But this means seizing a vast, privately owned industry, against all the traditions of American freedom and probably against the Constitution. Or you might order the workers to stay on the job, in the interests of the public welfare. But you know perfectly well you can't make men make steel, either under the law or any other way, if they just won't go back to work and do it.

Well, what would *you* do?

Compulsory arbitration?

Often a skillful third party can soothe hot tempers and help get labor and management together when they are negotiating a contract or settling a grievance. The federal government and most state governments provide "mediators" and "conciliators" who serve as impartial go-betweens in trying to get disputes settled without resort to strikes. Sometimes these men enter at the request of labor and management; sometimes they are sent by public officials who want to avoid work stoppages. Their work is generally unheralded and unspectacular, but they are successful in a great number of cases.

With the exception of a few cases (for example, railway labor disputes), the government has no legal power to enforce a settlement on the parties. Many observers believe it should have some such power, or that Congress should prescribe "compulsory arbitration," at least in disputes vitally affecting the public interest. Under compulsory arbitration, both management and labor would be bound to accept the decision of a third party, the arbitrator, if they could not resolve their own differences. No strike or employer lockout would be permitted.

Most unions and many employers oppose such a law. They want to be left alone to settle their own disputes. But can society afford the costly, disruptive strikes we now frequently face, or the inflationary wage settlements that often come out of long strikes during boom periods? These feelings are especially strong against public-sector strikes—by police, teachers, postmen, transit workers, and the like. But the case for compulsory arbitration is much weaker for smaller, run-of-the-mill labor disputes. How to define "big disputes where the public interest would require compulsory arbitration" is a tough problem, if you want to use compulsory arbitration only in those cases.

SHOULD THE GOVERNMENT GET OUT?

Ours is an economy of power groups. The unions and their leaders have great power. So do big employers. Wage setting has moved from the competitive marketplace to the industrywide bargaining table in many leading industries. The wage bargains in steel, autos, electrical equipment, and coal go far to set a pattern for the rest of the economy. How can the government stand aside and see its antiinflation program split open, the operation of the whole economy periled by disputes in these industries? Less than 1 percent of the nation's labor force is employed in trucking. Yet that 1 percent could probably bring the economy almost to a dead stop in a few weeks.

But if it is drawn in, what can government really do? Many observers think that government intervention, especially when it becomes habitual, does more harm than good. They argue that when both sides know the government will eventually step in, there is little chance of settling the dispute beforehand. This is particularly true, they say, in inflationary periods when both labor and management know they will ultimately get much of what they want, and the main question is how much prices will be pushed up for the consumer. One side or the other will nearly always feel it can get a better bargain by waiting to get government involved in the settlement. Thus, excessive government intervention in bargaining may hide the need for management and labor to accept basic responsibility in a free society, and may end up with more inflationary settlements too.

The American economy has come a long way from the highly competitive, individualistic system described by the classical economists. Concentrated economic power is here, like it or not. The problem is somehow to develop a framework within which economic power is responsibly channeled to the public good. The hard fact is that we cannot order huge groups of workers around in a democratic society. Wage setting must be by consensus when two powerful groups face each other across the bargaining table. And it must be by political as well as economic consensus once the government steps into the scene as a major participant in the process of wage setting.

REVIEW

Concepts to remember

This is mainly an applications and policy chapter, using the concepts from earlier chapters. But be sure you have the following clearly in mind:

collective bargaining   compulsory arbitration
capital substitution   union shop
mediation   right-to-work laws

For analysis and discussion

1. If you were a factory worker, and union members in the plant put pressure on you to join the union, would you join? Would you consider such pressures an infringement of your personal freedom of choice?
2. Should public-service unions (for example, teachers, firemen, and postal workers) have the same rights to strike as other unions? If not, what rights do they have to enforce their demands?
3. "Unions are justified where employers would otherwise be able to exploit employees, but nowhere else." Do you agree? Explain.

4. Would it be better to give employees the extra money rather than all the fringe benefits commonly included in union contracts, so that each person could decide for himself how to spend the money?

5. When the government intervenes in wage negotiations—for example, in autos or steel—what criteria should it use in deciding what wage settlement to urge?

6. Should compulsory arbitration be required by law in order to avoid strikes that involve government employees or otherwise affect the public interest? How would you define the public interest for this purpose?

7. Should labor unions be subject to the antitrust laws?

8. The Taft-Hartley Act requires unions and management to bargain "in good faith." Suppose an employer decides to make his best offer at the outset and thereafter refuses to improve the offer. Is he bargaining in good faith?

In 1975, the federal government defined as in "poverty" any four-person urban family earning less than $5,500. By this test, about 25 million Americans were poor.

If we figure that a full-time job involves about 2,000 hours of work a year, an hourly wage of $3.00 would provide a $6,000 annual income, just above the poverty level. The minimum wage currently (1976) prescribed by federal law is $2.30, but this is clearly inadequate to meet even the minimum poverty-level income standard.

Many have proposed, therefore, that Con-gress raise the legal minimum wage to at least $3.00, or better, $3.25 per hour to assure at least a bare minimum above-poverty income for all American workers. Less than that will clearly not provide a decent standard of living.

Do you favor this proposal? What would be the main effects of such legislation? Who would gain and who lose? (For simplicity, assume that total national expenditure is constant.)

33

PROPERTY INCOMES: RENT, INTEREST, AND CAPITAL

Most people obtain virtually all their income from wages, salaries, and transfer payments. But nearly all the rich, and an increasing share of the moderately well-to-do, get a lot of income from rent, interest, and profits—from property they own. In 1975, wages and salaries were $920 billion (76 percent) of the $1,210-billion total national income, while rents were $21 billion (2 percent), interest was $82 billion (7 percent), and corporation profits were $102 billion (8 percent).[1] The highest corporation salary reported was $776,000 for the head of International Telephone and Telegraph, but several hundred individuals reported taxable incomes of over $1 million, especially television, sport, and movie stars. Johnny Carson is said to get $3 million a year from NBC. But most of the very rich get most of their income from capital.

Ours is a "capitalist" economy. One of its central tenets is the right of each individual to accumulate property (capital) of his own—a house, a factory, land, stocks, bonds. And most capital produces income for its owner—rent on land, interest on bonds, dividends on stocks. Some of the income may be consumed directly by the owner—such as housing services received

[1]The rest of the national income goes to unincorporated businesses (farmers, lawyers, small shopkeepers, and the like) as a mixture of wages and profits.

by living in one's own house instead of renting. Thus, every homeowner is to that extent a capitalist, just as is a bondholder or stockholder. **Indeed, if we think of ourselves as owning our own productive capacities (human capital), we are all capitalists, with our incomes depending substantially on how much we have invested in human and nonhuman capital.**

This chapter deals with two types of income from nonhuman capital (rent and interest), leaving profits until Chapter 34. Substantially the same marginal-productivity, supply-and-demand theory explains the return on both human and nonhuman capital.

RENT

In everyday usage, "rent" is the price paid for the use of land, buildings, machinery, or other durable goods. This is the way we shall use the term, except in one later section where a special meaning is given to the term "economic rent."

What determines the rental income received by owners of land and other such durable productive resources? Although there are important institutional differences (we don't have a slave society in which we buy and sell human beings as we do land), the answer is much the same as what determines the wage income of labor—supply and demand, with demand based largely on the marginal productivity of the land or other asset. Whether the landlord is a greedy fellow or not is generally far less important than the powerful impersonal forces of supply and demand.

The *supply* of nonhuman productive resources, and hence of their services, varies widely from case to case. At one extreme, the supply of land at the corner of Fifth Avenue and 50th Street in New York City, where Saks Fifth Avenue and Rockefeller Center sit, is completely inelastic—there's just so much, and no more can be manufactured. At the other extreme, garden tools, a simple productive resource, can be reproduced readily, and their supply is highly elastic. Most cases lie somewhere in between. The supply of most productive resources is likely to be reasonably elastic *in the long run*—that is, given a long

period for adjustment. Even farm land can readily be improved through the use of fertilizer, drainage, and so forth, if it pays to do so. For practical purposes, this is similar to making more land—you still have the same number of acres, but the acres have increased productivity.

The *demand* for the services of property depends basically on how much the service rendered is worth to the user. The property's marginal productivity underlies the business demand for its services, as for labor. **Competitive bidding by businesses tends to draw each resource into its most productive use. Thus, each piece of land is rented to the highest bidder, and the high bidder must use the land where its marginal productivity is greatest to justify paying the high rent. Under competition, the rent will just equal the marginal productivity of the land. As with labor, monopsony or monopoly may lead to "exploitation" of resource owners, to inefficient allocation of resources, or to unemployment of some of the resources.**

An example

Take a simple example. What will the rent be on a ten-acre site on a highway near the outskirts of a city? Look at the demand side first. One demand may be for use in truck farming. How much renters will pay for this use will depend on the fertility of the soil, the water supply, and other such factors. Another demand may be for use as small individual business properties, such as restaurants, garden-supply stores, and so on. Here the amount of traffic passing by, the convenience of the location for potential customers, and other such factors will be especially important. Still another demand might be for use by a single supermarket, with surrounding parking area. Here again, traffic flows, convenience of location, availability of adequate parking space, and desirability of nearby neighbors might be especially important. Each potential renter would make some estimate of how much he could afford to pay in rent for the site—logically, up to its estimated marginal-revenue productivity for him.

Who will get the site, and at what rent? If there is active competition among the potential renters, the rent will be bid up until only the highest bidder is left. This will be the renter who estimates the marginal productivity of the site as being the highest. Thus, the site will be drawn into the use that promises the highest return to the renter, and through this mechanism into the use where consumers value it most highly. The rent will equal its marginal productivity in this most valuable use.

Can we be sure the rent will be bid up all the way to the estimated marginal productivity of the highest bidder? Not if the value to one user is substantially higher than to others. Suppose the site is ideal for a supermarket. Then the local Kroger's manager needs only to bid higher than the truck farmers and small shop operators, to whom the land is potentially worth less. Kroger's may get the site at a rent below its estimated marginal productivity as a supermarket site. But Kroger's won't if there's a local A&P or Safeway also in the market for sites.

"Economic rent"—a price-determined cost

Economists have one special definition of "rent" that differs from ordinary usage: **"Economic rent" is the payment for the use of a scarce, nonreproducible resource.** For example, the rent paid for one corner of Fifth Avenue and 50th Street in New York covers a mixture of "site value" and use of the building on the space, with all the improvements. If we isolate the site value of that corner—the land itself, exclusive of any improvements on it—we have a resource that is scarce and completely fixed in supply; the supply is perfectly inelastic.

The rent on such nonreproducible productive agents is determined exclusively by the demand for them. The supply curve is a vertical line. If there is no demand, there is no rent; the rent rises directly as demand rises, without relation to the original costs of producing the resource. Figure 33–1 illustrates the point. Since the supply is a fixed amount, SS is a vertical line. If the demand is D^1D^1, the rent will be $20 an acre. If demand is D^2D^2, rent is only $10 an acre. If demand is only D^3D^3, the land commands no rent at all.[2]

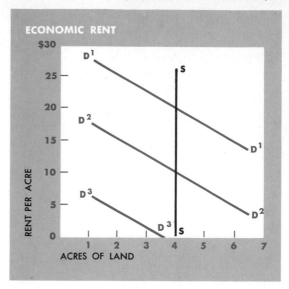

Figure 33–1
When the supply is a fixed amount, price (rent) is determined solely by demand.

Outside the site value of land, few cases of pure economic rent exist. But there are many cases with some element of economic rent, especially in the short run. For example, the great Wagnerian soprano, Birgit Nilsson, is unique today, and nonreproducible in the short run. The high fees she charges the Met and other opera houses can be considered a partial economic rent for the use of her great voice. Similarly, if a firm patents a new productive process, for the life of the patent the process is much like the site value of land; it cannot be reproduced (except by consent of the patent holder). Indeed, if a firm has a temporarily protected monopoly position, part of the monopoly profits may better be considered a temporary economic rent, or *quasi-rent*, on the monopoly position.[3]

---

[2] Years ago, Henry George argued that all rents should be confiscated through a "single tax," because they reflect a bonanza to landowners that arises as society's demand for the God-given, not man-made, land grows. Some cities—for example, Pittsburgh—still tax land more heavily than buildings, on the remnants of single-tax reasoning. A few disciples still advocate this as the basis for our entire tax system.

[3] Economists sometimes use the term "quasi rent" to describe the return on *temporarily* nonreproducible resources.

INTEREST

Most of us put our savings into financial assets, instead of buying real property directly. We buy bonds, or deposit the money in a bank or a savings and loan association. Our property is then a financial asset, and we collect the income from our capital in the form of interest. **Interest is the price paid for the use of money or credit, and indirectly for the capital or consumer goods that can be obtained with that money or credit.**

Why are interest rates what they are? Fundamentally, they depend on the marginal productivity of the real capital goods obtainable with the funds involved. (Temporarily, as we saw in Part 2, they may be heavily influenced by monetary policy and other special factors.) The same marginal-productivity, supply-and-demand framework is again the right one to use in answering the question.

Three special points about interest need to be made:

1. Interest is paid for the use of money, or credit, rather than directly for the use of productive resources. Money itself doesn't build buildings or dig ditches. But money does give its owner purchasing power to obtain men and machines that will build buildings and dig ditches, and demand for loan funds traces back in considerable part to their power to buy or rent real productive resources. Thus, fundamentally the marginal productivity of real capital goods determines the interest rate, as it does rents.

2. Interest is stated as a *rate* of return (4 percent) rather than as an absolute sum. To say that the interest rate is 4 percent is merely to say that the borrower pays $4 interest per year for each $100 borrowed. The statement in percentage terms as a rate permits ready comparison between the payments of different amounts for widely differing resources. You can easily compare the return on money invested in an office building, in a turret lathe, and in your own education, by converting all three returns into a percentage on the funds invested. For example, if the office building cost $1 million and provides

an annual net return of $50,000 after depreciation and other expenses, the rate is 5 percent. If the lathe cost $1,000 and provides an annual net return of $40, the rate is 4 percent. If a $1,000 investment in an electronics course will increase your annual income by $45, the rate of return is 4½ percent. According to these figures, funds invested in the office building provide a better return than funds invested in turret lathes or the electronics course.

3. There are hundreds of different interest rates. In 1975, for example, the government paid about 7 percent on long-term bonds. Short-term bank loans ranged from about 6 percent for well-established business concerns to 9 percent on mortgage loans to buy houses, and as much as 18 percent on small loans to individual borrowers. Some consumer loan agencies charged up to 40 percent per annum. You got no interest on demand deposits, but most banks and savings and loan institutions paid 5–7 percent on savings deposits. These different rates reflect differences in risk, locality, length of loan, cost of handling the loan, and a variety of other factors, as well as the "pure" interest rate that is included in each. To simplify matters, economists often talk about "the" interest rate. They mean the interest rate on a long-term, essentially riskless loan. The rate on long-term U.S. government bonds is often considered a close approximation. At mid-1975, therefore, we might have said "the interest rate" was about 7 percent. But don't make the mistake of assuming you could borrow money at this rate.

Nominal and real rates of interest in inflation

During inflation, the nominal (market) rate of interest exceeds the "real" rate. If you borrow $100 for one year at 6 percent and prices rise by 4 percent, in real purchasing power you pay only 2 percent interest, because the money you pay back will buy 4 percent less than when you borrowed it. Thus, economists say, the nominal interest rate is 6 percent but the real rate is only 2 percent. Conversely, if prices fall, the real rate will be higher than the money rate.

Presumably, if borrowers and lenders correctly anticipate inflation (say, 4 percent per annum), they will both take this into account in making their contracts. If the real productivity of capital is 3 percent, they will add on the 4 percent inflation allowance, making a 7 percent market rate. If their anticipation of inflation is perfect, the 7 percent nominal rate will be just high enough to produce the 3 percent real rate justified by the real productivity of capital. But we can never foresee inflation accurately, and the inflation allowance is correspondingly imperfect. Nonetheless, it is important to think of the real rate of interest if we want to make correct analyses of saving and investment decisions, in business or private affairs.

Interest and the stock of real capital

Fundamentally, interest is paid for the use (productivity) of real capital—machinery, factories, airplanes, houses. Assume for the moment there is no technical advance to increase the productivity of capital; growth in the capital stock means merely adding more units of the same capital goods—say, through saving and investing in more factories. Thus, in Figure 33–2, S^1 is the stock of capital now, S^2 next year. DD is the demand for real capital, dependent on its marginal productivity. Thus, as the capital stock grows, we would expect the interest rate to fall from i^1 to i^2, other things being equal. The demand is fixed and the supply increases.

Figure 33–2 can also show the effect of technical advance. Suppose that inventions occur that increase the productivity of capital—say, a new computer, or improved programs (software) for computer use. With higher marginal productivity, more capital will be demanded than before at the same price (interest rate). The DD curve will move to the right—say, to $D'D'$. Thus, with both more capital and technical progress, the interest rate here falls slightly, to i^3, but much less than without technical progress. Of course, if the technical progress is very large, it may dominate the growth in capital stock, so that the interest rate would rise in spite of the increased stock of capital. In fact, over the past century the two effects have been roughly offsetting; the real interest rate has fluctuated cyclically but without showing any clear long-term trend.

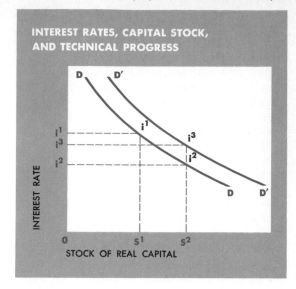

INTEREST RATES, CAPITAL STOCK, AND TECHNICAL PROGRESS

Figure 33–2
Given some level of technology and demand for capital DD, growth in the capital stock will reduce the interest rate from i^1 to i^2. Advancing technology partially offsets the growth in capital stock by increasing the demand for capital, and the resulting interest rate in second year is i^3.

The interest rate, resource allocation, and capital accumulation

The interest rate helps potential business and individual investors allocate their funds among the millions of potential investment opportunities in the economy. **When credit is allocated where the expected rate of return is highest, risk and other factors taken into account, it is optimally allocated from the consumer's viewpoint as well as from the investor's, because the highest returns will be found where consumer demand is relatively strongest.** Unless an investment promises a return high enough to pay the going rate of interest under a private-enterprise economy, it does not justify exploitation, by the test of the market. Money capital is the fluid embodiment of real productive resources. Thus, the credit market, by channeling funds into those investments where the potential return exceeds the interest rate, provides a most valuable service to private investors and to society as a whole.

The interest rate plays another, more subtle, role. It provides a rough measure of the relative advantages of current consumption and saving—of the present against the future. By saving, the individual or business can get a continuing return of, say, 6 percent annually. If that return is enough to justify foregoing consumption now, it is advantageous to save. Without the interest rate to indicate the return on saved funds, savers would have no standard by which to measure the relative advantages of current consumption and saving.

Similarly, the interest rate helps businessmen and government planners decide among projects of different capital intensity. Suppose we can produce product A either with lots of labor and a simple plant, or with little labor working with long-lived, expensive machinery. Which is better? Only by calculating the "capital cost" (the interest rate times the dollar investment discounted back to the present—see the following section) of each and comparing the expected total labor-plus-capital cost of the two alternatives can we accurately choose between the two methods.

Perhaps most important of all, the interest rate exerts a powerful influence on the rate of economic growth in a capitalist economy like ours. A low interest rate encourages investment and faster growth, because it is cheap for businessmen to borrow to expand their productive capacity. A high interest rate slows growth.[4]

Government policy and interest rates

Since the 1930s, the federal government has exerted substantial influence on interest rates, through both Treasury borrowing and Federal Reserve monetary policy. As Part 2 emphasized, the monetary authorities influence interest rates directly through purchase and sale of government securities, and indirectly through regulating bank reserves.

[4]Advanced texts in economic theory explain that in equilibrium, the interest rate must be equal to the marginal productivity of real capital, must equilibrate the loanable funds market, and must equilibrate the market for money (currency and deposits) so that everyone is just willing to continue holding the existing amount of money rather than spending it on goods and services or securities; and that it will simultaneously do all three.

Remember from Chapter 14 that Federal Reserve activities influence *money,* or nominal, interest rates more than *real* rates. Real interest rates are determined by the demand for and supply of real capital. If the Fed increases M but there is no change in the real forces at work, the result is likely to be inflation. Temporarily, more M will reduce short-term interest rates. But if substantial inflation develops, borrowers and lenders are likely to agree on adding an inflation allowance to the real interest rate. Nominal interest rates will then rise by the inflation allowance, but real rates are unchanged. In the mid-1970s, for example, the long-term nominal interest rate was about 9–10 percent on industrial bonds, but with 6–7 percent annual inflation, the real rate stayed near its long-term historical level of 3–4 percent.

VALUATION OF INCOME-PRODUCING PROPERTY

Income distribution is primarily concerned with the pricing of productive *services,* not with the prices of the productive agents themselves—land, machinery, buildings, and the stocks and bonds representing their ownership. But nonhuman income-producing assets are bought and sold daily in our economy, and the interest rate plays an important part in setting the prices at which they sell.

To estimate the price of an income-producing asset, we need to know (1) its net annual return, and (2) the going rate of interest.

Valuation of perpetual fixed income ("capitalization")

Take a simple hypothetical case. Suppose we have a mine that will *forever* produce ore worth $100 annually, net after all expenses are met. Suppose further that the going rate of interest on substantially riskless investments is 4 percent. What will the mine be worth?

To get the answer, we simply "capitalize" $100 at 4 percent. That is, we find that sum on which 4 percent interest would amount to $100 annually. The arithmetic is simple. Four percent of x (the unknown value) is $100. In equation form, this is $.04 \cdot x = 100$. Dividing the .04 into

100, we get $2,500 as the present value of the mine (or any other riskless asset that provides a $100 annual net return). Put another way, the formula is:

$$PV = \frac{\$ \text{ Return}}{\text{Interest rate}}$$

Can we be sure the mine will really sell for $2,500? No, but we can be sure it will sell for something near that. No one will be willing to pay a much higher price, because by investing $2,500 anywhere else at equal risk, he can get $100 annually. On the other hand, if the mine's price is much less than $2,500, people will find it a very attractive investment and the price will be bid up toward $2,500.

Valuation of depreciating assets

The principle involved in valuing nonperpetual assets is the same. Consider a machine that will last twenty years and whose marginal-revenue productivity (rent) per year is $60. The going rate of interest on comparable investments is 6 percent. Using the same approach as before, we might capitalize $60 at 6 percent, and find that $60 is 6 percent on $1,000.

But there's a catch. The $60 annual income lasts for only twenty years, because the machine wears out. Our problem then is, What is the present, or capitalized, value of an income stream of $60 at 6 percent over twenty years, rather than in perpetuity? Mathematicians and industrial engineers have worked out a series of tables giving the answer for all combinations of interest rates and time periods for such problems. The answer here is $688.

The basic reasoning runs like this: At the end of the first year, we get $60. At the end of the second year, we get another $60. And so on for the twenty years. Sixty dollars today is obviously worth $60, but $60 to be received, say, one year from today is clearly worth less than $60 today, since we do not have the use of it until a year hence. How much money today is equivalent to $60 a year from today? If the interest rate is 6 percent, $56.60 invested today at 6 percent will amount to just $60 a year from now. And we can make a similar calculation to get the amount

equal to $60 two years hence, and so on up to twenty years. If now we add together all these "present values" of $60 to be received at the end of each of the next twenty years, we will get how much we ought to be willing to pay now for the series of twenty annual $60 net returns anticipated from the machine. Adding these twenty present values together gives the $688 above, the present value of the income stream promised if we buy the machine.

So you'd better not pay more than about $688 for the machine if you don't want to get stung. It's easy to see why this amount is less than the $1,000 the machine would be worth if it provided the $60 annually in perpetuity. If you have to pay more than about $688, you could earn more on your money by investing it elsewhere at 6 percent for the twenty years.

One other point is needed to complete this example. Unless this is a patented machine, others like it can be produced. If the current cost of producing such machines, for example, is only $500, you can be pretty sure that even the $688 price won't last. At a price of $688, it will pay to produce more machines like this one. As more are produced, the price will gradually fall. Not until the price falls to $500 will a new equilibrium be established, where the price of the machine just covers its minimum cost of production. With a lot more machines, moreover, the marginal-revenue productivity of each will be lower, both because of the law of diminishing returns and because the product of the machine will have fallen in price, so that the net annual yield per machine will no longer be $60.

To summarize: (1) At any time, the capitalized present value of an income-producing asset will be based on its net yield and on the going rate of interest on investments of comparable risk. (2) In the long run, the value of any asset will tend to be equal to its cost of reproduction, although it may vary widely from this figure at any given time.

Valuation of corporate stocks: the stock market

The same general principle holds in valuing corporate stocks and bonds, which represent claims on income earned by the issuing companies. But don't take your nest egg and rush for the stock market with this new knowledge. Corporate securities are interesting illustrations of the capitalization principle especially because they point up so many of the pitfalls. So far, we've assumed that we knew the yield of each asset, its life, and the appropriate going rate of interest. But in the real world, all three of these are uncertain, especially on corporate stocks. The yield on most stocks fluctuates from year to year. There is no sure way of telling what it will be for any extended period in the future. Moreover, what rate of interest should we use in capitalizing? The appropriate one is the rate that prevails on other investments of comparable risk and other characteristics. But you pick it out.

Last, and most important, the market price of stocks is determined by thousands of other people who are all looking at the same imponderables as you. Many of them are in the market as speculators, looking for a quick dollar on the price rise rather than for a long-pull investment. There is no reproduction cost to set a stable base level that anyone can count on. The actual market price will reflect what all those people think is going to happen. So you're betting on what

other people will bet on, and they in turn are betting on what you and others will bet on.

The stock market is no place for neophytes. The capitalization principle can give you a rough steer and it can help you in comparing different securities. But the much-quoted statement of Bernard Baruch is relevant here:

If you are ready to give up everything else—to study the whole history and background of the market and all the principal companies whose stocks are on the board as carefully as a medical student studies anatomy—if you can do all that, and, in addition, you have the cool nerves of a great gambler, the sixth sense of a kind of clairvoyant, and the courage of a lion, you have a ghost of a chance.

The point of this section is not to warn you against investing in common stocks. On the contrary, overall, stocks have been a good investment over the long pull. Rather, the point is to stress the wide range of special factors at work in determining the actual market price of different income-producing assets. The analytical framework outlined in the simple cases above can help, but like all such models, it provides only a framework for analyzing any particular situation.

REVIEW

Concepts to remember

This is a difficult chapter. Recheck your understanding of the following concepts:

rent   "real" and "nominal" interest rates
economic rent   rate of return
quasi rent   capitalization
interest   "present value" of an income
"the interest rate"   stream

For analysis and discussion

1. How would you compare the rate of return on investment in yourself (human capital) through going to graduate school with the rate on investment in stocks or bonds (nonhuman capital)?
2. "Rent and wages are determined by substantially the same set of supply-and-demand forces, even though people are human and land is not." Do you agree? If not, what are the main differences?

3. "Rent is an unearned increment for any landowner, since he does not have to do any work for the rent he receives. Therefore, the government should confiscate land rents through special taxes." Do you agree? Explain.

4. "The profits made by a company on the basis of an exclusive patent are essentially rents, not profits." Do you agree or disagree?

5. Some economists predict persistent inflation over the years ahead. If they are correct, how would you expect this inflation to affect money and real rates of interest? Explain.

6. Other things equal, would you expect rapid technological advance to raise or lower the long-term rate of interest? Why?

7. Suppose the Federal Reserve tightens bank reserves and raises interest rates. Would this increase or decrease real investment, other things equal?

8. Find out the "carrying charge" on some article you are considering buying. Then calculate the interest rate you would be paying on the funds you in effect borrow from the seller. Would you be better off to borrow the money at a bank and pay cash? (See Case 28.)

9. Suppose you inherit an 80-acre tract of farmland. You are uncertain whether to sell it or to retain it and rent it out. How would you go about comparing the advantages of the two courses of action?

Interest rates aren't always what they seem to be. The following three cases may help you to protect yourself against some common mistakes, by looking at some situations that frequently arise in everyday life.

Installment charges You buy a $120 rug at the local furniture store. The store offers to let you pay over a full year, at $10 per month plus $1 per month additional carrying charge. (1) What is the actual interest rate the store is charging on the money it lends you over the year? (2) A local finance company will lend you the money at 15 percent on your unpaid balance. Should you borrow from them and pay cash for the rug, or buy on the installment plan?

ANALYSIS The store's offer looks like a 10 percent interest rate, a reasonable rate for such a loan, especially since it has to include something extra for the nuisance of keeping the books and maybe having to dun you for the money. But look again. The actual rate is far higher. You pay a dollar carrying charge each month, but the total amount you have on loan from the store goes down $10 each month. The last month, you owe them only $10; yet you are still paying interest at the rate of $1 a month, or $12 per year. The actual rate on your unpaid balance during the last month is 120 percent per annum. The average for the year is about 20 percent, twice the apparent rate, because the average loan to you is about half the purchase price of the rug. The actual rate for each month is calculated in the accompanying table. If you want to pay the smallest amount of interest, in this case go to the finance company at 15 percent.

General lesson: Compare carefully the actual interest rate included in installment carrying charges with what the money would cost you if you borrowed it directly elsewhere. This is not to suggest that installment sellers are crooked; they

Note: Because some of the necessary analysis is not included in this chapter, the suggestions for analysis are included here for this case.

	Unpaid balance	Interest ($1 monthly; $12 per year)	Interest rate on unpaid balance
1st month	$120	$12	10.0%
2nd month	110	12	10.9
3rd month	100	12	12.0
4th month	90	12	13.3
5th month	80	12	15.0
6th month	70	12	17.1
7th month	60	12	20.0
8th month	50	12	24.0
9th month	40	12	30.0
10th month	30	12	40.0
11th month	20	12	60.0
12th month	10	12	120.0

have to cover their costs of foregoing interest on the money they lend you, plus their operating expenses. But actual interest rates are often higher than they seem.

Bond yields You have about $1,000 to invest. You are considering an 8 percent corporation bond. It is a $1,000 face value bond, so the annual interest is $80. Its current market price is $1,100, and it is due in ten years. Your main alternative is putting the money into U.S. government bonds, which pay 6 percent, can be bought at face value ($1,000), and are also due in ten years. Assume that the two investments are equally safe and attractive on all other grounds. Which one should you choose?

ANALYSIS At first glance, the corporate bond seems to win hands down. But look again. You pay $1,100 for the bond, but you'll only get back $1,000 at the end of ten years. To get the true net yield, you need to "write off" $10 of the value of the bond each of the ten years, so your actual net annual yield would be only $70, rather than $80. Now you can calculate the exact yield on the corporate bond. It's $70 per year on $1,100 invested. This figures out to about 6.4 percent per annum, barely above the 6 percent offered on the government bond. If the risk on the two bonds is really identical, the corporate bond is the better buy. But if (as is likely in the real world) the corporate bond is riskier, the choice is not clear. Which you should prefer will depend on your attitude toward risk.

Inflation, risk, and growth Suppose again that you have $1,000 to invest. You can put it in a bank or a savings and loan account at 5 percent, buy 6 percent government bonds due in ten years, or buy Sears, Roebuck common stock at 100 to yield about 1.6 percent in dividends (4 percent in total earnings, including those plowed back into the company; the price–earnings ratio is 25 to 1). Of course you are not sure, but you judge that we face inflation of about 3 percent annually over the decade ahead. Which investment should you make?

ANALYSIS This is a trickier problem still, because it involves not only your risk aversion (as in the preceding case), but also probable inflation and the historically persistent growth in Sear's profitability. Inflation first: If prices rise 3 percent per year, the real rate of interest on the bank account is only 2 percent, on the government bond 3 percent, and the Sears dividend doesn't even cover the inflation loss. Better face it that your real return will be a good deal less than the nominal rates. Second, risk: There is virtually none on the bank or savings and loan account; their deposits are government-insured up to $40,000 per person, and you can withdraw your money whenever you want. On the government bond, there's no risk on repayment when the bond comes due, but the price may fluctuate

in the meantime, so you might have to sell at a loss if you want your money before ten years. Of course, there's also a possibility that the bond's price will rise in the meantime (for example, if market interest rates on comparable bonds fall—work out the capitalization for yourself), in which case you'd make a gain on your sale. On Sears, there's real risk. You have no guarantee at all that Sears will keep on paying its present dividend, or that the price–earnings ratio will stay as high as it is now. Everyone knows that Sears' earnings and dividends have risen persistently over the last three decades, and investors' present willingness to pay so much for a currently small dividend reflects their belief that Sears' earnings, dividends, and stock price will continue to grow in the future. Moreover, many investors figure that if inflation comes, Sears can pass along rising costs through higher prices, so money earnings will rise with the inflation rather than be eroded. If investors' expectations turn out to be seriously wrong on any of these points, Sears's high price–earnings multiple of about 25 to 1 is likely to fall, and you'll find that you can only sell your stock at a loss. But if the optimistic forecasts turn out to be right, Sears's earnings, dividends, and stock price will rise substantially.

What should you do with your money? Economic analysis can point up the issues and some consequences of various possible developments. But the best investment for you will depend on your assessment of the probability of these various developments and your attitude toward risk—and note that risk here is a far more complicated issue than just whether you will receive some stated number of dollars at a given time.

CHAPTER 34

PROFITS: THEORY, FACTS, AND FANTASY

In 1973–75, corporation profits before taxes averaged about $100 billion annually, about 9 percent of the national income. After payment of corporation income taxes, the comparable figures were $50 billion and 4.4 percent. If we add in unincorporated businesses (farmers, lawyers, doctors, small shopkeepers, and the like), the pretax profit figure is probably increased by $10–$20 billion; the amount can only be estimated roughly because we have no clear separation between profits on the one hand, and implicit wages, interest, and rent on the unincorporated businessmen's own labor and investments on the other. Indeed, a substantial part of reported corporate profits is also actually implicit interest on invested capital owned by the stockholders. Implicit interest is probably between a quarter and a half of total corporation pretax profits. Thus pure "economic" profits, after taxes and allowance for implicit interest, were probably small, or possibly even nonexistent, in 1973–75.

Nearly $50 billion in reported after-tax profits is enough to provide a lot of income to stockholders and unincorporated businessmen, but it's also only a small fraction of the total income received by the public. Whether profits are too big—an unconscionable exploitation of the workers, as Marxists and many others claim—or too low—an inadequate return to induce capitalists and risk takers to perform their proper social functions—is one of today's, and every day's, hottest issues.

Our look at the market system thus far has stressed two big roles for profits. They're the incentive to produce what consumers demand—the carrot that entices businessmen to perform their social function. And they're a major source of funds for the investment that makes the economy grow by the construction of new plant and equipment. Now it's time for a summary look at profits in their own right.

PROFITS ON THE MODERN SCENE

Potential profit indicates where society wants more resources used. Thus, the individual businessman who predicts most successfully what the consumer will want, who meets consumer demand most effectively, who handles his production most efficiently, and who buys his labor and materials most adroitly, will end up with the biggest profit. The inefficient producer who fails to respond to consumers' demands is likely to end up with red ink on his books. If a seller has a partial or complete monopoly, he may be able to maintain positive economic profits over a substantial period without innovations, real productive efficiency, or close response to consumer demands. But wherever other firms are free to enter the market, competition will tend to eliminate economic profits.[1] The pursuit of profits plays a central organizing role for the entire economy.

If you ask the man in the street, he probably won't be very sure just what profit does mean, but he'll almost certainly have an antagonistic attitude. Public-opinion polls show this time after time; most people think profits are too big. And it's highly likely he will have only a vague idea about how big profits actually are. So a further look at the facts may be in order.

The facts

Figure 34–1 summarizes the course of *corporate* profits before and after income taxes, since 1929. About half the total now goes to the government in corporation income taxes, before payment of dividends or reinvestment in the firm. Clearly, the size of profits looks a lot different before and after taxes. Remember too that over two-thirds of the huge growth since 1929 is inflation—prices have tripled.

The aggregate dollar figures don't mean much. They're too big. Everything in the economy has grown immensely since 1929. Have profits risen or fallen compared to other income shares? Are businesses making more or less profit these days per dollar of sales, or per dollar of investment? Figure 34–2 gives some of the answers.

The profit share in the national income has jumped all over the place in business cycles.

[1] Remember that elimination of *economic* profits by competition does not eliminate all accounting profits, since a substantial share of reported accounting profits is implicit interest on stockholders' investment in the firm.

Figure 34–1
Corporate profits have risen sharply but irregularly since the 1930s. Corporate income taxes now take somewhat less than half the total. Profits shown after inventory valuation adjustment. (Source: U.S. Department of Commerce.)

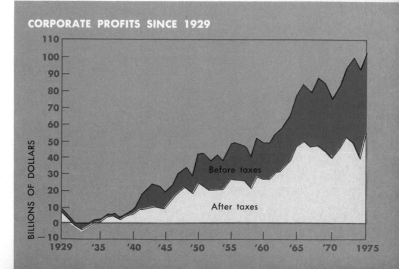

CORPORATE PROFITS SINCE 1929

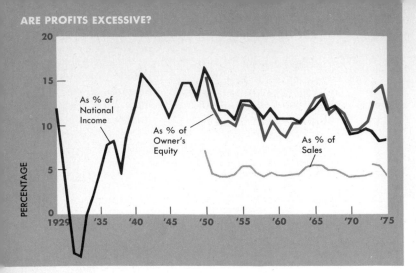

Figure 34-2
Corporate profits reached peaks during and after World War II. Since then, they have declined substantially and fluctuated irregularly at somewhat lower levels relative to national income, sales, and owners' equity. (Source: U.S. Department of Commerce. Profits as percentage of national income are before taxes for all manufacturing corporations. Note that new series after 1973 make data not fully comparable with earlier figures.)

Corporate profits were actually negative in 1931–32 (negative by a far larger amount, if we consider *economic* profits, eliminating implicit interest on stockholders' investment), and hit a peak of 17 percent of national income in 1950. Over the last quarter century, profits have declined substantially on all three bases shown. Lesson in statistics: Note how you can make the profit share look sharply rising or sharply falling, depending on whether you take the early 1930s or 1940s as your starting point.

Public-opinion surveys have repeatedly shown that the public holds wildly erroneous ideas about the size of corporate profits. Public estimates of after-tax profits as a proportion of sales have ranged all over the map, but have generally concentrated in the 25–35 percent range. This is some five to eight times the actual return of 4–5 percent over the last decade. If actual profit margins on sales had reached publicly guessed levels, total corporate profits before taxes in 1975 would have been over a half-trillion dollars, or nearly half the total GNP. Little wonder that many people believe that corporate profits could absorb the cost of almost any social reforms if only corporations were less greedy! And equally little wonder that many corporate executives are frustrated at how little the public understands business.

Last, a fact we wish we knew, but don't. Total reported corporate profits are a combination of implicit interest on stockholders' investment, monopoly or quasi-monopoly profits, and eco-

456

nomic profits arising largely out of dynamic change in the economy. Presumably, our attitude toward these three parts would be different if we could separate them. Types one and three look socially legitimate and useful, but not type two. But alas, we have only rough estimates of such a division.

THE TWO ROLES OF PROFITS

The preceding chapters have stressed profits as the carrot that lures businessmen and investors into meeting consumer demands, reducing costs, and innovating with new products. And losses are the stick that beats those who fail in their attempts. Part 2 stressed profits as a major source of financing new investment and growth for individual businesses and the economy. Let us now look more intensively at these critical roles of profits in our society, and at the theory of profits, preparatory to asking the final question: How big **should** profits be in the modern American economy?

Profits as an incentive

The primary social function of profits is to give businessmen an incentive to produce what consumers want, when and where they want it, at the lowest feasible cost. This includes innovation of new products and new methods.

The profit motive is at the center of a private-enterprise economy.

But a lot of questions are raised about just how the profit motive works as a practical matter. For example, most after-tax profits go to stockholders who have little to do with managing the businesses they own. Clearly, profits give them an incentive to invest, but professional managers (rather than owner-operators) now run most big businesses. Thus, some critics ask whether profit is still the most effective incentive to innovation and efficiency. The modern corporation president gets a salary plus a bonus dependent on profits, but as president he gets only a small fraction of 1 percent of the company's total profits. We rely on top management's urge to excel and to make large profits for the stockholders to produce the desired results, as well as on their personal enrichment from profits. We rely heavily on profits per se to draw investors' funds into the businesses where profit prospects are highest. The functions of management, entrepreneurship, and providing capital are thoroughly entangled in today's big firms.

Second, remember that it's the *expectation* of profits that must be there to make the system tick, not the achievement of profits. Never forget that this is a *profit-and-loss*, not just a profit, system. Every year, the big stick of losses pounds a large number of businesses that don't succeed in meeting the test of the market. Many a firm has gone broke.

In 1970–75, failures (bankruptcies) of incorporated businesses averaged nearly 1,000 per month. Total liabilities of these failures averaged $2 billion annually. Fewer than 25 percent of the businesses established during the immediate postwar years were still operating a decade later. Yet each year, new thousands rush in, confident that they have the knack to succeed where others have failed. Big-business failures are less common than failures among small firms. People who have $50 million or $100 million to venture are rare, and profitability calculations on such investments are made with a great deal of care. And failing big firms are often merged into other firms to avoid massive disasters. But even for big business, the story is far from one of unbroken success. Think of the auto industry, with its spectacular growth over the present century. The Oakland, Stanley Steamer, Maxwell, Hupmobile, and dozens of others were once as much household words as Ford and Pontiac are today. Yet only a few decades later, they are as extinct as the dodo. More recently, Douglas Aircraft, a multi-billion-dollar giant, was saved only by merger with McDonnell Aircraft; Lockheed Aircraft had to be bailed out by a quarter-billion-dollar government loan guarantee. The Penn Central Railroad and W. T. Grant stores were spectacular failures of big, nationally-known firms.

Hope springs eternal in American businessmen's and investors' breasts. Their mistakes lead to a good deal of waste in resources devoted to ventures that don't succeed. But their optimism gives the American economy much of the dynamic vigor that has pushed the American standard of living above its competitors. It is doubtful that dynamic progress in a private-enterprise system is possible without widespread losses from bad business guesses as well as widespread profits from good ones. But without the *expectation* of profits, the system will grind to a halt.

Profits as a source of investment and growth

Profits have a second major social function. Undistributed corporate profits (profits not paid out as dividends) are one important source of funds for business investment. In 1975, for example, they totaled $40 billion, and almost all were plowed back into new plant, equipment, and other such business uses. Corporation depreciation allowances are also considered by most businessmen as sources of funds for business investments (though, remember that a depreciation allowance is merely a bookkeeping charge, not actual money set aside). Because businesses seldom replace worn-out assets with identical assets, it is often hard to identify what is replacement and what is net new investment. Thus, business investment is often viewed gross (including replacement), as in the gross national product accounts. In 1975, depreciation charges totaled $90 billion, so net "internal" sources for corporate investment spending totaled about $130 billion.

THE THEORY OF PROFITS

Profits in a static economy

In a *static* economy, without technological advance, population change, capital accumulation, and changing consumer wants, only monopoly profits would continue in long-run equilibrium. Competition would gradually eliminate all other *economic* profits as resources were shifted into high-profit industries. Capitalization would bid up the prices and rents of especially productive resources. Throughout the economy, economic (although not accounting) profits would be eliminated when equilibrium was achieved, except for those industries where new businesses were prevented from entering. There, and there only, monopoly and oligopoly profits would continue indefinitely. In effect, monopoly and oligopoly profits would then be a kind of rent, or quasi-rent, on exclusive monopoly position.

Profits in a dynamic economy

However, continuous, unpredictable change is the dominant characteristic of the real world. Uncertainty confronts the entrepreneur or manager daily. He must somehow "guesstimate" the future demand for his product, his future costs, future changes in technology, future behavior of his competitors. Then he must keep an eagle eye out for how the government is going to behave—on taxes, spending, antitrust policy, labor relations, and international affairs. In the midst of all this, he needs to worry about keeping his costs below those of competitors, keeping the union at least tolerably happy, being sure that his sales organization is on its toes, and so on.

If he does all these things better than his competitors, and especially if he has a partial-monopoly position to help him, he'll end up with a good profit. If he misses on many of the important decisions, the red ink will appear. The biggest job of the modern entrepreneur is to live with and to make the best of uncertainty. If he doesn't thrive on this kind of life, he'd better save himself a big doctor bill for ulcers and go to work for someone else.

Insurable risk, uncertainty, and dynamic change. Many kinds of risk can be insured against. In this way, the uncertainty can be eliminated by incurring a known dollar cost. The best-known example is the risk of loss from fire. Without insurance, this uncertainty would be a major problem for any business concern. But the likelihood of fire loss is reasonably predictable for a large number of buildings of any given type, even though it is unpredictable for any given building. By pooling together the moderate insurance premiums on a large number of buildings, the insurance company has enough funds to pay off the fire losses on those few buildings that do burn each year. Long experience has reduced the likelihood of such occurrences to a scientific, statistical basis. Businesses can now convert this type of risk into a known cost through insurance.[2]

Professor Frank H. Knight has pointed out that insurable risks are thus really only another business cost to be included with other business costs, and that economic profits arise only from bona-fide cases of **uninsurable** uncertainty. Alas, the businessman can't go to his insurance agent and say, "I'm bringing out a new-style dishwasher; insure me against its being a flop." Economic profits beyond profits on monopoly positions, Knight argues, are thus analytically linked solely to a world of dynamic change and uninsurable uncertainty.

Since profits arise largely out of dynamic change and uncertainty, much of what happens to profits is outside the control of any individual manager or entrepreneur. The biggest profits arise in booms, the biggest losses in depressions. "Windfall profits" are widespread in a lusty boom; in a bad depression, the best management in the world has a tough time making ends meet. The manager who can foresee business fluctuations and adjust successfully to them is worth his weight in gold.

Shifting consumer demand for individual products is a second big area of change largely outside the control of the individual business-

---

[2]Very large firms may "self-insure." If a firm has hundreds of buildings itself, it may figure that the predictable likelihood of fire loss in any given year is less than the cost of buying commercial insurance on them.

man. Even General Motors is going to have a tough time making profits on automobiles if consumers decide to ride in helicopters instead. But the alert entrepreneur is far from helpless. He can change his product to keep in step with the times, and through his advertising he can influence what consumers want to buy.

Changes in costs are a third big area of uncontrollable uncertainty. What happens to the price of copper is outside the control of Westinghouse; yet copper represents one of the major costs in making electrical equipment. The same thing is true of many other costs. The businessman can bargain with his local union, but he isn't going to get much labor with a wage rate much below the rates that prevail elsewhere for similar work. Technological changes continually change costs.

Basically, it's the manager who does a good job of prediction under conditions of dynamic uncertainty, and who adjusts effectively to unforeseen conditions, who is likely to turn in good profits.

The profits of innovation. One noted economist, Joseph Schumpeter, has argued that profits boil down largely to payments for keeping a jump ahead of your competitors through innovation. The big profits come from big, successful innovations—the motor car, color TV, and so on.

Unfortunately, no one has yet figured out a sure way of telling in advance whether a new mousetrap or a new auto engine will prove a success. First, there is the technological problem of developing the idea into a usable process or product. When this is licked, there is still that capricious monarch of all he surveys—the consumer. Business history tells a fascinating story of the sure things that flopped, and of the thousand-to-one shots that have become the industrial giants of today.

Successful innovation in effect gives a temporary monopoly to the innovator, and often big profits. Like other monopoly profits, the economic profits of innovation persist only until competitors catch up and bring profits in the industry down to competitive levels. But innovations are often protected by 17-year patents. And a running start on your competitor is often more important than the legal protection of patents. The firm with the know-how and experience that go with a new product or new method is likely to have a new innovation at hand by the time competitors catch up on the last one. The continuing success of the industrial giants of today—General Electric, IBM, du Pont—rests as much on this kind of continuing innovation as on any other single factor.

HOW BIG SHOULD PROFITS BE?

Are profits too big? Is business too concerned with making profits, and not enough with social responsibilities, as a large majority of college students reported in a recent survey? How big do profits need to be to give the incentives they need to managers and investors to provide a dynamic, progressive, basically private-enterprise economy?

In principle, the answer is clear. Profits are big enough when businessmen and investors act as if they were big enough—when we get a satisfactory response to consumer demands in a dynamic economy, and the rate of economic growth we want. This answer puts the focus on the social functions of profits, not on the equity of the incomes received by profit makers, in contrast to much popular discussion about whether coupon clippers and dividend receivers are too rich.

The facts on profits were summarized above. In the past five years, corporate profits after taxes averaged about $45 billion, or about 4 percent of GNP. This is the amount society might consider taking away from profit receivers, if it considers profits too big. To judge the effects of such a profit transfer, we need first to remember, from above, that the total is made up of three quite different parts: (1) monopoly and quasi-monopoly profits, (2) returns (implicit interest) on stockholders' investments, and (3) true economic profits in a dynamic economy. Few economists would defend the first, but most evidence suggests it comprises a relatively small part of the total. If we oppose the second, we are essentially saying that savers should receive no interest on their investments. This is a position Marxists and many radicals hold and that we shall examine in the Appendix; this opposition would presumably apply equally to interest on bonds, bank deposits, and other savings. If we reduce the third part of profits, we question the need for profits as an incentive to businesses in both meeting consumer demands and investing for economic growth and higher living standards.

To assess these issues, we need to ask, Who gets the profits? Whose incentives are the crucial ones? The $10–$15 billion of profits in unincorporated businesses go to millions of individuals—doctors, lawyers, small shopkeepers, some poor, some rich. These are not the profits most critics challenge. Corporate profits go to some 25 million stockholders. On these, first remember that nearly half those profits are plowed back into the business involved, and hence do not show up in the current income of stockholders. Dividends actually paid out to stockholders averaged about $25 billion annually over the past five years—about 2 percent of GNP. Second, while there are over 25 million stockholders plus millions more who own stock indirectly through pension funds and insurance policies, most own only small amounts of stock, and their dividend incomes are a tiny proportion of their wages and salaries. In 1970, 20–30 percent of all wealth was held by the top 1 percent of families, and stockholdings of individuals were probably at least comparably concentrated. Third, a large and growing proportion of all stock is held by financial institutions (trust companies, banks, insurance companies, and pension funds), which in turn reflect the investments of millions of people, rich and poor. Fourth, the big incomes of corporate executives are primarily salaries, not profits, although many also receive bonuses based on the profits earned and own stock on which they receive dividends.

How big profits must be to get these diverse groups and individuals to perform their social functions of investing and entrepreneurship is obviously a complex question. Some fear that we have already so weakened the incentives to save and invest that America faces a major "capital shortage" over the next decade. They estimate that we will need perhaps $4.5 billion of new investment by 1985, and that present incentives will fall far short of providing this investment, especially if government borrowing soaks up much of the available savings. The result, they predict, will be slower growth, weak recoveries, and a persistent tendency toward inflation as the government creates new money to finance its own spending needs when private savings and taxes are not available.

The controversy is a complex one, and there is no way of predicting accurately whether the present system will produce the huge voluntary saving and investment needed to keep the economy growing at the desired rate with reasonably full employment and without inflation. Nearly everyone agrees that inadequate capital investment is at least conceivable, given present returns on business investment, tax rates, and probable levels of government spending. Estimates that the average *real* (inflation-adjusted) after-tax rate of return to private capital investment has declined from about 10 to 5 percent over the past decade strengthen the concern of the worriers.

Traditional Marxist doctrine and some modern radicals say the answer is easy. Profits and interest serve no social function; they should be zero. All property, except personal belongings, should be owned by the state, and state planners should decide what is to be produced, and how much of it. Only labor is productive, and there should be no return to property.

This answer obviously looks toward a communist system completely different from ours, and one with which few Americans agree. (We shall look at it briefly in the following Appendix and in detail in the final chapter.) Thus, it doesn't help much as a practical matter in answering our question on how big profits should be. The operationally important questions in America are whether we should tax away more corporation profits to provide money grants or subsidized services to other groups, and whether we should attempt to make stockholders pay out of profits for social improvements like cleaner air and water, jobs for the hard-core unemployed, and the like.

One may argue that investors would still invest as much if profit rates were lower; what else can they do with their money? Moreover, the cost of abstaining from consumption to save must be very low for rich investors; they have all they want and deserve no substantial reward for saving. Similarly, actual corporation decisions in responding to consumer demands are made by paid managers, whose incomes are mainly salaries, not profits; they would do just as well if profits were lower.

These arguments seem plausible to some, but experience suggests that they should be viewed with doubts. Even if you believe profit receivers *should* be content with less, try the case, "Profits for the Picking?" at the end of this chapter. It suggests that making profits pay for good causes may be much harder than it seems. And whether the system would function as well with substantially lower profits is far from clear. Investors do have other places to put their savings than in corporate equities; savers have a long history of searching out the investments that provide the best returns for them, shifting frequently from one to another as relative rates of return change. Perhaps they will feel they should readily give up part of their dividends to others less fortunate, without lessening their enthusiasm for risky, uncertain investments—but the stock market hasn't looked that way. Perhaps managers would do as well without a strong profit incentive, and certainly they have other important motives as well, but the drive for profits still looks like a powerful spur to getting goods and services produced efficiently in response to consumer dollars laid on the counter.

All this doesn't say that the present level of profits is just right. No one knows what is just right. But both the critics who are ready to throw out the profit incentive and the conservatives who say the American system is sinking because profits are too low have a lot of history to explain away, here and in other nations. The U.S. economy, relying heavily on profits as the carrot and losses as the stick, has been phenomenally successful in giving the masses the goods and services they seem to want—one of the world's highest standards of living. Every major high-per-capita-income nation in the world relies heavily on the profit motive in a market system.

Human motivation is a complex affair, and it varies widely from person to person. There are many incentives to good management and entrepreneurship. Pride in achievement, the social acclaim for success, the development of professional standards, the pure joy of risk taking—these and others like them may be powerful supplements to the monetary incentive of profits. Money is far from everything. And the billions of dollars we spend each year on gambling devices we know are loaded against us provide impressive evidence of our love for risk taking. With business innovation, there is no reason to suppose that the dice are loaded against entrepreneurs in the aggregate. Indeed, the long record of rapid growth in the economy points strongly the other way. Profits are just big enough when they induce entrepreneurs and investors to provide the social functions we want from them.

REVIEW

For analysis and discussion

1. Are current profits excessive? (See Figure 33–2.) What are the best criteria to judge whether profits are too large or too small?
2. What are the main functions of profits in the modern American economy? Should businessmen be proud, or apologetic, when they make record profits?
3. "By and large, continuing profits for any firm demonstrate it is doing a good job in satisfying consumer demand." Do you agree or disagree? Explain.
4. Go back to Case 1. Suppose that you and other consumer advocates want to be sure the cost of new auto safety features is borne by the manufacturers and not passed on to consumers. How would you accomplish this?

5. "So long as we let businessmen think they have a chance to make profits, it doesn't matter whether they actually make any profits or not." Is this a sound analysis of the incentive role of business profits?

6. Who actually gets the profits made by the American corporations? (Refer back to Chapter 4 for some of the relevant information.) If it is not primarily managers, how do profits serve their presumed incentive function?

7. Many economists say that Marxist criticism of capitalist profits as creating big incomes for stockholders is misplaced—that the main function of profits is as an incentive to get businesses to do what we (the consumers) want done, and that we should expect successful businesses to earn substantial profits for serving this social function. Who is right?

8. How much should a business firm spend on "social responsibilities" like reducing pollution, supporting universities, and hiring hard-core unemployed workers, rather than concentrating on maximizing profits? Who should (will) ultimately pay for such corporate activities—stockholders or customers?

In 1975, corporate profits after taxes were about $70 billion, dividends $33 billion. This total demonstrated to many the ability of corporations to absorb the costs of producing better products, providing better services, and paying higher wages without raising prices to consumers. Suppose we agree (although many stockholders would not) that profits are bigger than they need be, and we propose to make corporations more responsive to consumer and social needs, which we argue they can perfectly well afford to be with their huge profits. Using the theory of the preceding chapters, analyze the likely consequences of the following.

Consumerism—who pays? Ralph Nader and many others have recently complained vigorously that many drug manufacturers release inadequately tested drugs for public consumption. While the Food and Drug Administration sets minimum safety standards (see Chapter 28), these standards should be still higher. Drug producers should be made to do more thorough testing of new drugs before releasing them, since, as a practical matter, consumers have no way of judging for themselves what drugs are safe and what are not.

Another product recently subjected to widespread criticism as unsafe is the power lawn mower, which can be very efficient at mowing toes and fingers as well as grass, and which can hurl stones and other small objects out with the grass clippings at very dangerous velocities unless protective equipment is added. Require manufacturers to build more safety factors into mowers, insist the consumerists.

Should we pass new laws requiring manufacturers to do more extensive testing of drugs and to build safer power mowers? It looks like a good idea—safer products for consumers, and the manufacturer can well afford to do it out of those big profits. So we pass the law. Your economic theory should suggest what happens next: Costs are increased, manufacturers raise prices, and consumers have to pay more for drugs and power mowers. Maybe businesses *should* absorb

the higher costs out of profits, but it's unlikely that they will. They feel they need all the profits they are making, whether or not you agree, and if costs go up for everyone in the drug and mower industries, you can be pretty sure prices will too. Consumers get safer products, and pay for them. Whether they're better or worse off as a result depends on how much you think that extra safety is worth.

But suppose consumers are outraged at the greed of business in raising prices for such obviously needed consumer safety, and get Congress to pass a law forbidding drug and mower manufacturers to raise prices. Assuming the law is strictly enforced, what does your economic theory tell you will happen then? Right! Manufacturers will stop making the drugs and mowers on which they would now make a loss or smaller profit than on other products. Maybe they'll keep on for a while, but in the long run, capital will be transferred to other products where the potential profit rate is higher. If consumers want safer drugs and power mowers, they can get them, but in the long run only by paying their higher costs.

Consider another case. Recently, courts and juries have been holding sellers strictly responsible for damages to consumers from products that are in any way faulty. Juries have awarded large settlements to individuals injured in accidents presumably due to product defect. A Wisconsin man recently received $500,000 for the loss of a leg when a safety guard on a chain saw slipped after he thought he had fastened it firmly. The average award rose from $12,000 to $67,000 over the past five years in such seller-liability household chemical cases, from $38,000 to $98,000 in automobile cases. And the total number of such cases litigated rose from about 100,000 to 500,000 annually over the same period.

Fair enough! you may say. Consumers deserve safe, reliable products, and if businesses don't make them, let them pay. But get out your economic theory again. Where is all that money coming from? If the culprit is just one firm in an industry, its profits may indeed have to absorb the costs of coming up to industry standards. But if what consumers demand is higher safety and reliability standards for all, the result is probably higher costs, and if so almost certainly they'll be passed along in higher prices, in the long if not the short run. Same reasoning as above.

Some consumers say the insurance companies will have to pay the damages, so businesses won't have to charge consumers more. But that again is probably shortsighted. Insurance companies must also cover their costs to stay in business, and they push up rates quickly for any class of customers who show unusually large claims. Unless you can find an industry with a protected monopoly profit pool, it's unlikely that consumerism will get its better products and big consumer awards out of profits for very long; they'll be paid for in prices that cover full costs in the long run.

Now try the same reasoning on auto safety (where new legislation will add about $200 per car (about $2 billion total costs for the industry) annually by 1980—and on "clean air" and "clean water" legislation to force businesses to reduce pollution.

Wages and the profit pool Similar reasoning throws a sobering light on the perhaps ethically justifiable claim that workers getting very low wages should have more and wealthy dividend receivers less. Why not form a union or pass a law to raise their wages and let profits be squeezed? Go back to Chapters 30 and 31 for the answers. If profits rest on exploitation of workers, unions or minimum wage laws can shift income from profits to wages. And in high-profit oligopoly industries, perhaps some profits-to-wages shift may work. But wherever competitive pressures are strong, well-meaning attempts to get higher wages for workers out of profits will not succeed in the long run. Higher wage rates will mean not lower profits but higher prices and fewer jobs in the industry concerned.

All this does not mean that consumers shouldn't insist on safer, better products, or that workers shouldn't press for higher wages. Both may be worth what they cost. But economic analysis should help you avoid using fantasy rather than fact on how far society can solve its problems by drawing on a huge pool of profits just waiting to be tapped, however strongly you may feel that profits *should* bear the cost.

Note that this problem parallels closely the corporate "social responsibility" arguments that businesses should reduce pollution and the like, instead of just trying to make profits. Should corporations concentrate on doing social good instead of meeting consumer demands? If one company spends heavily on "social responsibilities" while others don't, what happens to its competitive position? If we pass a law requiring all companies to reduce pollution or help clean up the slums, who will pay?

APPENDIX

Marx, "radical economics," interest, and profits

Karl Marx, writing a century ago, developed an elaborate theory of the workings and ultimate downfall of capitalism. The central points were the following:

1. All history can be interpreted primarily in terms of economic issues and conflicts.
2. Value is created only by labor, and the labor time socially necessary for the production of any commodity will determine its value (price).
3. Capitalists (employers) do not pay workers the full value of the goods they produce. They take for themselves as profits and interest on their capital the "surplus value" above what they pay workers, using this surplus to support their own rich living and further accumulation of capital. Indeed, the dominant capitalist class will force the wages of the working class down to a subsistence level.
4. The operations of any economy can be understood best in terms of a class struggle between capitalists and workers, oppressors and oppressed, the rich and the poor. The capitalists also dominate governments. "The State," Marx wrote, "is nothing but the organized collective power of the possessing classes."
5. Out of this class struggle will emerge, eventually, the end of capitalism and the beginning of a communist society. The class struggle will develop "contradictions" in the capitalist system. Most important, unemployment and human misery will increase as the capitalists seize more and more surplus value and accumulate more capital, while the poor are increasingly unable to purchase the growing production of the capitalist society. Capital will be increasingly monopolized by a few huge firms, which imperialistically reach abroad for new opportunities to oppress workers in other nations and to further expand their own capital hoards. But in the end, the oppressed workers will rise in revolt, overthrow the capitalists, and establish a socialist or communist system.

Modern Marxists and radicals make many modifications on the argument, but this is the core.

Profits, interest, and wages   Marx declared profits and interest to be immoral—without social function, and obtained entirely by expropriating the surplus value produced by the workers. But modern economists point to crucial flaws in his "labor theory of value" on which the argument rests. The labor theory of value says that only labor is productive and that all prices will be proportional to labor inputs. Clearly, this is wrong; prices are basically determined by the forces of supply and demand in markets, as was explained in the preceding chapters. How will the labor theory of value explain the high price of a perfect pearl picked up with little labor by a passing beach walker? Or \$11/barrel OPEC oil, brought out of the ground at a labor cost of only a few cents? The argument that capital is not itself productive is equally fallacious, or a play on words. Without the capital they work with, total output with the same workers would clearly be less.

Similarly, most modern economists, including many in the USSR and Eastern Europe, agree that without the interest rate to help guide the choice between more- and less-roundabout means of production (for example, how much expensive machinery to use, compared to labor-intensive production), it is impossible to plan efficiently. For this reason, until recently, communist planners made major errors in production processes. Similarly, without profits as a guide and an incentive to efficient production, the communist nations have faced increasingly serious difficulties in getting central plans carried out. Recently, both interest and profits have been openly introduced into the USSR's and other communist countries' economic planning.

Marx and history   Marxists have for a century persistently proclaimed the death throes of capitalism. Capitalism has been uncooperative. Indeed, income and growth statistics (see Table 1–1) show the Western capitalist economies dominating the list, with the USSR the only communist nation in the top twenty countries. In the capitalist nations, the poor have not become poorer and more numerous; on the contrary, the bottom-quarter income recipients in the Western capitalist nations are notably better off economically than even the middle classes in the communist nations. Capitalist economies' income distributions have remained remarkably stable. Property income, depending on precisely how it is defined, has hovered around 20–25 percent of GNP in the United States (see Figure 30–4), and not far from that in other major Western capitalist nations. Profits have neither eroded from lack of mass purchasing power nor ballooned to sweep control over spendable income into capitalist hands. Aided by persistent technical progress, they have remained roughly constant as a rate of return on investment.

Modern monetary and fiscal policy appears to have tamed the worst excesses of the business cycle with its massive depressions. Wealth is certainly concentrated in the Western, democratic, capitalist nations, but the concentration is gradually diminishing. Although monopoly is a serious problem for many capitalist countries, it is not clear in America, for example, that the degree of monopoly has changed significantly in this century. The great middle classes look more and more stable and conservative, not increasingly ground down into an ever-hungrier proletariat. "The people" persistently refuse to vote to tax either profits and interest, or the rich per se, out of existence. The income tax and the "welfare state" have proved more attractive to the masses than has the sword in dealing with the rich.

What went wrong with the Marxist predictions? Today, many Marxists and other radicals say, "Just wait!" They say that capitalist statistics mask a growing sickness and economic instability, that modern capitalism with its profit motive is only temporarily shored up by wars and imperialism through which we live off the poor in other nations and at home.[3]

No one can know the future, but the Marxist arguments find limited support thus far in the data of history. Marx flatly denied any useful role for profits or interest in the operations of an economic system. But, as was indicated above, both have recently been introduced into Soviet economic planning and management of the economy.[4] Strikingly, to most modern "radicals" the problem of economic incentives is easily manageable. If everyone, especially the rich, would only be less greedy and share what they produced, economists' persistent concern with "scarcity" and more efficient use of resources would be seen to be fatuous. In any event, others say, government planning can do whatever needs to be done.

But all-powerful government planning has yet to demonstrate its superiority over profits and individual initiative. The optimal mix of planning and private economic incentives remains unsettled. But in a world with wants far in excess of the resources available to meet them, economic incentives lie inescapably at the heart of the problems faced by every society.[5]

[3] For some data on the "imperialism" issue, see Chapter 45.

[4] Although Marx was quite explicit about the death throes of capitalism, his writings are devoid of any picture of how he would see a true "Marxist" economy functioning after the revolution. Thus, it is hard to compare actual capitalist and communist developments with what Marx might have considered optimal. He predicted the gradual withering away of government after the workers' revolt, but failed to specify who would then run what parts of the economy and how. Clearly, the USSR, Communist China, and Cuba today are far from the governmentless economy Marx forecast.

[5] For a lively authoritative modern Marxist statement, see P. Baran and P. Sweezy, *Monopoly Capital* (New York: Modern Reader Paperbacks, 1966).

APPENDIX TO PART 4

Current research

Income distribution.   For the facts, begin with the *Economic Report of the President,* January 1974, Chapter 5. On the rich, see J. Smith and S. Franklin, "The Concentration of Personal Wealth," *American Economic Review,* May 1974; and H. Tuckman, *The Economics of the Rich* (New York: Random House, 1973).

Wages, unions, and collective bargaining.   Michigan's G.E. Johnson summarizes the impact of unions on relative wages, income inequality, and the rate of wage changes, in "Economic Analysis of Trade Unionism," *American Economic Review,* May 1975. A lively collection of analyses is assembled in *Unions, Management, and the Public,* E. Bakke, C. Kerr, and C. Anrod, eds. (New York: Harcourt Brace Jovanovich, 1967). Albert Rees and George Schultz's *Workers and Wages in an Urban Labor Market* (Chicago: University of Chicago Press, 1971) and P. Doerniger and M. Piore's *Internal Labor Markets and Manpower Analysis* (Lexington, 1971) illustrate other modern approaches to labor-market analysis.

There is a vast literature describing unions and the attitudes and behavior of organized labor groups. M. Perlman's *The Machinists* (Cambridge, Mass.: Harvard University Press, 1962) is a good example. Interesting studies of grass-roots union politics and policies are presented by L. Sayles and G. Strauss, *The Local Union* (New York: Harper & Row, 1961). The hottest collective-bargaining issue of this decade lies in the public sector. For a summary, see J. Stieber, *Public Employee Unionism* (Washington, D.C.: The Brookings Institution, 1973).

Discrimination.   *Still a Dream: The Changing Status of Blacks Since 1960,* by S. Levitan, W. Johnson, and R. Taggart (Cambridge, Mass.: Harvard University Press, 1975) provides a wide-ranging analysis of the current economic status of blacks. Both Richard Freeman, in *Brookings Papers in Economic Activity* (1973:1), and James Gwartney, "Changes in the Nonwhite/White Income Ratio," *American Economic Review,* December 1970, find substantial black economic progress; Lester Thurow's *Poverty and Discrimination* (Washington, D.C.: The Brookings Institution, 1969) reached less optimistic conclusions.

Research on economic discrimination against women is just beginning. For background information, see *Economic Report of the President,* January 1973, Chapter 4; and the colloquim on "What Economic Equality for Women Requires," *American Economic Review,* May 1972. Then see Victor Fuchs, "Recent Trends and Long-Run Prospects for Female Earnings," *American Economic Review,* May 1974, and the annual symposia on the problem in each May issue of that journal.

Among the few studies of the economic position of American Indians is Alan Sorkin, *American Indians and Federal Aid* (Washington, D.C.: The Brookings Institution, 1971); of Chicanos, Vernon Briggs, *Chicanos and Rural Poverty* (Baltimore: Johns Hopkins University Press, 1972).

Profits.   Debate over the division of the national income between wages and profits has been at the core of economics since its beginning. For a sample of recent work, see W. Nordhaus, "The Falling Share of Profits," *Brookings Papers on Economic Activity,* 1974:1; and G.L. Bach and J. Stephenson, "Inflation and the Redistribution of Wealth," *Review of Economics and Statistics,* February 1974—both somewhat technical.

PART **5** PUBLIC GOODS, income redISTRIBUTION, and THE PUBLIC SecTor

35 CHAPTER THE PUBLIC SECTOR

What should the government do in economic affairs? How much should it tax, and how much should it spend? The influential nineteenth-century English liberals argued that the primary function of the state was merely to set up and enforce certain "rules of the game" under which private enterprise could then be counted on to get goods efficiently produced and distributed. At the other extreme, the communists argue that all productive resources should be owned by the state, and that production and distribution should be directed in detail by the government.

The present attitude in America is somewhere in between, but much closer to the private-enterprise position. Most Americans believe in capitalism and a free, individual-initiative economy. Yet government action has grown far beyond the minimal regulatory duties prescribed by the laissez-faire advocates.

THE FOUR BIG FUNCTIONS OF GOVERNMENT

Modern government has four big economic functions. People may disagree widely on how far government should go on each front, but nearly everyone agrees that government needs to play all four roles.

Government as stabilizer: stably growing aggregate demand

Two centuries ago, Adam Smith didn't worry about booms and depressions, because they didn't exist. But with the emergence of our modern industrial society, economic instability became a major problem. There is no reason why aggregate spending (consumer plus business plus government) will automatically just match the growing output potential of the system at stable prices. Clearly, no private agency can assure the needed stable growth in aggregate demand. Government has to help, through monetary and fiscal policy, if we are to avoid the massive depressions and inflations that have marred the past. This was the topic of Part 2.

Government as policeman: the rules of the game

Even Adam Smith said that government has to act as policeman—to spell out some rules of the economic game and to see that people obey them. To live effectively together in a complex world, we have to agree that contracts will be respected. Equally important, competition must prevail in the marketplace to ensure the benefits of private enterprise, and only government can undertake this kind of regulation. The role of government in setting up and enforcing the rules of the competitive game was a main theme of Part 3. It's a vital role if a system like ours is to work effectively.

As indicated earlier, it's a complex question as to just how far government rules should go. Some, for ethical as well as economic reasons, would regulate minimum wages and working hours, the fares airlines can charge, wage bargains, and many other economic actions. Others demur. But nearly everyone agrees that where externalities bulk large, the marketplace will fail to produce the optimal output. If a paper mill produces dirty water and an objectionable odor as well as paper, government action is needed to see that paper buyers, in addition to paying the private costs of producing paper, pay for keeping the water and air clean. One way of doing this is for the government to forbid the pollution of water and air. Then the manufacturer's total cost will include pollution-control measures as well as labor, raw materials, and the like. Another approach is to impose a special tax on polluters and to use the funds to clean up the water or air. Either way, government action is needed. The line between simple government regulation and active intervention is often very fuzzy.

Government as provider of services: the public sector

There are some things a private-enterprise, profit-motivated system clearly will not provide adequately—national defense, highways, moon shots, police protection. Partly, these are instances of large externalities—social costs or benefits in addition to private costs and benefits. At the extreme are pure "public goods," such as the court system, where we clearly want the "product" but where there is no practical way of producing and selling it through the market. The critical point is the inability to withhold the benefits of the expenditure from anyone who wouldn't pay for them voluntarily. National defense is a public good.

In such cases, the government needs to act as a public store, providing the public good and collecting for it through taxes. Instead of relying on the private store to produce everything we want, we thus set up a public store alongside to handle what the private store can't or won't stock under the profit incentive. The public store is the "public sector," where we rely on political votes rather than the market to decide what to produce. The public sector allocates over 20 percent of all resources in the United States today, through taxes and government purchase of goods and services, although most of the actual production (say, of highways) is contracted out to the private sector. The taxes are the price we agree, through the political process, to pay.

Government as income redistributor: transfer payments

The fourth major economic function of government is to redistribute income—mainly

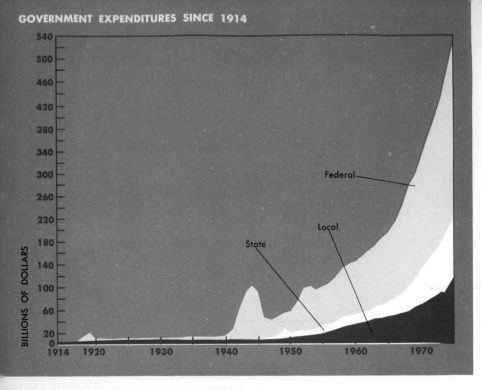

Figure 35-1
Federal spending has shot up during wars and again in recent peacetime years. State and local spending has grown rapidly since World War II. (Source: U.S. Treasury Department. Figures include social security.)

by taxing some persons and making transfer payments to others. The aged, the poor, farmers, the unemployed, and the vast middle-income classes—all receive large government transfer payments, financed mainly by taxes on others. Because the payments go mainly to middle- and lower-income groups, and our tax system is "progressive" (that is, the rich pay a higher percentage of their incomes than the poor do), this redistribution shifts income from upper- to lower-income groups. But, contrary to common belief, the great bulk of the redistribution is within the middle-income classes, who comprise the bulk of the population. They pay most of the taxes, and they get most of the government transfer payments—social security, housing subsidies, and the like. Government redistribution of money income is the second big activity of the public sector. It currently shifts about 15 percent of the total national income. Thus, the public store and income transfers together account for nearly a third of total economic activity. The public sector is a big part of the modern American economy (and of most other industrialized Western economies as well).

THE PUBLIC SECTOR TODAY

First, a look at the facts. In 1975, federal, state, and local governments spent over a half-trillion dollars, and their expenditures are rising every year. These expenditures have been roughly matched by growing tax collections. Thus, taxes, including social-security payroll taxes, are now about $2,500 a year for every man, woman, and child in the United States. Excluding military personnel, some fifteen million workers—one out of every six—are on government payrolls. You may not like having government so big, but there it is.

The growing role of government

It is useful to begin with some historical perspective. Look at Figure 35-1.

1. One major reason for the growth is war—past, present, and future. War is fabulously expensive. Today, $135 billion (one-third of the annual federal budget) is directly or indirectly attributable to past and future wars (including

veterans' benefits, interest on the national debt, and so on), although direct national-defense costs fell from 44 percent of the federal budget in 1968 to 25 percent in 1975.[1]

2. Partly, the increase is due to more people and higher prices. Since 1914, population has more than doubled and prices have quadrupled, so real government spending per capita has risen only about twentyfold, rather than the astronomical increase suggested by Figure 35–1—but twentyfold is a lot.

3. The biggest reason for the increase is that we have wanted our governments to do more for

[1] For the whole world, military budgets total nearly $300 billion, roughly equal to the total income of the poorest half of all mankind. In the last twenty years, the world has spent $3 trillion on military manpower and weapons. The United States and the USSR are the biggest spenders, but military outlays in 1975 totalled $40 billion in the poverty-ridden less-developed nations.

us—education, highways and streets, social security, welfare, sewers, moonshots, health. The nation's shift from a rural to an urban economy accounts for a big share of the state–local increase. But there's a lot more than just the cities involved. Now we want six-lane highways instead of dirt roads. Universal education and modern medical care are enormously expensive. And social security, unemployment insurance, health care, housing subsidies, and the like involve huge transfer payments, the fastest-growing part of the federal budget during recent years.

Figure 35–2 summarizes what governments spent in 1975 and the taxes they collected to pay the bills. The length of each bar shows the size of the tax or expenditure involved. Although Figure 35–2 speaks for itself, $500 billion deserves a closer look.

Figure 35–2
Federal, state, and local governments collected about $470 billion in taxes and spend about $525 billion (excluding intergovernmental grants) in 1975, including transfer payments. Chart does not include government-operated businesses, such as public utilities, but it does overstate net government outlays by including state–local spending of federal grants totaling $46 billion. (Source: U.S. Budget and Department of Commerce; preliminary estimates.)

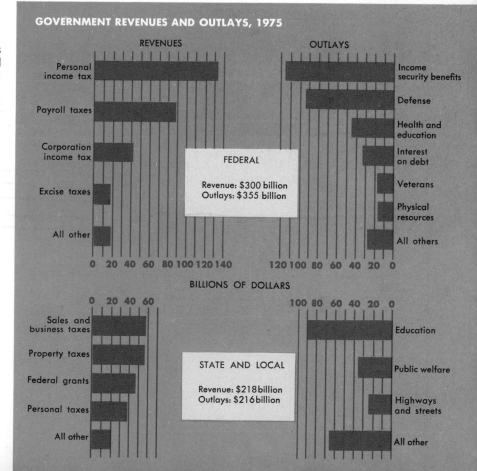

TOTAL GOVERNMENT SPENDING AND TAXES, 1975

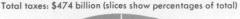

Total expenditures: $525 billion (slices show percentages of total)   Total taxes: $474 billion (slices show percentages of total)

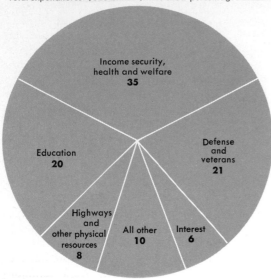 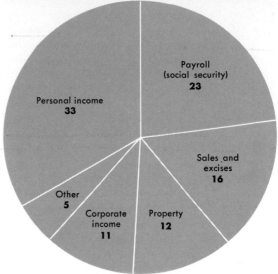

Figure 35-3
Income security, education, and national defense are the biggest government expenditures. Personal income and social-security payroll taxes provide over half the nation's tax revenues, sales and property taxes most of the rest. (Sources: U.S. Commerce and Treasury Departments; preliminary estimates.)

Government expenditures

Figure 35-3 combines government spending and taxes at all levels and shows the relative importance of each major tax and outlay.

On the expenditure side, three big recent developments deserve special attention.

1. First is the enormous growth in spending on "human resources"—social security, health, welfare, education, and the like. In earlier editions of this book, national defense dominated the total government spending picture. But no more! In 1973, federal income-security payments alone (mainly federal Social Security, welfare, and unemployment benefits) surpassed national defense, and when other human-resources spending is lumped in, the total is now nearly double that for national defense. Improvements

in Social Security benefits already built into the law will push benefits over $100 billion annually before 1980. The big increase has been in transfer payments—direct transfers of funds from taxpayer to beneficiaries, rather than government purchases of goods and services. Thus, the fourth of the big functions of government—redistribution of incomes—is increasingly dominating government budgets.

2. National defense, although it declined steadily in real terms and as a share of the total budget after the late 1960s, continues to be a huge cost, especially when veterans' benefits and other defense-related costs are included. Moreover, the total began to rise again in real as well as money terms after 1975, as military spending grew all over the world. (See footnote 1 above.) One B-1 bomber now costs $90 million, compared to only $700,000 for a World War II B-29. A new nuclear aircraft carrier in 1975 was estimated to cost over $1 billion, compared to only $6 million for a World War II carrier. Partly, this reflects inflation, but it mainly reflects the increasingly complex nature of modern war and defense.

3. The other big development of recent years

has been the rapid growth of state and local governments. Between 1960 and 1975, state and local spending rose from 10 to 15 percent of GNP. Today, state and local governments spend more ($210 billion) on goods and services than does the federal government ($123 billion, only $40 billion on nondefense). About twelve million people now work for state and local governments, only three million for the federal government. This distribution reflects the fact that the bulk of federal spending is on transfer payments (which require relatively few employees) and on goods and services contracted out to private industries (highways, aircraft, and so on), whereas state and local governments primarily provide services themselves (education, police protection, and the like).

Perhaps the biggest unsolved government finance problem today is the desperate plight of the central cities, which face spiraling costs of providing vital services (education, law and order, welfare, sanitation, and the like) at the same time that well-to-do businesses and individual taxpayers are moving to the suburbs, leaving a population that needs increasingly costly services but has little ability to pay taxes.

Taxes

Figure 35–3 also shows what taxes provided the revenue in 1975, combining federal, state, and local governments. Ours is increasingly a personal tax system. Over half of all taxes are raised that way—33 percent through personal income taxes alone, and 56 percent including payroll taxes. At the federal level, personal income and payroll taxes now bring in three-fourths of all revenue. Corporate-income, sales, excise, and property taxes account for most of the rest; property taxes still produce nearly all local-government revenue. If you feel you're taxed wherever you turn, you're right. We can't collect nearly a half-trillion dollars annually for our governments without making nearly everyone pay.

Who pays this half-trillion dollars of taxes? Chapter 38 is devoted to this question, but Figure 35–4 provides some *very rough* estimates of the burden of different taxes on families at different income levels in 1966. The burdens shown are for those who ultimately paid the taxes (for example, consumers when the cigarette tax or sales tax is passed on to them by retailers),

Figure 35–4
Most families pay about the same percentage of their incomes in taxes; the tax system is strongly progressive only for the 5 percent or so of families with incomes over $20,000. Most of the progression is provided by the personal and corporation income taxes. Data for 1966; estimates are subject to substantial disagreement. (Source: J. Pechman and B. Okner, *Who Bears the Tax Burden?* [Washington D.C.: The Brookings Institution, 1974], pp. 59 and 61.

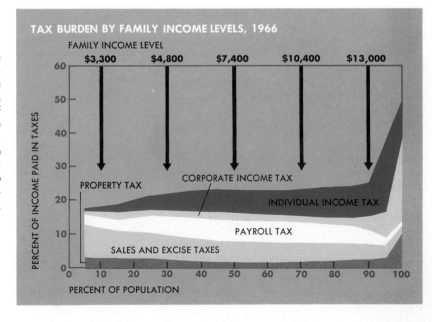

rather than the person who turns the money over to the government. For several taxes, we can only roughly estimate who bears the final burden, especially for the corporation income and property taxes. Different estimates that assume property taxes are mainly passed on to renters, for example, would show a substantially heavier tax burden on the very poor, and less on the rich. It is also important to recognize that the tax burdens are percentages of money income only; the poor, especially, get substantial additional transfer income in kind—for example, food stamps, subsidized housing, Medicaid, and the like—so the real burden of their taxes is less heavy than the picture suggests.

The estimates of Figure 35–4 suggest that the percentage tax burden was surprisingly similar in 1966 for the great bulk of American families, from very low incomes up to the top 5 percent or so who received incomes over $25,000. Only the very top of the income receivers in fact paid sharply progressive tax rates (that is, a higher percentage on large than on small incomes), and some other estimates (which allocate the burden of the corporation income and property taxes differently) show heavier burdens for the very poor and considerably less progression for the rich. The federal corporation and personal income taxes account for most of the system's progressivity; they took over 80 percent of the taxes paid by families with incomes above $50,000. Conversely, sales, excise, and payroll taxes are regressive; they take a larger proportion of low and middle than of high incomes.

Do these estimates still apply? Probably they are still roughly applicable, but you should shift all family incomes upward by 50 percent or so. Both inflation and growing real incomes have tended to move families up into higher tax brackets, especially for the personal income tax, where rates are sharply progressive at high income levels. But Congress has twice reduced personal income tax rates since 1966, mainly for lower and middle income taxpayers. In any event, the estimates should be viewed as only rough approximations. The problems of making such estimates are examined in more detail in Chapter 38.

REDISTRIBUTION OF INCOME THROUGH THE PUBLIC SECTOR

What is the net redistributional effect of these massive tax collections and public expenditures? Figure 35–5 provides a *very rough* set of estimates. The light bars show the benefits received from all government expenditures at different income levels, and the dark bars the taxes paid. While the tax system becomes sharply progressive only for high incomes, government benefits are a large percent of income for the poor but only a small percent for the rich. Thus, overall, the government redistributes income substantially from the rich to the poor. But the great mass of both tax payments and benefits are transfers within the big middle-income classes, as will be explained more fully in Chapter 36. The big redistribution is not from rich to poor, but from politically less-effective to more-effective middle-income groups.

It is important to recognize just what these rough estimates show. The tax burden estimates are similar to those in Figure 35–4, but note that Figure 35–5 shows no separate estimates for families above $15,000 income, so it doesn't show the sharp tax increases for high incomes or the more dramatic rich-to-poor shift when those families are shown separately. The benefit estimates are even rougher than those for tax burdens. They attempt to measure who gets the ultimate benefit from each government expenditure, including transfer payments. (That, incidentally, explains how benefits can be more than total income for the poor, since the usual annual family-income data exclude substantial non-money benefits like food stamps and Medicaid, which are included in the government benefits in Figure 35–5.) Estimating the final beneficiaries of old-age pensions, for example, is relatively easy. But for services such as national defense, education, police protection, and the like, only an arbitrary allocation is possible. The general picture shown by Figure 35–5 is almost certainly correct (remembering that all families over $15,000 are lumped together here), but don't take the details too seriously.

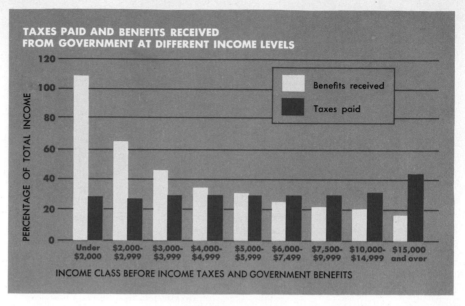

**TAXES PAID AND BENEFITS RECEIVED
FROM GOVERNMENT AT DIFFERENT INCOME LEVELS**

Benefits received

Taxes paid

PERCENTAGE OF TOTAL INCOME

INCOME CLASS BEFORE INCOME TAXES AND GOVERNMENT BENEFITS

Under $2,000 / $2,000-$2,999 / $3,000-$3,999 / $4,000-$4,999 / $5,000-$5,999 / $6,000-$7,499 / $7,500-$9,999 / $10,000-$14,999 / $15,000 and over

Figure 35–5
Low-income groups receive much more from government services and payments than they pay in taxes. The reverse is true for high-income groups. Estimates, for 1965, are rough. (Source: Tax Foundation.)

THE PUBLIC SECTOR
IN THE UNITED STATES AND ABROAD

How big is the public sector in the United States compared to that of other leading Western nations? Table 35–1 answers the question, and includes a few less-developed nations for comparative purposes. These figures show tax collections as a percentage of GNP in 1974, including taxes used to finance both real and transfer expenditures.

Taxes may seem heavy in the United States, but we are one of the lighter-taxed of the major developed nations. This reflects especially the broader range of social services provided by most West European governments. Note also the low figure for Japan, which maintains virtually no military establishment. Governments of poor, less-developed countries nearly all have relatively low taxes and expenditures.

Table 35–1
The public sector in different nations

Country	Taxes as percentage of GNP
Denmark	48
Sweden	44
Germany	37
France	37
United Kingdom	36
Canada	34
Italy	29
United States	28
Australia	24
Japan	23
Turkey	22
India	12

Source: Data for 1974, from Organization for Economic Cooperation and Development, except for India.

REVIEW

For analysis and discussion

1. What are the main economic functions of government?
2. Do governments spend too much? What are your criteria for deciding?
3. If a copy is available (for instance, in the *New York Times* about the third week of each January, or in *The Federal Budget in Brief*), read the president's most recent budget message to Congress. What are the major increases and decreases proposed from the preceding year? Do these changes seem desirable to you? What criteria have you used, implicitly or explicitly, in making these judgments?
4. Should the government do more to equalize the distribution of income? If you say yes, how do you justify your position to a doctor or businessman who is earning a large income and says he doesn't see why he should work hard to support others?
5. Locate your family income level on Figure 35–5. Assuming that these estimates are roughly accurate, do you feel that your income level is being treated fairly in the government's overall redistribution of income? Should you be taxed more heavily? Get more benefits from the government?
6. Recently, much concern has been expressed that in many areas, our educational facilities are inadequate, especially in the rural South. Should the federal government spend more money to improve these educational facilities—say, by building new schoolhouses, or making grants to raise teachers' salaries? If your answer is yes, who should pay? How much would you be willing to see your taxes raised to help pay for such new expenditures?

What should the public sector do? How much government will best serve the public interest? Who should get the benefits, and who should pay the taxes? To answer these questions, we need a theory of the public sector—a theory that will tell us when to turn to the public sector rather than relying on the private marketplace. This chapter provides such a theory: Where, public goods or important externalities are involved, or where we want to alter the distribution of income, we should turn to the public sector. Some people argue that government should also own and operate public utilities and other firms where economies of scale are too large to permit something approaching pure competition, but these issues were considered in Part 3 and are not reopened here. Last, the chapter compares the market and the political process as practical devices for reflecting the preferences of individuals in our society. For, as a practical matter, in using the public sector to achieve our goals, we face possible important "public-sector failures," just as we saw important "market failures" in the private sector.

WHAT SHOULD THE PUBLIC SECTOR DO?
Public goods and major externalities

As Part 3 emphasized, in the United States we have a strong tradition of trying private enterprise first, and turning to direct government operation only when private initiative clearly won't work. One major case of this sort is "public goods," which shades over into the case of major externalities of broad social concern.

Consider the case of national defense, or of the judicial system. Nearly everyone agrees that both are essential. Yet it is obviously impractical to rely on the private market to provide them; there is no feasible way to divide them up into salable units so that those who want to buy do so, while those who don't can be excluded from their use. If national defense is provided, Joe Nopay will get the benefit just as much as will those citizens who pay the bill. This is known as the "free-rider" problem. Where there is no way of keeping free riders from benefiting free, collective action to provide the "public good," with compulsory payment of the costs through taxes, seems the only practical way of providing the wanted good or service. Note that with a public good, moreover, the fact that A benefits does not lessen the possibility of B's doing so, while in a private-good case, if a unit of the good is sold to A, it will be unavailable to B. A lighthouse is another favorite economists' example. Once in place, the lighthouse rays are visible to all; there is no way of keeping free riders from benefiting; and the fact that A sees the light makes it no less useful to B.

The same principle can hold at a local level. Suppose a community is threatened by floods, which can be prevented by building a dam above the city. It may be clearly advantageous to all citizens to have the dam. Yet, without government intervention and taxation to pay the bills, the dam is unlikely to be built. The free-rider possibility will lead many citizens not to pay voluntarily, because once the dam is built, all are protected whether or not they paid. The dam is a public good.

Public financing and construction of facilities are often rationalized on public-goods reasoning when they don't really meet the crucial test above. For example, most big cities have sports arenas, often constructed partially or completely with public funds. The argument runs that big arenas are essential to draw major-league athletic teams, and such teams are a great benefit to the whole city. But in fact, only a small portion of the population of most cities attends such sporting events, and it is quite possible to keep the major benefits away from those who wouldn't pay enough for tickets to cover the full cost of the stadium; the stadium is not a true public good. Or take the case of public golf courses that operate on public subsidies. Citizens who enjoy athletics and exercise are clearly being subsidized by the general taxpayers, with a public-good rationalization that is, at best, only partially valid. Note that psuedopublic goods are not limited to athletics. Many cities also maintain publicly subsidized halls for symphony orchestras and ballets, which are attended by only a small fraction of the population, and an upper-income portion at that. Do the cultural gains benefit the city at large, so they could not be withheld from nonpayers, or do they benefit mainly those who attend the concerts and ballet performances? Is the free-rider problem there?

The line between public goods and private goods with major externalities is also sometimes hazy. For example, are highways a public good? In principle, no. Their use can be limited to those who pay; toll roads are an example. But some of the benefits accrue to those who never drive on the road—landowners, businesses, farmers, and others nearby who gain from the increased accessibility of their activities to others—and there is no practical way of shutting off these benefits once the road is built. We can say the highway is a quasi-public good, or we can call it a private good with major externalities. Education is a similar case. Think through the extent to which its public financing and operation depend on its being a public good or just a private good with major externalities. (See Case 30 at the end of this chapter for a futher exploration of the education case.)

For pure public goods and quasi-public goods where the product is very important and the externalities are both widespread and important, the common solution is for the government to take over production and distribution—national defense, education, streets, and space exploration are examples. Such services are generally financed by taxes and provided free (but not always—remember toll bridges, city transit systems, and partial tuition at state universities).[1] But **how much** the government should spend on any of these goods is less clear. In principle, government ought to increase production of each good up to the point where full marginal cost just equals full marginal benefit to society; but alas, there is no simple way of measuring either marginal cost or marginal benefits. Another alternative is simply to rely on a majority vote of the electorate, but as a practical matter, this is seldom feasible and, as we shall see, it would give dubious results even if it were feasible. What actually happens in the public sector in most cases, we shall examine presently.

Redistribution of income

The second big activity of the public sector is redistributing income, through money transfer payments and through transfers of real goods and services. Many people believe that the distribution of income produced by our largely individualistic, market-directed economy is too unequal. Even though the market may produce the most efficient use of our resources and the maximum total output consistent with our social and economic mores, the income-distribution result is ethically unacceptable. The spread between rich and poor is too wide.

This proposition is an ethical, or value, judgment, not one that follows from economic reasoning. But if one accepts it, direct government redistribution of money income from rich to poor is the simplest and most efficient way of attaining the ethically desired result. Without collective action to require the desired redistribution, it is unlikely to occur voluntarily with equitable treatment among the individuals paying and those receiving transfer payments. With government redistribution through taxes and transfer payments, all individuals could be left free to spend their after-tax and after-transfer-payment incomes as they wish, with markets responding to these expenditures. Welfare payments to the poor, financed by taxes on higher-income groups, are an example of such an in-

come transfer. Alternatively, government may intervene more directly with real transfers, especially where some additional ethical standard is involved. For example, we aid the poor partly in the form of food stamps and cheap public housing, presumably because we want to be sure they use their aid for these purposes rather than for automobiles, liquor, or other presumably less acceptable purposes. Figure 35–5 showed the substantial government redistribution of income from the rich to the poor.

But the most striking thing about government redistribution of income is that it is not primarily from the rich to the poor, but from some groups to others within the great mass of middle-income families—those in roughly the $5,000–$20,000 range, which includes most American families. Look back at Figures 35–4 and 35–5. The federal government alone now lists its cash "income-security" transfer payments at over $125 billion annually, enough to give the bottom fifth of the income distribution over $10,000 per family, even if they received no other income. Obviously, most of that money doesn't go to the poor. The big middle-income classes pay most of the taxes and receive most of the benefits from the government expenditures. Social-security and related income-security transfers are mainly from some middle-income groups to other middle-income groups, basically from workers to the elderly and other nonworkers. Similarly, federal government noncash housing subsidies mainly benefit middle-income home buyers and homeowners. Actual government redistribution of income as a practical matter is far from the common statement that we tax the rich to help the poor. Why, we shall explore in the following section.

Actually, income-redistribution and resource-allocation goals are often combined in the same government transfer programs. Poverty and education provide two examples. Income transfers to reduce poverty presumably rest largely on ethical grounds; yet, improving the lot of the poor can provide substantial positive externalities to the more fortunate, through higher future productivity, a more stable society, and the like. General free education is provided by government largely because education is considered a quasi-public good with large, widespread exter-

---

[1]For a pure public good, the proper economic charge is given unambiguously by the analysis of Part 3. Since the marginal cost of adding another user for national defense or our lighthouse is zero, the price should be set at zero; to exclude any users would be wasteful.

nalities. But it also involves a substantial element of income redistribution. We want to be sure poor children get a good education even though their families are unable to pay for it. But sometimes, combining the two objectives leads to perverse results. The farm-aid program over the past four decades is an example, as Chapter 23 pointed out.

THE MARKET VS. THE POLITICAL PROCESS

Government expenditure in a fully employed economy means a reallocation of resources or incomes—from taxpayers to recipients of government funds or services. The fundamental problem, here as in the private sector, is to use our limited resources most effectively to satisfy our wants.

Balancing costs and benefits in the public economy

In the process of deciding how much the government should spend, the principle of maximizing utility by equating returns at the margin suggests a rough guide to how big the public sector should be. Government expenditures should be increased up to the point where the marginal loss in giving up resources in the private sector just equals the marginal benefit from public expenditures. As long as the marginal gain is greater than the marginal loss, there is a net gain in overall welfare.

If society were a single unity, and *if* government were the all-comprehending brain of that unity, application of this principle would be feasible. The government could then weigh satisfactions lost against those gained. But in fact, there is no such all-comprehending brain. At best, we can make only the roughest sort of approximation. Yet, however rough its application, the marginal principle of economizing the use of scarce resources poses the question to ask in thinking about the right size for the public sector. And some progress has been made toward making such comparisons (see box).

Note that the chances of getting good government decision making on such issues go up as the size of the government unit goes down. At the local level, there is some chance that voters can weigh tax costs of proposed projects directly against potential benefits. And locally, there is a better chance than at state and national levels that legislators and administrators will be responsive to citizens' preferences.

Consumers' sovereignty and citizens' sovereignty

Does the political process or the market process do a better job of meeting people's desires on how our productive resources should be used? Allocation of resources through the private economy occurs primarily in response to consumers' money demands for goods and services. This is "consumers' sovereignty." In the public sector, we as citizens express our preferences for roads, rockets, and zoos by voting for representatives who in turn will, we hope, levy taxes and provide the government services we want. Thus, in the public sector, there is a "citizens' sovereignty," somewhat analogous to consumers' sovereignty in the private economy. But there are some very significant differences. Four, especially, deserve attention.

1. In the marketplace, voting for resource allocation is on a *one-dollar–one-vote* basis. In the public sector, in a democratic country, it is on a *one-person–one-vote* basis. Thus, in the private sector, the rich man has more votes than the poor man. In the public sector, a democratic system attempts, although not always successfully, to give each citizen equal voting power, regardless of whether he is rich or poor. Which way provides the better machinery for determining what to produce with our productive resources is a very fundamental question. Your answer will depend heavily on how well you think spendable incomes are distributed.

2. In the public sector, it is difficult for individuals to weigh specific benefits and costs, as we do daily in the private economy. In private life, Mr. X can consider carefully whether he prefers to spend $20 on football tickets, an electric razor, a new pair of shoes, or nothing at all. But when X votes to elect his representative, he has little opportunity to distinguish in detail between the things of which he approves and disapproves—he votes for one complex, ill-defined combination

COST–BENEFIT ANALYSIS
PLANNING–PROGRAMMING–BUDGETING

In recent years, economists have begun to tackle the problem of public-sector costs and benefits empirically through "cost–benefit analysis," an approach pioneered under Defense Secretary Robert McNamara in the 1960s but now applied widely. Should the government build a series of dams in the High Sierras to provide water for the cities and farms of California? To make a sound economic judgment, costs of alternative dams and water-distribution systems must be calculated, including possible ecological damage. Benefits must be estimated—for irrigation, for industrial use, for household use in cities, for electricity generated at the dam. For a multi-billion-dollar water system, the job of fully estimating the complex intermesh of costs and benefits is a difficult one. Massive changes in property values will result, and the calculations must cover many decades ahead. Effective cost–benefit analysis is one of the most difficult, but also potentially most valuable, branches of modern economics.

To extend cost–benefit analysis of proposed government programs, President Johnson instructed the Budget Bureau in the mid-1960s to push the spread of "Planning–Programming–Budgeting" (PPB) through the civilian agencies of the federal government. Should the post office automate its handling of mail? Should the Antipoverty Program spend more on retraining programs for the poor? PPB, utilizing cost–benefit analysis to help make government program decisions, is, in principle, the right move. But getting it used effectively in the political bureaucracy has proved a difficult undertaking.

At least, this kind of marginal cost–benefit analysis helps to avoid the nonsense often heard in public discussion of such issues. (1) For example, the assertion is often made that we "need" more police protection, or more classrooms; hence we should spend more for them. But such statements give no basis for intelligent economic judgment about whether the government should meet these "needs." To make that decision, the additional costs must be compared with the anticipated benefits. (2) Equally foolish is the common assertion that "we can afford" better schools and urban renewal; therefore we should have them. There are many things we "can afford." Their limit is set by our total productive resources. What and how resources should be used in the public sector can be decided rationally only by comparing expected marginal costs on each venture with expected marginal benefits.

against another when he chooses among candidates. And once he has voted, he has to take the package of virtues and failings rolled up in his representative—and to pay the taxes levied whether he thinks he gets his money's worth or not. Only when a specific decision is put to the voters is there an exception—for example, when a special bond issue to finance a new school must be approved by the voters. And even then, the individual has to accept the majority verdict. Consumers' sovereignty clearly gives him greater power both to indicate what he wants for his dollars, and to get it.

3. The public sector thus involves a big element of compulsion. Even with democratic processes, once our elected representatives decide we're going to put a man on Mars, you and I must pay the taxes to support the project, however foolish we may think it is. Not so in the private sector. There, I'm not forced to pay for something I don't want.

Admirers of the market process thus stress the ability of the market to give effective representation to majority votes while protecting minority interests. The market has a built-in protection for every interest. The rich man gets the most votes, but the little fellow has his say too, in proportion to how much he has to spend. One dollar counts one vote, and no man needs to spend a dollar on any product unless he personally decides it's worth a dollar to him.

4. As a practical matter, even in a democratic government like ours, few issues are decided on a simple town-meeting, majority-rule basis. As we

shall see, properly reflecting many diverse voters' interests is very difficult even in theory, and in operating politics, the legislative and administrative processes of government favor some groups over others. Our governments are more responsive to the folks back home than we often give them credit for. Representatives are elected from fairly small areas, which gives local minorities a chance to be heard. In legislatures, business is largely done by committees and in informal discussion, which work out compromises that can command majorities among legislators representing widely diverse interests. But the interest groups that are well organized generally fare well at the expense of the "little man," the consumer, the great unorganized masses. Such interest groups often have a lot at stake, and it pays them to work hard to influence legislation and government practices. Conversely, individual consumers and taxpayers often have too little at stake to justify a major investment of time and money to fight each special-interest group.

Moreover, without the test of the market, there is no assurance that any public service will actually render benefits greater than its cost, or that it will be dropped when the need for it is past. But here again, the case can be overstated. At least in the federal government, a new budget is enacted each year, with widespread publicity about major issues. The arguments aren't all on the side of either the private or the public sector.[2]

Often, advocates of bigger government stress how an ideal democracy would reflect the wishes of the people, in comparison with all the practical shortcomings of the market system. Conversely, private-sector enthusiasts often compare an ideal, perfectly competitive economy with the painful shortcomings of practical politics in action. Clearly, we ought to compare ideal with ideal, or the two sectors in practical operation, to make a meaningful judgment as to which will serve us better under what circumstances. Parts 3 and 4 stressed a number of important "market failures." The public sector, as a practical matter, may have comparable political failures.

[2] See, for example, *Economic Analysis and the Efficiency of Government*, Report of the Joint Economic Committee, U.S. Congress, 1970.

Private preferences and collective decisions

Consider a publicly owned, polluted lake surrounded by ten homes. The cost of cleaning up the lake is $10,000, and the potential benefit in improved fishing, swimming, and boating is calculated at $1,500 by each of the surrounding ten families. Clearly, collective action to eliminate the pollution is in the public interest. Perhaps informal negotiation will do the job, but the free-rider problem is likely to rear its ugly head. Certainly, with a larger number of families, transactions costs will be large and formal government action is likely to be the only feasible way of achieving the obviously desirable social result. Presumably, in a town meeting of the lakeside residents, a motion to levy an equally distributed tax of $1,000 per family to finance the cleanup would pass unanimously. Democratic government action looks impressive in solving the problem.

But now assume, probably more realistically, that different families attach different values to a cleaner lake, as in Table 36–1. Should the local government clean up the lake?

If we look only at the aggregate benefit, the government clearly ought to levy the tax and clean up the lake. And it is easy to predict that the vote will be 6 to 4 in favor of precisely that action. Has democratic government produced an efficient allocation of the community's resources? Maybe, but not from the viewpoint of families 7 through 10.

Now consider a more complex case. The cost of cleaning up the lake is the same, but the benefits are shown in Table 36–2. Here, the net village benefit is negative. Yet a clear majority stands to gain from the action. Should the lakeside government levy the tax and clean up the lake? Will it? How would you vote if you were family 1? Family 10?

If you believe in simple majority-rule democracy (or perhaps if you're an ardent ecologist), you will approve of the proposed government action here. But if you worry about protecting the "rights" of minorities, you will be uncomfortable. **In a real sense, the majorities in both Tables 36–1 and 36–2 are imposing externalities on their neighbors just as much as the dirty**

Table 36-1

Family	Tax cost	Benefit	Net gain
1	$ 1,000	$ 2,000	$1,000
2	1,000	2,000	1,000
3	1,000	2,000	1,000
4	1,000	2,000	1,000
5	1,000	2,000	1,000
6	1,000	2,000	1,000
7	1,000	500	−500
8	1,000	500	−500
9	1,000	500	−500
10	1,000	500	−500
	$10,000	$14,000	$4,000

Table 36-2

Family	Tax cost	Benefit	Net gain
1	$ 1,000	$1,100	$ 100
2	1,000	1,100	100
3	1,000	1,100	100
4	1,000	1,100	100
5	1,000	1,100	100
6	1,000	1,100	100
7	1,000	500	−500
8	1,000	400	−600
9	1,000	300	−700
10	1,000	200	−800
	$10,000	$8,000	− $2,000

steel mill did back in the earlier section. They are doing it through a "political failure" of the democratic process; the steel baron did it through a "market failure."

Interest groups and the "rational-ignorance effect." Now consider a case that will, at least at first, seem simpler. A chemical plant pollutes the air in a city, to the disadvantage of the residents. The air could be cleaned up to a level acceptable to 70 percent of the residents by plant changes costing $1 million. The other 30 percent demand still cleaner air, which would cost $2 million. There are 100,000 families, so the cost of the first improvement would be $10 per family, that of the second $20 per family. A benefit table like the preceding ones would show that virtually every family thinks it would be worth over $10 to get rid of the worst of the pollution. Should the government levy at least the $1 million tax and subsidize the chemical company to clean up to at least the minimum standards?

Absolutely not! you probably reply. Pass a law and make the factory clean up itself. That rich corporation has no right to pollute the clean air. Make the company pay for it out of profits, or pass the added costs along to its customers in higher prices. So you urge the city council to pass the antipollution measure without delay. Here, you can righteously insist that someone else pay the whole cost.

Will the council act? Not clear, is the answer. For the chemical company will surely point out that the higher costs will mean higher prices, less

sales, fewer jobs for the town's citizens. They may even shut the plant down, throwing everyone out of work, reducing sales of the city's merchants, and so on. The company will argue that it cannot compete against other companies that do not face such stringent clean-air laws. If the plant makes fertilizer that many of the citizens buy, their interests as consumers will also enter into the picture. Besides, the company may argue, the plant was there before most of the residents in the city, who thus knew about the bad-smelling air when they moved there. What do you predict the council will do?

As a practical matter, democratic governments seem highly responsive to pressure groups, often little concerned with the "public interest"—the welfare of the mass of the taxpaying voters. This is easy to explain in self-interest terms. Suppose a small group wants the city council to spend $100,000 on a new park that will benefit them especially. The cost to the typical taxpayer will be, say, $10. We can be sure the special-interest group will push hard for the park. But most voters, to whom the cost will be only $10 each if the measure passes, will pay little attention. For $10 it would be scarcely worth the cost of digging out information on the matter and taking time to urge council members to vote against it. (This is sometimes called the "rational-ignorance effect.") Thus, it is not surprising that the council may vote the subsidy to the special-interest group, even though it may be unjustifiable on grounds of the "public interest."

Note, too, that the rational-ignorance effect can go a long way toward explaining why some people don't bother to vote at all. This is one of the basic problems of democracy.

The politics of income redistribution. Last, turn to the question of how effectively collective action meets the wishes of the public in redistributing income. As we saw above, government does redistribute some income from the rich to the poor. But the bulk of income transfers are from more to less politically effective middle-class groups.

One theory is that the well-to-do use the state as a mechanism for making gifts to the poor. A second is that in a democracy, the poor are able to use their votes to get income transferred from the rich. Neither of these explains the modest rich-to-poor transfers, compared to those among the middle-classes. An alternative, self-interest theory is often advanced by those who face the facts as to what transfers government actually makes; most people look out for their own interests, some more effectively than others.

The simplest view is that the many poor outvote the few rich to transfer income from rich to poor. The bottom 51 percent can use their majority to take income away from the top 49 percent. But it is far from clear that the bottom 51 percent of the population works together in any such coalition; the top of that group are not poor by far, and their interests diverge substantially. The really poor are only 10 percent of the population, or 20 percent of the votes in the bottom-half coalition. Clearly, such a small minority cannot dominate the political coalition. Thus, who in the bottom 51 percent is going to get how much of the income taken from the upper half is likely to be a crucial issue in forming and maintaining a political coalition. Indeed, the upper-income 49 percent could become the majority merely by wooing over the top 2 percent of the lower coalition. Thus, not the poor, but the large lower- to middle-income group in the lower-half coalition is likely to end up as dominant in any bargaining process. Unless the ethical values of the rich lead them to coalesce with the poor, the resulting income transfers may well be *from* the well-to-do but primarily *to* the middle classes, which is roughly what we observe.

So far, we have assumed that government programs are made simply to accomplish transfers among income groups per se. But realistically, organized groups in the political process are usually centered differently—they are farmers, the elderly, homeowners, college students, owners of oil wells, and the like. The poor are not only relatively small in number but also generally not well organized politically. Collective action tends to shift income toward organized groups, mainly comprised of the middle classes, although often the stated rationale is to help the poor. And the taxes must come largely from those same middle classes, because that is where the bulk of the taxable income is. Social security, farmers' aid, housing subsidies, and higher education in state universities are all examples. In each case, tax funds are used to provide benefits primarily to the middle classes. Social-security benefits go mainly to those who have a record of past earnings; farm aid is paid largely on the size of the farmer's output; government housing subsidies are largely to those who can afford to buy their own homes; students at subsidized state universities come heavily from middle- and upper-income families.

Thus, as a practical matter, democratic government operates to a considerable extent through coalitions and organized interest groups. Only on major national issues does anything approaching a simple majority view of the public dominate. The same is true to a lesser extent at state and local levels. Ours is a pluralistic society, and nowhere is this evidenced more clearly than in the political process. In a huge, complex society, it is difficult to see how anything like the old New England town-meeting ideal of democracy can operate. Add to this the realistic fact of large bureaucracies as a way of running big government, and political failures in the public sector look as pervasive as market failures in the private sector.

Social choice: the problem of social balance

One last look at the central issue of consumers' versus citizens' sovereignty from another angle may be helpful. Those who say the public sector is too big have a basic presumption that individual freedom to spend in the marketplace should guide the allocation of resources; any other allocation of resources is presumptively inferior. But Professor Galbraith has made a forceful counterargument in his bestseller, *The Affluent Society*. He argues that such general distrust of government has led to a serious underallocation of resources to the public sector (leaving national defense aside). In the world's richest economy, we allocate less than 25 percent of GNP to satisfying all nondefense collective wants through public goods and services.

Galbraith argues that our economy is so rich that we can readily afford more and better public services, that we need them badly, and that the alternative is generally wasteful civilian consumption just to keep our economic machinery going. Yearly automobile model changes, plush night clubs, and mink coats are symbols of conspicuous consumption, meeting demands developed by pervasive advertising. Yet our public services are barely adequate. Our cities are marred by slums. Our streets are jammed. Our air and streams are polluted. Our police forces and local governments are often peopled by incompetents, so poorly paid as to be constant targets for graft. Few of our symphonies and art museums receive adequate public support. Somehow, he says, we have no effective machinery to translate the obvious need for greater public services into reality.

Why do we often assume that a dollar spent on taxes is wasted, while a dollar spent in the market provides a valuable return? Galbraith suggests that as taxpayers, each of us sees the cost of public services to himself, but the benefits are so widespread and generalized that it is hard for the individual to value them. But lots of taxpayers look at it differently, arguing that they prefer to judge for themselves where they can get a dollar's worth of results for each dollar they spend.

America can clearly "afford" more public services and the end to such negative externalities as pollution if we want them. The test of Galbraith's position lies in whether we collectively want them badly enough to pay for them, and by that test, it is far from clear that government should be bigger. Social cost–benefit analysis, program by program, is the basic foundation for rational decision making in the public as in the private sector.[3] Fundamentally, in our individualistic society, the public interest is what 200 million Americans say it is. But how best to get their diverse preferences registered and compromised is a very difficult problem.

[3] For an excellent summary of these issues, see Peter Steiner, "The Public Sector and the Public Interest," in *The Analysis and Evaluation of Public Expenditures* (Joint Economic Committee of Congress, 1969), Vol. I.

REVIEW

Concepts to remember

This chapter presents the basic theory of the public sector and introduces important new concepts. Be sure you understand the following:

public goods	cost–benefit analysis
free riders	"political failures"
citizens' sovereignty	"rational-ignorance effect"
balancing alternatives at the margin	

For analysis and discussion

1. Does consumers' sovereignty or citizens' sovereignty provide a better process for allocating society's productive resources?
2. As a practical matter, are the "market failures" of the private economy or the

"political failures" of the public economy more serious barriers to having individuals' preferences carried out effectively?

3. Chapter 36 suggests that we should rely on the public sector only where important externalities or public goods are involved, or where we want to alter the distribution of income. Is this the proper guiding principle? Can you list cases where it should not be followed?

4. How effectively do you expect democratic political processes to take care of minority interests? Would the market do better or worse?

5. Many argue that our national priorities should place a higher value on better public services—education, slum clearance, public health, and so on—than on more consumer goods. Analyze this argument.

6. What is cost–benefit analysis? How can it help in deciding what projects government should undertake?

7. a. Many people believe that there is always a presumption in favor of reducing government expenditures. Do you agree?

   b. Why, if at all, is the presumption above more defensible than a presumption that government spending to provide public services should be increased?

THE VOUCHER EDUCATION PLAN

Nearly everyone agrees on the importance of assuring all youngsters a good education, at least through the high school level. But many parents, and professional educators too, are dissatisfied with the educations provided by our public schools, which all children must attend unless they happen to be among the very few with parents rich enough to afford a private school. All the rest of us face a monopoly seller of public education, and many parents find school officials and teachers impervious to suggestions for change.

The "voucher education plan," with both conservative and liberal supporters, has gained considerable attention in recent years as a possible means of improving the situation. Its most extreme form shows the central issues most clearly, although less drastic alternatives are also feasible. Its essence is this: Abolish the public schools. Then let each state or community continue to collect in taxes the same amount it is now spending on public education, determined in the usual democratic political fashion. Instead of spending this sum on public schools, let it divide the total up and give a voucher of equal value (say, $1,000 annually, if that is what is now being spent) to the parents of each child, this voucher to be spent on education at any school of the parent's choice as long as the school meets minimum state standards.

A wide range of private, profit-seeking schools would spring up, seeking to obtain the business of different parents with different educational objectives for their children. While state standards would presumably require some subjects like reading and arithmetic for all beginners, high school curricula might range widely from college-preparatory to vocational focus. Instead of being faced with a monopoly school as now, consumers would be free to buy the education they want where they think they get the most for their voucher. Just as government decides how much national defense and how many highways we should have, but contracts out laying the concrete and building the bombers on a competitive basis, so the voucher plan would count on private enterprise to provide more varied, responsive education for children in response to the vouchers given to all parents.

This plan attempts to combine the best of the public and the private sectors. (1) Only the public sector can ensure that every child gets his minimum guaranteed level of education; this is essential on grounds of equity and attaining the positive externalities from widespread education. It is insured by the government voucher for each child. (2) But most evidence suggests that profit-seeking competitors (the private sector) do the best job of actually producing what consumers want to buy; so we should take advantage of this fact in education, one of the most important services we buy. Use the profit incentive to produce most efficiently the kinds of education we consumers want for our children. Who, the private-enterprise advocates ask, will try harder to educate our youngsters better—the local public-school principal and teachers, who are responsible only to the school board, or their counterparts who must satisfy you to get the dollars to stay in business? [4]

Are you in favor of the proposed voucher education plan to supplant the present public-education system? Does the plan offer a way to obtain the best of both the public and private sectors in providing education for our children?

---

[4] Introduction of any such plan would, of course, need to be spread out over a number of years, but disregard the transitional problems here to focus on the main issues.

CHAPTER 37 POVERTY, INEQUALITY, AND GOVERNMENT POLICY

Poverty is as old as history. America is rich, and by the standards of most of the world poverty has been virtually eliminated here. Most of our "poor" in New York live as well as the average worker in Moscow or Mexico City, vastly better than the Indian peasant. Even by our own standards, only about 10 percent of our people live in poverty. But even in our affluent society, there is an economic underworld of poverty, and most Americans agree on some collective (government) measures to level up these very low incomes at least somewhat. Partly, these measures involve redistributing income directly from the middle and upper classes to the poor; partly, they involve improving poor people's chances of earning higher incomes in the market economy. Often the antipoverty programs seem to miscarry, and most of the benefits go to politically effective sectors of the middle classes instead.

Even if poverty were eliminated by leveling up very low incomes at the bottom, the issue of inequality would remain. Chapter 30 presented the data on equality and inequality in modern America. Money incomes have become somewhat more equally distributed over the last century, and the great mass of American families now fall in the "middle" income range of $5,000 to $20,000. But the top fifth of all families still receive about 40 percent of all income, the top 5 percent about 15 percent of the total. In 1976, the federal government spent over $150 billion in "income-security" transfer payments (social security, welfare, unemployment insurance, Medicaid, and the like), mainly financed by taxes on the middle- and upper-income classes—a massive transfer of incomes through the public sector. Was the economic inequality that remained still too much? How much income inequality should there be? What would be the fairest and most efficient distribution of income in a society like ours?

Let us consider first the "poverty problem" and government measures to deal with it, then the broader question of how far the government should go to lessen overall inequality.

POVERTY—THE PROBLEM

There is no one accepted definition of poverty. The most widely used definition is that suggested by the Social Security Administration and used by the government in compiling its statistics. This definition says that, as of 1975, any urban four-person family receiving less than $5,500 in money income was considered "poor." For rural families, this figure is reduced by 30 percent. For larger or smaller families, the figure is adjusted appropriately.

These poverty-line figures were based on an extensive analysis of the living standards of lower-income families in the 1960s. They were arrived at by taking the cost of a reasonable but very moderate diet, and multiplying it by three. Each year, the figure is adjusted to take inflation into account; thus, the "real" level defined as poverty remains unchanged.[1]

What is considered poverty, however, changes with the times. Some people argue that there is a poverty problem only in the eyes of the do-gooders. Twenty years ago, the median money income of all families was about $4,600 (in 1975 prices). Then, $2,000 was widely considered the poverty level, and nearly half of all families then fell below what we now call the poverty level. As

Figure 37–1 shows, economic growth has steadily pushed most families above the minimal levels that seemed reasonable a generation or two ago. But our aspirations have risen with rising incomes. In 1975, there were about 25 million "poor" Americans, using the SSA definition— about 12 percent of the population.[2]

Who are the poor?

In 1962, Michael Harrington wrote a book, *The Other America,* that touched the conscience of many Americans. The other America, Harrington wrote, is the world of the poor in the midst of plenty—a world of desolation, of hopelessness, of bitterness and resentment, of slums, of discrimination. It is the world of blacks and Puerto Ricans living in the great city slums; of old men and women living alone in rented tenement rooms; of poor Southern farmers living in ramshackle huts without plumbing; of fatherless families whose mothers struggle to support their children; of failures and rejects for a dozen other reasons.

The poor, Harrington wrote, live in a subculture of their own. Most of them feel—with apathy or resentment—that no one cares. It is a world whose inhabitants are isolated from the mainstream of American life and alienated from its values. It is a world whose occupants are sometimes concerned with day-to-day survival, where minor illness is a tragedy. Last, it is a world turned in on itself in its values and its habits, a world in which the poverty of the parents is visited upon the children.

Each year, many families move up from the

[1] For a full description of Social Security Administration procedures and historical data, see U.S. Department of Commerce, *Poverty in the United States* (*Current Population Reports,* Series P-60, 1969).

[2] Using money income as a test can overstate the problem. Many poor people receive substantial transfers in kind (food stamps, housing subsidies, Medicaid, and the like) that make their real income higher than the money-income figures suggest (see Figure 35–5). The poor Southern farmer with an annual income of $3,000 and six children eats better off the land than the arithmetic suggests. Many elderly poor have accumulated assets, and draw on them to supplement their current incomes; thus, their actual consumption is well above the incomes they report. As a college student, you are probably another example. In many ways, consumption would be a better measure of poverty than is current money income, and such a measure would show an appreciable number of the "poor" families better off than they seem. But the SSA measure suffices as a reasonable approximation. (All 1975 figures are preliminary.)

ranks of the poor, and some families slide down below the imaginary line. But the great bulk of the poor stay poor.

To understand the problem of poverty, you must recognize that the poor differ widely. Five groups loom large.

Blacks. Although only 7 million of the 25 million poor in 1975 were nonwhite, over 30 percent of all black families are poor. Many poor black families live in the rural South; over 60 percent of black farmers are in the poverty group. But increasingly, they have moved to the Northern city slums. Those who live in the cities have incomes 30 percent below those of whites with comparable education. In the city slums, over half of black youths are high school dropouts. Over half of all poor blacks live in family units headed by females. Other minority groups are also poor (25 percent of all persons of Spanish origin were poor in 1975), but their numbers are far less than the blacks involved.

Farmers. About 17 percent of all farm families are poor, much higher than the urban rate. Rural poverty is concentrated in the South. A substantial portion of poor Southern farmers are the blacks mentioned above. Government aids to agriculture provide little help to poor farmers; the money goes largely to the big, well-capitalized farmers.

Old people. Old age often brings poverty rather than adequate retirement. About 1.3 million families in which the husband is over 65 are poor; this is about 15 percent of all such families, and the elderly account for nearly 20 percent of all the poor.

Fatherless families. Nearly half of all poor persons live in families with a female head, and 35 percent of all women left alone to provide for their children are poor; for nonwhites, the figure is 55 percent. The woman who has to earn her family's living faces many lost workdays and consequently job instability. The breakdown of the family is near the core of the difficult social problems of the city slums. Probably not one out of three black children in poor families who now reaches age 18 has lived all his life with both his parents. Nationwide, the number of children on public "welfare" has risen from less than one million to over eight million since 1950, with most of the increase during the 1960s, a decade of growing prosperity and falling unemployment. In New York City alone, over a million mothers and children were on welfare in 1975, out of a total population of under eight million.

Others. About one-third of all poor people do not fit into any of the groups above. They live in depressed areas; they have poor motivation; they have low intelligence; most have had little education; there is little demand for the jobs they can do. By the test of the market, they are failures, the rejects of our modern economy.

One generalization applies to all these groups. Most come from poor families and have been poor all their lives.

Why are the poor poor?

Why are the poor poor?

Inadequate aggregate demand and slow growth. When there is a recession, unemployment increases the proportion of the population below the poverty line. Conversely, prosperity brings more jobs, especially for marginal members of the labor force who are last to be taken on. A major depression is a catastrophe for the poor.

But only a small fraction (perhaps 10–15 percent) of the poor even in the recession year of 1975 were "unemployed," as measured by the unemployment statistics. Most unemployed are only temporarily out of work and find other jobs in a few weeks, or months at most. Thus, their annual incomes stay above the poverty level. Over half the poor are simply out of the labor market; children are the largest group. Many of the poor are elderly people, past their working years. Many in the slums have given up looking for work.

A closely related fact is that poverty piles up in periods of slow economic growth. Conversely, fast economic growth erodes poverty. This is shown dramatically by Figure 37–1.

Low productivity. The message of Chapter 31

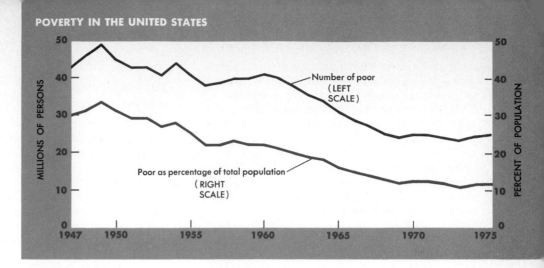

POVERTY IN THE UNITED STATES

Figure 37-1
Rapid economic growth persistently reduced the number of poor people in the United States after World War II until 1970. Since then, recessions have slowed this progress. (Source: U.S. Census Bureau.)

was that individual's incomes depend primarily on the marginal productivity of their labor and the capital they own. If this is correct, given a reasonable level of aggregate demand poor people in the labor market are by and large poor because their marginal-revenue productivity is low. They are poor because they are not worth more to employers in a profit-motivated economy. Or, if they are elderly, they are poor now because they did not adequately plan ahead or did not have an adequate life income to provide a reasonable retirement income through savings.

This is a harsh conclusion, and one that is only partially correct. But it has a strong core of truth. Over 60 percent of all poor families are headed by an individual with less than an eighth-grade education, only 20 percent by individuals who completed high school. Many older people, although seeking work, can offer only limited services in the market. Women attempting to support their children inescapably lose more time than others. Many of the adult poor have no skills, or have obsolete ones.

Market imperfections and discrimination. If there is effective competition among employers, this competition will bid the wage of each worker up to the value of his marginal product. And the value of his marginal product will be highest where he makes the greatest contribution to producing goods and services that consumers want to buy. Conversely, if there are market imperfections that prevent workers from finding employment where their productivity is highest,

or that prevent effective competition from forcing wages up to that level, society's resources are not most efficiently allocated, and workers do not earn the maximum incomes they could obtain in a competitive economy.

A major market imperfection, and a major cause of poverty for nonwhites, is discrimination—in education, jobs, access to medical care, on nearly every score. If employers, rationally or irrationally, refuse to bid for black workers on the same basis as they bid for white workers, it is to be expected that black incomes will be lower. In fact, black incomes average 30 to 35 percent lower than those for whites of the same years of education, areas of residence, and sex. Just how much of nonwhite poverty is accounted for by discrimination is sharply debated by the experts. Some estimates suggest about $15 billion as the minority-income shortfall due to discrimination, but this is only a very rough approximation.[3]

Many economists blame unions and the government itself for important job barriers. Many craft unions have de facto barriers against nonwhites for apprenticeships and union member-

[3]See for example, J. Kain, *Race and Poverty* (Englewood Cliffs, N.J.: Prentice-Hall, 1969); and L. Thurow, *Poverty and Discrimination* (Washington, D.C.: The Brookings Institution, 1969), especially Chaps. 7 and 9.

493

ship, and limit memberships for whites as well, thus in effect blocking them from higher-paying jobs. And the federal minimum wage law of $2.30 per hour as of 1976, however admirable its purpose, shuts many low-productivity workers out of jobs that might be there at lower wage rates for such workers, especially poorly educated, poverty-group teenagers. But on the whole, government has helped to reduce job discrimination, and union policies have apparently on balance helped as well.

Absence from the labor force and the vicious circle of poverty. Nearly 60 percent of all poor families are headed by individuals who are not in the labor force. Many of these are elderly people; others are discouraged youths and mothers of fatherless families who have given up looking for work. Over 40 percent of all poor persons are children. Thus, the problems of poverty, family instability, and insecurity in old age are inseparably intertwined. Others are out of the labor force for a variety of reasons—ill health, lack of motivation, family circumstances, or simply because they have given up hope of finding a job. "Welfare" has helped to break up poor families, because in many states no aid can be given to a family headed by a male of working age, so fathers leave in order to make their families eligible for welfare.

Beyond these economic causes, most observers add a socio-economic analysis. Poverty breeds poverty, in a vicious circle. A poor individual or family has a high probability of staying poor. The poor live largely in slums or in backward rural areas. Their children do not learn to read, to write, even to speak well. They grow up to apathy or resentment, and they go to poor schools with other poor children. They lag far behind children in middle-class schools, and their dropout rate is high—not surprisingly, for their is little in their culture to make them care about education. When the poor are sick, they stay sick longer because they have inadequate medical care. Thus, they find it harder to keep jobs. Broken homes are common. Often there is little motivation or hope to rise from the vicious circle of poverty, either for the young or for adults.

ANTIPOVERTY POLICIES: LEVELING UP THE BOTTOM

The preceding analysis, together with the macro and micro theory of earlier chapters, suggests two broad lines of attack on the poverty problem. One involves raising the demand for the services of the poor and their marginal productivity in the market. The other, facing the fact that many of the poor are inevitably out of the labor market, involves direct redistribution of income from the better-off to the poor. The former is obviously preferable, since it increases the real output of society, while the latter merely redistributes the existing level of output. History suggests that progress in reducing poverty comes mainly through increasing the size of the national GNP pie, not through slicing up a fixed pie so as to give the poor more and the rich less. One basic problem, as the data of Chapter 31 suggested, is that the incomes of the rich don't go very far when divided up among the masses; another is that most Americans show little enthusiasm for really radical surgery on high and middle incomes to raise the incomes of the poor.

Measures to increase total output and worker productivity

Increased aggregate demand and falling unemployment can help to lessen poverty, although they give jobs and higher incomes only to those who have a service to sell. The best estimates suggest that reduction of the overall unemployment rate from 4 percent to 3 percent would reduce the population below the poverty line by only about 1 percentage point. Nonetheless, a prosperous economy is a big help toward alleviating poverty, and it makes sense on other grounds as well. Prosperity helps reduce barriers against minority groups as labor markets tighten, provides more on-the-job training for marginal workers, and opens partial employment for the elderly. Macroeconomic theory tells us that we need not have depressions and mass unemployment if we maintain aggregate demand at the level needed to buy the high-employment output of the economy. Much poverty due to unemployment is a preventable waste.

As a closely related measure, accelerating economic growth over the long run (that is, faster growth in output per capita) provides a fundamental approach to eroding poverty. Over the 1950s and 1960s, economic growth reduced poverty by about 1 percent a year. If that rate could be maintained (remember that the 1960s included a cyclical upswing), poverty as it is now defined would be entirely eliminated in ten years. But the nearer poverty approaches zero, the harder it will be to make further gains. The remaining poor will be increasingly those insulated from labor markets—the aged, the disabled, what some have called the "hard-core poor."

Investment in human beings increases their productivity, just as does investment in nonhuman wealth. For many reasons, society's investment in the poor falls far short of its investment in most individuals who rise above poverty. The poor live in slums, in squalor. They receive short and poor education. They get little job training in schools—or on the job, because they so often find no employment. They receive inadequate medical care. If we want to raise the productivity of many of the poor, more investment in education and training is the first prescription of the preceding economic analysis.

Improving labor markets. Many of the poor are effectively isolated from jobs by lack of information, immobility, and inertia. This is especially true of the rural poor in the South. But it is also true in the slums of the great cities, where for thousands of unskilled and poorly educated teenagers and adults there is no practical channel into the jobs that are opening up elsewhere in the economy, even in the same city.

Better job-training programs, employment exchanges, guidance and counseling services, and the like could help those who suffer merely from inadequate information or are immobile because of financial difficulties. Better information, better education, and better training programs for both youth and adults make sense both to fight poverty and to improve the efficiency of our economic system. More subsidized day-care nurseries for poor working mothers could both improve their economic productivity and get underprivileged youngsters off to a better educational start.

Reduction of discrimination is essential to reducing poverty in minority groups. Substantial progress has been made. Over 40 percent of all black families received over $10,000 in 1974, compared to only 20 percent in 1960 (in constant 1974 dollars). For Northern black families headed by a male aged 25 to 34, incomes in 1974 were 95 percent those of comparable whites. But the black unemployment rate remains nearly twice that for whites. The number of black "professional and technical" employees more than doubled during the 1960s, compared to a 40 percent increase for whites. But the discrimination problem is still a massive one. Debate over how to eliminate racial discrimination in jobs, housing, education, everywhere, far transcends issues of how best to reduce poverty. The answers are at least as much political and social as they are economic.

Redistribution of money incomes

Direct money-income transfers (grants to the poor, financed by taxes on the nonpoor) are the other line of attack on the poverty problem. It recognizes that many poor people are out of the labor force. It has the virtue of letting us see the actual cost of the program. And it gives recipients of aid freedom to spend their incomes as they wish, in contrast to programs that force them to take aid through food stamps, housing subsidies, medical assistance, education, and the like. (Remember Case 4 on the food-stamp program, in comparing money grants with grants-in-kind; there are important arguments on both sides.) To raise the incomes of all today's "poor" to the SSA poverty level would require grants of about $12 billion, or about 1 percent of the GNP.

Fighting poverty by this approach does not raise society's total real income; it merely redistributes what we now produce without using the productive potential of many poor. Moreover, such direct cash grants to all the poor might raise serious problems on the incentive front, because individuals now working might prefer to take direct subsidies and avoid work. Thus, the actual cost of such a direct-subsidy approach to the poverty problem would probably be substantially larger than the $12 billion indicated.

At the extreme, if everyone in the poverty range who now works stopped, the total cost would obviously go up sharply and total GNP might drop temporarily. But it would still be a small percentage of GNP.

Welfare. "Welfare," or "relief," is the name generally applied to cash transfer payments by the government to the poor. Welfare has been the main form of direct government aid to the poor, and it has grown rapidly. In 1955, about 6 million people received $3 billion of welfare. By 1975, the totals were over 18 million recipients and $16 billion, with about half the money provided by the federal government and half by state and local governments.

The current "welfare" system, just about everyone agrees, is a mess. It has four big failings: (1) It excludes a lot of the poor people, because in many states, if there is an adult male in the family, even though he earns nothing or less than the poverty level, the family is not eligible for welfare. It also tends to break up families, because in those states, fathers tend to leave their families so the families can get welfare payments. Thus, only about half the poor receive any welfare payments. (2) The welfare system in effect imposes at least a 67 percent marginal tax rate on any welfare-family earnings, because welfare payments are reduced by two-thirds of any earnings from work. This is a direct incentive not to work. Worse, if work raises a family's income above the eligibility level for welfare, it may also lose its eligibility for Medicaid, food stamps, and housing allowances. (3) Benefits are very unequal because they are set by the individual states. They varied from $39 to $263 per person per month in the early 1970s, with the very low benefit payments in the deep South. (4) Costs of administering the complex welfare system have used up a substantial part of the funds allocated to helping the poor, and the administrative red tape has confused many poor people and kept them from receiving needed benefits.[4]

[4]An authoritative analysis of the welfare system, with detailed recommendations for changes, is provided by *Income Security for Americans*, Report of the Subcommittee on Fiscal Policy, Joint Economic Committee, December 5, 1974, based on a three-year study of the problem. See especially

The "negative income tax". Recently, a novel proposal to reform the welfare system has been advanced simultaneously by Milton Friedman, an adviser to Barry Goldwater and President Nixon, and James Tobin, an adviser to President Kennedy. It is to substitute a "negative income tax" for part or all of the present welfare system—to combine compassion with incentives by (1) guaranteeing *every* family or individual a basic minimum income (a negative income tax for the poor instead of the positive income tax we now pay if we have taxable incomes); and (2) permitting everyone to keep, say, half of all his earnings in addition, up to some moderate income level where he would slide over to a regular taxpayer status. It should be easy to see how the NIT flows directly from the economic analysis of the present chapter. It is widely favored by economists of a variety of political persuasions, because it does rest so directly on basic economic analysis of the situation and because it would minimize administrative complexity and waste. In 1969 and again in 1971, President Nixon proposed a modified version of the NIT in his new "Family Assistance Plan" to replace the present welfare system. But Congress turned the proposal down, for a variety of reasons, including some strictly political ones. One can argue over the details of the negative income tax, but it is hard to escape the basic economic analysis that underlies it. And widely diverse groups, including the prestigious big-business Committee for Economic Development, have come out for the plan.

Table 37-1 shows how the plan might work, assuming a guaranteed minimum income of $3,200 for a family of four and a marginal negative income tax rate of 50 percent, combined with the regular 1974 federal income tax.

If a family has no private income, it would receive from the government a $3,200 annual income (negative income tax), possibly in weekly or monthly checks—see columns 4 and 5. If the family earns $1,000, it keeps the $1,000, but its payment from the government drops by half

Chaps. 1, 8, and 9. For a vivid, perceptive picture of welfare in operation, see Susan Sheehan, "Welfare Mother," *The New Yorker*, Sept. 29, 1975.

Table 37–1

Negative income tax example[a] (family of four)

| Private income | UNDER 1972 TAX LAW | | | WITH NIT ADDED | |
	Tax (−)	After-tax income		Net benefit (+) or tax (−)	Income after NIT and tax
$ 0	$ 0	$ 0		$ + 3,200	$3,200
1,000	0	1,000		+ 2,700	3,700
2,000	0	2,000		+ 2,200	4,200
3,000	0	3,000		+ 1,700	4,700
4,000	− 140	3,860		+ 1,200	5,200
5,000	− 290	4,710		+ 700	5,700
6,000	− 450	5,550		+ 200	6,200
6,400[b]	− 511	5,889		0	6,400
7,000	− 603	6,397		− 300	6,700
7,920[c]	− 760	7,160		− 760	7,160
8,000	− 772	7,228		− 772	7,228

[a]On the assumption that the government would provide a minimum family income of $3,200, with a marginal income tax rate of 50 percent to supplement the regular tax system.
[b]End of government direct subsidy.
[c]Point of after-tax equality with 1974 tax system.

that amount. Net result: Its after-tax income is $3,700, up $500. Since each family can keep 50 percent of all earned income, its dollar aid from the government will not fall to zero until its earned income is $6,400. Moreover, since its marginal tax rate is not to exceed 50 percent, exact after-tax equality with the present tax system would not be reached until an income of $7,920, when it is back on the regular tax system, with a tax of $760.

How much would it cost? The minimum cost of the plan in Table 37–1 would be around $8 billion annually, assuming that no one stopped working because of the new NIT benefits. Probably some who now work would work less, and estimates of double the $8 billion look more realistic to some experts. Note that if we want the maximum work-incentive effect from the NIT, the cost will be still higher, since the marginal tax rate on earned income must be reduced for both the poor and the large numbers just above the poverty line. If we reduce the marginal tax rate to 25 percent to increase the work incentive, the total cost skyrockets—probably to $30 billion or more annually for the Table 37–1 plan. Obviously, the cost would also vary greatly for different minimum-income levels.

How much aid?   All this leaves unanswered the question of how much aid should be given to the poor, through income transfers or other measures. Table 37–2 summarizes *federal* aid to the poor in 1975. It understates the total, since it includes only programs specifically providing aid for poor people; it excludes, for example, the share of general social security benefits, education, unemployment payments, and the like that help the poor along with other beneficiaries. And it omits state and local programs for the poor, totaling at least $10 billion in 1975.

Table 37–2

Federal aid to the poor, 1975

	Amount (in billions)
Public assistance (welfare, etc.)	$ 8.9
Medicaid	7.0
Food (mainly food stamps)	5.1
Social Security supplements, veterans' and survivors' pensions, etc.	4.7
Housing	2.4
	$28.1

Is this too much, or too little? The answer will depend in considerable part on your notion of equity in the distribution of income. But it may depend also on issues of incentives—incentives for the poor to work, and incentives for those in higher-income groups who have to give up some of their earnings to help the poor. For some people, the ethical issues dominate—what minimum-income level *should* be provided for everyone, whether he works or not? For others, it's a straight economic cost–benefit comparison. How much will the "richer" 88 percent of the population above the poverty level gain by spending the money to get the other 12 percent out of poverty—through producing a more stable socio-political environment, checking the urban decay associated with poverty, increasing poor people's abilities to support themselves in the future, and the like?

Focusing more specifically on transfer payments, Table 37–3 summarizes the $177 billion of "income-security" benefits provided by the federal government in 1976. These massive transfers (in money, in kind, and in special tax concessions or loopholes) vastly exceed the transfers to the poor shown in Table 37–2. The great bulk of the income-security benefits, although often justified on grounds of helping the poor, are in fact largely transfers to the middle-income classes.

Table 37–3

Federal income-security benefits, 1976

	Amount (in billions)
Federal cash benefits:	
Social Security (OASDI)	$ 71.4
Unemployment insurance	17.9
Federal-employee benefits	16.5
Veterans' benefits	8.8
Public assistance	9.7
Railroad retirement	3.4
Other programs	1.2
Subtotal, cash benefits	$128.9
Federal outlays for in-kind benefits:	
Food and nutrition	8.0
Health care	25.3
Housing	2.3
Subtotal, in-kind benefits	$ 35.6
Special tax benefits:	
To the aged	6.4
To veterans	.7
To welfare recipients and working mothers	.3
To unemployed	3.8
To disabled	1.8
Subtotal, tax benefits	$ 13.0
Total benefits	$177.5

Source: *Special Analyses, Budget of the U.S. for Fiscal Years 1976 and 1977.*

INEQUALITY, EQUITY, AND EFFICIENCY

How equally should income be distributed in an economy like ours? Should the tax and transfer programs summarized in the preceding paragraphs be increased, modified, or eliminated? The answer will presumably depend in large part on your notion of what constitutes **equity**, in part on issues of **incentives and efficiency**.

Economic analysis offers reasonably objective criteria as to what ways of allocating our scarce resources are more efficient than others. These were summarized in Chapter 22, and we have used them throughout the book. They tell us what systems of income distribution will contribute most to an efficient allocation of resources in response to consumer demands. But economic analysis offers no comparably objec-

tive tests as to what distribution of income is most equitable. It comes down fundamentally to a question of personal values, not of objective analysis.

Most Americans subscribe to the basic proposition that "all men are created equal." From this, a basic presumption may evolve that all men should be economically equal—but this does not necessarily follow. Three different definitions of equity (or fairness) are commonly stated, or implied, in discussions of income equality and inequality.

1. **Everyone should have an equal start in the economic race. Thus, equality of opportunity is the central notion.** If, from an equal start, some obtain larger incomes than others (by working harder, being smarter, being luckier, or

producing more of what others will buy), so much the better for him. There's nothing unfair about that kind of inequality, in this view. This concept of equity implies government action to ensure equality of opportunity, but not government action to reduce inequality based on winning the economic race from a fair start. Whatever inequality arises from differing economic contributions to the general welfare, as measured by the market test (see number 3 below) is fair, if everyone has an equal start. Inequality reflecting personal choice (to be a minister rather than a lawyer) would be acceptable. Some questions, if you accept this concept: How should we ensure equal opportunity to babies born with white and black skins, into poor and rich families, in urban slums and on Western ranches? Will equal expenditure on education for all do the job? How much, if any, transfer of accumulated wealth from parents to children should be permitted?

2. **Everyone should have an equal income. Equality of results is what counts.** If you accept this notion of equity, the implications are clear. To produce an equitable society, government should tax the rich and subsidize the poor until all incomes are equal, however much or little each individual contributes to producing the income distributed. This is presumably the foundation of socialist doctrine: "From each according to his abilities, to each according to his needs."

One line of argument in support of the position is that the marginal utility of one dollar is always less to a rich man than to a poor man; therefore, total utility will be increased by taxing the rich and subsidizing the poor. But this is clearly unacceptable reasoning. We have no objective way of comparing the marginal utilities of different individuals, and many challenge the proposition. Consider a millionaire and a $5,000-a-year waiter. The first dollar transferred from the former to the latter may plausibly be assumed to hurt the millionaire less than it pleases the waiter. But what of the situation when the rich man has already paid out nearly half his income in taxes, while the waiter has now become rich beyond his wildest dreams? There is no objective way of comparing marginal utilities and disutilities between the two, but it now intuitively seems far from clear that the once-millionaire's marginal disutility is less

than the now-rich waiter's marginal utility from the transfer of one more dollar. One may prefer this concept of equity, but he should not kid himself that its preferability can be logically demonstrated by such reasoning.[5]

3. **Everyone should have the income he earns by contributing to consumer wants in a market-directed society, unless he voluntarily chooses to transfer part of it to others.** This can be combined with concept 1 above requiring an equal start for all in the economic race, since incomes reflect earnings on nonhuman capital as well as labor. Or it can be combined with the socialist proposition that all capital should be collectively owned; the concept would then imply that an income distribution that gives each individual what he earns by his own labor in a competitive market economy is fairest. The main thrust of this concept is that inequality is acceptable, indeed desirable on efficiency grounds, when it reflects merit in contributing to producing what others want to buy.

Worldwide movement toward the "welfare state" appears to imply widespread belief that it is "unfair" for some people to be as poor as they are and others as rich as they are. With government taxes nearing 50 percent of GNP in some Western European nations and about 30 percent in the United States (see Table 35–1), serious questions of conflict between equity and efficiency goals may arise, if they have not already done so. How much of a person's income can the state tax away without seriously reducing his incentive to earn more? In principle, we can have the *efficiency* of a market-directed, individual-incentive economy to get the goods and services that we want produced most efficiently, *and* the *equity* of whatever income distribution seems fairest, by transferring incomes from rich to poor once they have been earned in the market and letting the market respond to the spending of the redistributed income.[6] But if the required taxes seriously reduce incentives to earn, we face a painful choice between equity and

[5] Suppose a stock-market crash cuts the wealth and income of all rich people by half, but does not change this income of others. Clearly, incomes are now more equal. Is the result more equitable?

[6] For a micro example, see Case 30, "The Voucher Education Plan."

efficiency. Many observers believe they see serious strains on this score today in some of the major West European economies, especially the U.K. and Scandinavia. And the debate rages increasingly in the United States over each budget and tax-reform bill.

Last, it is important to reemphasize that the income redistribution brought about by government taxes and transfer payments is by no means limited to shifts from rich to poor. Indeed, perhaps an even more basic issue is how good a living current workers will be willing to provide in the future for nonworkers, such as children, the aged, and the unemployed. Our rapidly growing income-security program involves large payments by current workers (through payroll and income taxes) to support nonworkers, who may or may not be poor. Social Security benefits alone will approach $100 billion annually by 1980. Although Social Security is commonly thought of as insurance, with benefits financed by each individual's contributions while he is employed, its benefits bear no direct relationship to each individual's contributions, and no "reserve fund" has been built up, as with private insurance, that will finance future benefit payments. Instead, Social Security is a massive income-transfer program, from the working population to the elderly who no longer work. Fundamentally, payroll taxes on workers each year finance the payments to retired beneficiaries that year. The accumulated "reserve fund" totals less than one year's benefits. Today

and in the future, anything like the level of benefits specified by existing law will be feasible only if current workers pay the taxes to provide the benefits.

Today (as of 1977), each worker pays a payroll tax of about 6 percent on the first $16,800 of his earnings, and the employer pays a comparable tax (which is probably passed on to the worker), making a total of about 12 percent. Therefore, the typical worker whose wages are less than $16,800 pays 6 (or 12) percent of his total income, while those with incomes over $16,800 pay a smaller percentage of their total incomes. Thus the payroll tax, second in size only to the personal income tax, is regressive. On the other side, although most Social Security beneficiaries have only modest incomes, many have substantial total retirement incomes, from private benefits and their own savings as well as from Social Security, so some income transfer may be from lower to higher incomes. A roughly comparable case arises with much publicly-supported university education; the average family income of students is higher than that of the state's taxpayers, who finance a substantial part of each student's education.

What income transfers will be supported by the public as equitable and the growing clash between equity and efficiency will predictably be major questions of public policy over the decade ahead. More on them in the following case, and in Chapter 38.

REVIEW

For analysis and discussion

1. How unequal should incomes be? What criteria do you use in deciding?
2. Should government aid to the poor be primarily in money or in kind? Is your answer consistent with the analysis of individual utility maximization in Chapter 5?
3. "The simplest and cheapest approach to eliminating poverty would be simply to give a tax-financed cash subsidy to each poor individual big enough to raise his income above the poverty level, perhaps through the negative income tax. This would avoid the waste and misdirection of elaborate programs and would give each individual freedom to spend his income as he pleases." Do you agree? Why, or why not?

4. "A strong aggregate-demand policy to ensure high employment would solve the poverty problem and eliminate the need for the hodgepodge of government measures adopted over recent years." Do you agree?

5. What is your program to reduce or eliminate poverty in the United States?

6. How good a living can the current workers in our society afford to provide for nonworkers, such as children, the aged, and unemployed? What criteria do you use in answering?

7. What is your test of fairness in the distribution of income? Does it lead to any conflict with attaining the most efficient production of wanted goods and services?

8. Which of the "income-security benefits" listed in Table 37–3 do you consider justified? Which ones not? Would you be willing to pay $100 more in personal taxes to increase any of them?

HOW MUCH SOCIAL SECURITY CAN WE AFFORD?

The American Social Security system was set up in 1936, during the Great Depression, to provide some protection against poverty after retirement for wage and salary earners. The early benefits were about $30 a month for retired workers; these benefits were financed by a payroll tax of 2 percent on the first $3,000 of each worker's wages, matched by an equal tax on the employer. The plan was seen as a forced saving, or compulsory public retirement-insurance plan for workers who might not otherwise save enough to provide a living post-retirement income for themselves.

Since the 1930s, Congress has repeatedly extended the coverage of the system and raised benefits and taxes to finance them. In 1965, it added basic medical benefits for all participants over 65, through Medicare. (There are special provisions for wives, disabled workers, and other special cases.) Today, the Social Security system has become a financial giant, with nearly 100 million participants and tax collections and benefit payments of nearly $100 billion annually (the largest category in the federal budget). It covers nearly all private workers (most public employees are covered by parallel systems), and minimum cash-income payments are guaranteed for all aged poor. Social Security was originally conceived as roughly parallel to private insurance, accumulating a reserve fund with the payments made by participating individuals. But the insurance principle was soon discarded, and the system is now essentially a massive annual transfer of income from working taxpayers to nonworking retired workers and their families. Although there is a small reserve fund of about $40 billion, this equals less than one year's liabilities to retirees, while the present actuarial value of future liabilities to participants in the system is between $2 and $3 trillion.

Benefits vary somewhat according to how long the individual has worked, but a minimum income of about $3,000 is guaranteed to each poor couple whether or not they have contributed to the plan, and annual benefits total about $5,500 for a couple where the husband has worked for a long period at good pay in covered occupations. Most medical costs are covered for those over 65, with a minimum payment by the individual on each illness. Participants between 65 and 72 receive reduced benefits, however, if they continue to work and earn over $2,760; for each dollar earned over that amount, Social Security benefits are reduced by 50 cents.[7]

By law, both the taxes and the benefits are scheduled to rise as average real wages rise and as inflation occurs. In 1977, the annual tax per worker will total about $2,000 (including the employer share, which is passed on to the worker in most cases—see Chapter 38). By the time you retire at age 65, under present law you and your spouse will collect a retirement benefit of $3,150 per month—that's *per month*—assuming only a modest price inflation of 2.5 percent annually.

Recently three developments have led to widespread alarm concerning the state of the Social Security system. First, in spite of the large increases in annual tax collections, which are scheduled to continue to finance rising benefits, the system has recently been running substantial "deficits" of around $10 billion per year. Thus, unless either benefits are increased more slowly or taxes more rapidly, the reserve fund will be exhausted by about 1980.

Second is the heavy impact of payroll taxes as they have increased annually under the new benefit and tax schedules adopted by Congress in 1972. Benefits were "indexed" (tied to the rising cost of living) and tied also to the steadily rising level of real wages, which requires a rapid increase in annual taxes to meet these liabilities. Over the past decade, average monthly benefits have nearly tripled, and the annual tax burden per worker has risen from about $200 to $1,000 (double that, if the employer's share is included). And the annual tax increases must be even larger over the decade ahead under present law if inflation continues.

Third is the growing recognition that the

[7] For a brief summary of the system, see *Economic Report of the President*, 1976, pp. 111ff.

Social Security system is not an insurance plan at all, and that there is no accumulated reserve fund to guarantee each participant's benefits at retirement time. Worse, as was noted above, recently payments have been exceeding collections, so even the small reserve fund will be exhausted in a few years unless some action is taken. While full financial information on the system has been available to all, most Americans still think of it as insurance and view their retirement benefits as bought by their contributions during their working years. Recognition that future benefits are dependent on the willingness of Congress to levy the current taxes needed to pay the benefits has come as a major shock to many. What if congressmen (the voters) decide they are unwilling to levy the required heavy taxes on themselves, the workers, to support the retired nonworkers in the future?

As benefits and taxes rise, another range of questions has been widely debated. As was noted in the text, the payroll taxes used to finance Social Security are regressive. Critics argue that this regression should be reduced or eliminated by raising the $16,800 limit on taxable income, perhaps to cover all of each participant's income; or alternatively, by giving up the whole pretense of "insurance" and simply providing retirement and related medical payments for everybody out of general tax funds. If the president of General Motors has a salary of $800,000, they say, let him pay the 6 percent tax on all of it, making a tax of $48,000, which would still only be the same tax *rate* as that of the lower-income workers. A shift to general-tax-system financing would go even further, making the burden of financing retirement benefits progressive (see Figure 35–4). But opponents protest that retirement benefits are already limited to about $5,500 annually, no matter how much one contributes in taxes. To make the $800,000 businessman pay $48,000 annually when he will collect only the same modest retirement benefit as low-income workers seems a perversion of equity. Indeed, the higher-income person is likely to collect even less, since he is more likely to keep on earning above the permissible amount after age 65,

and hence to receive no retirement benefits at all until he is 72.

Still another line of attack on the present system is that it provides the wrong incentives to keep older people employed as happy, useful members of society. To get the full Social Security retirement benefits, people must now stop working at age 65. Maybe this made sense in a depression like the 1930s, when we were trying to spread the few jobs around, but now it merely helps to guarantee that the human resources of older people will be wasted, even though they may want to work.

One last set of facts: When Social Security was adopted, there were very few workers eligible for retirement benefits, and the ratio of taxpaying workers to beneficiaries was large. By the fifties, the ratio of workers to beneficiaries was about 4 to 1. Reflecting the low birthrates of the thirties and forties, the ratio of workers to older people has fallen steadily and is now about 3.2 to 1. If present demographic trends continue, in fifty years the ratio will be down to about 2 to 1.

What, if anything, should be done to reform the nation's Social Security system? In particular:

1. Are benefits too large, or too small? Should they be indexed to rise with inflation and with rising real wages?

2. Who should pay—the workers, or general taxpayers? Should taxes be directly related to the benefits each individual will receive on retirement, as in private insurance?

3. Should we abandon the position that Social Security is different from other government income transfers (welfare payments, unemployment insurance, food stamps, etc.), and simply merge it into the annual federal budget-making process?

4. How much work are you willing to do now to support the retired nonworkers in society? How much should the next generation be willing to do to support you when you reach 65?

5. Should the government accumulate a reserve fund from current workers' tax payments to finance future benefit payments, as private insurance companies do? (In answering, think back to Part 2 and the likely effects on aggregate demand, real output, and prices.)

CHAPTER 38

Taxes and Tax reform

Everyone complains about high taxes. But if we want public goods and services, we must get resources transferred from private to public use. If we assume full employment, taxes are the most straightforward way to get the necessary funds, since they take private incomes that would otherwise bid for the resources. With full employment, more government spending without more taxes means increased total spending and inflation; then resources are taken away from those whose incomes fall behind during inflation.

With government spending over a half-trillion dollars annually and headed higher, an efficient and equitable tax system is very important. The multi-billion-dollar federal budget may not mean much to you—the figures are too big. But the fact that when you leave college with an average, middle-class income of perhaps $12,000, you will start turning over to Uncle Sam and to state and local government units over $3,000 each year puts the dollars and cents in more meaningful terms.

GOOD AND BAD TAXES

Few subjects generate as much heat in popular discussion as taxes. But all too often, the heat is unaccompanied by light. You can't judge intelligently what are good and what are bad taxes until you've clarified the criteria by which you're judging. Since many people don't bother to clarify, it is little wonder that they often disagree violently on what taxes should be.

The same broad social objectives we've used before can be pointed up conveniently in three questions in analyzing the tax system:

1. **Progress.** Does the tax encourage or hinder investment, employment, and stable economic growth?

2. **Freedom and individual choice.** Does the tax hinder or aid the allocation of resources in accordance with consumer preferences? Does it interfere with the free choices of individuals and businesses in earning and spending?

3. **Equity.** How equitably is the tax burden distributed? Government taxing and spending significantly affect the distribution of income. Unless government tax collections exactly equal the benefits provided to each family, the issue is not *whether* the government will redistribute income, but *how*.

Progress: stable economic growth

Economic growth depends on an intricate complex of factors, but especially on technological advance, on saving and investment, on education, and on hard work by the labor force. (See Chapters 43 and 44.) Any tax is a drain on someone's income from work or investment, and in general, taxes will deter economic growth (although the related government expenditure may have an offsetting effect). But one tax **structure** may be less restrictive on (more conducive to) rapid growth than another.

Theory tells us that taxes that bear on profits and other returns from investment will discourage **growth**, compared to taxes that fall on personal income and consumption. Similarly, taxes that give special advantages to expenditures on investment, research and development, and education are an incentive to faster growth. We have learned over the past decade how to provide such incentives—the special "investment tax credit" of 1962, and more generous depreciation guidelines for plant and equipment are examples.

Tax contribution to **stability** is equally important. We want taxes that tend to keep after-tax incomes growing at a reasonably stable rate, not fluctuating sharply. Individual and corporate income taxes, for example, provide "built-in tax flexibility." When national income rises, these tax liabilities rise even more rapidly, because individual income tax rates are progressive and because corporate profits subject to taxes rise sharply in business expansion. The opposite is true when national income falls. This built-in flexibility tends to damp the swings in private incomes and spending. By contrast, a tax that is insensitive to income changes (for example, the property tax) makes no contribution to stabilizing private spending.[1]

Noninterference with free choices

If we want free private choices to determine the allocation of resources and the distribution of income, a "good" tax system should be neutral in the sense that it does not affect these results. But a tax system as pervasive as ours cannot be completely neutral. In a few cases—for example, taxes on tobacco and liquor—we consciously discourage the use of particular products through taxation. In these cases, the tax is used to bring resource allocation into line with our social preferences.

But in most cases, the distortions produced by taxes on individual commodities (excise taxes) are unfortunate. These distortions occur because higher taxes on particular commodities lead people to buy less of that commodity than they otherwise would, relative to other commodities. Or they lead people to work less in particular occupations than they would otherwise choose. By distorting resource use this way, a tax may produce a "deadweight" loss to the economy—a cost against which there is no offsetting gain. Such a cost is in excess of the resources given up by the private sector through taxation to finance public expenditures. The economy is misled into producing the wrong combination of goods.

[1] Remember, however, that built-in flexibility tends to damp down any changes in GNP, whether or not we are content with the existing level of employment. Thus, such built-in flexibility may produce undesirable as well as desirable results.

To minimize this deadweight loss while raising any given amount of revenue, we should use taxes that produce the smallest changes in private production and consumption behavior (excluding cases with externalities). A "head tax" (a lump-sum tax on each person regardless of income or expenditure) would rate high on this criterion. Because no one could avoid it, it would not affect his economic behavior much, if at all. Taxes on commodities with highly inelastic demand (for example, a salt tax) are similar, since people buy about as much of the product at the higher (taxed) price as before. Conversely, excise taxes on commodities with elastic demand are apt to be highly distorting in their effects.[2]

"Equity" in taxation

A tax system should be equitable as well as nondistorting and conducive to stable growth. Equity means different things to different people, and economics cannot say which is "right." But it can clarify the results of different taxes so you can better judge for yourself which seem most equitable.

Three different concepts of equity were outlined in the final section of the preceding chapter. A somewhat different statement is useful in considering tax policy.

The "ability-to-pay" principle. Taxation according to ability to pay is widely favored. This generally means that people with higher incomes should pay more than those with lower incomes. It rests on the underlying presumption that a more equal distribution of income would be more equitable.

Even if we agree on net income as the best measure of ability to pay, how much more should higher-income people pay? At what rate should different incomes be taxed? Some argue that the rate should be proportional—that is, the same percentage of each person's income. For example, the tax rate might be 1 percent, giving a $10 tax on $1,000; $100 on $10,000; $1,000 on $100,000. More argue that rates should be progressive—that is, a higher-percentage tax on

high incomes than on low (for example, $5 on $1,000; $100 on $10,000; $2,000 on $100,000). All ability-to-pay advocates argue against regressive taxation, which takes a larger percentage of income from the lower-income groups.

It is important to see that ability to pay as a base for taxation has no exactness or "absolute" validity. There is no objective way of deciding whether rates should be proportional or progressive, or, if progressive, how steeply progressive. As Chapter 37 stressed, there is no way of comparing objectively interpersonal disutilities of taxes paid by different people at different income levels. Although some presume that the marginal disutility of a dollar paid in taxes will always be less for a high- than a low-income taxpayer, such comparisons are not logically defensible, and even at an intuitive level, the proposition seems very doubtful as more taxes on the rich reduce their after-tax incomes to nearer the rising low incomes (see the final section of Chapter 37, for the reasoning).[3]

The "ability-to-pay" phrase is, nonetheless, convenient for working purposes, since in America there is general agreement that progressive taxation of income and inheritances represents the primary application of the ability-to-pay principle. When the term is used in this book, therefore, it will mean progressively higher tax rates as net income rises, without specifying the rate of progression. In the last analysis, the issue of how much progression is "equitable" is an ethical one. It boils down to the question of who should get how much of the national-income pie—a fundamental and explosive question. This issue of relative tax burdens at different income levels is often called the issue of "vertical" equity. Look back at Figure 35–4 for estimates of how progressive the present tax system is.

The benefit principle. The second concept of equity is that each individual should have the

---

[2]By this same criterion, to avoid distorting effects, marginal tax rates should be low relative to average rates; on this score, our progressive personal income tax rates low.

[3]Note that strict application of the principle would require that all taxes should be applied to the richest taxpayer first, until his income was just equal to the next richest; then to both of them till their incomes were reduced to just equal to the third richest; and so on until all after-tax incomes were equal.

income that he earns by helping to produce what consumers choose to buy. This implies that an equitable tax system will leave that distribution of income undisturbed, except insofar as each individual chooses to spend his money. It leads toward the proposition that people should be taxed only to pay for the benefits they choose to buy from the government. The public sector would roughly approximate the working of the market, except for cases of public goods and externalities.

One obvious problem is how the principle could be applied practically. If a city is putting in a new sewer, it's easy to see who the primary beneficiaries will be and to assess the cost against these property owners through a "special assessment." But how can the benefits derived from national defense, or highways, be divided up among the citizens?

Consider education, for example. Now we have free public schools for all. Suppose we put all education on a benefit-tax basis. Then each parent would have to pay a special school tax for each child he has in school—for example, $1,000 per child. This policy might be fine for the local banker and doctor. But how about the poor family on the other side of the tracks, with eight school-age children? The well-to-do could continue sending their youngsters to school (and more cheaply than now), but millions of poor children would be priced out of the market. Government activities like welfare would be completely ruled out by the benefit principle, since there would be little point in imposing special taxes on the poor just to return the funds to them.

Broad use of the benefit principle would thus be far more revolutionary than it sounds at first. It would mean, in effect, direct sale of government services to the user, and would preclude any redistribution of income through the public economy.

"Equal treatment of those equally situated". A third principle of equity states that persons equally situated should be taxed equally. This is a powerful guide to tax policy, and one that is accepted by most observers. But what is "equally situated"? Are two people with the same income always equally situated? For example, is a dis-

abled, retired man with an annual pension income of $5,000 equally situated with a healthy young man with the same income? Are both equally situated with the $5,000-a-year laborer who has a wife and ten children to support? Does it matter where the income comes from? For example, is a factory superintendent who earns $25,000 a year equally situated with someone who gains $25,000 on General Motors stock that has gone up in price between his buying and selling it? Our tax laws treat the first two identically, but apply a lower tax rate to the "capital gain" on the GM stock than to salary income. Should they? This is the issue of "horizontal" equity.

SHIFTING AND INCIDENCE OF TAXATION

Often, the person who hands the funds over to the government does not actually bear the burden of the tax. The federal tax on liquor, for example, is paid to the government by distillers; but it is largely "shifted" forward to consumers through higher prices. The final "incidence" of a tax may be far from the man who turns the money over to the government.

It is safe to assume that a taxpayer will shift a tax whenever he can. The question generally is, therefore, **When can a tax be shifted?** A tax can be shifted only when, as a result of the tax, the taxpayer is able to obtain a higher price for something he sells or to pay a lower price for something he buys. A price transaction of some sort is essential if shifting is to occur.

Generally, taxes do nothing to increase demand for taxed commodities (remember that we are examining the impact of the tax alone, apart from what is done with the money collected). But many taxes do raise costs and prices. If, as a result of a tax (for example, on cigarettes), the price is higher than it otherwise would have been, the tax has been shifted to that extent.

Because tax shifting depends on the prices charged and paid, it is largely an application of the general supply-and-demand analysis of Part 3. But a warning is necessary. A rise in price following the imposition of a tax in the real world is not necessarily proof that the tax has been shifted. The price rise may have come from some other cause. (Remember the fallacy of post hoc, propter hoc.) Empirical verification of tax shifting is very difficult, since it is hard to isolate one cause and its effects in the multitude of forces simultaneously at work in economic life. Analytically, however, we can trace through the effects of any tax assuming *"other things equal"*— that is, assuming the tax to be the only new element in the situation.

Three examples

Personal income tax. The personal income tax, which accounts for about a third of all tax revenues, is an example of a nonshiftable tax. The tax does not increase the demand for the services of the people taxed, nor does it decrease the supply of labor. (The latter statement is not quite accurate; some people may work less because their earnings are taxed, but there is little evidence that this effect is large in America. Even though the government takes some of your earnings, you still have more left when you work than when you don't, and for many people, keeping ahead of their neighbors is as important as absolute after-tax income level.) Thus, there is no way the taxed individual can raise his price to shift the tax forward, and there is no one onto whom he can shift it backward.

You may ask, How about unions? Won't they demand bigger wage increases if their taxes are raised? They may ask, but nothing has increased the demand for their labor to permit them to get a bigger wage increase. If they get more money after the tax, we must ask, why didn't they get it before? Price theory says the tax won't be shifted except possibly in cases of monopsony or oligopolies that are protected by barriers to entry. But in the dynamics of inflation and business cycles, the picture is less clear. Look back at Chapter 19.

Payroll taxes. Payroll taxes, levied on both workers and employers to finance Social Security benefits, are the second biggest and fastest-growing tax, totaling nearly $100 billion in 1976. The portion levied on the worker is like the income tax; it can't be shifted, for substantially the same reasons. But the part levied on the employer generally is shifted—back onto the worker. Consider the reasoning. The tax on the employer increases the effective wage cost of the employee.

Since cost per unit of output is now higher, unless the employer can reduce the wage rate he pays, he will have to raise prices, which will reduce output; and he will substitute machinery for labor, in order to keep maximizing his profits. If wage rates are flexible, wages will fall as the demand for labor falls. If wage rates are inflexible downward, some workers will be laid off. Either way, the burden is largely shifted onto the workers, although some of it may be shifted forward to consumers through higher prices.

A simple diagram makes clear that the incidence of both halves of the payroll tax is on the worker. In Figure 38–1, let D^L be the demand for labor and S^L its supply, fixed in amount. Part A shows that the wage will be W^1 without any tax. Now suppose a payroll tax is imposed on all workers, which they must pay to the government. Neither demand nor supply is changed, so the wage paid by employers is unchanged. Unhappily, workers' wages *after taxes* are only W^2, lower by the amount of the tax they must pay.

Part B starts with the same S^L and D^L curves, and the same wage, W^1. Now the government imposes the same wage tax *on employers*. Workers are worth no more than before to employers, so the employers' demand curve shifts down at all outputs by the amount of the tax, to D^{La}. Each worker now costs the old wage plus the tax, so employers will demand fewer workers at any wage level. If the wage is flexible, it will fall to a new equilibrium level at W^2, just as in Part A. In both cases, employment stays constant and the wage after tax is reduced just by the amount of the tax. It should be easy to see that the critical factor underlying the full incidence on workers is the fixed stock of labor, the perfectly inelastic labor-supply curve. The same result would follow for a tax imposed on the wage (or rent) of any other fixed resource. (If the wage rate is fixed at W^1, say by a union contract, work out for yourself what will happen to employment.)

If we want workers to bear the cost of old-age insurance and unemployment, payroll taxes may be a good means of financing Social Security. But putting half the tax on the employer, even though you *want* him to pay, doesn't necessarily mean that he *will* pay it.

Property taxes. Property taxes, the third most

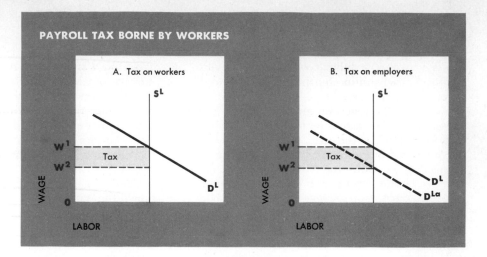

PAYROLL TAX BORNE BY WORKERS

A. Tax on workers

B. Tax on employers

Figure 38–1
Payroll taxes are generally borne by workers, whether
they are imposed on workers or on employers.

important revenue source, are levied on both residential and business property. They are often considered regressive on the theory that they are shifted to renters, but in part they fall on capital and are to that extent more progressive. Consider separately the main parts of the tax.

The part of the tax that falls on land mainly stays there—on the landowner. Note that the supply of land is fixed. The first effect of the tax is to reduce the net after-tax yield on the land. Thus, future buyers will be willing to pay less for the land after the tax. Since the capital value of the land has been reduced by the tax, we say the tax has been "capitalized." No future buyer of the land will invest unless the price falls enough to provide a net return *after taxes* equal to that obtainable on other comparable investments. The burden of the new tax is placed permanently on the owner at the time of first taxation; he has no way to shift it by transferring his investment and reducing the supply. Future owners buy free of the special land tax.

The part of the tax on residences is probably partly shifted, partly borne by capital. The tax will be gradually shifted to renters if the tax drives investment out of housing into other areas where taxes are lower, thereby reducing the supply and raising the rents on taxed buildings. This effect is plainly visible in big-city slums, where effective property-tax rates rise as buildings age but assessments are not reduced. Property owners just let their buildings depreciate and transfer their investment elsewhere. But in-

sofar as alternative investment opportunities are also taxed so property owners have no real alternative to keeping their investment in housing, they are stuck with the tax; it cannot be shifted.

One last point on the incidence of real-property taxes: Low-priced buildings are widely overassessed relative to high-priced ones; assessment practices are regressive. Thus, the actual incidence depends on a combination of basic tax and administrative factors.

Taxes on business property like inventories and machinery are business costs, quite similar to excise taxes on business products. They are usually shifted, but sometimes partly borne by owners of the business.

Put all these factors together and it is clear that the incidence of the property tax is complex. To the extent that it falls on renters, it makes the tax system more regressive for very low income receivers, who pay a large part of their incomes for rent. This would raise the average tax burden for very low incomes in Figure 35–4. But modern analysis is moving toward allotting more of the burden to capital.

TAX REFORM

Recent years have produced many complaints about the inequity of the present tax system. These charges have been leveled mainly against loopholes and special privileges allegedly enjoyed by the rich and powerful, and against the tax burdens borne by the poor and middle classes.

As Figure 35–4 showed, the tax system's progression comes largely from the federal personal and corporate income taxes, which mainly miss the poor and hit the rich with high marginal rates. Payroll taxes for Social Security, and state–local sales, excise, and (possibly) property taxes, produce the regressive offsets on the poor and middle-income classes. The result is a basically flat overall tax burden of around 25 percent for the lower- and middle-income classes (with perhaps a regressive burden on the very poor if the residential-property tax is largely shifted to renters). But, even though their tax rates are low, it is the great middle classes who in the aggregate pay the bulk of the taxes, because that's where the bulk of the income is. The cry of the radicals that we should make the rich pay the taxes and lift the burden from the back of the common man makes fine rhetoric, but it runs up against the fact that even a confiscatory 100 percent tax on all income over $1 million per family would yield only about $5 billion additional, compared to total federal tax collections approaching $400 billion. Thomas Jefferson's ideal of "a country made a paradise by the contribution of the rich alone" won't work any more—the country's too big and the rich don't have enough income. If the government needs big increases in tax revenue, they will have to come from the general public, not just a super-rich few. But that doesn't say we may not want tax reform to close some loopholes that especially help the rich.

Loopholes and "tax expenditures"

Oil depletion allowances, cattle ranches, and tax-exempt bonds make the headlines as tax loopholes. The federal Internal Revenue Code is full of special deductions, exemptions, and provisions that permit some citizens and businesses to pay less than others. For example, nearly all transfer payments, such as Social Security, unemployment payments, and "welfare" benefits, are exempt. Interest on state

and municipal bonds is exempt. Capital gains are taxed at lower rates than regular income. Taxes paid to states and localities, interest on mortgages and other borrowed money, and losses on personal businesses, like farming, can be deducted from taxable income. The aged and the blind are given other special exemptions. Poor families now get a complete exemption if their income is under about $6,000 for a family of four.

These legal loopholes can be looked at as much the same thing as federal government subsidies to the affected taxpayers. They are sometimes called "tax expenditures." Table 38–1 shows the magnitude of these federal tax expenditures, or loopholes. They totaled about $80 billion in 1976, $60 billion for individuals and $20 billion for corporations, according to rough Treasury estimates. This table does not include the additional personal deductions available to all taxpayers ($750 exemption for each individual), omission of imputed rent on owner-occupied homes, and the like. Addition of these further concessions would add another $30–$40 billion to the tax expenditures. It is obviously a hazy line that divides general reductions considered necessary to treat all fairly (like the $750 personal exemption) from "loopholes."

You may be struck by the fact that most of the big "loopholes" in Table 38–1 aren't quite what you expected. They're exemptions and deductions that obviously help you and most other middle-income taxpayers, not just the rich few—exemption of Social Security and unemployment benefits, deduction of property and sales taxes and of interest payments on mortgages, and the like. Some of the "loopholes" mainly benefit the rich (for example, the lower tax rates on capital gains and the exemption of interest on state and local bonds), who gain also from many of the others. But a big portion of the total goes to reduce the taxes of the vast middle and upper-middle classes. You read in the newspaper each year of a few super-rich individuals who somehow managed to pay very low income taxes, or no taxes at all (five millionaires in 1974). They managed this mainly by holding tax-exempt state and local bonds (where the exemption is intended mainly to help those governments borrow at lower interest rates), by

Table 38–1

Tax loopholes, or tax expenditures, 1976

	AMOUNTS (IN BILLIONS)	
	Corporations	*Individuals*
Deductibility of state–local taxes paid		$10.5
Exemption of Social Security and similar benefits		10.0
Investment tax credit	$ 6.9	
Exemption of contributions to pension funds		6.5
Deductibility of medical and health costs		5.7
Deductibility of consumer- and mortgage-interest payments		5.5
Lower tax rate on capital gains	.8	5.5
Corporate surtax exemption for smaller corporations	5.0	
Deductibility of charitable gifts	.5	4.2
Exemption of state–local bond interest	2.9	1.3
Other	4.3	8.4
Total	$19.9	$59.8

Source: *Special Analyses of the U.S. Budget for 1977.* "Loopholes" apply to the federal personal and corporation income taxes only. Totals shown are of dubious validity because of interactions among the loopholes shown, which would change amounts of some if others were eliminated.

having large deductible interest payments on money borrowed for personal business purposes (like cattle feeding), and by having large losses carried over from earlier years. But these are a tiny fraction of 1 percent of all high-income taxpayers, and to make them pay more will do more to assuage our feelings of inequity than to raise more money. The tax law now requires that such large-income receivers pay a minimum tax even though their exemptions and deductions would otherwise completely free them from tax.

Many Americans are outraged by such legal tax avoidance by the very rich. But big revenue gains from plugging loopholes will have to come from steps that affect a lot of taxpayers. The super-rich just don't have enough total income to pay a lot more of the total tax bill, even if their loopholes were closed. It is no accident that Congress shows little enthusiasm for closing the big loopholes, in spite of the vivid rhetoric about

their injustice to the common man. Most of the exemptions were put in to help special groups or causes—charitable deductions to help charities and schools, the Social Security exemption to help the elderly, and so on—and the many beneficiaries are understandably unenthusiastic about losing them. But it seems unlikely that Congress or the public would support annual cash subsidies of these amounts to the groups concerned if they were openly visible.[4]

[4]One special capital-gains loophole, which helps mainly the rich, seems especially difficult to justify. Property held till death can be transferred to heirs free of all capital-gains tax, however large the capital gain may be. For example, if you fortunately invested $1,000 in IBM stock fifty years ago, you are a millionaire now. If you die, leaving the stock to your children, they get it without paying any capital-gains tax on the million-dollar appreciation, either now or when they sell the stock (of course, they must pay regular estate taxes). By holding the asset to death, you completely escape taxes on the capital gains, and a similar avoidance is possible

Just about everyone agrees that the federal income tax code has become such a thicket of special provisions, understandable only to tax lawyers and accountants, that sweeping reform is desirable. Some observers propose eliminating all exemptions, and then applying a flat tax rate to all income, from whatever source received. Calculations vary, but with such a reform, a flat tax rate of about 18 percent would produce as much revenue as the present tax with its rates ascending to 70 percent. Few Americans would advocate a flat federal tax rate for all income levels, but the example highlights the position into which we have gotten ourselves through the increasing complexity of the tax code.

Shifting the mix of taxes

Figures 35–2 and 35–4 provided an overview of the taxes that now constitute our total tax system and how their burden falls on different income groups. Should we change the mix of taxes we use?

Federal personal and corporation income taxes are progressive in their impact. The personal tax now provides personal exemptions that, in effect, make all incomes below the "poverty" level free of federal income tax. Moreover, tax rates rise rapidly from a 14 percent minimum on income above exemptions to 70 percent on taxable income over $200,000, although since 1972 there has been a 50 percent ceiling on *earned* income; the higher rates apply to other income from dividends, interest, and the like. Although most wealthy families hold down their effective average rates well below these peaks by use of legal loopholes, the overall impact of the tax is still markedly progressive.[5] The incidence of the corporation income tax is less certain, but most of it is probably borne by capital (stockholders).

---

if you give the stock away prior to death. Many tax experts, even those who favor special lower rates on capital gains and permitting the owner to postpone taxes on capital gains until they are realized, favor making the estate recipients pay a capital-gains tax in such cases.

[5]Taxes will always be a lower percentage of total income than the peak marginal rates that apply to a family. Even though marginal rates reach 50 percent at the $44,000 income level, the actual average amount paid by families above that level was less than 35 percent in 1970.

Hence it too is generally, but erratically, progressive, because most, but by no means all, stock is held by wealthy owners; remember the pension funds. The corporate tax rate is 48 percent on all corporate profits over $25,000, and 22 percent on profits below that level to provide a lower rate for small businesses.

But, as Chapter 37 emphasized, the other big federal tax—the payroll tax to finance Social Security—is regressive. (See especially Case 31.) Because the payroll-tax burden is rising rapidly under the expanding Social Security system, many economists who favor more progression argue that reform of the payroll tax is our number one problem. Either the $16,800 limit on taxable income should be raised, or lower incomes should be tax-exempt, or Social Security should simply be paid for out of general tax revenues. But all these changes would move the Social Security system further away from its present special status toward becoming just part of the regular federal budget.

If you want more progression, you will probably favor heavier reliance on income taxes and reduced roles for payroll and sales taxes. You may argue that income taxes are also superior on grounds of minimal interference with the spending and earning behavior of individuals (you have to pay your tax, but you can spend what's left as you please), in contrast with government distortion of individual prices through other taxes. And income taxes are tops for built-in economic stabilization. Conversely, sales, excise, and property taxes raise some prices relative to others, thereby distorting the resource allocation that would come from free consumer spending. And neither property nor sales taxes have built-in stabilization effects comparable to those of income taxes.

But many people think the system is already too progressive, and that present peak income tax rates are confiscatory as well as serious deterents to work and risky investments. They argue that corporate profits are already double-taxed—as profits to the corporation, and again as income when stockholders receive them as dividends. If we assume that all the corporation income tax and half the property tax is borne by capital, in 1975 this $70 billion total alone took 40 percent of all returns to capital. **If we want to**

encourage investment and growth, we should lower taxes on capital, profits, and high incomes, not increase them. Tax reform is a complex and controversial issue.[6]

Taxes and inflation

Nearly everyone's real tax burden is increased by inflation unless Congress reduces tax rates. Inflation raises money incomes, thus moving previously tax-exempt income up into a taxable status and moving already-taxed income into higher tax brackets. If an exemption of $6,000 is required today to avoid taxes on poverty-level incomes, a doubling of prices (which we are now approaching over the past decade) means that this real exemption has fallen to $3,000. To continue the same real exemption, the dollar exemption level would have to be raised to $12,000. The typical family with a 20 percent preinflation marginal tax rate finds itself in higher and higher tax brackets, even though its real income is no higher.

Corporations' real taxes are similarly increased by inflation. Dollar profits rise, but the real purchasing power of those profits does not rise correspondingly, so the effective tax rate as a percent of real income rises. This situation is aggravated by standard corporate accounting practices, which overstate profits even further in inflation. Businesses can only charge depreciation equal to the original cost of their buildings and equipment. But with inflation, the cost of replacing the worn-out building or machine exceeds the original cost. Thus, businesses have undercharged their real costs, and must pay corporate income taxes on inflated "paper" profits. Similarly, inventories of materials bought today appreciate in price as inflation raises the price of the final product into which they are incorporated. Thus, the business, charging as a cost only the original low cost of the materials incorporated, records a juicy profit, and it pays a tax on this profit. But the profit is only a "paper" profit. When the firm replaces

the materials inventory for the next round of production, it must pay a new, higher price for the replacement inventory, roughly equal to the increase in product price that generated the inflation-period profit. Thus, again the firm has had to pay a real tax on inflation-period paper profits.

Inflation thus serves as a hidden tax increase on both individuals and businesses, draining off a larger share of the national income into the hands of the government without the unpleasant necessity of raising tax rates. If we want to avoid this presumably unintended effect, we should increase tax exemptions and raise tax brackets in proportion to inflation for individuals, thus maintaining the real effective tax rate for all taxpayers. And we should require, or at least permit, businesses to adjust their depreciation and inventory accounting practices to eliminate tax increases produced by purely inflation-induced paper profits. When inflation is slow, as during most of the post–World War II period, these inflation-induced tax increases are modest in size. But when inflation soars, as during the past decade, the distorting effects can be very large. For example, in 1974, $48 billion of $132 billion of reported corporate profits were such paper profits, unreal but subject to federal income tax.

Canada, Israel, and Brazil have changed their personal income tax laws to eliminate most of such inflation-induced real tax increases, and accountants in many nations are moving toward at least informing the public how much of stated profits are real and how much paper in inflation periods. U.S. tax law now permits corporations to use LIFO (last-in, first-out) accounting for inventories, which eliminates most of the overtaxing problem on inventories. But this country has taken no other specific steps to protect taxpayers against the tax effects of inflation. Alternatively, Congress has periodically passed tax-reduction bills, lowering rates or raising exemptions for some taxpayers. Perhaps the political rewards are higher that way.

How much taxation can we stand?

Hardly a day goes by but someone complains that we've reached the limit of our

---

[6]A more thorough, but controversial, analysis of the issues is provided by G. Break and J. Pechman, in *Federal Tax Reform: The Impossible Dream?* (Washington, D.C.: The Brookings Institution, 1975).

ability to pay taxes. Is there some definite limit to how much taxation the country can stand? Are we approaching it?

The general answer to both questions is no. But to answer more fully, we have to ask, What is the meaning of "what we can stand"? The usual connotation is that with more taxes, the system's growth would slow, people would stop working, there'd be no incentive for businessmen to invest. Faced with predictions of such a debacle, the economist asks, how will it come about, and why?

Economic analysis suggests that if more taxes are going to bring disaster, it will probably be through one or more of the following effects:

1. **Heavier taxes may reduce the incentive to work.** If the government takes too big a share of the income you earn, you may just quit working—or at least work less. But as long as something remains after taxes and most people still have much less than they want, the incentive to earn is a powerful one, even when earnings must be shared with the government. Still, for well-to-do people who feel less income pressure, the amount of work *may* fall off as tax rates rise. And this holds even for lower-income people, when it's a question of overtime work or a second job. The evidence we have doesn't settle the question. Most formal studies find little evidence that higher income taxes seriously reduce the work at any income level. But this runs contrary to many people's intuitive notions. And as Chapter 37 noted, high effective marginal tax rates certainly may reduce the incentive of the poor to give up government benefits and take relatively low-pay jobs.

2. **Heavier taxes may reduce the incentive to invest,** especially if the taxes fall heavily on profits. If taxes fall differentially on one type of investment, investors will flee from it in droves. But taxation on all corporate income leaves few alternatives to which investors can escape. They may turn to partnerships or individual enterprises, or to tax-exempt state and municipal bonds. But corporations are the only practical form of organization for most big businesses, and government bonds have limited appeal to profit-seeking investors. There's little evidence that wealthy individuals just consume more instead

of investing. More likely, they complain bitterly about the low return on investment, and go on investing—*if* profits are good (which is the most fundamental stimulus to investment). But Yale's Bill Nordhaus has found that the *real after-tax* rate of return on capital has fallen from 10 to 5 percent during the generally inflationary post–World War II years, which can hardly avoid being discouraging to investors.

3. **Heavier taxes may lead to legal tax "avoidance."** The law provides many loopholes for people who feel taxes heavily enough to hire a good tax lawyer. At last count, the Treasury listed about 100,000 tax counselors and tax lawyers whose business was to help on income tax returns. And the effort pays off. In spite of the 70 percent peak rate on incomes over $200,000, Treasury statistics show that less than 40 percent of all income above that level is collected in personal income taxes. What is worse, desire to avoid high tax rates often leads to distortions in investment and diversion of earning activities into special channels (like cattle feeding and oil drilling) that permit wealthy people to avoid peak tax rates under the law.

4. **Heavier taxes may lead to illegal tax "evasion."** The case of France is often cited, where for years the government has been able to collect only a modest fraction of the taxes due because of the expense and energy required to run down the individuals who just don't pay. By and large, we Americans report and pay our taxes without being pursued. But a recent National Bureau of Economic Research estimate suggested that 5 percent of all wages, and 30 percent of unincorporated-business incomes (farmers, doctors, lawyers, and so on) went unreported. How much harder it would become to collect taxes at higher rates nobody knows. Introduction of widespread employer reporting and computerized checking of tax returns has made tax evasion increasingly difficult for most people, and most dividend and interest income is probably now caught.

5. **Higher taxes may lead to inflation.** This seems a perverted argument, since modern fiscal policy rests on the premise that higher taxes check inflation. This argument is that if taxes get too high, everyone will raise his asking price to offset them—unions, businessmen, lawyers,

farmers, everyone. Careful thought will show that this behavior can result in continuing inflation only if the government helpfully puts in more money to support total purchasing power at the higher prices. But there are great pressures on government to do just that, if the price of inaction or restraint is unemployment and recession. Remember Chapter 19 and the "new" inflation.

What do all these points add up to? Not a conclusion that we can't stand any more taxation. Clearly, we can. Our standard of living is so high that we could readily divert more resources to the public sector and still have one of the highest private-consumption standards in the world. But they do point to some real dangers as the level of taxation climbs relative to the national income.

A "MODEL" TAX SYSTEM

What would your model tax system look like? What changes would you make in our tax system? This is one issue on which you, as a citizen, will repeatedly get a chance to say your piece. At federal, state, and local levels, tax changes are continually being made.

It's clear that different taxes look good on different criteria, and that what is considered a good tax system depends heavily on each individual's weighting of different objectives. Some economists recently proposed the following "model" tax system, which would make some drastic changes in the present system. It is presented only to stimulate you to think through your own views on what an ideal tax system would be.

Their "model" tax system would have four major taxes, for which they present the following argument:

1. A progressive personal income tax would account for at least two-thirds of all tax revenue. This would mean more than doubling present income-tax revenues. Much higher rates would reach down through the middle-income groups, and the bulk of the income-tax yield would necessarily come from these groups. This tax

places the burden directly on individuals where it ultimately must rest, and it makes clear who is paying how much. The exact rate structure would depend on our collective judgments on equity, together with recognition of the importance of adequate income incentives. The tax would be supplemented by progressive death and gift taxes. To encourage incentives and economic growth and to improve equitable treatment of similarly situated people, the present punitively high peak rates of the federal tax would be lowered to below 50 percent, but at the same time, many of the present loopholes for high-income taxpayers would be closed.

State income taxes would be added to the federal income tax, with the funds returned to the states concerned, in order to simplify tax reporting and collection procedures. Thus, the personal income tax base would be shared by federal and state governments, and there would be federal revenue sharing with local governments.

2. Both to stimulate economic growth and to reduce the present inequities between personal and corporation income taxes, present corporation income tax rates would be lowered substantially. The new tax would fall on all businesses, not merely corporations. Undistributed profits above generous reinvestment levels would be prorated out to stockholders for taxation, to avoid use of corporations as tax-avoidance devices; or stockholders might be permitted to deduct their share of corporation tax already paid from their taxable dividends, to avoid the present double taxation of profits.[7] (See Case 32.)

3. Taxes on real property would be continued at roughly present levels, not so much because the property tax is a good tax as because it is a major revenue source for local governments to which economic life has become well-adjusted, and because its removal would mean a large subsidy to present real-property owners.

4. There would be special "user charge" taxes that are clearly justifiable either to correct ex-

[7]Some would substitute a value-added tax for the business-income tax. The value-added tax (VAT) is similar to a general sales tax, but is partially collected at each stage of manufacture instead of all from the final consumer. It is used in most European nations.

ternalities or on the benefit principle. In this group would be (a) special assessments; (b) highway taxes (on fuel and on vehicles), with the revenue to be spent on highways and streets; and possibly (c) payroll taxes on the worker (not the employer) to finance Social Security benefits. All three have strong claim to use as benefit levies.

Could such a tax system yield adequate revenue to pay the governments' bills? The answer is clearly yes, because personal income tax rates could be set to produce any desired yield. But could it yield the revenue without impairing incentives to work and earn? This is a big question raised by critics of the income tax, which in this system would supplant hidden excise and sales taxes, plus part of present corporation taxes. Another way of putting the question is, Would we demand as many government services if we recognized individually what we have to pay for them?

Taxes are going to take over a quarter of the income you earn during the rest of your life if something like present conditions continue. So stop and ask yourself, What does *your* model tax system look like?

REVIEW

Concepts to remember

Public finance mainly involves the application of analytical concepts already learned in the preceding chapters. But it has some concepts and terms of its own that you need to have firmly installed in your economic tool kit:

benefit principle	vertical equity
ability-to-pay principle	horizontal equity
progressive taxation	incentive effects
regressive taxation	"tax expenditures"
"deadweight loss"	capital gain
incidence	tax capitalization
tax shifting	

For analysis and discussion

1. Are taxes too high? What is your criterion?
2. Can you suggest ways of minimizing the negative incentive effects of rising taxes as government expenditures grow?
3. Some tax experts argue that taxes should be highly visible (like the personal income tax) in order to make citizens keenly aware of the taxes they are paying. Others argue that indirect and hidden taxes (for example, excise and sales taxes) are better because taxpayers don't feel the burden so strongly and are less unhappy about the costs of government services. Analyze these arguments. What are the main issues, and where do you stand on them?
4. What are tax loopholes? Should all tax loopholes be closed by Congress? (See Table 38–1 in answering.)
5. Should all tax rates and exemptions be automatically changed to eliminate inflation's increase in real tax burdens? Do you see any disadvantages?
6. Suppose a new excise tax were imposed on the following products, at the producer's level:
   a. Steel (where there is mixed price leadership and competition, plus strong labor unions)

  b. Potatoes (where the market is highly competitive and little unionized labor is involved)
  c. Ladies' garments (where the market is highly competitive and there is a strong labor union)
  d. Refined oil and gasoline (where the market is oligopolistic and little strongly unionized labor is involved)

Explain in each case whether you would expect the incidence of the tax to be on the consumer, labor in the industry, the producing firm, or some combination. (Remember your price theory from Chapters 6 and 21–26.)

7. Assume a period of strong inflationary pressures as a result of government arms spending. Which of these alternatives would you consider the more equitable, and why?

  a. A general sales tax to balance the budget
  b. Inflation

8. Given a full-employment situation and the need for more taxes to finance increased government spending on national defense, what tax program would you propose to raise an additional $10 billion? Defend your program against likely criticism from those who would bear the major burden.

9. What is your model tax system?

The following editorial recently appeared in the *Wall Street Journal*.[8]

Growth and ethics   Treasury Secretary Simon's specific proposals to reform the taxation of corporate dividends, offered to the Ways and Means Committee last week, represent a milestone in an absolutely vital national debate that ranges far beyond the technicalities of the tax code. Ultimately the question is whether society should emphasize economic growth or redistribution of income.

Speeding economic growth is the purpose of Secretary Simon's proposals. There is an extraordinarily strong relationship between capital investment and productivity; see the accompanying chart. Various compilations of these statistics show that, with the possible exception of Great Britain, the United States has the lowest rate of capital investment in the developed world. It needs to boost capital formation in order to provide jobs for the baby-boom workers now entering the labor market, to make the

[8] The *Wall Street Journal*, August 5, 1975. Reproduced by permission.

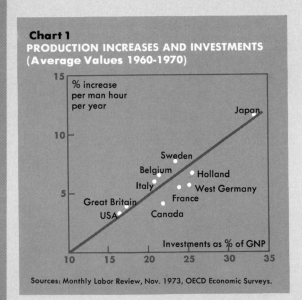

Chart 1
PRODUCTION INCREASES AND INVESTMENTS
(Average Values 1960-1970)

Sources: Monthly Labor Review, Nov. 1973, OECD Economic Surveys.

investments necessary for clean air and water, to pay the huge commitments of Social Security and private pensions, and to provide an increasing standard of living.

Secretary Simon proposes to boost capital formation by reducing the taxes on returns from capital. A greater after-tax return on investment will induce people to save more and invest more, thus providing the funds for future growth. Even in today's recession, an increase in after-tax return would provide a better yield on capital. It would not only speed the construction of productive resources for the future; it would also speed the rate at which existing resources are put back to work.

Specifically, the Secretary proposes to allow corporations a partial tax deduction for dividend payments, and to allow dividend recipients a partial tax credit. The effect would be to "integrate" the corporate and personal taxes, so that a shareholder would in effect be taxed as if he personally earned a pro rata share of the corporate earnings. At present, the income stream from the shareholder's invested capital is taxed twice, once through the corporate tax and again through the personal income tax on dividends.

Integration of corporate and personal taxes is already widespread in Europe. Indeed, the European Economic Committee has passed a resolution specifically urging all of its members to adopt such a system. It is one of a number of ways in which European nations tax returns from capital less heavily than does the United States. And their lower taxes on capital no doubt have much to do with their higher rates of capital formation.

When you want to reduce taxes on returns from capital, however, you are by definition talking about reducing the taxes of people who hold capital. Obviously, these will tend to be relatively wealthy people (though Secretary Simon pointed out that lower-income people living on savings would also receive some net benefit from his proposals). Thus the new proposals were immediately attacked as tax breaks for the rich. Rep. James Burke called them "a bonanza for the wealthy."

The nation is faced, then, with a trade-off between growth and redistribution. Does it want to split a smaller pie more equally or a larger pie less equally? We notice that for guidance on such matters, our liberal friends recently have been recommending *A Theory of Justice*, by Harvard philosopher John Rawls. The heart of his book is "the difference principle," which holds that inequality can be justified only if it works to the absolute benefit of the least advantaged.

For the record, we have little use for Professor Rawls' ideas, which stand in the dubious tradition of trying to draw morality from *a priori* principles rather than from reality as it exists. We do not believe a society can be meaningfully judged by any single criterion, and if forced to choose we would not pick Professor Rawls' criterion of equality but the ultimately opposing criterion of freedom. For all this, we do hope that his liberal followers apply his "difference principle" in judging Secretary Simon's proposals.

In helping the poor, economic growth has proved itself far more important than income redistribution. Even without changes in distribution over the last decade, growth has helped millions lift themselves out of poverty. In seeking more incentives for capital investment, Secretary Simon is pointing the way toward maintaining future growth. And an important result of those incentives, just as Mr. Rawls' recipe demands, will be a more rapid increase in the standard of living of the poor.

Do you favor or oppose Secretary Simon's proposal to integrate the personal and corporations income taxes, eliminating "double taxation" of dividends and reducing the effective tax rate on capital?

APPENDIX TO PART 5

Current research

Research on the fiscal-policy aspects of public finance was included in the appendix to Part 2. Here we concentrate on the allocative and distributional effects of government taxes and expenditures. As awareness has spread that the public sector accounts for between a fourth and a third of all economic activity, economic research on public-sector problems has burgeoned in recent years.

Government Expenditures. An excellent analysis of the main components of each year's federal budget is provided by The Brookings Institution in its annual *Setting National Priorities;* sample any major area, such as national defense. Murray Weidenbaum's *The Modern Public Sector* (New York: Basic Books, 1969) and J. Burkhead and J. Miner's *Public Expenditures* (Chicago: Aldine-Atherton, 1971) provide good, more traditional introductions to the whole area of public expenditures and public goods. *The Economics of Defense in a Nuclear Age,* by Charles Hitch and Roland McKean (Cambridge, Mass.: Harvard University Press, 1960), remains the best economic analysis of promoting efficiency in public expenditures, but there are many good studies of different aspects of the problem. On cost–benefit analysis, Stephen Enke's "Government-Industry Development of a Commercial Supersonic Transport," *American Economic Review,* May 1967, provides an accessible introduction; and the following articles on water resources and the federal antipoverty program in the same volume are examples of other applications. More advanced analyses are presented in the Joint Economic Committee's *The Analysis and Evaluation of Public Expenditures: The PPB System* (1969), Vol. 1, especially the articles by Steiner, Davis and Kamien, and Bonnen.

Transfer payments, poverty, and income redistribution. On antipoverty policy, James Tobin, one of the chief authors of the "negative income tax," provides a good introductory analysis in "Raising the Incomes of the Poor," in *Agenda for the Nation,* K. Gordon, ed. (Washington, D.C.: The Brookings Institution, 1968).

Then look at *Income Security for Americans: Recommendations,* the summary report of the Joint Economic Committee of Congress (December 5, 1974) on three years of intensive hearings and study on the problem; see especially pp. 1–17. Another excellent readable analysis is S. Lebergott, *Wealth and Want* (Princeton, N.J.: Princeton University Press, 1975).

The problem of transfer payments to achieve redistribution of income is a complex one. Most such programs are justified on the ground that they will help the poor, but the programs are not always what they seem. See Henry Aaron, *Shelters and Subsidies: Who Benefits from Federal Housing Policies?* (Washington, D.C.: The Brookings Institution, 1972); Charles Schultze, *The Distribution of Farm Subsidies* (Washington, D.C.: The Brookings Institution, 1971); L. Thurow, "Cash versus In-Kind Transfers," *American Economic Review,* May 1974; and E. Browning, "How Much More Equality Can We Afford?" *The Public Interest,* Spring 1976.

Social Security is by far the biggest income-transfer program of all and, as Case 37 indicates, seems guaranteed to generate controversy over the years ahead. See Martin Feldstein, "Toward a Reform of Social Security," *The Public Interest,* Summer 1975; and for a longer analysis, J. Pechman, H. Aaron and M. Taussig, *Social Security: Perspectives for Reform* (Washington, D.C.: The Brookings Institution, 1970).

Finally, one of the biggest income-transfer issues of the next decade is likely to be the financing of health programs. For stimulating overviews, see Victor Fuchs, *Who Shall Live?* (New York: Basic Books, 1974); and M. Feldstein, "A New Approach to National Health Insurance," *The Public Interest,* Spring 1971.

Taxes. Two recent studies by Joseph Pechman— *Who Bears the Tax Burden?* (with B. Okner; Washington, D.C.: The Brookings Institution, 1974), and *Federal Tax Reform: The Impossible Dream?* (with G. Break; Washington, D.C.: The Brookings Institution, 1975)—provide lively, if sometimes controversial, introductions to recent research on taxes. More intensive analyses of individual taxes are provided by H. Aaron, "A New View of Property Tax Incidence," *American Economic Review,* May 1974 (or, for more detail, his *Who Pays the Property Tax?* (Washington, D.C.: The Brookings Institution, 1975); and R. Goode, *The Individual Income Tax* (Washington, D.C.: The Brookings Institution, 1976). From a different perspective, the Tax Institute's *Tax Incentives* (Lexington, Mass.: D.C. Heath, 1971) collects several leading analyses of this tricky problem, including the "loopholes" issue. California's George Break looks further at the alleged deterrent effect of high personal income taxes on work, without finding much evidence of it, in "Income Taxes and Incentives to Work," *American Economic Review,* September 1967. For the revenue-sharing issue and state-local problems, see L. Ecker-Racz, *The Politics and Economics of State-Local Finance* (Englewood Cliffs, N.J.: Prentice-Hall, 1970).

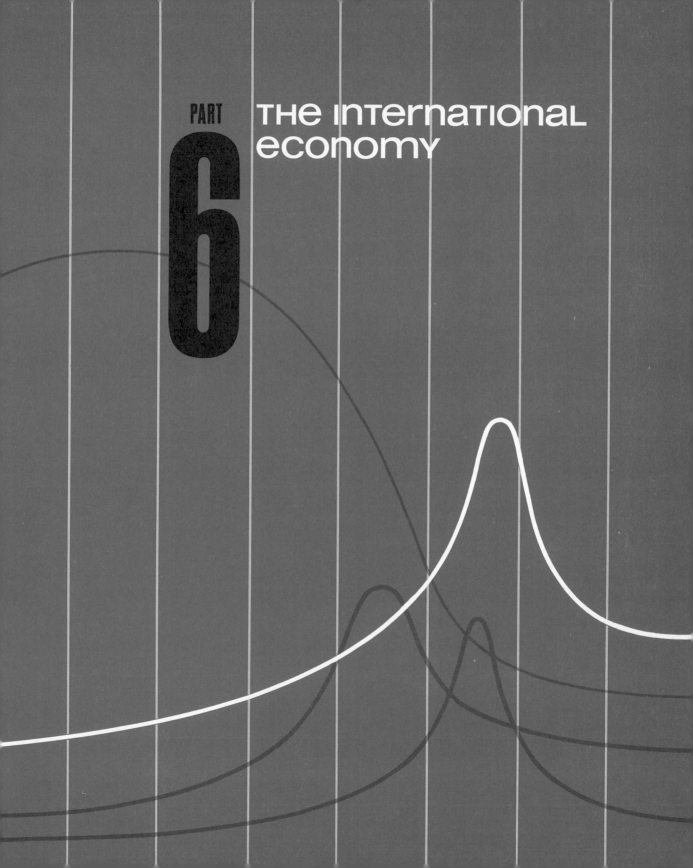

PART **6** THE INTERNATIONAL economy

CHAPTER 39 INTERNATIONAL TRADE AND LENDING

In the "one world" of today, the close interdependence among nations is painfully obvious. The big economic issues fill the newspapers. Should we "buy American" and shut out foreign goods? Do low foreign wages threaten our standard of living? Is the dollar weak, or strong?

Since prewar days, our sales of goods and services abroad have soared—from $4 billion in 1939 to $118 billion in 1975. Our imports grew from $3 billion to $100 billion over the same period. The best estimates indicate that perhaps five to seven million American workers owe their jobs directly to export sales, and exports come from every state in the union. Our exports of goods and services total only 8 percent of GNP, but to many industries, foreign trade is the blood of life—we export half our cotton crop and import almost all the tin and nickel we use. To most of the world, foreign trade is more urgent than it is to us. England must import most of her food or starve, and she can pay for these imports only by selling her exports abroad. And so it is with other nations—their living standards depend heavily on foreign trade.

In spite of the importance of foreign trade, governments have long followed policies that restrict rather than encourage such trade—tariffs, quotas, exchange controls. Prima facie, the case for international division of labor and exchange is as clear as it is in domestic affairs. On the surface, there would appear to be no reason

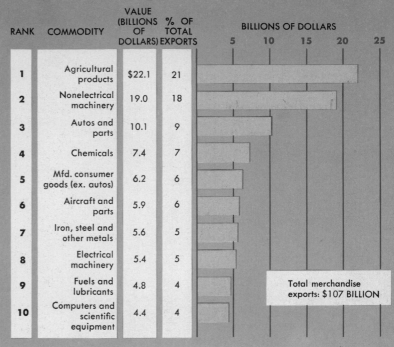

CHIEF MERCHANDISE EXPORTS OF THE UNITED STATES, 1975

RANK	COMMODITY	VALUE (BILLIONS OF DOLLARS)	% OF TOTAL EXPORTS
1	Agricultural products	$22.1	21
2	Nonelectrical machinery	19.0	18
3	Autos and parts	10.1	9
4	Chemicals	7.4	7
5	Mfd. consumer goods (ex. autos)	6.2	6
6	Aircraft and parts	5.9	6
7	Iron, steel and other metals	5.6	5
8	Electrical machinery	5.4	5
9	Fuels and lubricants	4.8	4
10	Computers and scientific equipment	4.4	4

Total merchandise exports: $107 BILLION

Figure 39–1
Agricultural products and high-technology manufactures (machinery, autos, and chemicals) dominate our exports. (Source: U.S. Department of Commerce.)

to suppose that human welfare could be improved by obstructing the processes of specialization and exchange. Why, then, have laymen and lawmakers so often distrusted foreign trade and favored the tariff? Why have nations so often flown in the face of apparent economic reason? Nowhere in economics is there a better opportunity to apply relatively simple economic analysis to popular fallacies.

THE BALANCE OF TRADE

First consider our exports and imports of commodities. Figure 39–1 summarizes the goods we exported in 1975. The figures speak for themselves. They show the huge sales abroad by many of our basic industries, especially high-technology manufactured goods and farm products. It's easy to see why a lot of American farmers, businessmen, and workers are in favor of foreign trade. Figure 39–2 shows the goods we imported in 1975. From this, it's easy to see why some businessmen and workers are opposed to foreign trade, which competes directly with them. Note the huge expenditure on oil imports,

reflecting the quadrupling of oil prices by the OPEC countries in 1974.

Figure 39–3 throws more light on this comparison. It shows exports and imports of goods and services as a percentage of GNP. During the prosperous 1920s, about 7 percent of all goods and services produced in the United States were exported. During the depression, this figure fell to around 4 percent. After World War II, the ratio rose sharply, then fell back, and has since climbed back up to 7 or 8 percent.

In recent years, the pattern of U.S. foreign trade has changed significantly. Overall, the U.S. share has declined from about 20 to 14 percent of total world exports. Our exports have been increasingly concentrated in farm products (where we use the most advanced technology and heavy capital investment) and in high-technology manufactured products (computers, automatic machine tools, aircraft, and the like). Markets for lower-technology manufactures (textiles, iron and steel, and consumer durables) have been increasingly usurped by other nations with lower labor costs than ours.

There is still another interesting way of looking at our foreign-trade picture: Who are our main

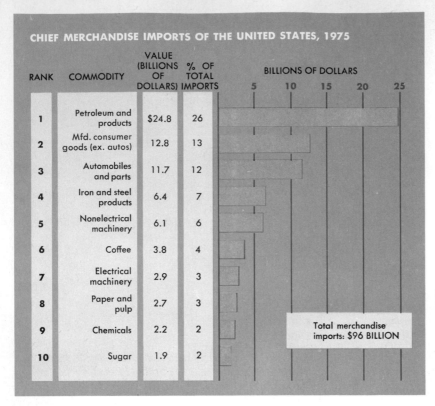

CHIEF MERCHANDISE IMPORTS OF THE UNITED STATES, 1975

RANK	COMMODITY	VALUE (BILLIONS OF DOLLARS)	% OF TOTAL IMPORTS
1	Petroleum and products	$24.8	26
2	Mfd. consumer goods (ex. autos)	12.8	13
3	Automobiles and parts	11.7	12
4	Iron and steel products	6.4	7
5	Nonelectrical machinery	6.1	6
6	Coffee	3.8	4
7	Electrical machinery	2.9	3
8	Paper and pulp	2.7	3
9	Chemicals	2.2	2
10	Sugar	1.9	2

Total merchandise imports: $96 BILLION

Figure 39-2
Petroleum dominates our imports, followed by lower-technology consumer goods, raw materials, and foods. (Source: U.S. Department of Commerce.)

customers and suppliers? Figure 39–4 provides the answer. Canada dominates the list, and all Western Hemisphere nations combined constitute about 40 percent of our customers. But the OPEC (oil-producing) countries have shot up in importance since their spectacular price increases in 1974. Western Europe and Japan are the other major trading partners. Trade with the so-called developing countries, except for oil, accounts for only about one-fifth of the total.

The commodities we buy and sell abroad are the most visible part of our foreign trade, and the part most directly related to American jobs. But in Figures 39–3 and 39–4, $12 billion of net sales of American services abroad (shipping, banking, and the like, plus net returns on U.S. investments abroad) were added to the $107 billion of merchandise exports. To get a complete picture of the international "balance of

Figure 39-3
U.S. exports of goods and services have exceeded imports, with rare exceptions. During recent years, both have risen substantially as percentages of GNP. (Source: U.S. Department of Commerce.)

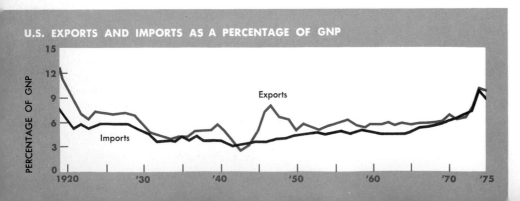

U.S. EXPORTS AND IMPORTS AS A PERCENTAGE OF GNP

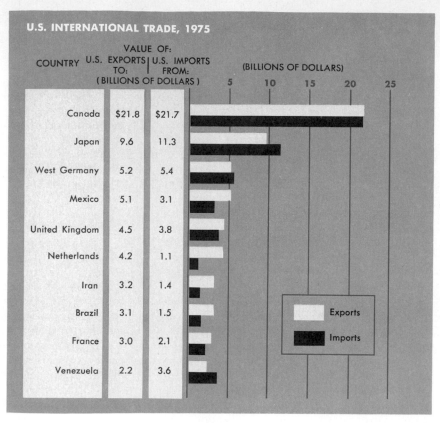

COUNTRY	VALUE OF: U.S. EXPORTS TO: (BILLIONS OF DOLLARS)	U.S. IMPORTS FROM: (BILLIONS OF DOLLARS)
Canada	$21.8	$21.7
Japan	9.6	11.3
West Germany	5.2	5.4
Mexico	5.1	3.1
United Kingdom	4.5	3.8
Netherlands	4.2	1.1
Iran	3.2	1.4
Brazil	3.1	1.5
France	3.0	2.1
Venezuela	2.2	3.6

Figure 39–4
Canada is by far our best customer, followed by Japan. The European Common Market and Latin America are about equally important. "Developing" countries accounted for nearly 40 percent of our imports with oil included, only about 15 percent without oil. (Source: U.S. Department of Commerce.)

payments," we will need to add "capital movements" (the transfer of short- and long-term monetary investments). But first, let us consider the basic analytical case for free international trade and lending.

THE CASE FOR INTERNATIONAL TRADE

Florida produces oranges; Iowa produces corn and hogs; Pittsburgh produces steel. Each sells its products to the others. When each specializes in what it does best, we produce more in total and we all have more to consume than if we each tried to be self-sufficient. In the same way, Brazil sells coffee to us, we sell computers to England, England sells cloth to Brazil. **When each nation specializes in what it does best and then exchanges with others, we produce more in total and we all end up consuming more than if we each tried to be self-sufficient.**

The advantages to all in the first case—to Florida, Iowa, and Pittsburgh—are obvious. No one would question them. For each area to try to live alone, barring trade with the others, would be foolish. The advantages to nations from specialization and exchange are identical; more is produced for all to consume. The case for free international trade is that simple and that powerful. By using its total resources most efficiently through specialization and exchange, the world can move all the way out to its combined production-possibilities frontier. But it seems very hard for voters and legislators to see and to remember this simple truth.

Interregional and international trade

Nations (like regions within a nation) vary greatly in efficiency in producing different goods, differences that persist largely because of international immobility of resources. These differences arise largely out of five considerations:

1. **Over the face of the earth, climatic and geographical conditions vary widely.** Brazil is admirably suited for raising coffee, the lower Nile valley for cotton production. Texas and Oklahoma are great oil-producing centers. Chile has rich nitrate deposits. Such geographical and climatic differences alone would justify world-wide specialization.

2. **Human capacities vary over the globe.** Some groups are large and strong, suited for physical labor. Others excel at dexterity and manual skills. Still others stand out in enterprise and organizational ability. These differences may be due to long-standing racial characteristics, or to the varying political, social, and economic environment. Whatever the causes, they constitute a reason why international specialization and trade will be beneficial.

3. **The accumulated supply of capital goods, as well as the kinds of capital, varies greatly from nation to nation.** In some countries, centuries of accumulation have produced large supplies of capital—railroads, buildings, machinery, and so forth. Examples are the United States and England. In other countries—for example, Greece and Nigeria—capital is scarce; they specialize in simple production that requires little elaborate equipment.

4. **The proportions among different resources vary widely among nations.** Australia has vast plains but relatively few people and capital goods. Therefore, she specializes in farm products that require a high proportion of natural resources to labor and capital goods. In England, land is scarce relative to human beings and capital. Therefore, she is best fitted for manufacturing and industry, even though her soil may be as good as Australia's for wheat growing.

5. **In addition to these "economic" considerations, great differences exist in the political** and social climates in different countries. In countries with stable government, vast industrial organizations requiring large long-period capital commitments are likely to grow. In less-developed, badly governed areas, conditions virtually prohibit mass-production industry. A hustling, mechanical-minded nation like the United States could hardly be expected to be satisfied again with a small-unit, predominantly rural economy, any more than we would expect South Sea islanders to be happy, efficient, auto makers.

The principle of comparative advantage

Given these differences among nations, it is clear that some international trade will be advantageous. But how far each nation should specialize and how much international trade is to its advantage is not so obvious. Disregard costs of transport between nations for the moment in answering that question.

The greatest possible advantage for all from trade will be obtained if each nation specializes in what it can do relatively most cheaply. In the simple case of Iowa and Florida, where the cost advantage of each in its representative products is clear and large, and with only two products, Iowa should raise all the corn, Florida all the oranges. The greatest total of corn plus oranges will be obtained in that way. But such money-cost comparisons don't provide much guidance when it comes to comparing costs between different nations with different monetary units, different proportions of the factors of production, different qualities of labor, and different productive techniques. Perhaps as between coffee and computers, Brazil has an "absolute" advantage in the former, the United States in the latter. But even in such an extreme case, it is hard to be precise on just why these absolute advantages exist and what they mean. When less-striking differences are considered, such as textiles in the United States and in England, the difficulty of such comparisons becomes insurmountable. Monetary comparisons mean little, because different monetary units are used in the two countries.

But fortunately, as David Ricardo demonstrated a century and a half ago, the advantages of international trade don't depend on such absolute cost calculations. Even if one nation were more efficient than another in the production of **everything**, it would still be to the advantage of both to specialize and engage in international trade. **Each, and both combined, will gain most when each specializes in producing those commodities for which its comparative, or relative, costs of production are lowest.**

Let us first illustrate this "principle of comparative advantage" with a case involving only two countries and two commodities—the United States and France, producing wheat and cloth. To simplify, let us assume that labor is the only factor of production (or that a day of labor is a shorthand measure of a bundle of land, labor, and capital used in producing things). Assume further that in the United States, one man-day can produce one bushel of wheat or one yard of cloth. Thus, in the United States we can obtain one bushel of wheat by giving up the production of one yard of cloth, and vice versa.[1]

Assume that in France, one day of labor also produces one bushel of wheat, but only a half yard of cloth. In this sense, American labor is more productive than French labor, but, as we shall see, this is not the critical factor. The critical factor is that in France, two bushels of wheat must be given up to produce one more yard of cloth. This situation is shown in Table 39–1.

First suppose that there is no trade between France and the United States; each country produces all its own wheat and cloth. Will it pay them to begin specializing and trading? The answer is yes. In the United States, we can obtain **one** more bushel of wheat by giving up one yard of cloth. But in France they can obtain **two** more bushels of wheat by giving up one yard of cloth. **Therefore, there will be an increase in total world output if the United States uses more of her labor to produce cloth while resources in France are shifted to raising wheat.**

A simple example may help demonstrate this point. Assume that there are 100 workers each in the United States and France. At the beginning,

in each country half are producing wheat and half cloth. Total world output is 100 bushels of wheat and 75 yards of cloth, as in Table 39–2.

Now suppose that we specialize completely in cloth and France specializes completely in wheat, as the principle suggests. As Table 39–3 shows, the result is 100 bushels of wheat and 100 yards of cloth, an increase of 25 yards of cloth to divide between us.

It might appear from these tables that the United States has an **absolute** advantage in efficiency over France, since in France it takes two man-days to produce a yard of cloth, whereas

Table 39–1

Comparative costs of production, in man-days

	U.S.	France
Wheat (1 bushel)	1	1
Cloth (1 yard)	1	2

Table 39–2
World output before specialization

U.S.
50 workers on wheat = 50 bushels
50 workers on cloth = 50 yards

France
50 workers on wheat = 50 bushels
50 workers on cloth = 25 yards

Table 39–3
World output after specialization

U.S.
100 workers on cloth = 100 yards

France
100 workers on wheat = 100 bushels

[1] Temporarily assume that wheat and cloth are industries of constant costs both here and abroad. That is, unit costs of production do not increase or decrease as output in the country changes. This is sometimes called the assumption of constant returns to scale.

here it takes only one. But it is easy to show that these absolute differences are not the critical point at all. Suppose, instead, that we had begun with the assumption that French labor was the more efficient—that one man-day in France would produce two bushels of wheat or one yard of cloth. Total world output can be larger because of the higher productivity of French labor. But work out the new example, and you will see that it pays each country to specialize where its comparative advantage is higher, just as before, and then to exchange part of its production.

The principle is that gain in total world output is possible from specialization and trade if the cost ratios of producing two commodities are different in different countries. This same principle would have applied in the example above had the cost ratios for producing wheat and cloth been 3 to 2 in the United States and 5 to 1 in France, or any other set of differing ratios. To repeat, absolute costs in the two countries are not relevant. It would make no difference, for example, if U.S. labor were vastly more efficient than French. Total output could be increased by further U.S. specialization in cloth, because our **comparative** advantage is greater in producing cloth. **This is the principle of comparative advantage: Total output will be maximized when each nation specializes in the lines where it has the greatest comparative advantage or the least comparative disadvantage.**[2]

From this statement we can also tell how far it is advantageous to carry specialization and trade. Gain from trade is possible until the cost ratios of producing the two commodities are the same in both the United States and France. With constant costs, complete specialization would occur; the cost ratios never become equal, because they are fixed by the constant-cost assumption. But now, realistically, drop the as-

sumption of constant costs. As production of cloth increases in the United States, the cost of producing cloth will rise relative to that of producing wheat. In France, as it produces more wheat, the cost of producing wheat will rise relative to that of producing cloth. Finally, at some levels of output, the cost ratios will become identical in the two countries. Thereafter, there is no advantage in further specialization and exchange, since no further increases in total output can be obtained. (Realistically, we should introduce transport costs between nations, which would correspondingly reduce the potential gains from international exchange.)

When the law of comparative advantage is generalized to many countries and thousands of products, no new principles are introduced, but the picture becomes more complex. Gain will still be maximized if each country specializes in those goods and services where its comparative advantage is greatest or its comparative disadvantage least, and if this specialization is carried to the point where the cost ratios involved are equal to those of other countries producing the same products. In any given country, production of many products will never take place, because the country's comparative disadvantage in their production is so great and because of international transportation costs. Most nations will find it advantageous to produce a variety of products.[3]

You may have noted that thus far we have said nothing about the division of the gains from international trade. For example, in the case of Table 39-3, will France or the United States get the extra 25 yards of cloth obtained by specialization, or will they be divided between the two nations? In most cases, the gain will be divided, based on a complex set of considerations, mainly the relative cost structures of the countries involved. In extreme cases, it is possible to demonstrate logically that all the gain would accrue to

---

[2]Note that we use this principle all the time in our domestic economic life. Suppose that in a business firm, the president is better at typing than any of the secretaries are. Should he do his own typing? Obviously not. He should specialize where his comparative advantage is greatest, in managing the firm, leaving the typing to his secretary even though she types more slowly than he does. Or suppose a fine surgeon is also the best driver in the community. Should he drive the hospital ambulance instead of spending all his available time in the hospital operating room?

[3]If this were an advanced treatise, we would introduce the fact that different industries in different countries may use differing ratios of labor to capital, and note that this raises interesting, intricate problems of exactly how far each country should go toward specialization in different industries. But these complications do not change the general principle of comparative advantage, and we need not become involved in them here.

one country, but this requires some highly unlikely assumptions.

The law of comparative advantage, free trade, and the price system

In world markets, the search for profits and the price system tend to bring about this international specialization and optimal allocation of resources in each country automatically. If we are relatively inefficient in producing coffee but very efficient in producing computers, American producers are going to have a tough time competing with Brazil in the world's coffee markets, but we'll beat out other computer manufacturers in the marketplace. Under an international free-trade system, in each country the greatest profits can be obtained by producing those commodities most desired by consumers at home and abroad where our costs are relatively lowest. If our comparative advantage is great in producing computers, this fact will be reflected in high returns to resources in the computer industry. If our comparative advantage is low in producing spices, American spice producers will be unable to pay wages high enough to bid resources away from the more efficient computer industry, since world prices for spices are set by relatively efficient East Indian production. Thus, under free trade, the resources of each nation would tend to be drawn into its most efficient industries. No one would manage or direct international trade. Each producer would simply try to maximize profits, and each buyer would simply buy where the price was lowest. **The central mechanism is the same as domestically with Adam Smith's "invisible hand." The principle of comparative advantage is central in both domestic and international trade.**

Worldwide multilateral trade

To provide the full advantages of international specializtion and exchange, trade must be multinational or "multilateral." That is, goods and services must move freely among all nations. This eliminates the necessity that the exports and imports between any two nations must be in balance, which would severely restrict the degree of international specialization. Vis-à-vis all other countries combined, a nation's exports and imports must roughly balance (omitting capital movements), but with multinational trade, this balance may result from a combination of export and import imbalances with different individual nations, taking full advantage of the individual-country comparative advantages involved.

This fact is illustrated by Figure 39–5, which shows the pattern of multinational trade among major areas of the world. The United States, for

THE COMPLEX PATTERN OF MULTILATERAL WORLD TRADE

Figure 39–5
The grey arrows show the directions of flow of exports where they exceed imports, while the blue arrows represent the net imports moving in the opposite directions. (Source: United Nations.)

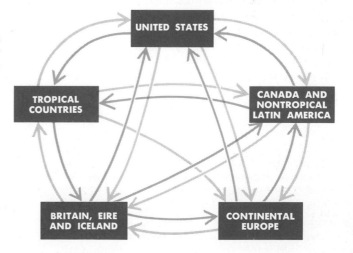

example, exports more to Europe, Canada, and nontropical Latin America than it imports from them. But our imports from the tropical nations exceed our exports to them. Our international trade is multinational, in fact much more complex than the patterns of exchange shown in Figure 39–5.

THE CASE FOR INTERNATIONAL LENDING

Society benefits when individuals and institutions save and invest, because useful capital goods are thereby accumulated. The saver gains individually from the return on his investment, and society gains from the increased efficiency of roundabout, mechanized production. **Both the saver and society gain most when savings are invested where their productivity is highest.**

In the domestic economy, we mainly trust the price system to allocate savings to the most desirable investments. Those who save invest their funds (either directly or through such institutions as banks) where the combination of safety, liquidity, and rate of return seems most attractive. Because the rate of return tends to be highest where investments fulfill the strongest consumer demands, savings are drawn into those industries where consumers most want output increased. Consumer choices direct the allocation of savings among investments.

Internationally, as domestically, society is generally best off if savings are allocated where their marginal productivity is greatest. International loans are "better" than domestic loans when the anticipated rate of return on them (including liquidity and risk allowance) is greater. For decades, both England and the New World gained from heavy loans by Britishers to the rapidly developing Western Hemisphere. British lenders gained by receiving good returns on their investments; U.S. borrowers gained by getting capital to combine with the plentiful natural resources of the New World. The overall result was a faster growth in world output, divided between the United States and Britain. Today, the United States is the big international lender, but the general result is similar. Internationally, as domestically, lending may be unwise if the loan is unsafe, or undesirably illiquid, and

the risk is often greater on international investments. But here again, national political boundaries do not invalidate basic economic principles: We gain as individuals and as nations from having savings invested where their marginal productivity is highest.

THE FOREIGN-TRADE MULTIPLIER AND DOMESTIC EMPLOYMENT

Thus far, we have implicitly assumed that full employment prevails, and that the problem is to allocate our fully employed resources most efficiently. But in the real world of intermittent underemployment and inflation, international trade can affect the level of domestic employment and output as well.

Export sales provide jobs, just as domestic sales do. Conversely, imports replace domestic jobs. Thus, the net excess of exports over imports ("net exports" in the GNP accounts) is one component of aggregate demand that calls forth production and employment. And like any other autonomous expenditure, such as private investment, it may have a multiplier effect on GNP. Thus, the net export balance produces jobs in its own right and also has a further multiplier effect tending to create additional jobs.

But this "foreign-trade multiplier" is smaller than the regular domestic-investment multiplier, because our increased exports, by increasing domestic income, will indirectly induce more imports into the United States. We import more when our incomes rise, and the foreign-trade multiplier is reduced by the extent to which induced imports offset the original export balance. Imports are a "leakage" parallel to saving and taxes when we add the foreign-trade multiplier to the domestic multipliers from Part 2.

This reasoning makes it easy to see why nations with unemployment want to increase their net export balances, by increasing exports and/ or reducing imports. Either way, the result will be more jobs at home. Creation by this country of a net export surplus is a way of exporting unemployment to the nation that buys more U.S. goods or has its exports to the United States cut. For this reason, it is often called a "beggar-my-neighbor" policy for increasing domestic employment.

But if any nation tries to export its unemployment in a world of widespread unemployment (as in the 1930s)—say, by raising its tariffs to shut out imports—it's easy to predict the result. Rather than importing unemployment, other nations will retaliate by raising their tariffs too. Obviously, it is not possible for all nations to increase their exports and none to increase their imports, for each export is someone else's import. Thus, the main result of import restrictions aimed at exporting unemployment is likely to be retaliation abroad and a shrinkage in the total volume of international trade with no more than transient gains to any nation. This was exactly the result in the 1930s, when snowballing trade restrictions cut world trade to a small fraction of its level during the 1920s, and everyone was worse off.

THE BALANCE OF PAYMENTS

Table 39–4 summarizes the complete U.S. balance of payments in 1975, including foreign investments and government foreign aid, as well as exports and imports of private goods and services. Basically, the table shows what we

Table 39–4
U.S. balance of international payments, 1975[a]

		Amount (in billions)
I. U.S. exports (payments due United States):		
Merchandise	$107.2	
Services	22.5	
Income from investments abroad	17.8	
Total exports		$147.5
II. U.S. imports (payments due to foreigners):		
Merchandise	−$98.1	
Services and U.S. travel abroad	−21.0	
Income on foreign investments here	−11.9	
Total imports		−131.0
III. Balance on goods and services		$16.5
IV. Private foreign investment in United States (long-term)	$9.7	
V. U.S. government grants and loans (net)	−10.2	
VI. U.S. private long-term investment and private remittance abroad	−14.6	
VII. Balance on current account and long-term capital		1.4
VIII. Nonliquid short-term private capital (net)	−$2.8	
IX. Errors and unrecorded transactions	4.6	
X. Liquidity balance		3.1
XI. Decrease in foreign private liquid claims on dollars (net)	−$5.6	
XII. Increase in foreign official claims on U.S. dollars	2.5	

[a] Some minor items are omitted and data are rounded to nearest $100 million, so figures may not add or subtract exactly. Minus sign shows payment from the United States.
Source: U.S. Department of Commerce. Preliminary data.

paid to foreigners and what they paid to us. The minus items are payments from the United States to foreigners; the other items, payments from foreigners to us. The three lines in the white background are the major balances. Item III shows that we exported $16.5 billion more goods and services than we imported. VII shows that when net U.S. long-term capital movements and grants to other nations are added, our net surplus fell to $1.4 billion; this is often called the balance on current account and long-term capial, or *"basic balance."* If we then add outflows of private nonliquid short-term capital and errors and omissions (probably mainly unreported short-term capital inflow), our total *liquidity balance* for 1975 was $3.1 billion, on line X. Foreigners' transactions requiring payments to us exeeded our transactions requiring payments to them by that amount.

This net liquidity balance due us was settled by private foreigners' reducing their dollar balances by $5.6 billion, partially offset by an increase of $2.5 in the dollar balances held here by foreign official institutions.

You may be struck by the fact that gold does not appear on the table. Until recently, foreigners might have chosen to convert part or all of their dollar balances into gold at the U.S. Treasury, but in 1973, the U.S. government announced it would no longer convert dollars into gold. Thus, the government now simply holds its gold stock as part of its monetary reserves. More on the rapidly changing role of gold in Chapter 42.

The balance of payments and the balance of trade

Table 39–4 points up the importance of being clear about the difference between the "balance of payments" and the "balance of trade." **The balance of payments includes all payments between the countries concerned (all of Table 39–4). The balance of trade includes only trade in goods and services (lines I and II of the table).**[4] Popular discussion, which gener-

---

[4] It is the difference between these two (item III in Table 39–4) that is the "net exports" figure shown separately in the GNP accounts. When not shown separately, it is usually included as part of gross private investment.

ally runs in terms of the balance of trade, is often confused because of the failure to consider the entire balance of payments. U.S. capital outflows (short- and long-term investments overseas) have been huge since World War II, and, even when netted against private investment flows to the United States, have frequently exceeded the balance-of-trade surplus, thus producing an overall U.S. balance-of-payments deficit.

During the 1920s and 1930s, we generally accumulated gold and short-term balances abroad, because payments were due us on balance. Since about 1950, by contrast, we have run a persistent balance-of-payments deficit. Thus, foreigners have steadily accumulated gold and dollar balances (U.S. bank deposits and short-term investments) here, as we have made large investments abroad and have annually given foreign nations a large amount of economic and military aid, pouring billions of dollars into other nations and the international monetary system. Since 1950, foreigners have taken about $16 billion in gold from us and increased their "dollar balances" by about $125 billion as a result of the United States's persistent payments deficits.

INTERNATIONAL COMMUNITY AND CONFLICT OF INTEREST

Free international trade and lending are in the interest of the world as a whole. This is the big lesson to be learned. Since World War II, the Western noncommunist world has moved persistently toward freer trade, with the United States a leader. And the results have been satisfying. Since 1950, world trade has more than tripled in real terms, rising from less than $60 billion to nearly $800 billion in 1975 in nominal terms. This is a substantially faster growth rate than in the domestic production of most of the individual countries.

For the most part, freer trade and lending also benefit each of the individual countries concerned while world output increases. But not always. It is possible, although unlikely, that an individual nation may temporarily increase its domestic employment by shutting out competing foreign goods and exporting its unemployment. But, even assuming full employment, some other possible conflicts of interest deserve attention, as qualifications to the general argument.

1. **Personal migration.** If the "economic welfare" of the world as a whole is our aim, then international migration probably should occur whenever real wages obtainable in one country are higher than in another. But for residents of the "advanced," high-wage countries, immigration of workers from low-wage countries might prove a major blow. Assume such an influx into the United States, and assume that the immigrants are substitutable for American workers. Work out the supply-and-demand analysis yourself. Worldwide average real wages would rise, but the influx of foreign workers would surely lower the incomes of present American workers. **Given the international distribution of resources,** the law of comparative advantage applies. But the law does not say that each nation must gain from an international shift of resources, even when the shift raises the world's average standard of living.

2. **Monopoly-type action by one country.** Just as a domestic monopolist can benefit himself by restricting output, so a country may be able to benefit itself by restricting trade. But the attempt may not always work. For one thing, the international monopolist must always face the potential competition of other countries. More important, any country's restrictions on imports are likely to provoke retaliatory restrictions by other countries, and then both are worse off.

The extreme cases of nations acting as monopolists are those where foreign trade is centralized under government control—Russia, for example. But to a smaller extent, other countries have also centralized their foreign-trade activities. Brazilian coffee is an example.

3. **Growth of less-developed areas.** When a rich country lends to less-developed areas, the lender *may* find itself worse off because of the loans. This result may occur if the new areas develop industries that compete with the lender's. More often, however, the new industries are not directly competitive. In any case, as the developing country sells abroad, it can begin to buy abroad, and the law of comparative advantage ultimately applies.

4. **War.** The most important potential conflict goes beyond economics. It centers around war and preparation for war. No nation wants to depend on potential enemies for vital raw materials and finished goods, or to help build up the strength of potential enemies. With this major exception, however, economic and political considerations point in the same direction. Wide-ranging international trade and finance are probably the soundest bases for lasting peace.

REVIEW

Concepts to remember

International economics is essentially fundamental economics applied to international economic activity. But it has some new terms and concepts that you need to understand to be able to operate effectively on international problems:

law of comparative advantage	foreign-trade multiplier
comparative costs	multilateral trade
balance of payments	capital movements
balance of trade	beggar-my-neighbor policies
liquidity deficit	

**For analysis
and discussion**

1. State the basic case for specialization, division of labor, and free exchange. Are there reasons why this case applies differently within a nation and across national boundaries?

2. What industries in your area are most affected by international trade? (See Tables 39–1 and 39–2.) How important is such trade to your immediate area?

3. Suppose U.S. imports were reduced by one-half due to new tariffs or import quotas. What effect would this probably have on jobs in export industries in your area? (See Table 39–1.)

4. Explain the difference between the balance of payments and the balance of trade. On which do the data in Figures 39–1 through 39–4 throw the most light?

5. "Anyone who believes in free trade ought to believe in free international migration of labor, unrestricted by immigration barriers." Do you agree? Why, or why not?

6. What is the principle of comparative advantage? How does it relate to your answer to question 1 above?

7. Why is multilateral trade more advantageous than bilateral trade?

8. If you were wealthy, would you invest any of your money abroad? Why, or why not?

9. Why is the foreign-trade multiplier different from the domestic-investment multiplier?

Frederic Bastiat was one of the liveliest of the nineteenth-century economic liberals. He delighted in little vignettes that exposed the essence of economic issues. The following, focused on the problem of gains from international trade, is one of these.

In Bastiat's tale, Robinson Crusoe and Friday are marooned on their island. Each morning, they hunt for six hours and bring back four baskets of game. In the evening, they work in the garden for six hours and obtain four baskets of vegetables.

One day a longboat lands on the Isle of Despair. A handsome foreigner disembarks and is admitted to the table of our two recluses. He tastes and highly praises the products of the garden, and, before taking leave of his hosts, he addresses them in these words:

"Generous islanders, I dwell in a land where game is much more plentiful than it is here, but where horticulture is unknown. It will be easy for me to bring you four baskets of game every evening, if you will give me in exchange only two baskets of vegetables."

At these words, Robinson and Friday withdraw to confer, and the debate they have is too interesting not to report here in full:

FRIDAY: Friend, what do you think of it?

ROBINSON: If we accept, we are ruined.

FRIDAY: Are you quite sure of that? Let us reckon up what it comes to.

ROBINSON: It has all been reckoned up, and there can be no doubt about the outcome. This competition will simply mean the end of our hunting industry.

FRIDAY: What difference does that make if we have the game?

ROBINSON: You are just theorizing! It will no longer be the product of our labor.

FRIDAY: No matter, since in order to get it, we shall have to part with some vegetables!

ROBINSON: Then what shall we gain?

FRIDAY: The four baskets of game cost us six hours of labor. The foreigner gives them to us in exchange for two baskets of vegetables, which take us only three hours to produce. Therefore, this puts three hours at our disposal.

ROBINSON: You ought rather to say that they are subtracted from our productive activity. That is the exact amount of our loss. *Labor is wealth,* and if we lose one-fourth of our working time, we shall be one-fourth less wealthy.

FRIDAY: Friend, you are making an enormous mistake. We shall have the same amount of game, the same quantity of vegetables, and—into the bargain—three more hours at our disposal. That is what I call progress, or there is no such thing in this world.

ROBINSON: You are talking in generalities! What shall we do with these three hours?

FRIDAY: We shall do *something else.*

ROBINSON: Ah! I have you there. You are unable to mention anything in particular. *Something else, something else*—that is very easy to say.

FRIDAY: We can fish; we can decorate our cabin; we can read the Bible.

ROBINSON: Utopia! Who knows which of these things we shall do, or whether we shall do any of them? . . . Moreover, there are political reasons for rejecting the selfish offers of the perfidious foreigner.

FRIDAY: Political reasons!

ROBINSON: Yes. First, he is making us these offers only because they are advantageous to him.

FRIDAY: So much the better, since they are so for us too.

ROBINSON: Then, by this traffic, we shall make ourselves dependent upon him.

FRIDAY: And he will make himself dependent on us. We shall have need of his game; and he, of our vegetables; and we shall all live in great friendship.

ROBINSON: You are just following some abstract system!

The dispute goes on for a long time and leaves each one, as often happens, unchanged in his convictions. However, since Robinson has great influence over Friday, he makes his view prevail; and when the foreigner comes to learn how his offer has been received, Robinson says to him:

"Foreigner, in order for us to accept your proposal, we must be very sure about two things:

"First, that game is not more plentiful on your island than on ours; for we want to fight only *on equal terms.*

"Second, that you will lose by this bargain. For, as in every exchange there is necessarily a gainer and a loser, we should be victimized if you were not the loser. What do you say?"

"Nothing," says the foreigner. And, bursting into laughter, he reembarks in his longboat."[5]

---

1. Who is right, Crusoe or Friday?
2. Do you see any fallacies in Friday's reasoning?
3. Is it true that in every exchange, there is necessarily a gaining and a losing party?

---

[5] Adapted from Frederic Bastiat, *Economic Sophisms* (New York: Van Nostrand Reinhold, 1964), pp. 245–48.

CASE 34
MULTINATIONAL CORPORATIONS

The years since World War II have seen a spectacular growth in the importance of multinational corporations, which have been called the most successful innovation in international relations since Adam Smith. "Multinational" corporations are companies with production and distribution facilities in several or many countries; often, ownership of the subsidiaries in different countries is shared with nationals of those countries. Thus, multinationals (sometimes called "transnationals") differ from the "international" companies that for many years have exported part of their production for sale abroad. In 1950, for example, U.S. direct investment abroad through multinationals was $11 billion; today, it is nearly $125 billion. Ford Motor Company, for example, has some 40 foreign-based subsidiaries, which produce and sell about 30 percent of its total output and provide jobs for about 30 percent of its 465,000 employees.

In 1974, the fifty largest industrial companies in the world, nearly all multinationals, had sales exceeding a half-trillion dollars, equal to about 10 percent of the world's total GNP. Exxon's sales are greater than the GNPs of most of the world's smaller nations. The table shows the fifteen largest industrial multinationals. Strikingly, eight of the top ten were oil companies, reflecting the huge increase in oil prices by the OPEC countries in that year. The other two were GM and Ford, by far the world's biggest auto companies. Eleven of the top fifteen were headquartered in the United States, but only 26 of the top 50 were American. British, German and Japanese companies were prominent on the list. The world's largest banks are similarly multinational, with a similar international-ownership flavor.

Why? Why have multinationals grown so? Why do they produce abroad rather than producing at home and exporting part of their products? Fundamentally, because it's cheaper the multinational way (although they may also produce abroad to get inside host-country tariff barriers and for other reasons). Adam Smith might disapprove of the huge size of some multi-

The largest multinationals, 1974

Company	Headquarters	Sales (in billions)
1. Exxon	New York	$42
2. Royal Dutch/Shell	London/The Hague	33
3. General Motors	Detroit	32
4. Ford	Dearborn, Mich.	24
5. Texaco	New York	23
6. Mobil Oil	New York	19
7. British Petroleum	London	18
8. Standard Oil of Calif.	San Francisco	17
9. National Iranian Oil	Tehran	17
10. Gulf Oil	Pittsburgh	16
11. Unilever	London	14
12. General Electric	Fairfield, Conn.	13
13. IBM	Armonk, N.Y.	13
14. International T&T	New York	11
15. Chrysler	Highland Park, Mich.	11

Source: *Fortune,* August 1975.

nationals, but he would surely commend their efficiency in shifting capital and production around the world to those areas where they promise the highest return. The multinational has proved a powerful ally of the principle of comparative advantage.

Fifty or a hundred years ago, most direct business investment abroad was from rich to poor countries, focused on exploiting natural resources, building railways, and developing manufacturing that used cheap local labor. The postwar multinational boom has fundamentally changed this pattern. Recent multinational investment has been predominantly in other developed countries—in Western Europe, Canada, Japan, and the United States. Immediately after World War II, about 55 percent of all U.S. direct investment abroad was in the less-developed ("Third World") countries. Today, 70 percent of the total is in the developed nations. Moreover, the nature of U.S. direct investment abroad has shifted dramatically toward high-technology products where research and development, high-skilled manpower, and sophisticated management are vital (for instance, petro-chemicals, electronics, and computers), away from the massive capital-using manufacturing and transportation industries. Recent large investments in

the less-developed nations are mostly in petroleum production and refining.

Some problems Are the multinationals good for everyone? Not necessarily. After World War II, they were welcomed nearly everywhere—in Western Europe as their investments helped rebuild war-torn economies, and in less-developed nations as they provided scarce capital needed to develop industrial capabilities. But as the war-torn economies regained their health and American-based multinationals took over more and more local industries—especially high-technology products that seemed vital to rapid economic growth and military preparedness—local sentiment began to shift against the multinationals, especially in France. A prominent French writer, Servan-Schreiber, created a sensation with his *American Challenge,* in which he predicted that the American-based multinationals might well become the world's greatest international power, after only the United States and the USSR. Three problems have received most attention.

The multinationals vs. nationalism. Huge multinational companies are fundamentally a challenge to the supremacy of national economic, and even political and military, power. When national interests of the host country conflict with those of the multinational company, which will dominate? The host country clearly has the legal power to require the multinational to obey national laws if it operates within the host's boundaries; at the extreme, the host can expropriate the multinational's properties and expel the company. But to do so may have high costs. Future investors will think twice before coming, and the expelled multinational may have skills, technology, and capital that the host country badly needs.

Recently, host nations have increasingly asserted their power over visiting multinationals. Wholesale expropriation of multinational oil properties is the most visible example; but smaller examples abound. If the multinational loses money on a plant (Hilton Hotels in Spain, Chrysler in France), decisions to slow or close down production may be denied by the host government, and the multinational can either maintain operations, temporarily absorbing the loss, or risk being taken over. Usually, multinationals find it expedient to give in to the host government, although often the solution is a bargained compromise. The cards are seldom all on one side. Companies like IBM, which has technology, management skills, and capital that are badly needed in many nations, bargain from a very strong position. But few nations are willing to see outside companies in a position to dominate their national economic and even military developments. It is a rare case now where the multinational can maintain 100 percent ownership of its direct investment abroad; domestic ownership of 51 percent of the local subsidiary's stock is an increasingly common requirement.

Balance-of-payments problems. When multinationals make profits abroad, they often want to bring them home to the stockholders. Even though the host country may know it is better off economically with than without the foreign investment, even if most or all of the profits are repatriated, this drain is sure to cause resentment—and when multinational investment is large, profit repatriation may mean a large annual balance-of-payments outflow for the host country.

Moreover, the multinational is almost certain to face difficult decisions on currency management. If it expects the host country's currency to weaken, shall it convert its holdings into dollars to avoid the loss—thereby, of course, increasing the probability that the host country's currency will weaken? If it does, the multinational will be seen as speculating against the host's currency. But if it does not, it is clearly imposing a loss on its stockholders that it could have avoided by selling the local currency. To whom is the multinational's subsidiary first responsible—the parent company, or the host nation?

The problem is even more complex. If an American-based multinational moves its production to Europe or Singapore, the American labor movement protests that this steals jobs from American workers and gives them to lower-wage foreign workers. At the same time, the capital outflow weakens the U.S. balance of payments. Worse, the multinational may begin to export goods from its new facility abroad back to the United States, which both competes with American-made products and increases the flow of dollars abroad. The offset, of course, is the flow of profits that will soon be established to the United States if the investment abroad has been a wise one. Whether the overall effect of American-based multinationals on the U.S. balance of payments is plus or minus is still a matter of debate. As to their effect on American jobs and wages and on the American standard of living, work it out for yourself, using the principle of comparative advantage. Or wait for Chapter 40, which deals specifically with such problems.

Tax problems and transfer pricing. When multinationals operate in many countries, and especially when they produce components and final products in different countries, they can substantially control where they make their profits by the "transfer prices" their components subsidiaries charge the final-assembly subsidiary. Since taxes vary widely among countries, multinationals often have a major incentive to set transfer prices that show the company's profits as being made largely in low-tax countries. This may be great for the company's stockholders and the low-tax country, but it is sure to raise hackles in the other countries to which the multinational pays few taxes. For example, the big American oil multinationals have long paid only small taxes to the United States, because a big part of the price paid to the oil-producing nations has been formally levied as a tax, not as a price for the oil. But here again, the problem is complex. Suppose the United States did not give multinational companies credit for income taxes paid abroad against their U.S. income tax liabilities. The companies could readily end up with tax rates over 100 percent. Would this be good for the companies and the United States? Would it be equitable?

Multinationals and the less-developed countries. The strongest criticisms of the multinationals come from the less-developed countries, which often see themselves as the victims of imperialist exploitation by multinationals based in the highly developed, rich nations. The imperialism charge raises complex issues, which we will consider in Chapter 45. As we shall see, by and large the multinationals have raised the living standards of the less-developed countries in which they have made direct investments, although they have sometimes made very large profits in the process, with most of the gain going to the multinational's stockholders and only a little to the host country. The principle again is that of comparative advantage. Even critics have stated that American multinationals have done more to raise LDC living standards than all our AID programs. But the overriding issue, as in the developed nations, is often that of nationalism, national pride, and resentment of foreign control. Economic analysis alone cannot solve the imperialism controversy.

Multinationals and a new world order? Today's huge multinational corporations seem to some the framework for a new world order. They see the managers of such corporations as true citizens of the world, international civil servants advancing the interests of the people of the world, not the individual interests of the nation-states that have so long dominated international affairs. Multinational rationalization of world production could, they argue, serve as the foundation for advancement of international economic efficiency and the world interest, replacing the narrow nation-state jealousies that have led to so much international friction and conflict in the past. But others counter that the multinationals constitute a threat to the common people. How can huge, oligopolistic corporations, dedicated to profit making as their primary goal, provide the basis for a stable world where the interests of individual citizens and groups are the ultimate good?

There are no simple right and wrong answers to most of the big questions raised by this case. We don't know whether big multinationals will prosper and grow, or whether they are being effectively checked by strong nationalist countertendencies. Nor can we say for sure whether their results are on balance good for mankind, or bad. But the central economic forces they represent are powerful ones, which clearly can contribute much to producing efficiently the goods and services that most countries and individuals want. For the multinationals to vanish would be a surprising development indeed.

Try a combination of analysis and speculation on the following questions:

1. Why would Adam Smith, if he were here today, approve or disapprove of the development of multinational corporations?

2. If an American-based multinational producing computers (say, IBM) invests in France by buying up a French computer company, what is the probable effect on U.S. investors? French investors? American workers? French workers? the U.S. standard of living? the French standard of living? (Use the principle of comparative advantage in thinking through your answers.)

3. Should America welcome investments here by foreign-based multinationals—say, by the National Iranian Oil Company? Would your answer be different if the foreign company planned to buy control of U.S. steel mills, computer companies, or banks?

4. Would you favor a plan whereby multinationals would become truly transnational—say, based on some independent island rather than in any existing nation?

5. If you managed the British subsidiary of an American-based multinational auto company and you strongly expected the British pound to be devalued against the dollar, would you continue to hold the pounds you now have, or would you convert them into dollars?

6. Should the world's nations try—say, through the UN—to agree on ways to encourage the rapid growth of multinational corporations? Is your answer different for the developed and the less-developed nations? If so, explain why.

CHAPTER 40

Tariffs, Import Quotas, and Free Trade

Adam Smith's *Wealth of Nations* in 1776 was a major attack on barriers to free international trade. The case for free trade internationally is the same as the case for free trade domestically, Smith argued. It is that specialization and division of labor with free exchange of the resulting products that makes possible a higher standard of living for everyone. Tariffs, import quotas, or other barriers to free international trade impede such mutually advantageous specialization and exchange and reduce living standards throughout the world, just as would barriers to free trade within a nation.

Yet from Smith's day to this, many have remained unconvinced. Support for tariffs and import quotas to "protect the American standard of living and the high wages of American workers" is still widespread. Why?

THE TARIFF

A tariff is a tax on imports, whose major goal is to restrict imports. Figure 40–1 shows average U.S. tariff rates on dutiable imports since 1820. From peak rates of about 60 percent under the Tariff Act of 1833 and the Smoot-Hawley Tariff of 1930, average tariff rates on covered products have been cut to below 10 percent in the last two decades, including a

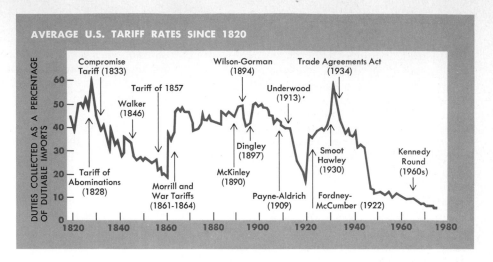

AVERAGE U.S. TARIFF RATES SINCE 1820

Figure 40-1
U.S. tariff rates have fluctuated with changing times and attitudes. Since 1934, they have been reduced sharply to the lowest levels in our history. (Source: U.S. Department of Commerce.)

last downward push by the "Kennedy round" in the 1960s. These figures understate the real restrictive effect of the tariff, because some products are shut out completely by the tariff, and they don't show up in Figure 40–1. But any way you look at it, major progress has been made in reducing U. S. tariff barriers since the early 1930s. The United States, after a spotty history of restrictionism, has been a leader in a worldwide push toward freer trade.

The history books are full of accounts of the tariff acts battled through Congress over nearly two centuries, and of the regional and political issues underlying them. Our job is to look objectively at the economics of tariffs—to apply the economic analysis of the preceding chapters to the major arguments advanced in support of tariffs. And the central principle to use is the law of comparative advantage.

Some partially valid arguments

Nations may use tariffs to stimulate the development of "infant industries," to ensure the continued operation of industries deemed essential to the national defense, and to stimulate more diversification of industries in order to avoid too much reliance on one or a few industries in foreign trade. All these arguments may be valid, if the nation wants to achieve these goals even though it incurs a lower standard of living at least temporarily by doing so. All involve shutting out lower-cost foreign

products, and hence paying higher prices for domestically produced products. A nation may choose to incur these costs to achieve other goals. But it should recognize the costs involved in doing so.

Over the last century in the United States, these partially valid arguments have carried little weight in tariff controversies. Let us now turn to the arguments that have been the important ones in support of the tariff. As we shall see, they turn out to be largely fallacious.

The favorable-balance-of-trade argument

Most naïve of all the tariff arguments is the desire for a "favorable balance of trade" for its own sake. It goes back to the old mercantilist desire to gain more gold and silver as national treasure. Two major fallacies are involved.

First, there is nothing generally favorable about a "favorable" balance of trade. A continued "favorable" balance means that we continually give foreigners more goods and services than they give us; we receive in exchange gold (often to be held idle at considerable storage expense) or investments abroad. Thus, it means a **reduced** standard of living for the country sending away goods and services, certainly in the

543

short run, and indefinitely if the "favorable" balance of trade continues without willingness to accept goods from abroad. We don't eat gold. Our standard of living is made up of the goods and services we obtain.

Second, a favorable balance of trade is impossible as a continuing policy, if we consider only the goods-and-services portion of the balance of payments. Foreigners can't buy from us unless they get dollars to pay for our products. The way they get dollars is by selling us their goods and services It is only by buying from foreigners that we can expect to sell to them.

There is no point more fundamental than this: We can sell abroad only if we buy abroad. It is basic to understanding the fallacy in nearly every argument for protective tariffs and other trade-restriction policies. Figure 40–2 shows where other countries obtained the dollars to buy our exports from 1929 to 1975 (U.S. exports are indicated by the heavy black line). Private investments abroad and government aid helped foreigners finance their purchases from us. **But our purchases of foreign goods and services have always been the big source of dollars with**

which foreigners bought our exports. To sell abroad, we must buy abroad. We cannot shut out foreign imports and continue to export.

The protect-home-industry argument

Perhaps the most popular argument for the tariff is that we need it to protect American industry against low-cost foreign competition.

A domestic industry asking for tariff protection argues that without protection, its market will be lost to foreign competitors. This will force the domestic industry out of business, throwing workers out of jobs. Suppose that the industry is right; if it does not receive protection it *will* lose its market to foreign competitors. What are the effects of giving the tariff protection the industry wants?[1]

---

[1] Often, industries seeking protective tariffs would be able to retain their markets without tariffs; tariffs enable them to raise domestic prices with lessened fear of foreign competition. Indeed, the tariff has been called "the mother of monopolies," because it helps domestic monopolies to exist by shutting out foreign competition.

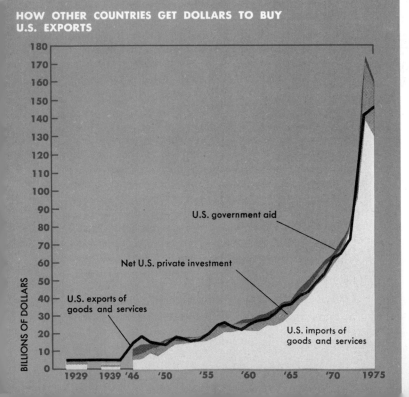

HOW OTHER COUNTRIES GET DOLLARS TO BUY U.S. EXPORTS

Figure 40–2
Other countries get dollars with which to buy U.S. exports mainly through our payments for imports. But net U.S. investments abroad and government foreign aid also provide a good many dollars. (Source: U.S. Department of Commerce. Military aid and exports excluded.)

The first effect is that domestic consumers must pay more for the protected product than if it had come in free. If sugar comes in over the tariff, consumers must pay the regular price of the foreign sugar plus the tariff duty. If the tariff shuts out foreign sugar, domestic consumers must pay a higher price for domestic sugar. We know it's higher because domestic producers cannot, without a tariff, produce and sell at a price low enough to meet foreign competition. If they could, they wouldn't need the tariff.

Second, domestic sugar producers are subsidized by the tariff; they are enabled to charge higher prices than would have been possible if foreign competition had not been shut out. It's clear that domestic producers are the great gainers from a tariff on their product.

In effect, therefore, a tariff is a subsidy to domestic producers, financed by consumers through higher prices for the protected product. Moreover, the more inefficient domestic producers are, the higher tariff they need to protect them against foreign competition and the larger subsidy they receive.

Indeed, industry's argument for a tariff is often for a "scientific" tariff that would just "equalize domestic and foreign costs of production." A suggestion in Congress that special taxes be levied on consumers to finance subsidies to producers, the size of each subsidy to be determined by the producer's inefficiency, would horrify everyone. Yet this is substantially the result of a "scientific" protective tariff designed to equalize foreign and domestic costs of production.

The same economist, Frederic Bastiat, who was responsible for Case 33, put the free-trade case against protection tellingly over a century ago, in his satirical "Petition of the Candlemakers." We need protection, said the candlemakers of Paris in their petition. Foreign competitors are bad enough, but it is the sun that is the most unfair competitor of all. Each day it shines and throws light over all, at no cost at all. If you only shut out the sun, pleaded the candlemakers, we can have a magnificent candle industry, giving jobs to untold numbers of workers.

Should we protect American domestic industry against cheap foreign competition today, using the same arguments that Bastiat's candlemakers did a century ago?

The protect-our-high-wages argument

American wages are among the highest in the world. Therefore, it is argued, unless we have a protective tariff, competition from low-wage nations will pull down high American wages to the level of wages abroad.

The "Petition of the Candlemakers" should suggest a fallacy here. Would the real wages of French workers have been raised by shutting out the sun? Would the French people have been better off? Look at the argument in detail.

First, why are wages now higher in the United States than in other countries? Fundamentally, because of the high productivity of American workers. Anything that raises their productivity makes it possible for them to receive higher real wages. And each worker can receive his highest-possible wage when he works where his marginal productivity is highest.

What happens when a tariff is passed to "protect" high American wages? The tariff shuts out foreign products and permits relatively inefficient American idustries to grow up where they otherwise could not have existed, giving new jobs to American workers. But, as a result, American exports will fall off, because foreign countries cannot buy from us unless we buy from them. (Remember Figure 40–2 above.) Therefore, fewer workers are employed in the export industries. **The net result is a shift of workers from relatively efficient export industries (where they would be situated under free trade) into less-efficient protected industries. As workers move to lower-marginal-productivity positions in protected industries, the wages they can receive in the new jobs are necessarily lower than they could have been before the shift. The long-run result of a protective tariff is to lower real wages, not to raise them. People earn the most when they work where they are most efficient.**[2]

[2] This is not to deny that a protective tariff on a particular product may raise the real wages of workers *in that industry* by increasing the demand for labor there, as long as there are immobilities in the domestic labor market that keep other workers from moving in to take advantage of the higher labor demand provided there by protection.

To be sure you understand this point, consider an extreme example cited by proponents of a tariff to protect American wages. Suppose that Japanese labor is paid only one-third as much as U.S. workers and we remove all tariffs on Japanese imports. Won't American workers be forced to take much lower wages to compete?

In analyzing this case, we first need to recognize that even though Japanese daily wages are much lower, it is not necessarily true that the labor costs of Japanese producers are correspondingly lower. The Japanese worker gets lower wages, but he also produces less in a day. Therefore, the labor cost per unit of output may be as much, or more, for the Japanese producer as for the American. For example, suppose the average hourly wage of Japanese industrial workers is $2, that in America $4. But suppose that, for example, in the chinaware industry, the hourly output per worker in Japan is 50 plates; then the labor cost per plate is 4 cents. If the hourly output per American worker is 100 plates, the labor cost per plate would be only 4 cents too. Wage cost per plate (per unit of output) is the one that counts.

The evidence is clear that although U.S. wages are high, U.S. unit costs are highly competitive in many industries. Our $100 billion worth of annual merchandise exports is impressive evidence. Wages and unit labor costs have risen rapidly everywhere in the Western world during the post–World War II period, but faster in nearly every other industrialized nation than in the United States. U.S. average hourly compensation in manufacturing in 1975 was $6.22, below the $6.32 figure for West Germany but well above France's $4.58, the U.K.'s $3.24, and Japan's $3.11. Fifteen years earlier, the U.S. average of $2.66 per hour was more than three times that in France and Germany, and nearly ten times that in Japan. Unit labor costs grew in the United States at about 5 percent a year over the last decade, in Germany, Japan, and France at 10–12 percent. Note that what happens to unit labor costs depends on both the rate of increase in wage rates and changes in labor productivity.[3]

Suppose, to continue the hypothetical example above, that even when productivity differences are taken into account, Japan can far undersell us on china plates, and that we remove the tariff on china. This move, of course, would throw workers in the American chinaware industry out of jobs. But since Japan would then be selling more to us, she could now buy more from us. She would buy from us those goods that we are able to produce most efficiently—say, computers. Workers thrown out of jobs in making china would gradually be drawn into the computer indutry. But since the United States is, by assumption, comparatively more efficient in producing computers than china, workers can

[3] For more complete data, see *International Economic Report of the President* for 1976, pp. 71–79.

"Don't be childish, man! Kicking Toyotas is no answer to our balance-of-trade gap." (Drawing by Donald Reilly; © 1971. The New Yorker Magazine, Inc.)

receive higher wages in the computer industry. Workers in the china industry would surely be temporarily unemployed and, if personally unadaptable, might never be reemployed. But the general public would gain by obtaining cheaper china, and more workers would be drawn into the high-productivity industries where wages are highest. Removal of an existing tariff may ruin protected producer groups; yet in the long run, average wages and the standard of living for the economy as a whole will be raised.

This reasoning, however, rides easily over some tough short-run adjustment problems. Higher average wages for the economy don't help the 50-year-old china maker thrown out of work by the new imports. Where will he get another equally good job, or even one at all? The offsetting new jobs, in industries producing for export may not come immediately. The Japanese may temporarily accumulate dollars, or spend them elsewhere. Sooner or later, our expanded imports will mean new export markets. But with these uncertainties and the pain felt in the displaced industries, it's easy to understand why some labor opposition to tariff cuts is bitter. Nor does the higher national standard of living help those china-company stockholders whose investment is destroyed by the cheap imports. The opposition comes from investors and businessmen as well as from workers.

The increased-employment argument

In the long run, it should be clear by now, a protective tariff neither increases nor decreases employment, but merely shifts resources from more-efficient to less-efficient industries. However, the short-run adjustments in moving toward the new long-run equilibrium may be slow and painful (as with any shift in demand). Removing an existing tariff may result in unemployment that may persist stubbornly if aggregate demand is weak.

But the protectionist argument claims more. **It says that, at least in the short run, raising tariffs will create more jobs as domestic firms begin selling to the customers who previously bought imported goods.** And the foreign-trade multiplier will amplify the creation of domestic jobs. Even though in the long run this may not increase total employment, temporarily the new tariff will raise exports relative to imports and create jobs.

But this is a short-sighted argument. Suppose America puts on a tariff to shut out foreign goods and to export our unemployment. What would you do if you were Belgium, or England, or France? You'd come right back with higher tariffs or quotas against American exports. And that's just what they did during the 1930s. If we can increase our exports relative to imports in a period of unemployment, this may temporarily raise employment and real GNP. But it's unlikely that higher tariffs will do the job, and likely that the main result will just be less trade for everyone.

Summary

From this analysis, we can draw a broad summary of the economic effects of tariffs. **In the long run,** a protective tariff lowers real wages and the standard of living. It diverts resources from self-sustaining export industries to less-efficient, protected domestic-consumption industries; and it forces consumers to pay higher prices.[4] **In the short run,** advantages may be gained from imposing new tariffs to aid infant industries or to reduce unemployment. However, new tariffs will increase domestic employment only if almost inevitable retaliatory steps are not taken by other nations.

Tariff making in the United States

If the protective tariff is open to such serious criticism, and if it benefits only particular groups at the cost of the rest of society, why have we had high protective tariffs so long. There are two chief answers.

First, public opinion on the tariff has been greatly influenced by self-seeking propaganda, and many citizens are uninformed on the nature of international trade. Groups seeking protection

---

[4]Even though as a practical matter, U.S. tariff reductions are nearly always advocated on the presumption of reciprocal reductions by other nations, the logic of comparative advantage shows that under most circumstances, even unilateral tariff reductions will benefit the country making them.

have presented their case effectively in Congress and to the general public, and the appeal to nationalism against foreigners is a potent rallying cry.

Second, the benefits of freer trade are widespread—lower prices, and more jobs in export industries tomorrow. But the costs are concentrated and direct—on the businessmen and workers who lose out to cheaper foreign imports. The threatened interests are alarmed, organized, and vocal. Consumers as a whole are not organized to speak effectively. Congress passes acts covering thousands of products, and most of the actual decisions are made by small subcommittees in the House and Senate. Each congressman is pressed by his constituents to vote for protection for the goods that they produce. Thus, the congressman from one state will vote for a tariff on shoes if his colleague from another state will vote for one on sugar. The tariff is the classic example of congressional logrolling. (Remember the "political failures" of Chapter 36.) Thus, the big tariff reductions since 1930 have come through congressional delegation of tariff-cutting authority to the president.

Recent trade-expansion legislation has included an important special provision. The International Trade Commission (formerly the Tariff Commission) can recommend to the president, where imports are a "substantial cause of serious harm" to a domestic industry, either imposition of tariffs, import quotas, or dollar "adjustment assistance" to workers and companies in the injured industry. If the president does not accept the recommendation of the commission, Congress can override him and impose the commission's recommendation directly. In 1975, for example, the commission recommended new import quotas on specialty steels, and President Ford imposed the recommended quota, against vigorous protests by free traders. But he refused to accept a divided commission recommendation for similar action on shoes (which total over $1 billion of imports annually), decreeing instead that adjustment assistance be made available to both displaced workers and companies that lost markets to imports. He emphasized that import restrictions would raise prices to American consumers. How much adjustment assistance is provided in such cases depends on both adminis-

tration proposals and congressional action in providing funds—to unemployed workers through grants similar to unemployment insurance, and to firms through loans and government technical assistance.

IMPORT QUOTAS AND EXPORT SUBSIDIES

The United States and most other major nations now use import quotas as well as tariffs to protect domestic producers. The United States now has import quotas for 67 major product categories, ranging from oil, steel, and textiles to minor consumer items like brooms. Japan and most European nations have roughly similar import quota structures.

Import quotas are more disruptive to free trade than are tariffs. With a quota, additional foreign goods cannot enter, no matter how much more efficient foreign producers may be. With a tariff, at least foreign goods may enter if their cost advantage is large enough to overcome the tariff barrier.

Bargaining on import quotas has become a more important means of adjusting competitive trade positions than are tariff negotiations. U.S. unions and businessmen in areas exposed to foreign competition have become strong advocates of tougher U.S. quotas, and have pressed for Japanese and West European agreements to limit exports to the United States. The provisions for more aid to injured U.S. workers and businesses are a move to buy off some opposition to freer trade, a move clearly justified to avoid imposing the full cost of socially desirable changes on a small sector of the economy.

Export subsidies are another device widely used to provide domestic producers a special advantage over foreign competitors in world markets. U.S. farm price-support programs are considered by many foreigners to provide, in effect, a large export subsidy to U.S. farm exporters. U.S. legislation also permits the use of "countervailing duties" against such subsidies given by foreign nations that sell in this country. Such contervailing duties have recently been levied on a variety of food imports from Europe. Moreover, the United States calculates its tariff duties on major chemical imports by pricing them at U.S. market levels, in effect imposing a higher tariff barrier; this is the controversial so-called "American selling price" provision. Conversely, some nations (especially Japan and many developing economies) use foreign-exchange controls to limit the purchase of particular products from foreigners.

Nontariff barriers to trade constitute the major current threat to continued progress toward free world trade.

THE EUROPEAN COMMON MARKET

After World War II, the spirit of internationalism was strong. All the victorious nations except the USSR moved to extend their wartime collaboration into economic cooperation that would reverse the restrictionist wave of the 1930s. Within the framework of the United Nations, the General Agreement on Tariffs and Trade (GATT) was created. It provides for regular discussion of means to reduce international trade barriers among members, and each member nation agrees to work toward freer trade practices, insofar as these practices are not in conflict with the country's national legislation.

But the biggest postwar move toward international economic cooperation is the European Common Market, and a major move it is. After earlier cooperation on coal, iron, and atomic energy, in 1958 six European nations—Belgium, France, Italy, Luxembourg, the Netherlands, and West Germany—banded together in the European Economic Community (EEC), generally called the Common Market. This precedent-shattering agreement has eliminated all tariff and similar trade barriers against one another and has gradually equalized all their restrictions on trade with nations outside the six, so they present a common tariff to the outside world. Barriers against internal movement of capital and labor are being abolished. Other economic policies will be "harmonized." A common antitrust policy is provided to eliminate long-time restrictions on competition, although here, considerable freedom is left for national differences. In essence, the Common Market is a new, huge, free-trade area.

In 1973, Denmark, Ireland, and the United Kingdom joined the Common Market. "The Nine" now have a total population of 260 million, larger than either the United States or the USSR. Their combined GNP was $1.3 trillion in 1975, far more than the USSR's and nearly 90 percent that of the United States. Combined, The Nine are by far the largest exporter and importer in the world; their 1975 exports and imports (including intercountry trade) were nearly $300 billion each, nearly triple those of the United States. Their combined international monetary reserves were $70 billion, far in excess of ours. The EEC is a huge economic bloc.

While the Common Market has been a powerful force toward free trade among its member countries, its push toward freer world trade is less clear. The Nine agree to have a common external tariff against other countries, but the agreement says nothing about the level of that external tariff. This situation confronts American business firms and American trade policy with a new challenge. American export markets inside the Common Market are in serious danger, because our products must pay the common external tariff while competitive prducts made within the Common Market pay no tariff. Intra–Common Market trade has grown far more than EEC trade with other nations. Recently the EEC has faced serious internal political and monetary strains that have slowed its progress. But we negotiate with the EEC on roughly equal economic terms.

America's response thus far has been a combination of public and private action. The U.S. government has bargained hard with the Common Market countries for lower tariffs against U.S. commodities (especially farm products) in exchange for larger European exports to the United States. But the private-market response has been stronger. Many American-based multinational companies have established plants or subsidiaries inside the Common Market, thus escaping the external tariff. Indeed, American investment by large multinational firms has grown so large that some European nations, especially France, have increasingly controlled U.S. direct investment there. (See Case 34.)

REVIEW

**For analysis
and discussion**

1. Recently, when France raised her import barriers against chickens, the United States raised its tariff on French brandy. Who gained and who lost by these actions? Are such retaliatory tariff increases good for the country making them?

2. What is the fallacy in the "Petition of the Candlemakers" for protection against the sun? Is the same fallacy present in other arguments for protective tariffs?

3. List the factors that explain the high wages received by American workers in the steel and chemical industries. Which, if any, would be affected and in which direction, if American tariffs were raised on steel and chemicals?

4. Presidents Kennedy, Nixon, and Ford all supported "adjustment assistance" for workers and firms that suffer because U.S. tariffs that previously protected them are removed. Do you agree? How large should such assistance be, and who should pay for it?

5. Are there any industries in the United States today that seem clearly to deserve tariff protection as "infant industries"?

6. Can you suggest any ways whereby, in a period of depression, the United States could raise its tariffs against foreign goods and avoid probable retaliation?

The following are excerpts from a statement of I.W. Abel, president, United Steelworkers and Industrial Union Department, AFL-CIO, in *Tariff and Trade Proposals*, Hearings before the House Ways and Means Committee, on May 22, 1970 (pp. 1776–81):

We are here today because many of our members have already been hurt by imports, and many more live in apprehension, with the fear that in the not too distant future they too will be elbowed out of a job by the growing flood of foreign imports. We are here to voice these deep-rooted concerns.

The world has changed. . . .

First, there has been a dramatic revival of the war-devastated economies, a revival which we helped. Japan is a most remarkable example of this recovery. . . . The Japanese expect—in five years—to be producing more steel than the United States. . . .

Another change is that technology has become international. It has become international because of improved communications and a sharp rise in United States investment in foreign countries—investment not only of money but of American technology.

Another startling new phenomenon on the world scene is the multinational corporation. . . .

As Fortune magazine has pointed out, these multinational firms like to buy cheap and sell dear—producing where costs are lowest and selling where prices are highest. The operations of American firms on the Mexican side of the border are another example of the problem of the multinational corporation. . . . They take advantage of Mexican law for its border area, U.S. tariff regulations, and low-wage Mexican labor, then ship the goods back to the United States, and sell them at U.S. prices. . . .

To put it bluntly, these American corporations which use components and complete units made overseas—at sweatshop wages—and sold here with no reduction in price—commit a kind of fraud against the American consumer.

In some circles, efforts are made to perpetuate the myth that American consumers benefit from such arrangements. But the truth is that in most cases, American consumers pay American prices. . . .

Delegate after delegate at our [last] convention arose to describe the impact of these new world trade conditions upon his members. . . .

In the textile industry, for example, we learned that imports more than doubled between 1964 and 1968. Today, the textile industry is up against the wall because of imports. The glass workers, too, are seriously concerned about imports. In one Pennsylvania county alone, imports have caused the loss of 1,500 jobs in the county's glass industry. . . .

Also in the electronics field, some 60 percent of black-and-white TV sets and 17 percent of the color TV sets last year were made in foreign countries, and virtually all transistors are now made overseas. . . .

The shoe workers, like the textile workers, are living in a nightmare of an increasing flood of imports that is washing out factories and jobs. Since 1955, the number of foreign-made shoes imported in 1969 were equivalent to the exportation and the loss of 65,000 job opportunities. . . .

Some will make the charge that we are putting on the cloak of protectionism. Those who do so fail to recognize that old concepts and labels of "free trade" and "protectionism" have become obsolete. They have been outdated in this new world of managed national economies, international technocracy, multinational corporations, and record U.S. investment overseas.

I would also say to those who charge us with seizing the banner of protectionism: We still believe in a healthy expansion of trade with other nations. But our support for the balanced expansion of trade does not mean we believe in the promotion of private greed at public expense. It does not mean that such expansion of trade should undercut unfairly the wages and working standards of Americans. . . .

That international trade is a two-way street is a truism which has long been neglected. The very countries, like Japan, which most strongly criticize our movement toward import restrictions, themselves are among the most protectionist in the world. That is, we open our markets to them while they close their markets to us.

Here are a few suggestions:

1. Industries, large and small, which have been seriously hurt by unrestricted tides of foreign imports include: textiles, including man-made fibers and rugs; autos, radios, TVs, and other consumer electronic products; shoes, sheet glass, furniture, pianos, apparel, ceramics, stainless-steel flatware, and so forth. The list is by no means complete, and it is growing.

   We believe these industries to be of basic importance to the American economy. We believe our more seriously affected industries must be assured of at least a modest share in the total economy's growth. This means that future import increases in such industries must be regulated and that their import growth, whether from foreign firms or from U.S.-owned offshore production facilities, must be proportionate to the total growth of the domestic market. . . .

   Sound policy also means we must adopt measures to limit and tax the export of capital which finances the establishment, acquisition, or expansion of U.S.-owned manufacturing facilities abroad.

2. Truth-in-import labeling legislation to identify the manufacturer and nation of origin of all imported products would serve an important purpose.

3. It is important that there be a clearly defined international crash program to quickly raise substandard wage levels to acceptable minimums, together with a longer-range program to raise such wages closer to our own domestic legal minimums within prescribed periods of time. There is a clear need for the creation of international fair labor standards, and the U.S. government should take aggressive leadership in such efforts. . . .

4. There should be more effective adjustment assistance for all workers displaced by a rise in imports, where it is a major or significantly contributing cause of such displacement. . . .

Your congressman is a member of the House Ways and Means Committee. Do you advise him to accept or to reject Mr. Abel's analysis and recommendations? Write him a letter explaining why. If you favor any of the recommendations, indicate what specific steps you believe Congress should take.

41

INTERNATIONAL ADJUSTMENTS AND THE BALANCE OF PAYMENTS

Domestic and international trade are essentially similar, but in foreign trade two different currencies are involved. This chapter explains first how international transactions are financed, and then how international economic adjustments occur under different international monetary systems.

FINANCING FOREIGN TRANSACTIONS

If you buy woolens from England, the English seller wants British pounds, not American dollars. You need to convert your dollars into pounds if you're going to buy his cloth. What do you do?

There is a continuous demand for this sort of currency conversion, and many big city banks stand ready to sell you pounds, or almost any other foreign currency, for dollars. If you go to your local bank to buy pounds, it will simply pass the transaction along to a big bank in the foreign-exchange business.

Suppose that you want to pay a Britisher £1,000 in British money for the woolen goods. You go to a bank—say, the Chase Manhattan in New York—to buy 1,000 British pounds. The Chase Manhattan is a regular dealer in foreign currencies. It sells you the pounds at the going rate—assume it's £1 for $2. You pay the Chase

Manhattan Bank $2,000 and get a special check, made out to the bearer, for £1,000. This special type of check is called "foreign exchange."

Then you send the check over to the British manufacturer. He takes it to his bank in London and gets his £1,000. His bank presents the check to the Chase Manhattan's London branch for payment, and the transaction is completed (except that we have omitted the small commission charged you by the Chase Manhattan on the deal). You have paid $2,000. The seller has received £1,000.[1]

The rate at which you can buy British pounds with American dollars is called the "exchange rate." When you buy pounds with dollars, you are purchasing foreign exchange. Foreign exchange is merely a claim on some foreign currency, and the rate of exchange is the number of units of one currency it takes to purchase one unit of another currency. If the franc–dollar exchange rate is 5 to 1, for example, then it takes five francs to buy one dollar; the price of one franc is 20 cents.

Like other prices, exchange rates are determined by supply and demand. Suppose American importers need large numbers of pounds to pay British manufacturers. When they try to buy these pounds with dollars, the increased demand will force up the price of pounds—say, to $2.10 for £1. Conversely, when Britishers want to make heavy payments here, they buy dollars. This bids up the price of dollars, and the exchange rate moves to, say, $1.90 to £1.

This situation can readily be represented by a simple supply-and-demand diagram, as in Figure 41–1. With the solid supply and demand curves, the price of a pound is $2. If demand increases to $D'D'$ (when Americans need more pounds to pay for their imports), the price of a pound goes up to $2.75, given the supply of pounds shown. Try for yourself to show the effect of an increased British demand for dollars to pay for movies imported from America.

There are always Americans buying British pounds with dollars, and Britishers buying dollars with pounds, which keeps things reasonably

<hr />

[1] This example is not exactly accurate. However, the actual procedure, although sometimes more complicated, follows the same general principle.

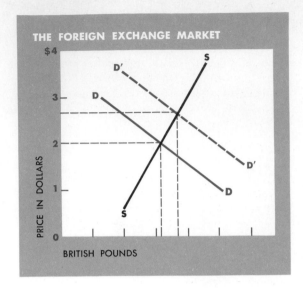

Figure 41–1
The supply and demand for British pounds looks just like the supply and demand for a commodity.

well in balance on both sides of the Atlantic. In both London and New York, there are regular foreign-exchange markets, in which foreign-exchange dealers buy and sell foreign currencies. As long as the total demand for pounds in New York equals the total demand for dollars in London, all transactions can be settled without any change in the exchange rate or any movement of reserves to settle a balance due either way. Here again, the marketplace does the complex job more or less automatically

EXCHANGE RATES AND INTERNATIONAL ADJUSTMENTS

Exchange rates are set by the demand for, and the supply of, the currencies in question, **except** where rates are somehow fixed by government decree. In a completely "free" exchange market, exchange rates would fluctuate freely ("float") in response to varying demands for the different currencies. With fluctuating demands for currencies, swings in foreign-exchange rates could be expected, a troublesome problem for international traders, who then cannot be sure how much any foreign currency will cost in terms of dollars. Thus, for many years under the gold standard and more recently under other types of government intervention, fluctuations in exchange rates have been limited by government action. We need now to explore how international trade operates under these different arrangements.

Under the gold standard

For many years before World War I and again during the 1920s, most important countries were "on the gold standard." During these periods, no direct control was exercised over exchange rates by governments, but through the gold standard, exchange fluctuations were held within narrow bounds.

Under the gold standard, each monetary unit "contained" (was convertible into) a fixed number of grains of gold. For example, the prewar dollar was 23.22 grains and the prewar British pound 113 grains of fine gold. Thus, the pound had 4.86 times as much gold as the dollar, a relationship that established a par of exchange between the currencies. And remember, from Chapter 18, that domestically the money supply varied roughly in proportion to changes in each nation's gold stock.

Under these circumstances, suppose that British importers needed more dollars to pay for imports from the United States. This would send the price of dollars up, so that £1 would buy less than $4.86 (say the exchange rate moved to 1 to 4.80). Then, instead of buying dollars and getting only $4.80 for £1, Britishers could simply convert their pounds into gold, send the gold to America, and there get $4.86 for the 113 grains of fine gold in each pound. Obviously, therefore, the exchange rate could not vary far from 4.86 to 1, or gold would be shipped instead of foreign exchange being used at all. Actually, shipping costs and interest losses in transit made it unprofitable to ship gold unless the exchange rate varied more than 3 cents either way from the 4.86-to-1 ratio. Hence, exchange rates could fluctuate within these "gold points" of 4.89 and 4.83, but no farther.

This stability of exchange rates was a great boon to international traders. They always knew just what foreign currencies would cost to make payments abroad and just what price they could get for foreign currencies received. Such stable exchanges may prevail without the gold standard, but as soon as one country is off the gold standard, the gold-standard **guarantee** of stable rates vanishes.

The gold standard also provided a more-or-less automatic procedure for keeping different countries "in balance" with one another. Suppose, under the gold standard, that the United States begins to buy more goods and services from France without a corresponding increase in exports to France. The United States will need an increasing number of francs to pay for its imports, and francs will become more expensive in terms of dollars. But as soon as the dollar–franc rate moves to the gold point, U.S. importers will begin to ship gold rather than francs to pay for their additional imports from France.

What happens when gold moves from America to France? In America, there is less gold backing for the money supply; currency and credit are contracted. In the absence of offsetting action, this movement will mean depressed prices, costs, and incomes here. In France, the reverse effect occurs. The new gold provides more bank deposits and more excess reserves. Currency and credit expand, with rising incomes, costs, and prices.

As these effects proceed, it will become easier for the French to buy here, harder for U.S. importers to buy from France. Frenchmen have larger incomes to spend on U.S. goods, and prices of U.S. goods are falling. Conversely, we have lower incomes to spend on French goods, and French prices are rising. This combination gradually shuts off the excess of U.S. imports from France, pulling the exports and imports of the two countries back into balance. When exports and imports are restored to balance, the gold flow ceases, and equilibrium has been restored in both American and French balances of payments.

But remember that gold flows tend to bring equilibrium only if they are permitted to affect prices, costs, and incomes in the countries involved—to generate booms and recessions. If central banks offset gold flows in trying to maintain stable economic growth domestically, gold flows' equilibrating effects are negated.

Under fluctuating ("floating") exchanges

How do international adjustments take place when exchange rates are free to fluctuate? Assume the same United States–France situation as before, with an American excess of imports. As before, Americans will buy francs to pay for their imports, and will thereby drive up the price of francs in terms of dollars. French goods become more expensive to us, and our goods become cheaper to France. French incomes rise because of their increased exports, without any such corresponding increase in America. These circumstances will gradually cut down on U.S. purchases from France, and will increase French purchases from us, until finally exports and imports between the two countries are restored to balance. As under the gold standard, there is an automatic tendency for the payments between the two countries to be brought back into equilibrium.

But the adjustment process is restricted to a smaller segment of each economy in the flexible-exchange case. The rising price of francs effectively raises the price of French exports to us, but it does so without raising French domestic prices generally in terms of dollars, as a gold inflow would have done by expanding the French money supply under the gold standard. Similarly, the falling dollar exchange rate effectively lowers the price of U.S. exports to French buyers, but it does so without imposing deflationary pressure on the whole U.S. economy, as a gold outflow from the United States would have done under the gold (fixed-exchange) standard.

All this makes a floating exchange standard sound very attractive. But it has one very important drawback. International traders and investors have to live in a world of uncertainty about the rates at which they convert their foreign receipts into domestic currency. More on this problem in Chapter 42.

Under intermediate arrangements

The international-gold-reserve standard. In the Great Depression of the 1930s, every major nation went off the gold standard. Facing massive unemployment, governments refused to accept the further deflation called for by gold losses. Exchange rates fluctuated. Country after country imposed controls on capital outflows to conserve its scarce gold. Together with widespread tariff increases designed to stimulate domestic employment, these capital controls increasingly stifled international trade and lending without, in retrospect, significantly helping any of the nations participating in the economic warfare.

Following World War II, everyone agreed that the folly of the 1930s must not be repeated. International cooperation, beginning with the Bretton Woods Conference of 1944, reintroduced stable exchange rates among the major currencies and gradually reduced restrictions on capital outflows. Finally, in 1958, substantially free convertibility of currencies at fixed exchange rates was restored among the major nations of the "free world," although some controls over capital movements were continued. Gold served as an international reserve for each country, which could use it to meet its international payments. Exchange rates were fixed by international agreement, and the various currencies were convertible into gold at fixed prices for official settlements, as under the old gold standard. But nations did not agree to tie their domestic monetary policies to gold flows, nor did central banks guarantee to buy gold from or sell it to private individuals and businesses. This intermediate arrangement was called an "international-gold-reserve standard."

How did adjustments to eliminate disequilibrium occur under the international-gold-reserve standard? Assume the same U.S.–French case, with U.S. imports exceeding exports. The deficit in the U.S. balance of payments will again lead to gold being transferred to France, or to a French accumulation of dollars. But now the United States need not accept a deflationary contraction of her money supply, nor France an inflationary expansion of hers, unless each country feels this would fit in with her domestic stabilization goals. Each nation attempts to balance its international and domestic goals.

A big country like the United States, if its gold reserves were large and its international trade was a small part of GNP, could afford to give dominant weight to domestic goals for a long time in the face of a balance-of-payments deficit and gold outflows. Indeed, most other countries were willing simply to accumulate dollars during the decades following World War II, when dollars were widely desired and were everywhere used as a medium of international payments. But smaller countries that depended heavily on foreign trade and whose currencies were not widely acceptable had little option; their prices and costs had to be closely in line with balance-of-payments needs or they would quickly exhaust their reserves and be unable to pay their bills. The international adjustment process was thus less direct and predictable than under either the gold standard or fluctuating exchange rates. The pressures for international adjustment built up on any country that continually ran a balance-of-payments deficit, and the nation would eventually run out of reserves to pay its international bills, as the United States nearly did in the early 1970s. But it is vital to recognize that any nation could postpone adjustment to international pressures, in order to pursue its own domestic policies, as long as its reserves held out.

Managed floats. Another intermediate arrangement, which was adopted by most "free-world" nations in 1973–74, evolved from the international-gold-reserve standard. It is a system of "managed floats." Governments found the rigors of fixed exchange rates increasingly objectionable; yet they recognized that each nation must somehow make the adjustments necessary to restore equilibrium when it faces large payments deficits. Thus, the more limited, efficient adjustment process with flexible rates seemed very attractive. But complete flexibility (a "clean float") left rates susceptible to day-to-day and week-to-week fluctuations that were troublesome to international traders. Thus, many nations moved to a modified floating-rate system (a "dirty float"), where their central banks and treasuries intervened to hold short-term rate fluctuations to modest levels, while leaving rates free to move where basic international adjustments were required. By this arrangement they hoped to avoid the economy-wide pressures of adjustments under fixed rates, and also to avoid many of the costs of sharply

fluctuating exchange rates. The trick in such a system, obviously, is to permit exchange rates to move freely enough to bring about the adjustments needed to correct payments disequilibria, while simultaneously keeping these rate fluctuations small enough to minimize disruptions to international traders and investors. The temptation is, of course, to keep rates too stable, thus blocking even the export-import sector adjustments required for international equilibrium. Time will tell how well the managed-float system works. More on this in Chapter 42.

CAPITAL MOVEMENTS, RESERVES, AND THE ADJUSTMENT PROCESS

Now introduce capital movements into the picture. U.S. investment abroad involves foreign payments, just as when we buy goods abroad. If Westinghouse decides to build a plant in the Netherlands, for example, it must have the Dutch guilders to pay its bills there. It uses dollars to buy guilders. If an individual American buys Royal Dutch Shell stock on the Dutch stock exchange, the same is true. In both cases, the Dutch end up with more dollars.

Long-term private capital investment tends to move in response to long-run profit prospects. In the postwar world, such capital flows have been enormous. U.S. long-term investment abroad totalled $160 billion by 1975, most of it made since World War II. Such capital transfers do not fluctuate sharply. However, individuals, businesses, and banks also shift *short-term* funds from nation to nation in search of the highest interest rates, and these shifts are often both huge and unpredictable. A big corporation or bank may have hundreds of millions of dollars in cash, and the interest gain from a difference of only a fraction of a percent for a few days is large. Some estimates place the total amount of such "hot money" in the modern world at over $200 billion, vastly more than the international reserves of any nation.

A rumor that a currency is "weak" (likely to depreciate vis-à-vis other currencies), or rising interest rates elsewhere, may thus trigger large short-term capital outflows. If the country has large reserves, it may simply pay out the gold or other currencies involved in the transfer. But few countries have large enough reserves to meet such hot-money drains. Thus, the result is likely to be either a suspension of gold payments (if the country is on the gold standard), or a sharp fall in the nation's currency vis-à-vis others.

Day-to-day transactions in exchange markets push the prices of different currencies up and down vis-à-vis one another. Under fixed-exchange-rate systems, it is the job of each central bank to intervene if the price of its currency deviates very far from parity. This it does by buying or selling its own currency or other currencies it holds as part of its international reserves.

For example, suppose there is a heavy demand for dollars by pound holders in London, and the price of pounds vis-à-vis dollars falls below its "parity" of $2.00—say, to $1.90. Then the Bank of England would "protect" the pound by buying pounds with dollars it holds as part of its international reserves. Conversely, if the pound were to rise above parity in the open market, the Bank of England would sell pounds, accumulating dollars or some other foreign currency. Thus, in order to protect its currency in a fixed-rate system, each central bank must have a big enough international reserve in other currencies or gold to be able to buy its own currency and maintain its price at parity if need be. If a nation runs out of reserves and other nations are unwilling to accumulate more of its currency, it must either borrow more reserves temporarily or "devalue" (that is, formally reduce the price of its currency in terms of gold or other currencies).

If a nation's currency is freely floating, market forces are permitted to determine its exchange value, and the central bank does not intervene. There is never a need to formally devalue a currency, since it appreciates or depreciates on a day-to-day basis in response to market pressures.

U.S. FOREIGN LENDING

A major development of the postwar financial world has been the massive growth of U.S. lending abroad. Our large postwar balance-of-payments deficits have been attributable mainly to our heavy private foreign investments and to government loans and foreign-aid programs (including military aid), since we had an export surplus on trade and services consistently until 1972. U.S. investors have acquired ownership of a huge volume of assets abroad—factories, oil refineries, assembly plants—through foreign securities and multinational corporations. Thus, it is important to look carefully at international capital movements if we are to understand recent international economic events.

Figure 41-2 shows how U.S. investment abroad has burgeoned since 1929. The three

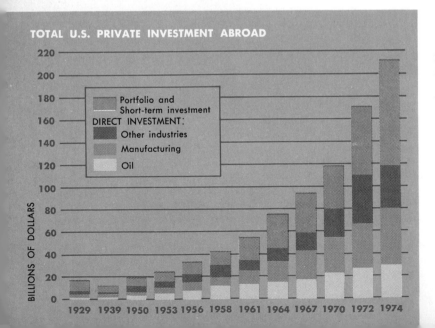

Figure 41-2
Since the 1930s, U.S. private investment abroad has soared. Petroleum is the biggest single industry, but manufacturing has grown much faster in recent years, and total manufacturing far exceeds oil investment. (Source: U.S. Department of Commerce.)

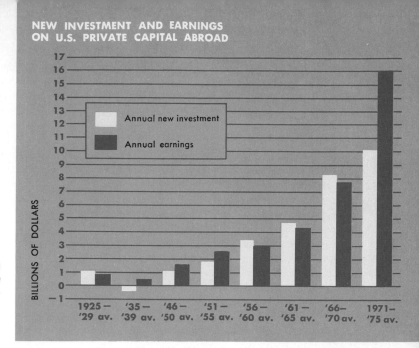

NEW INVESTMENT AND EARNINGS
ON U.S. PRIVATE CAPITAL ABROAD

☐ Annual new investment

■ Annual earnings

BILLIONS OF DOLLARS

1925— '35— '46— '51— '56— '61— '66— 1971–
'29 av. '39 av. '50 av. '55 av. '60 av. '65 av. '70 av. '75 av.

Figure 41-3
Annual new U.S. private investment abroad has grown rapidly, but returns on such investments abroad have grown even faster in recent years. (Source: U.S. Department of Commerce.)

lower areas in each bar are direct American investments. The area at the top is investment in foreign securities, including short-term investments. Even allowing for inflation, the rise has been phenomenal.

Figure 41-3 shows the picture in terms of annual new U.S. investment abroad and annual earnings on our investments abroad. The earnings bars show that our earnings each year on investments abroad now clearly exceed new investments abroad. Foreign investments are profitable business. As with domestic firms, a big part of new U.S. investment abroad each year consists of plowing back earnings on the investments already there. About three-fourths of U.S. private investment since World War II has been in the developed nations (mainly Canada and Western Europe), about one-fourth in the less-developed economies.

Figure 41-3 also suggests a central fact about foreign lending. To collect earnings and amortization on loans and investments abroad, we must either accept payment through importing goods and services or be prepared continually to reinvest the principal and earnings abroad. Government and private lending abroad has been a major factor in permitting us to continue our traditional export surplus of goods and serv-

ices. If we ever stop our annual net lending abroad, we will be able to collect our earnings and repayments on principal only by running a large net import surplus of goods and services.

Foreign investments in the United States have also risen recently, but they are far smaller than U.S. investments abroad.

THE UNITED STATES—WORLD CREDITOR

When capital movements are included, balance-of-payments equilibrium does not necessarily mean that exports should equal imports of goods and services. Growing nations tend to pass through four stages of economic development. Each requires a different payments position for balance-of-payments equilibrium.

1. **Early Borrower.** A less-developed country often borrows heavily abroad to obtain the capital goods it needs to develop its natural resources. For example, until about 1873 the United States was apparently a substantial capital importer from Europe. Imports of supplies, machinery, and consumption goods exceeded exports. In this stage, the trade balance must be

"unfavorable" (imports must exceed exports) if the needed goods and supplies are to be obtained, and this "unfavorable" balance is covered by borrowing.

2. **Mature Debtor.** After the 1870s, debt repayment by the United States began to exceed new borrowing, although we were still a heavy debtor. In this stage, exports tend to exceed imports—the trade balance is "favorable." Our net export balance transferred the real goods to other nations as we paid off our debts. As in stage 1, money transfers are only the first step. It is the real transfer of goods and services that counts.

3. **Early Creditor.** Stage 3 is entered when the nation shifts over to a net-creditor basis—when total investments abroad exceed foreign investments here. World War I and the 1920s thrust the United States abruptly into this stage, as we made heavy loans to our European allies. Government and private lending during and after World War II repeated the World War I experience with billions upon billions of dollars. Today, the United States is the great creditor nation of the world. In this stage, a continued export surplus is to be expected. This surplus transfers abroad in real form the loans we make as we increase our creditor position.

4. **Mature Creditor.** In stage 4, the creditor nation's outstanding loans are so great that current income on foreign investments more than offsets the net new loans being made abroad. In this stage, the trade balance must shift to an import surplus in order to transfer to the mature creditor nation the excess of its current return on investment over new loans being made abroad. England was a mature creditor early in this century; whether the United States has moved into that stage is debated by the experts. Our flow of interest and profits from overseas investments is growing rapidly, but so are our new investments abroad. Also, foreigners are investing large amounts in the United States, partially offsetting U.S. investments abroad. Only the years ahead will tell.

As a nation passes through these four stages, a changing trade balance is normal and essential. Whether a "favorable" balance of *trade* is in fact favorable depends basically on how well it fits in with the country's overall balance-of-payments position. Severe disequilibrium will result if the trade balance is maintained (by tariffs or other controls) in a position unsympathetic to general balance-of-payments equilibrium requirements.

REVIEW

Concepts to remember

This chapter adds a few more important concepts to the list at the end of Chapter 39.

foreign exchange
exchange rate
flexible ("floating") exchange rates
devaluation

international-gold-reserve standard
balance-of-payments equilibrium
managed float

For analysis and discussion

1. Explain how balance-of-payments disequilibrium tended to be eliminated under the gold standard, with fixed exchange rates. How is disequilibrium eliminated in a system of flexible exchange rates?

2. Using Figure 41–1, trace through the effects of the following, beginning from the equilibrium shown by *DD* and *SS:*

    a. General Motors decides to buy a British automobile plant to get production facilities there.

    b. British students come to study in America.

    c. British citizens decide to buy General Electric stock in America at the same time that American imports from England decline.

3. Suppose that you and many others decide to travel to France next summer. Trace through carefully the effect your trip might have on dollar–franc rates, gold flows, and prices in each country under:

    a. An international gold standard

    b. A flexible exchange-rate system

4. Domestically, free price movements serve to equilibrate supply and demand in the markets concerned. Since foreign exchange rates are substantially frozen under the gold standard, how can the gold standard be said to be an international equilibrating system?

5. The U.S. official international reserves of gold and foreign currencies in 1973 were about $13 billion. Yet potential "hot-money" dollar balances were said to be many times that amount. How does this help explain the U.S. move to floating rates in 1973?

6. Under a system of managed floats, how would you decide whether any fluctuation in dollar exchange rates should be offset by Federal Reserve action?

CHAPTER 42 CURRENT BALANCE-OF-PAYMENTS PROBLEMS

Over the past half century, international monetary crises have periodically been front-page news. Devaluation of the dollar and other currencies, gold shortages, first a world "dollar shortage" then a "dollar glut," U.S. balance-of-payments deficits, predictions of impending disaster. How worried, if at all, should we be about all these? Above all, what should we do about them?

One of the first things to recognize is that economic problems change rapidly. Two decades ago, the big international problem was the "dollar shortage" and too much of the world's gold accumulated in the United States. Then it was just the reverse. A few years ago, the great worry was that the OPEC (oil) countries would accumulate all the world's monetary reserves and take over control of the world monetary system. By the time you read this, the problem will probably have changed again. Thus, a brief look at history is a useful background for understanding the problems of today and tomorrow.

THE DOWNFALL OF THE GOLD STANDARD

Before 1914, the international gold standard ruled the international monetary scene. It was, in theory and to a substantial degree in practice, an "automatic" system. Central banks "managed" the money supply to a limited extent, but gold was the center of a "religion" of money. It was accepted by most economists and the public alike as an ultimate repository of value. In the rapidly expanding, reasonably flexible pre-1914 world, this gold standard supplied an important element of international-exchange stability, and the requisite domestic price and income adjustments were generally accomplished without excessively painful consequences.

The monetary disruptions of World War I were extreme. Wild inflations occurred in several European nations, serious inflation in all. Reestablishment of the international gold standard in the 1920s was thus fraught with difficulties. What should exchange rates be? Finally, new gold contents were prescribed for currencies in an endeavor to place these currencies in "equilibrium" balance-of-payments positions vis-à-vis the rest of the world. The Western world went back "on gold."

But the depression of the 1930s dealt the deathblow to the prewar gold standard. Losing gold in a period of growing unemployment meant even further deflationary contraction of national money supplies. First England in 1931, then all other major nations, "went off gold," devaluing their currencies relative to gold and to other currencies in order to avoid the domestic deflation implicit in adherence to the gold standard, and to encourage foreign purchases of their domestic products. The American dollar was devalued in 1934 to 59 percent of its earlier gold content. Eventually every major currency was devalued, exchange and capital movement controls were established, and domestic currencies were severed from gold flows.

In retrospect, three major factors led to the downfall of the gold standard:

1. The Great Depression of the 1930s made the domestic price of gold-standard orthodoxy too high to pay.

2. Downward cost-price rigidities served to aggravate the impact of price and income deflation, and to thwart the equilibrating forces previously at work under the gold-standard system. Unions, industrial monopolies, agricultural groups—all contributed to holding up prices when incomes fell in the depression.

3. With waning faith in the gold-standard religion, and with growing political instability, capital flights to "safer" countries became common. Huge "hot-money" drains were more than any nation could stand. The religion of gold worked admirably as long as no infidels entered the temple to whisper misgivings. Once doubt spread, however, capital flights never envisaged in a stable, well-behaved international system spelled doom to the gold standard in a rigid, depression-conscious world.

EXCHANGE DEPRECIATION AND EXCHANGE CONTROLS

Widespread desertion of the gold standard and currency devaluations failed to bring the expected results. One country acting alone could expand its exports by devaluation. But when everyone's currency was devalued, the actions just offset one another.

In retrospect, thus, the main result of the competitive depreciation race of the 1930s was disruption of international trade and investment, widespread friction and ill will, and few important gains to any of the competitors. As with tariff increases, exchange depreciation was a "beggar-my-neighbor" attempt to shift unemployment to other nations. And it was doomed to defeat by the virtual certainty of retaliation.

As exchange depreciation failed to eliminate the unemployment that plagued the Western world, crosscurrents of conflict and cooperation were everywhere apparent in international economic relations. New types of exchange controls proliferated. Nations set their exchange rates at varying levels, searching for the one to maximize their gain from foreign trade. Many countries, especially Nazi Germany, "blocked" the use of foreign exchange received from their foreign sales, and rationed the foreign exchange received to control its expenditure. Nearly every major nation introduced controls over capital exports.

THE INTERNATIONAL MONETARY FUND

To the nations mapping peacetime reconstruction at the end of World War II, the international monetary disruption and conflict of the 1930s were bitter memories. There was little sentiment for restoring the old gold standard. But there was widespread agreement on the need for reasonable exchange stability and for reduced restrictions on international trade and capital movements.

In 1945, some forty nations established the International Monetary Fund to help attain these goals; the total membership is now over a hundred.[1] The Fund now consists of about $47 billion of gold, SDRs, and member-country currencies made available for stabilization activities in accordance with the Fund's charter. Each country's contribution was based on its national income; the United States put up about one-third of the total. As world trade has grown, the size of the Fund has been increased four times. Voting control over the Fund is roughly in proportion to contributions to its capital; the U.S. share is down to about 25 percent.

The primary operating purposes of the Fund were to help member nations reestablish free convertibility among their currencies, and to maintain exchange-rate stability, coupled with reasonable flexibility to make any necessary long-run adjustments. In this respect, the philosophy of the Fund differed substantially from that of the old gold standard, whose keynote was exchange stability at all costs. The Fund could, in effect, thus lend foreign currencies to a country that was caught temporarily short of exchange. Whereas previously the likely alternative would have been devaluation or imposition of exchange controls, with the Fund's assistance it was easier to avoid such acts. More recently, the 1976 amendments to the Fund eliminated the major emphasis on exchange-rate stability, legitimatizing floating notes. The Fund from the outset did not prohibit controls over *capital* movements, for the reasons explained at the end of Chapter 41.[2]

With the worldwide adoption of floating exchange rates in the 1976 amendments, the Fund's role shifted to provision of more generous lending facilities (see below), and to facilitation of negotiations among member nations aimed at maintaining an effectively working, stable international system. Wide latitude is allowed to individual countries to adopt specific exchange arrangements of their own choosing, but proscriptions are retained against manipulation of exchange rates by one country to gain competitive advantages over others.

Special Drawing Rights

During the 1960s, the need for some collective means to increase international monetary reserves became increasingly clear. Newly mined gold became available erratically; gold moved in and out of private hoards in response to private speculation; and reliance on the U.S. balance-of-payments deficit was an obviously unsatisfactory way of obtaining reserves for other countries, as will be explained presently. Thus, in 1968, the leading free-world nations agreed to give the IMF power to create "Special

---

The Bank's operating head is from this country, in recognition of the United States's large contribution to the Bank's capital and the dominant demand for dollar loans. There are now seventy member nations, and total capital is about $25 billion. In 1976, the Bank announced plans to lend $7 billion to less-developed countries, a big increase over previous rates.

Although the IBRD may lend out its own capital, it operates primarily through two other channels—attaching its guarantee to private loans, and borrowing funds in the various member countries to finance its loans. For example, if Peru wants a loan to develop its industries and plans to spend most of the loan in the United States, the Bank will either try to arrange a direct loan for Peru from American lenders, attaching its own guarantee to the loan, or it will float a bond issue in the American market to obtain funds for the Peruvian loan. In either case, the U.S. representative on the Bank's board would have to approve, because every loan must be approved by the major country in which the loan is to be raised and spent, as well as by the Bank's officers, and the United States, as provider of over 20 percent of the Bank's capital, retains a veto power over most important decisions. The LDCs have steadily pushed for more control over Bank policies and for lower interest rates and easier credit conditions. Most observers feel the Bank has played a very useful, if modest, role in helping development in the LDCs.

---

[1] After participating in the planning, the Soviet-bloc countries did not join.

[2] Parallel to the International Monetary Fund, the same forty countries also established the $8-billion International Bank for Reconstruction and Development. It was set up to facilitate foreign lending for postwar reconstruction and for development of less-developed areas. The organization and management of the Bank roughly parallel those of the fund.

Drawing Rights"—in essence, new international reserves (often called "paper gold") created outright, much as new money might be printed. (The SDR is now defined as having the value of a "standard basket" of leading currencies, not in terms of dollars or gold). Member countries can then draw their shares of these new reserves as needed. New SDRs can be created only by an 85 percent vote of the Fund's shareholders, which gives both the United States and the Common Market countries (if they vote together) a veto over new issues. Countries' quotas correspond roughly to their general Fund borrowing quotas (the United States' is now about 25 percent of the total). But SDRs, unlike regular loans, need not be repaid to the Fund. About $3 billion of SDRs were issued in each of the first three years, beginning in 1970, with the expectation that more would be approved as needed. But no SDRs need be created if reserves are adequate.

SDRs are international money, spendable by the holder. Thus it is not surprising that many less-developed countries, which contributed very little to the IMF and hence had very small quotas, began in the 1970s to press increasingly for larger allocations of SDRs when new ones were created, and for larger borrowing facilities at the Fund. These claims were part of their general argument for more power in international organizations and a bigger share of the world's wealth. In these international negotiations, the line between monetary reform and redistribution of wealth from the richer to poorer nations became very hazy. The outcome in the 1976 Fund amendments was substantial increases in quotas for the LDCs, but retention of substantial control over the allocation of the Fund's resources by the developed nations that contributed most of the resources. It will be surprising if this controversy does not continue, with increasing pressure from the LDCs for both larger quotas and more voting power over IMF policies.

THE MODERN INTERNATIONAL MONETARY SYSTEM

To understand today's international monetary system, we need a little more history.

The dollar as a key currency

Western Europe, Russia, and Japan emerged from World War II physically devastated, with their foreign assets depleted, and heavily in debt. The United States emerged powerful, prosperous, unbombed, and a massive international creditor. Our real GNP more than doubled under the pressures of war from the depression of the late 1930s; we not only provided a large portion of the war material for our allies but simultaneously substantially raised the American standard of living in terms of consumer goods between 1940 and 1946. Until our allies used up their ability to pay, we sold war material and civilian supplies to them, and later provided many of them on loans and "lend-lease," rather than as gifts or our contributions to the common war. Thus, they ended the war heavily in debt to us.

In 1946, the reconstruction needs of Europe, Russia, and Japan were enormous. The unscathed American economy offered vast productive power to meet these needs. The resulting "dollar shortage" dominated the international scene. No nation seemed to have enough dollars to pay for the goods and services it needed from America. The Marshall Plan, under which we extended billions in reconstruction aid to allied nations, was one major answer to helping foreign nations rebuild and to alleviating this dollar shortage during the postwar years. Our exports of goods and services soared. But our total balance of payments was persistently in deficit, because of our even-larger investments and government aid abroad.

Each year, foreign nations received more payments from us than they made to us. With the option of taking gold or accumulating dollar balances, they mainly chose dollars through the 1950s. The dollar was better than gold. It could be freely exchanged for gold at $35 an ounce; one could earn interest on dollar balances held in New York banks or invested in short-term U.S. securities; much of what nations wanted to buy was available in the United States, and dollars were needed to pay; and throughout the free world, dollars were as acceptable as gold. **The dollar became the "key" currency of the**

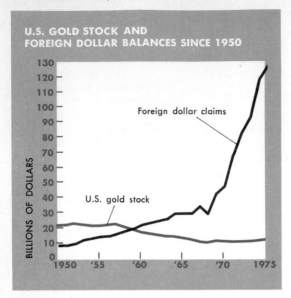

U.S. GOLD STOCK AND FOREIGN DOLLAR BALANCES SINCE 1950

Foreign dollar claims

U.S. gold stock

Figure 42-1
Since 1950, foreigners and foreign governments have accumulated large holdings of U.S. dollars and short-term claims on dollars, in addition to taking much of our World War II gold stock. Gold is valued at $42 per ounce after September 1973, although the free-market price has averaged $100–$150 since then. (Source: Federal Reserve Board.)

free world, widely used for both transactions and international reserve purposes.

Figure 42-1 shows the steady accumulation of short-term dollar balances by foreign nations after 1950 and the decline in the U.S. gold stock as foreign nations increasingly took some payments in gold.

Dollar shortage to dollar glut

By the mid-1950s, the rehabilitation of Europe and Japan was substantially complete, and their economies were booming. But the U.S. payments deficit continued. Foreign nations, with their own international-reserve balances substantially rebuilt, continued to increase their dollar balances, but with growing complaints. Although the United States was still carrying the major burden of defense spending for the free world and of providing economic aid

to the less-developed nations, increasing concern was voiced abroad over our continuing large payments deficit. With foreign dollar balances far exceeding the U.S. gold stock, it became increasingly clear that foreign attempts to convert dollars into gold would force this country off the international-gold-reserve standard; there simply wasn't enough U.S. gold to pay off our short-term dollar debts. Thus, when U.S. investors bought up European industries, in effect they paid with inconvertible U.S. dollars that the Europeans felt they had little option but to hold. To be sure, they could have simply bought more U.S. goods, but this would have undercut production and sales of their home industries; while they complained about the U.S. deficit, they were unwilling to give up their own payments-surplus positions that were the counterpart of the U.S. deficits. The dollar shortage of a decade earlier had become a dollar glut. Foreign central banks, which had long sought more dollars as the world's key currency, now had more than they wanted.

The unstable gold-and-dollar-reserve standard

Under the international-gold-and-dollar-reserve standard that evolved during the 1950s and 1960s, most nations held both gold and dollars as their basic international reserves, with the two convertible into one another. The international reserves for the world were thus supplied by gold and by short-term dollar balances, produced by the very U.S. balance-of-payments deficits that were so criticized.

As uncertainty grew as to the viability of the system, rumors developed intermittently that the dollar was "unsound." These rumors spread to other "weak" currencies, especially the pound and the franc at different times, and speculative "runs" developed against overvalued currencies that might be devalued. The U.S. payments deficit was widely criticized, and this country tried a variety of measures to expand U.S. exports, to increase American productivity, to reduce U.S. inflation, to limit imports, to restrict U.S. capital outflows, and to encourage foreign investments here. But the U.S. payments deficit steadily worsened.

The two-tier gold system and SDRs

In the face of this instability, two major modifications to the gold-and-dollar-reserve standard were agreed on by the major Western nations in 1968. First, SDRs were adopted to provide for more rational, managed growth in international reserves. Second, the major governments agreed to stop buying and selling gold vis-à-vis private holders and miners. This meant that private speculators could no longer count on getting gold for their dollars or other major currencies, but gold was continued as an official international reserve, exchanged by the major central banks to settle international balances at the established price of $35 per ounce. The amount of official monetary gold was thus substantially fixed at the amount held by the central banks, with additions to reserves to be provided mainly by SDRs, once the dollar deficit was eliminated. All other gold became, in effect, just another commodity, whose price was free to fluctuate in response to changing supply and demand conditions. This was called a "two-tier" gold system, because of the two separate (official and unofficial) markets for gold.

Dollar devaluation, inconvertibility, and floating rates

While the two-tier gold system worked well in insulating central banks from the whims of private gold speculators, the U.S. payments deficit rose, rather than falling, following 1968. Conversely, other nations (especially West Germany and Japan) ran large surpluses. Rumors spread of dollar devaluation and of mark and yen upward revaluations. There were repeated speculative "runs" on the dollar, in which private individual and business dollar holders converted their funds into other currencies (especially German marks and Japanese yen) that were expected to be valued upward relative to the dollar. In 1971, the German central bank had to buy up over $5 billion in only three days to keep the mark from rising above its agreed

"Then it's agreed. Until the dollar firms up, we let the clamshell float." (Drawing by Ed Fisher; © 1971. The New Yorker Magazine, Inc.)

parity with the dollar, and in 1973, even larger sums were shifted into marks and yen in speculation that the dollar would soon be devalued again.

Under these pressures, President Nixon twice (in 1971 and 1973) devalued the dollar relative to other leading currencies and to gold, in order to halt speculative runs on the dollar, to check the unwanted flow of dollars into Germany and Japan, and to reduce the U.S. balance-of-payments deficit. In terms of gold, the dollar was devalued about 20 percent; that is, the official price of gold was raised from $35 to $42.22 an ounce—although this was a largely formal act, because in 1973 the United States also announced that it would no longer convert dollars into gold even for other central banks. But the devaluation of the dollar vis-à-vis other leading currencies was real, increasing their buying power over U.S. exports and making their goods more expensive to us. Thus, although devaluation used to be defined primarily in terms of a currency's relationship to gold, this is no longer so; the more meaningful view of depreciation now is directly in terms of other currencies obtainable in exchange.

Last, as part of the revolutionary responses to the speculative currency runs of early 1973, most of the major Western trading nations agreed to let their currencies float temporarily against the dollar while they considered how the basic system should be reformed. But most governments and their central banks were unwilling to go all the way to freely floating rates. Most continued to intervene in exchange markets to keep rates from fluctuating too widely. The price of a nation's currency seems too important to most nations, controlling as it does the nation's ability to export and import, to be left solely to private market forces. Thus, the floats following the 1973 announcements were mostly "managed," or "dirty," floats, not "clean" ones with rates left completely to market forces.[3]

[3]Over the postwar period, numerous runs developed against other currencies, especially the British pound and the French franc, sometimes ending in devaluations. But these speculations were less disruptive to the whole system than were attacks on the key currency, the dollar.

THE CURRENT WORLD MONETARY SYSTEM

The post-1973 international monetary system was clearly in a state of transition. Moreover, the massive OPEC increase in oil prices in 1974 created a new crisis for the system. Oil-consuming nations were faced with the need to pay OPEC countries nearly $100 billion annually for oil, compared to less than $25 billion previously. Widespread fears were expressed that an unprecedented accumulation of international reserves by the OPEC countries, totaling hundreds of billions of dollars by 1980, would give them enormous power over other world economies and the international monetary system. (See Case 36.) Finally, in 1976, after years of negotiation, the leading Western industrial nations, with the reluctant concurrence of most less-developed nations, reached an interim agreement on a new structure for the world's monetary system. The major points of the so-called Jamaica agreement were:

1. The system of managed floating rates was formally accepted, recognizing each nation's right to determine its own domestic stabilization policies but stressing the common purpose of achieving international stability and growth.

2. The official price of gold was eliminated; plans were announced to sell promptly in the open market one-sixth of the IMF's holdings of gold (with the proceeds used to aid the less-developed countries) and to return another one-sixth to member nations; all IMF obligations to use gold were eliminated; and it was agreed that the total stock of gold held by the IMF and the ten leading industrial nations would not be increased. Member nations were left free to dispose of their gold as they wished.

3. IMF quotas were increased by a third, with an increased share going to the LDCs, so as to ease adjustment problems for nations facing payments difficulties; and steps were taken to establish SDRs as the principal reserve asset of the international monetary system, replacing both gold and dollars.

This new agreement moves the world to a system of managed floating exchanges, with

THE TOTAL U.S. INTERNATIONAL POSITION

All this may lead you to suspect that the U.S. is internationally bankrupt and the dollar of dubious value. Far from it! The dollar is backed fundamentally by the powerful U.S. economy, the most efficient and productive in the world. And our total foreign assets, once we add in our vast long-term investments overseas, far exceed our total liabilities, as is shown by the table below.

The United States is in much the position of any other banker. Although our basic position is excellent, our short-term liabilities substantially exceed our reserves and other short-term assets. Widespread confidence makes such systems work well. But we are a banker without deposit insurance. Internationally, there is no FDIC to insure deposits or Federal Reserve to assure liquidity to temporarily frozen assets in case a confidence crisis develops, although the IMF helps.

Total foreign assets and liabilities of the United States, January 1, 1975

	Amount (in billions)
Assets:	
Gold and foreign currency	$ 18
U.S. short-term private investments abroad	50
U.S. long-term private investments abroad	160
U.S. government claims abroad	36
Total assets abroad plus gold	$265
Liabilities:	
Short-term dollar balances of official organizations	$ 80
Short-term private dollar balances	50
Long-term foreign investments here	57
Total liabilities to foreigners	187
Excess of assets over liabilities	$ 78

Source: Department of Commerce and Federal Reserve Board.

wide freedom left to individual nations as to how to manage their exchange rates. (The Common Market countries, for example, have attempted to keep exchange rates among their own currencies fixed, while permitting them to fluctuate against other countries.) It thus attempts to realize most of the advatages of floating exchanges while maintaining agreement in principle on the need to cooperate for international stability, and to ensure a rational basis for determining the total supply of international reserves.

How well will the system work, and how long will it last? Its success will depend largely on how well it deals with four basic problems—adjustment, liquidity, confidence, and world inflation.

The adjustment problem

There is no escaping the fact that no nation can indefinitely run a balance-of-payments deficit (capital flows included) unless (1) it has an indefinitely large supply of international reserves, or (2) it is a key-currency country whose currency other nations will absorb and hold indefinitely—and even the United States found that neither of these two conditions lasted indefinitely. The real problem is, What is the most efficient, least painful way of eliminating major payments disequilibria?

Most economists agree now that a **rigidly fixed exchange-rate system,** whether or not tied to gold, has very high costs in tying different economies together and ruling out effective use of independent domestic stabilization policies. On the other hand, **flexible (floating) exchange rates** would automatically reflect excess demand or supply of any currency. As the price of that currency moved up or down, it would discourage or stimulate imports into the country, and conversely, exports—thus directly pulling the country's balance of payments back into equilibrium. Moreover, the floating exchange rate would **directly** affect the prices of the nation's exports and imports. There need be no economy-wide inflation or recession. No central bank or treasury needs to intervene to help achieve equilibrium; freely fluctuating exchange rates do the job automatically. Here again, it appears that the marketplace will do the right thing if we free it from restrictions.

What are the problems? There are three. First, many reject this solution because of the uncertainty it would create as to the future value of currencies. Creditors would never know what their future receipts would be in terms of their own currency. Traders, lenders, and borrowers alike would face serious uncertainties on all except the shortest-term transactions. While floating rates might make overall international adjustments easier, as a practical matter they might kill the goose that lays the golden eggs—trade and lending itself.

Economists have an answer. Just as in the markets for wheat and copper, organized "futures" markets in different currencies would develop in which importers and exporters could buy and sell currencies for delivery at the future date needed, thus eliminating the uncertainty produced by possibly fluctuating rates. They could "hedge" against the possibility of higher or lower prices for the foreign currency involved.

But there is a counteranswer. Many businessmen and bankers doubt that effective forward markets would actually develop in all major currencies, especially for long-term commitments. And both they and some economists fear that speculation on such forward markets might be destabilizing instead of stabilizing to rates themselves. With commodities, the cost of production provides a central level around which prices tend to move. With foreign-exchange rates, there is no cost of production to serve as a stabilizing force. Instead, if the dollar weakened, speculators might lose confidence in it and all decide to sell dollars at once, driving the dollar rate far down. Conclusion? At least for the last few years, world trade and investment seem to have prospered under *partly* flexible rates, and fluctuating rates appear to have worked roughly as predicted in restoring equilibria. But a tentative judgment is all that is justified so far.

Second, both theory and recent experience suggest that each nation's freedom to use domestic stabilization policy is less than it appears, especially when capital flows are included in the adjustment process. If, for example, a country's currency depreciates, this lowers its export prices in terms of other currencies but raises them relative to its domestic prices (because of the increased demand for the exports). If the domestic monetary authorities keep the money stock and aggregate demand unchanged, the result will be downward pressure on domestic prices since they must then fall to offset the rises in export prices, which are also part of the price level. But such deflation is just what the old fixed-rate standard prescribed, and most monetary authorities would probably insert new money to avoid it, thus facilitating domestic inflation as a consequence of its currency depreciation. Moreover, exchange depreciation would attract foreign investment, other things equal, since it would be cheaper for foreigners to buy the depreciated currency for investments—and this capital inflow would further stimulate domestic inflation. Fluctuating exchange rates only partly insulate the economy from international adjustment pressures.

Third, most governments feel that their exchange rate is too important a price to trust completely to the vagaries of the market. Hence, they insist on at least some intervention—on a *managed float.* Such limitations on free movements of exchange rates limit their power to induce equilibrating adjustments in the economies involved. But if the "management" is limited to smoothing short-term occilations, managed floating rates may provide most of the advantages of complete flexibility while avoiding some of the costs.

As was indicated above, the new system of managed floats has so far worked better than many critics forecast, including surviving the OPEC oil crisis. It has permitted nations to have widely varying rates of domestic inflation, which would have been impossible under a fixed-rate system. And it has provided enough flexibility to avoid major disequilibrium crises. But it is a somewhat jerry-built system, operating without full consensus among the nations as to the rules of the game; and it does not assure that national adjustments will be made to disequilibria that develop. It will take a number of years of experience before it can be judged a success. Many economists and financiers expect it to break apart under some crisis or other in the years ahead. The painful fact is that no one has discovered a surefire system for assuring basic balance-of-payments adjustments without unwanted pressure on domestic economies.[4]

The liquidity problem

World trade increased from $50 billion to over $800 billion between 1950 and 1975, requiring more reserves. International lending

[4]Some experts favor another compromise—the "sliding, or crawling, peg." This policy would recognize the need to keep exchange rates reasonably stable as a foundation for foreign trade and lending. But it would deviate from fixed exchanges in two ways. First, it would permit exchange rates to fluctuate moderately (say, by 2 to 5 percent on each side of parity) under market pressures, so they could do part of the equilibrating job. Second, if a currency consistently moved above or below par vis-à-vis other currencies, the par (peg) itself would automatically be adjusted gradually—say, by $\frac{1}{2}$ or 1 percent a quarter or half year. This sliding peg would be responsive to the fact that costs and prices do move differently in different nations, for example reflecting different rates of technological progress. But the changes would be gradual enough to retain most of the benefits from fixed rates.

The sliding peg wouldn't solve the basic dilemma if one nation got badly out of international equilibrium—say, because its technical progress is very slow, or because it tries to live beyond its international means by importing much more than it exports. But it would offer a more flexible system than fixed rates, without running the risks some see in a complete shift to a floating-rate system.

grew even faster. Yet the world's gold stock grew only slowly, and much of the new gold is needed for jewelry, industry, or other nonmonetary uses. Clearly, we cannot count on gold production to provide just the needed amount of new international monetary reserves each year.

The big post–World War II increase in international monetary reserves came from the persistent U.S. balance-of-payments deficits. But there is no reason to expect that the U.S. payments deficit will provide just the needed growth in international reserves.

Thus, adoption of the SDR plan in 1968 was a major step toward more rational collective action to gradually increase international monetary reserves. The plan is new and remains to be tested. The experts do not agree on just how fast reserves should be increased or how large they should be. Some argue that a generous supply is the best protection against crises for individual currencies and against undesirably drastic pressures on deficit countries to restore balance through precipitous action. Others argue that generous liquidity makes it too easy for deficit countries to avoid the painful steps needed to put their houses in order, and ensures worldwide inflation.

The dollar still plays a key role, reflecting U.S. dominance in world trade and finance, and there is no guarantee that U.S. deficits will not again swell international liquidity. Moreover, "Eurodollars" (see box) have further complicated the liquidity problem. But nearly everyone agrees that the SDRs are a sensible step in the direction of rational, managed growth of international reserves.

The confidence problem

When holders of any currency expect its value to fall in terms of other currencies, they tend to sell the currency in which they have lost confidence. In early 1973, for example, widespread suspicion that the dollar would be devalued against at least the mark and the yen led to massive conversion of dollars into those two currencies. To maintain existing exchange rates, the German and Japanese authorities bought huge quantities of dollars—some $6 billion in three days. But they did not want such huge

EURODOLLARS

Dollars are the transactions currency for much of the world's trade and investments, even when these do not involve U.S. exports or imports. For many years, foreign traders and investors held large dollar bank accounts in the United States to finance such transactions, and many still do. But recently the practice has developed of holding dollar deposits at banks outside the United States, especially in Western Europe. Such deposits are called "Eurodollars." The banks that hold such deposits and lend such dollars, often foreign branches of the big U.S. banks, are sometimes called Eurobanks—the banking counterparts of the multinational industrial corporations. The Eurodollar market has grown spectacularly over the last two decades, from zero to dollar deposits totaling over $200 billion. The total rises to over $300 billion if dollar deposits in other countries outside the United States (especially Canada and Japan) are added.

Eurodollars are spendable money, like bank deposits in the United States, although they are seldom used for transactions in the United States. They are used almost entirely for large transactions; the smallest deposits are usually $100,000. They constitute a massive addition to the total supply of world liquidity, and hence to world inflationary pressures. As with deposits in the United States, they can be created by banks in the act of making loans and investments. But Eurobanks are not under the control of the U.S. banking authorities. They have no reserve requirements nor (unlike domestic U.S. banks) any ceilings on the interest rates they can pay depositors. Thus, expansion possibilities for Eurodollars are limited only by the Eurobankers' need to be able to meet depositors' withdrawals. Eurobanks typically hold dollar deposits in the big New York banks as reserves for this purpose, with reserve ratios much lower than those set by the Federal Reserve for U.S. domestic banks. As long as depositors as a group do not transfer their Eurodollars outside the Eurobank group of institutions, the Eurobanks do not face reserve losses, and they can expand a large volume of deposits on limited dollar reserves in the United States. The past two decades have seen precisely such a Eurodollar expansion, largely outside the control of any of the world's monetary authorities.

quantities of dollars, and monetary officials of the leading nations agreed that the only short-run solution to the confidence crisis was a devaluation of the dollar against the mark, yen, and other strong currencies. Such negotiations are highly complex because of the infighting over the exact relationships to be established among the currencies involved (exchange rates go far to determine nations' international competitive positions).

In a fixed-exchange-rate system, major confidence crises were highly disruptive. No one knows, for example, how many dollars are held around the world that might be converted into other currencies if another dollar confidence crisis should develop. Some estimates put the total at $200 to $300 billion, held by banks, international businesses, wealthy individuals,

OPEC governments, and others. Whatever the exact figure, the total is so large that no central bank could hope to maintain the exchange rate between the dollar and its own currency if a substantial part of the dollars were sold against another currency en masse. This is the confidence problem, sometimes called the "hot-money" problem.

Willingness to let exchange rates fluctuate somewhat lessens this problem. Advocates of flexible rates claim that if speculators knew that rates might fluctuate widely, the wide fluctuations would in fact seldom occur, because the falling value of the attacked currency would soon eliminate the incentive to speculate against it. Certainly, this effect would tend to occur, but critics argue that rates might swing widely and disruptively before the self-correcting market forces checked them, and that this danger would seriously deter international traders and investors, who need to know what they can count on when they buy and sell abroad.

Thus, nearly all governments have rejected the freely-floating-rate "solution." During the 1960s, they turned to cooperation among central banks. The major central banks frequently cooperated to make huge loans to protect currencies under attack, and these sometimes did the job. This cooperation still prevails, although somewhat uncertainly from time to time. Reluctantly, many countries adopted capital controls against the inflow of unwanted hot money. The confidence problem is still an unresolved one for the international monetary system, although less serious now than under the old fixed-rate system.

The problem of world inflation

Persistent rapid inflation has plagued the Western world since World War II. The reasons have been many. Partly, special events like the formation of the OPEC oil cartel and the worldwide crop failures of 1972–73 shot up important individual prices. Partly, inflation has reflected the mixture of economic, social, and political forces emphasized in Chapter 19. Partly, nearly all nations have tended to create new money to finance spending increases on military and social programs. Not least, large U.S. balance-of-payments deficits have poured out new international reserves that have supported monetary expansion and increased spending in other nations. Recently, over $200 billion of new Eurodollars have swelled the world's money stock and the liquidity of individual nations. And inflations in different countries have been linked together through increasing international economic interdependence.

Economists disagree over the relative importance of these causes at different times. But there is little doubt that the huge growth in domestic money supplies and in international reserves have played a major role in producing demand-pull inflation and validating the rising costs and prices that constitute the cost-push element of inflation. The parallelism between money growth and rising prices has been close in almost all cases. The question is, Why have nearly all nations succumbed to the temptation of paying their bills through new money creation, when both economic theory and history so clearly predict the resulting inflation? The interacting political, social, and economic forces in the United States described in Chapter 19 appear to be broadly applicable to most other Western industrialized nations, and the big U.S. payments deficits clearly played an important role.

The inflation explosion of 1973–75 was a sobering experience for people and governments throughout the world. Reducing the United States's power to create new international reserves and buy up foreign assets by running large payments deficits was one of the major goals of the 1976 amendments to the Articles of the IMF. But the accompanying agreement to expand quotas simultaneously indicated the widespread tendency to turn to easy money and liquidity expansion as a way to raise living standards for some without facing up to the real burden this implies for others. In international finance even more than elsewhere, nations and individuals are reluctant to face up to the basic economic adage, "There's no such thing as a free lunch!" and the result is generally inflation.

THE ROLE OF GOLD

What is the future of gold in the world's monetary system? To answer, one needs a crystal ball, because so much of gold's present role depends on centuries-old tradition. Given the mixture of myth and reality that surrounds gold, the following seem probable.

1. Gold has declined greatly in monetary importance since the 1920s. It no longer limits domestic money creation in major nations, and most such nations (with France a strong exception) seem determined to continue the gradual elimination of gold as an official international reserve. It makes little sense to tie a nation's money stock or international liquidity to the vagaries of the mining industry in two nations (South Africa and the USSR) and of private speculators' wishes to hold gold. Nor is there an

obvious reason why we should pay South African miners to dig up gold at increasing expense so we can rebury it in Fort Knox, Kentucky.

2. As gold is demonetized, both national governments and the IMF will probably gradually sell off their stocks to the private market; U.S. and IMF sales began in 1975–76. But sales may be slow, partly because gold still has many supporters as a reserve metal and partly because to dump monetary gold rapidly on the open market would drive the price down sharply. Both nations and the IMF would like to get as much as possible for their gold if they sell it off. Thus, gold may continue as a part of international reserves for years to come.

3. The free market price of gold over the years ahead is uncertain. Today, it depends importantly on speculation that gold may be restored as a major monetary metal, valued at a new, higher price. How fast, if at all, the major nations sell off their gold stocks may go far to set world gold prices. Beyond these considerations, individuals and businesses may still want to hold gold as an asset (even though this has serious drawbacks, including the high cost of buying and holding gold and the fact that it yields no interest). Industrial, artistic, and medical demand for gold will presumably grow, while the new supply will depend on mining costs relative to the market price. Put all these factors together and make your own bet as to the future price.

4. There is a nonnegligible chance that gold will stage a comeback as a monetary metal. The gold mystique is strong, and SDRs are still far from accepted as "as good as gold" in many circles. A major financial crisis that destroys confidence in domestic monies and/or SDRs could strengthen the hand of conservatives who distrust "management" of money by governments, and of gold hoarders and producers like France, South Africa, and the USSR, who urge restoration of gold in the monetary system.

REVIEW

**Concepts
to remember**

This chapter reuses the central concepts of both domestic macroeconomics and Chapters 39–41, and adds the following important concepts and institutions:

International Monetary Fund   adjustment problem
Special Drawing Rights (SDRs)   sliding, or crawling, peg
two-tier gold system   liquidity problem
clean and dirty floats   confidence problem

**For analysis
and discussion**

1. Explain what it means when we say the dollar is "weak" or "strong."
2. What does it matter to the typical U.S. resident whether the dollar is weak or strong internationally?
3. Should the United States be concerned about running a balance-of-payments deficit? If we should be concerned, what should we do about it?
4. Under a system of floating rates, do countries need to hold larger or smaller international reserves than with fixed rates? Explain.
5. In your judgment, would this country be better off under a system of freely floating exchange rates than under the present system of managed floats? Explain.
6. What are SDRs? Are they "as good as gold" to the countries that get them through the IMF?
7. When new SDRs are created, who should get them?
8. Do we really need gold for domestic and international reserves? Explain.
9. How could we have a continuing balance-of-payments deficit during the 1960s when our exports exceeded our imports by a wide margin?

Few events in living memory have caused such anxiety and uncertainty as the OPEC[5] embargo of 1972–73 on oil shipments to the United States and other Western industrial nations, and the quadrupling of oil prices that followed. Domestically, long waiting lines at filling stations developed overnight; unheated schools and offices were commonplace; industries slowed or even shut down for lack of oil. But the anxiety concerning the impact on international monetary affairs was even more dramatic.

The OPEC countries controlled over half the world's known oil reserves; virtually every Western industrialized nation was dependent on them to a substantial extent to keep its economy operating. When the Arabs quadrupled the price of oil as the embargo was lifted, this meant that oil-importing nations saw their international oil bills soar from about $22 billion to nearly $100 billion annually, and they had little option but to pay. Simple arithmetic suggested that the earnings of the Arab states would rise almost instantaneously by $70 billion or more annually, and many predictions saw the price of oil raised further in the years to come. Many calculations placed the Arab accumulation of international reserves at from $300 billion to a trillion dollars by 1980. By comparison, the entire gold stock of all the free-world central banks was about $50 billion. U.S. Treasury Secretary George Shultz, a distinguished economist, observed, "It boggles the mind!"

The worries and dire predictions that filled the newspapers and the airwaves centered around five big questions:

[5]Organization of Petroleum Exporting Countries, dominated by the Arab nations.

1. Won't the Arab states drain a mass of money away from the other nations, bringing their economies to a grinding halt?

2. Even if the Arab states don't intend to impose disaster on the Western nations, will there be any feasible way of recycling all those funds back to the economies of the other nations?

3. Even if many of the funds are successfully recycled to the West, won't the OPEC countries hold enormous power over the world's financial and foreign-exchange markets, merely by shifting their huge reserves back and forth?

4. Won't the Arabs own a substantial share of the world's assets after a decade has gone by, through investing part or all of their huge earnings in the Western nations? The potential dollar amounts make the problem of multinational corporate power look picayune.

5. Even if all the problems above prove to be surmountable, won't the real burden of paying such high prices for essential oil bankrupt many of the world's poorer, less-developed nations—or lower their already pitifully low living standards below subsistence levels?

While everyone agreed that there were serious problems ahead, many experts in international economics suggested that Arab accumulations would be smaller than expected and that the results would be less calamitous than predicted. Using your newly acquired expertise in international economics from Chapters 39–42, how would you analyze the doomsday predictions listed above?

APPENDIX TO PART 6

Current research

Research in the area of international economic affairs has snowballed since World War II. The U.S. balance-of-payments deficit, attacks on the dollar, and the price of gold have been front-page news. Leaving aside our problems vis-à-vis the less-developed countries (covered in Part 8), the following sample may provide some impression of the lively probing into international economics in recent years.

U.S. and the world economy   The *International Economic Report of the President* each year presents a useful overview of the United States in the world economy. See especially Part I and sample the remainder as it interests you.

The balance of payments and gold   How to compromise effectively the international balance of payments and the domestic stabilization concerns of all nations is the most difficult problem faced on the international economic scene in recent years. A relatively simple beginning is provided by R. Aliber, *The International Money Game* (New York: Basic Books, 1973). Then try Milton Friedman, "The Advantages of Flexible Exchange Rates," and Henry Wallich, "In Defense of Fixed Exchange Rates," before the Joint Economic Committee, *Hearings on the U.S. Balance of Payments* (1963), pp. 451–59 and 495–99. Pitt's Marina Whitman provides an excellent historical and theoretical summary of recent developments in "The Payments Adjustment Process and the Exchange Regime: What Have We Learned?" *American Economic Review,* May 1975. M.A. Kriz's *Gold: Barbarous Relic or Useful Instrument?* (Princeton, N.J.: Princeton International Finance Section, 1967) reviews the changing role of gold over the years, culminating in its rejection in the Jamaica Agreements as the major international monetary reserve.

A useful analysis of "Eurodollars" and their role is provided by Milton Friedman, "The Euro-Dollar Market," Federal Reserve Bank of St. Louis *Review,* July 1971; and Fred Klopstock, "Money Creation in the Euro-Dollar Market," Federal Reserve Bank of New York *Review,* January 1970. *European Monetary Unification and Its Meaning for the United States,* L. Krause and W. Salant, eds. (Washington, D.C.: The Brookings Institution, 1973) combines the analysis of leading scholars.

International trade   Nations continue to impose barriers to free trade, in order to help their own economies. A broad and still up-to-date picture of research on U.S. tariff policy is provided by *Foreign Trade Policy,* a compendium for the Foreign Trade Policy Subcommittee of the House Committee on Ways and Means (1958). Many of the papers are partisan pleas by industry representatives, but the papers by Piquet, Salant, and Kravis are readable, analytical research pieces. Charles Kindleberger's *The Politics of International Economics and the Economics of International Politics* (New York: Basic Books, 1971) and M.A. Adelman's *The World Petroleum Market* (Baltimore: Johns Hopkins University Press, 1973) look at some of the hot international political-economic issues of this decade. "How the Japanese Mount That Export Blitz," *Fortune,* September 1970, explains some of the devices used by Japan in obtaining a bigger share of total markets.

The multinational corporation   One of the most controversial issues of modern international trade and investment is the role of multinational corporations. See Raymond Vernon, *Sovereignty at Bay: The Multinational Spread of U.S. Corporations* (New York: Basic Books, 1971); F. Bergsten, T. Horst, and T. Moran, *American Multinationals and American Interests* (Washington, D.C.: The Brookings Institution, 1976); and C. Kindleberger, *American Business Abroad* (New Haven, Conn.: Yale University Press, 1969). A highly critical, socialist view of the whole process is presented by Harry Magdoff in *The Age of Imperialism, Monthly Review Press,* 1969.

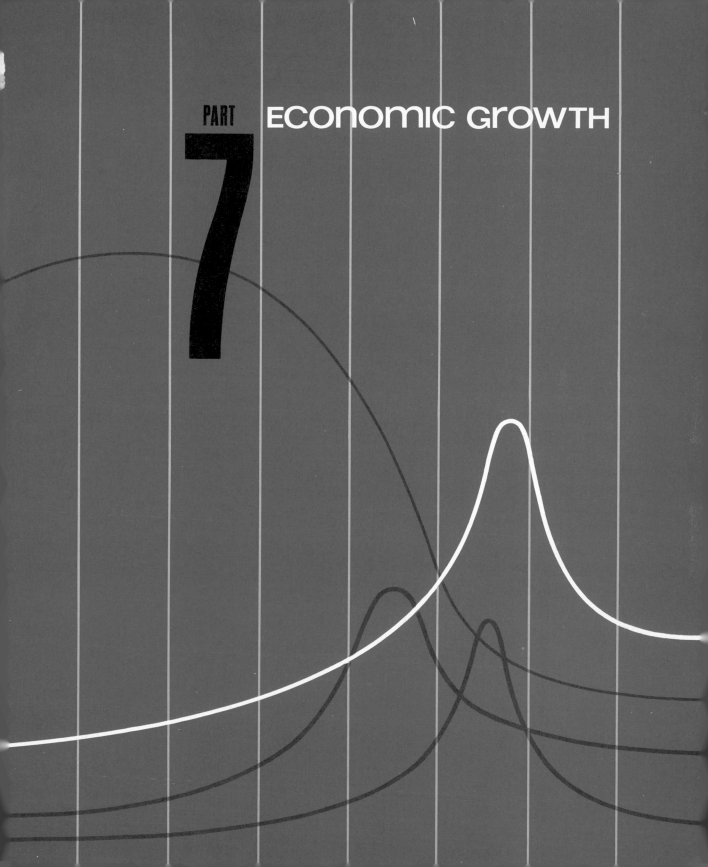

PART

7

ECONOMIC GROWTH

CHAPTER 43 THE THEORY OF economic GROWTH

For over half the world's population, the number one economic problem is getting enough to eat. By our standards, they are desperately poor. For them, economic growth—more output per capita—offers the only real hope of rising above a bare-subsistence level of food and shelter.

Even in the United States, there are millions of poor, miles of squalid slums—and few in our population of over 200 million do not continually hope for more income, for the better things in life. Thus, here too, economic growth is a central issue, although a far less pressing need than for the world's less-developed, poverty-stricken nations.

Today, many people argue that concern for the "quality of life" should replace our traditional stress on the quantity of GNP. Some advocate zero economic growth (ZEG). Extremists allege that technology has taken over society, and that man is now a mere slave to machines; their solution is often vague—to somehow slow technology and return to a simpler life. Others claim that mass starvation is just around the corner, because population is growing too fast.

This chapter begins with some facts on economic growth, but it is mainly concerned with the theory of growth. Why do economies grow as fast or as slowly as they do? Chapter 44 then uses this theoretical framework to explain growth in today's American economy; and Chapter 46 does the same for the less-developed economies, which contain the great bulk of the world's people.

SOME FACTS ON GROWTH
Economic growth defined

Economic growth means growth in the amount of goods and services produced—in total, or per capita. For some purposes, growth in total output is most important—for example, in assessing a nation's economic potential for war. But for most purposes, we are more interested in output per capita (or per family)—that is, growth in the ratio: $\dfrac{\text{total output}}{\text{population}}$. For output per capita provides a rough measure of the average standard of living of individuals in the economy. You will find "economic growth" used widely in both senses, but here, economic growth will mean growth in output per capita unless growth in total output is specified.

The two definitions can color the facts quite differently. If total output grows but population grows even faster, the standard of living of the typical individual falls. In this country, total output has risen on the average about 3.5 percent annually over the last century, while output per capita has risen only about 2.5 percent per annum as population grew about 1 percent per annum. In India, total output has recently grown too, at a rate not far behind ours, but population has grown nearly as fast as output. Hence there has been little change in output per capita, and the Indian standard of living today is little higher than it was a century ago.

Economic growth in perspective

Look back at Table 1–1 and then ahead to Table 46–1 to get a first picture of the results of such widely varying economic growth rates in the world today. The United States stands near the top, even though we are a new nation compared to most of the other leaders. The success story of the American economy (if we consider growth a "good") is written in these figures on our spectacular economic growth over a mere two or three centuries of world history.

What about comparative growth rates for major industrialized countries over the last century? Table 7–1 told the story. Growth rates have varied widely, and the national ordering is quite different from the nations' present ranks. Only a fraction of a percent can make a big difference when compounded over a century. When, for example, did the United States gain its present big advantage over France, the U.K., and the USSR? How about Japan, which began to industrialize very late? She now has the world's third largest GNP, behind only the United States and the USSR, and is growing far faster than either. Will she falter soon? Tables like these show why economic historians and economic theorists have a fascinating time explaining the facts.

One last introductory look at the facts. What about recent comparative growth rates? Table 43–1 provides the answer. Since World War II, we have grown nearly 50 percent faster than over the preceding century. But a number of other nations have done still better, especially Japan and West Germany. And the order is very different from those in Tables 1–1 and 7–1.

A word of warning is needed here, however. Growth figures for any short period are tricky, and the data in Table 43–1 reflect partly special conditions growing out of World War II.

Table 43–1
Comparative annual growth rates, 1950–74[a]

	GNP per Capita	GNP
Japan	9.8	10.6
West Germany	4.7	5.9
France	4.6	5.2
Italy	4.3	5.1
USSR	3.7	5.1
Sweden	3.3	3.9
Canada	3.3	4.5
United States	3.1	4.4
United Kingdom	2.3	2.6

[a]Estimates based on United Nations and International Monetary Fund data, in real terms.

The difference between growth and cycle upswings

It is important to distinguish between long-run growth rates and short-run swings reflecting business-cycle fluctuations. For example, output per capita usually rises rapidly as an economy moves from depression to high employment. But this is clearly a temporary factor, and should not be extrapolated out as a long-run growth rate. Thus, most economists look upon the long-run growth rate as something to be measured only over extended periods that cover at least the years from one cycle peak to another, and preferably several cycles. Alternatively, they look at the growth in the "full-employment capacity" of the economy—that is, its growing capacity to produce at "full employment" of men and machines.

THE THEORY OF ECONOMIC GROWTH

Why have some nations grown so fast and others not at all? Alas, there is no one simple theory that seems to explain everything. But there is growing consensus on some central factors in the growth process, and it is on these that we shall concentrate.

Supply and demand factors in economic growth

The classical economists had a simple answer to questions about economic growth. The basic productive factors were land, labor, and capital. Growth in total output depended on the combined expansion of these productive factors, reflecting especially enterprise, hard work, and thrift. And the growth in output per capita depended largely on the growth in population relative to the growth in land and capital available for production. They stressed the *supply* factors—the ones that move out the nation's production-possibilities curve.

Nearly two centuries later, the classical economists still look basically right. It is the "real" (supply) factors that matter most in economic growth—the accumulation of capital goods; growth in the size and efficiency of the labor force; the natural resources ("land") that a na-

tion has; and its research, education, and technical advance, which permit it to produce more with any given amount of capital, labor, and natural resources.

Beyond land, labor, capital, and technology, many historians and economists point to other, more tenuous factors—the energy and "drive" of a nation's people, the social and economic mobility of its classes, its economic institutions, its governmental and political stability. Although we set most of these forces aside for the moment, it is important not to forget them.

These "supply" factors matter most, but in a private-enterprise economy, money *demand* matters too. Unless aggregate demand is adequate to take goods off the market, they will not be produced for long. And unless prospective money demand promises reasonable returns on new investments, savings will not be invested in the new capital goods and research necessary for economic growth.

Summary: **On the supply side,** the problem of economic growth is to increase productive capacity—basically, through diverting resources from current consumption to investment in capital goods, research, education, and other activities that increase future productive capacity; through increasing the size and quality of the labor force; and through improving the economic and social-political organization of the society. **On the demand side,** the first problem is to be sure that there is always adequate total demand to induce high-level utilization of productive capacity. The second problem is to channel spending from consumption into saving and investment so that society's stock of capital goods and human resources will be built up to increase future output.

Adam Smith—progress through enterprise and thrift

How is it that in the last 200 years, only in a few now-industrialized nations of the Western world has man managed to rise rapidly from poverty to our present comfortable way of living? In 1776, Adam Smith, in his *Wealth of Nations,* first saw the central rationale of an individual-self-interest, market-directed economy. Would these forces of self-interest lead man to economic progress and an ever-better life? His answer was yes—because self-interest would produce not only hard work and enterprise, but also thrift and accumulation. As man saved part of what he produced, the savings of many individuals could mean new factories, new machines, better houses. Thus, thrift and accumulation, savings from the fruits of hard labor, were the foundations of economic growth—of progress toward a better life.

To be sure, more machinery and more capital would mean a larger demand for workers, and this in turn would lead to higher wages, so that profits—the special source of, and stimulus to, accumulation—would tend to be eaten away. But Smith saw no crisis in this process. He observed that higher wages and more food would lead to more people, and thus to more workers. This in turn would tend to push wages back down, lowering the costs to businessmen as it lowered the real wages of the worker. And so profits and accumulation would again become possible, with further progress.

Smith's was an optimistic world, of self-interest and of order. It was a world of progress for those who worked hard and saved, and for societies made up of such men. And Smith's analysis still has fundamental lessons to teach us today.

Malthus, Ricardo, and Marx— strife and diminishing returns

Two Englishmen, writing shortly after Smith, saw instead a gloomy world of conflict and strife—of workers, capitalists, and landlords climbing on each others' backs, each trying to increase his own share of the sustenance produced by society. T.R. Malthus and David Ricardo, two other great founders of modern economics, challenged the orderly world of Smith with disturbing predictions that still have a modern look, nearly two centuries later.

Malthus and the specter of famine. More people mean more productive power and more output. But more people also mean more mouths to feed, more backs to clothe. In 1798, Malthus, a young British minister, wrote his now famous *Essay on the Principle of Population.* He gloomily predicted that population would rise

far faster than the productive power associated with more people. Looking at rising birthrates, Malthus pointed out that the population could double every generation if each woman had only four surviving children, half of them girls who would produce more children in the next generation. Malthus felt that this might well result in a geometrical population increase—2, 4, 8, 16, 32, 64, and so on—with a doubling each generation.

But the world's land could not possibly increase its food output at this rate over the long run, Malthus argued. Thus, unless population growth was checked by moral restraint, or by such disasters as war or disease, it must ultimately be checked by recurrent famines as the population outran the food supply. The British standard of living was hardly above the subsistence level for much of the population; unless population growth slowed, the outlook for growth in output per capita and for a better life was bleak.

Ricardo and the "law of diminishing returns." David Ricardo, another famous British economist, provided a further intellectual justification for Malthus' fears. Ricardo first stated the law of diminishing returns. If the number of workers applied to any fixed supply of land is increased, the crops obtained from the land will increase, but output will increase at a slower rate than the rate at which workers are added.

The implications of this "law" for the standard of living of a growing population seemed clear. Given the world's supply of arable land, sooner or later food output per worker would fall when the point of diminishing returns was passed. And as population grew thereafter, food output **per capita** (more accurately, per worker) would decline steadily, even though total food output might continue to grow.

But at the same time that diminishing returns pressed down on the food available for individual workers, it would enrich the landlords. For as more and more workers sought sustenance from the land, the price of each piece of land (in sale or in rent) would rise. Ricardo, the economic theorist par excellence, explained through the law of diminishing returns precisely how fast rents would rise and wage rates fall as more workers were applied to the increasingly scarce land. Each factor of production would earn essentially its marginal contribution to total productivity—what we called in Part 4 its marginal productivity.

But what of capital accumulation, the path to progress in Smith's system? Ricardo saw the importance of thrift and accumulation in man's attempt to improve his lot. But here again, Ricardo wrote, the fact of diminishing returns rears its ugly head. As more and more capital is accumulated relative to scarce land, the return on capital (interest or profits) will be squeezed down more and more. In the end, it is the landlords who will wax ever richer, while both workers and capitalists find their individual returns (in the form of wages and of profits) squeezed to the barest minimum.

Were Malthus and Ricardo right? If history has proved them wrong in the nations of the Western world, where did they go astray? Have they been proved right in India and southeast Asia, where starvation is an ever-present threat for nearly a billion people? As with Smith, Malthus and Ricardo have lessons for today. Their arguments will reappear in the modern analysis of growth.

Marx and the collapse of capitalism. Fifty years later came Karl Marx, the gloomy prophet of the downfall of the capitalist system. Like his classical predecessors, Marx was interested in the grand dynamics—the progress of society or its road to collapse. But he saw no progress. Instead, he foresaw collapse, as capitalists seized ever-larger incomes while forcing the workers into degradation and eventually to revolt that would overthrow the capitalistic system.

Marx built an elaborate theoretical structure on the fallacy that labor is the source of **all** value. He said that any return to another productive resource, such as capital or land, is merely a misappropriation of the "surplus value" produced by labor. But we need not be concerned with the details of this argument.[1] To Marx, capital accumulation was again at the center of things. The desire for profit leads men to accumulate capital and to wring every ounce

of effort out of the workers who must labor for their bread. The class struggle is at the center of the economic process. Because capitalists are powerful and rich, whereas laborers are poor and divided, capitalists can push down the real wages of their workers to the point where workers can barely subsist. The higher profits lead to more and more capital accumulation, as Smith and Ricardo had predicted before him.

But to Marx, the end result of all this was quite different, although it had been hinted in the worryings of Parson Malthus. Capitalism will develop increasing crises, Marx wrote. Too much of society's income will go to the rich capitalists. Too little will be paid to the masses to permit them to buy the output of the new factories and machines. Thus, capitalism will face declining profit rates and increasingly severe crises and depressions, with resulting unemployment and chaos. Finally, the hungry workers, long ground under the heel of wealthy capitalists, will rise in revolt and overthrow the capitalist system. So, wrote Marx, will come the downfall of capitalism, brought on by the very process of capital accumulation that the classical economists had praised as the foundation of economic growth.

Clearly, Marx has been wrong in the Western world. Real wages have not been ground down over the long run. Both they and profits have risen rapidly in total, and real wages per worker are vastly higher now than 100 years ago. Interestingly, the real rate of return per dollar of capital invested (loosely, the profit rate or the interest rate) has apparently been about constant, although of course the total return to capital has grown enormously with the vast accumulation of capital. And apparently, modern monetary-fiscal policy has brought great depressions under control.

Let us now examine more analytically some of the issues exposed by Smith, Malthus, Ricardo, and Marx.

The deepening of capital and diminishing returns. It is relatively easy to explain the growth in total output of an economy as capital and labor grow. The production-possibilities curve moves out. Unless unbalanced "excessive" capital accumulation brings on the crises suggested

---

[1] See the Appendix to Chapter 34.

by Malthus and Marx, an increase in any or all of the factors of production will raise total output. Thus, more workers, more capital goods, or more natural resources will increase total production. (Note that increased natural resources are a real possibility in new nations; for example, until almost 1900, the United States had continuous access to more land through the open frontier westward.) But how to increase output **per capita** is a much more difficult problem. For more workers, given the law of diminishing returns, will produce more total output, but output per worker will fall, assuming that the stock of capital and land remain constant.

Disregard for a moment the supply of land (natural resources) as of decreasing importance in the advanced economies. Then, if the number of workers increases, at least a parallel increase in the stock of capital would appear to be the only hope for avoiding declining real wages as a result of the law of diminishing returns. People must save and the stock of capital must rise faster than population grows, if output per worker is to rise.

This is what economists call the "deepening" of capital—more capital per unit of labor. **It is this deepening of capital, the analysis of the preceding paragraphs suggests, that is the fundamental hope for progress.**

Let us now reconsider, more analytically, the effects of capital deepening in a simple system. Assume again that there is no land, merely labor and capital as productive factors. Suppose capital grows faster than the labor supply. What then happens to per capita output? The answer is given by Ricardo's law of diminishing returns. Total output will grow, but not in proportion to the growth in the capital stock. Thus, the return per unit of capital (the interest rate or profit rate) will fall as capital deepens. Here, labor is the relatively fixed factor (just as was land in Ricardo's case). Thus, the wage rate (the return to labor) will be bid up as labor becomes ever scarcer relative to capital; labor replaces the "greedy landlord" of Ricardo's system. But last, note that higher wage rates and lower interest rates in the system *do not* necessarily imply a higher percentage share of the total national output for labor. This is because there are more units of capital being used. The increased num-

ber of units may offset the lower return per unit of capital and may thus keep the aggregate share of capital in the national output from falling absolutely, or even relative to the share of labor.

It is important to be clear about the reasoning of the preceding paragraph. It is the foundation for much of the modern theory of growth, and for moving on to a new factor—technological progress.

The new look—technical advance and innovation

Why have Malthus, Ricardo, and Marx been proved wrong in nearly all the nations of the Western world, although they may be discomfortingly right for two billion people in the less-developed nations? Is the answer a simple one—that Adam Smith was basically right in his optimistic prediction of growth in private-enterprise economies, but that the less-developed nations have not yet heeded his advice?

Most modern economists say that Smith deserves credit for a powerful analysis of some of the basic forces. But something else has been added to give the victory to Smith's optimism over Malthus' and Ricardo's gloom. This is technical advance and its partner, innovation. **The revolution of science, technology, and education has saved us from diminishing returns!**

The basic fact is that total output has grown much faster than the combined inputs of the factors of production. Only part of the growth in total U.S. output since 1900 can be explained by the growth in capital and labor inputs, disregarding land as substantially fixed in quantity. Similar patterns apparently prevail in other advanced industrial nations. And, modern economics says, the main reason is technical progress and innovation. New machines, better management methods, computers to do the work of adding machines, new fertilizers to double the output of farms, new management techniques—these have more than offset the once-feared law of diminishing returns.

It is important to remember that technical change shows up in higher skills and better education for workers, scientists, and managers, as well as in new machines and methods. Modern computers drastically reduce business costs and make possible fantastic new scientific developments. Is the technical advance in the computers, or is it in the skills of the scientists who designed the computers and the programmers who apply them to new problems? Both, is the answer. Thus, technical advance is introduced through education and training (investment in human beings) as well as through new capital goods and techniques (investment in research and development and in nonhuman capital).

Technical progress has made Adam Smith right. It has gone far to prove that the pessimists were wrong, mainly because they overlooked the vast power of modern technical change. Joseph Schumpeter, a famous economist writing early in this century, first stressed innovation (in productive techniques and in new products) as the mainspring of economic growth. History appears to be bearing Schumpeter out, at least in the industrialized Western economies.

GROWTH IN THE DEVELOPED ECONOMIES

A satisfactory modern theory of growth for the developed Western economies like the United States must explain at least the following facts:

1. The strong, upward movement in real wages in the face of a rapidly growing population and labor force. (In the United States, population has tripled since 1900, while real wages have risen more than fivefold.)

2. A still more rapid increase in capital stock with a resultant deepening of capital, but (disregarding business-cycle fluctuations) with roughly stable long-term real interest and profit rates, contrary to the falling expectation given by the law of diminishing returns.

3. A slightly falling ratio of capital to total output for the economy in the face of the rapid deepening of capital, where the law of diminishing returns would lead us to suppose that the capital–output ratio would rise.

4. A surprisingly stable division of the total national product between wages and salaries on the one hand and returns to property (profits, interest, and rent) on the other—though with a gradual increase in the labor share in recent decades.

Supply factors: saving, investment, and technical progress

Modern growth theory stresses the fact that total output grows when capital and labor grow and technology improves, disregarding land as a relatively minor factor in highly developed countries.[2] In general, then, output *per capita* will grow only when capital grows faster than labor or when there is technical advance, or both. When capital is deepened, unless there is technical change, the law of diminishing returns will reduce the rate of return on capital and increase the real wage of labor. But with technical advance, the rate of return on capital need not fall; it may be stable or even rise while the real wage rises even more rapidly. What happens to the relative shares of capital and labor if the total national income depends on the relative rates of growth of the two.

Saving and investment (diversion of real resources from consumption to increase investment) is thus central to the growth process. For investment is required both for capital deepening and research and, in most instances, to incorporate technical advance. The larger the portion of its current output that a society devotes to investment, the faster capital will deepen and the faster output per capita will rise. Moreover, the more of its resources it devotes to investment in research and development and to education, the faster technical progress will occur.

Demand factors

Malthus and Marx warned of breakdowns in the growth process because aggregate demand might fall short of buying all the goods that could be produced as the stock of capital grows. This was a valid warning. We now recognize that aggregate demand must grow roughly

[2]Some economists like to summarize this relationship in a simple "production function" for the entire economy:

$$\text{Output} = a(A \cdot K \cdot L)$$

where K is the stock of capital, L is the stock of labor, and A is technical progress. Thus, output depends on the combined effect of all three. For a more complete discussion, see the appendix to this chapter.

in step with the productive capacity of the economy if unemployment and inflation are to be avoided. It is clear, further, that when aggregate demand does fall short and depression occurs, the ratio of investment to GNP, and therefore the rate of economic growth, declines.

Equally important, decisions on money spending or saving within the total are vital to a stable growth process. This is because they largely control the division of the national output between consumption on the one hand and saving–investment on the other. For a brainteaser on the saving–investment rate needed to just maintain stable growth in GNP, see the appendix to this chapter.

Growth and fluctuations

Schumpeter stressed the intimate relationship between growth and economic fluctuations. As we saw in Chapter 15, the bunching of real investment is the essence of a boom and of rapid growth. But this very process usually involves overshooting the amount of real productive capacity needed to meet consumer demands. When the overshoot becomes obvious, private investment is cut back and a recession occurs until a better balance between capacity and growing consumption is restored. Excessive expansion of credit helps to speed investment booms, supplementing the intended savings of the public and thus intensifying real overinvestment beyond a sustainable growth rate. On both real and monetary scores, the theory of growth and the theory of fluctuations are inseparable.

The eclectic consensus

Most modern economists thus look at the stock of capital, the stock of labor, and technical advance as a framework for analyzing growth in total output. The law of diminishing returns, partially or completely offset by technical advance and innovation, provides a powerful tool for understanding what happens to output per capita, and to the relative shares of capital and labor, in the growth process. The extent to which any growth is sustainable, rather than leading to overinvestment through excessive capital accumulation, depends partially on monetary-fiscal factors and partially on the bunching of real investment in the process. Throughout, there must be adequate demand to buy the growing full-employment output. This general theory helps to explain the basic facts on growth listed at the beginning of this section. It is a modern eclectic consensus that provides the foundation for the following chapters.

Other factors

One last preliminary word is needed. Many economists believe that this framework is too narrow to explain the basic forces of economic growth, in either the United States or less-developed nations. They say that private initiative and our free-enterprise economic institutions have played a major role in explaining our rapid growth. The *noneconomic* factors mentioned at the outset—the initiative of the people and their "drive," social and economic mobility in the system, the flexibility of economic and social institutions, religious traditions and ethical mores, and particularly the political stability of a nation—may be as important as the purely *economic* factors stressed in the preceding pages. Certainly, absence of these factors has seriously deterred growth in many of the less-developed nations.

REVIEW

Concepts to remember

Be sure you understand the following basic concepts introduced in this chapter. They are reused repeatedly in the following chapters. And remember especially your old friends, *saving* and *investment*.

economic growth
growth versus cycle upswings
supply (real) factors in growth

demand (money) factors in growth
technical advance
capital deepening

**For analysis
and discussion**

1. Does Adam Smith or Malthus–Ricardo provide a better explanation of economic growth over the past century in the United States? In India and the less-developed nations? If your answers are different, why?
2. Suppose you want to explain Japan's rapid economic growth. At what factors does the theory of Chapter 43 suggest you should look?
3. Can you explain why capital deepening is so important to economic progress?
4. Keynes stressed that increased saving could push the economy toward recession and unemployment, while this chapter stresses saving as a key to economic growth. Can you reconcile the two?
5. "Increased aggregate demand is a first-rate answer to the depression problem, but it can't help much to speed up long-term growth." Do you agree? Why, or why not?
6. Suppose you want to speed up the rate of economic growth in the United States. What does the theory of Chapter 43 suggest as promising measures?
7. Explain the relationship between business cycles and economic growth.
8. In what sense, if any, has modern technological advance repealed Ricardo's law of diminishing returns?
9. If the rate of population growth speeds up relative to the rate of capital accumulation, what effect, if any, would you predict on the shares of labor and capital in the national income?

APPENDIX

Some special points on economic growth

Growth theory raises a host of interesting problems. This "brain-teaser" appendix is intended for students who want to look a little further into the intricacies of the subject.

A simple growth model Shortly after World War II, Oxford's Sir Roy Harrod and MIT's Evsey Domar simultaneously developed a simple growth model that has since been widely used. It builds on the fact that investment (increase in the capital stock) is a prime cause of economic growth, and assumes for simplicity that the capital–output ratio is constant. Note that a constant capital–output ratio assumes away the existence of diminishing returns.

Let Y = output, K = capital stock, and designate changes in any variable by Δ. Suppose the constant capital–output ratio is β—for example, 3—so that 3 of additional capital means 1 of additional output. Suppose further that savings (S) are a constant proportion of income (Y). Let that proportion be σ. Last, let us assume full employment; that is, we are concerned with the growth in full-employment potential output for the economy.

Since β is fixed, we know how much Y will increase for any increase in K:

$$\Delta K = \beta \, \Delta Y$$

But ΔK in any year is simply net investment in that year, and we know that saving equals investment in any year. Thus:

$$\Delta K = I = S = \sigma Y$$

Now combine the equations, substituting σY for ΔK. Then:

$$\beta \Delta Y = \sigma Y$$

so

$$\frac{\beta \Delta Y}{Y} = \sigma$$

or

$$\frac{\Delta Y}{Y} = \frac{\sigma}{\beta}$$

Since $\Delta Y/Y$ is the growth rate, the full-employment growth rate for the economy is given by σ/β. Thus, if β is 3 and σ is 15 percent, the economy will grow at 5 percent per year: $.15/3 = .05$.

This model stresses some important relationships. But remember the simplified assumptions before you conclude that it will tell you just how much saving your favorite economy needs to grow at 5 percent annually. In the real world, we often don't know what the capital–output ratio for new capital will be, and the savings–income ratio also has a slippery way of sliding around. Moreover, we've abstracted from a lot of real-world factors, such as business savings, taxes, and the like.

How to maintain stable growth A difficult brain-teaser: Is there some rate of saving and investment out of total output that is necessary for "balanced" or "sustainable" growth, avoiding too rapid or too slow an increase of capital that might lead to an "over-supply" or "undersupply" of productive capacity? If there is a constant capital–output ratio given by technology, then we can show that there is indeed such a required rate. Suppose labor grows at 1 percent annually and technological advance at 2 percent, so the basic capacity of the system to produce grows at 3 percent. Suppose further that the fixed capital-output ratio is $3:1$. That is, $3 of additional capital will produce $1 of additional output.

Then, using the highly simplified Harrod-Domar model above, we can show that the economy must save and invest just 9 percent of its output to grow stably. Why? Begin with a total output of 100. The extra 9 units of capital ($\sigma = 9$ percent) will produce just the 3 additional units of output that match the 3 percent growth in potential output from more labor and technical change ($\beta = 3$). Less saving and investment would provide inadequate capital to produce the possible 3 percent annual growth in output, given the $3:1$ capital–output ratio. Larger saving and investment would pile up more capital than could be used in producing the 3 percent growth in output. In this model, a knife-edge saving rate is required for stable economic growth. But remember that this is only one model, based on extremely limited assumptions, so the conclusion may not directly apply to the real world.

Is technical progress "neutral"? Does technical progress tend to increase the share of Y going to labor or to capital, or is it "neutral" as between the two shares? Obviously, technical progress might be "labor-saving" or "capital-saving." That is, it might reduce or increase the relative amount of labor or capital needed to produce a given output. If the technical advance is labor-saving, so that less labor is now needed for a given output, we might predict that the labor share of Y would fall.

In fact, we observe in the real world that the labor and capital shares of national income have been surprisingly constant (abstracting from cyclical fluctuations), with a small tendency for the labor share to rise. Can we infer that technical progress has been "neutral" in the sense above? Consider two possible explanations.

First, it is possible that in the absence of technical change, the elasticity of substitution between K and L is 1. That is, if the wage rate falls relative to the cost of capital, businessmen will hire just enough more labor to offset the lower wage rate, and just enough less capital to offset the higher price per unit. Then the relative income shares of capital and labor will remain unchanged. We can write an aggregate "production function" to show this case, as follows:

$$\text{Output} = A(L^a \cdot K^{1-a})$$

where A is technical progress, L is the stock of labor, and K is the stock of capital. If this is the economy's production function, constant relative shares of total output for labor and capital are shown by the coefficients a and $1 - a$; a is the fraction of total output earned by labor, and $1 - a$ is the corresponding fraction for capital. This is sometimes called a Cobb-Douglas production function, after the economists who developed it to explain the apparent stability of relative income shares. If the elasticity of substitution between capital and labor is 1, the a and $1 - a$ will be constant shares of total output going to labor and capital, and A is "neutral" with respect to the relative shares going to labor and capital.[3]

Alternatively, it may be that without technical

---

[3]For a more complete account of the forces determining the incomes received by labor and capital, see Part 4, and Mathematical Appendix IV, which provides a rigorous analysis of the Cobb-Douglas production function.

change, the elasticity of substitution is not 1. Then, if investment produces a relatively faster growth in capital (as in the U.S. economy), the interest rate might fall enough and the wage rate might rise enough for the income share of capital to fall, that of labor to rise. Indeed, there seems little *a priori* reason to suppose that the elasticity of substitution between K and L is just 1. But if so, how shall we explain the surprising relative stability of income shares? The answer, some modern economists argue, is that technical progress is not neutral, but instead it provides a built-in mechanism for keeping income shares roughly constant. If, for example, this second case occurs, businessmen will be induced by the profit motive to shift their technical change (innovations) toward the labor-saving type. They do so because labor is becoming relatively more expensive, capital relatively cheaper. Moreover, it is argued, this inducement will be roughly enough to offset any tendency for the relative shares of capital and labor to shift.

Is this induced-innovation theory of stable income shares right? Or is innovation generally "neutral," so that the observed rough stability in income shares comes from an elasticity of substitution between K and L of about 1? We don't know. This is the kind of research project on which some modern economists work—both because it is intellectually challenging and because the conclusions may throw light on fundamental social issues.

44

ECONOMIC GROWTH IN THE UNITED STATES

Starting from nowhere only two centuries ago, the U.S. economy has produced results that are spectacular by any standards. Our 1975 GNP of $1.5 trillion was a quarter of the world's total, yet we have only 5 percent of the world's population. How have we done so well? And why have we fallen behind some other nations in the recent growth race?

THE U.S. RECORD

Figure 44–1 shows the record. Over the past century, total U.S. real GNP has risen fiftyfold. Over the same period, per capita GNP (in 1972 prices) rose from about $600 to $5,500, or nearly tenfold. Total output has grown at a rate of about 3.4 percent and per capita output at about 2.2 percent annually.

Let us now take a closer look at the anatomy of U.S. economic growth since 1900. Figure 44–2 shows the major variables in the growth process that were stressed in the theory of Chapter 43. Note that all curves are plotted on a ratio scale, so the slopes of the lines show comparative growth rates.

Note: This chapter provides mainly a descriptive picture of growth in the United States. Instructors preferring to stress an analytical approach may want to assign only the first three pages plus Chapter 45.

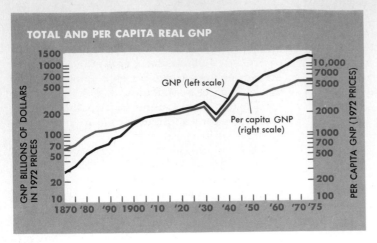

TOTAL AND PER CAPITA REAL GNP

Figure 44–1
Both total and per capita real GNP have risen persistently over the past century, faltering seriously only during the 1930s. Data are plotted only at five-year intervals to show the main growth trends. (Source: U.S. Department of Commerce.)

What can we see here? A rapid but jagged rate of growth in real GNP, reflecting a roughly similar rate of growth in the capital stock and a much slower growth in population. The theory of Chapter 43 would suggest rising real wages relative to the return on capital, and this is indeed what we see in the lower part of the chart. Further, the theory would predict that without technical progress, the rate of return on capital would fall absolutely. But interestingly, the return on capital (the interest rate), although fluctuating widely in the Great Depression, is

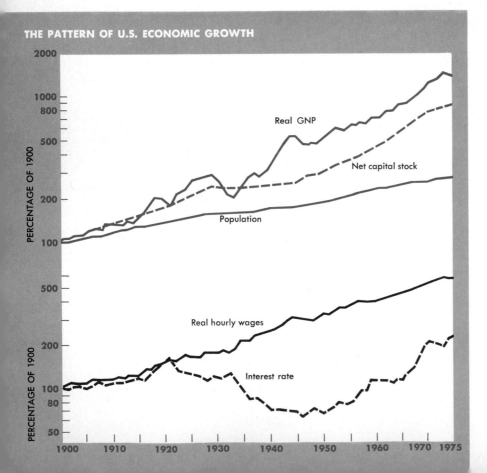

THE PATTERN OF U.S. ECONOMIC GROWTH

Figure 44–2
Since 1900, the capital stock has grown much faster than population and the labor force; GNP has grown faster than the combined inputs of capital and labor. Real wages and interest rates have moved about as would be expected from our theory of growth, recognizing the big role played by technological advance. Note that interest rates are not adjusted for price changes; real interest rates were much lower than those plotted for recent years. (Source: U.S. Department of Commerce, *Long Term Economic Growth, 1860–1965*; and *Economic Reports of the President*.)

roughly flat in trend. (Much of the recent rise is merely inflation.) Something, presumably technical advance, has buoyed up **both** real wages and the return to capital, as the theory suggests. Our growth theory from Chapter 43, with technical advance included, is confirmed by the evidence.

EXPLAINING U.S. GROWTH TO DATE

The sources of growth

What have been the main sources of economic growth in the United States? Table 44–1 gives one courageous expert's estimates of the quantitative importance of the big forces at work during this century. Although he doesn't pretend that these are more than approximations, they provide an interesting introduction to the rest of this chapter.

Note the significant differences between the pre- and post-1929 periods, although the figures are not strictly comparable. The increasing **quantity** of labor and capital goods dominates the pre-1929 picture. But since 1929, improvements in the **quality** of labor and capital (edu-

cation and technical advance incorporated in both real capital and human beings) have accounted for half our total growth, according to these estimates. And if we eliminate growth in the labor force (population) because it doesn't significantly raise output *per capita*, improvements in quality accounted for nearly two-thirds of the total increase.

These allocations are in dispute among research workers. Harvard's Zvi Griliches and Dale Jorgenson, using different methods, conclude that increased inputs account for more of the growth in output, leaving a smaller role for technical advance as a separate factor. Distinguishing between the contribution of more capital and that of improved technology is extremely difficult, because with advancing technology, new machines almost always have higher productivity than their predecessors. How much of the increased output shall we attribute to *more* capital, how much to *improved* capital? There is no undisputed way to draw the line. But almost all research experts agree that Denison's factors are the right ones to look at.[1]

To fill in this framework completely as an explanation of U.S. economic growth would require a separate book. The charts on the following pages summarize some of the main factors at work. They need only brief comments.

Natural resources

The United States has been rich in natural resources, and they help explain our record growth. But the most striking fact has been our success in substituting new resources for old as technology advances. In 1850, 65 percent of all energy came from animal and human power, only 35 percent from inanimate sources (water, petroleum, and so on). Today, only 1 percent of all power is furnished by humans and animals, 99 percent by inanimate sources.

Recently, there have been widespread fears that we will soon run out of natural resources, especially energy sources. We shall look at this issue carefully in Chapter 45. Figure 44–3 shows

Table 44–1
Sources of U.S. economic growth, 1909–69

	PERCENTAGE OF TOTAL GROWTH	
Source	*1909–29*	*1929–69*
Total growth in national real income	100	100
Increase in labor force[a]	35	24
Improved education and training	13	15
Increased stock of capital goods	23	15
Improved technology	19	35
Economies of scale[b]	10	11

[a] Adjusted for decreasing number of working hours per year.
[b] Economies of large-scale production with growing total size of the market.
Sources: Edward Denison, *The Sources of Economic Growth in the United States* (Committee for Economic Development, 1962), and *Accounting for U.S. Economic Growth, 1929–69* (The Brookings Institution, 1974). Figures before and after 1929 are not strictly comparable; see sources for details.

---

[1] Denison has done a similar analysis of growth in nine Western industrial nations, *Why Growth Rates Differ* (Washington, D.C.: The Brookings Institution, 1967).

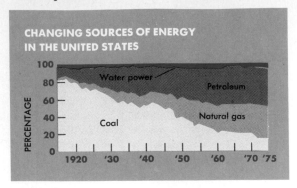

Figure 44–3
Petroleum and natural gas have increased as major sources of energy for the modern economy. Nuclear power is still a very small source. Will nuclear and solar power increase rapidly over the decades ahead?

the rapidly changing sources of energy used over the past half century. Will nuclear and solar energy be next?

Capital goods and capital accumulation

History suggests that the long-term economic growth rates of the major countries correspond roughly to the proportion of their total outputs that they save and invest. When we

Figure 44–4
Gross capital formation has risen enormously over the past century, but recently, both gross and net capital formation have been much smaller percentages of GNP than in earlier decades. (Sources: S. Kuznets, *Capital in the American Economy* [Princeton, N.J.: Princeton Univ. Press, 1961]; and Council of Economic Advisers.)

recognize that most technical advance also requires investment (in research and development, in human beings, and as a vehicle for introducing technical changes), the need to save and invest for economic growth becomes doubly obvious.

Throughout the nineteenth century, the United States was a high-saving and high-investment economy. It paced the world in economic growth. During the present century, although we have invested huge sums, the proportion of our national product devoted to investment has dropped substantially.[2]

Figure 44–4 tells the story. During the past decade, we have invested over $100 billion annually (in current dollars), a total exceeding the entire GNP of all except a half-dozen nations. The result is an enormous productive machine underlying our trillion-dollar GNP. Investment per employee in manufacturing is over $40,000. Our capital stock has grown sixfold since 1900.

Yet, as the right-hand part of Figure 44–4 shows, investment has trended down as a percentage of GNP. The United States now has the lowest investment ratio of all the major nations (See Table 45–4), so it should not be surprising that our growth rate recently has been well under those of such higher-saving nations as Japan and West Germany.

Technical change

Modern technology and innovation have long been the trademarks of American

[2]This is much less striking if we include consumers' durables as investment.

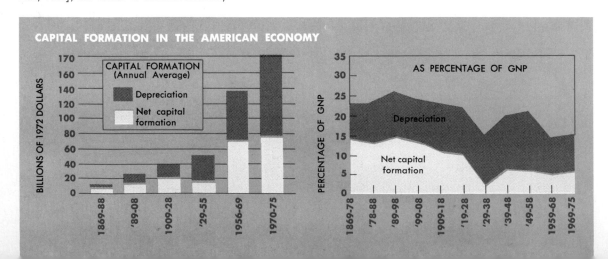

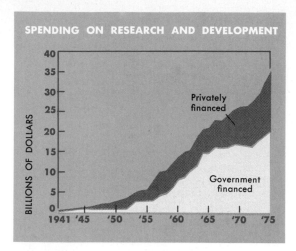

Figure 44-5
Research is the newest big industry in the United States, developed largely since World War II. It is about two-thirds government-financed. Total research spending adjusted for inflation has declined substantially since the 1960s. (Source: National Science Foundation.)

business. Behind this advance have been both a spirit of American entrepreneurship and an enormous increase in spending on research and development. Figure 44–5 tells the story. From only $1 billion annually in 1941, R&D spending has soared to nearly $40 billion annually, three-fourths the amount of total net private-business expenditures on plant and equipment. But the increase in real (inflation-adjusted) terms has been only half as much, and R&D, like investment spending on plant and equipment, has been falling in recent years as a percentage of GNP. Some experts predict that this will slow our rate of technological advance over the decades ahead unless we again step up our rate of R&D spending. Strikingly, about 60 percent of all R&D, and over 90 percent of *basic* research, is government-financed, although most of the work has been done in private industry, universities, and private research organizations.

Half of all the measured research in our history has occurred in the last 15 years. But the growth in federal financing of research slowed in the late 1960s; the flattening of the government portion of the total is clear in Figure 44–5. And when we allow for inflation, total *real* spending

on research has dropped by about 10 percent since 1967—reflecting cutbacks in government spending. About three-fourths of all government R&D is on military, space, and atomic-energy programs. Digital computers, many drugs, atomic energy, communications satellites, and modern aircraft are notable examples of major innovations originally financed by government research funds. Private industry has concentrated largely on developing the basic research of others into commercially profitable applications.

Population and the labor force

Denison allocates a quarter to a third of all growth in output to growth in the labor force. Population grew rapidly in the nineteenth century. But Figure 44–6 shows the persistent recent decline in its growth rate. While population is still growing by about two million annually, the present birthrate has dropped to roughly a zero-population-growth rate. However, even if this birthrate continues, it will take until after the year 2000 before we reach stability at around 250 million people, because of the large number of young people who have yet to pass through their child-bearing periods.

Figure 44–7 shows the persistent labor-force growth since 1900. Except for bulges during major wars, the growth has been a steady one,

Figure 44-6
The postwar baby boom produced a big increase in our population growth rate. But the rate has fallen dramatically since then. Each bar shows the percentage increase over the preceding decade. (Source: U.S. Census Bureau.)

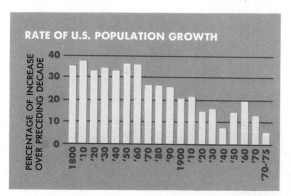

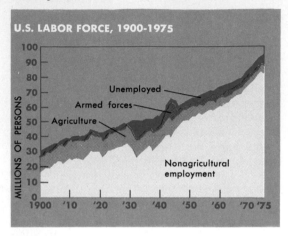

Figure 44-7
The U.S. labor force has grown steadily, with bulges during major wars. Most have taken nonagricultural jobs. Note the big unemployment pocket during the 1930s. (Source: U.S. Department of Labor.)

reflecting a combination of growing population and a gradual increase in the percentage of the population in the labor force. We have steadily increased the years of schooling before our youth enter the job market, and now most people retire earlier. Offsetting this drain, the proportion of women working has risen rapidly in recent decades. A century ago, few women worked at paid jobs. Once married, a girl retired sedately to her new home to keep the furniture dusted, get the meals ready on time, and raise a family. Today, about half of all women of working age and 45 percent of all such married women have paid jobs, and women make up 40 percent of the labor force.

A century ago, the average factory worker in the United States put in 75 hours a week—generally, ten hours or more a day, including Sundays. Today, he works only about forty hours. Over the decades, America has faced a continual choice between work and leisure. We have chosen a slow but steady increase in the amount of leisure. Short hours and long vacations may produce fewer cars and houses, but leisure, although not counted in GNP, has a real value for the persons enjoying it.

Investment in human capital

The growth of education in America has been phenomenal. In colonial days, few people received any formal education beyond elementary reading and writing. By 1870, only one in fifteen persons of high school age was attending school. Today, this figure is over 95 percent, with fourteen million students in some 25,000 high schools. Nearly half of all high school graduates now go on to college, while only a generation ago, a college education was a special privilege available only to the well-to-do.

Figure 44–8 shows the rapid growth in spending on education since 1900. During the first three decades of the century, the rate of growth in investment in human resources was more than twice that in nonhuman capital; the upward slope of the education line on the ratio chart is roughly twice that of the top line show-

Figure 44-8
Investment in education has grown faster than private investment in capital goods since 1900, and at a much more stable rate. (Sources: U.S. Departments of Commerce and of Health, Education and Welfare.)

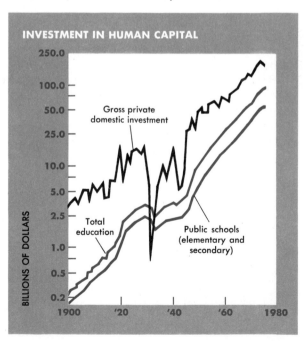

ing investment in capital goods. (*Query:* How long is the time lag between more education and a resulting increase in output per capita?)

Figure 44–8 indicates three other interesting facts: (1) The growth in spending on education has been much more stable than that on private investment in capital goods. (2) Since World War II, the rates of growth in investment in human and nonhuman resources have been roughly comparable, unlike the 1900–30 period. (3) The great bulk of our expenditure on education goes into elementary and secondary schools. Even with the recent big increase in college education, it still accounts for only a minor portion of our total investment in human capital.

Productivity

Average hourly or annual output per worker is often called worker "productivity." Thus, total output can be viewed as the number of workers times the average output per worker. But don't let the common practice of using "productivity" to mean output per man-hour mislead you into attributing all the increased output to workers. We could equally well do a productivity calculation showing output per unit of capital, by dividing total output by the number of units of capital employed.

Figure 44–9
The U.S. average annual gain in productivity has fluctuated, averaging 2.2 percent this century. (Data are for output per man-hour in the private sector.)

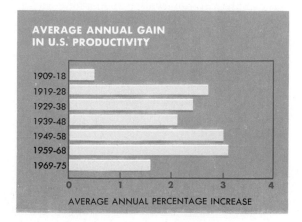

Figure 44–9 points up the wide fluctuations in productivity from decade to decade—and also its growth trend. Annual increases vary from as high as 12 percent (1919) to minus 8 percent (1917), although few years show a negative figure.

Moreover, the economy-wide figures cover up wide differences among industries. Since World War II, productivity gains have ranged from about 1 percent per annum in construction to about 6 percent in agriculture and public utilities. Occupational shifts may significantly affect the national average growth rate. The large-scale shift of workers from low-productivity agriculture to higher-productivity industry during the postwar period went far to explain the rapid growth rates achieved in Western Europe and Japan during those years.

Scale of market

Mass production is obviously more efficient than small-scale output in many industries. Steel, aluminum, automobiles, glass, and dozens of other major products must be produced on a massive scale to permit use of the expensive capital equipment and sophisticated techniques that characterize modern mass production and underlie low prices. Thus, an economy must have large markets if it is to take advantage of the economies of mass production.

Table 44–1 allocated 10 percent of our total growth this century to economies of scale. Other economists have come up with even larger estimates. The very fact that the American economy grew so fast and became so large gave it an edge for still faster growth, compared to the smaller economies of the world. Chalk up economies of scale as an important factor, and one on which the United States has had a big advantage.

Economic organization and social-political environment

How much of our economic growth is due to our individual-initiative, basically private-enterprise, free society? America's economic, political, and religious atmosphere has been peculiarly favorable to individual initiative, hard work, and the pursuit of material rewards. Success in business has been a mark of distinction. The "Protestant ethic," which looks upon work as good in itself, has been an important part of our mores. And the basic tradition of "each man for himself" has provided an inviting setting for individual attempts to move up the economic ladder. America's risk-taking entrepreneurs have clearly played a central role in our rapid growth. Experts trying to help the less-developed countries are increasingly impressed with the value of such traditions as a foundation for economic growth.

American economic institutions have shown unusual flexibility in adjusting to the needs of the growing economy. Banking and financial institutions developed rapidly in response to the need to accumulate savings for investment. Development of the modern corporation facilitated the accumulation of capital for business ventures without undue risk for nonmanagerial investors.

Reflecting this climate, government has been generally friendly to vigorous, open competition. Preservation of peace and order, protection of property rights, and provision of necessary government services all provided a strong foundation for economic activity.

How much credit should Denison have given these factors back in Table 44–1? He couldn't measure them, so he didn't put them in. Yet many observers feel they deserve much of the credit for our spectacular performance.

Aggregate demand

The preceding "real" factors fundamentally determine how fast an economy can grow. But stably growing aggregate demand to support full employment without inflationary booms is also important to stable growth in a market-directed economy. It is only since the 1930s that monetary-fiscal policy has been seriously mobilized to maintain a stably growing level of aggregate demand. The earlier growth in the money stock and aggregate demand, shown back in Chapter 13, came primarily from private financial behavior, not from government stabilization policy.

Whether the growth in the money stock was mainly cause or effect of the growth in real output, the end result has been somewhat faster growth in aggregate demand than in real output, with a resulting inflationary trend. Except during the long depression of the 1930s, deficient aggregate demand apparently has not seriously held back economic growth.

Some observers point to our repeated booms and depressions as evidence that misbehavior of aggregate demand has indeed slowed growth. One test would be the average level of unemployment of men and machines over the long pull. Here, the decade of the 1930s was our big failure, and growth was zero for the decade. On the average, we have had about 5 percent of our labor force unemployed over the past century—not a great success story, but not enough to seriously retard the nation's growth rate.

CONCLUSION

In retrospect, does the theory of Chapter 43 do a good job of helping us to understand U.S. economic growth? The answer appears to be yes. Growth in the United States has been a complex, shifting process. But this basic analytical framework can go a long way in pointing up the main forces, and in keeping you from getting bogged down in details.

REVIEW

For analysis and discussion

1. Has the U.S. record on economic growth been satisfactory over the period since World War II? What criteria do you use in making your judgment?
2. Make a list of the major factors likely to increase the labor force over the next twenty years, and those likely to decrease it. Which are apt to dominate?

3. How long should the workweek be? What are the major considerations in answering this question?
4. "Rising productivity (output per man-hour) is obviously the key to American growth. Thus, it is clear that the American worker deserves the big credit for our rapidly rising living standards." Do you agree with this statement by a labor leader? Explain.
5. Is Denison right (Table 44–1) in giving no weight to natural resources in explaining the causes of U.S. economic growth since 1909? Explain.
6. Most Americans feel that private initiative and our market system deserve great credit for our high standard of living compared to other nations. Suppose you meet a foreigner who disagrees. What arguments can you advance to convince him?
7. Critics of the law of diminishing returns argue that the law must be unimportant or invalid in the United States because the U.S. population has grown enormously over the past century while the stock of natural resources has been fixed, yet output of food per capita has risen greatly. Are the critics right?
8. "More rapid growth of population in the United States would mean a decline in our standard of living." Do you agree? Explain.

CHAPTER 45 GROWTH POLICY

Now, a look to the future. How fast *should* the American economy grow? Most living things—trees, animals, people—grow more slowly as they mature. Is this true of economies too? If so, should we expect our growth rate to slow down, or is the United States still a healthy, growing youngster?

The optimal rate of growth has become a controversial issue. Most Americans want a higher standard of living—more income and the things that income can buy. They want better houses, automatic washers and dryers, better education for their children, more entertainment and travel, and to get rid of the slums and poverty that mar American life. We must produce more if we are to have more. But zero economic growth (ZEG) has become a rallying cry of those who argue that modern technology and the economic growth it helps generate are dehumanizing society and destroying the environment. Our social values are perverted, the critics say. Not more GNP, but a higher quality of life should be our major goal.

Before examining the great growth controversy, it is important to distinguish between economic growth and population growth. Economic growth is growth in output, or output per capita. Population growth means more people—more mouths to feed—but not necessarily any more output. Thus, other things equal, economic growth means a higher standard of living, population growth a lower one.

Although as a practical matter economic and population growth often come together, it is important to separate them analytically. This chapter is primarily concerned with economic growth and with growth policy in industrially developed countries like the United States. Population growth typically slows as income per capita rises, and indeed, the American birthrate has recently fallen below a long-run ZPG level—about 2.1 children per family. Thus, fears of a "population bomb" now appear to have little force for the economically developed nations. But they are very real indeed for many of the less-developed nations, where population is growing rapidly and living standards are very low; these nations are the subject of Chapter 46.

THE GREAT GROWTH CONTROVERSY
The benefits of growth

The growth rate of the American economy will largely determine your standard of living during the rest of your life. Consider Table 45–1, which shows U.S. real GNP in 1985 and 2000, for growth rates of 3, 4, or 5 percent for the rest of this century (assuming no inflation).

Put simply, if GNP grows at 3 percent per annum, the average family's real income (assuming that real income per family continues to be about half of GNP per family) will be about twice as high by the year 2000 as it is now— about $25,000, compared to $14,000 in 1976. If we grow at 5 percent, this average family-income figure would soar to over $35,000 (in 1976

prices). Five percent would be high by historical standards, but it is the goal set by most West European nations in their recent planning. Even 4 percent, about our post–World War II rate, would yield an extra **trillion** dollars of real GNP **annually** by the year 2000, as compared to 3 percent. This **difference** is nearly two-thirds of our total GNP in 1976. The stakes in the growth game are huge!

These figures are so large as to be almost beyond comprehension. The benefits of growth as a practical matter can be illustrated by looking back at the growth in American living standards since 1900, when the economy's GNP has grown at about 3.5 percent annually.

The most obvious change is the dramatic reduction in hard, back-breaking physical labor—on the job, in housekeeping, and on the farm. In 1900, such labor was commonplace; today, very little remains. The average factory workweek has fallen from fifty-five to less than forty hours. In 1900, the typical housewife cooked on a wood or coal kitchen stove, which she fired several times a day. To do the weekly wash, she carried a huge tub of water to boil on top of the stove. Today, 99 percent of all families have refrigerators, 92 percent automatic washers, 41 percent automatic clothes dryers, 39 percent air conditioners. Today's family eats better (more meats, fruits, and dairy products), lives more comfortably, has hot running water and indoor plumbing, is healthier, and lives longer. Life expectancy today is seventy years, up from fifty. Today's average American goes more places and sees more things in a year than his 1900 counterpart did in a lifetime. All these facts are commonplace to us. But they are the envy of poorer nations, and they would have been utterly unbelievable to students in 1900.

Some argue that the United States is now so affluent that we no longer need to increase total output—that we have enough economic goods and services. But it is striking that this cry for ZEG should come just when the nation appears to be establishing a new set of enormously expensive "national priorities." Chapter 1 listed some of these. To raze and rebuild the nation's city slums would cost, it has been estimated, at least a quarter- to a half-trillion dollars. Twenty-five million Americans are still officially

Table 45–1

U.S. real GNP for alternative growth rates (in trillions, 1976 prices)

	1976	1985	2000
With 3 percent annual growth	$1.7	$2.2	$3.5
With 4 percent annual growth	1.7	2.4	4.4
With 5 percent annual growth	1.7	2.6	5.5

classified as poor—families receiving less than $5,500 annually. To reduce existing air and water pollution to 1975 legal standards will cost over a quarter-trillion dollars during the next decade, and most environmentalists consider these standards too low. Add better housing for those outside the slums, higher education standards, improved mass transportation, and so on, to say nothing of more private goods and services for most families, and it becomes painfully clear that, instead of a surplus of productive capacity, we face a massive resource crunch if we hope to make significant headway on our new national priorities and meet the personal aspirations of most people. Our aspirations have risen as fast as our ability to produce. Nor do they show any sign of slowing down.

If we add the vast needs for aid to the less-developed nations (with over two billion people living barely above the subsistence level), the need for economic growth seems overwhelming. Spreading the U.S. income equally over the world's four billion people would raise their average income by only about $300 annually, while pulling ours down to the same amount. It is no accident that neither the lower-income groups, the less-developed nations, nor economists are prominent in the ZEG movement. The main hope for a better life lies in more output, not in redistributing what there is now.

The costs of growth

Offset against these potential benefits of growth are two major types of costs. First, we can have more tomorrow only by consuming less today. Second, growth may involve undesirable side effects—air and water pollution, exhaustion of natural resources, overcrowded cities (caused by economic or population growth?), large organizations that dehumanize work and alienate people from "the system." Consider the costs in that order.

Less today for more tomorrow

Given full employment of resources, we can grow faster only by working harder or accepting less leisure and lower consumption now than we could otherwise have had. Rapid

technical advance can help, but remember that R&D takes resources too. Economists often say, "There's no such thing as a free lunch," to emphasize the fundamental economic problem.

Your inclination may be to say, "Of course we should save more today for a better tomorrow. We should sacrifice more for the benefit of our children and grandchildren." But don't be too quick. Even with the present growth rate, your children's per capita income a generation hence will be more than 50 percent higher than yours is today; that of your grandchildren two generations hence will be more than double the present level. Given these facts, some observers don't find the case for paying the cost of faster growth very impressive. Why, they ask, should we squeeze down on consumption now to make the future even richer? It's a good question.

Undesirable side effects of growth

Destruction of the environment, deterioration of the quality of life, and exhaustion of scarce natural resources are the major charges widely leveled against economic growth. It is clear that economic growth in the United States has helped produce the pollution of air, water, and quiet that plagues the land. Smog, dirty water, noise, and dirt are *real* and *objectionable*. Highways and streets are cluttered with unsightly neon signs, wires, and hot dog stands; parks are full of autos and empty beer cans. The facts are well known; there is little need to repeat them.

But as Chapter 29 pointed out, anger at pollution should not be permitted to confuse our analysis of what to do about it. While growth is responsible for some of today's pollution, to stop growth in order to stop pollution would be short-sighted, inefficient, and unnecessarily costly—cutting off our noses to spite our faces. For growth in total economic capacity can be used to produce what we want most. If it is cleaner air and water, we can produce more sewage disposal plants, quieter trucks, cleaner cars—and have capacity left to produce more of the other things we want, like better houses, health, education, comfortable living. Even if we spend the $287 billion estimated by the Council on Environmental Quality to clean up the envi-

POLLUTION, GROWTH, AND THE GNP ACCOUNTS

Many antipollution laws require businesses to invest in new equipment—for example, "scrubbers" to remove particles from smoke leaving factory chimneys. If such investment replaces ordinary profit-motivated investment, the rate of growth in GNP will be slowed, other things equal—because cleaner air and water are not counted as part of GNP. Suppose General Motors spends a million dollars on new scrubbers instead of on machine tools. The scrubbers show as investment in the GNP accounts, just as the machine tools would. But the resulting cleaner air does not count as GNP, whereas the additional cars produced by the new machine tools would. The growth in GNP is slower in the scrubber case. But it does not necessarily follow that the public is worse off. Remember that GNP is a far-from-perfect measure of economic welfare (see Case 7).

ronment over the 1970s, this will be less than half the total growth in GNP during the decade. To give up a half-trillion dollars of GNP to avoid the pollution it might create would be foolish. We would end up with no reduction in the present level of pollution and would have thrown away additional vast improvement in our economic living standards. Sensible pollution policy certainly is to enforce pollution reduction through government policy while encouraging the national growth that will permit us to pay for it without reducing our national standard of living to do so.

Other costs of growth—crowding as we move into cities, the rush of modern urban life, alienation of workers from their jobs, and the like—are harder to deal with through economic analysis alone. But economics can help. Look back at Table 8–6, which presented the estimates of Professors Tobin and Nordhaus of what has happened to total economic welfare as the economy has grown since 1929. Although the estimates are rough, Tobin and Nordhaus conclude that even when full account is taken of "undesirables" (like spending needed just to cope with the complexities of modern life) and "disamenities" (like the noise and dirt found in modern cities), net economic welfare roughly doubled between 1929 and 1965, while GNP was tripling. Thus, the costs of growth are real, but they certainly do not use up the total productive capacity associated with growth. **If we manage our affairs sensibly, we can have both a better, cleaner environment and the additional real benefits available from growth.**[1]

The allegation that growth dehumanizes work and alienates workers from their jobs obviously reaches beyond economics into psychology and sociology. But many of the alleged facts warrant a closer look. First, although some high-skill jobs have been eliminated by modern technology, there has been relatively little change in the overall skill-requirements pattern of the national job market. The modern computer, for example, has displaced mainly routine, low-skilled clerical jobs in banks and insurance companies. It has created mainly high-skill jobs in manufacturing, programming, and servicing computers. Perhaps the biggest modern job shift has been from manufacturing to services—store clerks, airline employees, beauty parlor operators. There have been enormous changes in jobs since frontier days, but whether today's jobs are less difficult, less interesting, and less challenging is far from clear. Similarly, it is far from clear whether big business necessarily leads to alienation and unhappiness. There is little doubt that some people find the modern corporation an oppressive, dull master. Others find it a comfortable, if unexciting, place to earn a good living. Still others find it an exciting, challenging environment where first-rate ability and hard work can bring big salaries and satisfying success. Unhappy workers didn't arrive with economic growth and the modern corporation. Moreover, don't forget that only about a quarter of all Americans work for the big corporations that are often alleged to dominate the American economy.

[1] Since Professor Tobin is widely acclaimed as one of the leading liberal economists of the day, there is little reason to suppose that these estimates may be slanted in favor of "the conservatives." He was one of President Kennedy's chief economic advisers.

Exhaustion of natural resources

Both population and economic growth use up natural resources. The American economy chews up an enormous volume of raw materials, and conservationists have long predicted dire consequences from our "extravagant" use of raw materials and energy reserves. But so far, new reserves and, more important, substitute materials and energy sources have been found as fast as our uses have grown. The substitution of artificial for natural rubber and of rayon, nylon, and other man-made fibers for silk are examples. Clearly, natural resources are not limitless, but technical ingenuity has more than overcome the major shortages to date. Most experts appear to take a middle position. We do indeed face problems ahead on some resources, but doomsday predictions are overdone.[2]

Nonetheless, fear is widespread that America will soon run out of natural resources, especially energy sources. No one can be sure of the future, but both history (the facts) and economic theory can help assess the danger.

What are the facts? First, U.S. per capita consumption of natural resources has grown steadily, with our rising standard of living. But over the past half century, growth in per capita consumption of all natural resources has been less than 1 percent per year while per capita real income has grown at over 2 percent; remember the large shift from manufactured goods to services. Consumption of minerals has grown about 1.5 percent per year since World War II. Second, if natural resources were becoming relatively scarce, one would expect their prices to rise relative to other prices. In general, with the exception of forest products, and (recently) oil and gas, the *relative* prices of most natural resources have *fallen*. This is shown vividly by Table 45–2 for leading minerals. Since 1900, for example, the price of labor has risen $4\frac{1}{2}$ times as fast as that of coal; the relative price of coal has fallen that much. Note especially the enormous decline in the relative prices of aluminum and petro-

Table 45–2

Prices of minerals compared to labor[a]
(1970 = 100)

	1900	1940	1970
Coal	459	189	100
Copper	785	121	100
Iron	620	144	100
Lead	788	204	100
Zinc	794	272	100
Aluminum	3,150	287	100
Petroleum	1,034	198	100

[a]Figures are the price per ton of the mineral divided by the hourly wage rate in manufacturing.
Source: W. Nordhaus, "Resources as a Constraint on Growth," *American Economic Review,* May 1974.

leum from 1900 to 1970. (But note also that the comparison shown may be "loaded" against those who worry about a shortage of natural resources, since it compares them not with other commodities but with wages, which have risen rapidly compared to the prices of virtually all commodities since 1900.)

Third, if the United States were suffering from natural-resource shortages, one would expect a rise in the proportion of such resources imported from abroad. There has recently been some increase, especially for oil, but relatively little change overall. All imports total less than 10 percent of total consumption. These facts do not support the doomsday predictions about natural-resource exhaustion that are so frequently made today.

One last way of looking at the problem is the experts' estimates of available natural resources. Table 45–3 shows estimates of the "known reserves" and the "ultimately recoverable resources" of major minerals compared to annual consumption. While the experts generally come out in the same ball park on "known reserves," they differ widely on "ultimately recoverable resources," because what is recoverable depends so heavily on how much we are willing to spend to recover it. There is little dispute that vast supplies exist far down in the earth and under the seas, but the cost of recovery is highly uncertain.

[2]Dire predictions of resource exhaustion are not new. In 1865, William Jevons, one of the world's leading economists, forecast (in *The Coal Question*) that economic progress would be stiffled by the exhaustion of coal reserves, now widely agreed to be perhaps the most ample energy source.

Table 45-3
Availability of major minerals

	Known reserves/ annual consumption	Ultimately recoverable resources/ annual consumption
Coal	2,736	5,119
Phosphorus	481	1,601
Iron	117	2,657
Molybdenum	65	630
Uranium	50	8,455
Copper	45	340
Sulphur	30	6,837
Aluminum	23	68,066
Zinc	21	618
Lead	10	162

Source: U.S. Geological Survey, *United States Mineral Resources* (Washington, 1973). This document provides a thorough, official study that recognizes both the problems and alternative solutions. See also the series of reports, *Toward a National Materials Policy,* by the National Commission on Materials Policy (Washington, D.C.: U.S. Government Printing Office, 1972).

These figures apply to world supplies. Many worries are focused on whether the United States will be able to get the resources it needs, even though they are available in other nations. We rely heavily on other nations for many natural resources, especially some critical but lesser-known materials. For example, we have relatively generous supplies of phosphates, iron, lead, copper, and vanadium. But we rely on other nations, mainly the less-developed countries, for columbium, cobalt, manganese, aluminum, and tin. No nation is anywhere near self-sufficient in all the minerals needed for a modern, industrialized economy.[3]

The ratio of rhetoric to reason is unfortunately high on questions of natural resources in the future of America. It is easy to overstress the likelihood that exhaustion of natural resources will seriously limit American growth in the foreseeable future. But it is easy,

too, to be shortsighted about the fact that our demands for many minerals and evergy sources are now growing fast relative to known reserves. Clearly, America will have to find substitutes or new sources on a large scale if we are to avoid serious shortages.

Last, a note on the underlying economic theory involved, which leads most economists to be less concerned about the danger of exhaustion of the natural resources needed for continued economic growth. What is the theory? When anything becomes relatively scarce in a market-directed economy, its price rises. This has three crucial effects. (1) It leads sellers to produce more of the product. If it is a natural resource, the higher price stimulates both more production from known sources and search for new sources. (2) It leads consumers to use less of the resource as it becomes more expensive, and to substitute other resources and products. (3) It stimulates the search for, or development of, substitute products. These three effects combined, in principle and in history, have consistently prevented exhaustion of natural resources from blocking continued economic growth.

Jevons' fear in 1865 that exhaustion of world coal reserves would check economic progress was noted above. We have found vast additional supplies of coal. Technical advance produced synthetic rubber in a brief period when natural rubber was shut off in World War II. Substitution possibilities are enormous. Better insulation and warmer clothes are substitutes for all types of fuel. Slower driving and smaller cars are substitutes for increasingly expensive gasoline. Aluminum turned out to be an effective substitute for copper in making transmission lines when the price of copper soared. Recycling is a substitute for mining new materials when prices get high enough. Business history records very few cases where exhaustion of a natural resource has shut off production of final products that consumers want to buy, when prices have been free to reflect the growing scarcity and to exercise the three effects listed above. The "shortages" that have disrupted economic life have been induced by price-fixing and other government measures that have made it impossible for the price system to do its job. Remember Chapters 6, 22, and 28.

[3] See the *International Economic Report of the President,* March 1976, p. 96, for the sources of all U.S. major mineral imports.

GROWTH POLICY—
INCREASING POTENTIAL SUPPLY

Suppose we want to grow faster. Leaving aside questions of how increased capacity should be allocated among different private and social priorities, can we increase the growth rate of total output? Many experts look at this question in two parts—first, how can we increase the amount of labor, and second, how can we increase the rate of growth in that labor's productivity? Since World War II, total man-hours of labor have grown at about 1.4 percent per annum, while productivity has grown at about 2.2 percent for the total public-plus-private economy, for a total GNP growth rate of 3.6 percent.

A menu for economic growth

Edward Denison, who made the estimates in Table 44–1, has also provided a menu for economic growth—a list of ten steps, which combined might raise the nation's annual growth in total output by 1 percentage point (for instance, from 3 to 4 percent per annum) over the next two decades. Each of the steps might account for .1 percent increase in the average growth rate. Remember that these estimates omit short-term business-cycle movements, and concern only the long-term growth in real productive capacity of the economy. Note also that an increase of 1 percentage point in the annual growth rate would be a big increase, of about 25–30 percent in the existing rate.

More work

Half of Denison's major proposals involve steps to increase the amount of work done by the working-age population. They are as follows:

1. **Double the rate of immigration of working-age adults.** (Note that this would not correspondingly increase per capita output.)

2. **Draw into the labor force one-tenth of all able-bodied adults (mainly women and young people) who would not otherwise be working.**

3. **Increase the average workweek for all workers by one hour.**

4. **Cut in half the time lost from work because of sickness and accidents.**

Most experts expect a gradual increase in labor-force participation by women, to be roughly offset by a shorter workweek, longer education for young people before they enter the labor force, and earlier retirement. The U.S. Department of Labor estimated that over the present decade, our labor force will grow at a high 1.6 percent annually, compared to only 1.3 percent over the preceding fifteen years, but that total annual working hours per working-age person will grow at only about 1.4 percent.

Ours is a free society. We believe that a housewife and her husband, not the government, should decide whether whe stays home or looks for a job. How many hours a week you work is largely up to you, your employer, and your union. The government may plead and explain the facts of economic growth. But short of national emergencies like war, there is little it can do to change the long-term trends of labor-force participation and the gradually lessening workweek. Indeed, government's main intervention has been through encouraging earlier retirement through social security, a shorter workweek through overtime rules, and low labor-force participation rates through free or cheap education. What would you suggest to accomplish proposals 2, 3, and 4?

5. **Reduce the average unemployment rate in the economy by 2 percentage points.** You should have your own menu of proposals on how to accomplish this after completing Part 2 above. Note that the one-year increase in output from reducing unemployment (say, from 5 to 3 percent) would mean a big increase in that year's growth, but once having been achieved, it would add little further to the growth rate over the next two decades, except through the higher investment rates that typically characterize high-employment periods.

Denison's other proposals involve ways to increase the annual growth in productivity (output per worker).

Saving and investment

6. **Increase the rate of net private saving and investment by about 25 percent.** This would mean an increase of some $15–$25

billion annually in private investment. While the United States saves and invests a huge amount annually, our private saving and investment as a percentage of GNP is the lowest of all major nations, and it appears to be falling. Table 45–4 tells the story.

7. **Increase government investment in productive assets by 50 percent annually.**

How could we induce such a large increase in private-plus-public investment? The main ways would be through monetary and fiscal policy. Lower interest rates would lead to more investment. Tax reform to shift the burden from high incomes and corporate profits onto lower incomes would reduce consumption and stimulate saving and investment. Government investment of funds obtained through taxation could raise the investment rate at least temporarily. But it is not clear how big a difference these monetary and fiscal policies would make.

Communist nations, like the USSR and China, directly allocate resources to investment through central planning and control. The central planners decide how many resources to invest, and hold consumption down by simply not producing consumption goods, but such dictatorial methods would be highly objectionable in a free society like ours.

Technical advance— research and development

8. **Increase by 10–15 percent the rate of technical advance.**

9. **Shorten by three years the lag between technical advances and their actual use in production.**

The importance of increasing the rate of growth in productivity is suggested by Table 45–4. Although the United States was long a leader in innovation and technical advance, the final column shows that our growth rate in productivity is now slower than that in other countries. By contrast, the extraordinary Japanese performance is largely attributable to their spectacular growth in productivity.

Although productivity reflects all the factors determining a nation's output except growth in the labor force, research and development spending and the effectiveness with which new knowledge is put to use are central forces determining the growth in total output. Following World War II, U.S. spending on R&D soared as a percentage of GNP (see Figure 44–4), with most of the spending financed by the federal government. Recently, this growth rate has slowed appreciably. No one knows just how long the lag is between R&D and its application, but clearly more spending on R&D would speed technical advance.

Private industry can probably be counted on to finance most developmental and applied research leading directly to salable products. There is no obvious way to increase such private spending on R&D, short of providing a government subsidy. Firms can already charge off most research expenses as direct costs and hence as full tax deductions. But the case for direct government support of *basic* research is strong. The results of truly basic research are unpredictable, and they seldom have direct commercial profitability. Even more important, if a company does make a major basic breakthrough, it is seldom able to protect its discovery for long from use by others. Thus, it is hard to see why many firms will spend much money on such basic research. But history records that it is the basic-research breakthroughs that have provided the foundation for the great scientific and practical benefits of our times.

Table 45–4

Private investment and productivity in major nations, 1960–74

	Investment as percent of GDP	Annual productivity increase in manufacturing
Japan	35	10.5
West Germany	25	5.8
France	26	5.9
Canada	22	4.3
United Kingdom	19	4.2
United States	18	3.3

Source: Organization for Economic Cooperation and Development. GDP is gross domestic product.

Government support for the rapid dissemination of new knowledge and techniques also makes sense, on the same grounds. The agricultural experiment stations and extension services established at state universities throughout the nation a century ago have played a major role in speeding innovation in American agriculture. Similar aid in manufacturing, services, and other areas might produce similar results.

Investment in human capital

10. **Increase by one and one-half years the average amount of education for all school-age members of the population, or improve the average quality of education by a corresponding amount.** Human beings are capital to a society, just as buildings and machines are. Modern research suggests that the return on investment in human capital (through formal education, training, and the like) is higher than the return on investment in capital goods. Both individuals and society would gain economically by spending more on education. In addition, we would get the large but immeasurable benefits of a better-educated population for a stable social-political system. The external economies again make a strong case for government action.

If education is such a good investment, why don't private individuals make the investment voluntarily? Many do. Beyond free education for all through high school, about half of all youths go on to college. Anyone who has done the arithmetic knows that a good education for his son is likely to be a better investment than buying stocks and bonds.

Nevertheless, most families and teenagers seem reluctant to borrow to make this investment in human capital. Moreover, our society frowns on slavery; thus there is no sure way a capitalist with spare funds can get back a big return if he wants to invest in John Jones' education instead of in a business venture. More publicly financed education would probably speed economic growth. Another approach would be to make adequate loan funds for education available to all, especially to low-income levels.

Many modern researchers argue that on-the-job training is the highest-return form of investment in human capital. Such training has a sure, quick payoff, unlike academic education that may or may not be put to immediate practical use. Some propose subsidies to businesses to provide such training for potential employees. Others argue that the best inducement is merely to assure prosperous times, and businesses will increase such training as they seek more workers in their own self-interest. Still others stress eliminating barriers to such private training—for example, the high legal minimum wage required for inexperienced young workers that makes it unprofitable for employers to invest in on-the-job training for them.

Improved economic efficiency

The preceding list includes the main possibilities Denison suggests for raising the nation's growth rate. Strikingly, it omits a number of measures often proposed—for example, changes in the tax structure, elimination of discrimination, and improvements in the efficiency of markets. The potential of tax structure reform he lists at only .02 percentage points, elimination of discrimination at .04. All potential improvements in the efficiency of labor and product markets combined might total over .1 percentage point, but none alone seems to Denison to have major potential. Other economists place more emphasis on elimination of monopoly restrictions by both unions and businesses, and on steps to improve information and mobility in labor markets, but quantification of that potential is extremely difficult.

The economic climate—initiative and enterprise

Denison warns that he has omitted some factors that may be important, because they are so hard to quantify. Individual initiative, the spirit of enterprise, open markets with active competition, economic and social mobility, and a generally favorable economic-social-political climate clearly deserve much credit for America's growth over the past two centuries. But how to make them contribute *more* to growth in the future is less clear.

Indeed, many observers believe they see a recent lessening of the contribution of these factors to American growth, especially beginning with the "liberal" social reforms and increased government intervention of the New Deal. They point to the spectacular productivity increases in postwar Germany and Japan as evidence that hard work, and high saving and investment, are still the main roads to rapid economic growth. By contrast, they see the modern American economy as increasingly comfortable, security-conscious, egalitarian, and critical of traditional American individualism and hard work.

Economic historians suspect that these—the economic and social mores of a nation—play a vital role indeed. But they are obviously difficult factors to change significantly through government growth policy.

GROWTH POLICY—THE DEMAND SIDE

Increasing our productive capacity (moving out the production-possibilities frontier) is the main requisite for faster economic growth. But in a largely private-enterprise economy, the demand side matters too. For businessmen will not long produce goods they cannot sell at a profit. On the other hand, excess aggregate demand will produce inflation and instability. What level of aggregate demand should monetary and fiscal policy encourage to ensure the desired rate of stable economic growth, avoiding both depressions and inflations?

What aggregate demand is needed for stable economic growth?

Assume that national productive capacity is growing 4 percent annually because of population growth, capital investment, and technological advance. If this is the desired rate, then aggregate demand should rise at about 4 percent a year (the same rate as productive capacity), and the division between consumption and investment spending should match the division between consumption and saving decisions (omitting government taxes and spending). More total spending will mean inflation. Less will mean underemployment and waste. A misallocation of spending between consumption and investment is likely to generate short-run

fluctuations that may become serious booms or depressions.

If we start, for example, with a trillion-dollar GNP, aggregate demand should increase about $40 billion next year to finance stable, high-employment growth without inflation. But note that in the following year, aggregate demand must grow by more—by $44 billion, or 4 percent of the new $1,040 billion GNP. And if the ratios of saving and government spending to GNP remain stable, private investment must also grow at 4 percent annually to ensure a stable growth.

In principle, there is no reason why we need to have a stable price level to achieve stable, full-employment growth. A stable, expected rate of inflation might be consistent with stable real growth. Or if, for example, total spending rises only 2 percent while capacity grows by 4 percent, full-employment output can still be achieved if the price level falls 2 percent. As a practical matter, however, as we saw in Part 2, substantial economy-wide price reductions without unemployment are unlikely in the modern American economy. With downward inflexibility of costs and prices, inadequate total spending means unemployment of men and machines. Thus, few economists now believe that aggregate demand can safely grow less than roughly in proportion to total capacity, and many believe it should grow faster because of basic inflationary pressures. As a practical matter, the combined inflation–unemployment dilemma considered in Chapter 19 seems to present the biggest problems in the management of aggregate demand.

Will private decisions provide the right amount of aggregate demand?

Will private consumption and investment-spending decisions provide just the right amount of aggregate demand year after year? Will private banks' lending decisions provide just the right growth in the money stock to support the needed growth in aggregate demand? Part 2 provided the answer loud and clear: It would be an economic miracle if millions of independent private spending and banking decisions produced just the right aggregate demand. The case for conscious stabilizing monetary and fiscal policies to keep aggregate demand growing on track is clear, although it is a far from simple job to carry them out successfully.

Capital and labor shares in stable growth

Even if aggregate demand grows stably, may not the investment–consumption balance get out of kilter? And a closely related question: What balance between wages and profits is required for stable, sustained growth?

The answer depends partly on how fast we want to grow. Fast growth requires a high-profit, high-investment economy. Wages and consumption shouldn't rise too fast.

But if profits and investment get *too* large relative to wages and consumption spending, excess capacity will develop and the boom will collapse. Indeed, when it comes to maintaining high-level employment, union leaders hammer away at one proposition: Wages are the biggest single source of buying power in our economy, and too-low wages are the major cause of depression. But don't be trapped by the common fallacy that business profits necessarily represent savings withdrawn from the income stream. Many business profits flow directly into investment spending, and there is no necessary reason to classify big profits as a deflationary force. What matters for economic health is total spending on consumption plus investment, not just consumption. Wages are purchasing power, but so are profits.

The investment–consumption balance issue is a thorny one. Economists have a variety of "growth models" that illustrate the relative paths of investment and consumption needed to ensure stable, sustainable growth under different conditions—different propensities to consume, different capital–output ratios, different rates of technical progress, and the like. One such simple model was represented in the appendix to Chapter 43. Nearly all these models, and historical experience, tell us that growth must be reasonably balanced if it is to be stable. Consumption and investment must be kept growing at *roughly* the same rates. If either investment or consumption gets too far out of line with the other, we're in for trouble. And although profits and wages are by no means identical with investment and consumption spending, *very roughly* the same balanced growth proposition holds for them.

A CONCLUDING NOTE

A provocative concluding note on national growth policy has been provided by Herbert Stein, a distinguished conservative economist:

We have had a good deal of talk about the desirability of economic growth. There have been national policies which contributed to growth but also many which retarded it. There has been no national determination of a desirable rate of growth, no effort to formulate a comprehensive program to achieve any specified rate of growth, and few policy decisions that were dominated by growth considerations. Growth in America has been the outcome of the efforts of millions of families to improve their own conditions and the conditions of their children, rather than the outcome of a national policy. The picture of a government of tyrannical Philistines forcing economic growth upon a citizenry of Henry David Thoreaus is fantasy. The spontaneous and decentralized origins of the growth suggest how difficult it would be to influence its rate very much, in either direction, by national policy.[4]

[4]From "An Economist Looks at the 1970s," speech at Rider College, Trenton, New Jersey, May 15, 1970, pp. 5–6. At the time, Stein was a member of President Nixon's Council of Economic Advisers.

REVIEW

For analysis and discussion

1. How fast should the American economy grow over the decade ahead? What measures would you propose to achieve your desired growth rate?

2. How much of your personal income are you willing to use over the next decade to build up the economic capacity of the nation for future production? Does the government have a right to dictate to you a rate different from the one you prefer?

3. Can you see how we can have continued economic growth and also a cleaner, more attractive environment? Explain.

4. Are economic growth and a better "quality of life" competitive or complementary? Explain.

5. Why do many economists who favor slower *population* growth simultaneously support faster *economic* growth?

6. Only about 3 percent of GNP is devoted to research and development. Would it be sound policy to double this amount? Who should decide? If the amount should be doubled, who should pay for it?

7. Can you suggest ways of increasing the nation's rate of saving and capital formation that do not impinge on the freedom of individuals and businesses to spend or to save their incomes as they please?

8. By 1986, the population of the United States may be 230 million. Assume that the same proportion (about 40 percent) of the population is in the labor force as in 1976, that the average propensity to consume out of GNP remains at about two-thirds; that output per worker rises about 2 percent per annum; and that the price level remains constant.

   a. What level of gross national expenditure will be required in 1986 to assure full employment? Explain.

   b. What level of private investment will be required, assuming that government expenditures on goods and services remain at their 1976 level of about $350 billion?

   c. Suppose that only 35 percent of the population is in the 1986 labor force. How would your answers to (a) and (b) change?

   d. Suppose now that the average workweek is reduced from forty to thirty hours. How would per capita real output compare with 1976, when population was 215 million?

9. Is Stein right in his last sentence, at the end of the text above?

Our modern economy runs on energy, and our energy use is doubling every twenty years or less.

Table 45–5 provides rough estimates of U.S. domestic energy "proven reserves" in 1976 and how long they are likely to last at currently forecasted use rates. Although our coal resources are almost unlimited, domestic oil and gas, the two most important current energy sources, may be exhausted in only ten years or so at currently expected use rates, assuming no further supplies are found. Little wonder that concern over a possible energy crisis has hit the headlines. Obviously, some big changes have to be made fast if we want to avoid becoming heavily reliant on foreign sources for our energy.

Whether we in fact face an energy crisis depends on both technological developments and the policies we adopt. Nearly everyone involved assumes that scientists will come up with major developments over the decades ahead, possibly in nuclear energy—using "fast breeder" technology that, amazingly, produces more fuel (plutonium) than it burns—or solar power. But these are unlikely to be commercially feasible on a large scale before 1990 or 2000.

There is no world shortage of energy sources. But as we become heavily dependent on the Middle East for our oil, we open ourselves to economic and political pressures, even black-mail, from those countries. The OPEC countries have already quadrupled oil prices since 1973; U.S. consumers are now paying them annually $25 billion for oil that five years ago cost us only $5 billion—and OPEC threatens to raise prices further. (See Case 36.) Indeed, the greatest danger of a major oil crisis in the next decade lies in the possibility that the Arab Mideastern oil-producing nations might cut off supplies to us for political reasons, or in the event of an Arab-Israeli war.

At home, we have plenty of coal, but most of it (except for some Western deposits) is high-sulfur coal, which causes substantial pollution; moreover, to obtain it would involve massive strip mining, which elicits further environmentalist cries of opposition. We have substantial undeveloped oil reserves, but many of them are offshore where drilling would risk oil spills, again drawing bitter environmentalist objection. Environmentalists for years successfully blocked construction of the Alaskan pipeline, and at least doubled its cost. Retreat from new antipollution rules for autos could reduce auto use of gasoline by perhaps 10 percent, but with substantial environmental costs. Both imported and domestically produced oil are under government price controls and allocation programs, designed to hold down oil-company profits and to see that scarce oil is equitably divided up among selling companies. Exploitation of our huge shale-oil reserves will be profitable only at oil prices well above their present levels; the huge investments required are apparently not now considered profitable, given existing uncertainty about future oil prices and government environmental regulations.

As with oil, the government could stimulate increased deep drilling for natural gas by decontrolling the prices gas companies are permitted to charge, but this suggestion brings widespread charges of a government sellout to the big gas companies. The price of natural gas has long been held down by the Federal Power Commission; this has, of course, encouraged its use and

Table 45–5

U.S. Energy Reserves, 1976

	Estimated reserves	Years' supply
Oil (billion barrels)	52	10
Natural gas (trillion cu. ft.)	3,000	11
Uranium (tons)	450,000	13
Shale oil (billion barrels)	160–600	35–120
Coal (trillion tons)	1.5	500

Source: U.S. Geological Service; estimates are for "proven" reserves.

discouraged drilling for new sources. Restoring the tax depletion allowances on gas and oil would have a similar effect, but these special allowances were just eliminated on tax-reform grounds. Nuclear power and development of fast-breeder technology are considered by many experts to be the most promising (cheapest and cleanest) solution for the next two decades, but environmentalists block construction of new nuclear plants on grounds of both inadequate safety provisions and environmental effects, and work to close down existing plants. The energy problem, like most others in economics, is a complex series of tradeoffs.

A different approach would involve persuading Americans not to use so much energy—to drive less, give up air conditioning, turn off their lights, and the like. But this does not seem very promising as a practical matter, unless we impose highly objectionable government regulations or permit sharply higher prices for energy. The mere thought of continuing peacetime national gas rationing for autos, for example, sends shivers up the backs of government administrators, as well it should.

Two approaches Just about everyone agrees that we need a unified national energy policy to replace our present hodgepodge of regulations. The problem is enormously complex, and any successful policy will surely have many facets. But two fundamental approaches dominate the discussion. One is increased government intervention and regulation—government controls over what forms of energy to produce where; how the energy should be distributed; who should get it, at what prices, and for what purposes. Avoiding windfall profits for the big oil companies through higher prices is an important goal in this approach.

The other approach calls for increased use of built-in individual incentives—letting the price system do a big part of the job. This would involve letting energy prices rise as demand grows relative to supply—in order to stimulate production, to reduce use of increasingly expensive fuels for less essential purposes, and to encourage development of substitutes. Under our public utility regulation, Americans have long had the cheapest gas and electricity in the world, and very cheap oil. Little wonder we use lots and face dwindling supplies relative to demand. Under this approach, producer profits might rise sharply with higher prices, although defenders point to the large number of companies competing at all stages of energy production and distribution as substantial protection against improperly high prices.

Many observers, of course, favor intermediate programs, to permit prices to rise with growing scarcities, but only to a limited extent. And either approach might be combined with international policies to minimize our exposure to exploitation by Mideastern oil nations.

What is your program to solve America's energy problem? (See the suggestions for analysis at the end of the book.)

APPENDIX

The limits to growth—doomsday models

In 1798, Malthus gloomily predicted recurrent famines for mankind, as population growth outran the ability of land to produce food. Every generation since then has had its prophets of doom, but recent years have seen a new brand of doomsday models, more persuasive to some because they are cast in mathematical form and spun out of computers. The best known of these is a recent model by a group of MIT engineers and scientists who, using a highly simplified computer model of world growth, find that growth must end soon, probably by the middle of the next century, and that our growth joyride will end with a bang, not a whimper.[5]

The authors pick up Malthus' stress on the tendency of population to outrun food supplies, and modernize it by adding two further propositions from ecology. First, we will soon exhaust the world's natural resources through the rapid growth of industrial production, and second, the same industrial production will strangle us in pollution. Using the trends of 1900–70 world experience, they combine these relationships in a simple computer model, and the resulting printouts tell us the limits to economic growth. The results follow directly from the assumptions that arable land and other natural resources are substantially fixed, while population and industrial production grow exponentially. Given these assumptions and no extenuating conditions, it is clear that growth in population and industrial output will run up against limits, and do so with force as exponential growth picks up speed. As the authors point out, any series that grows exponentially can become very big, very fast.[6]

The core of the Meadows analysis is summarized in Figure 45–1. The picture is self-explanatory. If population and industrial output continue to grow at exponential rates in the absence of checks, the world will rapidly exhaust its natural resources, including arable land, and pollution will rapidly become intolerable. Although industrial output and food will grow rapidly for a few more years, both will soon reach their peaks, probably around the end of this century. Growing hunger, shortages of raw materials, and pollution will soon thereafter combine to bring growth to a screeching halt, with widespread famine and strangulation from pollution, probably by the middle of the next century.

Meadows examines a number of alternative assumptions. For example, doubling the stock of natural resources (except arable land) only postpones the debacle a decade or so, because of the enormous increases in demands for food and industrial output produced by the exponential-growth assumptions; pollution and famine soon overtake us. Drastic steps to control pollution plus technological advance to extend the use of our natural resources could postpone doomsday, but we would not escape the famine problem. Figure 45–2 summarizes Meadows's results on what he presents as very optimistic assumptions—"unlimited" natural resources (except arable land) and "successful" drastic pollution controls. This permits a huge increase in industrial output with only a moderate increase in pollution, and it postpones the downturn in food output per capita. But Malthus is still there; famine eventually checks population, and industrial output per capita falls, since it is possible to extend our stock of natural resources only at rising real costs.

---

[5] D. Meadows et al, *The Limits to Growth* (New York: Universe Books, 1972). Strikingly, the authors excluded all economists and other social scientists from their team. The foundations of the analysis lie in J. Forrester, *World Dynamics* (Cambridge: Wright-Allen Press, 1971). Forrester is a well-known computer expert.

[6] They cite the old fable of the poor gypsy who saved the king's life, and when offered his choice of fabulous rewards, asked only for wheat from the king's granary to cover his chessboard—one grain on the first square, two on the second, four on the third, eight on the fourth, and so on. The king, no mathematician, was delighted to grant such a modest request. Do the arithmetic. The fifth square gets 16 grains, but as the doubling continues, the fortieth square requires one trillion grains—with twenty-four more squares to go on the chessboard.

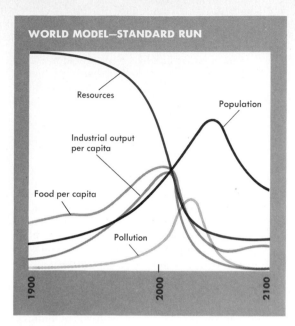

Figure 45–1
If recent trends continue, this model predicts massive starvation and deaths from pollution after about the middle of the twenty-first century. Living standards will also fall dramatically as resources are rapidly exhausted. (Adapted from D. Meadows et al., *The Limits to Growth* [New York: Universe Books, 1972], p. 124.)

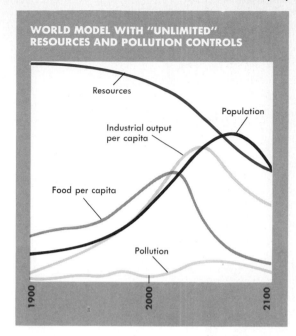

Figure 45–2
This model assumes that resources (except arable land) do not run out and that effective pollution controls are developed. Food and industrial output per capita nevertheless turn down early next century, and starvation limits population soon thereafter. This version might be termed the modern Malthus. (Adapted from Meadows et al., *The Limits to Growth*, p. 136.)

Is there any escape? Yes, Meadows says, if we immediately stop all growth in both population and the economy. This would imply no net investment, only a replacement of existing capital. If we also assume very successful efforts to control pollution and drastically extend the life of natural resources through recycling and technological advance, we should be able to achieve a stabilized world economy, with per capita real income about three times the present world average, as shown in Figure 45–3. But *only* if we immediately halt economic and population growth. Waiting a decade or two will be too late.

Although the Meadows-Forrester book received widespread acclaim by environmentalists, most economists expressed serious reservations. Why?

1. The price system appears nowhere in the Meadows analysis. Yet history demonstrates that when something becomes scarce, its relative price rises, with the three crucial results emphasized in the text—increased production and new modes of production; reduced con-

sumption; and development of substitutes. This has been the history of the industrial and technological revolutions. This is not to deny that supplies of some natural resources may be exhausted, but to suggest that this process will stimulate an effective search for substitutes and means of extending supplies. (Actually, in spite of the doomsday projections, the prices of most natural resources have thus far fallen, or risen little, relative to other goods and services—see Table 45-2.)

2. Meadows' assumptions on technological advance appear to be unduly pessimistic. Even his most optimistic models, assuming "unlimited natural resources," seem to many observers not much more optimistic than the actual performance of technical advance to date. This is especially true in the critical area of food and agriculture.

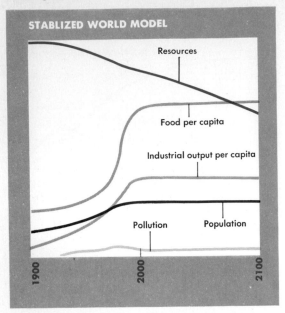

Figure 45-3
Only if we act immediately to halt population growth and net investment, adopt drastic resource conservation and antipollution measures, and substitute food and services for other kinds of production can we hope to achieve a sustainable equilibrium state. (Adapted from Meadows et al., *The Limits to Growth*, p. 165.)

3. Meadows assumes that as incomes rise, people continue to demand the same mix of goods and services as in the past. Thus, the demand for manufactured goods rises sharply. But all his-

torical evidence suggests that as societies grow more wealthy, they choose a rapidly growing share of services in the output mix they demand. Such a shift to services would alleviate the natural-resources and pollution problems.

4. Meadows's analysis assumes a blind continuation of population growth until it is checked by famine, even if world living standards rise dramatically. Again, history shows convincingly that population growth slows with affluence and rising living standards. Even Malthus recognized that voluntary restriction of births might occur to avoid famine, and modern birth-control methods are making this far easier. The extremity of Meadows's population assumption is indicated by the fact that beginning with two people, his system would blow up from overpopulation within 500 years. As one critic put it, apart from putting the Garden of Eden in the fifteenth century, what's new?

5. The Meadows analysis is entirely on a one-world basis. But we know that the growth issues are very different for different nations. Population growth rates, pollution, availability of raw materials and food, and other critical variables differ widely among nations, especially between the developed and less-developed countries. An analysis that fails to differentiate between the problems facing the United States and Western Europe on the one hand and Laos and India on the other is of limited use.[7]

[7] For a highly optimistic antidote to the Meadows analysis, see Herman Kahn and others, *The Next 200 Years* (New York: William Morrow, 1976), a forecast that also involves some dubious economic analysis.

APPENDIX TO PART 7

Current research

Growth in the developed nations   Edward Denison's *Accounting for U.S. Economic Growth* (Washington, D.C.: The Brookings Institution, 1974) is the place to begin, although it is primarily a reference work; Chapter 9 summarizes the results. For the European nations and Japan, see his *Why Growth Rates Differ* (Washington, D.C.: The Brookings Institution, 1967). The classical theoretical analysis underlying growth policy is James Tobin, "Economic Growth as an Objective of Government Policy," *American Economic Review,* May 1964, plus the following discussion by Herbert Stein. For perspective on growth in the long sweep of history, try Simon Kuznet's fascinating "Notes on the Pattern of U.S. Economic Growth," in *The Nation's Economic Objectives* (Chicago: University of Chicago Press, 1964). A quite different view of growth is given by A.D. Chandler, *Ford, G.M., and the Automobile Industry* (New York: Harcourt Brace Jovanovich, 1965), a case study of one major industry; and by Chapter 6 of W. Baumol's provocative little book, *Business Behavior, Value and Growth* (New York: Macmillan, 1967). Last, the role of technology in growth is thoroughly assessed by R.R. Nelson, M.J. Peck, and E. Kalachek in *Technology, Economic Growth, and Public Policy* (Washington, D.C.: The Brookings Institution, 1967); and by Edwin Mansfield in *Technological Change* (New York: Norton, 1971).

The great growth controversy   The controversy over growth, technology, and the quality of life has spawned a large literature. The attempt by Tobin and W. Nordham to measure changes in economic welfare, noted in Chapter 8 of the text, is one of the more imaginative pieces of recent research (*Economic Growth*, National Bureau of Economic Research, 1972). Another pioneering, more impressionistic study is Kenneth Boulding, *Beyond Economics* (Ann Arbor: University of Michigan Press, 1968). "The No-Growth Society," *Daedalus,* Fall 1973, assembles the views of experts on several elements of the issue. The direct attack on growth is led by E.J. Mishan in *Growth: The Costs We Pay* (London: Staples, 1969); for

a counterattack, see P. Passell and L. Ross, *The Retreat from Riches* (New York: Viking, 1973). If you want to look at the basic research model underlying the Meadows doomsday predictions described in the appendix to Chapter 45, see Jay Forrester, *World Dynamics* (Wright-Allen Press, 1971).

The basic economics underlying the problem of the optimal rate of utilization of scarce natural resources is laid out by Robert Solow in "The Economics of Resources or the Resources of Economics," *American Economic Review,* May 1974, and applied by William Nordhaus, "Resources as a Constraint on Growth," in the same volume, and N. Rosenberg, "Innovative Responses to Material Shortages," *American Economic Review,* May 1973.

The capital-shortage issue   Some economists and many others argue that we face a capital shortage, because we are not saving enough to provide resources for all the private and public investments we want to make. They worry especially when the government runs a big deficit in periods of high employment, thereby using funds, rather than providing savings through a surplus. The government will get the scarce savings, and private firms will face a capital shortage, the argument runs. Henry Wallich's "Is There a Capital Shortage?" in *Challenge,* September 1975, provides a perceptive analysis of the issues and the evidence. *Capital Needs in the Seventies,* by B. Bosworth, J. Duesenberry, and A. Carron (Washington, D.C.: The Brookings Institution, 1975), is a more detailed analysis along similar lines.

Speculation on growth   Many economists consider Meadows's *Limits to Growth* essentially a speculative story. Two other fascinating recent volumes on growth clearly rest primarily on impressions and speculation, plus political and sociological, rather than economic, analysis: Herman Kahn and others, *The Next 200 Years* (New York: Morrow, 1976); and Norman Macrae, *America's Third Century* (New York: Harcourt Brace Jovanovich, 1976). Try Kahn if you want a rosy antidote to Meadows, Macrae if you're ready for some gloomy doubts too.

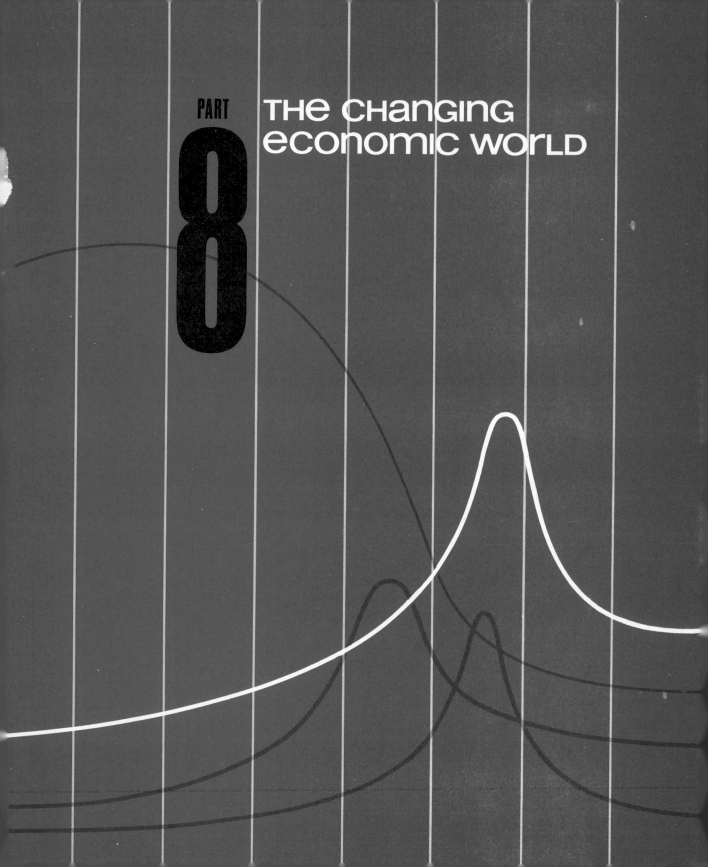

PART

8

THE CHANGING
economic world

CHAPTER 46

THE LESS-DEVELOPED COUNTRIES

For more than two billion people who live in the economically less-developed countries (LDCs), economic growth is a necessity if they are to escape from the bitter poverty that has been their lot through history. Per capita GNP in the United States in 1975 was $7,070. In the less-developed countries (sometimes called the "Third World") it averaged $225, and perhaps 30–40 percent of these people were living on less than $100 a year.

Table 46–1 classifies the nations of the world into three groups, depending on their per capita annual GNPs in 1973. **Highly developed** countries are those with per capita GNPs above $2,000. The **intermediate** group comprises countries where the figure was between $700 and $2,000. The **less-developed** nations are those with per capita GNPs below $700.

The figures in Table 46–1 are very rough. They probably substantially underestimate income levels in the poorer nations on two counts. First, incomes there may be relatively underestimated because so much home-produced food and clothing does not go through the market; accurate estimates are very difficult. Second, prices of the staples that form the standard of living of the masses there are generally very cheap compared to items bought by higher-income families. However, conversion of, say, Indian rupee incomes into U.S. dollars at the

Table 46–1

Countries grouped by 1974 per capita GNP—In U.S. dollars[a]

HIGHLY DEVELOPED COUNTRIES (ABOUT 1 BILLION PEOPLE)
(OVER $2,000 PER CAPITA)

In the Americas:		In Europe (cont.)	
United States	$6,640	Norway	5,280
Canada	6,080	Belgium	5,210
Puerto Rico	2,400	France	5,190
In Oceania and Asia:		Netherlands	4,880
Australia	4,760	Finland	4,130
New Zealand	4,100	Austria	4,050
Japan	3,800	East Germany	3,430
In Africa and the Middle East:		United Kingdom	3,360
Israel	3,380	Czechoslovakia	3,200
Libya	3,360	Italy	2,770
In Europe:		Poland	2,450
Sweden	$6,720	Ireland	2,370
Switzerland	6,650	USSR	2,300
West Germany	5,890	Hungary	2,140
Denmark	5,820		

INTERMEDIATE COUNTRIES (ABOUT 500 MILLION PEOPLE)
($700–2,000 PER CAPITA)

In the Americas:		In Europe:	
Argentina	$1,900	Greece	$1,970
Venezuela	1,710	Spain	1,960
Uruguay	1,060	Bulgaria	1,770
Panama	1,010	Portugal	1,540
Mexico	1,000	Yugoslavia	1,200
Brazil	900	In Africa and	
Chile	820	the Middle East:	
Peru	710	South Africa	1,200
		Lebanon	1,080
		Iran	1,060
		Iraq	970

LESS-DEVELOPED COUNTRIES (ABOUT 2½ BILLION PEOPLE)
(LESS THAN $700 PER CAPITA)

All of Africa except countries listed above	about $200	Communist China	$300
		India	130
All of the Americas except countries listed above	about 500	All of Asia except countries listed above	about 150

[a] Figures are estimated 1974 gross domestic product for each nation (rounded to nearest $10), converted to 1974 U.S. dollars at official exchange rates and divided by population. Alterations in exchange rates may change relative positions substantially from year to year.

Remember the text warning that data are very rough for the less-developed nations, and that figures for such nations are probably substantially understated by using official exchange rates—perhaps by as much as 100 percent. Estimates for communist-bloc countries are rougher than for others. Some small nations are omitted.

(Source: International Bank For Reconstruction and Development, *World Bank Atlas,* 1975.)

official exchange rate reflects prices of all internationally traded goods, many of which are not bought by low-income Indian families. Thus, the conversion implies higher dollar prices than poor families actually pay for most of what they consume. But even if the per capita incomes in the poor nations were doubled to adjust for these possible underestimates, the less-developed nations would still appear desperately poor. For most of the world, poverty is far and away the number one economic problem.[1]

Worse, this huge gap between rich and poor nations is widening rapidly, not closing. Table 46–2 tells the story for the United States and India since 1960. Although it shows the extremes, it suggests the rapid rate at which the Western industrial nations are pulling away from the less-developed world. A 2 percent annual increase on the U.S. base of $7,000 means a $140 increase in one year, equal to the *entire* per capita GNP in India. In India, the same 2 percent increase, if it could be achieved, would be less than $3 per capita.[2]

Why do these vast differences in standards of living exist? Why is the gap between the rich and the poor widening even further? The theory of economic growth presented in Chapter 43 can help answer these questions, and most of this chapter is devoted to applying that theory to the LDCs.

Development of these economically less-developed countries has become the most explosive socio-economic problem of our times. Pov-

Table 46–2
Per capita real GNP in the United States and India[a]

	1960	1975
United States	$4,000	$7,000
India	125	140

[a]Data in 1975 U.S. dollars. Figures for India are probably understated relative to United States, but the 1960–75 change is roughly accurate.

erty is a source of acute discontent for hundreds of millions of people, aroused by their leaders. In China and India alone, there are nearly 1.5 billion people. But in literally a hundred other nations, people are awakening to the fact that poverty and misery may not be the inescapable lot of the masses. A great change is moving Asia, Africa, and Latin America, a change compounded of growing nationalism and a desire for economic progress and power. A revolution of rising expectations—of economic progress, individual status, and national prestige and power—is sweeping the less-developed nations. We hear of it at every meeting of the United Nations and other international organizations. We are likely to hear more in the future.

THE ANATOMY OF UNDERDEVELOPMENT

Poverty is the central economic fact of the less-developed areas. But there are many differences among them. Some are primitive; others, like India and China, boast civilizations that are far older than those of the Western world. Some have generous natural resources; others are bitterly poor in the endowments of nature. Some have a high ratio of population to land; others have vast open spaces. The poverty of a beggar on the streets of Calcutta is different from that of the Bushman of Africa, or the desert nomad of the Middle East. But in spite of these differences, there are some strong resemblances. And the theory from Chapter 43 provides a useful framework for analyzing them.

[1]The country comparisons of Table 46–1 are also very sensitive to the exchange rates used to convert local currencies to dollars. Since the dollar depreciated substantially in 1973–75, especially relative to Western European and Japanese currencies, some estimates for later years place U.S. per capita GNP lower, especially relative to Switzerland, Sweden, and West Germany. Only limited weight should be placed on such international comparisons. The United Nations has released tentative new data, based on prices of only widely used commodities in each country, which show U.S. per capita income as substantially ahead of all other major countries (i.e., excluding some of the smaller oil-producing nations like Kuwait).

[2]Two good general references on the less-developed areas and their problems are E.E. Hagen, *The Economics of Development* (Homewood, Ill.: Richard D. Irwin, 1975), and J. Bhagwati, *Economics of the Under-developed Countries* (New York: McGraw-Hill, 1966).

Patterns of economic activity

First, a brief look at the economies of the less-developed nations as a backdrop for analysis of why they are poor, and of what can be done to raise their production.

Poverty and the dominance of low-productivity agriculture. In the less-developed countries, food is the main item of production and consumption. It has to be, for starvation hovers uncomfortably near. For the entire group of LDCs, about 70 percent of all production is food. In the United States, the comparable figure is below 20 percent. Although diets in most nations are adequate to preserve life, they are often inadequate to fend off disease or, even allowing for the small bodily stature of many peoples, to provide enough energy for continued hard work.

A mud or thatched hut and some simple clothing make up most of the rest of the consumption pattern. Remember that only around $5 per month per capita is left to cover everything except food. Hospitals, plumbing, highways, and other services that we take for granted have no place in such standards of living. The masses in these nations save little or nothing at all. In Calcutta, a teeming city, between a quarter- and a half-million people have no homes or jobs, so they simply wander the streets.

Because human labor is very cheap and capital scarce, hard work and laborious details are done by hand. Tractors and other mechanized farm equipment are scarce, and would often be unusable even if available, because of lack of fuel, maintenance facilities, and sufficient education to use them. Figure 46–1 shows vividly how little the poor nations rely on nonhuman energy (electricity, water, and minerals) compared to the developed nations. (In this and the following figures, income per capita is always shown on the vertical axis. Both income and energy use are plotted on ratio, or logarithmic, scales to facilitate relative comparisons.)

The nonagricultural population is often crowded into a few large cities, where small-scale industry, services for the wealthy, and government employment provide most of the jobs. Simple textiles are important in many less-developed economies; the cloth is used for clothing and home furnishings. In the more developed countries, modern large-scale industry (steel, chemicals, fertilizers, and the like) has begun to appear in the major cities.

Dual economies: limited development of markets. Thus, many LDCs are, in essence, "dual economies." One part is a money, market-oriented economy centered in a few large cities, with modern industry mixed with crowded slums. The other part is a subsistence-level, rural, barter-type economy of hand labor and primitive superstitions, comprising 75 percent or so of the population, substantially isolated from the markets and industry of the cities. To go from one to the other is to go from one world to another, from the dark ages to the present.

Transportation is crude. The highways of the cities rapidly dwindle to dirt roads and to mere paths a hundred miles away. Religious and cultural barriers fragment the nation. One can scarcely call them "economies"—for economic life as we know it exists only around the cities and towns. Without roads and communication, there is little chance for a market economy to develop.

In some nations, profitable one-product export economies have developed—copper in Chile, oil in Saudi Arabia. In many ways, these are the fortunate LDCs. But much of the investment to develop these export enclaves is often foreign, and resentment against foreign ownership and operation is common. Often it leads to nationalization, whether or not there is a native competence to operate the industry.

Unequal distribution of income. In most less-developed countries, income is very unequally distributed—far more unequally than in the highly developed, capitalist economies. There are often a few rich landholders, sometimes a few industrialists. The masses are dismally poor, mainly living just above the subsistence level on farms or in villages, often as tenant farmers who keep little of what they raise. There is no substantial "middle class" of shopkeepers, professional men, and skilled workers, which is a major portion of Western populations.

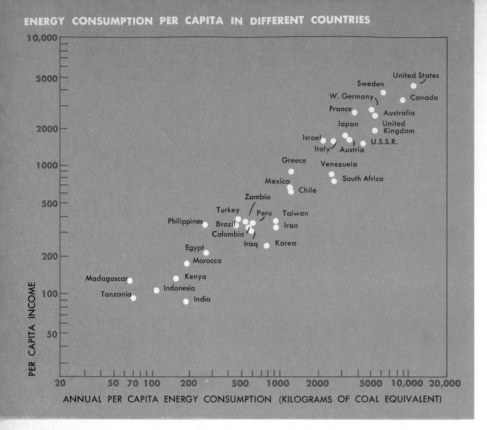

ENERGY CONSUMPTION PER CAPITA IN DIFFERENT COUNTRIES

Figure 46–1
Energy consumption per capita is closely correlated with the degree of economic development. (Source: United Nations. Data are for 1970.)

Weak governments. A few LDCs have well-established democratic institutions, but they are the exception. Governments are typically unstable, revolutions are commonplace. There can be little long-range planning of basic government services such as schools, highways, and the like. Equally important, there is no basis for long-run planning by investors and businessmen. Often governments are dominated by the entrenched "haves," who block social and political change that might endanger them.

Governments, which must provide leadership in development, are usually weakly staffed, reflecting the newness of the nations and the lack of education and traditions of honest civil service. Government jobs are often political perquisites, which mainly provide an accepted position for corruption. Confusion, red tape, and bungling often characterize government "programs." There is little chance for such governments to establish and administer effective tax systems to collect the funds needed to provide schools, highways, and sanitation. Overissue of

money and rampant inflation are commonplace.

So much for a general, if discouraging, overview. Now let us look more analytically at the problem, using the theory from Chapter 43. The theory predicts that low per capita output in the less-developed nations will reflect a high ratio of population to natural resources and to capital, a slow rate of capital accumulation and technical advance, an uneducated, low-productivity labor force, and a general environment unconducive to initiative, enterprise, and organized economic activity. And in fact, this is a reasonable description of most of the LDCs. Look now at these factors one at a time.

Natural resources

Lack of natural resources explains little of the plight of the less-developed nations. Switzerland has one of the world's highest per capita incomes on virtually no natural resources; Africa and Asia have some of the lowest on vast natural resources. The ratios of population to arable land for Switzerland, Belgium, and the Netherlands are about the same as those for Bolivia, Peru, and Egypt.

Nonetheless, plentiful natural resources can certainly help. The United States, Canada, and Australia all have rich resources and low ratios of population to land. Surely the vast western frontier helped to speed our early growth. Many poor nations would be much worse off without generous resources—the copper and nitrates of Chile, the oil of the Middle East. Perhaps climate, rather than natural resources in the usual sense, is critical. Most of the world's well-to-do nations lie in the temperate zone; none of them in the tropics. But within the temperate zone, there are wide variations in economic development. Nor does primary reliance on agriculture necessarily characterize poor nations. Denmark and New Zealand demonstrate that agricultural countries need not be poor. The poor nations are poor not because they are agricultural, but because productivity in their agriculture is so low.

Shortage of capital and primitive technology

The stock of capital explains much more. No less-developed country has a large stock of capital goods per capita; every well-to-do nation does. Modern factories, machinery and equipment, highways, hospitals—all are scarce in the LDCs. Without them, high output per capita is very difficult.

The reason is easy to see. When nations are poor, they find it hard to save. Saving in India or Somalia means cutting back an already pitifully low standard of living. Saving in America is easy. Yet without capital goods, the poor nation can never hope to raise the standard of living of the masses very much.

Capital investment of over $40,000 per factory worker in America was cited above. In the poorest nations, the comparable figure is only a few dollars. Gross capital formation is only 5–10 percent of gross national product in such poor nations as Paraguay and Nigeria. In the well-to-do nations it runs 15–20 percent, and in very rapidly growing nations, like Japan, up to 30–40 percent. It is easy for the rich to become richer. The poor, like the queen in *Through the Looking Glass,* must run as fast as they can merely to stay in the same place, as population grows constantly.

As a closely related factor, most less-developed countries have little modern technology. Human beings and beasts do virtually all the work in agriculture. Handicraft methods dominate in small-scale industry in the towns and cities. To the illiterate native of Tanzania or Yemen, Detroit's mass-production methods have little relevance. Where economic development is beginning, sometimes wild contrasts exist in the dual economies. In the cities of India and Venezuela, some of the world's most modern oil refineries and chemical plants loom against the sky. Fifty miles away, there is the most primitive agriculture, unchanged for a thousand years.

Overpopulation and the labor force

In one fundamental sense, overpopulation is the crux of the less-developed economies' problems. The population is so large that, given the natural resources and capital available, there is barely enough output per person to maintain life. And when total output increases because of improved technology or capital accumulation, population increases nearly as fast, so there is little improvement in the average standard of living. This is not the picture in all the LDCs, but it is in most.

In recent years, total production has risen at substantial rates in many LDCs, 4–5 percent per annum in Latin America, Africa, and southeast Asia. This is near the growth rate of total output in the industrialized countries. But population has grown nearly as fast as output.

In most less-developed economies, the annual birthrate is between 30 and 50 per thousand people; in the United States and Western Europe, the comparable rate has generally declined to around 15 to 20 per thousand. But in the LDCs, until recently, death rates typically ran from 25 to 35 per thousand, compared to 10 or below in the Western world. Thus, population growth rates in the two types of economies were roughly similar, running around 10 to 15 per thousand (1–1.5 percent per year).

Since World War II, Western methods of disease prevention have drastically reduced the death rate in many LDCs, especially the rate of

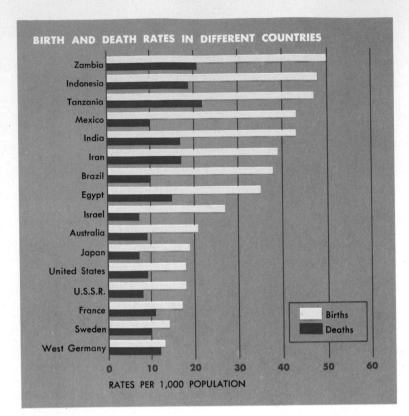

BIRTH AND DEATH RATES IN DIFFERENT COUNTRIES

Zambia
Indonesia
Tanzania
Mexico
India
Iran
Brazil
Egypt
Israel
Australia
Japan
United States
U.S.S.R.
France
Sweden
West Germany

Births
Deaths

0 10 20 30 40 50 60

RATES PER 1,000 POPULATION

Figure 46-2
The less-developed nations have the fastest-growing populations. For the whole world, the birthrate is about 34 per thousand and the death rate about 11. (Source: United Nations. Figures for 1970.)

infant mortality. DDT alone is estimated to have saved 50 million lives through checking the spread of infectious disease. During the 1950s, the death rate declined by 46 percent in Puerto Rico, 43 percent in Formosa, 23 percent in Jamaica. The result is a population explosion. In Latin America, Asia, and Africa, population is doubling every 20 to 25 years.

Figure 46-2 shows this contrast dramatically. Note the high birthrates in most less-developed countries, and the rapid rates of population growth implied by the big spread between their birth and death rates.

The world population problem is thus centered in the less-developed countries. In the developed nations of the Western world, population is generally stable or growing 1 percent or less per year. But given the explosive growth rates in the rest of the world, total world population may nearly double—from about 4 to 7.5 billion—in the next 25 years, whereas the last doubling took 45 years, and the one before that

80 years. If that high rate should continue, it would imply a world population of over thirty billion a century from now.

Such a population would make the earth into a human anthill, but we are unlikely to reach it or anything like it. Malthus's famine would probably check the growth before then, if nothing else did. Although food production has been rising rapidly, and there are still periodic food "surpluses" in developed nations that lead governments to support prices and restrict output, over half the world's population today has less than what most experts consider an "adequate" diet.

The population bomb is thus a real threat, not in the developed Western nations, but in the vast less-developed areas with over two billion people. Unless food production rises faster than in the past, many of their people will be hungry and undernourished if present population growth rates continue. Technical advance—the much-discussed "green revolution"—promises dramatically higher crop yields in some areas, but these results are still far from certain, and some combination of population control and increased food production is essential if many of the less-developed nations are to avoid disaster.[3]

The population problem is all the more serious because in many less-developed nations, much of the population is illiterate. New methods that involve even the simplest changes often meet barriers of superstition and inadequate understanding—for example, use of chemical fertilizers and crop rotation. In Africa, only about 25 percent of all children between five and eighteen go to school, about 40 percent in Asia. In the United States, the figure is over 95 percent. Figure 46–3 shows the high correlation between literacy and living standards.

[3]For authoritative analyses of the population and world food problems, see P. Hauser, ed., *The Population Dilemma* (Englewood Cliffs, N.J.: Prentice-Hall, 1969), and W.W. Cochrane, *The World Food Problem* (New York: Crowell Collier and Macmillan, 1969), which draw heavily on United Nations studies.

Environment and initiative

Rapid economic growth has occurred mainly in the Western world where the social and economic groundwork was laid centuries ago. Nowhere has there been rapid, continuing growth without reasonably stable government and financial and economic institutions. In all the major countries of the highly developed group of Table 46–1 except the USSR, the profit motive and individual initiative have played a central role.

On these scores, the problems faced by the less-developed economies are enormous. Apathy and ignorance characterize the great mass of their populations. Except for government leaders and small educated groups, there is often little effective impetus for economic development; and all too often, even the leaders appear more concerned with their own status than with economic progress for the masses. In central Africa, the medicine man or witch doctor is still the most influential member of many tribes. In some nations, manual labor is considered beneath the

Figure 46–3
The degree of literacy is strongly correlated with the extent of economic development, as both cause and effect. (Source: UNESCO. Income data for 1970; literacy data for various dates in the 1960s.)

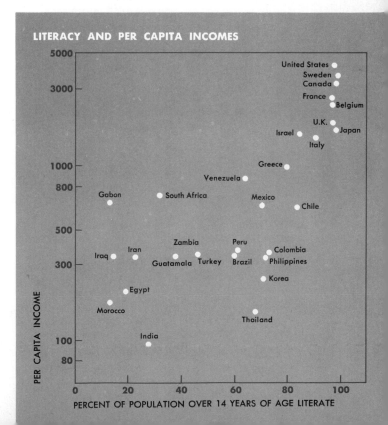

dignity of a man, and is left entirely to women. In many LDCs, few of the peasants own much, if any, land. They see little reason to work harder to produce more when most of it must be given up to the absentee landlord.

Many LDCs attempting to industrialize face backward-bending labor-supply curves. Ordinarily, higher wages will call forth more labor. But native workers, used to only low living standards and unacquainted with the Protestant work ethic, may be content with what seem to them adequate money incomes and simply stop working to take it easy or go spend their new wealth when they reach some weekly or monthly income level. Thus, offers of higher wages call forth less, not more, work, since workers reach the "big enough" income level sooner with higher wage rates. The labor-supply curve, as shown back in Figure 31–2, is backward-bending above some (often low) income level.

Thus, it is not surprising that the LDCs lack entrepreneurs—individuals with imagination and initiative to seize economic opportunities and to develop them. In the traditional societies, such attitudes and activities are often frowned upon. Caste systems bar occupational changes, and class hierarchies prevent vertical mobility. Things have been done the same way since time immemorial.

Nor can such nations expect to surge upward without what economists call an "infrastructure" of "social overhead capital"—highways, schools, communications, hospitals, sanitation. These all require capital and planning—and their benefits to the entire economy far exceed the individual benefits that individual investors might see. Enforced saving through government tax collections is the only practical way to finance them. Thus, stable, established governments, capable of collecting taxes and spending efficiently, are essential—but rare.

Absence of stable governments and established tax systems leads to persistent government deficits and to inflation. There are vast needs. But subsistence living standards make taxes very difficult to collect. The predictable result is government spending without corresponding taxes, and inflation in the market sector of their economies.

The resulting inflations are bad partly because of the inequities they work on the masses, who have no way to protect themselves from the higher prices of essentials. Inflation thus becomes a kind of "forced saving" that substitutes for tax collections. But worse, inflation and financial instability repel foreign investors, whose capital is desperately needed, and exacerbate balance-of-payments problems.

The vicious circle of poverty

The less-developed nations vary widely. But in most, the central problem seems to be a vicious circle of poverty. Incomes and living standards are so low that productivity is low and saving is impossible for the mass of the population. But without more capital goods, highways, and education, output per capita cannot be increased. If total output increases, population grows nearly as fast.

Throughout the LDCs, a significant part of the farm population is "surplus" in the sense that it could be removed from the farms of the countries concerned without any reduction in *total* farm output. But to move this surplus population to productive employment seems impossible. What will keep them from starving until they become established in industrial jobs? How can uneducated people be made into effective industrial workers? Who will provide the factory equipment, and the capital to establish new concerns? How could the newly made industrial goods be sold either domestically or abroad without an established market and without adequate transportation and commercial facilities?

Last, government planning and taxation are required to enforce saving and to channel investment into socially desirable uses; yet governments are weak, inefficient, unstable. Inefficient bureaucracies bungle rules and frustrate businessmen with red tape. Inflations and financial instability are commonplace. It seems that everywhere they turn, the LDCs face insoluble dilemmas. Their leaders may know the prescriptions of the theory of Chapter 43, but what shall they do?

POLICY FOR ECONOMIC DEVELOPMENT

How can the LDCs break out of the vicious circle of poverty and take off into self-sustaining growth? There is no simple answer.

Indeed, there may be no answer at all for some of them. The main approaches suggested by the experts follow the lines of the theory suggested above.

Environment and institutions for economic development

It is striking that every one of the top ten countries in the highly developed group of Table 46–1 is either in Western Europe or has inherited much of Western European culture and traditions. Max Weber, a famous sociologist, in his *Protestant Ethic and the Spirit of Capitalism,* argued that the rapid economic development of Western Europe was linked intimately with what he called the "Protestant ethic"—the belief that work is good for its own sake and that the individual should be free to seek after his own welfare through work.

Weber emphasized the institutions of capitalistic society that have accompanied rapid economic development in the West: (1) private ownership and control of the means of production; (2) freedom of the market from such restrictions as guild monopolies, social-class barriers, and government price-fixing; (3) the reign of calculable law, enabling people to know in advance what rules they operate under in economic life; (4) freedom of individuals to work for wages; (5) "commercialism" of economic life through a market system of wages and prices to mobilize and allocate productive resources; and (6) speculation and risk taking (which had been largely forbidden in the preceding feudal and guild societies).

Were the Protestant ethic and the institutions of capitalism essential to the rapid economic growth of today's richest countries? The facts fit Weber's description reasonably well, but there are important exceptions.

Everyone agrees that sustained rapid economic growth is unlikely without a stable government, law, and order. Without them, neither domestic nor foreign investors are willing to risk their funds; the essential economic infrastructure of highways, communications, and other public utilities is unlikely to come. But revolution and instability have been common in the LDCs. Struggles for power by competing factions have been common. Illiterate, superstitious people

find it hard to make democracy work effectively after they wrest power from rich dictators or foreign rulers. But difficult as it may be, establishment of stable government appears to be a *sine qua non* for the takeoff into economic growth.

Development of individual initiative and an entrepreneurial class, plus acceptance of a market economy, also seems very important (although China may be a counterexample). Individuals who take leadership, who see potential gains in taking risks, who manage to mobilize capital, who have the drive to push ahead through difficulties and to organize the work of others play a key role in most successful development. Often, immigrants from a different culture, who are materialistic, experimental, industrious, and ambitious for their families, have provided entrepreneurial leadership.

Equally important, and perhaps most difficult, a spirit of greater initiative must be instilled in the masses. Apathy and ignorance lead to acceptance of poverty and the status quo—to acceptance of the life of one's parents and their parents before them. No other problem seems more frustrating to the planners trying to pull economies up from poverty.

How initiative, a market, and an entrepreneurial class develop in traditional tribal or village societies is far from clear. Sociologists, economists, and anthropologists have studied dozens of cases and find no single explanation. In some instances (Japan, for example), an entrepreneurial class seems to develop from pressures of social and cultural change. Dissatisfied groups outside the ruling elite see trading and business as a way to rise to higher status. In other cases (Egypt, for example), the spirit of entrepreneurship is imported through colonial rule, which is later thrown off. Increasing awareness of the outside world seems everywhere to be important. In many cases, the development of an entrepreneurial class has been a revolt against prevailing tribal or village mores, a social as well as an economic revolution.

Capital accumulation and industrialization

As our theory would lead us to expect, substantial capital accumulation has marked every major case of rapid economic development. To rise from poverty, every na-

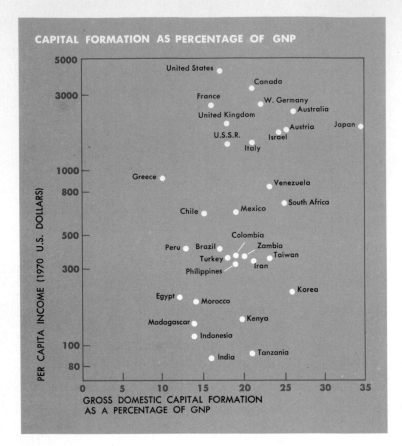

CAPITAL FORMATION AS PERCENTAGE OF GNP

Figure 46-4
High per capita incomes and high rates of capital formation generally go together, as interacting cause and effect. But there are exceptions; note Japan. (Source: United Nations. Data for 1970.)

tion faces the central problem of increasing saving and investment as a share of total output. Figure 46-4 shows the wide variation among countries in the ratio of gross investment to GNP. Although a few nations with very high investment ratios have relatively low per capita incomes (for example, Yugoslavia), they are now growing rapidly. The United States has a moderate savings–investment ratio but also a relatively slow rate of growth over recent years; we had a high savings ratio during the nineteenth century.

There is some evidence that it takes about $3–$4 of new capital goods to increase current income by $1 annually in these countries (a "capital–output ratio" of $3:1$ or $4:1$). With a $4:1$ marginal capital–output ratio, an economy that saves 4 percent of its income to accumulate capital will, other things equal, increase its national income by 1 percent annually. Then, if population grows at, say, 1 percent annually, per

capita income is just held constant. To raise its living standard, the economy must either save more or slow its population growth. Any saving rate below 4 percent of income will mean decreasing per capita incomes.

This relationship between the capital–output ratio and the rate of saving is illustrated by Table 46-3. If 4 percent of total income is saved, there will be a 1.33 percent annual increase in output in case the capital–output ratio is $3:1$, but only a 1 percent increase if the ratio is $4:1$. Obviously, both higher savings ratios and lower capital–output ratios are good for economic growth. A few countries have apparently managed a capital–output ratio of $2:1$, which has permitted them to expand output rapidly with modest savings ratios.

Many LDCs have turned to government investment programs (financed by taxes or inflationary money-issue) to force more saving and investment, especially in economic infrastruc-

Table 46-3

Capital-output and savings ratios

	ANNUAL INCREASE IN OUTPUT (PERCENTAGE) WITH:	
Savings-income ratio	Capital-output ratio = 3:1	Capital-output ratio = 4:1
.04	1.33	1.0
.05	1.67	1.25
.10	3.33	2.5
.15	5.0	3.75

tures—roads, schools, and dams that aid development throughout the nation. When the mass of the population is barely above the subsistence level, to obtain more voluntary saving is very difficult. Recent research emphasizes the importance of developing financial institutions to gather together small savings and channel them to useful investments.

Foreign investment and imperialism

Some nations—for example, India and the Middle East—have obtained substantial portions of their growth capital from abroad, through both private investment and government aid. The United Nations estimates that the annual provision of capital by the developed to the less-developed nations rose from $2 billion in 1950 to $26 billion in 1974. About 40 percent was loans or grants from other nations or international agencies; 60 percent was private investment from the developed nations. Ten billion dollars came from the United States. In 1976, the IMF sold off one-sixth of its gold stock, and provided the proceeds to the LDCs.

Poor nations desperately need capital from abroad. Economic analysis says that there will be benefit to both borrower and foreign lender if the expected rate of return on the capital in the developing nation exceeds that which the lender can obtain elsewhere. Nonetheless, many developing nations have invited foreign private investment only with stringent restrictions. With burgeoning national pride, they want no part of foreign control, and they distrust foreign investors who may try to exploit them. The memories of many decades of colonialism are still strong. Thus, as badly as they need foreign capital, many of the poor nations have hedged foreign capital and companies around with restrictive controls reaching into day-to-day operations.

Are these fears of foreign imperialism and multinational corporations irrational? Over the past century, some foreign investors have exploited native resources and workers, making large profits with little concern for the welfare of the less-developed nations. This economic domination was often paralleled by ruthless political and social repression of native populations. Although native living standards may well have been higher than they would have been with no foreign capital at all, bitter resentment was a predictable consequence.

But since the emergence of national independence for nearly all people since World War II, the pendulum has swung. Foreign companies (for example, in petroleum) that formerly paid only 25 percent of their profits to local nations for the privilege of extracting natural resources have seen their shares fall to 50 percent, and lower. Restrictions on foreign operations have been steadily tightened. Outright expropriation, often with limited compensation, has become common. Prospective foreign businesses have often been turned away because offers were considered inadequate, sometimes with the result that nothing happens—no foreign capital, no jobs for native people.

Socialist doctrine says that foreign "imperialist" investment will bleed the less-developed economy by withdrawing the profits it extorts from the native population. But, although this may sometimes occur, two counterarguments are important. First, although withdrawal of profits and interest has grown steadily with the cumulation of foreign investments in the LDCs, reinvested earnings plus new U.S. investments in the LDCs has been even larger, so net U.S. investment in the LDCs has grown persistently.

Second, even if *all* profits were withdrawn by the foreign investor, the developing nation might well gain from the investment. Remember the desperate need for capital to raise output and provide jobs for the surplus native population. If native workers take jobs voluntarily in the foreign business, they presumably prefer that to their other alternatives. If local customers voluntarily buy the foreign product, they presumably prefer it to other alternatives, even though its price may have yielded a large profit to the foreign company. Hard-boiled realism would ask, Whether I like the foreigner or not, am I better off with his capital invested here, or without it? Clearly, the developing nation would be still better off if part or all of the profits were reinvested there. But what if the alternative is no foreign investment at all?[4]

Most of the developing nations have attempted to compromise this dilemma. They seek foreign capital, but on terms they dictate. Some compromises have been effective in attracting foreign capital; others have not. To the outsider, restrictions that lead foreign investors to turn away may seem shortsighted, for the less-developed nation ends up with its restrictions and no capital for development. But fear of foreign exploitation is understandably strong in many of the less-developed nations.

Technical advance and education

Technological advance and development of an educated, skilled labor force have played a central role in the development of the Western economies. How can the poor nations achieve such technical advance?

Their problem may look easy—just borrow the technology of more advanced nations. The USSR after World War II adopted industrial methods and techniques wholesale from the West. Japan has adopted foreign technology even more effectively. But such importation often requires heavy capital investment; skilled laborers, technicians, and managers; and mass markets to justify many modern methods—conditions not met in most poor nations.

Think, for example, how you would go about introducing modern technology into Somalia, an emerging African nation of about three million people, most of them illiterate nomads. Literacy:

[4]For a more complete analysis, see R. Vernon, *Sovereignty at Bay* (New York: Basic Books, 1971); and C. Kindleberger, *American Business Abroad* (New Haven, Conn.: Yale University Press, 1969), Chap. 5.

perhaps 15 percent. Total college graduates in the country: about two hundred. Per capita income: about $80 a year. Politics: longstanding bitter rivalry among tribal groups.

In fact, the biggest promise for technical change probably lies in agriculture rather than in industry. Primitive, low-productivity agriculture is the greatest millstone around the necks of the poor economies. Improving productivity in agriculture has led the way in nearly every case of growth. Here, technology can be introduced in small stages, and with modest capital costs—simple tools, fertilizers, improved irrigation.

Most technological advance requires an educated labor force and willingness to accept change. Thus, mass education and development of a core of skilled technicians and teachers are goals of virtually every LDC. Investment in education may not pay a fast return. But Figure 46–3 speaks for itself. The long-run payoff is big.

Steps toward mass education in some LDCs have been spectacular since World War II. But schools are expensive and teachers are very scarce. Thus, educational efforts have been concentrated on the young. It will be generations before half the population in many of the less-developed nations is even literate. For example, Indonesia, with 110 million people, has only two national universities.

Population policy

Until most LDCs slow their rates of population growth, they are unlikely to escape far from Malthus's dire predictions. Even high growth rates in aggregate output cannot outdistance high rates of population growth.

Many LDCs' first reaction to Western suggestions that population growth be limited was resentment. They accused the developed nations of plotting to hold down the numbers of the poor who might overtake them, of advocating genocide for the Third World peoples. And some of this resentment remains. But the pressure of exploding populations has made the point unmistakably, and increasing numbers of the LDCs are inaugurating population-limitation programs. India, whose population is growing by 15 million people annually, provides a vivid example. For over a decade, the Gandhi government has included large expenditures for birth control in its annual budgets. In 1976, some of the individual Indian states adopted experimental legislation requiring sterilization of couples who have more than two children, although with many exceptions in the law. The national government withdrew housing benefits from large families, increased outlays on education, and threatened increasingly drastic measures.

But population limitation is easier said than done, and the programs of the LDCs have had limited success. Providing effective bases for family planning among hundreds of millions of illiterate, widely scattered people is very difficult. Religious barriers appear to be less formidable than was previously believed. But in most poor societies, the family is the main economic and social unit, and parents must look to their children for support in old age. Some people in the poor nations now recognize that with modern death rates, they need not have seven or eight children to be reasonably sure three or four will survive, and perhaps birth control will be more readily accepted. But overturning centuries-old beliefs and practices is not easy, and progress is far from certain.

Balanced versus unbalanced growth

In the less-developed nations and among the experts, the debate rages as to whether poor nations can grow faster by concentrating on the development of either industry or agriculture alone, or by striving to develop both sectors in balance.

Sooner or later, industrialization is necessary for full economic development. Every high-income nation in Table 46–1 has a major industrial and commercial sector. Transport and steel play prominent roles in industrialization. Adequate transport facilities and communication permit specialization and underlie mass production and mass markets. Steel is used in nearly every facet of modern industrial activity, and every growing nation longs for its own modern steel mill, as a symbol of national pride.

Moreover, if a nation can develop its own industry, it can then substitute domestic products for essential but expensive imported goods (machinery, fertilizer, food), for which there is

never enough foreign exchange. Thus, "import substitution" is always an alluring goal for the developing nations. Getting more foreign exchange to pay for imports is a top priority of nearly every LDC.

However, large industrial plants in the developing nations have often proved costly and inefficient, with their products costing far more than the imports for which they are supposed to substitute. Thus, they generally require heavy subsidies and tariff or import protection to get started. Often, little foreign exchange is saved.

Thus, mounting experience suggests that improving agricultural productivity is the first need if LDCs are to break out of their vicious circle. With 70–80 percent of the population in agriculture, that's where the first problem is. A more efficient agriculture could produce more food for domestic use and export. More workers would be freed for gradual transfer to other jobs.

Some simple arithmetic dramatizes the importance of improving farm productivity. Suppose a nation wants to increase total output 5 percent annually but finds it impossible to raise agricultural productivity. If the "modern," nonagricultural sector produces 20 percent of total output, *its* productivity would have to increase 25 percent a year in order to provide the desired overall 5 percent increase. Such a spectacular performance is hardly likely.

Thus, allocation of scarce capital to raising agricultural output makes sense. Improving agricultural efficiency through fertilizer, simple tools, and improved methods requires little capital compared to mass industrialization. It requires less social disruption, less transfer of people, less infrastructure than does movement to a modern industrial sector.

The crucial role of foreign trade

As the preceding section indicates, nearly every LDC faces a critical shortage of foreign exchange to pay for essential imports of food, fertilizer, and capital goods. The LDCs can get foreign exchange only by selling their own exports, unless they can borrow abroad, attract foreign investors, or obtain gifts from the developed nations or international institutions.

Typically, LDCs can compete effectively in

world export markets only when they have supplies of scarce natural resources (oil, nitrates, copper, bauxite, and so on), special advantages in agriculture (as with coffee in Brazil, long-staple cotton in Egypt), or relatively efficient, labor-intensive, simple manufactured products where they can take advantage of their plentiful, cheap labor (cotton textiles). Thus, developed-country markets for these products (especially minerals and other raw materials) are essential to the development of many LDCs, and they have understandably exerted increasing pressure through international organizations on the richer nations to guarantee markets for such products at high prices. They have also attempted cartel arrangements, like OPEC, to achieve the same purposes. Import substitution through industrialization, as noted above, is an ever-beguiling possibility, but one that often, alas, turns out to be costly rather than helpful. The need to export is a never-ending pressure on most LDCs. (See Case 38.)

Economic planning or the price system?

Many Americans, seeing the success of our essentially private-enterprise, market-directed economy, argue that the LDCs should rely on private initiative and the marketplace. But this view has found little sympathy in the LDCs. There is so much to be done and so little time to do it. These nations do not trust the "unseen hand" of Adam Smith to guide the complex process of growth, to assess the long-range importance of alternative uses of resources. They want roads, schools, fertilizers, and industrial plants **now.** Thus, government intervention on a wide scale is the active agent in less-developed nations. The main issue is whether it shall involve complete government control over economic life (as in Communist China) or merely government direction of broad lines of activity with wide scope left to private initiative (as in India).

Nearly everywhere, it is agreed that government must provide infrastructure. Even where most of the economy stays private, basic investment priorities have become the province of the government. Nearly everywhere, foreign exchange is under government control, so that scarce foreign currencies are used for high-priority imports rather than for private luxuries.

But in recent years, the experts have turned back to the crucial importance of individual initiative, and the role of self-interest in providing that initiative. There is disenchantment with government planning to solve all the problems. Many government planners and native bureaucrats have proved incompetent; corruption is commonplace. Some LDCs now try to regulate the behavior of individuals to a degree unknown in the Western world since mercantilism. All foreign trade and use of foreign exchange is regulated in detail; new businesses require government licenses. Rents, wages, and basic commodity prices are controlled; internal shipments of grains and other basic commodities require government permits. The amount of red tape horrifies both native entrepreneurs and foreign businessmen. With the best of intentions, such complex regulations plus widespread incompetence in their administration can stifle business rather than speed development.[5] Many countries are learning that government control per se is no answer to the real problems of development, even though government planning is needed to supplement markets and individual initiative. Only Communist China and Cuba have adhered rigidly to a communist complete-planning approach, and even they make substantial use of markets.

Monetary-fiscal policy and economic growth

Part 2 stressed aggregate demand and expansionary monetary-fiscal policy to eliminate underemployment and to stimulate investment. Why don't the governments of the poor nations use deficit-financed spending to set up factories and lure the surplus farm population away from disguised unemployment into useful work, thereby increasing output and improving everyone's welfare?

The answer is that the main result would be

---

[5] See P.T. Bauer, *United States AID and Indian Economic Development* (American Enterprise Foundation, 1969), and W. Dick, "Authoritarian versus Nonauthoritarian Approaches to Economic Development," *Journal of Political Economy,* July 1974. But Communist China has developed rapidly under economy-wide planning; see below.

inflation rather than increased output. As in the United States, raising the long-term growth rate is basically a *real* "supply" problem, not one of inadequate demand.

Suppose the government of Peru or Afghanistan prints money to lure workers into industry. There are no idle factories where output can be increased by calling the unemployed back to work. The critical shortage is real capital (factories, machinery, transport), not aggregate money demand. The situation is very different from the depression period in advanced countries, with vast unused productive capacity.

With this barrier to increasing real output, government spending without corresponding tax collections is likely to lead mainly to inflation as spending rises and output does not. Rapid inflation may endanger the stability of the government. Sound government finances are the first thing outside investors look for. And inflated domestic costs and prices make it harder to sell in world markets, a major blow when foreign exchange is badly needed to finance imports. **To repeat, the problems of the less-developed economies are basically *real* problems.**

Two important cases: India and China

One third of all the people in the world live in two countries: India (600 million) and China (900 million). And these countries exemplify dramatically different approaches to economic development.[6]

In many respects, India and China face similar problems. They are both vast land masses, heavily populated in many areas but with great reaches of mountains and wasteland. Both, in 1950, had per capita incomes below $100. In both, about 80 percent of the total population is

[6] Informative overviews of the two economies in action are provided by *China: A Reassessment of the Economy* (Joint Economic Committee of Congress, 1975), especially Introduction and Chapter 1; G. Myrdal, *Asian Drama* (New York: Pantheon, 1968); and J. Mellor, *The New Economics of Growth* (Ithaca, N.Y.: Cornell University Press, 1976). More informal pictures by two distinguished American economists are J. Tobin, "The Economy of China: A Tourist's View," and L. Reynolds, "China's Economy: A View from the Grass Roots," in *Challenge*, March 1973 and March 1974, respectively.

engaged in agriculture. And both, since World War II, have undertaken vigorous planned programs of economic development.

India. In her first five "five-year plans," covering 1951 to 1979, India has chosen an essentially democratic approach. This has left considerable freedom to private enterprise under government planning, while using government projects in such major areas as irrigation, transportation, and steel. Over one-third of total investment has been private, and in spite of India's claim to be a "socialist" state, the great bulk of her economic activity remains in private hands. Government taxes and spending remain only about half as large a percentage of GNP as in the United States and Western European nations. The plans pushed both industrialization and agricultural productivity—primarily the former at first, with more stress on agriculture recently. Industrial investment concentrated on both small-scale industry, such as textiles, and on larger projects, such as power development, fertilizers, coal, and heavy manufacturing. The plans called for increased capital accumulation in both agriculture and industry, plus added government services.

Results of the plans have been mixed. Real national income rose 3–4 percent per annum and population about 2.5 percent, giving perhaps a 1 percent annual increase in per capita income—a pitifully small $1 a year. It is not clear that the living standard of many Indian peasants is much higher than it was a thousand years ago. Industrial improvement is more encouraging. Industrial production has quadrupled since 1950, and the 1979 goal in the fifth plan is another 50 percent increase. Net investment rose from about 5 to 10 percent of net national product, and saving is apparently rising.

But the achievements have fallen far short of India's optimistic goals, and per capita income has been basically flat in the 1970s. Moreover, unemployment has risen from probably ten to twenty million people in the cities, perhaps many more; no one has reliable statistics. Agriculture has been the great problem sector. And all the plans would have foundered had not large-scale foreign aid, mainly from America, eased India's desperate foreign-exchange shortages as she tried to finance the imports required for food and capital investment. Heavy military expenditures, reflecting concern over Indian relations with both China and Pakistan, have cut the supply of civilian-type goods.

The current plan calls for a 5.5 percent annual growth in output and a large increase in both public and private investment. It emphasizes manufacturing, energy sources, and agriculture, plus fertilizers and irrigation.

India has wavered uncertainly as to the amount of government control she wants. In the second and third plans, government regulation of investment, foreign trade, and other aspects of economic activity became more and more detailed. Complaints of bureaucratic red tape and corruption multiplied, from Indians, foreign businesses in India, and potential investors. The major shortfalls of the third plan were attributed by many to this increasing bureaucracy and government inefficiency. The public sector and detailed government planning are thus less prominent in the later plans. Detailed industry targets have been replaced by planning estimates, except for a few key industries. More stress is placed on encouraging initiative of individual farmers.

The hopeful view is that India is on the verge of her takeoff into self-sustaining growth. But her successes have been modest, and the plans have made little progress in raising per capita incomes—especially because population-control programs have fallen far short of hopes. Bureaucracy, indecision, and red tape frustrate foreign visitors who try to help the Indians. Today, India remains a restless giant, unsure of the success of her individualistic, humanistic program of mixed public and private enterprise.

China. China's first five-year plan, covering 1952–57, called for drastic increases in industrialization, collectivization of agriculture, and ruthless suppression of consumption to obtain the resources required for capital accumulation. The plan centralized economic control in the Communist government. It called for rapid increases in agricultural output and mass transfer of agricultural population into industry. High government taxes on the masses and "profits" on

government-monopolized necessities were used to seize a larger portion of total income for government investment, and large-scale external aid was received from the USSR. Hard work and long hours were forced on the Chinese people. The result was a substantial pickup in the rate of economic growth, which had been zero or negative during the preceding war decade.

The second five-year plan called for a further "great leap forward" with the primary focus on heavy industry, although food targets were also upped substantially. In 1958, government seizure of huge land masses and forced concentration of millions of agricultural families in huge "communes" virtually abolished individual family units. Women were pressed into all areas of work, and children were placed in state nurseries. Communist dictation of thought patterns made George Orwell's *1984* seem very real indeed.

But Mao's great leap forward turned out to be China's great failure. After an initial surge, industrial output collapsed. In the years 1959–61, both industrial and agricultural output fell radically—food production apparently by nearly one-half, as bad weather compounded the troubles. The strains of the previous decade's massive conversion to industry and of the Communists' ruthless abolition of traditional family values apparently forced a massive retreat from the "communes" policy that had seized all private land and forced families into closely regulated agricultural communes. Some land was returned to individual family ownership, and some degree of family life was restored. More stress was placed on food production, and industrialization plans were revised downward radically.

Since the failure of the great leap forward, China has followed a more moderate development policy. The 1960s were devoted to restoring more orderly growth, and it was not until the mid-1960s that food and industrial production again reached the levels of a decade earlier. China's forward progress was again interrupted by the "cultural revolution" of 1967–69, which involved a massive social and political revolution to assure the dominance of Maoist thought. By 1970, more regular economic planning was again restored, and apparently industrial output has grown rapidly since then. Over the entire 1952–75 period, real GNP has apparently grown at an average of about 5 percent annually, with large swings above and below that figure.

Today, China is the world's most completely communist nation—a rapidly growing, dual economy with substantially more progress in the industrial than the agricultural sector. The impressive growth in industrial output, absolutely and relative to India, is shown in Table 46–4. Visitors are impressed by the hard work of the Chinese people, by the clean cities, and by their obviously improving standard of living. China has launched space satellites, built atomic bombs, and mounted a major military force. She is clearly no longer a typical less-developed nation.

But China is still a very poor nation, and the differences between the cities and agriculture are great. Eighty percent of all Chinese live on the land, and most still spend their lives at backbreaking labor, with little help from modern machinery, or even animals. As in most LDCs, farm incomes are apparently only about one-third to one-half those in the cities. The farm sector, the backbone of the Chinese economy, is organized into people's communes, which are both local government subdivisions and economic units for production, including some nonagricultural output. The communes vary in size from 5,000 to 40,000 people. They are in turn divided into production brigades of about 1,000 members, and these into production teams of 150–200. The team is responsible for cultivating its assigned land, and for carrying out all the associated activities; the Maoists emphasize the importance of group participative decision making at this level. Part of the output is allocated to local public and social services, and taxes are paid to the central government. Each team is given delivery goals for sales to the state at state-established prices. As long as it meets these goals, it is apparently free to consume what it wants of what more it produces. Peasants are allowed small plots for their own cultivation, and there are small private markets for this output, as in most other communist economies, reflecting what are termed "spontaneous forces" fo the rural economy.

Although communism stresses equality of incomes, there are substantial income differentials. The average factory worker's wage is about 60 yuan per month, while a beginning, low-output worker gets about half that amount. (A yuan equals about 45 cents in U.S. money.) High-skilled workers get about 100 yuan, while engineers and technicians earn up to 130–140 yuan. Some physicians and surgeons apparently earn 200–300 yuan. Thus, incomes are considerably more equal than in the Western capitalist socie-

Table 46–4

Economic growth in India and China

	INDIA		CHINA	
	1950	1974	1950	1974
GNP (in 1974 U.S. dollars)	24	79	60	220
GNP per capita (in 1974 U.S. dollars)	90	130	90	240
Industrial production (1950 = 100)	100	465	100	972
Electric power (million kilowatt hrs.)	4	59	5	108
Cement (million tons)	1	14	1	32
Steel (million tons)	1	7	1	24
Cotton cloth (billion meters)	1	4	2	8
Grain (million tons)	55	102	135	255
Fertilizers (million tons)	.1	11	.1	25

Source: United Nations. Data are based on reports by Indian and Chinese governments. Figures are rough estimates and may be overstated in some cases.

ties, because there are no high incomes from capital, but high-skilled experts may still earn ten times what common workers do, and perhaps twenty times as much as farm workers. The Chinese apparently find that monetary rewards can be important, as have the Russians and other communist societies.

All universities were closed for three years during the "cultural revolution," and they are still only partially reopened. Students are chosen from the workers apparently without regard to intellectual achievement; highly educated individuals are periodically sent off to work in the fields; and production decisions are made collectively in the communes and factories—although always within the central plan. How many skilled scientists, engineers, doctors, and the like will be developed in the future remains to be seen. There is some evidence that the central leadership has carefully protected a few intellectual leaders (for example, in the fields of physics and computer science) to ensure continued rapid progress in those fields.

Many Western observers question whether China's economic progress is worth the loss of individual freedom and the thought control it imposes on the Chinese people; and they question whether such conformist behavior is consistent with continuing economic and intellectual vitality. But communist supporters counter that results are what count, and that it is entirely proper for everyone to be governed by Maoist doctrine.

The future of the less-developed nations

Clearly, many of the less-developed nations are economies in motion. During the 1960s, labelled by the UN as the "decade of development," real GNP for all developing countries combined grew at a surprising 5.6 percent per annum. Some countries—Lybia (oil), Greece, Taiwan, Israel, Iran (oil), Korea, and Brazil—averaged 7 percent or better. Oil-producing LDCs are the big success stories of the 1970s. While special factors, like oil, explain some of the spectacular success, the overall picture is reasonably encouraging.

Most nations are learning from experience. A leading American economist has summarized the lessons of development policy over the past two decades:

Both the practical and theoretical emphasis is now more on agriculture and less exclusively on industry, more on human and relatively less on physical capital investment, more on private enterprise and less on state industries, more on reducing birthrates and less on increasing national output, and more on cultural and technological change instead of making foreign loans and grants called "capital." The lack of real managers and technical specialists is seen as especially acute in the recently decolonized nations. The importance of efficient and honest government is becoming more appreciated.[7]

There is no chance that the LDCs will catch up with developed-nation per capita incomes in the foreseeable future. Even on the most optimistic assumptions of annual growth rates in the LDCs, the absolute gap between rich and poor nations is widening at a breakneck pace. A 2 percent **annual increase** on $7,000 (roughly the present U.S. per capita figure) is $140, roughly the **total** present annual per capita income in India. Even if the Indian growth rates were to be double ours (say, 4 percent per capita as against 2 percent)—a **most** unlikely situation—by the end of the century, U.S. per capita income would still be nearly $10,000, Indian less than $500. Clearly, the less-developed nations can raise their living standards. But even if success surpasses their wildest dreams, the absolute gap between the "haves" and "have-nots" in our ever-smaller world seems certain to widen spectacularly over the years ahead.

What would you advise Mme. Gandhi, Prime Minister of India, to do to raise the standard of living of the Indian people?

U.S. POLICY

Mankind is passing through the most pervasive revolution it has ever known—the revolt of two-thirds of the world's people against the poverty, misery, and degradation of their present conditions of life, and against the domi-

[7] Stephen Enke, "Economists and Development," *Journal of Economic Literature,* December 1969, p. 1135.

nation of the industrialized, wealthy Western powers. The speed and force of this revolution are hard to perceive, sitting in the comfort of an American home or classroom. But they may well do more than any other force to determine the kind of world in which we will live a half century hence.

What should American policy be? As the proud leader of a democratic, humanitarian tradition, what should we do? What interests do we have in the less-developed nations, many of whose names we scarcely recognize?

First, an unhappy, resentful world of LDCs will be politically unstable. Rising living standards can give hope to the world's undernourished billions, even though they certainly cannot guarantee friendship or quiesence.

Second, we have economic interests. It would be foolish to overstress this element. Trade with *all* the LDCs amounts to only about 2 percent of U.S. GNP. But trade with the LDCs looks favorable for both us and them. We need their raw materials, and they need our food and manufactures.

Third, and perhaps most important, many Americans feel that we have a humanitarian interest in the relief of starvation, the lessening of disease and misery, and the improvement of education and living standards of the billions of people in the less-developed areas. There but for the grace of God go I, they say. We are very rich and they are very poor, and they need our help. Others disagree, especially when the time comes to pay the taxes to finance help to the LDC. Here, obviously, is a moral issue on which you must make up your own mind.

Channels of American aid

If we want to help, for political, economic, or humanitarian reasons, we should first ask the question, Can we really make any difference? The task of helping one or two billion people to a better life is a huge one. And the preceding pages surely show that the task is not simply one of providing more dollars of foreign aid.

Yet we should remember some facts. The total income of all the billion people in the non-Communist less-developed nations in 1975 was less than $250 billion. The GNP of the United States was $1.5 trillion. In 1975, we spent nearly $100 billion on military purposes; total arms spending in the world was about $300 billion. Elimination of these war expenditures could have doubled the living standard of each of the billion people.

The United States and the other developed nations have the economic ability to help significantly. What have we done? What should we do?

In 1974, total government loans, grants, and private investments from the developed countries to the LDCs totaled $27 billion, including $10 billion from the United States. About 60 percent was private long-term investment, presumably made in search of profits. The rest was government aid, either bilaterally or through international organizations. The U.S. $10 billion was $3.5 billion government aid, including "Food for Peace," with the remainder private investment, mainly in Latin America and the Middle East. (These totals do not include military aid.) Although the United States dominated total grants and investments, our $3.5 billion of government aid was only about .25 of one percent of our GNP, below the .4 percent average for all other developed nations.

Since World War II, U.S. government loans and gifts to other nations have totaled $175 billion, about two-thirds in military aid and one-third in civilian aid. India has received by far the largest amount of civilian aid (nearly $10 billion), followed by South Vietnam, South Korea, and Pakistan. While most such aid was originally on a government-to-government basis, in recent years U.S. official aid has been channeled increasingly through international institutions, such as the World Bank, the Inter-American, Asian, and African Development Banks, and the OECD Development Assistance Committee.

After the postwar burst of enthusiasm for aid to the less-developed economies came the sobering recognition that many of the crucial problems were internal ones. "Technical assistance" programs to help local governments and local peoples help themselves thus grew in popularity, partly because they seem to work well, partly because they are far cheaper than mass capital-investment grants. Assistance in establishing better schools, efficient local government admin-istration, sanitation and public health projects, and better farming techniques are examples. U.S. and multinational technical-assistance pro-grams stress training natives to take over essen-tial jobs themselves at the earliest possible mo-ment. In most cases, U.S. technical assistance has been provided on a matching basis, with half the cost of the joint programs being borne by local governments. Technical assistance is a bright spot in our foreign-aid program.

In order to grow, most LDCs must sell basic products abroad if they are to secure foreign exchange with which to finance needed imports. Many of their economies are centered around one or two basic products—oil, rubber, nitrates, coffee, tin. Trade barriers that shut these prod-ucts out of American markets strike a serious blow to the economies concerned. Contrary to the "imperialism" argument that we are bleed-ing the LDCs of their natural resources, those nations bitterly resent barriers to their sales in U.S. markets. The United States has led the way in reducing tariff barriers and in helping to provide stable international markets for such basic commodities.

The LDCs and a new world order?

Not long ago, most LDCs were polite suppliants for development aid from the richer nations. But no more! Third World countries want a new international economic order, with a massive sharing of the world's wealth. Using a variety of international organizations in which they can now outvote the highly developed na-tions, the LDCs have demanded vastly increased low-interest loan facilities with funds provided by the richer nations; an indefinite moratorium on existing debts owed to the developed nations; international cartel-like commodity price-stabi-lization agreements covering raw materials, with prices guaranteed by the developed nations;

preferential tariff treatment in Western markets; freer transfer of technology. Much of the flavor is conveyed by a quotation from a recent U.N. speech by President Hourari Boumedienne of Algeria:

Europe and the U.S. have plundered the natural wealth of the Third World. We should consider what-ever contribution the industrialized countries make to be a simple restitution of a tiny part of the debt contracted by their odious exploitation.

What should be the response of the United States and other developed nations to such de-mands? We have repeatedly led the way toward establishment of new international organizations to support Third World development, especially through international lending plans. But in case after case, the Third World countries have de-manded more generous aid programs than the United States has supported, and have amassed the votes, on a one-country-one-vote basis, to substitute theirs for the Western nations' propos-als. Since the charters of world financial organi-zations generally allocate votes roughly on the basis of contributions, the Third World nations cannot force contributions by the Western na-tions. Nor can they force us to participate in commodity price-support agreements and the like. But the successful OPEC escalation of oil prices strengthened their hand, and the industri-alized countries find themselves increasingly outvoted by the Third World nations, usually with the support of the Communist bloc.

Economic analysis can tell you a lot about the problem of raising living standards for the world's impoverished billions. It can give some guidance on how our help can do the most lasting good. But the problem of aid is moral and political as much as economic. It is one of the biggest issues on which this nation will re-peatedly take a stand over the decades ahead. How, and how much, shall we aid the Third World?

REVIEW

**For analysis
and discussion**

1. How well do the theories of Adam Smith and Malthus explain the plight of the less-developed nations? Has modern growth theory (from Chapter 43) added much to their analyses?
2. To develop rapidly, a nation must save and invest a substantial portion of its income. What steps would you advise the Indian government to take to increase India's saving rate when the majority of the population is on the brink of starvation?
3. Suppose the U.S. government sends you to a less-developed nation to assess its development prospects over the next decade. What would be the key information you would seek for your report?
4. Nearly everyone agrees that slower population growth is essential to reducing poverty in the LDCs. Suppose you were prime minister of India or Kenya; how would you bring this about?
5. Development of an entrepreneurial class seems critical for nations trying to break out of the vicious circle of poverty. If you were a government official in Peru or Zaire, what would you do about this problem?
6. Modern economics tells us to pump in purchasing power in order to eliminate unemployment when depression occurs in the Western world. How well will this policy work in the less-developed nations?
7. Will the gap between U.S. and less-developed nations' living standards narrow or widen over the next quarter century?
8. Are large-scale U.S. purchases of raw materials from the LDCs a sign of U.S. exploitation at work, or a major aid to development through providing badly needed foreign exchange?

Basic commodity prices (of agricultural products and minerals) have long fluctuated sharply, reflecting sharp variations in supply and fluctuating (often inelastic) demands. During the 1930s, nearly all basic commodity prices nosedived, and a number of international intergovernmental commodity agreements were established (for example, on sugar and coffee), somewhat parallel to the New Deal agricultural price and income stabilization programs in the United States (see Chapter 23). Under these agreements, producing countries agreed to maintain reasonably stable output levels, and both producing and consuming governments agreed to keep prices reasonably stable by export and import controls, stockpiles, and production-control plans. Without such agreements, the LDCs, which were the primary producing countries, suffered wild fluctuations in their supplies of foreign exchange, and considerable sympathy existed in the United States and world wide for the plight of such low-income producers. In some cases (for example, the European aluminum cartel), private producers formed cartels to stabilize prices at profitable levels, but these were generally short-lived through the depression years.

During the World War II inflations, commodity prices shot up, and since then, international commodity agreements have had a checkered history. In general, producing countries have sought them in depressed times, and output and trade restrictions have withered in boom periods. By the early 1970s, most such plans had been abandoned.

In 1973, the international coffee agreement expired, as Brazilian producers held out for higher coffee prices than the United States (the number one consumer) was willing to accept. Two-thirds of the world's coffee is produced by Brazil, Colombia, the Ivory Coast, and Angola, with the rest scattered among several countries, many of them in Latin America. Brazil and other producing countries argued that they desperately needed the foreign exchange provided by good coffee prices, and they reminded the

United States and other developed nations of their promises to aid in economic development. They were also keenly aware of the spectacular success of the OPEC countries in quadrupling oil prices.[8] The United States said that the concessions demanded by the producers were just too much, and other major consumers agreed.

When the international agreement regulating prices, exports, and imports expired, the four main producers formed a cartel, and by mid-1974, world coffee prices hit an all-time peak, reflecting in part at least the major producers' agreement to hold 20 percent of the 1974–75 crop off the world market. But a year later, coffee prices were back down to their 1973 levels and falling. While Brazil was holding back coffee to support the higher prices, several of the smaller exporters, which had never stockpiled coffee before, couldn't resist the temptation to capitalize on the high prices, and started selling heavily. The weather was good, and coffee surpluses piled up. Farmers in Angola, uncertain about the revolution in Portugal, also decided that the best policy was to take profits when they could be had, and finally Colombia also broke ranks. As Chapter 26 emphasized, cartel prices are hard to maintain without close control over supply.

By mid-1975, top Brazilian and Colombian officials were back in the United States, exploring the possibility of renewing a worldwide coffee pact.

Put yourself in two different roles in this case:

1. Suppose you were a Brazilian or Colombian government official. What position would you take?

   a. Let your individual coffee producers battle it out in the free market, winning customers away from other nations as best they could by price cuts or other competitive moves?

   b. Try to re-form the coffee cartel among the

[8] Several other international cartels (bauxite, phosphates, bananas, copper, and tin) were activated at about the same time.

major producers, building in stronger safeguards against price cutters?

c. Try to get the United States, other larger consumers, and other producers to join in a new international coffee agreement in the hope that it would both stabilize coffee prices and keep them at a moderately higher level than would be produced by cutthroat competition?

Whichever position you take, specify the arguments you would use to convince others to support it, and explain how you would implement the plan.

2. Suppose you are the U.S. assistant secretary of state for economic affairs. Would you support formation of a new international coffee agreement? Explain your recommendation to a congressional committee, including details on how you would compromise the interests of the U.S. consumer and the LDC producer. If you oppose renewal of the coffee agreement, indicate how you would explain this country's position to Brazil, Colombia, and other Latin American producers when we so strongly claim that we want to be a good neighbor and help the Latin American nations to develop economically.

CHAPTER 47

AN OVerview: comparative economic systems

What type of economic system serves man best? On the evidence of Tables 1–1 and 46–1, it is private-enterprise, market-directed capitalism. Of the top ten nations in real income per capita, every one has basically this type of economy. But all have recently mixed in a liberal dose of government planning and regulation. Moreover, one-third of the world's people live in Communist nations (mainly China and the USSR), and Soviet Russia is the world's second great industrial and military power. Many of the smaller nations are still hovering as to the type of economy they prefer.

At the end of a long book, devoted mainly to our type of largely private-enterprise system, it is well to look briefly at how other types of economic systems work. Russia is perhaps the most interesting comparison, because it is the world's second most powerful economy and because it exemplifies modern socialism in action in a developed, industrial economy, a major alternative to our type of economic organization. But a look at Japan is also appropriate, because it has been the world's great economic success story since World War II and because it exemplifies a more planned capitalist economy than does the United States. Add to these China, India, and the other LDCs from Chapter 46 and you have the spectrum of economic systems currently on trial, although there are many variations among the other nations.

| Private ownership | { Japan
{ U.S. ————————————————India————————————————————USSR—China | Public ownership |
| Price-directed | U.S. ——————Japan——————India——————USSR——————China | Centrally planned |

CAPITALISM AND COMMUNISM

To look at the economic side of any "ism" alone is to miss its essence.[1] Communism has become inseparably associated with political and economic dictatorship because we see them together in Russia and Mainland China, today's predominant Communist countries. Yet in its original form, Marxian socialism was highly democratic in spirit. Karl Marx's famous *Das Kapital,* the foundation of modern communism, provided a detailed critique of capitalism, but he was conveniently vague when it came to blueprinting the communist economy. Still, one thing is sure. Marx wasn't looking for any political or economic dictatorship except the dictatorship of the proletariat—of the whole working class.

From an **economic** viewpoint, there are two big differences between capitalism and communism. **Under private-enterprise capitalism as we know it, most productive resources are privately owned, and economic activity is largely directed by the interaction of supply and demand in the market. Under communism, conversely, most productive resources are publicly owned, and economic activity is directed largely by central planning; this type of economy is often called a "command economy."** The two critical questions, then, are: (1) Are productive resources privately or publicly owned, and (2) is economic activity directed by individual choice and the price system or by government planning?

Obviously, both are matters of degree. Not all productive resources are privately owned under American capitalism—governments own land,

[1] There are many volumes on comparative economic systems and on the "isms." Two readable ones are G. Grossman, *Economic Systems,* 2nd ed. (Englewood Cliffs, N.J.: Prentice-Hall, 1974); and W. Ebenstein, *Today's Isms* (Englewood Cliffs, N.J.: Prentice-Hall, 1970), which stresses the political-economic mix.

highways, dams, buildings, and so on. Nor are all resources publicly owned in Russia. Also, an economy can have private ownership of resources and nevertheless be centrally planned. The American economy during World War II was a partial example. Hitler's fascism in Germany was a more complete example. India makes substantial use of central planning today, with primarily private ownership of resources.

Thus, economic systems fall along a spectrum on both these conditions, something like the arrangement shown in the diagram. The location of the countries is only approximate, but it is intended to suggest the variation on the two scores. The American and Russian systems differ widely on both. They are thus especially worth careful comparison. But don't forget that most of the world's economies lie in between, on one or both of the spectrums shown. Nor is Russia at the extreme of communism; today, China is a purer example.

The following pages include an analysis and evaluation of how the Soviet economy operates—and a running comparison with the way the American economy accomplishes the same tasks. There is also a final brief look at Japan as an in-between economy. A major purpose is to help you focus your own understanding and evaluation of the American economy.

HOW DOES THE SOVIET ECONOMY WORK?
Objectives

The modern Soviet economy rests on the doctrines of Marx. "From each according to his abilities, to each according to his needs," was Marx's foundation for communist society. The rule of the masses, with productive resources owned by the state and used for the common benefit of all, remains, on paper, the foundation of the modern communist economies—of China as well as the USSR.

The goals stressed by modern Communist leaders look very much like those stated by Americans—improved living standards, economic growth, more leisure, freedom, security, elimination of poverty. From these words, it is hard to distinguish Russia from the Western democratic societies.

In fact, the USSR appears to most outsiders to be a "command" economy, with the big commands issued by a small group of Communist officials over whom the people have little control. Centralization of political power in Russia is especially significant for our economic survey, because all basic economic plans and policies are made by the controlling political group. Even after recent steps to decentralize planning and control, among the major nations the Soviet economy is still the most highly planned and controlled, save that of Communist China. In America, we leave everyone relatively free to use his private property and his income as he wishes within the law, and we accept the outcome as being by and large the best one for the public welfare. The Russian leaders decide what they want to happen economically, and they use a comprehensive system of plans and controls to make it happen.

So much for Russia's stated objectives and approach. How do the Soviets go about solving the four big problems that all economies face?[2]

(1) Deciding what to produce and
(2) Getting it produced

In the USSR, the central planners decide what is to be produced. After the Russian revolution of 1917–18, the Communists made an almost fatal mistake. They assumed that central economic control was easy—that all they had to do was to confiscate private productive resources, tell people what to produce, and everything would go along nicely. It didn't! Russian total output in 1919–20 dropped back to near the 1890 level. The Russian peasants didn't see why they should produce just to have their crops taken away and given to someone else. There

[2] Two good studies of the Russian economy are Robert Campbell, *Soviet Economic Power* (Boston: Houghton Mifflin, 1973); and Alex Nove, *The Soviet Economy* (New York: Praeger, 1968).

was virtually no modern industrial capacity. The economy was thrown into chaos.

The central planners made many mistakes, but they learned. After years of experimentation and a series of "five-year plans" for economic development since 1928, the Soviets have developed this general pattern:

First, the basic policy decisions are made by the central Communist authorities—which industries to develop, which to let lag, how much to allocate for consumption, how much for industrial expansion, how much for the military. Then the lower-level planners map out detailed directions for units in the economy to follow in implementing these decisions. Last, these plans have to be carried out by millions of officials, managers, and workers throughout Russia.

This process has been modified many times. In recent decades, the Communists have become increasingly aware of the problems of centrally planning and controlling a vast economy, and since Stalin's death in 1952, controls have been substantially liberalized. Especially since 1965, the Soviets have admitted having serious problems with their top-heavy planning mechanism, and they have both substantially decentralized authority to plant and industry managers and placed more reliance on market prices and consumer demands to guide production. But the big decisions are still made by the central planners.

Making the plan

The broad goals for the economy are set by the Praesidium and the Central Committee of the Communist party. Since 1928, the goals have been contained in a series of comprehensive five-year plans. The tenth plan, for 1976–80, calls for an annual growth rate of 6 percent in industrial production and $4\frac{1}{2}$ to 5 percent in national income. While early plans concentrated on military output and industrial growth, recently more weight has been given to satisfying consumer wants.

Within these broad objectives, the plan for each year is developed by the Gosplan (State Planning Commission), working with a huge Central Statistical Administration, which provides data on available resources and productive capacities. Their job is immense. Suppose you had to plan only aircraft. How would you plan production of all the hundreds of thousands of components that go into a modern airplane, scheduling each to be on hand when it was needed? Now back up and decide how you would plan the production of all the sub-components to produce the parts you need for the airplanes. By now you'll be up in the millions of individual decisions, just for one major product. And the complexities multiply geometrically when you add other products, because of all the interlinkages between materials, labor, and manufacturing facilities needed. It's this vast complex of decisions that we leave to supply and demand in the marketplace in our private-enterprise economy. And this complexity has led the Soviets into more and more trouble as their economy has grown. How do they do it now?

First, they don't start from scratch each year. They use last year as a bench mark, which greatly simplifies the task. Second, the Gosplan apparently focuses each year primarily on some fifty basic products and industries that are of critical importance in attaining the prime goals of the overall plan.[3] They apparently then construct for some 1,500 major commodities (industries) a materials balance, a labor balance, and a geographical balance. These show the materials, labor, and other resources needed to produce the desired output throughout the economy. By combining these balances for all major products, they have a reasonably complete picture of the overall materials, labor, facilities, and regional balances for the entire economy. From this "input-output" model, they can see roughly where there are likely to be material shortages, where labor surpluses, and so on, and they can then adjust accordingly.

Once the broad outline of an annual plan is completed, it is sent to regional and industry councils throughout the economy. They check their quotas against the productive capacities in their region or industry to see whether the plan appears feasible. If they think the quotas are too high, or if they believe their tentative allocations of materials and equipment would be inade-

[3]During World War II, when the U.S. industrial economy was extensively but by no means completely planned, the whole planning process hinged largely on allocation of three major materials—steel, copper, and aluminum.

quate to meet them, they have the right to protest—and they do! Local plant managers often argue that the goals are too high and that inadequate raw materials and machinery are being allocated to meet them. The local workers may protest that they are already speeded up to the limit of their capacity. Then it's a subject for negotiation with the regional and industry-level planners, and after that between them and the national planners at the Gosplan. The Soviet planning process involves a lot of talk. Some observers have called it the most gigantic collective-bargaining process in history.

Finally, all this information gets reflected back to Moscow, where the Gosplan must settle on the final plan so that everything balances out for the whole economy. The planners do the best they can, using some modern mathematical and electronic computer techniques, and making adjustments to accommodate the major goals.

The final stage, after the plan has been approved by top Communist officials, is to send it back down to the regional and industry councils for implementation.

We know the planners make mistakes. Plans are continuously adjusted. If the small-machinery plan runs into labor shortages while that for electric light globes turns up a surplus, the planners don't wait until next year to make an adjustment. This doesn't make for a quiet life among Gosplan employees or for managers throughout the economy, and the number of adjustments has apparently snowballed in recent years as the Russian economy has grown in complexity. Complaints from below have become increasingly bitter. Industry plans are changed dozens of times a year. These crises have led the pragmatic rulers in the Kremlin to consider delegating more responsibility and freedom to local managers in carrying out the broad goals handed down from above.

Carrying out the plan

The annual plan is a *physical* blueprint for the use of productive resources and the production of intermediate and final goods for the year. How do the Soviets get their plans carried out? In essence, by telling people what to do and by paying them for doing it.

Managerial incentives.   Under the early plans, each plant manager received a production *quota*, together with detailed information on the supply of materials he would receive, the equipment that would be allocated to him, the labor he was to use, and so on. Then it was up to him to get the final product out. His job was to meet the quota, not to question why. If he exceeded his quota, he was praised by the party and received substantial economic rewards, including money, better housing, a car, paid vacations, and other benefits not available except through the official reward system. These are powerful incentives in a low-consumption society. On the other hand, if his plant ended the year below quota, or if he required more labor and materials than were allocated to him, the rewards went the other way.

The Soviets are thoroughly aware of the importance of good managers to the success of their plans. Managers are among the highest-paid. They receive medals and public commendation for exceeding quotas. The Soviets are also harsh critics when managerial performance falls short. Good managers are very important under communism, the Soviets have found, just as they are under capitalism.

But the Soviets have had major problems on managerial incentives. Because rewards depended mainly on meeting physical output quotas, managers concealed production possibilities in order to get lower quotas, hoarded materials, and avoided doing too well lest quotas be raised for next year. There was no penalty for wasteful use of materials or manpower as long as it didn't violate the plan.

"Blat" (using influence with higher-ups in industry) and "tolkachi" (special purchasing agents from plants who go around buying up scarce materials and parts outside the plan) are well known, if technically illegal, parts of the Russian industrial scene. Russian managers have learned to make their own performances look good by hoarding labor and materials, bootlegging scarce materials outside the plan, and even fudging the basic performance reports on which they are judged. This is not utterly different from the American case, where local managers sometimes try to make their own units look good by devices that reduce rather than increase total corporate profits. Either way, it's tough to make middle managers stick to top-level plans. But in America, the dollars and cents on the income statement at year-end, the percentage return on investment, and the per-share earnings for the stockholders provide visible measures that facilitate evaluation of management performance.

Innovation has been another special managerial problem. New ideas involve risks, and the Soviet system has lacked effective rewards for risk taking. In the Soviet climate, doing reasonably well is more conducive to the manager's peace of mind than taking a chance on a new idea that may flop. There's nothing like the American private-enterprise entrepreneur out to make a million (or go broke) in a gamble on a new product or new method. Soviet criticism of managers for lack of imaginative innovation has been bitter.

"Profits" and the new look in Soviet planning.   As the central planning process increasingly bogged down and as inefficiences piled up at the local level, in the 1960s the Soviets began to question whether more reliance on a kind of "profit motive" for individual managers couldn't help the planners avoid the local wastes of physical planning and increase total output. In 1965, the Communists announced an experiment that freed managers in the shoe and food-processing industries from planned quotas, and directed them to maximize their profits, much as in America, with their own bonuses based on the profits they made. Each manager was substantially free to set the price of his product and the wages he paid, and to choose his own production methods. The profits themselves, above the special awards to the successful manager, of course reverted to the state. In the following years, apparently about one-third of all consumer-goods production was shifted to such a plan.

But the new look inevitably raised basic issues. Local managers free to bid resources away from others came into conflict with central-plan goals. Thus, in 1973 another major reform was announced. Recognizing that dispersion of authority to 50,000 local managers didn't work satisfactorily under the general planning process, the Soviets combined much of the economy into intermediate-level industry corporations, or production associations, for major industries. Managers of these industry production centers apparently have some freedom to attempt to maximize "profits" for their industries, and they assumed much of the planning function for their industries. Most individual plants have become, in effect, operating divisions of the new corporations, with the decision-making powers granted to factory managers in 1965 now given to the corporations. The central planning ministries set basic goals for these industries, determine investment and technological improvements, and establish overall policies.

The problem of how much decentralization of decision-making and operating authority is optimal remains unsettled in the USSR. The problem is similar to that faced by a large American corporation like GM. In America, decentralizing decision making and authority to local "profit centers," under only broad rules from headquarters, is now widely accepted as the best way to maintain local managerial initiative and to couple the advantages of central corporate planning with local, firsthand management. But in the USSR, Gosplan still makes the basic plans and the blueprints for carrying them out for most of the economy.

Labor incentives and labor unions. How do the Soviets get the workers to carry out their plans? Just as in the United States, money is the big incentive, but it is supplemented by continuous emphasis on national pride and party loyalty for members.

The planners decide how much should be paid for each type of work, and they do it so as to get the plan carried out effectively. The biggest pay goes to scientists, artists, inventors, and managers who overproduce their quotas. About 75 percent of all industrial workers are on "piece rates," whereby each worker gets paid according to how much he turns out. This is a much higher percentage than in the United States. Money wages thus play much the same role in pulling labor into jobs and stimulating good performance as they do in America, **except** that in Russia they are set by the planners to channel workers where the planners want them, rather than by market supply and demand. It is striking that money incentives—differential pay for workers turning out more output—are used more strongly than in such capitalist countries as the United States. And resulting pay differentials for **workers** are **wider** in the USSR than here, where union pressures have tended to lessen them.

How free are Soviet workers to work where they wish? Substantially free, given the immobility inevitably associated with low incomes and limited geographical mobility—except for farm workers, who are needed to expand farm output, and workers who have been "recruited" for special projects or have received special training or education at state expense. The complaints of managers about labor turnover suggest that labor moves from job to job with considerable freedom; labor turnover was reported at 20 percent in the early 1970s. The main coercion used to hold workers in particular jobs is preference on desirable housing, which may be lost if the worker leaves. With a nationwide housing shortage, this is a powerful incentive.

Most Soviet workers belong to unions. But they are quite different from unions in America. Soviet unions have nothing to do with setting wages. The unions are worker organizations that are expected to help in implementing government plans. As such, they apparently have a substantial role in urging workers to meet quotas and in channeling labor from surplus to shortage occupations. But they are more like workmen's clubs than like the unions we know. Make your own comparison with the role of unions in America, where there is far more union power—and far more conflict.

Checking on performance: the Gosbank and the state control commission. The Gosplan also makes up a complete set of "value" (or financial) plans to parallel the basic physical plans. Using these financial plans, the Gosbank (state banking system) provides money to managers to pay for labor and materials to carry out the production plans. For example, if the annual plan calls for ten million pairs of shoes, the Gosbank provides shoe-plant managers just enough rubles to pay for the labor, leather, and so on, allocated to the production of those shoes. It does the same for all other products. And managers must deposit their receipts in the Gosbank, except for cash payments made to workers. Except for wages and citizens' purchases of consumer goods, transactions in Russia are made by check through the Gosbank.

The Gosbank plays two significant roles. First, it provides a financial control over managers. If they run out of money, this is a sign they are buying more than the inputs allocated to them under the physical plan. And because they can get materials and labor only by paying for them, the control is close and effective. When the manager deposits his receipts in the Gosbank, this provides an automatic check on whether he has produced the amount specified in the plan. How much this financial control is being relaxed under the 1973 reforms remains to be seen. Second, the Gosbank provides a regular banking function, transferring funds, advancing working capital, and creating money for the economy.

Thus, in some respects, the Gosbank with its local branches is like banks in the United States. But it is strictly government-operated, and its main goal is to help implement the physical plan. It advances new checking accounts (creates money) when they are needed to facilitate production, and it reduces funds to industries that have been absorbing too much labor or material.

How does this checking on performance compare with the private-enterprise process? In America, too, the availability of funds exercises a basic control over what is done and who does it. In America, the firm continuously gets funds from selling its product; thus, consumers (rather than the government) exercise a continuous check on whether any firm is doing its job effectively. If a firm wants to expand, it must either have stored up its own profits or it must go to the competitive capital market for funds. There, its project is evaluated by bankers, private investors, and other lenders against alternative demanders of funds. If the firm's prospects look good, it will get loans; if they look bad, it will have trouble raising funds. The capital market controls who can expand and who cannot.

Which process is more effective? It obviously depends on your point of view. Who should check on whom? The Soviet procedure gives direct control to the planners through the Gosbank and the control commission. In America, we place most of our faith in the impersonal market, where consumers, lenders, and business firms are counted on to look out for their own capital and incomes and thereby to get resources allocated most effectively. The socialists say that under capitalism, capital is rationed out by monopolistic lenders to big, favored borrowers. But even fewer officials decide who gets the capital to expand in the USSR. Think back to the chapters on monopoly and competition and on the American banking system to decide how much weight to give this criticism.

The recalcitrant problem of agriculture. Agriculture has been the Communists' knottiest problem. Their early attempts to collectivize Russian agriculture, carried through by bloody force during the 1920s and 1930s, met bitter and sullen resistance. Forced to work on collective farms, farmers produced less than before and kept crops and animals for themselves rather than turning them over to the authorities for export to the cities. Frustrated Communist planners tried one tack, then another—but with little success in meeting expanded food goals for the rapidly growing industrial population or in freeing farm labor for industrial jobs.

In theory, a collective farm is a cooperative, democratic association of farmers who have pooled their land, tools, and labor to make a large farm, which they operate in common. Proceeds are shared in proportion to the quantity and quality of work they do. Large-scale operation produces the economies of large-scale mechanized farming, eliminating the waste and inefficiency that for centuries characterized Russian agriculture.

It sounds fine, but not to the peasants. Soviet planners found crops vanishing into farm consumption and total production declining. Bloody reprisals brought only temporary compliance and smoldering resentment. Over millions of acres and widely scattered farmers, effective control was impossible.

There are now some 100,000 collective and state farms, compared to perhaps 25 million small peasant farms four decades ago. About 5,000 of these are huge state farms of many thousand acres, operated outright as "business" firms by the Ministry of Agriculture in much the same pattern as prevails for industrial production. The rest are collective farms, ranging from a few "communes" (which involve complete sharing of property, labor, and results) to many cases where the collective farm is scarcely more than a sharing of major machinery and some exchange of labor. In most cases, part of the land is farmed collectively but each family retains a small plot for its own individual operation. These private plots make up only 5–10 percent of the total land under cultivation, but they apparently produce nearly one-third of total farm output of vegetables, eggs, meat, milk, and other products that are suited to labor-intensive production and that can be sold in small lots on uncontrolled markets, which exist throughout Russia.

Payments to farmers are calculated on a complicated basis. For work on collective farms, they receive partly payment in kind and partly money income that varies above a guaranteed minimum depending on how much they produce. Apparently about a third of total output is delivered directly to the state, about a third is used on the farms for further output (seed, feed for animals, and so on), and about a third is given to the farmers themselves. A substantial portion of the last finds its way onto the free market for food consumption in the cities. This supply is augmented by products from the millions of small family holdings, as indicated above. Private initiative is far from dead in Russian agriculture.

In any case, agricultural output has persistently lagged far behind the plan goals, in spite of one reform after another. Most outsiders estimate that since 1950, Soviet farm output has grown no more than 2 or 3 percent a year, if that much. Several times, Russia, historically a large wheat exporter, had to import large quantities of wheat for food. Food output per capita has barely held stable over the last decade.

The importance of agriculture in Russia is great. A quarter of the Russian labor force is in agriculture—over 30 million compared to only 3 million in the United States. Yet U.S. total farm output exceeds Russia's. One American farmer can feed nearly 60 people, one Russian farmer only seven. Low productivity in agriculture is the Communists' number one production problem.

(3) Deciding how income is to be distributed

Marxist doctrine says, To each according to his need. The Soviet leaders today season this liberally with, To each according to how hard he works and how much he contributes. Incomes are more equally distributed than in the United States, because in Russia income **from property** is very limited, whereas many of the highest American incomes are from dividends, interest, and capital gains on private property. There are no millionaires in modern Russia. But money incomes derived **from work** are about as unequally distributed in Russia as in America. This inequality reflects the strong use of incentive payments to achieve the central planners' goals.

Artists, scientists, professors, managers, and government officials receive the highest incomes, including special supplements in premium housing, use of government autos, paid vacations, and so on. As in America, common labor is at the bottom of the totem pole—except for farmers, many of whom in Russia take much of their incomes in kind from their farms. Within the ranks of factory workers and comparable laborers, apparently the spread between the lowest and highest monthly incomes is nearly one to eight, *wider* than in America.

The Soviets adjust wage rates up and down frequently for different occupations and industries, to help implement the overall plan. The planners may be good Marxists on paper, but their behavior on wages suggests that they have learned a good deal about the power of monetary incentives.

Government services and income redistribution. Although it uses money incentives freely to stimulate production and to allocate resources, the state provides widespread free social services to help the masses. Soviet authorities claim that one-third of the income of low-income groups is provided by free government services. Nearly all housing is government-owned, and rents are extremely low; on the average, Soviet citizens apparently pay only about 2–3 percent of their income for housing, far under the 15–25 percent common in America. A Moscow two-bedroom apartment rents for $20–$30 a month—if you can find one. Russian housing is generally bad, but it's very cheap. Paid vacations, government nurseries, special grants to large families, free education, and extensive health services all supplement money incomes.

But to evaluate these government services, we have to ask, Who pays for them? A general sales (turnover) tax accounts for over half of all government income. Profits on state enterprises provide most of the rest. Direct personal taxes (mainly an income tax) take only 8 percent of personal income. All told, government collections and expenditures comparable to our combined federal-state-local government taxes and expenditures are apparently about 35–40 percent of GNP, although estimates vary substantially.

The turnover tax and state profits vary widely from product to product and from year to year. Increases and decreases in the tax are used to adjust the prices of individual products up and down to discourage or to stimulate consumption. This way, the planners make consumer demand match the goods produced, somewhat as free-market prices provide this adjustment in the United States. This tax, therefore, substantially offsets the apparent big government supplement to low incomes.

On the other hand, the Soviets use especially low prices on some major commodities in addition to housing to subsidize low-income consumers. This means that such goods are sold below "cost." Prices are set very high on such luxuries as autos. Here again, pricing is used to promote the goals that seem important to the planners.

(4) Deciding between current consumption and economic growth

In America, the choice between current consumption and economic growth depends on consumer and business saving, business investment decisions, private educational and research decisions, and government tax and investment behavior. In Russia, the decision is made and implemented by the central planners. And their choice has been in favor of rapid industrialization and growth, at the expense of current consumption.

Since the early 1920s, Russia's GNP has grown at about 4 percent annually, about the same as the U.S. rate. Soviet growth during the 1950s was spectacular—about double that rate—but it has slowed down persistently since then. To press its postwar growth, the USSR allocated an extraordinarily large portion of its output to capital formation, and Soviet military expenditures now exceed ours, although their GNP is only about 55 percent of ours. Soviet consumption was so repressed that per capita real consumption was no higher in 1958 than it had been in 1928; only since about 1960 has the average Russian benefited much through higher consumption from the last half century of economic growth. But this Soviet policy produced an average annual increase of 10 percent in the Russian capital stock, which went far to account for rapid Soviet growth—aided by her ability to borrow a large amount of technology from the West, and a rapid growth in the labor force.

The decline in Russian growth since 1960 has reflected in substantial part a decline in the capital accumulation rate, as more resources were allocated to satisfying consumer wants. Even with central planning and control rather than individual choice and the price system, Russia faces the same fundamental problem in growth as does any other economy—she must divert scarce resources from consumption to investment, improve her technology, and step up the ability and performance of her labor force. There is no other way, for either communism or capitalism. As post-Stalin liberalization has opened up the Soviet economy to Western standards and Western ideas, the pressure has intensified on Communist leaders for more consumption goods.[4]

How fast the Russian economy grows depends on the decisions of the central planners, but it also depends on fundamental political forces—on how long the population will be con-

---

[4]Under Marxist doctrine, only labor is truly productive. Thus, interest on money or real capital plays no role in communist doctrine. Western economists properly point out that this position, if followed, will lead Soviet planners to improper decisions in allocating resources—to waste capital if they underprice it. But the pragmatic Soviet planners (who are smart fellows too) are now slipping the interest rate into their calculations through the back door.

tent to see most of the increased output go into capital expansion and military products. In the American economy, the public speaks on this division continuously, through its own savings–spending behavior and through its directions to congressmen on government spending and taxes. Under the Soviet system, there is little evidence that the man in the street has much voice in the decisions. Yet the Soviet leaders constantly face the need to keep the masses reasonably content if they are to stay in power. Recent increases in consumption-goods output attest to this concern.

No reliable estimates of total Soviet expenditure on research are available, but apparently, with a national income about half ours, Russia spends about as much as we do on basic research.

Government monetary and fiscal policy and economic stabilization

The Soviet central planners do not program men or machines into unemployment. If there is unemployment, it is because planning has gone awry or because someone is not behaving according to plan. And there has been very little official unemployment in the USSR. But there is still the problem of keeping total spending power roughly equal to goods available for purchase. If buying power gets too large, inflationary pressures will mount. If buying power is too low, prices must be cut or unsold inventories will pile up.

The Soviets manage this balance largely through the turnover tax (fiscal policy) and the Gosbank (monetary policy), the same two tools we use. In Russia, most of the burden falls on the turnover tax. If total demand is excessive, the turnover tax is raised all along the line, or on those products where demand seems most excessive, raising prices and siphoning off income to the government. If total demand is inadequate, turnover taxes are lowered. In a real sense, the Russians have adopted "functional finance" as the core of their stabilization and allocation mechanism.

In spite of this plan, inflation has been a persistent problem for the Soviets. The Russians are human beings too, and when there isn't enough to go around, they apparently tend to

plan a little more resources for all the demands than there are to parcel out. The result is a demand pressure that tends to bid up prices all along the line as shortages occur; black markets spring up everywhere. The basic pressures that make for inflation—shortage of goods relative to the purchasing power provided by incomes paid out—are the same in communist and capitalist societies.

COMMUNISM AND CAPITALISM IN PERSPECTIVE

How well have communism and capitalism done in the USSR and the United States? To answer, we must specify criteria for judgment. It may be convenient to use the five suggested in Chapter 1, but if you prefer others, use your own.

Progress—rising living standards

Which economic system has provided the higher standard of living for its people? However you measure, the United States is far out in front. In 1975, the U.S. GNP was $1.5 trillion. The USSR's, with a vastly larger area and forty million more people, was only about 55 percent as large. Per capita GNP, a more significant measure of individual economic well-being, was $7,000 in the United States, $2,700 in the USSR. Such comparisons may be substantially off because of measurement problems and currency-conversion difficulties. Some observers put Russian per capita incomes as high as half ours, but not more.

The Soviets have made impressive headway since they took over in the 1920s. Table 47–1 presents data comparing U.S. and USSR performance on a variety of scores. While total USSR output is less than 60 percent of ours, in 1975 (a recession year in the United States), Soviet steel, coal, and oil production surpassed ours, reflecting the longtime Soviet emphasis on expanding industrial output. But on food, consumer goods, and indeed just about everything else, the U.S. lead is large. Some important variables are hard to summarize in a simple table. Soviet housing is appallingly poor. Over a third

Table 47–1

How the giants compare (1975)

	United States	USSR
Gross national product (bil. U.S. dollars)	1,500	870
Per capita GNP (U.S. dollars)	7,070	2,700
Grain production (bil. bushels)	10	5.6
Electricity (bil. kw-hours)	1.9	1.0
Steel production (mil. tons)	117	155
Crude-oil production (mil. barrels)	3,056	3,440
Coal production (mil. tons)	643	770
Telephones per capita	.64	.06
National defense (bil. U.S. dollars)	90	95 (est.)
Refrigerators per family	.99	.25
Autos per hundred people	50	2
TV sets per family	2	.7
Doctors per 100,000 population	178	365
Average workweek (hours)	36.3	40.6
Months' earnings to buy a car	4.3	51
Annual hard liquor consumed per adult (qts.)	4.5	8

of all city families still live in a single room, sharing a kitchen and bath with others. Food for the masses is adequate, but has little variety. Life in the USSR is repeatedly described as drab.

Although the Soviets publish higher figures, most Western observers place the Soviet growth rate in real GNP at 6–6½ percent from World War II to the 1960s. Since then, the rate has dropped gradually, to around 4 percent for the 1970s; and even the official Russian plan only calls for 4½–5 percent for the last half of this decade, about that expected by the West European non-Communist countries. In perspective, the earlier rapid communist growth reflected very high investment while consumption was suppressed; a large increase in the industrial labor force as workers shifted from low-productivity agriculture and most women entered the labor force; and widespread borrowing of technology from the Western economies. But a more open society has recently led to more consumers goods and lower investment. By the 1960s, over 90 percent of the able-bodied population, including women, was either in the labor force or going to school; the labor force grew from 97 million in 1950 to 135 million in 1975; further increases will be difficult. As Soviet industry caught up in technology with other nations, this

source of growth also faded. Explanation of the high Soviet growth rate in past years thus appears to be much like that for capitalist countries, and the reasons for the recent Soviet slow-down also look much like those found in maturing capitalist nations. With the end of their special growth advantages, the Soviet rate of growth will depend heavily on their ability to maintain high growth in productivity (output per man-hour).

One last comparison. Some critics argue that GNP per capita is an inadequate measure of economic well-being. They are right. GNP doesn't take into account leisure, such real costs as pollution, and a variety of other factors, noted in Chapter 8. But as best we can tell, the USSR is no better off than we are on these unmeasured factors. Their press and their officials complain about water, air, and noise pollution, much as we do. Inclusion of leisure in GNP would clearly *worsen* Russia's relative position. Although the industrial workweek is about the same in both countries, a much larger proportion of the total population, including women, works in Russia. No other non-GNP factor would appear to change the relative standard of living comparison much; if we could construct a Russian measure of net economic welfare, it would probably relate to GNP about the way ours does.

Individualism and consumer control—
dispersion of economic power

Clearly, the American economy produces the biggest economic pie for consumers and for growth. How does it rate in giving the individual citizen control over what is produced, over the allocation of productive resources?

In Russia, the Communist central planners, not the consumers, decide what is to be produced. Consumers have substantially free choice in spending their money—but they can spend it only on goods available and at the prices set by the planners. The American system surely responds more directly to consumer demands if we take their dollar votes as guides. About three-fourths of our GNP is allocated through the private economy, pretty much in response to consumers' dollar demands. Our market system responds to consumer demands far from perfectly. Varying degrees of monopoly and monopsony through the economy impede allocation of resources in accord with the purely competitive ideal. Businesses influence what consumers "want" through advertising and other selling techniques. Social costs and social benefits not mirrored in market prices and costs distort resource allocation. But overall, consumer choice is *the* powerful director of economic production in our basically market-directed, unplanned economy. And our democracy, although far from perfect in meeting the one-man-one-vote ideal, surely comes closer than the Soviets do to democratic control over resources allocated through the public sector.

Equity and inequality

Which system does a better job in slicing up the national economic pie equitably among competing claimants? Much depends on how you define *equity*. Is more equality of income always more equitable? Or does equity mean equality of opportunity, rather than results? Or are incomes in proportion to services rendered the equitable ideal?

By substantially eliminating incomes from property, the Communists have eliminated most of the very high incomes of capitalistic systems. *Worker* money incomes, on the other hand, are more unequally distributed than in the United States, but then somewhat equalized by subsidized government services and pricing policies. This fact reflects the heavy emphasis placed on both monetary work incentives and government assurance of essentials by the Communists.

American incomes are somewhat unequal—more so than in some countries, less so than in others. America has a few very rich, and a lower tenth who are poor by our standards, although well-off by the standards of most nations. But the emergence of a huge, reasonably well-to-do middle class is the most striking development of recent American economic history. The clash between equality of economic results and equality of economic opportunity is one of the most basic in modern America. While more equality of incomes is a widespread American goal, many Americans prefer a mixture of more equality of opportunity and reward for services rendered, stressing that issues of equity and economic incentives are inseparable in the real world. If we want to live comfortably and be able to level up very low incomes, effective incentives to work and invest are essential, they argue. Remember the Russian experience that individual money rewards seem to be a more powerful economic incentive than the Communists used to admit. Any income redistribution that reduces total output is very hard to defend. Table 46–1 showed how growth in the Western market-directed economies has dominated all distributional issues. Even the poor at the bottom of the income scale in the highly productive Western economies have higher incomes than the middle-income citizens in the command-type economies. Individual initiative motivated by individual reward has been the foundation of most successful economic growth in the nineteenth- and twentieth-century world.

Individual freedom

The American economy provides almost complete freedom on where to work, where to live, how to spend your money, and other economic choices. The freedom to go into business for yourself is completely unmatched in the Soviet system. American unions are a powerful device for equalizing the economic power of employers and employees. Government taxes are heavy, and to this extent economic freedom may be said to be curtailed—although less so than in Russia and in other highly developed nations.

How much "economic freedom" the Soviet economy provides for the individual depends on what you mean by the phrase. Today, the Soviet citizen has considerable freedom to move to another job and to spend his income on whatever he can find to buy. But the government determines what goods will be available for purchase and indirectly tells him where he should work. America has nothing like the Soviet insistence that workers stay on farms in spite of low incomes there. Further, Russian unions have no voice in determining the wages at which the citizens will work. Nor have the Soviets shown concern for their minorities and dissenters that compares favorably with the American record. Concern for human rights goes far beyond economics, but the economic component is an important one.

Security

Is economic security freedom from the fear of unemployment? of arbitrary discharge? of poverty and disaster in old age or ill health? Is economic security separable from political security?

How economic security is defined will partly determine the rating of the American and Soviet systems on this score. By one test, the Soviet citizen is secure economically. He is assured of a minimum of public services and of a job if he works reasonably hard and conforms to the rules of the leaders in power. In a planned economy, workers aren't planned into unemployment (although Westerners observe that misdirected planning often involves large-scale waste of misallocated workers). The Soviets believe their system provides more economic security than does capitalism, where (to them) the worker lives in constant fear of discharge by the all-powerful capitalist and of unemployment in periodic depressions.

The United States has moved a long way toward similar security (see Chapter 37). Our Social Security system, including Medicare and Medicaid, now offers protection against most types of economic insecurity likely to strike older individuals. And private pension plans are now widespread. But beyond these, the great protection to economic security in the American system is the jobs and high per capita incomes that make it possible for workers to look out for themselves. Still, the capitalist system has some unwanted insecurity that will persist until we learn to eliminate recessions and inflations, a problem not unique to America.

How much security *should* an economic system provide? Many Americans believe the system ought to deal out big rewards to those who work hard and "produce," and that those who don't produce have no right to guaranteed economic security. This is the incentive that has made the American economic system a success, they argue, and to substitute guaranteed economic security would undermine the very foundation of the system. But most voters disagree, arguing that elimination of unnecessary insecurity will make our system work better—and even if it didn't, we can now well afford the cost of reasonable economic security.

PLANNING WITH PRIVATE ENTERPRISE: THE NEW LOOK?

Most of the world's economies lie somewhere between America's private enterprise and Russia's communism. Some, like Japan, are basically private enterprise but with extensive government–industry cooperation and joint planning. Others, like Yugoslavia, are near the communist end of the spectrum, but with a new twist that allows widespread individual initiative and market guidance, with collective ownership of productive resources. Still others, like Sweden and Denmark, are experimenting with limited joint government–private planning and extensive equalization of incomes through government real and money transfers. Most of the world's economies can only be classified as mixed, and to most Americans these mixtures (not communism) are the likely alternatives if we want to change. Japan may be worth special attention, because of her spectacular rise to third place among the world's economies during the postwar years.

JAPAN

Japan is the economic success story of the postwar world. Her growth rate since World War II has been a spectacular 10 percent, and she grew at a rapid, although slower, rate over the preceding century. Before the Meiji era, beginning in 1868, Japan was an isolated, backward, feudal economy. To analyze the Japanese growth performance since would take a book itself. Here, we are primarily interested in the role played by Japan's economic organization—a type of mixed economy that is uniquely Japanese.

Growth experts suggest that Japan's recent performance reflects an unusual set of forces, woven together in a planned national growth policy. (1) Her postwar saving–investment rate has averaged a huge 30–35 percent of GNP, producing an annual growth of 12 percent in the capital stock, while consumption grew relatively slowly. (2) There was a massive shift of labor from low-productivity agriculture to industry, producing a nearly 4 percent annual growth in the nonagricultural labor force. (3) Japan was extraordinarily effective in adapting new technology from the United States and West European economies. (4) She devoted virtually no resources to national defense, and very few to the "welfare" programs that burgeoned in other Western democracies, so taxes were low. (5) She began from a very low post–World War II level. (6) Both laborers and management demonstrated an extraordinarily high level of hard work and skill development. (7) Business–government joint efforts proved especially effective in selling Japanese exports. (8) An unusual program of joint government–industry planning and operations facilitated growth as the nation's number one economic objective. This peculiarly Japanese combined growth effort is worth examination, including some reasons why it seems already to be giving way to more traditional problems.

National commitment to growth

Japan (government officials, industrialists, bankers, workers, just about everyone) has been committed to rapid growth as a keystone of national economic policy. Just how this commitment was achieved is unclear to most Westerners, but it provided the framework for the entire interlinked, coordinated Japanese growth effort. Many outsiders have reported the Japanese extraordinary commitment to common goals, their hard work, and their focus on achieving the goals they set. Private goals are important; the national goal of growth seems even more so.

Government–business relations

The relations between big business and government are very close, peculiarly Japanese, and difficult to describe in Western terms. The giant industrial combines that dominate the economy (*zaibatsu*) both compete vigorously and work together and with the government on plans for domestic and (especially) foreign markets. Japanese profit rates have been high. Direct government intervention in day-to-day business activities has been moderate, probably less than in the United States, although the Japanese government does operate the railroads, the major airline, telecommunications, and the cigarette and salt monopolies. But the government ministries and the Bank of Japan on the one hand and the major business groups on the other comprise a planning net, which interacts closely on major economic decisions for the economy.

Broad economic plans are developed by the Economic Planning Agency, working with business organizations. Some 300 consultative committees of government and trade-association officials work out detailed implementation of these plans. All Japanese industry is organized into trade associations, which in turn combine into a prestigious federation of economic organizations, which represents all industry. Neither government nor business is monolithic. Different government ministries and different industries have different needs and approaches, and the overall plan for the economy carries less weight than do individual industry plans. Yet, as compared to all Western economies, Japanese business and government plan and operate closely together; some American businessmen call the result "Japan, Inc.," as if the nation were one big integrated economic firm.

Japan's spectacular success in world markets shows this cooperation most clearly. The Japanese export offensive produced a 15 percent annual increase in exports during the 1960s. The Japanese Supreme Trade Council is headed by the premier himself; top business executives and government officials personally set export goals. The government backs corporations with special tax incentives and credit facilities. Cartels of Japanese exporters are encouraged to fix prices and make collaborative plans for invading foreign markets. Giant trading companies market Japanese products throughout the world, sometimes at prices substantially below Japanese domestic prices. At the same time, the government has imposed import quotas on a wide range of products and limits foreign investment in Japan in many industries to protect Japanese firms. Little wonder that businessmen in the United States and Europe complain that competing with Japanese exports seems almost impossible, and that they in turn need government help to let them compete on even terms.

Monetary-financial policies for growth

Adequate financing is a first requirement for capital investment. Japanese firms finance most (up to 85 percent) of their investment through bank loans, an extraordinarily high figure. This heavy debt ratio leaves them badly exposed in case the banks ever run short of funds and call their loans. The banks in turn operate with nearly 100 percent of their deposits offset by loans. How can the economy operate so precariously? The answer is that the Bank of Japan (fundamentally, the Japanese government) stands firmly committed to financing rapid growth and to providing the reserves needed to support it through bank loans. This financing system works especially well for the giant *zaibatsu*. Each industrial group is tied closely to a major bank or financial group, which is directly responsible for ensuring finance to the wide-ranging industrial activities of the group, and which also helps to see that financial resources within the *zaibatsu* are channeled to those activities that promise the highest yield.

Because only a few *zaibatsu* dominate much of Japanese industry, it is easy for them and the big banks to work directly with the government and the Bank of Japan in making their plans for expansion and national economic growth. The monetary support for rapid growth has produced persistent inflation, but it is a cornerstone of the Japanese growth policy.

Employment practices and work habits

Japan is the only non-Western economy to industrialize so successfully, but in the process, she has become only partly Westernized. When the typical Japanese factory worker, clerk, or minor manager is employed, it is for life. His salary depends almost entirely on age, education, and seniority, not on his job or productivity. In effect, he becomes a member of that business family for the rest of his life, with both benefits and responsibilities. Strikingly, the system produces high labor productivity. Workers identify closely with their companies, and the Japanese tradition of hard, careful work is strong. Although union membership is about as widespread as in the United States, and union leaders are often left-wing, strikes are rare and generally mild. Since pay and status do not depend on job assignments, managers have great freedom in moving workers among jobs, and employment flexibility is high, in spite of the apparent rigidity of the traditional arrangement. Union work rules and "featherbedding" are almost unknown. Clearly, this employment system can work only with continuing high-level employment; firms would go bankrupt rapidly if they had to keep on paying workers when markets vanished. Again, the system depends on the government's commitment and ability to maintain high employment and rapid growth.

The future of Japanese growth

Has Japan found the key to success through its own brand of mixed economy? The record is impressive, but the OPEC oil crisis and worldwide recession of 1974 hit Japan hard, and for the first time since World War II, her real GNP growth rate fell precipitously, from $+10$ to -2 percent. Domestic sales, exports, and profits all nosedived. Two large industrial firms actually failed and some workers lost their jobs, partly because the central bank sharply reduced the growth rate in the money stock from 30 to 10 percent in order to restrain the inflation that reached 25 percent per annum. Retrenchment became the order of the day. Businessmen, financiers, and government officials were shaken.

Although Japan recovered quickly from her recession, most experts predict slower growth for the future. Inflation has proved a persistent problem to the Japanese as they operate their high-pressure economy. Consumers increasingly press for a bigger share of the growing national output, and the personal savings rate is falling. Workers are less content to follow traditional patterns of work, promotion, and pay. Large supplies of excess farm labor are no longer available. Technology can no longer be borrowed wholesale from the West. Pollution and urban crowding will require investment resources, as in the United States. Stronger retaliation by other nations in foreign markets seems likely. Leftist critics challenge big-business–government domination of economic life, and demand more welfare benefits for the poor. Japan, although still growing lustily, is very unlikely to overtake the United States in total or per capita output, as some journalists have predicted by extrapolating postwar growth rates.[5]

ASPIRATIONS AND ACHIEVEMENTS

Looking back over two centuries, any reasonable observer must be impressed with the achievements of the American economy. But strikingly, our aspirations have risen as fast as our achievements. What was only a hope fifty years ago is taken for granted today, as we insist on ever-higher performance. As fast as total output has grown, our aspirations have grown even

[5] The best study of the postwar Japanese economy is H. Patrick and H. Rosovsky, eds., *Asia's New Giant: How the Japanese Economy Works* (Washington, D.C.: The Brookings Institution, 1976). R. Johnson and W. Ouchi, "Made in America (under Japanese Management)," *Harvard Business Review*, September 1974, provides a fascinating analysis of the effectiveness of traditional Japanese personnel practices, in Japan and in the United States.

faster—for health, national defense, education, housing, consumer goods, electric power, entertainment, travel, care for the aged, clean air and water, consumer protection, minimum incomes, leisure. The list could go on and on.

If America faces a crucial economic problem today, perhaps this is it—that our aspirations (our income demands) exceed our ability to meet them, given our productive resources and the constraints we impose on how we use them. Perhaps it is a "divine discontent" that drives us on to work harder and produce more. Perhaps it is excessive concern with physical things rather than with the quality of life. Perhaps as we become ever more affluent, we will find our wants shifting toward those goods and services that to many exemplify the better life and that require fewer physical resources.

But in the meantime, this excess of demands makes economic scarcity still the number one problem of the American and the world economy, generates social and political frictions that threaten domestic stability and international peace, and jeopardizes the ability of aggregate-demand measures to ensure both high employment and stable prices. Closely related is the fact that many Americans now support "welfare" and income-maintenance programs aimed at ensuring more equal incomes for all, in contrast to our traditional emphasis on equality of opportunity. How we resolve the potential clash between economic incentives and the new concept of equity is one of the major unanswered questions of American democratic capitalism— and probably of the other Western industrial democracies as well. Indeed, the big economic problems facing the United States today are strikingly similar to those facing the other major democracies. The need to provide adequate monetary demand, which was the great economic lesson of the 1930s, is no longer a major problem. The supply side of the aggregate-demand–supply equation is again the central problem in modern economic policy.

Some nations, like Sweden and Denmark, appear to have compromised these competing socio-economic claims effectively, at least for the time being. Others, like the United Kingdom, currently face disruptive economic and social tensions that may precipitate major changes in the country's traditional political and economic arrangements. Some thoughtful observers question whether democratic capitalism can survive the strains of excess claims by powerful competing groups, and suggest that more authoritarian political and economic systems are inevitable. But others point to the great achievements of the modern democratic economies as the path toward higher living standards and a higher quality of life for all, if we will only sensibly combine individual incentives with government planning and more equal distribution of the world's great wealth.

CONVERGENCE OF ECONOMIC SYSTEMS?

Each nation has tried its own approach to economic "rationalization" over the postwar period. Sweden has combined private management with moves to share control between owners and workers, and with extensive government welfare programs to reduce income inequality. Britain has moved toward a pervasive government-sponsored "incomes policy" prescribing growth rates for wages and profits, although without detailed government planning. Even West Germany, commonly considered far over on the private-enterprise side, has done a lot of behind-the-scenes planning. During two postwar decades, 56 percent of Germany's net investment was financed by the government—directly, or indirectly through government loans and special tax privileges to industries that followed policies consistent with the plans for German growth.

Some observers say that these experiments are the new look for the democratic societies—planning combined with private enterprise. Others take a dimmer view. They fear that such planning will be an entering wedge for more government control over the private economy. At first, the plan is voluntary. But after a while, when some private firms or unions decide not to play the roles assigned them under the plan, it is a short step to government mandatory controls. And informal planning sooner or later requires agreement on an "incomes policy," which specifies the shares of the growing GNP that should go to labor and to profits. Cooperative planning has repeatedly collapsed when unions and firms refuse to accept the wage and price holddowns provided in the official plans. What then? is an unsolved problem.

Economists debate whether capitalist and communist economies are converging on a middle ground. No one argues that all nations will soon have identical mixed economies. It is unlikely that Sweden, Russia, Yugoslavia, Japan, and the United States will soon look the same. But after a survey of European economies, Stanford's J.E. Howell and UCLA's Neil Jacoby advance the following two hypotheses:

1. Optimum performance by advanced economies requires a judicious and probably changing blend of central economic management and decentralized competitive market direction.
2. There is an increasing appearance of convergence among the economic management systems of advanced countries.[6]

Time will tell whether Howell and Jacoby are right. Do their hypotheses point the optimal path for the United States?

CONCLUSION

Since the beginning of recorded history, men have sought the perfect society. In the books that fill the libraries, many of these utopias promise peace and plenty for all. But it is a long step from dream to reality. In the real world, the utopias that look best in the writing sometimes turn sour for quite unforseen reasons.

Over the years, some economists have worked out the details of an "ideal" democratic economy. In it, resources would be allocated in accordance with consumer market demands, individuals would be free to work and spend as they wish, state-owned capital resources would be devoted to producing what consumers want, and the proceeds from state enterprises would be distributed among the people to provide as

[6] *European Economics: East and West* (New York: World Publishing Company, 1967).

much income equality as the public desired. This is much like the utopia of the early socialists, with state ownership of resources and operation of enterprise, with political democracy, and with economic implementation through the price system. Its advocates claim it combines the best features of private enterprise and of socialism.

But in the real world, are centralized economic control and democratic freedom in fact compatible? The Russian official blueprint looks surprisingly like this model, but in operation it looks very different. Wise observers have noted that dispersion of economic and political power are usually handmaidens to each other—that centralized economic power and political democracy seldom live long together. If this is true, the attempt to plan and centrally control economic activity toward the goals we want may be a false dream, likely to lead to political and economic slavery rather than to organized plenty.

The economic system must be our servant, not our master, in an effective society. If the society has fundamentally democratic, individualistic ideals, most people must be at heart satisfied with the way the system works—not in detail and all the time, but by and large. Lewis Carroll, in *Alice in Wonderland*, puts his finger tellingly on the basic problem:

. . . the Dodo suddenly called out, "The race is over!" and they all crowded around it, panting, and asking, "But who has won?"

This question the Dodo could not answer without a great deal of thought, and it stood for a long time with one finger pressed upon its forehead . . . while the rest waited in silence. At last Dodo said, "*Everybody* has won, and *all* must have prizes."

In a working democratic society, most must win, and most must have prizes. What shall the prizes be, and how can the economic system keep everyone satisfied with his reward? The American economy provides prizes in abundance, compared with the other nations of the world. And its ability to adapt, without revolution, to the changing demands of the people has been one of its most impressive qualities. Any reasonable evaluation must count it highly successful. But to be pleased should not make us smug. The American economic system is far from perfect. And it will change further over the years ahead, as it adapts to shifting demands and objectives.

You should now be able to do a good share of your own thinking on how the American economy should steer over the years ahead. Economic analysis alone cannot give you answers to the hard problems we face. But it can help greatly to illuminate the way in a changing world.

REVIEW

For analysis and discussion

1. In the light of your study of the American economic system and alternative systems, make a careful list of the major defects, if any, you see in the American system. What, if any, reforms do you think are needed, and how feasible do you think each of your reforms is?
2. During the past half century, the economic climate of the world has shifted toward central economic planning. What factors do you think have been most important in bringing about this change?
3. Recently, the USSR has apparently moved toward a limited profit motive for managers. If this experiment is broadened, do you think it will be compatible with basic planning for the rest of the economy? Explain your answer.
4. Since World War II, four of the nations showing the highest growth rates have been Russia (a Communist state), West Germany (a basically private-enterprise econ-

omy), Japan (a mixed capitalist economy with extensive government intervention), and Yugoslavia (a modified socialist country). How do you account for this fact? Does it indicate that the two types of economic organization are equally fitted for producing continued, rapid growth?

5. In Russia, wages are set by the central planners to keep total purchasing power about in line with the supply of goods to be bought. Would some variant of this plan be a good approach to our problem of avoiding creeping, wage-push inflation? If you think so, defend your answer against the likely attack of a union member.

6. Make a list of those attributes of present-day communist Russia that seem most objectionable to you. How many of these attributes are economic, how many social, how many political?

7. Do you believe the United States should adopt some of the cooperative government–business planning approaches of Japan? What would be the main advantages and disadvantages?

8. What does your economic utopia look like?

APPENDIX TO PART 8

Current research

The less-developed economies. There is a flood of research on the less-developed economies, why they are less-developed, and how they might grow faster. For a starter, try two classics: Albert Hirschman, *Journeys Toward Progress* (Garden City, N.Y.: Doubleday, 1963), on Latin America; or Gunnar Myrdahl, *Asian Drama* (1-vol. ed.) (New York: Twentieth Century Fund, 1971). Derek Healey sums up recent experience in "Development Policy: New Thinking about an Interpretation," *Journal of Economic Literature,* September 1972. On **Communist China,** see *China: A Reassessment of the Economy,* A Compendium of Papers Prepared for the Joint Economic Committee, 1975, especially pp. 1–51. More informal pictures are given by two distinguished American economists: J. Tobin, "The Economy of China: A Tourist's View," and L. Reynolds, "China's Economy: A View from the Grass Roots," in *Challenge,* March 1973 and 1974, respectively. A recent look at **India** is Wilfred Malenbaum's *Modern India's Economy* (Philadelphia: University of Pennsylvania Press, 1971). The World Bank has published studies of the economies of nearly all the LDCs. Last, on the controversial issue of whether the LDCs face an imminent starvation threat, balanced analyses are presented by S. Cochrane, *The World Food Problem* (New York: Thomas Y. Crowell, 1969), and P. Hauser, ed., *The Population Dilemma* (Englewood Cliffs, N.J.: Prentice-Hall, 1969).

The USSR. Two good accounts of Soviet economic planning and performance, in addition to those cited in the chapter, are N. Spulber, *The Soviet Economy* (New York: Norton, 1969), and H. Sherman, *The Soviet Economy* (Boston: Little, Brown, 1969). Marshall Goldman writes of a problem we share with the Soviets, in *The Spoils of Progress: Environmental Pollution in the Soviet Union* (Cambridge, Mass.: M.I.T. Press, 1973); and a noted Soviet economist, T.S. Khachatourov, explains their approach to planning in "Long-Term Planning and Forecasting in the USSR," *American Economic Review,* May 1972. At a more advanced level, A. Bergson's *Planning and Productivity under Soviet Socialism* (New York: Columbia University Press, 1968) provides an authoritative analysis of the planning process; and R. Powell's "Economic Growth in the USSR," *Scientific American,* December 1968, shows how skilled researchers probe such a difficult area.

Comparisons among communist systems. Peter Wiles edits an interesting symposium on the outlook for different national adaptations of communist planning, in *The Prediction of Communist Economic Performance* (New York: Cambridge University Press, 1971). N. Spulber, in *The Economics of Socialism* (Bloomington: Indiana University Press, 1971), puts more stress on ideological differences in comparing different Communist countries. For more detailed studies of individual countries, see C. Mesa-Logo, ed., *Revolutionary Change in Cuba* (Pittsburgh, Pa.: University of Pittsburgh Press, 1971), a volume of somewhat uneven studies on an economy for which we have little reliable information; and D.D. Milenkovitch, *Plan and Market in Yugoslav Economic Thought* (New Haven, Conn.: Yale University Press, 1971).

Cutting across the Soviet and Western "mixed" economies, two studies, *The Red Executive* and *The European Executive* (New York: Doubleday, 1960 and 1963), by Wisconsin's David Granick, draw an intriguing, still-relevant parallel between managerial problems and behavior in the two types of economies.

Last, although to us many of its articles smack more of propaganda than of research, sample the publication, *Problems of Economics,* a monthly translation into English of current papers by leading Soviet economists on all phases of Russian economics and the performance of the Soviet economy.

Other Mixed Economies. On Japan, the best study is the Patrick-Rosovsky volume cited in footnote 5 of Chapter 47. A brief summary is given by R. Komiya, "Economic Planning in Japan," *Challenge,* May 1975. A brief review of how they do it in France is provided by John Sheahan, "Planning in France," *Challenge,* March 1975. For Sweden, A. Lindbeck's *Swedish Economic Policy* (University of California Press, 1974) is an authoritative, more advanced study.

MATHEMATICAL APPENDIXES

In economics, as in many other disciplines, mathematics has important uses. Mathematics provides a convenient, concise language for stating complicated ideas and relationships. It facilitates the analysis of complicated interrelationships and helps in reaching "correct" conclusions from sets of assumptions or premises. It provides a language for stating "models" or theories in a precise way that makes them testable by rigorous statistical analysis of empirical data ("econometrics").

Since an increasing number of college students know some mathematics, these brief appendixes use mathematics (through elementary calculus) to state precisely and rigorously some of the concepts and arguments developed verbally or graphically in the text. Each appendix relates directly to the chapter or section of the text indicated. If you know some mathematics, and especially if you find the language of mathematics a helpful one, the following appendixes may prove a useful supplement to the verbal and graphical exposition of the same ideas in the relevant chapters.

The appendixes show, in very elementary form, how mathematical language and mathematical reasoning can simplify and illuminate the (sometimes complex) interrelationships with which economic analysis must deal. Although a half century ago there were virtually no economists interested in applying mathematical analysis to economic problems, today use of mathematics in economics has become com-

Note: These appendixes were prepared in collaboration with Professor Michael Lovell of Wesleyan University.

monplace; and, as the appendix to Chapter 11 indicates, *econometrics* (the use of mathematically stated models as the basis for quantitative measurement in analysis of economic variables) has become the fastest growing branch of modern economics. The following appendixes give a small indication of how mathematics can help in stating clearly and precisely some of the important concepts and relationships in economics.[1]

[1]If you find these appendixes interesting and want to investigate mathematical economics a bit further, R.G.D. Allen, *Mathematical Economics* (New York: Macmillan, 1956) provides an excellent introduction for students who know calculus. Lawrence Klein's *Introduction to Econometrics* (Englewood Cliffs, N.J.: Prentice-Hall, 1974) is a comparable introduction to the field of econometrics, although it is designed primarily for readers who have also had a course in elementary statistics.

APPENDIX I (to Chapter 5)

DEMAND FUNCTIONS AND ELASTICITY OF DEMAND

The demand curve for any commodity shows how many units will be bought at each price. Looked at another way, it represents the function indicating how price responds to changes in the quantity of a commodity offered for sale, given buyer preferences and incomes, and may be denoted as $p(q)$. [This function might also be denoted by p, or by $f(q)$.] It will be assumed that this function is differentiable.

As is explained in Chapter 5, demand curves are ordinarily negatively sloped; that is, $dp/dq < 0$. This information does not tell precisely how the total revenue obtained by the sellers will respond to changes in price and quantity sold, but simple analysis of the demand function can provide an answer to this important question.

Total revenue, denoted by $r(q)$, is simply price times quantity:

$$r(q) = p(q)q \qquad (I.1)$$

Differentiating with respect to quantity yields

$$\frac{dr}{dq} = p(q) + \frac{dp}{dq}q \qquad (I.2)$$

This derivative, which economists call **marginal revenue,** may be either positive or negative (remember, $dp/dq < 0$). Selling more at a lower price will reduce total revenue if the fall in price is not offset by the increase in the quantity of the commodity purchased; that is, if the demand is inelastic. (Note that this is the same as saying that a reduction in price will increase the number of units sold less than proportionately.)

What level of output with its resulting price would maximize **total revenue** (but not necessarily profits)? We can tell by examining the demand function with the aid of a few rules of elementary calculus. Remember that a necessary condition for a maximum is

that the first derivative of revenue with respect to quantity be zero.

$$\frac{dr}{dq} = p(q) + \frac{dp}{dq}q = 0 \qquad (I.3)$$

This maximum can be defined in terms of the elasticity of the demand function. Economists, following the reasoning on elasticity in Chapter 5, customarily denote elasticity more precisely as[2]

$$\eta = -\frac{dq}{dp} \cdot \frac{p}{q} \qquad (I.4)$$

Thus, when elasticity of demand is unity, revenue is maximized.

If demand is inelastic ($\eta < 1$), note that a reduction in the quantity of the commodity offered on the market would increase total revenue. Thus, a businessman with control over his selling price and output would be foolish to produce at a point where the demand for his commodity is inelastic, for then he could obtain more revenue by producing and selling less!

It is easy to determine graphically the elasticity of demand. Consider the demand curve q^*p^*, first graph below. To find the elasticity of demand at any point a (corresponding to price p and quantity q) we note that $-dq/dp = (q^* - q)/p$; hence

$$\eta = -\frac{dq}{dp} \cdot \frac{p}{q} = \left(\frac{q^* - q}{p}\right)\frac{p}{q} = \frac{q^* - q}{q} \qquad (I.5)$$

From the last equality we see that for a linear demand curve, the elasticity of demand is simply the

[2]If, as for the individual seller under perfect competition, $\frac{dq}{dp} = \infty$, then we say elasticity is infinite.

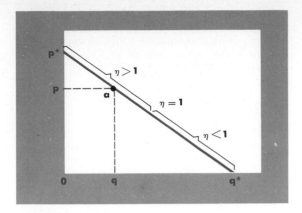

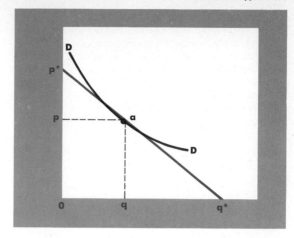

ratio of the excess of the quantity that could have been sold at a zero price over actual sales [i.e., $(q^* - q)$, divided by quantity sold (q)]. Note that, although this demand curve has a constant slope, it is not characterized by a constant elasticity. The elasticity changes along the curve. If q^* units were sold at zero price, the elasticity of demand would be zero; for higher prices, less is sold and elasticity increases without bound as the price approaches p^*.

To determine the elasticity of demand at some point on a nonlinear demand curve, such as point a on curve DD on the second graph, draw a straight line tangent to the demand curve at that point, and from it determine the location of point q^*. Since at point a the demand curve and the tangent line have the same slope, as well as the same p and q values, they also have the same elasticity at that point; hence, formula I.5 again applies.

$$\eta = \frac{q^* - q}{q}$$

Is it possible for a demand curve to have constant elasticity throughout its entire length? Yes. Suppose that $q = \alpha p^\beta$, $\beta < 0$; then

$$dq/dp = (\beta\, \alpha p^{\beta-1}) = \beta\,\frac{q}{p}$$

and

$$\eta = -\left(\beta\,\frac{q}{p}\right)\frac{p}{q} = -\beta$$

That is, the parameter $-\beta$ of the demand curve is the elasticity of demand. For example, a rectangular hyperbola has a constant elasticity equal to 1.

APPENDIX II (to Chapters 10 and 11)

GNP DETERMINATION AND THE MULTIPLIER

Chapters 10 and 11 present a simple algebraic model showing how, in an economy assuming no government or foreign trade, private investment and the marginal propensity to consume interact to determine the level of GNP. This appendix first states the model quite generally in mathematical terms, and then develops more rigorously "the multiplier" and the way in which it helps explain the impact of changes in investment on GNP. This is the reasoning from the text put in mathematical language.

A. The income-determination model. In Chapter 10, two consumption functions were presented. In one, consumption (C) was simply a fixed proportion of GNP, Y. In the other, a somewhat more general form was used:[3]

$$C = a + bY \qquad (II.1)$$

[3]You will remember from the text discussion that

$$0 < b < 1$$

(Of course, if $a = 0$, then this reduces to the simpler consumption function.) As in Chapter 10, since all of GNP is either consumed or invested (I),

$$Y = C + I \qquad \text{(II.2)}$$

Now substitute the consumption function into this last equation in order to obtain

$$Y = a + bY + I \qquad \text{(II.3)}$$

Next, subtract bY from both sides.

$$Y - bY = (1 - b)Y = a + I \qquad \text{(II.4)}$$

Dividing both sides by the marginal propensity to save, $1 - b$, gives us

$$Y = \left(\frac{1}{1 - b}\right)(a + I) \qquad \text{(II.5)}$$

as the equilibrium level of GNP, in which consumption is at the level prescribed by the consumption function (equation II.1) for the given level of I and the resulting level of Y. In particular, if $a = 40$, $b = .6$, and $I = 100$ (as in Chapter 10), this last equation reveals that gross national product must be 350.

$$\left(\frac{1}{1 - .6}\right)(40 + 100) = 350$$

B. The multiplier. The multiplier tells us what happens as a result of a rise in investment to a new level (I^*). Clearly, GNP will rise, and as people receive more income, consumption will rise as well. Let Y^* denote the new equilibrium level of income and C^* the new equilibrium level of consumption, when the increase in I has exercised its full effect.

Since these new equilibrium values, Y^* and C^*, must satisfy both equations II.1 and II.5, the same line of reasoning as before implies that

$$Y^* = \left(\frac{1}{1 - b}\right)(a + I^*) \qquad \text{(II.5*)}$$

Subtracting equation II.5 from this last expression yields

$$Y^* - Y = \left(\frac{1}{1 - b}\right)(I^* - I) \qquad \text{(II.6)}$$

The expression in large parentheses, the reciprocal of the marginal propensity to save, is the multiplier. It tells us by how much the change in investment ($I^* - I$) must be multiplied in order to determine the change that it will induce in GNP.

C. Addition of government spending and taxes. Government spending and taxes can readily be introduced into this multiplier analysis. Government spending, G, then represents purchases of one part of the current GNP. Consequently, we must rewrite equation II.2 to read

$$Y = C + I + G \qquad \text{(II.7)}$$

In addition, we must now recognize a distinction between gross national product and disposable income. Specifically, let T denote tax revenue, and suppose that consumption depends on disposable (after-tax) income, so that $C = a + b(Y - T)$. Then

$$Y = a + b(Y - T) + G + I \qquad \text{(II.8)}$$

Proceeding as before, we obtain

$$Y = \left(\frac{1}{1 - b}\right)(a - bT + G + I)$$

as the equation explaining the equilibrium level of GNP as determined by private investment, consumption behavior, government expenditure, and taxes. Note that for any given tax take, government spending and investment both have the same multiplier. On the other hand, the effect of an increase in taxes is to change GNP by a negative "tax multiplier" of $-b/(1 - b)$. Thus, if government expenditure and taxes both increase by \$3 billion, we would have

$$Y^* = \left(\frac{1}{1 - b}\right)[a - b(T + 3)$$
$$+ (G + 3) + I] = Y + 3$$

That is, income increases by the same amount as taxes and government spending, which in Chapters 11 and 16 is called the "balanced-budget multiplier."

D. Dynamics of the multiplier. This exercise tells us nothing about the nature of the adjustment process. Let us now consider the dynamic process by which Y rises as a result of the increase in I. This corresponds to the discussion of successive rounds of consumption spending out of rising income in Chapter 11. Let time be measured in discrete units—say, months—and suppose that the level of consumption during the current month depends upon the income earned in the immediately preceding month. Thus

$$C_t = a + bY_{t-1} \qquad \text{(II.9)}$$

where the subscripts serve to indicate the time period.

Now let us suppose that the marginal propensity to consume, b, is .75; that $a = 20$: and that initially, at time zero, investment is 67.5, $G = T = 0$, and income $Y_0 = 350$. From equation II.9 we find that, in period one, consumption will be

$$C_1 = 20 + .75 \cdot 350 = 282.5$$

If investment were to remain constant at 67.5, there would be no tendency for GNP to change from 350. (Check that $C_1 + I_1 = Y_1 = 350$.) This is the sense in which the economy is said to be in **equilibrium.** But suppose that instead, investment increases by 10, to 77.5. Our initial equilibrium is disturbed, and the economy will gradually adjust to the disturbance. The nature of the adjustment process is suggested by the following:

Period	$I_t - I_0$	$C_t - C_0$	$Y_t - Y_0$
1	10		10
2	10	7.5	17.5
3	10	13.1	23.1
4	10	17.3	27.3
⋮	⋮	⋮	⋮
	10	30	40

Each increase in income induces additional consumption in the next period, which constitutes additional income to the seller of goods or services, and so on ad infinitum. Will the process stop? The total increase in income is

$$10 + 7.5 + 5.6 + 4.2 + \cdots$$

But this is readily seen to be a sum of an infinite number of terms. More generally, of course, for any arbitrary marginal propensity to consume, the change in income resulting from a change in investment will be

$$\Delta I + b\Delta I + b^2\Delta I + b^3\Delta I + \cdots$$
$$= \Delta I(1 + b + b^2 + b^3 + \cdots) \quad \text{(II.10)}$$

The conditions under which such a sum will be finite can be determined if we recall the procedure for deriving the sum of a geometric series. Let S_n be the first n terms in such a series,

$$S_n = 1 + b + b^2 + \cdots + b^n \quad \text{(II.11)}$$

Multiplying by b gives

$$bS_n = b + b^2 + \cdots + b^{n+1} \quad \text{(II.12)}$$

Subtracting equation II.12 from II.11 yields

$$S_n - bS_n = (1 - b)S_n = 1 - b^{n+1}$$

Consequently,

$$S_n = \frac{1 - b^{n+1}}{1 - b} \quad \text{(II.13)}$$

It is now obvious that

$$\lim_{n \to \infty} S_n = \frac{1}{1 - b} \quad \text{(II.14)}$$

if and only if the marginal propensity to consume is less than unity. This limiting expression is, of course, the multiplier of equation II.6. If the marginal propensity to consume were greater than unity, something that is conceivable but not likely except in temporary special cases, GNP would increase without bounds in response to an increase in private investment spending, at least under the simple assumptions used here.[4]

More advanced analysis would recognize that rising GNP and business sales might well induce a further rise in investment spending, and thus increase the stimulative effect of any of the above assumed increases in I or G. Such further "induced" investment is often called the "accelerator" effect, and is considered more completely in Chapter 15. See especially the second appendix to that chapter for a simple mathematical model incorporating both multiplier and accelerator effects.

[4]Readers interested in the complexities of dynamic analysis will note that equation II.6 correctly tells us that equilibrium GNP will decrease as a result of an increase in investment spending if the marginal propensity to consume is greater than unity; that is, if, somehow, GNP did decline to the level suggested by that equation, it would remain there indefinitely. But if $b \leq 1$, this equilibrium is *unstable,* and with the passage of time, GNP will diverge further and further from its equilibrium as a result of the increased consumption induced by the augmented level of investment spending. This, however, while it is analytically interesting, is extremely unlikely, since empirical studies show that the marginal propensity to consume is less than unity except under very special circumstances.

APPENDIX III (to Chapters 20–21)

COST CURVES AND PROFIT MAXIMIZATION

To determine what level of output will maximize profits, production costs in relation to demand considerations must be analyzed. This appendix mathematically analyzes this interrelationship.

A. Key cost concepts. In Chapter 20, the dependence of production costs upon the level of output was examined in detail, and a number of basic concepts were explained. Table 20–1 reported hypothetical cost figures for a firm producing a single commodity. In such cases, the **total cost function,** $c(q)$, reveals how the total costs incurred by the firm depend on the level of output; we assume that the function is differentiable. Other cost concepts discussed in the text may be expressed in terms of $c(q)$, as shown in the following list:

Fixed costs:	$c(0)$
Variable costs:	$c(q) - c(0)$
Total unit cost:	$c(q)/q$
Variable unit cost:	$[c(q) - c(0)]/q$
Fixed unit cost:	$c(0)/q$
Marginal cost:	$\dfrac{dc(q)}{dq}$

B. Maximizing profits. Profit, at any level of output, $\pi(q)$, is simply the excess of total revenue over total cost,

$$\pi(q) = r(q) - c(q) \qquad (\text{III.1})$$

where $r(q)$ is the total revenue function discussed in Mathematical Appendix I; the three curves are plotted in Figure 21–1. From elementary calculus we know that if profits are maximized at some level of output $q > 0$, it is necessary that

$$\frac{\partial \pi(q)}{\partial q} = \frac{\partial r(q)}{\partial q} - \frac{\partial c(q)}{\partial q} = 0 \qquad (\text{III.2})$$

Equation III.2 implies:

$$\frac{\partial r(q)}{\partial q} = \frac{\partial c(q)}{\partial q} = 0 \qquad (\text{III.3})$$

This mathematically states the fundamental proposi-

tion that a necessary condition for profit maximization at $q > 0$ is that marginal cost equals marginal revenue.

It is essential to note that condition III.2 does not necessarily yield a level of output, q, at which profits will be positive. In the short run, before the firm can liquidate its fixed investment, it may be worthwhile to operate at a loss rather than shut down. Remember that zero output involves fixed cost, $c(0)$, in the short run. Would a zero output minimize losses (negative profits) when there are fixed costs? Not if

$$\pi(q) = r(q) - c(q) > \pi(0) = -c(0) \qquad (\text{III.4})$$

or equivalently:

$$r(q) - [c(q) - c(0)] > 0 \qquad (\text{III.5})$$

In other words, the firm will produce a positive output at a loss if revenue exceeds total **variable** costs. Dividing both sides of III.5 by q yields, since $r(q)/q = p$, an equivalent condition:

$$p - [c(q) - c(0)]/q > 0 \qquad (\text{III.6})$$

This is the condition (in Chapter 21) that the firm will minimize losses by shutting down altogether only if there is no positive level of output where price would exceed average variable cost.

C. Some observations on competitive equilibrium. Under competitive conditions, the output of the individual firm constitutes an insignificant contribution to the total market sales of the commodity. Consequently, the price the firm receives for its output is unaffected by variation in the quantity it offers for sale; its demand curve is horizontal $(dp/dq = 0)$, and from equation I.2 we have marginal revenue equal to price $(dr/dq = p)$. Hence, equation III.3 implies that if firms maximize profits under competitive conditions, they produce at the point where marginal cost equals price.

This constitutes a basic proposition of economic theory that explains the general presumption of economists in favor of competition: When firms maximize profits under competitive conditions, the increment to total cost incurred in producing the last unit sold is exactly equal to the price, which is precisely as it should be. For the price reflects the consumer's evaluation of the benefits he will obtain from the purchase of that last unit; if the benefits were less, he wouldn't buy the unit, and if they were greater, he would buy more units.

Chapter 22 points out that in long-run competitive equilibrium, price is equal to the minimum point on the total-unit-cost curve. This must be the case, for a higher price would encourage new firms to enter the industry in search of profits, while a lower price would yield continued losses and induce firms to leave the industry. But if price is to be equal to the minimum point on the total-unit-cost curve, can we be sure it also equals marginal cost, as required under competition (condition III.3, with $dr/dq = p$)? It is easy to show that the answer is, necessarily, yes. If output is at the minimum total-unit-cost level, then

marginal cost will be equal to total unit cost. To establish this proposition, we note that the condition that output be at the minimum total-unit-cost level implies:

$$\frac{d\left[\dfrac{c(q)}{q}\right]}{dq} = \frac{\dfrac{dc(q)}{dq}}{q} - \frac{c(q)}{q^2} = 0$$

Multiplying through by q yields:

$$\frac{dc(q)}{dq} = \frac{c(q)}{q}$$

Thus, marginal cost is equal to average cost if output is at the firm's lowest average-unit-cost point. The marginal-cost curve cuts the average-cost curve at the latter's minimum point.

APPENDIX IV (to Chapters 30–31)

PRODUCTION FUNCTIONS AND THE DISTRIBUTION OF INCOME

Most firms have alternative ways to produce any given output. Thus, within limits, the services of machinery may be substituted for labor in the production of steel, or vice versa. A "production function," which states the relationship between various combinations of inputs and the resulting outputs (products), can be a helpful concept for exploring the way in which technological considerations influence the distribution of income among different factors of production (labor, capital, and so on).

A. Simple production functions. For simplicity, suppose that only two factors of production, labor (L) and machinery (M), are used in producing a commodity. The output (q) produced each period depends on the quantity of labor and machinery services employed. We assume that this production function can be described by a differentiable function of the two inputs:

$$q = f(L, M) \qquad (IV.1)$$

Such functions can be estimated empirically from business and engineering production data or derived from engineering or physical principles.

We wish to determine the optimal (highest-profit) mix of labor and machinery to produce any output. We will maximize profits (π) by maximizing the excess of revenue over cost. If we assume that labor

and machinery services are purchased on competitive markets at prices w and p_m, we have:

$$\pi = r(q) - wL - p_m M \qquad (IV.2)$$

or, substituting from IV.1,

$$\pi(L, M) = r[f(L, M)] - wL - p_m M \quad (IV.3)$$

If the optimal quantity of labor is indeed being employed, it must be impossible to increase profits by either increasing or decreasing the amount of labor used. Consequently, a necessary condition for profit maximization is that:

$$\frac{\partial \pi(L, m)}{\partial L} = \frac{dr}{dq} \cdot \frac{\partial q}{\partial L} - w = 0 \qquad (IV.4)$$

Similarly, if the optimal quantity of machinery services is being employed,

$$\frac{\partial \pi(L, m)}{\partial M} = \frac{dr}{dq} \cdot \frac{\partial q}{\partial m} - p_m = 0 \qquad (IV.5)$$

As Chapters 30 and 31 indicate, economists call

$$\frac{\partial r}{\partial q} \cdot \frac{\partial q}{\partial L}$$

the **marginal-revenue product** of labor. Thus, equation IV.4 shows that to maximize profits, a firm hiring on a competitive market must hire additional workers just to the point where the marginal-revenue product of labor equals the wage rate.

It follows from IV.4 and IV.5 that

$$\frac{\partial q / \partial m}{p_m} = \frac{\partial q / \partial L}{w} \qquad \text{(IV.6)}$$

The economist calls

$$\frac{\partial q}{\partial L}$$

the marginal productivity of labor; similarly,

$$\frac{\partial q}{\partial m}$$

is the marginal productivity of machinery services. Equation IV.6 thus shows that under profit-maximizing equilibrium conditions in competitive markets, each factor of production is rewarded in proportion to its marginal productivity.

B. The Cobb-Douglas production function: an example. As an illustration, let us consider a much discussed conjecture of Professors C.W. Cobb and Paul H. Douglas (later U.S. senator) that the total industrial output of the American economy may be described by a simple production function of the form:

$$q(L, M) = aL^{\lambda}M^{1-\lambda} \qquad \text{(IV.7)}$$

Statistical investigations have disclosed that a function of this form fits the historical data quite closely when $\lambda = .75$. Note that this function is characterized by **constant returns to scale**; that is, if the initial inputs are all multiplied by some scale factor, $\rho > 0$, then output will also increase by ρ; more precisely:

$$q(\rho L, \rho M) = \rho q(L, M) \text{ for all } \rho \geqslant 0 \quad \text{(IV.8)}$$

What are the implications of the Cobb-Douglas analysis for the shares of labor and machinery (capital) in the national income? Not only did Cobb-Douglas find that equation IV.7 provides a reasonable explanation of how capital and labor contribute to the generation of industrial output. They also found that this function, in conjunction with equation IV.4, embodying the assumption of competition, helps to explain an important observed fact—that labor income (wages and salaries) has been a roughly stable percentage of total income over many decades.

Their explanation of the rough constancy of labor's share can be appreciated if we first observe that the marginal productivity of labor is

$$\frac{\partial q}{\partial L} = \lambda a L^{\lambda-1} M^{1-\lambda} = \lambda \frac{Q}{L} \qquad \text{(IV.9)}$$

Similarly, the marginal productivity of capital services is

$$\frac{\partial q}{\partial M} = (1 - \lambda) a L^{\lambda} M^{-\lambda} = (1 - \lambda) \frac{Q}{M} \text{ (IV.10)}$$

If output is sold on a competitive market at price p (so that $dr/dq = p$), then condition IV.4 implies:

$$p\lambda \frac{Q}{L} = w \qquad \text{(IV.11)}$$

Hence

$$\frac{Lw}{Qp} = \lambda \qquad \text{(IV.12)}$$

Now remember that Lw is labor income, while Qp is the value of total output; consequently, equation IV.12 implies that the ratio of labor income to total income, labor's share, is equal to the parameter λ of the Cobb-Douglas production function.

SUGGESTIONS FOR analysis of cases

This section includes suggestions to help you with the analysis of each case in the book. The cases are primarily designed to get you to use the concepts and principles in the chapter that each case follows. You will generally benefit the most if you work each case through for yourself, or in discussion with others, before you check against these suggestions.

In some cases, especially the earlier ones, the suggestions are quite explicit and detailed. In others, especially the later ones, they are brief, often consisting more of questions you should be asking yourself than of specific suggestions on how to proceed and what principles to use. Even in the former, you will seldom find simple "answers" to the cases. The purpose is to get you to think through your own answers, and many of the cases are designed so that there is no one "right" answer that is unambiguously superior to all others. In many cases, you will have to combine your value judgments with economic analysis. (Case 1 is a good example.) Especially on such cases, but on the others as well, you will usually gain by discussing the problem and your answer with other students, in or out of class. One of the tricks in thinking through such real-world cases is to be sure that you see the problem from different points of view, and your friends are almost certain to see some of the cases from different angles from the one that appears to you. But never forget that a major goal is to practice your economic analysis. Even though your value judgments differ, you should be able to agree on the relevant economic concepts and principles, and on the economic analysis involved.

CASE 1: HOW MUCH FOR AUTO SAFETY?   Auto passenger safety legislation poses sharply the issue of priorities and resource allocation by individual choice through the market as against collective action through the political process and government regulation. Supporters of the legislation say that everyone "should" be protected against death or serious injury in case of accident; obviously, the protection is worth far more than $100 in case of a serious accident, and the only way to be sure everyone will have it is for Congress to make it mandatory on all new cars.

Opponents counter that each individual should be free to decide for himself how much the protection is worth to him, and to buy only as much auto safety as he wants to pay for. They argue that this case is quite different from other auto safety legislation that is designed to protect innocent people against injury by others, such as speed laws, requirements for operating head- and taillights, and so on. Everyone agrees that laws are needed to protect innocent people against injury by others, but seat belts and air bags protect only their users. They do nothing to lessen the risk of injury for others. And opponents of the legislation point out that car purchasers could buy a lot of other things with the $1–$2 billion they are required to spend on seat belts, air bags, and other safety features—things they might value more highly, such as ski trips to Squaw Valley, new clothes, T-bone steaks, health insurance, or any of thousands of other goods and services available on the market.

Thinking through this controversy should help you sort out the issues as to when individual free choice in the market, and when "collective" (governmental) action that is binding on everyone, should control our priorities. In the process, consider the following two related questions: (1) Should Congress pass a law requiring everyone who goes out in below-freezing weather to wear warm clothing? (2) Should Congress pass a law requiring steel mills to reduce the amount of smoke and dirt they emit? How, if at all, do these two cases differ from each other and from the auto passenger safety case? (*Hint:* How does the action affect innocent third parties in each case?)

CASE 2: CAMPUS PARKING.   Stanford faces the central problem that is always faced when the supply of some desirable good is limited (scarce): how to allocate the scarce good or service among those who want it. At Stanford, the past method has combined tradition and "command" (by the central administration) to solve the problem. Five additional alternatives are suggested in the case, and obviously there are a substantial number of further possible combinations and permutations. In deciding which is best, it may be useful to use at least two criteria—equity and efficiency.

On the first, what is your criterion of equity? Should everyone have an equal chance at the best spaces, regardless of his status? Should seniority on the campus count? age? distance of residence from the central campus? How about ability and willingness to pay? Who should decide on these, and how?

On the efficiency criterion, what are the crucial points? Is it most important to ensure that professors get to class on time? Should preference be given to those who come in car pools? to those who stay all day, in contrast to in-and-outers for just two or three classes? Is willingness to pay for a sticker a good measure of how badly any individual needs a close-in parking space? If not, what is a better criterion? Would a parking charge be an efficient way of discouraging professors, staff, and students who now drive to work although they live nearby and could readily walk or bicycle? Should you overallocate spaces to be sure they aren't wasted when some sticker-holders don't come every day?

The text suggests four main approaches to rationing scarce resources: market prices, tradition, command, and a democratic ("community") decision process. Think through who would get the spaces under each arrangement, and how the results would meet your criteria of equity and efficiency. Far from least important, which should dominate, equity or efficiency, if there is a conflict between the two—for example, if you believe everyone should have an equal chance at the best spaces but know that to follow that policy would make professors late frequently and would give spaces to some people who live close by and who would only use the spaces part of each day?

Last, *how* should Stanford *determine* its parking policy (as distinct from what you believe the policy should be)—by decision of the president, by vote of those concerned, or some other way? If by voting, who should get to vote, and how, if at all, should minority interests be protected? Stanford's problem, if you look at it closely, is very similar to the nation's problem when it must decide how to allocate its scarce productive resources. Would you apply your conclusions on the parking problem to the allocation of Jaguar sports cars, raincoats, and education on the national scene?

CASE 3: GENERAL ELECTRIC COMPANY.   The suggestions for analysis of this case are given in the appendix to Chapter 4.

CASE 4: CASH OR FOOD STAMPS FOR THE POOR?   The main economic issue here is, Which form of aid is more efficient? That is, which increases the well-being of the poor more, $162 worth of food stamps monthly, or $162 in cash? Economic analysis cannot decide the ethical issue of how much, if any, aid should be given, or whether those giving the aid have an ethical right to determine in which form it should be given. But economic analysis can help judge the consequences of different policies.

If a poor family is given cash, we can assume it will spend the money along with its other income to maximize its satisfaction by allocating its income so that the last dollar spent on each good yields about the same marginal utility. If, instead, the family receives food stamps, its freedom to allocate its income is restricted. If the amount of the food stamps is less than the amount that would have been spent on food anyhow, the food stamps would be equivalent to cash because the household would be able to spend the money saved on food for anything else it wanted (including more food). But if the food stamps are more than the family would otherwise have spent on food, under the food-stamp program the family consumes more food than it prefers relative to other goods; it is forced to take a lower total satisfaction than it could have obtained from an all-cash income. On the grounds of economic efficiency, cash aid is likely to be better than food stamps.

But many people do not believe that economic efficiency is the most important consideration in this case. They believe that Congress does know better than the poor what is best for them. Or they are simply not interested in maximizing the satisfaction of the poor; they just want to assure poor people, especially children, a minimum diet. And they doubt that many recipients will resist the temptation to waste the money on nonessentials, instead of adequately feeding their youngsters. These are matters of ethics, however, not economics. Chapter 5 does not have much to say about ethics, but it is important to separate clearly the ethical from the economic arguments. You should also recognize that in making the actual decision, Congress must decide on both types of issues.

Make up your own mind. Then ask yourself whether your arguments hold equally for cash aid versus in-kind subsidies of public housing, health services, and public education.

CASE 5: CONSUMER CREDIT AND USURY LAWS. Simple supply-and-demand analysis can help on this problem. The new laws are fixing a price ceiling (interest rate) on loans, below the free-market price. Suppose the supply and demand curves for consumer credit in your state are as on the following chart. Then the free-market interest rate would be 20 per-

cent per year, and $300 million would be offered and borrowed per month. The supply curve, sloping upward, says that lenders would offer more at higher interest rates, less at lower ones. Why? Because at higher interest rates on consumer loans, it will pay to divert more credit from other potential borrowers, and because at higher rates, it will pay to lend to higher-risk borrowers. The demand curve, sloping downward, says that more will be borrowed at lower than at higher rates. Obviously the "finance charge" (of which the interest rate is a big part) helps determine whether or not people can afford a new refrigerator or a new car. The lower the interest rate, the lower the monthly payments and the effective price of the product to people who buy on credit rather than paying cash.

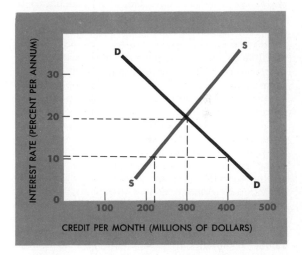

Suppose, now, the state legislature decrees that no lender shall charge consumers more than 1 percent monthly—12 percent per year. At that rate, lenders will lend only $225 million monthly, but consumers will want to borrow $400 million. Clearly, there is a large excess demand—$175 million of unsatisfied consumer wants for credit. There's a "shortage" of credit for consumers. The first effect of the new law is that some consumers get cheaper credit, but some who were previously borrowing at 20 percent now get nothing. Seventy-five million dollars less is lent and an additional $100 million of demand goes unsatisfied. We can be sure there are going to be a lot of angry consumers who get a friendly but firm "no" from auto dealers, banks, finance companies, department stores, and credit-card companies. And the lenders are not going to be very happy about alienating their present and potential customers.

But the law is the law. Who gets the limited

supply of consumer credit at 1 percent a month? Probably the well-established, low-risk customers of the lenders. But pity the consumer who applies for a new credit card, or charge account, or finance-company loan in your state, especially if his income is low and he does not look like a top-notch credit risk. If you were a lender, you would stick with your established, sure-pay customers for what credit you have to lend—and that is just what lenders did in Arkansas, Minnesota, Washington, and Wisconsin. If the free price system does not decide who gets the available credit, lenders will have to ration it out on some other basis—unhappy customers or not.

What other effects would you expect? Rejected borrowers who live near the state boundary can reasonably be expected to take their business next door where credit is available. This is not calculated to make your home-state merchants very happy. Some borrowers and lenders may cheat a little—some of those rejected potential borrowers may offer to slip the finance man, auto dealer, or credit-card manager a little something on the side to get credit, or a new credit card. "Black markets" can develop in credit just as they did in butter and gasoline when they were price-fixed. For sure, angry consumers turned away will complain bitterly to their legislators that they are being treated unfairly—they were supposed to get cheaper credit, but in fact they are getting none. It is those greedy moneylenders trying to gouge them again, especially the poor, minority groups, and others who need the credit most if they are to buy.

Next, and a bit outside our assumptions, the whole supply curve (SS) is likely to move to the left—because big consumer lenders, like the nationwide finance companies, may essentially drop out of business in your state. Why suffer the criticisms and take the lower interest rates there if they can make more money with happier customer relationships in other states? Move the SS curve to the left and see what that does to the problem.

Who has gained and who has lost from the new law? Should your state legislature be next to put a 1 percent monthly ceiling on customer credit rates?

Last, apply your analysis to Senator Tunney's proposal. For a relevant news account, see "When Usury Laws Backfire against Borrowers," *Business Week*, August 17, 1974.

CASE 6: THE COSTS OF UNEMPLOYMENT AND IN-FLATION.   The analysis of Chapter 7 is directly applicable to this controversy. There are several issues:

1. Is the official concept of unemployment the best one? The AFL-CIO criticism is voiced by many observers. Is the present concept seriously misleading?

Would alternative concepts be better? Be sure you understand just what the current unemployment statistics measure.

2. What are the actual costs of unemployment and of inflation today? The chapter suggests that simplistic answers are likely to be misleading for both. Go back and review the main sections of the chapter on the effects of each, focusing on the "moderate" levels of both inflation and unemployment that prevail in America now. How you balance them off will depend partly on your personal values as well as on just who is hurt how much by each.

3. Beyond the immediate costs of unemployment and inflation, how much danger of further inflation do we incur if the government stimulates more spending now to fight unemployment? You can't answer this question satisfactorily until you've studied all of Part 2, but the Burns and Heller comments suggest the issues. Note that Burns not only warns about the danger of restimulating inflation, but also suggests that such stimulus will fail to produce more jobs if it rekindles inflationary expectations and higher prices.

4. The problem confronting the political candidate is a tough one. Unemployment surely hurts the unemployed worker who cannot find a job more than inflation hurts most citizens. But serious unemployment hits only a small percentage of all workers; private and public unemployment insurance and other benefits soften the blow for many of the unemployed; and the duration of unemployment is brief for most. On the inflation side, if inflation does not reduce the nation's real output (note that Heller argues that more spending will only increase jobs and real output), it will merely redistribute income and wealth, not hurt us economically as a nation. But every individual has to pay higher prices in inflation, and few of us recognize that our parallel salary increases reflect inflation rather than our own hard work and virtue. The 1975 mail to Washington complained more about inflation than about unemployment, although the intensity of feeling often went the other way. By the time you read this, the national election results of November 1976 will have answered the question of which was the best way to get elected.

CASE 7: SHOULD GNP MEASURE SOCIAL WELFARE? There are no suggestions for analysis on this case because Dr. Okun's statement effectively lays out the arguments on both sides of the issue. But be sure you look back at the Nordhaus-Tobin analysis of "net economic welfare" in the latter part of the chapter, as you think through the issue.

CASE 8: DOES CAPITALISM NEED WAR FOR PROSPERITY?   Scarcity, aggregate demand, and government fiscal policy are the keys to the answer. First, resources are scarce relative to human wants. The huge amounts of manpower, steel, electronics, and other resources now used for defense could, if freed, help provide better housing, education, civilian goods, and health services for the nation. Even $50 billion would fall far short of meeting our new national priorities. To continue to waste the resources on unneeded national defense would be stupid indeed when there are so many other unfilled human wants.

But wouldn't the cutback merely throw millions into unemployment? Not if the government uses fiscal policy effectively. The first lesson of macroeconomics is that in the short run, aggregate output and employment are determined basically by the level of aggregate demand. If we cut aggregate demand drastically, we can certainly expect employment to fall. A $50 billion cut in government spending would directly cut aggregate demand by about 3 percent (GNP is about $1.6 trillion), but if the multiplier is, say, 2, the total drop in aggregate demand would be closer to $100 billion. This would be enough to raise unemployment by five to six million people, including those discharged from the armed services; the unemployment rate would soar by perhaps 5 percent.

But it would be a shortsighted government indeed that permitted this shrinkage of aggregate demand. One obvious alternative is to increase nondefense spending by $50 billion, thereby keeping the government's contribution to aggregate demand unchanged, and use the resources to meet the new, much-discussed national priorities, such as health, the environment, urban reconstruction, and education. The negative multiplier is thereby avoided, and no new unemployment is engendered.

Another alternative, more attractive if you want to keep government small and let people spend their incomes as they wish, is to cut taxes. Suppose we cut taxes by $50 billion. This gives the public $50 billion of additional disposable income. But note that it will probably not fully offset the cut in government spending, because the public's marginal propensity to consume will be less than 1; they will probably save some of the additional disposable income. To assure $50 billion of induced consumer spending to offset the government cut, the government will need to reduce taxes by *more* than $50 billion. Precisely how much more will depend on the public's marginal propensity to consume. In other words, to reduce both government spending and taxes by $50 billion would probably produce a negative balanced budget multiplier of 1, or thereabouts.

Are tax cuts or increased government nonmilitary spending better means of avoiding unemployment? Either can do the job, as indicated above. Your preference will presumably depend on how highly you value dollars spent by the government on the new social priorities, as compared with letting people make their own individual decisions as to how to spend their incomes in the market. If you like allocating resources primarily through the marketplace, advise your congressman to cut taxes. If you believe we need a bigger public sector, with more spending on highways, environmental control, public health, and the like, advise him to vote for more spending on those projects.

Two warnings on this simple exercise in fiscal policy analysis: First, we have entirely disregarded the transitional problems of getting all the people who are thrown out of defense jobs shifted to civilian jobs, either in the industries where government civilian spending rises or where consumers decide to spend their new disposable income. This may pose serious problems, including a lot of transitional unemployment and big losses for defense-industry businesses, even if the total number of jobs in the economy stays unchanged.

Second, we have completely neglected the monetary factors at work, as we did in the preceding chapter. As we shall see in Chapters 13 and 18, the government has another powerful approach to controlling aggregate demand—monetary policy, which it exercises by changing the amount of money in the economic system. Without considering monetary factors, we are seeing only part of the picture, and with money in, the problem becomes more complex. Remember that we've temporarily made the problem too simple by focusing only on fiscal policy.

CASE 9: INTEREST RATES, INVESTMENT, AND INFLATION.   Chairman Patman is right that interest is a cost that must be covered by the price charged by businesses for their products. It makes up a small fraction of the cost of most products, although it is a substantial part in a few cases. And he is of course right that the interest cost on any given amount of federal debt would be lower if interest rates had been kept lower.

The opposing economists are right that interest is a peculiarly important price (cost), in that it helps regulate the amount of investment businesses make, and investment plays an especially important role (directly and through the multiplier) in determining the level of aggregate demand and inflation.

The truth is thus not entirely on either side, but Congressman Patman finds little support among economists of either political persuasion for his extreme position favoring low interest rates even in high-employment, inflationary periods. The case for low interest rates is strong on both scores when there is widespread unemployment and little danger of inflation. But when there is substantially full employment, the small direct effect of higher interest rates in raising costs and prices is far more than overcome by high interest rates' strong deterrent effect on new business investment, as spelled out in Chapter 12. The higher interest rates would also deter consumer borrowing to buy durables, although many economists consider this a weaker restraint on total spending. In high-employment periods, the small interest cost saving to the government through holding interest rates down by creating more money is quickly overcome by the higher prices it must pay on its huge purchases of goods and services, to say nothing of the higher costs to the general public as the price level is bid up through excess aggregate demand. Thus, in such periods, the government is likely to have to borrow more if interest rates are held down and more inflation results, leading to a larger, not a smaller, national debt.

("Monetarists," whose position is presented in the following two chapters, would take an even stronger anti-Patman position, because they believe the impact of more money on aggregate demand is even more direct and powerful than the income-expenditure theory of Chapters 10–12 suggests.)

CASE 10: MONEY AND THE GREAT GERMAN HYPER-INFLATION. Chapter 13 provides the analytical tools needed to understand the role of money in the great German hyperinflation.

1. In a direct sense, the vast increase in money caused the German inflation. But it is important to ask also, Why did the government so overissue paper marks? The answer is, because of the very difficult economic and political situation in postwar, defeated Germany, caused in no small part by the extremely heavy reparations burdens imposed by the Allies. To understand the dilemma, ask yourself what you would have done to pay the enormous bills had you been the government, or the German people. (*Answer:* Raise taxes to cover all your payments?) The German case illustrates the close linkage among basic economic conditions, government spending and finance, the stock of money, and inflation. The power of governments to create money is central in most big inflations.

2. Clearly, the German inflation is consistent with the general predictions of the quantity theory. Rapidly increasing M resulted in rapidly rising prices (although it is perhaps equally accurate to say that rapidly rising prices resulted in rapidly increasing M,

as the government had to print ever-larger amounts of marks to pay its bills at the higher prices). Data on real output for the same period would make it possible to do a more detailed analysis.

3. There could be two explanations of why prices rose faster than M increased: V might have increased, or T (real output) might have decreased. Actually, the main reason was that V rose rapidly as the public spent its money faster and faster to beat expected rising prices. In portfolio-balancing terms, the return on money became negative, as people increasingly expected more inflation. Thus, as soon as people received more money, they converted it into real goods or financial assets (for example, common stocks of prosperous companies or foreign currencies) whose prices would rise at least roughly in step with inflation. The faster prices rose, the greater was the incentive to spend money promptly, and the larger V became. (Compare the increases in M and P in Table 13–1.)

4. Both the equation of exchange and portfolio balancing are useful in understanding the German inflation. The equation has the virtue of pointing up the four main variables one needs to consider. Portfolio balancing concentrates on the demand for money relative to other assets and provides a more detailed analysis than does V, but it doesn't remind us of the nonmonetary variables; it assumes you'll think of the forces controlling M and T independently. Let your taste be your guide.

CASE 11: HOW TO FIGHT UNEMPLOYMENT? This case raises a number of problems. First, do you prefer fiscal or monetary policy, or some combination of both? If you choose fiscal policy, note the problem you will face unless M is simultaneously increased. Without more M, interest rates will rise, because the government has to borrow $20 billion to finance the deficit and because people will demand more money to hold as their incomes rise. Fiscal action with no increase in M seems unlikely to produce the full desired multiplier effect.

On the other hand, if you choose monetary policy alone, how will you get the money to the public so that it will increase their spending as desired? Merely to buy up government bonds with the new money will increase neither the public's wealth nor its disposable income. Although the bond buying would reduce interest rates and perhaps thus indirectly stimulate investment, this result looks uncertain when businessmen are facing a depressed economy. But if you want to pay out the money directly to increase the public's wealth and disposable income—say, by unemployment relief or other direct gifts—this implies using fiscal policy—having the government spend the money, running a deficit and financing it with the newly created money. Clearly, you're likely to need more new M to increase GNP by $40 billion if you buy up bonds than if you pay the new money out through fiscal policy as new wealth to the public.

If you choose fiscal policy—say, with a supporting increase in M—should it be increased expenditures or tax cuts? Here, the answer will depend heavily on your personal values—whether you prefer having individual spending in the marketplace decide what is produced, or government action to produce things that the free market doesn't seem to provide. (Part 5 provides a detailed analysis of this issue.) But either way, here you should recognize that to get the desired increase in aggregate demand, a dollar of government spending and a dollar of tax cuts are not identical. In technical terms, the expenditure and tax multipliers are different. Go back to Chapter 11 for the explanation. Basically, it is because the government expenditure directly increases GNP while the tax cut merely increases disposable income. Either way, past experience suggests a lot of uncertainty about the public's short-run marginal propensity to consume. Although the average propensity to consume out of disposable income has been quite stable at reasonably high income levels, MPC has varied widely over periods of several quarters, especially when the public thinks the income increase may be only temporary. And remember that business saving and business taxes constitute additional leakages that reduce the multiplier.

Conclusion: There's no simple "right" answer. Make your own judgment. Most economists would opt for a combined strategy, using both fiscal and monetary policy, but just how much of each is a matter for expert professional judgment, on which your congressman is unlikely to get complete agreement. (More details to come in Chapters 16–19.)

CASE 12: THE IMPACT OF INVENTORIES. Both Ms. Golden and the two economists she quotes are right. The big recession of 1974–75 was in large part an inventory recession, straight out of the textbooks. In 1973 and 1974, inventories (especially of automobiles) piled up rapidly, first as dealers sought cars to meet a booming demand, and then involuntarily as consumer demand collapsed in the oil crisis but new cars kept coming off the production lines. By early 1975, dealers' and manufacturers' auto inventories were far out of line with sales, and both moved vigorously to reduce inventories, the manufacturers by cutting back production and the dealers by selling off their stocks on hand. It was this big inventory reduction, plus similar but smaller cutbacks in other products,

that reduced GNP sharply in early 1975. Auto sales sagged, but new-car production was cut even further.

But the inventory reduction was a good omen for the future. As long as inventories were far too large for current sales, manufacturers were not going to produce many new cars. Thus, it was necessary to reduce auto inventories before we could expect unemployed auto workers to be called back to their jobs. The medicine of inventory liquidation was painful, but the faster it worked, the sooner the economy would be ready for renewed auto production and a healthy upswing.

CASE 13: ARE WE GOING BROKE? The TV commentator's argument runs head-on into much of the analysis in the preceding pages. To point up the issues, ask yourself the following questions. (Your answers ought to help you decide how convincing the arguments are.)

1. Is the public debt just like private debt? Is the nation one big family so that what is true for one family is equally true for the nation as a whole? (The fallacy of composition.)

2. Are the reasons governments run deficits the same as those for why families go into debt?

3. When the government runs a deficit, are we "going on a binge" now that we will have to pay for in the future? Who pays for the binge in the future if the debt is continuously refunded?

4. What is the best measure of how well-off the nation is economically? Is the size of the public debt part of this measure?

5. Are you carrying a $10,000 bag of stones on your back?

6. Is it bad for individuals and businesses to go into debt? (Note Figure 16–6.)

7. What do you think the commentator really wants the government to do? Pay off the debt by running big budget surpluses? If not, what? Would you advise your congressman to follow his advice?

8. What criteria would you use in deciding when the public debt is too big, and when it should be reduced by running a current budget surplus to be used for debt retirement?

CASE 14: FEDERAL RESERVE INDEPENDENCE. The issues in this cases are suggested in Chapter 18, especially the section on "Federal Reserve Independence," and by the arguments advanced in the case itself on the side of restricting Federal Reserve independence. In considering the issues, ask yourself:

1. What are the proper goals of monetary policy?

2. Who is best suited to state those goals?

3. Given the goals of policy, what are the best ways of getting Federal Reserve action that will achieve these goals?

4. Who is most likely to carry out these procedures most effectively on a day-to-day basis?

5. How much discretionary power should be left to the Fed in adapting to unforeseen, day-to-day developments?

6. Is the Federal Reserve significantly different from other government agencies (the Treasury Department, Justice Department, Commerce Department, etc.) in what we want it to accomplish, so that it should be set up as a quasi-independent operating agency, rather than as a regular cabinet-type department of the government?

7. In election years, should the Fed make money a little easier than usual to assure good times and help the administration in power get reelected?

CASE 15: INDEXING—LEARNING TO LIVE WITH INFLATION. This case is a complex one. Note that economist A rests his argument entirely on preventing the redistributional inequities involved in inflation, while economist B deals with both that issue and the macroeconomic stabilization problem.

On the redistributional issue, look back at Chapter 7, which presents some of the facts relevant to the case. Unanticipated inflation does have substantial redistributional effects that seem inequitable to most observers. Complete indexing would, in principle, avoid these inequities. But as economist B points out, complete indexing would involve an enormously complex adjustment by our economic system, probably involving vast governmental control. Short of that, which most Americans may be unwilling to contemplate seriously, economist A might argue that businesses and individuals "ought" to go to an indexed basis in their private transactions. Indeed, many of them have. Some six million workers are now covered by union contracts that directly tie their wages to increases in the cost of living. And the interest rate that borrowers and lenders agree on clearly has an inflation allowance added on to the basic rate when rising prices are anticipated. Moreover, prices of assets like stocks, bonds, land, and houses are highly sensitive to inflation, so that a kind of indexing occurs automatically through the marketplace. But these market adjustments are erratic, and they would eliminate inequity only if everybody were equally well equipped to anticipate future infla-

tion and to protect himself against it by bargaining in the marketplace. This is clearly not the case; we surely cannot count on the marketplace to fully protect the less-educated, less-informed, and lower-income groups in the population.

Some economists, therefore, propose a middle ground. They argue that indexing could be introduced to protect three big groups that need help most, without getting involved in the enormous complexities of total indexing. First, older people out of the labor market because of retirement should be protected, primarily by indexing Social Security benefits. This has already been done. Second, the government should issue at least some bonds on an indexed basis so small investors could invest their savings in these securities without danger of losing the savings through inflation. For example, U.S. savings bonds might be issued on an indexed basis, with an upper limit of perhaps $50,000 per buyer if we want to avoid extending the protection to all government securities. Third, the tax system should be substantially indexed. It is difficult to defend the equity of the government's benefiting by secretly taking resources away from the taxpayers through inflation, when government monetary-fiscal policy plays a central role in producing the very inflation that does the stealing. These three reforms would go a long way toward removing the worst inequities of modern inflation, and would leave the marketplace free to produce as much market indexing as individual buyers and sellers want to put into their transactions. (The government has already gone further than these proposals on one score; wages and salaries of virtually all government employees are now indexed. But taxes are not, nor are government bonds.)

On the impact of indexing on economic stabilization, the issues are still more complex. If indexing increased the sensitivity of inflation expectations to actual inflation, it would speed any upward spiral of inflation that got started. That is, if people calculate their income demands in real terms, they would presumably simply add to the indexed wage or price a further allowance to increase their share of the national income pie over their automatically protected indexed share. Conversely, it can be argued that if people were assured that their existing shares would be protected by indexing, they might be more content with those real shares, and not feel obliged to fight so hard to increase or protect them. We simply don't know. The crucial factors here are anticipations of further inflation and the extent to which different income groups would try to increase their income shares by demanding more real income in the market and through the political process under different circumstances; see the analysis of "the new inflation" in Chapter 19. Many economists believe that indexing would somewhat increase the likelihood that inflation would escalate once started, but there is substantial disagreement on the issue.

A few other nations have tried indexing on a large scale. Brazil is the best-known example, but Israel has also made widespread use of indexing. Unfortunately, the conditions in each country are so different that it is difficult to generalize from the experience of any one country as to how indexing might work in others. Most observers feel that indexing has worked fairly well in Brazil, but under circumstances that would not be feasible in the United States. Brazil has used government-controlled indexing specifically to lag wages and thereby divert resources from workers to the government in order to finance more rapid economic growth.

For further simple examinations of the issues, see G. L. Bach, *The New Inflation,* Chapter 5; and R.A. Krieger, "Inflation and the 'Brazilian Solution,'" *Challenge,* September 1974.

CASE 16: POLLY POET'S PROBLEM. Professor Poet's first inclination is to say that if she can get anything more than $405 per month, she'll be better off to rent the house. She's stuck with paying $405 anyway, so anything she gets above that will help her all-too-small bank account. But one of her friends points out that this seems wrong, because there will clearly be more wear and tear on the house and furnishings if a renter lives in the house: The minimum rent to charge is $485.

Actually, neither Polly nor her friend is right, if you think it through. The right answer is, rent for anything over $40, if all that matters are the costs listed in the table. The reasoning, which is far from intuitively obvious, is this.

Suppose Polly keeps the house empty. She is clearly out $405 per month, the amount of her inescapable costs; they are sunk costs. If she rents the house, how much additional (marginal) cost does she incur? The answer is $40, the additional wear and tear on the place. Suppose she rents the house for $45 per month. Her costs are then $445 per month, or $40 higher. But when she uses the $45 rent to apply on the $445, she has only $400 left to pay out-of-pocket on her inescapable $405 sunk costs. She's $5 better off than with the house empty, even at such a low rent.

Obviously, she will be still better off if she can rent for more than $45, which presumably she can for such a nice house. If she can get $345 rent, for example, she can apply it against the $445 of costs, thus leaving only $100 she must pay out of her own bank account on her sunk costs. If she can rent for more than $445,

of course, she will actually make a profit on her house for the year, covering all her costs and having something left over.

Principle: If your additional cost from renting (your marginal cost) is more than covered by your additional income (marginal revenue), you'll be better off by renting, even though you don't cover all your sunk costs. Marginal cost is the key concept here, and marginal cost doesn't include sunk costs.

How much rent should she ask for her house? *Answer:* As much as she can get, as long as it's $40 or more.

CASE 17: AIRLINE TAKES THE MARGINAL ROUTE. The main lesson is pointed up in the box in Chapter 21. As long as the marginal cost is below marginal revenue, it pays Continental Airlines to increase its output (add more flights), even though the extra income (marginal revenue) may not cover the full average cost of production. Continental's total profit is larger with the flights in question than without them. Mr. Whelan gets an A in Economics I.

But there is a second lesson, too, which Mr. Whelan recognizes in the tenth paragraph. Some flights can add to total profits even though they do not cover *full* costs, but clearly, for all flights together income must cover full costs if the firm is to make a profit and to stay in business. Those marginal Continental flights are good business because the company has the planes, airport docks, reservation clerks, and other needed facilities on hand anyway. For purposes of this analysis, these are *fixed* (*sunk*) costs; they go on whether or not Continental adds the marginal flights in question. As Whelan says, the out-of-pocket (marginal) approach comes into play only after the airline's basic schedule has been set—but income from some flights obviously has to cover all those costs if the company is to make a profit.

CASE 18: EGGS, COPPER, AND COFFEE. The California case is a microcosm of the problems raised by federal farm policy on major products. The analysis in the chapter should be directly applicable. Make up your own mind after you have analyzed the gains and costs to producers, consumers, and any others concerned.

Existence of the California Egg Advisory Board to monitor policies of the egg producers raises a question that will be considered at length in Chapters 26 and 28—how effective government agencies and boards are likely to be in compromising the interests of consumers and producers in such cases. Looking ahead, the answer is: Mixed, but not very effective in many cases. The urgent problems of producers tend to override the less concentrated concerns of consumers. Such industry agreements to restrict production are generally called cartels, and often government-monitored cartels have worked effectively for the producers involved (for instance, in agriculture) where purely private agreements would have been both illegal and unworkable.

The international copper and coffee cartels raise the same issues as do the domestic ones involving eggs or hi-fis, except that the consumers and producers are in different countries in the various cases—leaving aside balance-of-payments considerations from international transactions until Part 6. (See Case 38.)

The hi-fi producers' proposal, again, raises the same issues. Should farmers be treated differently from nonfarm businesses by the government and by consumers? Most hi-fi producers are relatively small firms. Would you want to distinguish between large and small businesses in judging such cases? If so, why? (Use the analysis of Chapter 22 here.)

CASE 19: HOMETOWN ELECTRIC COMPANY—PUBLIC UTILITY REGULATION. This is a tough problem, with which public utility commissions and economists have been unhappily wrestling for a long time. First, an unsatisfactory alternative: If we just let Hometown Electric set the price it wants, that will be about 6.9 cents, and Hometown will make a juicy profit of about $33,000 monthly. But marginal cost is only about 2.5 cents at that output, so price would be far above marginal cost, the condition for a socially optimum allocation of resources. Thus, consumers would be getting too little electricity and paying too much for it.

How about following the social optimum rule from Chapter 22 of price = marginal cost, and setting price at 5.5 cents (where MC intersects the demand curve on Figure 24–2)? At that price, consumers would buy over 1,600,000 kilowatts, and the company would make a profit of about $20,000. Looks reasonable, but there may be a problem. Does the $20,000 provide the company with a fair rate of return on its investment, so that it will keep its capital invested in producing electricity here, and expand if demand rises? We can't tell from the limited data here, but if the price doesn't provide a fair rate of return, we can expect resources to be pulled out and future shortages of electricity in Hometown.

Suppose the $20,000 *is* below the normal rate of return on Hometown's investment. How can we get the socially optimum price and output without a long-run outflow of resources because of inadequate profits? One answer is, have the government (all consumers) pay a lump-sum benefit to Hometown to bring its rate of return up to the market rate. This would be ideal economics, but no government unit has yet faced up to the political problems of explaining to the voters and the taxpayers the case for such a tax-financed subsidy to public utilities, especially when the underlying consumer-demand data would only be roughly estimated.

As a practical matter, most regulatory commissions have substituted a second-best rule. They say to the utility: We'll give you an exclusive franchise; you produce as efficiently as possible, and charge the lowest price that will give you a fair return on your investment. Of course, this price may or may not be near marginal cost; in industries where demand is small relative to the most efficient scales of production, price may be far above MC although approximately the same as average cost for that output. Moreover, this approach runs into two knotty problems: How shall we measure the company's investment, and what is a "fair" rate of return? For example, the investment figure varies greatly during inflations depending on whether we use the original cost of investment less depreciation or the higher replacement cost (because of the inflation). On rate of return, commissions and courts vary, often arbitrarily setting 6, 7, or 8 percent. Many lawyers and economists make a living arguing the proper rate in these cases.

Last, none of these plans offers anything about how to keep the company efficient and on its toes, to minimize costs without the pressure of competition.

What is your answer—both as to the optimum price and how to assure efficient operation and a continued adequate supply of electricity in Hometown? Not least important, how would you decide what is an "adequate" supply of electricity for Hometown?

CASE 20: ADVERTISING AND CONSUMERISM. The concepts and analysis of the preceding chapters should help you decide on the proposed legislation. Try answering the following questions:

1. Who would gain? What would be the benefits to them?

2. Who would lose? What would be the costs to them? (Look at different groups of consumers and businesses.)

3. Would paragraphs 1 and 2 infringe the freedom of speech or freedom of individuals to seek profits as long as they do no harm to others?

4. How should the FTC decide what advertising is "useful" to consumers? what advertising is "misleading"? (If you don't think these terms are sufficiently clear, can you suggest better ones?)

5. Would you be concerned about concentration of power in the hands of the FTC?

6. Would consumers have more or less influence than now over what businesses produce?

7. Would you expect the price of newspapers and magazines to change if the legislation passed? How?

8. Would you expect TV programming and financing arrangements to change? How?

9. If triple damage suits under paragraph 3 involved large settlements, who would you expect to bear the cost? in the short run? in the long run?

10. If you see problems with this proposal, can you suggest an alternative that you think the country needs?

CASE 21: THE BATTLE OF THE SUPERMARKETS. This case illustrates both the managerial and the social problems of oligopoly. The questions at the end of the case point up some of the main issues. Questions 1–6 focus on management problems in this oligopoly; so viewed, this case is much like the ones you will face if you go on to a graduate school of business. Questions 7–9 focus on the social issues; who will gain and who will lose, what is the public interest here, and what, if any, government intervention is called for?

A&P's situation is a classic example of the problem faced by an oligopolistic market leader that is losing its share of the market. The A&P management surely knew that their price cutting would bring retaliation; presumably they decided that, nonetheless, this was their best chance of retaining their market share without such a serious price war that profits would be more than temporarily eroded. Possibly they were surprised at the vigor of the price war they started; many have criticized their managerial strategy. But it's not clear what other steps they could have taken to improve their deteriorating position; they had tried the obvious measures such as more advertising, improved service, and the like.

The problem of the competitive chains is equally easy to understand, but no easier to solve. If they didn't meet the cuts, they would almost surely lose business to A&P, which would thus achieve its goal, at least in part. But meeting the cuts would clearly produce a price war, which would help no one's profits and would probably be hard to stop—and this is precisely what happened. One approach would have been to fight back through advertising and other sales techniques, instead of cutting prices. And advertising budgets did rise. But this raises costs, and there's no guarantee that you can convince housewives to buy your products if they can get substan-

tially the same thing cheaper down the street. Or you might just sit it out in the hope that A&P will soon see the costs of cutting its own prices and profits. Do you have a better alternative?

Note, too, the strong market pressures in such a case toward open (illegal) or covert collusion. If there were now some way to stop the price war, all firms would clearly be better off, especially some of the weaker ones that face extinction if their losses continue for long. But the law against price collusion is clear, and who dares risk being the leader in putting his prices back up to a profitable level and leaving them there to establish a new pattern without some assurance the others will go along? Only a strong, acknowledged price leader would dare to do so, and it's not obvious just which firm that is in this complex case. All things considered, from a managerial point of view, the case provides strong support for a price policy of leaving well enough alone in an oligopoly, as the text suggests is common practice in such markets.

Turning to the social issues, consumers seem to be the big gainers from the price war. But if the war ends up bankrupting many smaller, weaker firms, the long-run result is less clear. (Remember, that's what some smaller firms say A&P is trying to do.) With fewer firms, there's less certainty of effective competition to hold down prices in the future. Moreover, after taking a "bath" like this, you can be sure that every firm is going to think a long time before it risks starting another price war. And new investment in the industry is going to be unattractive unless there are both reasonably stable competitive relationships and reasonable returns on investment. The demand for food is growing steadily; unless investment in food retailing continues to grow, services to consumers will deteriorate.

Last, investors are part of society too. Price wars that benefit consumers can also bankrupt investors. Remembering that, what is "the public interest" in this case?

By 1975, A&P sales had fallen $3.7 billion behind Safeway's total of about $10 billion; and A&P reported a net *loss* of $10 million for the year, compared to Safeway's profits of $135 million. Profits for the industry as a whole were still depressed, only back up to about 0.8 cents per dollar of sales. (Safeway earned about 1.3 cents per dollar of sales.)

If you want to check how A&P and the grocery industry have come out by the time you use this case, up-to-date sales and profit figures can be obtained from the July issue of *Fortune* each year, which provides summary information on each of the fifty largest retailing companies for the preceding year; or from Moody's or Standard & Poor's investment manuals, probably available in your library.

CASE 22: SOME MANAGERIAL APPLICATIONS. These little cases are designed to illustrate the application of economic concepts and principles in relatively simple business situations. Because each example includes an explanation of the principles and concepts involved and how they apply, no further suggestions for analysis are needed.

CASE 23: U.S. VERSUS VON'S GROCERIES. Just how many firms are needed to ensure the benefits of competition under different conditions is a complex issue. The purpose of this case is to pose this problem in a particular situation, and to let you see how the Supreme Court goes about analyzing such cases when it must decide them under the law. Although it is important to understand something of how the Court applies the broadly stated law to particular cases, the main purpose is to induce you to think through for yourself what would best serve the public interest here, using your economic analysis to do so.

In arriving at your answer, consider the following questions:

1. What do we want competition to accomplish for us?

2. How many grocery firms does it take in the Los Angeles market to ensure the benefits of competition? (Note the total number of firms in the Los Angeles market, the share of market covered by the merger, and the actual overlap in the markets served by Von's and Shopping Bag.)

3. How shall we balance the lower costs of supermarkets against the potentially greater competition among more small, but higher-cost, stores? Who or what should decide how many grocery stores there should be in Los Angeles?

4. Should the purpose of antitrust be to protect competition or small competitors?

CASE 24: WHAT TO DO ABOUT APPLIANCES? This case provides a sample of the issues faced when society decides to regulate sellers and their products to provide consumer protection. For each alternative, ask, What would it cost, and whom would it benefit? Would the costs ultimately be borne by sellers or by consumers? Is there a danger that all consumers would be forced to buy higher-quality products and services than they want to pay for? Fundamentally, for a wise decision we would presumably need a social cost–benefit comparison for each proposal, and some basis for deciding how to compromise the freedom of the individual to make his own decisions on what to buy against the possible advantages to many buyers of being assured that appliances will meet at least minimum standards when they are unable to make satisfactory technical judgments themselves. Even if there is a net social gain for society from adopting new regulation, should society override the preferences of a minority who object? Last, as a practical matter, can you count on a government agency to carry out effectively the directions you would give in legislation? If you favor new regulations, try to state concretely how you would define the standards you advocate.

CASE 25: THE $66 BILLION MISTAKE. If you are an ardent environmentalist, you may be understandably wary of a proposal on auto-pollution control by one of the major oil companies. Clearly, you have no basis for judging the accuracy of Mobil's $66 billion estimate, and that is not the main point of the case. The $66 billion has been disputed, as has been the exact nature of the rising cost curve in Chart 2. If you prefer, assume that the $66 billion extra cost is only $33 billion and that the Chart 2 curve rises only half as fast between the California and national standards, figures that even Mobil critics would agree are reasonable. In analyzing the proposals, it may be useful to focus on these three broad questions (using whichever cost figure you prefer).

1. How clean is clean enough? Is meeting the 1976 clean-air standards for auto emissions worth $66 (or $33) billion over the next ten years? Note that economics can give no one "right" answer to this question; each person must decide for himself whether having air that is clean is worth the alternatives foregone. Marginalism and alternative cost are the key concepts here. Mobil is right in stressing the other things we could get with our $66 billion if we settle for the California standards on air cleanliness. But be careful about the figures; Mobil's $66 billion extra cost is spread over ten years, while most of the alternatives given are for one year.

2. Accepting the need for government controls, should the direct-regulation approach be used, as Mobil suggests, or would we be better served by an effluent-charge approach (for example, a special charge per unit of emission from each car, perhaps based on the type of car and mileage driven annually, or a special tax on gasoline)? Should every car owner pay the same amount (by buying an emission-control system for his car), regardless of how much and where he drives? Regulation versus stress on individual incentives is a big issue here.

3. If Congress accepts the Mobil proposal for large, modern mass-transit systems, who should pay the bill—the general taxpayer (as Mobil suggests),

car drivers, mass-transit riders, local taxpayers in the areas served? What principle do you use in deciding who should pay?

CASE 26: THE VALUE OF A COLLEGE EDUCATION.   The changing college scene during the past quarter century is readily amenable to analysis with the tools of elementary economics. The supply of college graduates, which had lagged badly during the Great Depression and World War II, increased enormously over the postwar decades. But the demand for highly trained people, as the economy returned to peacetime prosperity, grew even faster. These shifting relationships produced rapidly rising incomes for college graduates, both absolutely and relative to other wage and salary earners. Supply and demand worked just as we would expect.

Rapidly rising prices for college graduates had the expected two effects. First, they stimulated a further growth in supply; and second, they led buyers to economize on the use of these increasingly expensive resources and to substitute less expensive ones where this was possible. Thus, the supply grew even faster, but demand grew more slowly (and even fell in business-cycle recession years). As the expected rate of return on investment in human capital through going to college fell relative to other forms of investment, many young people and their families, not surprisingly, decided that getting a college education simply wasn't worth it. Others decided that differential rates of return on investment in different types of college education were good guides to investment policy. The expected rate of return fell precipitously in the humanities, teaching, many social sciences, and other areas where there seemed to be no growth in demand; it continued to rise in such areas as medicine, business, law, and engineering. Faulkner scholars and Italian linguists ended up driving taxis and waiting on tables. Allowing for inflation, the starting *real* incomes of college graduates in 1974 were actually lower than those of a decade earlier. (Law by the 1970s began to exhibit the same overreaction pattern. Earnings of law graduates rose rapidly during the early postwar years, then leveled off, and then fell in real terms in the 1970s as the supply of graduates soared.) Draw the supply and demand curves.

But, as the final paragraph of the case suggests, self-interest in the market has a way of taking over. As supply outgrew demand, unemployment rose and incomes of college graduates fell, relatively and even absolutely in real terms. No planners were needed to tell high school graduates what to do. They looked at the world and decided for themselves. A lot said it was still worthwhile to go to college, especially if they picked the right fields; investment in human capital still promised a high payoff in some fields, such as medicine. But others voted with their feet. They turned to trade schools and junior colleges, or directly to the job market. Rapidly rising costs in higher education brought rising tuition rates and related costs of college, and it didn't take a trained mathematician to see that the effective real rate of return on dollars put into college education was falling.

Would self-interest do the job of adjusting the supply of college graduates to the demand for them if educators and government planners did nothing? Should society (acting through government) subsidize students to take more courses in the liberal arts, humanities, and general education than their own perceived self-interests would lead them to do? The answer to this last question depends partly on economics but even more on the values we place on having well-educated, cultivated people as neighbors and voters in our society. This problem is explored in more detail in Part 5 of the text.

CASE 27. THE ECONOMICS OF MINIMUM WAGE LAWS.   Minimum wage legislation is an example of government price-fixing, with the legal minimum price (wage) above the market-clearing level. Draw a demand and a supply curve for labor, with the market equilibrium wage at, say, $2.50. Now set the minimum wage at $3.00, and assume the law is enforced rigorously. What are the likely results?

1. Clearly, there will now be an excess supply of labor—some previously employed workers will lose their jobs, and new labor-force entrants will seek jobs at the higher wage. In marginal-productivity language, the wage has gone up without any increase in labor's marginal productivity, so it will pay profit-seeking businesses to hire fewer workers.

What will happen to the unemployed workers? They may stay unemployed, or look for work in industries not covered by the minimum wage law. If they do the latter, they force wages down in the uncovered industries, since the supply of labor is increased without any increase in demand.

Who is helped by the new law? Those who keep their jobs in the covered industries. This will presumably include some who were previously earning less than $3.00, but the new law will not increase the wages of those who were earning more than $3.00 before the new legislation if markets are competitive. Who is hurt? Obviously, those who lose their jobs, plus newcomers to the labor force who would have been hired into covered industries at a lower wage but whose marginal productivity is less than $3.00. Those hurt will be mainly unskilled workers, teenagers, minority workers—the very low-income people the law was designed to help. It will no longer pay businesses or others to hire workers whose marginal productivity is less than $3.00.

2. If employers were "exploiting" labor before the law by paying wages below labor's marginal productivity, the minimum wage might simply boost wages without reducing employment. Wages would then get more of the consumer's dollar, profits less. This is the situation implicitly assumed in most of the ardent arguments for minimum wage legislation.

3. Even if there is no exploitation of labor, the law's upward pressure on wage rates may drive employers to more efficient methods, thereby absorbing the higher wages without reducing employment. This, too, is a favorite argument of minimum wage advocates. How often it works this way is not clear from the evidence. It depends mainly on how efficiently businessmen have been running their businesses without the pressures of the minimum wage law. If businesses were maximizing profits before, the results are as described in the first paragraph above. If some businesses were failing to produce as cheaply as possible, the new minimum wage may simply push them to more efficient methods, which offset the higher wage costs. This latter case obviously implies the absence of effective competition. It is the other situation implicitly assumed by many minimum wage advocates.

4. Minimum wage laws tend to redistribute incomes—from employers to labor, and mainly from workers who get pushed out to those who keep their jobs at higher pay. What happens to the total labor share in the national income depends basically on the elasticity of demand for labor. If employers' aggregate demand for labor is inelastic, the law will mean higher total wage payments. Unfortunately, we don't know what the general elasticity of demand for labor is, although we do know that higher wages induce the substitution of capital for labor over extended periods. The impact of a minimum wage law is uneven, operating mainly against low-productivity workers wherever they are.

5. While the analysis above is correct, as a practical matter the minimum wage law has probably had only a limited effect thus far on the American economy. It has repeatedly been repealed by inflation. By the time the original 30-cents-per-hour minimum went into effect, market wages in most covered industries had already risen above that level. Wages in some industries, especially in the South, lagged behind the minimum figures, but many of these were in industries not covered by the law—agriculture, services, local shops, and so on. Further inflation and rising wages robbed each increase in the legal minimum of much of its intended impact. If inflation continues, it would erode the effect of the new $3.00 minimum, as in the past—although even then, the $3.00 floor would affect low-wage pockets throughout the economy, and such low-productivity groups as unskilled workers and teenagers. Recent legislation has broadened the coverage to include most occupations.

Given this analysis, what is your answer on the proposed $3.00 minimum wage? How effectively would it deal with the poverty problem? Clearly, it is likely to have conflicting results for different groups. Congress can specify the minimum wage businesses must pay if they hire workers, but it cannot require businesses to hire all the workers who want jobs at that wage. Where you come out on the legislation will presumably depend largely on which effects you think would predominate, and how you weight the welfare of different groups in the economy.

CASE 28: NOMINAL AND ACTUAL INTEREST RATES. Suggestions for analysis are given with the case at the end of Chapter 33.

CASE 29: PROFITS FOR THE PICKING? Suggestions for analysis are given with the case in Chapter 34.

CASE 30: THE VOUCHER EDUCATION PLAN. At first, the idea of turning education over to profit-seeking business may shock you, but the plan has won many advocates, and modified experiments are being conducted in several states under the auspices of the U.S. Office of Education.

Analytically, the voucher plan has two quite separate parts. First, it relies on the public sector to guarantee a minimum level of education for all children. This is in part an income redistribution activity; without the government guarantee through free vouchers for all, the poor would not be able to afford this much education, which under the voucher plan, as now, would be financed by general tax receipts that come more heavily from higher-income groups. Partly, the guarantee also rests on the widespread belief in positive externalities from general education. Most Americans believe that we have a better society when everyone has at least a minimum level of education.

Second, the plan relies on the private market to provide most efficiently the education parents want for their children. Advocates argue that it makes sense for private entrepreneurs to provide education, just as they produce clothing, hotels, highways, airplanes, food, and a wide variety of other goods and services. This is what the private sector has shown it can do best—produce efficiently the goods and services consumers offer to buy in the market. Just because we need the government to guarantee a minimum level of education for all is no reason we should expect the government to actually produce the education, especially not in a monopoly status such as the present public education system provides.

What are the main objections to the plan? First, and perhaps most important, many Americans feel that many (other?) parents really aren't competent to decide what is the best schooling for their youngsters, and that they would be easy picking for unscrupulous businessmen selling poor education. Make up your own mind. This raises the same issues as the food-stamp plan back in Case 5. Should government give the poor money and let them decide how much to spend on food (education); give them vouchers but leave them free to decide what food (education) to buy; or prescribe in detail what food (education) they shall receive?

Second, some critics say the plan wouldn't guarantee the same education for everybody, poor and rich. They are correct; it would not. Nor does it claim to, any more than the present system does. Rich parents would still have the option, as now, of spending more than the voucher on education for their youngsters. But the voucher plan would guarantee the same *minimum* for each youngster within the area involved. If you stop to think about it, further legislation forbidding richer parents to spend more than the minimum on their children would be hard to justify, under the voucher plan or now, unless you favor eliminating all differences in income per se.

Third, isn't education too important to entrust to profit-seeking businesses? Would you make the same argument about food, drugs, medical services? Education is important, just as are many other goods and services now produced by private businesses. The issue is not how important the product is, but what kind of enterprise is likely to produce what consumers want most efficiently (at the lowest cost and price). We rely on private firms to train their employees in routine and highly technical skills; is education of youngsters more difficult? If so, why should non-profit-seeking schools be able to do it better? If the public feels there are some skills that should be guaranteed for all, let the state mandate them for all schools eligible to receive the vouchers. But, say the plan's supporters, be wary of getting too much government regulation into the picture lest you destroy the private initiative that the plan seeks.

Fourth, wouldn't many areas be too small to support enough schools to provide alternative programs to compete for parents' dollars? The answer is yes. Some would, just as some are now too small to support adequate schools. The youngster who lives in a small village out in the mountains isn't going to get the best education either way. It's a problem society must face, possibly with special subsidies, under any educational system.

Fifth, couldn't the plan be used to finance church schools, violating the constitutional separation of church and state? And sixth, might not it permit development of racially segregated schools? Voucher supporters answer that safeguards can and should be built in to forbid both religious and racial misuse of the plan, by refusal to certify such schools under the voucher plan. Indeed, they argue, the proposed voucher plan should speed integration by breaking present ties between the school attended and residential location.

As a practical matter, the voucher plan is a long way from supplanting the present public school system. But it poses sharply the problem of where and how the private and public sectors can most effectively serve the public. Thinking it through is a valuable exercise. And don't think it's completely farfetched. Many government scholarships and fellowships for college and postgraduate education are given now in the form of vouchers, usable at any approved school. There are many partial voucher arrangements that may be attractive even though the complete plan may seem to go too far.

CASE 31: HOW MUCH SOCIAL SECURITY CAN WE AFFORD? This case raises an interesting combination of economic and ethical issues. Fundamentally, the problem is that we face limited resources, and that the more fully we use these resources, the larger will be the economy's total output. When people retire, they cease to add to society's output but continue as consumers. The earlier we require or permit people to retire, the smaller is the total real output on which we all depend for our standards of living.

How much of any total output should be transferred to retired nonworkers is both an economic and an ethical issue. It is an economic issue because it may well affect the incentives of younger people to work, and hence affect society's total output. It is an ethical issue as to how much of their work younger people are willing to devote to supporting older nonworkers, who, it must be remembered, as parents earlier supported the present workers through their years of education.

The financing pattern used for Social Security determines who pays, again both an ethical and an economic (incentives) issue. It is also a political issue. If we throw Social Security into the regular annual federal budget process, will the result be higher or lower taxes and benefits for older people? Many supporters of the present system urge that it be kept in its present special status to avoid its becoming a political football, with annual battles over both taxes and benefits leading to unpredictable results and highly disruptive uncertainties for retired people.

The last question calls for use of your macroeconomics from Part 2. If the government were to accumulate a huge insurance-type reserve fund to finance future benefit payments, what would be the impact on current output and prices? If the fund were held uninvested, this would clearly impose a massive deflationary pressure on the economy—it would be an enormous annual government surplus. Suppose, therefore, the government set out to invest the fund, channeling it back into the income stream. In what would it invest? If in ventures like schools and highways, how would these be liquidated when the funds were later needed for benefit payments? Who would be the buyers to provide the funds needed then by the government? Alternatively, if the government invested the fund in business ventures, it would soon find itself massively engaged in the private business sector. The volume of funds is so huge that it would soon find itself dominating many markets and moving rapidly toward a socialist economy. Or if the government simply used the fund to cover part of its current budget expenditures, from a macroeconomic point of view there would be little change from the present pay-as-you-go system; no fund would be accumulated. If you think through the macroeconomic alternatives, it's easy to see why the government rapidly drifted into the present modified annual-income-transfer financing pattern.

If people view their Social Security taxes as savings, they will save less through private channels. Funds for private investment projects are therefore less than they would be without the present Social Security system. This may help explain why the U.S. private saving and investment rate is a lower percentage of GNP than it was earlier, and why the U.S. growth rate may be slowing. Thus, how we handle Social Security may have a significant effect on our economic growth.

CASE 32: SHOULD TAXES ON CORPORATE PROFITS BE REDUCED? This case raises both micro and macro issues, issues of both equity and incentives. The following questions may help organize your analysis:

On the incentives-growth issue:

1. Would reducing the effective tax rate on returns to capital (say, by integrating the personal and corporation income taxes to eliminate "double taxation") stimulate more investment and faster national economic growth? The answer is given partly by the macro analysis of Part 2, partly by the micro analysis of the behavior of the individual firm in Part 3 and this chapter. Note also the evidence of Figure 37–1. The question will be examined in more detail in Part 7, on "Economic Growth."

On the equity issue:

2. If the answer to the preceding question is yes, will the increase in GNP be enough to increase the incomes of the lower- and middle-income classes, even though the first effect is to increase the after-tax incomes of the well-to-do?

3. Is more equality in after-tax incomes under the present tax system more "equitable" than would be the more unequal but higher absolute incomes for both rich and poor with a larger GNP, stimulated by a lower tax rate on investment income?

4. If personal and corporation income taxes were integrated, as Secretary Simon proposes, corporate profits would be taxed to the individual stockholder as earned, whether or not they are paid out in dividends. The corporate income tax rate is proportional at about 50 percent for all large corporations, while personal income tax rates rise to a 70 percent maximum on very large incomes. Would the proposed change make the combined taxes more or less progressive? Is your answer changed by the fact that many corporate stocks are held by pension funds accumulated to pay future retirement benefits to lower- and middle-income workers?

CASE 33: ROBINSON CRUSOE, FRIDAY, AND THE GAINS FROM TRADE. No suggestions for analysis should be necessary on this case. The analysis is presented directly in the middle portion of Chapter 39. It has also been presented repeatedly in the domestic sections of the text (Parts 1, 3, and 4) dealing with the advantages of specialization and exchange among freely consenting individuals or businesses.

CASE 34: MULTINATIONAL CORPORATIONS. As the case suggests, answers to many of the questions here are open to debate. The fundamental thrust of the multinationals toward a more efficient allocation of world resources and against the restrictionism of nation-states is clear. Use the principle of comparative advantage, with specialization and exchange, as the central analysis. Multinationals will tend to increase total world output, and there will be more to divide up among all the nations involved.

But the balance-of-payments questions are more complex, and the question of how the increased total output is divided among the nations is uncertain. With Chapter 39, try tracing the effects of multinational investment and profit flows on the international payments of the different nations involved. But to explore this issue fully, you need the more complete analysis of Chapter 42.

On the most explosive issue of nationalism versus multinational pressures, you're on your own. Economic analysis can suggest results, but it can only help to provide the answers.

CASE 35: IMPORTS: BANE OR BOON? This case requires no extended suggestions for analysis. For the most part, Mr. Abel's statement is in head-on opposition to the reasoning supporting freer trade in Chapter 39, with one important exception. Abel argues that the presumed advantages of free trade are not obtained when multinational corporations use cheap labor to manufacture abroad and then sell here, because they retain all the lower-cost advantages for themselves as profits. Consumers, he argues, do not benefit.

If Abel is right, clearly the presumed consumer gain from free international trade would be short-circuited. How would you check up on his allegation? Note that there are two ways. One would be to look at profits of multinational firms compared to others; this would not be definitive, because many other factors also influence company profits. The other is to use your theory, which tells you to ask whether substantial competition exists in the areas discussed by Abel. If there is competition, and other firms selling in the United States are free to duplicate low-cost production overseas, we can be reasonably sure the multinational firms won't be able to hold onto their excess profits because competition will force prices down toward costs of production.

Should the U.S. government limit imports in all industries to a constant proportion of total domestic consumption? On the basis of Mr. Abel's statement, under what conditions do you believe he would favor free trade? What steps do you believe the U.S. government might take to "raise substandard wage levels abroad to acceptable minimums," so that there would be "fair competition" between U.S. and overseas workers?

CASE 36: ARAB OIL AND THE INTERNATIONAL MONETARY SYSTEM. The international economists were right that the dire predictions of disaster were overdone—although there were some real problems to be faced. The problem provides a nice exercise in basic analysis of international trade and finance. Consider the five questions in order.

1. This prediction involves a crude fallacy that you should have detected easily. U.S. payments for Arab oil were not made in dollar bills, or even gold.

They were made by check, giving the Arab sellers increased dollar balances at New York banks. The Arabs might have demanded gold in exchange for their dollars (although we would probably have refused, and such a demand would simply have led sooner to the formal end of dollar convertibility). The meaning of the Arabs' "draining" dollars or other reserves out of the United States is thus unclear. Certainly they would not have taken billions of dollars of currency to the Middle East and hoarded them there. What would the Arabs do with the dollars—just look at them? Their interest was clearly better served by either spending the dollars or keeping them invested in bank accounts, securities, or real assets. From the U.S. point of view, if the Arabs were so irrational as to want physical dollars to hoard at home, the Federal Reserve could readily print up some more currency to fill the gap in the United States.

2. The same reasoning suggests the answer to question 2. There was no shipment of dollars to the Arabs, which then had to be shipped back to the United States. The Arabs received payment in the form of bank checks, which could be deposited in banks in the United States or elsewhere (say, in London). While Arab decisions to keep all their deposits in, say, London rather than New York could raise serious U.S.–U.K. balance-of-payments problems, the dollars (Western currencies) were automatically recycled to the Western nations; they never left the Western world.

Once they received dollars in payment, the Arabs, of course, had a choice as to how to use them. Since most of the OPEC nations are poor, it was reasonable to expect that they would want to spend most of them on goods and services to build up their economies and raise their standards of living—and that is precisely how most of them have used their big earnings increases. Alternatively, they could invest the funds (through direct investment or by buying securities) in other nations; the United States and Western Europe offer the largest opportunities. Or they could hold the funds in liquid form—in bank accounts or short-term securities like Treasury bills. But whichever of these they choose, the Western payments are recycled to the Western nations.

3. If the OPEC nations choose to build up their holdings of international reserves (Western nations' currencies and gold) instead of investing or spending the funds on current goods and services, they do to that extent have reserves they could shift from nation to nation, somewhat like the "hot-money" shifts described earlier in the text. But what would the Arabs stand to gain from such behavior? As large holders of

foreign currencies and foreign investments, they have rapidly become a part of the international monetary system, with much the same interests in its stability as the Western industrial nations have. To bring financial disruption to the United States would destroy the value of the dollars held by the Arabs at the same time it disrupted the U.S. financial structure. Nonetheless, the major Western nations in 1974 devised an oil "safety net" (special lending facility) to supplement the IMF's lending facilities specifically in case any of them should face serious financial disruption from OPEC actions. To date, it has not been necessary to use these special lending facilities.

4. How much of the world's assets the Arabs hold by 1980 will depend on how well they can maintain the cartel price of oil at its present high level, on how much oil they sell, and on how much of their earnings they spend buying current goods and services from other nations. A few countries (notably Kuwait and Saudi Arabia) are so small and such large oil producers that they simply cannot currently spend their huge earnings on any feasible steps to raise their living standards. Their investments abroad can, therefore, be expected to rise to large figures. But most OPEC nations are poor, and have managed to escalate their purchases abroad nearly as fast as their earnings have grown. Indeed, Iran within two years had so increased its foreign expenditures for current consumption and building roads, cities, and the like, that its international balance of payments was in deficit. Estimates of the accumulation of all OPEC countries' international assets by 1980 now cluster around $150 to $250 billion. Massive Arab ownership of the Western economies' assets looks a good deal less likely than in the first doomsday predictions, but some OPEC nations may well end up with very large investments in Western nations and power in international monetary markets.

5. The real burden of OPEC's high prices is their reduction of living standards in oil-consuming nations. U.S. consumers, for example, must now pay about $25 billion annually to the OPEC countries for the oil we use, compared to about $5 billion previously. The Arabs therefore have $20 billion more annually to buy part of our currently produced GNP or our assets through direct or portfolio (security) investments. The Arabs get a bigger share of our current output; we get a smaller one. And so it is for other countries that must buy OPEC oil.

For the United States and other high-income countries, this reduced standard of living is painful, but tolerable. For other nations that depend more heavily on foreign oil (for example, Japan), the cost is correspondingly greater; and for very poor, less-developed nations like India and Bangladesh, the result may be disaster. Oil is essential to development, for power and for making fertilizer, but such nations have no foreign exchange to pay the new higher prices. Thus, they must either do without the desperately needed oil or cut back their imports of food or other imports to pay for it. They are already heavily in debt, so borrowing to finance the higher oil bills is increasingly difficult, or impossible. To ease this problem, the Western nations established through the International Monetary Fund a special oil lending facility to provide low-cost loans for oil imports, and the OPEC countries have made some such loans available directly, although mainly to other Arab or politically sympathetic countries. The burden of the oil cartel is concentrated most heavily on the poor, less-developed nations.

CASE 37: THE ENERGY PROBLEM. In considering the two major alternative approaches to the energy crisis, be concrete as to what would be done under each. Specifically, if you choose the first, what new government steps would you suggest to increase energy production without permitting higher prices—or large direct subsidies to producers, which amount to much the same thing, since we are nearly all both taxpayers and energy buyers. How would you make gas and oil companies drill more domestic wells if you hold prices below profitable levels and raise costs by antipollution regulations? How would you induce power companies to build the new plants you need where you want them?

If you choose the individual-incentive (price-system) route, would you free energy prices from all government controls? (Remember that electricity and gas are widely considered public utilities.) If you propose only limited price increases, how big must they be to get the three desired effects from the price system? Would you limit oil, gas, and coal company profits? How about electrical utilities? (See Case 19.) Whichever approach you favor, how would you deal with the ever-present tradeoff between energy and ecology? What are your most fundamental goals?

Nowhere is the fundamental economic problem of tradeoffs more central than here. The tradeoffs are all too painfully evident. We can have cleaner air and water *if* we accept less energy or more expensive energy. We can have wanted energy *if* we pay more for it and *if* we forego some of our environmental goals. How much dirtier air should we accept to keep down the prices of gas, oil, and electricity—for example, by using more coal with modified clean-air standards? There's no such thing as a free lunch, is the number one lesson of economics. In thinking through your solution, you should find the following concepts from earlier chapters useful:

Alternative cost—tradeoffs.

Marginalism—comparison of alternatives at the margin, rather than on an all-or-nothing basis.

Rising marginal costs—The more energy we want, the more it will cost to find and produce each additional unit; similarly with rising standards for cleanliness and the environment. How clean is clean enough when the cost in terms of energy prices rises rapidly?

Importance of economic incentives—How can we make individuals and businesses act "in the public interest" if the action is not in their own self-interests? (For example, how shall we convince consumers to economize on natural gas, and gas companies to drill for more, if the price of natural gas is held down?)

Importance of technical advance.

Interdependence—Any move on one part of the energy problem is likely to affect other parts. If we raise the price of natural gas but keep oil under control, users will shift to oil and create an oil "shortage," which in turn will lead to price increases by foreign oil producers. Similarly, if we reject nuclear energy, this will put upward pressure on coal prices, raise the demand for coal-fueled electricity plants, and create more locational problems as to what states and localities will permit "dirty" coal-burning plants to be built in their jurisdictions. Try to think through the interdependencies involved in your solution, and decide whether you want them worked out by government planners or the price system.

CASE 38: COFFEE, CARTELS, AND THE U.S. DEVELOPMENT AID. Here it is the end of the course, and you should be able to be on your own at last. For the central issues and concepts to use, look back at Chapters 23, 26, and 42, plus Cases 18, 21, and 36, in addition to Chapter 46. This case, like the preceding one, provides an opportunity to use a substantial part of the tool kit you've been accumulating, and it leaves an important role for the differing value judgments that so often loom large in economic policy decisions.

Name Index

SUBJECT INDEX